ORGANIZATIONAL BEHAVIOR

CONCEPTS ■ CONTROVERSIES ■ APPLICATIONS

SEVENTH EDITION

STEPHEN P. ROBBINS

San Diego State University

PRENTICE HALL
ENGLEWOOD CLIFFS, NJ 07632

Library of Congress Cataloguing-in-Publication Data

Robbins, Stephen P.,
Organizational behavior:concepts, controversies, and applications/Stephen P. Robbins.
p. cm.
Includes bibliographical references and index.
ISBN 0-13-192519-9
1. Organizational behavior. I. Title.
HD58.7.R62 1995
658.3—dc20 94-46765
CIP

Acquisitions Editor: *David Shafer*
Associate Editor: *Lisamarie Brassini*
Production Editor: *Edith Pullman*
Managing Development Editor: *Steven Rigolosi*
Interior and Cover Design: *Delgado Design, Inc.*
Design Director: *Linda Fiordilino and Patricia H. Wosczyk*
Photo Development: *Nancy Moudry*
Photo Research: *Doris Milligan*
Photo Coordinator: *Melinda Reo*
Prepress and Manufacturing Buyer: *Vincent Scelta*
Editorial Assistant: *Nancy Proyect*

A Simon & Schuster Company
Englewood Cliffs, New Jersey 07632

Printed in the United States of America

10 9 8 7 6 5 4 3 2 1

ISBN 0-13-192519-9

Prentice-Hall International (UK) Limited, *London*
Prentice-Hall of Australia Pty. Limited, *Sydney*
Prentice-Hall Canada Inc., *Toronto*
Prentice-Hall Hispanoamericana, S.A., *Mexico*
Prentice-Hall of India Private Limited, *New Delhi*
Prentice-Hall of Japan, Inc., *Tokyo*
Simon & Schuster Asia Pte. Ltd., *Singapore*
Editora Prentice-Hall do Brasil, Ltda., *Rio de Janeiro*

LEARNING ABOUT YOURSELF EXERCISE

Helps you increase your self–awareness through the use of assessment questionnaires.

WORKING WITH OTHERS EXERCISE

Helps develop your interpersonal competencies through group–based activities.

ETHICAL DILEMMA EXERCISE

Presents situations that require you to assess and evaluate your ethical standards.

CASE INCIDENT

Presents a realistic case application.

tion." But favoring women and minorities isn't necessarily against the law. The courts allow organizations to take race into account in hiring, for instance, to remedy past discrimination.

When organizations are adding new people, they're looking for women, Latinos, Asian-Americans, and African-Americans. This seems to be especially true among professional and managerial workers. In 1983 white men held 63.5 percent of those jobs in the United States. In 1993 they were down to 53 percent. Among the upper ranks, white women have been the major beneficiaries of men's loss of dominance.

Managers—many of them white males themselves—face a dilemma. To make their organizations more diverse, they are certain to hire and promote women and minorities over other white males. In so doing, they risk angering those passed over. But if these managers fail to embrace diversity, they not only perpetuate past injustices, but risk leaving their organizations less globally competitive. What should they do? What do *you* think?

Based on M. Galen, "White, Male, and Worried," *Business Week* (January 31, 1994), pp. 50–55; M.L. Ganga, "Changing of the Guard," *Los Angeles Times* (February 7, 1994), p. 59; and J.S. Lublin, "Firms Designate Some Openings for Women Only," *Wall Street Journal* (February 7, 1994), p. B1.

CASE INCIDENT

Xerox of Mexico

Paul Hunt grew up in Houston and got his degree in business management from Texas A&M in 1988. Upon graduation, Paul took a job with the Xerox Corporation in Dallas as a human resource specialist. During his first two years, he split his time between recruiting on college campuses and establishing a

VIDEO CASE

Presents a case based on an ABC News video, including questions for analysis and discussion.

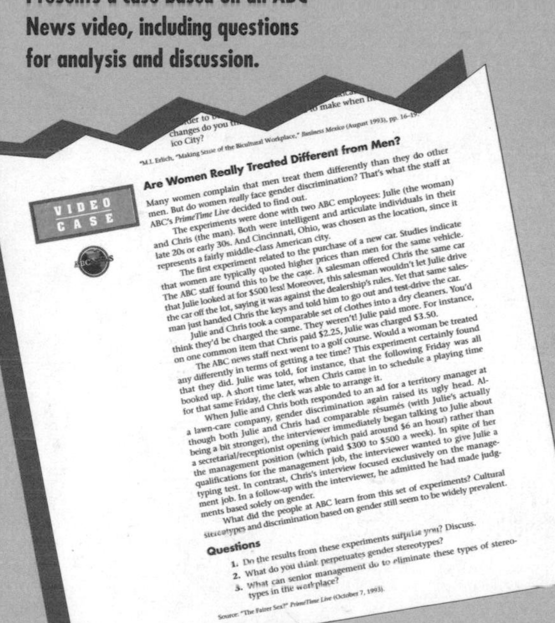

VIDEO CASE

Are Women Really Treated Different from Men?

Many women complain that men treat them differently than they do other men. But do women *really* face gender discrimination? That's what the staff at ABC's *PrimeTime Live* decided to find out.

The experiments were done with two ABC employees: Julie (the woman) and Chris (the man). Both were intelligent and articulate individuals in their late 20s or early 30s. And Cincinnati, Ohio, was chosen as the location, since it represents a fairly middle-class American city.

The first experiment related to the purchase of a new car. Studies indicate that women are typically quoted higher prices than men for the same vehicle. The ABC staff found this to be the case. A salesman offered Chris the same car that Julie looked at for $500 less! Moreover, this salesman wouldn't let Julie drive the car off the lot, saying it was against the dealership's rules. Yet that same salesman just handed Chris the keys and told him to go out and test-drive the car.

Julie and Chris took a comparable set of clothes into a dry cleaners. You'd think they'd be charged the same. They weren't! Julie paid more. For instance, on one common item that Chris paid $2.25, Julie was charged $3.50.

The ABC news staff next went to a golf course. Would a woman be treated any differently in terms of getting a tee time? This experiment certainly found that they did. Julie was told, for instance, that the following Friday was all booked up. A short time later, when Chris came in to schedule a playing time for that same Friday, the clerk was able to arrange it.

When Julie and Chris both responded to an ad for a territory manager at a lawn-care company, gender discrimination again raised its ugly head. Although both Julie and Chris had comparable résumés (with Julie's actually being a bit stronger), the interviewer immediately began talking to Julie about a secretarial/receptionist opening (which paid around $6 an hour) rather than the management position (which paid $300 to $500 a week). In spite of her qualifications for the management job, the interviewer wanted to give Julie a typing test. In contrast, Chris's interview focused exclusively on the management job. In a follow-up with the interviewer, he admitted he had made judgments based solely on gender.

What did the people at ABC learn from this set of experiments? Cultural stereotypes and discrimination based on gender still seem to be widely prevalent.

Questions

1. Do the results from these experiments surprise *you*? Discuss.
2. What do you think perpetuates gender stereotypes?
3. What can senior management do to eliminate these types of stereotypes in the workplace?

Source: "The Fairer Sex?" *PrimeTime Live* (October 7, 1993).

ROB PANCO CASE

Helps you integrate chapters and sections through a real–life case found at the end of each section.

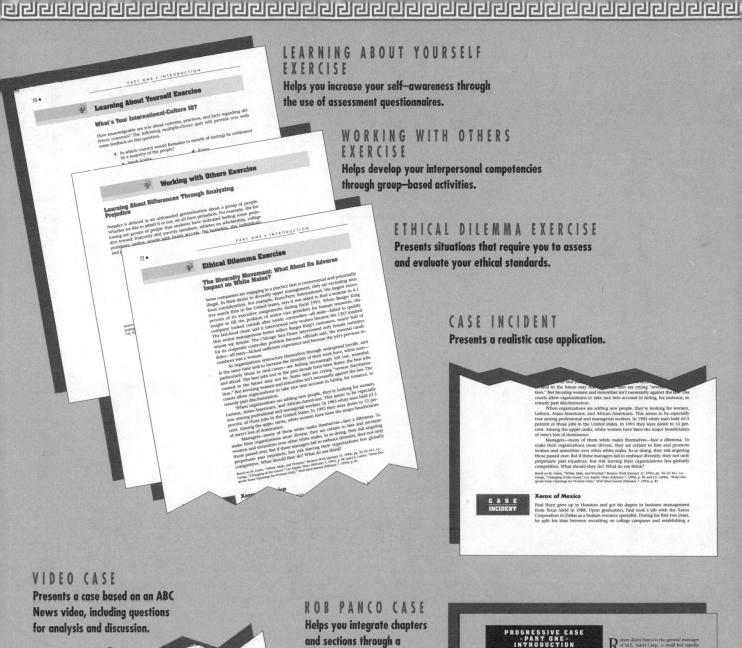

PROGRESSIVE CASE
PART ONE
INTRODUCTION

ROB PANCO: THE EVOLUTION OF A MANAGER*

Robert (Rob) Panco is the general manager of M.E. Aslett Corp., a small but rapidly growing New Jersey-based packager of educational and professional reference books. Aslett handles book projects from conception all the way up to, but excluding, the printing stage. The company's clients include Grolier Encyclopedia, World Book International, Prentice Hall, Harcourt Brace, and McGraw-Hill.

What career path did Rob Panco take to get to where he is today? What challenges and problems related to OB has he encountered in his career? This progressive case (which appears at the end of each section of this book) will provide answers to these questions.

You will find this case valuable for at least two reasons. First, it'll help you integrate many of the OB concepts introduced in this book. Unfortunately, textbooks have to be linear—moving sequentially through an artificially created set of independent chapters. The real world, however, is a juggling act of overlapping and highly interdependent activities. This case will make this interdependence clearer and help demonstrate how individual, group, and organization-system factors overlap. Second, this progressive case will show you the applicability of OB concepts to actual management practice. Most textbook examples or cases are short and designed to illustrate only one or two points. As an integrated and progressive story, the Rob Panco case will show you how one real-life manager has dealt with dozens of OB issues.

Figure I-1 on the next page provides a brief description of Rob Panco's background and career progression. But résumés leave a lot out. So let's begin by talking a bit about Rob's early life and career experiences.

If you had asked Rob during his senior year in high school what he planned on doing with his life, he'd have answered: "I'm going to be a professional musician." Toward that end, he had trained as a string bass player. When he went off to college—Duquesne University in Pittsburgh—it was with the intention to pursue his music interests. But things don't always work out as planned. During his first year, Rob came face to face with reality: There were lots of string bass players more talented than he was. If he pursued his passion, he could be a music teacher at best. Rob wanted more so he decided to change majors. He chose to work toward a degree in business, with specialization in marketing and management.

Why pursue a career in business? Rob wasn't sure. It might have been the influence of his father, who opened a State Farm insurance agency after spending 22 years in the U.S. Navy. Or it might have been the positive experiences he'd had working part-time in high school. From the age of 14 to 18, Rob worked evenings, weekends, and summers at a weekly newspaper. "I took the job initially to make money. I wanted to buy a $1400 string bass." He started by sweeping floors and washing presses. But, over time, he learned most of the jobs at the paper. For instance, he set type, pasted up ads, and perfected the skills of maintaining complex printing equipment. After graduating from high school, Rob continued working summers at the newspaper. This job may have laid the groundwork for his job today in the publishing industry.

*Some facts, incidents, and quotes included in this progressive case have been slightly modified by the author to enhance student discussion and analysis.

77

Brief Contents

CONTENTS

PART TWO • THE INDIVIDUAL 80

PREFACE

It seems just like yesterday that I began outlining what would become the first edition of this book. That "yesterday" is now 20 years ago and some 400,000 copies later! But just as companies—the late E.F. Hutton, Eastern Airlines, and Western Union come immediately to mind—can't rest on their laurels, neither can textbook authors. So I put a great deal of time and effort into the planning and execution of this seventh edition.

The following highlights the major changes between the sixth and seventh editions:

- *Topic coverage.* There are new chapters on work teams (Chapter 9) and technology and the design of work (Chapter 15). I've combined the chapters on organization structure and organization design into a single, more focused chapter. Topics new to this edition include TQM, reengineering, ESOPs, employee involvement, and organizational learning. I've also significantly rewritten and/or expanded coverage on the following topics: innovation, negotiation, coping with temporariness, and work stress.
- *Improved integration.* Globalization, ethics, diversity, and TQM are integrated throughout the text rather than isolated in stand-alone boxes. A new feature—the Rob Panco progressive case—has been added to the end of each section to help readers synthesize and integrate the content of that section and previous sections. Rob Panco was chosen to illustrate the application of OB concepts because of his ability to honestly discuss difficult issues and his diverse experience. Rob's openness provides insights into a manager's job rarely revealed in textbook cases. Additionally, the fact that Rob's experience covers diverse organizations—a university, a mega-corporation, and a small business—makes this case interesting to students interested in not-for-profit institutions and entrepreneurship as well as corporate management.
- *Increased focus on applications.* The two box themes in this edition address application of OB concepts. The "OB in the News" boxes recreate articles from business periodicals to show the relevance of OB concepts to daily business activities. The "From Concepts to Skills" boxes illustrate how readers can translate OB concepts into effective on-the-job skills. Other features in this edition that faciliate application include new chapter summaries that consider implications for management practice, "Learning About Yourself," "Working With Others," and "Ethical Dilemma" end-of-chapter exercises, and two cases per chapter (one being a video case). Consistent with the objective of making this edition more applications-focused, you'll also find that the chapter on

research methods and model building (Chapter 2 in the last edition) has been reformatted. The discussion of research methods in OB is now included as an appendix, while the discussion on developing an OB model has been abbreviated and included in Chapter 1.

Users of past editions of this text will find that the basic structure of the book and the writing style remain unchanged. The book continues to be organized around three levels of analysis: the individual, the group, and the organization system. The writing style still maintains a conversational tone, with a heavy reliance on examples to illustrate the application of concepts. And the Point-Counterpoint debates—which have been a popular feature of this text since its inception—are again included to help students build their critical-thinking skills. In this edition, four of the debates are totally new and a number have been rewritten and updated.

Finally, you'll find that the research base of this seventh edition has been completely updated. I've combed the academic journals and business periodicals published since the last edition so that I could include the latest research findings and examples from business practice.

Supplements

INSTRUCTOR'S MANUAL Includes chapter outlines and synopsis. Point-Counterpoint summary and analysis, answers to discussion questions, teaching guide for in-text exercises, teaching notes for cases, and video guide.

TEST ITEM FILE Over 2,500 test questions including Multiple Choice, True/False, Scenario based Multiple Choice, and Discussion. Answer Key includes page references and is annotated according to orientation (factual or applied) and level of difficulty (easy, moderate, or challenging). New to this edition are questions covering the boxed material, video cases, Point-Counterpoint, and the Progressive Case.

PRENTICE HALL TEST MANAGER The test item file is designed for use with The Prentice Hall Test Manager, a computerized package that allows users to custom design, save, and generate classroom tests. Available on a 3.5" IBM disc, the test manager also permits professors to edit, add or delete questions from the test item file and to export files to various word processing programs, including WordPerfect and Microsoft Word.

OVERHEAD TRANSPARENCIES Over 100 original four-color acetates of illustrations not found in the text.

ELECTRONIC TRANSPARENCIES The overhead transparencies collection on disc for classroom use. Available from your Prentice Hall representative or America Online.

ABC NEWS/PRENTICE HALL VIDEO LIBRARY 18 video clips that correlate with the end of chapter cases found in the text.

THE PRENTICE HALL ORGANIZATIONAL BEHAVIOR/MANAGEMENT LASER DISC An additional collection of videos and over 2,000 stills from all of PH's Management and OB texts. Free upon adoption of Robbins: OB 7/e.

Acknowledgments

Textbooks are a team project. While my name is on the cover of this book, literally hundreds of people have contributed to this text and its previous editions.

A number of colleagues have been kind enough to review the previous edition and/or the revised manuscript and offer suggestions for improvement. This book is a whole lot better because of insights and suggestions provided by:

Professor Jeffrey Kane, University of North Carolina, Greensboro, NC
Professor Tom Clark, Xavier University, Cincinnati, OH
Professor Ernie Bourgeois, Castleton State College, Castleton, VT
Professor Susan Aaron Moller, City University, Bellevue, WA
Professor Kathleen Ganley, Robert Morris College, Corapolis, PA
Professor Carol Carnevale, Empire State College, Saratoga Springs, NY
Professor Judy Nixon, University of Tennessee, Chattanooga, TN
Professor Gary Blau, Temple University, Philadelphia, PA
Professor Sandra Robinson, New York University, New York, NY
Professor Maureen Fleming, The University of Montana, Missoula, MT
Professor Eric Stephan, Brigham Young University, Provo, UT
Professor Ram Subramanian, Grand Valley State University, Allendale, MI

Regardless of how good the manuscript is that I turn in, it's only three or four floppy disks until my friends at Prentice Hall swing into action. Then PH's crack team of editors, production personnel, designers, marketing specialists, and sales representatives turn those couple of million digital characters into a bound textbook and see that it gets into faculty and students' hands. My thanks on this project go to David Shafer, Natalie Anderson, Nancy Proyect, Jim Boyd, Bill Oldsey, Edie Pullman, Jo-Ann Deluca, Steven Rigolosi, Nancy Moudry, Doris Milligan, Lisa Delgado, Pat Wosczyk, Linda Fiordilino, Belen Poltorak, and all my friends at Prentice-Hall of Canada, Prentice Hall of Australia, and Simon & Schuster Asia who have been so supportive of this book over its many editions. A special thank you is also extended to Rob Panco. Rob's openness and honesty helped to make the integrative case a truly unique addition to this book. Finally, I want to thank the good people at Apple Computer. This was the first book I've worked on using a computer. I confess that I didn't give up my typewriter voluntarily. I was *told* by Prentice Hall that all my manuscripts, beginning with this one, would have to be submitted on disk. My hopes of making it through my whole writing career without having to use a computer were crushed. PH gave me a Mac for Christmas of 1993. Surprisingly, my computer-fears were unfounded. I now understand why Macs are so popular. I've found mine to be stupid-proof. The writing flow and transitions in this book are better than in the previous editions largely due to my Mac. Keep up the good work, Apple-people!

Stephen P. Robbins

ABOUT THE AUTHOR

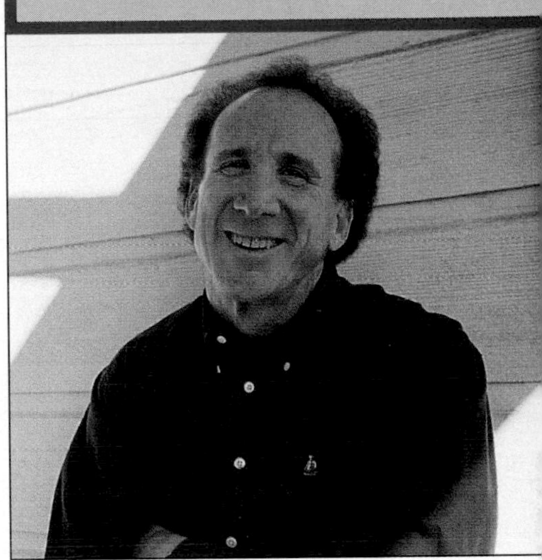

STEPHEN P. ROBBINS received his Ph.D. from the University of Arizona. He previously worked for the Shell Oil Company and Reynolds Metals Company. Since completing his graduate studies, Dr. Robbins has taught at the University of Nebraska at Omaha, Concordia University in Montreal, the University of Baltimore, Southern Illinois University at Edwardsville, and San Diego State University. Dr. Robbins' research interests have focused on conflict, power, and politics in organizations, as well as the development of effective interpersonal skills. His articles on these and other topics have appeared in such journals as *Business Horizons*, the *California Management Review, Business and Economic Perspectives, International Management, Management Review, Canadian Personnel and Industrial Relations*, and *The Journal of Management Education*.

In recent years, Dr. Robbins has been spending most of his professional time writing textbooks. His other Prentice Hall books include *Management*, 5th edition (with Mary Coulter); *Fundamentals of Management* (with David De Cenzo); *Essentials of Organizational Behavior*, 4th edition; *Training in InterPersonal Skills*, 2nd edition (with Phillip Hunsaker); *Organization Theory*, 3rd edition; and *Supervision Today!* These books are used at more than 1,000 U.S. colleges and universities, as well as hundreds of schools in Canada, Australia, New Zealand, Singapore, Hong Kong, Malaysia, China, the Philippine Islands, Mexico, the Netherlands, and Scandinavia.

In Dr. Robbins' "other life," he participates in masters' track competitions. Since turning 50 in 1993, he has won four U.S. national indoor age-group titles and set world records at both 60 and 200 meters. He has also broken the outdoor world records at 100 and 200 meters, won national titles at both distances, and became "the world's fastest human—age 50 and over" when he won the 100 meters at the 10th World Veteran Games in Miyazaki, Japan. Robbins was chosen as U.S. track athlete of the year for his age group in 1993 and 1994.

◆PART ONE◆
INTRODUCTION

CHAPTER 1

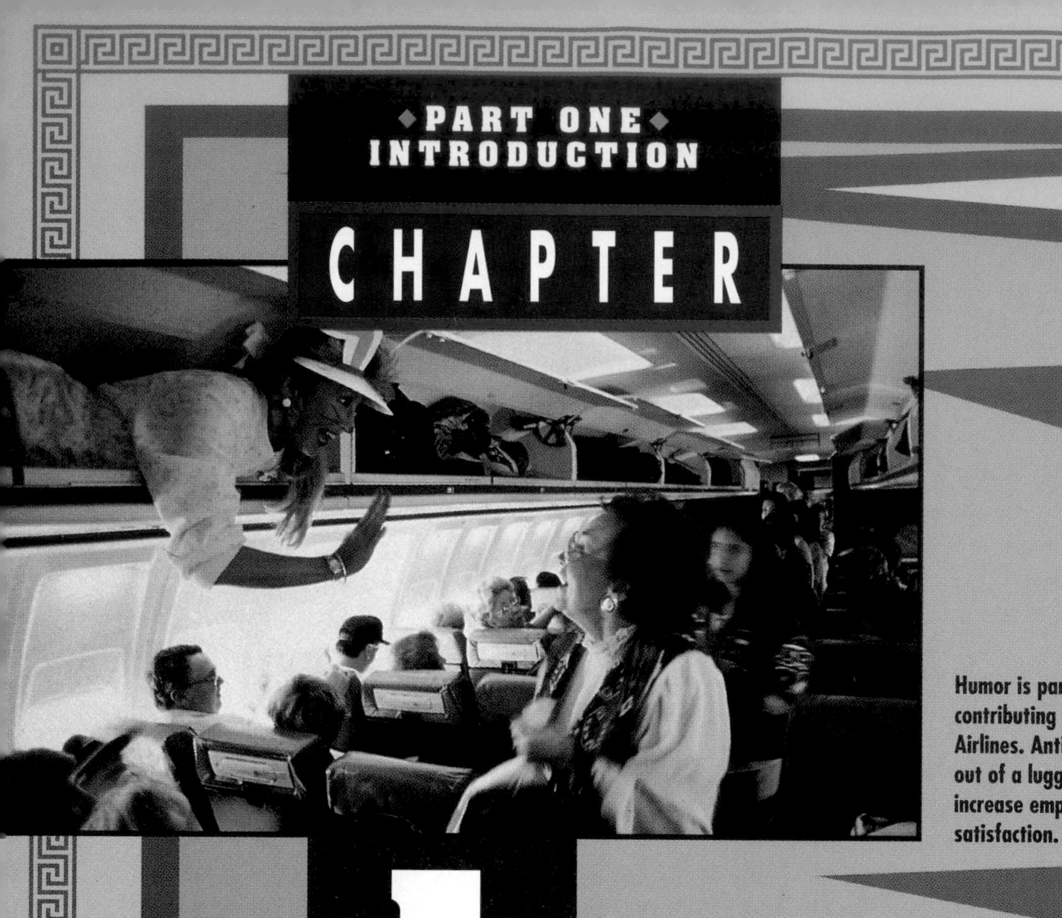

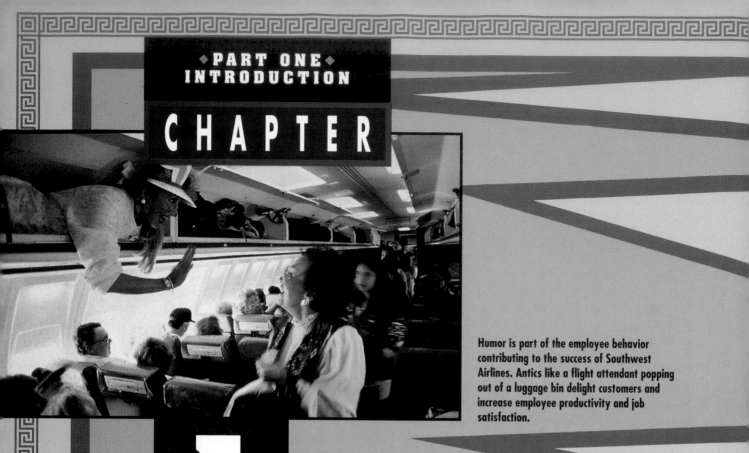

Humor is part of the employee behavior contributing to the success of Southwest Airlines. Antics like a flight attendant popping out of a luggage bin delight customers and increase employee productivity and job satisfaction.

WHAT IS ORGANIZATIONAL BEHAVIOR?

CHAPTER OUTLINE

LEARNING OBJECTIVES

After studying this chapter, you should be able to:

1. Define organizational behavior (OB).
2. Describe what managers do.
3. Explain the value of the systematic study of OB.
4. List the major challenges and opportunities for managers to use OB concepts.
5. Identify the contributions made by major behavioral science disciplines to OB.
6. Describe why managers require a knowledge of OB.
7. Explain the need for a contingency approach to the study of OB.
8. Identify the three levels of analysis in this book's OB model.

It's not what we don't know that gives us trouble,
it's what we know that ain't so.
W. ROGERS

Meet David Kwok. A 1987 graduate of the University of California at Los Angeles, with a major in cognitive science, David works for a company called The Princeton Review that prepares students to take college and graduate school admission tests. Although he is only 29 years old, David directs more than 100 instructors at Princeton Review's Los Angeles office.

"My academic training in artificial intelligence didn't really prepare me for my biggest job challenge—understanding and motivating people," says David. "For instance, nothing at UCLA really emphasized how to get people psyched up. For me, people are the unknown part of the equation that determines how effective I am in my job. Other tasks, like scheduling or customer relations, give me very few headaches. What I've learned is that when things go wrong, it's almost always a people problem. I've worked hard to make our teaching staff feel like a small family and to learn techniques for getting them motivated. But it's been on-the-job training for me. I didn't learn any of this in school."

David Kwok has learned what most managers learn very quickly: A large part of the success in any management job is developing good interpersonal or people skills. Lawrence Weinbach, chief executive at the accounting firm of Arthur Andersen & Co., puts it this way: "Pure technical knowledge is only going to get you to a point. Beyond that, interpersonal skills become critical."[1] As the items in the following three paragraphs attest, this recognition of the importance of developing managers' interpersonal skills seems to be spreading.

The chief executive of Chrysler Corporation, Robert Eaton, sees his work force as an asset that provides his company with a sustainable competitive advantage. "The only way we can beat the competition is with people," says Eaton. "That's the only thing anybody has. Your culture and how you motivate and empower and educate your people is what makes the difference."[2] The head of Starbucks, the rapidly growing Seattle-based coffee retailer, concurs: "Our only sustainable competitive advantage is the quality of our work force."[3]

A study of 191 top executives at six Fortune 500 companies sought an answer to the question: Why do managers fail? The single biggest reason for failure, according to these executives, is poor interpersonal skills.[4] The Center for Creative Leadership in Greensboro, North Carolina, estimates that half of all managers and 30 percent of all senior managers have some type of difficulty with people.[5] Consistent with these findings are surveys that have sought to determine what job skills college recruiters consider most important for job effectiveness of MBA graduates.[6] These surveys consistently identify interpersonal skills as most important.

In the 1990s, we've come to understand that technical skills are necessary, but insufficient, for succeeding in management. In today's increasingly competitive and demanding workplace, managers can't succeed on their technical skills alone. They've also got to have good people skills. This book has been written to help both managers and potential managers develop those people skills.

What Managers Do

Let's begin by briefly defining the terms *manager* and the place where managers work—the *organization*. Then let's look at the manager's job; specifically, what do managers do?

Managers get things done through other people. They make decisions, allocate resources, and direct the activities of others to attain goals. Managers do their work in an **organization**. This is a consciously coordinated social unit, composed of two or more people, that functions on a relatively continuous basis to achieve a common goal or set of goals. Based on this definition, manufacturing and service firms are organizations and so are schools, hospitals, churches, military units, retail stores, police departments, and local, state, and federal government agencies. The people who oversee the activities of others and who are responsible for attaining goals in these organizations are their managers (although they're sometimes called *administrators*, especially in not-for-profit organizations).

managers
Individuals who achieve goals through other people.

organization
A consciously coordinated social unit, composed of two or more people, that functions on a relatively continuous basis to achieve a common goal or set of goals.

Management Functions

In the early part of this century, a French industrialist by the name of Henri Fayol wrote that all managers perform five management functions: They plan, organize, command, coordinate, and control.[7] Today, we've condensed these down to four: planning, organizing, leading, and controlling.

If you don't know where you're going, any road will get you there. Since organizations exist to achieve goals, someone has to define these goals and the means by which they can be achieved. Management is that someone. The **planning** function encompasses defining an organization's goals, establishing an overall strategy for achieving these goals, and developing a comprehensive hierarchy of plans to integrate and coordinate activities.

Managers are also responsible for designing an organization's structure. We call this function **organizing**. It includes the determination of what tasks are to be done, who is to do them, how the tasks are to be grouped, who reports to whom, and where decisions are to be made.

Every organization contains people, and it is management's job to direct and coordinate these people. This is the **leading** function. When managers

planning
Includes defining goals, establishing strategy, and developing plans to coordinate activities.

organizing
Determining what tasks are to be done, who is to do them, how the tasks are to be grouped, who reports to whom, and where decisions are to be made.

leading
Includes motivating subordinates, directing others, selecting the most effective communication channels, and resolving conflicts.

What do managers do? This team of managers at First Brands Corporation develops and implements plans for the growth of Glad® food protection products. Their strategies for growth include growing existing businesses through new product introductions, expanding international operations and exports, and increasing profit margins by improving the company's product mix and reducing operating costs. Here, the management team plans the advertising strategy for Glad-Lock® Zipper Bags.

motivate subordinates, direct the activities of others, select the most effective communication channel, or resolve conflicts among members, they are engaging in leading.

Table 1-1 Mintzberg's Managerial Roles

Role	Description	Examples
Interpersonal		
Figurehead	Symbolic head; required to perform a number of routine duties of a legal or social nature	Ceremonies, status requests, solicitations
Leader	Responsible for the motivation and direction of subordinates	Virtually all managerial activities involving subordinates
Liaison	Maintains a network of outside contacts who provide favors and information	Acknowledgment of mail, external board work
Informational		
Monitor	Receives wide variety of information; serves as nerve center of internal and external information of the organization	Handling all mail and contacts categorized as concerned primarily with receiving information
Disseminator	Transmits information received from outsiders or from other subordinates to members of the organization	Forwarding mail into organization for informational purposes; verbal contacts involving information flow to subordinates such as review sessions
Spokesperson	Transmits information to outsiders on organization's plans, policies, actions, and results; serves as expert on organization's industry	Board meetings; handling contacts involving transmission of information to outsiders
Decisional		
Entrepreneur	Searches organization and its environment for opportunities and initiates projects to bring about change	Strategy and review sessions involving initiation or design of improvement projects
Disturbance handler	Responsible for corrective action when organization faces important, unexpected disturbances	Strategy and review sessions involving disturbances and crises
Resource allocator	Making or approving significant organizational decisions	Scheduling; requests for authorization; budgeting; the programming of subordinates' work
Negotiator	Responsible for representing the organization at major negotiations	Contract negotiation

Source: Adapted from *The Nature of Managerial Work* by H. Mintzberg. Copyright © 1973 by H. Mintzberg. Reprinted by permission of Harper Collins Publishers.

The final function managers perform is **controlling**. After the goals are set, the plans formulated, the structural arrangements delineated, and the people hired, trained, and motivated, there is still the possibility that something may go amiss. To ensure that things are going as they should, management must monitor the organization's performance. Actual performance must be compared with the previously set goals. If there are any significant deviations, it is management's job to get the organization back on track. This monitoring, comparing, and potential correcting is what is meant by the controlling function.

controlling
Monitoring activities to ensure they are being accomplished as planned and correcting any significant deviations.

So, using the functional approach, the answer to the question of what managers do is that they plan, organize, lead, and control.

Management Roles

In the late 1960s, a graduate student at MIT, Henry Mintzberg, undertook a careful study of five executives to determine what these managers did on their jobs. Based on his observations of these managers, Mintzberg concluded that managers perform ten different highly interrelated roles, or sets of behaviors, attributable to their jobs.[8] As shown in Table 1-1, these ten roles can be grouped as being primarily concerned with interpersonal relationships, the transfer of information, and decision making.

INTERPERSONAL ROLES All managers are required to perform duties that are ceremonial and symbolic in nature. When the president of a college hands out diplomas at commencement or a factory supervisor gives a group of high school students a tour of the plant, he or she is acting in a *figurehead* role. All managers have a *leadership* role. This role includes hiring, training, motivating, and disciplining employees. The third role within the interpersonal grouping is the *liaison* role. Mintzberg described this activity as contacting outsiders who provide the manager with information. These may be individuals or groups inside or outside the organization. The sales manager who obtains information from the personnel manager in his or her own company has an internal liaison relationship. When that sales manager has contacts with other sales executives through a marketing trade association, he or she has an outside liaison relationship.

INFORMATIONAL ROLES All managers will, to some degree, receive and collect information from organizations and institutions outside their own. Typically, this is done through reading magazines and talking with others to learn of changes in the public's tastes, what competitors may be planning, and the like. Mintzberg called this the *monitor* role. Managers also act as a conduit to transmit information to organizational members. This is the *disseminator* role. Managers additionally perform a *spokesperson* role when they represent the organization to outsiders.

DECISIONAL ROLES Finally, Mintzberg identified four roles that revolve around the making of choices. In the *entrepreneur* role, managers initiate and oversee new projects that will improve their organization's performance. As *disturbance handlers*, managers take corrective action in response to previously unforeseen problems. As *resource allocators*, managers are responsible for allocating human, physical, and monetary resources. Lastly, managers perform a *negotiator* role, in which they discuss and bargain with other units to gain advantages for their own unit.

Management Skills

Still another way of considering what managers do is to look at the skills or competencies they need to successfully achieve their goals. Robert Katz has identified three essential management skills: technical, human, and conceptual.[9]

technical skills
The ability to apply specialized knowledge or expertise.

TECHNICAL SKILLS **Technical skills** encompass the ability to apply specialized knowledge or expertise. When you think of the skills held by professionals such as civil engineers, tax accountants, or oral surgeons, you typically focus on their technical skills. Through extensive formal education, they have learned the special knowledge and practices of their field. Of course, professionals don't have a monopoly on technical skills and these skills don't have to be learned in schools or formal training programs. All jobs require some specialized expertise and many people develop their technical skills on the job.

human skills
The ability to work with, understand, and motivate other people, both individually and in groups.

HUMAN SKILLS The ability to work with, understand, and motivate other people, both individually and in groups, describes **human skills**. Many people are technically proficient but interpersonally incompetent. They might, for example, be poor listeners, unable to understand the needs of others, or have difficulty managing conflicts. Since managers get things done through other people, they must have good human skills to communicate, motivate, and delegate.

conceptual skills
The mental ability to analyze and diagnose complex situations.

CONCEPTUAL SKILLS Managers must have the mental ability to analyze and diagnose complex situations. These are **conceptual skills**. Decision making, for instance, requires managers to spot problems, identify alternatives that can correct them, evaluate these alternatives, and select the best one. Managers can be technically and interpersonally competent, yet still fail because of an inability to rationally process and interpret information.

Effective vs. Successful Managerial Activities

Fred Luthans and his associates looked at the issue of what managers do from a somewhat different perspective.[10] They asked this question: Do managers who move up most quickly in an organization do the same activities and with the same emphasis as those managers who do the best job? You would tend to think that those managers who were the most effective in their jobs would also be the ones who were promoted fastest. But that's not what appears to happen.

Luthans and his associates studied more than 450 managers. What they found was that these managers all engaged in four managerial activities:

1. *Traditional management*: Decision making, planning, and controlling.
2. *Communication*: Exchanging routine information and processing paperwork.
3. *Human resource management*: Motivating, disciplining, managing conflict, staffing, and training.
4. *Networking*: Socializing, politicking, and interacting with outsiders.

The "average" manager studied spent 32 percent of his or her time in traditional management activities, 29 percent communicating, 20 percent in human resource management activities, and 19 percent networking. However, the amount of time and effort that different managers spent on these four activities varied a great deal. Specifically, as shown in Figure 1-1, managers who

Figure 1-1
Allocation of Activities by Time

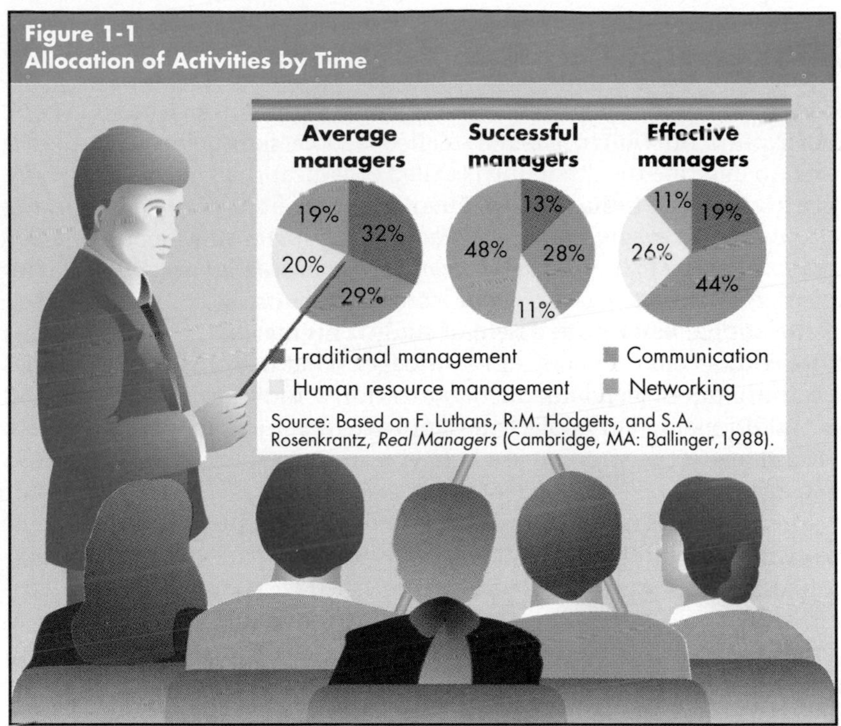

Source: Based on F. Luthans, R.M. Hodgetts, and S.A. Rosenkrantz, *Real Managers* (Cambridge, MA: Ballinger, 1988).

were *successful* (defined in terms of the speed of promotion within their organization) had a very different emphasis than managers who were *effective* (defined in terms of the quantity and quality of their performance and the satisfaction and commitment of their subordinates). Networking made the biggest relative contribution to manager success; human resource management activities made the least relative contribution. Among effective managers, communication made the largest relative contribution and networking the least.

This study adds important insights to our knowledge of what managers do. On average, managers spend approximately 20 to 30 percent of their time on each of the four activities: traditional management, communication, human resource management, and networking. However, successful managers don't give the same emphasis to each of these activities as do effective managers. In fact, their emphases are almost the opposite. This challenges the historical assumption that promotions are based on performance, vividly illustrating the importance that social and political skills play in getting ahead in organizations.

A Review of the Manager's Job

One common thread runs through the functions, roles, skills, and activities approaches to management: Each recognizes the paramount importance of managing people. As David Kwok found out when he became a manager at The Princeton Review, regardless of whether it's called "the leading function," "interpersonal roles," "human skills," or "human resource management and networking activities," it's clear that managers need to develop their people skills if they're going to be effective and successful in their job.

Enter Organizational Behavior

We've made the case for the importance of people skills. But neither this book nor the discipline on which it rests is called people skills. The term that is widely used to describe the discipline is called organizational behavior.

organizational behavior (OB)
A field of study that investigates the impact that individuals, groups, and structure have on behavior within organizations, for the purpose of applying such knowledge toward improving an organization's effectiveness.

Organizational behavior (frequently abbreviated as OB) is *a field of study that investigates the impact of individuals, groups, and structure on behavior within organizations for the purpose of applying such knowledge toward improving an organization's effectiveness*. That's a lot of words, so let's break it down.

Organizational behavior is a field of study. This means it is a distinct area of expertise with a common body of knowledge. What does it study? It studies three determinants of behavior in organizations: individuals, groups, and structure. Additionally, OB applies the knowledge gained about individuals, groups, and the effect of structure on behavior in order to make organizations work more effectively.

To sum up our definition, OB is concerned with the study of what people do in an organization and how that behavior affects the performance of the organization. And because OB is specifically concerned with employment-related situations, you should not be surprised to find that it emphasizes behavior as related to jobs, work, absenteeism, employment turnover, productivity, human performance, and management.

There is increasing agreement on the components or topics that constitute the subject area of OB. While there is still considerable debate about the relative importance of each, there appears to be general agreement that OB includes the core topics of motivation, leader behavior and power, interpersonal communication, group structure and process, learning, attitude development and perception, change processes, conflict, job design, and work stress.[11]

Replacing Intuition with Systematic Study

Each of us is a student of behavior. Since our earliest years, we have watched the actions of others and have attempted to interpret what we see. Whether or not you have explicitly thought about it before, you have been "reading" people almost all your life. You watch what others do and try to explain to yourself why they have engaged in their behavior. Additionally, you've attempted to predict what they might do under different sets of conditions.

Generalizations About Behavior

You have already developed some generalizations that you find helpful in explaining and predicting what people do and will do. But how did you arrive at these generalizations? You did so by observing, sensing, asking, listening, and reading. That is, your understanding comes either directly from your own experience with things in the environment, or secondhand, through the experience of others.

How accurate are the generalizations you hold? Some may represent extremely sophisticated appraisals of behavior and may prove highly effective in explaining and predicting the behavior of others. However, most of us also carry with us a number of beliefs that frequently fail to explain why people do what they do.[12] To illustrate, consider the following statements about work-related behavior:

1. Happy workers are productive workers.
2. All individuals are most productive when their boss is friendly, trusting, and approachable.
3. Interviews are effective selection devices for separating job applicants who would be high-performing employees from those who would be low performers.
4. Everyone wants a challenging job.
5. You have to scare people a little to get them to do their jobs.
6. Everyone is motivated by money.
7. Most people are much more concerned with the size of their own salaries than with others'.
8. The most effective work groups are devoid of conflict.

How many of these statements do you think are true? For the most part, they are all false, and we touch on each later in this text. But whether these statements are true or false is not really important at this time. What is important is to be aware that many of the views you hold concerning human behavior are based on intuition rather than fact. As a result, a systematic approach to the study of behavior can improve your explanatory and predictive abilities.

Consistency vs. Individual Differences

Casual or commonsense approaches to obtaining knowledge about human behavior are inadequate. In reading this text, you will discover that a systematic approach will uncover important facts and relationships, and provide a base from which more accurate predictions of behavior can be made.

Underlying this systematic approach is the belief that behavior is not random. It is caused and directed toward some end that the individual believes, rightly or wrongly, is in his or her best interest.

> Behavior generally is predictable if we know how the person perceived the situation and what is important to him or her. While people's behavior may not appear to be rational to an outsider, there is reason to believe it usually is intended to be rational and it is seen as rational by them. An observer often sees behavior as nonrational because the observer does not have access to the same information or does not perceive the environment in the same way.[13]

Certainly there are differences between individuals. Placed in similar situations, all people do not act alike. However, certain fundamental consistencies underlie the behavior of all individuals that can be identified and then modified to reflect individual differences.

These fundamental consistencies are very important. Why? Because they allow predictability. When you get into your car, you make some definite and usually highly accurate predictions about how other people will behave. In North America, for instance, you would predict that other drivers will stop at stop signs and red lights, drive on the right side of the road, pass on your left, and not cross the solid double line on mountain roads. Notice that your predictions about the behavior of people behind the wheels of their cars are almost always correct. Obviously, the rules of driving make predictions about driving behavior fairly easy.

Psychologists at the Center for Creative Leadership systematically study the behavior of managers in a controlled environment. Through one-way glass, they observe, videotape, and evaluate managers' leadership skills. They also gather data by surveying the managers and their co-workers, bosses, and subordinates. The goal of this scientific study: to teach managers how to lead others in their organizations effectively.

What may be less obvious is that there are rules (written and unwritten) in almost every setting. Therefore, it can be argued that it's possible to predict behavior (undoubtedly not always with 100 percent accuracy) in supermarkets, classrooms, doctors' offices, elevators, and in most structured situations. To illustrate further, do you turn around and face the doors when you get into an elevator? Almost everyone does, yet did you ever read you're supposed to do this? Probably not! Just as I make predictions about automobile drivers (where there are definite rules of the road), I can make predictions about the behavior of people in elevators (where there are few written rules). In a class of 60 students, if you wanted to ask a question of the instructor, I would predict you would raise your hand. Why don't you clap, stand up, raise your leg, cough, or yell, "Hey, over here!"? The reason is that you have learned raising your hand is appropriate behavior in school. These examples support a major contention in this text: Behavior is generally predictable, and the **systematic study** of behavior is a means to making reasonably accurate predictions.

systematic study
Looking at relationships, attempting to attribute causes and effects, and drawing conclusions based on scientific evidence.

When we use the phrase "systematic study," we mean looking at relationships, attempting to attribute causes and effects, and basing our conclusions on scientific evidence, that is, on data gathered under controlled conditions and measured and interpreted in a reasonably rigorous manner. (See Appendix B for a basic review of research methods used in studies of organizational behavior.)

intuition
A feeling not necessarily supported by research.

Systematic study replaces **intuition** or those gut feelings about "why I do what I do" and "what makes others tick." Of course, a systematic approach does not mean those things you have come to believe in an unsystematic way are necessarily incorrect. Some of the conclusions we make in this text, based on reasonably substantive research findings, will only support what you always knew was true. But you will also be exposed to research evidence that runs counter to what you may have thought was common sense. In fact, one of the challenges of teaching a subject like organizational behavior is to overcome the notion, held by many, that "it's all common sense."[14] You will find that many of the so-called commonsense views you hold about human behavior are, on closer examination, wrong. Moreover, what one person considers "common sense" frequently runs counter to another's version of "common sense." Are leaders born or made? What is it that motivates people at work nowadays? You probably have answers to such questions, and individuals who have not reviewed the research are likely to differ on their answers. The point is that one of the objectives of this text is to encourage you to move away from your intuitive views of behavior toward a systematic analysis, in the belief that such analysis will improve your accuracy in explaining and predicting behavior.

Challenges and Opportunities for OB

Understanding organizational behavior has never been more important for managers. A quick look at a few of the dramatic changes now taking place in organizations supports this claim. For instance, the typical employee is getting older; more and more women and nonwhites are in the workplace; corporate restructuring and cost cutting are severing the bonds of loyalty that historically tied many employees to their employers; and global competition is requiring employees to become more flexible and to learn to cope with rapid change and innovation.

In short, there are a lot of challenges and opportunities today for managers to use OB concepts. In this section, we review some of the more critical issues confronting managers for which OB offers solutions—or at least some meaningful insights toward solutions.

Improving Quality and Productivity

Tom Rossi manages in a tough business. He runs a light bulb plant in Mattoon, Illinois, for General Electric. His business has seen tough competition from manufacturers in the United States, Europe, Japan, and even China. To survive, he's had to cut fat, increase productivity, and improve quality. And he's succeeded. Between 1988 and 1993, the Mattoon plant has averaged annual cost productivity improvements of approximately 8 percent. By focusing on continuous improvement, streamlining processes, and cost cutting, GE's Mattoon plant has remained viable and profitable.[15]

More and more managers are confronting the challenges that Tom Rossi is facing. They are having to improve their organization's productivity and the quality of the products and services they offer. Toward improving quality and productivity, they are implementing programs like total quality management and reengineering—programs that require extensive employee involvement.

total quality management (TQM) A philosophy of management that is driven by the constant attainment of customer satisfaction through the continuous improvement of all organizational processes.

We discuss **total quality management (TQM)** at a number of places throughout this book. As Table 1-2 describes, TQM is a philosophy of manage-

Table 1-2 What Is Total Quality Management?

1. *Intense focus on the customer.* The customer includes not only outsiders who buy the organization's products or services, but also internal customers (such as shipping or accounts payable personnel) who interact with and serve others in the organization.
2. *Concern for continual improvement.* TQM is a commitment to never being satisfied. "Very good" is not good enough. Quality can always be improved.
3. *Improvement in the quality of everything the organization does.* TQM uses a very broad definition of quality. It relates not only to the final product but how the organization handles deliveries, how rapidly it responds to complaints, how politely the phones are answered, and the like.
4. *Accurate measurement.* TQM uses statistical techniques to measure every critical performance variable in the organization's operations. These performance variables are then compared against standards or benchmarks to identify problems, the problems are traced to their roots, and the causes are eliminated.
5. *Empowerment of employees.* TQM involves the people on the line in the improvement process. Teams are widely used in TQM programs as empowerment vehicles for finding and solving problems.

ment that is driven by the constant attainment of customer satisfaction through the continuous improvement of all organizational processes.[16] TQM has implications for OB because it requires employees to rethink what they do and become more involved in workplace decisions.

reengineering
Reconsiders how work would be done and the organization structured if they were being created from scratch.

In times of rapid and dramatic change, it's sometimes necessary to approach improving quality and productivity from the perspective of "How would we do things around here if we were starting over from scratch?" That, in essence, is the approach of **reengineering**. It asks managers to reconsider how work would be done and their organization structured if they were starting over.[17] To illustrate the concept of reengineering, consider a manufacturer of roller skates. His product is essentially a shoe with wheels beneath it. The typical roller skate was a leather boot with shoelaces, attached to a steel platform that held four wooden wheels. If our manufacturer took a continuous improvement approach to change, he would look for small incremental improvements that he could introduce in his product. For instance, he might consider adding hooks to the upper part of the boot for speed lacing; or changing the weight of leather used for improved comfort; or using different ballbearings to make the wheels spin more smoothly. Now most of us are familiar with in-line skates. They represent a reengineering approach to rollerskates. The goal was to come up with a skating device that could improve skating speed, mobility, and control. Rollerblades fulfilled those goals in a completely different type of shoe. The upper was made of injected plastic, made popular in skiing. Laces were replaced by easy-close clamps. And the four wheels, set in pairs of two, were replaced by four to six in-line plastic wheels. The reengineered result, which didn't look much like the traditional roller skate, proved universally superior. The rest, of course, is history. In-line skates have revolutionized the roller skate business.

Our point is that today's contemporary managers understand the success of any efforts at improving quality and productivity must include their employees. These employees will not only be a major force in carrying out changes but increasingly will participate actively in planning those changes. OB offers important insights into helping managers work through these changes.

Improving People Skills

We opened this chapter by demonstrating how important people skills are to managerial effectiveness. We said, "This book has been written to help both managers and potential managers develop those people skills."

As you proceed through this text, we present relevant concepts and theories that can help you explain and predict the behavior of people at work. In addition, you'll also gain insights into specific people skills that you can use on the job. For instance, you'll learn how to be an effective listener, the proper way to give performance feedback, how to delegate authority, and how to create effective teams. Moreover, you'll have the opportunity to complete exercises that will give you insights into your own behavior, the behavior of others, and practice at improving your interpersonal skills.

Managing Work Force Diversity

One of the most important and broad-based challenges currently facing U.S. organizations is adapting to people who are different. The term we use for describing this challenge is work force diversity.

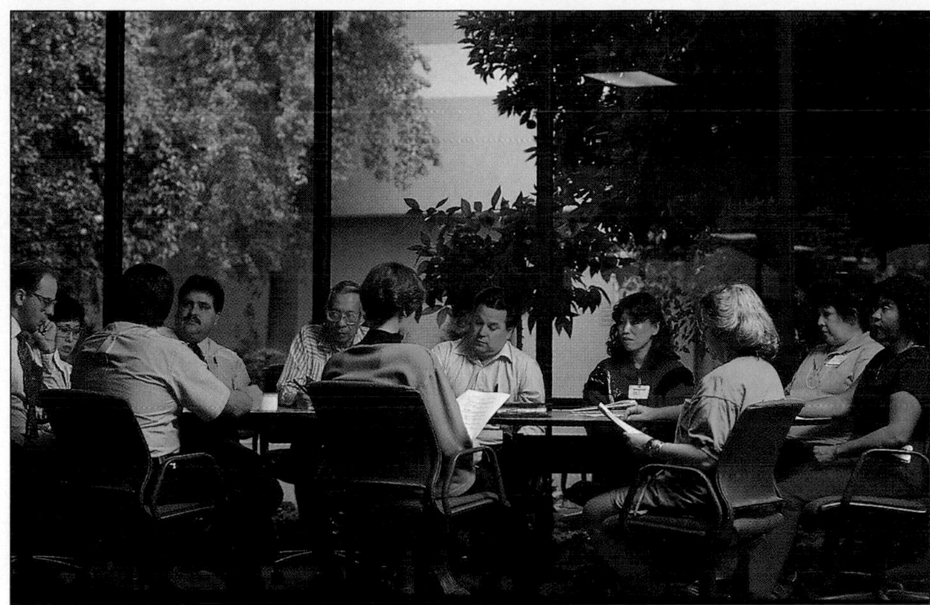

Honeywell's diverse global work force includes employees who speak 29 languages and represent 47 cultures and 90 ethnic backgrounds. Honeywell strives to create an environment that values individual differences, removes barriers to equal opportunity, and empowers employees to develop their talents fully. Among the advisory councils that the company has formed to identify and resolve common issues are the American Asian Council, American Indian Council, Black Employee Network, Council of Employees with Disabilities, Hispanic Council, Older Workers League, Committee of Vietnam Veterans, Women's Council, and Work and Family Council.

Work force diversity means that organizations are becoming more heterogeneous in terms of gender, race, and ethnicity. But the term encompasses anyone who varies from the so-called norm. In addition to the more obvious groups—women, African-Americans, Hispanic-Americans, Asian-Americans—it also includes the physically disabled, gays and lesbians, and the elderly.

work force diversity
The increasing heterogeneity of organizations with the inclusion of different groups.

We used to take a melting pot approach to differences in organizations, assuming people who were different would somehow automatically want to assimilate. But we now recognize that employees don't set aside their cultural values and lifestyle preferences when they come to work. The challenge for organizations, therefore, is to make themselves more accommodating to diverse groups of people by addressing their different lifestyles, family needs, and work styles. The melting pot assumption is being replaced by one that recognizes and values differences.[18]

◆One of the most important and broad-based challenges currently facing U.S. organizations is adapting to people who are different.

Haven't organizations always included members of diverse groups? Yes, but they were a small percentage of the work force and were, for the most part, ignored by large organizations. Moreover, it was assumed these minorities would seek to blend in and assimilate. The bulk of the pre-1980s work force were male Caucasians working full time to support a nonemployed wife and school-aged children. Now such employees are the true minority! Currently, 45 percent of the U.S. labor force are women. Minorities and immigrants make up 22 percent.[19] As a case in point, Hewlett-Packard's work force is 19 percent minorities and 40 percent women.[20] A Digital Equipment Corp. plant in Boston provides a partial preview of the future. The factory's 350 employees include men and women from 44 countries who speak 19 languages. When plant management issues written announcements, they are printed in English, Chinese, French, Spanish, Portuguese, Vietnamese, and Haitian Creole.

Work force diversity has important implications for management practice. Managers will need to shift their philosophy from treating everyone alike to recognizing differences and responding to those differences in ways that will

◆◆◆◆ OB in the News ◆◆◆◆

Work-Force Study Finds Divisions of Race and Gender Are Deep

A broad survey of American workers depicts a work force that is deeply divided by race and gender. The survey, funded by the Families and Work Institute, covered 2,958 wage and salaried workers.

One of the survey's more interesting findings is that younger workers don't seem any better equipped to cope with a more diverse workplace than their older coworkers. Employees under 25 show no greater preference than older employees for working with people of other races, ages, or ethnic groups. Just over half of surveyed workers of all ages said they prefer working with people of the same race, sex, gender, and education.

Employees who had greater experience living or working with people of other races, ethnic groups, and ages showed a stronger preference for diversity in the workplace. Unfortunately, few employees have such experience. The study found that even workers under 25 had little contact in the neighborhoods where they grew up with people of different ethnic and cultural backgrounds.

(Work-Force Study Finds Divisions of Race and Gender Are Deep. From the *Wall Street Journal* (September 3, 1993), p. B1.

ensure employee retention and greater productivity—while, at the same time, not discriminating. Diversity, if positively managed, can increase creativity and innovation in organizations as well as improve decision making by providing different perspectives on problems.[21] When diversity is not managed properly, there is potential for higher turnover, more difficult communication, and more interpersonal conflicts. We discuss work force diversity in greater detail in Chapter 2.

Responding to Globalization

Management is no longer constrained by national borders. Burger King is owned by a British firm and McDonald's sells hamburgers in Moscow. Exxon, a so-called American company, receives almost 75 percent of its revenues from sales outside the United States. Toyota makes cars in Kentucky; General Motors makes cars in Brazil; and Ford (which owns part of Mazda) transfers executives from Detroit to Japan to help Mazda manage its operations. These examples illustrate that the world has become a global village. In turn, managers have to become capable of working with people from different cultures.

Globalization affects a manager's people skills in at least two ways. First, if you're a manager you're increasingly likely to find yourself in a foreign assignment. You'll be transferred to your employer's operating division or subsidiary in another country. Once there, you'll have to manage a work force that is likely to be very different in needs, aspirations, and attitudes from the ones you were used to back home. Second, even in your own country, you're going to find yourself working with bosses, peers, and subordinates who were born and raised in different cultures. What motivates you may not motivate them. While your style of communication may be straightforward and open, they may find this style uncomfortable and threatening. This suggests that if you're going to be able to work effectively with these people, you'll need to understand their

Japan's electronic giant Matsushita Electric Company, maker of Panasonic and National brands, operates more than 150 plants in 38 countries throughout Southeast Asia, North America, Europe, the Middle East, Latin America, and Africa. In managing its overseas network of factories that employ 99,000 workers, Matsushita adapts its organizational practices to each country. At its plants in Malaysia, it accommodates the cultural differences of Muslim Malays, ethnic Chinese, and Indian employees by offering Chinese, Malaysian, and Indian food in company cafeterias. It accommodates Muslim religious customs by providing special prayer rooms at each plant and allowing two prayer sessions per shift. Shown here are Muslim Malays during a midday prayer break.

culture, how it has shaped them, and learn to adapt your management style to these differences. In the next chapter, we provide some frameworks for understanding differences between national cultures. Further, as we discuss OB concepts throughout this book, we focus on how cultural differences might require managers to modify their practices.

Empowering People

If you pick up any popular business periodical nowadays, you'll read about the reshaping of the relationship between managers and those they're supposedly responsible for managing. You'll find managers being called coaches, advisers, sponsors, or facilitators.[22] In many organizations, employees have become associates.[23] And there's a blurring between the roles of managers and workers. Decision making is being pushed down to the operating level, where workers are being given the freedom to make choices about schedules, procedures, and solving work-related problems. In the 1980s, managers were encouraged to get their employees to *participate* in work-related decisions.[24] Now, managers are going considerably further by allowing employees full control of their work. Self-managed teams, where workers operate largely without bosses, have become the rage of the 1990s.[25]

What's going on is that managers are empowering employees. They are putting employees in charge of what they do. And in so doing, managers are having to learn how to give up control and employees are having to learn how to take responsibility for their work and make appropriate decisions. In later chapters of this book we show how **empowerment** is changing leadership styles, power relationships, the way work is designed, and the way organizations are structured.

empowerment
Putting employees in charge of what they do.

Stimulating Innovation and Change

Whatever happened to W. T. Grant, Gimbel's, and Eastern Airlines? All these giants went bust! Why have other giants like General Motors, Sears, Westinghouse, Boeing, and AT&T implemented huge cost-cutting programs and eliminated thousands of jobs? To *avoid* going bust!

Today's successful organizations must foster innovation and master the art of change or they will become candidates for extinction. Victory will go to those organizations that maintain their flexibility, continually improve their quality, and beat their competition to the marketplace with a constant stream of innovative products and services. Domino's single-handedly brought on the demise of thousands of small pizza parlors whose managers thought they could continue doing what they had been doing for years. Fox Television has successfully stolen a major portion of the under-25 viewing audience from their much larger network rivals through innovative programming like *The Simpsons* and *Beverly Hills 90210*.

An organization's employees can be the impetus for innovation and change, or they can be a major stumbling block. The challenge for managers is to stimulate employee creativity and tolerance for change. The field of organizational behavior provides a wealth of ideas and techniques to aid in realizing these goals.

Coping with "Temporariness"

Managers have always been concerned with change. What's different nowadays is the length of time between change implementations. It used to be that managers needed to introduce major change programs once or twice a decade. Today, change is an ongoing activity for most managers. The concept of continuous improvement, for instance, implies constant change.

Managing in the past could be characterized by long periods of stability, interrupted occasionally by short periods of change. Managing today would be more accurately described as long periods of ongoing change, interrupted occasionally by short periods of stability! The world that most managers and employees face today is one of permanent "temporariness." The actual jobs that workers perform are in a permanent state of flux. So workers need to continually update their knowledge and skills to perform new job requirements.[26] For example, production employees at companies like Caterpillar, Chrysler, and Reynolds Metals now need to know how to operate computerized production equipment. That was not part of their job description 15 years ago. Work groups are also increasingly in a state of flux. In the past, employees were assigned to a specific work group and that assignment was relatively permanent. There was a considerable amount of security in working with the same people day in and day out. That predictablity has been replaced by temporary work groups, teams that include members from different departments and whose members change all the time, and the increased use of employee rotation to fill constantly changing work assignments. Finally, organizations themselves are in a state of flux. They continually reorganize their various divisions, sell off poor-performing businesses, downsize operations, and replace permanent employees with temporaries.[27]

Today's managers and employees must learn to cope with temporariness. They have to learn to live with flexibility, spontaneity, and unpredictability. The study of OB can provide important insights into helping you better understand a work world of continual change, how to overcome resistance to change, and how best to create an organizational culture that thrives on change.

Declining Employee Loyalty

Corporate employees used to believe their employers would reward their loyalty and good work with job security, generous benefits, and pay increases. But

◆◆◆◆ OB in the News ◆◆◆◆

The Flexible Work Force

It's one of the fastest growing trends in business today. We're talking about the use of "contingent" workers—temporary, subcontracted, part-time, and leased employees.

Just how large the contingent work force has gotten is difficult to accurately measure. Conservative estimates, however, put the number at about 25 percent of the labor force. Interestingly, these employees are not just the stereotypical clerks, secretaries, and laborers commonly supplied by temporary-help agencies. Increasingly, temporary employees also include technical professionals such as engineers, financial analysts, doctors, and lawyers.

The appeal of temporary employees is obvious. In a rapidly changing and uncertain business environment, managers want flexibility. Reluctant to add full-time, permanent workers to their payrolls, they look to contingent workers as a means of turning labor costs from a fixed expense to a variable expense. Using contingent workers gives an organization the ability to respond to changing market conditions quickly. For instance, by using contingent employees, Apple Computer can quickly adjust its work force as the demand for Macintoshs rise and fall. In addition, temporary workers allows an organization to save on health and vacation benefits, avoid ending up with retirees and pensions, and lessens the chance of legal action because there are fewer regulations that cover contingent employees.

We can expect to see an increased use of contingent workers by employers. It provides organizations with a fluid work force that can be swelled or deflated like an accordian at a moment's notice.

Critics of this trend, especially unions, argue that contingent workers don't have the benefits, security, and job protection that permanent employees have. And this argument is valid. On the other hand, proponents note that employers must be able to quickly respond to changing market conditions. The use of contingent workers helps meet that goal. Additionally, it's often overlooked that the concept of permanent jobs with large corporations is a relatively recent phenomenon. At the beginning of this century, half of all Americans were self-employed. In essence, what's happening is that we're returning to an earlier pattern when employees were free agents, carrying their skills with them from job to job.

The Flexible Work Force. From *Training* (December 1993), pp. 23–30

beginning in the mid-1980s, in response to global competition, unfriendly takeovers, leveraged buyouts, and the like, corporations began to discard traditional policies on job security, seniority, and compensation. They sought to become "lean and mean" by closing factories, moving operations to lower cost countries, selling off or closing down less profitable businesses, eliminating entire levels of management, and replacing permanent employees with temporaries. Importantly, this is not just a North American phenomenon. European companies are doing the same. Barclays, the big British bank, has recently cut staff levels by 20 percent. And a number of German firms have trimmed their work force and management ranks. Siemens, the electronic engineering conglomerate, shed more than 3,000 jobs in 1993 alone; steelmaker Krupp-Hoesch has cut its management hierarchy from five to three levels; and Mercedes-Benz has trimmed its number of levels from seven to five.

Figure 1-2
Changing Views of Loyalty
1993 vs. 1988

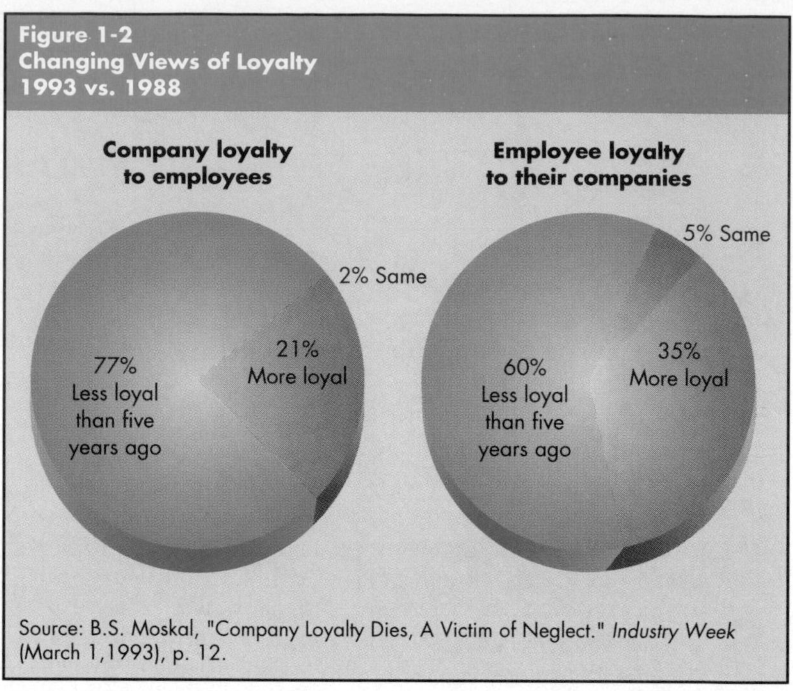

Source: B.S. Moskal, "Company Loyalty Dies, A Victim of Neglect." *Industry Week* (March 1,1993), p. 12.

These changes have resulted in a sharp decline in employee loyalty.[28] In a 1993 survey of workers, for instance, 77 percent said there is less loyalty between companies and employees than in 1988.[29] Employees perceive that their employers are less committed to them and, as a result, employees respond by being less committed to their companies (see Figure 1-2).

An important OB challenge will be for managers to devise ways to motivate workers who feel less committed to their employers while maintaining their organizations' global competitiveness.

Improving Ethical Behavior

In an organizational world characterized by cutbacks, expectations of increasing worker productivity, and tough competition in the marketplace, it's not altogether surprising that many employees feel pressured to cut corners, break rules, and engage in other forms of questionable practices.

ethical dilemma
Situations where an individual is required to define right and wrong conduct.

Members of organizations are increasingly finding themselves facing **ethical dilemmas**, situations where they are required to define right and wrong conduct.[30] For example, should they blow the whistle if they uncover illegal activities taking place in their company? Should they follow orders they don't personally agree with? Do they give an inflated performance evaluation to an employee they like, knowing that such an evaluation could save that employee's job? Do they allow themselves to play politics in the organization if it will help their career advancement?

What constitutes good ethical behavior has never been clearly defined. And in recent years the line differentiating right from wrong has become even more blurred. Employees see people all around them engaging in unethical practices—elected officials indicted for padding their expense accounts or taking bribes; high-powered lawyers, who know the rules, are found to be avoiding payment of Social Security taxes for their household help; successful executives who use insider information for personal financial gain; employees in other companies participating in massive cover-ups of defective military weapons. When caught, they hear these people giving excuses like "Everyone does it," or "You have to seize every advantage nowadays," or "I never thought I'd get caught."

Managers and their organizations are responding to this problem from a number of directions.[31] They're writing and distributing codes of ethics to guide employees through ethical dilemmas. They're offering seminars, workshops, and similar training programs to try to improve ethical behaviors. They're providing in-house advisers who can be contacted, in many cases anonymously, for assistance in dealing with ethical issues. And they're creating protection mechanisms for employees who reveal internal unethical practices.

Today's manager needs to create an ethically healthy climate for his or her employees, where they can do their work productively and confront a minimal degree of ambiguity regarding what constitutes right and wrong behaviors. We discuss ethics in several places in this book—for example, as it relates to decision making and politics in organizations. To help you define and establish your personal ethical standards, you'll find ethical dilemma exercises at the conclusion of each chapter. By confronting ethical issues you might not have thought about before, and sharing your ideas with classmates, you can gain insights into your own ethical viewpoints, those of others, and the implications of various choices.

> ◆ Today's manager needs to create an ethically healthy climate for his or her employees, where they can do their work productively and confront a minimal degree of ambiguity regarding what constitutes right and wrong behavior.

Contributing Disciplines to the OB Field

Organizational behavior is an applied behavioral science that is built on contributions from a number of behavioral disciplines. The predominant areas are psychology, sociology, social psychology, anthropology, and political science.[32] As we shall learn, psychology's contributions have been mainly at the individual or micro level of analysis; the other four disciplines have contributed to our understanding of macro concepts such as group processes and organization. Figure 1-3 overviews the major contributions to the study of organizational behavior.

Psychology

Psychology is the science that seeks to measure, explain, and sometimes change the behavior of humans and other animals. Psychologists concern themselves with studying and attempting to understand individual behavior. Those who have contributed and continue to add to the knowledge of OB are learning theorists, personality theorists, counseling psychologists, and, most important, industrial and organizational psychologists.

Early industrial/organizational psychologists concerned themselves with problems of fatigue, boredom, and other factors relevant to working conditions that could impede efficient work performance. More recently, their contributions have been expanded to include learning, perception, personality, training, leadership effectiveness, needs and motivational forces, job satisfaction, decision-making processes, performance appraisals, attitude measurement, employee selection techniques, job design, and work stress.

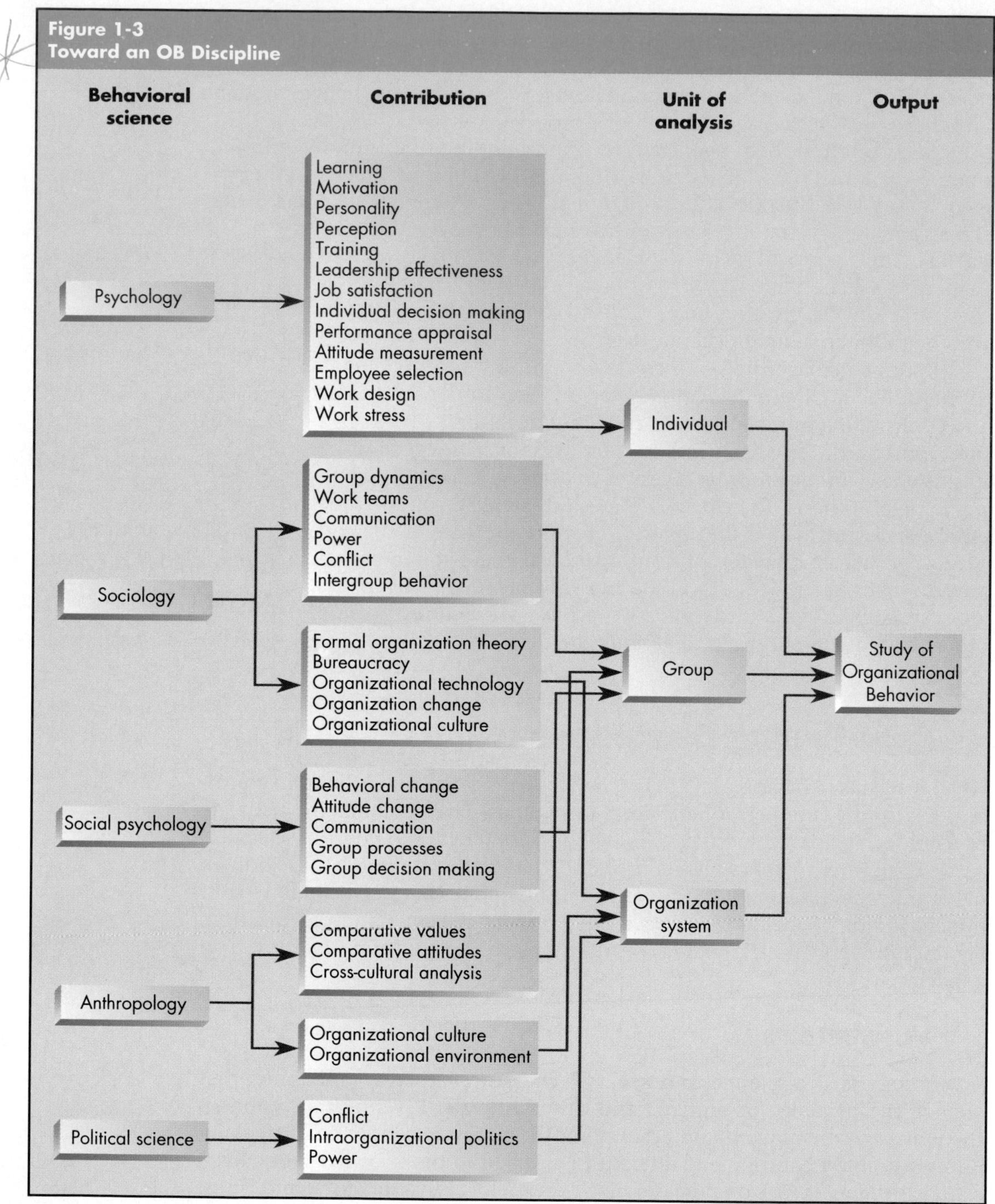

Sociology

Whereas psychologists focus their attention on the individual, sociologists study the social system in which individuals fill their roles; that is, sociology studies people in relation to their fellow human beings. Specifically, sociologists have made their greatest contribution to OB through their study of group behavior in organizations, particularly formal and complex organizations. Some of the areas within OB that have received valuable input from sociologists are group dynamics, design of work teams, organizational culture, formal organization theory and structure, organizational technology, bureaucracy, communications, power, conflict, and intergroup behavior.

Social Psychology

Social psychology is an area within psychology, but blends concepts from both psychology and sociology. It focuses on the influence of people on one another. One of the major areas receiving considerable investigation from social psychologists has been change—how to implement it and how to reduce barriers to its acceptance. Additionally, we find social psychologists making significant contributions in the areas of measuring, understanding, and changing attitudes; communication patterns; the ways in which group activities can satisfy individual needs; and group decision-making processes.

Anthropology

Anthropologists study societies to learn about human beings and their activities. Their work on cultures and environments, for instance, has helped us understand differences in fundamental values, attitudes, and behavior between people in different countries and within different organizations. Much of our current understanding of organizational culture, organizational environments, and differences between national cultures is the result of the work of anthropologists or those using their methodologies.

"I'm a social scientist, Michael. That means I can't explain electricity or anything like that, but if you ever want to know about people I'm your man."

Figure 1-4
Drawing by Handelsman in *The New Yorker*. Copyright © 1986 by The New Yorker Magazine. Reprinted by permission.

Political Science

Although frequently overlooked, the contributions of political scientists are significant to the understanding of behavior in organizations. Political scientists study the behavior of individuals and groups within a political environment. Specific topics of concern here include structuring of conflict, allocation of power, and how people manipulate power for individual self-interest.

Twenty-five years ago, little of what political scientists were studying was of interest to students of organizational behavior. But times have changed. We have become increasingly aware that organizations are political entities; if we are to be able to accurately explain and predict the behavior of people in organizations, we need to bring a political perspective to our analysis.

There Are Few Absolutes in OB

There are few, if any, simple and universal principles that explain organizational behavior. There are laws in the physical sciences—chemistry, astronomy, physics—that are consistent and apply in a wide range of situations. They allow scientists to generalize about the pull of gravity or to confidently send astronauts into space to repair satellites. But as one noted behavioral researcher aptly concluded, "God gave all the easy problems to the physicists." Human beings are very complex. They are not alike, which limits the ability to make simple, accurate, and sweeping generalizations. Two people often act very differently in the same situation, and the same person's behavior changes in different situations. For instance, not everyone is motivated by money, and you behave differently at church on Sunday than you did at the beer party the night before.

> ◆God gave all the easy problems to the physicists.

That doesn't mean, of course, that we can't offer reasonably accurate explanations of human behavior or make valid predictions. It does mean, however, that OB concepts must reflect situational or contingency conditions. We can say that *x* leads to *y*, but only under conditions specified in *z* (the **contingency variables**). The science of OB was developed by using general concepts and then altering their application to the particular situation. So, for example, OB scholars would avoid stating that effective leaders should always seek the ideas of their subordinates before making a decision. Rather, we find that in some situations a participative style is clearly superior, but in other situations, an autocratic decision style is more effective. In other words, the effectiveness of a particular leadership style is contingent on the situation in which it is utilized.

contingency variables
Situational factors; variables that moderate the relationship between the independent and dependent variables and improve the correlation.

As you proceed through this text, you'll encounter a wealth of research-based theories about how people behave in organizations. But don't expect to find a lot of straightforward cause–effect relationships. There aren't many! Organizational behavior theories mirror the subject matter with which they deal. People are complex and complicated, and so too must be the theories developed to explain their actions.

Consistent with the contingency philosophy, you'll find point–counterpoint debates at the conclusion of each chapter. These debates are included to reinforce the fact that within the OB field there are many issues over which there is significant disagreement. By directly addressing some of the more controversial issues using the point–counterpoint format, you get the opportunity to explore different points of view, discover how diverse perspectives complement and oppose each other, and gain insight into some of the debates currently taking place within the OB field.[33]

So at the end of one chapter, you'll find the argument that leadership plays an important role in an organization's attaining its goals, followed by the argument that there is little evidence to support this claim. Similarly, at the end of other chapters, you'll read both sides of the debate on whether money is a motivator, clear communication is always desirable, bureaucracies have become obsolete, and other controversial issues. These arguments are meant to demonstrate that OB, like many disciplines, has disagreements over specific findings, methods, and theories. Some of the point–counterpoint arguments are more provocative than others, but each makes some valid points you should find thought provoking. The key is to be able to decipher under what conditions each argument may be right or wrong.

Coming Attractions: Developing an OB Model

We conclude this chapter by presenting a general model that defines the field of OB, stakes out its parameters, and identifies its primary dependent and independent variables. The end result will be a coming attraction of the topics making up the remainder of this book.

An Overview

A **model** is an abstraction of reality; a simplified representation of some real-world phenomenon. A mannequin in a retail store is a model. So, too, is the accountant's formula: assets = liabilities + owners' equity. Figure 1-6 presents the skeleton on which we will construct our OB model. It proposes three levels of analysis in OB. As we move from the individual level to the organization systems level, we add systematically to our understanding of behavior in organizations. The three basic levels are analogous to building blocks—each level is constructed on the previous level. Group concepts grow out of the foundation laid in the individual section; we overlay structural constraints on the individual and group in order to arrive at organizational behavior.

model
Abstraction of reality; simplified representation of some real-world phenomenon.

The Dependent Variables

Dependent variables are the key factors you want to explain or predict. What are the primary dependent variables in OB? Scholars tend to emphasize

dependent variable
A response that is affected by an independent variable.

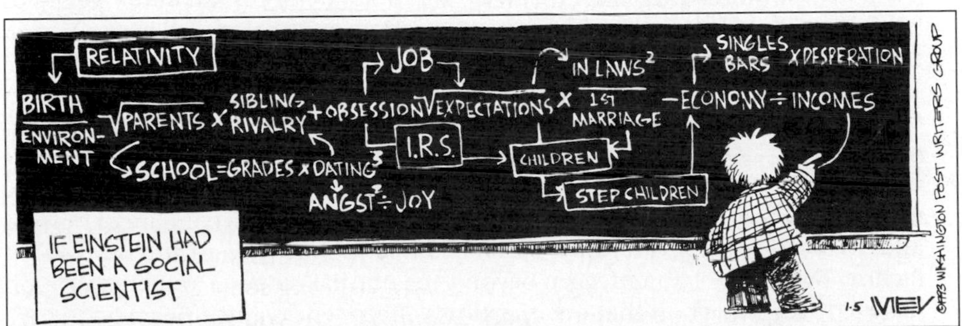

Figure 1-5
"Non-Sequitur" by Wiley in *The Washington Post*, January 5, 1993. Copyright © 1993, Washington Post Writers Group. Reprinted with permission.

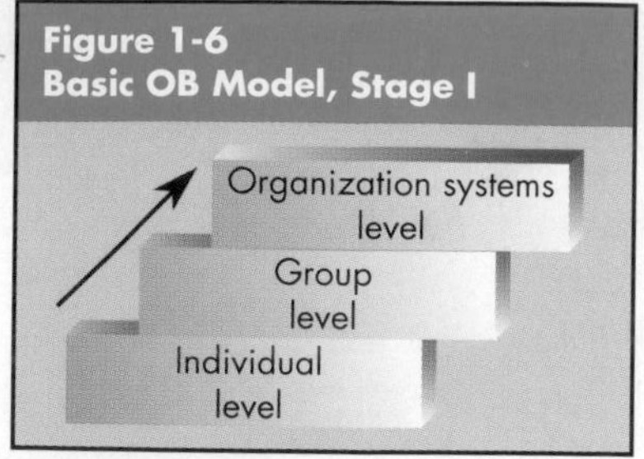

Figure 1-6
Basic OB Model, Stage I

productivity, absenteeism, turnover, and job satisfaction. Because of their wide acceptance, we use these four as the critical determinants of an organization's human resources effectiveness. However, there is nothing magical about these dependent variables. They merely show that OB research has strongly reflected managerial interests over those of individuals or of society as a whole. Let's review these terms to ensure we understand what they mean and why they have achieved the distinction of being OB's primary dependent variables.

productivity
A performance measure including effectiveness and efficiency.

effectiveness
Achievement of goals.

efficiency
The ratio of effective output to the input required to achieve it.

PRODUCTIVITY An organization is productive if it achieves its goals, and does so by transferring inputs to outputs at the lowest cost. As such, **productivity** implies a concern for both **effectiveness** and **efficiency**.

A hospital, for example, is *effective* when it successfully meets the needs of its clientele. It is *efficient* when it can do this at a low cost. If a hospital manages to achieve higher output from its present staff by reducing the average number of days a patient is confined to a bed or by increasing the number of staff–patient contacts per day, we say the hospital has gained productive efficiency. A business firm is effective when it attains its sales or market share goals, but its productivity also depends on achieving these goals efficiently. Measures of such efficiency may include return on investment, profit per dollar of sales, and output per hour of labor.

We can also look at productivity from the perspective of the individual employee. Take the cases of Mike and Al, who are both long-distance truckers. If Mike is supposed to haul his fully loaded rig from New York to its destination in Los Angeles in 75 hours or less, he is effective if he makes the 3,000-mile trip within this time period. But measures of productivity must take into account the costs incurred in reaching the goal. That's where efficiency comes in. Let's assume that Mike made the New York to Los Angeles run in 68 hours and averaged 7 miles per gallon. Al, on the other hand, made the trip in 68 hours also, but averaged 9 miles per gallon (rigs and loads are identical). Both Mike and Al were effective—they accomplished their goal—but Al was more efficient than Mike because his rig consumed less gas and, therefore, he achieved his goal at a lower cost.

In summary, one of OB's major concerns is productivity. We want to know what factors will influence the effectiveness and efficiency of individuals, of groups, and of the overall organization.

absenteeism
Failure to report to work.

ABSENTEEISM The annual cost of **absenteeism** has been estimated at over $40 billion for U.S. organizations and $12 billion for Canadian firms.[34] At the job level, a one-day absence by a clerical worker can cost an employer up to $100 in reduced efficiency and increased supervisory workload.[35] These figures indicate the importance to an organization of keeping absenteeism low.

It is obviously difficult for an organization to operate smoothly and to attain its objectives if employees fail to report to their jobs. The work flow is disrupted, and often important decisions must be delayed. In organizations that rely heavily on assembly-line technology, absenteeism can be considerably more than a disruption—it can result in a drastic reduction in quality of output, and, in some cases, it can bring about a complete shutdown of the production facility. But levels of absenteeism beyond the normal range in any organization have a direct impact on that organization's effectiveness and efficiency.

Are *all* absences bad? Probably not! While most absences impact negatively on the organization, we can conceive of situations where the organization may benefit by an employee voluntarily choosing not to come to work.

For instance, fatigue or excess stress can significantly decrease an employee's productivity. In jobs where an employee needs to be alert—surgeons and airline pilots are obvious examples—it may well be better for the organization if the employee does not report to work rather than show up and perform poorly. The cost of an accident in such jobs could be prohibitive. Even in managerial jobs, where mistakes are less spectacular, performance may be improved when managers absent themselves from work rather than make a poor decision under stress. But these examples are clearly atypical. For the most part, we can assume that organizations benefit when employee absenteeism is reduced.

TURNOVER A high rate of **turnover** in an organization means increased recruiting, selection, and training costs. How high are those costs? A conservative estimate would be about $15,000 per employee.[36] It can also mean a disruption in the efficient running of an organization when knowledgeable and experienced personnel leave and replacements must be found and prepared to assume positions of responsibility. All organizations, of course, have some turnover. If the right people are leaving the organization—the marginal and submarginal employees—turnover can be positive. It may create the opportunity to replace an underperforming individual with someone with higher skills or motivation, open up increased opportunities for promotions, and add new and fresh ideas to the organization.[37] But turnover often means the loss of people the organization doesn't want to lose. For instance, one study covering 900 employees who had resigned their jobs found that 92 percent earned performance ratings of "satisfactory" or better from their superiors.[38] So when turnover is excessive, or when it involves valuable performers, it can be a disruptive factor, hindering the organization's effectiveness.

turnover
Voluntary and involuntary permanent withdrawal from the organization.

JOB SATISFACTION The final dependent variable we will look at is **job satisfaction**, which we define simply, at this point, as the difference between the amount of rewards workers receive and the amount they believe they should receive. (We expand considerably on this definition in Chapter 5.) Unlike the previous three variables, job satisfaction represents an attitude rather than a behavior. Why, then, has it become a primary

job satisfaction
A general attitude toward one's job; the difference between the amount of rewards workers receive and the amount they believe they should receive.

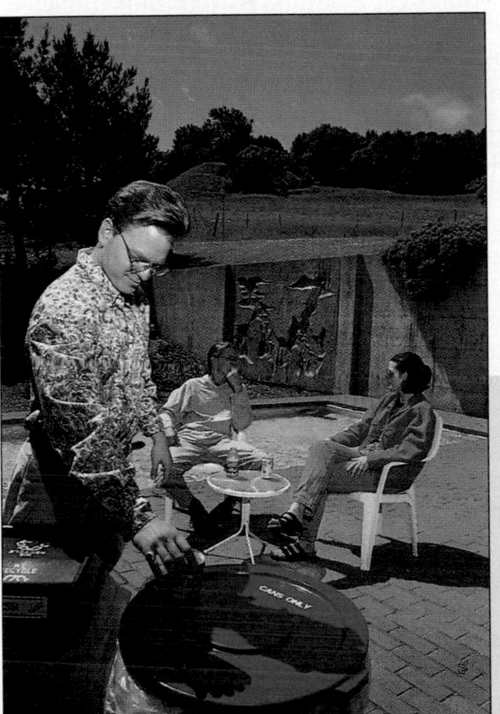

Job satisfaction is a top objective at Birkenstock Footwear Sandals. When employees wanted the company to become more environmentally conscious, Birkenstock allowed a group of them to spend an hour each week working on environmental projects. These included developing an in-house environmental library, compiling a guide to nontoxic resources, and organizing monthly meetings with other businesses to share ideas on conservation products and issues. By giving employees the chance to participate in causes they believe in, Birkenstock has created a motivated and loyal work force that rates high on job satisfaction and productivity and low on turnover.

dependent variable? For two reasons: its demonstrated relationship to performance factors and the value preferences held by many OB researchers.

The belief that satisfied employees are more productive than dissatisfied employees has been a basic tenet among managers for years. While much evidence questions this assumed causal relationship, it can be argued that advanced societies should be concerned not only with the quantity of life—that is, concerns such as higher productivity and material acquisitions—but also with its quality. Those researchers with strong humanistic values argue that satisfaction is a legitimate objective of an organization. Not only is satisfaction negatively related to absenteeism and turnover, but, they argue, organizations have a responsibility to provide employees with jobs that are challenging and intrinsically rewarding. Therefore, although job satisfaction represents an attitude rather than a behavior, OB researchers typically consider it an important dependent variable.

The Independent Variables

independent variable
The presumed cause of some change in the dependent variable.

What are the major determinants of productivity, absenteeism, turnover, and job satisfaction? Our answer to that question brings us to the **independent variables**. Consistent with our belief that organizational behavior can best be understood when viewed essentially as a set of increasingly complex building blocks, the base or first level of our model lies in understanding individual behavior.

INDIVIDUAL-LEVEL VARIABLES It has been said that "Managers, unlike parents, must work with used, not new, human beings—human beings whom others have gotten to first."[39] When individuals enter an organization, they're a bit like used cars. Each is different. Some are "low mileage"—they have been treated carefully and have had only limited exposure to the realities of the elements. Others are "well worn," having experienced a number of rough roads. This metaphor indicates that people enter organizations with certain characteristics that will influence their behavior at work. The more obvious of these are personal or biographical characteristics such as age, gender, and marital status; personality characteristics; values and attitudes; and basic ability levels. These characteristics are essentially intact when an individual enters the work force, and, for the most part, management can do little to alter them. Yet they have a very real impact on employee behavior. Therefore, each of these factors—biographical characteristics, personality, values and attitudes, and ability—are discussed as independent variables in Chapters 3 and 5.

Four other individual-level variables have been shown to affect employee behavior: perception, individual decision making, learning, and motivation. These topics are introduced and discussed in Chapters 3, 4, 6, and 7.

GROUP-LEVEL VARIABLES The behavior of people in groups is more than the sum total of each individual acting in his or her own way. The complexity of our model is increased when we acknowledge that people's behavior when they are in groups is different from their behavior when they are alone. Therefore, the next step in the development of an understanding of OB is the study of group behavior.

Chapter 8 lays the foundation for an understanding of the dynamics of group behavior. This chapter discusses how individuals in groups are influenced by the patterns of behavior they are expected to exhibit, what the group considers to be acceptable standards of behavior, and the degree to which group members are attracted to each other. Chapter 9 translates our under-

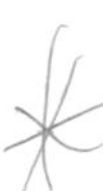

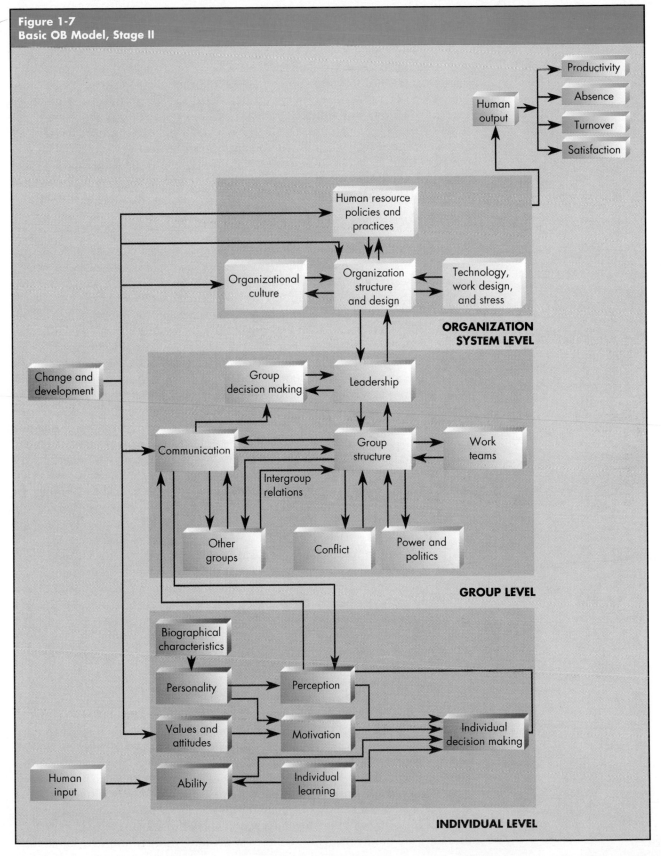

Figure 1-7
Basic OB Model, Stage II

standing of groups to the design of effective work teams. Chapters 10 through 13 demonstrate how communication patterns, leadership styles, power and politics, intergroup relations, and levels of conflict affect group behavior.

ORGANIZATION SYSTEM-LEVEL VARIABLES Organizational behavior reaches its highest level of sophistication when we add formal structure to our previous knowledge of individual and group behavior. Just as groups are more than the sum of their individual members, so are organizations more than the sum of their member groups. The design of the formal organization, technology and work processes, and jobs; the organization's human resource policies and practices (that is, selection processes, training programs, performance appraisal methods); the internal culture; and levels of work stress all have an impact on the dependent variables. These are discussed in detail in Chapters 14 through 17.

Toward a Contingency OB Model

Our final model is shown in Figure 1-7. It shows the four key dependent variables and a large number of independent variables, organized by level of analysis, that research indicates have varying impacts on the former. As complicated as this model is, it still does not do justice to the complexity of the OB subject matter, but it should help explain why the chapters in this book are arranged as they are and help you explain and predict the behavior of people at work.

For the most part, our model does not explicitly identify the vast number of contingency variables because of the tremendous complexity that would be involved in such a diagram. Rather, throughout this text we introduce important contingency variables that will improve the explanatory linkage between the independent and dependent variables in our OB model.

Note that we've added the concepts of change and development to Figure 1-7, acknowledging the dynamics of behavior and recognizing that there are ways for change agents or managers to modify many of the independent variables if they are having a negative impact on the key dependent variables. Specifically, in Chapter 18 we discuss the change process and techniques for changing employee attitudes, improving communication processes, modifying organization structures, and the like.

Also note that Figure 1-7 includes linkages between the three levels of analysis. For instance, organization structure is linked to leadership. This is meant to convey that authority and leadership are related—management exerts its influence on group behavior through leadership. Similarly, communication is the means by which individuals transmit information; thus, it is the link between individual and group behavior.

Summary and Implications for Managers

Managers need to develop their interpersonal or people skills if they're going to be effective in their job. Organizational behavior (OB) is a field of study that investigates the impact which individuals, groups, and structure have on behavior within organizations, then applies that knowledge to make organizations work more effectively. Specifically, OB focuses on how to improve productivity, reduce absenteeism and turnover, and increase employee job satisfaction.

We all hold a number of generalizations about the behavior of people. While some of these generalizations provide valid insights into human behavior, many are often erroneous. OB uses systematic study to improve behavioral predictions that would be made from intuition alone. But because people are different, we need to look at OB in a contingency framework, using situational variables to moderate cause-effect relationships.

Organizational behavior offers a number of challenges and opportunities for managers. It can help improve quality and employee productivity by showing managers how to empower their people as well as design and implement change programs. It offers specific insights to improve a manager's people skills. OB recognizes differences and helps managers see the value of work force diversity and practices that may need to be made when managing in different countries. In times of rapid and ongoing change, OB can help managers learn to cope in a world of "temporariness" and declining employee loyalty. Finally, OB can offer managers guidance in creating an ethically healthy work climate.

For Review

1. "Behavior generally is predictable." Do you agree or disagree? Explain.
2. Define *organizational behavior.* How does this compare with *management*?
3. What is an *organization*? Is the family unit an organization? Explain.
4. Identify and contrast the three general management roles.
5. What is *TQM*? How is it related to OB?
6. In what areas has psychology contributed to OB? Sociology? Social psychology? Anthropology? Political science? What other academic disciplines may have contributed to OB?
7. "Since behavior is generally predictable, there is no need to formally study OB." Why is this statement wrong?
8. What are the three levels of analysis in our OB model? Are they related? If so, how?
9. If job satisfaction is not a behavior, why is it considered an important dependent variable?
10. What are *effectiveness* and *efficiency*, and how are they related to organizational behavior?

For Discussion

1. Contrast the research comparing effective managers with successful managers. What are the implications from this research for practicing managers?
2. "The best way to view OB is through a contingency approach." Build an argument to support this statement.
3. Why do you think the subject of OB might be criticized as being "only common sense," when one would rarely hear such a criticism of a course in physics or statistics?
4. An increasing number of managers are now acknowledging that an understanding of OB may be more important than any other business discipline in contributing to an organization's overall success or failure. But few managers were saying this 20 years ago. What's changed?
5. On a scale of 1 to 10 that measures the sophistication of a scientific discipline in predicting phenomena, mathematical physics would probably be a 10. Where do you think OB would fall on this scale? Why?

Point

The Case for a Structural Explanation of Organizational Behavior

If you want to really understand the behavior of people at work, you need to focus on social structure. Why? As one noted scholar put it, "The fundamental fact of social life is precisely that it is social—that human beings do not live in isolation but associate with other human beings."*

Far too much emphasis is placed on studying individual characteristics of people. We're not saying here that values, attitudes, personalities, and similar personal characteristics are irrelevant to understanding organizational behavior. Rather, our position is that you gain considerably more insight if you look at the structured relationships between individuals in organizations and how these relationships constrain and enable certain actions to occur.

Organizations come with a host of formal and informal control mechanisms that, in effect, largely shape, direct, and constrain members' behavior. Let's look at a few examples.

Almost all organizations have formal documentation that limits and shapes behavior like policies, procedures, rules, job descriptions, and job instructions. This formal documentation sets standards of acceptable and unacceptable behavior. If you know an organization's major policies and have a copy of a specific employee's job description, you have a major leg up in being able to predict a good deal of that specific employee's on-the-job behavior.

Almost all organizations differentiate roles horizontally. By that I mean they create unique jobs and departments. Toni is a sales representative for H.J. Heinz, calling on supermarkets. Frank also works for Heinz, but on an assembly line where he monitors machines that fill pickle relish jars. The structure of these jobs alone allow me to predict that Toni will have a great deal more autonomy in deciding what she is going to do in her job and how she is going to do it than Frank does.

Organizations also differentiate roles vertically by creating levels of management. In so doing, they create boss-subordinate relationships that constrain subordinate behavior. In our nonwork lives we don't have bosses who can tell us what to do, evaluate us, and even fire us. But most of us do at work. And remember, bosses evaluate employee performance and typically control the allocation of rewards. So if I know what behaviors your boss prefers, I can gain insight into what behaviors you're more likely to exhibit.

When you join an organization, you're expected to adapt to its norms of acceptable behavior. These rules don't have to be written down to be powerful and controlling. An organization, for instance, may not have a formal dress code but employees are expected to "dress appropriately," which means adapting to the implied dress code norms. Merrill Lynch expects its brokers to dress appropriately: Men wear coats and ties and women wear similarly professional attire. Along the same lines, Microsoft's norms emphasize long work hours—60- to 70-hour workweeks are not unusual. These expectations are understood by employees, and employees modify their behavior accordingly.

The point we're trying to make here is that you shouldn't forget the *organizational* part of organizational behavior. While it doesn't sound very nice, organizations are instruments of domination. They put people into job "boxes" that constrain what they can do and individuals with whom they can interact. To the degree that employees accept their boss's authority and the limits the organization places on their role, then they become constraints that limit the behavioral choices of organization members.

*P.M. Blau, *Inequality and Heterogeneity* (New York: Free Press, 1977), p. 1.

Some points in this argument are based on J. Pfeffer, "Organization Theory and Structural Perspectives on Management," *Journal of Management* (December 1991), pp. 789–803.

counterPoint

The Case for a Psychological Explanation of Organizational Behavior

The concept of an "organization" is an artificial notion. Organizations have physical properties like buildings, offices, and equipment, but this tends to gloss over the obvious fact that organizations are really nothing other than aggregates of individuals. As such, organizational actions are just the combined actions of individuals. In this section, we argue that much of organizational behavior can be viewed as the collection of efforts by a set of quasi-independent actors.

Let me begin by acknowledging that organizations place constraints on employee behavior. However, in spite of these constraints, every job possesses a degree of discretion—areas where rules, procedures, job descriptions, supervisory directives, and other formal constraints do not apply. Generally speaking, the higher one moves in the organization, the more discretion he or she has. Lower level jobs tend to be more programmed than middle management jobs; and middle-managers have less discretion than do senior managers. But *every job* comes with some autonomy. And it is this autonomy that allows different people to do different things in the same job.

Casual observation leads all of us to the obvious conclusion that no two people in the same job behave in exactly the same way. Even in highly programmed jobs, like assembly-line work in an automobile factory or processing claims in an insurance company, employee behavior varies. Why? Individual differences! College students certainly understand and act on this reality when they choose classes. If three instructors are all teaching Accounting 101 at the same time of day, most students will question their friends to find out the differences among the instructors. Even though they teach the same course as described in the college catalog, the instructors enjoy a considerable degree of freedom in how they meet their course objectives. Students know this and they try to acquire accurate information that will allow them to select among the three. So in spite of the fact that the instructors are teaching the same course and the content of that course is explicitly defined in the organization's formal documentation (the college catalog), the students (and all the rest of us) know that the behavior of the three instructors will undoubtedly vary widely.

People go about doing their jobs in different ways. They differ in their interactions with their bosses and coworkers. They vary in terms of work habits—promptness in completing tasks, conscientiousness in doing quality work, cooperation with coworkers, ability to handle stressful situations, and the like. They vary by level of motivation and the degree of effort they're willing to exert on their job. They vary in terms of the creativity they display in doing their work. And they vary in terms of the importance they place on factors such as security, recognition, advancement, social support, challenging work assignments, and willingness to work overtime. What explains these variations? Individual psychological characteristics like values, attitudes, perceptions, motives, and personalities.

The end result is that, in the quest to understand employee productivity, absenteeism, turnover, and satisfaction, you have to recognize the overwhelming influence that individual psychological factors play.

Some points in this argument are based on B.M. Staw, "Dressing Up Like an Organization: When Psychological Actions can Explain Organizational Action," *Journal of Management* (December 1991), pp. 805–19.

Learning About Yourself Exercise

How Does Your Ethical Behavior Rate?*

Below are 15 statements. Identify the frequency of which you do, have done, or would do these things in the future when employed full time. Place the letter R, O, S, or N on the line before each statement.

R = Regularly; O = Occasionally; S = Seldom; N = Never

___ **1.** I come to work late and get paid for it.
___ **2.** I leave work early and get paid for it.
___ **3.** I take long breaks/lunches and get paid for it.
___ **4.** I call in sick to get a day off when I'm not sick.
___ **5.** I use the company phone to make personal long-distance calls.
___ **6.** I do personal work on company time.
___ **7.** I use the company copier for personal use.
___ **8.** I mail personal things through the company mail.
___ **9.** I take home company supplies or merchandise.
___ **10.** I give company supplies or merchandise to friends, or allow friends to take them without saying anything.
___ **11.** I put in for reimbursement for meals, travel, or other expenses I did not actually eat or make.
___ **12.** I use the company car for personal business.
___ **13.** I take my spouse/friend out to eat and charge it to the company expense account.
___ **14.** I take my spouse/friend on business trips and charge the expense to the company.
___ **15.** I accept gifts from customers/suppliers in exchange for giving them business.

Turn to page A-26 for scoring directions and key.

*Source: R.N. Lussier, *Human Relations in Organizations: A Skill Building Approach*, 2nd ed. (Homewood, IL: Irwin, 1993), p. 297.

Working With Others Exercise

Work Force Diversity Exercise*

Purpose To learn about the different needs of a diverse work force.

Time Required Approximately 40 minutes.

Participants and Roles Divide the class into six groups of approximately equal size. Each group is assigned one of the following roles:

Nancy is 28 years old. She is a divorced mother of three children, aged 3, 5, and 7. She is the department head. She earns $33,000 a year on her job and receives another $3,600 a year in child support from her ex-husband.

Ethel is a 72-year-old widow. She works 25 hours a week to supplement her $7,000-a-year pension. Based on her hourly wage of $7.50, she earns $9,375 a year.

John is a 34-year-old black male born in Trinidad, but now a U.S. resident. He is married and the father of two small children. John attends college at night and is within a year of earning his bachelor's degree. His salary is $22,000 a year. His wife is an attorney and earns approximately $40,000 a year.

Lu is a 26-year-old physically impaired male Asian-American. He is single and has a master's degree in education. Lu is paralyzed and confined to a wheelchair as a result of an auto accident. He earns $27,000 a year.

Maria is a single 22-year-old Hispanic. Born and raised in Mexico, she came to the United States only three months ago. Maria's English needs considerable improvement. She earns $17,000 a year.

Mike is a 16-year-old white male high school sophomore who works 15 hours a week after school. He earns $6.25 an hour, or approximately $4,700 a year.

The members of each group are to assume the character consistent with their assigned role.

Background Our six participants work for a company that has recently installed a flexible benefits program. Instead of the traditional "one benefit package fits all," the company is allocating an additional 25 percent of each employee's annual pay to be used for discretionary benefits. Those benefits and their annual cost are as follows.

Supplementary health care for employee:

Plan A (No deductible and pays 90 percent) = $3,000
Plan B ($200 deductible and pays 80 percent) = $2,000
Plan C ($1,000 deductible and pays 70 percent) = $500

Supplementary health care for dependents (same deductibles and percentages as above):

Plan A = $2,000
Plan B = $1,500
Plan C = $500

Supplementary dental plan = $500

Life insurance:

Plan A ($25,000 coverage) = $500
Plan B ($50,000 coverage) = $1,000
Plan C ($100,000 coverage) = $2,000
Plan D ($250,000 coverage) = $3,000

Mental health plan = $500
Prepaid legal assistance = $300

Vacation = 2 percent of annual pay for each week, up to 6 weeks a year

Pension at retirement equal to approximately 50% of final annual earnings = $1,500

4-day workweek during the three summer months (available only to full-time employees) = 4 percent of annual pay

Day-care services (after company contribution) = $2,000 for all of an employee's children

Company-provided transportation to and from work = $750

College tuition reimbursement = $1,000

Language class tuition reimbursement = $500

The Task

1. Each group has 15 minutes to develop a flexible benefits package that consumes 25 percent (and no more!) of their character's pay.
2. After completing step 1, each group appoints a spokesperson who describes to the entire class the benefits package they have arrived at for their character.
3. The entire class then discusses the results. How have the needs, concerns, and problems of each participant influenced his or her decision? What do these results suggest for trying to motivate a diverse work force?

*Special thanks to Professor Penny Wright for her suggestions during the development of this exercise.

Ethical Dilemma Exercise

Can a Business Firm Be Too Ethical?

"A couple of years ago, we were competing on a government contract," recalls Norman Augustine," CEO of Martin Marietta Corp. "The low bid would win. Two days before we were to submit the bid, we got a brown paper bag with our competitor's bid in it." Managers didn't think twice about what they should do. They turned the price sheet over to the U.S. government and informed its competitor about what had happened. Consistent with what management perceived as good ethical practices, the company did not change its bid. And what was the result? Martin Marietta lost the contract, some of its employees lost their jobs, and company stockholders lost money. Is it possible that Martin Marietta's management was *too* ethical?

What happens to a company in a highly competitive industry where hardball practices are the norm? If it behaves too nobly, might it consistently lose out to its more aggressive competitors? Or what about companies that spend heavily to achieve safety or environmental standards that are above what the law mandates? Doesn't that lower company profits?

One school of thought is that the subject of ethics deals with principles—standards of right or wrong. So it's not possible to be too ethical. How can you have too much principle? While high ethical standards might hurt a company's performance in the short term, it will pay dividends over the long haul.

Companies with high principles—such as Johnson & Johnson, Merck, Hallmark Cards, Delta Airlines, PepsiCo—develop positive public images that result in long-term profits.

The counterargument is that there can be too much of a good thing. For example, studies that have sought to link corporate social responsibility and profits have found a curvilinear relationship. Profitability rises as one moves from companies that exhibit little or no social responsibility to those that demonstrate a moderate degree. But profitability falls off for the most socially responsible firms. Just as management can spend too much money on advertising, on computers, or on research and development, it can also overspend on social responsibility. Control Data Corp. represents an illustration. Control Data built factories in riot-torn inner cities in the late 1960s and 1970s. It hired minority men and women with little formal education and few qualifications and allowed them to rise through the ranks and become managers. But the onslaught of Japanese competition in the mid-1980s led to huge losses. Some argue that Control Data's management dedicated too much of its time and energy, and the company's resources, to doing good. And its traditional business suffered.

What do *you* think? Can a business firm be *too* ethical?

Source: Based on A.W. Singer, "Can a Company Be Too Ethical?" *Across the Board* (April 1993), pp. 17–22.

Rosenbluth International Travel, Inc.

CASE INCIDENT

Rosenbluth International Travel, Inc., isn't like your typical travel agency. First of all, it's huge. It employs 3,000 people in 582 offices in the United States, England, and Asia. You probably never heard of them because 96 percent of their business comes from some 1,500 corporate clients like Du Pont, Merck, Chevron, Eastman Kodak, Scott Paper, and General Electric. The company has experienced explosive growth: In the late 1970s, it was a local Philadelphia travel agency with sales of $20 million. Sales in 1992 hit $1.5 billion. What explains the company's success? Its president and chief executive

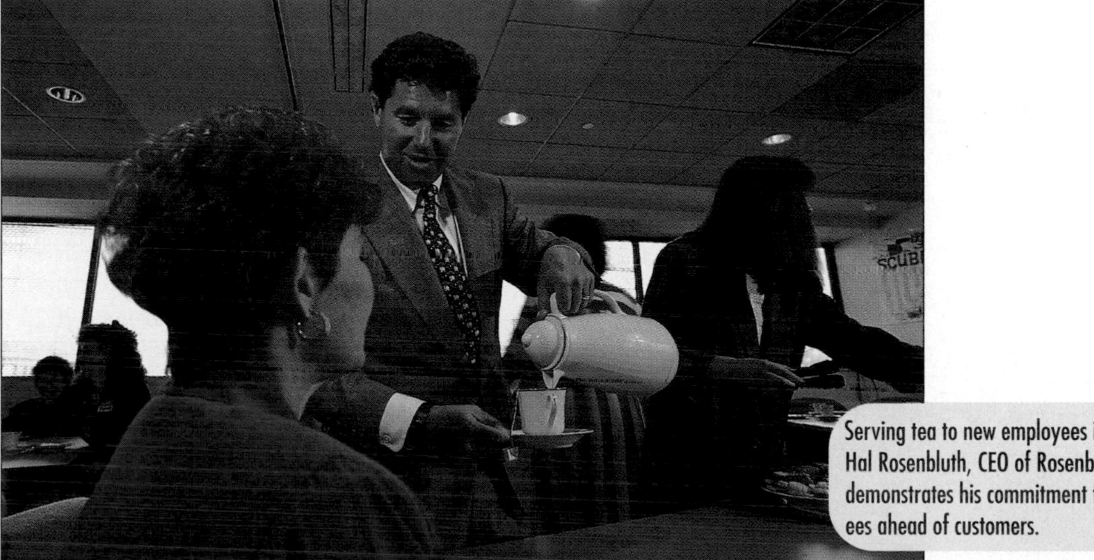

Serving tea to new employees is one way that Hal Rosenbluth, CEO of Rosenbluth International, demonstrates his commitment to putting employees ahead of customers.

officer, Hal F. Rosenbluth, says it's the company's commitment to service achieved by putting its employees ahead of its customers. Yes, you read right. When was the last time you heard of a company putting its people before the customer? According to Rosenbluth, "When people are worried about typical workplace obstacles like fear, frustration, and bureaucracy, they can't focus on the customer. They must worry about themselves. Only when people know what it feels like to be first in the eyes of their employer can they impart the same feeling to their customers."

Rosenbluth believes he has a responsibility to make work a pleasant and happy experience, so he has things like the Happiness Barometer Group. This is made up of 18 employees, randomly selected from various offices, who provide feedback on how people are feeling about their jobs. Surveys are also sent to all employees twice a year to measure their degree of happiness with their jobs. Results from these surveys are tallied and shared with everyone in the company. The travel business, according to Rosenbluth, is stressful: "It's like being an air traffic controller, one call after another." As a result, turnover in the industry tends to be high—sometimes up to 45 or 50 percent a year. Yet Rosenbluth's turnover is only 6 percent. His hiring and training programs help explain why.

Job candidates are carefully screened to find people who will fit into the agency. Rosenbluth wants team players and people with an upbeat attitude. According to Rosenbluth, "Companies can all buy the same machines and tools. It's people who apply them creatively. In the end, people are the one true competitive advantage a company can have, so it's crucial to find the right people. . . . We look for nice people; everything else can be taught. You can't tell someone, 'Thursday, begin caring.' In our selection process, we let kindness, compassion, and enthusiam carry more weight than years on the job, salary history, and other traditional resume fare." Entry-level candidates undergo three to four hours of interviewing. For senior positions, Rosenbluth personally gets to know each applicant. For instance, he invited a sales executive candidate and his wife to go on a vacation with Rosenbluth and his wife. "On the third day of a vacation, things start to come out."

Once hired, the new employee becomes acclimated to the agency very quickly. Instead of filling out forms on the first day, the new employee takes a role in skits meant to convey that Rosenbluth wants his people to laugh and have fun. But the skits are also learning experiences. New employees may be asked to play out an experience they've had with negative service, for example. Then the experience is analyzed to learn how the episode could be turned into great service. All new employees go through two to eight weeks of training, partly to allow managers to assess whether they will fit into Rosenbluth's high-energy team-focused environment. People who need the individual limelight are released.

One of Rosenbluth's more unusual qualities is putting the employee ahead of the customer. On rare occasions, he has even gone so far as to help a corporate client find another travel agency. He notes that usually these are firms that mistreat their own people, so they mistreat his employees on the phone. "I think it's terrible to ask one of our [employees] to talk with someone who's rude to them every fifteen minutes."

Source: Based on "Many Happy Returns," *INC.*, (October 1990), pp. 31–44; "First Impressions," *INC.*, (December 1991), p. 157; "A People-First Philosophy in Action," *At Work* (January-February 1993), pp. 13–14; and R. Levering and M. Moskowitz, "The Ten Best Companies to Work for in America," *Business and Society Review* (Spring 1993), pp. 35–36.

Questions

1. Would you want to work for Rosenbluth International Travel? Why or why not?
2. If Rosenbluth's approach to managing people is so effective, why do so many organizations try hard to create a serious work climate?
3. Do you think happy workers are more productive?

The Workplace of the 1990s

An increasing number of Americans see themselves as overworked, underpaid, and just fed up with the way their employers are treating them. They're having to work longer hours for less pay. And the job security they enjoyed just 10 or 15 years ago seems like a distant memory. The workplace that used to be "one big happy family" is now the scene of stressed-out workers who fear for their jobs. As a case in point, IBM, which had a "no-layoff" policy through the late 1980s, has since discarded that policy and laid off hundreds of thousands of its employees.

In order to cut costs and improve productivity, most major corporations have instituted massive layoffs—on a magnitude not seen since the Great Depression of the 1930s. One in five employees today fears losing his or her job.

To improve competitiveness, firms are asking those employees who survive the layoffs to work longer hours and often for less pay than they made previously. The result is a work force that is tired and burned out. A recent poll of workers found that 80 percent of those surveyed described their employers as requiring them to work "very hard"; 65 percent had to work "very fast"; and 42 percent complained of being "used up" by the end of the workday.

To add insult to injury, employers are also increasingly replacing laid off workers with part-time employees because the latter gives management more flexibility and often cost a lot less. Today, one out of every four workers is temporary.

Layoffs, pressures for higher productivity, and replacement of permanent workers with temporaries are undermining employee loyalty. For instance, only one of four employees today say they're committed to their organization. As employers have demonstrated by their actions that employees are expendable, employees are responding with a dramatic decline in loyalty to those employers.

The new workplace climate is highly threatening to people. When employees are asked what's important to them, factors like a better work environment, flexible jobs, and understanding bosses are near the top of the list. But it is just these factors that are being undermined in many organizations as management tries to increase productivity.

Questions

1. Compare the competitive environment facing major corporations in the 1960s with that environment in the 1990s.
2. Contrast how these changes in the environment are affecting employees.
3. Is it possible for large companies to be competitive and, at the same time, create a workplace that provides employee security? High employee loyalty?

Source: "American Workers Trying to Survive in the '90s," *Nightline* (September 6, 1993).

Suggestions for Further Reading

BRIEF, A.P., and J.M. DUKERICH, "Theory in Organizational Behavior: Can It Be Useful?" in L.L. Cummings and B.M. Staw (eds.), *Research in Organizational Behavior*, Vol. 13 (Greenwich, CT: JAI Press, 1991), pp. 327–52.

COATES, J.F., J. JARRAT, and J.B. MAHAFFIE, *Future Work* (San Francisco: Jossey–Bass, 1990).

MARTOCCHIO, J.J., "The Financial Cost of Absence Decisions," *Journal of Management* (March 1992), pp. 133–52.

O'REILLY, C.A., III, "Organizational Behavior: Where We've Been, Where We're Going," in M.R. Rosenzweig and L.W. Porter (eds.), *Annual Review of Psychology*, Vol. 42 (Palo Alto, CA: Annual Reviews, 1991), pp. 427–58.

PETERS, T., *Liberation Management* (New York: Knopf, 1992).

PETTIT, J.D., JR., B.C. VAUGHT, and R.L. TREWATHA, "Interpersonal Skill Training: A Prerequisite for Success," *Business* (April–June 1990), pp. 8–14.

PFEFFER, J., *Competitive Advantage Through People: Unleashing the Power of the Work Force* (Boston: Harvard Business School Press, 1994).

PIPER, T.R., M.C. GENTILE, and S.D. PARKS, *Can Ethics Be Taught?* (Boston: Harvard Business School Press, 1993).

PRITCHARD, R.D., "Organizational Productivity," in M.D. Dunnette and L.M. Hough (eds.), *Handbook of Industrial & Organizational Psychology*, 2nd ed., Vol. 3 (Palo Alto, CA: Consulting Psychologists Press, 1992), pp. 443–71.

SIMS, R.R., "The Challenge of Ethical Behavior in Organizations," *Journal of Business Ethics*, (July 1992), pp. 505–13.

Notes

1 D. Milbank, "Managers Are Sent to 'Charm Schools' to Discover How to Polish Up Their Acts," *Wall Street Journal* (December 14, 1990), p. B1.

2 S. Sherman, "Are You as Good as the Best in the World?" *Fortune* (December 13, 1993), p. 96.

3 M. Rothman, "Into the Black," *INC.* (January 1993), p. 59.

4 C. Hymowitz, "Five Main Reasons Why Managers Fail," *Wall Street Journal* (May 2, 1988), p. 25.

5 Milbank, "Managers Are Sent to 'Charm Schools' to Discover How to Polish Up Their Acts."

6 S.A. Waddock, "Educating Tomorrow's Managers," *Journal of Management Education* (February 1991), pp. 69–96; and K.F. Kane, "MBAs: A Recruiter's-Eye View," *Business Horizons* (January-February 1993), pp. 65–71.

7 H. Fayol, *Industrial and General Administration* (Paris: Dunod, 1916).

8 H. Mintzberg, *The Nature of Managerial Work* (New York: Harper & Row, 1973).

9 R.L. Katz, "Skills of an Effective Administrator," *Harvard Business Review* (September-October 1974), pp. 90–102.

10 F. Luthans, "Successful vs. Effective Real Managers," *Academy of Management Executive* (May 1988), pp. 127–32; and F. Luthans, R.M. Hodgetts, and S.A. Rosenkrantz, *Real Managers* (Cambridge, MA: Ballinger, 1988).

11 See, for instance, J.E. Garcia and K.S. Keleman, "What Is Organizational Behavior Anyhow?" paper presented at the Organizational Behavior Teaching Conference, Columbia, MO, June 1989.

12 See, for instance, A. Kohn, "You Know What They Say . . ." *Psychology Today* (April 1988), pp. 36–41.

13 E.E. Lawler III and J.G. Rhode, *Information and Control in Organizations* (Pacific Palisades, CA: Goodyear, 1976), p. 22.

14 R. Weinberg and W. Nord, "Coping with 'It's All Common Sense,'" *Exchange*, Vol. VII, No. 2 (1982), pp. 29–33; R.P. Vecchio, "Some Popular (But Misguided) Criticisms of the Organizational Sciences," *Organizational Behavior Teaching Review*, Vol. 10, No. 1 (1986–87), pp. 28–34; and M.L. Lynn, "Organizational Behavior and Common Sense: Philosophical Implications for Teaching and Thinking," paper presented at the 14th Annual Organizational Behavior Teaching Conference, Waltham, MA, May 1987.

15 J.S. McClenahen, "The Edge of Light,"*Industry Week* (January 3, 1994), p. 11.

16 See, for instance, M. Sashkin and K.J. Kiser, *Putting Total Quality Management to Work* (San Francisco: Berrett-Koehler, 1993).

17 M. Hammer and J. Champy, *Reengineering the Corporation: A Manifesto for Business Revolution* (New York: HarperBusiness, 1993).

18 See, for instance, R.R. Thomas, Jr., "From Affirmative Action to Affirming Diversity," *Harvard Business Review* (March-April 1990), pp. 107–17; B. Mandrell and S. Kohler-Gray, "Management Development That Values Diversity," *Personnel* (March 1990), pp. 41–47; J. Dreyfuss, "Get Ready for the New Work Force," *Fortune* (April 23, 1990), pp. 165–81; and I. Wielawski, "Diversity Makes Both Dollars and Sense," *Los Angeles Times* (May 16, 1994), p. II-3.

19 See S. Pedigo, "Diversity in the Workforce: Riding the Tide of Change," *The Wyatt Communicator* (Winter 1991), pp. 4–11.

20 Dreyfuss, "Get Ready for the New Work Force," p. 168.

21 See, for instance, P.L. McLeod and S.A. Lobel, "The Effects of Ethnic Diversity on Idea Generation in Small Groups," paper presented at the Annual Academy of Management Conference, Las Vegas, August 1992.

[22] B. Dumaine, "The New Non-Manager Managers," *Fortune* (February 22, 1993), pp. 80–84.

[23] J. Weber, "No Bosses. And Even 'Leaders' Can't Give Orders," *Business Week* (December 10, 1990), pp. 196–97.

[24] M. Sashkin, "Participative Management Is an Ethical Imperative," *Organizational Dynamics* (Spring 1984), pp. 5–22.

[25] J. Hillkirk, "Self-Directed Work Teams Give TI Lift," *USA Today* (December 20, 1993), p. 8B.

[26] M. Kaeter, "The Age of the Specialized Generalist," *Training* (December 1993), pp. 48–53; and N. Templin, "Auto Plants, Hiring Again, Are Demanding Higher-Skilled Labor," *Wall Street Journal* (March 11, 1994), p. A1.

[27] See, for example, C. Ansberry, "Workers Are Forced to Take More Jobs with Few Benefits," *Wall Street Journal* (March 11, 1993), p. A1; D. Lamb, "Portrait of the Recession: Disposable Workers, Jobs," *Los Angeles Times* (May 15, 1993), p. 1; M. Calabresi, J. Van Tassel, M. Riley, and J.R. Szczesny, "Jobs in an Age of Insecurity," *Time* (November 22, 1993), pp. 32–39; and B. Geber, "The Flexible Work Force," *Training* (December 1993), pp. 23–30.

[28] See B.S. Moskal, "Company Loyalty Dies, A Victim of Neglect," *Industry Week* (March 1, 1993), pp. 11–12; and F.F. Reichheld, "Loyalty-Based Management," *Harvard Business Review* (March-April 1993), pp. 64–73.

[29] Cited in B.S. Moskal, "Company Loyalty Dies."

[30] K. Davis and W.C. Frederick, *Business and Society: Management, Public Policy, Ethics*, 5th ed. (New York: McGraw-Hill, 1984), p. 76.

[31] R.R. Sims, "The Challenge of Ethical Behavior in Organizations," *Journal of Business Ethics* (July 1992), pp. 505–13.

[32] See, for example, M.J. Driver, "Cognitive Psychology: An Interactionist View"; R.H. Hall, "Organizational Behavior: A Sociological Perspective"; and C. Hardy, "The Contribution of Political Science to Organizational Behavior," all in J.W. Lorsch (ed.), *Handbook of Organizational Behavior* (Englewood Cliffs, NJ: Prentice Hall, 1987), pp. 62–108.

[33] D. Tjosvold, "Controversy for Learning Organizational Behavior," *Organizational Behavior Teaching Review*, Vol. XI, No. 3 (1986–87), pp. 51–59; and L.F. Moore, D.C. Limerick, and P.J. Frost, "Debating the Issue: Increasing Understanding of the 'Close Calls' in Organizational Decision Making," *Organizational Behavior Teaching Review*, Vol. XIV, No. 1 (1989–90), pp. 37–43.

[34] S.R. Rhodes and R.M. Steers, *Managing Employee Absenteeism* (Reading, MA: Addison-Wesley, 1990).

[35] Cited in "Expensive Absenteeism," *Wall Street Journal* (July 29, 1986), p. 1.

[36] M. Mercer, "Turnover: Reducing the Costs," *Personnel* (December 1988), pp. 36–42; and R. Darmon, "Identifying Sources of Turnover Cost," *Journal of Marketing* (April 1990), pp. 46–56.

[37] See, for example, D.R. Dalton and W.D. Todor, "Functional Turnover: An Empirical Assessment," *Journal of Applied Psychology* (December 1981), pp. 716–21; and G.M. McEvoy and W.F. Cascio, "Do Good or Poor Performers Leave? A Meta-Analysis of the Relationship Between Performance and Turnover," *Academy of Management Journal* (December 1987), pp. 744–62.

[38] Cited in "You Often Lose the Ones You Love," *Industry Week* (November 21, 1988), p. 5.

[39] H.J. Leavitt, *Managerial Psychology*, rev. ed. (Chicago: University of Chicago Press, 1964), p. 3.

CHAPTER 2

The Coca-Cola Company operates in 196 countries and earns more than 80 percent of its profits from non-U.S. sales. On a global basis, the company holds 45 percent of the world market in carbonated drinks.

RESPONDING TO GLOBAL AND CULTURAL DIVERSITY

CHAPTER OUTLINE

- Pervasiveness of Diversity
- Welcome to the Global Village
- Facing the International Challenge
- The Relevant Question: Are National Cultures Becoming More Homogeneous?
- Assessing Differences Between Countries
- The Reality of Culture Shock
- Inside the Organization: The Challenge of Work Force Diversity
- Managing Diversity in Organizations

LEARNING OBJECTIVES

After studying this chapter, you should be able to:

1. Define a multinational corporation.
2. Describe the effects of regional cooperative arrangements on managing global enterprises.
3. Contrast *parochialism* and *ethnocentrism.*
4. List the six basic dimensions along which cultures vary in Kluckhohn and Strodtbeck's framework.
5. Describe Hofstede's four cultural dimensions.
6. Characterize the United States on Hofstede's dimensions.
7. Contrast affirmative action with the work force diversity movement.
8. List the common characteristics in a comprehensive work force diversity program.

Japanese and American management is 95 percent the same, and differs in all important respects.
—S. Honda

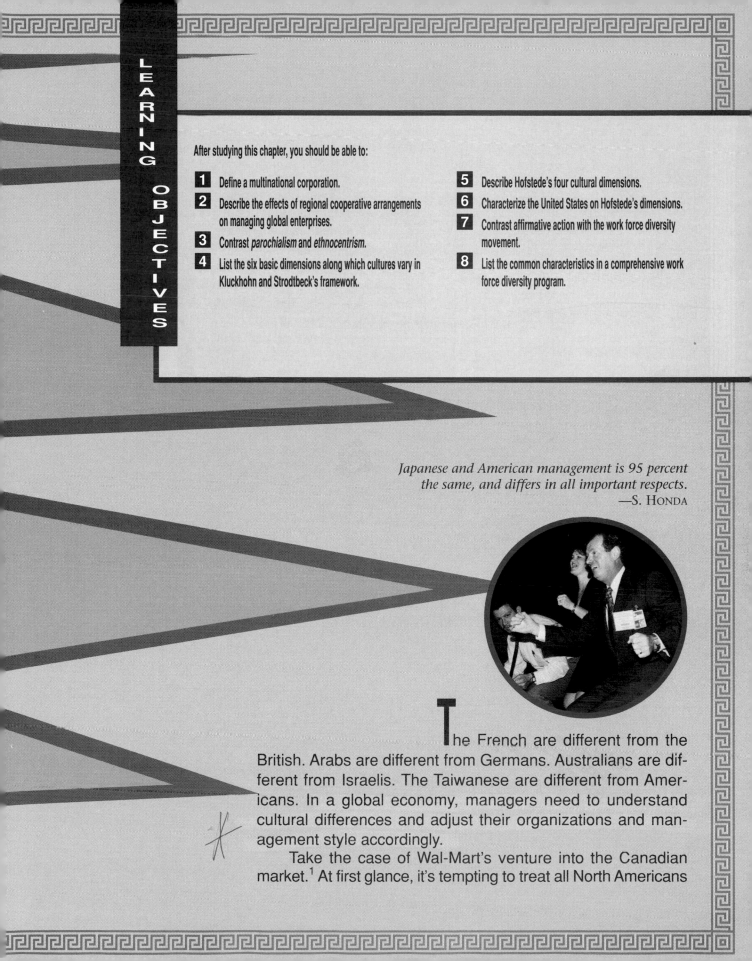

The French are different from the British. Arabs are different from Germans. Australians are different from Israelis. The Taiwanese are different from Americans. In a global economy, managers need to understand cultural differences and adjust their organizations and management style accordingly.

Take the case of Wal-Mart's venture into the Canadian market.[1] At first glance, it's tempting to treat all North Americans alike. Most Canadians, after all, live within a couple of hundred miles of the U.S. border. The two countries share a common language and are each other's largest trading partners. Yet Wal-Mart is learning that Canadians *aren't* just like their American counterparts.

Wal-Mart prides itself on its team spirit and family-like culture. Employees at U.S. Wal-Mart stores, for instance, know that every morning begins with the same routine: managers leading the troops in singing a rousing version of "The Star-Spangled Banner," followed by spelling the company name in unison ("Give me a W, give me an A, give me an L . . ."), hollerin' that the customer is number 1, and screamin' their store number. This is all part of a process called "Wal-Martization," where employees enthusiastically buy into a corporate philosophy that blends team spirit, self-esteem, and the relentless pursuit of higher sales.

Unfortunately, Canadians don't share Americans' extroversion or upbeat positive attitude. Wal-Mart's U.S. management learned this firsthand when it bought 122 Woolco stores in Canada and began turning them into Wal-Marts. Management thought all they'd have to do to Canadianize the morning ritual was change the national anthem and then they'd be off and running. Surprise! Wal-Mart executives found themselves face to face with a national culture where senior managers who proselytize about values and vision are considered odd. And overt expressions of enthusiasm are seen as embarrassing. In Calgary, for example, new Wal-Mart employees refused to sing Canada's national anthem at the morning rally and were reluctant to participate in company cheers. Wal-Mart's management is learning, with a few humbling mistakes along the way, that its U.S. practices don't automatically transfer to other cultures.

The Wal-Mart example illustrates the need for managers to adjust their style and practices to reflect national differences. Later in this chapter, we provide a framework for assessing these national differences and then show you what changes, if any, you might need to make when managing in a different country.

Pervasiveness of Diversity

This chapter looks at differences from two levels of analysis. First, we build on our theme that people from different countries have common characteristics that differentiate them from people in other countries. This is the *inter*national level of analysis. Then we look at the importance of differences within any specific country. We call this *intra*national diversity.

International Diversity

The phrase "When in Rome, do as the Romans do" captures the essence of why it's important to understand international diversity. Differences between countries are real. Those managers who understand this and can adjust their styles appropriately when working with people from other countries will be more effective than those who assume "all people are the same."

Managers who are knowledgeable about national differences will understand appropriate practices in a specific country. For instance, they would know that the British protect their privacy, so avoid asking the English personal questions. In contrast, asking personal questions in Greece is acceptable—it's a sign of showing interest. In Denmark, they would use professional titles when addressing people; but avoid it in Greece where such formality is frowned upon. In Japan, all business transactions begin by the formal exchanging of business cards; but knowledgeable managers know not to expect this practice in Italy. Italians don't use business cards much. While August may be like any other month in most countries, managers should know not to do business during this month in France. The French go en masse on vacation during August. And while the British are sticklers for schedules and promptness, managers who understand national differences wouldn't be surprised if a Spaniard turned up 20 or 30 minutes late for an appointment. Punctuality is not highly valued in the Spanish culture.[2]

Unfortunately, it's a lot easier to say "When in Rome, do as the Romans do" than it is to know exactly what it is that "the Romans do." In other words, you can know that Greeks, Danes, and Spaniards are different from you, but can you accurately identify what it is that makes them different? Understanding the characteristics common to people *within* a given country is important if you're going to successfully manage in a global economy.

Intranational Diversity

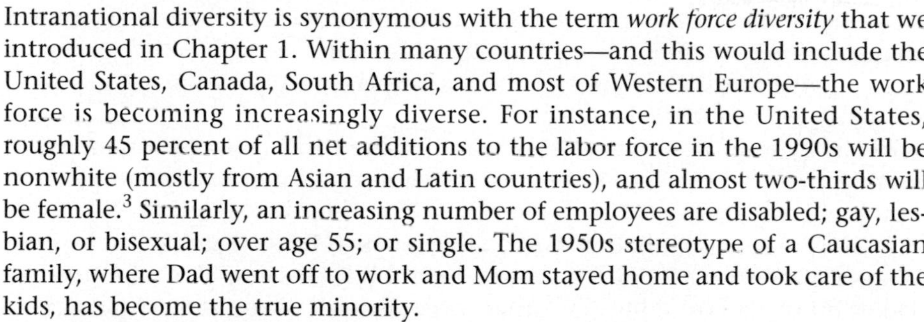

Intranational diversity is synonymous with the term *work force diversity* that we introduced in Chapter 1. Within many countries—and this would include the United States, Canada, South Africa, and most of Western Europe—the work force is becoming increasingly diverse. For instance, in the United States, roughly 45 percent of all net additions to the labor force in the 1990s will be nonwhite (mostly from Asian and Latin countries), and almost two-thirds will be female.[3] Similarly, an increasing number of employees are disabled; gay, lesbian, or bisexual; over age 55; or single. The 1950s stereotype of a Caucasian family, where Dad went off to work and Mom stayed home and took care of the kids, has become the true minority.

Few generalizations apply to today's workers. They come in all shapes, sizes, and categories. We show later in this chapter that effective managers are learning the value which diversity can bring to their organization and the importance of modifying organizational practices so as to better manage diversity.

Welcome to the Global Village

A number of respected observers of world affairs have been arguing for more than a decade that our world has become a global village. Transportation and communication capabilities—for example, supersonic jets, international telephone and computer networks, and worldwide news broadcasts via satellite—make it easier to talk with or visit people on other continents than it was for our ancestors of a century ago to do the same with friends in a neighboring village. Distance and national borders are rapidly disappearing as a major barrier to business transactions. With the advent of the global village, identifying the "home country" of a company and its product has become a lot more difficult. For instance, Honda is supposedly a Japanese firm, but it builds its Accords in Ohio. Ford, which has its headquarters in Detroit, builds its Mercury Tracers in Mexico. "All-

> ◆Distance and national borders are rapidly disappearing as a major barrier to business transactions.

"Tonight's program 'America, America' is being brought to you by a grant from the Sony and Nissan corporations."

Figure 2-1
Source: From the *Wall Street Journal*, September 5, 1990. With permission, Cartoon Features Syndicate.

American" firms like IBM, Mobil, Citicorp, Motorola, Gillette, and Coca-Cola get more than half of their revenues from operations outside the United States; other "All-American" firms such as CBS Records, General Tire, and Pillsbury are actually foreign owned.

The reality of the global village can be demonstrated by looking at the growing impact of multinational corporations and the rise of regional cooperative arrangements between countries.

Multinational Corporations

Most of the firms currently listed in the Fortune 500 are **multinational corporations**—companies that maintain significant operations in two or more countries simultaneously.

While international businesses have been around for centuries, multinationals are a relatively recent phenomenon. They are a natural outcome of the global economy. Multinationals use their worldwide operations to develop global strategies. Rather than confining themselves to their domestic borders, they scan the world for competitive advantages. The result? Manufacturing, assembly, sales, and other functions are being strategically located to give firms advantages in the marketplace. A photocopying machine, for instance, might be designed in Toronto, have its microprocessing chips made in Taiwan, its physical case manufactured in Japan, be assembled in South Korea, and then be sold out of warehouses located in Melbourne, London, and Los Angeles.

multinational corporations
Companies that maintain significant operations in two or more countries simultaneously.

How big are multinationals? In a list in which nations are ranked by gross national product (GNP) and industrial firms by total sales, 37 of the first 100 names on the list would be industrial corporations.[4] Exxon's sales, as a case in point, exceed the GNPs of such countries as Indonesia, Nigeria, Argentina, and Denmark.

A global computer network gives Texas Instruments a competitive edge in speeding new products to market. A company unit named Tiris (Texas Instruments Registration and Identification System) produces transponders, tiny James Bond-type communications devices for security and identification purposes. Tiris is managed out of Bedford, England; develops product designs in the Netherlands and Germany; and manufactures and assembles products in Japan and Malaysia. Employees at all these locations send text, diagrams, and designs to each other using TI's computer network, giving Tiris an 18- to 24-month lead over competitors. Shown here holding reels of transponders are assembly workers in Kuala Lumpur, Malaysia.

Managers of multinationals confront a wealth of challenges. They face diverse political systems, laws, and customs. But these differences create both problems and opportunities. It's obviously more difficult to manage an operation that spans 15,000 miles and whose employees speak five different languages than one located under a single roof where a common language is spoken. Differences additionally create opportunities, and that has been the primary motivation for corporations to expand their worldwide operations.

Regional Cooperative Arrangements

National boundaries are also being blurred by the creation of regional cooperative arrangements. The most notable of these, so far, is the European Union, made up of 15 West European countries, and NAFTA, which reduces trade barriers between the United States, Mexico, and Canada. The reunification of Germany and the fall of communism also appears to be setting the stage for internation cooperative agreements among Eastern European countries.

THE EUROPEAN UNION The year 1993 marked the creation of a United States of Europe. There are 335 million people in the 15 nations making up the **European Union**—France, Denmark, Belgium, Greece, Ireland, Italy, Luxembourg, the Netherlands, Portugal, Spain, the United Kingdom, Austria, Finland, Sweden, and Germany. Before 1993 these countries individually had border controls, border taxes, border subsidies, nationalistic policies, and protected industries. Now they are a single market. Gone are national barriers to travel, employment, investment, and trade. In their place are a free flow of money, workers, goods, and services. A driver hauling cargo from Amsterdam to Lisbon is now able to clear four border crossings and five countries merely by showing a single piece of paper. In 1992 that same driver needed two pounds of documents.

European Union
Common market made up of 15 nations: France, Denmark, Belgium, Greece, Ireland, Italy, Luxembourg, the Netherlands, Portugal, Spain, the United Kingdom, Austria, Finland, Sweden, and Germany.

The primary motivation for these 15 nations to unite was the desire to strengthen their position against the industrial might of the United States and Japan. When they were separate countries creating barriers against one another, their industries were unable to develop the economies of scale enjoyed by the United States and Japan. The new European Union, however, allows European firms to tap into a single market that is larger than either the domestic markets of the United States or Japan. This reduction in trade barriers also encourages non–Western European companies to invest in these countries to take advantage of new opportunities. Finally, European multinationals have new clout in attacking American, Japanese, and other worldwide markets.

NAFTA The United States and Canada established a free-trade agreement in the early 1990s. This agreement phased out tariffs on most goods traded between the two countries. The **North American Free Trade Agreement (NAFTA)**, which took effect on January 1, 1994, added Mexico to create the world's largest and richest trading market, with about 370 million people and $6.5 trillion worth of goods and services annually.[5]

North American Free Trade Agreement (NAFTA)
Agreement that phases out tariffs on most goods traded among the United States, Canada, and Mexico.

Prior to NAFTA, Mexican tariffs averaged about 250 percent of comparable U.S. duties. This restricted U.S. exports to Mexico. NAFTA immediately eliminated tariffs on more than half of the approximately 9,000 goods traded between the United States and Mexico, and provided for phasing out of the others in varying time lengths of as long as 15 years.

NAFTA underscores the economic interdependence of the United States, Mexico, and Canada. While the three countries have separate political systems and cultural histories, their geographic proximity to each other encouraged an economic partnership to better compete in the global marketplace.

NAFTA is giving U.S. exporters of telecommunications equipment a big boost. AT&T is exporting $150 million worth of the fiber-optic cable made in this Atlanta, Georgia, factory to Mexico. Over 8,300 miles of AT&T's fiber-optic cable and switching equipment will connect 54 Mexican cities and towns. NAFTA is also helping AT&T compete in Mexico, where Mexican subsidiaries of Ericsson of Sweden and Alcatel of France have had a lock on the market.

THE NEW EASTERN EUROPE The Cold War is over, communism is rapidly disappearing, and capitalism is spreading throughout the world. In the last several years, Germany has been reunited, countries like Poland and Romania have introduced democratic governments, and the former Soviet Union has become a set of independent states trying to implement market-based reforms.

In terms of the changing global environment, the spread of capitalism makes the world a smaller place. Business has new markets to conquer. Additionally, well-trained and reliable workers in countries like Hungary and the Czech Republic and Slovakia provide a rich source of low-cost labor. The implementation of free markets in Eastern Europe further underscores the growing interdependence between countries of the world and the potential for goods, labor, and capital to easily move across national borders.

WHAT'S NEXT? A PACIFIC RIM BLOC? With the culmination of a European common market and a North American free-trade zone, can a Pacific Rim trading bloc be far away?

At this point, it's not more than speculation. But the creation of a Pacific Rim bloc—which might include countries such as Japan, China, Australia, Taiwan, Thailand, and South Korea—would make a more self-reliant region, better able to provide both raw materials and markets within the region. Moreover, a unified Pacific Rim would have increased clout in trading with North America and Europe.

Facing the International Challenge

national culture
Primary values and practices that characterize a particular country.

A global economy presents challenges to managers that they never had to confront when their operations were constrained within national borders. They face different legal and political systems. They confront different economic climates and tax policies. But they also must deal with varying **national cultures**—the primary values and practices that characterize particular countries—many of which are nothing like those in which they have spent their entire lives.

If this were an economics text, we would carefully dissect the economic implications for managers of a global economy. But this book is about organizational behavior and understanding people at work. Therefore, let's look at why managers, especially those born and raised in the United States, often find managing people in foreign lands so difficult.

American Biases

Americans have been singled out as suffering particularly from **parochialism**; that is, they view the world solely through their own eyes and perspective.[6] People with a parochial perspective do not recognize that other people have different ways of living and working. We see this most explicitly in Americans' knowledge of foreign languages. While it is not uncommon for Europeans to speak three or four languages, Americans are almost entirely monolingual. The reasons probably reflect the huge domestic market in the United States, the geographical separation of the United States from Europe and Asia, and the reality that English has become the international business language in many parts of the world.

parochialism
Narrow view of the world; an inability to recognize differences between people.

Americans have also been frequently criticized for holding **ethnocentric views**.[7] They believe their cultural values and customs are superior to all others. This may offer another explanation for why Americans don't learn foreign languages. Many think their language is superior and that it's the rest of the world's responsibility to learn English.

ethnocentric views
Beliefs that one's cultural values and customs are superior to all others.

No shortage of stories illustrate the problems created when American managers failed to understand cultural differences. Consider the following examples.

> An American manager, recently transferred to Saudi Arabia, successfully obtained a million-dollar contract from a Saudi manufacturer. The manufacturer's representative had arrived at the meeting several hours late, but the American executive considered it unimportant. The American was certainly surprised and frustrated to learn later that the Saudi had no intention of honoring the contract. He had signed it only to be polite after showing up late for the appointment.
>
> An American executive operating in Peru was viewed by Peruvian managers as cold and unworthy of trust because, in face-to-face discussions, the American kept backing up. He did not understand that in Peru the custom is to stand quite close to the person with whom you are speaking.
>
> An American manager in Japan offended a high-ranking Japanese executive by failing to give him the respect his position deserved. The American was introduced to the Japanese executive in the latter's office. The American assumed the executive was a low-level manager and paid him little attention because of the small and sparsely furnished office he occupied. The American didn't realize the offices of top Japanese executives do not flaunt the status symbols of their American counterparts.[8]

U.S. parochialism and ethnocentrism may not have been debilitating in the post–World War II period, when the United States accounted for 75 percent of the world's gross national product. But it is a "life threatening disease" today, when U.S. firms produce only about 22 percent of the world's GNP.[9] The point is that the world is not dominated by U.S. economic power anymore, and unless U.S. managers conquer their parochialism and ethnocentrism, they will not be able to take full advantage of the new global opportunities.

◆Unless U.S. managers conquer their parochialism and ethnocentrism, they will not be able to take full advantage of the new global opportunities.

◆◆◆◆ OB in the News ◆◆◆◆

Under Japanese Bosses, Americans Find Work Both Better and Worse

Setex Inc. is a Japanese American joint venture that manufactures car seats in southwestern Ohio.

The company gets high marks from its blue-collar workers for the way they're treated. The factory is immaculate, well lit, ergonomically designed, and air conditioned. Every worker (or "associate") is part of a team. And the team members build camaraderie and avoid boredom by rotating jobs every two hours, moving through all 18 assembly jobs in a few days. Setex's American managers, however, aren't as positive when they talk about their Japanese bosses and use of Japanese management practices. The American managers particularly complain about Setex's decision processes, the lack of feedback from their Japanese superiors, cross-cultural communication barriers, and the long hours the Japanese executives expect their American managers to put in.

The U.S. managers say they aren't allowed to make decisions or fully use their talents. The Japanese approach to decision making—shared consensus building—frustrates American managers used to individual responsibility and recognition. Aggressive, ambitious Americans often feel out of place.

American managers complain about a lack of feedback from their Japanese bosses. Even when their work is outstanding, some managers contend they're not promoted simply because they're not Japanese.

Communication presents another problem. Language differences, for example, hinder mutual understanding. The English spoken by the Japanese is sometimes difficult for Americans to understand. And Japanese terminology often confuses Americans. For instance, one American manager asked, "What difference does it make if you call someone an hourly worker or an associate?" But to the Japanese, it matters! Add the fact that the Japanese bosses occasionally talk among themselves in Japanese and fax messages back and forth to Japan in their native language, and the non-Japanese-speaking Americans begin to feel left out of the loop.

The Japanese managers come from a culture that stresses company teamwork, harmony, and consensus. They see the workplace as an extended family. As such, they expect their American managers to place the company ahead of their personal lives. While Americans typically look forward to time off with their families, the Japanese spend long hours after work socializing together and piling up years of unused vacation time. Setex's American managers find it hard to adjust to jobs that seem to consume their entire lives.

Source: Based on T.F. O'Boyle in *Wall Street Journal* (November 27, 1991), p. A1.

The Foreign Born in America

Don't assume that Americans are alone in blundering on foreign soil. Cultural ignorance goes two ways. Foreign owners now control more than 12 percent of all American manufacturing assets and employ over 3 million American workers. In one recent year alone, foreign investors acquired nearly 400 American businesses, worth a total of $60 billion.[10] However, these foreign owners are facing the same challenges and making many of the same mistakes that American executives have long made overseas.[11]

Americans, for instance, are used to stability. When new owners with different management styles take over a U.S. company, American workers often feel threatened by high uncertainty, yet this is often ignored by foreign managers. Some foreign owners, especially those from relatively homogeneous cultures, have the outmoded, stereotypical attitudes toward women and minorities that build ill will. Many American employees complain they feel left out of the established personal networks in traditional European and Asian corporations that acquire American firms. Japanese managers, as a case in point, work 10- to 12-hour days and then socialize until midnight. A lot of important business is done at these social gatherings, but American managers are excluded, and this exclusion creates feelings of hurt and distrust. The Japanese way of dealing with people also confounds Americans. Communication, for example, is often more difficult. Americans value directness—they tend to say exactly what they mean. The Japanese are more subtle and see this directness as rude and abrasive. The Japanese emphasis on group consensus is another practice that doesn't fit well in the United States. Americans, used to making decisions fast, get frustrated by what they interpret as unnecessary delays.[12]

The Relevant Question: Are National Cultures Becoming More Homogeneous?

It can be argued that the creation of a true global village is making the concern over cultural differences irrelevant. Today, when Cable News Network (CNN) is watched in over 140 countries, Levis are as popular in Moscow as in Dallas, and a significant portion of students in American graduate business programs are foreigners who expect to return to their homelands to practice management, it may be naive to think that cultural differences are very important. If they are, they are so only in the near term. In the long run, the global village will become a single homogeneous culture—that is, a world melting pot in which cross-cultural differences will all but disappear.

Are national cultures becoming more homogeneous? In some ways, yes. Consider these Chinese couples, who prefer Western-style dancing over *t'ai chi*, the traditional meditative morning exercise. In the workplace, however, significant cultural differences challenge foreign companies operating in China. Managers face China's rigidly hierarchical culture, where the idea of younger managers telling older workers what to do is unheard of and employees work in state-controlled companies that provide no incentives for advancement.

Is this argument correct? Are national cultures becoming more homogeneous? At one level, they are.[13] Research demonstrates that organization strategies, structures, and technologies are becoming more alike. However, there are still differences among people within organizations in different cultures.[14] In other words, national culture continues to be a powerful force in explaining a large proportion of organizational behavior. In further support of this viewpoint, research comparing employees in 40 countries concluded that national culture explained approximately 50 percent of the differences in these employees' attitudes and behavior.[15]

If people were becoming more homogeneous, we could take a culture-free approach to organizational behavior. But such an approach does not appear to be justified at present, for the following reasons: (1) There are differences in OB across national cultures. (2) These differences explain a large proportion of the variance in attitudes and behaviors. (3) And for now at least, and probably for a number of years to come, these differences are not decreasing at any significant rate. On the last point we might speculate that, despite the tremendous increase in cross-cultural communication, there continues to be unique country-specific traditions and customs that shape the attitudes and behaviors of the people in those countries.

Assessing Differences Between Countries

American children are taught early the values of individuality and uniqueness. In contrast, Japanese children are taught to be team players, to work within the group, and to conform. A significant part of American students' education is to learn to think, to analyze, and to question. Their Japanese counterparts are rewarded for recounting facts. These different socialization practices reflect different cultures and, not surprisingly, result in different types of employees. The average American worker is more competitive and self-focused than the Japanese worker. Predictions of employee behavior based on samples of American workers are likely to be off target when they are applied to a population of employees—like the Japanese—who perform better in standardized tasks, as part of a work team, with group-based decisions and rewards.

It's relatively easy to get a reading of the Japanese culture—dozens of books and hundreds of articles have been written on the subject. But how do you gain an understanding of Venezuela's or Denmark's national culture? Or if you were an American employed by National Semiconductor in California and got transferred to their company in Israel, how would you learn about Israeli culture? A popular notion is that you should talk with people from the country in question—for instance, Venezuelans, Danes, or Israelis. Evidence suggests, however, that this rarely works.[16] Why? Because people born and raised in a country are fully programmed in the ways of its culture by the time they're adults. They understand how things are done and can work comfortably within their country's unwritten norms, but they can't explain their culture to someone else. It is pervasive, but it is hidden. Most people are unaware of just how their culture has shaped them. Culture is to people as water is to fish. It's there all the time but the fish are oblivious to it. So one of the frustrations of moving into a different culture is that the "natives" are often the least capable of explaining its unique characteristics to an outsider.

To illustrate the difficulty of accurately describing the unique qualities of one's own culture, if you're an American, raised in the United States, ask yourself, What are Americans like? Think about it for a moment and then see how many of the points in Table 2-1 you identified correctly.

Although foreign culture is difficult to fathom from what its natives tell you, there is an expanding body of research that can tell us how cultures vary and what the key differences are between, say, the United States and Venezuela. Let's look at the two best known of these research frameworks.

The Kluckhohn-Strodtbeck Framework

One of the most widely referenced approaches for analyzing variations among cultures is the Kluckhohn-Strodtbeck framework.[17] It identifies six basic cultural dimensions: relationship to the environment, time orientation, nature of people, activity orientation, focus of responsibility, and conception of space. In this section, we review each of these dimensions.

Table 2-1 What Are Americans Like?

Americans are very informal. They don't tend to treat people differently even when there are great differences in age or social standing.

Americans are direct. They don't talk around things. To some foreigners, this may appear as abrupt or even rude behavior.

Americans are competitive. Some foreigners may find Americans assertive or overbearing.

Americans are achievers. They like to keep score, whether at work or at play. They emphasize accomplishments.

Americans are independent and individualistic. They place a high value on freedom and believe that individuals can shape and control their own destinies.

Americans are questioners. They ask a lot of questions, even of someone they have just met. Many of these questions may seem pointless ("How ya doing?") or personal ("What kind of work do you do?").

Americans dislike silence. They would rather talk about the weather than deal with silence in a conversation.

Americans value punctuality. They keep appointment calendars and live according to schedules and clocks.

Americans value cleanliness. They often seem obsessed with bathing, eliminating body odors, and wearing clean clothes.

Source: Based on M. Ernest (ed.), *Predeparture Orientation Handbook: For Foreign Students and Scholars Planning to Study in the United States* (Washington, DC: U.S. Information Agency, Bureau of Cultural Affairs, 1984), pp. 103–105; A. Bennett, "American Culture Is Often a Puzzle for Foreign Managers in the U.S.," *Wall Street Journal* (February 12, 1986), p. 29; "Don't Think Our Way's the Only Way," *The Pryor Report* (February 1988), p. 9; and B. J. Wattenberg, "The Attitudes Behind American Exceptionalism," *U.S. News & World Report* (August 7, 1989), p. 25.

RELATIONSHIP TO THE ENVIRONMENT Are people *subjugated* to their environment, in *harmony* with it, or able to *dominate* it? In many Middle Eastern countries, people see life as essentially preordained. When something happens, they tend to see it as "God's will." In contrast, Americans and Canadians believe they can control nature. They're willing to spend billions of dollars each year on cancer research, for instance, because they think cancer's cause can be identified, a cure found, and the disease eventually eradicated.

In between these two extreme positions is a more moderate view that seeks harmony with nature. In many Far Eastern countries, for example, people's way of dealing with the environment is to work around it.

You should expect these different perspectives toward the environment to influence organizational practices. Take the setting of goals as an example. In a subjugation society, goal setting is not likely to be very popular. Why set goals if you believe people can't do much toward achieving them? In a harmony society, goals are likely to be used, but deviations are expected and penalties for failing to reach the goals are likely to be minimal. In a domination society, goals are widely applied, people are expected to achieve them, and the penalties for failure tend to be quite high.

TIME ORIENTATION Does the culture focus on the *past, present,* or *future?* Societies differ in the value they place on time. For instance, Western cultures perceive time as a scarce resource. "Time is money" and must be used efficiently. Americans focus on the present and the near future. You see evidence of this in the short-term orientation of performance appraisals. In the typical North American organization, people are evaluated every six months or once a

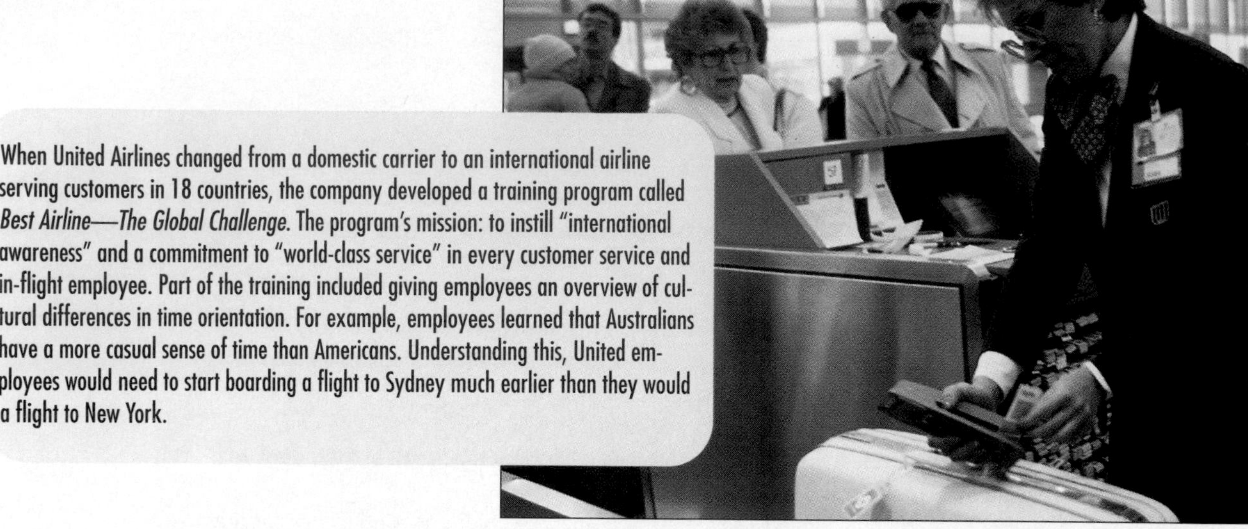

When United Airlines changed from a domestic carrier to an international airline serving customers in 18 countries, the company developed a training program called *Best Airline—The Global Challenge*. The program's mission: to instill "international awareness" and a commitment to "world-class service" in every customer service and in-flight employee. Part of the training included giving employees an overview of cultural differences in time orientation. For example, employees learned that Australians have a more casual sense of time than Americans. Understanding this, United employees would need to start boarding a flight to Sydney much earlier than they would a flight to New York.

year. The Japanese, in contrast, take a longer term view and this is reflected in their performance appraisal methods. Japanese workers are often given ten years or more to prove their worth.

Some cultures take still another approach to time: They focus on the past. Italians, for instance, follow their traditions and seek to preserve their historical practices.

Knowledge of different cultures' time orientations can provide you with insights into the importance of deadlines, whether long-term planning is widely practiced, the length of job assignments, and what constitutes lateness. It can explain, for instance, why Americans are obsessed with making and keeping appointments. It also suggests why not every society is as likely to be enamored of timesaving devices—such as day planners, overnight mail delivery, car phones, electronic mail, and fax machines—as North Americans are.

NATURE OF PEOPLE Does a culture view people as *good*, *evil*, or some *mix* of these two? In many developing countries, people see themselves as basically honest and trustworthy. North Korea, on the other hand, takes a rather evil view of human nature. North Americans tend to be somewhere in between. They see people as basically good, but are cautious so as not to be taken advantage of.

You can readily see how a culture's view of the nature of people might influence the dominant leadership style of its managers. A more autocratic style is likely to rule in countries that focus on the evil aspects of people. Participation or even a laissez-faire style should prevail in countries that emphasize trusting values. In mixed cultures, leadership is likely to emphasize participation but provide close controls that can quickly identify deviations.

ACTIVITY ORIENTATION Some cultures emphasize *doing* or action. They stress accomplishments. Some cultures emphasize *being* or living for the moment. They stress experiencing life and seeking immediate gratification of desires. Still other cultures focus on *controlling*. They stress restraining desires by detaching oneself from objects.

North Americans live in doing-oriented societies. They work hard and expect to be rewarded with promotions, raises, and other forms of recognition for their accomplishments. Mexico, in contrast, is being oriented. The afternoon siesta is consistent with the slower pace and enjoying-the-moment orientation of the culture. The French have a controlling orientation and put emphasis on rationality and logic.

An understanding of a culture's activity orientation can give you insights into how its people approach work and leisure, how they make decisions, and the criteria they use for allocating rewards. For instance, in cultures with a dominant being orientation, decisions are likely to be emotional. In contrast, doing and controlling cultures are likely to emphasize pragmatism and rationality, respectively, in decision making.

FOCUS OF RESPONSIBILITY Cultures can be classified according to where responsibility lies for the welfare of others. Americans, for instance, are highly *individualistic*. They use personal characteristics and achievements to define themselves. They believe a person's responsibility is to take care of himself or herself. Countries like Malaysia and Israel focus more on the *group*. In an Israeli kibbutz, for example, people share chores and rewards. Emphasis is on group harmony, unity, and loyalty. The British and French follow another orientation by relying on *hierarchical* relationships. Groups in these countries are hierarchically ranked and a group's position remains essentially stable over time. Hierarchical societies tend to be aristocratic.

This dimension of culture has implications for the design of jobs, approaches to decision making, communication patterns, reward systems, and selection practices in organizations. For instance, selection in individualistic societies emphasizes personal accomplishments. In group societies, working well with others is likely to be of primary importance. In hierarchical societies, selection decisions are made on the basis of a candidate's social ranking. This dimension helps to explain the popularity in the United States of the résumé, which lists personal achievements, and the negative connotation attached to nepotism (hiring one's relatives).[18]

CONCEPTION OF SPACE The final dimension in the Kluckhohn-Strodtbeck framework relates to ownership of space. Some cultures are very open and conduct business in *public*. At the other extreme are cultures that place a great deal of emphasis on keeping things *private*. Many societies *mix* the two and fall somewhere in between.

Japanese organizations reflect the public nature of their society. There are, for instance, few private offices. Managers and operative employees work in the same room with no partitions separating their desks. North American firms also reflect their cultural values. They use offices and privacy to reflect status. Important meetings are held behind closed doors. Space is frequently given over for the exclusive use of specific individuals. In societies that have a mixed orientation, there is a blend of the private and public. For instance, there might be a large office where walls are only 5 or 6 feet high, thus creating "limited privacy." These differences in the conception of space have obvious implications for organizational concerns such as work design and communication.

SUMMARY Table 2-2 on the next page summarizes the six cultural dimensions in the Kluckhohn-Strodtbeck framework and the possible variations for each. As a point of reference, the jagged line in the table identifies where the United States tends to fall along these dimensions.

Table 2-2 Variations in Kluckhohn-Strodtbeck's Value Dimensions

Value Dimension	Variations		
Relationship to the environment	Domination	Harmony	Subjugation
Time orientation	Past	Present	Future
Nature of people	Good	Mixed	Evil
Activity orientation	Being	Controlling	Doing
Focus of responsibility	Individualistic	Group	Hierarchical
Conception of space	Private	Mixed	Public

Note: The jagged line identifies where the United States tends to fall along these dimensions.

The Hofstede Framework

A more comprehensive analysis of cultural diversity has been done by Geert Hofstede.[19] In contrast to most of the previous organizational studies, which either included a limited number of countries or analyzed different companies in different countries, Hofstede surveyed over 116,000 employees in 40 countries who all worked for a single multinational corporation. This database eliminated any differences that might be attributable to varying practices and policies in different companies. So any variations that he found between countries could reliably be attributed to national culture.

What did Hofstede find? His huge database confirmed that national culture had a major impact on employees' work-related values and attitudes. More important, Hofstede found that managers and employees vary on four dimensions of national culture: (1) individualism versus collectivism; (2) power distance; (3) uncertainty avoidance; and (4) quantity versus quality of life. (Actually, Hofstede called this fourth dimension masculinity versus femininity, but we've changed his terms because of their strong sexist connotation.)

individualism
National culture attribute describing a loosely knit social framework in which people emphasize only the care of themselves and their immediate family.

collectivism
National culture attribute that describes a tight social framework in which people expect others in groups of which they are a part to look after them and protect them.

INDIVIDUALISM VS. COLLECTIVISM **Individualism** refers to a loosely knit social framework in which people are chiefly supposed to look after their own interests and those of their immediate family. This is made possible because of the large amount of freedom that such a society allows individuals. Its opposite is **collectivism**, which is characterized by a tight social framework in which people expect others in groups to which they belong (such as an organization) to look after them and protect them when they are in trouble. In exchange for this security, they feel they owe absolute loyalty to the group.

Hofstede found that the degree of individualism in a country is closely related to that country's wealth. Rich countries like the United States, Great Britain, and the Netherlands are very individualistic. Poor countries like Colombia and Pakistan are very collectivist.

power distance
National culture attribute describing the extent to which a society accepts the idea that power in institutions and organizations is distributed unequally.

POWER DISTANCE People naturally vary in their physical and intellectual abilities. This, in turn, creates differences in wealth and power. How does a society deal with these inequalities? Hofstede used the term **power distance** as a measure of the extent to which a society accepts the fact that power in institutions and organizations is distributed unequally. A high-power-distance society accepts wide differences in power in organizations. Employees show a great deal of respect for those in authority. Titles, rank, and status carry a lot of weight. When negotiating in high-power-distance countries, companies find it helps to send representatives with titles at least as high as those with whom they're bargaining. Countries high in power distance include the Philippines, Venezuela, and India. In contrast, a low-power-distance society plays down inequalities as much as possible. Superiors still have authority, but employees are not fearful or in awe of the boss. Denmark, Israel, and Austria are examples of countries with low-power-distance scores.

UNCERTAINTY AVOIDANCE We live in a world of uncertainty. The future is largely unknown and always will be. Societies respond to this uncertainty in different ways. Some socialize their members into accepting it with equanimity. People in such societies are more or less comfortable with risks. They're also relatively tolerant of behavior and opinions that differ from their own because they don't feel threatened by them. Hofstede describes such societies as having low **uncertainty avoidance**; that is, people feel relatively secure. Countries that fall into this category include Singapore, Switzerland, and Denmark.

uncertainty avoidance
National culture attribute describing the extent to which a society feels threatened by uncertain and ambiguous situations and tries to avoid them.

A society high in uncertainty avoidance is characterized by a high level of anxiety among its people, which manifests itself in nervousness, stress, and aggressiveness. Because people feel threatened by uncertainty and ambiguity in these societies, mechanisms are created to provide security and reduce risk. Organizations are likely to have more formal rules, there will be less tolerance for deviant ideas and behaviors, and members will strive to believe in absolute truths. Not surprisingly, in organizations in countries with high uncertainty avoidance, employees demonstrate relatively low job mobility and lifetime employment is a widely practiced policy. Countries in this category include Japan, Portugal, and Greece.

QUANTITY VS. QUALITY OF LIFE The fourth dimension, like individualism and collectivism, represents a dichotomy. Some cultures emphasize the **quantity of life** and value assertiveness and the acquisition of money and material things. Other cultures emphasize the **quality of life**, the importance of relationships, and show sensitivity and concern for the welfare of others.

quantity of life
National culture attribute describing the extent to which societal values are characterized by assertiveness and materialism.

quality of life
National culture attribute that emphasizes relationships and concern for others.

Hofstede found that Japan and Austria scored high on the quantity dimension. In contrast, Norway, Sweden, Denmark, and Finland scored high on the quality dimension.

THE UNITED STATES AND OTHER COUNTRIES ON HOFSTEDE'S DIMENSIONS Comparing the 40 countries on the four dimensions, Hofstede found U.S. culture to rank as follows:

- Individualism vs. collectivism = Highest among all countries on individualism
- Power distance = Below average
- Uncertainty avoidance = Well below average
- Quantity vs. quality = Well above average on quantity

These results are not inconsistent with the world image of the United States. The below average score on power distance aligns with what one might expect in a country with a representative type of government with democratic ideals. In this category, the United States would rate below nations with a small ruling class and a large powerless set of subjects, and above those nations with very strong commitments to egalitarian values. The well-below-average ranking on uncertainty avoidance is also consistent with a representative type of

Table 2-3 Examples of Hofstede's Cultural Dimensions

Country	Individualism/ Collectivism	Power Distance	Uncertainty Avoidance	Quantity of Life[a]
Australia	Individual	Small	Moderate	Strong
Canada	Individual	Moderate	Low	Moderate
England	Individual	Small	Moderate	Strong
France	Individual	Large	High	Weak
Greece	Collective	Large	High	Moderate
Italy	Individual	Moderate	High	Strong
Japan	Collective	Moderate	High	Strong
Mexico	Collective	Large	High	Strong
Singapore	Collective	Large	Low	Moderate
Sweden	Individual	Small	Low	Weak
United States	Individual	Small	Low	Strong
Venezuela	Collective	Large	High	Strong

[a]A weak quantity-of-life score is equivalent to a high quality-of-life score.

Source: Based on G. Hofstede, *Cultures and Organizations: Software of the Mind* (London: McGraw-Hill, 1991), pp. 23–138.

government having democratic ideals. Americans perceive themselves as being relatively free from threats of uncertainty. The individualistic ethic is one of the most frequently used stereotypes to describe Americans, and, based on Hofstede's research, the stereotype seems well founded. The United States was ranked as the single most individualistic country in his entire set. Finally, the well-above-average score on quantity of life is also no surprise. Capitalism—which values aggressiveness and materialism—is consistent with Hofstede's quantity characteristics.

We haven't the space here to review the results Hofstede obtained for all 40 countries, although a dozen examples are presented in Table 2-3. Since our concern is essentially with identifying similarities and differences among cultures, let's briefly identify those countries that are most and least like the United States on the four dimensions.

The United States is strongly individualistic but low on power distance. This same pattern was exhibited by England, Australia, Sweden, the Netherlands, and New Zealand. Those least similar to the United States on these dimensions were Venezuela, Colombia, Pakistan, Singapore, and the Philippines.

The United States scored low on uncertainty avoidance and high on quantity of life. The same pattern was shown by Ireland, the Philippines, New Zealand, India, and South Africa. Those least similar to the United States on these dimensions were Chile, Portugal, and the former Yugoslavia republic of Macedonia.

The Reality of Culture Shock

culture shock
Confusion, disorientation, and emotional upheaval caused by being immersed in a new culture.

Any move from one country to another will create a certain amount of confusion, disorientation, and emotional upheaval.[20] We call this **culture shock**. The transfer of an executive from the United States to Canada, for example, would require about as little adjustment as one could possibly make. Why? Be-

◆◆◆◆ OB in the News ◆◆◆◆

Aren't Canadians Just Like Their Neighbors to the South?

Most Americans don't see much difference between themselves and Canadians. Yet many Canadians resent the assumption by Americans that they're just like their southern neighbors.[21] For example, in one survey, 79 percent of Canadians polled stated that they consider themselves to be different from Americans. However, there was no consensus among those respondents as to what exactly makes Canadians unique.

Studies indicate that Canadians *perceive* themselves as more collective, traditional, and readier to accept government authority with passivity than Americans. Canadians see Americans as more aggressive, individualistic, and violent. In contrast, Canadians see themselves as more concerned about the environment and the poor than their southerly neighbors. They also see themselves as more modest, open, honest, and fair.

But perceptions can be erroneous. For instance, a number of Canadian companies, run by Canadians, are highly fierce competitors in the American market. These include Bombardier Inc., Labatt Brewing Co., Northern Telecom, the Seagram Co., and Cineplex Odeon Corporation. Many of the executives at these firms are as (or more) aggressive than their American counterparts.

Two facts suggest that Canadians are more egalitarian than Americans. First, Canadians are far more supportive of unions. In the United States, only 16 percent of workers belong to labor unions, compared to 37 percent in Canada. Second, the pay differences between top managers and first-line supervisors are much greater in the United States. CEOs in the United States earn approximately nine times more than first-line supervisors. In Canada, they earn only five times more.

On close examination of the research, the most meaningful conclusion that can be drawn is that Canada is a more regionalized nation than the United States and that English-speaking Canadians (anglophones) and Americans seem to be more alike in their styles of communication and influence than anglophones and French-speaking Canadians (francophones). Research evidence indicates, for instance, that francophones take a more competitive approach to negotiations than do either Americans or anglophone Canadians.

Canadians are different from Americans, but the differences are nebulous rather than substantive. In fact, the differences between French-speaking and English-speaking Canadians are probably more significant than the difference between English-speaking Canadians and Americans.

cause the United States and Canada have relatively similar profiles in terms of Hofstede's four cultural dimensions. Even so, there would be some culture shock. The executive would still have to adjust to differences that would include the form of representative government (Canadians have a parliamentary system, much like the one in Great Britain); language (Canada is a bilingual—English- and French-speaking—country); and even holidays (the Canadian Thanksgiving is in early October). However, culture shock will obviously be

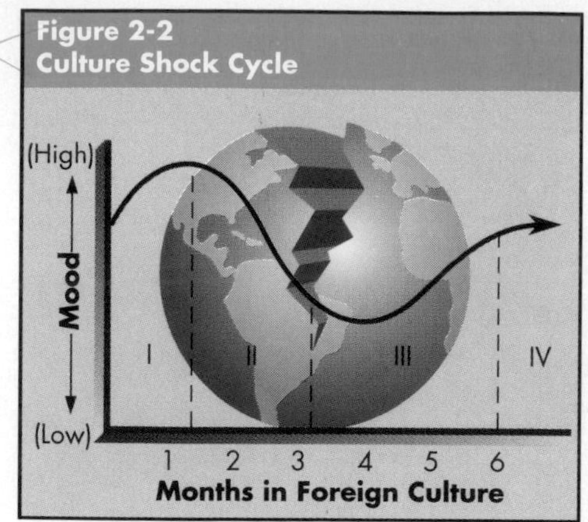

Figure 2-2
Culture Shock Cycle

more severe when individuals move to cultures that are most unlike their old environment.

The adjustment to a foreign country has been found to follow a U-shaped curve that contains four distinct stages.[22] This is shown in Figure 2-2.

Stage I is one of novelty. The newcomer is excited and optimistic. His or her mood is high. For the temporary visitor to a foreign country, this stage is all that is experienced. A person who spends a week or two on vacation in a strange land considers cultural differences to be interesting, even educational. However, the employee who makes a permanent, or relatively permanent, move experiences euphoria and then disillusionment. In Stage II, the "quaint" quickly becomes "obsolete," and the "traditional," "inefficient." The opportunity to learn a new language turns into the reality of struggling to communicate. After a few months, the newcomer hits bottom. At Stage III, any and all of the culture's differences have become blatantly clear. The newcomer's basic interpretation system, which worked fine at home, now no longer functions. He or she is bombarded by millions of sights, sounds, and other cues that are uninterpretable. Frustration and confusion are highest and mood lowest in Stage III. Finally, the newcomer begins to adapt, and the negative responses related to culture shock dissipate. In Stage IV, the newcomer has learned what is important and what can be ignored about the new culture.

What are the implications of this model? There are at least two. First, if you're a newcomer in a foreign land or you are managing a newcomer, expect culture shock. It's not abnormal. To some degree, everyone goes through it. Second, culture shock follows a relatively predictable pattern. Expect early euphoria, followed by depression and frustration. However, after about four to six months, most people adjust to their new culture. What was previously different and strange becomes understandable.

Inside the Organization: The Challenge of Work Force Diversity

We now turn toward looking at differences between people inside the organization. That is, we turn to the subject of work force diversity. What we find is that the makeup of organizations is changing to reflect the increasing heterogeneity of the overall population. Moreover, work force diversity is bringing to organizations people with skills, experiences, and outlooks that, in the past, were frequently excluded or underutilized. A few examples can illustrate this latter point.

Leigh Compton and her mother have several things in common. Both graduated in the top 1 percent of their Chicago-area high school graduating classes. Both also then went to the University of Illinois and received degrees in biology. But when Leigh's mother graduated in 1962, she saw few opportunities for female scientists in corporate America. So instead of going on to graduate school, as she preferred, she took a job as a high school science teacher, and business lost a valuable resource. Leigh, graduating in 1985, saw no such barriers. She went on to earn her master's and doctorate at Northwestern and is now a successful project manager at Genentech.

Jack O'Malley spent 42 years as a tool and die designer. He retired in 1992 with a nice pension. Yet, within six months, he was bored to death. Even though he was 67 years old, he was hired as a full-time designer by a small firm in St. Louis. Said the firm's owner, "It's almost impossible for us to find experienced tool designers like Jack. They're few and far between. Our diversity-recruitment program has specifically targeted seniors. They've got a wealth of experience and they come highly motivated."

Jim Kordosky has ten years of experience repairing expensive imported cars. He wants to work, but as a widower with three young children, his family responsibilities make a full-time job impossible. Because his employer, the German Auto Clinic, has adjusted its policies to allow employees to choose permanently reduced workdays, Jim is able to balance his family and work responsibilities.

Tina Thompson has Down's syndrome, yet holds a full-time job. She was hired by McDonald's, a company with one of corporate America's most progressive work force diversity programs. Tina's shift manager describes her as one of the hardest working and most conscientious employees she has ever had.

Skilled, experienced, and enthusiastic employees like Leigh, Jack, Jim, and Tina are a scarce resource. As we show in this section, those organizations that learn to effectively manage diversity—gender, race, ethnicity, age, able-bodiness, sexual preferences, and the like—will win the competition to hire and keep those individuals who are different.

The Changing Workplace

During the next decade, new-worker growth in the United States will be occurring most rapidly among women and Hispanics. This is going to result in reshaping the overall labor force. By the year 2005, women will likely hold 50 percent of all jobs in the United States. And as Figure 2-3 illustrates, minorities will hold more than one out of four jobs. While these small percentage changes may not seem important, they are! They indicate that the white-male working population is aging and the younger faces in organizations will belong to women, African-Americans, Latinos, and Asian-Americans.

Figure 2-3
The Changing U.S. Labor Force

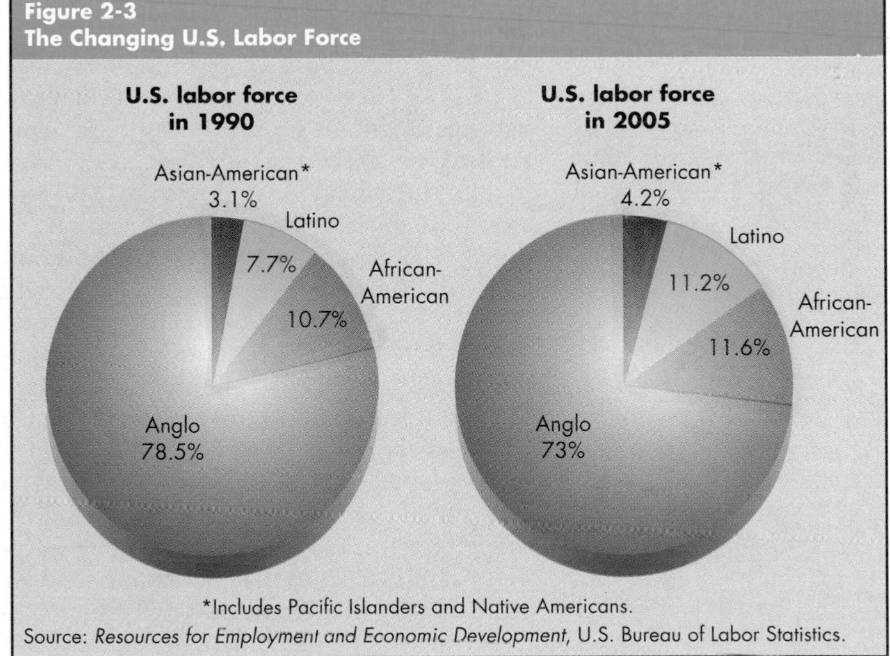

*Includes Pacific Islanders and Native Americans.
Source: *Resources for Employment and Economic Development*, U.S. Bureau of Labor Statistics.

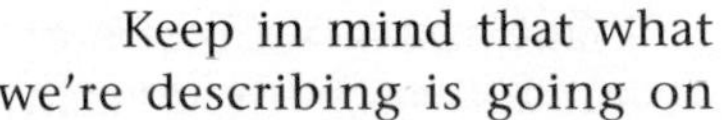

Keep in mind that what we're describing is going on all over the world, not just in the United States. Take Western Europe as an example. Eight million legal immigrants and an estimated 2 million illegal immigrants now live in the 15 nations of the European Union. A particularly large influx of Muslims and Africans in recent years has been changing the religious and racial composition of these countries.[23] And in Asia, the big challenge in organizations is adjusting to the rapid increase in the number of women employees, especially in the managerial ranks.[24] Although still a distinct minority, women are making significant inroads into managerial positions throughout Asia. For instance, in Hong Kong, women made up less than 7 percent of the total managers and administrators in 1971. In 1991 they were up to 20 percent. In Malaysia, between 1980 and 1988, women's share of administrative and managerial jobs doubled from 6 to 12 percent. And even in Japan, long hostile to corporate women, females are increasing their presence in management. In 1981 just 1.5 percent of the section chiefs in companies with more than 100 employees were women. Today that figure has nearly doubled to 2.9 percent. That's still very small, but representative of significant change for corporate Japan.[25]

Origins of the Diversity Movement

Many organizations trace the beginnings of their diversity programs to the Hudson Institute's famous *Workforce 2000* report published in 1987.[26] That report was the first to detail the extensive changes that would be forthcoming in the composition of the work force. Among its more important conclusions were that the work force would include significantly higher representation by females, minorities, and immigrants; would grow more slowly than it had in the past; and would require increased skill demands of workers. But the diversity movement more accurately has its roots in civil rights legislation and affirmative action.[27]

affirmative action programs
Programs that enhance the organizational status of members of protected groups.

Beginning with the Civil Rights Act in 1964, U.S. federal laws began to aggressively seek to prohibit discrimination based on race, color, religion, national origin, or gender. In response, many organizations implemented **affirmative action programs** to ensure that decisions and practices enhanced the employment, upgrading, and retention of members from protected groups, such as minorities and females. By taking affirmative action, organizations not only sought to refrain from discriminating, but actively sought to enhance the status of members from protected groups.

Affirmative action efforts became more pervasive and more aggressive in the late 1960s and early 1970s as the federal government began holding employers accountable for eliminating ethnic and gender imbalances in hiring. The result was that jobs became open to qualified women and minorities that had been completely shut out to them before.[28] But many of these women and minorities became dissatisfied because of what they perceived to be slow progress and resistance from the organizations' white-male majority. Even though organizations were hiring more women and minorities, there were still significant barriers to their acceptance and promotion. Additionally, it soon became evident that the turnover rate among women and minorities was considerably higher than among white males.[29] Something was wrong and it needed to be fixed. It was in this climate of trying to make organizations more "friendly" to people who were different that essentially gave the diversity movement its momentum. Diversity efforts would not only seek to bring in the disenfranchised—women, ethnic minorities, seniors, the disabled, gays and lesbians, and the like—but also to integrate them into the day-to-day workings of the organization.

From "Everyone's the Same" to "Acknowledging Differences" to "Valuing Differences"

The last 30 years has seen an evolution in the way organizations have looked at their employees (see Figure 2-4). As we noted in Chapter 1, the melting pot approach historically dominated the way management thought about the transition employees had to make upon entering an organization. Management assumed that people would automatically assimilate and become part of a homogeneous group. Regardless of who you were or where you came from, you would quickly become an IBMer, Ford employee, or whatever, depending on the firm that employed you. It sounded nice, but as we noted previously, people who were different still found barriers to their acceptance and promotion. In addition, people weren't necessarily willing to throw away 20 or 30 years of unique cultural experiences when they joined an organization. They were not only different from the majority but they had no desire to be like the majority! So, while management may have wished people to all be the same, the fact was that they weren't and didn't want to be.

Figure 2-4
The Evolution in the Ways Organizations Have Looked at Their Employees

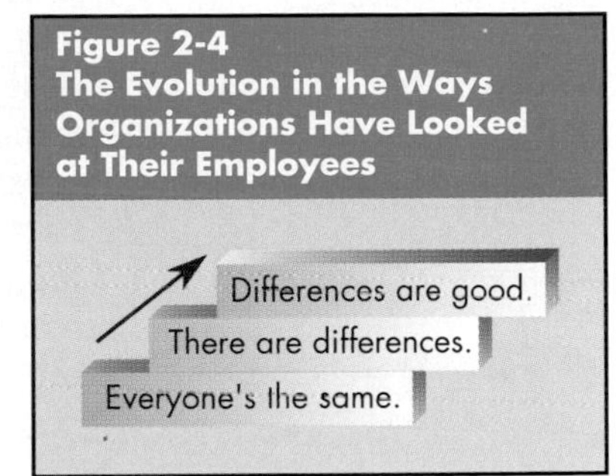
Differences are good.
There are differences.
Everyone's the same.

The period from the late 1960s through the late 1980s was characterized by acknowledging differences. Affirmative action programs were consistent with the belief that management had to redress past inequities and open

◆◆◆◆ OB in the News ◆◆◆◆

Hewlett-Packard Discovers Diversity Is Good for Business

Betty A. Sproule, a marketing research manager at Hewlett-Packard, credits the company's new mentoring program for helping her make decisions faster and improving her time-management skills. This program was designed to ensure that women and minorities get the preparation needed to move smoothly into senior-level positions and to train supervisors to manage their culturally diverse work groups.

H-P's overall commitment to managing diversity began in 1988 as a replacement to an affirmative action workshop that focused strictly on compliance with U.S. laws governing equal opportunity. The diversity program was developed after an in-house survey found that minority employees were less satisfied with pay, benefits, and promotional opportunities than their nonminority counterparts.

The basic three-day program is required for all managers and covers topics such as awareness of attitudes and prejudices, sexual harassment, workers with disabilities, legal issues, corporate objectives, and management responsibilities. In addition, a select group of managers, such as Sproule, are chosen to participate in an accelerated development program. Each participant is paired with a mentor who acts as a role model and a source for discussing job-related problems.

While the diversity program has not resulted in a dramatic increase in women and minorities moving into top level jobs, it has had some success. Worldwide, senior management positions at Hewlett-Packard are now filled 13 percent by women and 8 percent by minorities. But the program has had other positive benefits. Turnover among women and minorities has slowed. And as one executive noted, "It gives you a flood of different ideas. I have had staffs of all males. They are not as effective as a team as is a mixture of employees with diverse backgrounds."

Source: *Los Angeles Times* (May 17, 1993), p. 16.

the door for those who had previously been kept out. But again, as we noted previously, awareness of differences wasn't enough. People of diverse backgrounds had real problems adapting to organizations that were built with a white-male perspective and that had no mechanisms for adjusting to people of diversity.

Most U.S. organizations have responded by going beyond *acknowledging* differences to *valuing* differences. Managers and employees are encouraged to pay attention to both individual differences and group-member differences, to raise their level of comfort with differences, and to capitalize on differences as a major asset to the organization's productivity.[30] By valuing differences, organizations can channel the unique qualities that various individuals bring to the workplace to increase creativity and innovation, improve decision making, and gain insights into marketplaces characterized by diversity (such as women's, African-American, and global markets). The next section on managing diversity describes some of the specific programs organizations are implementing that are consistent with the valuing diversity perspective.

Managing Diversity in Organizations

United Parcel Service (UPS) has taken a rather unique approach to managing diversity. They're giving their managers a crash course in hard times.[31] The company believes its managers aren't truly able to understand someone's problems unless they're in their shoes. So each year, UPS assigns 40 middle- and upper-level managers to month-long community internships that require them to live and work in poor communities. In McAllen, Texas, they assist poor Mexican Americans and Latin American refugees. In Chicago, they live in a church and work with young people and their families. In Chattanooga, Tennessee, they provide aid to poor families, the disabled, and the severely retarded. In New York, they help unwed teenage mothers find jobs, they visit mental patients, and teach poor children. All of this is intended to help UPS managers better understand employees and customers from diverse backgrounds. One group of nine UPS managers, for instance, recently put in 60-hour weeks in McAllen, Texas, setting up a mobile library for migrant children, laid the plans for a sewing shop to provide jobs, and developed a video at a local clinic to educate indigent patients about health and nutrition.

The UPS program is unconventional. When we look at what companies like American Express, Avon Products, Corning, Digital Equipment, Johnson & Johnson, McDonald's, Xerox, and other prominent proponents of diversity are doing, we find a number of common characteristics. For the most part, their programs tend to emphasize flexible work arrangements, generous child- and elder-care benefits, and diversity training.[32]

Flexible Work Arrangements

Successfully managing diversity means organizations must increase their flexibility.[33] How do they do this? By offering employees the opportunity to work at home, providing flexible hours and compressed workweeks, allowing employees to share jobs and work part time, permitting leaves of absences, and the like.

John Hancock Mutual Life Insurance Company is a leader in providing employees with family-friendly benefits. Its on-site child care center, including a room for ill children, serves employees' families in Boston. A special hotline provides information, support, and referral to employees who need advice regarding child care, adoption, or problems their children are having in school. John Hancock has learned that benefits that help families also help productivity and profits.

Flexibility is frequently assumed to be only of interest to women who are trying to balance family and work responsibilities. But that's not the case. Job sharing, for example, is often appealing to full-time students, working at home might appeal to single parents of either sex, senior citizens might prefer part-time work to full-time responsibilities, and fathers are increasingly desirous of taking leaves from work to take care of newborn children.

Child- and Elder-Care Benefits

For many parents, the ultimate determinant of whether they are able to work or not is the availability of child care. Fel-Pro, one of the world's largest makers of gaskets for automobiles and industrial uses, is a model of what a company can do for the children of its employees.[34] When children of Fel-Pro employees turn 2, they are eligible to attend the professionally staffed Fel-Pro day-care center located adjacent to the company's plant. After the children start school, Fel-Pro sends professionally trained caregivers to the home to take care of them if they get sick. If a child is having difficulty in school, the company provides testing and individual tutoring for a modest cost. And the company runs a summer day camp for children of employees. Buses pick up kids at the factory every weekday morning during the summer and returns them every evening.

As the population ages, an increasing number of employees find themselves with responsibility for caring for parents or grandparents.[35] Employees who spend time worrying about elder care have less time for, and are less focused on, work-related issues. So many organizations are widening child-care concerns to cover all dependents including elderly family members.

Diversity Training

The centerpiece of most diversity programs is training. Diversity training programs are generally intended to provide a vehicle for increasing awareness and examining stereotypes. Participants learn to value individual differences, increase their cross-cultural understanding, and confront stereotypes.

The typical program lasts from half a day to three days in length and includes role playing, exercises, lectures, discussions, and group experiences. For example, Xerox has worked with Cornell University's theater department to create a set of short plays that increase awareness of work-related racial and gender conflicts. The show has been presented to more than 1,300 Xerox managers.[36] A training exercise at Hartford Insurance that sought to increase sensitivity to aging asked participants to repond to the following four questions:

1. If you didn't know how old you are, how old would you guess you are? In other words, how old do you feel inside?
2. When I was 18, I thought middle age began at age ____.
3. Today, I think middle age begins at age ____.
4. What would be your first reaction if someone called you an older worker?[37]

Answers to these questions were then used to analyze age-related stereotypes. In another program designed to raise awareness of the power of stereotypes, each participant was asked to write an anonymous paper detailing all groups—women, born-again Christians, blacks, gays, Hispanics, men—to which they had attached stereotypes.[38] They were also asked to explain why they'd had trouble working with certain groups in the past. Based on responses, guest speakers were brought into the class to shatter the stereotypes directed at each group. This was followed by extensive discussion.

Summary and Implications for Managers

The country in which a person is raised shapes and constrains his or her behavior. Given that the world has become a global village, we therefore need to take into consideration national culture as a potent force in explaining and predicting behavior.

Most of the concepts that currently make up the body of knowledge we call *organizational behavior* have been developed by Americans using American subjects within domestic contexts. A comprehensive study, for instance, of more than 11,000 articles published in 24 management and organizational behavior journals over a ten-year period revealed that approximately 80 percent of the studies were done in the United States and had been conducted by Americans.[39] Follow-up studies continue to confirm the lack of cross-cultural considerations in management and OB research.[40] What this means is that not all the concepts we present in future chapters are universally applicable to managing people around the world.

Given this U.S. bias, how should managers approach the findings in this book? First, they should find out where the person or people whose behavior they're trying to understand come from. Second, they should evaluate that country using one or both of the cultural differences frameworks presented in this chapter. Third, they need to compare the national culture in question against the data for the United States and identify relevant differences. This is necessary because most of the research in OB has been conducted on Americans in the United States. Finally, they should modify the concepts about to be introduced in this book that explain and predict employee behavior to reflect these differences.

How about managerial implications for work force diversity? First, managers have to sensitize themselves to the difficulties that people of diversity face in organizations. Then they must play a proactive role in fostering a work climate that supports and values diversity. This means actively seeking out input on the needs of women and minorities. It means supporting policies and practices that make it easier for people of diversity to perform their jobs. And it means encouraging the development of diversity training programs and the participation of all organization members in them.

For Review

1. What is the argument in support of the proposition that the world has become a global village?
2. Is the variance between national cultures increasing, decreasing, or staying about the same?
3. Why is a country's national culture so hard to identify and understand?
4. Describe the United States in terms of Americans' relationship to the environment, time orientation, activity orientation, and conception of space. Describe it in terms of Hofstede's four major criteria.
5. In which countries are employees *most* like those in the United States? *Least* like those in the United States?
6. What is *culture shock*? How could you use the four-stage culture shock model to better understand employee behavior?
7. What's the origin of the work force diversity movement?
8. Contrast "acknowledging differences" with "valuing differences."
9. Give four examples of work arrangements that increase flexibility for employees.
10. What would a diversity training program look like? What objectives might it seek to achieve?

For Discussion

1. How do you think managing people in Finland might be different for an individual who was born and raised in Mexico?
2. How will regional cooperative agreements affect management practices in Canada? Germany? Australia?
3. You've been transferred to Tokyo to manage your company's Japanese operations because of your high job performance and the fact that you studied Japanese for three years in college. Discuss the changes you will need to make in order to effectively oversee your Japanese staff.
4. Women and minorities have been in the work force since the late 1940s. Why has work force diversity become such a hot topic in the 1990s?
5. Management practitioners, consultants, and scholars have tended in recent years to look at the positive aspects of work force diversity. Are there any negative aspects? If so, what are they? How can they be minimized?

Point

Cross-Cultural Training Doesn't Work

Academics seem to take it as a truism that the expanding global marketplace has serious implications for management practice. As a result, they have become strong advocates for the necessity of cross-cultural training. But most corporations don't provide cross-cultural training for employees. Studies indicate, for instance, that only 30 percent of American managers who are sent on foreign assignments scheduled to last from one to five years receive any cross-cultural training before their departure.

Why don't most organizations provide their managers with cross-cultural training? We propose two possible explanations. One is that top managers believe that "managing is managing," so *where* it is done is irrelevant. The other explanation is that top management doesn't believe that cross-cultural training is effective.

Contrary to the evidence presented in this chapter, many senior managers continue to believe that managerial skills are perfectly transferable across cultures. A good manager in New York or Los Angeles, for instance, should be equally effective in Paris or Hong Kong. In organizations where this belief dominates, you won't find any concern with cross-cultural training. Moreover, there is likely to be little effort made to select candidates for foreign assignments based on their ability to fit into, or adapt to, a specific culture. Selection decisions for overseas postings in these organizations are primarily made using a single criterion: the person's domestic track record.

It's probably fair to say that most senior managers today recognize that cultural differences do affect managerial performance. But their organizations still don't provide cross-cultural training because these managers doubt the effectiveness of this training. They argue that people can't learn to manage in a foreign culture after only a few weeks or months of training. An understanding of a country's culture is something one assimilates over many years based on input from many sources. It is not something that lends itself to short-term learning, no matter how intensive a training program might be.

Given the previous arguments, it would be surprising to find organizations offering cross-cultural training. We submit that top executives of organizations typically take one of three approaches in dealing with the selection of managerial personnel for staff foreign assignments. One approach is to ignore cultural differences. They don't worry about them, and make their selection decisions based solely on individuals' previous managerial records. Another approach is to hire nationals to manage foreign operations. Since cross-cultural training isn't effective, when a firm such as IBM needs an executive to fill a key post in Italy, it might be best served by hiring an Italian. This solution has become even easier for North American firms in recent years as the number of foreigners in American and Canadian business schools has increased. For instance, there are now literally thousands of Italians, Arabs, Germans, Japanese, and other foreign nationals who have graduate business degrees from American universities, understand American business practices, and have returned to their homelands. The third solution to the problem is to either hire nationals or intensively train people to be expert advisers to management. AT&T, as a case in point, sent one executive and his family to Singapore for a lengthy stay to soak up the atmosphere and learn about the Singaporian way of doing business. He then returned to New York as the resident expert on Singapore. When problems involving that country arise, he is called on to provide insight.

The evidence in this argument is drawn from J.S. Black and M. Mendenhall, "Cross-Cultural Training Effectiveness: A Review and a Theoretical Framework for Future Research," *Academy of Management Review* (January 1990), pp. 113–36; and A. Kupfer, "How to Be a Global Manager," *Fortune* (March 14, 1988), p. 52.

counterPoint

Cross-Cultural Training Is Effective

Yes, it's true that most corporations don't provide cross-cultural training. And that's a mistake! Clearly, the ability to adapt to the cultural differences in a foreign assignment is important to managerial success. Moreover, contrary to what many managers believe, cross-cultural training is very effective. Let's elaborate on this second point.

A comprehensive review of studies that specifically looked at the effectiveness of cross-cultural training shows overwhelming evidence that this training fosters the development of cross-cultural skills and leads to higher performance. Training has been shown to improve an individual's relationships with host nationals, to allow that person to adjust more rapidly to a new culture, and to improve his or her work performance. In addition, training significantly reduces expatriate failure rates. For instance, without training, 68 out of every 100 Americans transferred to Saudi Arabia will come home early because of their inability to cross the cultural chasm. Shell Oil, however, put 800 American employees through training before sending them to a petrochemical operation in Saudi Arabia and only 3 didn't survive the cultural adjustment.

While these results are impressive, they don't say anything about the type of training the employee received. Does that make a difference?

A variety of training techniques are available to prepare people for foreign work assignments. They range from documentary programs that merely expose people to a new culture through written materials on the country's sociopolitical history, geography, economics, and cultural institutions, to intense interpersonal-experience training, where individuals participate in role-playing exercises, simulated social settings, and similar experiences to "feel" the differences in a new culture.

One research study looked at the effectiveness of these two approaches on a group of American managers. These managers, who worked for an electronic products firm, were sent on assignment to Seoul, South Korea. Twenty of them received no training, 20 got only the documentary program, and 20 received only interpersonal-experience training. The training activities were all completed in a three-day period. All participants, no matter which group they were in, received some language training, briefings covering company operations in South Korea, and a cursory three-page background description of the country. The results of this study confirmed the earlier evidence that cross-cultural training works. Specifically, the study found that managers who received either form of training were better performers and perceived less need to adjust to the new culture than those who received no such training. Additionally, neither method proved superior to the other.

In another study with civilian employees in a U.S. military agency, participants were grouped so they received either a documentary orientation, experiential training, some combination of the two, or no training at all. Findings from this study again confirmed the value of cross-cultural training. Either type of training proved to be more effective than no training in improving cross-cultural knowledge and behavioral performance, and the combination approach was found to be most effective.

The evidence in this argument is drawn from J.S. Black and M. Mendenhall, "Cross-Cultural Training Effectiveness: A Review and a Theoretical Framework for Future Research," *Academy of Management Review* (January 1990), pp. 113–36; P.C. Earley, "Intercultural Training for Managers: A Comparison of Documentary and Interpersonal Methods," *Academy of Management Journal* (December 1987), pp. 685–98; S. Caudron, "Surviving Cross-Cultural Shock," *Industry Week* (July 6, 1992), pp. 35–38; J.S. Lublin, "Companies Use Cross-Cultural Training to Help Their Employees Adjust Abroad," *Wall Street Journal* (August 4, 1992), p. B1; and J.K. Harrison, "Individual and Combined Effects of Behavior Modeling and the Cultural Assimilator in Cross-Cultural Management Training," *Journal of Applied Psychology* (December 1992) pp. 952–62.

Learning About Yourself Exercise

What's Your International-Culture IQ?

How knowledgeable are you about customs, practices, and facts regarding different countries? The following multiple-choice quiz will provide you with some feedback on this question.

1. In which country would *Ramadan* (a month of fasting) be celebrated by a majority of the people?

a. Saudi Arabia
b. India
c. Singapore
d. Korea
e. All of the above

2. On first meeting your prospective Korean business partner, Lo Kim Chee, it would be best to address him as:

a. Mr. Kim
b. Mr. Lo
c. Mr. Chee
d. Bud
e. Any of the above are readily accepted

3. In Brazil, your promotional material should be translated into what language?

a. French
b. Italian
c. Spanish
d. No need to translate it
e. None of the above

4. In Japan it is important to:

a. Present your business card only after you have developed a relationship with your Japanese host
b. Present your business card with both hands
c. Put your company name on the card, but never your position or title
d. All of the above
e. None of the above

5. Which one of the following sports is the most popular worldwide?

a. Basketball
b. Baseball
c. Tennis
d. Futbol
e. Golf

6. For an American businessperson, touching a foreign businessperson would be least acceptable in which one of the following countries?

a. Japan
b. Italy
c. Slovenia
d. Venezuela
e. France

7. Which of the following would be an appropriate gift?

a. A clock in China
b. A bottle of liquor in Egypt
c. A set of knives in Argentina
d. A banquet in China
e. None of the above would be appropriate

8. Which one of the following countries has the most rigid social hierarchy?
   a. United Kingdom
   b. United States
   c. Japan
   d. India
   e. Germany

9. Traditional western banking is difficult in which one of the following countries because their law forbids both the giving and taking of interest payments?
   a. Brazil
   b. Saudi Arabia
   c. Mongolia
   d. India
   e. Greece

10. The capital of Canada is:
   a. Toronto
   b. Ottawa
   c. Vancouver
   d. Ontario
   e. Montreal

Turn to page A-26 for scoring directions and key.

Source: Professor David Hopkins, University of Denver, 1991. With permission.

Working with Others Exercise

Learning About Differences Through Analyzing Prejudice

Prejudice is defined as an unfounded generalization about a group of people. Whether we like to admit it or not, we all have prejudices. For example, the following are groups of people that students have indicated feeling some prejudice toward: fraternity and sorority members, athletes on scholarship, college professors, surfers, people with heavy accents, the homeless, shy individuals, and people with assertive personalities.

1. Select a prejudice you hold.

2. Individually, take approximately 15 minutes and analyze this prejudice:
   a. Why did you develop it?
   b. What functions, if any, does it currently serve?
   c. Do you want to keep it? Explain your answer.
   d. How could you go about removing it from your worldview?

3. Form groups of three to five each. Group members should share their analysis from step 2 and discuss how people can go about reducing prejudices they hold toward those from different cultures.

Source: This exercise is based on an assignment described in M. Mendenhall, "A Painless Approach to Integrating 'International' into OB, HRM, and Management Courses," *Organizational Behavior Teaching Review*, Vol. XIII, No. 3 (1988–89), p. 29.

Ethical Dilemma Exercise

The Diversity Movement: What About Its Adverse Impact on White Males?

Some companies are engaging in a practice that is controversial and potentially illegal. In their desire to diversify upper management, they are excluding men from consideration. For example, Korn/Ferry International, the largest executive search firm in the United States, says it was asked to find a woman in 4.1 percent of its executive assignments during fiscal 1993. When Burger King sought to fill the position of senior vice president for human resources, the company looked outside after inside contenders—all male—failed to qualify. The fast-food chain said it interviewed only women because the CEO insisted that senior management better reflect Burger King's customers, nearly half of whom are female. The Chicago Sun-Times interviewed only female outsiders for its corporate controller position because, officials said, the internal candidates—all men—lacked sufficient experience and because the job's previous incumbent was a woman.

As organizations restructure themselves through widespread layoffs, and at the same time seek to increase the diversity of their work force, white men—particularly those in mid-career—are feeling increasingly left out, resentful, and afraid. The best jobs lost in the past decade have been theirs; the best jobs created in the future may not be. Some men are crying "reverse discrimination." But favoring women and minorities isn't necessarily against the law. The courts allow organizations to take race into account in hiring, for instance, to remedy past discrimination.

When organizations are adding new people, they're looking for women, Latinos, Asian-Americans, and African-Americans. This seems to be especially true among professional and managerial workers. In 1983 white men held 63.5 percent of those jobs in the United States. In 1993 they were down to 53 percent. Among the upper ranks, white women have been the major beneficiaries of men's loss of dominance.

Managers—many of them white males themselves—face a dilemma. To make their organizations more diverse, they are certain to hire and promote women and minorities over other white males. In so doing, they risk angering those passed over. But if these managers fail to embrace diversity, they not only perpetuate past injustices, but risk leaving their organizations less globally competitive. What should they do? What do *you* think?

Based on M. Galen, "White, Male, and Worried," *Business Week* (January 31, 1994), pp. 50–55; M.L. LaGanga, "Changing of the Guard," *Los Angeles Times* (February 7, 1994), p. S9; and J.S. Lublin, "Firms Designate Some Openings for Women Only," *Wall Street Journal* (February 7, 1994), p. B1.

Xerox of Mexico

Paul Hunt grew up in Houston and got his degree in business management from Texas A&M in 1988. Upon graduation, Paul took a job with the Xerox Corporation in Dallas as a human resource specialist. During his first two years, he split his time between recruiting on college campuses and establishing a training program for maintenance engineers. In 1990 Paul was promoted to assistant manager for human resources-western region. The company moved him to the western regional office in Denver.

Paul's annual performance appraisals were consistently high. The company believed he had strong advancement potential. Although Paul was ambitious and made no attempt to hide his desire to move into higher management, even he was a bit surprised when he was called to Xerox's Connecticut headquarters in September 1993 and offered the position of director of human resources for Xerox of Mexico. If he accepted the position, Paul would oversee a staff of 20 people in Mexico City and be responsible for all human resource activities—hiring, compensation, labor relations, and so on—for the company's Mexican operations. He was told that the combination of his outstanding job performance ratings and his ability to speak Spanish (Paul had taken four years of Spanish in high school and another 12 hours of advanced coursework in college) led the company to select him for the promotion.

Paul accepted the offer. Why not? It was an important promotion, meant a large increase in pay, and provided an opportunity to live in a foreign country. But he knew he would have some serious adjustments to make. That became abundantly clear when he read an article describing the differences between the United States and Mexico.* Here were a few of the observations made in the article:

- Mexicans tend to accept the inherent worth of friends and colleagues without demanding specific performance or achievement. Americans believe that one demonstrates integrity or dignity through actions. In the United States, the one who wins is obviously the "better person"; in Mexico every individual is special whether the winner or not.
- In the United States, a person should not look for any special favors or exemptions from the rules. No one is above the law. In Mexico, rules, policies, and procedures are sometimes overlooked. Given their belief in the uniqueness of each individual, it stands to reason that people, rather than abstract principles, should be respected. Following rules in Mexico is often considered the most ineffective way to get things done.
- A strong tendency in Mexico is to shun open confrontation due to fear of losing face and having to acknowledge disagreements. Negative or disappointing information is either withheld or modified to avoid being offensive. In contrast, Americans place greater emphasis on stating the facts, regardless of the impact.
- When an American executive agrees to do something, it is a matter of personal honor and professional integrity to fulfill that commitment. For many Mexicans, a commitment is an intention—a statement of a desirable outcome, not a promise to fulfill an agreed upon arrangement.
- Mexicans have a different perception of time from Americans. Mexicans have a loose notion of what being "on time" means, interruptions are handled without much stress, and there is little expectation that plans will proceed in a logical order. In contrast, Americans believe appointments and deadlines should be scheduled tightly and respected as much as possible; interruptions are annoying and inefficient; and "on time" literally means "on time."

Questions

1. Using the two frameworks presented in this chapter, how would you describe Mexico's national culture?
2. Contrast the culture in Mexico to the culture in which Paul grew up.
3. In order to be effective in managing his Mexican staff, what specific changes do you think Paul will need to make when he arrives in Mexico City?

*M.I. Erlich, "Making Sense of the Bicultural Workplace," *Business Mexico* (August 1993), pp. 16–19.

VIDEO CASE

Are Women Really Treated Different from Men?

Many women complain that men treat them differently than they do other men. But do women *really* face gender discrimination? That's what the staff at ABC's *PrimeTime Live* decided to find out.

The experiments were done with two ABC employees: Julie (the woman) and Chris (the man). Both were intelligent and articulate individuals in their late 20s or early 30s. And Cincinnati, Ohio, was chosen as the location, since it represents a fairly middle-class American city.

The first experiment related to the purchase of a new car. Studies indicate that women are typically quoted higher prices than men for the same vehicle. The ABC staff found this to be the case. A salesman offered Chris the same car that Julie looked at for $500 less! Moreover, this salesman wouldn't let Julie drive the car off the lot, saying it was against the dealership's rules. Yet that same salesman just handed Chris the keys and told him to go out and test-drive the car.

Julie and Chris took a comparable set of clothes into a dry cleaners. You'd think they'd be charged the same. They weren't! Julie paid more. For instance, on one common item that Chris paid $2.25, Julie was charged $3.50.

The ABC news staff next went to a golf course. Would a woman be treated any differently in terms of getting a tee time? This experiment certainly found that they did. Julie was told, for instance, that the following Friday was all booked up. A short time later, when Chris came in to schedule a playing time for that same Friday, the clerk was able to arrange it.

When Julie and Chris both responded to an ad for a territory manager at a lawn-care company, gender discrimination again raised its ugly head. Although both Julie and Chris had comparable résumés (with Julie's actually being a bit stronger), the interviewer immediately began talking to Julie about a secretarial/receptionist opening (which paid around $6 an hour) rather than the management position (which paid $300 to $500 a week). In spite of her qualifications for the management job, the interviewer wanted to give Julie a typing test. In contrast, Chris's interview focused exclusively on the management job. In a follow-up with the interviewer, he admitted he had made judgments based solely on gender.

What did the people at ABC learn from this set of experiments? Cultural stereotypes and discrimination based on gender still seem to be widely prevalent.

Questions

1. Do the results from these experiments surprise you? Discuss.
2. What do you think perpetuates gender stereotypes?
3. What can senior management do to eliminate these types of stereotypes in the workplace?

Source: "The Fairer Sex?" *PrimeTime Live* (October 7, 1993).

Suggestions for Further Reading

ALBA, R.D., *Ethnic Identity* (London: Yale University Press, 1990).

CHAN, H.L., "Preparing Managers to Work in China," *Journal of Management Education* (December 1992), pp. 54–60.

COX, T., JR., and S. BLAKE, "Managing Cultural Diversity: Implications for Organizational Competitiveness," *Academy of Management Executive* (August 1991), pp. 45–56.

FAGENSON, E.A. (ed.), *Women in Management: Challenges in Managerial Diversity* (Newbury Park, CA: Sage, 1993).

GANNON, M.J., AND ASSOCIATES, *Understanding Global Cultures* (Thousand Oaks, CA: Sage, 1994).

HARRIS, P.R., and R.T. MORAN, *Managing Cultural Differences*, 3rd ed. (Houston: Gulf Publishing, 1991).

HURH, W., and K. KIM, "The Success Image of Asian-Americans: Its Validity and Its Practical and Theoretical Implications," *Ethnic and Racial Studies*, Vol. 12, No. 4 (1989), pp. 512–38.

LOBEL, S.A., "Sexuality at Work: Where Do We Go from Here?" *Journal of Vocational Behavior* (February 1993), pp. 136–52.

MORRISON, A.N., and M. VON GLINOW, "Women and Minorities in Management," *American Psychologist* (February 1990), pp. 200–208.

POWELL, G.N., *Women & Men in Management*, 2nd ed. (Thousand Oaks, CA: Sage, 1993).

Notes

[1] D. McMurdy, "Battling Bentonville," *MacLean's* (May 2, 1994), p. 36.

[2] These examples are from H.J. LaFleche, "When in Rome . . .", *TWA Ambassador* (October 1990), p. 69.

[3] Cited in T. Cox, Jr., *Cultural Diversity in Organizations* (San Francisco: Berrett-Koehler, 1993), p. 3.

[4] World Bank, *World Development Report: 1986* (Washington, DC: Author, 1986); and "The International 500," *Forbes* (July 19, 1993), pp. 126–90.

[5] A.G. Holzinger, "NAFTA Opens a New Era," *Nation's Business* (January 1994), p. 24.

[6] N.J. Adler, *International Dimensions of Organizational Behavior*, 2nd ed. (Boston: Kent, 1991), p. 11.

[7] R. Knotts, "Cross-Cultural Management: Transformations and Adaptations," *Business Horizons* (January-February 1989), p. 32.

[8] See D.A. Ricks, M.Y.C. Fu, and J.S. Arpas, *International Business Blunders* (Columbus, OH: Grid, 1974); A. Bennett, "American Culture Is Often a Puzzle for Foreign Managers in the U.S.," *Wall Street Journal* (February 12, 1986); and C.F. Valentine, "Blunders Abroad," *Nation's Business* (March 1989), p. 54.

[9] Reported in N.A. Boyacigiller and N.J. Adler, "The Parochial Dinosaur: Organizational Science in a Global Context," *Academy of Management Review* (April 1991), pp. 264–65.

[10] W. McWhirter, "I Came, I Saw, I Blundered," *Time* (October 9, 1989), p. 72.

[11] Ibid., pp. 72–77.

[12] See H.W. Lane and D.G. Simpson, "Bribery in International Business: Whose Problem Is It?" in H.W. Lane and J.J. DiStefano (eds.), *International Management Behavior: From Policy to Practice* (Scarborough, Ontario: Nelson Canada, 1988), pp. 236–47; and J.B. Ford and E.D. Honeycutt, Jr., "Japanese National Culture as a Basis for Understanding Japanese Business Practices," *Business Horizons* (November-December 1992), pp. 27–34.

[13] J. Child, "Culture, Contingency and Capitalism in the Cross-National Study of Organizations," in L.L. Cummings and B.M. Staw (eds.), *Research in Organizational Behavior*, Vol. 3 (Greenwich, CT: JAI Press, 1981), pp. 303–56.

[14] Ibid.

[15] G. Hofstede, *Culture's Consequences: International Differences in Work Related Values* (Beverly Hills, CA: Sage, 1980).

[16] The following is based on M. Hornblower and R.T. Zintl, "Racism," *Time* (August 12, 1991), pp. 36–38.

[17] F. Kluckhohn and F.L. Strodtbeck, *Variations in Value Orientations* (Evanston, IL: Row, Peterson, 1961).

[18] Boyacigiller and Adler, "The Parochial Dinosaur," p. 274.

[19] See Hofstede, *Culture's Consequences*; G. Hofstede, "The Cultural Relativity of Organizational Practices and Theories," *Journal of International Business Studies* (Fall 1983), pp. 75–89; G. Hofstede, *Cultures and Organizations: Software of the Mind* (London: McGraw-Hill, 1991); and G. Hofstede, "Cultural Constraints in Management Theories," *Academy of Management Executive* (February 1993), pp. 81–94.

[20] See, for example, R.G. Linowes, "The Japanese Manager's Traumatic Entry into the United States: Understanding the American-Japanese Cultural Divide," *Academy of Management Executive* (November 1993), pp. 21–40.

[21] This box is based on K. Freed, "Canadians New Pride in Own Identity," *Los Angeles Times* (January 22, 1986), p. 1; M. McDonald, "Pride and Patriotism," *Maclean's* (July 7, 1986), pp. 10–13; N.J. Adler and J.L. Graham, "Business Negotiations: Canadians Are Not Just Like Americans," *Canadian Journal of Administrative Sciences* (September 1987), pp. 211–38; A. Phillips, "Defining Identity," *Maclean's* (January 4, 1988), pp. 44–45; D. Baer, E. Grabb, and W.A. Johnston, "The Values of Canadians and Americans: A Critical Analysis and Reassessment," *Social Forces* (March 1990), pp.

693–713; F. Livsey, "Employee Compensation and Benefits: Canada vs. U.S.," *Business Quarterly* (Spring 1990), pp. 20–26; and S.P. Robbins and R. Stuart-Kotze, *Management: Canadian Fourth Edition* (Scarborough, Ontario: Prentice Hall Canada, 1994), pp. 1–11.

[22] This section is based on the work of J.T. Gullahorn and J.E. Gullahorn, "An Extension of the U-Curve Hypothesis," *Journal of Social Sciences* (January 1963), pp. 34–47.

[23] Lane and DiStefano, *International Management Behavior*, pp. 4–5.

[24] Z. Abdoolcarim, "How Women Are Winning at Work," *Asian Business* (November 1993), pp. 24–29.

[25] Ibid.

[26] W.B. Johnston and A.E. Packer, *Workforce 2000: Work and Workers for the 21st Century* (Indianapolis: Hudson Institute, 1987).

[27] See L.S. Gottfredson, "Dilemmas in Developing Diversity Programs," in S.E. Jackson and associates (eds.), *Diversity in the Workplace* (New York: Guilford Press, 1992), pp. 280–83.

[28] Ibid.

[29] See B.R. Bergmann and W.R. Krause, "Evaluating and Forecasting Progress in Racial Integration of Employment," *Industrial and Labor Relations Review* (April 1968), pp. 399–409; and F. Schwartz, "Management Women and the New Facts of Life," *Harvard Business Review* (January-February 1989), pp. 65–76.

[30] B.A. Walker and W.C. Hanson, "Valuing Differences at Digital Equipment Corporation," in S.E. Jackson and associates (eds.), *Diversity in the Workplace*, pp. 119–20.

[31] K. Murray, "Listening to the Other America," *New York Times* (April 25, 1993), p. F25.

[32] See, for example, E.W. Morrison and J.M. Herlihy, "Becoming the Best Place to Work: Managing Diversity at American Express Travel Related Services," in S.E. Jackson and associates (eds.), *Diversity in the Workplace*, pp. 203–26; L.A. Hollister, N.E. Day, and P.T. Jesaitis, "Diversity Programs: Key to Competitiveness or Just Another Fad?" *Organization Development Journal* (Winter 1993), pp. 49–58; and B.P. Noble, "Making a Case for Family Programs," *New York Times* (May 2, 1993), p. F25.

[33] D.T. Hall and V.A. Parker, "The Role of Workplace Flexibility in Managing Diversity," *Organizational Dynamics* (Summer 1993), pp. 5–18.

[34] R. Levering and M. Moskowitz, "The Ten Best Companies to Work for in America," *Business and Society Review* (Spring 1993), pp. 31–32.

[35] S. Shellenbarger, "The Aging of America Is Making 'Elder Care' a Big Workplace Issue," *Wall Street Journal* (February 16, 1994), p. A1.

[36] L.E. Wynter, "Theatre Program Tackles Issues of Diversity," *Wall Street Journal* (April 18, 1991), p. B1.

[37] B. Hynes-Grace, "To Thrive, Not Merely Survive," in *Textbook Authors Conference Presentations* (Washington, DC: October 21, 1992); sponsored by the American Association of Retired Persons; p. 12.

[38] "Teaching Diversity: Business Schools Search for Model Approaches," *Newsline* (Fall 1992), p. 21.

[39] N.J. Adler, "Cross-Cultural Management Research: The Ostrich and the Trend," *Academy of Management Review* (April 1983), pp. 226–32.

[40] L. Godkin, C.E. Braye, and C.L. Caunch, "U.S.-Based Cross Cultural Management Research in the Eighties," *Journal of Business and Economic Perspectives*, Vol. 15 (1989), pp. 37–45; and T.K. Peng, M.F. Peterson, and Y.P. Shyi, "Quantitative Methods in Cross-National Management Research: Trends and Equivalence Issues," *Journal of Organizational Behavior*, Vol. 12 (1991), pp. 87–107.

PROGRESSIVE CASE
◆PART ONE◆
INTRODUCTION

ROB PANCO: THE EVOLUTION OF A MANAGER*

Robert (Rob) Panco is the general manager of M.E. Aslett Corp., a small but rapidly growing New Jersey-based packager of educational and professional reference books. Aslett handles book projects from conception all the way up to, but excluding, the printing stage. The company's clients include Grolier Encyclopedia, World Book International, Prentice Hall, Harcourt Brace, and McGraw-Hill.

What career path did Rob Panco take to get to where he is today? What challenges and problems related to OB has he encountered in his career? This progressive case (which appears at the end of each section of this book) will provide answers to these questions.

You will find this case valuable for at least two reasons. First, it'll help you integrate many of the OB concepts introduced in this book. Unfortunately, textbooks have to be linear—moving sequentially through an artificially created set of independent chapters. The real world, however, is a juggling act of overlapping and highly interdependent activities. This case will make this interdependence clearer and help demonstrate how individual, group, and organization-system factors overlap. Second, this progressive case will show you the applicability of OB concepts to actual management practice. Most textbook examples or cases are short and designed to illustrate only one or two points. As an integrated and progressive story, the Rob Panco case will show you how one real-life manager has dealt with dozens of OB issues.

Figure I-1 on the next page provides a brief description of Rob Panco's background and career progression. But résumés leave a lot out. So let's begin by talking a bit about Rob's early life and career experiences.

If you had asked Rob during his senior year in high school what he planned on doing with his life, he'd have answered: "I'm going to be a professional musician." Toward that end, he had trained as a string bass player. When he went off to college—Duquesne University in Pittsburgh—it was with the intention to pursue his music interests. But things don't always work out as planned. During his first year, Rob came face to face with reality: There were lots of string bass players more talented than he was. If he pursued his passion, he could be a music teacher at best. Rob wanted more so he decided to change majors. He chose to work toward a degree in business, with specialization in marketing and management.

Why pursue a career in business? Rob wasn't sure. It might have been the influence of his father, who opened a State Farm insurance agency after spending 22 years in the U.S. Navy. Or it might have been the positive experiences he'd had working part-time in high school. From the age of 14 to 18, Rob worked evenings, weekends, and summers at a weekly newspaper. "I took the job initially to make money. I wanted to buy a $1400 string bass." He started by sweeping floors and washing presses. But, over time, he learned most of the jobs at the paper. For instance, he set type, pasted up ads, and perfected the skills of maintaining complex printing equipment. After graduating from high school, Rob continued working summers at the newspaper. This job may have laid the groundwork for his job today in the publishing industry.

*Some facts, incidents, and quotes included in this progressive case have been slightly modified by the author to enhance student discussion and analysis.

Figure I-1

Résumé
ROBERT PANCO, JR.
446 Sheridan Avenue
New Brunswick, NJ 07114
(908) 792-1722

Education

M.B.A., Duquesne University (Pittsburgh, PA), 1984
B.S., Business Administration, Duquesne University.
Major: Marketing/Management; Minor: Economics, 1982

Professional Experience

5/93-present	General Manager, M.E. Aslett Corp., New Jersey
10/92-4/93	Business Manager, M.E. Aslett Corp.
9/90-9/92	Project Manager/Consultant, AT&T Bell Laboratories, New Jersey
5/89-9/90	Senior Marketing Manager, AT&T Network Systems Regional Marketing, Maryland
10/88-4/89	Marketing Manager, AT&T Network Systems Regional Marketing
5/87-9/88	Market Planner, AT&T Network Systems Network Market Planning, New Jersey
6/86-4/87	Associate Market Planner, AT&T Network Systems Network Market Planning
6/83-6/86	Senior Consultant, Small Business Development Center; Duquesne University, Division of Continuing Education

Personal

Birthdate: January 20, 1960
Marital Status: Married, no children

During his undergraduate college years, Rob gained experience selling shoes at Tom McAn, working in a Hallmark card store, and in similar jobs. It wasn't unusual for him to carry 18 units and work 30 hours a week during the school year. (He needed the money, but he also enjoyed working.) Rob also assumed leadership roles in campus activities. He was on the Student Activity Board (SAB) and singlehandedly fought to bring jazz concerts to campus. These concerts eventually became one of the SAB's few profit-making enterprises. But Rob's heavy schedule had a price. "My grades were never as high as they should have been," says Rob. "I was a B student when I should have been making A's."

After earning his undergraduate degree, and facing a weak job market, Rob entered graduate school to work on an MBA. Again, he combined studying with an outside job. In his first year, he spent 20 hours a week supervising students at the university's Student Union. In his second year, he spent 30 hours a week working in the university's Small Business Development Center. Both these jobs were valuable because they allowed Rob to apply what he was learning in his MBA program. Clearly, a pattern was emerging. This was a guy who wasn't happy unless he was keeping very busy.

Rob stayed at the Small Business Development Center for two years after earning his MBA. Then he left for a job at AT&T in New Jersey. In his first job there, he did market research on new products. After six months, he got his first promotion. A year later, he was chosen to head a temporary market-research project team made up of five peers. "This was a very challenging job," says Rob. "These people worked under my direction but reported to their departmental bosses. I had no real authority, yet I was responsible for the project. Ironically, it was a lot like my experience in running concerts in college. The people I oversaw were all volunteers. Managing peers and volunteers is very similar."

Rob's success in managing this project team led to his nomination and selection to AT&T's Leadership Continuity Program. This is a select group of individuals who show promise for significantly higher managerial responsibilities. As part of this program, Rob linked up with a senior executive who would become an informal mentor, participated in two continuing education programs a year, and gained favored status on future job assignments. In May 1989, Rob was transferred to Maryland as a senior marketing manager. Eighteen months later he returned to New Jersey as a project manager.

In October 1992, Rob joined M.E. Aslett as the company's business manager. Seven months later he took over his current job as general manager. He now oversees the firm's operations—the production manager, network administrator, copy editors, proofreaders, desktop publishers, and color separators all report directly to him. Aslett experienced sales growth of 22 percent a year between 1992 and 1994 and now has sales in the multimillions.

When asked about his philosophy toward managing people, Rob says: "You can't take honesty away. Don't mislead people. Be open and tell the truth." But he also mentions something that occasionally gets him into trouble: "I assume that other people love their work as much as I do. I like to learn, to keep moving forward. For instance, I set self-improvement goals for myself every quarter. I sometimes forget that other people aren't like me."

The comment that "other people aren't like me" prompted questions about work force diversity at Aslett. "We have more women working here than men," Rob says. "And several of our people are single parents. In addition, we employ a couple of people from Great Britain, an African-American, and a Jamaican. For a company with only 20 people, I think we have a pretty diverse group."

When asked about his career goals, Rob is equally forthcoming. "I want to grow. I want to learn new things. I like working hard, but as long as I'm learning, I enjoy it. I want to do things that are fun."

Questions

1. How do you think Rob's early life experiences have influenced his career choices and his philosophy toward managing people?
2. Review Rob's current job in terms of managerial functions, roles, and skills.
3. What challenges might Rob face with his diverse work force at Aslett that he might not have to deal with in a homogeneous work force?
4. What do you think Rob means when he says that "managing peers and volunteers is very similar"?
5. How might Rob's job be different today than it would have been ten years ago? How might it be different ten years from now?

PART TWO
THE INDIVIDUAL

CHAPTER

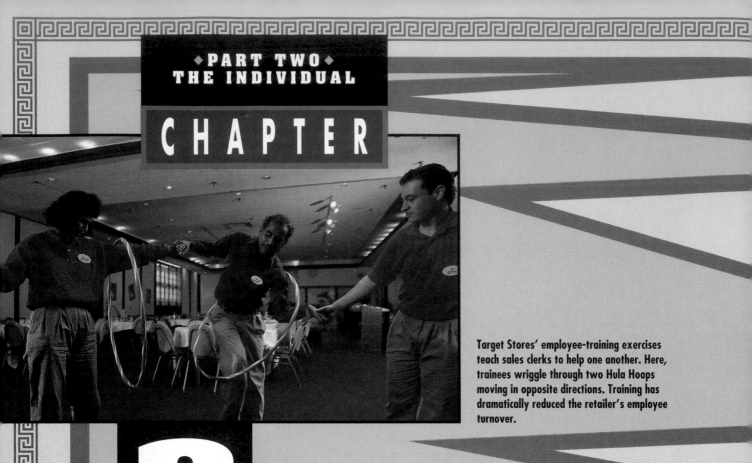

Target Stores' employee-training exercises teach sales clerks to help one another. Here, trainees wriggle through two Hula Hoops moving in opposite directions. Training has dramatically reduced the retailer's employee turnover.

3

FOUNDATIONS OF INDIVIDUAL BEHAVIOR

CHAPTER OUTLINE

LEARNING OBJECTIVES

After studying this chapter, you should be able to:

1. Define the key biographical characteristics.
2. Identify two types of ability.
3. Explain the factors that determine an individual's personality.
4. Describe the impact of job typology on the personality–job performance relationship.
5. Summarize how learning theories provide insights into changing behavior.
6. Distinguish among the four schedules of reinforcement.
7. Clarify the role of punishment in learning.

I ain't much, baby—but I'm all I've got.
J. LAIR

Barry Sherman doesn't lack for critics. It seems like everyone in the Canadian pharmaceutical industry has something negative to say about him. For instance, the CEO of Novopharm Ltd. calls him "bombastic" and a "strange individual." A leading Toronto physician and drug entrepreneur says "Barry Sherman is the only person I've ever met with no redeeming features." Canada's leading business magazine calls him "obsessed," "a nonstop agitator," "cantankerous," "isolated," and "the renegade who doesn't care what others think."[1]

Who is Barry Sherman? Why does he have so many enemies? And what in his past might explain the behaviors that have earned him his nasty reputation?

Sherman is the 52-year-old founder and president of the generic drug maker Apotex Inc. His company has sales of $500 millon a year and employs 2,000 people. The company has made him a very rich man.

Apotex is the leading generic drug maker in Canada. It has grown by busting brand-name patents and selling them for a fraction of the price. While the brand-name drug manufacturers hate Sherman—after all, he's ripping off their products without spending any of the huge amounts of money they have on research to develop these drugs—Sherman sees his company as the good guys and the brand-name firms as the bad guys. According to him, they try to "extort out of somebody who's in pain, or whose life is threatened."

It's important to understand that Barry Sherman is no fool. He didn't just stumble into his success. He was always bright and a top student. He went to the University of Toronto to study engineering physics and graduated first in his class. Then he attended the Massachusetts Institute of Technology and earned a master's in astronautics and a Ph.D. in systems engineering. He earned both his graduate degrees in two and a half years—about half the normal time. After graduation, he teamed up with a group of investors to buy a small generic drug business that his uncle had been running. Six years later, he sold out and founded Apotex. In spite of the company's impressive growth and the riches it has provided him, Sherman has no intentions of resting on his laurels. He is expanding Apotex into the brand-name business by investing in research and development. "Our objective is to be the largest pharmaceutical firm in the world in 20 years." If history is any guide, Sherman won't let anything—or anyone—stand in his way. He's a no-compromise fighter. He is prepared to take on the multinational drug companies, his generic competitors, the federal government, and whoever else thinks they can stop him. At the time of this writing, he had 80 court cases pending against competitors and government agencies.

What makes Barry Sherman the type of aggressive, entrepreneurial executive that he is? Here are some clues. His father died suddenly when he was 10 years old, leaving his upper-middle-class family's future uncertain. His mother had to go to work right away, they had to take boarders into their house to make ends meet, and Barry helped out by getting a part-time job as a stock boy in a discount store. During the summers, Barry worked at his uncle's small generic drug company. In high school, he was shy and isolated. He was smart, and he knew it, and he never cared much about what other people thought of him. But he exhibited, even then, a tremendously strong drive to succeed. He graduated as the province of Ontario's top student.

Barry Sherman's aggressiveness, competitiveness, and independence are personality characteristics that he developed at an early age. But Barry Sherman isn't unique. *All* our behavior is somewhat shaped by our personalities and the learning experiences we've encountered. In this chapter we look at four individual-level variables—biographical characteristics, ability, personality, and learning—and consider their effect on employee performance and satisfaction.

Biographical Characteristics

As we discussed in Chapter 1, this text is essentially concerned with finding and analyzing those variables that have an impact on employee productivity, absence, turnover, and satisfaction. The list of these variables—as shown in Figure 1-7 on page 29—is long and contains a number of complicated concepts.

Many of these concepts—motivation level, say, or power relations or organizational culture—are hard to assess. It might be valuable, then, to begin by looking at factors that are easily definable and readily available—data that can be obtained, for the most part, simply from information available in an employee's personnel file. What factors would these be? Obvious characteristics would be an employee's age, gender, marital status, number of dependents, and length of service with an organization. Fortunately, a sizable amount of research has specifically analyzed many of these **biographical characteristics**.

biographical characteristics Personal characteristics—such as age, sex, and marital status—that are objective and easily obtained from personnel records.

Age

The relationship between age and job performance is likely to be an issue of increasing importance during the next decade for at least three reasons. First, there is a widespread belief that job performance declines with increasing age. Regardless of whether it's true or not, a lot of people believe it and act on it. Second is the reality that the work force is aging. For instance, workers 55 and older are the fastest growing sector of the labor force—between 1990 and 2005, their ranks are expected to jump 43.7 percent.[2] The third reason is recent American legislation that, for all intents and purposes, outlaws mandatory retirement. Most workers today no longer have to retire at age 70.

Now let's take a look at the evidence. What effect does age actually have on turnover, absenteeism, productivity, and satisfaction?

The older you get, the less likely you are to quit your job. That is the overwhelming conclusion based on studies of the age–turnover relationship.[3] Of course, this conclusion should not be too surprising. As workers get older, they have fewer alternative job opportunities. In addition, older workers are less likely to resign because their longer tenure tends to provide them with higher wage rates, longer paid vacations, and more attractive pension benefits.

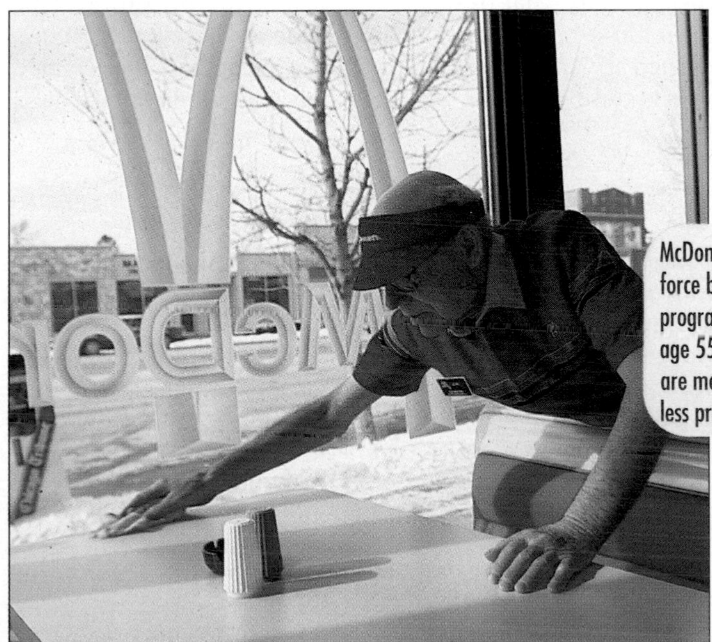

McDonald's embraces the benefits of a diverse work force by hiring older workers. Through its McMasters programs it recruits, trains, and develops people over age 55. Studies indicate that, in general, older workers are more stable and (contrary to popular belief) no less productive than their younger co-workers.

It's tempting to assume that age is also inversely related to absenteeism. After all, if older workers are less likely to quit, wouldn't they also demonstrate higher stability by coming to work more regularly? Not necessarily! Most studies do show an inverse relationship, but closer examination finds that the age–absence relationship is partially a function of whether the absence is avoidable or unavoidable.[4] Generally, older employees have lower rates of avoidable absence than do younger employees. However, they have higher rates of unavoidable absence. This is probably due to the poorer health associated with aging and the longer recovery period that older workers need when injured.

How does age affect productivity? There is a widespread belief that productivity declines with age. It is often assumed an individual's skills—particularly speed, agility, strength, and coordination—decay over time, and that prolonged job boredom and lack of intellectual stimulation all contribute to reduced productivity. The evidence, however, contradicts these beliefs and assumptions. For instance, from 1988 to 1991, a large hardware chain staffed one of its stores solely with employees over 50 and compared its results with those of five stores with younger employees. The store staffed by the over-50 employees was significantly more productive (measured in terms of sales generated against labor costs) than two of the other stores and held its own with the other three.[5] A recent comprehensive review of the research found that age and job performance were unrelated.[6] Moreover, this seems to be true for almost all types of jobs, professional and nonprofessional. The natural conclusion is that the demands of most jobs, even those with heavy manual labor requirements, are not extreme enough for any declines in physical skills due to age to have an impact on productivity; or if there is some decay due to age, it is offset by gains due to experience.

Our final concern is the relationship between age and job satisfaction. On this issue, the evidence is mixed. Most studies indicate a positive association between age and satisfaction, at least up to age 60.[7] Other studies, however, have found a U-shaped relationship.[8] Several explanations could clear up these results, the most plausible being that these studies are intermixing professional and nonprofessional employees. When the two types are separated, satisfaction tends to continually increase among professionals as they age, whereas it falls among nonprofessionals during middle age and then rises again in the later years.

Gender

Few issues initiate more debates, myths, and unsupported opinions than whether females perform as well on jobs as males do. In this section, we review the research on this issue.

The evidence suggests that the best place to begin is with the recognition that few, if any, important differences between males and females affect *their job performance*. There are, for instance, no consistent male–female differences in problem-solving ability, analytical skills, competitive drive, motivation, sociability, or learning ability.[9] While psychological studies have found that women are more willing to conform to authority, and that men are more aggressive and more likely than women to have expectations of success, these differences are minor. Given the significant changes that have taken place in the last 25 years in terms of increasing female participation rates in the work force and rethinking what constitutes male and female roles, you should operate on the assumption that there is no significant difference in job productivity between males and females. Similarly, no evidence indicates an employee's gender affects job satisfaction.[10]

But what about absence and turnover rates? Are females less stable employees than males? First, on the question of turnover, the evidence is mixed.[11] Some have found females to have higher turnover rates; others have found no difference. There doesn't appear to be enough information from which to draw meaningful conclusions. The research on absence, however, is a different story. The evidence consistently indicates that women have higher rates of absenteeism than men do.[12] The most logical explanation for this finding is that the research was conducted in North America, and North American culture has historically placed home and family responsibilities on the female. When a child is ill or someone needs to stay home to wait for the plumber, it has been the woman who has traditionally taken time off from work. However, this research is undoubtedly time bound.[13] The historical role of the woman in child caring and as secondary breadwinner has definitely changed since the 1970s; and a large proportion of men nowadays are as interested in day care and the problems associated with child care in general as are women.

Marital Status

There are not enough studies to draw any conclusions about the effect of marital status on productivity. But consistent research indicates that married employees have fewer absences, undergo less turnover, and are more satisfied with their jobs than their unmarried coworkers.[14]

Marriage imposes increased responsibilities that may make a steady job more valuable and important. But the question of causation is not clear. It may very well be that conscientious and satisfied employees are more likely to be married. Another offshoot of this issue is that research has not pursued other statuses besides single or married. Does being divorced or widowed have an impact on an employee's performance and satisfaction? What about couples who live together without being married? These questions need investigating.

Number of Dependents

Again, we don't have enough information relating to employee productivity,[15] but quite a bit of research has been done on the relationship between the number of dependents an employee has and absence, turnover, and job satisfaction.

Strong evidence indicates that the number of children an employee has is positively correlated with absence, especially among females.[16] Similarly, the evidence seems to point to a positive relationship between number of dependents and job satisfaction.[17] In contrast, studies relating number of dependents and turnover produce mixed results.[18] Some indicate that children increase turnover; others show they result in lower turnover. At this point, the evidence regarding turnover is just too contradictory to permit us to draw conclusions.

Tenure

The last biographical characteristic we look at is tenure. With the exception of the issue of male–female differences, probably no issue is more subject to myths and speculations than the impact of seniority on job performance.

Extensive reviews of the seniority–productivity relationship have been conducted.[19] While past performance tends to be related to output in a new position, seniority by itself is not a good predictor of productivity. In other words, holding all other things equal, there is no reason to believe that people who have been on a job longer are more productive than those with less seniority.

The research relating tenure to absence is quite straightforward. Studies consistently demonstrate seniority to be negatively related to absenteeism.[20] In fact, in terms of both absence frequency and total days lost at work, tenure is the single most important explanatory variable.[21]

As with absence, tenure is also a potent variable in explaining turnover. "Tenure has consistently been found to be negatively related to turnover and has been suggested as one of the single best predictors of turnover."[22] Moreover, consistent with research suggesting past behavior is the best predictor of future behavior,[23] evidence indicates that tenure on an employee's previous job is a powerful predictor of that employee's future turnover.[24]

The evidence indicates that tenure and satisfaction are positively related.[25] In fact, when age and tenure are treated separately, tenure appears to be a more consistent and stable predictor of job satisfaction than chronological age.

Ability

Contrary to what we were taught in grade school, we weren't all created equal. Most of us are to the left of the median on some normally distributed ability curve. Regardless of how motivated you are, it is unlikely you can act as well as Meryl Streep, run as fast as Linford Christie, write horror stories as well as Stephen King, or sing as well as Whitney Houston. Of course, just because we aren't all equal in abilities does not imply that some individuals are inherently inferior to others. What we're acknowledging is that everyone has strengths and weaknesses in terms of ability that make him or her relatively superior or inferior to others in performing certain tasks or activities.[26] From management's standpoint, the issue isn't whether or not people differ in terms of their abilities. They do! The issue is knowing how people differ in abilities and using that knowledge to increase the likelihood an employee will perform his or her job well.

◆Contrary to what we were taught in grade school, we weren't all created equal.

ability
An individual's capacity to perform the various tasks in a job.

What does *ability* mean? As we use the term, **ability** refers to an individual's capacity to perform the various tasks in a job. It is a current assessment of what one can do. An individual's overall abilities are essentially made up of two sets of factors: intellectual and physical abilities.

Intellectual Abilities

intellectual ability
That required to do mental activities.

Intellectual abilities are those needed to perform mental activities. IQ tests, for example, are designed to ascertain one's general intellectual abilities. So, too, are popular college admission tests like the SAT and ACT and graduate admission tests in business (GMAT), law (LSAT), and medicine (MCAT). The seven most frequently cited dimensions making up intellectual abilities are number aptitude, verbal comprehension, perceptual speed, inductive reasoning, deductive reasoning, spatial visualization, and memory.[27] Table 3-1 describes these dimensions.

Jobs differ in the demands they place on incumbents to use their intellectual abilities. Generally speaking, the more information processing demands that exist in a job, the more general intelligence and verbal abilities will be necessary to perform the job successfully.[28] Of course, a high IQ is not a prerequi-

Table 3-1 Dimensions of Intellectual Ability

Dimensions	Description	Job Example
Number aptitude	Ability to do speedy and accurate arithmetic	Accountant: Computing the sales tax on a set of items
Verbal comprehension	Ability to understand what is read or heard and the relationship of words to each other	Plant manager: Following corporate policies
Perceptual speed	Ability to identify visual similarities and differences quickly and accurately	Fire Investigator: Identifying clues to support a charge of arson
Inductive reasoning	Ability to identify a logical sequence in a problem and then solve the problem	Market researcher: Forecasting demand for a product in the next time period
Deductive reasoning	Ability to use logic and assess the implications of an argument	Supervisor: Choosing between two different suggestions offered by employees
Spatial visualization	Ability to imagine how an object would look if its position in space were changed	Interior decorator: Redecorating an office
Memory	Ability to retain and recall past experiences	Salesperson: Remembering the names of customers

site for all jobs. In fact, for many jobs—where employee behavior is highly routine and there are little or no opportunities to exercise discretion—a high IQ may be unrelated to performance. However, a careful review of the evidence demonstrates that tests which assess verbal, numerical, spatial, and perceptual abilities are valid predictors of job proficiency across all levels of jobs.[29] So tests that measure specific dimensions of intelligence have been found to be strong predictors of job performance.

The major dilemma faced by employers who use mental ability tests for selection, promotion, training, and similar personnel decisions is that they may have a negative impact on racial and ethnic groups.[30] The evidence indicates that some minority groups score, on the average, as much as one standard deviation lower than whites on verbal, numerical, and spatial ability tests.

Physical Abilities

To the same degree that intellectual abilities play a larger role in complex jobs with demanding information processing requirements, specific **physical abilities** gain importance for successfully doing less skilled and more standardized jobs. For example, jobs in which success demands stamina, manual dexterity, leg strength, or similar talents require management to identify an employee's physical capabilities.

physical ability
That required to do tasks demanding stamina, dexterity, strength, and similar skills.

Research on the requirements needed in hundreds of jobs has identified nine basic abilities involved in the performance of physical tasks.[31] These are described in Table 3-2. Individuals differ in the extent to which they have each of these abilities. Not surprisingly, there is also little relationship between them: A high score on one is no assurance of a high score on others. High employee performance is likely to be achieved when management has ascertained the extent to which a job requires each of the nine abilities and then ensures that employees in that job have those abilities.

The Ability–Job Fit

Our concern is with explaining and predicting the behavior of people at work. In this section, we have demonstrated that jobs make differing demands on people and that people differ in the abilities they possess. Employee performance, therefore, is enhanced when there is a high ability–job fit.

The specific intellectual or physical abilities required for adequate job performance depend on the ability requirements of the job. So, for example, airline pilots need strong spatial-visualization abilities; beach lifeguards need both strong spatial-visualization and body coordination; senior executives need verbal abilities; high-rise construction workers need balance; and journalists with weak reasoning abilities would likely have difficulty meeting minimum job performance standards. Directing attention at only the employee's abilities or the ability requirements of the job ignores that employee performance depends on the interaction of the two.

What predictions can we make when the fit is poor? As alluded to previously, if employees lack the required abilities, they are likely to fail. If you're hired as a word processor and you can't meet the job's basic keyboard typing re-

Table 3-2 Nine Basic Physical Abilities

Strength Factors	
1. Dynamic strength	Ability to exert muscular force repeatedly or continuously over time
2. Trunk strength	Ability to exert muscular strength using the trunk (particularly abdominal) muscles
3. Static strength	Ability to exert force against external objects
4. Explosive strength	Ability to expend a maximum of energy in one or a series of explosive acts
Flexibility Factors	
5. Extent flexibility	Ability to move the trunk and back muscles as far as possible
6. Dynamic flexibility	Ability to make rapid, repeated flexing movements
Other Factors	
7. Body coordination	Ability to coordinate the simultaneous actions of different parts of the body
8. Balance	Ability to maintain equilibrium despite forces pulling off balance
9. Stamina	Ability to continue maximum effort requiring prolonged effort over time

Source: Reprinted from the June 1979 issue of *Personnel Administrator*, copyright 1979, The American Society for Personnel Administration; 606 North Washington Street; Alexandria, Virginia 22314, pp. 82–92.

quirements, your performance is going to be poor irrespective of your positive attitude or your high level of motivation. When the ability–job fit is out of sync because the employee has abilities that far exceed the requirements of the job, our predictions would be very different. Job performance is likely to be adequate, but there will be organizational inefficiencies and possible declines in employee satisfaction. Given that pay tends to reflect the highest skill level that employees possess, if an employee's abilities far exceed those necessary to do the job, management will be paying more than it needs to. Abilities significantly above those required can also reduce the employee's job satisfaction when the employee's desire to use his or her abilities is particularly strong and is frustrated by the limitations of the job.

Personality

Why are some people quiet and passive, while others are loud and aggressive? Are certain personality types better adapted for certain job types? What do we know from theories of personality that can help us explain and predict the behavior of people like Barry Sherman, the head of Apotex, described at the opening of this chapter? In this section, we attempt to answer such questions.

What Is Personality?

When we talk of personality, we don't mean a person has charm, a positive attitude toward life, a smiling face, or is a finalist for "Happiest and Friendliest" in this year's Miss America contest. When psychologists talk of personality, they mean a dynamic concept describing the growth and development of a person's whole psychological system. Rather than looking at parts of the

From Concepts to Skills

Self-Awareness: Do You Know Yourself?

A famous cartoonist once attended a cocktail party with some friends. Someone asked him to draw a caricature of everyone present, which he proceeded to do with a few skilled strokes of his pencil. When the sketches were passed around for the guests to identify, everyone recognized the other persons, but hardly anyone recognized the caricature of himself.[32]

Many of us are like the people at that cocktail party. We really don't know ourselves. But you can expand your self-awareness. And when you do, you'll better understand your personal strengths and weaknesses, how you're perceived by others, and gain insights into why others respond to you as they do.

A major component in gaining self-understanding is finding out how you rate on key personality characteristics. Later in our discussion of personality, we review six major personality attributes: locus of control, Machiavellianism, self-esteem, self-monitoring, risk taking, and the Type A personality. Included with the review is a series of self-awareness questionnaires designed to tap these personality characteristics. Individually, these questionnaires will give you insights into how you rate on each attribute. In aggregate, they will help you better understand who you are.

person, personality looks at some aggregate whole that is greater than the sum of the parts.

The most frequently used definition of personality was produced by Gordon Allport nearly 60 years ago. He said personality is "the dynamic organization within the individual of those psychophysical systems that determine his unique adjustments to his environment."[33] For our purposes, you should think of **personality** as the sum total of ways in which an individual reacts and interacts with others. This is most often described in terms of measurable personality traits that a person exhibits.

personality
The sum total of ways in which an individual reacts and interacts with others.

Personality Determinants

An early argument in personality research was whether an individual's personality was the result of heredity or environment. Was the personality predetermined at birth, or was it the result of the individual's interaction with his or her environment? Clearly, there is no simple black-and-white answer. Personality appears to be a result of both influences. Additionally, today we recognize a third factor—the situation. Thus, an adult's personality is now generally considered to be made up of both hereditary and environmental factors, moderated by situational conditions.

HEREDITY Heredity refers to those factors that were determined at conception. Physical stature, facial attractiveness, sex, temperament, muscle composition and reflexes, energy level, and biological rhythms are characteristics that are generally considered to be either completely or substantially influenced by who your parents were, that is, by their biological, physiological, and inherent psychological make-up. The heredity approach argues that the ultimate explanation of an individual's personality is the molecular structure of the genes, located in the chromosomes.

Three different streams of research lend some credibility to the argument that heredity plays an important part in determining an individual's personality. The first looks at the genetic underpinnings of human behavior and temperament among young children. The second addresses the study of twins who were separated at birth. The third examines the consistency in job satisfaction over time and across situations.

Recent studies of young children lend strong support to the power of heredity.[34] Evidence demonstrates that traits such as shyness, fear, and distress are most likely caused by inherited genetic characteristics. This suggests that some personality traits may be built into the same genetic code that affects factors like our height and hair color.

Researchers have studied more than 100 sets of identical twins who were separated at birth and raised separately.[35] If heredity played little or no part in determining personality, you'd expect to find few similarities between the separated twins. But the researchers found a lot in common. For almost every behavioral trait, a significant part of the variation among the twins turned out to be associated with genetic factors. For instance, one set of twins who had been separated for 39 years and raised 45 miles apart were found to drive the same model and color car, chain-smoked the same brand of cigarette, owned dogs with the same name, and regularly vacationed within three blocks of each other in a beach community 1,500 miles away. Researchers have found that genetics accounts for about 50 percent of the personality differences and more than 30 percent of the variation in occupational and leisure interests.

Further support for the importance of heredity can be found in studies of individual job satisfaction. Research has uncovered an interesting phenomenon: Individual job satisfaction is remarkably stable over time. Even when employers or occupations change, job satisfaction remains relatively stable during one's lifetime.[36] This result is consistent with what you would expect if satisfaction is determined by something inherent in the person rather than by external environmental factors.

If personality characteristics were *completely* dictated by heredity, they would be fixed at birth and no amount of experience could alter them. If you were relaxed and easygoing as a child, for example, that would be the result of your genes, and it would not be possible for you to change these characteristics. But personality characteristics are not completely dictated by heredity.

ENVIRONMENT Among the factors that exert pressures on our personality formation are the culture in which we are raised, our early conditioning, the norms among our family, friends, and social groups, and other influences we experience. The environment we are exposed to plays a substantive role in shaping our personalities.

For example, culture establishes the norms, attitudes, and values that are passed along from one generation to the next and create consistencies over time. An ideology that is intensely fostered in one culture may have only moderate influence in another. For instance, North Americans have had the themes of industriousness, success, competition, independence, and the Protestant work ethic constantly instilled in them through books, the school system, family, and friends. North Americans, as a result, tend to be ambitious and aggressive relative to individuals raised in cultures that have emphasized getting along with others, cooperation, and the priority of family over work and career.

Careful consideration of the arguments favoring either heredity or environment as the primary determinant of personality forces the conclusion that both are important. Heredity sets the parameters or outer limits, but an individual's full potential will be determined by how well he or she adjusts to the demands and requirements of the environment.

The cultural environment in which people are raised plays a major role in shaping personality. In India, children learn from an early age the values of hard work, frugality, and family closeness. This photo of the Harilela family illustrates the importance that Indians place on close family ties. Six Harilela brothers own real estate and hotels throughout Asia. Not only do the brothers work together, but their six families and that of a married sister also live together in a Hong Kong mansion.

SITUATION A third factor, the situation, influences the effects of heredity and environment on personality. An individual's personality, while generally stable and consistent, does change in different situations. The different demands of different situations call forth different aspects of one's personality. We should not, therefore, look at personality patterns in isolation.[37]

While it seems only logical to suppose that situations will influence an individual's personality, a neat classification scheme which would tell us the impact of various types of situations has so far eluded us. "Apparently we are not yet close to developing a system for clarifying situations so they might be systematically studied."[38] However, we do know that certain situations are more relevant than others in influencing personality.

> What is of interest taxonomically is that situations seem to differ substantially in the constraints they impose on behavior, with some situations—e.g., church, an employment interview—constraining many behaviors and others—e.g., a picnic in a public park—constraining relatively few.[39]

Furthermore, although certain generalizations can be made about personality, there are significant individual differences. As we see, the study of individual differences has come to receive greater emphasis in personality research, which originally sought out more general, universal patterns.

Personality Traits

personality traits
Enduring characteristics that describe an individual's behavior.

The early work in the structure of personality revolved around attempts to identify and label enduring characteristics that describe an individual's behavior. Popular characteristics include shy, aggressive, submissive, lazy, ambitious, loyal, and timid. These characteristics, when they are exhibited in a large number of situations, are called **personality traits**.[40] The more consistent the characteristic and the more frequently it occurs in diverse situations, the more important that trait is in describing the individual.

EARLY SEARCH FOR PRIMARY TRAITS Efforts to isolate traits have been hindered because there are so many of them. In one study, 17,953 individual traits were identified.[41] It is virtually impossible to predict behavior when such a large number of traits must be taken into account. As a result, attention has been directed toward reducing these thousands to a more manageable number.

One researcher isolated 171 traits but concluded they were superficial and lacking in descriptive power.[42] What he sought was a reduced set of traits that

Figure 3-1
Source: PEANUTS reprinted by permission of UFS, Inc.

would identify underlying patterns. The result was the identification of 16 personality factors, which he called the *source* or *primary traits*. They are shown in Table 3-3. These 16 traits have been found to be generally steady and constant sources of behavior, allowing prediction of an individual's behavior in specific situations by weighing the characteristics for their situational relevance.

THE MYERS-BRIGGS TYPE INDICATOR One of the most widely used personality frameworks is called the **Myers-Briggs Type Indicator (MBTI)**.[43] It is essentially a 100-question personality test that asks people how they usually feel or act in particular situations.

Myers-Briggs Indicator (MBTI)
A personality test that taps 4 characteristics and classifies people into one of 16 personality types.

Based on the answers individuals give to the test, they are classified as extroverted or introverted (E or I), sensing or intuitive (S or N), thinking or feeling (T or F), and perceiving or judging (P or J), which are then combined into 16 personality types. (These are different from the 16 primary traits in Table 3-3.) To illustrate, let's take several examples. INTJs are visionaries. They usually have original minds and great drive for their own ideas and purposes. They're characterized as skeptical, critical, independent, determined, and often stubborn. ESTJs are organizers. They're practical, realistic, matter-of-fact, with a natural head for business or mechanics. They like to organize and run activities. The ENTP type is a conceptualizer. He or she is quick, ingenious, and good at many things. This person tends to be resourceful in solving challenging problems, but may neglect routine assignments. A recent book that profiled 13 contemporary businesspeople who created supersuccessful firms like Apple Computer, Federal Express, Honda Motors, Microsoft, Price Club, and Sony found that all 13 are intuitive thinkers (NTs).[44] This is particularly interesting, since intuitive thinkers represent only about 5 percent of the population.

More than 2 million people a year take the MBTI in the United States alone. Organizations using the MBTI include Apple Computer, AT&T, Citicorp, Exxon, GE, 3M Co., plus many hospitals, educational institutions, and even the U.S. armed forces.

Table 3-3 Sixteen Primary Traits

1.	Reserved	vs.	Outgoing
2.	Less intelligent	vs.	More intelligent
3.	Affected by feelings	vs.	Emotionally stable
4.	Submissive	vs.	Dominant
5.	Serious	vs.	Happy-go-lucky
6.	Expedient	vs.	Conscientious
7.	Timid	vs.	Venturesome
8.	Tough-minded	vs.	Sensitive
9.	Trusting	vs.	Suspicious
10.	Practical	vs.	Imaginative
11.	Forthright	vs.	Shrewd
12.	Self-assured	vs.	Apprehensive
13.	Conservative	vs.	Experimenting
14.	Group-dependent	vs.	Self-sufficient
15.	Uncontrolled	vs.	Controlled
16.	Relaxed	vs.	Tense

Ironically, no hard evidence supports the MBTI as a valid measure of personality. However, this doesn't seem to deter its use in a wide range of organizations.

THE BIG 5 MODEL While the MBTI may lack valid supporting evidence, that can't be said for the five-factor model of personality—more typically called the "Big Five."[45]

In recent years, an impressive body of research supports that five basic personality dimensions underlie all others. The Big Five factors are:

extraversion
A personality dimension describing someone who is sociable, talkative, and assertive.

agreeableness
A personality dimension that describes someone who is good-natured, cooperative, and trusting.

conscientiousness
A personality dimension that describes someone who is responsible, dependable, persistent, and achievement oriented.

emotional stability
A personality dimension that characterizes someone who is calm, enthusiastic, secure (positive) to tense, nervous, depressed, and insecure (negative).

openness to experience
A personality dimension that characterizes someone who is imaginative, artistically sensitive, and intellectual.

- **Extraversion**: Sociable, talkative, assertive
- **Agreeableness**: Good-natured, cooperative, and trusting
- **Conscientiousness**: Responsible, dependable, persistent, and achievement oriented
- **Emotional stability**: Calm, enthusiastic, secure (positive) to tense, nervous, depressed, and insecure (negative)
- **Openness to experience**: Imaginative, artistically sensitive, and intellectual

In addition to providing a unifying personality framework, research on the Big Five also has found important relationships between these personality dimensions and job performance.[46] Five categories of occupations were looked at: professionals (including engineers, architects, accountants, attorneys), police, managers, sales, and semiskilled and skilled employees. Job performance was defined in terms of performance ratings, training proficiency (performance during training programs), and personnel data such as salary level. The results showed that conscientiousness predicted job performance for all five occupational groups. For the other personality dimensions, predictability depended on both the performance criterion and occupational group. For instance, extraversion predicted performance in managerial and sales positions. This makes sense, since these occupations involve high social interaction. Similarly, openness to experience was found to be important in predicting training proficiency, which, too, seems logical. What wasn't so clear was why emotional stability wasn't related to job performance. Intuitively it would seem that people who are calm and secure would do better on almost all jobs than people who were anxious and insecure. The researchers suggested the answer might be that only people who score fairly high on emotional stability retain their jobs. So the range among those people studied, all of whom were employed, would tend to be quite small.

Major Personality Attributes Influencing OB

In this section, we want to more carefully evaluate a number of specific personality attributes that have been found to be powerful predictors of behavior in organizations. The first of these is related to where one perceives the locus of control in one's life. The others are Machiavellianism, self-esteem, self-monitoring, propensity for risk taking, and Type A personality. In this section, we briefly introduce these attributes and summarize what we know about their ability to explain and predict employee behavior.

LOCUS OF CONTROL Some people believe they are masters of their own fate. Other people see themselves as pawns of fate, believing that what happens to them in their lives is due to luck or chance. The first type, those who believe they

Increase Your Self-Awareness: Assess Your Locus of Control

Instructions: Read the following statements and indicate whether you agree more with choice A or choice B.

A	B	
1. Making a lot of money is largely a matter of getting the right breaks.	1. Promotions are earned through hard work and persistence.	___
2. I have noticed a direct connection between how hard I study and the grades I get.	2. Many times the reactions of teachers seem haphazard to me.	___
3. The number of divorces indicates that more and more people are not trying to make their marriages work.	3. Marriage is largely a gamble.	___
4. It is silly to think that one can really change another person's basic attitudes.	4. When I am right I can convince others.	___
5. Getting promoted is really a matter of being a little luckier than the next person.	5. In our society a person's future earning power depends on his or her ability.	___
6. If one knows how to deal with people they are really quite easily led.	6. I have little influence over the way other people behave.	___
7. The grades I make are the result of my own efforts; luck has little or nothing to do with it.	7. Sometimes I feel I have little to do with the grades I get.	___
8. People like me can change the course of world affairs if we make ourselves heard.	8. It is only wishful thinking to believe that one can readily influence what happens in our society at large.	___
9. A great deal that happens to me is probably a matter of chance.	9. I am the master of my fate.	___
10. Getting along with people is a skill that must be practiced.	10. It is almost impossible to figure out how to please some people.	___

Source: Adapted from Julian B. Rotter, "External Control and Internal Control," *Psychology Today* (June 1971), p. 42. Copyright 1971 by the American Psychological Association. Adapted with permission.

Scoring Key:
Give yourself 1 point for each of the following selections: 1B, 2A, 3A, 4B, 5B, 6A, 7A, 8A, 9B, and 10A. Scores can be interpreted as follows:

8–10 = High internal locus of control
6–7 = Moderate internal locus of control
5 = Mixed
3–4 = Moderate external locus of control
1–2 = High external locus of control

control their destinies, have been labeled **internals**, whereas the latter, who see their lives as being controlled by outside forces, have been called **externals**.[47]

internals
Individuals who believe that they control what happens to them.

externals
Individuals who believe that what happens to them is controlled by outside forces such as luck or chance.

A large amount of research comparing internals with externals has consistently shown that individuals who rate high in externality are less satisfied with their jobs, have higher absenteeism rates, are more alienated from the work setting, and are less involved on their jobs than are internals.[48]

Why are externals more dissatisfied? The answer is probably because they perceive themselves as having little control over those organizational outcomes that are important to them. Internals, facing the same situation, attribute organizational outcomes to their own actions. If the situation is unattractive, they believe they have no one else to blame but themselves. Also, the dissatisfied internal is more likely to quit a dissatisfying job.

locus of control
The degree to which people believe they are masters of their own fate.

The impact of **locus of control** on absence is an interesting one. Internals believe that health is substantially under their own control through proper habits, so they take more responsibility for their health and have better health habits. This leads to lower incidences of sickness and, hence, lower absenteeism.[49]

We shouldn't expect any clear relationship between locus of control and turnover. The reason is that there are opposing forces at work. "On the one hand, internals tend to take action and thus might be expected to quit jobs more readily. On the other hand, they tend to be more successful on the job and more satisfied, factors associated with less individual turnover."[50]

Increase Your Self-Awareness: How Machiavellian Are You?

Instructions: For each statement, circle the number that most closely resembles your attitude.

Statement	Disagree A Lot	Disagree A Little	Neutral	Agree A Little	Agree A Lot
1. The best way to handle people is to tell them what they want to hear.	1	2	3	4	5
2. When you ask someone to do something for you, it is best to give the real reason for wanting it rather than giving reasons that might carry more weight.	1	2	3	4	5
3. Anyone who completely trusts anyone else is asking for trouble.	1	2	3	4	5
4. It is hard to get ahead without cutting corners here and there.	1	2	3	4	5
5. It is safest to assume that all people have a vicious streak, and it will come out when they are given a chance.	1	2	3	4	5
6. One should take action only when it is morally right.	1	2	3	4	5
7. Most people are basically good and kind.	1	2	3	4	5
8. There is no excuse for lying to someone else.	1	2	3	4	5
9. Most people more easily forget the death of their father than the loss of their property.	1	2	3	4	5
10. Generally speaking, people won't work hard unless they're forced to do so.	1	2	3	4	5

Source: R. Christie and F. L. Geis, *Studies in Machiavellianism*. © Academic Press 1970. Reprinted by permission.

Scoring Key:
To obtain your Mach score, add the number you have circled on questions 1, 3, 4, 5, 9, and 10. For the other four questions, reverse the numbers you have checked: 5 becomes 1, 4 is 2, 2 is 4, and 1 is 5. Total your ten numbers to find your score. The higher your score, the more Machiavellian you are. Among a random sample of American adults, the national average was 25.

The overall evidence indicates that internals generally perform better on their jobs, but that conclusion should be moderated to reflect differences in jobs. Internals search more actively for information before making a decision, are more motivated to achieve, and make a greater attempt to control their environment. Externals, however, are more compliant and willing to follow directions. Therefore, internals do well on sophisticated tasks—which includes most managerial and professional jobs—that require complex information processing and learning. Additionally, internals are more suited to jobs that require initiative and independence of action. In contrast, externals should do

Increase Your Self-Awareness: How's Your Self-Esteem?

Instructions: Answer each of the following questions *frankly* and *honestly*. Next to each question write a 1, 2, 3, 4, or 5 depending on which statement best describes you:

1 = This statement describes you *very often*.
2 = This statement describes you *fairly often*.
3 = This statement describes you *sometimes*.
4 = This statement describes you *once in a great while*.
5 = This statement describes you *practically never*.

____ 1. How often do you have the feeling that there is nothing that you can do well?
____ 2. When you talk in front of a class or group of people your own age, how often do you feel worried or afraid?
____ 3. How often do you feel that you have handled yourself well at a social gathering?
____ 4. How often do you have the feeling that you can do everything well?
____ 5. How often are you comfortable when starting a conversation with people you don't know?
____ 6. How often do you feel self-conscious?
____ 7. How often do you feel that you are a successful person?
____ 8. How often are you troubled with shyness?
____ 9. How often do you feel inferior to most people you know?
____ 10. How often do you feel that you are a worthless individual?
____ 11. How often do you feel confident that your success in your future job or career is assured?
____ 12. How often do you feel sure of yourself when among strangers?
____ 13. How often do you feel confident that some day people will look up to you and respect you?
____ 14. In general, how often do you feel confident about your abilities?
____ 15. How often do you worry about how well you get along with other people?
____ 16. How often do you feel that you dislike yourself?
____ 17. How often do you feel so discouraged with yourself that you wonder whether anything is worthwhile?
____ 18. How often do you worry about whether other people like to be with you?
____ 19. When you talk in front of a class or a group of people of your own age, how often are you pleased with your performance?
____ 20. How often do you feel sure of yourself when you speak in a class discussion?

Source: Developed by A.H. Eagly and adapted from J.R. Robinson and P.R. Shaver, *Measures of Social Psychological Attitudes* (Ann Arbor, MI: Institute of Social Research, 1973), pp. 79–80. With permission.

Scoring Key:
Add up your scores from the left column for the following ten items: 1, 2, 6, 8, 9, 10, 15, 16, 17, and 18. For the other ten items, reverse your scoring (i.e., a 5 becomes a 1; a 4 becomes a 2).

The higher your score, the higher your self-esteem.

well on jobs that are well structured and routine and where success depends heavily on complying with the direction of others.

Machiavellianism
Degree to which an individual is pragmatic, maintains emotional distance, and believes that ends can justify means.

MACHIAVELLIANISM The personality characteristic of **Machiavellianism** (Mach) is named after Niccolò Machiavelli, who wrote in the sixteenth century about how to gain and manipulate power. An individual high in Machiavellianism is pragmatic, maintains emotional distance, and believes that ends can justify means. "If it works, use it" is consistent with a high-Mach perspective.

A considerable amount of research has been directed toward relating high- and low-Mach personalities to certain behavioral outcomes.[51] High-Machs manipulate more, win more, are persuaded less, and persuade others more than do low-Machs.[52] Yet these high-Mach outcomes are moderated by situational factors. It has been found that high-Machs flourish (1) when they interact face to face with others rather than indirectly; (2) when the situation has a minimum number of rules and regulations, thus allowing latitude for improvisation; and (3) where emotional involvement with details irrelevant to winning distracts low-Machs.[53]

Should we conclude that high-Machs make good employees? That answer depends on the type of job and whether you consider ethical implications in evaluating performance. In jobs that require bargaining skills (such as labor negotiation) or where there are substantial rewards for winning (as in commissioned sales), high-Machs will be productive. But if ends can't justify the means, if there are *absolute* standards of behavior, or if the three situational factors noted in the previous paragraph are not in evidence, our ability to predict a high-Mach's performance will be severely curtailed.

self-esteem
Individuals' degree of liking or disliking for themselves.

SELF-ESTEEM People differ in the degree to which they like or dislike themselves. This trait is called **self-esteem**.[54]

The research on self-esteem (SE) offers some interesting insights into organizational behavior. For example, self-esteem is directly related to expectations for success. High-SEs believe they possess more of the ability they need in order to succeed at work. Individuals with high SE will take more risks in job selection and are more likely to choose unconventional jobs than people with low SE.

The most generalizable finding on self-esteem is that low-SEs are more susceptible to external influence than high-SEs. Low-SEs depend on the receipt of positive evaluations from others. As a result, they are more likely to seek approval from others and more prone to conform to the beliefs and behaviors of those they respect than are high-SEs. In managerial positions, low-SEs tend to be concerned with pleasing others and, therefore, are less likely to take unpopular stands than are high-SEs.

Not surprisingly, self-esteem has also been found to be related to job satisfaction. A number of studies confirm that high-SEs are more satisfied with their jobs than low-SEs.

self-monitoring
A personality trait that measures an individual's ability to adjust his or her behavior to external, situational factors.

SELF-MONITORING A personality trait that has recently received increased attention is called **self-monitoring**.[55] It refers to an individual's ability to adjust his or her behavior to external, situational factors.

Individuals high in self-monitoring show considerable adaptability in adjusting their behavior to external situational factors. They are highly sensitive to external cues and can behave differently in different situations. High self-monitors are capable of presenting striking contradictions between their public

Increase Your Self-Awareness: Are You a High Self-Monitor?

Indicate the degree to which you think the following statements are true or false by circling the appropriate number; for example, if a statement is always true, you would circle the 5 next to that statement.

5 = Certainly always true
4 = Generally true
3 = Somewhat true, but with exceptions
2 = Somewhat false, but with exceptions
1 = Generally false
0 = Certainly always false

1. In social situations, I have the ability to alter my behavior if I feel that something else is called for.	5	4	3	2	1	0
2. I am often able to read people's true emotions correctly through their eyes.	5	4	3	2	1	0
3. I have the ability to control the way I come across to people, depending on the impression I wish to give them.	5	4	3	2	1	0
4. In conversations, I am sensitive to even the slightest change in the facial expression of the person I'm conversing with.	5	4	3	2	1	0
5. My powers of intuition are quite good when it comes to understanding others' emotions and motives.	5	4	3	2	1	0
6. I can usually tell when others consider a joke in bad taste, even though they may laugh convincingly.	5	4	3	2	1	0
7. When I feel that the image I am portraying isn't working, I can readily change it to something that does.	5	4	3	2	1	0
8. I can usually tell when I've said something inappropriate by reading the listener's eyes.	5	4	3	2	1	0
9. I have trouble changing my behavior to suit different people and different situations.	5	4	3	2	1	0
10. I have found that I can adjust my behavior to meet the requirements of any situation I find myself in.	5	4	3	2	1	0
11. If someone is lying to me, I usually know it at once from that person's manner of expression.	5	4	3	2	1	0
12. Even when it might be to my advantage, I have difficulty putting up a good front.	5	4	3	2	1	0
13. Once I know what the situation calls for, it's easy for me to regulate my actions accordingly.	5	4	3	2	1	0

Source: R. D. Lennox and R. N. Wolfe, "Revision of the Self-Monitoring Scale," *Journal of Personality and Social Psychology* (June 1984), p. 1361. Copyright 1984 by the American Psychological Association. Reprinted by permission.

Scoring Key:
To obtain your score, add up the numbers circled, except reverse scores for questions 9 and 12. On those, a circled 5 becomes a 0, 4 becomes 1, and so forth. High self-monitors are defined as those with scores of approximately 53 or higher.

persona and their private self. Low self-monitors can't disguise themselves this way. They tend to display their true dispositions and attitudes in every situation; hence there is high behavioral consistency between who they are and what they do.

Increase Your Self-Awareness: Are You a Risk Taker?

For each of the following situations, indicate the minimum odds of success you would demand before recommending that one alternative be chosen over another. Try to place yourself in the position of the central person in each of the situations.

1. Mr. B, a 45-year-old accountant, has recently been informed by his physician that he has developed a severe heart ailment. The disease would be sufficiently serious to force Mr. B to change many of his strongest life habits—reducing his workload, drastically changing his diet, giving up favorite leisure-time pursuits. The physician suggests that a delicate medical operation could be attempted which, if successful, would completely relieve the heart condition. But its success could not be assured, and in fact, the operation might prove fatal.

Imagine you are advising Mr. B. Listed below are several probabilities or odds that the operation will prove successful. Check the *lowest probability* that you would consider acceptable for the operation to be performed.

____ Place a check here if you think Mr. B should *not* have the operation no matter what the probabilities.
____ The chances are 9 in 10 that the operation will be a success.
____ The chances are 7 in 10 that the operation will be a success.
____ The chances are 5 in 10 that the operation will be a success.
____ The chances are 3 in 10 that the operation will be a success.
____ The chances are 1 in 10 that the operation will be a success.

2. Mr. D is the captain of College X's football team. College X is playing its traditional rival, College Y, in the final game of the season. The game is in its final seconds, and Mr. D's team, College X, is behind in the score. College X has time to run one more play. Mr. D, the captain, must decide whether it would be best to settle for a tie score with a play which would be almost certain to work or, on the other hand, should he try a more complicated and risky play which could bring victory if it succeeded, but defeat if not.

Imagine you are advising Mr. D. Listed below are several probabilities or odds that the risky play will work. Check the *lowest probability* that you would consider acceptable for the risky play to be attempted.

____ Place a check here if you think Mr. D should *not* attempt the risky play no matter what the probabilities.
____ The chances are 9 in 10 that the risky play will work.
____ The chances are 7 in 10 that the risky play will work.
____ The chances are 5 in 10 that the risky play will work.
____ The chances are 3 in 10 that the risky play will work.
____ The chances are 1 in 10 that the risky play will work.

3. Ms. K is a successful businesswoman who has participated in a number of civic activities of considerable value to the community. Ms. K has been approached by the leaders of her political party as a possible congressional candidate in the next election. Ms. K's party is a minority party in the district, although the party has won occasional elections in the past. Ms. K would like to hold political office, but to do so would involve a serious financial sacrifice, since the party has insufficient campaign funds. She would also have to endure the attacks of her political opponents in a hot campaign.

Imagine you are advising Ms. K. Listed below are several probabilities or odds of Ms. K's winning the election in her district. Check the *lowest probability* that you would consider acceptable to make it worthwhile for Ms. K to run for political office.

____ Place a check here if you think Ms. K should *not* run for political office no matter what the probabilities.
____ The chances are 9 in 10 that Ms. K would win the election.
____ The chances are 7 in 10 that Ms. K would win the election.
____ The chances are 5 in 10 that Ms. K would win the election.
____ The chances are 3 in 10 that Ms. K would win the election.
____ The chances are 1 in 10 that Ms. K would win the election.

(continued)

4. Ms. L, a 30-year-old research physicist, has been given a five-year appointment by a major university laboratory. As she contemplates the next five years, she realizes she might work on a difficult long-term problem which, if a solution could be found, would resolve basic scientific issues in the field and bring high scientific honors. If no solution were found, however, Ms. L would have little to show for her five years in the laboratory, and this would make it hard for her to get a good job afterward. On the other hand, she could, as most of her professional associates are doing, work on a series of short-term problems where solutions would be easier to find, but where the problems are of lesser scientific importance.

Imagine you are advising Ms. L. Listed below are several probabilities or odds that a solution would be found to the difficult long-term problem that Ms. L has in mind. Check the *lowest probability* that you would consider acceptable to make it worthwhile for Ms. L to work on the more difficult long-term problem.

____ The chances are 1 in 10 that Ms. L would solve the long-term problem.
____ The chances are 3 in 10 that Ms. L would solve the long-term problem.
____ The chances are 5 in 10 that Ms. L would solve the long-term problem.
____ The chances are 7 in 10 that Ms. L would solve the long-term problem.
____ The chances are 9 in 10 that Ms. L would solve the long-term problem.
____ Place a check here if you think Ms. L should *not* choose the long-term difficult problem, no matter what the probabilities.

Source: Adapted from N. Kogan and M.A. Wallach, *Risk Taking: A Study in Cognition and Personality* (New York: Holt, Rinehart and Winston, 1964), pp. 256–61.

Scoring Key:
The previous series of situations were based on a longer questionnaire. As such, your results are meant to indicate a general orientation toward risk rather than to act as a precise measure. To calculate your risk-taking score, add up the chances you were willing to take and divide by 4. For any of the situations in which you would not take the risk regardless of the probabilities, give yourself a 10. The lower your number, the more risk taking you are.

The research on self-monitoring is in its infancy, so predictions must be guarded. However, preliminary evidence suggests that high self-monitors tend to pay closer attention to the behavior of others and are more capable of conforming than are low self-monitors.[56] We might also hypothesize that high self-monitors will be more successful in managerial positions where individuals are required to play multiple, and even contradicting, roles. The high self-monitor is capable of putting on different "faces" for different audiences.

RISK TAKING People differ in their willingness to take chances. This propensity to assume or avoid risk has been shown to have an impact on how long it takes managers to make a decision and how much information they require before making their choice. For instance, 79 managers worked on simulated personnel exercises that required them to make hiring decisions.[57] High-risk-taking managers made more rapid decisions and used less information in making their choices than did the low-risk-taking managers. Interestingly, the decision accuracy was the same for both groups.

While it is generally correct to conclude that managers in organizations are risk aversive,[58] there are still individual differences on this dimension.[59] As a result, it makes sense to recognize these differences and even to consider aligning risk-taking propensity with specific job demands. For instance, a high-risk-taking propensity may lead to more effective performance for a stock trader in a brokerage firm because this type of job demands rapid decision making. On the other hand, this personality characteristic might prove a major obstacle to an accountant who performs auditing activities. The latter job might be better filled by someone with a low-risk-taking propensity.

Type A personality
Aggressive involvement in a chronic, incessant struggle to achieve more and more in less and less time and, if necessary, against the opposing efforts of other things or other people.

TYPE A PERSONALITY Do you know any people who are excessively competitive and always seem to be experiencing a chronic sense of time urgency? If so, it's a good bet these people have a **Type A personality**.[60] A Type A individual is "*aggressively* involved in a *chronic, incessant* struggle to achieve more and more in less and less time, and if required to do so, against the opposing efforts of other things or other persons."[61] In the North American culture, such characteristics tend to be highly prized and positively associated with ambition and the successful acquisition of material goods.

Type A's

1. are always moving, walking, and eating rapidly;
2. feel impatient with the rate at which most events take place;
3. strive to think or do two or more things simultaneously;
4. cannot cope with leisure time; and
5. are obsessed with numbers, measuring their success in terms of how much of everything they acquire.

In contrast to the Type A personality is the Type B, who is exactly opposite. Type B's are "rarely harried by the desire to obtain a wildly increasing number of things or participate in an endless growing series of events in an ever decreasing amount of time."[62]

Type B's

1. never suffer from a sense of time urgency with its accompanying impatience;
2. feel no need to display or discuss either their achievements or accomplishments unless such exposure is demanded by the situation;

Increase Your Self-Awareness: Are You a Type A?

Circle the number on the scale below that best characterizes your behavior for each trait.

1. Casual about appointments	1 2 3 4 5 6 7 8	Never late
2. Not competitive	1 2 3 4 5 6 7 8	Very competitve
3. Never feel rushed	1 2 3 4 5 6 7 8	Always rushed
4. Take things one at a time	1 2 3 4 5 6 7 8	Try to do many things at once
5. Slow doing things	1 2 3 4 5 6 7 8	Fast (eating, walking, etc.)
6. Express feelings	1 2 3 4 5 6 7 8	"Sit" on feelings
7. Many interests	1 2 3 4 5 6 7 8	Few interests outside work

Source: Adapted from R.W. Bortner, "Short Rating Scale as a Potential Measure of Pattern A Behavior," *Journal of Chronic Diseases* (June 1969), pp. 87–91. With permission.

Scoring Key:
Total your score on the seven questions. Now multiply it by 3. A total of 120 or more indicates you're a hard-core Type A. Scores below 90 indicates you're a hard-core Type B. The following gives you more specifics:

Points	*Personality Type*
120 or more	A+
106–119	A
100–105	A−
90–99	B+
Less than 90	B

3. play for fun and relaxation, rather than to exhibit their superiority at any cost; and
4. can relax without guilt.

Type A's operate under moderate to high levels of stress. They subject themselves to more or less continuous time pressure, creating for themselves a life of deadlines. These characteristics result in some rather specific behavioral outcomes. For example, Type A's are fast workers. This is because they emphasize quantity over quality. In managerial positions, Type A's demonstrate their competitiveness by working long hours and, not infrequently, making poor decisions because they make them too fast. Type A's are also rarely creative. Because of their concern with quantity and speed, they rely on past experiences when faced with problems. They will not allocate the time that is necessary to develop unique solutions to new problems. They rarely vary in their responses to specific challenges in their milieu; hence their behavior is easier to predict than that of Type B's.

Are Type A's or Type B's more successful in organizations? In spite of the hard work of Type A's, the Type B's are the ones who appear to make it to the top. Great salespersons are usually Type A's; senior executives are usually Type B's. Why? The answer lies in the tendency of Type A's to trade off quality of effort for quantity. Promotions in corporate and professional organizations "usually go to those who are wise rather than to those who are merely hasty, to those who are tactful rather than to those who are hostile, and to those who are creative rather than to those who are merely agile in competitive strife."[63]

Personality and National Culture

There are certainly no common personality types for a given country. You can, for instance, find high and low risk takers in almost any culture. Yet a country's culture should influence the dominant personality characteristics of its population. Let's build this case by looking at two personality attributes: locus of control and the Type A personality.

In Chapter 2, we introduced a "person's relationship to the environment" as a value dimension that separates national cultures. We noted that North Americans believe they can dominate their environment whereas people in other societies, such as Middle Eastern countries, believe life is essentially preordained. Notice the close parallel to internal and external locus of control. We should expect a larger proportion of internals in the American and Canadian work force than in the Saudi Arabian or Iranian work force.

The prevalence of Type A personalities will be somewhat influenced by the culture in which a person grows up. Type A's exist in every country, but there will be more in capitalistic countries where achievement and material success are highly valued. For instance, it is estimated that about 50 percent of the North American population is Type A.[64] This shouldn't be too surprising. The United States and Canada both have a high emphasis on time management and efficiency. Both have a "doing" activity orientation, which stresses accomplishments. And both focus on quantity of life, with its emphasis on acquisition of money and material goods.

Matching Personalities and Jobs

In the previous discussion of personality attributes, our conclusions were often qualified to recognize that the requirements of the job moderated the relationship between possession of the personality characteristic and job performance. This concern with matching the job requirements with personality characteristics is best articulated in John Holland's **personality–job fit theory**.[65] The theory is based on the notion of fit between an individual's personality characteristics and his or her occupational environment. Holland presents six personality types and proposes that satisfaction and the propensity to leave a job depend on the degree to which individuals successfully match their personalities to a congruent occupational environment.

personality-job fit theory
Identifies 6 personality types and proposes that the fit between personality type and occupational environment determines satisfaction and turnover.

Each one of the six personality types has a congruent occupational environment. Table 3-4 describes the six types and their personality characteristics, and gives examples of congruent occupations.

Holland has developed a Vocational Preference Inventory questionnaire that contains 160 occupational titles. Respondents indicate which of these occupations they like or dislike, and these answers are used to form personality profiles. Utilizing this procedure, research strongly supports the hexagonal diagram in Figure 3-2.[66] This figure shows that the closer two fields or orientations are in the hexagon, the more compatible they are. Adjacent categories are quite similar; those diagonally opposite are highly dissimilar.

What does all this mean? The theory argues that satisfaction is highest and turnover lowest where personality and occupation are in agreement. Social

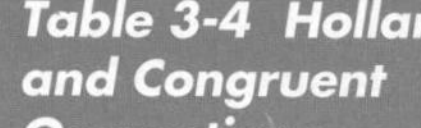

Table 3-4 Holland's Typology of Personality and Congruent Occupations

Type	Personality Characteristics	Congruent Occupations
Realistic: Prefers physical activities that require skill, strength, and coordination	Shy, genuine, persistent, stable, conforming, practical	Mechanic, drill press operator, assembly-line worker, farmer
Investigative: Prefers activities that involve thinking, organizing, and understanding	Analytical, original, curious, independent	Biologist, economist, mathematician, news reporter
Social: Prefers activities that involve helping and developing others	Sociable, friendly, cooperative, understanding	Social worker, teacher, counselor, clinical psychologist
Conventional: Prefers rule-regulated, orderly, and unambiguous activities	Conforming, efficient, practical, unimaginative, inflexible	Accountant, corporate manager, bank teller, file clerk
Enterprising: Prefers verbal activities where there are opportunities to influence others and attain power	Self-confident, ambitious, energetic, domineering	Lawyer, real estate agent, public relations specialist, small business manager
Artistic: Prefers ambiguous and unsystematic activities that allow creative expression	Imaginative, disorderly, idealistic, emotional, impractical	Painter, musician, writer, interior decorator

individuals should be in social jobs, conventional people in conventional jobs, and so forth. A realistic person in a realistic job is in a more congruent situation than is a realistic person in an investigative job. A realistic person in a social job is in the most incongruent situation possible. The key points of this model are that (1) there do appear to be intrinsic differences in personality among individuals, (2) there are different types of jobs, and (3) people in job environments congruent with their personality types should be more satisfied and less likely to voluntarily resign than people in incongruent jobs.

Figure 3-2 Relationships Among Occupational Personality Types

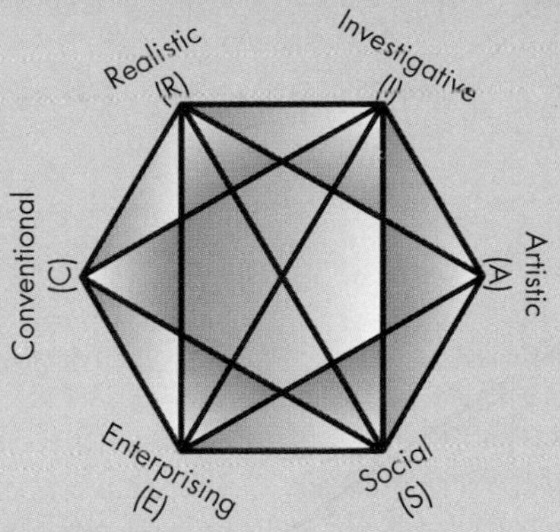

Source: J.L. Holland, *Making Vocational Choices: A Theory of Vocational Personalities and Work Environments*, 2nd ed. (Englewood Cliffs, NJ: Prentice Hall, 1985). Used by permission. The model originally appeared in J.L. Holland et al., *An Empirical Occupational Classification Derived from a Theory of Personality and Research*, ACT Research Report No. 29 (Iowa City: The American College Testing Program, 1969).

Learning

The last topic we introduce in this chapter is learning. It is included for the obvious reason that almost all complex behavior is learned. If we want to explain and predict behavior, we need to understand how people learn.

A Definition of Learning

What is *learning*? A psychologist's definition is considerably broader than the layperson's view that "it's what we did when we went to school." In actuality, each of us is continuously going "to school." Learning occurs all of the time. A generally accepted definition of **learning**, therefore, is *any relatively permanent change in behavior that occurs as a result of experience*. Ironically, we can say that changes in behavior indicate learning has taken place and that learning is a change in behavior.

learning
Any relatively permanent change in behavior that occurs as a result of experience.

Obviously, the foregoing definition suggests we never see someone learning. We can see changes taking place, but not the learning itself. The concept is theoretical and, hence, not directly observable:

> You have seen people in the process of learning, you have seen people who behave in a particular way as a result of learning and some of you (in fact, I guess the majority of you) have "learned" at some time in your life. In other words, we infer that learning has taken place if an individual behaves, reacts, responds as a result of experience in a manner different from the way he formerly behaved.[67]

Our definition has several components that deserve clarification. First, learning involves change. This may be good or bad from an organizational point of view. People can learn unfavorable behaviors—to hold prejudices or to restrict their output, for example—as well as favorable behaviors. Second, the change must be relatively permanent. Temporary changes may be only reflexive and fail to represent any learning. Therefore, this requirement rules out behavioral changes caused by fatigue or temporary adaptations. Third, our definition is concerned with behavior. Learning takes place where there is a change in actions. A change in an individual's thought processes or attitudes, if accompanied by no change in behavior, would not be learning. Finally, some form of experience is necessary for learning. This may be acquired directly through observation or practice. Or it may result from an indirect experience, such as that acquired through reading. The crucial test still remains: Does this experience result in a relatively permanent change in behavior? If the answer is "Yes," we can say that learning has taken place.

Theories of Learning

How do we learn? Three theories have been offered to explain the process by which we acquire patterns of behavior: classical conditioning, operant conditioning, and social learning.

classical conditioning
A type of conditioning where an individual responds to some stimulus that would not invariably produce such a response.

CLASSICAL CONDITIONING **Classical conditioning** grew out of experiments to teach dogs to salivate in response to the ringing of a bell, conducted at the turn of the century by a Russian physiologist, Ivan Pavlov.[68]

A simple surgical procedure allowed Pavlov to measure accurately the amount of saliva secreted by a dog. When Pavlov presented the dog with a piece of meat, the dog exhibited a noticeable increase in salivation. When Pavlov withheld the presentation of meat and merely rang a bell, the dog had no salivation. Then Pavlov proceeded to link the meat and the ringing of the bell. After repeatedly hearing the bell before getting the food, the dog began to salivate as soon as the bell rang. After a while, the dog would salivate merely at the sound of the bell, even if no food was offered. In effect, the dog had learned to respond—that is, to salivate—to the bell. Let's review this experiment to introduce the key concepts in classical conditioning.

The meat was an *unconditioned stimulus*; it invariably caused the dog to react in a specific way. The reaction that took place whenever the unconditioned stimulus occurred was called the *unconditioned response* (or the noticeable increase in salivation, in this case). The bell was an artificial stimulus, or what we call the *conditioned stimulus*. While it was originally neutral, after the bell was paired with the meat (an unconditioned stimulus), it eventually produced a response when presented alone. The last key concept is the *conditioned response*. This describes the behavior of the dog salivating in reaction to the bell alone.

Using these concepts, we can summarize classical conditioning. Essentially, learning a conditioned response involves building up an association between a conditioned stimulus and an unconditioned stimulus. Using the paired stimuli, one com-

THE FAR SIDE By GARY LARSON

Unbeknownst to most students of psychology, Pavlov's first experiment was to ring a bell and cause his dog to attack Freud's cat.

Figure 3-3
Source: THE FAR SIDE copyright 1990 & 1991 FARWORKS, INC./Dist. by UNIVERSAL PRESS SYNDICATE. Reprinted with permission. All rights reserved.

pelling and the other one neutral, the neutral one becomes a conditioned stimulus and, hence, takes on the properties of the unconditioned stimulus.

Classical conditioning can be used to explain why Christmas carols often bring back pleasant memories of childhood—the songs being associated with the festive Christmas spirit and initiating fond memories and feelings of euphoria. In an organizational setting, we can also see classical conditioning operating. For example, at one manufacturing plant, every time the top executives from the head office were scheduled to visit, the plant management would clean up the administrative offices and wash the windows. This went on for years. Eventually, employees would turn on their best behavior and look prim and proper whenever the windows were cleaned—even in those occasional instances when the cleaning was not paired with the visit from the top brass. People had learned to associate the cleaning of the windows with the visit from the head office.

Classical conditioning is passive. Something happens and we react in a specific way. It is elicited in response to a specific, identifiable event. As such it can explain simple reflexive behaviors. But most behavior—particularly the complex behavior of individuals in organizations—is emitted rather than elicited. It is voluntary rather than reflexive. For example, employees choose to arrive at work on time, ask their boss for help with problems, or goof off when no one is watching. The learning of these behaviors is better understood by looking at operant conditioning.

operant conditioning
A type of conditioning in which desired voluntary behavior leads to a reward or prevents a punishment.

OPERANT CONDITIONING **Operant conditioning** argues that behavior is a function of its consequences. People learn to behave to get something they want or avoid something they don't want. Operant behavior means voluntary or learned behavior in contrast to reflexive or unlearned behavior. The tendency to repeat such behavior is influenced by the reinforcement or lack of reinforcement brought about by the consequences of the behavior. Reinforcement, therefore, strengthens a behavior and increases the likelihood it will be repeated.

What Pavlov did for classical conditioning, the late Harvard psychologist B. F. Skinner did for operant conditioning.[69] Building on earlier work in the field, Skinner's research extensively expanded our knowledge of operant conditioning. Even his staunchest critics, who represent a sizable group, admit his operant concepts work.

Behavior is assumed to be determined from without—that is, learned—rather than from within—reflexive or unlearned. Skinner argued that by creating pleasing consequences to follow specific forms of behavior, the frequency of that behavior will increase. People will most likely engage in desired behaviors if they are positively reinforced for doing so. Rewards, for example, are most effective if they immediately follow the desired response. Additionally, behavior that is not rewarded, or is punished, is less likely to be repeated.

You see illustrations of operant conditioning everywhere. For example, any situation in which it is either explicitly stated or implicitly suggested that reinforcements are contingent on some action on your part involves the use of operant learning. Your instructor says that if you want a high grade in the course you must supply correct answers on the test. A commissioned salesperson wanting to earn a sizable income finds it contingent on generating high sales in her territory. Of course, the linkage can also work to teach the individual to engage in behaviors that work against the best interests of the organization. Assume your boss tells you that if you will work overtime during the next

American Express Company uses positive reinforcement to reward 10,000 employees in its consumer-card and consumer-lending groups. Designed to bring out the best in employees, the incentive pay plan links employee pay to three corporate goals—customer satisfaction, employee productivity, and shareholder wealth creation. Employees are rewarded with bonuses.

three-week busy season, you will be compensated for it at the next performance appraisal. However, when performance appraisal time comes, you find you are given no positive reinforcement for your overtime work. The next time your boss asks you to work overtime, what will you do? You'll probably decline! Your behavior can be explained by operant conditioning: If a behavior fails to be positively reinforced, the probability that the behavior will be repeated declines.

SOCIAL LEARNING Individuals can also learn by observing what happens to other people and just by being told about something, as well as by direct experiences. So, for example, much of what we have learned comes from watching models—parents, teachers, peers, motion picture and television performers, bosses, and so forth. This view that we can learn through both observation and direct experience has been called **social-learning theory**.[70]

social-learning theory
People can learn through observation and direct experience.

While social-learning theory is an extension of operant conditioning—that is, it assumes behavior is a function of consequences—it also acknowledges the existence of observational learning and the importance of perception in learning. People respond to how they perceive and define consequences, not to the objective consequences themselves.

The influence of models is central to the social-learning viewpoint. Four processes have been found to determine the influence that a model will have on an individual. As we show later in this chapter, the inclusion of the following processes when management sets up employee training programs will significantly improve the likelihood the programs will be successful:

1. *Attentional processes.* People only learn from a model when they recognize and pay attention to its critical features. We tend to be most influenced by models that are attractive, repeatedly available, important to us, or similar to us in our estimation.
2. *Retention processes.* A model's influence will depend on how well the individual remembers the model's action after the model is no longer readily available.
3. *Motor reproduction processes.* After a person has seen a new behavior by observing the model, the watching must be converted to doing. This process then demonstrates that the individual can perform the modeled activities.
4. *Reinforcement processes.* Individuals will be motivated to exhibit the modeled behavior if positive incentives or rewards are provided. Behaviors that are reinforced will be given more attention, learned better, and performed more often.

◆◆◆◆ OB in the News ◆◆◆◆

Apprenticeship Programs at Siemens

Siemens AG, the German electronics giant, has introduced a highly successful apprenticeship program at its Stromberg-Carlson operation in Boca Raton, Florida, that is built largely on social-learning concepts.

Nineteen Americans were chosen for the two-and-a-half-year program. The first year combines academic training at a local community college with hands-on training at the Siemens training center. In the second year, apprentices receive on-the-job training at the company's Lake Mary, Florida, manufacturing facility. When completed, each apprentice will have earned an associate's degree in telecommunications engineering technology and will be a certified Siemens technician.

The early results from the Boca Raton program are highly encouraging. These apprentices have posted the highest scores worldwide on the corporation's first-year apprenticeship final exams, which required them to design, build, and evaluate a working electronics project in one day.

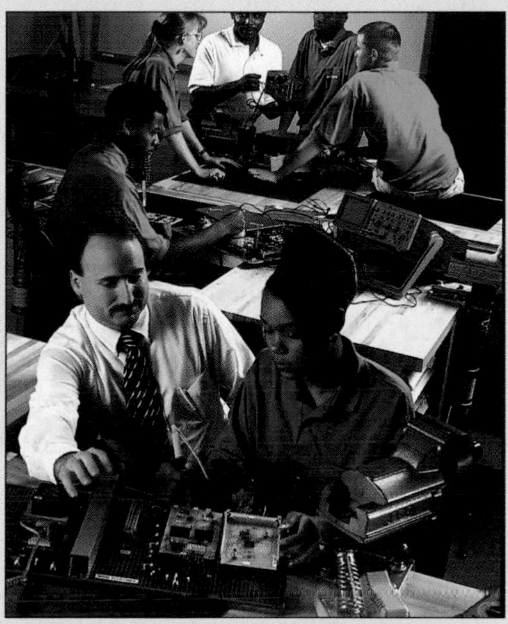

A German *meister*, or expert instructor, and his apprentices illustrate the social learning view that we can learn through both observation and direct experience.

Apprenticeships that blend learning in the classroom with shop-floor experience have long been a staple of German work force training. It is frequently referred to as that country's secret to high productivity. The Boca Raton program demonstrates that German-style apprenticeships can be successfully applied in the United States.

Based on J.F. McKenna, "Siemens' Yanks Make the Grade," *Industry Week* (January 3, 1994), p. 30.

Shaping: A Managerial Tool

Because learning takes place on the job as well as prior to it, managers are concerned with how they can teach employees to behave in ways that most benefit the organization. When we attempt to mold individuals by guiding their learning in graduated steps, we are **shaping behavior**.

shaping behavior
Systematically reinforcing each successive step that moves an individual closer to the desired response.

Consider the situation in which an employee's behavior is significantly different from that sought by management. If management only reinforced the individual when he or she showed desirable responses, very little reinforcement might be taking place. In such a case, shaping offers a logical approach toward achieving the desired behavior.

We *shape* behavior by systematically reinforcing each successive step that moves the individual closer to the desired response. If an employee who has chronically been a half hour late for work comes in only 20 minutes late, we can reinforce this improvement. Reinforcement would increase as responses more closely approximate the desired behavior.

METHODS OF SHAPING BEHAVIOR There are four ways in which to shape behavior: through positive reinforcement, negative reinforcement, punishment, and extinction.

When a response is followed with something pleasant, it is called *positive reinforcement*. This would describe, for instance, the boss who praises an employee for a job well done. When a response is followed by the termination or withdrawal of something unpleasant, it is called *negative reinforcement*. If your college instructor asks a question and you don't know the answer, looking through your lecture notes is likely to preclude your being called on. This is a negative reinforcement because you have learned that looking busily through your notes prevents the instructor from calling on you. *Punishment* is causing an unpleasant condition in an attempt to eliminate an undesirable behavior. Giving an employee a two-day suspension from work without pay for showing up drunk is an example of punishment. Eliminating any reinforcement that is maintaining a behavior is called *extinction*. When the behavior is not reinforced, it tends to gradually be extinguished. College instructors who wish to discourage students from asking questions in class can eliminate this behavior in their students by ignoring those who raise their hands to ask questions. Hand raising will become extinct when it is invariably met with an absence of reinforcement.

Both positive and negative reinforcement result in learning. They strengthen a response and increase the probability of repetition. In the preceding illustrations, praise strengthens and increases the behavior of doing a good job because praise is desired. The behavior of looking busy is similarly strengthened and increased by its terminating the undesirable consequence of being called on by the teacher. Both punishment and extinction, however, weaken behavior and tend to decrease its subsequent frequency.

Reinforcement, whether it is positive or negative, has an impressive record as a shaping tool. Our interest, therefore, is in reinforcement rather than in punishment or extinction. A review of research findings on the impact of reinforcement on behavior in organizations concluded that

1. Some type of reinforcement is necessary to produce a change in behavior.
2. Some types of rewards are more effective for use in organizations than others.

3. The speed with which learning takes place and the permanence of its effects will be determined by the timing of reinforcement.[71]

Point 3 is extremely important and deserves considerable elaboration.

SCHEDULES OF REINFORCEMENT The two major types of reinforcement schedules are *continuous* and *intermittent*. A **continuous reinforcement** schedule reinforces the desired behavior each and every time it is demonstrated. For example, in the case of someone who has historically had trouble arriving at work on time, every time he is *not* tardy his manager might compliment him on his desirable behavior. In an intermittent schedule, on the other hand, not every instance of the desirable behavior is reinforced, but reinforcement is given often enough to make the behavior worth repeating. This latter schedule can be compared to the workings of a slot machine, which people will continue to play even when they know it is adjusted to give a considerable return to the gambling house. The intermittent payoffs occur just often enough to reinforce the behavior of slipping in coins and pulling the handle. Evidence indicates that the intermittent or varied form of reinforcement tends to promote more resistance to extinction than does the continuous form.[72]

continuous reinforcement
A desired behavior is reinforced each and every time it is demonstrated.

An **intermittent reinforcement** can be of a ratio or interval type. *Ratio schedules* depend on how many responses the subject makes. The individual is reinforced after giving a certain number of specific types of behavior. *Interval schedules* depend on how much time has passed since the last reinforcement. With interval schedules, the individual is reinforced on the first appropriate behavior after a particular time has elapsed. A reinforcement can also be classified as fixed or variable. Intermittent techniques for administering rewards can, therefore, be placed into four categories, as shown in Figure 3-4.

intermittent reinforcement
A desired behavior is reinforced often enough to make the behavior worth repeating, but not every time it is demonstrated.

When rewards are spaced at uniform time intervals, the reinforcement schedule is of the **fixed-interval** type. The critical variable is time, and it is held constant. This is the predominant schedule for almost all salaried workers in North America. When you get your paycheck on a weekly, semimonthly, monthly, or other predetermined time basis, you are rewarded on a fixed-interval reinforcement schedule.

fixed-interval schedule
Rewards are spaced at uniform time intervals.

If rewards are distributed in time so reinforcements are unpredictable, the schedule is of the **variable-interval** type. When an instructor advises her class of a number of pop quizzes given during the term (the exact number of which is unknown to the students), and the quizzes will account for 20 percent of the term grade, she is using such a variable-interval schedule. Similarly, a series of randomly timed unannounced visits to a company office by the corporate audit staff is an example of a variable-interval schedule.

variable-interval schedule
Rewards are distributed in time so that reinforcements are unpredictable.

fixed-ratio schedule
Rewards are initiated after a fixed or constant number of responses.

In a **fixed-ratio** schedule, after a fixed or constant number of responses are given, a reward is initiated. For example, a piece-rate incentive plan is a fixed-ratio schedule—the employee receives a reward based on the number of work pieces generated. If the piece rate for a zipper installer in a dressmaking factory is $5 a dozen, the reinforcement (money in this case) is fixed to the number of zippers sewn into garments. After every dozen is sewn in, the installer has earned another $5.

variable-ratio schedule
The reward varies relative to the behavior of the individual.

When the reward varies relative to the behavior of the individual, he or she is said to be reinforced on a **variable-ratio** schedule. Salespeople on commission are examples of individuals on such a reinforcement schedule. On some occasions, they may make a sale after only two calls on potential customers. On other occasions, they might need to make 20 or more calls to

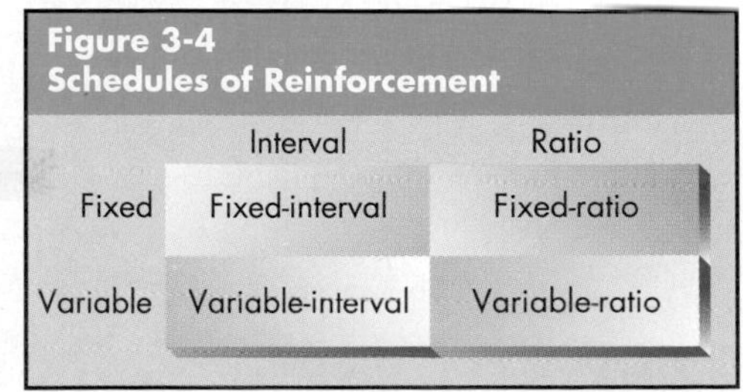
Figure 3-4
Schedules of Reinforcement

	Interval	Ratio
Fixed	Fixed-interval	Fixed-ratio
Variable	Variable-interval	Variable-ratio

secure a sale. The reward, then, is variable in relation to the number of successful calls the salesperson makes. Figure 3-5 visually depicts the four categories of intermittent schedules.

REINFORCEMENT SCHEDULES AND BEHAVIOR Continuous reinforcement schedules can lead to early satiation, and under this schedule behavior tends to weaken rapidly when reinforcers are withheld. However, continuous reinforcers are appropriate for newly emitted, unstable, or low-frequency responses. In contrast, intermittent reinforcers preclude early satiation because they don't follow every response. They are appropriate for stable or high-frequency responses.

FIGURE 3-5
Intermittent Schedules of Reinforcement

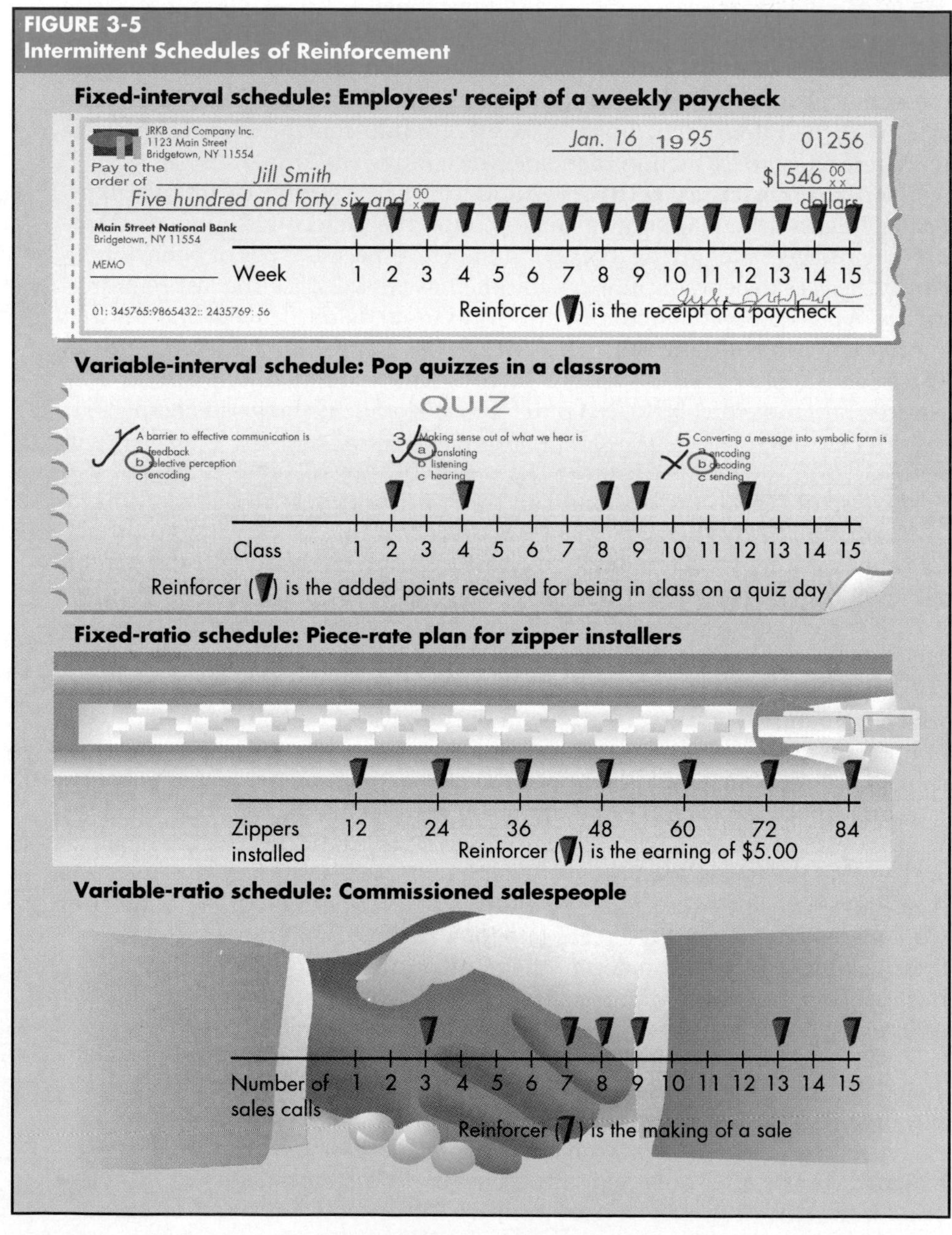

In general, variable schedules tend to lead to higher performance than fixed schedules. For example, as we noted previously, most employees in organizations are paid on fixed-interval schedules. But such a schedule does not clearly link performance and rewards. The reward is given for time spent on the job rather than for a specific response (performance). In contrast, variable-interval schedules generate high rates of response and more stable and consistent behavior because of a high correlation between performance and reward and because of the uncertainty involved: The employee tends to be more alert because there is a surprise factor.

Some Specific Organizational Applications

We have alluded to a number of situations where learning theory could be helpful to managers. In this section, we briefly look at six specific applications: reducing absenteeism through the use of lotteries, substituting well pay for sick pay, disciplining problem employees, developing effective employee training programs, creating mentoring programs for new employees, and applying learning theory to self-management.

USING LOTTERIES TO REDUCE ABSENTEEISM Management can design programs to reduce absenteeism utilizing learning theory. For example, New York Life Insurance Co. created a lottery that rewarded employees for attendance.[73] Each quarter the names of all those headquarters employees with no absences are placed in a drum. In a typical quarter, about 4,000 of the company's 7,500 employees have their names placed in the drum. The first 10 names pulled earn a $200 bond, the next 20 earn a $100 bond, and 70 more receive a paid day off. At the end of the year, another lottery is held for those with 12 months of perfect attendance. Twelve prizes are awarded—two employees receive $1,000 bonds and ten more earn five days off with pay.

This lottery follows a variable-ratio schedule. A good attendance record increases an employee's probability of winning, yet having perfect attendance is no assurance an employee will be rewarded by winning one of the prizes. Consistent with the research on reinforcement schedules, this lottery resulted in lower absence rates. In its first ten months of operation, for instance, absenteeism was 21 percent lower than for the comparable period in the preceding year.

WELL PAY VS. SICK PAY Most organizations provide their salaried employees with paid sick leave as part of the employee's fringe benefit program. But ironically, organizations with paid sick leave programs experience almost twice the absenteeism of organizations without such programs.[74] The reality is that sick leave reinforces the wrong behavior—absence from work.

Organizations should have programs that encourage employees to be on the job by discouraging unnecessary absences. When employees receive ten paid sick days a year, it is the unusual employee who isn't sure to use them all up, regardless of whether or not he or she is sick. This suggests that organizations should reward attendance, not absence.

◆Sick leave programs reinforce the wrong behavior.

As a case in point, one Midwest organization implemented a well-pay program that paid a bonus to employees who had no absence for any given four-week period and then only paid for sick leave after the first eight hours of absence.[75] Evaluation of the well-pay program found that it produced increased savings to the organization, reduced absenteeism, increased productivity, and improved employee satisfaction.

Forbes magazine used the same approach to cut its health-care costs.[76] It rewarded those employees who stayed healthy and didn't file medical claims by paying them the difference between $500 and their medical claims, then doubling the amount. So if someone submitted no claims in a given year, he or she would receive $1,000 ($500 × 2). By rewarding employees for good health, Forbes cut its major medical and dental claims by over 30 percent.

EMPLOYEE DISCIPLINE Every manager will, at some time, have to deal with an employee who drinks on the job, is insubordinate, steals company property, arrives consistently late for work, or engages in similar problem behaviors. Managers will respond with disciplinary actions such as oral reprimands, written warnings, and temporary suspensions. Research on discipline shows that the manager should act immediately to correct the problem, match the severity of the punishment to the severity of the "crime," and ensure that the employee sees the link between the punishment and the undesirable behavior.[77] But our knowledge about punishment's effect on behavior indicates that the use of discipline carries costs. It may provide only a short-term solution and result in serious side effects.

Disciplining employees for undesirable behaviors only tells them what *not* to do. It doesn't tell them what alternative behaviors are preferred. The result is that this form of punishment frequently leads to only short-term suppression of the undesirable behavior rather than its elimination. Continued use of punishment, rather than positive reinforcement, also tends to produce a conditional fear of the manager. As the punishing agent, the manager becomes associated in the employee's mind with adverse consequences. Employees respond by "hiding" from their boss. Hence the use of punishment can undermine manager–employee relations.

The popularity of discipline undoubtedly lies in its ability to produce fast results in the short run. Managers are reinforced for using discipline because it produces an immediate change in the employee's behavior. But over the long run, when used without positive reinforcement of desirable behaviors, it is likely to lead to employee frustration, fear of the manager, reoccurrences of the problem behaviors, and increases in absenteeism and turnover.

DEVELOPING TRAINING PROGRAMS It's estimated that more than 90 percent of all private organizations have some type of systematic training program and more than $44 billion a year is spent on training initiatives.[78] Can these or-

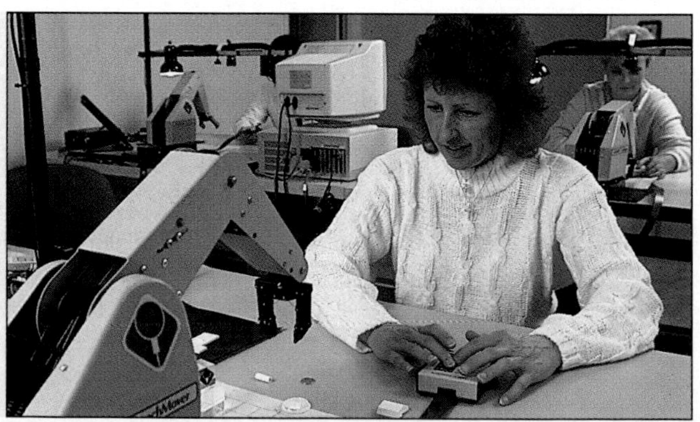

Learning theory helps organizations design training programs. Motorola, which spends $120 million a year on training and education, conducts its worldwide programs from Motorola University at corporate headquarters in Schaumburg, Illinois. Motorola says every $1 it invests in training returns $30 in productivity gains within three years. In a recent five-year period, Motorola cut costs by $3.3 billion by training employees to simplify processes and reduce waste. In the same period, sales per employee doubled and company profits increased 47 percent. The Motorola employee shown here applies the training she received to her job of programming robots.

ganizations draw from our discussion of learning in order to improve the effectiveness of their training programs? Certainly.

Social-learning theory offers such a guide. It tells us that training should offer a model to grab the trainee's attention; provide motivational properties; help the trainee file away what he or she has learned for later use; provide opportunities to practice new behaviors; offer positive rewards for accomplishments; and, if the training has taken place off the job, allow the trainee some opportunity to transfer what he or she has learned to the job.

CREATING MENTORING PROGRAMS It's the unusual senior manager who, early in his or her career, didn't have an older, more experienced mentor higher up in the organization. This mentor took the protégé under his or her wing and provided advice and guidance on how to survive and get ahead in the organization. Mentoring, of course, is not limited to the managerial ranks. Union apprenticeship programs, for example, do the same thing by preparing individuals to move from unskilled apprentice status to that of skilled journeyman. A young electrician apprentice typically works under an experienced electrician for several years to develop the full range of skills necessary to effectively execute his or her job.

A successful mentoring program will be built on modeling concepts from social-learning theory. That is, a mentor's impact comes from more than merely what he or she explicitly tells a protégé. Mentors are role models. Protégés learn to convey the attitudes and behaviors that the organization wants by emulating the traits and actions of their mentors. They observe and then imitate. Top managers who are concerned with developing employees who will fit into the organization and with preparing young managerial talent for greater responsibilities should give careful attention to who takes on mentoring roles. The creating of formal mentoring programs—where young individuals are officially assigned a mentor—allows senior executives to manage the process and increases the likelihood that protégés will be molded the way top management desires.

SELF-MANAGEMENT Organizational applications of learning concepts are not restricted to managing the behavior of others. These concepts can also be used to allow individuals to manage their own behavior and, in so doing, reduce the need for managerial control. This is called **self-management**.[79]

self-management
Learning techniques that allow individuals to manage their own behavior so that less external management control is necessary.

Self-management requires an individual to deliberately manipulate stimuli, internal processes, and responses to achieve personal behavioral outcomes. The basic processes involve observing one's own behavior, comparing the behavior with a standard, and rewarding oneself if the behavior meets the standard.

So how might self-management be applied? To illustrate, a group of state government blue-collar employees received eight hours of training in which they were taught self-management skills.[80] They were then shown how the skills could be used for improving job attendance. They were instructed on how to set specific goals for job attendance, both short term and intermediate term. They learned how to write a behavioral contract with themselves and identify self-chosen reinforcers. Finally, they learned the importance of self-monitoring their attendance behavior and administering incentives when they achieved their goals. The net result for these participants was a significant improvement in job attendance.

Summary and Implications for Managers

This chapter has looked at four individual variables: biographical characteristics, ability, personality, and learning. Let's now summarize what we found and consider their importance for the manager who is trying to understand organizational behavior.

BIOGRAPHICAL CHARACTERISTICS Biographical characteristics are readily available to managers. For the most part, they represent data contained in almost every employee's personnel file. After reviewing the evidence, the most important conclusions we can draw are that age seems to have no relationship to productivity; older workers and those with longer tenure are less likely to resign; and married employees have fewer absences, less turnover, and report higher job satisfaction than do unmarried employees.

ABILITY Ability directly influences an employee's level of performance and satisfaction through the ability–job fit. Given management's desire to get a compatible fit, what can be done?

First, an effective selection process will improve the fit. A job analysis will provide information about jobs currently being done and the abilities that individuals need to perform the jobs adequately. Applicants can then be tested, interviewed, and evaluated to the degree to which they possess the necessary abilities. Second, promotion and transfer decisions affecting individuals already in the organization's employ should reflect the abilities of candidates. As with new employees, care should be taken to assess critical abilities that incumbents will need in the job and to match those requirements with the organization's human resources. Third, the fit can be improved by fine-tuning the job to better match an incumbent's abilities. Often modifications can be made in the job that, while not having a significant impact on the job's basic activities, better adapts it to the specific talents of a given employee. Examples of this are changing some of the equipment used and reorganizing tasks within a group of employees. A final alternative is to provide training for employees. This is applicable to both new workers and present job incumbents. For the latter, training can keep their abilities current or provide new skills as times and conditions change.

PERSONALITY A review of the personality literature offers general guidelines that can lead to effective job performance. As such, it can improve hiring, transfer, and promotion decisions. Because personality characteristics create the parameters for people's behavior, they give us a framework for predicting behavior. For example, individuals who are shy, introverted, and uncomfortable in social situations would probably be ill suited as salespeople. Individuals who are submissive and conforming might not be effective as advertising "idea" people.

Can we predict which people will be high performers in sales, research, or assembly-line work based on their personality characteristics alone? The answer is no. But a knowledge of an individual's personality can aid in reducing mismatches, which, in turn, can lead to reduced turnover and higher job satisfaction.

Personality tests help Will Knecht (left) place people in the jobs they can do most effectively. Knecht is vice-president of Wendell August Forge, which makes metal giftware. His business requires a variety of workers—crafts workers, artists, salespeople, and customer-service employees. The personality test Knecht uses measures traits such as patience, exactitude, and independence, characteristics related to the job success of master craftsman Ty Thompson (right). Knecht uses personality testing in hiring, promoting, and training employees and in selecting complementary employees to form teams.

We can look at certain personality characteristics that tend to be related to job success, test for these traits, and use this data to make selection more effective. A person who accepts rules, conformity, and dependence and rates low on openness to experience is likely to feel more comfortable in, say, a structured assembly-line job, as an admittance clerk in a hospital, or as an administrator in a large public agency than as a researcher or an employee whose job requires a high degree of creativity.

LEARNING Any observable change in behavior is, by definition, prima facie evidence that learning has taken place. What we want to do, of course, is ascertain if learning concepts provide us with any insights that would allow us to explain and predict behavior.

Positive reinforcement is a powerful tool for modifying behavior. By identifying and rewarding performance-related behaviors, management increases the likelihood they will be repeated.

Our knowledge about learning further suggests that reinforcement is a more effective tool than punishment. Punished behavior tends to be only temporarily suppressed rather than permanently changed, and the recipients of punishment tend to become resentful of the punisher. Although punishment eliminates undesired behavior more quickly than negative reinforcement does, its effect is only temporary and it may later produce unpleasant side effects such as lower morale and higher absenteeism or turnover. Managers, therefore, are advised to use reinforcement rather than punishment.

Finally, managers should expect that employees will look to them as models. Managers who are constantly late to work, or take two hours for lunch, or help themselves to company office supplies for personal use, should expect employees to read the message they're sending and model their behavior accordingly.

For Review

1. Which biographical characteristics best predict productivity? Absenteeism? Turnover? Satisfaction?
2. Describe the specific steps you would take to ensure that an individual has the appropriate abilities to do a given job satisfactorily.
3. What constrains the power of personality traits to precisely predict behavior?
4. What behavioral predictions might you make if you knew that an employee had (a) an external locus of control? (b) a low Mach score? (c) low self-esteem? (d) a Type A personality?
5. What is the Myers-Briggs Type Indicator?
6. What were the six personality types identified by Holland?
7. How might employees actually learn unethical behavior on their jobs?
8. Contrast classical conditioning, operant conditioning, and social learning.
9. Describe the four types of intermittent reinforcers.
10. What are the drawbacks to a manager using discipline with a problem employee?

For Discussion

1. "Heredity determines personality." (a) Build an argument to support this statement. (b) Build an argument against this statement.
2. "The type of job an employee does moderates the relationship between personality and job productivity." Do you agree or disagree with this statement? Discuss.
3. One day your boss comes in and he's nervous, edgy, and argumentative. The next day he is calm and relaxed. Does this suggest that personality traits aren't consistent from day to day?
4. Learning theory can be used to explain behavior and to control behavior. Can you distinguish between the two objectives? Can you give any ethical or moral arguments why managers should not seek control over others' behavior? How valid do you think these arguments are?
5. What have you learned about "learning" that could help you explain the behavior of students in a classroom if (a) the instructor gives only one test—a final examination at the end of the course? (b) the instructor gives four exams during the term, all of which are announced on the first day of class? (c) the student's grade is based on the results of numerous exams, none of which are announced by the instructor ahead of time?

Point

The Value of Traits in Explaining Attitudes and Behavior

The essence of trait approaches in OB is that employees possess stable personality characteristics—such as dependency, anxiety, and sociability—that significantly influence their attitudes toward, and behavioral reactions to, organizational settings. People with particular traits tend to be relatively consistent in their attitudes and behavior over time and across situations.

Of course, trait theorists recognize that all traits are not equally powerful. *Cardinal traits* are defined as being so strong and generalized that they influence every act a person performs. For instance, a person who possesses dominance as a cardinal trait is domineering in virtually all of his or her actions. The evidence indicates that cardinal traits are relatively rare. More typical are *primary traits*. These are generally consistent influences on behavior, but they may not show up in all situations. So a person may be generally sociable but not display this primary trait in, say, large meetings. Finally, *secondary traits* are attributes that do not form a vital part of the personality but come into play only in particular situations. An otherwise assertive person may be submissive, for example, when confronted by his or her boss. For the most part, trait theories have focused on the power of primary traits to predict employee attitudes and behavior.

Trait theories do a fairly good job of meeting the average person's face validity test. That is, they appear to be a reasonably accurate way to describe people. Think of friends, relatives, and acquaintances you've known for a number of years. Do they have traits that have remained essentially stable over time? Most of us would answer this question in the affirmative. If Cousin Anne was shy and nervous when we last saw her ten years ago, we'd be surprised to find her outgoing and relaxed now.

In an organizational context, researchers have found that a person's job satisfaction in one given year was a significant predictor of his or her job satisfaction five years later, even when changes in occupational status, pay, occupation, and employer were controlled for.* This led the researchers to conclude that individuals possess a predisposition toward happiness, which significantly affects their job satisfaction in all types of jobs and organizations.

A final point regarding the function of traits in organizations: Managers must have a strong belief in the power of traits to predict behavior. Otherwise, they would not bother testing and interviewing prospective employees. If they believed that situations determined behavior, they would hire people almost at random and structure the situation properly. But the employee selection process in many organizations throughout the industrialized world places a great deal of emphasis on how applicants perform in interviews and on tests. Pretend you are an interviewer and ask yourself: What am I looking for in job candidates? If you answered with terms like *conscientious*, *hardworking*, *ambitious*, *confident*, *independent*, and *dependable*, you're a trait theorist!

*B. M. Staw and J. Ross, "Stability in the Midst of Change: A Dispositional Approach to Job Attitudes," *Journal of Applied Psychology* (August 1985), pp. 469–80.

counterPoint

The Limited Power of Traits in Organizations

Few people would dispute the point that there are some stable individual attributes that affect experience in and reactions to the workplace. But trait theorists go beyond this generality and argue that individual behavior consistencies are widespread and account for much of the differences in behavior among people.

Two important problems arise when using traits to explain a large proportion of behavior in organizations. First, a substantial amount of evidence shows that organizational settings are strong situations that have a large impact on employee attitudes and behavior. Second, a growing body of research indicates that individuals are highly adaptive and personality traits change in response to organizational situations. Let's elaborate on each of these problems.

It has been well known for some time that the effects of traits are likely to be strongest in relatively weak situations and weakest in relatively strong situations. Organizational settings tend to be strong situations. Why? First, they have formal structures with rules, regulations, policies, and reward systems that define acceptable behavior and punish deviant behaviors. Second, they have informal norms that dictate appropriate behaviors. These formal and informal constraints lead employees to adopt attitudes and behaviors that are consistent with their organizational roles, thus minimizing the effects of personality traits.

By arguing that employees possess stable traits which lead to cross-situational consistency in their attitudes and behaviors, trait theorists are implying that individuals do not really adapt to different situations. But a growing body of evidence indicates that an individual's traits are changed by the organizations that individual participates in. Thus, instead of remaining stable over time, an individual's personality is changed by all the organizations in which he or she has taken part. If the individual's personality changes as a result of exposure to organizational settings, in what sense can that individual be said to have traits that persistently and consistently affect his or her reactions to those very settings? Moreover, people demonstrate their situational flexibility when they change roles as they participate in different organizations. Employees often belong to many organizations. Bob is a corporate accountant during the day, presides over church meetings two nights a week, and coaches his daughter's soccer team on weekends. Most of us are like Bob; we belong to multiple organizations that often include very different kinds of members. We adapt to these different situations. Instead of being the prisoners of a rigid and stable personality framework as trait theorists propose, we regularly adjust our behavior and attitudes to reflect the requirements of various situations.

Based on A. Davis-Blake and J. Pfeffer, "Just a Mirage: The Search for Dispositional Effects in Organizational Research," *Academy of Management Review* (July 1989), pp. 385–400.

Learning About Yourself Exercise

How Important is Success to You?

Answer each of the following items as honestly as you can by circling the most appropriate number.

	Strongly Disagree				Strongly Agree
1. When something good happens to me, I often get the feeling that it won't last.	1	2	3	4	5
2. I usually feel good when I win an argument.	5	4	3	2	1
3. I seldom tell my friends when I excel at something.	1	2	3	4	5
4. When my boss or instructor praises my work, I often feel unworthy.	1	2	3	4	5
5. I like competitive sports and games.	5	4	3	2	1
6. I have gotten this far in school largely through luck.	1	2	3	4	5
7. I like receiving praise for a job well done.	5	4	3	2	1
8. I like to stay in the background on group projects.	1	2	3	4	5
9. When a project or job is going well, I often feel I will do something to mess things up.	1	2	3	4	5
10. I think I have a "winning attitude" in my approach to new assignments.	5	4	3	2	1

Turn to page A-26 for scoring directions and key.

Source: R.M. Steers and J.S. Black, *Organizational Behavior*, 5th ed. (New York: HarperCollins, 1994), p. 653.

Working With Others Exercise

Positive and Negative Reinforcement

This ten-step exercise takes approximately 20 minutes.

EXERCISE OVERVIEW (STEPS 1–4)

1. Two volunteers are selected to receive reinforcement from the class while performing a particular task. The volunteers leave the room.

2. The instructor identifies an object for the student volunteers to locate when they return to the room. (The object should be unobstrusive but clearly visible to the class. Examples that have worked well include a small triangular piece of paper that was left behind when a notice was torn off a classroom bulletin board, a smudge on the chalkboard, and a chip in the plaster of a classroom wall).

3. The instructor specifies the reinforcement contingencies that will be in effect when the volunteers return to the room—for negative reinforcement students should hiss and boo when the first volunteer is moving away from the object, and cheer and applaud when the second volunteer is getting closer to the object.
4. The instructor should assign a student to keep a record of the time it takes each of the volunteers to locate the object.

VOLUNTEER 1 (STEPS 5 AND 6)

5. Volunteer 1 is brought back into the room and is instructed that "Your task is to locate and touch a particular object in the room and the class has agreed to help you. You may not use words or ask questions. You may begin."
6. Volunteer 1 continues to look for the object until it is found while the class assists by giving negative reinforcement.

VOLUNTEER 2 (STEPS 7 AND 8)

7. Volunteer 2 is brought back into the room and is instructed that "Your task is to locate and touch a particular object in the room and the class has agreed to help you. You may not use words or ask questions. You may begin."
8. Volunteer 2 continues to look for the object until it is found while the class assists by giving positive reinforcement.

CLASS REVIEW

9. The timekeeper presents the results on how long it took each volunteer to find the object.
10. The class discusses the following:
    a. What was the difference in behavior of the two volunteers?
    b. What are the implications of this exercise to reinforcement schedules in organizations?

Source: Based on an exercise developed by Larry Michaelson of the University of Oklahoma. With permission.

Ethical Dilemma Exercise

Reinforcement and Unethical Behavior

An employee's ethical behavior depends on both his or her values and the ethical climate within the organization.* Good people can be encouraged to do bad things when their organization's reward system positively reinforces wrong behaviors. When an organization praises, promotes, gives large pay increases, and offers other desirable rewards to employees who lie, cheat, and misrepresent, its employees learn that unethical behaviors pay off.

Regardless of what management says is important, people in organizations pay attention to how actual rewards are handed out. This helps explain why some college faculty pay little attention to their students and teaching responsibilities. Despite the importance that all college administrators claim teaching carries, many colleges ignore good teaching and confer tenure, promotions, and other rewards on those who do research. Faculty who engage in research at the expense of their teaching are not bad people. They are merely people whose behavior has been shaped by their organization's reward system.

It has been noted that an organization's rewards can encourage employee practices which run counter to society's ethical norms.** For instance, North American norms encourage openness, honesty, and candor; yet organizations often reward those employees who resort to secrecy and lying to get their jobs done. Similarly, following the rules is part of North American culture, but many organizations give out promotions to those who achieve their goals by disregarding the rules.

In recent years, considerable national attention has focused on the corruption in U.S. college sports programs. Athletes' high school grades are altered to allow them admission. Cash payments are made to star athletes by college boosters. Jobs are provided by boosters to parents of prized recruits. Athletes are discouraged by their coaches from taking the English, math, and science courses they need to graduate out of fear that poor grades in these courses will jeopardize their eligibility to play the sport they were recruited for. On what can these unethical (and sometimes illegal) practices be blamed? The pressure on coaches to win! College presidents want the revenues that come from filled arenas and appearances in postseason competitions, and these are only possible when teams win. So coaches who produce winning teams get rewarded with extended contracts and fat compensation packages. Coaches who lose games—no matter how successful they may be in "building character"—get fired!

Give an example of a work-related situation where you observed unethical behavior that was encouraged or supported by the organization's reward system. What, if anything, could management have done to discourage this behavior or encourage ethical behavior in that situation?

*L. K. Trevino, "Ethical Decision Making in Organizations: A Person–Situation Interactionist Model," *Academy of Management Review* (July 1986), pp. 601–17; and L.K. Trevino and S.A. Youngblood, "Bad Apples in Bad Barrels: A Causal Analysis of Ethical Decision-Making Behavior," *Journal of Applied Psychology* (August 1990), pp. 378–85.

**E. Jansen and M. A. Von Glinow, "Ethical Ambivalence and Organizational Reward Systems," *Academy of Management Review* (October 1985), pp. 814–22.

Predicting Performance

Alix Maher is the new admissions director at a small, highly selective New England college. She has a bachelor's degree in education and a recent master's in educational administration. But she has no prior experience in college admissions.

Alix's predecessor, in conjunction with the college's admissions committee (made up of five faculty members), had given the following weights to student selection criteria: high school grades (40 percent); Scholastic Aptitude Test (SAT) scores (40 percent); extracurricular activities and achievements (10 percent); and the quality and creativity of a written theme submitted with the application (10 percent).

Alix has serious reservations about using SAT scores. In their defense, she recognizes that the quality of high schools varies greatly, so the level of student performance that receives an "A" in American history at one school might earn only a "C" at a far more demanding school. And Alix is aware that the people who design the SATs, the Educational Testing Service, argue forcibly that these test scores are valid predictors of how well a person will do in college. Yet, Alix has several concerns:

1. The pressure of the SAT exam is very great and many students suffer from test anxiety. The results, therefore, may not be truly reflective of what a student knows.
2. Evidence indicates that coaching improves scores by between 40 and 150 points. Test scores, therefore, may adversely affect the chances of acceptance for students who cannot afford the $500 or $600 to take test-coaching courses.
3. Are SATs really valid? Or do they discriminate against minorities, the poor, and those who have had limited access to cultural growth experiences?

As Alix ponders whether she wants to recommend changing the college's selection criteria and weights, she is reminded of a recent conversation she had with a friend who is an industrial psychologist with a Fortune 100 company. He told her that his company regularly uses intelligence tests to help select from among job applicants. For instance, after the company's recruiters interview graduating seniors on college campuses and identify possible hirees, they give the applicants a standardized intelligence test. Those who fail to score at least in the 80th percentile are eliminated from the applicant pool.

Alix thinks that if intelligence tests are used by billion-dollar corporations to screen job applicants, why shouldn't colleges use them? Moreover, since one of the objectives of a college should be to get its graduates placed in good jobs, maybe SAT scores should be given even higher weight than 40 percent in the selection decision. After all, she wonders, if SATs tap intelligence and employers want intelligent job applicants, why not make college selection decisions predominantly on the basis of SAT scores? Or should her college replace the SAT with a pure intelligence test like the Wechsler Adult Intelligence Scale?

Questions

1. What do you think SATs measure: aptitude, innate ability, achievement potential, intelligence, ability to take tests, or something else?
2. If the best predictor of future behavior is past behavior, what should college admissions directors use to identify the most qualified applicants?
3. If you were Alix, what would you do? Why?

Why Do Some People Have a "Winning" Personality?

It's as American as apple pie. It's winning. Listen to what a few people have to say on the subject of winning and losing.

Jim Otto, former football player: "You show me a good loser, and I'll show you a loser. And that's the way I feel about it."

James Carville, political consultant: "You know what they say, 'I've won and I've lost, and winning is better.'"

John McKissick, the winningest high school football coach in the United States: "Winning is our way of life, it's the American way of life, and it's a measure of success in any endeavor you choose. Winning is positive, losing is negative, failure is negative."

Grace Little, the number one seller of Tupperware in the United States: "I get letters, a lot, from people around the nation, cards, and just excitement, general excitement. When I'm at a convention, a lot of people will flock around me."

Natalie Weinstein, an aspiring young gymnast: "On the bulletin board it says, 'If you're not working, somewhere, somehow, someone is, and she'll best you.'"

What drives these people? Are they different from you and me? Mark Delzell, a tennis coach, says he can tell the difference between a winner and loser. "By their eyes. The intensity, the energy, the excitement they bring to the drilling like this, or to match play, or even the physical conditioning, you can see the excitement."

No one goes through life without losing. As one coach so perfectly noted after losing the first game in a 25-game season, "At least it takes all the pressure off for an undefeated season!" Even if you've never been beaten in competition, nature and old age have a way of slowing everyone down. But competitive people tend to be competitive as long as they're alive. They *always* want to be number one. Political consultant Ed Rollins calls it "an addiction."

A common insight made by highly successful and competitive people is that they don't learn from winning. Regardless of how many wins they have and how few the losses, it's the losses they learned from and they remember. "Losses stay with you a lot longer than victories do," says football star Emmitt Smith. "They stay with you a lot longer than some of the games that you remember where you went out and excelled."

Questions

1. Do you think "the desire to win" is a personality characteristic? Do you think it's in a person's genes or is it environmentally determined?
2. To what degree do you think winning (or "not losing") is a cultural manifestation? Is this a uniquely American attribute? What other cultures share it? What cultural factors might explain its development?
3. "Be careful what you wish for because you might get it." People who value winning over everything are often let down after they get their win. What implications, if any, could this have for understanding employee behavior?
4. Would you want to have employees with a high competitive drive? A high need to win at any cost? Support your position.

Source: "Winning and Losing, Competitive Spirit," *Nightline* (February 18, 1994).

Suggestions for Further Reading

ACKERMAN, P.L., and L.G. HUMPHREYS, "Individual Differences Theory in Industrial and Organizational Psychology," in M.D. Dunnette and L.M. Hough (eds.), *Handbook of Industrial and Organizational Psychology*, 2nd ed., Vol. 1 (Palo Alto, CA: Consulting Psychologists Press, 1990), pp. 223–82.

BALDWIN, T.T., "Effects of Alternative Modeling Strategies on Outcomes of Interpersonal-Skills Training," *Journal of Applied Psychology* (April 1992), pp. 147–154.

BALL, G.A., L.K. TREVINO, and H.P. SIMS, JR., "Just and Unjust Punishment: Influences on Subordinate Performance and Citizenship," *Academy of Management Journal* (April 1994), pp. 299–322.

CALDWELL, D.F., and C.A. O'REILLY, III, "Measuring Person–Job Fit with a Profile–Comparison Process," *Journal of Applied Psychology* (December 1990), pp. 648–57.

EDWARDS, J.R., "Person–Job Fit: A Conceptual Integration, Literature Review, and Methodological Critique," in C.L. Cooper and I.T. Robertson (eds.), *International Review of Industrial and Organizational Psychology*, Vol. 6 (Chichester, England: Wiley, 1991), pp. 283–357.

FROILAND, P., "Action Learning," *Training* (January 1994), pp. 27–34.

GOLDBERG, L.R., "The Structure of Phenotypic Personality Traits," *American Psychologist* (January 1993), pp. 26–34.

GEORGE, J.M., "The Role of Personality in Organizational Life: Issues and Evidence," *Journal of Management* (June 1992), pp. 185–213.

SCHMIT, M.J. and A.M. RYAN, "The Big Five in Personnel Selection: Factor Structure in Applicant and Nonapplicant Populations," *Journal of Applied Psychology* (December 1993), pp. 966–74.

WEISS, H.M., "Learning Theory and Industrial and Organizational Psychology," in M.D. Dunnette and L.M. Hough (eds.), *Handbook of Industrial and Organizational Psychology*, 2nd ed., Vol. 1 (Palo Alto, CA: Consulting Psychologists Press, 1990), pp. 171–221.

Notes

[1] Based on R. McKenzie, "A Hard Pill to Swallow," *Canadian Business* (February 1994), pp. 44–50.

[2] Reported in M. Galen, "Myths About Older Workers Cost Business Plenty," *Business Week* (December 20, 1993), p. 83.

[3] L.W. Porter and R. Steers, "Organizational, Work and Personal Factors in Employee Turnover and Absenteeism," *Psychological Bulletin* (January 1973), pp. 151–76; W.H. Mobley, R.W. Griffeth, H.H. Hand, and B.M. Meglino, "Review and Conceptual Analysis of the Employee Turnover Process," *Psychological Bulletin* (May 1979), pp. 493–522; S.R. Rhodes, "Age–Related Differences in Work Attitudes and Behavior: A Review and Conceptual Analysis," *Psychological Bulletin* (March 1983), pp. 328–67; J.D. Werbel and A.G. Bedeian, "Intended Turnover as a Function of Age and Job Performance," *Journal of Organizational Behavior*, Vol. 10 (1989), pp. 275–81; and D.R. Davies, G. Matthews, and C.S.K. Wong, "Ageing and Work," in C.L. Cooper and I.T. Robertson (eds.), *International Review of Industrial and Organizational Psychology*, Vol. 6 (Chichester, England: Wiley, 1991), pp. 183–87.

[4] Rhodes, "Age-Related Differences," pp. 347–49; R.D. Hackett, "Age, Tenure, and Employee Absenteeism," *Human Relations* (July 1990), pp. 601–19; and D.R. Davies, G. Matthews, and C.S.K. Wong, "Ageing and Work," pp. 183–87.

[5] Cited in K. Labich, "The New Unemployed," *Fortune* (March 8, 1993), p. 43.

[6] G.M. McEvoy and W.F. Cascio, "Cumulative Evidence of the Relationship Between Employee Age and Job Performance," *Journal of Applied Psychology* (February 1989), pp. 11–17.

[7] A.L. Kalleberg and K.A. Loscocco, "Aging, Values, and Rewards: Explaining Age Differences in Job Satisfaction," *American Sociological Review* (February 1983), pp. 78–90; R. Lee and E.R. Wilbur, "Age, Education, Job Tenure, Salary, Job Characteristics, and Job Satisfaction: A Multivariate Analysis," *Human Relations* (August 1985), pp. 781–91; and D.R. Davies, G. Matthews, and C.S.K. Wong, "Ageing and Work," pp. 176–83.

[8] K.M. Kacmar and G.R. Ferris, "Theoretical and Methodological Considerations in the Age–Job Satisfaction Relationship," *Journal of Applied Psychology* (April 1989), pp. 201–207; and G. Zeitz, "Age and Work Satisfaction in a Government Agency: A Situational Perspective," *Human Relations* (May 1990), pp. 419–38.

[9] See, for example, E. Maccoby and C. Nagy Jacklin, *The Psychology of Sex Differences* (Stanford, CA: Stanford University Press, 1974); A.H. Eagly and L.L. Carli, "Sex Researchers and Sex–Typed Communications as Determinants of Sex Differences in Influenceability: A Meta–Analysis of Social Influence Studies," *Psychological Bulletin* (August 1981), pp. 1–20; J.S. Hyde, "How Large Are Cognitive Gender Differences?" *American Psychologist* (October 1981), pp. 892–901; and P. Chance, "Biology, Destiny, and All That," *Across the Board* (July–August 1988), pp. 19–23.

[10] R.P. Quinn, G.L. Staines, and M.R. McCullough, *Job Satisfaction: Is There a Trend?* (Washington, DC: U.S. Government Printing Office, Document 2900–00195, 1974).

[11] T.W. Mangione, "Turnover—Some Psychological and Demographic Correlates," in R.P. Quinn and T.W. Mangione (eds.), *The 1969–70 Survey of Working Conditions* (Ann Arbor:

University of Michigan, Survey Research Center, 1973); and R. Marsh and H. Mannari, "Organizational Commitment and Turnover: A Predictive Study," *Administrative Science Quarterly* (March 1977), pp. 57–75.

[12] R.J. Flanagan, G. Strauss, and L. Ulman, "Worker Discontent and Work Place Behavior," *Industrial Relations* (May 1974), pp. 101–23; K.R. Garrison and P.M. Muchinsky, "Attitudinal and Biographical Predictors of Incidental Absenteeism," *Journal of Vocational Behavior* (April 1977), pp. 221–30; G. Johns, "Attitudinal and Nonattitudinal Predictors of Two Forms of Absence from Work," *Organizational Behavior and Human Performance* (December 1978), pp. 431–44; and R.T. Keller, "Predicting Absenteeism from Prior Absenteeism, Attitudinal Factors, and Nonattitudinal Factors," *Journal of Applied Psychology* (August 1983), pp. 536–40.

[13] See, for instance, M. Tait, M.Y. Padgett, and T.T. Baldwin, "Job and Life Satisfaction: A Reevaluation of the Strength of the Relationship and Gender Effects as a Function of the Date of the Study," *Journal of Applied Psychology* (June 1989), pp. 502–507.

[14] Garrison and Muchinsky, "Attitudinal and Biographical Predictors"; C.J. Watson, "An Evaluation and Some Aspects of the Steers and Rhodes Model of Employee Attendance," *Journal of Applied Psychology* (June 1981), pp. 385–89; Keller, "Predicting Absenteeism"; J.M. Federico, P. Federico, and G.W. Lundquist, "Predicting Women's Turnover as a Function of Extent of Met Salary Expectations and Biodemographic Data," *Personnel Psychology* (Winter 1976), pp. 559–66; Marsh and Mannari, "Organizational Commitment"; and D.R. Austrom, T. Baldwin, and G.J. Macy, "The Single Worker: An Empirical Exploration of Attitudes, Behavior, and Well-Being," *Canadian Journal of Administrative Sciences* (December 1988), pp. 22–29.

[15] One of the few studies that has looked at family responsibilities found that increasing numbers of dependents had no adverse effect on productivity, as measured by work effort and size of merit increase. See S.A. Lobel and L. St. Clair, "Effects of Family Responsibilities, Gender, and Career Identity Salience on Performance Outcomes," *Academy of Management Journal* (December 1992), pp. 1057–69.

[16] Porter and Steers, "Organizational, Work, and Personal Factors"; N. Nicholson and P.M. Goodge, "The Influence of Social, Organizational and Biographical Factors on Female Absence," *Journal of Management Studies* (October 1976), pp. 234–54; P.M. Muchinsky, "Employee Absenteeism: A Review of the Literature," *Journal of Vocational Behavior* (June 1977), pp. 316–40; and R.M. Steers and S.R. Rhodes, "Major Influences on Employee Attendance: A Process Model," *Journal of Applied Psychology* (August 1978), pp. 391–407.

[17] Porter and Steers, "Organizational, Work, and Personal Factors"; Federico, Federico, and Lundquist, "Predicting Women's Turnover"; and Marsh and Mannari, "Organizational Commitment."

[18] A.S. Gechman and Y. Wiener, "Job Involvement and Satisfaction as Related to Mental Health and Personal Time Devoted to Work," *Journal of Applied Psychology* (August 1975), pp. 521–23.

[19] M.E. Gordon and W.J. Fitzgibbons, "Empirical Test of the Validity of Seniority as a Factor in Staffing Decisions," *Journal of Applied Psychology* (June 1982), pp. 311–19; M.E. Gordon and W.A. Johnson, "Seniority: A Review of Its Legal and Scientific Standing," *Personnel Psychology* (Summer 1982), pp. 255–80; and M.A. McDaniel, F.L. Schmidt, and J.E. Hunter, "Job Experience Correlates of Job Performance," *Journal of Applied Psychology* (May 1988), pp. 327–30.

[20] Garrison and Muchinsky, "Attitudinal and Biographical Predictors"; N. Nicholson, C.A. Brown, and J.K. Chadwick-Jones, "Absence from Work and Personal Characteristics," *Journal of Applied Psychology* (June 1977), pp. 319–27; and Keller, "Predicting Absenteeism."

[21] P.O. Popp and J.A. Belohlav, "Absenteeism in a Low Status Work Environment," *Academy of Management Journal* (September 1982), p. 681.

[22] H.J. Arnold and D.C. Feldman, "A Multivariate Analysis of the Determinants of Job Turnover," *Journal of Applied Psychology* (June 1982), p. 352.

[23] R.D. Gatewood and H.S. Feild, *Human Resource Selection* (Chicago: Dryden Press, 1987).

[24] J.A. Breaugh and D.L. Dossett, "The Effectiveness of Biodata for Predicting Turnover," paper presented at the National Academy of Management Conference, New Orleans, August 1987.

[25] A.G. Bedeian, G.R. Ferris, and K.M. Kacmar, "Age, Tenure, and Job Satisfaction: A Tale of Two Perspectives," *Journal of Vocational Behavior* (February 1992), pp. 33–48.

[26] L.E. Tyler, *Individual Differences: Abilities and Motivational Directions* (Englewood Cliffs, NJ: Prentice-Hall, 1974).

[27] M.D. Dunnette, "Aptitudes, Abilities, and Skills," in M.D. Dunnette (ed.), *Handbook of Industrial and Organizational Psychology* (Chicago: Rand McNally, 1976), pp. 478–83.

[28] D. Lubinski and R.V. Dawis, "Aptitudes, Skills, and Proficiencies," in M.D. Dunnette and L.M. Hough (eds.), *Handbook of Industrial and Organizational Psychology*, 2nd ed., Vol. 3 (Palo Alto, CA: Consulting Psychologists Press, 1992), pp. 30–33.

[29] J.E. Hunter and R.F. Hunter, "Validity and Utility of Alternative Predictors of Job Performance," *Psychological Bulletin* (January 1984), pp. 72–98; J. E. Hunter, "Cognitive Ability, Cognitive Aptitudes, Job Knowledge, and Job Performance," *Journal of Vocational Behavior* (December 1986), pp. 340–62; and W.M. Coward and P.R. Sackett, "Linearity of Ability–Performance Relationships: A Reconfirmation," *Journal of Applied Psychology* (June 1990), pp. 297–300.

[30] Hunter and Hunter, "Validity and Utility," pp. 73–74.

[31] E.A. Fleishman, "Evaluating Physical Abilities Required by Jobs," *Personnel Administrator* (June 1979), pp. 82–92.

[32] Cited in R. Bolton, *People Skills* (Englewood Cliffs, NJ: Prentice-Hall, 1979), p. 260.

[33] G.W. Allport, *Personality: A Psychological Interpretation* (New York: Holt, Rinehart and Winston, 1937), p. 48.

[34] Reported in R.L. Hotz, "Genetics, Not Parenting, Key to Temperament, Studies Say," *Los Angeles Times* (February 20, 1994), p. A1.

[35] See T.J. Bouchard, Jr., D.T. Lykken, M. McGue, N.L. Segal, and A. Tellegen, "Sources of Human Psychological Differ-

ences—The Minnesota Study of Twins Reared Apart," *Science* (October 12, 1990), pp. 223–38; T.J. Bouchard, Jr., and M. McGue, "Genetic and Rearing Environmental Influences on Adult Personality: An Analysis of Adopted Twins Raised Apart," *Journal of Personality*, Vol. 58, (1990), pp. 263–92; and D.T. Lykken, T.J. Bouchard, Jr., M. McGue, and A. Tellegen, "Heritability of Interests: A Twin Study," *Journal of Applied Psychology* (August 1993), pp. 649–61; and R.D. Arvey and T.J. Bouchard, Jr., "Genetics, Twins, and Organizational Behavior," in B.M. Staw and L.L. Cummings (eds.), *Research in Organizational Behavior*, Vol. 16 (Greenwich, CT: JAI Press, 1994), pp. 65–66.

[36] See B.M. Staw and J. Ross, "Stability in the Midst of Change: A Dispositional Approach to Job Attitudes," *Journal of Applied Psychology* (August 1985), pp. 469–80; and B.M. Staw, N.E. Bell, and J.A. Clausen, "The Dispositional Approach to Job Attitudes: A Lifetime Longitudinal Test," *Administrative Science Quarterly* (March 1986), pp. 56–77.

[37] R.C. Carson, "Personality," in M.R. Rosenzweig and L.W. Porter (eds.), *Annual Review of Psychology*, Vol. 40 (Palo Alto, CA: Annual Reviews, 1989), pp. 228–29.

[38] L. Sechrest, "Personality," in M.R. Rosenzweig and L.W. Porter (eds.), *Annual Review of Psychology*, Vol. 27 (Palo Alto, CA: Annual Reviews, 1976), p. 10.

[39] Ibid.

[40] See A.H. Buss, "Personality as Traits," *American Psychologist* (November 1989), pp. 1378–88.

[41] G.W. Allport and H.S. Odbert, "Trait Names, A Psycholexical Study," *Psychological Monographs*, No. 47 (1936).

[42] R.B. Cattell, "Personality Pinned Down," *Psychology Today* (July 1973), pp. 40–46.

[43] See A.J. Vaccaro, "Personality Clash," *Personnel Administrator* (September 1988), pp. 88–92; and R.R. McCrae and P.T. Costa, Jr., "Reinterpreting the Myers-Briggs Type Indicator from the Perspective of the Five-Factor Model of Personality," *Journal of Personality* (March 1989), pp. 17–40.

[44] G.N. Landrum, *Profiles of Genius* (New York: Prometheus, 1993).

[45] J.M. Digman, "Personality Structure: Emergence of the Five-Factor Model," in M.R. Rosenzweig and L.W. Porter (eds.), *Annual Review of Psychology*, Vol. 41 (Palo Alto, CA: Annual Reviews, 1990), pp. 417–40; and O.P. John, "The 'Big Five' Factor Taxonomy: Dimensions of Personality in the Natural Language and in Questionnaires," in L.A. Pervin (ed.), *Handbook of Personality Theory and Research* (New York: Guilford Press, 1990), pp. 66–100.

[46] M.R. Barrick and M.K. Mount, "The Big Five Personality Dimensions and Job Performance: A Meta-Analysis," *Personnel Psychology*, Vol. 44 (1991), pp. 1–26; and M.R. Barrick and M.K. Mount, "Autonomy as a Moderator of the Relationships Between the Big Five Personality Dimensions and Job Performance," *Journal of Applied Psychology* (February 1993), pp. 111–18.

[47] J.B. Rotter, "Generalized Expectancies for Internal versus External Control of Reinforcement," *Psychological Monographs*, Vol. 80, No. 609 (1966).

[48] See P.E. Spector, "Behavior in Organizations as a Function of Employee's Locus of Control," *Psychological Bulletin* (May 1982), pp. 482–97; and G.J. Blau, "Locus of Control as a Potential Moderator of the Turnover Process," *Journal of Occupational Psychology* (Fall 1987), pp. 21–29.

[49] Keller, "Predicting Absenteeism."

[50] Spector, "Behavior in Organizations," p. 493.

[51] R.G. Vleeming, "Machiavellianism: A Preliminary Review," *Psychological Reports* (February 1979), pp. 295–310.

[52] R. Christie and F.L. Geis, *Studies in Machiavellianism* (New York: Academic Press, 1970), p. 312.

[53] Ibid.

[54] Based on J. Brockner, *Self-Esteem at Work* (Lexington, MA: Lexington Books, 1988), Chapters 1–4.

[55] See M. Snyder, *Public Appearances/Private Realities: The Psychology of Self–Monitoring* (New York: Freeman, 1987).

[56] Ibid.

[57] R.N. Taylor and M.D. Dunnette, "Influence of Dogmatism, Risk-Taking Propensity, and Intelligence on Decision–Making Strategies for a Sample of Industrial Managers," *Journal of Applied Psychology* (August 1974), pp. 420–23.

[58] I.L. Janis and L. Mann, *Decision Making: A Psychological Analysis of Conflict, Choice, and Commitment* (New York: Free Press, 1977).

[59] N. Kogan and M.A. Wallach, "Group Risk Taking as a Function of Members' Anxiety and Defensiveness," *Journal of Personality* (March 1967), pp. 50–63.

[60] M. Friedman and R.H. Rosenman, *Type A Behavior and Your Heart* (New York: Knopf, 1974).

[61] Ibid., p. 84.

[62] Ibid., pp. 84–85.

[63] Ibid., p. 86.

[64] Ibid.

[65] J.L. Holland, *Making Vocational Choices: A Theory of Vocational Personalities and Work Environments*, 2nd ed. (Englewood Cliffs, NJ: Prentice-Hall, 1985).

[66] See, for example, A.R. Spokane, "A Review of Research on Person–Environment Congruence in Holland's Theory of Careers," *Journal of Vocational Behavior* (June 1985), pp. 306–43; D. Brown, "The Status of Holland's Theory of Career Choice," *Career Development Journal* (September 1987), pp. 13–23; J.L. Holland and G.D. Gottfredson, "Studies of the Hexagonal Model: An Evaluation (or, The Perils of Stalking the Perfect Hexagon)," *Journal of Vocational Behavior* (April 1992), pp. 158–70; and T.J. Tracey and J. Rounds, "Evaluating Holland's and Gati's Vocational-Interest Models: A Structural Meta-Analysis," *Psychological Bulletin* (March 1993), pp. 229–46.

[67] W. McGehee, "Are We Using What We Know About Training?—Learning Theory and Training," *Personnel Psychology* (Spring 1958), p. 2.

[68] I.P. Pavlov, *The Work of the Digestive Glands*, trans. W. H. Thompson (London: Charles Griffin, 1902).

[69] B.F. Skinner, *Contingencies of Reinforcement* (East Norwalk, CT: Appleton-Century-Crofts, 1971).

[70] A. Bandura, *Social Learning Theory* (Englewood Cliffs, NJ: Prentice-Hall, 1977).

[71] T.W. Costello and S. S. Zalkind, *Psychology in Administration* (Englewood Cliffs, NJ: Prentice-Hall, 1963), p. 193.

[72] F. Luthans and R. Kreitner, *Organizational Behavior Modification and Beyond*, 2nd ed. (Glenview, IL: Scott, Foresman, 1985).

[73] A. Halcrow, "Incentive! How Three Companies Cut Costs," *Personnel Journal* (February 1986), p. 12.

[74] D. Willings, "The Absentee Worker," *Personnel and Training Management* (December 1968), pp. 10–12.

[75] B.H. Harvey, J.F. Rogers, and J.A. Schultz, "Sick Pay vs. Well Pay: An Analysis of the Impact of Rewarding Employees for Being on the Job," *Public Personnel Management Journal* (Summer 1983), pp. 218–24.

[76] M.S. Forbes, Jr., "There's a Better Way," *Forbes* (April 26, 1993), p. 23.

[77] A. Belohlav, *The Art of Disciplining Your Employees* (Englewood Cliffs, NJ: Prentice-Hall, 1985).

[78] Cited in R.D. Bretz, Jr. and R.E. Thompsett, "Comparing Traditional and Integrative Learning Methods in Organizational Training Programs," *Journal of Applied Psychology* (December 1992), p. 941.

[79] See, for instance, C.C. Manz and H.P. Sims, "Self–Management as a Substitute for Leadership: A Social Learning Theory Perspective," *Academy of Management Review* (July 1980), pp. 361–67.

[80] G.P. Latham and C.A. Frayne, "Self–Management Training for Increasing Job Attendance: A Follow–Up and a Replication," *Journal of Applied Psychology* (June 1989), pp. 411–16.

CHAPTER 4

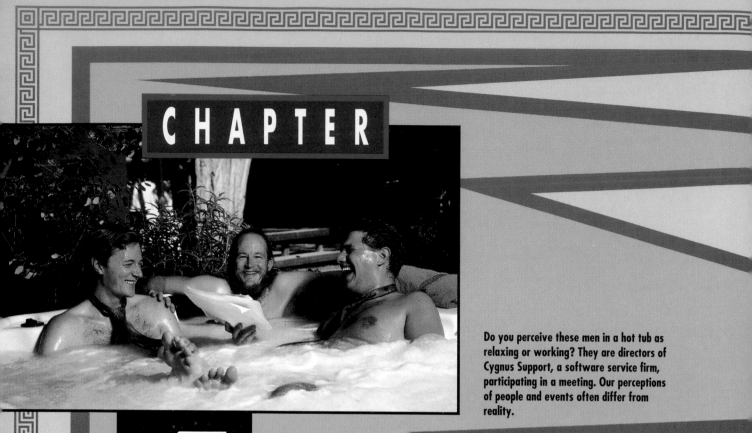

Do you perceive these men in a hot tub as relaxing or working? They are directors of Cygnus Support, a software service firm, participating in a meeting. Our perceptions of people and events often differ from reality.

PERCEPTION AND INDIVIDUAL DECISION MAKING

CHAPTER OUTLINE

LEARNING OBJECTIVES

After studying this chapter, you should be able to:

1. Explain how two people can see the same thing and interpret it differently.
2. List the three determinants of attribution.
3. Explain how perception affects the decision–making process.
4. Outline the six steps in the optimizing decision process.
5. Explain how individuals satisfice.
6. Describe the implicit favorite model of decision making.
7. Identify the conditions in which individuals are most likely to use intuition in decision making.
8. Describe three different criteria for making ethical choices.

First umpire: "Some's balls and some's strikes and I calls 'em as they is."
Second umpire: "Some's balls and some's strikes and I calls 'em as I sees 'em."
Third umpire: "Some's balls and some's strikes but they ain't nothin' till I calls 'em."
H. CANTRIL

Pictured here is an executive for a large company. From the picture, can you tell if he is working or goofing off? Probably not! Yet this executive's boss makes judgments about him all the time. Whether the boss perceives him, in this instance, as "sitting around staring at a wall" or as "engaged in deep thinking" will depend on a number of factors. For example, how long has the boss known him? What's his past performance record? Has he engaged in this practice previously? How do other people in similar jobs behave? Answers to questions like these will go a long way toward shaping the boss's interpretation of the executive's behavior.

This example reminds us that we don't *see* reality. We *interpret* what we see and call it reality. You will probably complete an evaluation form on the course you're currently taking and the instructor who is teaching it. If the class is large enough, it's almost a sure bet there will be some range of answers in evaluating your instructor. It's not that unusual for an instructor to be rated "excellent" by some students and "unsatisfactory" by other students in the same class. The instructor's teaching behavior, of course, is a constant. Even though the students see the same instructor, they perceive his or her effectiveness differently. Apparently, perception is like beauty, in that it lies "in the eye of the beholder."

What Is Perception and Why Is It Important?

perception
A process by which individuals organize and interpret their sensory impressions in order to give meaning to their environment.

Perception can be defined as a process by which individuals organize and interpret their sensory impressions in order to give meaning to their environment. However, as we have noted, what one perceives can be substantially different from objective reality. It need not be, but there is often disagreement. For example, it is possible that all employees in a firm may view it as a great place to work—favorable working conditions, interesting job assignments, good pay, an understanding and responsible management—but, as most of us know, it is very unusual to find such agreement.

Why is perception important in the study of OB? Simply because people's behavior is based on their perception of what reality is, not on reality itself. The world as it is perceived is the world that is behaviorally important.

Factors Influencing Perception

How do we explain that individuals may look at the same thing yet perceive it differently? A number of factors operate to shape and sometimes distort perception. These factors can reside in the *perceiver*, in the object or *target* being perceived, or in the context of the *situation* in which the perception is made.

The Perceiver

When an individual looks at a target and attempts to interpret what he or she sees, that interpretation is heavily influenced by personal characteristics of the individual perceiver. Have you ever bought a new car and then suddenly noticed a large number of cars like yours on the road? It's unlikely that the number of such cars suddenly expanded. Rather, your own purchase has influenced your perception so you are now more likely to notice them. This is an example of how factors related to the perceiver influence what he or she perceives. Among the more relevant personal characteristics affecting perception are attitudes, motives, interests, past experience, and expectations.

Sandy likes small classes because she enjoys asking her teachers a lot of questions. Scott prefers large lectures. He rarely asks questions and likes the anonymity that goes with being lost in a sea of bodies. On the first day of classes this term, Sandy and Scott find themselves walking into the university auditorium for their introductory course in psychology. They both recognize that they will be among some 800 students in this class. But given the different attitudes held by Sandy and Scott, it shouldn't surprise you to find they interpret what they see differently. Sandy sulks, while Scott's smile does little to hide his relief in being able to blend unnoticed into the large auditorium. They both see the same thing, but they interpret it differently. A major reason is that they hold divergent *attitudes* concerning large classes.

Unsatisfied needs or *motives* stimulate individuals and may exert a strong influence on their perceptions. This was dramatically demonstrated in research on hunger.[1] Individuals in the study had not eaten for varying numbers of hours. Some had eaten an hour earlier; others had gone as long as 16 hours without food. These subjects were shown blurred pictures, and the results indicated that the extent of hunger influenced the interpretation of the blurred pictures. Those who had not eaten for 16 hours perceived the blurred images as pictures of food far more frequently than did those subjects who had eaten only a short time earlier.

This same phenomenon has application in an organizational context as well. It would not be surprising, for example, to find that a boss who is insecure perceives a subordinate's efforts to do an outstanding job as a threat to his or her own position. Personal insecurity can be transferred into the perception that others are out to "get my job," regardless of the intention of the subordinates. Likewise, people who are devious are prone to see others as also devious.

It should not surprise you that a plastic surgeon is more likely to notice an imperfect nose than a plumber is. The supervisor who has just been reprimanded by her boss for the high level of lateness among her staff is more likely to notice lateness by an employee tomorrow than she was last week. If you are preoccupied with a personal problem, you may find it hard to be attentive in class. These examples illustrate that the focus of our attention appears to be influenced by our *interests*. Because our individual interests differ considerably, what one person notices in a situation can differ from what others perceive.

Just as interests narrow one's focus, so do one's *past experiences*. You perceive those things to which you can relate. However, in many instances, your past experiences will act to nullify an object's interest.

Objects or events that have never been experienced before are more noticeable than those that have been experienced in the past. You are more likely to notice a machine you have never seen before than a standard filing cabinet that is exactly like a hundred others you have previously seen. Similarly, you are more likely to notice the operations along an assembly line if this is the first time you have seen an assembly line. In the late 1960s and early 1970s, women and minorities in managerial positions were highly visible because, historically, these positions were the province of white males. Today, these groups are more widely represented in the managerial ranks, so we are less likely to notice that a manager is female, African-American, Asian-American, or Latino.

Finally, *expectations* can distort your perceptions in that you will see what you expect to see. If you expect police officers to be authoritative, young people to be unambitious, personnel directors to "like people," or individuals holding public office to be "power hungry," you may perceive them this way regardless of their actual traits.

The Target

Characteristics in the target that is being observed can affect what is perceived. Loud people are more likely to be noticed in a group than quiet ones. So, too, are extremely attractive or unattractive individuals. Motion, sounds, size, and other attributes of a target shape the way we see it.

Because targets are not looked at in isolation, the relationship of a target to its background influences perception, as does our tendency to group close things and similar things together.

What we see depends on how we separate a figure from its general background. For instance, what you see as you read this sentence is black letters on a white page. You do not see funny-shaped patches of black and white because you recognize these shapes and organize the black shapes against the white background. Figure 4-1 dramatizes this effect. The object on the left may at first look like a beige vase. However, if beige is taken as the background, we see two blue profiles. At first observation, the group of objects on the right appears to be some blue modular figures against a beige background. Closer inspection will reveal the word "FLY" once the background is defined as blue.

Figure 4-1
Figure-Ground Illustrations

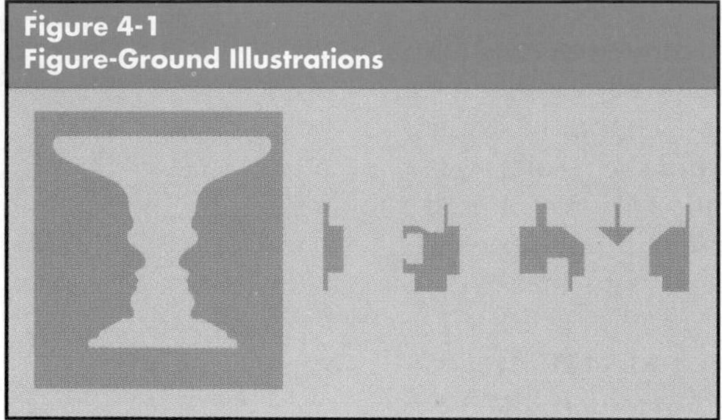

Objects that are close to each other will tend to be perceived together rather than separately. As a result of physical or time proximity, we often put together objects or events that are unrelated. Employees in a particular department are seen as a group. If two people in a four-member department suddenly resign, we tend to assume their departures were related when, in fact, they may be totally unrelated. Timing may also imply dependence when, for example, a new sales manager is assigned to a territory and, soon after, sales in that territory skyrocket. The assignment of the new sales manager and the increase in sales may not be related—the increase may be due to the introduction of a new product line or to one of many other reasons—but there is a tendency to perceive the two occurrences as related.

Persons, objects, or events that are similar to each other also tend to be grouped together. The greater the similarity, the greater the probability we will tend to perceive them as a common group. Women, blacks, or members of any other group that has clearly distinguishable characteristics in terms of features or color will tend to be perceived as alike in other, unrelated, characteristics as well.

The Situation

The context in which we see objects or events is important. Elements in the surrounding environment influence our perceptions.

I may not notice a 25-year-old female in an evening gown and heavy makeup at a nightclub on Saturday night. Yet that same woman so attired for my Monday morning management class would certainly catch my attention (and that of the rest of the class). Neither the perceiver nor the target changed between Saturday night and Monday morning, but the situation is different.

Similarly, you are more likely to notice your subordinates goofing off if your boss from the head office happens to be in town. Again, the situation affects your perception. The time at which an object or event is seen can influence attention, as can location, light, heat, or any number of situational factors. Figure 4-2 summarizes the factors influencing perception.

Figure 4-2
Factors that Influence Perception

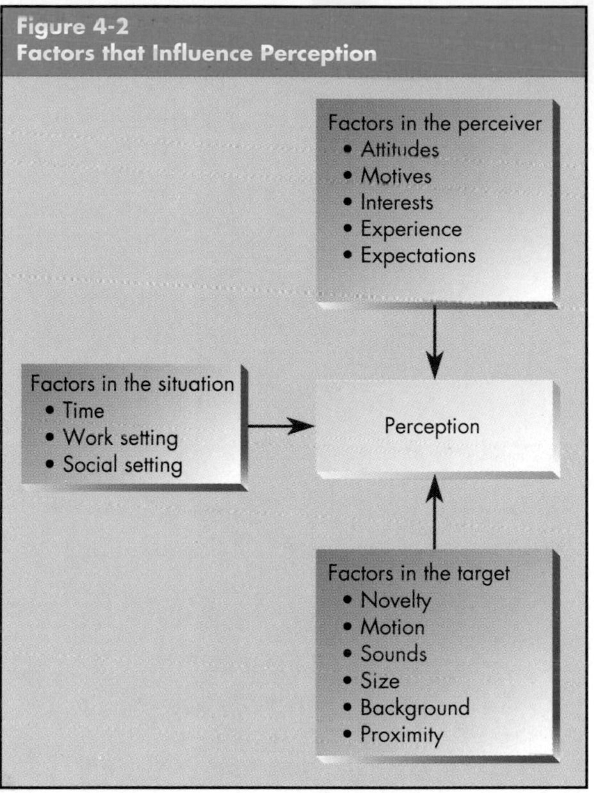

Person Perception: Making Judgments About Others

Now we turn to the most relevant application of perception concepts to OB: the issue of *person perception*.

Attribution Theory

Our perceptions of people differ from our perceptions of inanimate objects like desks, machines, or buildings because we make inferences about the actions of people that we don't make about inanimate objects. Nonliving objects are subject to the laws of nature, but they have no beliefs, motives, or intentions. People do. The result is that when we observe people, we attempt to develop explanations of why they behave in certain ways. Our perception and judgment of a person's actions, therefore, will be significantly influenced by the assumptions we make about the person's internal state.

attribution theory
When individuals observe behavior, they attempt to determine whether it is internally or externally caused.

Attribution theory has been proposed to develop explanations of the ways in which we judge people differently, depending on what meaning we attribute to a given behavior.[2] Basically, the theory suggests that when we observe an individual's behavior, we attempt to determine whether it was internally or externally caused. That determination, however, depends largely on three factors: (1) distinctiveness, (2) consensus, and (3) consistency. First, let's clarify the differences between internal and external causation and then we will elaborate on each of the three determining factors.

Internally caused behaviors are those believed to be under the personal control of the individual. *Externally* caused behavior is seen as resulting from outside causes; that is, the person is seen as forced into the behavior by the situation. If one of your employees is late for work, you might attribute his lateness to his partying into the wee hours of the morning and then oversleeping. This would be an internal attribution. But if you attribute his arriving late to a major automobile accident that tied up traffic on the road this employee regularly uses, then you would be making an external attribution.

Distinctiveness refers to whether an individual displays different behaviors in different situations. Is the employee who arrives late today also the source of complaints by coworkers for being a goof-off? What we want to know is if this behavior is unusual or not. If it is, the observer is likely to give the behavior an external attribution. If this action is not unusual, it will probably be judged as internal.

If everyone who is faced with a similar situation responds in the same way, we can say the behavior shows *consensus*. Our late employee's behavior would meet this criterion if all employees who took the same route to work were also late. From an attribution perspective, if consensus is high, you would be expected to give an external attribution to the employee's tardiness, whereas if other employees who took the same route made it into work on time, your conclusion as to causation would be internal.

Finally, an observer looks for *consistency* in a person's actions. Does the person respond the same way over time? Coming in ten minutes late for work is not perceived in the same way for the employee for whom it is an unusual case (she hasn't been late for several months) as for the employee for whom it is part of a routine pattern (she is regularly late two or three times a week). The more consistent the behavior, the more the observer is inclined to attribute it to internal causes.

Figure 4-3 summarizes the key elements in attribution theory. It would tell us, for instance, that if your employee—Kim Randolph—generally performs at about the same level on other related tasks as she does on her current task (low distinctiveness), if other employees frequently perform differently—better or worse—than Kim does on that current task (low consensus), and if Kim's performance on this current task is consistent over time (high consistency), you or anyone else who is judging Kim's work is likely to hold her primarily responsible for her task performance (internal attribution).

Figure 4-3
Attribution Theory

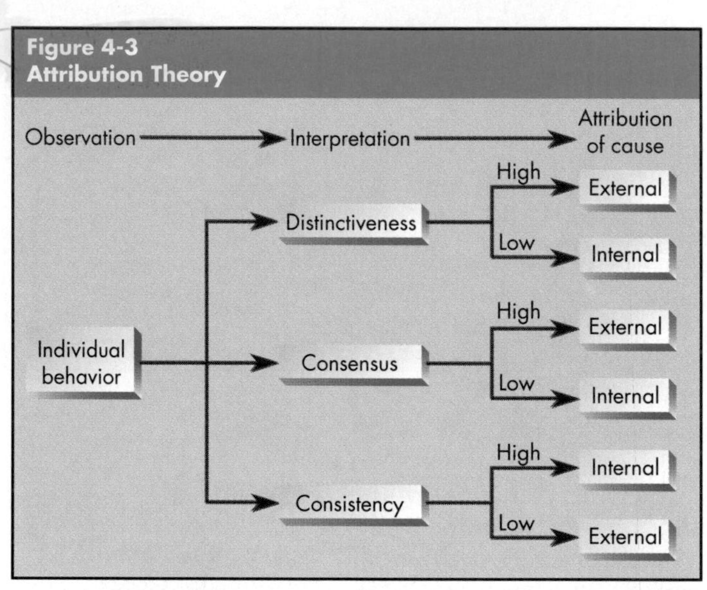

One of the more interesting findings from attribution theory is that there are errors or biases that distort attributions. For instance, substantial evidence suggests that when we make judgments about the behavior of other people, we have a tendency to underestimate the influence of external factors and overestimate the influence of internal or personal factors.[3] This is called the **fundamental attribution error** and can explain why a sales manager is prone to attribute the poor performance of her sales agents to laziness rather than the innovative product line introduced by a competitor. Individuals tend to attribute their own successes to internal factors like ability or effort while putting the blame for failure on external factors like luck. This is called the **self-serving bias** and suggests that feedback provided to employees in performance reviews will be predictably distorted by recipients depending on whether it is positive or negative.

fundamental attribution error
The tendency to underestimate the influence of external factors and overestimate the influence of internal factors when making judgments about the behavior of others.

self-serving bias
The tendency for individuals to attribute their own successes to internal factors while putting the blame for failures on external factors.

Are these errors or biases that distort attributions universal across different cultures? While we can't answer that question definitively, some preliminary evidence indicates cultural differences. For instance, a study of Korean managers found that, contrary to the self-serving bias, they tended to accept responsibility for group failure "because I was not a capable leader" instead of attributing it to group members.[4] Attribution theory was developed largely in the United States based on experiments with Americans. But the Korean study suggests caution in making attribution theory predictions outside the United States, especially in countries with strong collectivist traditions.

Frequently Used Shortcuts in Judging Others

We use a number of shortcuts when we judge others. Perceiving and interpreting what others do is burdensome. As a result, individuals develop techniques

The self-serving bias of attribution theory doesn't apply in all cultures. In countries that value collectivism more than individualism, managers take responsibility for group failure rather than blame other people or external factors. An example is Masatochi Ito, founder of Japan's Ito-Yokado supermarket chain, shown here bowing out as president of the company he founded. Ito exited the firm in the wake of embarrassing stock-related scandals, accepting responsibility for the unethical actions of his employees.

for making the task more manageable. These techniques are frequently valuable—they allow us to make accurate perceptions rapidly and provide valid data for making predictions. However, they are not foolproof. They can and do get us into trouble. An understanding of these shortcuts can be helpful toward recognizing when they can result in significant distortions.

SELECTIVE PERCEPTION Any characteristic that makes a person, object, or event stand out will increase the probability it will be perceived. Why? Because it is impossible for us to assimilate everything we see—only certain stimuli can be taken in. This explains why, as we noted earlier, you're more likely to notice

◆◆◆◆ OB in the News ◆◆◆◆

Managers Explain What Has Helped and Hindered Their Advancement

Industry Week magazine surveyed 1,300 middle managers in medium-sized and large companies with at least 500 employees on a number of issues.

Two questions were particularly relevant because they address attribution issues: To what do you attribute your success to date? And what do you think has most hampered your advancement to even higher levels in your company?

Most managers attributed their advancement to their knowledge and on-the-job accomplishments. More than 80 percent of these middle managers ranked these as being the biggest factors in their promotion into management.

When asked what most hindered their advancement to even higher levels of management, 56 percent of the managers said it was because they hadn't built relationships with the "right" people. This was followed by 23 percent saying that they were most hindered by insufficient education, intelligence, or knowledge of their business area.

These results are exactly what you'd expect based on attribution theory.

Specifically, consistent with the self-serving bias, these managers attributed their success to internal factors (their knowledge and on-the-job accomplishments) and placed the blame for their failures on external factors (the implied politics in knowing the right people).

Based on D.R. Altany, "Torn Between Halo and Horns," *Industry Week* (March 15, 1993), p. 19.

cars like your own or why some people may be reprimanded by their boss for doing something that when done by another employee goes unnoticed. Since we can't observe everything going on about us, we engage in **selective perception**. A classic example shows how vested interests can significantly influence what problems we see.

selective perception
People selectively interpret what they see based on their interests, background, experience, and attitudes.

Dearborn and Simon performed a perceptual study in which 23 business executives read a comprehensive case describing the organization and activities of a steel company.[5] Six of the 23 executives were in the sales function, 5 in production, 4 in accounting, and 8 in miscellaneous functions. Each manager was asked to write down the most important problem he found in the case. Eighty-three percent of the sales executives rated sales important; only 29 percent of the others did so. This, along with other results of the study, led the researchers to conclude that the participants perceived aspects of a situation that related specifically to the activities and goals of the unit to which they were attached. A group's perception of organizational activities is selectively altered to align with the vested interests they represent. In other words, where the stimuli are ambiguous, as in the steel company case, perception tends to be influenced more by an individual's base of interpretation (that is, attitudes, interests, and background) than by the stimulus itself.

But how does selectivity work as a shortcut in judging other people? Since we cannot assimilate all we observe, we take in bits and pieces. But these bits and pieces are not chosen randomly; rather, they are selectively chosen according to our interests, background, experience, and attitudes. Selective perception allows us to "speed–read" others, but not without the risk of drawing an inaccurate picture. Because we see what we want to see, we can draw unwarranted conclusions from an ambiguous situation. If a rumor is going around the office that your company's sales are down and large layoffs may be coming, a routine visit by a senior executive from headquarters might be interpreted as the first step in management's identification of people to be fired, when in reality such an action may be the furthest thing from the mind of the senior executive.

HALO EFFECT When we draw a general impression about an individual based on a single characteristic, such as intelligence, sociability, or appearance, a **halo effect** is operating. This phenomenon frequently occurs when students appraise their classroom instructor. Students may isolate a single trait such as enthusiasm and allow their entire evaluation to be tainted by how they judge the instructor on this one trait. Thus an instructor may be quiet, assured, knowledgeable, and highly qualified, but if his style lacks zeal, he will be rated lower on a number of other characteristics.

halo effect
Drawing a general impression about an individual based on a single characteristic.

The reality of the halo effect was confirmed in a classic study where subjects were given a list of traits like intelligent, skillful, practical, industrious, determined, and warm and asked to evaluate the person to whom these traits applied.[6] Based on these traits, the person was judged to be wise, humorous, popular, and imaginative. When the same list was modified to substitute cold for warm in the trait list, a completely different set of perceptions was obtained. Clearly, the subjects were allowing a single trait to influence their overall impression of the person being judged.

The propensity for the halo effect to operate is not random. Research suggests it is likely to be most extreme when the traits to be perceived are ambiguous in behavioral terms, when the traits have moral overtones, and when the perceiver is judging traits with which he or she has had limited experience.[7]

CONTRAST EFFECTS An old adage among entertainers who perform in variety shows advises, Never follow an act that has kids or animals in it. Why? The common belief is that audiences love children and animals so much, you will look bad in comparison. In a similar vein, your author remembers when he was a college freshman required to give a presentation in a speech class. I was scheduled to speak third that morning. After both of the first two speakers stammered, stumbled, and forgot their lines, I suddenly got a rush of confidence because I figured that even though my talk might not go too well, I'd probably get a pretty good grade. I was counting on the instructor raising my evaluation after contrasting my speech to those that immediately preceded it.

These two examples demonstrate how **contrast effects** can distort perceptions. We don't evaluate a person in isolation. Our reaction to one person is often influenced by other persons we've recently encountered.

contrast effects
Evaluations of a person's characteristics that are affected by comparisons with other people recently encountered who rank higher or lower on the same characteristics.

An illustration of how contrast effects operate is an interview situation in which one sees a pool of job applicants. Distortions in any given candidate's evaluation can occur as a result of his or her place in the interview schedule. The candidate is likely to receive a more favorable evaluation if preceded by mediocre applicants, and a less favorable evaluation if preceded by strong applicants.

PROJECTION It is easy to judge others if we assume they are similar to us. For instance, if you want challenge and responsibility in your job, you assume others want the same. Or you're honest and trustworthy, so you take it for granted that other people are equally honest and trustworthy. This tendency to attribute one's own characteristics to other people—which is called **projection**—can distort perceptions made about others.

projection
Attributing one's own characteristics to other people.

People who engage in projection tend to perceive others according to what they themselves are like rather than according to what the person being observed is really like. When observing others who actually are like them, these

"I do not hate you. You're projecting."

Figure 4-4
Drawing by William Steig; © 1987 The New Yorker Magazine. Reprinted by permission.

observers are quite accurate—not because they are perceptive, but rather because they always judge people as being similar to themselves, so when they finally find someone who is, they are naturally correct. When managers engage in projection, they compromise their ability to respond to individual differences. They tend to see people as more homogeneous than they really are.

stereotyping
Judging someone on the basis of one's perception of the group to which that person belongs.

STEREOTYPING When we judge someone on the basis of our perception of the group to which he or she belongs, we are using the shortcut called **stereotyping**. F. Scott Fitzgerald engaged in stereotyping in his reported conversation with Ernest Hemingway when he said, "The very rich are different from you and me." Hemingway's reply, "Yes, they have more money," indicated that he refused to generalize characteristics about people based on their wealth.

Generalization, of course, is not without advantages. It's a means of simplifying a complex world and it permits us to maintain consistency. It's less difficult to deal with an unmanageable number of stimuli if we use stereotypes. As an example, assume you're a sales manager looking to fill a sales position in your territory. You want to hire someone who is ambitious, hardworking, and who can deal well with adversity. You've had good success in the past by hiring individuals who participated in athletics during college. So you focus your search by looking for candidates who participated in collegiate athletics. In so doing, you've cut down considerably on your search time. Further, to the extent that athletes *are* ambitious, hardworking, and able to deal with adversity, the use of this stereotype can improve your decision making. The problem, of course, is when we inaccurately stereotype.[8] All college athletes are *not* necessarily ambitious, hardworking, or good at dealing with adversity, just as all accountants are *not* quiet and introspective.

In organizations, we frequently hear comments that represent stereotypes based on gender, age, nationality, and even weight: "Women won't relocate for a promotion"; "men aren't interested in child care"; "older workers can't learn new skills"; "Asian immigrants are hardworking and conscientious"; "overweight people lack discipline." From a perceptual standpoint, if people expect to see these stereotypes, that is what they will perceive, whether it's accurate or not.

Peggy Witte is chair and CEO of Canada's Royal Oak Mines. Women like Witte in top management positions often suffer from sex-role stereotypes. With determination and hard work, Witte built a successful gold-mining firm from scratch in a male-dominated industry where old-timers believe that allowing a woman to go underground in a mine brings bad luck. Research studies indicate that successful managers, male or female, share certain traits and skills that lead to their success. Witte is a skilled miner and first-rate metallurgist and helped devise a new gold-recovery technology in Canada that makes low-grade ore bodies more profitable. She uses her financial and negotiation skills to acquire old mines with poor ore reserves and transform them into profitable operations. In this photo, Witte discusses strategy with other Royal Oak managers.

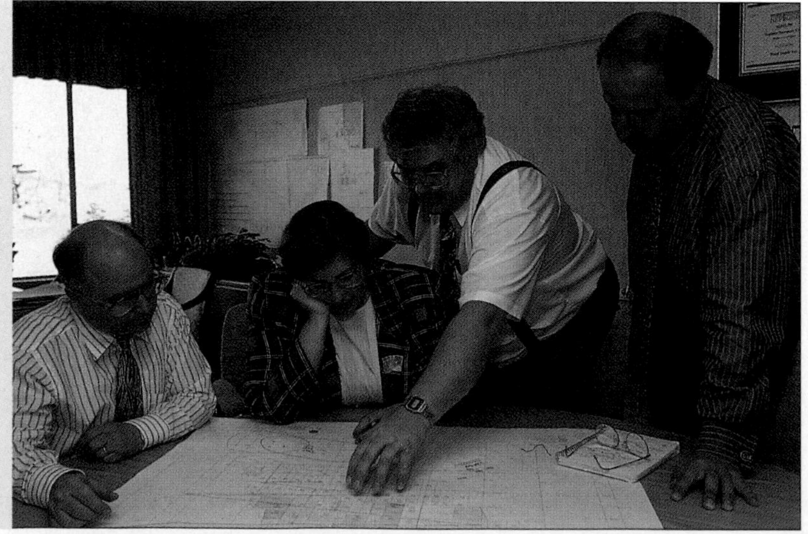

Obviously, one of the problems of stereotypes is they are so widespread, despite the fact that they may not contain a shred of truth or may be irrelevant. Their being widespread may only mean that many people are making the same inaccurate perception based on a false premise about a group.

Specific Applications in Organizations

People in organizations are always judging each other. Managers must appraise their subordinates' performances. We evaluate how much effort our coworkers are putting into their jobs. When a new person joins a department, he or she is immediately sized up by the other department members. In many cases, these judgments have important consequences for the organization. Let's briefly look at a few of the more obvious applications.

EMPLOYMENT INTERVIEW A major input into who is hired and who is rejected in any organization is the employment interview. It's fair to say that few people are hired without an interview. But the evidence indicates that interviewers often make inaccurate perceptual judgments. Additionally, interrater agreement among interviewers is often poor; that is, different interviewers see different things in the same candidate and thus arrive at different conclusions about the applicant.

Interviewers generally draw early impressions that become very quickly entrenched. If negative information is exposed early in the interview, it tends to be more heavily weighted than if that same information comes out later.[9] Studies indicate that most interviewers' decisions change very little after the first four or five minutes of the interview. As a result, information elicited early in the interview carries greater weight than does information elicited later, and a "good applicant" is probably characterized more by the absence of unfavorable characteristics than by the presence of favorable characteristics.

Importantly, who you think is a good candidate and who I think is one may differ markedly. Because interviews usually have so little consistent structure and interviewers vary in terms of what they are looking for in a candidate, judgments of the same candidate can vary widely. If the employment interview is an important input into the hiring decision—and it usually is—you should recognize that perceptual factors influence who is hired and eventually the quality of an organization's labor force.

PERFORMANCE EXPECTATIONS An impressive amount of evidence demonstrates that people will attempt to validate their perceptions of reality, even when these perceptions are faulty.[10] This is particularly relevant when we consider performance expectations on the job.

The terms **self-fulfilling prophecy** or pygmalion effect have evolved to characterize the fact that people's expectations determine their behavior. Or, in other words, if a manager expects big things from his people, they're not likely to let him down. Similarly, if a manager expects people to perform minimally, they'll tend to behave so as to meet these low expectations. Thus the expectations become reality.

self-fulfilling prophecy
When one person inaccurately perceives a second person and the resulting expectations cause the second person to behave in ways consistent with the original perception.

An interesting illustration of the self-fulfilling prophecy is a study undertaken with 105 soldiers in the Israeli Defense Forces who were taking a 15-week combat command course.[11] The four course instructors were told that one-third of the specific incoming trainees had high potential, one-third had normal potential, and the rest's potential was unknown. In reality, the trainees were randomly placed into these categories by the researchers. The results confirmed the existence of a self-fulfilling prophecy. Those trainees whom instructors were told had high potential scored significantly higher on objective achievement tests, exhibited more positive attitudes, and held their leaders in higher regard. The instructors of the supposedly high potential trainees got better results from them because the instructors expected it!

PERFORMANCE EVALUATION Although the impact of performance evaluations on behavior is discussed fully in Chapter 16, we point out here that an employee's performance appraisal very much depends on the perceptual process.[12] An employee's future is closely tied to his or her appraisal—promotions, pay raises, and continuation of employment are among the most obvious outcomes. The performance appraisal represents an assessment of an employee's work. While this can be objective (for example, a salesperson is appraised on how many dollars of sales she generates in her territory), many jobs are evaluated in subjective terms. Subjective measures are easier to implement, they provide managers with greater discretion, and many jobs do not readily lend themselves to objective measures. Subjective measures are, by definition, judgmental. The evaluator forms a general impression of an employee's work. To the degree that managers use subjective measures in appraising employees, what the evaluator perceives to be "good" or "bad" employee characteristics/behaviors will significantly influence the appraisal outcome.

EMPLOYEE EFFORT An individual's future in an organization is usually not dependent on performance alone. In many organizations, the level of an employee's effort is given high importance. Just as teachers frequently consider how hard you try in a course as well as how you perform on examinations, so often do managers. And, as illustrated in the opening photograph at the beginning of this chapter, assessment of an individual's effort is a subjective judgment susceptible to perceptual distortions and bias. If it is true, as some claim, that "more workers are fired for poor attitudes and lack of discipline than for lack of ability,"[13] then appraisal of an employee's effort may be a primary influence on his or her future in the organization.

EMPLOYEE LOYALTY Another important judgment that managers make about employees is whether they are loyal to the organization. In spite of the

AMP, Inc., a producer of electrical and electronic connection devices, is implementing its Journey for Excellence continuous improvement program worldwide to improve quality and productivity, eliminate waste, and reduce costs. Gaining the commitment of AMP's 28,000 employees at 175 facilities in 36 countries is essential to the program's success. In this photo, plant employees at AMP Mexico sign their names to the Journey for Excellence, symbolizing their loyalty to the company.

general decline in employee loyalty noted in Chapter 1, few organizations appreciate employees, especially those in the managerial ranks, openly disparaging the firm. Further, in some organizations, if the word gets around that an employee is looking at other employment opportunities outside the firm, that employee may be labeled as disloyal and cut off from all future advancement opportunities. The issue is not whether organizations are right in demanding loyalty, but that many do, and that assessment of an employee's loyalty or commitment is highly judgmental. What is perceived as loyalty by one decision maker may be seen as excessive conformity by another. An employee who questions a top management decision may be seen as disloyal by some, yet caring and concerned by others. As a case in point, **whistle-blowers**—individuals who report unethical practices by their employer to authorities inside and/or outside the organization—typically act out of loyalty to their organization but are perceived by management as troublemakers.[14]

whistle-blowers
Individuals who report unethical practices by their employers to authorities inside and/or outside the organization.

The Link Between Perception and Individual Decision Making

Individuals in organizations make **decisions**. That is, they make choices from among two or more alternatives. Top managers, for instance, determine their organization's goals, what products or services to offer, how best to organize corporate headquarters, or where to locate a new manufacturing plant. Middle- and lower-level managers determine production schedules, select new employees, and decide how pay raises are to be allocated. Of course, making decisions is not the sole province of managers. Nonmanagerial employees also make decisions that affect their jobs and the organizations they work for. The more obvious of these decisions might include whether to come to work or not on any given day, how much effort to put forward once at work, and whether to comply with a request made by the boss. Additionally, an increasing number of organizations in recent years have been empowering their nonmanagerial employees with job-related decision-making authority that historically was reserved for managers alone. Individual decision making, therefore, is an important part of organizational behavior. But how individuals in organizations make decisions, and the quality of their final choices, are largely influenced by their perceptions.

decisions
The making of choices from among two or more alternatives.

◆How individuals in organizations make decisions, and the quality of their final choices, are largely influenced by their perceptions.

Decision making occurs as a reaction to a **problem**. A discrepancy exists between some *current* state of affairs and some *desired* state, requiring consideration of alternative courses of action. So if your car breaks down and you rely on it to get to school, you have a problem that requires a decision on your part. Unfortunately, most problems don't come neatly packaged with a label "problem" clearly displayed on them. One person's *problem* is another person's *satisfactory state of affairs*. One manager may view her division's 2 percent decline in quarterly sales to be a serious problem requiring immediate action on her part. In contrast, her counterpart in another division of the same company, who also had a 2 percent sales decrease, may consider that quite satisfactory. So the awareness that a problem exists and a decision needs to be made is a perceptual issue.

problem
A discrepancy between some current state of affairs and some desired state.

Moreover, every decision requires interpretation and evaluation of information. Data is typically received from multiple sources and it needs to be screened, processed, and interpreted. What data, for instance, is relevant to the decision and what isn't? The perceptions of the decision maker will answer this question. Alternatives will be developed and the strengths and weaknesses of each will need to be evaluated. Again, because alternatives don't come with red flags identifying themselves as such or with their strengths and weaknesses clearly marked, the individual decision maker's perceptual process will have a large bearing on the final outcome.

The Optimizing Decision-Making Model

optimizing model
A decision-making model that describes how individuals should behave in order to maximize some outcome.

Let's begin by describing how individuals *should* behave in order to maximize some outcome. We call this the **optimizing model** of decision making.[15]

Steps in the Optimizing Model

Table 4-1 outlines the six steps an individual should follow, either explicitly or implicitly, when making a decision.

STEP 1: ASCERTAIN THE NEED FOR A DECISION The first step requires recognition that a decision needs to be made. The existence of a problem—or, as we stated previously, a disparity between some desired state and the actual condition—brings about this recognition. If you calculate your monthly expenses and find you're spending $50 more than you allocated in your budget, you have ascertained the need for a decision. There is a disparity between your desired expenditure level and what you're actually spending.

STEP 2: IDENTIFY THE DECISION CRITERIA Once an individual has determined the need for a decision, the criteria that will be important in making the decision must be identified. For illustration purposes, let's consider the case of a high school senior confronting the problem of choosing a college. The concepts derived from this example may be generalized to any decision a person might confront.

For the sake of simplicity, let's assume our high school senior has already chosen to attend college (versus other, noncollege options). We know the need for a decision is precipitated by graduation. Once she has recognized this need for a decision, the student should begin to list the criteria or factors that will be relevant to her decision. For our example, let's assume she has identified the following criteria about the colleges she is considering attending: annual cost, availability of financial aid, admission requirements, status or reputation, size, geographic location, curricula offering, male–female ratio, quality of social life, and the physical attractiveness of the campus. These criteria represent what the decision maker thinks is relevant to her decision. Note that, in this step, what

Table 4-1 Steps in the Optimizing Decision-Making Model

1. Ascertain the need for a decision.
2. Identify the decision criteria.
3. Allocate weights to the criteria.
4. Develop the alternatives.
5. Evaluate the alternatives.
6. Select the best alternative.

is *not* listed is as important as what *is*. For example, our high school senior did not consider factors such as where her friends were going to school, availability of part-time employment, and whether freshmen are required to reside on campus. To someone else making a college selection decision, the criteria used might be considerably different.

This second step is important because it identifies only those criteria the decision maker considers relevant. If a criterion is omitted from this list, we treat it as irrelevant to the decision maker.

STEP 3: ALLOCATE WEIGHTS TO THE CRITERIA The criteria listed in the previous step are not all equally important. It's necessary, therefore, to weight the factors listed in step 2 in order to prioritize their importance in the decision. All the criteria are relevant, but some are more relevant than others.

How does the decision maker weight criteria? A simple approach would merely be to give the most important criteria a number—say ten—and then assign weights to the rest of the criteria against this standard. So the result of steps 2 and 3 is to allow decision makers to use their personal preferences both to prioritize the relevant criteria and to indicate their relative degree of importance by assigning a weight to each. Table 4-2 lists the criteria and weights our high school senior is using in her college decision.

STEP 4: DEVELOP THE ALTERNATIVES The fourth step requires the decision maker to list all the viable alternatives that could possibly succeed in resolving the problem. No attempt is made in this step to appraise the alternatives, only to list them. To return to our example, let's assume our high schooler has identified eight potential colleges—Alpha, Beta, Delta, Gamma, Iota, Omega, Phi, and Sigma.

STEP 5: EVALUATE THE ALTERNATIVES Once the alternatives have been identified, the decision maker must critically evaluate each one. The strengths and weaknesses of each alternative will become evident when they are compared against the criteria and weights established in steps 2 and 3.

The evaluation of each alternative is done by appraising it against the weighted criteria. In our example, the high school senior would evaluate each college using every one of the criteria. To keep our example simple, we assume

Table 4-2 Criteria and Weights in Selection of a College

Criteria	Weights
Availability of financial aid	10
School's reputation	10
Annual cost	8
Curricula offering	7
Geographic location	6
Admission requirements	5
Quality of social life	4
School size	3
Male-female ratio	2
Physical attractiveness of the campus	2

a ten means the college is rated as "most favorable" on that criterion. The results from evaluating the various alternative colleges are shown in Table 4-3.

Keep in mind that the ratings given the eight colleges shown in Table 4-3 are based on the assessment made by the decision maker. Some assessments can be made in a relatively objective fashion. If our decision maker prefers a small school, one with an enrollment of 1,000 is obviously superior to one with 10,000 students. Similarly, if a high male–female ratio is sought, 3:1 is clearly higher than 2:1. But the assessment of criteria such as reputation, quality of social life, and the physical attractiveness of the campus reflects the decision maker's values. The point is that most decisions contain judgments. They are reflected in the criteria chosen in step 2, the weights given to these criteria, and the evaluation of alternatives. This explains why two people faced with a similar problem—such as selecting a college—may look at two totally different sets of alternatives or even look at the same alternatives but rate them very differently.

Table 4-3 represents an evaluation of eight alternatives only against the decision criteria. It does not reflect the weighting done in step 3. If one choice had scored ten on every criterion, there would be no need to consider the weights. Similarly, if the weights were all equal, you could evaluate each alternative merely by summing up the appropriate column in Table 4-3. For instance, Omega College would be highest, with a total score of 84. But our high school senior needs to multiply each alternative against its weight. The result of this process is shown in Table 4-4. The summation of these scores represents an evaluation of each college against the previously established criteria and weights.

STEP 6: SELECT THE BEST ALTERNATIVE The final step in the optimizing decision model is the selection of the best alternative from among those enumerated and evaluated. Since *best* is defined in terms of highest total score, the

Table 4-3 Evaluation of Eight Alternatives Against the Decision Criteria[a]

	ALTERNATIVES							
Criteria	**ALPHA College**	**BETA College**	**DELTA College**	**GAMMA College**	**IOTA College**	**OMEGA College**	**PHI College**	**SIGMA College**
Availability of financial aid	5	4	10	7	7	8	3	7
School's reputation	10	6	6	6	9	5	9	6
Annual cost (low cost preferred)	5	7	8	8	5	10	5	8
Curricula offering	6	10	8	9	8	8	9	8
Geographic location	6	7	10	10	6	9	10	7
Admission requirements (in terms of likelihood of acceptance)	7	10	10	10	8	10	8	10
Quality of social life	10	5	7	7	3	7	10	8
School size	10	7	7	7	9	7	9	4
Male–female ratio	2	2	8	8	8	10	2	8
Physical attractiveness of the campus	8	10	6	3	4	10	5	9

[a] The colleges that achieved the highest rating for a criterion are given ten points.

Table 4-4 Evaluation of College Alternatives

	ALTERNATIVES							
Criteria (and weight)	**ALPHA College**	**BETA College**	**DELTA College**	**GAMMA College**	**IOTA College**	**OMEGA College**	**PHI College**	**SIGMA College**
Availability of financial aid (10)	50	40	100	70	70	80	30	70
School's reputation (10)	100	60	60	60	90	50	90	60
Annual cost (8)	40	56	64	64	40	80	40	64
Curricula offering (7)	42	70	56	63	56	56	63	56
Geographic location (6)	36	42	60	60	36	54	60	42
Admission requirements (5)	35	50	50	50	40	50	40	50
Quality of social life (4)	40	20	28	28	12	28	40	32
School size (3)	30	21	21	21	27	21	27	12
Male–female ratio (2)	4	4	16	16	16	20	4	16
Physical attractiveness of the campus (2)	16	20	12	6	8	20	10	18
Totals	393	373	467	438	395	459	404	420

selection is quite simple. The decision maker merely chooses the alternative that generated the largest total score in step 5. For our high school senior, that means Delta College. Based on the criteria identified, the weights given to the criteria, and the decision maker's evaluation of each college on each of the criteria, Delta College scored highest and thus becomes the best.

Assumptions of the Optimizing Model

The steps in the optimizing model contain a number of assumptions. It's important to understand these assumptions if we're to determine how accurately the optimizing model describes actual individual decision making.

The assumptions of the optimizing model are the same as those that underlie the concept of **rationality**. Rationality refers to choices that are consistent and value maximizing. Rational decision making, therefore, implies that the decision maker can be fully objective and logical. The individual is assumed to have a clear goal, and all of the six steps in the optimizing model are assumed to lead toward the selection of the alternative that will maximize that goal. Let's take a closer look at the assumptions inherent in rationality and, hence, the optimizing model.

rationality
Choices that are consistent and value-maximizing.

GOAL ORIENTED The optimizing model assumes there is no conflict over the goal. Whether the decision involves selecting a college to attend, determining whether or not to go to work today, or choosing the right applicant to fill a job vacancy, it is assumed the decision maker has a single well-defined goal he or she is trying to maximize.

ALL OPTIONS ARE KNOWN It is assumed the decision maker can identify *all* the relevant criteria and can list *all* viable alternatives. The optimizing model portrays the decision maker as fully comprehensive in his or her ability to assess criteria and alternatives.

PREFERENCES ARE CLEAR Rationality assumes the criteria and alternatives can be assigned numerical values and ranked in a preferential order.

PREFERENCES ARE CONSTANT The same criteria and alternatives should be obtained every time because, in addition to the goal and preferences being clear, it is assumed the specific decision criteria are constant and the weights assigned to them are stable over time.

FINAL CHOICE WILL MAXIMIZE THE OUTCOME The rational decision maker, following the optimizing model, will choose the alternative that rates highest. This most preferred solution will, based on step 6 of the process, give the maximum benefits.

Predictions from the Optimizing Model

Using the preceding assumptions, we would predict that the individual decision maker would have a clear and specific goal; a fully comprehensive set of criteria that determine the relevant factors in the decision; and a precise ranking of the criteria, which will be stable over time. We further assume the decision maker will select the alternative that scores highest after all options have been evaluated (see Figure 4-5).

In terms of the college selection decision introduced earlier, the optimizing model would predict the high school student could identify every factor that might be important in her decision. Each of these factors would be weighted in terms of importance. All of the colleges that could possibly be viable options would be identified and evaluated against the criteria. Remember, because all alternatives are assumed to be considered, our decision maker might be looking at hundreds of colleges. Also, even if this activity took six

Figure 4-5
The Optimizing Model

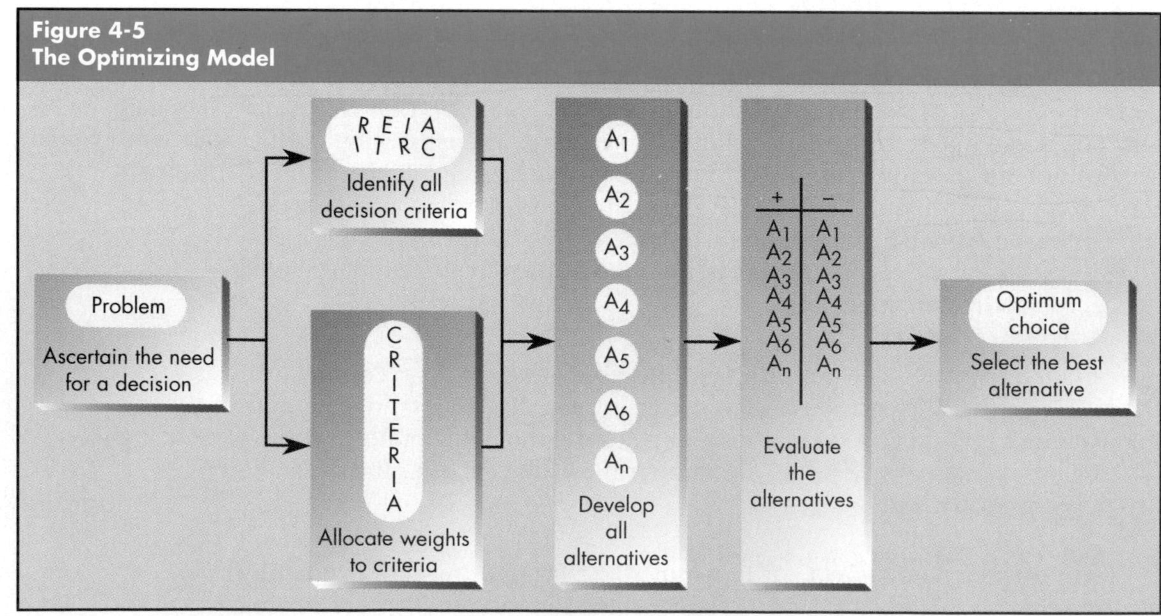

From Concepts to Skills

Creative Problem Solving

Most of us have unleashed creative potential that we can use when confronted with a decision-making problem. The challenge is to get out of the psychological ruts we all get into and to learn how to use the creative problem-solving talent we have.

For software maker Microsoft, creative problem solving is vital to success in developing innovations. The manager of Microsoft's Windows NT development team unleashes team members' creative potential by letting them throw around ideas on a basketball court at company headquarters. Trained in attribute listing, team members are encouraged to voice crazy ideas, which are never rejected outright and sometimes result in meaningful projects.

Let's begin with the obvious. People differ in their inherent creativity. Einstein, Picasso, and Mozart were individuals of exceptional creativity. What personality characteristics do the exceptionally creative share? Generally they are independent, risk taking, persistent, and highly motivated. They're also nonconformists who can be hard to get along with. Additionally, highly creative individuals prefer complex and unstructured tasks.[16] Disorder doesn't make them anxious.

How widespread is *exceptional* creativity? Not very! A study of lifetime creativity of 461 men and women found that fewer than 1 percent were exceptionally creative.[17] But 10 percent were highly creative and about 60 percent were somewhat creative. This suggests that most of us have creative potential, if we can learn to unleash it.

You can use several proven techniques to improve your ability as a creative problem solver. These include attribute listing, lateral thinking, and synectics.

In *attribute listing*, what you do is turn off all judgmental processes. You state the general characteristics of the problem and then generate as many alternatives as possible. No ideas are rejected, no matter how ridiculous they may appear at first glance. In fact, you should specifically try to reach for wild and extreme alternatives. Once you've completed your extensive list, the constraints of the problem are imposed so as to leave only viable alternatives.

Creativity can be stimulated by replacing traditional vertical thinking with zig zag or *lateral thinking*. Vertical thinking is highly rational. It's a stepwise process, with each step following the previous step in an unbroken sequence. It must be correct at every step. In addition, vertical thinking selects and deals only with what is relevant. In contrast, lateral thinking isn't sequential. Rather than developing a pattern, you try to restructure a pattern. For example, you might tackle a problem from the solution end rather than the starting end, and back into various beginning states. As a manager, for instance, you could conceptualize what your department might look like in terms of tasks, people, and work layout in the year 2010—then back into various scenarios about how it got to look like that.

Synectics uses analogies and inverted rationale to make the strange familiar and the familiar strange. It operates on the assumption that most problems aren't new. The challenge is to view the problem in a new way. So you have to try to abandon the familiar or routine ways you look at things. For instance, most of us think of hens laying eggs. But how many of us have considered that a hen is only an egg's way of making another egg? One of the most famous examples where analogy resulted in a creative breakthrough was Alexander Graham Bell's observation that it might be possible to take concepts that operate in the ear and apply them to his "talking box." He noticed that the massive bones in the ear are operated by a delicate thin membrane. He wondered why, then, a thicker and stronger piece of membrane shouldn't be able to move a piece of steel. Out of that analogy, the telephone was conceived.

months to complete, the criteria and weights would not vary over time. If the college's reputation was most important in September, it would still be so in March. Further, if Beta College was given a score of six on this criterion in September, six months later the assessment would be the same. Finally, since every factor that is important in the decision has been considered and given its proper weight, and since every alternative has been identified and evaluated against the criteria, the decision maker can be assured the college that scores highest in the evaluation is the best choice. There are no regrets because all information has been obtained and evaluated in a logical and consistent manner.

Alternative Decision-Making Models

Do individuals actually make their decisions the way the optimizing model predicts? Sometimes. When decision makers are faced with a simple problem having few alternative courses of action, and when the cost of searching out and evaluating alternatives is low, the optimizing model provides a fairly accurate description of the decision process.[18] Buying a pair of shoes or a new personal computer might be examples of decisions where the optimizing model would apply. But many decisions, particularly important and difficult ones—the kind a person hasn't encountered before and for which no standardized or programmed rules exist to provide guidance—don't involve simple and well-structured problems. Rather, they're characterized by complexity, relatively high uncertainty (all the alternatives, for example, are unlikely to be known), and goals and preferences that are neither clear nor consistent. This category of decision would include choosing a spouse, considering whether to accept a new job offer in a different city, selecting among job applicants for a vacancy in your department, developing a marketing strategy for a new product, deciding where to build an additional manufacturing plant, and determining the proper time to take your small company public by selling stock in it. In this section, we review three alternatives to the optimizing model: the satisficing or bounded rationality model, the implicit favorite model, and the intuitive model.

The Satisficing Model

satisficing model
A decision-making model where a decision maker chooses the first solution that is "good enough"; that is, satisfactory and sufficient.

bounded rationality
Individuals make decisions by constructing simplified models that extract the essential features from problems without capturing all their complexity.

The essence of the **satisficing model** is that, when faced with complex problems, decision makers respond by reducing the problems to a level at which they can be readily understood. This is because the information processing capability of human beings makes it impossible to assimilate and understand all the information necessary to optimize. Since the capacity of the human mind for formulating and solving complex problems is far too small to meet all the requirements for full rationality, individuals operate within the confines of **bounded rationality**. They construct simplified models that extract the essential features from problems without capturing all their complexity.[19] Individuals can then behave rationally within the limits of the simple model.

How does bounded rationality work for the typical individual? Once a problem is identified, the search for criteria and alternatives begins. But the list of criteria is likely to be far from exhaustive. The decision maker will identify a limited list made up of the more conspicuous choices. These are the choices that are easy to find and tend to be highly visible. In most cases, they will represent familiar criteria and the tried-and-true solutions. Once this limited set of alternatives is identified, the decision maker will begin reviewing them. But the review will not be comprehensive. That is, not all the alternatives will be carefully evaluated. Instead, the decision maker will begin with alternatives that differ only in a relatively small degree from the choice currently in effect. Following along familiar and well-worn paths, the decision maker proceeds to review alternatives only until he or she identifies an alternative that satisfices—one that is satisfactory and sufficient. So the satisficer settles for the first solution that is "good enough," rather than continuing to search for the optimum. The first alternative to meet the "good enough" criterion ends the search, and the decision maker can then proceed toward implementing this acceptable course of action. This is illustrated in Figure 4-6.

One of the more interesting aspects of the satisficing model is that the order in which alternatives are considered is critical in determining which alternative is selected. If the decision maker were optimizing, all alternatives would eventually be listed in a hierarchy of preferred order. Since all the alternatives would be considered, the initial order in which they were evaluated would be irrelevant. Every potential solution would get a full and complete

Figure 4-6
The Satisficing Model

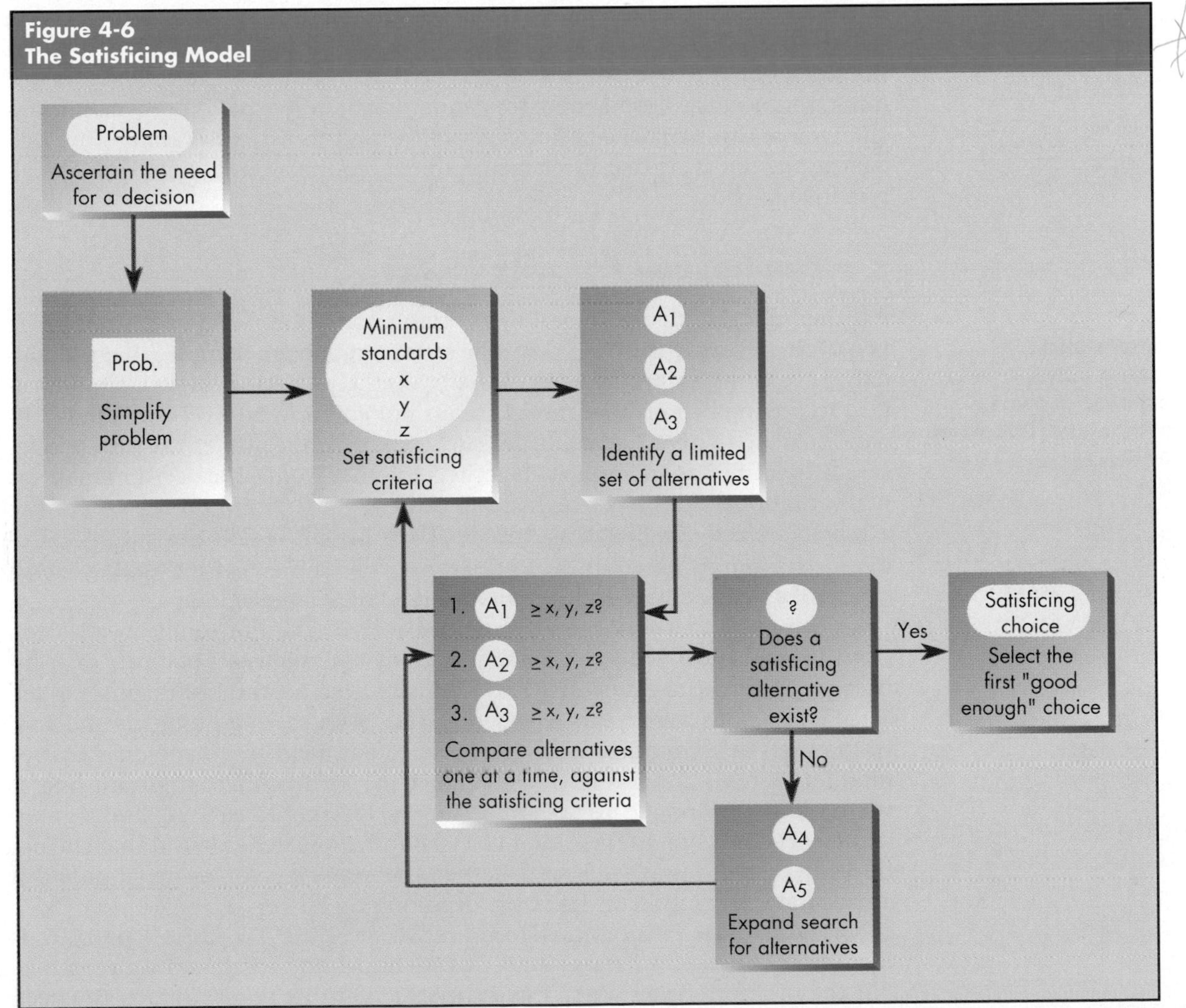

evaluation. But this is not the case with satisficing. Assuming a problem has more than one potential solution, the satisficing choice will be the first acceptable one the decision maker encounters. Since decision makers use simple and limited models, they typically begin by identifying alternatives that are obvious, ones with which they are familiar, and those not too far from the status quo. Those solutions that depart least from the status quo and meet the decision criteria are most likely to be selected. This may help to explain why many decisions that people make don't result in the selection of solutions radically different from those they have made before. A unique alternative may present an optimizing solution to the problem; however, it will rarely be chosen. An acceptable solution will be identified well before the decision maker is required to search very far beyond the status quo.

Using the satisficing model, how might we predict that the high school senior introduced earlier would make her college choice? Obviously, she will not consider all of the more than 2,000 colleges in the United States or the multitude of others in foreign countries. Based on schools she's heard about from friends and relatives, plus possibly a quick look through a guide to colleges, she will typically select a half-a-dozen or a dozen colleges to which she will send for catalogs, brochures, and applications. Based on a cursory appraisal of the materials she receives from the colleges, and using her rough decision criteria, she will look for a school that meets her minimal requirements. When she finds one, the decision search will be over. If none of the colleges in this initial set meet the "good enough" standards, she will expand her search to include more diverse colleges. But even following this extended search, the first college she uncovers that meets her minimal requirements will become the alternative of choice.

The Implicit Favorite Model

implicit favorite model
A decision-making model where the decision maker implicitly selects a preferred alternative early in the decision process and biases the evaluation of all other choices.

Another model designed to deal with complex and nonroutine decisions is the **implicit favorite model**.[20] Like the satisficing model, it argues that individuals solve complex problems by simplifying the process. However, simplification in the implicit favorite model means not entering into the difficult "evaluation of alternatives" stage of decision making until one of the alternatives can be identified as an implicit "favorite." In other words, the decision maker is neither rational nor objective. Instead, early in the decision process, he or she implicitly selects a preferred alternative. Then the rest of the decision process is essentially a decision confirmation exercise, where the decision maker makes sure his or her implicit favorite is indeed the "right" choice.

The implicit favorite model initially evolved from research on job decisions by graduate management students at the Massachusetts Institute of Technology. Clearly, these students knew and understood the optimizing model. They had spent several years repeatedly using it for solving problems and analyzing cases in accounting, finance, management, marketing, and quantitative methods courses. Moreover, the job choice decision was an important one. If there was a decision where the optimizing model should be used, and a group experienced in using it, this should be it. But the researcher found that the optimizing model was not followed. Rather, the implicit favorite model provided an accurate description of the actual decision process.

The implicit favorite model is outlined in Figure 4-7. Once a problem is identified, the decision maker implicitly identifies an early favorite alternative. But the decision maker doesn't end the search at this point. In fact, the deci-

Figure 4-7
The Implicit Favorite Model

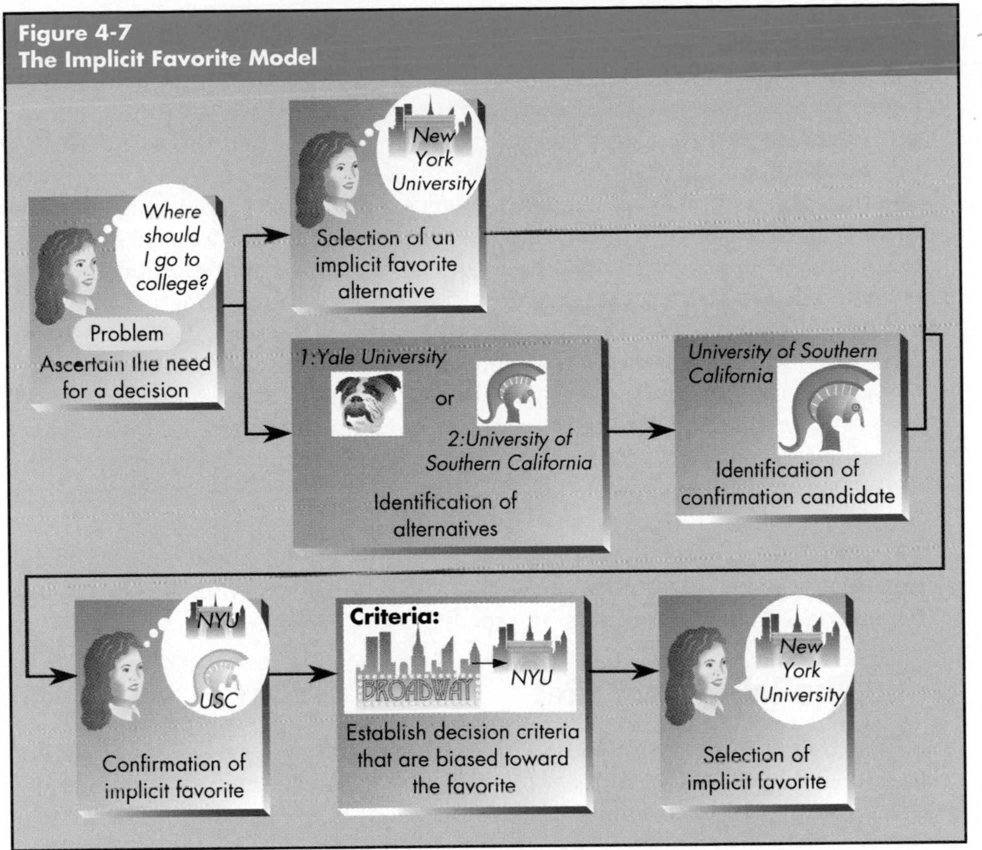

sion maker is often unaware he or she has already identified an implicit favorite and that the rest of the process is really an exercise in prejudice. So more alternatives will be generated. This is important, for it gives the appearance of objectivity. Then the confirmation process begins. The alternative set will be reduced to two—the choice candidate and a confirmation candidate. If the choice candidate is the only viable option, the decision maker will try to obtain another acceptable alternative to become the confirmation candidate, so he or she will have something to compare against. At this point, the decision maker establishes the decision criteria and weights. A great deal of perceptual and interpretational distortion is taking place, with the selection of criteria and their weight being "shaped" to ensure victory for the favored choice. And, of course, that's exactly what transpires. The evaluation demonstrates unequivocally the superiority of the choice candidate over the confirmation candidate.

If the implicit favorite model is at work, the search for new alternatives ends well before the decision maker is willing to admit having made his or her decision. In the job search with MIT students, the researcher found he was able to accurately predict 87 percent of the career jobs taken two to eight weeks before the students would admit they had reached a decision.[21] This points to a decision process that is influenced a lot more by intuitive feelings than by rational objectivity.

Recent research provides strong support for several of the primary tenets of the implicit favorite model. Considerable evidence suggests that individuals frequently make an early commitment to one alternative and don't evaluate the strengths and weaknesses of the various alternatives until *after* having made their final choice.[22]

Using the implicit favorite model, let's look at how our high school senior might go about choosing which college to attend. Early in the process, she will find that one of the colleges seems intuitively right for her. However, she may not reveal this to others, nor be aware of it herself. She'll review catalogs and brochures on a number of schools, but eventually reduce the set to two. One of these two, of course, will be her implied favorite. She'll then focus in on the relevant factors in her decision. Which college has the better reputation? Where will she have the better social life? Which campus is more attractive? Her evaluations of criteria such as these are subjective judgments. Her assessment, though, won't be fair and impartial. Rather, she'll distort her judgments to align with her intuitive preference. Since "the race is fixed," the winner is a foregone conclusion. Our high school student won't necessarily choose the optimum alternative, nor can we say her choice will satisfice. Remember, she distorted her evaluations to get the results she wanted, so there is no guarantee her final selection will reflect the assumptions of bounded rationality. What we can say is that, if she follows the implicit favorite model, she'll choose the college that was her early preference, regardless of any relevant facts that may have surfaced later in the decision process.

The Intuitive Model

Joe Garcia has just committed his corporation to spend in excess of $40 million to build a new plant in Atlanta to manufacture electronic components for satellite communication equipment. A vice president of operations for his firm, Joe had before him a comprehensive analysis of five possible plant locations developed by a site location consulting firm he had hired. This report ranked the Atlanta location third among the five alternatives. After carefully reading the report and its conclusions, Joe decided against the consultant's recommendation. When asked to explain his decision, Joe said, "I looked the report over very carefully. But in spite of its recommendation, I felt the numbers didn't tell the whole story. Intuitively, I just sensed that Atlanta would prove to be the best bet over the long run."

Intuitive decision making, like that used by Joe Garcia, has recently come out of the closet and into some respectability. Experts no longer automatically assume that using intuition to make decisions is irrational or ineffective.[23] There is growing recognition that rational analysis has been overemphasized and that, in certain instances, relying on intuition can improve decision making.

What do we mean by intuitive decision making? There are a number of ways to conceptualize intuition.[24] For instance, some consider it a form of extrasensory power or sixth sense, and some believe it is a personality trait that a limited number of people are born with. For our purposes, we define **intuitive decision making** as an unconscious process created out of distilled experience. It doesn't necessarily operate independently of rational analysis; rather, the two complement each other.

intuitive decision making
An unconscious process created out of distilled experience.

> ◆Intuition isn't independent of rational analysis. The two complement each other.

Research on chess playing provides an excellent example of how intuition works.[25] Novice chess players and grand masters were shown an actual, but unfamiliar, chess game with about 25 pieces on the board. After five or ten seconds, the pieces were removed and each was asked to reconstruct the pieces by position. On average, the grand master could put 23 or 24 pieces in their correct squares; the novice was able to replace only 6. Then the exercise was changed. This time the pieces were placed randomly on the board. Again, the novice got only about six correct, but so did the grand master! The second exercise demonstrated that the grand master didn't have any better memory than the novice. What he did have was the ability, based on the experience of having played thousands of chess games, to recognize patterns and clusters of

◆◆◆◆ OB in the News ◆◆◆◆

Too Many Facts Spoil the Decision

Every management decision has an element of risk in it. As a result, managers frequently try to minimize that risk by seeking additional facts. Good managers, however, learn when they have sufficient information to make a decision. They recognize they'll never have *all* the facts they want. And while the search for additional data can reduce or eliminate risk or even show a problem doesn't really exist, delays have costs. Opportunities can be missed while waiting for additional information. It is analogous to the fearful marksman: "Ready, aim, aim, aim, aim . . ." He just can't pull the trigger!

If it were possible to have so many facts that the risk element of decision making were totally eliminated, the question could be asked: Why do we need managers?

It's easy to fault decisions after the fact. All of us have 20-20 hindsight. It's self-evident today that we should have bought Microsoft stock back in 1988! Everyone knows now the error of Coca-Cola executives who, in 1985, decided to withdraw Coke's original formula and replace it with a new formula. The public outcry eventually led Coca-Cola's management to reintroduce the original version as "Coke Classic."

On television newscasts, programs such as *Nightline,* and at news conferences, U.S. Attorney General Janet Reno publicly accepted responsibility for her decision to storm the Branch Davidian compound rather than putting the blame on the F.B.I., which planned the attack.

U.S. Attorney General Janet Reno took a lot of flak for her decision to have federal agents storm the Branch Davidian compound in Waco, Texas, and the resulting deaths of dozens of people. In spite of the criticism, she publicly proclaimed, "I had all the information I needed to make a decision." Whether that was true or not, she exhibited effective management skills in two ways: (1) she decided she had enough information to make a decision, and (2) she went ahead and made the decision.

Decision making is not just an analysis of facts. There is a strong element of gut feel in the process, especially when it comes to knowing when you have reached that point where you have sufficient facts on which to base a decision with a minimum of risk. This gut feel often separates the effective from the ineffective manager.

Source: Based on H. Gittler in *Industry Week* (January 3, 1994), p. 46.

pieces that occur on chessboards in the course of games. Studies further show that chess professionals can play 50 or more games simultaneously, where decisions often must be made in only seconds, and exhibit only a moderately lower level of skill than when playing one game under tournament conditions, where decisions take half an hour or longer. The expert's experience allows him or her to recognize a situation and draw on previously learned information associated with that situation to quickly arrive at a decision choice. The result is that the intuitive decision maker can decide rapidly with what appears to be very limited information.

When are people most likely to use intuitive decision making? Eight conditions have been identified: (1) when a high level of uncertainty exists; (2) when there is little precedent to draw on; (3) when variables are less scientifically predictable; (4) when "facts" are limited; (5) when facts don't clearly point the way to go; (6) when analytical data are of little use; (7) when there are several plausible alternative solutions to choose from, with good arguments for each; and (8) when time is limited and there is pressure to come up with the right decision.[26]

Is there a standard model that people follow when using intuition? Individuals seem to follow one of two approaches. They apply intuition to either the front end or the back end of the decision-making process.[27]

When intuition is used at the front end, the decision maker tries to avoid systematically analyzing the problem, but instead gives intuition free rein. The idea is to try to generate unusual possibilities and new options that might not normally emerge from an analysis of past data or traditional ways of doing things. A back-end approach to using intuition relies on rational analysis to identify and allocate weights to decision criteria, as well as to develop and evaluate alternatives. Once this is done, the decision maker stops the analytical process in order to "sleep on the decision" for a day or two before making the final choice.

Although intuitive decision making has gained in respectability since the early 1980s, don't expect people who use it—especially in North America, Great Britain, and other cultures where rational analysis is the approved way of making decisions—to acknowledge they are doing so. People with strong intuitive abilities don't usually tell their colleagues how they reached their conclusions. Since rational analysis is considered more socially desirable, intuitive ability is often disguised or hidden. As one top executive commented, "Sometimes one must dress up a gut decision in 'data clothes' to make it acceptable or palatable, but this fine-tuning is usually after the fact of the decision."[28]

Current Issues in Decision Making

We conclude this chapter by reviewing three current issues in decision making: improving ethical decision-making; how decision-making styles vary in different countries; and the tendency for people to continue to commit resources to a previous decision in spite of evidence that the original decision was a mistake.

Improving Ethical Decision Making

No contemporary discussion of decision making would be complete without inclusion of ethics. Why? Because ethical considerations should be an important criterion in organizational decision making. In this section, we present three different ways to frame decisions and look at the factors that shape an individual's ethical decision-making behavior.

THREE ETHICAL DECISION CRITERIA An individual can use three different criteria in making ethical choices.[29] The first is the *utilitarian* criterion, in which decisions are made solely on the basis of their outcomes or consequences. The goal of **utilitarianism** is to provide the greatest good for the greatest number. This view tends to dominate business decision making. It is consistent with goals like efficiency, productivity, and high profits. By maximizing profits, for instance, a business executive can argue he is securing the greatest good for the greatest number—as he hands out dismissal notices to 15 percent of his employees.

utilitarianism
Decisions are made so as to provide the greatest good for the greatest number.

◆Utilitarianism dominates business decision making.

Another ethical criterion is to focus on *rights*. This calls on individuals to make decisions consistent with fundamental liberties and privileges as set forth in documents like the Bill of Rights. An emphasis on rights in decision making means respecting and protecting the basic rights of individuals, such as the right to privacy, to free speech, and to due process. For instance, use of this criterion would protect whistle-blowers when they report unethical or illegal practices by their organization to the press or government agencies on the grounds of their right to free speech.

A third criterion is to focus on *justice*. This requires individuals to impose and enforce rules fairly and impartially so there is an equitable distribution of benefits and costs. Union members typically favor this view. It justifies paying people the same wage for a given job, regardless of performance differences, and using seniority as the primary determination in making layoff decisions.

Each of these three criteria has advantages and liabilities. A focus on utilitarianism promotes efficiency and productivity, but it can result in ignoring the rights of some individuals, particularly those with minority representation in the organization. The use of rights as a criterion protects individuals from injury and is consistent with freedom and privacy, but it can create an overly legalistic work environment that hinders productivity and efficiency. A focus on justice protects the interests of the underrepresented and less powerful, but it can encourage a sense of entitlement that reduces risk taking, innovation, and productivity.

Decision makers, particularly in for-profit organizations, tend to feel safe and comfortable when they use utilitarianism. A lot of questionable actions can be justified when framed as being in the best interests of "the organization" and stockholders. But many critics of business decision makers argue that this perspective needs to change.[30] Increased concern in society about individual rights and social justice suggests the need for managers to develop ethical standards based on nonutilitarian criteria. This presents a solid challenge to today's managers because making decisions using criteria such as individual rights and social justice involves far more ambiguities than using utilitarian criteria such as effects on efficiency and profits. This helps explain why managers are increasingly finding themselves criticized for their actions. Raising prices, selling products with questionable effects on consumer health, closing down plants, laying off large numbers of employees, moving production overseas to cut costs, and similar decisions can be justified in utilitarian terms. But that may no longer be the single criterion by which good decisions should be judged.

FACTORS INFLUENCING ETHICAL DECISION-MAKING BEHAVIOR What accounts for unethical behavior in organizations? Is it immoral individuals or a work environment that promotes unethical activity? The answer is *both*! The evidence indicates that ethical or unethical actions are largely a function of both the individual's characteristics and the environment in which he or she works.[31]

stages of moral development An assessment of a person's capacity to judge what is morally right.

Figure 4-8 presents a model for explaining ethical or unethical behavior. **Stages of moral development** is an assessment of a person's capacity to judge what is morally right.[32] The higher one's moral development, the less dependent he or she is on outside influences and, hence, the more he or she will be predisposed to behave ethically. For instance, most adults are at a midlevel of moral development—they're strongly influenced by peers and will follow an organization's rules and procedures. Those individuals who have progressed to the higher stages place increased value on the rights of others, regardless of the majority's opinion, and are likely to challenge organizational practices they believe are personally wrong.

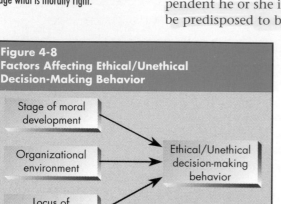

Figure 4-8
Factors Affecting Ethical/Unethical Decision-Making Behavior

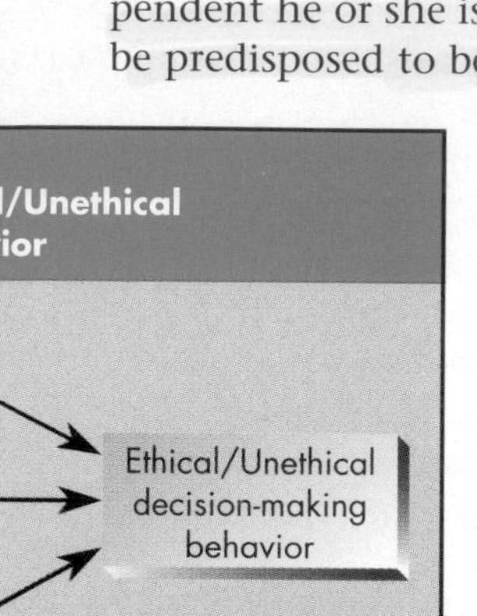

We discussed *locus of control* in Chapter 3. It's a personality characteristic that taps the extent to which people believe they are responsible for the events in their lives. Research indicates that people with an external locus of control (i.e., what happens to them in life is due to luck or chance) are less likely to take responsibility for the consequences of their behavior and are more likely to rely on external influences. Internals, on the other hand, are more likely to rely on their own internal standards of right or wrong to guide their behavior.

The *organizational environment* refers to an employee's perception of organizational expectations. Does the organization encourage and support ethical behavior by rewarding it or discourage unethical behavior by punishing it? Written codes of ethics, high moral behavior by senior management, realistic performance expectations, performance appraisals that evaluate means as well as ends, visible recognition and promotions for individuals who display high moral behavior, and visible punishment for those who act unethically are some examples of an organizational environment that is likely to foster high ethical decision making.

In summary, people who lack a strong moral sense are much less likely to make unethical decisions if they are constrained by an organizational environment that frowns on such behaviors. Conversely, very righteous individuals can be corrupted by an organizational environment that permits or encourages unethical practices.

Decision Making in Different Cultures

Who makes a decision, when it's made, and the importance placed on rationality vary in organizations around the world.[33] Therefore, we need to take national culture into consideration when we discuss an individual's approach to decision making.

Our knowledge of power-distance differences, for example, tells us that in high-power-distance cultures, such as India, only very senior-level managers make decisions. But in low-power-distance cultures, such as Sweden, low-ranking employees expect to make most of their own decisions about day-to-day operations. Our knowledge that cultures vary in terms of time orientation

Who makes decisions in an organization varies from culture to culture. In Indonesia, all decisions are made by top managers, respectfully called *bapak*, which translates as "father." Indonesia is a paternalistic society, where people are very polite, soft-spoken, and influenced by ancient myths that provide models for exemplary behavior. In Indonesian culture, avoiding confrontation and maintaining harmony are far more important than working quickly and efficiently. Employees shown here at the port of Jakarta perform their work, never daring to challenge or influence the decisions of their *bapak*.

helps us understand why managers in Egypt will make decisions at a much slower and more deliberate pace than their American counterparts. Even the assumption of rationality is culturally biased. A North American manager might make an important decision intuitively, but he or she knows it is important to appear to proceed in a rational fashion. This explains why, in the implicit favorite model, the decision maker develops a confirmation candidate. It reassures the decision maker that he or she is seeking to be rational and objective by reviewing alternative options. In countries such as Iran, where rationality is not deified, efforts to appear rational are not necessary.

We can also assess cultural influences in terms of the six steps in the optimizing decision model. To illustrate, let's look at just two of those steps: ascertaining the need for a decision and developing alternatives.

Based on a society's activity orientation, some cultures emphasize solving problems; others focus on accepting situations as they are. The United States falls in the former category; Thailand and Indonesia are examples of cultures that fall into the latter. Because problem-solving managers believe they can and should change situations to their own benefit, American managers might identify a problem long before their Thai or Indonesian counterparts would choose to recognize it as such. We can also use differences in time orientation to project the type of alternatives that decision makers might develop. Because Italians value the past and traditions, managers in that culture will tend to rely on tried-and-proven alternatives to problems. In contrast, the United States and Australia are more aggressive and now oriented; managers in these countries are more likely to propose unique and creative solutions to their problems.

Escalation of Commitment or "Throwing Good Money After Bad"

A popular strategy in playing blackjack is supposed to "guarantee" you can't lose: When you lose a hand, double your next bet. While this strategy or decision rule may seem innocent enough, if you start with $5 and lose six hands in a row (a not uncommon occurrence for many of us), you'll be wagering $320 on your seventh hand merely to recoup your losses and win $5!

A friend of mine had been dating a woman for about four years. Although he admitted things weren't going too well in the relationship, he informed me he was going to marry the woman. A bit surprised by this decision, I asked him why. He responded, "I have a lot invested in this relationship!"

escalation of commitment
An increased commitment to a previous decision in spite of negative information.

The blackjack strategy and marriage decision just described illustrate a phenomenon called **escalation of commitment**. Specifically, it is defined as an increased commitment to a previous decision in spite of negative information.

It has been well documented that individuals escalate commitment to a failing course of action when they view themselves as responsible for the failure.[34] That is, they "throw good money after bad" to demonstrate their initial decision wasn't wrong and to avoid having to admit they made a mistake.

Maybe the most frequently cited example of the escalation of commitment phenomenon was President Lyndon Johnson's decisions regarding the Vietnam War. Despite continued information that bombing North Vietnam was not bringing the war any closer to conclusion, his solution was to increase the tonnage of bombs dropped. More recently, the premier of Ontario, David Peterson, committed an additional $4 billion to complete the Darlington nuclear plant in spite of evidence that original energy consumption forecasts used to justify building the plant were overly optimistic. Peterson became increasingly preoccupied with funds that already had been spent to construct the megaproject: "I don't think anybody can look at a situation with . . . $7 billion in the ground and just cavalierly write it off."[35] But that's probably what he should have done as the final price tag ballooned to $14 billion and energy consumption diminished.

Escalation of commitment has broad implications for managerial decisions in organizations. Many an organization has suffered large losses because a manager was determined to prove his or her original decision was right by continuing to commit resources to what was a lost cause from the beginning.

Summary and Implications for Managers

Perception

Individuals behave in a given manner based not on the way their external environment actually is but, rather, on what they see or believe it to be. An organization may spend millions of dollars to create a pleasant work environment for its employees. However, in spite of these expenditures, if an employee believes his or her job is lousy, that employee will behave accordingly. It is the employee's perception of a situation that becomes the basis on which he or she behaves. The employee who perceives his or her supervisor as a hurdle reducer and an aid to help him or her do a better job and the employee who sees the same supervisor as "big brother, closely monitoring every motion, to ensure that I keep working" will differ in their behavioral responses to their supervisor. The difference has nothing to do with the reality of the supervisor's actions; the difference in employee behavior is due to different perceptions.

The evidence suggests that what individuals *perceive* from their work situation will influence their productivity more than will the situation itself. Whether a job is actually interesting or challenging is irrelevant. Whether a manager successfully plans and organizes the work of his or her subordinates and actually helps them structure their work more efficiently and effectively is far less important than how subordinates perceive his or her efforts. Similarly, issues like fair pay for work performed, the validity of performance appraisals, and the adequacy of working conditions are not judged by employees in a way that assures common perceptions, nor can we be assured that individuals will interpret conditions about their jobs in a favorable light. Therefore, to be able to influence productivity, it is necessary to assess how workers perceive their jobs.

Absenteeism, turnover, and job satisfaction are also reactions to the individual's perceptions. Dissatisfaction with working conditions or the belief that there is a lack of promotion opportunities in the organization are judgments based on attempts to make some meaning out of one's job. The employee's conclusion that a job is good or bad is an interpretation. Managers must spend time understanding how each individual interprets reality and, where there is a significant difference between what is seen and what exists, try to eliminate the distortions. Failure to deal with the differences when individuals perceive the job in negative terms will result in increased absenteeism and turnover and lower job satisfaction.

Individual Decision Making

Individuals think and reason before they act. It is because of this that an understanding of how people make decisions can be helpful for explaining and predicting their behavior.

Under some decision situations, people follow the optimizing model. But for most people, and most nonroutine decisions, this is probably more the exception than the rule. Few important decisions are simple or unambiguous enough for the optimizing model's assumptions to apply. So we find individuals looking for solutions that satisfice rather than optimize, injecting biases and prejudices into the decision process, and relying on intuition.

The alternative decision models we presented can help us explain and predict behaviors that would appear irrational or arbitrary if viewed under optimizing assumptions. Let's look at a couple of examples.

Employment interviews are complex decision activities. The interviewer finds himself or herself inundated with information. Research indicates that interviewers respond by simplifying the process.[36] Most interviewers' decisions change very little after the first four or five minutes of the interview. In a half-hour interview, the decision maker tends to make a decision about the suitability of the candidate in the first few minutes and then uses the rest of the interview time to select information that supports the early decision. In so doing, interviewers reduce the probability of identifying the highest performing candidate. They bias their decision toward individuals who make favorable first impressions.

Evaluating an employee's performance is a complex activity. Decision makers simplify the process by focusing on visible and easy-to-measure criteria.[37] This may explain why factors such as neatness, promptness, enthusiasm, and a positive attitude are often related to good evaluations. It also explains why quantity measures typically override quality measures. The former category is easier to appraise. This effort at satisficing encourages individuals to take on visible problems rather than important ones.

What can we say regarding ethics? For individuals already employed, managers can influence only the employee's work environment. So managers should overtly seek to convey high ethical standards to employees through the actions the managers take. By what managers say, do, reward, punish, and overlook, they set the ethical tone for their employees. When hiring new employees, managers have an opportunity to weed out ethically undesirable applicants. The selection process—for instance, interviews, tests, and background checks—should be viewed as an opportunity to learn about an individual's level of moral development and locus of control. This then can be used to identify individuals whose ethical standards might be in conflict with those of the organization or who are particularly vulnerable to negative external influences.

Finally, managers must guard against the tendency to escalate commitments to decisions to avoid having to admit they made a mistake. This applies to individual managers and to those who report to them. Decision making comes with risks and sometimes you make the wrong choice. It's often less costly to admit a decision error when it first surfaces rather than escalating commitment to that decision based on unrealistic hopes it may eventually prove to have been correct.

For Review

1. Define *perception*.
2. What is attribution theory? What are its implications for explaining organizational behavior?
3. What factors do you think might create the fundamental attribution error?
4. How does selectivity affect perception? Give an example of how selectivity can create perceptual distortion.
5. What is *stereotyping*? Give an example of how stereotyping can create perceptual distortion.
6. Give some positive results of using shortcuts when judging others.
7. What is the optimizing decision-making model? Under what conditions is it applicable?
8. Explain the satisficing model. How widely applicable do you think this model is?
9. Contrast the implicit favorite model to the satisficing model.
10. Describe the three criteria individuals can use in making ethical decisions.

For Discussion

1. "That you and I agree on what we see suggests we have similar backgrounds and experiences." Do you agree or disagree? Discuss.
2. In what work-related situations do you think it is important to be able to determine whether others' behavior stems primarily from internal or external causes?
3. "For the most part, individual decision making in organizations is an irrational process." Do you agree or disagree? Discuss.
4. What factors do you think differentiate good decision makers from poor ones? Relate your answer back to the six-step optimizing model.
5. Have you ever increased your commitment to a failed course of action? If so, analyze the follow-up decision to increase your commitment and explain why you behaved as you did.

Point

When Hiring Employees: Emphasize the Positive

Hiring new employees requires managers to become salespeople. They have to emphasize the positive, even if it means failing to mention the negative aspects in the job. While there is a real risk of setting unrealistic expectations about the organization and about the specific job, that's a risk managers have to take. As in dealing with any salesperson, it is the job applicant's responsibility to follow the dictum *caveat emptor*—let the buyer beware!

Why should managers emphasize the positive when discussing a job with a prospective candidate? They have no choice! First, there is a dwindling supply of qualified applicants for many job vacancies; and second, this approach is necessary to meet the competition.

The massive restructuring and downsizing of organizations that began in the late 1980s has drawn attention to corporate layoffs. What has often been overlooked in this process is the growing shortage of qualified applicants for literally millions of jobs. Through the foreseeable future, managers will find it increasingly difficult to get qualified people who can fill jobs such as legal secretary, nurse, accountant, salesperson, maintenance mechanic, computer repair specialist, software programmer, social worker, physical therapist, environmental engineer, telecommunications specialist, and airline pilot. But managers will also find it harder to get qualified people to fill entry-level minimum wage jobs. There may be no shortage of physical bodies, but finding individuals who can read, write, perform basic mathematical calculations, and have the proper work habits to effectively perform these jobs isn't so easy. There is a growing gap between the skills workers have and the skills employers require. So managers need to *sell* jobs to the limited pool of applicants. And this means presenting the job and the organization in the most favorable light possible.

Another reason management is forced to emphasize the positive with job candidates is because that is what the competition is doing. Other employers also face a limited applicant pool. As a result, to get people to join their organizations, they are forced to put a positive spin on their descriptions of their organizations and the jobs they seek to fill. In this competitive environment, any employer who presents jobs realistically to applicants—that is, openly provides the negative aspects of a job along with the positive—risks losing most or all of his or her most desirable candidates.

counterPoint

When Hiring Employees: Balance the Positive with the Negative

Regardless of the changing labor market, managers who treat the recruiting and hiring of candidates as if the applicants must be sold on the job and exposed to only positive aspects set themselves up to have a work force that is dissatisfied and prone to high turnover.

Every applicant acquires, during the selection process, a set of expectations about the organization and about the specific job he or she hopes to be offered. When the information an applicant receives is excessively inflated, a number of things happen that have potentially negative effects on the organization. First, mismatched applicants who would probably become dissatisfied with the job and soon quit are less likely to select themselves out of the search process. Second, the absence of negative information builds unrealistic expectations. If hired, the new employee is likely to become quickly disappointed. And inaccurate perceptions lead to premature resignations. Third, new hires are prone to become disillusioned and less committed to the organization when they come face to face with the negatives in the job. Employees who feel they were tricked or misled during the hiring process are unlikely to be satisfied workers.

To increase job satisfaction among employees and reduce turnover, applicants should be given a realistic job preview, with both unfavorable and favorable information, before an offer is made. For example, in addition to positive comments, the candidate might be told there are limited opportunities to talk with coworkers during work hours or that erratic fluctuations in workload create considerable stress on employees during rush periods.

Research indicates that applicants who have been given a realistic job preview hold lower and more realistic expectations about the job they'll be doing and are better prepared for coping with the job and its frustrating elements. The result is fewer unexpected resignations by new employees. In a tight labor market, retaining people is as critical as hiring them in the first place. Presenting only the positive aspects of a job to a recruit may initially entice him or her to join the organization, but it may be a marriage that both parties will quickly regret.

Information in this argument comes from J.A. Breaugh, "Realistic Job Previews: A Critical Appraisal and Future Research Directions," *Academy of Management Review* (October 1983), pp. 612–19; S.L. Premack and J.P. Wanous, "A Meta-Analysis of Realistic Job Preview Experiments," *Journal of Applied Psychology* (November 1985), pp. 706–20; B.M. Meglino, A.S. DeNisi, S.A. Youngblood, and K.J. Williams, "Effects of Realistic Job Previews: A Comparison Using an Enhancement and a Reduction Preview," *Journal of Applied Psychology* (May 1988), pp. 259–66; and R.J. Vandenberg and V. Scarpello, "The Matching Model: An Examination of the Processes Underlying Realistic Job Previews," *Journal of Applied Psychology* (February 1990), pp. 60–67.

Learning About Yourself Exercise

Decision-Making Style Questionnaire

PART I

Circle the response that comes closest to how you usually feel or act. There are no right or wrong responses to any of these items.

1. I am more careful about
   a. people's feelings
   b. their rights

2. I usually get on better with
   a. imaginative people
   b. realistic people

3. It is a higher compliment to be called
   a. a person of real feeling
   b. a consistently reasonable person

4. In doing something with other people, it appeals more to me
   a. to do it in the accepted way
   b. to invent a way of my own

5. I get more annoyed at
   a. fancy theories
   b. people who do not like theories

6. It is higher praise to call someone
   a. a person of vision
   b. a person of common sense

7. I more often let
   a. my heart rule my head
   b. my head rule my heart

8. I think it is a worse fault
   a. to show too much warmth
   b. to be unsympathetic

9. If I were a teacher, I would rather teach
   a. courses involving theory
   b. fact courses

PART II

Which word in the following pairs appeals to you more? Circle a or b.

10. a. Compassion
   b. Foresight

11. a. Justice
   b. Mercy

12. a. Production
   b. Design

13. a. Gentle
    b. Firm
14. a. Uncritical
    b. Critical
15. a. Literal
    b. Figurative
16. a. Imaginative
    b. Matter–of–fact

Turn to page A-26 for scoring directions and key.

Source: Adapted from the Myers-Briggs Type Indicator and a scale developed by D. Hellriegel, J. Slocum, and R.W. Woodman, *Organizational Behavior*, 3rd ed. (St. Paul, MN: West, 1983), pp. 127–41; and reproduced in J. M. Ivancevich and M. T. Matteson, *Organizational Behavior and Management*, 2nd ed. (Homewood, IL: BPI/Irwin, 1990), pp. 538–39.

Working With Others Exercise

Evaluating Your Interpersonal Perception

1. On a piece of paper, write down how you would describe *yourself* on the following dimensions:
   a. Friendliness
   b. Mood
   c. Sense of humor
   d. Career motivation
   e. Interpersonal skills
   f. Desire to be accepted by others
   g. Independence
2. Now form groups of three to five members. Evaluate each of the *other members* in your group (as best you can) on the same seven dimensions.
3. Going around the group so each member gets to participate, describe what each of you have written about Member A. After you have all provided your perceptions, Member A will share his or her own self-perceptions. Then do the same with Member B, and so forth, until all group members have received feedback and shared their own impressions.
4. The exercise concludes by each member analyzing the similarities and differences between their perceptions of themselves on the seven dimensions and how they're perceived by the other members of their group.

Ethical Dilemma Exercise

Five Ethical Decisions: What Would You Do?

Assume you're a middle manager in a company with about a thousand employees. How would you respond to each of the following situations?

1. A close business associate has asked you for preferential treatment on an upcoming contract and has offered you a generous sum of money for your time and trouble. Do you accept his offer?
2. You have the opportunity to steal $100,000 from your company with absolute certainty that you would not be detected or caught. Would you do it?
3. Your company policy on reimbursement for meals while traveling on company business is that you will be repaid for your out-of-pocket costs, not to exceed $50 a day. You don't need receipts for these expenses—the company will take your word. When traveling, you tend to eat at fast-food places and rarely spend in excess of $15 a day. Most of your colleagues put in reimbursement requests in the range of $40 to $45 a day regardless of what their actual expenses are. How much would you request for your meal reimbursements?
4. Your kids will be going back to school next week. You have access to your department's office supplies. No one would know if you took any for personal use. Would you take pens, pencils, writing pads, or the like, from the office and give them to your kids?
5. You've discovered that one of your closest friends at work has stolen a large sum of money from the company. Would you: Do nothing? Go directly to an executive to report the incident before talking about it with the offender? Confront the individual before taking action? Make contact with the individual with the goal of persuading that person to return the money?

Several of these scenerios are based on D.R. Altany, "Torn Between Halo and Horns," *Industry Week* (March 15, 1993), pp. 15–20.

"I Don't Make Decisions"

CASE INCIDENT

I met Ted Kelly for the first time at a cocktail party. He was the plant manager at a large chemical refinery in town. About ten minutes into our conversation, I asked him about his leadership style.

Ted: "I don't make decisions at my plant."

Author: "You use democratic leadership?"

Ted: "No, I said I don't make decisions! My subordinates are paid to make decisions. No point in my doing their jobs."

I didn't really believe what I was hearing. I guess Ted sensed that, so he invited me to visit his plant. I asked him when I could come over. "Any time you like, except Mondays between 1 and 3 P.M."

The middle of the next week, I popped in on Ted unannounced. He had no secretary. He was lying on his sofa, half asleep. My arrival seemed to jar him awake. He offered me a seat.

Our conversation began by my inquiring exactly what he did every day. "You're looking at it. I sleep a lot. Oh yeah, I read the four or five memos I get from head office every week." I couldn't believe what I was hearing. Here was a 50-year-old obviously successful executive telling me he doesn't do anything. He could tell I wasn't buying his story.

"If you don't believe what I'm saying, check with my subordinates," he told me. He said he had six department managers working for him. I asked him to choose one I could talk with.

"No, I can't do that. Remember, I don't make decisions. Here—these are the names and numbers of my department managers. You call them."

I did just that. I picked Peter Chandler, who headed up quality control. I dialed his number. I told him that I wanted to talk to him about his boss's leadership style. He said, "Come on over. I've got nothing to do anyway."

When I arrived at Pete's office, he was staring out the window. We sat down and he began to laugh. "I'll bet Ted's been telling you about how he doesn't make decisions." I concurred. "It's all true," he injected. "I've been here for almost three years and I've never seen him make a decision."

I couldn't figure out how this could be. "How many people do you have working here?" I asked.

Peter: "About two hundred."

Author: "How does this plant's operating efficiency stack up against the others?"

Peter: "Oh, we're number one out of the eighteen refineries. This is the oldest refinery in the company, too. Our equipment may be outdated, but we're as efficient as they come."

Author: "What does Ted Kelly do?"

Peter: "Beats me. He attends the staff meetings on Monday afternoon from 1 to 3, but other than that, I don't know."

Author: "I get it. He makes all the decisions at that once-a-week staff meeting?"

Peter: "No. Each department head tells what key decisions he has made last week. We then critique each other. Ted says nothing. The only thing he does at those meetings is listen and pass on any happenings up at headquarters."

I wanted to learn more, so I went back to Ted's office. I found him clipping his fingernails. What followed was a long conversation in which I learned the following facts:

The two-hour weekly staff meeting is presided over by one of the department heads. They choose among themselves who will be their leader. It's a permanent position. Any problem that has come up during the week, if it can't be handled by a manager, will first be considered by several of the managers together. Only if the problem is still unresolved will it be taken to the leader. All issues are resolved at that level. They are never taken to Ted Kelly's level.

The performance record at Kelly's plant is well known in the company. Three of the last four new plant managers have come out of Kelly's plant. When recommending candidates for a plant management vacancy, Ted always selects the department head who presides over the staff meetings, so there is a great deal of competition to lead the meetings. Additionally, because of Kelly's plant record for breeding management talent, whenever there is a vacancy for a department manager at Kelly's plant, the best people in the company apply for it.

Questions

1. Why does Ted Kelly's decision–making style work?

2. Is Ted Kelly abrogating his decision–making responsibilities? Explain.

3. Would you like to work for Ted Kelly? Why?

4. Would you want Ted Kelly working for you? Why?

Source: Based on A. E. Carlisle, "MacGregor," *Organizational Dynamics* (Summer 1976), pp. 50–62.

What Do Those Wall Street People Do?

First trader: "I think today's going to be an up day."
Second trader: "I suspect the market will be lower today."
Third trader: "At the close of business today, I think that the market will be unchanged from yesterday's close."

These three quotes support two facts. First, one of these traders is going to be correct. Second, you can't predict the stock market (although tens of millions of investors try). In April 1994 ABC News's Ted Koppel spent a day trying to figure out what the traders, analysts, and brokers on Wall Street were doing. Koppel was particularly interested in getting some insights into predicting market and interest rate movements.

Jim Jacobsen, a floor trader, told Koppel:

> What's going to happen today will depend upon what's coming in the future, in the next four hours of the day, not what's happened in the past. Now, none of us, to my knowledge, have the ability to very accurately predict the future in a very positive fashion. We act on what we think will happen, but certainly not on what we know will happen, or if we know what happens, then we have an insider problem, which is a different . . . a different breed of cat.

What's Jacobsen saying? Basically, he's saying you can't accurately predict future market movements. And if you know something as a result of insider information, that's illegal.

Dennis Kelly, a vice president at a Wall Street firm:

> We have a tremendous amount of volatility. Whenever I make a decision out of fear, or out of confusion, it tends to be the wrong decision. What you've got now is a situation where sheer emotion is dictating what's going to happen in the marketplace on a very short-term basis. I don't think there's anybody in the history of our country that can predict accurately interest rates on a short-term basis, and obviously the stock market as well. So you take all your intuition, all your education, all your experience, and put it together, and try to match that with the emotional state of that individual client at that point in time.

Noted Wall Street economist Henry Kaufman explains to Koppel his predictions on interest rates and the implications for equity markets:

> First of all, the volatility that we've seen over the last week or two is going to continue to reoccur from time to time, probably even with greater magnitude. I suspect that over the next three or four years, the direction of interest rates is going to be upwards. The long-term government bond, which at the present time is roughly at 6, may go to the 7.25 range, before it peaks out in three or four years from now, at perhaps 9 to 10 percent, and short-term interest rates may go perhaps up to 7 percent. . . . I think, over a period of time, this means bond prices will go down, and as we move on over the next three, four years we will diminish the positive prospects for the equity market, and they will be under some duress, and in three, four years from now we'll have somewhat lower equity prices than are prevailing today. There'll be pressure from interest rates, earnings will come under pressure, and we'll see a cyclical decline.

It's interesting that while all the experts seem to agree that you can't predict the market's movements, especially in the short term, that doesn't stop them from making predictions and selling advice to clients. Moreover, no matter which way the market moves on any given day, you can pick up the next day's newspaper, turn to the business section, and you'll see some "expert" confidently explaining why the market did what it did yesterday.

Questions

1. Analyze this case using attribution theory.
2. "Comments in this case support that decision making on Wall Street is completely intuitive." Do you agree or disagree? Discuss.

Source: "A Day in the Life of Wall Street," *Nightline* (April 7, 1994).

Suggestions for Further Reading

BAZERMAN, M.H., *Judgment in Managerial Decision Making*, 3rd ed. (New York: Wiley, 1994).

CRANT, J.M., and T.S. BATEMAN, "Assignment of Credit and Blame for Performance Outcomes," *Academy of Management Journal* (February 1993), pp. 7–27.

FALKENBERG, L., "Improving the Accuracy of Stereotypes Within the Workplace," *Journal of Management* (March 1990), pp. 107–18.

KAUFMAN, B.E., "A New Theory of Satisficing," *The Journal of Behavioral Economics* (Spring 1990), pp. 35–51.

KNOUSE, S.B. and R.A. GIACALONE, "Ethical Decision-Making in Business: Behavioral Issues and Concerns," *Journal of Business Ethics* (May 1992), pp. 369–77.

LANGLEY, A., "In Search of Rationality: The Purposes Behind the Use of Formal Analysis in Organizations," *Administrative Science Quarterly* (December 1989), pp. 598–631.

MUMBY, D.K., and L.L. PUTNAM, "The Politics of Emotion: A Feminist Reading of Bounded Rationality," *Academy of Management Review* (July 1992), pp. 465–86.

SKIDD, D.R., "Revisiting Bounded Rationality," *Journal of Management Inquiry* (December 1992), pp. 343–47.

STRUTHERS, C.W., N.L. COLWILL, and R.P. PERRY, "An Attributional Analysis of Decision Making in a Personnel Selection Interview," *Journal of Applied Social Psychology* (May 1992), pp. 801–18.

ZEY, M., (ed.), *Decision Making: Alternatives to Rational Choice* (Newbury Park, CA: Sage, 1992).

Notes

[1] D.C. McClelland and J.W. Atkinson, "The Projective Expression of Needs: The Effect of Different Intensities of the Hunger Drive on Perception," *Journal of Psychology*, Vol. 25 (1948), pp. 205–22.

[2] H.H. Kelley, "Attribution in Social Interaction," in E. Jones et al. (eds.), *Attribution: Perceiving the Causes of Behavior* (Morristown, NJ: General Learning Press, 1972).

[3] See L. Ross, "The Intuitive Psychologist and His Shortcomings," in L. Berkowitz (ed.), *Advances in Experimental Social Psychology*, Vol. 10 (Orlando, FL: Academic Press, 1977), pp. 174–220; and A.G. Miller and T. Lawson, "The Effect of an Informational Option on the Fundamental Attribution Error," *Personality and Social Psychology Bulletin* (June 1989), pp. 194–204.

[4] S. Nam, *Cultural and Managerial Attributions for Group Performance*, unpublished doctoral disseration, University of Oregon. Cited in R.M. Steers, S.J. Bischoff, and L.H. Higgins, "Cross-Cultural Management Research," *Journal of Management Inquiry* (December 1992), pp. 325–26.

[5] D.C. Dearborn and H.A. Simon, "Selective Perception: A Note on the Departmental Identification of Executives," *Sociometry* (June 1958), pp. 140–44. Some of the conclusions

in this classic study have recently been challenged in J.P. Walsh, "Selectivity and Selective Perception: An Investigation of Managers' Belief Structures and Information Processing," *Academy of Management Journal* (December 1988), pp. 873–96.

[6] S.E. Asch, "Forming Impressions of Personality," *Journal of Abnormal and Social Psychology* (July 1946), pp. 258–90.

[7] J.S. Bruner and R. Tagiuri, "The Perception of People," in E. Lindzey (ed.), *Handbook of Social Psychology* (Reading, MA: Addison–Wesley, 1954), p. 641.

[8] See, for example, C.M. Judd and B. Park, "Definition and Assessment of Accuracy in Social Stereotypes," *Psychological Review* (January 1993), pp. 109–28.

[9] See, for example, E.C. Webster, *Decision Making in the Employment Interview* (Montreal: McGill University, Industrial Relations Center, 1964).

[10] See, for example, L. Jussim, "Self-Fulfilling Prophecies: A Theoretical and Integrative Review," *Psychological Review* (October 1986), pp. 429–45; R.H.G. Field and D.A. Van Seters, "Management by Expectations (MBE): The Power of Positive Prophecy," *Journal of General Management* (Winter 1988), pp. 19–33; and D. Eden, *Pygmalion in Management* (Lexington, MA: Lexington, 1990).

[11] D. Eden and A.B. Shani, "Pygmalion Goes to Boot Camp: Expectancy, Leadership, and Trainee Performance," *Journal of Applied Psychology* (April 1982), pp. 194–99.

[12] See, for example, R.D. Bretz, Jr., G.T. Milkovich, and W. Read, "The Current State of Performance Appraisal Research and Practice: Concerns, Directions, and Implications," *Journal of Management* (June 1992), pp. 323–24; and P.M. Swiercz, M.L. Icenogle, N.B. Bryan, and R.W. Renn, "Do Perceptions of Performance Appraisal Fairness Predict Employee Attitudes and Performance?" in D.P. Moore (ed.), *Proceedings of the Academy of Management* (Atlanta, 1993), pp. 304–08.

[13] D. Kipnis, *The Powerholders* (Chicago: University of Chicago Press, 1976).

[14] See J.P. Near and M.P. Miceli, "Whistle-Blowers in Organizations: Dissidents or Reformers?" in L.L. Cummings and B.M. Staw (eds.), *Research in Organizational Behavior*, Vol. 9 (Greenwich, CT: JAI Press, 1987), pp. 321–68.

[15] For a comprehensive review of the optimizing model and its assumptions, see E.F. Harrison, *The Managerial Decision-Making Process*, 2nd ed. (Boston: Houghton Mifflin, 1981), pp. 53–57, 81–93.

[16] Cited in E.T. Smith, "Are You Creative?" *Business Week* (September 30, 1985), p. 81.

[17] Cited in C.G. Morris, *Psychology: An Introduction*, 8th ed. (Englewood Cliffs, NJ: Prentice Hall, 1993), p. 341.

[18] D.L. Rados, "Selection and Evaluation of Alternatives in Repetitive Decision Making," *Administrative Science Quarterly* (June 1972), pp. 196–206.

[19] See H.A. Simon, *Administrative Behavior*, 3rd ed. (New York: Free Press, 1976); and J. Forester, "Bounded Rationality and the Politics of Muddling Through," *Public Administration Review* (January-February 1984), pp. 23–31.

[20] See P.O. Soelberg, "Unprogrammed Decision Making," *Industrial Management Review* (Spring 1967), pp. 19–29; and D.J. Power and R.J. Aldag, "Soelberg's Job Search and Choice Model: A Clarification, Review, and Critique," *Academy of Management Review* (January 1985), pp. 48–58.

[21] Soelberg, "Unprogrammed Decision Making."

[22] E. Langer and R.C. Schank (eds.), *Beliefs, Reasoning, and Decision Making* (Hillsdale, NJ: Erlbaum, 1994).

[23] W.H. Agor, "The Logic of Intuition: How Top Executives Make Important Decisions," *Organizational Dynamics* (Winter 1986), p. 5; W.H. Agor (ed.), *Intuition in Organizations* (Newbury Park, CA: Sage, 1989); O. Behling and N.L. Eckel, "Making Sense Out of Intuition," *Academy of Management Executive* (February 1991) pp. 46–47; and V. Johnson, "Intuition in Decision-Making," *Successful Meetings* (February 1993), pp. 148–51.

[24] Behling and Eckel, "Making Sense Out of Intuition," pp. 46–54.

[25] As described in H.A. Simon, "Making Management Decisions: The Role of Intuition and Emotion," *Academy of Management Executive* (February 1987), pp. 59–60.

[26] Agor, "The Logic of Intuition," p. 9.

[27] Ibid., pp. 12–13.

[28] Ibid., p. 15.

[29] G.F. Cavanagh, D.J. Moberg, and M. Valasquez, "The Ethics of Organizational Politics," *Academy of Management Journal* (June 1981), pp. 363–74.

[30] See, for example, T. Machan (ed.), *Commerce and Morality* (Totowa, NJ: Rowman and Littlefield, 1988).

[31] L.K. Trevino, "Ethical Decision Making in Organizations: A Person-Situation Interactionist Model," *Academy of Management Review* (July 1986), pp. 601–17; and L.K. Trevino and S.A. Youngblood, "Bad Apples in Bad Barrels: A Causal Analysis of Ethical Decision-Making Behavior," *Journal of Applied Psychology* (August 1990), pp. 378–85.

[32] L. Kohlberg, *Essays in Moral Development: The Philosophy of Moral Development*, Vol. 1 (New York: Harper & Row, 1981); and L. Kohlberg, *Essays in Moral Development: The Psychology of Moral Development*, Vol. 2 (New York: Harper & Row, 1984).

[33] N.J. Adler, *International Dimensions of Organizational Behavior*, 2nd ed. (Boston: Kent, 1991), pp. 160–68.

[34] See, for instance, B.M. Staw, "The Escalation of Commitment to a Course of Action," *Academy of Management Review* (October 1981), pp. 577–87; and D.R. Bobocel and J.P. Meyer, "Escalating Commitment to a Failing Course of Action: Separating the Roles of Choice and Justification," *Journal of Applied Psychology* (June 1994), pp. 360–63.

[35] S. McKay, "When Good People Make Bad Choices," *Canadian Business* (February 1994), pp. 52–55.

[36] E.C. Mayfield in N. Schmitt's "Social and Situational Determinants of Interview Decisions: Implications for Employment Interviews," *Personnel Psychology*, (Spring 1976), p. 81.

[37] G.P. Huber, *Managerial Decision Making* (Glenview, IL: Scott, Foresman, 1980), p. 215.

CHAPTER 5

These Pep Boys employees' enthusiasm demonstrates an attitude that fits with their company's philosophy of giving customers extraordinary "Banner Service." Employees work hard to ensure that customers drive away happy with their car repair and maintenance service.

VALUES, ATTITUDES, AND JOB SATISFACTION

CHAPTER OUTLINE

Values

Attitudes

Job Satisfaction

LEARNING OBJECTIVES

After studying this chapter, you should be able to:

1. Explain the source of an individual's value system.
2. List the dominant values in today's work force.
3. Summarize the relationship between attitudes and behavior.
4. Identify the role consistency plays in attitudes.
5. Explain what determines job satisfaction.
6. State the relationship between job satisfaction and behavior.
7. Describe the current level of job satisfaction among Americans in the workplace.
8. Identify four employee responses to dissatisfaction.

When you prevent me from doing anything I want to do, that is persecution; but when I prevent you from doing anything you want to do, that is law, order, and morals.

G.B. SHAW

Richard Melman's Lettuce Entertain You Enterprises Inc. is becoming the preeminent operator of unique restaurants in America.[1] His restaurants offer cuisines ranging from seafood to Italian and from Greek to Spanish. And he covers the full range of ambiance—from Ed Debevic's 1950s-style diner to Chicago's elegant Pump Room. Lettuce, in fact, has turned dining into theater by developing restaurant chains such as Lawrence of Oregano, Scoozi's, Need Some Dim Some, and Tucci Benucch. Behind these restaurants, however, is a cadre of happy, loyal employees. To Melman's credit, he has worked hard to inspire his 4,000 employees.

Melman runs Lettuce as tightly as McDonald's, but without the stifling standardization. His restaurants thrive on individuality. Equity stakes, extensive employee training, generous benefits, and expanding promotion opportunities have kept the company devoutly entrepreneurial while developing employee loyalty that is unusual in an industry notorious for high turnover. Employees participate in each concept's development. Chefs, managers, designers, and artists are all involved in concocting a "history" of each new eatery. Each restaurant also has its own set of partners, usually longtime Lettuce employees rewarded with the opportunity of ownership.

Melman trusts his workers to be partners because Lettuce has trained them. Nobody is promoted unless he or she has prepared a replacement, and many people started at the bottom and rose through management. For instance, Luis Garcia started at Tucci Benucch in 1987 as a dishwasher who spoke no English. Lettuce adjusted his work schedule so Garcia could take English classes and promoted him through a series of jobs. Today he's a manager at Tucci.

For Melman, treating employees well is simply good business. "If people are happy and able to make a decent living, you can have teamwork," he says. "That falls apart when individuals are unhappy."

Is Melman right? Do happy workers *really* make better employees? It makes intuitive sense that satisfied workers would be more productive, loyal, and committed, but is it true? We answer this and a number of other questions related to values, attitudes, and job satisfaction in this chapter.

Values

Is capital punishment right or wrong? How about racial quotas in hiring—are they right or wrong? If a person likes power, is that good or bad? The answers to these questions are value laden. Some might argue, for example, that capital punishment is right because it is an appropriate retribution for crimes like murder and treason. However, others might argue, just as strongly, that no government has the right to take anyone's life.

values
Basic convictions that a specific mode of conduct or end-state of existence is personally or socially preferable to an opposite or converse mode of conduct or end-state of existence.

value system
A hierarchy based on a ranking of an individual's values in terms of their intensity.

Values represent basic convictions that "a specific mode of conduct or end-state of existence is personally or socially preferable to an opposite or converse mode of conduct or end-state of existence."[2] They contain a judgmental element in that they carry an individual's ideas about what is right, good, or desirable. Values have both content and intensity attributes. The content attribute says that a mode of conduct or end-state of existence is *important*. The intensity attribute specifies *how important* it is. When we rank an individual's values in terms of their intensity, we obtain that person's **value system**. All of us have a hierarchy of values that forms our value system. This system is identified by the relative importance we assign to such values as freedom, pleasure, self-respect, honesty, obedience, and equality.

Importance of Values

Values are important to the study of organizational behavior because they lay the foundation for the understanding of attitudes and motivation and because they influence our perceptions. Individuals enter an organization with precon-

ceived notions of what "ought" and what "ought not" to be. Of course, these notions are not value free. On the contrary, they contain interpretations of right and wrong. Further, they imply that certain behaviors or outcomes are preferred over others. As a result, values cloud objectivity and rationality.

Values generally influence attitudes and behavior.[3] Suppose you enter an organization with the view that allocating pay on the basis of performance is right, whereas allocating pay on the basis of seniority is wrong or inferior. How are you going to react if you find the organization you have just joined rewards seniority and not performance? You're likely to be disappointed—and this can lead to job dissatisfaction and the decision not to exert a high level of effort, since "it's probably not going to lead to more money anyway." Would your attitudes and behavior be different if your values aligned with the organization's pay policies? Most likely.

Sources of Our Value Systems

Where do our value systems come from? A significant portion is genetically determined. The rest is attributable to factors like national culture, parental dictates, teachers, friends, and similar environmental influences.

Studies of twins reared apart demonstrate that about 40 percent of the variation in work values is explained by genetics.[4] So the values of your biological parents play an important part in explaining what your values will be. Still, the majority of the variation in values is due to environmental factors.

When we were children, why did many of our mothers tell us "you should always clean your dinner plate"? Why is it that, at least historically in North America, achievement has been considered good and being lazy has been considered bad? The answer is that, in every culture, certain values have developed over time and are continuously reinforced. Achievement, peace, cooperation, equity, and democracy are societal values that are considered desirable in North America. These values are not fixed, but when they change, they do so very slowly.

A significant portion of the values we hold are established in our early years—from parents, teachers, friends, and others. Many of your early ideas of what is right and wrong were probably formulated from the views expressed by your parents. Think back to your early views on such topics as education, sex, and politics. For the most part, they were the same as those expressed by your parents. As you grew up and were exposed to other value systems, you may have altered a number of your values. For example, in high school, if you joined a social club whose values included the conviction that "every person should carry a gun," there is a good probability you changed your value system to align with that of the members of the club, even if it meant rejecting your parents' value that "only gang members carry guns, and gang members are bad."

Interestingly, values are relatively stable and enduring.[5] This has been explained as a result of both their genetic component and the way in which they're learned.[6] Concerning this second point, we were told as children that certain behaviors or outcomes were always desirable or always undesirable. There were no gray areas. You were told, for example, that you should be honest and responsible. You were never taught to be just a little bit honest or a little bit responsible. It is this absolute, or black-or-white learning of values, when combined with a significant portion of genetic imprinting, that more or less assures their stability and endurance.

The process of questioning our values, of course, may result in a change. We may decide these underlying convictions are no longer acceptable. More often, our questioning merely acts to reinforce those values we hold.

Types of Values

Can we classify values? The answer is: Yes! In this section, we review three approaches to developing value typologies.

ALLPORT AND ASSOCIATES One of the earliest efforts to categorize values was made by Allport and his associates.[7] They identified six types of values:

1. *Theoretical*: Places high importance on the discovery of truth through a critical and rational approach
2. *Economic*: Emphasizes the useful and practical
3. *Aesthetic*: Places the highest value on form and harmony
4. *Social*: Assigns the highest value to the love of people
5. *Political*: Places emphasis on acquisition of power and influence
6. *Religious*: Is concerned with the unity of experience and understanding of the cosmos as a whole

Allport and his associates developed a questionnaire that described a number of different situations and asked respondents to preference-rank a fixed set of answers. Based on their replies, the researchers were able to rank respondents in terms of the importance they gave to each of the six types of values and to identify a value system for each respondent.

Using this approach, it's been found that people in different occupations place different importance on the six value types. For instance, one study compared ministers, purchasing agents, and industrial scientists.[8] Not surprisingly, religious leaders rated religious values most important and economic values least important. Economic values, on the other hand, were found to be of highest importance to purchasing executives.

terminal values
Desirable end-states of existence; the goals that a person would like to achieve during his or her lifetime.

instrumental values
Preferable modes of behavior or means of achieving one's terminal values.

ROKEACH VALUE SURVEY Milton Rokeach created the Rokeach Value Survey (RVS).[9] The RVS consists of two sets of values, with each set containing 18 individual value items. One set, called **terminal values**, refers to desirable end-states of existence. These are the goals a person would like to achieve during his or her lifetime. The other set, called **instrumental values**, refers to preferable modes of behavior, or means of achieving the terminal values. Table 5-1 gives common examples for each of these sets.

Several studies confirm that the RVS values vary among groups.[10] As with Allport's findings, people in the same occupations or categories (e.g., corporate managers, union members, parents, students) tend to hold similar values. For instance, one study comparing corporate executives, members of the steelworkers' union, and members of a community activist group found a good deal of overlap among the three groups,[11] but also some very significant differences (see Table 5-2). The activists had value preferences that were quite different from those of the other two groups. They ranked equality as their most important terminal value; executives and union members ranked this value 14 and 13, respectively. Activists ranked "helpful" as their second highest instrumental value. The other two groups both ranked it 14. These differences are important,

Table 5-1 Terminal and Instrumental Values in Rokeach Value Survey

Terminal Values	Instrumental Values
A comfortable life (a prosperous life)	Ambitious (hardworking, aspiring)
An exciting life (a stimulating, active life)	Broad-minded (open–minded)
A sense of accomplishment (lasting contribution)	Capable (competent, effective)
A world at peace (free of war and conflict)	Cheerful (lighthearted, joyful)
A world of beauty (beauty of nature and the arts)	Clean (neat, tidy)
Equality (brotherhood, equal opportunity for all)	Courageous (standing up for your beliefs)
Family security (taking care of loved ones)	Forgiving (willing to pardon others)
Freedom (independence, free choice)	Helpful (working for the welfare of others)
Happiness (contentedness)	Honest (sincere, truthful)
Inner harmony (freedom from inner conflict)	Imaginative (daring, creative)
Mature love (sexual and spiritual intimacy)	Independent (self-reliant, self-sufficient)
National security (protection from attack)	Intellectual (intelligent, reflective)
Pleasure (an enjoyable, leisurely life)	Logical (consistent, rational)
Salvation (saved, eternal life)	Loving (affectionate, tender)
Self-respect (self-esteem)	Obedient (dutiful, respectful)
Social recognition (respect, admiration)	Polite (courteous, well mannered)
True friendship (close companionship)	Responsible (dependable, reliable)
Wisdom (a mature understanding of life)	Self-controlled (restrained, self-disciplined)

Source: M. Rokeach, *The Nature of Human Values* (New York: Free Press, 1973).

since executives, union members, and activists all have a vested interest in what corporations do. "When corporations and critical stakeholder groups such as these [other] two come together in negotiations or contend with one another over economic and social policies, they are likely to begin with these built-in differences in personal value preferences. . . . Reaching agreement on any specific issue or policy where these personal values are importantly implicated might prove to be quite difficult."[12]

CONTEMPORARY WORK COHORTS Your author has integrated a number of recent analyses of work values into a four-stage model that attempts to capture the unique values of different cohorts, or generations in the U.S. work force.[13] (No assumption is made that this framework would universally apply across all cultures.)[14] Table 5-3 proposes that employees can be segmented by the era in which they entered the work force. Because most people start work between the ages of 18 and 23, the eras also correlate closely with the chronological age of employees.

Workers who grew up influenced by the Great Depression, World War II, U.S. leadership in world manufacturing, the Andrew Sisters, and the Berlin blockade entered the work force from the mid-1940s through the late 1950s believing in the Protestant work ethic. Once hired, they tended to be loyal to their employer. In terms of the terminal values on the RVS, these employees

Table 5-2 Mean Value Rankings of Executives, Union Members, and Activists (Top Five Only)

EXECUTIVES		UNION MEMBERS		ACTIVISTS	
Terminal	**Instrumental**	**Terminal**	**Instrumental**	**Terminal**	**Instrumental**
1. Self-respect	1. Honest	1. Family security	1. Responsible	1. Equality	1. Honest
2. Family security	2. Responsible	2. Freedom	2. Honest	2. A world of peace	2. Helpful
3. Freedom	3. Capable	3. Happiness	3. Courageous	3. Family security	3. Courageous
4. A sense of accomplishment	4. Ambitious	4. Self-respect	4. Independent	4. Self-respect	4. Responsible
5. Happiness	5. Independent	5. Mature love	5. Capable	5. Freedom	5. Capable

Source: Based on W.C. Frederick and J. Weber, "The Values of Corporate Managers and Their Critics: An Empirical Description and Normative Implications," in W.C. Frederick and L.E. Preston (eds.), *Business Ethics: Research Issues and Empirical Studies* (Greenwich, CT: JAI Press, 1990), pp. 123–44.

are likely to place the greatest importance on a comfortable life and family security.

Employees who entered the work force during the 1960s through the mid-1970s were influenced heavily by John F. Kennedy, the civil rights movement, the Beatles, the Vietnam War, and baby-boom competition. They brought with them a large measure of the hippie ethic and existential philosophy. They are more concerned with the quality of their lives than with the amount of money and possessions they can accumulate. Their desire for autonomy has directed their loyalty toward themselves rather than toward the organization that employs them. In terms of the RVS, freedom and equality rate high.

Individuals who entered the work force from the mid-1970s through the late 1980s reflect the society's return to more traditional values, but with far greater emphasis on achievement and material success. As a generation, they were strongly influenced by Reagan conservatism, the defense buildup, dual-

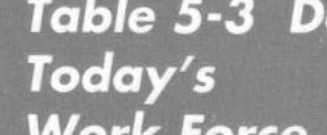

Table 5-3 Dominant Values in Today's Work Force

Stage	Entered the Work Force	Approximate Current Age	Dominant Work Values
I. Protestant work ethic	Mid-1940s to late 1950s	55–75	Hard work, conservative; loyalty to the organization
II. Existential	1960s to mid-1970s	40–55	Quality of life, nonconforming, seeks autonomy; loyalty to self
III. Pragmatic	Mid-1970s to late 1980s	30–40	Success, achievement, ambition, hard work; loyalty to career
IV. Generation X	1990 to present	Under 30	Flexibility, job satisfaction, leisure time; loyalty to relationships

career households, and $150,000 starter homes. Born toward the end of the baby-boom period, these workers are pragmatists who believe that ends can justify means. They see the organizations that employ them merely as vehicles for their careers. Terminal values like a sense of accomplishment and social recognition rank high with them.

Our final category encompasses what has become known as generation X. Their lives have been shaped by globalization, economic stagnation, the fall of communism, MTV, AIDS, and computers. They value flexibility, life options, and the achievement of job satisfaction. Family and relationships are very important to this cohort. Money is important as an indicator of career performance, but they are willing to trade off salary increases, titles, security, and promotions for increased leisure time and expanded lifestyle options. In search of balance in their lives, these more recent entrants into the work force are less willing to make personal sacrifices for the sake of their employer than previous generations were. On the RVS, they rate high on true friendship, happiness, and pleasure.

◆The lives of generation X have been shaped by globalization, economic stagnation, the fall of communism, MTV, AIDS, and computers.

An understanding that individuals' values differ but tend to reflect the societal values of the period in which they grew up can be a valuable aid in explaining and predicting behavior. Employees in their thirties and sixties, for instance, are more likely to be conservative and accepting of authority than their existential coworkers in their forties. And workers under 30 are more likely than the other groups to balk at having to work weekends and more prone to leave a job in midcareer to pursue another that provides more leisure time.

Values, Loyalty, and Ethical Behavior

Did a decline in business ethics set in sometime in the late 1970s? The issue is debatable.[15] Nevertheless, a lot of people think so. If there has been a decline in ethical standards, perhaps we should look to our four-stage model of work co-

Patagonia, manufacturer of products for outdoor enthusiasts, succeeds in creating a work environment attractive to younger workers. About 40 percent of Patagonia's employees are in their twenties. Patagonia meets their needs by providing a nontraditional office environment where everyone works in open spaces rather than in offices. It offers employees a flexible work hours policy and the option of working at the office for five hours a day and at home for three hours. In addition, employees may take a personal leave of absence of as much as four months each year to enjoy extended leisure-time activities. Patagonia donates 1 percent of its sales to various environmental groups, demonstrating a social conscience in tune with young employees' values and engendering their loyalty to the company.

hort values (see Table 5-3) for a possible explanation. After all, managers consistently report that the actions of their bosses is the most important factor influencing ethical and unethical behavior in their organizations.[16] Given this fact, the values of those in middle and upper management should have a significant bearing on the entire ethical climate within an organization.

Through the mid-1970s, the managerial ranks were dominated by Protestant work-ethic types (stage I) whose loyalties were to their employer. When faced with ethical dilemmas, their decisions were made in terms of what was best for their organization. Beginning in the mid-to-late 1970s, individuals with existential values began to rise into the upper levels of management. They were soon followed by pragmatic types. By the late 1980s, a large portion of middle and top management positions in business organizations were held by people from stages II and III.

The loyalty of existentials and pragmatics are to self and careers, respectively. Their focus is inward and their primary concern is with "looking out for Number 1." Such self-centered values would be consistent with a decline in ethical standards. Could this help explain the alleged decline in business ethics beginning in the late 1970s?

The potential good news in this analysis is that recent entrants to the work force, and tomorrow's managers, appear to be less self-centered. Since their loyalty is to relationships, they are more likely to consider the ethical implications of their actions on others around them. The result? We might look forward to an uplifting of ethical standards in business over the next decade or two merely as a result of changing values within the managerial ranks.

Attitudes

attitudes
Evaluative statements or judgments concerning objects, people, or events.

Attitudes are evaluative statements—either favorable or unfavorable—concerning objects, people, or events. They reflect how one feels about something. When I say "I like my job," I am expressing my attitude about work.

Attitudes are not the same as values, but the two are interrelated. You can see this by looking at the three components of an attitude: cognition, affect, and behavior.[17]

cognitive component of an attitude
The opinion or belief segment of an attitude.

affective component of an attitude
The emotional or feeling segment of an attitude.

behavioral component of an attitude
An intention to behave in a certain way toward someone or something.

The belief that "discrimination is wrong" is a value statement. Such an opinion is the **cognitive component** of an attitude. It sets the stage for the more critical part of an attitude—its **affective component**. Affect is the emotional or feeling segment of an attitude and is reflected in the statement "I don't like Jon because he discriminates against minorities." Finally, and we discuss this issue at considerable length later in this section, affect can lead to behavioral outcomes. The **behavioral component** of an attitude refers to an intention to behave in a certain way toward someone or something. So, to continue our example, I might choose to avoid Jon because of my feeling about him.

Viewing attitudes as made up of three components—cognition, affect, and behavior—is helpful toward understanding their complexity and the potential relationship between attitudes and behavior. But for clarity's sake, keep in mind that the term *attitude* essentially refers to the affect part of the three components.

Sources of Attitudes

Attitudes, like values, are acquired from parents, teachers, and peer group members. We are born with certain genetic predispositions.[18] Then, in our early years, we begin modeling our attitudes after those we admire, respect, or maybe even fear. We observe the way family and friends behave, and we shape our attitudes and behavior to align with theirs. People also imitate the attitudes of popular individuals and those they admire and respect. If the "right thing" is to favor eating at McDonald's, you're likely to hold that attitude.

In contrast to values, your attitudes are less stable. Advertising messages, for example, attempt to alter your attitudes toward a certain product or service: If the people at Ford can get you to hold a favorable feeling toward their cars, that attitude may lead to a desirable behavior (for them)—your purchase of a Ford product.

In organizations, attitudes are important because they affect job behavior. If workers believe, for example, that supervisors, auditors, bosses, and time-and-motion engineers are all in conspiracy to make employees work harder for the same or less money, then it makes sense to try to understand how these attitudes were formed, their relationship to actual job behavior, and how they might be changed.

Types of Attitudes

A person can have thousands of attitudes, but OB focuses our attention on a very limited number of job-related attitudes. These job-related attitudes tap positive or negative evaluations that employees hold about aspects of their work environment. Most of the research in OB has been concerned with three attitudes: job satisfaction, job involvement, and organizational commitment.[19]

JOB SATISFACTION The term *job satisfaction* refers to an individual's general attitude toward his or her job. A person with a high level of job satisfaction holds positive attitudes toward the job; a person who is dissatisfied with his or her job holds negative attitudes about the job. When people speak of employee attitudes, more often than not they mean job satisfaction. In fact, the two are frequently used interchangeably. Because of the high importance OB researchers have given to job satisfaction, we review this attitude in considerable detail later in this chapter.

JOB INVOLVEMENT The term **job involvement** is a more recent addition to the OB literature.[20] While there isn't complete agreement over what the term means, a workable definition states that job involvement measures the degree to which a person identifies psychologically with his or her job and considers his or her perceived performance level important to self-worth.[21] Employees with a high level of job involvement strongly identify with and really care about the kind of work they do.

job involvement
The degree to which a person identifies with his or her job, actively participates in it, and considers his or her performance important to self-worth.

High levels of job involvement have been found to be related to fewer absences and lower resignation rates.[22] However, it seems to more consistently predict turnover than absenteeism, accounting for as much as sixteen percent of the variance in the former.[23]

ORGANIZATIONAL COMMITMENT The third job attitude we discuss is **organizational commitment**. It's defined as a state in which an employee identifies with a particular organization and its goals, and wishes to maintain membership in the organization.[24] So high *job involvement* means identifying with one's specific job; high *organizational commitment* means identifying with one's employing organization.

organizational commitment
The degree to which an employee identifies with a particular organization and its goals, and wishes to maintain membership in the organization.

Turnover of professional employees in the health care industry is extremely high, especially for registered nurses, whose high-stress jobs have a high burnout rate. Children's Medical Center of Dallas makes huge efforts to motivate its staff to stay. Joan McGuigan, a registered nurse in the emergency room at Children's, is fiercely loyal to her organization. Although she knows she could make more money at other hospitals, McGuigan drives an hour to her job at the inner-city medical center. Children's inspires loyalty among its professional employees by giving them a sense of purpose, recognizing their contributions, involving them in decision making, and giving them freedom to operate as an independent practice.

As with job involvement, the research evidence demonstrates negative relationships between organizational commitment and both absenteeism and turnover.[25] In fact, studies demonstrate that an individual's level of organizational commitment is a better indicator of turnover than the far more frequently used job satisfaction predictor, explaining as much as 34 percent of the variance.[26] Organizational commitment is probably a better predictor because it is a more global and enduring response to the organization as a whole than is job satisfaction.[27] An employee may be dissatisfied with his or her particular job and consider it a temporary condition, yet not be dissatisfied with the organization as a whole. But when dissatisfaction spreads to the organization itself, individuals are more likely to consider resigning.

Attitudes and Consistency

Did you ever notice how people change what they say so it doesn't contradict what they do? Perhaps a friend of yours has consistently argued that the quality of American cars isn't up to that of the imports and that he'd never own anything but a foreign import. But his dad gives him a late model American-made car, and suddenly they're not so bad. Or, when going through sorority rush, a new freshman believes sororities are good and that pledging a sorority is important. If she fails to make a sorority, however, she may say, "I recognized that sorority life isn't all it's cracked up to be, anyway!"

◆Did you ever notice how people change what they say so it doesn't contradict what they do?

Research has generally concluded that people seek consistency among their attitudes and between their attitudes and their behavior. This means that individuals seek to reconcile divergent attitudes and align their attitudes and behavior so they appear rational and consistent. When there is an inconsistency, forces are initiated to return the individual to an equilibrium state where attitudes and behavior are again consistent. This can be done by altering either the attitudes or the behavior or by developing a rationalization for the discrepancy.

For example, a recruiter for the ABC Company, whose job it is to visit college campuses, identify qualified job candidates, and sell them on the advantages of ABC as a place to work, would be in conflict if he personally believes

◆◆◆◆ OB in the News ◆◆◆◆

How Do Tobacco Executives Live with Themselves?

How do tobacco executives explain their responsibility for a product that kills more than 420,000 Americans a year? How do they reject the overwhelming evidence connecting smoking with lung and throat cancer, emphysema, and heart disease? By insisting that direct causation has not been proved? These executives are quick to point out to critics that their product is legal, they don't encourage nonsmokers to take up smoking, and what they are really promoting is freedom of choice.

Philip Morris is both the largest tobacco company in America and the largest consumer products company in the world. In 1992 it had sales of $59 billion and was the largest taxpayer in the United States. It directly employs 161,000 people worldwide. A *New York Times* reporter spent time interviewing several Philip Morris executives. One of them was Steven C. Parrish, 44, general counsel and senior vice president for external affairs, Philip Morris, U.S.A. He and his wife have a daughter, 11, and a son, 4. For the record, he does smoke cigarettes.

After graduating from the University of Missouri, Parrish joined a Kansas City law firm and later became a partner in the firm. In his law practice he represented Philip Morris on a highly visible case where the tobacco company was sued for contributing to the death of a woman by lung cancer. Soon after that case Philip Morris approached Parrish about working for the company full time.

"I took the job because I liked being a trial lawyer. I enjoy the ego rush you get when you're up and performing in court. And there's something about being an in-house lawyer that had always intrigued me. Philip Morris is a great company in terms of its business success, its reputation, and all that sort of thing. The people really impressed me. And I really like representing the tobacco workers, who run the machinery and make the cigarettes. Really good people—the kind I thought I'd represent when I was growing up [in a small Missouri town]. I also had always wanted to live on the East Coast . . . I didn't have any qualms about joining a tobacco company.

"But I wouldn't be honest with you if I didn't tell you that when I see Sam Donaldson, for example, on *This Week with David Brinkley*, as he did a few months ago, say 'I don't see how an executive with a tobacco company can look himself in the mirror in the morning' . . .It troubles me. The day that happened I was sitting on a couch with my wife and kids. We'd just gotten home from church. I love that show, so as soon as we get home I flip it on, and there's Sam Donaldson saying that. And it was upsetting. If I could just sit down with Sam Donaldson—he's not going to change his attitudes about smoking, but doggone, he'd probably realize that I'm not a bad guy. I've got two little kids. I worry about all the issues that a parent worries about—drugs, AIDS, violence, all that stuff.

"Obviously, one way to deal with that is to say: 'O.K., I'm not going to work for a cigarette company. Then they wouldn't be saying those things about me.' But I feel good about what I do, both in how I go about my job and what my role in the company is, so I try not to let it bother me. But anybody would be hurt if somebody says you are a merchant of death and you shouldn't be able to look yourself in the mirror in the morning. I wish they wouldn't say things like that.

"A year or two ago, my daughter came home from school, and said, 'I have a homework assignment I need you to help me with. Tomorrow we're going to talk about drugs like marijuana, cocaine, and alcohol. We're also going to talk about cigarettes and whether they're addictive. I want to know what you think about cigarettes.' And I told her that a lot of people believe cigarette smoking is addictive but I don't believe it. And I told her the Surgeon General says some 40 million people have quit smoking on their own. But if she asked me about the health consequences, I would tell her that I certainly don't think it's safe to smoke. It's a risk factor for lung cancer. For heart disease. But it's a choice. We're confronted with choices all the time. Still, I'd have to tell her that it might be a bad idea. I don't know. But it might be.

"You might say that we ought to do everything we can do reasonably to make sure that nobody ever smokes another cigarette. But you wouldn't say that people who work for tobacco companies can't look themselves in the mirror because they're somehow lesser human beings than people who work for a drug company or a steel company."

Based on R. Rosenblatt, *New York Times Magazine* (March 20, 1994), pp. 34–41.

the ABC Company has poor working conditions and few opportunities for new college graduates. This recruiter could, over time, find his attitudes toward the ABC Company becoming more positive. He may, in effect, brainwash himself by continually articulating the merits of working for ABC. Another alternative would be for the recruiter to become overtly negative about ABC and the opportunities within the firm for prospective candidates. The original enthusiasm that the recruiter may have shown would dwindle, probably to be replaced by open cynicism toward the company. Finally, the recruiter might acknowledge that ABC is an undesirable place to work, but think that, as a professional recruiter, his obligation is to present the positive side of working for the company. He might further rationalize that no place is perfect to work at; therefore, his job is not to present both sides of the issue, but rather to present a rosy picture of the company.

Cognitive Dissonance Theory

Can we additionally assume from this consistency principle that an individual's behavior can always be predicted if we know his or her attitude on a subject? If Mr. Jones views the company's pay level as too low, will a substantial increase in his pay change his behavior, that is, make him work harder? The answer to this question is, unfortunately, more complex than merely a "Yes" or "No."

cognitive dissonance
Any incompatibility between two or more attitudes or between behavior and attitudes.

Leon Festinger, in the late 1950s, proposed the theory of **cognitive dissonance**.[28] This theory sought to explain the linkage between attitudes and behavior. Dissonance means an inconsistency. Cognitive dissonance refers to any incompatibility that an individual might perceive between two or more of his or her attitudes, or between his or her behavior and attitudes. Festinger argued that any form of inconsistency is uncomfortable and that individuals will attempt to reduce the dissonance and, hence, the discomfort. Therefore, individuals will seek a stable state where there is a minimum of dissonance.

Of course, no individual can completely avoid dissonance. You know that cheating on your income tax is wrong, but you fudge the numbers a bit every year, and hope you're not audited. Or you tell your children to brush after

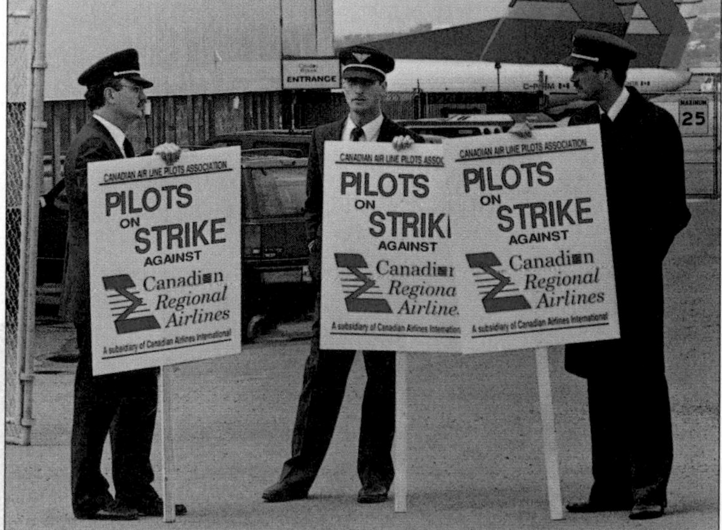

These striking pilots at Canadian Regional Airlines claim to love their work. How, then, can they strike their employer and picket for higher wages? Group pressure from peers and union officials contribute toward dissonance reduction, allowing the pilots to have a positive attitude toward their work and still engage in picketing.

every meal, but *you* don't. So how do people cope? Festinger would propose that the desire to reduce dissonance would be determined by the *importance* of the elements creating the dissonance, the degree of *influence* the individual believes he or she has over the elements, and the *rewards* that may be involved in dissonance.

If the elements creating the dissonance are relatively unimportant, the pressure to correct this imbalance will be low. However, say that a corporate manager—Mrs. Smith—believes strongly that no company should pollute the air or water. Unfortunately, Mrs. Smith, because of the requirements of her job, is placed in the position of having to make decisions that would trade off her company's profitability against her attitudes on pollution. She knows that dumping the company's sewage into the local river (which we assume here for the sake of argument is legal) is in the best economic interest of her firm. What will she do? Clearly, Mrs. Smith is experiencing a high degree of cognitive dissonance. Because of the importance of the elements in this example, we cannot expect Mrs. Smith to ignore the inconsistency. She can follow several paths to deal with her dilemma. Mrs. Smith can change her behavior (stop polluting the river). Or she can reduce dissonance by concluding that the dissonant behavior is not so important after all ("I've got to make a living, and in my role as a corporate decision maker, I often have to place the good of my company above that of the environment or society"). A third alternative would be for Mrs. Smith to change her attitude ("There is nothing wrong in polluting the river"). Still another choice would be to seek out more consonant elements to outweigh the dissonant ones ("The benefits to society from our manufacturing our products more than offset the cost to society of the resulting water pollution").

The degree of influence that individuals believe they have over the elements will have an impact on how they will react to the dissonance. If they perceive the dissonance to be an uncontrollable result—something over which they have no choice—they are less likely to be receptive to attitude change. If, for example, the dissonance-producing behavior is required as a result of the boss's directive, the pressure to reduce dissonance would be less than if the behavior was performed voluntarily. Although dissonance exists, it can be rationalized and justified.

Rewards also influence the degree to which individuals are motivated to reduce dissonance. High rewards accompanying high dissonance tend to reduce the tension inherent in the dissonance. The rewards act to reduce dissonance by increasing the consistency side of the individual's balance sheet.

These moderating factors suggest that just because individuals experience dissonance they will not necessarily move directly toward consistency, that is, toward reduction of this dissonance. If the issues underlying the dissonance are of minimal importance, if an individual perceives that the dissonance is externally imposed and is substantially uncontrollable by him or her, or if rewards are significant enough to offset the dissonance, the individual will not be under great tension to reduce the dissonance.

What are the organizational implications of the theory of cognitive dissonance? It can help to predict the propensity to engage in attitude and behavioral change. If individuals are required, for example, by the demands of their job to say or do things that contradict their personal attitude, they will tend to modify their attitude in order to make it compatible with the cognition of what they have said or done. Additionally, the greater the dissonance—after it has been moderated by importance, choice, and reward factors—the greater the pressures to reduce it.

Measuring the A-B Relationship

We have maintained throughout this chapter that attitudes affect behavior. The early research work on attitudes assumed they were causally related to behavior; that is, the attitudes people hold determine what they do. Common sense, too, suggests a relationship. Isn't it logical that people watch television programs they say they like or that employees try to avoid assignments they find distasteful?

However, in the late 1960s, this assumed relationship between attitudes and behavior (A–B) was challenged by a review of the research.[29] Based on an evaluation of a number of studies that investigated the A–B relationship, the reviewer concluded that attitudes were unrelated to behavior or, at best, only slightly related.[30] More recent research has demonstrated that the A–B relationship can be improved by taking moderating contingency variables into consideration.

MODERATING VARIABLES One thing that improves our chances of finding significant A–B relationships is the use of both specific attitudes and specific behaviors.[31] It is one thing to talk about a person's attitude toward "preserving the environment" and another to speak of his or her attitude toward recycling. The more specific the attitude we are measuring, and the more specific we are in identifying a related behavior, the greater the probability we can show a relationship between A and B. If you ask people today whether they are concerned about preserving the environment, most will probably say "Yes." That doesn't mean, however, that they separate out recyclable items from their garbage. The correlation between a question that asks about concern for protecting the environment and recycling may be only +.20 or so. But as you make the question more specific—by asking, for example, about the degree of personal obligation one feels to separate recyclable items—the A–B relationship is likely to reach +.50 or higher.

Another moderator is social constraints on behavior. Discrepancies between attitudes and behavior may occur because the social pressures on the individual to behave in a certain way may hold exceptional power.[32] Group pressures, for instance, may explain why an employee who holds strong antiunion attitudes attends prounion organizing meetings.

Still another moderating variable is experience with the attitude in question.[33] The A–B relationship is likely to be much stronger if the attitude being evaluated refers to something with which the individual has experience. For instance, most of us will respond to a questionnaire on almost any issue. But is my attitude toward starving fish in the Amazon any indication of whether I'd donate to a fund to save these fish? Probably not! Getting the views of college students with no work experience on job factors that are important in determining whether they would stay put in a job is an example of an attitude response that is unlikely to predict much in terms of actual turnover behavior.

SELF-PERCEPTION THEORY While most A–B studies yield positive results[34]—that attitudes do influence behavior—the relationship tends to be weak before adjustments are made for moderating variables. But requiring specificity, an absence of social constraints, and experience in order to get a meaningful correlation imposes severe limitations on making generalizations about the A–B relationship. This has prompted some researchers to take another direction—to look at whether behavior influences attitudes. This view, called **self-perception theory**, has generated some encouraging findings. Let's briefly review the theory.[35]

self-perception theory
Attitudes are used after the fact to make sense out of an action that has already occurred.

When asked about an attitude toward some object, individuals recall their behavior relevant to that object and then infer their attitude from their past behavior. So if an employee was queried on her feelings about being a payroll clerk at Exxon, she would likely think, "I've had this same job at Exxon as a payroll clerk for ten years, so I must like it!" Self-perception theory, therefore, argues that attitudes are used, *after the fact*, to make sense out of an action that has already occurred rather than as devices that precede and guide action.

Self-perception theory has been well supported.[36] While the traditional attitude–behavior relationship is generally positive, it is also weak. In contrast, the behavior–attitude relationship is quite strong. So what can we conclude? It seems we're very good at finding reasons for what we do, but not so good at doing what we find reasons for.[37]

An Application: Attitude Surveys

The preceding review should not discourage us from using attitudes to predict behavior. In an organizational context, most of the attitudes management would seek to inquire about would be ones with which employees have some experience. If the attitudes in question are specifically stated, management should obtain information that can be valuable in guiding their decisions relative to these employees. But how does management get information about employee attitudes? The most popular method is through the use of **attitude surveys**.[38]

attitude surveys
Eliciting responses from employees through questionnaires about how they feel about their jobs, work groups, supervisors, and/or the organization.

Table 5-4 illustrates what an attitude survey might look like. Typically, attitude surveys present the employee with a set of statements or questions. Ideally, the items are tailored to obtain the specific information that management desires. An attitude score is achieved by summing up responses to individual

Table 5-4 Sample Attitude Survey

Answer each of the following statements using the following rating scale:

5 = Strongly agree
4 = Agree
3 = Undecided
2 = Disagree
1 = Strongly disagree

Statement	Rating
1. This company is a pretty good place to work.	___
2. I can get ahead in this company if I make the effort.	___
3. This company's wage rates are competitive with those of other companies.	___
4. Employee promotion decisions are handled fairly.	___
5. I understand the various fringe benefits the company offers.	___
6. My job makes the best use of my abilities.	___
7. My work load is challenging but not burdensome.	___
8. I have trust and confidence in my boss.	___
9. I feel free to tell my boss what I think.	___
10. I know what my boss expects of me.	___

questionnaire items. These scores can then be averaged for job groups, departments, divisions, or the organization as a whole.

Results from attitude surveys frequently surprise management. For instance, Michael Gilliland owns and operates a chain of 12 food markets.[39] He and his management team developed a ten-item job satisfaction questionnaire, which they administer to all employees twice a year. Recently Gilliland was surprised to find the worst complaints coming from employees at the store with the best working conditions and the most benefits. Careful analysis of the results uncovered that, although the manager at this store was well liked, employees were frustrated because he was behind on their performance reviews and had failed to fire a particularly unproductive employee. As one of Gilliland's associates put it, "We'd assumed it would be the happiest store, but it wasn't."

A corporatewide attitude survey at BP Exploration revealed that employees were unhappy with the way their direct superiors managed them.[40] In response, management introduced a formal upward appraisal system that allows the company's 12,000 employees to evaluate their boss's managerial performance. Now managers pay a lot more attention to the needs of their employees because their employees' opinions play an important part in determining the manager's future in the organization.

From Concepts to Skills

Changing Attitudes

Can you change unfavorable employee attitudes? Sometimes! It depends on who you are, the strength of the employee attitude, the magnitude of the change, and the technique you choose to try to change the attitude.[41]

Employees are most likely to respond to change efforts made by someone who is liked, credible, and convincing. If people like you, they're more apt to identify and adopt your message. Credibility implies trust, expertise, and objectivity. So you're more likely to change an employee's attitude if that employee sees you as believable, knowledgeable about what you're talking about, and unbiased in your presentation. Finally, successful attitude change is enhanced when you present your arguments clearly and persuasively.

It's easier to change an employee's attitude if he or she isn't strongly committed to it. Conversely, the stronger the belief about the attitude, the harder it is to change it. In addition, attitudes that have been expressed publicly are more difficult to change because it requires one to admit he or she has made a mistake.

It's easier to change attitudes when that change isn't very significant. To get an employee to accept a new attitude that varies greatly from his or her current position requires more effort. It may also threaten other deeply held attitudes and create increased dissonance.

All attitude change techniques are not equally effective across situations. Oral persuasion techniques are most effective when you use a positive, tactful tone; present strong evidence to support your position; tailor your argument to the listener; use logic; and support your evidence by appealing to the employee's fears, frustrations, and other emotions. But people are more likely to embrace change when they can experience it. The use of training sessions where employees share and personalize experiences, and practice new behaviors, can be powerful stimulants for change. Consistent with self-perception theory, changes in behavior can lead to changes in attitudes.

Using attitude surveys on a regular basis provides managers with valuable feedback on how employees perceive their working conditions. Consistent with our discussion of perceptions in Chapter 4, the policies and practices that management views as objective and fair may be seen as inequitable by employees in general or by certain groups of employees. That these distorted perceptions have led to negative attitudes about the job and organization should be important to management. This is because employee behaviors are based on perceptions, not reality. Remember, the employee who quits because she believes she is underpaid—when, in fact, management has objective data to support that her salary is highly competitive—is just as gone as if she had actually been underpaid. The use of regular attitude surveys can alert management to potential problems and employees' intentions early so that action can be taken to prevent repercussions.[42]

Attitudes and Work Force Diversity

Managers are increasingly concerned with changing employee attitudes to reflect shifting perspectives on racial, gender, and other diversity issues. A comment to a coworker of the opposite sex that 15 years ago might have been taken as a compliment can today become a career-limiting episode.[43] As such, organizations are investing in training to help reshape attitudes of employees.

In 1993 a survey of U.S. organizations with 100 or more employees found that 47 percent of them sponsored some sort of diversity training.[44] Some examples: Police officers in Escondido, California, receive 36 hours of diversity training each year. Pacific Gas & Electric Co. requires a minimum of four hours of training for its 12,000 employees. The Federal Aviation Administration sponsors a mandatory eight-hour diversity seminar for its Western-Pacific-region employees.

What do these diversity programs look like, and how do they address attitude change?[45] They almost all include a self-evaluation phase. People are pressed to examine themselves and to confront ethnic and cultural stereotypes they might hold. Then participants typically take part in group discussions or panels with representatives from diverse groups. So, for instance, a Hmong man might describe his family's life in Southeast Asia, and explain why they

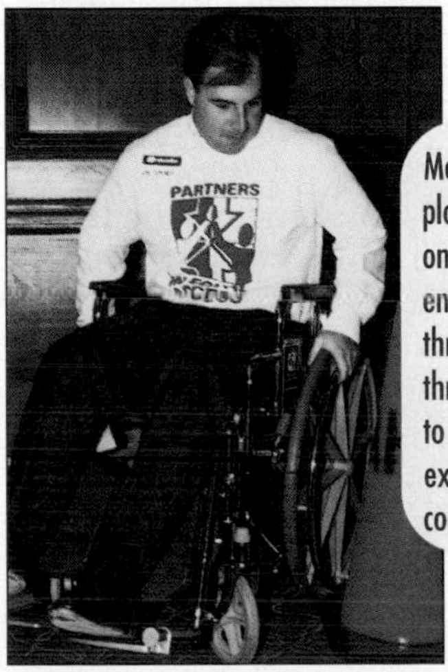

Meridian Bancorp Inc. provides diversity training to sensitize employees to the needs of disabled co-workers and bank customers. In one training exercise, employees who are not disabled (such as the employee shown here), sit in a wheelchair and try to maneuver through an obstacle course. In other exercises, employees try to read through a pair of eyeglasses smeared with petroleum jelly and listen to audio tapes with plugged ears. These exercises allow employees to experience what it might be like to have a disability and help to dispel common myths and stereotypes associated with disabilities.

resettled in California; or a lesbian might describe how she discovered her sexual identity, and the reaction of her friends and family when she came out.

Additional activities designed to change attitudes include arranging for people to do volunteer work in community or social service centers in order to meet face to face with individuals and groups from diverse backgrounds and using exercises that let participants feel what it's like to be different. For example, when participants see the film *Eye of the Beholder*, where people are segregated and stereotyped according to their eye color, participants see what it's like to be judged by something they have no control over.

Job Satisfaction

We have already discussed job satisfaction briefly—earlier in this chapter as well as in Chapter 1. We want to dissect the concept more carefully here. How do we measure job satisfaction? Are most workers today satisfied with their jobs? What determines job satisfaction? What is its effect on employee productivity, absenteeism, and turnover rates? We answer each of these questions in this section.

Measuring Job Satisfaction

We previously defined job satisfaction as an individual's general attitude toward his or her job. This definition is clearly a very broad one.[46] Yet this is inherent in the concept. Remember, a person's job is more than just the obvious activities of shuffling papers, waiting on customers, or driving a truck. Jobs require interaction with coworkers and bosses, following organizational rules and policies, meeting performance standards, living with working conditions that are often less than ideal, and the like.[47] This means an employee's assessment of how satisfied or dissatisfied he or she is with his or her job is a complex summation of a number of discrete job elements. How, then, do we measure the concept?

The two most widely used approaches are a *single global rating* and a *summation score* made up of a number of job facets. The single global rating method is nothing more than asking individuals to respond to one question, such as "All things considered, how satisfied are you with your job?" Respondents then reply by circling a number between 1 and 5 that corresponds with answers from "Highly Satisfied" to "Highly Dissatisfied." The other approach—a summation of job facets—is more sophisticated. It identifies key elements in a job and asks for the employee's feelings about each. Typical factors that would be included are the nature of the work, supervision, present pay, promotion opportunities, and relations with coworkers.[48] These factors are rated on a standardized scale and then added up to create an overall job satisfaction score.

Is one of the foregoing approaches superior to the other? Intuitively, it would seem that summing up responses to a number of job factors would achieve a more accurate evaluation of job satisfaction. The research, however, doesn't support this intuition.[49] This is one of those rare instances in which simplicity wins out over complexity. Comparisons of one-question global ratings with the more lengthy summation-of-job-factors method indicate that the former is more valid. The best explanation for this outcome is that the concept of job satisfaction is inherently so broad, the single question actually becomes a more inclusive measure.

The Status of Job Satisfaction in the Workplace Today

Are American workers satisfied with their jobs? The answer to this question, based on numerous studies, seems to be "Yes." Moreover, the numbers are surprisingly constant over time. Let's take a closer look at what we know.

Regardless of what studies you choose to look at, when employees are asked if they are satisfied with their jobs, the results tend to be very similar: Between 70 and 80 percent of American workers report they are satisfied with their jobs.[50] Older workers report the highest satisfaction (92 percent for those age 65 and over), but even young people—under age 25—report high levels of satisfaction (73 percent).[51]

While there was some concern in the late 1970s that satisfaction was declining across almost all occupational groups,[52] recent reinterpretations of these data and additional longitudinal studies indicate that job satisfaction levels have held steady for decades—through economic recessions as well as prosperous times.[53]

These results don't mean that people are satisfied with *all* aspects of their job. As Table 5-5 illustrates, fewer than half of employees report they are satisfied with advancement opportunities, recognition, and pay.

How does one explain these generally positive results? Taken literally, we can say that whatever it is people want from their jobs, they seem to be getting it and have been for quite some time, at least if we believe what people say in job satisfaction surveys. But if we dig a little deeper, we might question this literal interpretation. For instance, based on our knowledge of cognitive dissonance theory, we might expect employees to resolve inconsistencies between dissatisfaction with their jobs and their staying with those jobs by not reporting the dissatisfaction. Also, when employees are asked whether they would again choose the same work or whether they would want their children to follow in their footsteps, typically less than half answer in the affirmative.[54] So maybe employees aren't as satisfied with their jobs as the numbers would suggest.

Table 5-5 Responses on Dimensions of Job Satisfaction

The following represents the percentage of workers responding they were satisfied when asked: How satisfied are you with these aspects of your job?

	PERCENTAGE OF WORKERS SAYING THEY WERE SATISFIED			
Dimension	**1984**	**1988**	**1990**	**1992**
Type of work	78	80	77	79
Coworkers	76	77	77	76
Benefits	81	77	74	71
Being treated with respect and fairness	64	62	60	58
Job security	63	64	59	58
Chances to contribute ideas	54	55	56	54
Pay	57	50	47	46
Recognition for performance	44	48	45	39
Advancement opportunities	33	36	34	27

Source: International Survey Research Corp., Employee Satisfaction Surveys, Chicago, 1984, 1988, 1990, 1992. As reported in *INC.* (November 1992), p. 102.

Another explanation for the high stability of job satisfaction findings over time can be attributed to genetics.[55] Analysis of satisfaction data for a selected sample of individuals over a 50-year period found that individual results were consistently stable over time, even when these people changed the employer for whom they worked and their occupation. It may well be that many of the work-related variables we think cause job satisfaction aren't that important. Rather, most individuals' disposition toward life—positive or negative—is established by adolescence, holds over time, carries over into their disposition toward work, and—at least among Americans—is generally upbeat.

What Determines Job Satisfaction?

We now turn to the question: What work-related variables determine job satisfaction? An extensive review of the literature indicates that the more important factors conducive to job satisfaction are mentally challenging work, equitable rewards, supportive working conditions, and supportive colleagues.[56]

MENTALLY CHALLENGING WORK Employees tend to prefer jobs that give them opportunities to use their skills and abilities and offer a variety of tasks, freedom, and feedback on how well they are doing. These characteristics make work mentally challenging. Jobs that have too little challenge create boredom, but too much challenge creates frustration and feelings of failure. Under conditions of moderate challenge, most employees will experience pleasure and satisfaction.[57]

EQUITABLE REWARDS Employees want pay systems and promotion policies that they perceive as being just, unambiguous, and in line with their expectations. When pay is seen as fair based on job demands, individual skill level, and community pay standards, satisfaction is likely to result. Of course, not everyone seeks money. Many people willingly accept less money to work in a preferred location or in a less demanding job or to have greater discretion in the work they do and the hours they work. But the key in linking pay to satisfaction is not the absolute amount one is paid; rather, it is the perception of fairness. Similarly, employees seek fair promotion policies and practices. Promotions provide opportunities for personal growth, more responsibilities, and increased social status. Individuals who perceive that promotion decisions are made in a fair and just manner, therefore, are likely to experience satisfaction from their jobs.[58]

SUPPORTIVE WORKING CONDITIONS Employees are concerned with their work environment for both personal comfort and facilitating doing a good job. Studies demonstrate that employees prefer physical surroundings that are not dangerous or uncomfortable. Temperature, light, noise, and other environmental factors should not be at either extreme—for example, having too much heat or too little light. Additionally, most employees prefer working relatively close to home, in clean and relatively modern facilities, and with adequate tools and equipment.

SUPPORTIVE COLLEAGUES People get more out of work than merely money or tangible achievements. For most employees, work also fills the need for social interaction. Not surprisingly, therefore, having friendly and supportive coworkers leads to increased job satisfaction. The behavior of one's boss

Ronna Adams says she felt like "Queen for a Day" on her 20th-year anniversary with Walgreen's. While she was having a celebratory lunch, co-workers prepared a giant surprise party for Ronna, a bookkeeper. Research indicates that supportive colleagues like Ronna's leads to increased job satisfaction. In an industry noted for high turnover, supportive colleagues contribute to keeping Walgreen's resignations low. One-third of Walgreen's employees have five or more years of company service and 7 percent have over 15 years.

also is a major determinant of satisfaction. Studies generally find that employee satisfaction is increased when the immediate supervisor is understanding and friendly, offers praise for good performance, listens to employees' opinions, and shows a personal interest in them.

DON'T FORGET THE PERSONALITY–JOB FIT In Chapter 3, we presented Holland's personality–job fit theory. As you remember, one of Holland's conclusions was that high agreement between an employee's personality and occupation results in a more satisfied individual. His logic was essentially this: People with personality types congruent with their chosen vocations should find they have the right talents and abilities to meet the demands of their jobs; are thus more likely to be successful on those jobs; and, because of this success, have a greater probability of achieving high satisfaction from their work. Studies to replicate Holland's conclusions have been almost universally supportive.[59] It's important, therefore, to add this to our list of factors that determine job satisfaction.

The Effect of Job Satisfaction on Employee Performance

Managers' interest in job satisfaction tends to center on its effect on employee performance. Researchers have recognized this interest, so we find a large number of studies that have been designed to assess the impact of job satisfaction on employee productivity, absenteeism, and turnover. Let's look at the current state of our knowledge.

SATISFACTION AND PRODUCTIVITY A number of reviews were done in the 1950s and 1960s covering dozens of studies that sought to establish the relationship between satisfaction and productivity.[60] These reviews could find no consistent relationship. In the 1990s, though the studies are far from unambiguous, we can make some sense out of the evidence.

The early views on the satisfaction–performance relationship can be essentially summarized in the statement "a happy worker is a productive worker." Much of the paternalism shown by managers in the 1930s, 1940s, and 1950s—forming company bowling teams and credit unions, having company picnics, providing counseling services for employees, training supervisors to be sensitive to the concerns of subordinates—was done to make workers happy. But belief in the happy worker thesis was based more on wishful thinking than hard evidence. A careful review of the research indicates that if there is a positive relationship between satisfaction and productivity, the correlations are consistently low—in the vicinity of +0.14.[61] However, introduction of moderating variables has improved the relationship.[62] For example, the relationship is stronger when the employee's behavior is not constrained or controlled by outside factors. An employee's productivity on machine-paced jobs, for instance, is going to be much more influenced by the speed of the machine than his or her level of satisfaction. Similarly, a stockbroker's productivity is largely constrained by the general movement of the stock market. When the market is moving up and volume is high, both satisfied and dissatisfied brokers are going to ring up lots of commissions. Conversely, when the market is in the doldrums, the level of broker satisfaction is not likely to mean much. Job level also seems to be an important moderating variable. The satisfaction–performance correlations are stronger for higher level employees. Thus we might expect the relationship to be more relevant for individuals in professional, supervisory, and managerial positions.

Another point of concern in the satisfaction–productivity issue is the direction of the causal arrow. Most of the studies on the relationship used research designs that could not prove cause and effect. Studies controlled for this possibility indicate the more valid conclusion is that productivity leads to satisfaction rather than the other way around.[63] If you do a good job, you intrinsically feel good about it. Additionally, assuming the organization rewards productivity, your higher productivity should increase verbal recognition, your pay level, and probabilities for promotion. These rewards, in turn, increase your level of satisfaction with the job.

The most recent research provides renewed support for the original satisfaction–performance relationship.[64] When satisfaction and productivity data is gathered for the organization as a whole, rather than at the individual level, we find that organizations with more satisfied employees tended to be more effective than organizations with less satisfied employees. If this conclusion can be reproduced in additional studies, it may well be that the reason we haven't gotten strong support for the *satisfaction causes productivity thesis* is that studies have focused on individuals rather than the organization and that individual-level measures of productivity don't take into consideration all the interactions and complexities in the work process.

SATISFACTION AND ABSENTEEISM We find a consistent negative relationship between satisfaction and absenteeism, but the correlation is moderate—usually less than 0.40.[65] While it certainly makes sense that dissatisfied employees are more likely to miss work, other factors have an impact on the relationship and reduce the correlation coefficient. For example, remember our discussion of sick pay versus well pay in Chapter 3. Organizations that provide liberal sick leave benefits are encouraging all their employees—including those who are highly satisfied—to take days off. Assuming you have a reasonable number of varied interests, you can find work satisfying and yet still take off work to enjoy a three-day weekend, tan yourself on a warm summer day, or watch the World Series on television if those days come free with no penalties. Also, as with productivity, outside factors can act to reduce the correlation.

An excellent illustration of how satisfaction directly leads to attendance, where there is a minimum impact from other factors, is a study done at Sears, Roebuck.[66] Satisfaction data were available on employees at Sears's two headquarters in Chicago and New York. Additionally, it is important to note that Sears's policy was not to permit employees to be absent from work for avoidable reasons without penalty. The occurrence of a freak April 2 snowstorm in Chicago created the opportunity to compare employee attendance at the Chicago office with attendance in New York, where the weather was quite nice. The interesting dimension in this study is that the snowstorm gave the Chicago employees a built-in excuse not to come to work. The storm crippled the city's transportation, and individuals knew they could miss work this day with no penalty. This natural experiment permitted the comparison of attendance records for satisfied and dissatisfied employees at two locations—one where you were expected to be at work (with normal pressures for attendance) and the other where you were free to choose with no penalty involved. If satisfaction leads to attendance, where there is an absence of outside factors, the more satisfied employees should have come to work in Chicago while dissatisfied employees should have stayed home. The study found that, on this April 2 day, absenteeism rates in New York were just as high for satisfied groups of workers as for dissatisfied groups. But in Chicago, the workers with high satisfaction scores had much higher attendance than did those with lower satisfaction levels. These findings are exactly what we would have expected if satisfaction is negatively correlated with absenteeism.

SATISFACTION AND TURNOVER Satisfaction is also negatively related to turnover, but the correlation is stronger than what we found for absenteeism.[67] Yet, again, other factors such as labor market conditions, expectations about alternative job opportunities, and length of tenure with the organization are important constraints on the actual decision to leave one's current job.[68]

Evidence indicates that an important moderator of the satisfaction–turnover relationship is the employee's level of performance.[69] Specifically,

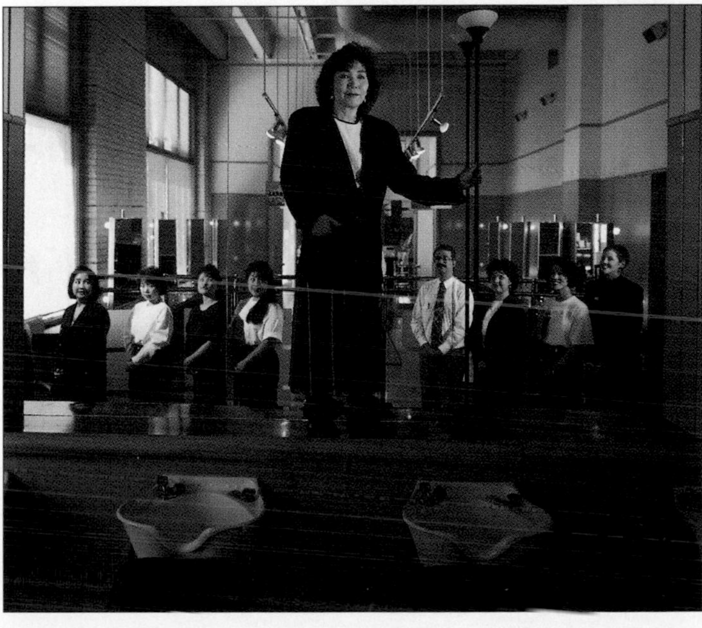

Increased job satisfaction has helped Kay Hirai, owner of Studio 904 hair salons, reduce turnover. Because they are paid in commissions and tips, stylists are highly individualistic and tend to guard their clients. Hirai has her stylists work as empowered teams and pays them a salary—no tips or commissions—plus benefits such as medical and dental coverage, paid vacation, and sick days. Each Monday Hirai closes her salons and trains stylists in new styles and techniques, how to work in teams, and how to deliver exceptional service. She posts daily, weekly, and monthly financial results and distributes 25 percent of her profits to employees as bonuses every two weeks. Stylists are happy because they're not competing with co-workers, the salons' client base of 4,500 is growing by 170 a month, and Hirai says stylists don't pass through Studio 904 "like it was a revolving door."

level of satisfaction is less important in predicting turnover for superior performers. Why? The organization typically makes considerable efforts to keep these people. They get pay raises, praise, recognition, increased promotional opportunities, and so forth. Just the opposite tends to apply to poor performers. Few attempts are made by the organization to retain them. There may even be subtle pressures to encourage them to quit. We would expect, therefore, that job satisfaction is more important in influencing poor performers to stay than superior performers. Regardless of level of satisfaction, the latter are more likely to remain with the organization because the receipt of recognition, praise, and other rewards gives them more reasons for staying.

Consistent with our previous discussions regarding the stability of an individual's job satisfaction level over time, we shouldn't be surprised to find that a person's general disposition toward life also moderates the satisfaction–turnover relationship.[70] Specifically, some individuals generally gripe more than others and such individuals, when dissatisfied with their jobs, are less likely to quit than those who are more positively disposed toward life. So if two workers report the same level of job dissatisfaction, the one most likely to quit is the one with the highest predisposition to be happy or satisfied in general.

How Employees Can Express Dissatisfaction

One final point before we leave the issue of job satisfaction: Employee dissatisfaction can be expressed in a number of ways.[71] For example, rather than quit, employees can complain, be insubordinate, steal organizational property, or shirk a part of their work responsibilities. Figure 5-1 offers four responses that differ from one another along two dimensions: constructiveness/destructiveness and activity/passivity. They are defined as follows:[72]

exit
Dissatisfaction expressed through behavior directed toward leaving the organization.

Exit: Behavior directed toward leaving the organization. Includes looking for a new position as well as resigning.

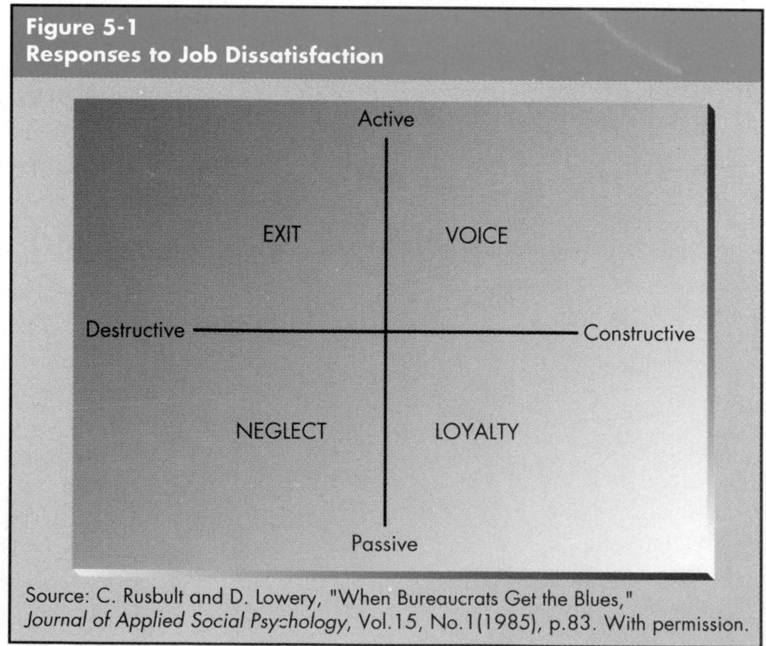

Figure 5-1
Responses to Job Dissatisfaction

Source: C. Rusbult and D. Lowery, "When Bureaucrats Get the Blues," *Journal of Applied Social Psychology*, Vol.15, No.1(1985), p.83. With permission.

Voice: Actively and constructively attempting to improve conditions. Includes suggesting improvements, discussing problems with superiors, and some forms of union activity.

Loyalty: Passively but optimistically waiting for conditions to improve. Includes speaking up for the organization in the face of external criticism and trusting the organization and its management to "do the right thing."

Neglect: Passively allowing conditions to worsen. Includes chronic absenteeism or lateness, reduced effort, and increased error rate.

voice
Dissatisfaction expressed through active and constructive attempts to improve conditions.

loyalty
Dissatisfaction expressed by passively waiting for conditions to improve.

neglect
Dissatisfaction expressed through allowing conditions to worsen.

Exit and neglect behaviors encompass our performance variables—productivity, absenteeism, and turnover. But this model expands employee response to include voice and loyalty, constructive behaviors that allow individuals to tolerate unpleasant situations or to revive satisfactory working conditions. It helps us understand situations, such as those sometimes found among unionized workers, where low job satisfaction is coupled with low turnover.[73] Union members often express dissatisfaction through the grievance procedure or through formal contract negotiations. These voice mechanisms allow the union members to continue in their jobs while convincing themselves they are acting to improve the situation.

Summary and Implications for Managers

Why is it important to know an individual's values? Although they don't have a direct impact on behavior, values strongly influence a person's attitudes. So knowledge of an individual's value system can provide insight into his or her attitudes.

Given that people's values differ, managers can use the Rokeach Value Survey to assess potential employees and determine if their values align with the dominant values of the organization. An employee's performance and satisfaction are likely to be higher if his or her values fit well with the organization. For instance, the person who places high importance on imagination, independence, and freedom is likely to be poorly matched with an organization that seeks conformity from its employees. Managers are more likely to appreciate, evaluate positively, and allocate rewards to employees who fit in, and employees are more likely to be satisfied if they perceive they do fit. This argues for management to strive during the selection of new employees to find job candidates who not only have the ability, experience, and motivation to perform, but also a value system that is compatible with the organization's.

Managers should be interested in their employees' attitudes because attitudes give warnings of potential problems and because they influence behavior. Satisfied and committed employees, for instance, have lower rates of turnover and absenteeism. Given that managers want to keep resignations and absences down—especially among their more productive employees—they will want to do those things that will generate positive job attitudes.

Managers should also be aware that employees will try to reduce cognitive dissonance. More important, dissonance can be managed. If employees are required to engage in activities that appear inconsistent to them or are at odds with their attitudes, the pressures to reduce the resulting dissonance are lessened when the employee perceives the dissonance is externally imposed and is beyond his or her control or if the rewards are significant enough to offset the dissonance.

For Review

1. Contrast the Protestant work ethic, existential, pragmatic, and generation X typologies with the terminal values identified in the Rokeach Value Survey.
2. Contrast the cognitive and affective components of an attitude.
3. What is cognitive dissonance and how is it related to attitudes?
4. What is self-perception theory? How does it increase our ability to predict behavior?
5. What contingency factors can improve the statistical relationship between attitudes and behavior?
6. What role do genetics and personality play in determining an individual's job satisfaction?
7. Are happy workers productive workers?
8. What is the relationship between job satisfaction and absenteeism? Turnover? Which is the stronger relationship?
9. How can managers get employees to more readily accept working with colleagues who are different from themselves?
10. Contrast exit, voice, loyalty, and neglect as employee responses to job dissatisfaction.

For Discussion

1. "Thirty-five years ago, young employees we hired were ambitious, conscientious, hardworking, and honest. Today's young workers don't have the same values." Do you agree or disagree with this manager's comments? Support your position.
2. Do you think there might be any positive and significant relationship between the possession of certain personal values and successful career progression in organizations like Merrill Lynch, the AFL-CIO, and the city of Cleveland's police department? Discuss.
3. "Managers should do everything they can to enhance the job satisfaction of their employees." Do you agree or disagree? Support your position.
4. Discuss the advantages and disadvantages of using regular attitude surveys to monitor employee job satisfaction.
5. Most people indicate they're reasonably satisfied with their jobs. Why? How might you go about determining if such satisfaction is real or only apparent?

Point

The Importance of High Job Satisfaction

The importance of job satisfaction is obvious. Managers should be concerned with the level of job satisfaction in their organizations for at least three reasons: (1) there is clear evidence that dissatisfied employees skip work more often and are more likely to resign; (2) it has been demonstrated that satisfied employees have better health and live longer; and (3) satisfaction on the job carries over to the employee's life outside the job.

We reviewed the evidence between satisfaction and withdrawal behaviors in this chapter. That evidence was fairly clear. Satisfied employees have lower rates of both turnover and absenteeism. If we consider the two withdrawal behaviors separately, however, we can be more confident about the influence of satisfaction on turnover. Specifically, satisfaction is strongly and consistently negatively related to an employee's decision to leave the organization. Although satisfaction and absence are also negatively related, conclusions regarding the relationship should be more guarded.

An often overlooked dimension of job satisfaction is its relationship to employee health. Several studies have shown that employees who are dissatisfied with their jobs are prone to health setbacks ranging from headaches to heart disease. Some research even indicates that job satisfaction is a better predictor of length of life than is physical condition or tobacco use. These studies suggest that dissatisfaction is not solely a psychological phenomenon. The stress that results from dissatisfaction apparently increases one's susceptibility to heart attacks and the like. For managers, this means that even if satisfaction didn't lead to less voluntary turnover and absence, the goal of a satisfied work force might be justifiable because it would reduce medical costs and the premature loss of valued employees by way of heart disease or strokes.

Our final point in support of job satisfaction's importance is the spin-off effect that job satisfaction has for society as a whole. When employees are happy with their jobs, it improves their lives off the job. In contrast, the dissatisfied employee carries that negative attitude home. In wealthy countries such as the United States, Canada, Great Britain, Australia, or Japan, doesn't management have a responsibility to provide jobs from which employees can receive high satisfaction? Some benefits of job satisfaction accrue to every citizen in society. Satisfied employees are more likely to be satisfied citizens. These people will hold a more positive attitude toward life in general and make for a society of more psychologically healthy people.

The evidence is impressive. Job satisfaction is important. For management, a satisfied work force translates into higher productivity due to fewer disruptions caused by absenteeism or good employees quitting, as well as into lower medical and life insurance costs. Additionally, there are benefits for society in general. Satisfaction on the job carries over to the employee's off-the-job hours. So the goal of high job satisfaction for employees can be defended in terms of both dollars and cents and social responsibility.

counterPoint

Job Satisfaction Has Been Overemphasized

Few issues have been more blown out of proportion than the importance of job satisfaction at work. Let's look closely at the evidence.

No consistent relationship indicates that satisfaction leads to productivity. And, after all, isn't productivity the name of the game? Organizations are not altruistic institutions. Management's obligation is to use efficiently the resources that it has available. It has no obligation to create a satisfied work force if the costs exceed the benefits. As one executive put it, "I don't care if my people are happy or not! Do they produce?"

It would be naive to assume that satisfaction alone would have a major impact on employee behavior. As a case in point, consider the issue of turnover. Certainly a number of other factors have an equal or greater impact on whether an employee decides to remain with an organization or take a job somewhere else—length of time on the job, financial situation, and availability of other jobs, to name the most obvious. If I'm 55 years old, have been with my company 25 years, perceive few other opportunities in the job market, and have no other source of income besides my job, does my unhappiness have much impact on my decision to stay with the organization? No!

Did you ever notice who seems to be most concerned with improving employee job satisfaction? It's usually college professors and researchers! They've chosen careers that provide them with considerable freedom and opportunities for personal growth. They place a very high value on job satisfaction. The problem is that they impose their values on others. Because job satisfaction is important to them, they suppose it's important to everyone. To a lot of people, a job is merely the means to get the money they need to do the things they desire during their nonworking hours. Assuming you work 40 hours a week and sleep 8 hours a night, you still have 70 hours or more a week to achieve fulfillment and satisfaction in off-the-job activities. So the importance of job satisfaction may be oversold when you recognize there are other sources—outside the job—where the dissatisfied employee can find satisfaction.

A final point against overemphasizing job satisfaction: Consider the issue in a contingency framework. Even if satisfaction was significantly related to performance, it's unlikely the relationship would hold consistently across all segments of the work force. In fact, evidence demonstrates that people differ in terms of the importance that work plays in their lives. To some, the job is their central life interest. But for the majority of people, their primary interests are off the job. Non-job-oriented people tend not to be emotionally involved with their work. This relative indifference allows them to accept frustrating conditions at work more willingly. Importantly, the majority of the work force probably falls into this non-job-oriented category. So while job satisfaction might be important to lawyers, surgeons, and other professionals, it may be irrelevant to the average worker because he or she is generally apathetic about the job's frustrating elements.

Learning About Yourself Exercise

What Do You Value?

Below are 16 items. Rate how important each one is to you on a scale of 0 (not important) to 100 (very important). Write the number on the line to the left of each item.

Not important				Somewhat important				Very important		
0	10	20	30	40	50	60	70	80	90	100

90 1. An enjoyable, satisfying job.
60 2. A high-paying job.
90 3. A good marriage.
60 4. Meeting new people; social events.
30 5. Involvement in community activities.
60 6. My religion.
50 7. Exercising, playing sports.
80 8. Intellectual development.
80 9. A career with challenging opportunities.
60 10. Nice cars, clothes, home, etc.
90 11. Spending time with family.
60 12. Having several close friends.
20 13. Volunteer work for not-for-profit organizations, like the cancer society.
60 14. Meditation, quiet time to think, pray, etc.
60 15. A healthy, balanced diet.
50 16. Educational reading, TV, self-improvement programs, etc.

Turn to page A-27 for scoring directions and key.

Source: R.N. Lussier, *Human Relations in Organizations: A Skill Building Approach*, 2nd ed. (Homewood, IL: Richard D. Irwin, 1993). With permission.

Working With Others Exercise

Assessing Work Attitudes

Objective
To compare attitudes about the work force.

Time
Approximately 30 minutes.

Procedure
Answer the following five questions:

1. *Generally*, American workers (pick one)
___ a. are highly motivated and hardworking
___ b. try to give a fair day's effort
___ c. will put forth effort if you make it worthwhile
___ d. try to get by with a low level of effort
___ e. are lazy and/or poorly motivated

2. The people I have worked with (pick one)
   ___ a. are highly motivated and hardworking
   ___ b. try to give a fair day's effort
   ___ c. will put forth effort if you make it worthwhile
   ___ d. try to get by with a low level of effort
   ___ e. are lazy and/or poorly motivated
3. Compared to foreign workers, American workers are (pick one)
   ___ a. more productive
   ___ b. equally productive
   ___ c. less productive
4. Over the past twenty years, American workers have (pick one)
   ___ a. improved in overall quality of job performance
   ___ b. remained about the same in quality of job performance
   ___ c. deteriorated in overall quality of job performance
5. If you have a low opinion of the U.S. work force, give the one step (or action) that could be taken that would lead to the most improvement.

Evaluation

1. Break into groups of three to five members each. Compare your answers to the five questions.
2. For each question where one or more members disagree, discuss why each member chose his or her answer.
3. After this discussion, members are free to change their original answer. Did any in your group do so?
4. Your instructor will provide data from other student attitude responses to these questions, then lead the class in discussing the implications or accuracy of these attitudes.

Source: Based on D. R. Brown, "Dealing with Student Conceptions and Misconceptions About Worker Attitudes and Productivity," *Journal of Management Education* (May 1991), pp. 259–64.

Ethical Dilemma Exercise

Dissatisfaction and Whistle-blowing

As briefly introduced in Chapter 4, whistle-blowing refers to disclosing illegal, immoral, or illegitimate practices to authorities inside and/or outside the organization. Most cases described in the media involve someone who informs an outsider—a newspaper reporter, a government official, a public pressure group—about an assumed injustice, irresponsible action, or violation of law engaged in by an organization or by an employee of an organization. For instance, several engineers at Morton Thiokol complained, wrote memos, and "blew the whistle" to draw attention to design flaws in the O-rings that went into the space shuttle *Challenger*. Their cries were ignored and the result was the tragic loss of seven astronauts. When an MIT scientist exposed false research data in a scientific article coauthored by a Nobel laureate, she was fired from her job. These examples of whistle blowing illustrate it is an active, but risky and controversial, response to dissatisfaction.

What makes whistle-blowing risky and controversial? First are the possible negative repercussions for the whistle-blower, who is often punished for tarnishing the organization's reputation or embarrassing some key people in the organization. That punishment can be as extreme as being fired and blackballed, making it almost impossible for the whistle-blower to find another job in the industry. Second is the question of the whistle-blower's motives. Is he or she acting altruistically, that is, strictly to benefit others without regard to repercussions or retaliation? Or does the whistle-blower intend to gain personal rewards? For instance, an employee at Singer Corp. was awarded $7.5 million by a court for providing evidence that a unit of Singer cheated the Pentagon out of $77 million.

Do you think whistle-blowing reflects disloyalty to the organization? Would you ever blow the whistle if you were aware of an illegal or unethical practice by your employer? What kind of actions would you consider worth blowing the whistle over?

Binney & Smith

Binney & Smith (B&S) operates a plant in Lindsay, Ontario, to produce crayons. Their Crayola brand is familiar to almost every preschooler and young grade schooler in North America.

In 1992 the production goals for the Lindsay plant were doubled, to 4 million 16-stick boxes of assorted color crayons. Little more than a year earlier, the plant produced about a quarter of that volume. Maybe somewhat surprisingly, employees have been very receptive to these much higher production goals. These employees, most of whom have been with the company for at least ten years, indicate they're more excited about their jobs and more satisfied with their working lives than ever before.

Workers at B&S traditionally knew their own jobs well, and many of these jobs were repetitive and unchallenging. For instance, one job is to run the machine that glues labels to crayon sticks—172 labels per minute. The label gluing machine operator was an expert at his job but knew little about the other jobs in the plant. But to get the increased production, management redesigned the label gluing machine operator's job and almost everybody else's too.

Workers in the Lindsay plant now do their jobs in teams and are encouraged to learn the jobs of everyone else on their team. Team members regularly rotate jobs to increase their skills and reduce boredom. These teams have taken on the responsibility for solving their work problems. And employees in the plant now also have taken charge of tracking production, changing layouts as needed to solve quality problems, and conceiving and implementing cost reduction ideas like recycling waste.

Employees receive no financial or material rewards for accepting these new changes. What they do get is increased recognition, the opportunity to learn new tasks, and greater control over their work. The results have been extremely encouraging for both employees and management. Employees have increased job satisfaction and self-esteem. And the plant has more than doubled its profit in the first year of these new changes. Additionally, employees at Lindsay now have greater job security than they had before because the plant has eliminated the 15 to 25 percent cost disadvantage it previously labored under compared to the company's sister plants in the United States.

Questions

1. How does the B&S experience in its Lindsay plant compare with the evidence on the satisfaction–productivity relationship described in this chapter? Explain why it might confirm or contradict the research.
2. B&S's historical turnover rate has been very low. Why do you think that is? Shouldn't a plant with boring and repetitive jobs like gluing 172 labels a minute on crayon sticks have high absenteeism and turnover?
3. Explain why, in spite of tremendously high new production goals, B&S employees seem more satisfied with their jobs than ever.

Source: Based on J. Wells, "Winning Colours," *Report on Business Magazine* (July 1992); cited in S.P. Robbins and R. Stuart-Kotze, *Management: Canadian Fourth Edition* (Scarborough, Ontario: Prentice Hall Canada, 1994), p. 449.

Between Two Worlds

Karen Gunn is a full-time mediator of cultural differences. She works for the Korean American Community Services agency and her job is to try to improve relations between Koreans and African Americans in Chicago's inner city.

Karen was hired by Korean merchants to try to change the negative attitudes and stereotypes that many Koreans and African Americans have about each other. And it's no easy job. A great number of animosities have developed between these two groups.

According to African Americans, Korean businesspeople look down on blacks. They believe that Koreans think all blacks are criminals, that they're poor, and that they steal. "They follow you all through the stores," says a black woman, "like you're going to steal something, and I think it's uncalled for." Gunn found that some blacks believe the Korean merchants even have some secret source of funding, or that they were wealthy in Korea. For the most part, this isn't true. The reality is that most of the Korean merchants had limited funds when they arrived in the United States.

Part of the problem between the two groups is cultural differences. In the Korean culture, "You don't look a person in the eye. You don't smile. Expressions, emotions are not something that are readily shown, not at all," says Gunn. Also, Koreans don't like to touch people they don't know well. So, for instance, Koreans may seem standoffish when giving change. "Blacks interpret these behaviors as being rude."

Gunn (herself an African American) points out, however, that part of the resentment of blacks toward Korean merchants is just the fact that they aren't black. "Before the Korean merchant, it was the Jewish merchant. Before it was the Jewish merchant, it was someone else. To constantly have your community run by someone else is a sign of dependence upon others, as if you can't do it for yourselves. And a lot of people take offense at that because we can do it by ourselves or for ourselves."

What is Karen Gunn doing to try to change attitudes? "I'm asking them to respect each other enough to sit down and listen to the other." Her goal is gentle persuasion, to make sure Korean merchants treat black customers with respect. She inspects the quality of merchandise, the service, and things like a merchant's exchange policy to ensure it is equitable and within the law. She's trying to educate each group about their differences and encouraging them to be a little bit more tolerant.

Karen Gunn's work seems to be making a difference. Says a Chicago alderman, "The gap was wide, and it's closer together now. On a scale of 1 to 10, the gap was at 10 in the 1980s. Now it's like 5 or 4."

Questions

1. How were the negative attitudes described here formed?
2. Does cognitive dissonance apply to this situation? Explain.
3. What specific suggestions, in addition to what Karen is already doing, would you make to help Karen change the attitudes of Korean and African Americans about each other?

Source: "Between Two Worlds," *DYO* (July 5, 1993).

Suggestions for Further Reading

CONNOR, P.E., and B.W. BECKER, "Personal Values and Management: What Do We Know and Why Don't We Know More?" *Journal of Management Inquiry* (March 1994), pp. 67–73.

JUDGE, T.A., and C.L. HULIN, "Job Satisfaction as a Reflection of Disposition: A Multiple Source Causal Analysis," *Organizational Behavior and Human Decision Processes* (December 1993), pp. 388–421.

JUDGE, T.A., and S. WATANABE, "Another Look at the Job Satisfaction-Life Satisfaction Relationship," *Journal of Applied Psychology* (December 1993), pp. 939–48.

MAWHINNEY, T.C., "Job Satisfaction as a Management Tool and Responsibility," *Journal of Organizational Behavior Management* (Winter 1989), pp. 187–91.

MEGLINO, B.M., E.C. RAVLIN, and C.L. ADKINS, "The Measurement of Work Value Congruence: A Field Study Comparison," *Journal of Management* (March 1992), pp. 33–43.

MEINDL, J.R., R.G. HUNT, and W. LEE, "Individualism-Collectivism and Work Values: Data from the United States, China, Taiwan, Korea, and Hong Kong," in G.R. Ferris and K.M. Rowland (eds.), *Research in Personnel and Human Resource Management* (Greenwich, CT: JAI Press, 1989), pp. 57–59.

MISUMI, J., "Attitudes to Work in Japan and the West," *Long Range Planning* (August 1993), pp. 66–71.

MOSKAL, B.S., "A Shadow Between Values and Reality," *Industry Week* (May 16, 1994), pp. 23–26.

SMITH, P.C., "In Pursuit of Happiness: Why Study General Job Satisfaction?" in C.J. Cranny, P.C. Smith, and E.F. Stone (eds.), *Job Satisfaction* (New York: Lexington Books, 1992), pp. 5–19.

STAW, B.M., and S.G. BARSADE, "Affect and Managerial Performance: A Test of the Sadder-But-Wiser vs. Happier-and-Smarter Hypothesis," *Administrative Science Quarterly* (June 1993), pp. 304–31.

Notes

[1] This is based on L. Therrien, "Why Rich Melman is Really Cooking," *Business Week* (November 2, 1992), pp. 127–28.

[2] M. Rokeach, *The Nature of Human Values* (New York: Free Press, 1973), p. 5.

[3] See, for instance, J.H. Barnett and M.J. Karson, "Personal Values and Business Decisions: An Exploratory Investigation," *Journal of Business Ethics* (July 1987), pp. 371–82.

[4] L.M. Keller, T.J. Bouchard, Jr., R.D. Arvey, N.L. Segal, and R.V. Dawis, "Work Values: Genetic and Environmental Influences," *Journal of Applied Psychology* (February 1992), pp. 79–88.

[5] M. Rokeach and S.J. Ball-Rokeach, "Stability and Change in American Value Priorities, 1968–1981," *American Psychologist* (May 1989), pp. 775–84.

[6] M. Rokeach, *The Nature of Human Values*, p. 6.

[7] G.W. Allport, P.E. Vernon, and G. Lindzey, *Study of Values* (Boston: Houghton Mifflin, 1951).

[8] R. Tagiuri, "Purchasing Executive: General Manager or Specialist?" *Journal of Purchasing* (August 1967), pp. 16–21.

[9] Rokeach, *The Nature of Human Values*.

[10] J.M. Munson and B.Z. Posner, "The Factorial Validity of a Modified Rokeach Value Survey for Four Diverse Samples," *Educational and Psychological Measurement* (Winter 1980), pp. 1073–79; and W.C. Frederick and J. Weber, "The Values of Corporate Managers and Their Critics: An Empirical Description and Normative Implications," in W.C. Frederick and L.E. Preston (eds.), *Business Ethics: Research Issues and Empirical Studies* (Greenwich, CT: JAI Press, 1990), pp. 123–44.

[11] Frederick and Weber, "The Values of Corporate Managers and Their Critics."

[12] Ibid., p. 132.

[13] See, for example, D.J. Cherrington, S.J. Condie, and J.L. England, "Age and Work Values," *Academy of Management Journal* (September 1979), pp. 617–23; J.A. Raelin, "The '60s Kids in the Corporation: More Than Just 'Daydream Believers,' " *Academy of Management Executive* (February 1987), pp. 21–30; W. Shapiro, "A Generation Takes Power," *Time* (November 16, 1992), pp. 57–60; L. Zinn, "Move Over, Boomers," *Business Week* (December 14, 1992), pp. 74–82; A. Harmon, "For GenX, the *Angst* Is On-Line," *Los Angeles Times* (April 28, 1993), p. A1; S. Ratan, "Generational Tension in the Office: Why Busters Hate Boomers," *Fortune* (October 4, 1993), pp. 56–70; P. O'Toole, "Redefining Success," *Working Woman* (November 1993), pp. 49–55, 100; and B. Filipczak, "It's Just a Job: Generation X at Work," *Training* (April 1994), pp. 21–27.

[14] As noted to your author by R. Volkema and R.L. Neal, Jr., of American University, this model may also be limited in its application to minority populations and recent immigrants to North America.

[15] R.E. Hattwick, Y. Kathawala, M. Monipullil, and L. Wall, "On the Alleged Decline in Business Ethics," *Journal of Behavioral Economics* (Summer 1989), pp. 129–43.

[16] B.Z. Posner and W.H. Schmidt, "Values and the American Manager: An Update Updated," *California Management Review* (Spring 1992), p. 86.

[17] S.J. Breckler, "Empirical Validation of Affect, Behavior, and Cognition as Distinct Components of Attitude," *Journal of Personality and Social Psychology* (May 1984), pp. 1191–1205.

[18] See R.D. Arvey and T.J. Bouchard, Jr., "Genetics, Twins, and Organizational Behavior," in B.M. Staw and L.L. Cummings (eds.), *Research in Organizational Behavior*, Vol. 16 (Greenwich, CT: JAI Press, 1994), pp. 66–68 for evidence demonstrating a genetic basis for attitude development and expression.

[19] P.P. Brooke Jr., D.W. Russell, and J.L. Price, "Discriminant Validation of Measures of Job Satisfaction, Job Involvement, and Organizational Commitment," *Journal of Applied Psychology* (May 1988), pp. 139–45.

[20] See, for example, S. Rabinowitz and D.T. Hall, "Organizational Research in Job Involvement," *Psychological Bulletin* (March 1977), pp. 265–88; G.J. Blau, "A Multiple Study Investigation of the Dimensionality of Job Involvement," *Journal of Vocational Behavior* (August 1985), pp. 19–36; and N.A. Jans, "Organizational Factors and Work Involvement," *Organizational Behavior and Human Decision Processes* (June 1985), pp. 382–96.

[21] Based on G.J. Blau and K.R. Boal, "Conceptualizing How Job Involvement and Organizational Commitment Affect Turnover and Absenteeism," *Academy of Management Review* (April 1987), p. 290.

[22] G.J. Blau, "Job Involvement and Organizational Commitment as Interactive Predictors of Tardiness and Absenteeism," *Journal of Management* (Winter 1986), pp. 577–84; and K. Boal and R. Cidambi, "Attitudinal Correlates of Turnover and Absenteeism: A Meta Analysis," paper presented at the meeting of the American Psychological Association, Toronto, Canada, 1984.

[23] G. Farris, "A Predictive Study of Turnover," *Personnel Psychology* (Summer 1971), pp. 311–28.

[24] Blau and Boal, "Conceptualizing," p. 290.

[25] See, for instance, P.W. Hom, R. Katerberg, and C.L. Hulin, "Comparative Examination of Three Approaches to the Prediction of Turnover," *Journal of Applied Psychology* (June 1979), pp. 280–90; H. Angle and J. Perry, "Organizational Commitment: Individual and Organizational Influence," *Work and Occupations* (May 1983), pp. 123–46; and J.L. Pierce and R.B. Dunham, "Organizational Commitment: Pre-Employment Propensity and Initial Work Experiences," *Journal of Management* (Spring 1987), pp. 163–78.

[26] Hom, Katerberg, and Hulin, "Comparative Examination"; and R.T. Mowday, L.W. Porter, and R.M. Steers, *Employee Or-*

ganization Linkages: The Psychology of Commitment, Absenteeism, and Turnover (New York: Academic Press, 1982).

[27] L.W. Porter, R.M. Steers, R.T. Mowday, and P.V. Boulian, "Organizational Commitment, Job Satisfaction, and Turnover Among Psychiatric Technicians," *Journal of Applied Psychology* (October 1974), pp. 603–609.

[28] L. Festinger, *A Theory of Cognitive Dissonance* (Stanford, CA: Stanford University Press, 1957).

[29] A.W. Wicker, "Attitude versus Action: The Relationship of Verbal and Overt Behavioral Responses to Attitude Objects," *Journal of Social Issues* (Autumn 1969), pp. 41–78.

[30] Ibid., p. 65.

[31] T.A. Heberlein and J.S. Black, "Attitudinal Specificity and the Prediction of Behavior in a Field Setting," *Journal of Personality and Social Psychology* (April 1976), pp. 474–79.

[32] H. Schuman and M.P. Johnson, "Attitudes and Behavior," in A. Inkeles (ed.), *Annual Review of Sociology* (Palo Alto, CA: Annual Reviews, 1976), pp. 161–207.

[33] R.H. Fazio and M.P. Zanna, "Direct Experience and Attitude-Behavior Consistency," in L. Berkowitz (ed.), *Advances in Experimental Social Psychology* (New York: Academic Press, 1981), pp. 161–202.

[34] L.R. Kahle and H.J. Berman, "Attitudes Cause Behaviors: A Cross-Lagged Panel Analysis," *Journal of Personality and Social Psychology* (March 1979), pp. 315–21; and C.L. Kleinke, "Two Models for Conceptualizing the Attitude-Behavior Relationship," *Human Relations* (April 1984), pp. 333–50.

[35] D.J. Bem, "Self-Perception Theory," in L. Berkowitz (ed.), *Advances in Experimental Social Psychology*, Vol. 6 (New York: Academic Press, 1972), pp. 1–62.

[36] See, for example, C.A. Kiesler, R.E. Nisbett, and M.P. Zanna, "On Inferring One's Belief from One's Behavior," *Journal of Personality and Social Psychology* (April 1969), pp. 321–27.

[37] R. Abelson, "Are Attitudes Necessary?" in B.T. King and E. McGinnies (eds.), *Attitudes, Conflicts, and Social Change* (New York: Academic Press, 1972), p. 25.

[38] See, for example, G.E. Lyne, "How to Measure Employee Attitudes," *Training and Development Journal* (December 1989), pp. 40–43; and P. Hise, "The Motivational Employee-Satisfaction Questionnaire," *INC.* (February 1994), pp. 73–75.

[39] P. Hise, "The Motivational Employee-Satisfaction Questionnaire."

[40] I. Barmash, "More Substance Than Show," *Across the Board* (May 1993), pp. 43–45.

[41] This box is based on P.G. Zimbardo, E.B. Ebbesen and C. Maslach, *Influencing Attitudes and Changing Behavior* (Reading, MA: Addison-Wesley, 1977); R.E. Petty and J.T. Cacioppo, *Attitudes and Persuasion: Central and Peripheral Routes to Persuasion* (New York: Springer-Verlag, 1984); and A. Bednar and W.H. Levie, "Attitude-Change Principles," in C. Fleming and W.H. Levie (eds.), *Instructional Message Design: Principles from the Behavioral and Cognitive Sciences*, 2nd ed. (Englewood Cliffs, NJ: Educational Technology Publications, 1993).

[42] See G. Gallup, "Employee Research: From Nice to Know to Need to Know," *Personnel Journal* (August 1988), pp. 42–43; and T. Lammers, "The Essential Employee Survey," *INC.* (December 1992), pp. 159–61.

[43] M. Crawford, "The New Office Etiquette," *Canadian Business* (May 1993), pp. 22–31.

[44] Cited in A. Rossett and T. Bickham, "Diversity Training: Hope, Faith and Cynicism," *Training* (January 1994), p. 40.

[45] This section is based on A. Rossett and T. Bickham, "Diversity Training," pp. 40–46.

[46] For problems with the concept of job satisfaction, see R. Hodson, "Workplace Behaviors," *Work and Occupations* (August 1991), pp. 271–90.

[47] The Wyatt Company's 1989 national WorkAmerica study identified 12 dimensions of satisfaction: work organization, working conditions, communications, job performances and performance review, coworkers, supervision, company management, pay, benefits, career development and training, job content and satisfaction, and company image and change.

[48] See J.L. Price and C.W. Mueller, *Handbook of Organizational Measurement* (Marshfield, MA: Pitman, 1986), pp. 223–27.

[49] V. Scarpello and J.P. Campbell, "Job Satisfaction: Are All the Parts There?" *Personnel Psychology* (Autumn 1983), pp. 577–600.

[50] See, for instance, studies cited in A.F. Chelte, J. Wright, and C. Tausky, "Did Job Satisfaction Really Drop During the 1970s?" *Monthly Labor Review* (November 1982), pp. 33–36; "Job Satisfaction High in America, Says Conference Board Study," *Monthly Labor Review* (February 1985), p. 52; and C. Hartman and S. Pearlstein, "The Joy of Working," *INC.* (November 1987), pp. 61–66. See also "Wyatt WorkAmerica," published by The Wyatt Company, 1990.

[51] "Job Satisfaction High in America," p. 52.

[52] G.L. Staines and R.P. Quinn, "American Workers Evaluate the Quality of Their Jobs," *Monthly Labor Review* (January 1979), pp. 3–12.

[53] Chelte, Wright, Tausky, "Did Job Satisfaction Really Drop?"; and B.M. Staw, N.E. Bell, and J.A. Clausen, "The Dispositional Approach to Job Attitudes: A Lifetime Longitudinal Test," *Administrative Science Quarterly* (March 1986), pp. 56–77.

[54] R.L. Kahn, "The Meaning of Work: Interpretation and Proposals of Measurement," in A. Campbell and P.E. Converse (eds.), *The Human Meaning of Social Change* (New York: Russell Sage Foundation, 1972).

[55] For the data and arguments on this issue, see Staw, Bell, and Clausen, "The Dispositional Approach to Job Attitudes"; R.D. Arvey, T.J. Bouchard, Jr., N.L. Segal, and L.M. Abraham, "Job Satisfaction: Environmental and Genetic Components," *Journal of Applied Psychology* (April 1989), pp. 187–92; B. Gerhart, "How Important Are Dispositional Factors as Determinants of Job Satisfaction? Implications for Job Design and Other Personnel Programs," *Journal of Ap-*

plied Psychology (August 1987), pp. 366–73; A. Davis-Blake and J. Pfeffer, "Just a Mirage: The Search for Dispositional Effects in Organizational Research," *Academy of Management Review* (July 1989), pp. 385–400; R.D. Arvey, G.W. Carter, and D.K. Buerkley, "Job Satisfaction: Dispositional and Situational Influences," in C.L. Cooper and I.T. Robertson (eds.), *International Review of Industrial and Organizational Psychology*, Vol. 6 (Chichester, England: Wiley, 1991), pp. 359–83; R. Cropanzano and K. James, "Some Methodological Considerations for the Behavioral Genetic Analysis of Work Attitudes," *Journal of Applied Psychology* (June 1990), pp. 433–39; T.J. Bouchard, Jr., R.D. Arvey, L.M. Keller, and N.L. Segal, "Genetic Influences on Job Satisfaction: A Reply to Cropanzano and James," *Journal of Applied Psychology* (February 1992), pp. 89–93; and R.D. Arvey and T.J. Bouchard, Jr., "Genetics, Twins, and Organizational Behavior," in B.M. Staw and L.L. Cummings (eds.), *Research in Organizational Behavior.*

[56] E.A. Locke, "The Nature and Causes of Job Satisfaction," in M.D. Dunnette (ed.), *Handbook of Industrial and Organizational Psychology* (Chicago: Rand McNally, 1976), pp. 1319–28.

[57] R.A. Katzell, D.E. Thompson, and R.A. Guzzo, "How Job Satisfaction and Job Performance Are and Are Not Linked," in C.J. Cranny, P.C. Smith, and E.F. Stone (eds.), *Job Satisfaction* (New York: Lexington Books, 1992), pp. 195–217.

[58] L.A. Witt and L.G. Nye, "Gender and the Relationship Between Perceived Fairness of Pay or Promotion and Job Satisfaction," *Journal of Applied Psychology* (December 1992), pp. 910–17.

[59] See, for example, D.C. Feldman and H.J. Arnold, "Personality Types and Career Patterns: Some Empirical Evidence on Holland's Model," *Canadian Journal of Administrative Science* (June 1985), pp. 192–210.

[60] A.H. Brayfield and W.H. Crockett, "Employee Attitudes and Employee Performance," *Psychological Bulletin* (September 1955), pp. 396–428; F. Herzberg, B. Mausner, R.O. Peterson, and D.F. Capwell, *Job Attitudes: Review of Research and Opinion* (Pittsburgh: Psychological Service of Pittsburgh, 1957); V.H. Vroom, *Work and Motivation* (New York: Wiley, 1964); G.P. Fournet, M.K. Distefano, Jr., and M.W. Pryer, "Job Satisfaction: Issues and Problems," *Personnel Psychology* (Summer 1966), pp. 165–83.

[61] Vroom, *Work and Motivation*; and M.T. Iaffaldano and P.M. Muchinsky, "Job Satisfaction and Job Performance: A Meta-Analysis," *Psychological Bulletin* (March 1985), pp. 251–73.

[62] See, for example, J.B. Herman, "Are Situational Contingencies Limiting Job Attitude–Job Performance Relationship?" *Organizational Behavior and Human Performance* (October 1973), pp. 208–24; and M.M. Petty, G.W. McGee, and J.W. Cavender, "A Meta-Analysis of the Relationship Between Individual Job Satisfaction and Individual Performance," *Academy of Management Review* (October 1984), pp. 712–21.

[63] C.N. Greene, "The Satisfaction–Performance Controversy," *Business Horizons* (February 1972), pp. 31–41; E.E. Lawler III, *Motivation in Organizations* (Monterey, CA: Brooks/Cole, 1973); and Petty, McGee, and Cavender, "A Meta-Analysis of the Relationship Between Individual Job Satisfaction and Individual Performance."

[64] C. Ostroff, "The Relationship Between Satisfaction, Attitudes, and Performance: An Organizational Level Analysis," *Journal of Applied Psychology* (December 1992), pp. 963–74.

[65] Locke, "The Nature and Causes of Job Satisfaction," p. 1331; S.L. McShane, "Job Satisfaction and Absenteeism: A Meta-Analytic Re-Examination," *Canadian Journal of Administrative Science* (June 1984), pp. 61–77; R.D. Hackett and R.M. Guion, "A Reevaluation of the Absenteeism-Job Satisfaction Relationship," *Organizational Behavior and Human Decision Processes* (June 1985), pp. 340–81; K.D. Scott and G.S. Taylor, "An Examination of Conflicting Findings on the Relationship Between Job Satisfaction and Absenteeism: A Meta-Analysis," *Academy of Management Journal* (September 1985), pp. 599–612; and R.D. Hackett, "Work Attitudes and Employee Absenteeism: A Synthesis of the Literature," paper presented at 1988 National Academy of Management Conference, Anaheim, CA, August 1988.

[66] F.J. Smith, "Work Attitudes as Predictors of Attendance on a Specific Day," *Journal of Applied Psychology* (February 1977), pp. 16–19.

[67] Brayfield and Crockett, "Employee Attitudes"; Vroom, *Work and Motivation*; J. Price, *The Study of Turnover* (Ames: Iowa State University Press, 1977); and W.H. Mobley, R.W. Griffeth, H.H. Hand, and B.M. Meglino, "Review and Conceptual Analysis of the Employee Turnover Process," *Psychological Bulletin* (May 1979), pp. 493–522.

[68] See, for example, C.L. Hulin, M. Roznowski, and D. Hachiya, "Alternative Opportunities and Withdrawal Decisions: Empirical and Theoretical Discrepancies and an Integration," *Psychological Bulletin* (July 1985), pp. 233–50; and J.M. Carsten and P.E. Spector, "Unemployment, Job Satisfaction, and Employee Turnover: A Meta-Analytic Test of the Muchinsky Model," *Journal of Applied Psychology* (August 1987), pp. 374–81.

[69] D.G. Spencer and R.M. Steers, "Performance as a Moderator of the Job Satisfaction-Turnover Relationship," *Journal of Applied Psychology* (August 1981), pp. 511–14.

[70] T.A. Judge, "Does Affective Disposition Moderate the Relationship Between Job Satisfaction and Voluntary Turnover?" *Journal of Applied Psychology* (June 1993), pp. 395–401.

[71] S.M. Puffer, "Prosocial Behavior, Noncompliant Behavior, and Work Performance Among Commission Salespeople," *Journal of Applied Psychology* (November 1987), pp. 615–21; J. Hogan and R. Hogan, "How to Measure Employee Reliability," *Journal of Applied Psychology* (May 1989), pp. 273–79; and C.D. Fisher and E.A. Locke, "The New Look in Job Satisfaction Research and Theory," in C.J. Cranny, P.C. Smith, and E.F. Stone (eds.), *Job Satisfaction*, pp. 165–94.

[72] See D. Farrell, "Exit, Voice, Loyalty, and Neglect as Responses to Job Dissatisfaction: A Multidimensional Scaling Study," *Academy of Management Journal* (December 1983),

pp. 596 606; C.E. Rusbult, D. Farrell, G. Rogers, and A.G. Mainous III, "Impact of Exchange Variables on Exit, Voice, Loyalty, and Neglect: An Integrative Model of Responses to Declining Job Satisfaction," *Academy of Management Journal* (September 1988), pp. 599–627; M.J. Withey and W.H. Cooper, "Predicting Exit, Voice, Loyalty, and Neglect," *Administrative Science Quarterly* (December 1989), pp. 521–39; and D. Farrell, C. Rusbult, Y-H Lin, and P. Bernthall, "Impact of Job Satisfaction, Investment Size, and Quality of Alternatives on Exit, Voice, Loyalty, and Neglect Responses to Job Dissatisfaction: A Cross-Legged Panel Study," in L.R. Jauch and J.L. Wall (eds.), *Proceedings of the 50th Annual Academy of Management Conference* (San Francisco: 1990), pp. 211–15.

[73] R.B. Freeman,"Job Satisfaction as an Economic Variable," *American Economic Review* (January 1978), pp. 135–41.

CHAPTER 6

Mary Kay Cosmetics motivates its salesforce by recognizing their achievements during an annual sales rally. High achievers are feted in a crowning ceremony and win trips, jewelry, cars, and other prizes for their hard work.

BASIC MOTIVATION CONCEPTS

CHAPTER OUTLINE

LEARNING OBJECTIVES

After studying this chapter, you should be able to:

1. Outline the motivation process.
2. Describe Maslow's need hierarchy.
3. Contrast Theory X and Theory Y.
4. Differentiate motivators from hygiene factors.
5. List the characteristics that high achievers prefer in a job.
6. Summarize the types of goals that increase performance.
7. State the impact of underrewarding employees.
8. Clarify the key relationships in expectancy theory.

When someone says, "It's not the money, it's the principle," it's the money!
—ANONYMOUS

Lincoln Electric is a Cleveland-based firm that employs about 2,400 people and generates 90 percent of its sales from manufacturing arc-welding equipment and supplies. Founded in 1895, the company's legendary profit-sharing incentive system and resultant productivity record are the envy of the manufacturing world.[1]

Factory workers at Lincoln receive piece-rate wages with no guaranteed minimum hourly pay. After working for the firm for two years, employees begin to participate in the year-end bonus plan. Determined by a formula that considers the company's gross profits, the employees' base piece rate, and merit rating, it may be the most lucrative bonus system for factory workers in American manufacturing. The average size of the bonus over the past 55 years has been 95.5 percent of base wages!

The company has a guaranteed employment policy, which it put in place in 1958. Since that time, it has not laid off a single worker. In return for job security, however, employees agree to several things. During slow times, they will accept reduced work periods. They also agree to accept work transfers, even to lower paid jobs, if that is necessary to maintain a minimum of 30 hours of work per week.

You'd think the Lincoln Electric system would attract quality people, and it does. For instance, the company recently hired four Harvard MBAs to fill future management slots. But, consistent with company tradition, they started out, like everyone else, doing piecework on the assembly line.

Lincoln Electric's profit-sharing incentive system has provided positive benefits for the company as well as for its employees. One company executive estimates that Lincoln's overall productivity is about double that of its domestic competitors. The company has earned a profit every year since the depths of the 1930s Depression and has never missed a quarterly dividend. And Lincoln has one of the lowest employee turnover rates in U.S. industry.

Lincoln Electric has successfully integrated employment security, financial incentives, job flexibility, and high productivity standards into a system that motivates its employees. Most organizations haven't been so successful. This may explain why the concept of motivation is probably the most researched and discussed topic in the organizational sciences.

A cursory look at most organizations quickly suggests that some people work harder than others. Who among us, for instance, hasn't seen an individual with outstanding abilities outperformed by someone with clearly inferior talents? Why do some people appear to be highly motivated, while others are not? We try to answer this latter question in this and the following chapter.

What is Motivation?

Maybe the place to begin is to say what motivation isn't. Many people incorrectly view motivation as a personal trait—that is, some have it and others don't. In practice, some managers label employees who seem to lack motivation as lazy. Such a label assumes an individual is always lazy or is lacking in motivation. Our knowledge of motivation tells us this just isn't true. What we know is that motivation is the result of the interaction of the individual and the situation. Certainly, individuals differ in their basic motivational drive. But the same employee who is quickly bored when pulling the lever on his drill press may pull the lever on a slot machine in Las Vegas for hours on end without the slightest hint of boredom. You may read a complete novel at one sitting, yet find it difficult to stay with a textbook for more than 20 minutes. It's not necessarily you—it's the situation. So as we analyze the concept of motivation, keep in mind that level of motivation varies both between individuals and within individuals at different times.

motivation
The willingness to exert high levels of effort toward organizational goals, conditioned by the effort's ability to satisfy some individual need.

We define **motivation** as the willingness to exert high levels of effort toward organizational goals, conditioned by the effort's ability to satisfy some individual need. While general motivation is concerned with effort toward *any* goal, we narrow the focus to *organizational* goals in order to reflect our singular interest in work-related behavior. The three key elements in our definition are effort, organizational goals, and needs.

The effort element is a measure of intensity. When someone is motivated, he or she tries hard. But high levels of effort are unlikely to lead to favorable job performance outcomes unless the effort is channeled in a direction that benefits the organization.[2] Therefore, we must consider the quality of the effort as well as its intensity. Effort that is directed toward, and consistent with, the organization's goals is the kind of effort we should be seeking. Finally, we treat motivation as a need-satisfying process. This is depicted in Figure 6-1.

need
Some internal state that makes certain outcomes appear attractive.

A **need**, in our terminology, means some internal state that makes certain outcomes appear attractive. An unsatisfied need creates tension that stimulates drives within the individual. These drives generate a search behavior to find particular goals that, if attained, will satisfy the need and lead to the reduction of tension.

Figure 6-1
The Motivation Process

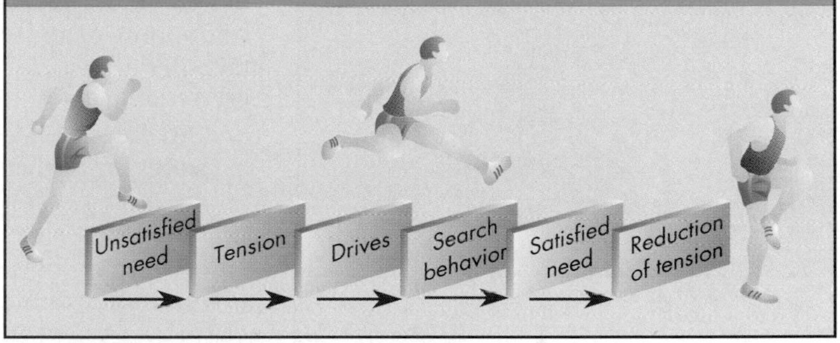

So we can say that motivated employees are in a state of tension. To relieve this tension, they exert effort. The greater the tension, the higher the effort level. If this effort successfully leads to the satisfaction of the need, tension is reduced. But since we are interested in work behavior, this tension reduction effort must also be directed toward organizational goals. Therefore, inherent in our definition of motivation is the requirement that the individual's needs be compatible and consistent with the organization's goals. Where this does not occur, we can have individuals exerting high levels of effort that actually run counter to the interests of the organization. This, incidentally, is not so unusual. For example, some employees regularly spend a lot of time talking with friends at work in order to satisfy their social needs. There is a high level of effort, only it's being unproductively directed.

Early Theories of Motivation

The 1950s were a fruitful period in the development of motivation concepts. Three specific theories were formulated during this time, which, although heavily attacked and now questionable in terms of validity, are probably still the best known explanations for employee motivation. These are the hierarchy of needs theory, Theories X and Y, and the motivation-hygiene theory. As you'll see later in this chapter, we have since developed more valid explanations of motivation, but you should know these early theories for at least two reasons: (1) they represent a foundation from which contemporary theories have grown, and (2) practicing managers regularly use these theories and their terminology in explaining employee motivation.

Hierarchy of Needs Theory

hierarchy of needs theory
There is a hierarchy of five needs—physiological, safety, social, esteem, and self-actualization—and as each need is sequentially satisfied, the next need becomes dominant.

It's probably safe to say that the most well-known theory of motivation is Abraham Maslow's **hierarchy of needs**.[3] He hypothesized that within every human being there exists a hierarchy of the following five needs.

1. *Physiological*: Includes hunger, thirst, shelter, sex, and other bodily needs
2. *Safety*: Includes security and protection from physical and emotional harm
3. *Social*: Includes affection, belongingness, acceptance, and friendship
4. *Esteem*: Includes internal esteem factors such as self-respect, autonomy, and achievement; and external esteem factors such as status, recognition, and attention
5. **Self-actualization**: The drive to become what one is capable of becoming; includes growth, achieving one's potential, and self-fulfillment

self-actualization
The drive to become what one is capable of becoming.

Figure 6-2
Maslow's Hierarchy of Needs

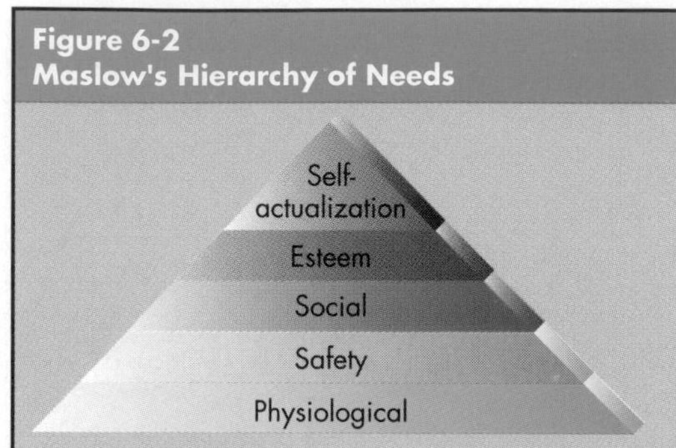

As each of these needs becomes substantially satisfied, the next need becomes dominant. In terms of Figure 6-2, the individual moves up the steps of the hierarchy. From the standpoint of motivation, the theory would say that although no need is ever fully gratified, a substantially satisfied need no longer motivates. So if you want to motivate someone, according to Maslow, you need to understand what level of the hierarchy that person is currently on and focus on satisfying those needs at or above that level.

Maslow separated the five needs into higher and lower orders. Physiological and safety needs were described as **lower order** and social, esteem, and self-actualization as **higher order needs**. The differentiation between the two orders was made on the premise that higher order needs are satisfied internally (within the person), whereas lower order needs are predominantly satisfied externally (by pay, union contracts, and tenure, for example). In fact, the natural conclusion to be drawn from Maslow's classification is that in times of economic plenty, almost all permanently employed workers have their lower order needs substantially met.

lower-order needs
Needs that are satisfied externally; physiological and safety needs.

higher-order needs
Needs that are satisfied internally; social, esteem, and self-actualization needs.

Maslow's need theory has received wide recognition, particularly among practicing managers. This can be attributed to the theory's intuitive logic and ease of understanding. Unfortunately, however, research does not generally validate the theory. Maslow provided no empirical substantiation, and several studies that sought to validate the theory found no support for it.[4]

Old theories, especially ones that are intuitively logical, apparently die hard. One researcher reviewed the evidence and concluded that "although of great societal popularity, need hierarchy as a theory continues to receive little empirical support."[5] Further, the researcher stated that the "available research should certainly generate a reluctance to accept unconditionally the implication of Maslow's hierarchy."[6] Another review came to the same conclusion.[7] Little support was found for the prediction that need structures are organized along the dimensions proposed by Maslow, that unsatisfied needs motivate, or that a satisfied need activates movement to a new need level.

Theory X and Theory Y

Douglas McGregor proposed two distinct views of human beings: one basically negative, labeled **Theory X**, and the other basically positive, labeled **Theory Y**.[8] After viewing the way in which managers dealt with employees, McGregor concluded that a manager's view of the nature of human beings is based on a certain grouping of assumptions and that he or she tends to mold his or her behavior toward subordinates according to these assumptions.

Theory X
The assumption that employees dislike work, are lazy, dislike responsibility, and must be coerced to perform.

Theory Y
The assumption that employees like work, are creative, seek responsibility, and can exercise self-direction.

According to Theory X, the four assumptions held by managers are as follows:

1. Employees inherently dislike work and, whenever possible, will attempt to avoid it.
2. Since employees dislike work, they must be coerced, controlled, or threatened with punishment to achieve goals.
3. Employees will avoid responsibilities and seek formal direction whenever possible.
4. Most workers place security above all other factors associated with work and will display little ambition.

In contrast to these negative views about the nature of human beings, McGregor listed four positive assumptions, which he called Theory Y:

1. Employees can view work as being as natural as rest or play.
2. People will exercise self-direction and self-control if they are committed to the objectives.
3. The average person can learn to accept, even seek, responsibility.
4. The ability to make innovative decisions is widely dispersed throughout the population and is not necessarily the sole province of those in management positions.

What are the motivational implications if you accept McGregor's analysis? The answer is best expressed in the framework presented by Maslow. Theory X assumes that lower order needs dominate individuals. Theory Y assumes that higher order needs dominate individuals. McGregor himself held to the belief that Theory Y assumptions were more valid than Theory X. Therefore, he proposed such ideas as participative decision making, responsible and challenging jobs, and good group relations as approaches that would maximize an employee's job motivation.

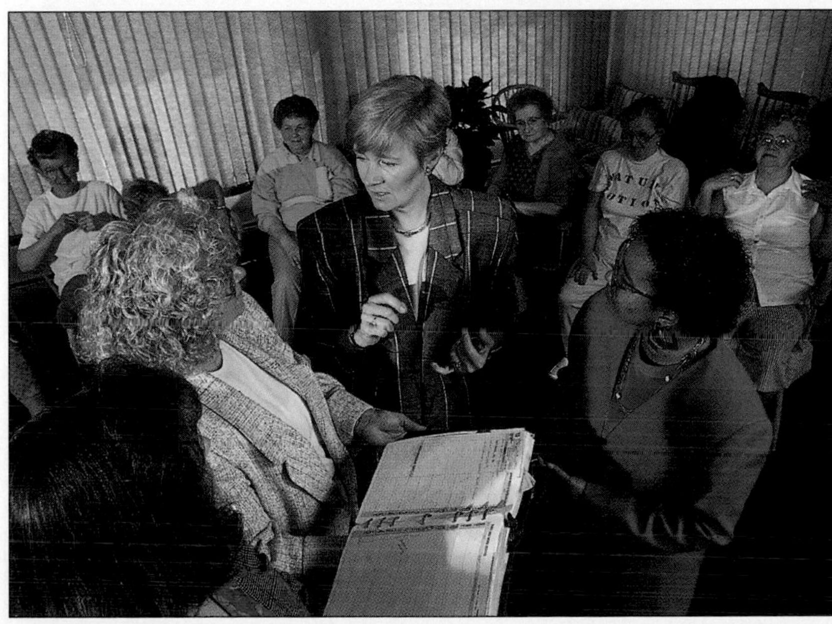

Mary Tjosvold (center), chief executive officer of Mary T. Inc., believes in Theory Y. She says, "Those of us who run a business realize the employees have the most power." Her company of 600 employees provides residential social services for people with disabilities. Tjosvold uses employee teams to service customers and gives team members decision-making responsibility. For example, the quality-assurance team directs its own activity, draws up its own budgets and schedules, and decides its own disciplinary actions. Tjosvold trusts her employees to implement programs that meet the company's high standards. Her employees respond by accepting responsibility and exercising self-direction.

Unfortunately, no evidence confirms that either set of assumptions is valid or that accepting Theory Y assumptions and altering one's actions accordingly will lead to more motivated workers. As will become evident later in this chapter, either Theory X or Theory Y assumptions may be appropriate in a particular situation.

Motivation-Hygiene Theory

motivation-hygiene theory
Intrinsic factors are related to job satisfaction, while extrinsic factors are associated with dissatisfaction.

The **motivation-hygiene** theory was proposed by psychologist Frederick Herzberg.[9] In the belief that an individual's relation to his or her work is a basic one and that his or her attitude toward this work can very well determine the individual's success or failure, Herzberg investigated the question, "What do people want from their jobs?" He asked people to describe, in detail, situations when they felt exceptionally *good* and *bad* about their jobs. These responses were tabulated and categorized. Factors affecting job attitudes as reported in 12 investigations conducted by Herzberg are illustrated in Figure 6-3.

From the categorized responses, Herzberg concluded that the replies people gave when they felt good about their jobs were significantly different from

Figure 6-3
Comparison of Satisfiers and Dissatisfiers

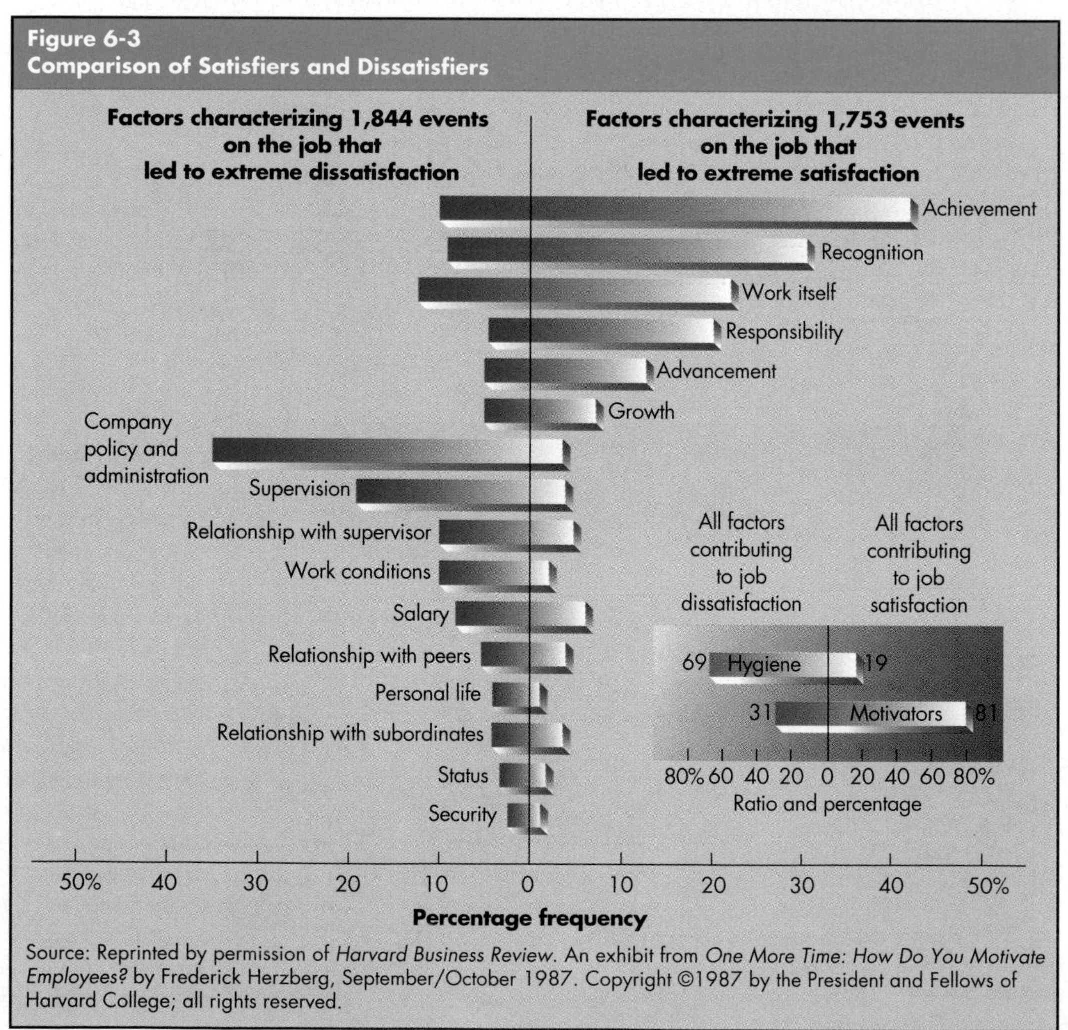

Source: Reprinted by permission of *Harvard Business Review*. An exhibit from *One More Time: How Do You Motivate Employees?* by Frederick Herzberg, September/October 1987.

the replies given when they felt bad. As seen in Figure 6-3, certain characteristics tend to be consistently related to job satisfaction (factors on the right side of the figure), and others to job dissatisfaction (the left side of the figure). Intrinsic factors, such as achievement, recognition, the work itself, responsibility, advancement, and growth, seem to be related to job satisfaction. When those questioned felt good about their work, they tended to attribute these characteristics to themselves. On the other hand, when they were dissatisfied, they tended to cite extrinsic factors, such as company policy and administration, supervision, interpersonal relations, and working conditions.

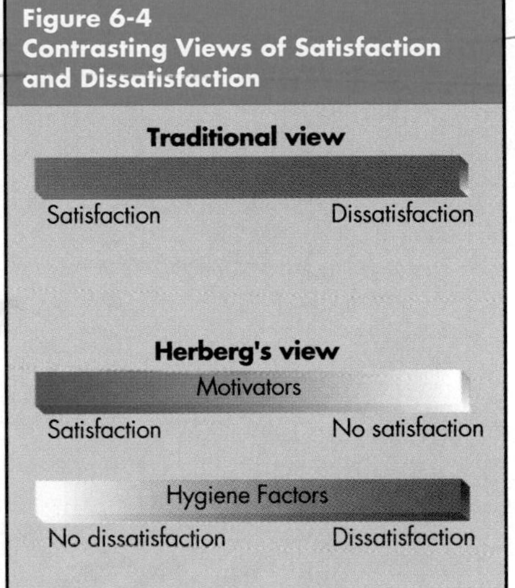

Figure 6-4
Contrasting Views of Satisfaction and Dissatisfaction

The data suggest, says Herzberg, that the opposite of satisfaction is not dissatisfaction, as was traditionally believed. Removing dissatisfying characteristics from a job does not necessarily make the job satisfying. As illustrated in Figure 6-4, Herzberg proposes that his findings indicate the existence of a dual continuum: The opposite of "Satisfaction" is "No Satisfaction," and the opposite of "Dissatisfaction" is "No Dissatisfaction."

According to Herzberg, the factors leading to job satisfaction are separate and distinct from those that lead to job dissatisfaction. Therefore, managers who seek to eliminate factors that create job dissatisfaction can bring about peace, but not necessarily motivation. They will be placating their work force rather than motivating them. As a result, such characteristics as company policy and administration, supervision, interpersonal relations, working conditions, and salary have been characterized by Herzberg as **hygiene factors**. When they are adequate, people will not be dissatisfied; however, neither will they be satisfied. If we want to motivate people on their jobs, Herzberg suggests emphasizing achievement, recognition, the work itself, responsibility, and growth. These are the characteristics that people find intrinsically rewarding.

hygiene factors
Those factors—such as company policy and administration, supervision, and salary—that, when adequate in a job, placate workers. When these factors are adequate, people will not be dissatisfied.

The motivation-hygiene theory is not without its detractors. The criticisms of the theory include the following:

1. The procedure that Herzberg used is limited by its methodology. When things are going well, people tend to take credit themselves. Contrarily, they blame failure on the external environment.
2. The reliability of Herzberg's methodology is questioned. Since raters have to make interpretations, it is possible they may contaminate the findings by interpreting one response in one manner while treating another similar response differently.
3. The theory, to the degree it is valid, provides an explanation of job satisfaction. It is not really a theory of motivation.
4. No overall measure of satisfaction was utilized. In other words, a person may dislike part of his or her job, yet still think the job is acceptable.
5. The theory is inconsistent with previous research. The motivation-hygiene theory ignores situational variables.
6. Herzberg assumes a relationship between satisfaction and productivity. But the research methodology he used looked only at satisfaction, not at productivity. To make such research relevant, one must assume a high relationship between satisfaction and productivity.[10]

Regardless of criticisms, Herzberg's theory has been widely read, and most managers are familiar with his recommendations. The increased popularity

◆◆◆◆ OB in the News ◆◆◆◆

Thanks for the Recognition, but Where's the Money?

Prior to the late 1980s, pay raises were as predictable and constant as the arrival of Christmas—they came every year. Not anymore! Raises are being replaced by one-shot bonuses or stock. And praise that used to show up in a paycheck is increasingly delivered in the unbankable form of plaques, theater tickets, and thank you notes from the boss. Federal Express, for instance, sent out over 50,000 of such notes in one recent year.

As traditional raises grow fewer and farther between, or even disappear altogether, "attaboys" are taking their place. In a 1993 survey of 3,200 companies, it was found that noncash recognition rewards were being used by 60 percent of the firms, up from 20 percent in 1988. This same survey also showed that 14 percent of the companies were using one-shot bonuses instead of annual raises. These bonuses save companies money because they do not become part of the employee's permanent wage base.

Why is recognition increasingly replacing the annual pay increase? Fierce competition from low-wage countries means companies have to keep costs in line. And one way to do that is to curtail pay raises or at least link them to increases in productivity. Another key factor has been the slow growth in job formation. The supply-demand imbalance has created a buyer's market, so employers are less concerned about losing good people if they don't hand out annual pay increases.

Based on J. Fierman, "When Will You Get a Raise?," *Fortune* (July 12, 1993), pp. 34–36.

since the mid-1960s of vertically expanding jobs to allow workers greater responsibility in planning and controlling their work can probably be largely attributed to Herzberg's findings and recommendations.

Contemporary Theories of Motivation

The previous theories are well known but, unfortunately, have not held up well under close examination. However, all is not lost.[11] A number of contemporary theories have one thing in common: Each has a reasonable degree of valid supporting documentation. Of course, this doesn't mean the theories we are about to introduce are unquestionably right. We call them contemporary theories not because they necessarily were developed recently, but because they represent the current state of the art in explaining employee motivation.

ERG Theory

ERG theory
There are three groups of core needs: existence, relatedness, and growth.

Clayton Alderfer of Yale University has reworked Maslow's need hierarchy to align it more closely with the empirical research. His revised need hierarchy is labeled **ERG theory**.[12]

Alderfer argues that there are three groups of core needs—existence, relatedness, and growth—hence the label ERG theory. The *existence* group is concerned with providing our basic material existence requirements. It includes the items that Maslow considered physiological and safety needs. The second group of needs are those of *relatedness*—the desire we have for maintaining important interpersonal relationships. These social and status desires require interaction with others if they are to be satisfied, and they align with Maslow's social need and the external component of Maslow's esteem classification. Finally, Alderfer isolates *growth* needs—an intrinsic desire for personal development. These include the intrinsic component from Maslow's esteem category and the characteristics included under self-actualization.

Besides substituting three needs for five, how does Alderfer's ERG theory differ from Maslow's? In contrast to the hierarchy of needs theory, the ERG theory demonstrates that (1) more than one need may be operative at the same time, and (2) if the gratification of a higher level need is stifled, the desire to satisfy a lower level need increases.

Maslow's need hierarchy is a rigid steplike progression. ERG theory does not assume a rigid hierarchy where a lower need must be substantially gratified before one can move on. A person can, for instance, be working on growth even though existence or relatedness needs are unsatisfied; or all three need categories could be operating at the same time.

ERG theory also contains a frustration-regression dimension. Maslow, you'll remember, argued that an individual would stay at a certain need level until that need was satisfied. ERG theory counters by noting that when a higher order need level is frustrated, the individual's desire to increase a lower level need takes place. Inability to satisfy a need for social interaction, for instance, might increase the desire for more money or better working conditions. So frustration can lead to a regression to a lower need.

In summary, ERG theory argues, like Maslow, that satisfied lower order needs lead to the desire to satisfy higher order needs; but multiple needs can be operating as motivators at the same time, and frustration in attempting to satisfy a higher level need can result in regression to a lower level need.

ERG theory is more consistent with our knowledge of individual differences among people. Variables such as education, family background, and cultural environment can alter the importance or driving force that a group of needs holds for a particular individual. The evidence demonstrating that people in other cultures rank the need categories differently—for instance, natives of Spain and Japan place social needs before their physiological requirements[13]—would be consistent with the ERG theory. Several studies have supported the ERG theory,[14] but there is also evidence that it doesn't work in some organizations.[15] Overall, however, ERG theory represents a more valid version of the need hierarchy.

McClelland's Theory of Needs

You've got one beanbag and five targets set up in front of you. Each target is progressively farther away and, hence, more difficult to hit. Target A is a cinch. It sits almost within arm's reach of you. If you hit it, you get $2. Target B is a bit farther out, but about 80 percent of the people who try can hit it. It pays $4. Target C pays $8, and about half the people who try can hit it. Very few people can hit Target D, but the payoff is $16 if you do. Finally, Target E pays $32, but it's almost impossible to achieve. Which target would you try for? If you selected C, you're likely to be a high achiever. Why? Read on.

In Chapter 3 we introduced the need to achieve as a personality characteristic. It is also one of three needs proposed by David McClelland and his associates as being important in organizational settings for understanding

McClelland's theory of needs
Achievement, power, and affiliation are three important needs that help to understand motivation.

achievement need
The drive to excel, to achieve in relation to a set of standards, to strive to succeed.

power need
The desire to make others behave in a way that they would not otherwise have behaved in.

affiliation need
The desire for friendly and close interpersonal relationships.

motivation.[16] **McClelland's theory of needs** focuses on three needs: achievement, power, and affiliation. They are defined as follows:

- **Need for achievement**: The drive to excel, to achieve in relation to a set of standards, to strive to succeed
- **Need for power**: The need to make others behave in a way they would not have behaved otherwise
- **Need for affiliation**: The desire for friendly and close interpersonal relationships

Some people have a compelling drive to succeed. They're striving for personal achievement rather than the rewards of success per se. They have a desire to do something better or more efficiently than it has been done before. This drive is the achievement need (*nAch*). From research into the achievement need, McClelland found that high achievers differentiate themselves from others by their desire to do things better.[17] They seek situations where they can attain personal responsibility for finding solutions to problems, where they can receive rapid feedback on their performance so they can tell easily whether they are improving or not, and where they can set moderately challenging goals. High achievers are not gamblers; they dislike succeeding by chance. They prefer the challenge of working at a problem and accepting the personal responsibility for success or failure rather than leaving the outcome to chance or the actions of others. Importantly, they avoid what they perceive to be very easy or very difficult tasks. They want to overcome obstacles, but they want to feel their success (or failure) is due to their own actions. This means they like tasks of intermediate difficulty.

> ◆High achievers avoid what they perceive to be very easy or very difficult tasks.

High achievers perform best when they perceive their probability of success as being 0.5, that is, where they estimate they have a 50-50 chance of success. They dislike gambling with high odds because they get no achievement

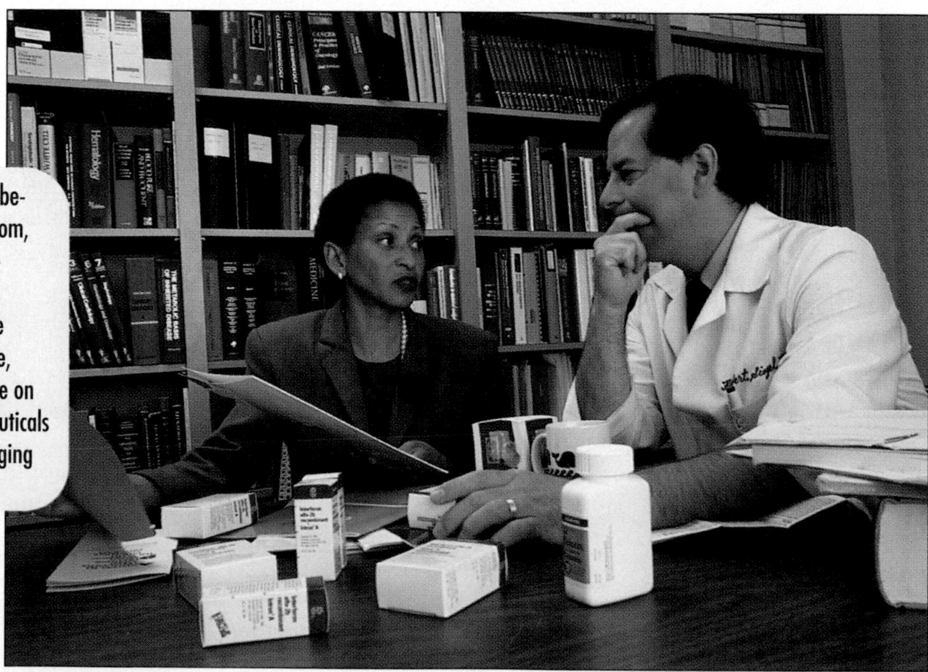

High achievers do well in sales positions because their jobs provide them with freedom, personal responsibility for outcomes, immediate feedback on their performance, and the opportunity to take on moderate risks. Schering-Plough selects salespeople, such as the woman shown here, who take on the challenging task of selling pharmaceuticals in a highly competitive and rapidly changing industry.

satisfaction from happenstance success. Similarly, they dislike low odds (high probability of success) because then there is no challenge to their skills. They like to set goals that require stretching themselves a little. When there is an approximately equal chance of success or failure, there is the optimum opportunity to experience feelings of accomplishment and satisfaction from their efforts.

The need for power (*nPow*) is the desire to have impact, to be influential, and to control others. Individuals high in *nPow* enjoy being in charge, strive for influence over others, prefer to be placed into competitive and status-oriented situations, and tend to be more concerned with prestige and gaining influence over others than with effective performance.

The third need isolated by McClelland is affiliation (*nAff*). This need has received the least attention from researchers. Affiliation can be likened to Dale Carnegie's goals—the desire to be liked and accepted by others. Individuals with a high affiliation motive strive for friendship, prefer cooperative situations rather than competitive ones, and desire relationships involving a high degree of mutual understanding.

How do you find out if someone is, for instance, a high achiever? There are questionnaires that tap this motive,[18] but most research uses a projective test in which subjects respond to pictures.[19] Each picture is briefly shown to the subject and then he or she writes a story based on the picture. As an example, the picture may show a male sitting at a desk in a pensive position, looking at a photograph of a woman and two children that sits at the corner of the desk. The subject will then be asked to write a story describing what is going on, what preceded this situation, what will happen in the future, and the like. The stories become, in effect, projective tests that measure unconscious motives. Each story is scored and a subject's ratings on each of the three motives is obtained.

Relying on an extensive amount of research, some reasonably well-supported predictions can be made based on the relationship between achievement need and job performance. Although less research has been done on power and affiliation needs, there are consistent findings here, too.

First, as shown in Figure 6-5, individuals with a high need to achieve prefer job situations with personal responsibility, feedback, and an intermediate degree of risk. When these characteristics are prevalent, high achievers will be strongly motivated. The evidence consistently demonstrates, for instance, that high achievers are successful in entrepreneurial activities such as running their own businesses and managing a self-contained unit within a large organization.[20]

Figure 6-5
Matching Achievers and Jobs

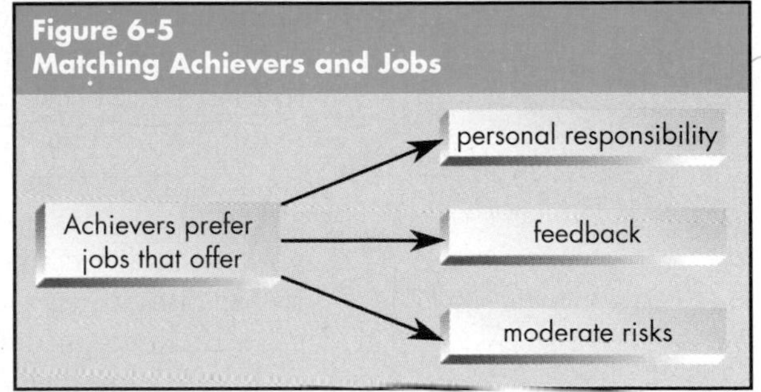
Achievers prefer jobs that offer
personal responsibility
feedback
moderate risks

Second, a high need to achieve does not necessarily lead to being a good manager, especially in large organizations. People with a high achievement need are interested in how well they do personally and not in influencing others to do well. High-*nAch* salespeople do not necessarily make good sales managers, and the good general manager in a large organization does not typically have a high need to achieve.[21]

Third, the needs for affiliation and power tend to be closely related to managerial success. The best managers are high in their need for power and low in their need for affiliation.[22] In fact, a high-power motive may be a requirement for managerial effectiveness.[23] Of course, what is the cause and what is the effect is arguable. It has been suggested that a high-power need may occur simply as a function of one's level in a hierarchical organization.[24] The latter argument proposes that the higher the level an individual rises to in the organization, the greater is the incumbent's power motive. As a result, powerful positions would be the stimulus to a high-power motive.

Lastly, employees have been successfully trained to stimulate their achievement need. Trainers have been effective in teaching individuals to think in terms of accomplishments, winning, and success; and then helping them to learn how to *act* in a high achievement way by preferring situations where they have personal responsibility, feedback, and moderate risks. So if the job calls for a high achiever, management can select a person with a high *nAch* or develop its own candidate through achievement training.[25]

Cognitive Evaluation Theory

In the late 1960s one researcher proposed that the introduction of extrinsic rewards, such as pay, for work effort that had been previously intrinsically rewarding due to the pleasure associated with the content of the work itself would tend to decrease the overall level of motivation.[26] This proposal—which has come to be called the **cognitive evaluation theory**—has been extensively researched, and a large number of studies have been supportive.[27] As we show, the major implications for this theory relate to the way in which people are paid in organizations.

cognitive evaluation theory Allocating extrinsic rewards for behavior that had been previously intrinsically rewarded tends to decrease the overall level of motivation.

Historically, motivation theorists have generally assumed that intrinsic motivations such as achievement, responsibility, and competence are independent of extrinsic motivators like high pay, promotions, good supervisor relations, and pleasant working conditions. That is, the stimulation of one would not affect the other. But the cognitive evaluation theory suggests otherwise. It argues that when extrinsic rewards are used by organizations as payoffs for superior performance, the intrinsic rewards, which are derived from individuals doing what they like, are reduced. In other words, when extrinsic rewards are given to someone for performing an interesting task, it causes intrinsic interest in the task itself to decline.

Why would such an outcome occur? The popular explanation is that the individual experiences a loss of control over his or her own behavior so the previous intrinsic motivation diminishes. Further, the elimination of extrinsic rewards can produce a shift—from an external to an internal explanation—in an individual's perception of causation of why he or she works on a task. If you're reading a novel a week because your English literature instructor requires you to, you can attribute your reading behavior to an external source. However, after the course is over, if you find yourself continuing to read a novel a week, your natural inclination is to say, "I must enjoy reading novels, because I'm still reading one a week!"

If the cognitive evaluation theory is valid, it should have major implications for managerial practices. It has been a truism among compensation specialists for years that if pay or other extrinsic rewards are to be effective motivators, they should be made contingent on an individual's performance. But, cognitive evaluation theorists would argue, this will only tend to decrease the internal satisfaction that the individual receives from doing the job. We have substituted an external stimulus for an internal stimulus. In fact, if cognitive evaluation theory is correct, it would make sense to make an individual's pay noncontingent on performance in order to avoid decreasing intrinsic motivation.

We noted earlier that the cognitive evaluation theory has been supported in a number of studies. Yet it has also met with attacks, specifically on the methodology used in these studies[28] and in the interpretation of the findings.[29] But where does this theory stand today? Can we say that when organizations use extrinsic motivators like pay and promotions to stimulate workers' performance they do so at the expense of reducing intrinsic interest and motivation in the work being done? The answer is not a simple "Yes" or "No."

While further research is needed to clarify some of the current ambiguity, the evidence does lead us to conclude that the interdependence of extrinsic and intrinsic rewards is a real phenomenon.[30] But its impact on employee motivation at work, in contrast to motivation in general, may be considerably less than originally thought. First, many of the studies testing the theory were done with students, not paid organizational employees. The researchers would observe what happens to a student's behavior when a reward that had been allocated is stopped. This is interesting, but it does not represent the typical work situation. In the real world, when extrinsic rewards are stopped, it usually means the individual is no longer part of the organization. Second, evidence indicates that very high intrinsic motivation levels are strongly resistant to the detrimental impacts of extrinsic rewards.[31] Even when a job is inherently interesting, there still exists a powerful norm for extrinsic payment.[32] At the other extreme, on dull tasks extrinsic rewards appear to increase intrinsic motivation.[33] Therefore, the theory may have limited applicability to work organizations because most low-level jobs are not inherently satisfying enough to foster high intrinsic interest and many managerial and professional positions offer intrinsic rewards. Cognitive evaluation theory may be relevant to that set of organizational jobs that falls in between—those that are neither extremely dull nor extremely interesting.

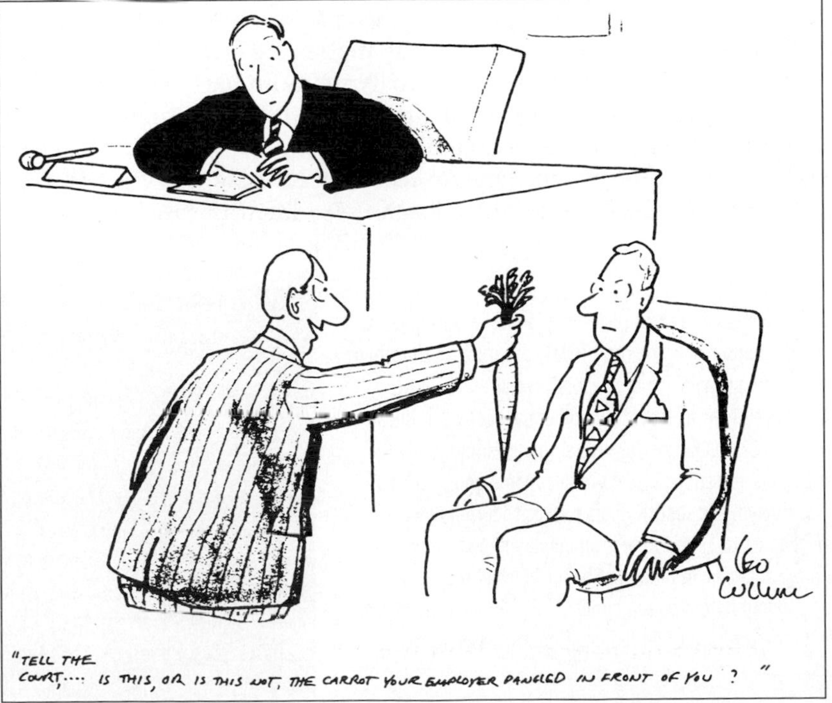

Leo Cullum
"TELL THE COURT,.... IS THIS, OR IS THIS NOT, THE CARROT YOUR EMPLOYER DANGLED IN FRONT OF YOU ? "

Figure 6-6

Source: Drawing by Leo Cullum as it was reprinted within *The Harvard Business Review*. Copyright © by Leo Cullum. Reprinted by permission of Leo Cullum.

Goal-Setting Theory

Gene Broadwater, coach of the Hamilton High School cross-country team, gave his squad these last words before they approached the line for the league championship race: "Each one of you is physically ready. Now, get out there and do your best. No one can ever ask more of you than that."

You've heard the phrase a number of times yourself: "Just do your best. That's all anyone can ask for." But what does "do your best" mean? Do we ever know if we've achieved that vague goal? Would the cross-country runners have recorded faster times if Coach Broadwater had given each a specific goal to shoot for? Might you have done better in your high school English class if your parents had said, "You should strive for 85 percent or higher on all your work in English" rather than telling you to "do your best"? The research on **goal-setting theory** addresses these issues, and the findings, as you will see, are impressive in terms of the effect of goal specificity, challenge, and feedback on performance.

goal-setting theory
The theory that specific and difficult goals lead to higher performance.

In the late 1960s Edwin Locke proposed that intentions to work toward a goal are a major source of work motivation.[34] That is, goals tell an employee what needs to be done and how much effort will need to be expended.[35] The evidence strongly supports the value of goals. More to the point, we can say that specific goals increase performance; that difficult goals, when accepted, result in higher performance than do easy goals; and that feedback leads to higher performance than does nonfeedback.[36]

Specific hard goals produce a higher level of output than does the generalized goal of "do your best." The specificity of the goal itself acts as an internal stimulus. For instance, when a trucker commits to making 12 round-trip hauls between Toronto and Buffalo, New York, each week, this intention gives him a specific objective to reach for. We can say that, all things being equal, the trucker with a specific goal will outperform his counterpart operating with no goals or the generalized goal of "do your best."

If factors like ability and acceptance of the goals are held constant, we can also state that the more difficult the goal, the higher the level of performance. However, it's logical to assume that easier goals are more likely to be accepted. But once an employee accepts a hard task, he or she will exert a high level of effort until it is achieved, lowered, or abandoned.

People will do better when they get feedback on how well they are progressing toward their goals because feedback helps identify discrepancies be-

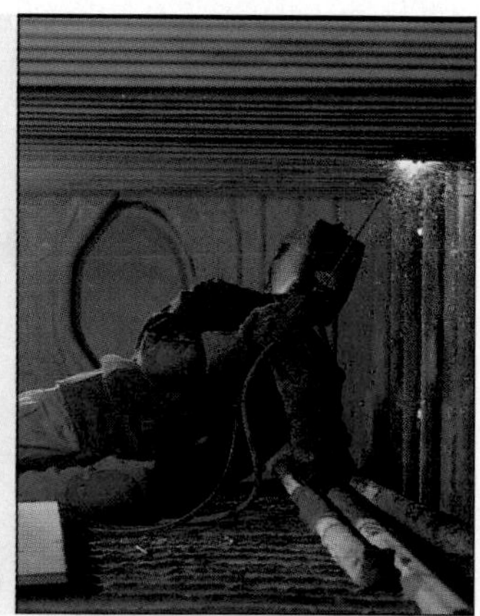

Detroit Edison involves its electric utility employees in setting goals. Under its goals, measures, and targets (GMT) program, each company unit defines team and invididual goals, performance measures, and specific expectations to ensure that all employees work toward the same results. Detroit Edison rewards employees financially for their contributions in meeting broad organizational goals such as customer satisfaction and specific goals such as reducing power plant production costs. Shown here is an employee-generated, cost-reduction project. Employees replaced boiler tubes at a company power plant, saving Detroit Edison about $228,000 over the lowest bid by an outside contractor and reaping financial rewards for employees.

tween what they have done and what they want to do; that is, feedback acts to guide behavior. But all feedback is not equally potent. Self-generated feedback—where the employee is able to monitor his or her own progress—has been shown to be a more powerful motivator than externally generated feedback.[37]

If employees have the opportunity to participate in the setting of their own goals, will they try harder? The evidence is mixed regarding the superiority of participative over assigned goals.[38] In some cases, participatively set goals elicited superior performance; in other cases, individuals performed best when assigned goals by their boss. But a major advantage of participation may be in increasing acceptance of the goal itself as a desirable one to work toward.[39] As we noted, resistance is greater when goals are difficult. If people participate in goal setting, they are more likely to accept even a difficult goal than if they are arbitrarily assigned it by their boss. The reason is that individuals are more committed to choices in which they have a part. Thus, although participative goals may have no superiority over assigned goals when acceptance is taken as a given, participation does increase the probability that more difficult goals will be agreed to and acted upon.

Are there any contingencies in goal-setting theory or can we take it as a universal truth that difficult and specific goals will always lead to higher performance? In addition to feedback, three other factors have been found to influence the goals–performance relationship: goal commitment, adequate self-efficacy, and national culture. Goal-setting theory presupposes that an individual is *committed* to the goal, that is, determined not to lower or abandon the goal. This is most likely to occur when goals are made public, when the individual has an internal locus of control, and when the goals are self-set rather than assigned.[40] **Self-efficacy** refers to an individual's belief that he or she is capable of performing a task.[41] The higher your self-efficacy, the more confidence you have in your ability to succeed in a task. So, in difficult situations, we find that people with low self-efficacy are more likely to lessen their effort or give up altogether whereas those with high self-efficacy will try harder to master the challenge.[42] In addition, individuals high in self-efficacy seem to respond to negative feedback with increased effort and motivation; those low in self-efficacy are likely to lessen their effort when given negative feedback.[43] Lastly, goal-setting theory is culture bound. It's well adapted to countries like the United States and Canada because its key components align reasonably well with North American cultures. It assumes subordinates will be reasonably independent (not too high a score on power distance), that managers and subordinates will seek challenging goals (low in uncertainty avoidance), and that performance is considered important by both (high in quantity of life). So don't expect goal setting to necessarily lead to higher employee performance in countries such as Portugal or Chile, where the opposite conditions exist.

self-efficacy
The individual's belief that he or she is capable of performing a task.

Our overall conclusion is that intentions—as articulated in terms of hard and specific goals—are a potent motivating force. Under the proper conditions, they can lead to higher performance. However, no evidence supports the idea that such goals are associated with increased job satisfaction.[44]

Reinforcement Theory

A counterpoint to goal-setting theory is **reinforcement theory**. The former is a cognitive approach, proposing that an individual's purposes direct his or her action. In reinforcement theory, we have a behavioristic approach, which

reinforcement theory
Behavior is a function of its consequences.

argues that reinforcement conditions behavior. The two are clearly at odds philosophically. Reinforcement theorists see behavior as being environmentally caused. You need not be concerned, they would argue, with internal cognitive events; what controls behavior are reinforcers—any consequence that, when immediately following a response, increases the probability that the behavior will be repeated.

Reinforcement theory ignores the inner state of the individual and concentrates solely on what happens to a person when he or she takes some action. Because it does not concern itself with what initiates behavior, it is not, strictly speaking, a theory of motivation. But it does provide a powerful means of analysis of what controls behavior, and it is for this reason that it is typically considered in discussions of motivation.[45]

We discussed the reinforcement process in detail in Chapter 3. We showed how using reinforcers to condition behavior gives us considerable insight into how people learn. Yet we cannot ignore the fact that reinforcement has a wide following as a motivational device. In its pure form, however, reinforcement theory ignores feelings, attitudes, expectations, and other cognitive variables that are known to impact behavior. In fact, some researchers look at the same experiments that reinforcement theorists use to support their position and interpret the findings in a cognitive framework.[46]

Reinforcement is undoubtedly an important influence on behavior, but few scholars are prepared to argue it is the only influence. The behaviors you engage in at work and the amount of effort you allocate to each task are affected by the consequences that follow from your behavior. If you are consistently reprimanded for outproducing your colleagues, you will likely reduce your productivity. But your lower productivity may also be explained in terms of goals, inequity, or expectancies.

Equity Theory

Jane Pearson graduated last year from State University with a degree in accounting. After on-campus interviews with a number of organizations, she accepted a position with one of the nation's largest public accounting firms and was assigned to their Boston office. Jane was very pleased with the offer she received: challenging work with a prestigious firm, an excellent opportunity to gain important experience, and the highest salary any accounting major at State was offered last year—$2,950 a month. But Jane was the top student in her class; she was ambitious and articulate and fully expected to receive a commensurate salary.

Twelve months have passed since Jane joined her employer. The work has proved to be as challenging and satisfying as she had hoped. Her employer is extremely pleased with her performance; in fact, she recently received a $200-a-month raise. However, Jane's motivational level has dropped dramatically in the past few weeks. Why? Her employer has just hired a fresh college graduate out of State University, who lacks the one-year experience Jane has gained, for $3,200 a month—$50 more than Jane now makes! It would be an understatement to describe Jane in any other terms than irate. Jane is even talking about looking for another job.

Jane's situation illustrates the role that equity plays in motivation. Employees make comparisons of their job inputs and outcomes relative to those of others. We perceive what we get from a job situation (outcomes) in relation to what we put into it (inputs), and then we compare our outcome-input ratio with the outcome-input ratio of relevant others. This is shown in Table 6-1. If

Table 6-1 Equity Theory

Ratio Comparisons	Perception
$O/IA < O/IB^a$	Inequity due to being underrewarded
$O/IA = O/IB$	Equity
$O/IA > O/IB$	Inequity due to being overrewarded

[a] Where O/IA represents the employee; and O/IB represents relevant others.

we perceive our ratio to be equal to that of the relevant others with whom we compare ourselves, a state of equity is said to exist. We perceive our situation as fair—that justice prevails. When we see the ratio as unequal, we experience equity tension. J. Stacy Adams has proposed that this negative tension state provides the motivation to do something to correct it.[47]

The referent that an employee selects adds to the complexity of **equity theory**. Evidence indicates that the referent chosen is an important variable in equity theory.[48] There are four referent comparisons an employee can use:

equity theory
Individuals compare their job inputs and outcomes with those of others and then respond so as to eliminate any inequities.

1. *Self-inside*: An employee's experiences in a different position inside his or her current organization
2. *Self-outside*: An employee's experiences in a situation or position outside his or her current organization
3. *Other-inside*: Another individual or group of individuals inside the employee's organization
4. *Other-outside*: Another individual or group of individuals outside the employee's organization

So employees might compare themselves to friends, neighbors, coworkers, colleagues in other organizations, or past jobs they themselves have had. Which referent an employee chooses will be influenced by the information the employee holds about referents as well as by the attractiveness of the referent. This has led to focusing on four moderating variables—gender, length of tenure, level in the organization, and amount of education or professionalism.[49] Research shows that both men and women prefer same-sex comparisons. The research also demonstrates that women are typically paid less than men in comparable jobs and have lower pay expectations than men for the same work. So a female who uses another female as a referent tends to result in a lower comparative standard. This leads us to conclude that employees in jobs that are not sex segregated will make more cross-sex comparisons than those in jobs which are either male or female dominated. This also suggests that if women are tolerant of lower pay it may be due to the comparative standard they use.

Employees with short tenure in their current organizations tend to have little information about others inside the organization, so they rely on their own personal experiences. However, employees with long tenure rely more heavily on coworkers for comparison. Upper-level employees, those in the professional ranks, and those with higher amounts of education tend to be more cosmopolitan and have better information about people in other organizations. Therefore, these types of employees make more other-outside comparisons.

Based on equity theory, when employees perceive an inequity they can be predicted to make one of six choices:[50]

1. Change their inputs (for example, don't exert as much effort)
2. Change their outcomes (for example, individuals paid on a piece-rate basis can increase their pay by producing a higher quantity of units of lower quality)
3. Distort perceptions of self (for example, "I used to think I worked at a moderate pace but now I realize that I work a lot harder than everyone else.")
4. Distort perceptions of others (for example, "Mike's job isn't as desirable as I previously thought it was.")
5. Choose a different referent (for example, "I may not make as much as my brother-in-law, but I'm doing a lot better than my Dad did when he was my age.")
6. Leave the field (for example, quit the job)

Equity theory recognizes that individuals are concerned not only with the absolute amount of rewards they receive for their efforts, but also with the relationship of this amount to what others receive. They make judgments as to the relationship between their inputs and outcomes and the inputs and outcomes of others. Based on one's inputs, such as effort, experience, education, and competence, one compares outcomes such as salary levels, raises, recognition, and other factors. When people perceive an imbalance in their outcome–input ratio relative to others, tension is created. This tension provides the basis for motivation, as people strive for what they perceive as equity and fairness.

◆ Equity theory recognizes that individuals are concerned not only with the absolute amount of rewards for their efforts, but also with the relationship of this amount to what others receive.

Specifically, the theory establishes four propositions relating to inequitable pay:

Professional athletes, like baseball player Barry Bonds, perceive pay equity by comparing inputs such as skill and ability with their performance measures against the input-outcome ratio of other athletes who play similar positions. Bonds, who has won the Gold Glove award for three consecutive years, excels in his position as left fielder for the San Francisco Giants. He also ranks high in hitting home runs, batting runs in, stealing bases, and other offensive play categories. After signing a six-year, $42.75 million contract, Bonds is baseball's highest-paid player. Of his pay, Bonds says, "I'm worth it." Giants owner Peter Magowan agrees. He says, "Barry is the best player in the game. If he is the best player, then he has to be paid the most."

1. *Given payment by time, overrewarded employees produce more than equitably paid employees.* Hourly and salaried employees generate high quantity or quality of production in order to increase the input side of the ratio and bring about equity.
2. *Given payment by quantity of production, overrewarded employees produce fewer, but higher quality, units than equitably paid employees.* Individuals paid on a piece-rate basis increase their effort to achieve equity, which can result in greater quality or quantity. However, increases in quantity only increase inequity, since every unit produced results in further overpayment. Therefore, effort is directed toward increasing quality rather than increasing quantity.
3. *Given payment by time, underrewarded employees produce less or poorer quality of output.* Effort is decreased, which brings about lower productivity or poorer quality output than equitably paid subjects.
4. *Given payment by quantity of production, underrewarded employees produce a large number of low-quality units in comparison with equitably paid employees.* Employees on piece-rate pay plans can bring about equity because trading off quality of output for quantity results in an increase in rewards with little or no increase in contributions.

These propositions have generally been supported, with a few minor qualifications.[51] First, inequities created by overpayment do not seem to have a very significant impact on behavior in most work situations. Apparently, people have a great deal more tolerance of overpayment inequities than of underpayment inequities, or are better able to rationalize them. Second, not all people are equity sensitive. For example, a small part of the working population actually prefers that their outcome-input ratio be less than the referent comparison. Predictions from equity theory are not likely to be very accurate with these so-called benevolent types.

It's also important to note that while most research on equity theory has focused on pay, employees seem to look for equity in the distribution of other organizational rewards. For instance, it's been shown that the use of high-status job titles as well as large and lavishly furnished offices may function as outcomes for some employees in their equity equation.[52]

Finally, recent research has been directed at expanding what is meant by equity or fairness. Historically, equity theory focused on **distributive justice** or the perceived fairness of the *amount* and *allocation* of rewards among individuals. But equity should also consider **procedural justice**—the perceived fairness of the *process* used to determine the distribution of rewards. The evidence indicates that distributive justice has a greater influence on employee satisfaction than procedural justice whereas procedural justice tends to affect an employee's organizational commitment, trust in his or her boss, and intention to quit.[53] So managers should consider openly sharing information on how allocation decisions are made, following consistent and unbiased procedures, and engaging in similar practices to increase the perception of procedural justice. And by increasing the perception of procedural fairness, employees are likely to view their bosses and the organization as positive even if they're dissatisfied with pay, promotions, and other personal outcomes.

distributive justice
Perceived fairness of the amount and allocation of rewards among individuals.

procedural justice
The perceived fairness of the process used to determine the distribution of rewards.

In conclusion, equity theory demonstrates that, for most employees, motivation is influenced significantly by relative rewards as well as by absolute rewards. But some key issues are still unclear.[54] For instance, how do employees handle conflicting equity signals, such as when unions point to other employee groups who are substantially *better off*, while management argues how much things have *improved*? How do employees define inputs and outcomes? How do they combine and weigh their inputs and outcomes to arrive at totals? When and how do the factors change over time? Yet, regardless of these problems, equity theory continues to offer us some important insights into employee motivation.

Expectancy Theory

expectancy theory
The strength of a tendency to act in a certain way depends on the strength of an expectation that the act will be followed by a given outcome and on the attractiveness of that outcome to the individual.

Currently, one of the most widely accepted explanations of motivation is Victor Vroom's **expectancy theory**.[55] Although it has its critics,[56] most of the research evidence is supportive of the theory.[57]

Expectancy theory argues that the strength of a tendency to act in a certain way depends on the strength of an expectation that the act will be followed by a given outcome and on the attractiveness of that outcome to the individual. In more practical terms, expectancy theory says an employee is motivated to exert a high level of effort when he or she believes effort will lead to a good performance appraisal; a good appraisal will lead to organizational rewards like a bonus, a salary increase, or a promotion; and the rewards will satisfy the employee's personal goals. The theory, therefore, focuses on three relationships (see Figure 6-7).

1. *Effort–performance relationship*: The probability perceived by the individual that exerting a given amount of effort will lead to performance.
2. *Performance–reward relationship*: The degree to which the individual believes that performing at a particular level will lead to the attainment of a desired outcome.
3. *Rewards–personal goals relationship*: The degree to which organizational rewards satisfy an individual's personal goals or needs and the attractiveness of those potential rewards for the individual.[58]

Figure 6-7
Expectancy Theory

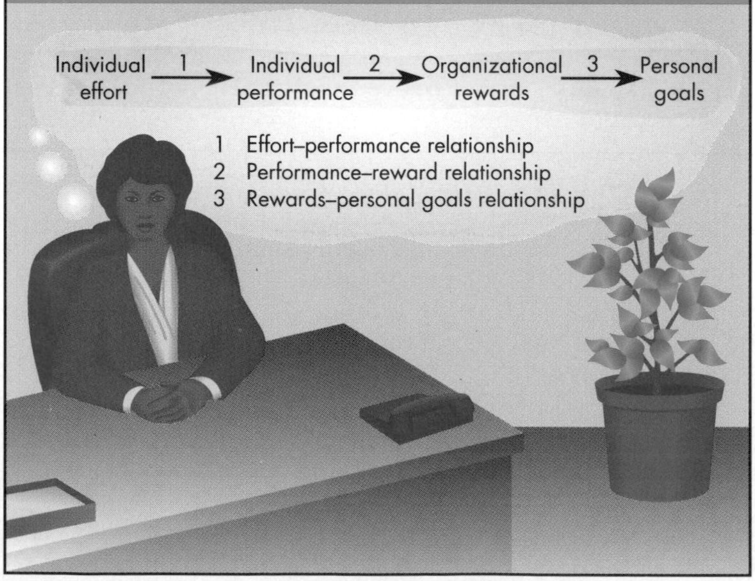

Expectancy theory helps explain why a lot of workers aren't motivated on their jobs and merely do the minimum necessary to get by. This is evident when we look at the theory's three relationships in a little more detail. We present them as questions employees need to answer in the affirmative if their motivation is to be maximized.

◆Expectancy theory helps explain why a lot of workers aren't motivated on their jobs and merely do the minimum necessary to get by.

First, *if I give a maximum effort, will it be recognized in my performance appraisal*? For a lot of employees, the answer is no. Why? Their skill level may be deficient, which means no matter how hard they try, they're not likely to be a high performer. The organization's performance appraisal system may be designed to assess nonperformance factors like loyalty, initiative, or courage, which means more effort won't necessarily result in a higher evaluation. Still another possibility is that the employee, rightly or wrongly, perceives that her boss doesn't like her. As a result, she expects to get a poor appraisal regardless of her level of effort. These examples suggest that one possible source of low employee motivation is the belief, by the employee, that no matter how hard she works, the likelihood of getting a good performance appraisal is low.

Second, *if I get a good performance appraisal, will it lead to organizational rewards*? Many employees see the performance–reward relationship in their job as weak. The reason, as we elaborate on in Chapters 7 and 16, is that organizations reward a lot of things besides just performance. For example, when pay is allocated to employees based on factors such as seniority, being cooperative, or for "kissing up" to the boss, employees are likely to see the performance–reward relationship as being weak and demotivating.

Last, *if I'm rewarded, are they the rewards I find personally attractive*? The employee works hard in hope of getting a promotion, but gets a pay raise instead. Or the employee wants a more interesting and challenging job, but receives only a few words of praise. Or the employee puts in extra effort to be relocated to the company's Paris office but instead is transferred to Chicago. These examples illustrate the importance of the rewards being tailored to individual employee needs. Unfortunately, many managers are limited in the rewards they can distribute, which makes it difficult to individualize rewards. Moreover, some managers incorrectly assume that all employees want the same thing, thus overlooking the motivational effects of differentiating rewards. In either case, employee motivation is submaximized.

In summary, the key to expectancy theory is the understanding of an individual's goals and the linkage between effort and performance, between performance and rewards, and, finally, between the rewards and individual goal satisfaction. As a contingency model, expectancy theory recognizes that there is no universal principle for explaining everyone's motivations. Additionally, just because we understand what needs a person seeks to satisfy does not ensure that the individual himself perceives high performance as necessarily leading to the satisfaction of these needs.

Referring back to this chapter's opening vignette on Lincoln Electric, notice how this company has successfully applied the key elements from expectancy theory. The effort–performance relationship is strengthened by a clear and objective system for evaluating an employee's performance. Lincoln tightly links the appraisal to rewards by basing piece-rate wages and bonuses on employee productivity and company profits. Finally, because the company's bonus and security system has been in place so long, Lincoln tends to attract and hire individuals who value the rewards it provides—job security, job flexibility, and lucrative financial benefits.

◆◆◆◆ OB in the News ◆◆◆◆

How Do You Motivate American Workers to Improve Quality?

A recent study compared the attitudes and behavior of American workers with their Japanese counterparts on the issue of quality improvement. The findings were illuminating, especially in terms of applying total quality management in U.S. organizations. Highlights from the study include the following:

- Unlike Japanese workers, Americans aren't interested in incremental improvements to increase quality. They want to achieve major breakthroughs. Implications for motivation: Ask for big leaps rather than tiny steps.
- Change is a threat to Americans when imposed from above but can be positive if workers feel they can control it. Implications for motivation: Managers should talk to employees about the general goal and get them to suggest the changes necessary to achieve it.
- The Japanese are methodical and rational in their relentless drive to improve things. Americans are more emotional. Implications for motivation: Get U.S. workers to feel they have a personal stake or are achieving things individually.
- Americans learn by making mistakes. It doesn't work for managers to demand that workers get it right the first time. Implications for motivation: Be tolerant of mistakes and create mechanisms for spreading news of mistakes and the lessons learned from them.

Based on "Quality: What Motivates American Workers?" *Business Week* (April 12, 1993), p. 93

Does expectancy theory work? Attempts to validate the theory have been complicated by methodological, criterion, and measurement problems. As a result, many published studies that purport to support or negate the theory must be viewed with caution. Importantly, most studies have failed to replicate the methodology as it was originally proposed. For example, the theory proposes to explain different levels of effort from the same person under different circumstances, but almost all replication studies have looked at different people. Correcting for this flaw has greatly improved support for the validity of expectancy theory.[59] Some critics suggest the theory has only limited use, arguing that it tends to be more valid for predicting in situations where effort–performance and performance–reward linkages are clearly perceived by the individual.[60] Since few individuals perceive a high correlation between performance and rewards in their jobs, the theory tends to be idealistic. If organizations actually rewarded individuals for performance rather than according to such criteria as seniority, effort, skill level, and job difficulty, then the theory's validity might be considerably greater. However, rather than invalidating expectancy theory, this criticism can be used in support of the theory, for it explains why a large segment of the work force exerts low levels of effort in carrying out their job responsibilities.

Don't Forget Ability and Opportunity

Robin and Chris both graduated from college a couple of years ago with their degrees in elementary education. They each took jobs as first grade teachers, but in different school districts. Robin immediately confronted a number of obstacles on the job: a large class (42 students), a small and dingy classroom, and inadequate supplies. Chris's situation couldn't have been more different. He had only 15 students in his class, plus a teaching aide for 15 hours each week, a modern and well-lighted room, a well-stocked supply cabinet, six Macintosh computers for students to use, and a highly supportive principal. Not surprisingly, at the end of their first school year, Chris had been considerably more effective as a teacher than Robin.

The preceding episode illustrates an obvious but often overlooked fact. Success on a job is facilitated or hindered by the existence or absence of support resources.

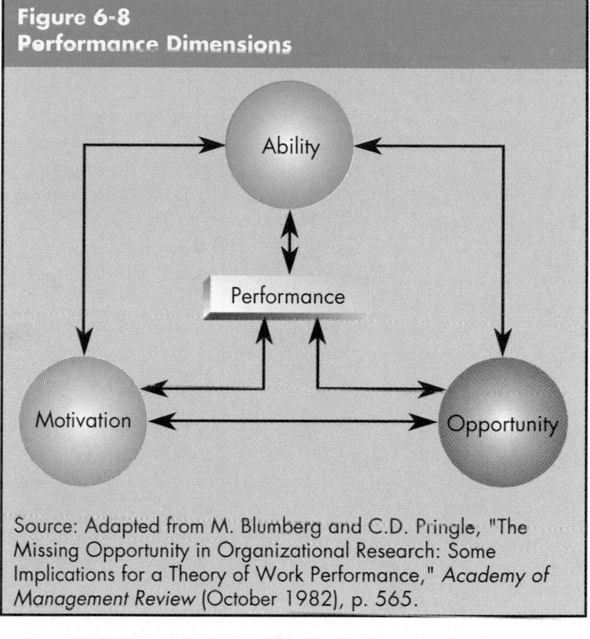

Figure 6-8
Performance Dimensions

Source: Adapted from M. Blumberg and C.D. Pringle, "The Missing Opportunity in Organizational Research: Some Implications for a Theory of Work Performance," *Academy of Management Review* (October 1982), p. 565.

A popular, although arguably simplistic, way of thinking about employee performance is as a function of the interaction of ability and motivation; that is, performance = $f(A \times M)$. If either is inadequate, performance will be negatively affected. This helps to explain, for instance, the hardworking athlete or student with modest abilities who consistently outperforms his or her more gifted, but lazy, rival. So, as we noted in Chapter 3, an individual's intelligence and skills (subsumed under the label "ability") must be considered in addition to motivation if we are to be able to accurately explain and predict employee performance. But a piece of the puzzle is still missing. We need to add **opportunity to perform** to our equation—performance = $f(A \times M \times O)$.[61] Even though an individual may be willing and able, there may be obstacles that constrain performance. This is shown in Figure 6-8.

opportunity to perform
High levels of performance are partially a function of an absence of obstacles that constrain the employee.

When you attempt to assess why an employee may not be performing to the level you believe he or she is capable of, take a look at the work environment to see if it's supportive. Does the employee have adequate tools, equipment, materials, and supplies; does the employee have favorable working conditions, helpful coworkers, supportive rules and procedures to work under, sufficient information to make job-related decisions, adequate time to do a good job, and the like? If not, performance will suffer.

Integrating Contemporary Theories of Motivation

We've looked at a lot of motivation theories in this chapter. The fact that a number of these theories have been supported only complicates the matter. How simple it would have been if, after presenting half-a-dozen theories, only one was found valid. But these theories are not all in competition with one another! Because one is valid doesn't automatically make the others invalid. In fact, many of the theories presented in this chapter are complementary. So the challenge is now to tie these theories together to help you understand their interrelationships.

Figure 6-9 presents a model that integrates much of what we know about motivation. Its basic foundation is the expectancy model shown in Figure 6-7. Let's work through Figure 6-9.

Figure 6-9
Integrating Contemporary Theories of Motivation

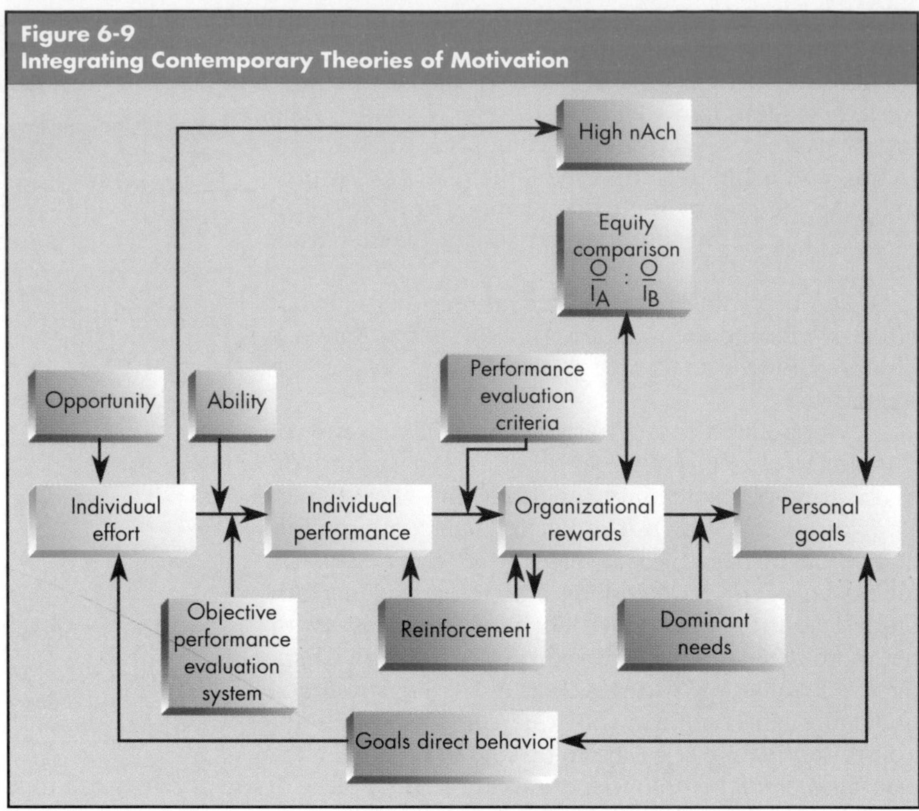

We begin by explicitly recognizing that opportunities can aid or hinder individual effort. The individual effort box also has another arrow leading into it. This arrow flows out of the person's goals. Consistent with goal-setting theory, this goals–effort loop is meant to remind us that goals direct behavior.

Expectancy theory predicts that an employee will exert a high level of effort if he or she perceives a strong relationship between effort and performance, performance and rewards, and rewards and satisfaction of personal goals. Each of these relationships, in turn, is influenced by certain factors. For effort to lead to good performance, the individual must have the requisite ability to perform, and the performance appraisal system that measures the individual's performance must be perceived as being fair and objective. The performance–reward relationship will be strong if the individual perceives it is performance (rather than seniority, personal favorites, or other criteria) that is rewarded. If cognitive evaluation theory were fully valid in the actual workplace, we would predict here that basing rewards on performance should decrease the individual's intrinsic motivation. The final link in expectancy theory is the rewards–goals relationship. ERG theory would come into play at this point. Motivation would be high to the degree that the rewards an individual received for his or her high performance satisfied the dominant needs consistent with his or her individual goals.

A closer look at Figure 6-9 will also reveal that the model considers the achievement need and reinforcement and equity theories. The high achiever is not motivated by the organization's assessment of his or her performance or organizational rewards, hence the jump from effort to personal goals for those with a high *nAch*. Remember, high achievers are internally driven as long as the jobs they are doing provide them with personal responsibility, feedback, and moderate risks. So they are not concerned with the effort–performance, performance–rewards, or rewards–goal linkages.

Reinforcement theory enters our model by recognizing that the organization's rewards reinforce the individual's performance. If management has designed a reward system that is seen by employees as paying off for good performance, the rewards will reinforce and encourage continued good performance. Rewards also play the key part in equity theory. Individuals will compare the rewards (outcomes) they receive from the inputs they make with the outcome–input ratio of relevant others (O/Ia:O/Ib), and inequities may influence the effort expended.

Caveat Emptor: Motivation Theories are Culture Bound

In our discussion of goal setting, we said care needs to be taken in applying this theory because it assumes cultural characteristics that are not universal. This is true for many of the theories presented in this chapter. Most current motivation theories were developed in the United States by Americans and about Americans.[62] Maybe the most blatant pro-American characteristics inherent in these theories is the strong emphasis on what we defined in Chapter 2 as individualism and quantity of life. For instance, both goal-setting and expectancy theories emphasize goal accomplishment as well as rational and individual thought. Let's take a look at how this bias has affected several of the motivation theories introduced in this chapter.

Maslow's need hierarchy argues that people start at the physiological level and then move progressively up the hierarchy in this order: physiological, safety, social, esteem, and self-actualization. This hierarchy, if it has any application at all, aligns with American culture. In countries like Japan, Greece, and

While managers must be careful in applying motivation theories across cultures, Switzerland-based Nestlé, the world's largest branded food company, hires high achievers to sell its products in markets that span the globe. Cultural differences aside, Nestlé salespeople are motivated by growth, achievement, responsibility, and recognition. In Thailand, Nestlé formed the Red Hot Sales Force (shown here) to sell its products to the American-style supermarkets and superstores sprouting up in developing nations. College-educated and fluent in English, the Red Hot team is trained in Western-style management practices. Nestlé challenges these high achievers to succeed in maintaining profit and market share growth as competition in Thailand intensifies.

Mexico, where uncertainty avoidance characteristics are strong, security needs would be on top of the need hierarchy. Countries that score high on quality-of-life characteristics—Denmark, Sweden, Norway, the Netherlands, and Finland—would have social needs on top.[63] We would predict, for instance, that group work will motivate employees more when the country's culture scores high on the quality criterion.

Another motivation concept that clearly has an American bias is the achievement need. The view that a high achievement need acts as an internal motivator presupposes two cultural characteristics—a willingness to accept a moderate degree of risk (which excludes countries with strong uncertainty avoidance characteristics) and a concern with performance (which applies almost singularly to countries with strong quantity-of-life characteristics). This combination is found in Anglo-American countries like the United States, Canada, and Great Britain.[64] On the other hand, these characteristics are relatively absent in countries such as Chile and Portugal.

But don't assume there aren't *any* cross-cultural consistencies. For instance, the desire for interesting work seems important to almost all workers, regardless of their national culture. In a study of seven countries, employees in Belgium, Britain, Israel, and the United States ranked "interesting work" number one among 11 work goals. And this factor was ranked either second or third in Japan, the Netherlands, and Germany.[65] Similarly, in a study comparing job preference outcomes among graduate students in the United States, Canada, Australia, and Singapore, growth, achievement, and responsibility were rated the top three and had identical rankings.[66] Both of these studies suggest some universality to the importance of intrinsic factors in motivation-hygiene theory.

Summary and Implications for Managers

The theories we've discussed in this chapter do not all address our four dependent variables. Some, for instance, are directed at explaining turnover; others emphasize productivity. The theories also differ in their predictive strength. In this section, we (1) review the key motivation theories to determine their relevance in explaining our dependent variables, and (2) assess the predictive power of each.[67]

NEED THEORIES We introduced four theories that focused on needs: Maslow's hierarchy, motivation-hygiene, ERG, and McClelland's needs theories. The strongest of these is probably the last, particularly regarding the relationship between achievement and productivity. If the other three have any value at all, that value relates to explaining and predicting job satisfaction.

GOAL-SETTING THEORY Few dispute that clear and difficult goals lead to higher levels of employee productivity. This evidence leads us to conclude that goal-setting theory provides one of the more powerful explanations of this dependent variable. The theory, however, does not address absenteeism, turnover, or satisfaction.

REINFORCEMENT THEORY This theory has an impressive record for predicting factors like quality and quantity of work, persistence of effort, absenteeism, tardiness, and accident rates. It does not offer much insight into employee satisfaction or the decision to quit.

EQUITY THEORY Equity theory deals with all four dependent variables. However, it is strongest when predicting absence and turnover behaviors and weak when predicting differences in employee productivity.

EXPECTANCY THEORY Our final theory focused on performance variables. It has proved to offer a relatively powerful explanation of employee productivity, absenteeism, and turnover. But expectancy theory assumes that employees have few constraints on their decision discretion. It makes many of the same assumptions as the optimizing model about individual decision making (see Chapter 4). This acts to restrict its applicability.

For major decisions, like accepting or resigning from a job, expectancy theory works well because people don't rush into decisions of this nature. They're more prone to take the time to carefully consider the costs and benefits of all the alternatives. But expectancy theory is not a very good explanation for more typical types of work behavior, especially for individuals in lower level jobs, because such jobs come with considerable limitations imposed by work methods, supervisors, and company policies. We would conclude, therefore, that expectancy theory's power in explaining employee productivity increases where the jobs being performed are more complex and higher in the organization (where discretion is greater).

Summary

Table 6-2 summarizes what we know about the power of the more well-known motivation theories to explain and predict our four dependent variables. Although based on a wealth of research, it also includes some subjective judgments. However, it does provide a reasonable guide through the motivation theory maze.

Table 6-2 Power of Motivation Theories[a]

	THEORIES				
Variable	Need	Goal-Setting	Reinforcement	Equity	Expectancy
Productivity	3[b]	5	3	3	4[c]
Absenteeism			4	4	4
Turnover				4	5
Satisfaction	2			2	

[a] Theories are rated on a scale of 1 to 5, 5 being highest.
[b] Applies to individuals with a high need to achieve.
[c] Limited value in jobs where employees have little discretionary choice.

Source: Based on F.J. Landy and W.S. Becker, "Motivation Theory Reconsidered," in L.L. Cummings and B.M. Staw (eds.), *Research in Organizational Behavior*, Vol. 9 (Greenwich, CT: JAI Press, 1987), p. 33.

For Review

1. Define motivation. Describe the motivation process.
2. What are the implications of Theories X and Y for motivation practices?
3. Compare and contrast Maslow's hierarchy of needs theory with (a) Alderfer's ERG theory and (b) Herzberg's motivation-hygiene theory.
4. Describe the three needs isolated by McClelland. How are they related to worker behavior?
5. Explain cognitive evaluation theory. How applicable is it to management practice?
6. What's the role of self-efficacy in goal setting?
7. Contrast distributive and procedural justice.
8. Identify the variables in expectancy theory.
9. Explain the formula: Performance $= f(A \times M \times O)$ and give an example.
10. What consistencies among motivation concepts, if any, apply cross culturally?

For Discussion

1. "The cognitive evaluation theory is contradictory to reinforcement and expectancy theories." Do you agree or disagree? Explain.
2. "Goal setting is part of both reinforcement and expectancy theories." Do you agree or disagree? Explain.
3. Analyze the application of Maslow's and Herzberg's theories to an African or Caribbean nation where more than a quarter of the population is unemployed.
4. Can an individual be too motivated, so his or her performance declines as a result of excessive effort? Discuss.
5. Identify three activities you really enjoy (for example, playing tennis, reading a novel, going shopping). Next, identify three activities you really dislike (for example, going to the dentist, cleaning the house, staying on a restricted calorie diet). Using the expectancy model, analyze each of your answers to assess why some activities stimulate your effort while others don't.

Point

Money Motivates!

The importance of money as a motivator has been consistently downgraded by most behavioral scientists. They prefer to point out the value of challenging jobs, goals, participation in decision making, feedback, cohesive work groups, and other nonmonetary factors as stimulants to employee motivation. We argue otherwise here—that money is *the* crucial incentive to work motivation. As a medium of exchange, it is the vehicle by which employees can purchase the numerous need-satisfying things they desire. Further, money also performs the function of a scorecard, by which employees assess the value the organization places on their services and by which employees can compare their value to others.*

Money's value as a medium of exchange is obvious. People may not work only for money, but take the money away and how many people would come to work? A recent study of nearly 2,500 employees found that while these people disagreed over what was their number one motivator, they unanimously ranked money as their number two.** This study reaffirms that for the vast majority of the work force, a regular paycheck is absolutely necessary in order to meet their basic physiological and safety needs.

As equity theory suggests, money has symbolic value in addition to its exchange value. We use pay as the primary outcome against which we compare our inputs to determine if we are being treated equitably. That an organization pays one executive $80,000 a year and another $95,000 means more than the latter's earning $15,000 a year more. It is a message, from the organization to both employees, of how much it values the contribution of each.

In addition to equity theory, both reinforcement and expectancy theories attest to the value of money as a motivator. In the former, if pay is contingent on performance, it will encourage workers to high levels of effort. Consistent with expectancy theory, money will motivate to the extent that it is seen as being able to satisfy an individual's personal goals and is perceived as being dependent upon performance criteria.

The best case for money as a motivator is a review of studies done by Ed Locke at the University of Maryland.*** Locke looked at four methods of motivating employee performance: money, goal setting, participation in decision making, and redesigning jobs to give workers more challenge and responsibility. He found that the average improvement from money was 30 percent; goal setting increased performance 16 percent; participation improved performance by less than 1 percent; and job redesign positively impacted performance by an average of 17 percent. Moreover, every study Locke reviewed that used money as a method of motivation resulted in some improvement in employee performance. Such evidence demonstrates that money may not be the *only* motivator, but it is difficult to argue that it *doesn't* motivate!

*K.O. Doyle, "Introduction: Money and the Behavioral Sciences," *American Behavioral Scientist* (July 1992), pp. 641–57.

**S. Caudron, "Motivation? Money's Only No. 2," *Industry Week* (November 15, 1993), p. 33.

***E.A. Locke et al., "The Relative Effectiveness of Four Methods of Motivating Employee Performance," in K.D. Duncan, M.M. Gruneberg, and D. Wallis (eds.), *Changes in Working Life* (London: Wiley, 1980), pp. 363–83.

counterPoint

Money Doesn't Motivate Most Employees Today!

Money can motivate *some* people under *some* conditions. So the issue isn't really whether or not money *can* motivate. The more relevant question is: Does money motivate most employees in the work force today to higher performance? The answer to this question, we'll argue, is "No."

For money to motivate an individual's performance, certain conditions must be met. First, money must be important to the individual. Second, money must be perceived by the individual as being a direct reward for performance. Third, the marginal amount of money offered for the performance must be perceived by the individual as being significant. Finally, management must have the discretion to reward high performers with more money. Let's take a look at each of these conditions.

Money is not important to all employees. High achievers, for instance, are intrinsically motivated. Money should have little impact on these people. Similarly, money is relevant to those individuals with strong lower order needs; but for most of the work force, their lower order needs are substantially satisfied.

Money would motivate if employees perceived a strong linkage between performance and rewards in organizations. Unfortunately, pay increases are far more often determined by community pay standards, the national cost-of-living index, and the organization's current and future financial prospects than by each employee's level of performance.

For money to motivate, the marginal difference in pay increases between a high performer and an average performer must be significant. In practice, it rarely is. For instance, a high-performing employee who currently is earning $35,000 a year is given a $200-a-month raise. After taxes, that amounts to about $35 a week. But this employee's $35,000-a-year coworker, who is an average performer, is rarely passed over at raise time. Instead of getting a 7 percent raise, he is likely to get half of that. The net difference in their weekly paychecks is probably less than $20. How much motivation is there in knowing that if you work really hard you're going to end up with $20 a week more than someone who is doing just enough to get by? For a large number of people, not much!

Our last point relates to the degree of discretion that managers have in being able to reward high performers. Where unions exist, that discretion is almost zero. Pay is determined through collective bargaining and is allocated by job title and seniority, not level of performance. In nonunionized environments, the organization's compensation policies will constrain managerial discretion. Each job typically has a pay grade. So a systems analyst III can earn between $3,825 and $4,540 a month. No matter how good a job that analyst does, her boss cannot pay her more than $4,540 a month. Similarly, no matter how poorly someone does in that job, he will earn at least $3,825 a month. In most organizations, managers have a very small area of discretion within which they can reward their higher performing employees. So money might be theoretically capable of motivating employees to higher levels of performance, but most managers aren't given enough flexibility to do much about it.

Learning About Yourself Exercise

What Motivates You?

For each of the following 15 statements, circle the number that most closely agrees with how you feel. Consider your answers in the context of your current job or past work experience.

	Strongly Disagree				Strongly Agree
1. I try very hard to improve on my past performance at work.	1	2	3	4	5
2. I enjoy competition and winning.	1	2	3	4	5
3. I often find myself talking to those around me about nonwork matters.	1	2	3	4	5
4. I enjoy a difficult challenge.	1	2	3	4	5
5. I enjoy being in charge.	1	2	3	4	5
6. I want to be liked by others.	1	2	3	4	5
7. I want to know how I am progressing as I complete tasks.	1	2	3	4	5
8. I confront people who do things I disagree with.	1	2	3	4	5
9. I tend to build close relationships with co-workers.	1	2	3	4	5
10. I enjoy setting and achieving realistic goals.	1	2	3	4	5
11. I enjoy influencing other people to get my way.	1	2	3	4	5
12. I enjoy belonging to groups and organizations.	1	2	3	4	5
13. I enjoy the satisfaction of completing a difficult task.	1	2	3	4	5
14. I often work to gain more control over the events around me.	1	2	3	4	5
15. I enjoy working with others more than working alone.	1	2	3	4	5

Turn to page A-27 for scoring directions and key.

Source: Based on R. Steers and D. Braunstein, "A Behaviorally Based Measure of Manifest Needs in Work Settings," *Journal of Vocational Behavior* (October 1976), p. 254; and R. N. Lussier, *Human Relations in Organizations: A Skill Building Approach* (Homewood, IL: Richard D. Irwin, 1990), p. 120.

Working with Others Exercise

What Do People Want from Their Jobs?

Each class member begins by completing the following questionnaire:

Rate the 12 job factors listed below according to how important each is to you. Place a number on a scale of 1 to 5 on the line before each factor.

Very important		Somewhat important		Not important
5	4	3	2	1

_____ 1. An interesting job
_____ 2. A good boss
_____ 3. Recognition and appreciation for the work I do
_____ 4. The opportunity for advancement
_____ 5. A satisfying personal life
_____ 6. A prestigious or status job
_____ 7. Job responsibility
_____ 8. Good working conditions
_____ 9. Sensible company rules, regulations, procedures, and policies
_____ 10. The opportunity to grow through learning new things
_____ 11. A job I can do well and succeed at
_____ 12. Job security

This questionnaire taps the two dimensions in Herzberg's motivation-hygiene theory. To determine if hygiene or motivating factors are important to you, place the numbers 1–5 that represent your answers below.

Hygiene factors score	Motivational factors score
2. ____	1. ____
5. ____	3. ____
6. ____	4. ____
8. ____	7. ____
9. ____	10. ____
12. ____	11. ____
Total points ____	Total points ____

Add up each column. Did you select hygienes or motivators as being most important to you?

Now break into groups of five or six and compare your questionnaire results: (a) How similar are your scores? (b) How close did your group's results come to those found by Herzberg? (c) What motivational implications did your group arrive at based on your analysis?

This exercise is based on R.N. Lussier, *Human Relations in Organizations: A Skill Building Approach*, 2nd ed. (Homewood, IL: Richard D. Irwin, 1993). With permission.

Ethical Dilemma Exercise

Is "Motivation" Merely "Manipulation" in Fine Dress Clothes?

Managers are concerned with the subject of motivation because they're concerned with learning how to get the most effort from their employees. Is this ethical? For example, when managers link rewards to productivity, aren't they manipulating employees?

"To manipulate" is defined as "(1) to handle, manage, or use, especially with skill, in some process of treatment or performance; (2) to manage or influence by artful skill; (3) to adapt or change to suit one's purpose or advantage."

Aren't one or more of these definitions compatible with the notion of managers skillfully seeking to influence employee productivity for the benefit of the manager and the organization? If so, isn't that why managers want to become proficient at motivating others?

Do managers have the right to seek control over their employees? Does anyone, for that matter, have the right to control others? Does control imply manipulation? Does manipulation mean merely getting others to do what you want? Does it mean making others behave the way you want? Does it connote fraud or deceit?

What do *you* think?

Responding to a Labor Shortage: Nissan vs. USA Truck

CASE INCIDENT

Nissan Motor Company has a problem. It can't find enough people in Japan to fill its factories.

Young people in Japan are rejecting assembly-line work. They see it as monotonous, fast paced, and tiring. They'd rather work in a service job where the working conditions are cleaner and safer. Even among the young people who do try auto work, as many as 30 percent quit in their first year.

The worker shortage has meant long overtime hours, with many employees working 12-hour days and on Saturdays. Not only do employees dislike the long hours, management has become frustrated by the high costs of overtime and hiring temporary workers.

What can Nissan's management do? Whatever solutions they come up with, they realize this is no short-term problem. Japan's population is aging. Its low birthrate means the population of 18-year-olds is expected to drop from roughly 2 million now to 1.5 million by the end of the decade. Moreover, automakers are being pressed by the Japanese government to reduce the average number of hours worked to bring Japan more in line with other industrialized nations.

USA Truck, Inc., had a similar problem to Nissan. This Arkansas long hauler of goods such as tire fabric and auto parts for companies like Goodyear and General Motors faced a shortage of truck drivers due to high turnover. When new management took over the company in 1989, they decided to address the problem head on. They went directly to their 600 drivers and asked them for advice about how the company could reduce turnover. This became the first of regular quarterly meetings between company management and senior drivers.

USA Truck keeps valued employees like experienced driver Carlton Curry, age 32, by treating them fairly. Curry says of his company, "It's first class here." He works long hours but is well compensated. In a recent year, Curry made $50,000, more than a lot of middle managers his age.

USA Truck's new management got an earful from the drivers. While the pay was good (often $50,000 a year or more), the drivers complained about the long hours—70-hour weeks aren't unusual—and spending two to four weeks on the road at a time. When the drivers asked for antilock brakes and air-ride suspensions, management installed them. When USA built a drivers' dormitory at its West Memphis, Arkansas, terminal, the drivers suggested putting in private shower stalls instead of a communal bathing area; it was done. Drivers wanted to get home more often from their long, cross-country trips; so USA added the time a driver had been on the road to the information provided to dispatchers assigning loads and cut average tours from six to two weeks.

The changes at USA Truck have significantly improved morale and cut turnover among drivers. But the jobs are still hard. Management demands on-time deliveries because, unlike most long-haul truckers, USA guarantees delivery not just to the day but to the hour (and charges a small premium to shippers for this service). So while management has demonstrated increased respect for its employees, it has not let up on its expectations from drivers. For instance, drivers who are late just twice in a year are out of a job.

Questions

1. Analyze Nissan's problem using motivation-hygiene theory.
2. What other theories of motivation might provide Nissan management with insights into solving their problem?
3. Contrast USA Truck's approach to the labor shortage problem with Nissan's approach. Use the motivation theories in this chapter to facilitate your analysis.
4. Make a comprehensive list of various actions Nissan might take to deal with its labor shortage.
5. Which of the actions listed in question 4 would you recommend they pursue? Why?

Based on A. Pollack, "Assembly-Line Amenities for Japan's Auto Workers," *New York Times* (July 20, 1992), p. A1; and R.L. Sullivan, "'It's First Class Here, Man,'" *Forbes* (March 14, 1994), pp. 102–4

Perks That Come with Being a State Governor

Why would any sane person spend millions of dollars trying to get a four-year job that pays $85,000 a year? That's what candidates for state governorships typically have to spend to get into office. Are these candidates crazy? Or is there something else—power, other forms of compensation—that motivates these people.

It's estimated that 39 percent of the trips Gov. Douglas Wilder of Virginia took in state transportation between 1990 and 1992 were for political or personal reasons.

Forty-five of 50 governors receive free housing. And typically it is not subsistence-level housing. Jim Edgar, governor of Illinois, resides in a 99-room, 45,000 square foot mansion, with a staff of 14—courtesy of state taxpayers. Kentucky's governor Brereton Jones is provided with a mansion and a staff that includes seven housekeepers and three chefs.

Many governors also use their position to approve remodeling of their official residences. William Donald Schaefer, Maryland's governor, spent $1.7 million of taxpayers' money to remodel his state's mansion. And Schaefer has 17 state troopers permanently assigned to him at a cost of more than a million dollars a year.

Some states allow their governors to supplement their salaries with income from speeches. New York's Mario Cuomo recently made $273,700 in one year from just giving speeches.

At least 19 states provide expense accounts for their governor's use. In New Mexico, for instance, the state's head gets $80,000 to cover everything from official entertainment to personal items.

By far the largest source of extra money for the nation's governors comes from unspent campaign contributions they can solicit even while in office. Virginia's Wilder kept $124,500 from his last campaign and has $900,000 left over from an inaugural fund that he hasn't told anyone what he plans to do with.

Not all states pamper their governors. Idaho, for instance, provides little in terms of perks for its chief executive. Cecil Andrus, Idaho's governor, lives in his own three bedroom, two bath home; drives himself to work; travels coach fare; and has no security detail.

Questions

1. Do you think perks provided to governors by state taxpayers are motivators or hygiene factors? Explain.
2. Using expectancy theory, explain how nonfinancial rewards might act as motivators.
3. What do you think motivates individuals to seek public office, even in cases where they have to spend large sums from their own personal assets to get elected?

Source: "Their Excellencies," *PrimeTime* (September 16, 1993).

Suggestions for Further Reading

CROPANZANO, R., K. JAMES, and M. CITERA, "A Goal Hierarchy Model of Personality, Motivation, and Leadership," in L.L. Cummings and B.M. Staw (eds.), *Research in Organizational Behavior*, Vol. 15 (Greenwich, CT: JAI Press, 1993), pp. 267–322.

HARDER, J.W., "Equity Theory versus Expectancy Theory: The Case of Major League Baseball Free Agents," *Journal of Applied Psychology* (June 1991), pp. 458–64.

JACKSON, L.A., P.D. GARDNER, and L.A. SULLIVAN, "Explaining Gender Differences in Self-Pay Expectations: Social Comparison Standards and Perceptions of Fair Pay," *Journal of Applied Psychology* (October 1992), pp. 651–63.

KANFER, R., "Motivation Theory and Industrial and Organizational Psychology," in M.D. Dunnette and L.M. Hough (eds.), *Handbook of Industrial and Organizational Psychology*, 2nd ed., Vol. 1 (Palo Alto, CA: Consulting Psychologists Press, 1990), pp. 75–170.

KATZELL, R.A., and D.E. THOMPSON, "Work Motivation: Theory and Practice," *American Psychologist* (February 1990), pp. 144–53.

KILBOURNE, L.M., and A.M. O'LEARY-KELLY, "A Reevaluation of Equity Theory: The Influence of Culture," *Journal of Management Inquiry* (June 1994), pp. 177–88.

STEERS, R.M., and L.W. PORTER, *Motivation and Work Behavior*, 5th ed. (New York: McGraw-Hill, 1991).

TUBBS, M.E., D.M. BOEHNE, and J.G. DAHL, "Expectancy, Valence, and Motivational Force Functions in Goal-Setting Research: An Empirical Test," *Journal of Applied Psychology* (June 1993), pp. 361–73.

WOFFORD, J.C., V.L. GOODWIN, and S. PREMACK, "Meta-Analysis of the Antecedents of Personal Goal Level and the Antecedents and Consequences of Goal Commitment," *Journal of Management* (September 1992), pp. 595–615.

WRIGHT, P.M., "An Examination of the Relationships Among Monetary Incentives, Goal Level, Goal Commitment, and Performance," *Journal of Management* (December 1992), pp. 677–93.

Notes

[1] Based on "Why This 'Obsolete' Company Is a 'Great Place to Work,'" *International Management* (April 1986), pp. 46–51; S.J. Modic, "Fine-Tuning a Classic," *Industry Week* (March 6, 1989), pp. 15–18; C. Wiley, "Incentive Plan Pushes Production," *Personnel Journal* (August 1993), pp. 86–87; and K. Chilton, "Lincoln Electric's Incentive System: Can It Be Transferred Overseas?" *Compensation & Benefits Review* (November-December 1993), pp. 21–30.

[2] R. Katerberg and G.J. Blau, "An Examination of Level and Direction of Effort and Job Performance," *Academy of Management Journal* (June 1983), pp. 249–57.

[3] A. Maslow, *Motivation and Personality* (New York: Harper & Row, 1954).

[4] See, for example, E.E. Lawler III and J.L. Suttle, "A Causal Correlation Test of the Need Hierarchy Concept," *Organizational Behavior and Human Performance* (April 1972), pp. 265–87; D.T. Hall and K.E. Nougaim, "An Examination of Maslow's Need Hierarchy in an Organizational Setting," *Organizational Behavior and Human Performance* (February 1968), pp. 12–35; and J. Rauschenberger, N. Schmitt, and J.E. Hunter, "A Test of the Need Hierarchy Concept by a Markov Model of Change in Need Strength," *Administrative Science Quarterly* (December 1980), pp. 654–70.

[5] A.K. Korman, J.H. Greenhaus, and I.J. Badin, "Personnel Attitudes and Motivation," in M.R. Rosenzweig and L.W. Porter (eds.), *Annual Review of Psychology* (Palo Alto, CA: Annual Reviews, 1977), p. 178.

[6] Ibid., p. 179.

[7] M.A. Wahba and L.G. Bridwell, "Maslow Reconsidered: A Review of Research on the Need Hierarchy Theory," *Organizational Behavior and Human Performance* (April 1976), pp. 212–40.

[8] D. McGregor, *The Human Side of Enterprise* (New York: McGraw-Hill, 1960). For an updated analysis of Theory X and Theory Y constructs, see R.J. Summers and S.F. Cronshaw, "A Study of McGregor's Theory X, Theory Y and the Influence of Theory X, Theory Y Assumptions on Causal Attributions for Instances of Worker Poor Performance," in S.L. McShane (ed.), *Organizational Behavior*, ASAC 1988 Conference Proceedings, Vol. 9, Part 5. Halifax, Nova Scotia, 1988, pp. 115–23.

[9] F. Herzberg, B. Mausner, and B. Snyderman, *The Motivation to Work* (New York: Wiley, 1959).

[10] R J. House and L.A. Wigdor, "Herzberg's Dual-Factor Theory of Job Satisfaction and Motivations: A Review of the Evidence and Criticism," *Personnel Psychology* (Winter 1967), pp. 369–89; D.P. Schwab and L.L. Cummings, "Theories of Performance and Satisfaction: A Review," *Industrial Relations* (October 1970), pp. 403–30; and R.J. Caston and R. Braito, "A Specification Issue in Job Satisfaction Research," *Sociological Perspectives* (April 1985), pp. 175–97.

[11] D. Guest, "What's New in Motivation," *Personnel Management* (May 1984), pp. 20–23.

[12] C.P. Alderfer, "An Empirical Test of a New Theory of Human Needs," *Organizational Behavior and Human Performance* (May 1969), pp. 142–75.

[13] M. Haire, E.E. Ghiselli, and L.W. Porter, "Cultural Patterns in the Role of the Manager," *Industrial Relations* (February 1963), pp. 95–117.

[14] C.P. Schneider and C.P. Alderfer, "Three Studies of Measures of Need Satisfaction in Organizations," *Administrative Science Quarterly* (December 1973), pp. 489–505.

[15] J.P. Wanous and A. Zwany, "A Cross-Sectional Test of Need Hierarchy Theory," *Organizational Behavior and Human Performance* (May 1977), pp. 78–97.

[16] D.C. McClelland, *The Achieving Society* (New York: Van Nostrand Reinhold, 1961); J.W. Atkinson and J.O. Raynor, *Motivation and Achievement* (Washington, DC: Winston, 1974); D.C. McClelland, *Power: The Inner Experience* (New York: Irvington, 1975); and M.J. Stahl, *Managerial and Technical Motivation: Assessing Needs for Achievement, Power, and Affiliation* (New York: Praeger, 1986).

[17] McClelland, *The Achieving Society*.

[18] See, for example, A. Mehrabian, "Measures of Achieving Tendency," *Educational and Psychological Measurement* (Summer 1969), pp. 445–51; H.J.M. Hermans, "A Questionnaire Measure of Achievement Motivation," *Journal of Applied Psychology* (August 1970), pp. 353–63; and J.M. Smith, "A Quick Measure of Achievement Motivation," *British Journal of Social and Clinical Psychology* (June 1973), pp. 137–43.

[19] See W.D. Spangler, "Validity of Questionnaire and TAT Measures of Need for Achievement: Two Meta-Analyses," *Psychological Bulletin* (July 1992), pp. 140–54.

[20] D.C. McClelland and D.G. Winter, *Motivating Economic Achievement* (New York: Free Press, 1969).

[21] McClelland, *Power*; McClelland and D.H. Burnham, "Power Is the Great Motivator," *Harvard Business Review* (March–April 1976), pp. 100–10; and R.E. Boyatzis, "The Need for Close Relationships and the Manager's Job," in D.A. Kolb, I.M. Rubin, and J.M. McIntyre (eds.), *Organizational Psychology: Readings on Human Behavior in Organizations*, 4th ed. (Englewood Cliffs, NJ: Prentice-Hall, 1984), pp. 81–86.

[22] Ibid.

[23] J.B. Miner, *Studies in Management Education* (New York: Springer, 1965).

[24] D. Kipnis, "The Powerholder," in J.T. Tedeschi (ed.), *Perspectives in Social Power* (Chicago: Aldine, 1974), pp. 82–123.

[25] D. McClelland, "Toward a Theory of Motive Acquisition," *American Psychologist* (May 1965), pp. 321–33; and D. Miron and D.C. McClelland, "The Impact of Achievement Motivation Training on Small Businesses," *California Management Review* (Summer 1979), pp. 13–28.

[26] R. de Charms, *Personal Causation: The Internal Affective Determinants of Behavior* (New York: Academic Press, 1968).

[27] E.L. Deci, *Intrinsic Motivation* (New York: Plenum, 1975); R.D. Pritchard, K.M. Campbell, and D.J. Campbell, "Effects of Extrinsic Financial Rewards on Intrinsic Motivation," *Journal of Applied Psychology* (February 1977), pp. 9–15; E.L. Deci, G. Betly, J. Kahle, L. Abrams, and J. Porac, "When Trying to Win: Competition and Intrinsic Motivation," *Personality and Social Psychology Bulletin* (March 1981), pp. 79–83; and P.C. Jordan, "Effects of an Extrinsic Reward on Intrinsic Motivation: A Field Experiment," *Academy of Management Journal* (June 1986), pp. 405–12.

[28] W.E. Scott, "The Effects of Extrinsic Rewards on 'Intrinsic Motivation': A Critique," *Organizational Behavior and Human Performance* (February 1976), pp. 117–19; B.J. Calder and B.M. Staw, "Interaction of Intrinsic and Extrinsic Motivation: Some Methodological Notes," *Journal of Personality and Social Psychology* (January 1975), pp. 76–80; and K.B. Boal and L.L. Cummings, "Cognitive Evaluation Theory: An Experimental Test of Processes and Outcomes," *Organizational Behavior and Human Performance* (December 1981), pp. 289–310.

[29] G.R. Salancik, "Interaction Effects of Performance and Money on Self-Perception of Intrinsic Motivation," *Organizational Behavior and Human Performance* (June 1975), pp. 339–51; and F. Luthans, M. Martinko, and T. Kess, "An Analysis of the Impact of Contingency Monetary Rewards on Intrinsic Motivation," *Proceedings of the Nineteenth Annual Midwest Academy of Management* (St. Louis: 1976), pp. 209–21.

[30] J.B. Miner, *Theories of Organizational Behavior* (Hinsdale, IL: Dryden Press, 1980), p. 157.

[31] H.J. Arnold, "Effects of Performance Feedback and Extrinsic Reward upon High Intrinsic Motivation," *Organizational Behavior and Human Performance* (December 1976), pp. 275–88.

[32] B.M. Staw, "Motivation in Organizations: Toward Synthesis and Redirection," in B.M. Staw and G.R. Salancik (eds.), *New Directions in Organizational Behavior* (Chicago: St. Clair, 1977), p. 76.

[33] B.J. Calder and B.M. Staw, "Self-Perception of Intrinsic and Extrinsic Motivation," *Journal of Personality and Social Psychology* (April 1975), pp. 599–605.

[34] E.A. Locke, "Toward a Theory of Task Motivation and Incentives," *Organizational Behavior and Human Performance* (May 1968), pp. 157–89.

[35] P.C. Earley, P. Wojnaroski, and W. Prest, "Task Planning and Energy Expended: Exploration of How Goals Influence Performance," *Journal of Applied Psychology* (February 1987), pp. 107–14.

[36] G.P. Latham and G.A. Yukl, "A Review of Research on the Application of Goal Setting in Organizations," *Academy of Management Journal* (December 1975), pp. 824–45; E.A. Locke, K.N. Shaw, L.M. Saari, and G.P. Latham, "Goal Setting and Task Performance," *Psychological Bulletin* (January 1981), pp. 125–52; A.J. Mento, R.P. Steel, and R.J. Karren, "A Meta-Analytic Study of the Effects of Goal Setting on Task Performance: 1966–1984," *Organizational Behavior and Human Decision Processes* (February 1987), pp. 52–83; M.E. Tubbs "Goal Setting: A Meta-Analytic Examination of the Empirical Evidence," *Journal of Applied Psychology* (August 1986), pp. 474–83; P.C. Earley, G.B. Northcraft, C. Lee, and T.R. Lituchy, "Impact of Process and Outcome Feedback on the Relation of Goal Setting to Task Performance," *Academy of Management Journal* (March 1990), pp. 87–105; and E.A. Locke and G.P. Latham, *A Theory of Goal Setting and Task Performance* (Englewood Cliffs, NJ: Prentice Hall, 1990).

[37] J.M. Ivancevich and J.T. McMahon, "The Effects of Goal Setting, External Feedback, and Self-Generated Feedback on Outcome Variables: A Field Experiment," *Academy of Management Journal* (June 1982), pp. 359–72.

[38] See, for example, G.P. Latham, M. Erez, and E.A. Locke, "Resolving Scientific Disputes by the Joint Design of Crucial Experiments by the Antagonists: Application to the Erez-Latham Dispute Regarding Participation in Goal Setting," *Journal of Applied Psychology* (November 1988), pp. 753–72.

[39] M. Erez, P.C. Earley, and C.L. Hulin, "The Impact of Participation on Goal Acceptance and Performance: A Two-Step Model," *Academy of Management Journal* (March 1985), pp. 50–66.

[40] J.R. Hollenbeck, C.R. Williams, and H.J. Klein, "An Empirical Examination of the Antecedents of Commitment to Difficult Goals," *Journal of Applied Psychology* (February 1989), pp. 18–23. See also J.C. Wofford, V.L. Goodwin, and S. Premack, "Meta-Analysis of the Antecedents of Personal Goal Level and of the Antecedents and Consequences of Goal Commitment," *Journal of Management* (September 1992), pp. 595–615; and M.E. Tubbs, "Commitment as a Moderator of the Goal-Performance Relation: A Case for Clearer Construct Definition," *Journal of Applied Psychology* (February 1993), pp. 86–97.

[41] A. Bandura, "Self-Efficacy: Toward a Unifying Theory of Behavioral Change," *Psychological Review* (May 1977), pp. 191–215; and M.E. Gist, "Self-Efficacy: Implications for Organizational Behavior and Human Resource Management," *Academy of Management Review* (July 1987), pp. 472–85.

[42] E.A. Locke, E. Frederick, C. Lee, and P. Bobko, "Effect of Self-Efficacy, Goals, and Task Strategies on Task Performance," *Journal of Applied Psychology* (May 1984), pp. 241–51; and M.E. Gist and T.R. Mitchell, "Self-Efficacy: A Theoretical Analysis of Its Determinants and Malleability," *Academy of Management Review* (April 1992), pp. 183–211.

[43] A. Bandura and D. Cervone, "Differential Engagement in Self-Reactive Influences in Cognitively-Based Motivation," *Organizational Behavior and Human Decision Processes* (August 1986), pp. 92–113.

[44] See J.C. Anderson and C.A. O'Reilly, "Effects of an Organizational Control System on Managerial Satisfaction and Performance," *Human Relations* (June 1981), pp. 491–501; and J.P. Meyer, B. Schacht-Cole, and I.R. Gellatly, "An Examination of the Cognitive Mechanisms by Which Assigned Goals Affect Task Performance and Reactions to Performance," *Journal of Applied Social Psychology*, Vol. 18, No. 5 (1988), pp. 390–408.

[45] R.M. Steers and L.W. Porter, *Motivation and Work Behavior*, 2nd ed. (New York: McGraw-Hill, 1979), p. 13.

[46] E.A. Locke, "Latham vs. Komaki: A Tale of Two Paradigms," *Journal of Applied Psychology* (February 1980), pp. 16–23.

[47] J.S. Adams, "Inequity in Social Exchanges," in L. Berkowitz (ed.), *Advances in Experimental Social Psychology* (New York: Academic Press, 1965), pp. 267–300.

[48] P.S. Goodman, "An Examination of Referents Used in the Evaluation of Pay," *Organizational Behavior and Human Performance* (October 1974), pp. 170–95; S. Ronen, "Equity Perception in Multiple Comparisons: A Field Study," *Human Relations* (April 1986), pp. 333–46; R.W. Scholl, E.A. Cooper, and J.F. McKenna, "Referent Selection in Determining Equity Perception: Differential Effects on Behavioral and Attitudinal Outcomes," *Personnel Psychology* (Spring 1987), pp. 113–27; and T.P. Summers and A.S. DeNisi, "In Search of Adams' Other: Reexamination of Referents Used in the Evaluation of Pay," *Human Relations* (June 1990), pp. 497–511.

[49] C.T. Kulik and M.L. Ambrose, "Personal and Situational Determinants of Referent Choice," *Academy of Management Review* (April 1992), pp. 212–37.

[50] See, for example, E. Walster, G.W. Walster, and W.G. Scott, *Equity: Theory and Research* (Boston: Allyn & Bacon, 1978); and J. Greenberg, "Cognitive Reevaluation of Outcomes in Response to Underpayment Inequity," *Academy of Management Journal* (March 1989), pp. 174–84.

[51] P.S. Goodman and A. Friedman, "An Examination of Adams' Theory of Inequity," *Administrative Science Quarterly* (September 1971), pp. 271–88; R.P. Vecchio, "An Individual-Differences Interpretation of the Conflicting Predictions Generated by Equity Theory and Expectancy Theory," *Journal of Applied Psychology* (August 1981), pp. 470–81; J. Greenberg, "Approaching Equity and Avoiding Inequity in Groups and Organizations," in J. Greenberg and R.L. Cohen (eds.), *Equity and Justice in Social Behavior* (New York: Academic Press, 1982), pp. 389–435; R.T. Mowday, "Equity Theory Predictions of Behavior in Organizations," in R.M. Steers and L.W. Porter (eds.), *Motivation and Work Behavior*, 4th ed. (New York: McGraw-Hill, 1987), pp. 89–110; E.W. Miles, J.D. Hatfield, and R.C. Huseman, "The Equity Sensitive Construct: Potential Implications for Worker Performance," *Journal of Management* (December 1989), pp. 581–88; and R.T. Mowday, "Equity Theory Predictions of Behavior in Organizations," in R. Steers and L.W. Porter (eds.), *Motivation and Work Behavior*, 5th ed. (New York: McGraw-Hill, 1991), pp. 111–31.

[52] J. Greenberg and S. Ornstein, "High Status Job Title as Compensation for Underpayment: A Test of Equity Theory," *Journal of Applied Psychology* (May 1983), pp. 285–97; and J. Greenberg, "Equity and Workplace Status: A Field Experiment," *Journal of Applied Psychology* (November 1988), pp. 606–13.

[53] See, for example, R.C. Dailey and D.J. Kirk, "Distributive and Procedural Justice as Antecedents of Job Dissatisfaction and Intent to Turnover," *Human Relations* (March 1992), pp. 305–16; and D.B. McFarlin and P.D. Sweeney, "Distributive and Procedural Justice as Predictors of Satisfaction with Personal and Organizational Outcomes," *Academy of Management Journal* (August 1992), pp. 626–37.

[54] P.S. Goodman, "Social Comparison Process in Organizations," in B.M. Staw and G.R. Salancik (eds.), *New Directions in Organizational Behavior* (Chicago: St. Clair, 1977), pp. 97–132; and J. Greenberg, "A Taxonomy of Organizational Justice Theories," *Academy of Management Review* (January 1987), pp. 9–22.

[55] V.H. Vroom, *Work and Motivation* (New York: Wiley, 1964).

[56] See, for example, H.G. Heneman III and D.P. Schwab, "Evaluation of Research on Expectancy Theory Prediction of Employee Performance," *Psychological Bulletin* (July 1972), pp. 1–9; T.R. Mitchell, "Expectancy Models of Job Satisfaction, Occupational Preference and Effort: A Theoretical, Methodological and Empirical Appraisal," *Psychological Bulletin* (No-

vember 1974), pp. 1053–77; and L. Reinharth and M.A. Wahba, "Expectancy Theory as a Predictor of Work Motivation, Effort Expenditure, and Job Performance," *Academy of Management Journal* (September 1975), pp. 502–37.

[57] See, for example, L.W. Porter and E.E. Lawler III, *Managerial Attitudes and Performance* (Homewood, IL: Richard D. Irwin, 1968); D.F. Parker and L. Dyer, "Expectancy Theory as a Within-Person Behavioral Choice Model: An Empirical Test of Some Conceptual and Methodological Refinements," *Organizational Behavior and Human Performance* (October 1976), pp. 97–117; and H.J. Arnold, "A Test of the Multiplicative Hypothesis of Expectancy-Valence Theories of Work Motivation," *Academy of Management Journal* (April 1981), pp. 128–41.

[58] Vroom refers to these three variables as expectancy, instrumentality, and valence, respectively.

[59] P.M. Muchinsky, "A Comparison of Within- and Across-Subjects Analyses of the Expectancy-Valence Model for Predicting Effort," *Academy of Management Journal* (March 1977), pp. 154–58.

[60] R.J. House, H.J. Shapiro, and M.A. Wahba, "Expectancy Theory as a Predictor of Work Behavior and Attitudes: A Re-evaluation of Empirical Evidence," *Decision Sciences* (January 1974), pp. 481–506.

[61] L.H. Peters, E.J. O'Connor, and C.J. Rudolf, "The Behavioral and Affective Consequences of Performance-Relevant Situational Variables," *Organizational Behavior and Human Performance* (February 1980), pp. 79–96; M. Blumberg and C.D. Pringle, "The Missing Opportunity in Organizational Research: Some Implications for a Theory of Work Performance," *Academy of Management Review* (October 1982), pp. 560–69; D.A. Waldman and W.D. Spangler, "Putting Together the Pieces: A Closer Look at the Determinants of Job Performance," *Human Performance*, Vol. 2 (1989), pp. 29–59; and J. Hall, "Americans Know How to Be Productive If Managers Will Let Them," *Organizational Dynamics* (Winter 1994), pp. 33–46.

[62] N. J. Adler, *International Dimensions of Organizational Behavior*, 2nd ed. (Boston: PWS-Kent, 1991), p. 152.

[63] G. Hofstede, "Motivation, Leadership, and Organization: Do American Theories Apply Abroad?" *Organizational Dynamics* (Summer 1980), p. 55.

[64] Ibid.

[65] I. Harpaz, "The Importance of Work Goals: An International Perspective," *Journal of International Business Studies* (First Quarter 1990), pp. 75–93.

[66] G.E. Popp, H.J. Davis, and T.T. Herbert, "An International Study of Intrinsic Motivation Composition," *Management International Review* (January 1986), pp. 28–35.

[67] This section is based on F.J. Landy and W.S. Becker, "Motivation Theory Reconsidered," in L.L. Cummings and B.M. Staw (eds.), *Research in Organizational Behavior*, Vol. 9 (Greenwich, CT: JAI Press, 1987), pp. 24–35.

CHAPTER 7

At General Mills, when employees do a great job they get a big reward. This team of Yoplait yogurt managers earned bonuses of up to $50,000 each for exceeding growth goals.

MOTIVATION: FROM CONCEPTS TO APPLICATIONS

CHAPTER OUTLINE

company in the United States.[1] It's hard to find an organization where rank-and-file employees have such a direct influence on company policies.

The firm has an elaborate three-tier system to resolve differences and set all employee policies and guidelines. At the first level are work teams. Everyone at Donnelly, whether in the factory or in an office, belongs to one. The teams elect representatives to serve on the second-tier equity committees. These committees meet monthly to settle disputes and interpret personnel policies. These committees, in turn, elect members to the Donnelly Committee, the third—and highest—tier. This 15-member committee, which includes a representative from the company's senior management team, makes final decisions on company policies. It even recommends an annual wage and benefits package to the company's board of directors.

Donnelly practices true workplace democracy. Instead of majority rule, all decisions by these committees must be unanimous so as to avoid the formation of divisive groups. Involving all employees in decisions is obviously time consuming. For instance, the committees recently spent three months studying the question of drug testing. But the company is committed to workplace democracy and strongly believes the benefits far exceed the costs.

Employee involvement at Donnelly doesn't stop with only participation in decisions. Employees also participate in a company bonus system. Quarterly bonuses are paid to all employees once the company's return on investment reaches 5.2 percent. Over the past seven years, these bonuses have ranged from a low of 1 percent to a high of 7 percent.

Donnelly is committed to creating an organization that respects and listens to its employees, offers full participation, provides equity to all, and allows everyone to share in the company's success. And while workplace democracy may intimidate managers at more traditional, autocratically run organizations, it certainly works well for Donnelly. Although their major customers—automakers—have been laying off thousands of employees in recent years, Donnelly has grown and expanded. Since 1985, sales have tripled and its work force doubled.

In this chapter, we focus on how to apply motivation concepts. We want to link theories to practice. It's one thing to be able to regurgitate motivation theories, but it's often another to see how, as a manager, you could use them.

In the following pages, we review a number of motivation techniques and programs that have gained varying degrees of acceptance in practice. For example, we discuss employee involvement programs along the lines of the one used at Donnelly. And for each of the techniques and programs we review, we specifically address how they build on one or more of the motivation theories covered in the previous chapter.

Management by Objectives

Goal-setting theory has an impressive base of research support. But as a manager, how do you make goal setting operational? The best answer to that question is: Install a management by objectives (MBO) program.

What Is MBO?

management by objectives (MBO)
A program that encompasses specific goals, participatively set, for an explicit time period, with feedback on goal progress.

Management by objectives emphasizes participatively set goals that are tangible, verifiable, and measurable. It's not a new idea. In fact, it was originally proposed by Peter Drucker more than 40 years ago as a means of using goals to motivate people rather than to control them.[2] Today, no introduction to basic management concepts would be complete without a discussion of MBO.

LEARNING OBJECTIVES

After studying this chapter, you should be able to:

1. Identify the four ingredients common to MBO programs.
2. Outline the typical five-step problem-solving model in OB Mod.
3. Explain why managers might want to use employee involvement programs.
4. Define quality circles.
5. Explain how ESOPs can increase employee motivation.
6. Describe the link between skill-based pay plans and motivation theories.
7. Explain how flexible benefits turn benefits into motivators.
8. Describe the influence of comparable worth on female employees.
9. Contrast the challenges in motivating professional employees versus low-skilled employees; professional employees versus temporary workers.

Set me anything to do as a task, and it is inconceivable the desire I have to do something else.
G. B. SHAW

Have you ever heard of the Donnelly Corporation? Probably not. But it's a good bet you use one or more of their products. For instance, the rearview mirror in your car was undoubtedly made by Donnelly, since they control more than 90 percent of this market. The company is the major supplier of glass products to automobile manufacturers.

What's interesting about the Donnelly Corporation is that it has been described as possibly "the most democratic

MBO's appeal undoubtedly lies in its emphasis on converting overall organizational objectives into specific objectives for organizational units and individual members. MBO operationalizes the concept of objectives by devising a process by which objectives cascade down through the organization. As depicted in Figure 7-1, the organization's overall objectives are translated into specific objectives for each succeeding level (that is, divisional, departmental, individual) in the organization. But because lower unit managers jointly participate in setting their own goals, MBO works from the bottom up as well as from the top down. The result is a hierarchy of objectives that links objectives at one level to those at the next level. And for the individual employee, MBO provides specific personal performance objectives. Each person, therefore, has an identified specific contribution to make to his or her unit's performance. If all the individuals achieve their goals, then their unit's goals will be attained and the organization's overall objectives become a reality.

Four ingredients are common to MBO programs: goal specificity, participative decision making, an explicit time period, and performance feedback.[3]

The objectives in MBO should be concise statements of expected accomplishments. It's not adequate, for example, to merely state a desire to cut costs, improve service, or increase quality. Such desires have to be converted into tangible objectives that can be measured and evaluated. To cut departmental costs *by 7 percent*, to improve service by ensuring that all telephone orders are processed *within 24 hours of receipt*, or to increase quality by keeping returns to *less than 1 percent of sales* are examples of specific objectives.

Figure 7-1
Cascading of Objectives

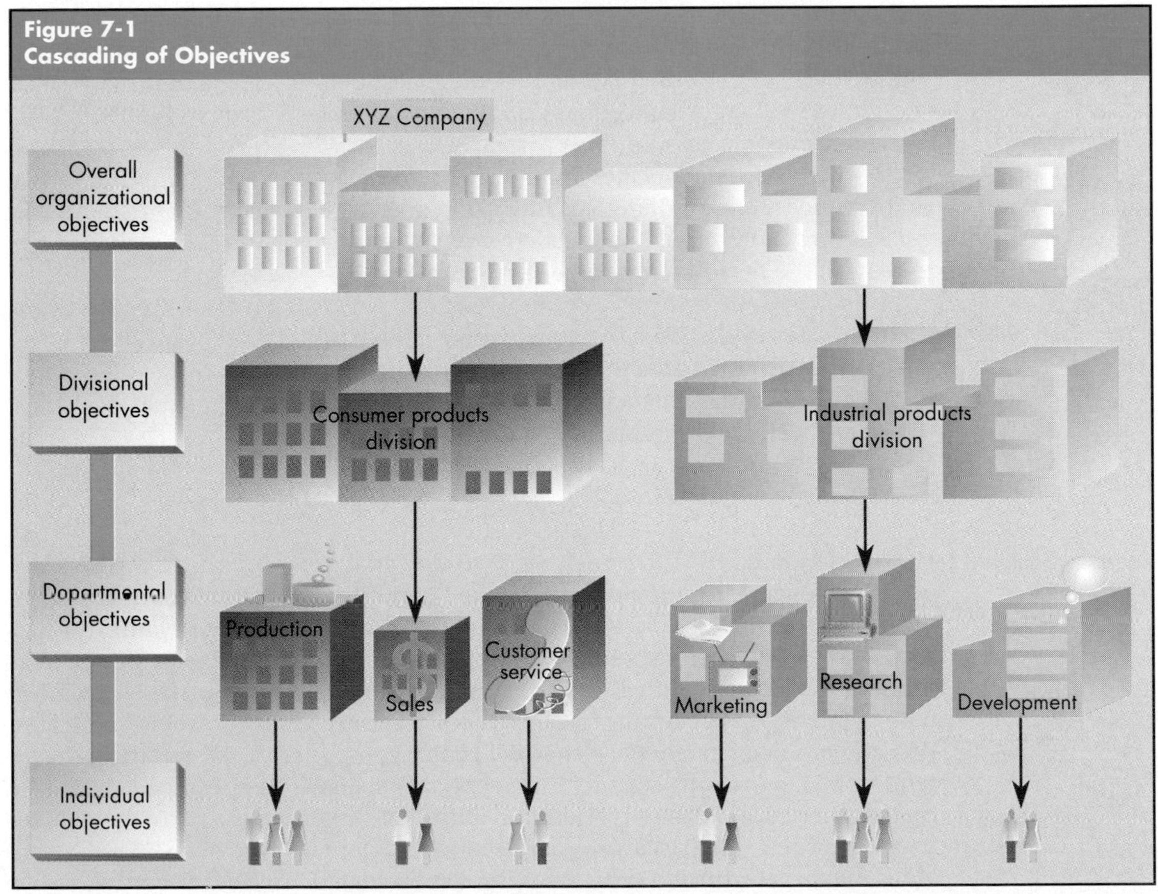

The objectives in MBO are not unilaterally set by the boss and then assigned to subordinates. MBO replaces imposed goals with participatively determined goals. The superior and subordinate jointly choose the goals and agree on how they will be measured.

Each objective has a specific time period in which it is to be completed. Typically the time period is three months, six months, or a year. So managers and subordinates not only have specific objectives, but also stipulated time periods in which to accomplish them.

The final ingredient in an MBO program is feedback on performance. MBO seeks to give continuous feedback on progress toward goals. Ideally, this is accomplished by giving ongoing feedback to individuals so they can monitor and correct their own actions. This is supplemented by periodic managerial evaluations, when progress is reviewed. This applies at the top of the organization as well as at the bottom. The vice president of sales, for instance, has objectives for overall sales and for each of his or her major products. He or she will monitor ongoing sales reports to determine progress toward the sales division's objectives. Similarly, district sales managers have objectives, as does each salesperson in the field. Feedback in terms of sales and performance data is provided to let these people know how they are doing. Formal appraisal meetings also take place at which superiors and subordinates can review progress toward goals and further feedback can be provided.

Linking MBO and Goal-Setting Theory

Goal-setting theory demonstrates that hard goals result in a higher level of individual performance than do easy goals, that specific hard goals result in higher levels of performance than do no goals at all or the generalized goal of "do your best," and that feedback on one's performance leads to higher performance. Compare these findings with MBO.

MBO directly advocates specific goals and feedback. MBO implies, rather than explicitly states, that goals must be perceived as feasible. Consistent with goal setting, MBO would be most effective when the goals are difficult enough to require the person to do some stretching.

The only area of possible disagreement between MBO and goal-setting theory relates to the issue of participation: MBO strongly advocates it whereas goal setting demonstrates that assigning goals to subordinates frequently works just as well. The major benefit to using participation, however, is that it appears to induce individuals to establish more difficult goals.

MBO in Practice

How widely used is MBO? Reviews of studies that have sought to answer this question suggest it's a popular technique. You'll find MBO programs in many business, health-care, educational, government, and nonprofit organizations.[4]

MBO's popularity should not be construed to mean it always works. In a number of documented cases MBO has been implemented but failed to meet management's expectations.[5] A close look at these cases, however, indicates that the problems rarely lie with MBO's basic components. Rather, the culprits tend to be factors such as unrealistic expectations regarding results, lack of top management commitment, and an inability or unwillingness by management to allocate rewards based on goal accomplishment. Nevertheless, MBO provides managers with the vehicle for implementing goal-setting theory.

OB in the News

Many Managers Still Complain About a Lack of Clear Job Goals

A recent survey of U.S. managers by *Industry Week* provides some interesting insights into the prevalence of job goals.

First the good news. Overall, 75 percent of those surveyed said "yes," they have clear goals for their jobs. The bad news is that negative responses increased at each lower managerial level. Among top managers, 80 percent said they have clear goals. The number drops to 70 percent among middle managers and falls to just 61 percent for supervisors.

Clarity of performance standards also tends to fall off as the level of management moves down. Sixty-one percent of senior managers say they have clear performance standards in their jobs. Only 53 and 51 percent of middle-level managers and supervisors, respectively, thought they had clear performance standards.

Two other findings from the survey seem relevant, since they are key elements of MBO. When asked to rate their immediate managers on a 1 to 7 scale (negative to positive), the use of participative methods rated 4.62 and providing feedback on performance rated 4.27.

To the degree these results are applicable to managerial ranks in general, it certainly appears there is considerable room for improvement in providing managers with clear goals and performance standards and feedback on performance. In addition, if these are the results obtained when managers are surveyed, what would the responses have been if operating employees had been polled? For example, if goal clarity declines with level in the organization, it seems reasonable to conclude that maybe 50 percent or more of rank-and-file employees perceive an absence of clear job goals.

Based on D.W. Sommer and M. Frohman, "American Management (Still) Missing Some Basics," *Industry Week* (July 20, 1992), pp. 36–37.

Behavior Modification

A now classic study took place a number of years ago with freight packers at Emery Air Freight (now part of Federal Express).[6] Emery's management wanted packers to use freight containers for shipments whenever possible because of specific economic savings. When packers were queried as to the percentage of shipments containerized, the standard reply was 90 percent. An analysis by Emery found, however, that the container utilization rate was only 45 percent. In order to encourage employees to use containers, management established a program of feedback and positive reinforcements. Each packer was instructed to keep a checklist of his or her daily packings, both containerized and noncontainerized. At the end of each day, the packer computed his or her container utilization rate. Almost unbelievably, container utilization jumped to more than 90 percent on the first day of the program and held to that level. Emery reported that this simple program of feedback and positive reinforcements saved the company $2 million over a three-year period.

OB Mod
A program where managers identify performance-related employee behaviors and then implement an intervention strategy to strengthen desirable performance behaviors and weaken undesirable behaviors.

This program at Emery Air Freight illustrates the use of behavior modification, or what has become more popularly called **OB Mod**.[7] It represents the application of reinforcement theory to individuals in the work setting.

What Is OB Mod?

The typical OB Mod program, as shown in Figure 7-2, follows a five-step problem-solving model: (1) identification of performance-related behaviors; (2) measurement of the behaviors; (3) identification of behavioral contingencies; (4) development and implementation of an intervention strategy; and (5) evaluation of performance improvement.[8]

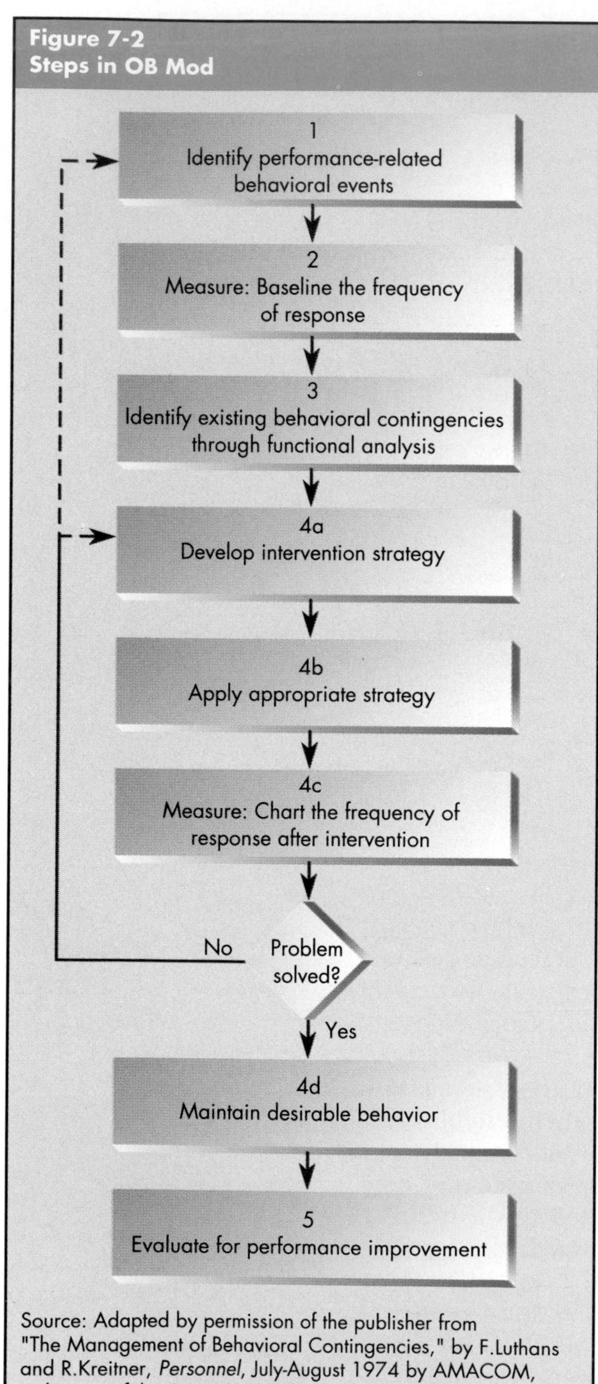

Figure 7-2
Steps in OB Mod

Source: Adapted by permission of the publisher from "The Management of Behavioral Contingencies," by F.Luthans and R.Kreitner, *Personnel*, July-August 1974 by AMACOM, a division of the American Management Association, p.13. All rights reserved.

Everything an employee does on his or her job is not equally important in terms of performance outcomes. The first step in OB Mod, therefore, is to identify the critical behaviors that make a significant impact on the employee's job performance. These are those 5 to 10 percent of behaviors that may account for up to 70 or 80 percent of each employee's performance. Using containers whenever possible by freight packers at Emery Air Freight is an example of a critical behavior.

The second step requires the manager to develop some baseline performance data. This is obtained by determining the number of times the identified behavior is occurring under present conditions. In our freight packing example at Emery, this would have revealed that 45 percent of all shipments were containerized.

The third step is to perform a functional analysis to identify the behavioral contingencies or consequences of performance. This tells the manager the antecedent cues that emit the behavior and the consequences currently maintaining it. At Emery Air Freight, social norms and the greater difficulty in packing containers were the antecedent cues. This encouraged the practice of packing items separately. Moreover, the consequences for continuing this behavior, prior to the OB Mod intervention, were social acceptance and escaping more demanding work.

Once the functional analysis is complete, the manager is ready to develop and implement an intervention strategy to strengthen desirable performance behaviors and weaken undesirable behaviors. The appropriate strategy will entail changing some element of the performance–reward linkage—structure, processes, technology, groups, or the task—with the goal of making high-level performance more rewarding. In the Emery example, the work technology was altered to require the keeping of a checklist. The checklist plus the computation, at the end of the day, of a container utilization rate acted to reinforce the desirable behavior of using containers.

The final step in OB Mod is to evaluate performance improvement. In the Emery intervention, the immediate improvement in the container utilization rate demonstrated that behavioral change took place.

That it rose to 90 percent and held at that level further indicates that learning took place. That is, the employees underwent a relatively permanent change in behavior.

Linking OB Mod and Reinforcement Theory

Reinforcement theory relies on positive reinforcement, shaping, and recognizing the impact of different schedules of reinforcement on behavior. OB Mod uses these concepts to provide managers with a powerful and proven means for changing employee behavior.

OB Mod in Practice

OB Mod has been used by a number of organizations to improve employee productivity and to reduce errors, absenteeism, tardiness, and accident rates.[9] Organizations like General Electric, Weyerhauser, the city of Detroit, Dayton-Hudson Stores, and Xerox report impressive results using OB Mod.[10] For instance, a few years back, frustrated by customer complaints, Xerox's top management changed the basis for its executive bonus plan from traditional quotas to long-term customer satisfaction.[11] The company now surveys 40,000 customers worldwide every month to determine the percentage who are satisfied with Xerox products and service. At the start of each year, top management looks at the previous year's results and develops a goal. In 1989 the target was 86 percent. Each succeeding year the goal has gone up; it is now 100 percent.

Seattle Pacific Supply Co., an apartment supply firm with only 11 employees, has used OB Mod to significantly improve employee performance.[12] Every day the company books $5,500 in sales, all employees receive an extra half hour's pay. If daily sales hit $15,000, everyone gets another six hours of wages. The previous year's sales provide the basis for Pacific's bonus targets. Paid out once a month, the bonuses accrue daily and in a typical month amount to an extra 20 hours of salary for each employee. Since Pacific scrapped its monthly incentive program in favor of this daily performance appraisal, company sales have increased more than 50 percent, turnover has dropped to almost zero, and daily sales targets have been hit four out of five days a week.

Convex Computer Corporation, a Texas-based supercomputer manufacturer with 1,200 employees, reinforces employee accomplishments through recognition.[13] On a quarterly basis, the company's vice president of operations recognizes individuals who have been nominated by their managers as having gone "above and beyond the call of duty." Annually, individual employees may nominate their peers for the Customer Service Award, which recognizes such categories as risk taking, innovation, cost reduction, and overall customer service. And at the departmental level, recognition takes the form of team or departmental T-shirts, coffee mugs, banners, and pictures. Supervisors use movie tickets, Friday afternoon bowling get-togethers, paid time off, and cash awards to acknowledge such achievements as three months of defect-free assembly, five years of perfect attendance, and completing a project ahead of time.

OB Mod has also proven effective in sports organizations. Researchers, for instance, helped a midwestern university hockey team win more games by significantly increasing the number of legal body blocks or hits by team members.[14] These legal hits are crucial for winning collegiate games because they give the offense more total time with the puck, more shots on goal, and, usually, more goals. Over a two-year period, using OB Mod techniques, the team's mean hit rate increased 141 percent and its win-loss-tie record went from 13-21-2 to 23-15-2.

The philosophy behind OB Mod additionally appears to be affecting many managers in the way they relate to their employees—in the kind and quantity of feedback they give, the content of performance appraisals, and the type and allocation of organizational rewards.

Despite the positive results that OB Mod has demonstrated, it is not without its critics.[15] Is it a technique for manipulating people? Does it decrease an employee's freedom? If so, is such action on the part of managers unethical? And do nonmonetary reinforcers like feedback, praise, and recognition get stale after a while? Will employees begin to see these as ways for management to increase productivity without providing commensurate increases in their pay? There are no easy answers to questions such as these.

Employee Involvement Programs

As described at the beginning of this chapter, the Donnelly Corporation uses committees of elected representatives to make all key decisions affecting Donnelly employees. At a General Electric lighting plant in Ohio, work teams perform many tasks and assume many of the responsibilities once handled by their supervisors. In fact, when the plant was faced with a recent decline in the demand for the tubes it produces, the workers decided first to slow production and eventually to lay themselves off. Marketing people at USAA, a large insurance company, meet in a conference room for an hour every week to discuss ways in which they can improve the quality of their work and increase productivity. Management has implemented many of their suggestions. Childress Buick, an automobile dealer in Phoenix, allows their salespeople to negotiate and finalize deals with customers without any approval from management. The laws of Germany, France, Denmark, Sweden, and Austria require compa-

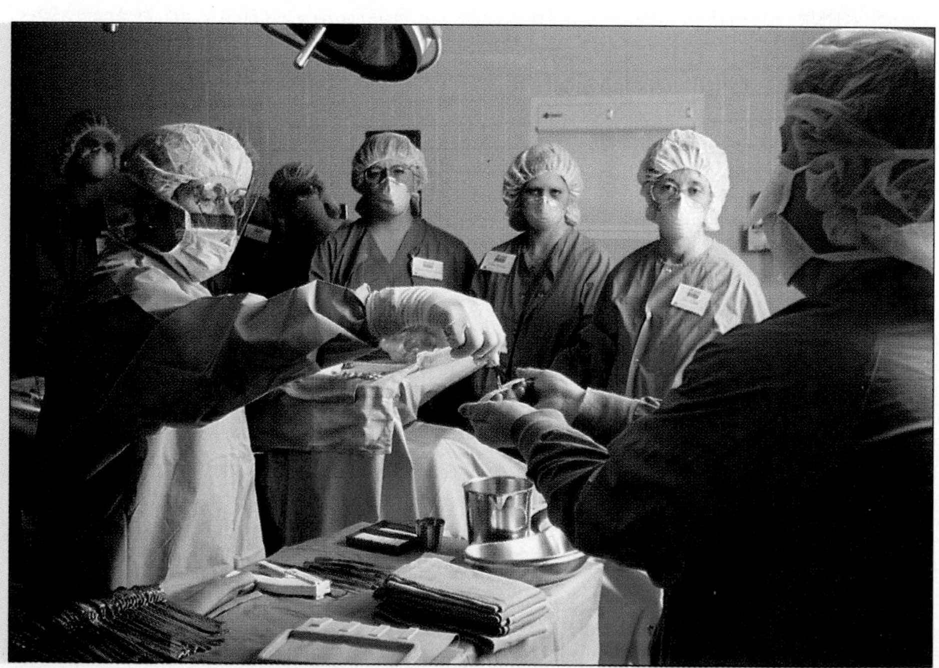

3M involves employees by letting them see how the products they make are used by customers. At a 3M medical and surgical products plant, all 750 employees, from production-line workers to senior executives, participate in a program called Pulse. Employees (shown here with name tags) put on scrubs and watch how doctors and nurses in operating rooms of local hospitals use the surgical tapes, drapes, prep solutions, and other products 3M employees make. This face-to-face interaction with customers increases employee commitment to 3M's goal of delivering products that completely satisfy customers.

nies to have elected representatives from their employee groups as members of their board of directors.[16]

The common theme through the examples just cited is that they all illustrate employee involvement programs. In this section, we clarify what we mean by employee involvement, describe some of the various forms it takes, consider the motivational implications of these programs, and show some applications.

What Is Employee Involvement?

Employee involvement has become a convenient catchall term to cover a variety of techniques.[17] For instance, it encompasses such popular ideas as employee participation or participative management, workplace democracy, empowerment, and employee ownership. Our position, although each of these ideas has some unique characteristics, is they all have a common core—that of employee involvement.

So what specifically do we mean by **employee involvement**? We define it as a participative process that uses the entire capacity of employees and is designed to encourage increased commitment to the organization's success.[18] The underlying logic is that by involving workers in those decisions that affect them and by increasing their autonomy and control over their work lives, employees will become more motivated, more committed to the organization, more productive, and more satisfied with their jobs.

employee involvement
A participative process that uses the entire capacity of employees and is designed to encourage increased commitment to the organization's success.

Does that mean participation and employee involvement are synonyms for each other? No. Participation is a more limited term. It's a subset within the larger framework of employee involvement. All of the employee involvement programs we describe include some form of employee participation, but the term *participation*, per se, is too narrow and limiting.

Examples of Employee Involvement Programs

In this section we review four forms of employee involvement: participative management, representative participation, quality circles, and employee stock ownership plans.

PARTICIPATIVE MANAGEMENT The distinct characteristic common to all **participative management** programs is the use of joint decision making. That is, subordinates actually share a significant degree of decision-making power with their immediate superiors.

participative management
A process where subordinates share a significant degree of decision-making power with their immediate superiors.

Participative management has, at times, been promoted as a panacea for poor morale and low productivity. One author has even argued that participative management is an ethical imperative.[19] But participative management is not appropriate for every organization or every work unit. For it to work, there must be adequate time to participate, the issues in which employees get involved must be relevant to their interests, employees must have the ability (intelligence, technical knowledge, communication skills) to participate, and the organization's culture must support employee involvement.[20]

Why would management want to share its decision-making power with subordinates? There are a number of good reasons. As jobs have become more complex, managers often don't know everything their employees do. So participation allows those who know the most to contribute. The result can be better decisions. The interdependence in tasks that employees often do today also requires consultation with people in other departments and work units. This increases the need for teams, committees, and group meetings to resolve issues that affect them jointly. Participation additionally increases commitment to decisions. People are less likely to undermine a decision at the time of its implementation if they shared in making that decision. Finally, participation provides intrinsic rewards for employees. It can make their jobs more interesting and meaningful.

Dozens of studies have been conducted on the participation–performance relationship. The findings, however, are mixed.[21] When the research is looked at carefully, it appears that participation typically has only a modest influence on variables such as employee productivity, motivation, and job satisfaction. Of course, that doesn't mean the use of participative management can't be beneficial under the right conditions. What it says, however, is that the use of participation is no sure means for improving employee performance.

representative participation
Workers participate in organizational decision making through a small group of representative employees.

REPRESENTATIVE PARTICIPATION Almost every country in Western Europe has some type of legislation requiring companies to practice **representative participation**. That is, rather than participate directly in decisions, workers are represented by a small group of employees who actually participate. Representative participation has been called "the most widely legislated form of employee involvement around the world."[22] The goal of representative participation is to redistribute power within an organization, putting labor on a more equal footing with the interests of management and stockholders.

works councils
Groups of nominated or elected employees who must be consulted when management makes decisions involving personnel.

board representatives
A form of representative participation; employees sit on a company's board of directors and represent the interests of the firm's employees.

The two most common forms that representative participation takes are works councils and board representatives.[23] **Works councils** link employees with management. They are groups of nominated or elected employees that must be consulted when management makes decisions involving personnel. For example, in the Netherlands, if a Dutch company is taken over by another firm, the former's works council must be informed at an early stage, and if the council objects, it has 30 days to seek a court injunction to stop the takeover.[24] **Board representatives** are employees who sit on a company's board of directors and represent the interests of the firm's employees. In some countries, large companies may be legally required to make sure employee representatives have the same number of board seats as stockholder representatives.

The overall influence of representative participation on working employees seems to be minimal.[25] For instance, the evidence suggests that works councils are dominated by management and have little impact on employees or the organization. And while this form of employee involvement might increase the motivation and satisfaction of those individuals who are doing the representing, little evidence indicates that this trickles down to the operating employees who they represent. Overall, "The greatest value of representative participation is symbolic. If one is interested in changing employee attitudes or in improving organizational performance, representative participation would be a poor choice."[26]

quality circle
A work group of employees who meet regularly to discuss their quality problems, investigate causes, recommend solutions, and take corrective actions.

QUALITY CIRCLES "Probably the most widely discussed and undertaken formal style of employee involvement is the quality circle."[27] The quality circle concept is frequently mentioned as one of the techniques Japanese firms utilize that has allowed them to make high-quality products at low costs. Originally begun in the United States and exported to Japan in the 1950s, the quality circle became quite popular in North America and Europe during the 1980s.[28]

What is a **quality circle**? It's a work group of eight to ten employees and supervisors who have a shared area of responsibility. They meet regularly—

typically once a week, on company time and on company premises—to discuss their quality problems, investigate causes of the problems, recommend solutions, and take corrective actions. They take over the responsibility for solving quality problems, and they generate and evaluate their own feedback. But management typically retains control over the final decision regarding implementation of recommended solutions. Of course, it is not presumed that employees inherently have this ability to analyze and solve quality problems. Therefore, part of the quality circle concept includes teaching participating employees group communication skills, various quality strategies, and measurement and problem analysis techniques. Figure 7-3 describes a typical quality circle process.

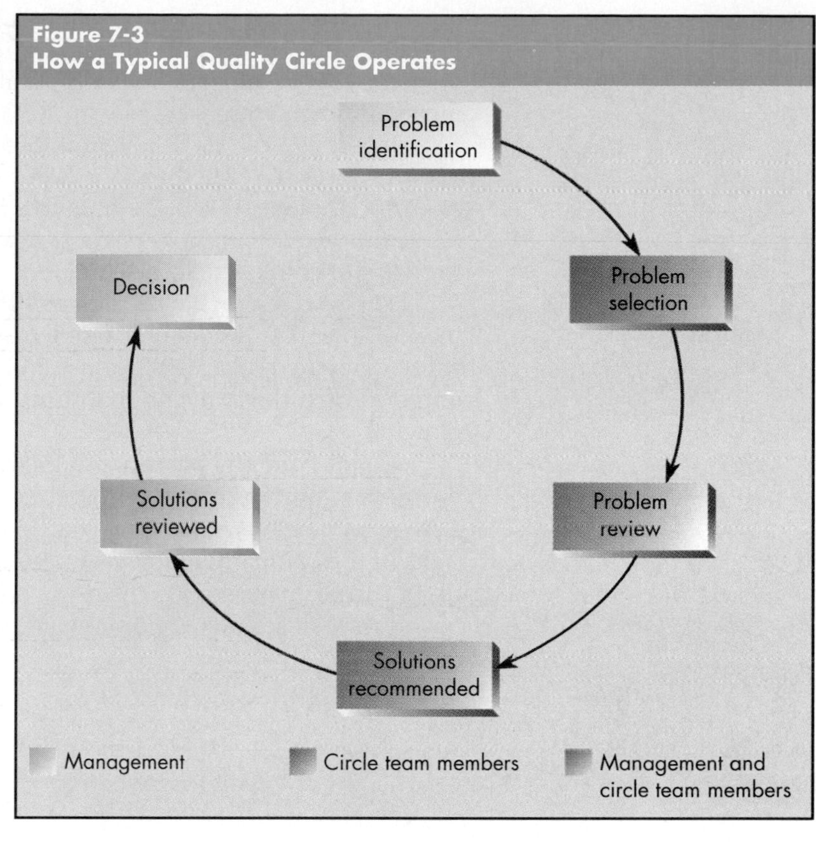

Figure 7-3
How a Typical Quality Circle Operates

Do quality circles improve employee productivity and satisfaction? A review of the evidence indicates they are much more likely to positively affect productivity. They tend to show little or no effect on employee satisfaction; and while many studies report positive results from quality circles on productivity, these results are by no means guaranteed.[29] The failure of many quality circle programs to produce measurable benefits has also led to a large number of them being discontinued.

One author has gone as far as to say that although quality circles were the management fad of the 1980s, they've "become a flop."[30] He offers two possible explanations for their disappointing results. First is the little bit of time that actually deals with employee involvement. "At most, these programs operate for one hour per week, with the remaining 39 hours unchanged. Why should changes in 2.5 percent of a person's job have a major impact?"[31] Second, the ease of implementing quality circles often worked against them. They were seen as a simple device that could be added on to the organization with few changes required outside the program itself. In many cases, the only significant involvement by management was funding the program. So quality circles became an easy way for management to get on the employee involvement bandwagon. And, unfortunately, the lack of planning and top management commitment often contributed to quality circle failures.

EMPLOYEE STOCK OWNERSHIP PLANS The final employee involvement approach we discuss is **employee stock ownership plans (ESOPs)**.[32]

employee stock ownership plans (ESOPs)
Company-established benefit plans in which employees acquire stock as part of their benefits.

Employee ownership can mean a number of things from employees owning some stock in the company where they work to the individuals working in the company owning and personally operating the firm. Employee stock ownership plans are company-established benefit plans in which employees acquire stock as part of their benefits. Approximately 20 percent of Polaroid, for example, is owned by its employees. Fifty-five percent of United Airlines is owned by its employees. Avis Corporation and Weirton Steel are 100 percent owned by their employees.[33]

In the typical ESOP, an employee stock ownership trust is created. Companies contribute either stock or cash to buy stock for the trust and allocate the stock to employees. While employees hold stock in their company, they usually cannot take physical possession of their shares or sell them as long as they're still employed at the company.

The research on ESOPs indicates that they increase employee satisfaction. In addition, they frequently result in higher performance. For instance, one study compared 45 ESOPs against 238 conventional companies.[34] The ESOPs outperformed the conventional firms both in terms of employment and sales growth.

ESOPs have the potential to increase employee job satisfaction and work motivation. But for this potential to be realized, employees need to psychologically experience ownership.[35] That is, in addition to merely having a financial stake in the company, employees need to be kept regularly informed on the status of the business and also have the opportunity to exercise influence over the business. When these conditions are met, "employees will be more satisfied

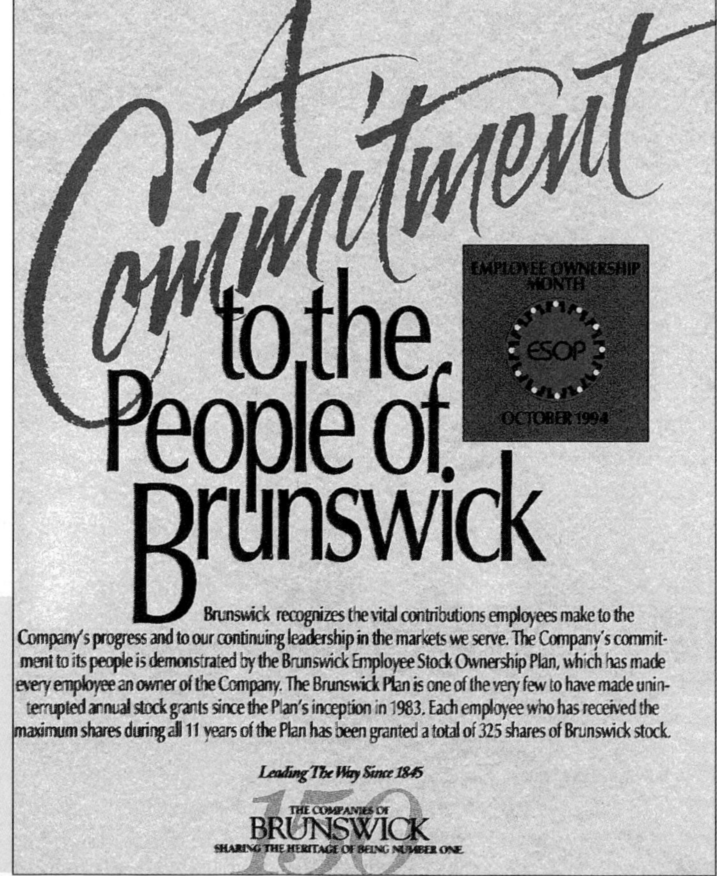

Brunswick Corporation creates a sense of financial ownership among its employees by making every eligible employee a shareholder. Under Brunswick's ESOP, the company makes annual contributions to a trust for eligible employees in the form of common shares of the firm. Each year Brunswick celebrates the special status of employee-owners during Employee Ownership Week with a series of events and displays such as the poster shown here.

◆◆◆◆ OB in the News ◆◆◆◆

"I'm not only a reservation agent, I'm an owner!"

Avis became famous for its ads that made a virtue of its second-place status: "We're No. 2—We try harder." Since becoming an ESOP, Avis just might have to change that ad to something like "Now we're No. 1, but we still try harder!"

In 1987 Avis became an ESOP and its 12,500 employees became the owners. With the change to employee ownership, the company has turned its work force into a highly motivated team. Employee ownership has proven particularly effective in motivating workers to provide extra effort in customer service.

"Right now Avis is on a roll," says a prominent security analyst in the rental car industry. "The ESOP has really improved their morale and productivity and service." In the first year after converting to an ESOP, all internal measures of service quality set records. For example, on-time arrivals of airport buses rose from 93 percent to 96 percent. Service-related customer complaints were rising at the time of the employee buyout, but dropped 35 percent after the ESOP was in place.

Avis has put together a structure to convert employee motivation into higher productivity. The essence of that structure is employee participation groups. These groups comprise representatives from each class of worker, from mechanics to rental agents. They meet at least monthly at each Avis location. Out of these group meetings have come a number of ideas. An employee in Reno, Nevada, suggested setting aside cars for nonsmokers. Another thought renters might appreciate tips on local traffic laws. A sales staffer suggested the sales force could use an internal charge card instead of American Express when renting Avis cars on the road, which saved the transaction fee paid to American Express as well as the concession fee Avis pays to the airport for every paid rental.

Employees don't just make suggestions—they follow up. Says the company's Fort Lauderdale district manager, "In many cases people get prices on materials for some idea they've had and come back to the committee and say, 'Hey, should we do it?' And we make the decision as a group. We're not sitting there as managers and employees. We're sitting there as a group of employees in Fort Lauderdale, asking how we can provide better service."

Based on D. Kirkpatrick, "How the Workers Run Avis Better," *Fortune* (December 5, 1988), pp. 103–14.

with their jobs, more satisfied with their organizational identification, motivated to come to work, and motivated to perform well while at work."[36]

Linking Employee Involvement Programs and Motivation Theories

Employee involvement draws on a number of the motivation theories discussed in Chapter 6. For instance, Theory Y is consistent with participative management; Theory X aligns with the more traditional autocratic style of managing people. In terms of motivation-hygiene theory, employee involvement programs could provide employees with intrinsic motivation by increasing opportunities for growth, responsibility, and involvement in the work itself. Similarly, the opportunity to make and implement decisions, and then seeing them work out, can help satisfy an employee's needs for responsibility, achievement, recognition, growth, and enhanced self-esteem. So employee involvement is compatible with ERG theory and efforts to stimulate the achievement need.

Employee Involvement Programs in Practice

Germany, France, Holland, and the Scandinavian countries have firmly established the principle of industrial democracy in Europe, and other nations, including Japan and Israel, have traditionally practiced some form of representative participation for decades. Participative management and representative participation were much slower to gain ground in North American organizations. But nowdays, employee involvement programs that stress participation have become the norm. While some managers continue to resist sharing decision-making power, the pressure is on managers to give up their autocratic decision-making style in favor of a more participative, supportive, coachlike role.

What about quality circles? How popular are they in practice? The names of companies that have used quality circles reads like a Who's Who of corporate America: Hewlett-Packard, Digital Equipment, Westinghouse, General Electric, Texas Instruments, Inland Steel, Xerox, Eastman Kodak, Polaroid, Procter & Gamble, Control Data, General Motors, Ford, IBM, Martin Marietta, Motorola, American Airlines, TRW.[37] But, as we noted, the success of quality circles has been far from overwhelming. They were popular in the 1980s, largely because they were easy to implement. In the 1990s many organizations have dropped their quality circles and replaced them with more comprehensive team-based structures (which we discuss in Chapter 9).

And what about ESOPs? They have become the most popular form of employee ownership. They've grown from just a handful in 1974 to around 10,000 now, covering more than 10 million employees. Many well-known companies, including Anheuser-Busch, Lockheed, Procter & Gamble, and Polaroid, have implemented ESOPs.[38] But so too have many not-so-well-known companies. Phelps County Bank, in Rolla, Missouri, for instance, employs only 55 people. While the bank's ESOP has been in place for 13 years, the average employee's ownership balance exceeds $70,000. Connie Beddoe, a teller who annually earns less than $20,000, has managed to save almost three times that amount through her ESOP after seven years at the bank.[39]

Variable-Pay Programs

Rogan Corporation, a small manufacturer of plastic knobs, set up a program seven years ago to cut its labor costs.[40] Management set a specific goal for labor costs as a percentage of sales. When costs drop below this goal, employees get to keep the difference. In the most recent year of the program, employees got 17 percent added to their annual salaries as a bonus.

For over 25 years, Nucor Steel has had an incentive compensation plan in place that pays bonuses to employees based on the company's profitability.[41] Originally intended to provide workers with an additional 15 to 20 percent to their base salaries, actual bonus payouts have been as high as 80 to 150 percent of base.

P. Roy Vagelos, CEO of pharmaceutical giant Merck & Co., took an 11 percent reduction in salary and bonus in 1993.[42] This is because his pay package is closely tied to his company's performance, and Merck's profits fell by 11 percent in 1993.

Bob Baker is no CEO. He's just a petroleum geologist at Tri-C Resources, a small oil exploration firm.[43] But like Vagelos at Merck, Baker's pay is also tied to performance, in this case discovering profitable oil and gas sites. In 1993 Baker helped Tri-C find nearly 40 profitable gas sites on a 140,000-acre ranch in southern Texas. He got a $7,500 bonus for each of the dozen sites he was primarily responsible for discovering, plus 0.25 percent of the revenue from all 40 wells. Including performance incentives from about 45 other still-producing wells he had previously discovered, Baker earned about $150,000 in 1993. That's more than triple his base salary of $48,000.

The common thread in each of the previous examples is that they all illustrate variable-pay programs.

What Are Variable-Pay Programs?

Piece-rate plans, wage incentives, profit sharing, bonuses, and gain sharing are all forms of **variable-pay programs**. What differentiates these forms of compensation from more traditional programs is that instead of paying a person only for time on the job or seniority, a portion of an employee's pay is based on some individual and/or organizational measure of performance. Unlike more traditional base-pay programs, variable pay is not an annuity. There is no guarantee that just because you made $60,000 last year you'll make the same amount this year. With variable pay, earnings fluctuates up and down with the measure of performance.[44]

variable-pay programs
A portion of an employee's pay is based on some individual and/or organizational measure of performance.

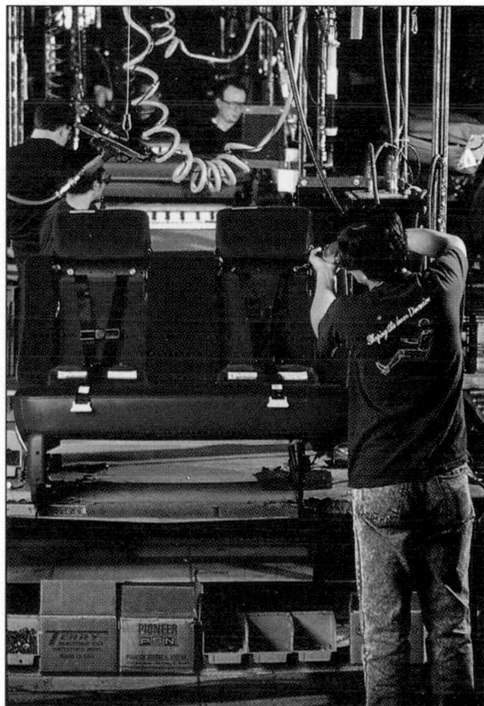

Canada's Magna International, a supplier of 4,000 automotive parts, is one of the growing number of firms giving bonuses to lower-ranking employees. Magna's founder Frank Stronach recently added a proviso to the company's constitution stating that each production worker share equally in 10 percent of pretax profits every year. The bonus incentive motivates Magna's nonunion work force to design, build, and produce components that help the company retain its preferred supplier status for every major automaker in North America. As Chrysler's largest components supplier, Magna developed the car seat shown here.

It is precisely the fluctuation in variable pay that has made these programs attractive to management. It turns part of an organization's fixed labor costs into a variable cost, thus reducing expenses when performance declines. Additionally, by tying pay to performance, earnings recognize contribution rather than being a form of entitlement. Low performers find, over time, that their pay stagnates; high performers enjoy pay increases commensurate with their contribution.

Four of the more widely used of the variable-pay programs are piece-rate wages, bonuses, profit sharing, and gain sharing. Piece-rate wages have been around for nearly a century. They

piece-rate pay plans
Workers are paid a fixed sum for each unit of production completed.

profit-sharing plans
Organization-wide programs that distribute compensation based on some established formula designed around a company's profitability.

gainsharing
An incentive plan where improvements in group productivity determines the total amount of money that is allocated.

have long been popular as a way to compensate production workers. In **piece-rate pay plans**, workers are paid a fixed sum for each unit of production completed. When an employee gets no base salary and is paid only for what he or she produces, this is a pure piece-rate plan. People who work ballparks selling peanuts and soda pop frequently are paid this way. They might get to keep 25 cents for every bag of peanuts they sell. If they sell 200 bags during a game, they make $50. If they sell only 40 bags, their take is a mere $10. The harder they work and the more peanuts they sell, the more they earn. Many organizations use a modified piece-rate plan, where employees earn a base hourly wage plus a piece-rate differential. So a legal typist might be paid $6 an hour plus 20 cents per page. Such modified plans provide a floor under an employee's earnings while still offering a productivity incentive.

Bonuses can be paid exclusively to executives or to all employees. For instance, annual bonuses in the millions of dollars are not uncommon in American corporations. Robert A. Watson, for example, received a $10 million incentive bonus in 1993 for his success in dismantling Westinghouse's financial operation.[45] Increasingly, bonus plans are taking on a larger net within organizations to include lower ranking employees. Additionally, these plans tend to combine individual, group, and organizationwide performance variables. At AT&T, for instance, the biggest piece of an individual's bonus is based on overall corporate performance. But at Scott Paper, approximately 70 percent is tied to the performance of an individual's department or division, with the remaining 30 percent linked to individual success. Bonuses amounting to 10 to 25 percent of base salary are not unusual at Scott.[46]

Profit-sharing plans are organizationwide programs that distribute compensation based on some established formula designed around a company's profitability. These can be direct cash outlays or, particularly in the case of top managers, allocated as stock options. When you read about executives like Michael Eisner, the CEO at Disney, earning over $200 million in one year, almost all of this comes from cashing in stock options previously granted based on company profit performance.

The variable-pay program that has gotten the most attention in recent years is undoubtedly **gainsharing**.[47] This is a formula-based group incentive plan. Improvements in group productivity—from one period to another— determine the total amount of money allocated. And the division of productivity savings can be split between the company and employees in any number of ways, but 50-50 is fairly typical.

Isn't gainsharing the same thing as profit sharing? They're similar but not the same thing. By focusing on productivity gains rather than profits, gainsharing rewards specific behaviors that are less influenced by external factors. Employees in a gainsharing plan can receive incentive awards even when the organization isn't profitable.

Do variable-pay programs work? Do they increase motivation and productivity? The answer is a qualified "yes." Gainsharing, for example, has been found to improve productivity in a majority of cases and often has a positive impact on employee attitudes. An American Management Association study of 83 companies who used gainsharing also found, on average, that grievances dropped 83 percent, absences fell 84 percent, and lost-time accidents decreased by 69 percent.[48] The downside of variable pay, from an employee's perspective, is its unpredictability. With a straight base salary, employees know what they'll be earning. Adding in merit and cost of living, they can make fairly accurate predictions about what they'll be making next year and the year after. They can finance cars and homes based on reasonably solid assumptions. That's more difficult to do with variable pay. Your group's performance might slip this year or a recession may undermine your company's profits. Depending how your variable pay is determined, these can cut your pay. Moreover, people begin to take repeated annual performance bonuses for granted. A 15 or 20 percent bonus, received three years in a row, begins to become expected in the fourth year. If it doesn't materialize, management will find itself with some disgruntled employees.

Linking Variable-Pay Programs and Expectancy Theory

Variable pay is probably most compatible with expectancy theory predictions. Specifically, individuals should perceive a strong relationship between their performance and the rewards they receive if motivation is to be maximized. If rewards are allocated completely on nonperformance factors—such as seniority or job title—then employees are likely to reduce their effort.

The evidence supports the importance of this linkage, especially for operative employees working under piece-rate systems. For example, one study of 400 manufacturing firms found that those companies with wage incentive plans achieved 43 to 64 percent greater productivity than those without such plans.[49]

Group and organizationwide incentives reinforce and encourage employees to sublimate personal goals for the best interests of their department or the organization. Group-based performance incentives are also a natural extension for those organizations that are trying to build a strong team ethic. By linking rewards to team performance, employees are encouraged to make extra efforts to help their team succeed.

Variable-Pay Programs in Practice

Variable pay is a concept that is rapidly replacing the annual cost of living raise. One reason, as just cited, is its motivational power—but don't ignore the cost implications. Bonuses, gainsharing, and other variable-based reward programs avoid the fixed expense of permanent salary boosts.

> ◆ Variable pay is rapidly replacing the annual cost of living raise.

Pay for performance has been in vogue for compensating managers for more than a decade. The new trend has been expanding this practice to nonmanagerial employees. In 1989, 44 percent of companies had pay-for-performance plans for employees other than senior management. That had increased to 51 percent by 1991.[50]

A 1993 survey of 382 medium-size and large companies found that approximately three-quarters use variable pay to boost productivity.[51] Another survey found that 14 percent of U.S. companies used performance-based bonuses to completely replace the annual raise in 1993, and that increased to 21 percent in 1994.[52]

Gainsharing's popularity seems to be narrowly focused among large unionized manufacturing companies.[53] It is currently being used in about 2,000 companies including such major firms as Bell & Howell, American Safety Razor, Champion Spark Plug, Cincinnati Milacron, Eaton, Firestone Tire, Hooker Chemical, and Mead Paper.[54]

Among firms that haven't introduced performance-based compensation programs, common concerns tend to surface.[55] Managers fret over what should

Mayflower Transit was the first company in the moving industry to join the trend of tying nonmanagerial employee pay to performance. In 1989, Mayflower introduced a pay-for-performance plan for its van operators who are independent contractors. Operators are rated on safety, on-time delivery, claims, and customer satisfaction, which is gauged directly from customer evaluations on survey forms. This approach to compensation has significantly contributed to improved customer satisfaction by motivating operators to give customers exceptional service during the stressful moving process.

constitute performance and how it should be measured. They have to overcome the historical attachment to cost of living adjustments and the belief they have an obligation to keep all employees' pay in step with inflation. Other barriers include salary scales keyed to what the competition is paying, traditional compensation systems that rely heavily on specific pay grades and relatively narrow pay ranges, and performance appraisal practices that produce inflated evaluations and expectations of full rewards. Of course, from the employees' standpoint, the major concern is a potential drop in earnings. Pay for performance means employees have to share in the risks as well as the re-

◆◆◆◆ OB in the News ◆◆◆◆

Gainsharing Works at Whirlpool

Things have changed a lot in the last few years at the Whirlpool Corporation factory in Benton Harbor, Michigan. "Productivity used to be a dirty word around here," says the union president of Machinists Local 1918. "People thought they'd have to work harder without getting anything for it." They were wrong. Thanks to improved productivity at this aging tooling and plating plant—defined in terms of output per hour of work—each of the plant's 265 employees recently earned an extra $2,700 a year through gainsharing. This lifted their average compensation to more than $26,400.

When the plan went into effect in 1988, things were in pretty bad shape. Productivity in the plant was extremely low and employees didn't seem to care. "If a machine broke, you just sat down" until someone came along sooner or later and fixed it, says Bill Bonfoey, a 31-year Whirlpool veteran. Workers hid inferior parts, he adds, so "an inspector wouldn't see them."

In the plan's first four years, Benton Harbor's productivity has surged more than 19 percent and the number of parts rejected has sunk to a world-class 10 per million from 837 per million. Moreover, this was achieved with no regular wage or cost of living increases. Yet, because of gainsharing, the average worker's pay at the factory actually increased nearly 12 percent.

Based on R. Wartzman, "A Whirlpool Factory Raises Productivity—and Pay of Workers," *Wall Street Journal* (May 4, 1992), p. A1.

wards of their employer's business. This, incidentally, explains why Du Pont's fiber division dropped its variable-pay plan.[56] Introduced in 1989, the division's 20,000 workers agreed to smaller than average annual raises in exchange for the opportunity to receive performance bonuses that might add an additional 12 percent to their salaries. First-year bonuses amounted to only 3 percent and disappeared completely the next year. Employee morale sunk to new lows so management scuttled the plan in 1991 and raised salaries by 4 percent.

Skill-Based Pay Plans

Organizations hire people for their skills, then typically put them in jobs and pay them based on their job title or rank. So the director of corporate sales earns $120,000 a year, the regional sales managers make $75,000, and the district sales managers get $60,000. But if organizations hire people because of their competencies, why don't they pay them for those same competencies? Some organizations do.

Workers at American Steel & Wire can boost their annual salaries by up to $12,480 by acquiring as many as 10 skills. At AT&T's Universal Card service center in Jacksonville, Florida, the best paid customer representatives have rotated through four to six trouble-shooting assignments over two or three years, becoming adept at solving any billing, lost card, or other problem a credit card holder runs into. New employees at a Quaker Oats's pet food plant in Topeka, Kansas, start at $8.75 an hour, but can reach a top rate of $14.50 when they master 10 to 12 skills like operating lift trucks and factory computer controls. Salomon Brothers, a major brokerage firm, is using a skills-based pay system to turn narrowly trained and independent specialists into well-rounded product experts and to encourage them to be team players.[57]

What Are Skill-Based Pay Plans?

Skill-based pay is an alternative to job-based pay. Rather than having an individual's job title define his or her pay category, **skill-based pay** (sometimes called competency-based pay) sets pay levels on the basis of how many skills employees have or how many jobs they can do.[58] For instance, at the Polaroid Corporation, the highest pay you can earn as a machine operator is $14 an hour. But the company has a skill-based pay plan. So if machine operators can broaden their competencies to include additional skills like material accounting, maintenance of equipment, and quality inspection, they can earn up to 10 percent more. If they can learn some of their supervisor's skills, they can earn even more.[59]

skill-based pay
Pay levels are based on how many skills employees have or how many jobs they can do.

What's the appeal of skill-based pay plans? From management's perspective, it's flexibility. Filling staffing needs is easier when employee skills are interchangeable. This is particularly true in the 1990s as many organizations cut the size of their work force. Downsizing requires more generalists and fewer specialists. Skill-based pay encourages employees to acquire a broader range of skills. But there are other benefits to skill-based pay. It facilitates communication across the organization because people gain a better understanding of others' jobs. It lessens dysfunctional "protection of territory" behavior. Where skill-based pay exists, you're less likely to hear the phrase, "It's not my job!" Skill-based pay additionally helps meet the needs of ambitious employees who confront minimal advancement opportunities. These people can increase their earnings and knowledge without a promotion in job title. Finally, skill-based pay appears to lead to performance improvements. A broad-based survey of Fortune 1000 firms found that 60 percent of those with skill-based pay rated their plans as successful or very successful in increasing organizational performance; only 6 percent considered them unsuccessful or very unsuccessful.[60]

What about the downside of skill-based pay? People can "top out," learning all the skills the program calls for them to learn. This can frustrate employees after they've become challenged by an environment of learning, growth, and continual pay raises. Skills can become obsolete. When this happens, what should management do? Cut employee pay or continue to pay for skills that are no longer relevant? There is also the problem created by paying people for acquiring skills for which there may be no immediate need. This happened at IDS Financial Services.[61] The company found itself paying people more money even though there was little immediate use for their new skills. IDS eventually dropped its skill-based pay plan and replaced it with one that equally balances individual contribution and gains in work-team productivity. Finally, skill-based plans don't address level of performance. They deal only with the issue of whether someone can perform the skill. For some skills—such as checking quality or leading a team—level of performance may be equivocal. While it's possible to assess how well employees perform each of the skills and combine that with a skill-based plan, that is not an inherent part of skill-based pay.

Linking Skill-Based Pay Plans to Motivation Theories

Skill-based pay plans are consistent with several motivation theories. Because they encourage employees to learn, expand their skills, and grow, they are consistent with ERG theory. Among employees whose lower order needs are substantially satisfied, the opportunity to experience growth can be a motivator.

Paying people to expand their skill levels is also consistent with research on the achievement need. High achievers have a compelling drive to do things better or more efficiently. By learning new skills or improving the skills they already hold, high achievers will find their jobs more challenging.

There is also a link between reinforcement theory and skill-based pay. Skill-based pay encourages employees to develop their flexibility, to continue to learn, to cross-train, to be generalists rather than specialists, and to work cooperatively with others in the organization. To the degree that management wants employees to demonstrate such behaviors, skill-based pay should act as a reinforcer.

Skill-based pay may additionally have equity implications. When employees make their input-outcome comparisons, skills may provide a fairer input criterion for determining pay than factors such as seniority or education. To the degree that employees perceive skills as the critical variable in job performance, the use of skill-based pay may increase the perception of equity and help optimize employee motivation.

Skill-Based Pay in Practice

A number of studies have investigated the use and effectiveness of skill-based pay. The overall conclusion, based on these studies, is that skill-based pay is expanding and that it generally leads to higher employee performance and satisfaction.

Employees of McDonnell Douglas Helicopter Company, shown here in a company lab testing parts for an Apache helicopter, helped develop and implement a skill-based pay system that pays them for what they can do, what they know, and what they can contribute. To receive a pay increase, employees must learn and demonstrate a new skill that meets specific quality and time standards and that is directly related to their job. The skill-based plan benefits employees by giving them control of the process that determines their compensation. It benefits managers by giving them a better sense of employees' abilities, enabling them to develop progression paths for individual workers. For McDonnell Douglas, replacing its automatic wage progression with skill-based pay has contributed to significant productivity improvements.

The Fortune 1000 study mentioned earlier found a significant increase in skill-based pay plans between 1987 and 1990.[62] In 1990, 51 percent of large U.S. corporations used skill-based pay with at least some employees, an increase of more than 25 percent in just three years. But in the typical company that adopted skill-based pay, it applied to less than 20 percent of employees. Another study, covering a broader range of organizations, confirmed this trend. Among the 1,800 companies polled, 10 percent were using skill-based pay in 1993; however, 25 percent were expecting to have such a plan in place within a year.[63]

A survey of 27 companies that pay employees for learning extra skills found 70 to 88 percent reported higher job satisfaction, product quality, or productivity. Some 70 to 75 percent cited lower operating costs or turnover.[64]

Additional research has discovered some other interesting trends. The increased use of skills as a basis for pay appears particularly strong among organizations facing aggressive foreign competition and those companies with shorter product life cycles and speed-to-market concerns.[65] Also, skill-based pay is moving from the shop floor to the white-collar work force, and sometimes as far as the executive suite.[66]

Skilled-based pay appears to be an idea whose time has come. As one expert noted, "Slowly, but surely, we're becoming a skill-based society where your market value is tied to what you can do and what your skill set is. In this new world where skills and knowledge are what really counts, it doesn't make sense to treat people as jobholders. It makes sense to treat them as people with specific skills and to pay them for those skills."[67]

Flexible Benefits

Todd Evans and Allison Murphy both work for PepsiCo, but they have very different needs in terms of fringe benefits. Todd is married, has three young children, and a wife who is at home full time. Allison, too, is married, but her husband has a high-paying job with the federal government, and they have no children. Todd is concerned about having a good medical plan and enough life insurance to support his family if he wasn't around. In contrast, Allison's husband already has her medical needs covered on his plan, and life insurance is a low priority for both her and her husband. Allison is more interested in extra vacation time and long-term financial benefits like a tax-deferred savings plan.

What Are Flexible Benefits?

flexible benefits
Employees tailor their benefit program to meet their personal needs by picking and choosing from a menu of benefit options.

Flexible benefits allow employees to pick and choose from among a menu of benefit options. The idea is to allow each employee to choose a benefit package that is individually tailored to his or her own needs and situation. It replaces the traditional "one-benefit-plan-fits-all" programs that have dominated organizations for more than 50 years.[68]

The average organization provides fringe benefits worth approximately 40 percent of an employee's salary. But traditional benefit programs were designed for the typical employee of the 1950s—a male with a wife and two children at home. Less than 10 percent of employees now fit this stereotype. Twenty-five percent of today's employees are single, and a third are part of two-income families without any children. As such, these traditional programs don't meet the needs of today's more diverse work force. Flexible benefits, however, do meet these diverse needs. An organization sets up a flexible spending account for each employee, usually based on some percentage of his or her salary, and then a price tag is put on each benefit. Options might include inexpensive medical plans with high deductibles; expensive medical plans with low or no deductibles; hearing, dental, and eye coverage; vacation options; extended disability; a variety of savings and pension plans; life insurance; college tuition reimbursement plans; and extended vacation time. Employees then select benefit options until they have spent the dollar amount in their account.

Linking Flexible Benefits and Expectancy Theory

Giving all employees the same benefits assumes all employees have the same needs. Of course, we know this assumption is false. So flexible benefits turn the benefits' expenditure into a motivator.

Consistent with expectancy theory's thesis that organizational rewards should be linked to each individual employee's goals, flexible benefits individualize rewards by allowing each employee to choose the compensation package that best satisfies his or her current needs. That flexible benefits can turn the traditional homogeneous benefit program into a motivator was demonstrated at one company: Eighty percent of the organization's employees changed their benefit packages when a flexible plan was put into effect.[69]

Flexible Benefits in Practice

In 1991 about 38 percent of large U.S. companies had flexible benefits programs.[70] Flexible benefits are even becoming routinely available in companies with fewer than 50 employees.[71]

Let's look at the benefits and drawbacks. For employees, flexibility is attractive because they can tailor their benefits and levels of coverage to their own needs. The major drawback, from the employee's standpoint, is that the costs of individual benefits often go up, so fewer total benefits can be purchased.[72] For example, low-risk employees keep the cost of medical plans low for everyone. As they are allowed to drop out, the high-risk population occupies a larger segment and the cost of medical benefits go up. From the organization's standpoint, the good news is that flexible benefits often produce savings. Many organizations use the introduction of flexible benefits to raise deductibles and premiums. Moreover, once in place, costly increases in items like health insurance premiums often have to be substantially absorbed by the employee. The bad news for the organization is that these plans are more cumbersome for management to oversee, and administering the programs is often expensive.

Comparable Worth

Is it fair that two people do jobs that are equally demanding, require the same amount of education and training, and have similar responsibilities, yet one receives significantly less pay than the other? Of course not! But such situations are actually not that uncommon, with women being the ones earning the lesser amounts. What's the source of this inequity? Some economists would argue it merely reflects the market forces of supply and demand. Another interpretation—and one gaining an increasing audience—is that these differences are the result of gender-based wage discrimination.

It is not unusual for female-dominated jobs (i.e., elementary school teacher, nurse, librarian) to pay less than male-dominated jobs (i.e., truck driver, lumberjack, chef), even though they are of equal or greater comparable value. This inequity has stimulated considerable interest in the concept of comparable worth.

What Is Comparable Worth?

Comparable worth holds that jobs equal in value to an organization should be equally compensated, whether or not the work content of those jobs is similar.[73] That is, if the positions of secretary and draftsman (historically viewed as female and male jobs, respectively) require similar skills and make comparable demands on employees, they should pay the same, regardless of external market factors. Specifically, comparable worth argues that jobs should be evaluated and scored on four criteria: skill, effort, responsibility, and working conditions.

comparable worth
A doctrine that holds that jobs equal in value to an organization should be equally compensated, whether or not the work content of those jobs is similar.

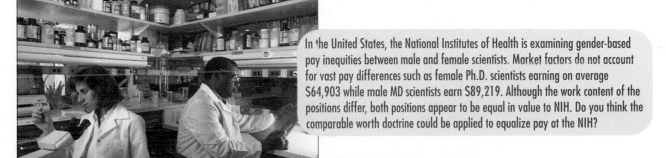

In the United States, the National Institutes of Health is examining gender-based pay inequities between male and female scientists. Market factors do not account for vast pay differences such as female Ph.D. scientists earning on average $64,903 while male MD scientists earn $89,219. Although the work content of the positions differ, both positions appear to be equal in value to NIH. Do you think the comparable worth doctrine could be applied to equalize pay at the NIH?

The criteria should be weighted and given points, with the points then used to value and compare jobs.

Comparable worth is a controversial idea. It assumes that totally dissimilar jobs can be accurately compared, that pay rates based on supply and demand factors in the job market are frequently inequitable and discriminatory, and that job classes can be identified and objectively rated.

Comparable Worth and Equity Theory

Comparable worth expands the notion of "equal pay for equal work" to include jobs that are dissimilar but of comparable value. As such, it is a direct application of equity theory.

As long as women in traditionally lower paid female-dominated jobs compare themselves solely to other women in female-dominated jobs, they are unlikely to perceive gender-based pay inequities. But when other referents are chosen, inequities often become quickly evident. This is because so-called women's jobs have been historically devalued. Take the following case. You went to a university for six years, earned a master's of library science degree, and over the past four years have taken on increased responsibilities as a reference librarian for a public library in the city of Seattle. Your current pay is $2,460 a month. Your younger brother also works for the city of Seattle, but as a driver on a sanitation truck. He's a high school graduate with no college education and has also held his job for four years. He makes $2,625 a month. If you were that librarian, wouldn't you be likely to compare your pay to your brother's and to conclude you are being underpaid?

◆Comparable worth expands the notion of "equal pay for equal work" to include jobs that are dissimilar but of comparable value.

To the degree that job classes reflect historical gender discrimination and create pay inequities, comparable worth provides a potential remedy. And job classes in the United States do reflect gender discrimination! For instance, a study of state workers in Washington gave clerical supervisors more points than chemists, although the chemists were paid 41 percent more; and gave retail clerks higher points than truck drivers, but the drivers earned 30 percent more.[74] For women in these discriminated job classes, the application of the comparable worth concept should reduce inequities and increase work motivation.

Comparable Worth in Practice

Women earn, on average, about 75 cents for each dollar that men earn. Part of this difference can be explained in market terms. For instance, the average number of years of professional job preparation is 4.2 for males and 0.4 for females. Males also have, on average, 12.6 years of job seniority compared to only 2.4 for females.[75] Yet even after objective differences are accounted for, a good portion of the variance remains. It is this variance that comparable worth is addressing.

In the United States, the comparable worth issue has been almost exclusively related to jobs in the public sector. Twenty states have specifically enacted legislation or adopted policies aggressively implementing comparable worth standards in the state civil service. A number of other states are currently examining their work forces for gender-based pay inequities.[76] In the private sector, the most important and visible activity is currently taking place in Ontario, Canada.

The province of Ontario (which has a population of over 9 million) passed the Pay Equity Act in 1987. It defined male and female job classes, established criteria by which they were to be valued, and mandated equality of pay between classes of comparable worth in both the public and the private sectors. Because of the projected cost to Canadian employers, the law provided a five-year phase-in period.

The impact of this legislation cannot be underestimated. For instance, retailer T. Eaton Co. has 15,000 employees in 580 jobs within Ontario. Evaluating and comparing these jobs required four full-time employees and cost the company several million dollars a year in salary adjustments.[77] A regional distributor in Canada pays its "pickers"—mostly men—about $30,000 a year for filling orders by picking warehouse stock from bins. Female typists in nearby offices do jobs that are equally demanding but are paid only $18,000. Their salaries will be increased to at least $30,000.[78]

Ontario may be merely the first of many provinces in Canada to adopt a private sector comparable worth law. Other provinces in Canada are moving in a similar direction.

Because of the high costs associated with correcting pay inequities, business firms don't look favorably on the notion of comparable worth. When comparable worth legislation is introduced, business executives typically organize and lobby hard against it. Their arguments focus on the importance of allowing market forces to determine pay levels. Advocates of comparable worth counter with statistics showing that cultural forces and societal pay systems have created gender-based discrimination in certain job classes and that only legislation can provide a near-term solution to the problem.

Special Issues in Motivation

Various groups provide specific challenges in terms of motivation. In this section we look at some of the unique problems faced in trying to motivate professional employees, temporary workers, and the diverse work force.

Motivating Professionals

The typical employee of the 1990s is more likely to be a highly trained professional with a college degree than a blue-collar factory worker. These professionals receive a great deal of intrinsic satisfaction from their work. They tend to be well paid. So what, if any, special concerns should you be aware of when trying to motivate a team of engineers at Intel, a software designer at Microsoft, or a group of CPAs at Price Waterhouse?

Professionals are typically different from nonprofessionals.[79] They have a strong and long-term commitment to their field of expertise. Their loyalty is more often to their profession than to their employer. To keep current in their field, they need to regularly update their knowledge. And their commitment to their profession means they rarely define their workweek in terms of 8 to 5 and five days a week.

> ◆Money and promotions are typically low on the priority list of professionals.

So what motivates professionals? Money and promotions typically are low on their priority list. Why? They tend to be well paid and they enjoy what they do. In contrast, job challenge tends to be ranked high. They like to tackle problems and find solutions. Their chief reward in their job is the work itself. Professionals also value support. They want others to think what they're working on is important. While this may be true for all employees, because professionals tend to be more focused on their work as their central life interest, nonprofessionals typically have other interests outside of work that can compensate for needs not met on the job.

The preceding description implies a few guidelines to keep in mind if you're trying to motivate professionals. Provide them with ongoing challenging projects. Give them autonomy to follow their interests and allow them to structure their work in ways they find productive. Reward them with educational opportunities—training, workshops, attending conferences—that allow them to keep current in their field. And ask questions and engage in other actions that demonstrate to them you're sincerely interested in what they're doing.

Motivating Temporary Workers

We noted in Chapter 1 that one of the more comprehensive changes taking place in organizations is the addition of temporary or contingent employees. As downsizing has eliminated millions of "permanent" jobs, an increasing number of new openings are for part-time, contract, and other forms of temporary workers. In 1994, 25 percent of all working Americans were temporaries. By 2000, fully half will be temps. These contingent employees don't have the security or stability that permanent employees have. As such, they don't identify with the organization or display the commitment that other employees do. Temporary workers also are typically provided with little or no health care, pensions, or similar benefits.[80]

There is no simple solution for motivating temporary employees. For that small set of temps who prefer the freedom of their temporary status—some students, working mothers, seniors—the lack of stability may not be an issue. Additionally, temporariness might be preferred by those highly compensated doctors, engineers, accountants, and financial planners who don't want the demands of a stable job. But these are the exceptions. For the most part, temporary employees are so involuntarily.

What will motivate involuntarily temporary employees? An obvious answer is the opportunity for permanent status. In those cases where permanent employees are selected from the pool of temporaries, temporaries will often work hard in hopes of becoming permanent. A less obvious answer is the opportunity for training. The ability of a temporary employee to find a new job is largely dependent on his or her skills. If the employee sees the job he or she is doing for you can help develop salable skills, then motivation is increased. From an equity standpoint, you should also consider the repercussions of mixing permanent and temporary workers where pay differentials are significant. When temps work alongside permanent employees who earn more, and get benefits too, for doing the same job, the performance of temps is likely to suffer. Separating such employees or converting all employees to a variable-pay or skill-based pay plan might help lessen this problem.

Motivating the Diversified Work Force

Not everyone is motivated by money. Not everyone wants a challenging job. The needs of women, singles, immigrants, the physically disabled, senior citizens, and others from diverse groups are not the same as a white American male with three dependents. A couple of examples can make this point clearer.

Employees who are attending college typically place a high value on flexible work schedules. Such individuals may be attracted to organizations that offer flexible work hours, job sharing, or temporary assignments. A father may prefer to work the midnight to 8 A.M. shift in order to spend time with his children during the day when his wife is at work.

If you're going to maximize your employees' motivation, you've got to understand and respond to this diversity. How? The key word to guide you should be flexibility. Be ready to design work schedules, compensation plans, benefits, physical work settings, and the like, to reflect your employees' varied needs. This might include offering child care, flexible work hours, and job sharing for employees with family responsibilites. Or flexible leave policies for immigrants who want to occasionally make extensive return trips to their homelands. Or work teams for employees who come from countries with a strong collectivist orientation. Or allowing employees who are going to school to vary their work schedule from semester to semester.

Summary and Implications for Managers

We've presented a number of motivation theories and applications in this and the previous chapter. While it's always dangerous to synthesize a large number of complex ideas into a few simple guidelines, the following suggestions summarize the essence of what we know about motivating employees in organizations.

RECOGNIZE INDIVIDUAL DIFFERENCES Employees have different needs. Don't treat them all alike. Moreover, spend the time necessary to understand what's important to each employee. This will allow you to individualize goals, level of participation, and rewards to align with individual needs.

USE GOALS AND FEEDBACK Employees should have hard, specific goals, as well as feedback on how well they are faring in pursuit of those goals.

ALLOW EMPLOYEES TO PARTICIPATE IN DECISIONS THAT AFFECT THEM Employees can contribute to a number of decisions that affect them: setting work goals, choosing their own fringe benefit packages, solving productivity and quality problems, and the like. This can increase employee productivity, commitment to work goals, motivation, and job satisfaction.

LINK REWARDS TO PERFORMANCE Rewards should be contingent on performance. Importantly, employees must perceive a clear linkage. Regardless of how closely rewards are actually correlated to performance criteria, if individuals perceive this correlation to be low, the result will be low performance, a decrease in job satisfaction, and an increase in turnover and absenteeism statistics.

CHECK THE SYSTEM FOR EQUITY Rewards should also be perceived by employees as equating with the inputs they bring to the job. At a simplistic level, this means that experience, skills, abilities, effort, and other obvious inputs should explain differences in performance and, hence, pay, job assignments, and other obvious rewards.

For Review

1. Relate goal-setting theory to the MBO process. How are they similar? Different?
2. How does OB Mod influence employee motivation?
3. Explain the roles of employees and management in quality circles.
4. What are the pluses of variable-pay programs from an employee's viewpoint? From management's viewpoint?
5. Contrast job-based and skill-based pay.
6. What motivates professional employees?
7. What motivates temporary employees?
8. What can you do as a manager to increase the likelihood your employees will exert a high level of effort?

For Discussion

1. How might a college instructor use OB Mod to improve learning in the classroom?
2. Identify five different criteria by which organizations can compensate employees. Based on your knowledge and experience, do you think performance is the criterion most used in practice? Discuss.
3. "Performance can't be measured, so any effort to link pay with performance is a fantasy. Differences in performance are often caused by the system, which means the organization ends up rewarding the circumstances. It's the same thing as rewarding the weatherman for a pleasant day." Do you agree or disagree with this statement? Support your position.
4. What drawbacks, if any, do you see in implementing flexible benefits? (Consider this question from the perspective of both the organization and the employee.)
5. "The competitive marketplace acts as an efficient means of ensuring that pay equity is achieved." Do you agree or disagree with this statement? Support your position.
6. Your text argues for recognizing individual differences. It also suggests paying attention to members of diversity groups. Is this contradictory? Discuss.

Point

The Case for Pay Secrecy

"Oh, and one last point," said the director of human resources to the new hiree. "We treat salary information as a private matter around here. What you make is your business and no one else's. We consider it grounds for termination if you tell anyone what you make."

This policy of pay secrecy is the norm in most organizations, although in the majority of cases, it's communicated informally. The message trickles down and new employees quickly learn from their boss and peers not to inquire about what other people make or to openly volunteer their own salary. However, in some companies, pay secrecy is a formal policy. For instance, at GM's Electronic Data Systems (EDS) Corp. unit, new hirees sign a form acknowledging several policies, one of which states that employees are allowed to disclose their salaries, but if such disclosure leads to disruption, they can be fired. It doesn't take a genius to predict this policy effectively stifles discussion of pay at EDS.

For those raised in democratic societies, it may be tempting to surmise something inherently wrong with pay secrecy. On the other hand, if it's wrong, why do the vast majority of successful corporations in democracies follow the practice? There are a number of logical reasons why organizations practice pay secrecy and why they are likely to continue to do so.

First, pay is privileged information to both the organization and the individual employee. Organizations hold many things privileged—manufacturing processes, product formulas, new-product research, marketing strategies—and U.S. courts have generally supported the argument that pay rightly belongs in this category. Salary information has been held to be confidential and the property of management. Employees who release such data can be discharged for willful misconduct. Moreover, most employees want their pay kept secret. They are as comfortable discussing their specific pay as they are providing details of their sex life to strangers. Employees have a right to privacy, and this includes ensuring their pay is kept secret.

Second, pay secrecy lessens the opportunity for comparisons among employees and the exposure of perceived inequities. No pay system will ever be perceived as fair by everyone. One person's "merit" is another person's "favoritism." Knowledge of what other employees are making only highlights perceived inequities and causes disruptions.

Third, pay differences are often perfectly justified, yet only for subtle, complicated, or difficult-to-explain reasons. For instance, people doing similar jobs were hired under different market conditions. Or two managers have similar titles, although one supervises 10 people while the other supervises 20. Or one person earns more today than a coworker because of responsibilities held or contributions made to the organization in a different job several years earlier.

Fourth, pay secrecy saves embarrassing underpaid and underperforming employees. By definition, half of an organization's work force is going to be below average. What kind of organization would be so cold and insensitive as to publicly expose those in the lower half of the performance distribution?

Finally, pay secrecy gives managers more freedom in administering pay because every pay differential doesn't have to be explained. A policy of openness encourages managers to minimize differences and allocate pay more evenly. Since employee performance in an organization tends to follow a normal distribution, only through pay secrecy can managers feel comfortable in giving large rewards to high performers and little or no rewards to low performers.

Based on J. Solomon, "Hush Money," *Wall Street Journal* (April 18, 1990), pp. R22–R24; and K. Tracy, M. Renard, and G. Young, "Pay Secrecy: The Effects of Open and Secret Pay Policies on Satisfaction and Performance," in A. Head and W.P. Ferris (eds.), *Proceedings of the 28th Annual Meeting of the Eastern Academy of Management* (Hartford, CT, May 1991), pp. 248–51.

counterPoint

Let's Make Pay Information Open to All!

Open pay policies make good sense. They already exist for employees of most public institutions and for top executives in all publicly held corporations. A few private sector companies have also seen the benefits that can accrue from making the pay of all employees public knowledge. For instance, the computer maker NeXT Inc. has lists of all its employees' salaries hanging in company offices for anyone to consult.

Why do open pay policies make good sense? We can articulate at least five reasons.

First, such pay policies open communication and build trust. As an executive at NeXT stated, "Anything less than openness doesn't establish the same level of trust." If the organization can be open about such a sensitive issue as pay, it makes employees believe management can be trusted about other concerns that are not so sensitive. In addition, if an organization's pay system is fair and equitable, employees report greater satisfaction with pay and with pay differentials where pay is open.

Second, an employee's right to privacy needs to be balanced against his or her right to know. Laws to protect an employee's right to know have become more popular in recent years, especially in the area of hazardous working conditions. The case can be made that the right to a free flow of information includes the right to know what others in one's organization earn.

Third, pay secrecy is often supported by organizations not to prevent embarrassment of employees, but to prevent embarrassment of management. Pay openness threatens exposing system inequities caused by a poorly developed and administered pay system. An open pay system not only says to employees that management believes its pay policies are fair, but is itself a mechanism for increasing fairness. When true inequities creep into an open pay system, they are much more likely to be quickly identified and corrected than when they occur in pay secrecy systems. Employees will provide the checks and balances on management.

Fourth, what management calls "freedom" in administering pay is really a euphemism for "control." Pay secrecy allows management to substitute favoritism for performance criteria in pay allocations. To the degree we believe organizations should reward good performance rather than good political skills, open pay policies take power and control away from managers. When pay levels and changes are public knowledge, organizational politics is less likely to surface.

Finally, and maybe most importantly, pay secrecy obscures the connection between pay and performance. Both equity and expectancy theories emphasize the desirability of linking rewards to performance. To maximize motivation, employees should know how the organization defines and measures performance, and the rewards attached to differing levels of performance. Unfortunately, when pay information is kept secret, employees make inaccurate perceptions. Even more unfortunately, those inaccuracies tend to work against increasing motivation. Specifically, research has found that people overestimate the pay of their peers and their subordinates and underestimate the pay of their superiors. So where pay is kept secret, actual differences tend to be discounted, which reduces the motivational benefits of linking pay to performance.

Based on E.E. Lawler III, "Secrecy About Management Compensation: Are There Hidden Costs?" *Organizational Behavior and Human Performance* (May 1967), pp. 182–89; J. Solomon, "Hush Money," *Wall Street Journal* (April 18, 1990), pp. R22–R24; and K. Tracy, M. Renard, and G. Young, "Pay Secrecy: The Effects of Open and Secret Pay Policies on Satisfaction and Performance," in A. Head and W.P. Ferris (eds.), *Proceedings of the 28th Annual Meeting of the Eastern Academy of Management* (Hartford, CT, May 1991), pp. 248–51.

Learning About Yourself Exercise

How Equity Sensitive Are You?

The following questions ask what you'd like your relationship to be with any organization for which you might work. For each question, divide 10 points between the two answers (A and B) by giving the most points to the answer that is most like you and the fewest points to the answer least like you. You can, if you like, give the same number of points to both answers. And you can use zeros if you'd like. Just be sure to use all 10 points on each question. Place your points in the blank next to each letter.

In any organization where I might work:

1. It would be more important for me to:
   5 A. Get from the organization
   5 B. Give to the organization
2. It would be more important for me to:
   6 A. Help others
   4 B. Watch out for my own good
3. I would be more concerned about:
   4 A. What I receive from the organization
   6 B. What I contribute to the organization
4. The hard work I would do should:
   8 A. Benefit the organization
   2 B. Benefit me
5. My personal philosophy in dealing with the organization would be:
   4 A. If you don't look out for yourself, nobody else will
   6 B. It's better to give than to receive

Turn to page A-28 for scoring directions and key.

Source: Courtesy of Prof. Edward W. Miles, Georgia State University, and Dean Richard C. Huseman, University of Central Florida. With permission.

Working With Others Exercise

Goal-Setting Task

Purpose This exercise will help you learn how to write tangible, verifiable, measurable, and relevant goals as might evolve from an MBO program.

Time Approximately 20 to 30 minutes.

Instructions

1. Break into groups of three to five.
2. Spend a few minutes discussing your class instructor's job. What does he or she do? What defines good performance? What behaviors will lead to good performance?

3. Each group is to develop a list of five goals that, although not established participatively with your instructor, you believe might be developed in an MBO program at your college. Try to select goals that seem most critical to the effective performance of your instructor's job.
4. Each group will select a leader who will share his or her group's goals with the entire class. For each group's goals, class discussion should focus on their (a) specificity, (b) ease of measurement, (c) importance, and (d) motivational properties.

Ethical Dilemma Exercise

Are American CEOs Paid Too Much?

Critics describe the astronomical pay packages given to American CEOs as "rampant greed." They note, for instance, that during the 1980s, CEO compensation jumped by 212 percent while factory workers saw their pay increase by just 53 percent. During the same decade, the average earnings per share of the Standard & Poor's 500 companies grew by only 78 percent. In 1993 the average salary and bonus for a chief executive of a major U.S. corporation was $3,841,273. That was 149 times the average factory worker's pay of $25,317!

While the CEO average was undoubtedly skewed by people like Michael Eisner at Disney ($203 million), Sanford Weill at Travelers ($53 million), and Joseph Hyde III at Autozone ($32 million), high levels of executive pay seems to be widespread in the United States. For instance, a survey examined the compensation of the two highest paid executives at 361 large U.S. corporations. A record number—501 of these 722 executives—earned more than $1 million in pay during 1993.

How do you explain these astronomical pay packages? Some say this represents a classic economic response to a situation in which the demand is great for high-quality top executive talent and the supply is low. Other arguments in favor of paying executives $1 million a year or more are the need to compensate people for the tremendous responsibilities and stress that go with such jobs, the motivating potential that seven- and eight-figure annual incomes provide to senior executives and those who might aspire to be, and the influence of senior executives on the company's bottom line.

Executive pay is considerably higher in the United States than in most other countries. American CEOs typically make two or three times as much as their counterparts in Europe and Asia. In 1992, for instance, the 20 highest paid U.S. chief executives of publicly traded companies earned 167 percent more than their German counterparts and 820 percent more than their Japanese counterparts. Critics of executive pay practices in the United States argue that CEOs choose board members they can count on to support ever-increasing pay for top management. If board members fail to play along, they risk losing their positions, their fees, and the prestige and power inherent in board membership.

Is high compensation of U.S. executives a problem? If so, does the blame for the problem lie with CEOs or with the shareholders and boards that knowingly allow the practice? Are American CEOs greedy? Are these CEOs acting unethically? What do you think?

Source: J. Castro, "How's Your Pay?," *Time* (April 15, 1991), pp. 40–41; J.M. Pennings, "Executive Reward Systems: A Cross-National Comparison," *Journal of Management Studies* (March 1993), pp. 261–80; R. Morais, G. Eisenstodt, and S. Kichen, "The Global Boss' Pay: Where (and How) the Money Is," *Forbes* (June 7, 1993), pp. 90–98; and J.A. Byrne, "That Eye-Popping Executive Pay," *Business Week* (April 25, 1994), pp. 52–58.

"What Am I Going to Do About Stella McCarthy?"

CASE INCIDENT

Jim Murray had worked as a cost accountant at Todd Brothers Chevrolet for nearly three years. When his boss retired in the spring of 1994, Ross Todd, the company's president, asked Jim to take over the accounting department. As the company controller, Jim supervises four people: Stella McCarthy, Judy Lawless, Tina Rothschild, and Mike Sohal.

Six months have passed since Jim took over his new job. As he expected, Judy, Tina and Mike have been easy to work with. All have been in their jobs for at least four years. They know their jobs backward and forward. And they require very little of Jim's time.

Stella McCarthy, unfortunately, is a completely different story. Stella was hired about three months before Jim got his promotion. Her age and education aren't significantly different from his other three employees—she's in her early 30s with an undergraduate degree in accounting. But in recent weeks she has become his number one headache.

Stella's job is to handle general accounting records. She also acts as the accounting department's link to the service department. Stella provides advice and support to service on anything having to do with credit, cost control, the computer system, and the like.

The first sign of a problem began three weeks ago. Stella called in sick on both Monday and Tuesday. When she showed up for work on Wednesday morning, she looked like she hadn't slept in days. Jim called her into his office and, in an informal manner, began trying to find out what was going on. Stella was open. She admitted she hadn't been ill. She called in sick because she didn't have the emotional strength to come to work. She volunteered that her marriage was in trouble. Her husband had a serious drinking problem but wouldn't seek help. He had lost his third job in as many months on that last Friday. She was concerned about her children and her finances. Stella has a 7-year-old son from a previous marriage and twin daughters who are 3. Jim tried to console Stella. He encouraged her to keep her spirits up and reminded her that the company's health plan provides six free sessions of counseling. He suggested she consider using them.

Since that initial encounter, little seems to have changed with Stella. She's used up three more days of sick leave. When she comes to the office, it's clear her mind is somewhere else. She is spending an inordinate amount of time on the telephone, and Jim suspects it's almost all related to personal matters. Twice in the past week, Jim has noticed Stella crying at her desk.

Yesterday was the third working day of the new month. Stella should have completed the closing of last month's books yesterday, an important part of her job. This morning, soon after Stella arrived, Jim asked her where the closing numbers were. Stella got up and, with tears welling in her eyes, went to the ladies' room. Jim saw last month's books on Stella's desk. He opened them up. They were incomplete. Stella had missed her deadline, and Jim wasn't sure when he would have the final figures to give to Ross Todd.

Questions

1. Do any motivation techniques appear relevant to helping Jim deal with Stella? If so, what are they?
2. From an ethical perspective, how far do you think Jim should go in dealing with Stella's personal problems?
3. If you were Jim, what would you do?

Executive Compensation As a Motivator

It's a basic tenet of most contemporary motivation programs: Link rewards to performance. How, then, has it happened in recent years that dozens of executives' paychecks have gone up while their companies profits have gone down?

The answer seems to be lack of CEO accountability. Shareholders, who actually own the company, by law have no direct say in how much their chief executive is paid. The decision lies with the company's board of directors. But the typical board is made up of individuals handpicked by the CEO. As such, there are few checks and balances to prevent excessive compensation of CEOs.

Among the top 30 corporations in the United States, the average CEO compensation is now more than $3 million. But is $3 million too much for running a company with 100,000 or more employees? Is it too much when baseball players earn $5 million, singers make $30 million, or a movie producer like Steven Speilberg pulls down more than $170 million?

A study of the largest 1,000 companies in corporate America found that only 4 percent of the difference in executive pay could be attributed to differences in performance. This seems to support the premise that performance has little bearing on executive compensation. What, then, is it related to? Some argue that it's based substantially on the industry in which the firm operates. The entertainment industry, for example, pays considerably more than the utility industry. Others suggest that pay is a function of organization size: Larger companies pay more than smaller ones. Still others claim that compensation is purely a function of a CEO's power and control of his or her board. Those with the most power get the most bucks.

Questions

1. Can you make an argument, in terms of motivation, to justify increases in CEO pay when his or her organization's profits decline?
2. How would you structure a CEO's compensation to maximize both executive motivation and shareholder interest?
3. Should there be a ratio—say 20:1 or 30:1—between a CEO's pay and the lowest paid employee in his or her company that defines an upper limit to any executive's compensation?
4. How do you think excessive CEO compensation affects low-level employees in terms of motivation?

Source: "The U.S.'s Overpaid Executives," *Nightline* (April 17, 1992).

Suggestions for Further Reading

BANAS, P.A., "Employee Involvement: A Sustained Labor/Management Initiative at Ford Motor Company," in J.P. Campbell and R.J. Campbell (eds.), *Productivity in Organizations: New Perspectives from Industrial and Organizational Psychology* (San Francisco: Jossey-Bass, 1988), pp. 388–416.

CONNER, P.E., "Decision-Making Participation Patterns: The Role of Organizational Context," *Academy of Management Journal* (March 1992), pp. 218–31.

FIERMAN, J., "The Perilous New World of Fair Pay," *Fortune* (June 13, 1994), pp. 57–64.

HARDER, J.W., "Play for Pay: Effects of Inequity in a Pay-for-Performance Context," *Administrative Science Quarterly* (June 1992), pp. 321–35.

LAWLER, E.E., "Gainsharing Theory and Research: Findings and Future Directions," in W.A. Pasmore and R.W. Woodman (eds.), *Research in Organizational Change and Development*, Vol. 2 (Greenwich, CT: JAI Press, 1988), pp. 323–44.

LEANA, C.A., R.S. AHLBRANDT, and A.J. MURRELL, "The Effects of Employee Involvement Programs on Unionized Workers' Attitudes, Perceptions, and Preferences in Decision Making," *Academy of Management Journal* (October 1992), pp. 861–73.

LEDFORD, G.E., E.E. LAWLER, and S.A. MOHRMAN, "The Quality Circle and Its Variations," in J.P. Campbell and R.J. Campbell (eds.), *Productivity in Organizations: New Perspectives from Industrial and Organizational Psychology* (San Francisco: Jossey-Bass, 1988), pp. 255–94.

PAUL, R.J., and J.B. TOWNSEND, "Managing the Older Worker—Don't Just Rinse Away the Gray," *Academy of Management Executive* (August 1993), pp. 67–74.

RUSSELL, R., and V. RUS (eds.), *International Handbook of Participation in Organizations: Ownership and Participation*, Vol. II (Oxford, England: Oxford University Press, 1992).

VERESPEJ, M.A., "New Responsibilities? New Pay!" *Industry Week* (August 15, 1994), pp. 11–22.

Notes

[1] This section is based on R. Levering and M. Moskowitz, "The Ten Best Companies to Work for in America," *Business and Society Review* (Spring 1993), p. 29.

[2] P.F. Drucker, *The Practice of Management* (New York: Harper & Row, 1954).

[3] See, for instance, S.J. Carroll and H.L. Tosi, *Management by Objectives: Applications and Research* (New York, Macmillan, 1973); and R. Rodgers and J.E. Hunter, "Impact of Management by Objectives on Organizational Productivity," *Journal of Applied Psychology* (April 1991), pp. 322–36.

[4] See, for instance, F. Schuster and A.F. Kendall, "Management by Objectives, Where We Stand—a Survey of the Fortune 500," *Human Resource Management* (Spring 1974), pp. 8–11; R.C. Ford, F.S. MacLaughlin, and J. Nixdorf, "Ten Questions About MBO," *California Management Review* (Winter 1980), p. 89; C.H. Ford, "MBO: An Idea Whose Time Has Gone?" *Business Horizons* (December 1979), p. 49; T.J. Collamore, "Making MBO Work in the Public Sector," *Bureaucrat* (Fall 1989), pp. 37–40; G. Dabbs, "Nonprofit Businesses in the 1990s: Models for Success," *Business Horizons* (September-October 1991), pp. 68–71; and R. Rodgers and J.E. Hunter, "A Foundation of Good Management Practice in Government: Management by Objectives," *Public Administration Review* (January-February 1992), pp. 27–39.

[5] See, for instance, Ford, "MBO: An Idea Whose Time Has Gone?"; R. Rodgers and J.E. Hunter, "Impact of Management by Objectives on Organizational Productivity," *Journal of Applied Psychology* (April 1991), pp. 322–36; and R. Rodgers, J.E. Hunter, and D.L. Rogers, "Influence of Top

Management Commitment on Management Program Success," *Journal of Applied Psychology* (February 1993), pp. 151–55.

[6] At Emery Air Freight: Positive Reinforcement Boosts Performance," *Organizational Dynamics* (Winter 1973), pp. 41–50.

[7] F. Luthans and R. Kreitner, *Organizational Behavior Modification and Beyond: An Operant and Social Learning Approach* (Glenview, IL: Scott, Foresman, 1985).

[8] F. Luthans and R. Kreitner, "The Management of Behavioral Contingencies," *Personnel* (July-August 1974), pp. 7–16.

[9] Luthans and Kreitner, *Organizational Behavior Modification and Beyond*, Chapter 8.

[10] See W.C. Hamner and E.P. Hamner, "Behavior Modification on the Bottom Line," *Organizational Dynamics* (Spring 1976), pp. 12–24; and "Productivity Gains from a Pat on the Back," *Business Week* (January 23, 1978), pp. 56–62.

[11] M.P. Heller, "Money Talks, Xerox Listens," *Business Month* (September 1990), pp. 91–92.

[12] "One Day at a Time," *INC.* (November 1990), p. 146.

[13] S. Navarette, "Multiple Forms of Employee Recognition," *At Work* (July-August 1993), p. 9.

[14] D.C. Anderson, C.R. Crowell, M. Doman, and G. S. Howard, "Performance Posting, Goal Setting, and Activity-Contingent Praise as Applied to a University Hockey Team," *Journal of Applied Psychology* (February 1988), pp. 87–95.

[15] See, for example, E. Locke, "The Myths of Behavior Mod in Organizations," *Academy of Management Review* (October 1977), pp. 543–53.

[16] B. Saporito, "The Revolt Against 'Working Smarter,'" *Fortune* (July 21, 1986), pp. 58–65; "Quality Circles: Rounding up Quality at USAA," *AIDE Magazine* (Fall 1983), p. 24; and J. Finegan, "People Power," *INC.* (July 1993), pp. 62–63.

[17] J.L. Cotton, *Employee Involvement* (Newbury Park, CA: Sage, 1993), pp. 3, 14.

[18] Ibid., p. 3.

[19] M. Sashkin, "Participative Management Is an Ethical Imperative," *Organizational Dynamics* (Spring 1984), pp. 5–22.

[20] R. Tannenbaum, I.R. Weschler, and F. Massarik, *Leadership and Organization: A Behavioral Science Approach* (New York: McGraw-Hill, 1961), pp. 88–100.

[21] E. Locke and D. Schweiger, "Participation in Decision Making: One More Look," in B.M. Staw (ed.), *Research in Organizational Behavior*, Vol. 1, (Greenwich, CT: JAI Press, 1979); E.A. Locke, D.B. Feren, V.M. McCaleb, K.N. Shaw, and A.T. Denny, "The Relative Effectiveness of Four Methods of Motivating Employee Performance," in K.D. Duncan, M.M. Gruneberg, and D. Wallis (eds.), *Changes in Working Life* (London: Wiley, 1980), pp. 363–88; K.L. Miller and P.R. Monge, "Participation, Satisfaction, and Productivity: A Meta-Analytic Review," *Academy of Management Journal* (December 1986), pp. 727–53; J.A. Wagner III and R.Z. Gooding, "Effects of Societal Trends on Participation Research," *Administrative Science Quarterly* (June 1987), pp. 241–62; J.A. Wagner III and R.Z. Gooding, "Shared Influence and Organizational Behavior: A Meta-Analysis of Situational Variables Expected to Moderate Participation-Outcome Relationships," *Academy of Management Journal* (September 1987), pp. 524–41; J.L. Cotton, D.A. Vollrath, K.L. Froggatt, M.L. Lengnick-Hall, and K.R. Jennings, "Employee Participation: Diverse Forms and Different Outcomes," *Academy of Management Review* (January 1988), pp. 8–22; D.I. Levine, "Participation, Productivity, and the Firm's Environment," *California Management Review* (Summer 1990), pp. 86–100; C.R. Leana, E.A. Locke, and D.M. Schweiger, "Fact and Fiction in Analyzing Research on Participative Decision Making: A Critique of Cotton, Vollrath, Froggatt, Lengnick-Hall, and Jennings," *Academy of Management Review* (January 1990), pp. 137–46; J.W. Graham and A. Verma, "Predictors and Moderators of Employee Responses to Employee Participation Programs," *Human Relations* (June 1991), pp. 551–68; J.L. Cotton, *Employee Involvement*; and J.A. Wagner III, "Participation's Effects on Performance and Satisfaction: A Reconsideration of Research Evidence," *Academy of Management Review* (April 1994), pp. 312–30.

[22] J.L. Cotton, *Employee Involvement*, p. 114

[23] See, for example, M. Poole, "Industrial Democracy: A Comparative Analysis," *Industrial Relations* (Fall 1979), pp. 262–72; IDE International Research Group, *European Industrial Relations* (Oxford, England Clarendon, 1981); E.M. Kassalow, "Employee Representation on U.S., German Boards," *Monthly Labor Review* (September 1989), pp. 39–42; T.H. Hammer, S.C. Currall, and R.N. Stern, "Worker Representation on Boards of Directors: A Study of Competing Roles," *Industrial and Labor Relations Review* (Winter 1991), pp. 661–80; and P. Kunst and J. Soeters, "Works Council Membership and Career Opportunities," *Organization Studies* (1991), pp. 75–93.

[24] J.D. Kleyn and S. Perrick, "Netherlands," *International Financial Law Review* (February 1990), pp. 51–56.

[25] J.L. Cotton, *Employee Involvement*, pp. 129–30, 139–40.

[26] Ibid., p. 140.

[27] Ibid., p. 59.

[28] See, for example, G.W. Meyer and R.G. Stott, "Quality Circles: Panacea or Pandora's Box?" *Organizational Dynamics* (Spring 1985), pp. 34–50; M.L. Marks, P.H. Mirvis, E.J. Hackett, and J.F. Grady, Jr., "Employee Participation in a Quality Circle Program: Impact on Quality of Work Life, Productivity, and Absenteeism," *Journal of Applied Psychology* (February 1986), pp. 61–69; E.E. Lawler III and S.A. Mohrman, "Quality Circles: After the Honeymoon," *Organizational Dynamics* (Spring 1987), pp. 42–54; R.P. Steel and R.F. Lloyd, "Cognitive, Affective, and Behavioral Outcomes of Participation in Quality Circles: Conceptual and Empirical Findings," *Journal of Applied Behavioral Science*, Vol. 24, No. 1 (1988), pp. 1–17; T.R. Miller, "The Quality Circle Phenomenon: A Review and Appraisal," *SAM Advanced Management Journal* (Winter 1989), pp. 4–7; K. Buch and R. Spangler, "The Effects of Quality Circles on Performance and Promotions," *Human Relations* (June 1990), pp. 573–82; P.R. Liverpool, "Employee Participation in Decision-Making: An Analysis of the Perceptions of Members and Nonmembers of Quality Circles," *Journal of Business and Psychology* (Summer 1990), pp. 411–22; and E.E. Adams, Jr., "Quality Circle Performance," *Journal of Management* (March 1991), pp. 25–39.

[29] J.L. Cotton, *Employee Involvement*, p. 76.

[30] Ibid., p. 78.

[31] Ibid., p. 87.

[32] See K.M. Young (ed.), *The Expanding Role of ESOPs in Public Companies* (New York: Quorum, 1990); J.L. Pierce and C.A. Furo, "Employee Ownership: Implications for Management," *Organizational Dynamics* (Winter 1990), pp. 32–43; J. Blasi and D.L. Druse, *The New Owners: The Mass Emergence of Employee Ownership in Public Companies and What It Means to American Business* (Champaign, IL: Harper Business, 1991); F.T. Adams and G.B. Hansen, *Putting Democracy to Work: A Practical Guide for Starting and Managing Worker-Owned Businesses* (San Francisco: Berrett-Koehler, 1993); and A.A. Buchko, "The Effects of Employee Ownership on Employee Attitudes: An Integrated Causal Model and Path Analysis," *Journal of Management Studies* (July 1993), pp. 633–56.

[33] J.L. Pierce and C.A. Furo, "Employee Ownership" and W. Cole and W.A. McWhirter, "Fly It? They Own It," *Time* (July 25, 1994), p. 46.

[34] C.M. Rosen and M. Quarrey, "How Well Is Employee Ownership Working?" *Harvard Business Review* (September-October 1987), pp. 126–32.

[35] J.L. Pierce and C.A. Furo, "Employee Ownership."

[36] Ibid., p. 38.

[37] T.R. Miller, "The Quality Circle Phenomenon," p. 5.

[38] J.L. Pierce and C.A. Furo, "Employee Ownership," p. 32.

[39] Cited in T. Ehrenfeld, "Cashing In," *INC.* (July 1993), pp. 69–70.

[40] Ibid.

[41] S.E. Gross and J.P. Bacher, "The New Variable Pay Programs: How Some Succeed, Why Some Don't," *Compensation & Benefits Review* (January-February 1993), p. 52.

[42] J.A. Byrne, "That Eye-Popping Executive Pay," *Business Week* (April 25, 1994), p. 52.

[43] G. Fuchsberg, "What's My Cut?" *Wall Street Journal* (April 13, 1994), p. R8.

[44] Based on S.E. Gross and J.P. Bacher, "The New Variable Pay Programs," p. 51; and J.R. Schuster and P.K. Zingheim, "The New Variable Pay: Key Design Issues," *Compensation & Benefits Review* (March-April 1993), p. 28.

[45] J.A. Byrne, "That Eye-Popping Executive Pay," p. 58.

[46] K. Hannon, "Variable-Pay Programs: Where the Real Raises Are," *Working Woman* (March 1994), p. 50.

[47] See, for instance, S.E. Markham, K.D. Scott, and B.L. Little, "National Gainsharing Study: The Importance of Industry Differences," *Compensation & Benefits Review* (January-February 1992), pp. 34–45; C.L. Cooper, B. Dyck, and N. Frohlich, "Improving the Effectiveness of Gainsharing: The Role of Fairness and Participation," *Administrative Science Quarterly* (September 1992), pp. 471–90; and W. Imberman, "Boosting Plant Performance with Gainsharing," *Business Horizons* (November-December 1992), pp. 77–79.

[48] See J.L. Cotton, *Employee Involvement*, pp. 89–113; and W. Imberman, "Boosting Plant Performance with Gainsharing," p. 79.

[49] M. Fein, "Work Measurement and Wage Incentives," *Industrial Engineering* (September 1973), pp. 49–51.

[50] Cited in J.S. Lublin, "A New Track," *Wall Street Journal* (April 22, 1992), p. R5.

[51] Cited in K. Hannon, "Variable-Pay Programs," p. 48.

[52] Ibid., p. 50.

[53] D. Beck, "Implementing a Gainsharing Plan: What Companies Need to Know," *Compensation & Benefits Review* (January-February 1992), p. 23.

[54] W. Imberman, "Boosting Plant Performance with Gainsharing."

[55] Cited in "Pay for Performance," *Wall Street Journal* (February 20, 1990), p. 1.

[56] F.R. Bleakley, "Many Companies Try Management Fads, Only to See Them Flop," *Wall Street Journal* (July 6, 1993), p. A6.

[57] These examples are cited in A. Gabor, "After the Pay Revolution, Job Titles Won't Matter," *New York Times* (May 17, 1992), p. F5; "Skill-Based Pay Boosts Worker Productivity and Morale," *Wall Street Journal* (June 23, 1992), p. A1; and L. Wiener, "No New Skills? No Raise," *U.S. News & World Report* (October 26, 1992), p. 78.

[58] E.E. Lawler, III, G.E. Ledford, Jr., and L. Chang, "Who Uses Skill-Based Pay, and Why," *Compensation & Benefits Review* (March-April 1993), p. 22.

[59] M. Rowland, "For Each New Skill, More Money," *New York Times* (June 13, 1993), p. F16.

[60] E.E. Lawler, III, G.E. Ledford, Jr., and L. Chang, "Who Uses Skill-Based Pay, and Why."

[61] "Tensions of a New Pay Plan," *New York Times* (May 17, 1992), p. F5.

[62] E.E. Lawler, III, G.E. Ledford, Jr., and L. Chang, "Who Uses Skill-Based Pay, and Why."

[63] F.R. Bleakley, "Many Companies Try Management Fads, Only to See Them Flop."

[64] "Skill-Based Pay Boosts Worker Productivity and Morale."

[65] E.E. Lawler, III, G.E. Ledford, Jr., and L. Chang, "Who Uses Skill-Based Pay, and Why."

[66] M. Rowland, "It's What You Can Do That Counts," *New York Times* (June 6, 1993), p. F17.

[67] Ibid.

[68] See, for instance, "When You Want to Contain Costs and Let Employees Pick Their Benefits: Cafeteria Plans," *INC.* (December 1989), p. 142; "More Benefits Bend with Workers' Needs," *Wall Street Journal* (January 9, 1990), p. B1; R. Thompson, "Switching to Flexible Benefits," *Nation's Business* (July 1991), pp. 16–23; and A.E. Barber, R.B. Dunham, and R.A. Formisano, "The Impact of Flexible Benefits on Employee Satisfaction: A Field Study," *Personnel Psychology* (Spring 1992), pp. 55–75.

[69] E.E. Lawler III, "Reward Systems," in Hackman and Suttle (eds.), *Improving Life at Work*, p. 182.

[70] Thompson, "Switching to Flexible Benefits," p. 17.

[71] "When You Want to Contain Costs and Let Employees Pick Their Benefits."

[72] H. Bernstein, "New Benefit Schemes Can Be Deceiving," *Los Angeles Times* (May 14, 1991), p. D3.

[73] D. Grider and M. Shurden, "The Gathering Storm of Comparable Worth," *Business Horizons* (July-August 1987), pp. 81–86.

[74] Cited in S.E. Rhoads, "Pay Equity Won't Go Away," *Across the Board* (July/August 1993), p. 41.

[75] Cited in T.J. Patten, *Fair Play* (San Francisco: Jossey-Bass, 1988), p. 31.

[76] Ibid., pp. 74–81.

[77] Cited in K.A. Kovach and P.E. Millspaugh, "Comparable Worth: Canada Legislates Pay Equity," *Academy of Management Executive* (May 1990), p. 97.

[78] J. Solomon, "Pay Equity Gets a Tryout in Canada—and U.S. Firms Are Watching Closely," *Wall Street Journal* (December 28, 1988), p. B1.

[79] See, for instance, M. Alpert, "The Care and Feeding of Engineers," *Fortune* (September 21, 1992), pp. 86–95.

[80] See, for example, L. Morrow, "The Temping of America," *Time* (March 29, 1993), pp. 40–47; B. Geber, "The Flexible Work Force," *Training* (December 1993), pp. 23–30; M. Barrier, "Now You Hire Them, Now You Don't," *Nation's Business* (January 1994), pp. 30–31; and J. Fierman, "The Contingency Work Force," *Fortune* (January 24, 1994), pp. 30–36.

PROGRESSIVE CASE ◆PART TWO◆ THE INDIVIDUAL

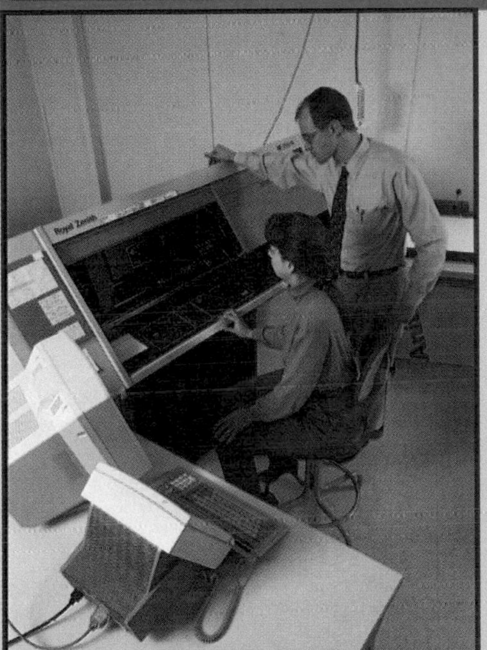

ROB PANCO: MANAGING INDIVIDUALS

Before you can understand others, you need to understand yourself. With that in mind, Rob Panco was asked to describe his strengths and weaknesses. "On the positive side, I'm very opportunistic. I'm good at exploiting opportunities. I'm a positive person. I'm realistic. Broad-minded. I can deal with different opinions and change my mind when I need to. I'm also driven to succeed." When asked to identify his faults, Rob said, "I take too much responsibility for other people's performance and happiness. I want to provide my people with safety nets. Sometimes people perform best when they work without a net. Nurturing is good, but too much isn't. This tendency creates problems when I delegate assignments. On one side, sometimes I don't provide enough instructions with my delegation. This is particularly a problem with younger project leaders. On the other side, I'm frequently paranoid when I delegate something. I'm afraid that it'll get screwed up. I worry a lot. I think this reflects the fact that I'm not always 100 percent sure of myself. I go through phases of insecurity. I feel overly responsible for people. Friends describe me as having confidence without arrogance. But I have a lot of responsibility here and I probably worry too much about people making mistakes and screwing things up."

Our discussion with Rob then turned to the topics of selecting new employees, his decision-making style, his views on motivation, the importance he places on measuring employee attitudes, and ethical dilemmas in his job.

"To find an ideal job candidate, I always start by looking at the specific job to be done. Essentially, I break jobs into one of two categories. For entry-level jobs, I look for people who show promise and are trainable. I can then mold them into the type of employee we want here. For experienced workers and managers, I'm more concerned with the fit between them and us. Their attitudes and ways of doing things are established so I need to be sure they fit well with our organization. For example, I'm currently interviewing candidates to fill the position of production manager. I'm looking for four things in this position. First, they have to have the ability to do the functional task. Second, they need raw talent. By that I mean they have to show me evidence they can successfully apply their ability. Third, I want some evidence of professional ambition. And fourth, I look at people's personal dynamics. Will they fit into our culture? Personality wise, the kind of people I want here are those with enthusiasm, team players—I don't want any heroes—and individuals committed to growth."

"Of course, like everyone, I've made some mistakes in hiring," Rob admitted. "I had to let one person go recently. He was late a lot. He lacked motivation. I had hired Dan right out of high school and I thought I could shape him into a real good employee. He was OK for about six months. Then the problems started. He wanted to leave at exactly 5 P.M. to be with his friends. He was resistant to new technologies. I encouraged him to take advantage of our training opportunities, but he wasn't interested. I talked with him about these problems on a monthly basis. I even talked with Hank, who Dan sort of modeled himself after. Hank told me that Dan lacked motivation and was hurting company morale. This confirmed to me that Dan didn't fit in. So I let him go. In another instance, I hired a woman as my financial assistant who did marvelously in the interview, had good references, and exactly the experience I was looking for. But Anne was just lethargic. She was slow, inaccurate, and her productivity was unsatisfactory. I had to fire her. Interestingly, I went back to Anne's original file and reviewed her application, references, and my interview notes. Nothing suggested she wouldn't be a top performer. Sometimes you just can't predict how an employee is going to turn out!"

"This discussion of hiring makes a good segue to the topic of decision making. I consider myself very rational. I'm a fact-based decision maker. Two things I think characterize my decision making. First, I'm flexible. I listen to others. I may not agree with you but I'm open to letting you sell me on your position. I believe in others giving me input. But we don't make decisions by committee around here. Second, I follow what I call my '12-hour rule.' I never rush big decisions that have a lasting impact. If people ask me right after a proposal what I'm going to do, I'll say 'I don't know yet.' I like to sleep on the decision and then make a commitment."

Motivating employees is a key issue for most managers and Rob is no exception. "I may be wrong, but I think money is less of a factor in the '90s than it was in the 1980s. Now quality of work life is a prime motivator. At our place, no one earns less than $25,000 a year. So everyone has their basic financial needs met. Let me quality my earlier comment. For people in the $25,000 to $32,000 range, money matters. It's less important for people who make over $35,000. And today, with so many dual-career couples, people just aren't going to jump through hoops in order to get an extra $1,000 or $2,000 salary increase. Also keep in mind that times have changed. The 10 percent annual cost-of-living raise is becoming extinct. We rely more on annual bonuses based on company and personal performance. Last year, for instance, bonuses ranged from 1 to 10 percent of a person's salary. Additionally, I look for creative ways to motivate people. As an example, I gave one person two days off with pay as a reward for an outstanding job. Most people appreciate recognition, so I use that. One employee got a write-up in a local paper for her success in fund-raising for charity. I put that article up on the wall in the lunch room. I also try to modify work schedules to reflect individual differences. I work with my single parents to give them leaves and schedules that help them meet their personal needs. Oh yeah, and we give all employees ten holidays a year. Only six of them are universally taken by everybody. The other four are floating days. Individuals can choose which holidays they want to take. Some take Martin Luther King Day as their holiday. One former military guy takes Veteran's Day. Several of our Jewish employees take Rosh Hashanah and/or Yom Kippur.

"The most recent motivation problem I had to confront was with an employee, Jim, who felt he was being inequitably treated relative to another worker. Jim is exempt from overtime, but he was putting in extra hours. Another coworker was also putting in extra hours but was earning overtime pay of time-and-a-half. I didn't think Jim's complaint was justified. His basic pay was higher than his coworker. And he seemed to downplay that he had recently received project-specific bonuses that reflected the long hours he had been putting in."

M.E. Aslett doesn't use attitude surveys. Rob talked about three means by which he keeps track of employee attitudes. "I tap employee attitudes informally. There are two people who regularly come in to my office, talk with me, and give me feedback on what people are thinking and saying. These people are very open with me. They speak their mind. And they're pretty accurate at tapping into the mood." Rob gets formal feedback on attitudes through project debriefings and performance reviews. Most projects at Aslett are done in teams. At the completion of a project, he debriefs the group. "I have to admit I don't get that much out of these debriefings," says Rob, "but it's a good motivating tool. It gives people a feeling of contributing." Finally, Rob uses the feedback from performance reviews and evaluations to monitor how employees feel about factors such as supervision, their job, and the organization itself.

When Rob was asked to identify ethical dilemmas he's faced, he mentioned two. A publisher wanted him to publish a book Rob felt was obviously outdated. Since he would be the editor of record, he didn't want to be associated with such a project. A second had to do with laying off a full-time employee and then rehiring someone to fill that slot but on a temporary basis. He wasn't sure whether such a decision, which made good business sense, was ethically appropriate.

Questions

1. To what degree do you think a manager like Rob should feel responsible for an employee's performance and happiness?
2. What do you think of the four criteria Rob used in the selection of a production manager? What personality characteristics, if any, do you think might be related to success in this job?
3. How well did Rob handle his problems with Dan?
4. What pluses does Rob's "12-hour rule" provide? How about negatives?
5. What theories can help explain Rob's motivation practices? Do you have any suggestions on how he might additionally motivate his work force?
6. What do you think of the means by which Rob keeps tabs on employee attitudes?
7. Is it unethical to fire a full-time employee and replace him or her with a temporary? What obligations, if any, does an employer have to a permanent employee?

◆PART THREE◆
THE GROUP

CHAPTER

Success in the growing worldwide market for MagneTek's electrical products requires speed and flexibility. The use of teams allows MagneTek to adapt quickly to changes in the size, schedule, and complexity of customer orders.

8

FOUNDATIONS OF GROUP BEHAVIOR

CHAPTER OUTLINE

- Defining and Classifying Groups
- Stages of Group Development
- Sociometry: Analyzing Group Interaction
- Toward Explaining Group Behavior
- External Conditions Imposed on the Group
- Group Member Resources
- Group Structure
- Group Processes
- Group Tasks
- Group Decision Making
- Should Management Seek Cohesive Work Groups?

LEARNING OBJECTIVES

After studying this chapter, you should be able to:

1. Differentiate between formal and informal groups.
2. Compare two models of group development.
3. Identify the key factors in explaining group behavior.
4. Explain how role requirements change in different situations.
5. Describe how norms exert influence on an individual's behavior.
6. Define *social loafing* and its effect on group performance.
7. Explain the influence of group demography on member behavior.
8. Contrast the effectiveness of interacting, brainstorming, nominal, Delphi, and electronic meeting groups.
9. Identify the benefits and disadvantages of cohesive groups.

One of the truly remarkable things about work groups is that they can make 2 + 2 = 5. Of course, they also have the capability of making 2 + 2 = 3.

S.P.R.

The pulp and paper products industry in Canada has been under cost pressures since the mid-1980s. One particular player in this industry, MacMillan Bloedel Ltd. (MacBlo), has responded by closing mills, shutting down machines, and cutting its work force down from 25,000 to 13,000. These efforts at downsizing have helped MacBlo, but the company still continues to post annual losses.[1]

If you think these cutbacks at MacBlo haven't set well with the company's unions, you'd be right. In fact, the company and its unions have a long history of antagonism. Three times during the 1980s, union locals hit the company with wildcat strikes. Each time the company sued the offending local and won cash awards and workplace concessions. The regional vice president of one union—the Communications, Energy, and Paperworkers Union of Canada—says, "There is not a great trust relationship here."

MacBlo's management, led by CEO Robert Findlay (see photo on p. 293), is trying to change its labor relations climate by getting workers more involved in company decision making. Its woodlands and mill managers now share detailed financial data and production plans in regular meetings with workers. Joint union–management committees have been created to solicit suggestions for improving productivity. And some division managers are even taking union representatives along on sales trips so they can see, firsthand, the industry's competitive conditions.

Management's efforts to improve relations with its union members haven't met with a great deal of success. Union leaders openly question management's motives. They claim that joint committees just dupe union members into making suggestions that increase productivity at the cost of jobs. And they use examples like the company's plan in March 1993 to discontinue bus service at one of the mills, which precipitated a one-day wildcat strike by 725 loggers, as evidence that the company just doesn't care about its employees.

The labor–management problems at MacMillan Bloedel illustrate the importance of understanding groups in the workplace. The behavior of individuals in groups is something more than the sum total of each acting in his or her own way. In other words, when individuals are in groups, they act differently than they do when they're alone. So, for instance, the employee who would individually accept change and cooperate with management might become belligerent and try to hinder that change if he or she is a union member and the union seeks to maintain the status quo.

Union members are just one example of a work group. As we show in this chapter, organizations are made up of a number of formal and informal groups. An understanding of these groups is critical to explaining organizational behavior.

Defining and Classifying Groups

group
Two or more individuals, interacting and interdependent, who have come together to achieve particular objectives.

formal group
A designated work group defined by the organization's structure.

informal group
A group that is neither formally structured nor organizationally determined; appears in response to the need for social contact.

A **group** is defined as two or more individuals, interacting and interdependent, who have come together to achieve particular objectives. Groups can be either formal or informal. By **formal groups**, we mean those defined by the organization's structure, with designated work assignments establishing tasks. In formal groups, the behaviors that one should engage in are stipulated by and directed toward organizational goals. The three members making up an airline flight crew are an example of a formal group. In contrast, **informal groups** are alliances that are neither formally structured nor organizationally determined. These groups are natural formations in the work environment that appear in response to the need for social contact. Three employees from different departments who regularly eat lunch together are an example of an informal group.

It's possible to subclassify groups as command, task, interest, or friendship groups.[2] Command and task groups are dictated by the formal organization, whereas interest and friendship groups are informal alliances.

A **command group** is determined by the organization chart. It is composed of the subordinates who report directly to a given manager. An elementary school principal and her 12 teachers form a command group, as do the director of postal audits and his five inspectors.

command group
A manager and his or her immediate subordinates.

Task groups, also organizationally determined, represent those working together to complete a job task. However, a task group's boundaries are not limited to its immediate hierarchical superior. It can cross command relationships. For instance, if a college student is accused of a campus crime, it may require communication and coordination among the dean of academic affairs, the dean of students, the registrar, the director of security, and the student's adviser. Such a formation would constitute a task group. It should be noted that all command groups are also task groups, but because task groups can cut across the organization, the reverse need not be true.

task group
Those working together to complete a job task.

People who may or may not be aligned into common command or task groups may affiliate to attain a specific objective with which each is concerned. This is an **interest group**. Employees who band together to have their vacation schedule altered, to support a peer who has been fired, or to seek increased fringe benefits represent the formation of a united body to further their common interest.

interest group
Those working together to attain a specific objective with which each is concerned.

Groups often develop because the individual members have one or more common characteristics. We call these formations **friendship groups**. Social alliances, which frequently extend outside the work situation, can be based on similar age, support for "Big Red" Nebraska football, having attended the same college, or the holding of similar political views, to name just a few such characteristics.

friendship group
Those brought together because they share one or more common characteristics.

Informal groups provide a very important service by satisfying their members' social needs. Because of interactions that result from the close proximity of work stations or task interactions, we find workers playing golf together, riding to and from work together, lunching together, and spending their breaks around the water cooler together. We must recognize that these types of interactions among individuals, even though informal, deeply affect their behavior and performance.

No single reason explains why individuals join groups. Since most people belong to a number of groups, it's obvious that different groups provide different benefits to their members. Table 8-1 summarizes the most popular reasons why people join a group.

Stages of Group Development

For 20 years or more, we thought most groups follow a specific sequence in their evolution and that we knew what that sequence was. But we were wrong. Recent research indicates no standardized pattern of group development. In this section, we review the better known five-stage model of group development, and then the recently discovered punctuated-equilibrium model.

The Five-Stage Model

From the mid-1960s, it was believed groups pass through a standard sequence of five stages.[3] As shown in Figure 8-1, these five stages have been labeled forming, storming, norming, performing, and adjourning.

The first stage, **forming**, is characterized by a great deal of uncertainty about the group's purpose, structure, and leadership. Members are testing the

forming
The first stage in group development, characterized by much uncertainty.

Table 8-1 Why Do People Join Groups?

Security
By joining a group, individuals can reduce the insecurity of standing alone. People feel stronger, have fewer self-doubts, and are more resistant to threats when they are part of a group.

Status
Inclusion in a group that is viewed as important by others provides recognition and status for its members.

Self-Esteem
Groups can provide people with feelings of self-worth. That is, in addition to conveying status to those outside the group, membership can also give increased feelings of worth to the group members themselves.

Affiliation
Groups can fulfill social needs. People enjoy the regular interaction that comes with group membership. For many people, these on-the-job interactions are their primary source for fulfilling their needs for affiliation.

Power
What cannot be achieved individually often becomes possible through group action. There is power in numbers.

Goal Achievement
There are times when it takes more than one person to accomplish a particular task—there is a need to pool talents, knowledge, or power in order to get a job completed. In such instances, management will rely on the use of a formal group.

waters to determine what types of behavior are acceptable. This stage is complete when members have begun to think of themselves as part of a group.

storming
The second stage in group development, characterized by intragroup conflict.

The **storming** stage is one of intragroup conflict. Members accept the existence of the group, but resist the constraints the group imposes on individuality. Further, there is conflict over who will control the group. When this stage is complete, a relatively clear hierarchy of leadership exists within the group.

norming
The third stage in group development, characterized by close relationships and cohesiveness.

The third stage is one in which close relationships develop and the group demonstrates cohesiveness. There is now a strong sense of group identity and camaraderie. This **norming** stage is complete when the group structure solidifies and the group has assimilated a common set of expectations of what defines correct member behavior.

performing
The fourth stage in group development, when the group is fully functional.

The fourth stage is **performing**. The structure at this point is fully functional and accepted. Group energy has moved from getting to know and understand each other to performing the task at hand.

Figure 8-1
Stages of Group Development

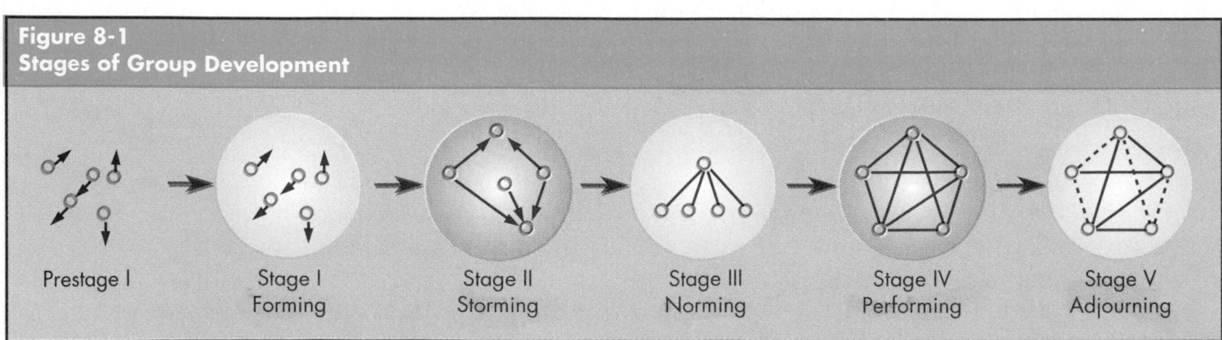

For permanent work groups, performing is the last stage in their development. However, for temporary committees, teams, task forces, and similar groups that have a limited task to perform, there is an **adjourning** stage. In this stage, the group prepares for its disbandment. High task performance is no longer the group's top priority. Instead, attention is directed toward wrapping up activities. Responses of group members vary in this stage. Some are upbeat, basking in the group's accomplishments. Others may be depressed over the loss of camaraderie and friendships gained during the work group's life.

adjourning
The final stage in group development for temporary groups, characterized by concern with wrapping up activities rather than task performance.

Many interpreters of the five-stage model have assumed a group becomes more effective as it progresses through the first four stages. While this assumption may be generally true, what makes a group effective is more complex than this model acknowledges. Under some conditions, high levels of conflict are conducive to high group performance. So we might expect to find situations where groups in Stage II outperform those in Stages III or IV. Similarly, groups do not always proceed clearly from one stage to the next. Sometimes, in fact, several stages go on simultaneously, as when groups are storming and performing at the same time. Groups even occasionally regress to previous stages. Therefore, even the strongest proponents of this model do not assume all groups follow its five-stage process precisely or that Stage IV is always the most preferable.

Another problem with the five-stage model, in terms of understanding work-related behavior, is that it ignores organizational context.[4] For instance, a study of a cockpit crew in an airliner found that, within ten minutes, three strangers assigned to fly together for the first time had become a high-performing group. What allowed for this speedy group development was the strong organizational context surrounding the tasks of the cockpit crew. This context provided the rules, task definitions, information, and resources needed for the group to perform. They didn't need to develop plans, assign roles, determine and allocate resources, resolve conflicts, and set norms the way the five-stage model predicts. Since much group behavior in organizations takes place within a strong organizational context, it would appear the five-stage development model may have limited applicability in our quest to understand work groups.

The Punctuated-Equilibrium Model

Studies of more than a dozen field and laboratory task force groups confirmed that groups don't develop in a universal sequence of stages.[5] But the timing of when groups form and change the way they work is highly consistent. Specifically, it's been found that (1) the first meeting sets the group's direction; (2) the first phase of group activity is one of inertia; (3) a transition takes place at the end of the first phase, which occurs exactly when the group has used up half its allotted time; (4) the transition initiates major changes; (5) a second phase of inertia follows the transition; and (6) the group's last meeting is characterized by markedly accelerated activity. These findings are shown in Figure 8-2.

Figure 8-2
The Punctuated-Equilibrium Model

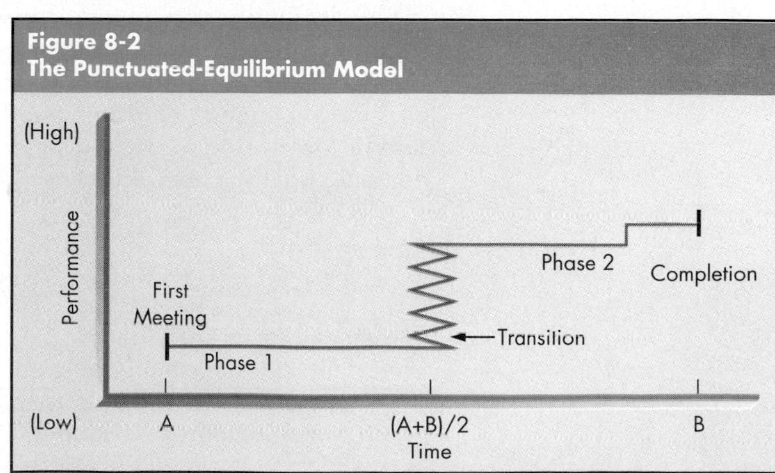

The first meeting sets the group's direction. A framework of behavioral patterns and assumptions through which the group will approach its project emerges in this first meeting. These lasting patterns can appear as early as the first few seconds of the group's life.

Once set, the group's direction becomes written in stone and is unlikely to be reexamined throughout the first half of the group's life. This is a period of inertia—that is, the group tends to stand still or become locked into a fixed course of action. Even if it gains new insights that challenge initial patterns and assumptions, the group is incapable of acting on these new insights in Phase 1.

One of the more interesting discoveries made in these studies was that each group experienced its transition at the same point in its calendar—precisely halfway between its first meeting and its official deadline—despite the fact that some groups spent as little as an hour on their project while others spent six months. It was as if the groups universally experienced a midlife crisis at this point. The midpoint appears to work like an alarm clock, heightening members' awareness that their time is limited and they need to get moving.

This transition ends Phase 1 and is characterized by a concentrated burst of changes, dropping of old patterns, and adoption of new perspectives. The transition sets a revised direction for Phase 2.

Phase 2 is a new equilibrium or period of inertia. In this phase, the group executes plans created during the transition period.

The group's last meeting is characterized by a final burst of activity to finish its work.

We can use this model to describe some of your experiences with student teams created for doing group term projects. At the first meeting, a basic timetable is established. Members size up one another. They agree they have nine weeks to do their project. The instructor's requirements are discussed and debated. From that point, the group meets regularly to carry out its activities. About four or five weeks into the project, however, problems are confronted. Criticism begins to be taken seriously. Discussion becomes more open. The group reassesses where it's been and aggressively moves to make necessary changes. If the right changes are made, the next four or five weeks find the group developing a first-rate project. The group's last meeting, which will probably occur just before the project is due, lasts longer than the others. In it, all final issues are discussed and details resolved.

In summary, the punctuated-equilibrium model characterizes groups as exhibiting long periods of inertia interspersed with brief revolutionary changes triggered primarily by their members' awareness of time and deadlines. Or, to use the terminology of the five-stage group development model, the group begins by combining the forming and norming stages, then goes through a period of low performing, followed by storming, then a period of high performing, and, finally, adjourning.

Sociometry: Analyzing Group Interaction

Shirley Goldman knew the formal work groups in the branch bank she managed. The tellers made up one group, the loan processors another, administrative support personnel still another, and the task force she had created for suggesting ways to improve customer service was a fourth. What Shirley didn't feel as confident about were the informal groups in her branch. Who were in these groups? Who were their informal leaders? How might these groups be affecting communication in the bank or creating potential conflicts? To get answers to these questions, Shirley decided to use a technique she learned in business school. Called **sociometry**, it's an analytical tool for studying group interactions.[6]

sociometry
An analytical technique for studying group interactions.

Sociometry seeks to find out who people like or dislike and whom they would or would not wish to work with. How do you get that information? Through the use of interviews or questionnaires. For instance, employees might be asked (1) Who, within the organization, would you like to associate with in the process of carrying out your job? or (2) Name several organization members with whom you would like to spend some of your free time.

This information can then be used to create a **sociogram**, a diagram that graphically maps the preferred social interactions obtained from the interviews or questionnaires. Before we actually work through an example, let's define some key terms you need to know when discussing and analyzing a sociogram:[7]

sociogram
A diagram that graphically maps the preferred social interactions obtained from interviews or questionnaires.

- **Social networks**. Specific set of linkages among a defined set of individuals.
- **Clusters**. Groups that exist within social networks.
- **Prescribed clusters**. Formal groups like departments, work teams, task forces, or committees.
- **Emergent clusters**. Informal, unofficial groups.
- **Coalitions**. Cluster of individuals who temporarily come together to achieve a specific purpose.
- **Cliques**. More permanent informal groupings that involve friendship.
- **Stars**. Individuals with the most linkages in a network.
- **Liaisons**. Individuals who connect two or more clusters but are not members of any cluster.
- **Bridges**. Individuals who serve as a linking pin by belonging to two or more clusters.
- **Isolates**. Individuals who aren't connected to the network.

social networks
A specific set of linkages among a defined set of individuals.

clusters
Groups that exist within social networks.

prescribed clusters
Formal groups like departments, work teams, task forces, or committees.

emergent clusters
Informal, unofficial groups.

coalitions
A cluster of individuals who temporarily come together to achieve a specific purpose.

cliques
Relatively permanent informal groups that involve friendship.

stars
Individuals with the most linkages in a network.

liaisons
Individuals in a social network who connect two or more clusters but are not members of any cluster.

bridges
Individuals in a social network who serve as linking pins by belonging to two or more clusters.

isolates
Individuals who are not connected to a social network.

Shirley Goldman has just completed a sociometric survey of the 11 people who work in her Bank of America branch in Sacramento, California. She has had each employee fill out a questionnaire identifying with whom they would like to spend more time. Now Shirley has translated those preferences into the simplified sociogram shown in Figure 8-3. Each employee is shown as a circle. The arrow from B to A means B chose A. The two-headed arrow connecting A and D means both chose each other.

What information can Shirley deduce from this sociogram? A is the star. F is an isolate. D is a bridge. There don't appear to be any liaisons. In addition to the four prescribed clusters, two emergent clusters seem to exist. And without more information, Shirley can't tell if these emergent clusters are coalitions or cliques.

So what, if anything, can Shirley do with this information? It can help her predict communication patterns. For instance, D is likely to act as an information conduit between the tellers and the administrative support group. Similarly, Shirley shouldn't be surprised that F is out of the gossip loop and tends to rely almost exclusively on formal communication to know what's happening in the branch. If Shirley was going on vacation and needed to pick

Figure 8-3
Simplified Sociogram of the Sacramento Branch of Bank of America

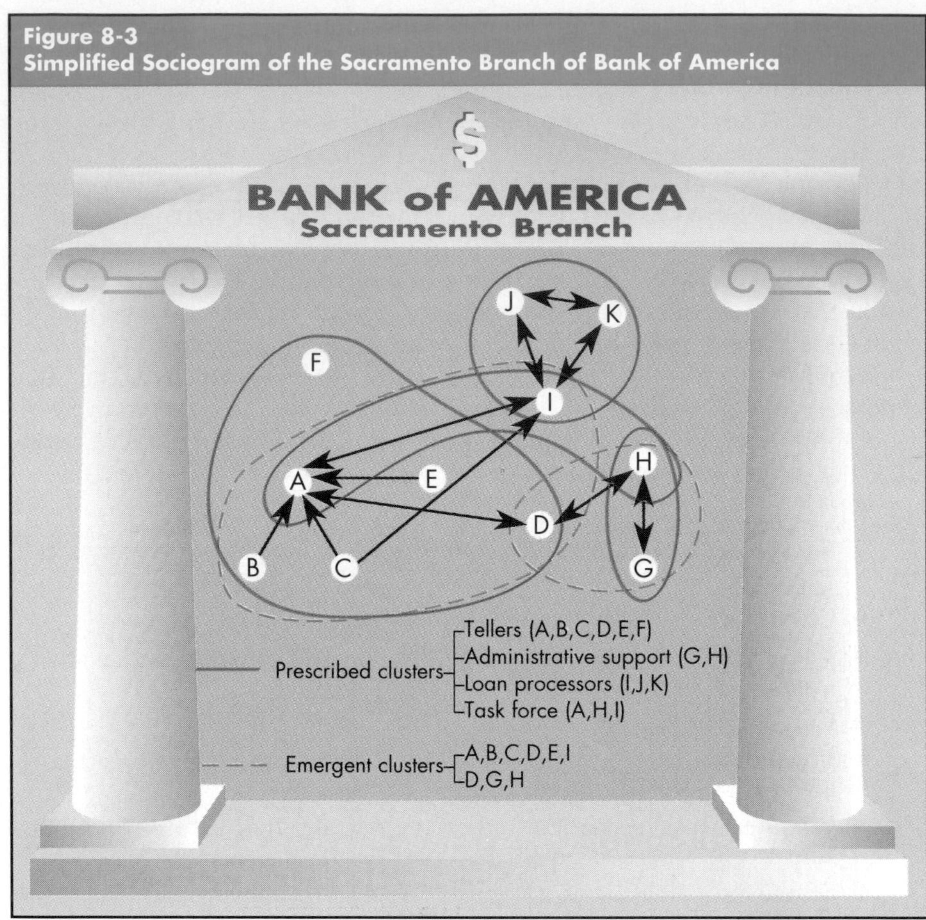

someone to temporarily run the branch, a good choice might be A, since this person seems to be well liked. When conflicts occur between the tellers and administrative support group, a bridge like D might be the best person to help resolve them.

Before we leave the topic of sociometry, some research relating to turnover, conflict, and diversity should be briefly mentioned. First, turnover is likely to be linked to emergent clusters.[8] Employees who perceive themselves as members of common clusters tend to act in concert—they're likely to stay or quit as a group. Second, strong interpersonal relationships between members tends to be associated with lower conflict levels.[9] So since members of emergent clusters tend to interact more with each other, there should be less conflict among these members. Finally, women and minorities tend to form coalitions and cliques, and are less likely than their white male counterparts to become liaisons or bridges.[10]

Toward Explaining Work Group Behavior

Why are some group efforts more successful than others? The answer to that question is complex, but it includes variables such as the ability of the group's members, the size of the group, the level of conflict, and the internal pressures on members to conform to the group's norms. Figure 8-4 presents the major components that determine group performance and satisfaction.[11] It can help you sort out the key variables and their interrelationships.

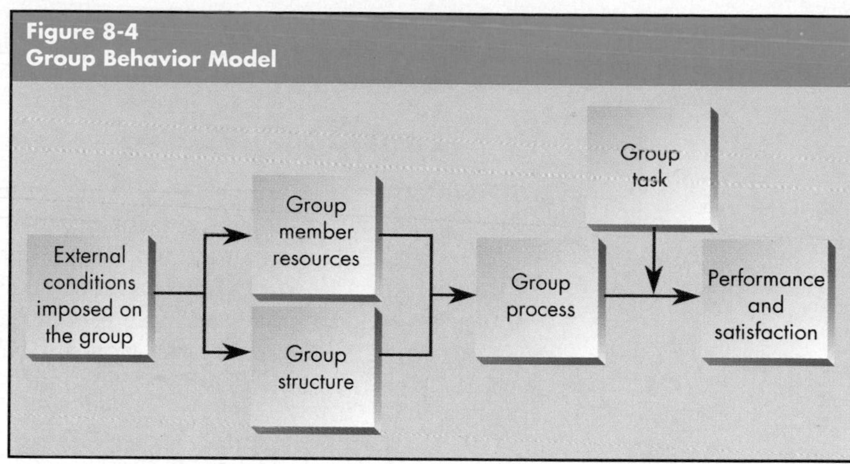

Figure 8-4
Group Behavior Model

Work groups don't exist in isolation. They are part of a larger organization. A research team in Dow's plastic products division, for instance, must live within the rules and policies dictated from the division's headquarters and Dow's corporate offices. So every work group is influenced by external conditions imposed from outside it. The work group itself has a distinct set of resources determined by its membership. This includes such things as intelligence and motivation of members. It also has an internal structure that defines member roles and norms. These factors—group member resources and structure—determine interaction patterns and other processes within the group. Finally, the group process–performance/satisfaction relationship is moderated by the type of task the group is working on. In the following pages, we elaborate on each of the basic boxes identified in Figure 8-4.

External Conditions Imposed on the Group

To begin understanding the behavior of a work group, you need to view it as a subsystem embedded in a larger system.[12] That is, when we realize groups are a subset of a larger organization system, we can extract part of the explanation of the group's behavior from an explanation of the organization to which it belongs.

Organization Strategy

An organization's overall strategy, typically put into place by top management, outlines the organization's goals and the means for attaining these goals. It might, for example, direct the organization toward reducing costs, improving quality, expanding market share, or shrinking the size of its overall operations. The strategy an organization is pursuing, at any given time, will influence the power of various work groups, which, in turn, will determine the resources the organization's top management is willing to allocate to it for performing its tasks. To illustrate, an organization that is retrenching through selling off or closing down major parts of its business is going to have work groups with a shrinking resource base, increased member anxiety, and the potential for heightened intragroup conflict.[13]

Authority Structures

Organizations have authority structures that define who reports to whom, who makes decisions, and what decisions individuals or groups are empowered to make. This structure typically determines where a given work group is placed in the organization's hierarchy, the formal leader of the group, and formal relationships between groups. So while a work group might be led by someone who emerges informally from within the group, the formally designated leader—appointed by management—has authority that others in the group don't have.

Formal Regulations

Organizations create rules, procedures, policies, and other forms of regulations to standardize employee behavior. Because McDonald's has standard operating procedures for taking orders, cooking hamburgers, and filling soda containers, the discretion of work group members to set independent standards of behavior is severely limited. The more formal regulations that the organization imposes on all its employees, the more the behavior of work group members will be consistent and predictable.

Organizational Resources

Some organizations are large and profitable, with an abundance of resources. Their employees, for instance, will have modern high-quality tools and equipment to do their jobs. Other organizations aren't as fortunate. When organizations have limited resources, so do their work groups. What a group actually accomplishes is, to a large degree, determined by what it is capable of accomplishing. The presence or absence of resources such as money, time, raw materials, and equipment—which are allocated to the group by the organization—has a large bearing on the group's behavior.

Personnel Selection Process

Members of any work group are, first, members of the organization of which the group is a part. Members of a cost-reduction task force at Boeing first had to be hired as employees of the company. So the criteria an organization uses in its selection process will determine the kinds of people that will be in its work groups.

Performance Evaluation and Reward System

Another organizationwide variable that affects all employees is the performance evaluation and reward system.[14] Does the organization provide employees with challenging, specific performance objectives? Does the organization reward the accomplishment of individual or group objectives? Since work groups are part of the larger organizational system, group members' behavior will be influenced by how the organization evaluates performance and what behaviors are rewarded.

Organizational Culture

Every organization has an unwritten culture that defines standards of acceptable and unacceptable behavior for employees. After a few months, most employees understand their organization's culture. They know things like how to dress for work, whether rules are rigidly enforced, what kinds of questionable behaviors are sure to get them into trouble and which are likely to be overlooked, the importance of honesty and integrity, and the like. While many organizations have subcultures—often created around work groups—with an additional or modified set of standards, they still have a dominant culture that conveys to all employees those values the organization holds dearest. Members of work groups have to accept the standards implied in the organization's dominant culture if they are to remain in good standing.

Physical Work Setting

Finally, we propose that the physical work setting imposed on the group by external parties has an important bearing on work group behavior.[15] Architects, industrial engineers, and office designers make decisions regarding the size and physical layout of an employee's work space, the arrangement of equipment, illumination levels, and the need for acoustics to cut down on noise distractions. These create both barriers and opportunities for work group interaction. It's obviously a lot easier for employees to talk or goof off if their work stations are close together, there are no physical barriers between them, and their supervisor is in an enclosed office 50 yards away.

Group Member Resources

A group's potential level of performance depends, to a large extent, on the resources its members individually bring to the group. In this section, we look at two resources that have received the greatest amount of attention: abilities and personality characteristics.

Abilities

Part of a group's performance can be predicted by assessing the task-relevant and intellectual abilities of its individual members. Sure, it's true we occasionally read about the athletic team composed of mediocre players who, because of excellent coaching, determination, and precision teamwork, beat a far more talented group of players. But such cases make the news precisely because they represent an aberration. As the old saying goes, "The race doesn't always go to the swiftest nor the battle to the strongest, but that's the way to bet." A group's performance is not merely the summation of its individual members' abilities. However, these abilities set parameters for what members can do and how effectively they will perform in a group.

What predictions can we make regarding ability and group performance? First, evidence indicates that individuals who hold crucial abilities for attaining the group's task tend to be more involved in group activity, generally contribute more, are more likely to emerge as the group leaders, and are more satisfied if their talents are effectively utilized by the group.[16] Second, intellectual ability and task-relevant ability have both been found to be related to overall group performance.[17] However, the correlation is not particularly high, suggesting that other factors, such as the size of the group, the type of tasks being performed, the actions of its leader, and level of conflict within the group, also influence performance.

Personality Characteristics

A great deal of research has explored the relationship between personality traits and group attitudes and behavior. The general conclusion is that attributes tending to have a positive connotation in our culture tend to be positively related to group productivity, morale, and cohesiveness. These include traits such as sociability, self-reliance, and independence. In contrast, negatively evaluated characteristics such as authoritarianism, dominance, and unconventionality tend to be negatively related to the dependent variables.[18] These personality traits affect group performance by strongly influencing how the individual will interact with other group members.

Is any one personality characteristic a good predictor of group behavior? The answer to that question is "No." The magnitude of the effect of any *single* characteristic is small, but taking personality characteristics *together*, the consequences for group behavior are of major significance.

Group Structure

◆Groups are not unorganized mobs. They have a structure that shapes the behavior of members.

Work groups are not unorganized mobs. They have a structure that shapes the behavior of members and makes it possible to explain and predict a large portion of individual behavior within the group as well as the performance of the group itself. What are some of these structural variables? They include formal leadership, roles, norms, group status, group size, and composition of the group.

Formal Leadership

Almost every work group has a formal leader. He or she is typically identified by titles such as unit or department manager, supervisor, foreman, project leader, task force head, or committee chair. This leader can play an important part in the group's success, so much so, in fact, that we have devoted an entire chapter to the topic of leadership. In Chapter 11, we review the research on leadership and the effect of leaders on individual and group performance variables.

Roles

role
A set of expected behavior patterns attributed to someone occupying a given position in a social unit.

Shakespeare said, "All the world's a stage, and all the men and women merely players." Using the same metaphor, all group members are actors, each playing a **role**. By this term, we mean a set of expected behavior patterns attributed to someone occupying a given position in a social unit. The understanding of role behavior would be dramatically simplified if each of us chose one role and played it out regularly and consistently. Unfortunately, we are required to play a number of diverse roles, both on and off our jobs. As we see, one of the tasks in understanding behavior is grasping the role a person is currently playing.

For example, Bill Patterson is a plant manager with Electrical Industries, a large electrical equipment manufacturer in Phoenix. He has a number of roles he fulfills on that job—for instance, Electrical Industries employee, member of middle management, electrical engineer, and the primary company spokesperson in the community. Off the job, Bill Patterson finds himself in still more roles: husband, father, Catholic, Rotarian, tennis player, member of the Thunderbird Country Club, and president of his homeowners' association. Many of these roles are compatible; some create conflicts. For instance, how does Bill's religious involvement influence his managerial decisions regarding layoffs, expense account padding, and providing accurate information to government agencies? A recent offer of promotion requires Bill to relocate, yet his family very much wants to stay in Phoenix. Can the role demands of his job be reconciled with the demands of his husband and father roles?

The issue should be clear: Like Bill Patterson, we all are required to play a number of roles, and our behavior varies with the role we are playing. Bill's behavior when he attends church on Sunday morning is different from his behavior on the golf course later that same day. So different groups impose different role requirements on individuals.

ROLE IDENTITY Certain attitudes and actual behaviors consistent with a role create the **role identity**. People have the ability to shift roles rapidly when they recognize that the situation and its demands clearly require major changes. For instance, when union stewards were promoted to supervisory positions, it was found their attitudes changed from prounion to promanagement within a few months of their promotion. When these promotions had to be rescinded later because of economic difficulties in the firm, it was found the demoted supervisors had once again adopted their prounion attitudes.[19]

role identity
Certain attitudes and behaviors consistent with a role.

ROLE PERCEPTION One's view of how one is supposed to act in a given situation is a **role perception**. Based on an interpretation of how we believe we are supposed to behave, we engage in certain types of behavior.

role perception
An individual's view of how he or she is supposed to act in a given situation.

Where do we get these perceptions? We get them from stimuli all around us—friends, books, movies, television. Many current law enforcement officers learned their roles from reading Joseph Wambaugh novels or watching Dirty Harry movies. Tomorrow's lawyers will be influenced by the actions of attorneys in the O.J. Simpson double-murder trial. Of course, the primary reason that apprenticeship programs exist in many trades and professions is to allow beginners to watch an expert, so they can learn to act as they are supposed to.

ROLE EXPECTATIONS **Role expectations** are defined as how others believe you should act in a given situation. How you behave is determined to a large extent by the role defined in the context in which you are acting. The role of a U.S. senator is viewed as having propriety and dignity, whereas a football coach is seen as aggressive, dynamic, and inspiring to his players. In the same context, we might be surprised to learn the neighborhood priest moonlights during the week as a bartender because our role expectations of priests and bartenders tend to be considerably different. When role expectations are concentrated into generalized categories, we have role stereotypes.

role expectations
How others believe a person should act in a given situation.

In the workplace, it can be helpful to look at the topic of role expectations through the perspective of the **psychological contract**. An unwritten agree-

psychological contract
An unwritten agreement that sets out what management expects from the employee, and vice versa.

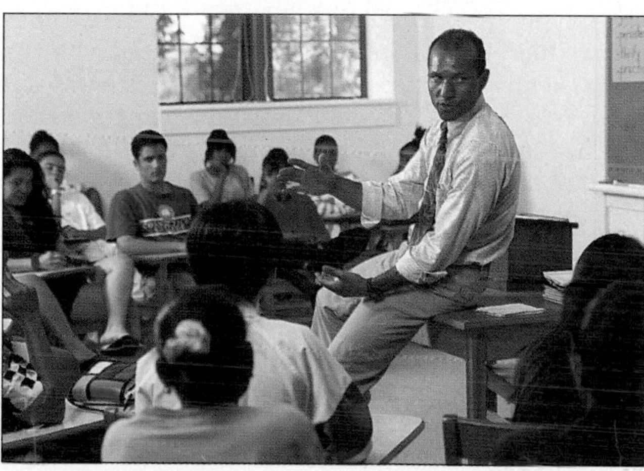

Pfizer Inc, a research-based, global health care company, expects employees to be "part of the cure" by helping to improve the quality of people's lives, both on and off the job. In the research laboratory, Pfizer expects its scientists to discover and develop innovative products that help people enjoy healthier and more productive lives. In the community, this scientist assumes the role of an educator, conducting seminars for high school students about careers in science and math.

ment exists between employees and their employer. This psychological contract sets out mutual expectations—what management expects from workers, and vice versa.[20] In effect, this contract defines the behavioral expectations that go with every role. Management is expected to treat employees justly, provide acceptable working conditions, clearly communicate what is a fair day's work, and give feedback on how well the employee is doing. Employees are expected to respond by demonstrating a good attitude, following directions, and showing loyalty to the organization.

What happens when role expectations as implied in the psychological contract are not met? If management is derelict in keeping up its part of the bargain, we can expect negative repercussions on employee performance and satisfaction. When employees fail to live up to expectations, the result is usually some form of disciplinary action up to and including firing.

The psychological contract should be recognized as a "powerful determiner of behavior in organizations."[21] It points out the importance of accurately communicating role expectations. In Chapter 17, we discuss how organizations socialize employees in order to get them to play out their roles in the way management desires.

role conflict
A situation in which an individual is confronted by divergent role expectations.

ROLE CONFLICT When an individual is confronted by divergent role expectations, the result is **role conflict**. It exists when an individual finds that compliance with one role requirement may make more difficult the compliance with another. At the extreme, it would include situations in which two or more role expectations are mutually contradictory.

Our previous discussion of the many roles Bill Patterson had to deal with included several role conflicts—for instance, Bill's attempt to reconcile the expectations placed on him as a husband and father with those placed on him as an executive with Electrical Industries. The former, as you will remember, emphasizes stability and concern for the desire of his wife and children to remain in Phoenix. Electrical Industries, on the other hand, expects its employees to be responsive to the needs and requirements of the company. Although it might be in Bill's financial and career interests to accept a relocation, the conflict comes down to choosing between family and career role expectations.

All of us have faced and will continue to face role conflicts. The critical issue, from our standpoint, is how conflicts imposed by divergent expectations within the organization impact on behavior. Certainly they increase internal tension and frustration. There are a number of behavioral responses one may engage in. For example, one can give a formalized bureaucratic response. The conflict is then resolved by relying on the rules, regulations, and procedures that govern organizational activities. For instance, an employee faced with the conflicting requirements imposed by the corporate controller's office and his own plant manager decides in favor of his immediate boss—the plant manager. Other behavioral responses may include withdrawal, stalling, negotiation, or, as we found in our discussion of dissonance in Chapter 5, redefining the facts or the situation to make them appear congruent.

AN EXPERIMENT: ZIMBARDO'S SIMULATED PRISON One of the more illuminating role experiments was done by Stanford University psychologist Philip Zimbardo and his associates.[22] They created a "prison" in the basement of the Stanford psychology building; hired at $15 a day two dozen emotionally stable, physically healthy, law-abiding students who scored "normal average" on extensive personality tests; randomly assigned them the role of either "guard" or "prisoner"; and established some basic rules. The experimenters then stood back to see what would happen.

At the start of the planned two-week simulation, there were no measurable differences between those individuals assigned to be guards and those chosen to be prisoners. Additionally, the guards received no special training in how to be prison guards. They were told only to "maintain law and order" in the prison and not to take any nonsense from the prisoners: Physical violence was forbidden. To simulate further the realities of prison life, the prisoners were allowed visits from relatives and friends. But while the mock guards worked eight-hour shifts, the mock prisoners were kept in their cells around the clock and were allowed out only for meals, exercise, toilet privileges, head-count lineups, and work details.

It took the "prisoners" little time to accept the authority positions of the guards, or the mock guards to adjust to their new authority roles. After the guards crushed a rebellion attempt on the second day, the prisoners became increasingly passive. Whatever the guards dished out, the prisoners took. The prisoners actually began to believe and act as if they were, as the guards constantly reminded them, inferior and powerless. And every guard, at some time during the simulation, engaged in abusive, authoritative behavior. For example, one guard said, "I was surprised at myself. . . . I made them call each other names and clean the toilets out with their bare hands. I practically considered the prisoners cattle, and I kept thinking: 'I have to watch out for them in case they try something.'" Another guard added, "I was tired of seeing the prisoners in their rags and smelling the strong odors of their bodies that filled the cells. I watched them tear at each other on orders given by us. They didn't see it as an experiment. It was real and they were fighting to keep their identity. But we were always there to show them who was boss."

The simulation actually proved too successful in demonstrating how quickly individuals learn new roles. The researchers had to stop the experiment after only six days because of the pathological reactions that the participants were demonstrating. And remember, these were individuals chosen precisely for their normalcy and emotional stability.

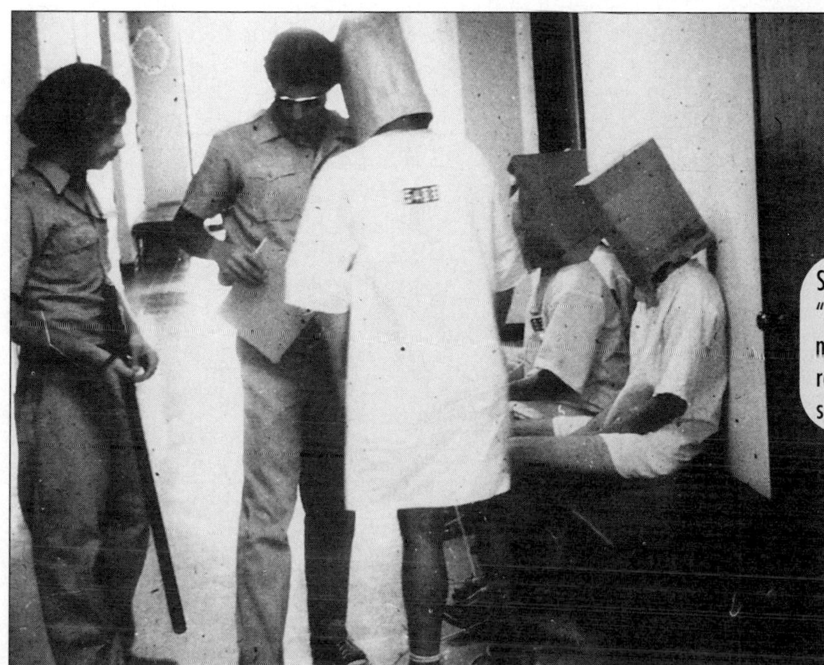

Students at Stanford University playing roles of "guard" and "prisoner" in a simulated prison experiment demonstrate how quickly individuals learn new roles different from their personalities and without any special training.

What should you conclude from this prison simulation? The participants in this prison simulation had, like the rest of us, learned stereotyped conceptions of guard and prisoner roles from the mass media and their own personal experiences in power and powerlessness relationships gained at home (parent–child), in school (teacher–student), and in other situations. This, then, allowed them easily and rapidly to assume roles very different from their inherent personalities. In this case, we saw that people with no prior personality pathology or training in their roles could execute extreme forms of behavior consistent with the roles they were playing.

Norms

Did you ever notice that golfers don't speak while their partners are putting on the green or that employees don't criticize their bosses in public? Why? The answer is: Norms!

norms
Acceptable standards of behavior within a group that are shared by the group's members.

All groups have established **norms**, that is, acceptable standards of behavior shared by the group's members. Norms tell members what they ought and ought not to do under certain circumstances. From an individual's standpoint, they tell what is expected of you in certain situations. When agreed to and accepted by the group, norms act as a means of influencing the behavior of group members with a minimum of external controls. Norms differ among groups, communities, and societies, but they all have them.[23]

Formalized norms are written up in organizational manuals setting out rules and procedures for employees to follow. By far, the majority of norms in organizations are informal. You don't need someone to tell you that throwing paper airplanes or engaging in prolonged gossip sessions at the water cooler are unacceptable behaviors when the "big boss from New York" is touring the office. Similarly, we all know that when we're in an employment interview discussing what we didn't like about our previous job, there are certain things we shouldn't talk about (difficulty in getting along with coworkers or our supervisor), but it's very appropriate to talk about other things (inadequate opportunities for advancement or unimportant and meaningless work). Evidence suggests that even high school students recognize that in such interviews certain answers are more socially desirable than others.[24]

COMMON CLASSES OF NORMS A work group's norms are like an individual's fingerprints—each is unique. Yet there are still some common classes of norms that appear in most work groups.[25]

Probably the most widespread norms deal with *performance-related processes*. Work groups typically provide their members with explicit cues on how hard they should work, how to get the job done, their level of output, appropriate communication channels, and the like. These norms are extremely powerful in affecting an individual employee's performance—they are capable of significantly modifying a performance prediction that was based solely on the employee's ability and level of personal motivation.

A second category of norms encompasses *appearance factors*. This includes appropriate dress, loyalty to the work group or organization, when to look busy, and when it's acceptable to goof off. Some organizations have formal dress codes. However, even in their absence, norms frequently develop to dictate the kind of clothing that should be worn to work. Presenting the appearance of loyalty is important in many work groups and organizations. For instance, in many organizations, especially among professional employees and those in the executive ranks, it is considered inappropriate to be openly looking for another job.

Another class of norms concerns *informal social arrangements*. These norms come from informal work groups and primarily regulate social interactions within the group. With whom group members eat lunch, friendships on and off the job, social games, and the like, are influenced by these norms.

A final category of norms relates to *allocation of resources*. These norms can originate in the group or in the organization and cover pay, assignment of difficult jobs, and allocation of new tools and equipment.

THE "HOW" AND "WHY" OF NORMS *How* do norms develop? *Why* are they enforced? A review of the research allows us to answer these questions.[26]

Norms typically develop gradually as group members learn what behaviors are necessary for the group to function effectively. Of course, critical events in the group might short-circuit the process and act quickly to solidify new norms. Most norms develop in one or more of the following four ways: (1) *Explicit statements made by a group member*, often the group's supervisor or a powerful member. The group leader might, for instance, specifically say that no personal phone calls are allowed during working hours or that coffee breaks are to be kept to ten minutes. (2) *Critical events in the group's history*. These set important precedents. A bystander is injured while standing too close to a machine and, from that point on, members of the work group regularly monitor each other to ensure that no one other than the operator gets within 5 feet of any machine. (3) *Primacy*. The first behavior pattern that emerges in a group frequently sets group expectations. Friendship groups of students often stake out seats near each other on the first day of class and become perturbed if an outsider takes "their" seats in a later class. (4) *Carry-over behaviors from past situations*. Group members bring expectations with them from other groups of which they have been members. This can explain why work groups typically prefer to add new members who are similar to current ones in background and experience. This is likely to increase the probability that the expectations they bring are consistent with those already held by the group.

But groups don't establish or enforce norms for every conceivable situation. The norms the group will enforce tend to be those that are important to it. But what makes a norm important? (1) *If it facilitates the group's survival*. Groups don't like to fail, so they look to enforce those norms that increase their chances for success. This means they'll try to protect themselves from interference from other groups or individuals. (2) *If it increases the predictability of group members' behaviors*. Norms that increase predictability enable group members to anticipate each other's actions and to prepare appropriate responses. (3) *If it reduces embarrassing interpersonal problems for group members*. Norms are important if they ensure the satisfaction of their members and prevent as much interpersonal discomfort as possible. (4) *If it allows members to express the central values of the group and clarify what is distinctive about the group's identity*. Norms that encourage expression of the group's values and distinctive identity help solidify and maintain the group.

CONFORMITY As a member of a group, you desire acceptance by the group. Because of your desire for acceptance, you are susceptible to conforming to the group's norms. Considerable evidence shows that groups can place strong pressures on individual members to change their attitudes and behaviors to conform to the group's standard.[27]

Do individuals conform to the pressures of all the groups they belong to? Obviously not, because people belong to many groups and their norms vary. In some cases, they may even have contradictory norms. So what do people do? They conform to the important groups to which they belong or hope to belong. The important groups have been referred to as *reference* groups and are characterized as ones where the person is aware of the others; the person defines himself or herself as a member, or would like to be a member; and the person feels the group members are significant to him or her.[28] The implication, then, is that *all* groups do not impose equal conformity pressures on their members.

conformity
Adjusting one's behavior to align with the norms of the group.

The impact that group pressures for **conformity** can have on an individual member's judgment and attitudes was demonstrated in the now classic studies by Solomon Asch.[29] Asch made up groups of seven or eight people, who sat in a classroom and were asked to compare two cards held by the experimenter. One card had one line; the other had three lines of varying length. As shown in Figure 8-5, one of the lines on the three-line card was identical to the line on the one-line card. Also as shown in Figure 8-5, the difference in line length was quite obvious; under ordinary conditions, subjects made fewer than 1 percent errors. The object was to announce aloud which of the three lines matched the single line. But what happens if the members in the group begin to give incorrect answers? Will the pressures to conform result in an unsuspecting subject (USS) altering his or her answer to align with the others? That was what Asch wanted to know. So he arranged the group so that only the USS was unaware the experiment was fixed. The seating was prearranged: The USS was placed so as to be the last to announce his or her decision.

Figure 8-5
Examples of Cards Used in Asch Study

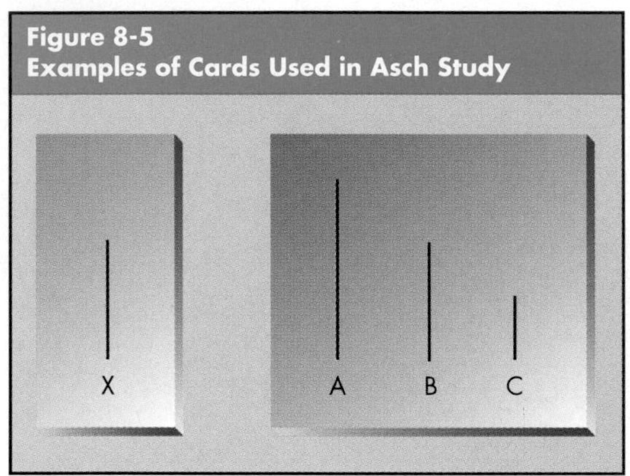

The experiment began with several sets of matching exercises. All the subjects gave the right answers. On the third set, however, the first subject gave an obviously wrong answer—for example, saying "C" in Figure 8-5. The next subject gave the same wrong answer, and so did the others until it got to the unknowing subject. He knows "B" is the same as "X," yet everyone said "C." The decision confronting the USS is this: Do you publicly state a perception that differs from the preannounced position of the others in your group? Or do you give an answer that you strongly believe is incorrect in order to have your response agree with that of the other group members?

The results obtained by Asch demonstrated that over many experiments and many trials, subjects conformed in about 35 percent of the trials; that is, the subjects gave answers they knew were wrong but that were consistent with the replies of other group members.

What can we conclude from this study? The results suggest that group norms press us toward conformity. We desire to be one of the group and avoid being visibly different. We can generalize further to say that when an individual's opinion of objective data differs significantly from that of others in the group, he or she is likely to feel extensive pressure to align his or her opinions to conform with that of the others.

Status

While teaching a college course on adolescence, the instructor asked the class to list things that contributed to status when they were in high school. The list was long and included being an athlete or a cheerleader and being able to cut class without getting caught. Then the instructor asked the students to list things that didn't contribute to status. Again, it was easy for the students to create a long list: getting straight A's, having your mother drive you to school, and so forth. Finally, the students were asked to develop a third list—those things that didn't matter one way or the other. There was a long silence. At last one student in the back row volunteered, "In high school, nothing didn't matter."[30]

status
A socially defined position or rank given to groups or group members by others.

Status—that is, a socially defined position or rank given to groups or group members by others—permeates society far beyond the walls of high school. It would not be extravagant to rephrase the preceding quotation to read, "In the status hierarchy of life, nothing doesn't matter." We live in a class-structured society. Despite all attempts to make it more egalitarian, we have made little progress toward a classless society. Even the smallest group develops roles, rights, and rituals to differentiate its members. Status is an important factor in understanding human behavior because it is a significant motivator and has major behavioral consequences when individuals perceive a disparity between what they believe their status to be and what others perceive it to be.

FORMAL AND INFORMAL STATUS Status may be formally imposed by a group—that is, organizationally imposed through titles or amenities. This is the status that goes with being crowned "the heavyweight champion of the world" or receiving the "teacher-of-the-year" award. We are all familiar with the trappings of high organizational status—large offices with impressive views, fancy titles, high pay, preferred work schedules, and so on. Whether or not management acknowledges the existence of a status hierarchy, organizations are filled with amenities that are not uniformly available and, hence, carry status value. More often, we deal with status in an informal sense. Status may be informally acquired by such characteristics as education, age, gender, skill, and experience (see Table 8-2). Anything can have status value if others in the group evaluate it as status conferring. Keep in mind that informal status is not necessarily less important than the formal variety.

Table 8-2 Occupational Status: How U.S. Jobs Rate (Based on 740 Occupations)

Top 30

1.	Surgeon	16.	Engineer
2.	Physician	17.	Board member (large corporation)
3.	College president	18.	Minister
4.	Astronaut	19.	Pharmacist
5.	Mayor of a large city	20.	Owner of a manufacturing plant
6.	Lawyer	21.	Registered nurse
7.	College professor	22.	High school teacher
8.	Architect	23.	Colonel in the army
9.	Environmental scientist	24.	Accountant
10.	Biologist	25.	Air traffic controller
11.	Airline pilot	26.	Professional athlete
12.	Psychiatrist	27.	Electrical engineer
13.	Dentist	28.	Public grade school teacher
14.	Justice of a municipal court	29.	Manager of an automobile plant
15.	Priest	30.	Meterologist

Source: From "How U.S. Jobs Rate" originally developed by K. Niakao and J. Treas and reprinted in *Industry Week*, March 1, 1993. Copyright © 1993 by Penlon Publishing, Inc. Reprinted by permission.

In his classic restaurant study, William F. Whyte demonstrated the importance of status.[31] Whyte proposed that people work together more smoothly if high-status personnel customarily originate action for lower status personnel. He found a number of instances in which the initiating of action by lower status people created a conflict between formal and informal status systems. In one instance he cited, waitresses were passing their customers' orders directly on to countermen—which meant that low-status servers were initiating action for high-status cooks. By the simple addition of an aluminum spindle to which the order could be hooked, a buffer was created between the lower status waitresses and the higher status countermen, allowing the latter to initiate action on orders when they felt ready.

Whyte also noted that in the kitchen, supply men secured food supplies from the chefs. This was, in effect, a case of low-skilled employees initiating action to be taken by high-skilled employees. Conflict was stimulated when supply men, either explicitly or implicitly, urged the chefs to "get a move on." However, Whyte observed that one supply man had little trouble with the chefs because he gave the order and asked that the chef call him when it was ready, thus reversing the initiating process. In his analysis, Whyte suggested several changes in procedures that aligned interactions more closely with the accepted status hierarchy and resulted in substantial improvements in worker relations and effectiveness.

STATUS AND NORMS Status has been shown to have some interesting effects on the power of norms and pressures to conform. For instance, high-status members of groups often are given more freedom to deviate from norms than are other group members.[32] High-status people also are better able to resist conformity pressures than their lower status peers. An individual who is highly valued by a group but who doesn't much need or care about the social rewards the group provides is particularly able to pay minimal attention to conformity norms.[33]

The previous findings explain why many star athletes, famous actors, top-performing salespeople, and outstanding academics seem oblivious to appearance or social norms that constrain their peers. As high-status individuals, they're given a wider range of discretion. But this is true only as long as the high-status person's activities aren't severely detrimental to group goal achievement.[34]

STATUS EQUITY It is important for group members to believe the status hierarchy is equitable. When inequity is perceived, it creates disequilibrium that results in various types of corrective behavior.[35]

The concept of equity presented in Chapter 6 applies to status. People expect rewards to be proportionate to costs incurred. If Dana and Anne are the two finalists for the head nurse position in a hospital, and it is clear that Dana has more seniority and better preparation for assuming the promotion, Anne will view the selection of Dana to be equitable. However, if Anne is chosen because she is the daughter-in-law of the hospital director, Dana will believe an injustice has been committed.

The trappings that go with formal positions are also important elements in maintaining equity. When we believe there is an inequity between the perceived ranking of an individual and the status accoutrements that person is given by the organization, we are experiencing status incongruence. Examples of this kind of incongruence are the more desirable office location being held

Do you think it's fair that firms lay off employees and mandate companywide cost-reduction programs yet own expensive jets for top managers' business trips? Of all executive perks, travel on "royal barges" such as Canadair's $19 million Challenger 601 shown here carries the highest status. Firms owning private aircraft believe the status of traveling in a corporate jet is congruent with top executives' formal positions. They contend private jets are essential for conducting global business and increase executives' security, flexibility, efficient use of time, and responsiveness to domestic and foreign customers.

by a lower ranking individual and paid country club membership being provided by the company for division managers but not for vice presidents. Pay incongruence has long been a problem in the insurance industry, where top sales agents often earn two to five times more than senior corporate executives. As a result it is very hard for insurance companies to entice agents into management positions. Our point is that employees expect the things an individual has and receives to be congruent with his or her status.

Groups generally agree within themselves on status criteria and, hence, there is usually high concurrence in group rankings of individuals. However, individuals can find themselves in a conflict situation when they move between groups whose status criteria are different or when they join groups whose members have heterogeneous backgrounds. For instance, business executives may use personal income or the growth rate of their companies as determinants of status. Government bureaucrats may use the size of their budgets. Professional employees may use the degree of autonomy that comes with their job assignment. Blue-collar workers may use years of seniority. Academics may use the number of grants received or articles published. In groups made up of heterogeneous individuals or when heterogeneous groups are forced to be interdependent, status differences may initiate conflict as the group attempts to reconcile and align the differing hierarchies. As we see in the next chapter, this can be a particular problem when management creates teams made up of employees from across varied functions within the organization.

Size

Does the size of a group affect the group's overall behavior? The answer to this question is a definite "Yes," but the effect depends on what dependent variables you look at.[36]

The evidence indicates, for instance, that smaller groups are faster at completing tasks than are larger ones. However, if the group is engaged in problem solving, large groups consistently get better marks than their smaller counterparts. Translating these results into specific numbers is a bit more hazardous, but we can offer some parameters. Large groups—with a dozen or more members—are good for gaining diverse input. So if the goal of the group is fact finding, larger groups should be more effective. On the other hand, smaller groups are better at doing something productive with that input.

◆Large groups are good for gaining diverse input, but smaller groups are better at doing something productive with that input.

Groups of approximately seven members, therefore, tend to be more effective for taking action.

social loafing
The tendency for individuals to expend less effort when working collectively than when working individually.

One of the most important findings related to the size of a group has been labeled **social loafing**. Social loafing is the tendency for individuals to expend less effort when working collectively than when working individually. It directly challenges the logic that the productivity of the group as a whole should at least equal the sum of the productivity of each individual in that group.

A common stereotype about groups is that the sense of team spirit spurs individual effort and enhances the group's overall productivity. In the late 1920s, a German psychologist named Ringelmann compared the results of individual and group performance on a rope-pulling task.[37] He expected that the group's effort would be equal to the sum of the efforts of individuals within the group. That is, three people pulling together should exert three times as much pull on the rope as one person, and eight people should exert eight times as much pull. Ringelmann's results, however, did not confirm his expectations. Groups of three people exerted a force only two-and-a-half times the average individual performance. Groups of eight collectively achieved less than four times the solo rate.

Replications of Ringelmann's research with similar tasks have generally supported his findings.[38] Increases in group size are inversely related to individual performance. More may be better in the sense that the total productivity of a group of four is greater than that of one or two people, but the individual productivity of each group member declines.

What causes this social loafing effect? It may be due to a belief that others in the group are not carrying their fair share. If you see others as lazy or inept, you can reestablish equity by reducing your effort. Another explanation is the dispersion of responsibility. Because the results of the group cannot be attributed to any single person, the relationship between an individual's input and the group's output is clouded. In such situations, individuals may be tempted to coast on the group's efforts. In other words, there will be a reduction in efficiency where individuals think their contribution cannot be measured.

The implications for OB of this effect on work groups are significant. Where managers utilize collective work situations to enhance morale and teamwork, they must also provide means by which individual efforts can be identified. If this is not done, management must weigh the potential losses in productivity from using groups against any possible gains in worker satisfaction.[39] However, this conclusion has a Western bias. It's consistent with individualistic cultures, like the United States and Canada, that are dominated by self-interest. It is not consistent with collective societies where individuals are motivated by in-group goals. For instance, in studies comparing employees from the United States with employees from the People's Republic of China and Israel (both collectivist societies), the Chinese and Israelis showed no propensity to engage in social loafing. In fact, the Chinese and Israelis actually performed better in a group than when working alone.[40]

The research on group size leads us to two additional conclusions: (1) groups with an odd number of members tend to be preferable to those with an even number; and (2) groups made up of five or seven members do a good job of exercising the best elements of both small and large groups.[41] Having an odd number of members eliminates the possibility of ties when votes are taken. And groups made up of five or seven members are large enough to form a majority and allow for diverse input, yet small enough to avoid the negative outcomes often associated with large groups, such as domination by a few members, development of subgroups, inhibited participation by some members, and excessive time taken to reach a decision.

Composition

Most group activities require a variety of skills and knowledge. Given this requirement, it would be reasonable to conclude that heterogeneous groups—those composed of dissimilar individuals—would be more likely to have diverse abilities and information and should be more effective. Research studies generally substantiate this conclusion.[42]

When a group is heterogeneous in terms of gender, personalities, opinions, abilities, skills, and perspectives, there is an increased probability that the group will possess the needed characteristics to complete its tasks effectively.[43] The group may be more conflict laden and less expedient as diverse positions are introduced and assimilated, but the evidence generally supports the conclusion that heterogeneous groups perform more effectively than do those that are homogeneous.

But what about diversity created by racial or national differences? The evidence indicates that these elements of diversity interfere with group processes, at least in the short term.[44] Cultural diversity seems to be an asset on tasks that call for a variety of viewpoints. But culturally heterogeneous groups have more difficulty in learning to work with each other and solving problems. The good news is that these difficulties seem to dissipate with time. While newly formed culturally diverse groups underperform newly formed culturally homogeneous groups, the differences disappear after about three months. The reason is that it takes diverse groups a while to learn how to work through disagreements and different approaches to solving problems.

An offshoot of the composition issue has recently received a great deal of attention by group researchers. This is the degree to which members of a group share a common demographic attribute, such as age, gender, race, educational level, or length of service in the organization, and the impact of this attribute on turnover. We call this variable **group demography**.

group demography
The degree to which members of a group share a common demographic attribute, such as age, sex, race, educational level, or length of service in the organization, and the impact of this attribute on turnover.

We discussed individual demographic factors in Chapter 3. Here we consider the same type of factors, but in a group context. That is, it is not whether a person is male or female or has been employed with the organization a year rather than ten years that concerns us now, but rather the individual's attribute in relationship to the attributes of others with whom he or she works. Let's work through the logic of group demography, review the evidence, and then consider the implications.

Groups and organizations are composed of **cohorts**, which we define as individuals who hold a common attribute. For instance, everyone born in 1960 is of the same age. This means they also have shared common experiences. People born in 1960 have experienced the women's movement, but not the Korean conflict. People born in 1945 shared the Vietnam War, but not the Great Depression. Women in organizations today who were born before 1945 matured prior to the women's movement and have had substantially different experiences from women born after 1960. Group demography, therefore, suggests that such attributes as age or the date that someone joins a specific work group or organization should help us predict turnover. Essentially, the logic goes like

cohorts
Individuals who, as part of a group, hold a common attribute.

These members of Pepsi-Cola International's marketing team in Great Britain share a common demographic attribute. They're all young. Pepsi's plan is to dramatically increase its international soft drink sales. To execute its plan, Pepsi is banking on youthful cohorts who have a passion for change, can embrace risk, act quickly, innovate constantly, and aren't afraid to break the rules of soft drink marketing. Shafi Saxena (seated center) left a marketing job she held for four years to join the Pepsi team. "I wanted to work in a faster-moving place," she says. At 28, Saxena oversees Pepsi's new Max cola in Great Britain.

this: Turnover will be greater among those with dissimilar experiences because communication is more difficult. Conflict and power struggles are more likely, and more severe when they occur. The increased conflict makes group membership less attractive, so employees are more likely to quit. Similarly, the losers in a power struggle are more apt to leave voluntarily or be forced out.

Several studies have sought to test this thesis, and the evidence is quite encouraging.[45] For example, in departments or separate work groups where a large portion of members entered at the same time, there is considerably more turnover among those outside this cohort. Also, where there are large gaps between cohorts, turnover is higher. People who enter a group or an organization together, or at approximately the same time, are more likely to associate with one another, have a similar perspective on the group or organization, and thus be more likely to stay. On the other hand, discontinuities or bulges in the group's date-of-entry distribution is likely to result in a higher turnover rate within that group.

The implication of this line of inquiry is that the composition of a group may be an important predictor of turnover. Differences per se may not predict turnover. But large differences within a single group will lead to turnover. If everyone is moderately dissimilar from everyone else in a group, the feelings of being an outsider are reduced. So it's the degree of dispersion on an attribute, rather than the level, that matters most.

We can speculate that variance within a group in respect to attributes other than date of entry, such as social background, gender differences, and levels of education, might similarly create discontinuities or bulges in the distribution that will encourage some members to leave. To extend this idea further, the fact that a group member is a female may, in itself, mean little in predicting turnover. In fact, if the work group is made up of nine women and one man, we'd be more likely to predict that the lone male would leave. In the executive ranks of organizations, however, where females are in the minority, we would predict that this minority status would increase the likelihood that female managers would quit.

◆◆◆◆ OB in the News ◆◆◆◆

Work Force Diversity and Cliques

Leslie Meltzer Aronzon, a Los Angeles investment broker, remembers the incident well. It was right after she and four colleagues had been in an intense negotiating session with an important client. As they were walking along discussing their potential responses, the conversation came to an abrupt halt. Aronzon's associates had all veered off and disappeared into the men's room. When the men came out of the rest room, "they had decided what we should do." The incident again reminded Aronzon that she was a woman in a mostly male profession.

"A lot of guys in my office hang out together on weekends and share information. They even call each other with tips," Aronzon said. "They don't discriminate against me consciously, but they do discriminate."

Paul Muniz, a claims processor for a Los Angeles insurance firm, notices how people of similar backgrounds tend to congregate together at work. "My best friends at work tend to be other people from Mexico. You see Latinos clustering together, Vietnamese people together, black people together." Muniz says that he and his friends speak Spanish to one another because "we feel we can express ourselves better in Spanish. But I try to be careful not to overdo it, because sometimes people who don't speak Spanish think we're saying something important that they should be in on."

Workplace cliques are perfectly natural and usually understandable, but inherently exclusive. And despite today's emphasis on diversity awareness, they are phenomena that corporate America cannot control.

It can be like high school all over again, except that at work, people break into cliques according to age, marital status, gender, race, and position rather than looks, athletic ability, and popularity with the opposite sex.

Still, cliques can affect you as deeply at the workplace as they did in high school, determining not only your lunch crowd and your access to gossip, but such critical matters as your assignments, promotions, and salary. And unlike high school cliques, which thankfully disintegrate at graduation, office crowds don't meet such neat and convenient ends.

Based on S. Christian, "Out of the 'In' Crowd," *Los Angeles Times* (May 16, 1994), p. II- 7.

Group Processes

The next component of our group behavior model considers the processes that go on within a work group—the communication patterns used by members for information exchanges, group decision processes, leader behavior, power dynamics, conflict interactions, and the like. Chapters 10 through 13 elaborate on many of these processes.

Why are processes important to understanding work group behavior? One way to answer this question is to return to the topic of social loafing. We found that 1 + 1 + 1 doesn't necessarily add up to 3. In group tasks where each member's contribution is not clearly visible, there is a tendency for individuals to decrease their effort. Social loafing, in other words, illustrates a process loss as a result of using groups. But group processes can also produce positive results. That is, groups can create outputs greater than the sum of their inputs. Figure 8-6 illustrates how group processes can impact on a group's actual effectiveness.[46]

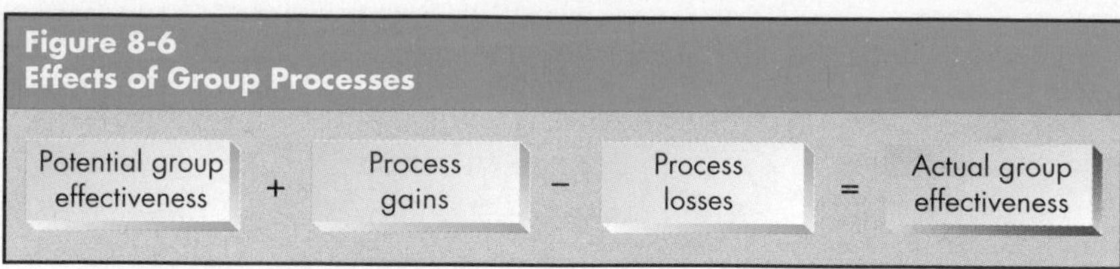

Figure 8-6
Effects of Group Processes

synergy
An action of two or more substances that results in an effect that is different from the individual summation of the substances.

Synergy is a term used in biology which refers to an action of two or more substances that results in an effect different from the individual summation of the substances. We can use the concept to better understand group processes.

Social loafing, for instance, represents negative synergy. The whole is less than the sum of the parts. On the other hand, research teams are often used in research laboratories because they can draw on the diverse skills of various individuals to produce more meaningful research as a group than could be generated by all of the researchers working independently. That is, they produce positive synergy. Their process gains exceed their process losses.

Another line of research that helps us better understand group processes is the social facilitation effect.[47] Have you ever noticed that performing a task in front of others can have a positive or negative effect on your performance? For instance, you privately practice a complex springboard dive at your home pool for weeks. Then you do the dive in front of a group of friends and you do it better than ever. Or you practice a speech in private and finally get it down perfect, but you bomb when you have to give the speech in public.

The **social facilitation effect** refers to this tendency for performance to improve or decline in response to the presence of others. While this effect is not entirely a group phenomenon—people can work in the presence of others and not be members of a group—the group situation is more likely to provide the conditions for social facilitation to occur. The research on social facilitation tells us that the performance of simple routine tasks tends to be speeded up and made more accurate by the presence of others. Where the work is more complex, requiring closer attention, the presence of others is likely to have a negative effect on performance.[48] So what are the implications of this research in terms of managing process gains and losses? The implications relate to learning and training. People seem to perform better on a task in the presence of others if that task is very well learned, but poorer if it is not well learned. So process gains will be maximized by training people for simple tasks in groups and training people for complex tasks in individual private practice sessions.

Group Tasks

Imagine, for a moment, two groups at a major oil company. The job of the first is to consider possible location sites for a new refinery. The decision is going to affect people in many areas of the company—production, engineering, marketing, distribution, personnel, purchasing, real estate development, and the like—so key people from each of these areas will need to provide input into the decision. The job of the second group is to coordinate the building of the refinery after the site has been selected, the design finalized, and the financial arrangements completed. Research on group effectiveness tells us that management would be well advised to use a larger group for the first task than for the second.[49] The reason is that large groups facilitate pooling of information. The addition of a diverse perspective to a problem-solving committee typically results in a process gain. But when a group's task is coordinating and implementing a decision, the process loss created by each additional member's presence is likely to be greater than the process gain he or she makes. So the size–performance relationship is moderated by the group's task requirements.

The preceding conclusions can be extended: The impact of group processes on the group's performance and member satisfaction is also moderated by the tasks the group is doing. The evidence indicates that the complexity and interdependence of tasks influence the group's effectiveness.[50]

Tasks can be generalized as either simple or complex. Complex tasks are ones that tend to be novel or nonroutine. Simple ones are routine and standardized. We would hypothesize that the more complex the task, the more the group will benefit from discussion among members on alternative work methods. If the task is simple, group members don't need to discuss such alternatives. They can rely on standardized operating procedures for doing the job. Similarly, if there is a high degree of interdependence among the tasks that group members must perform, they'll need to interact more. Effective communication and minimal levels of conflict, therefore, should be more relevant to group performance when tasks are interdependent.

These conclusions are consistent with what we know about information-processing capacity and uncertainty.[51] Tasks that have higher uncertainty—those that are complex and interdependent—require more information processing. This, in turn, puts more importance on group processes. So just because a group is characterized by poor communication, weak leadership, high levels of conflict, and the like, it doesn't necessarily mean it will be low performing. If the group's tasks are simple and require little interdependence among members, the group still may be effective.

Group Decision Making

The belief—characterized by juries—that two heads are better than one has long been accepted as a basic component of North American and many other countries' legal systems. This belief has expanded to the point that, today, many decisions in organizations are made by groups, teams, or committees. In this section, we review group decision making.

Groups vs. the Individual

Decision-making groups may be widely used in organizations, but does that imply group decisions are preferable to those made by an individual alone? The answer to this question depends on a number of factors. Let's begin by looking at the advantages and disadvantages that groups afford.[52]

ADVANTAGES OF GROUPS Individual and group decisions each have their own set of strengths. Neither is ideal for all situations. The following identifies the major advantages that groups offer over individuals in the making of decisions:

1. *More complete information and knowledge.* By aggregating the resources of several individuals, we bring more input into the decision process.

2. *Increased diversity of views*. In addition to more input, groups can bring heterogeneity to the decision process. This opens up the opportunity for more approaches and alternatives to be considered.
3. *Increased acceptance of a solution*. Many decisions fail after the final choice has been made because people do not accept the solution. However, if people who will be affected by a decision and who will be instrumental in implementing it are able to participate in the decision itself, they will be more likely to accept it and encourage others to accept it. This translates into more support for the decision and higher satisfaction among those required to implement it.
4. *Increased legitimacy*. North American and many other capitalistic societies value democratic methods. The group decision-making process is consistent with democratic ideals and, therefore, may be perceived as being more legitimate than decisions made by a single person. When an individual decision maker fails to consult with others before making a decision, the decision maker's complete power can create the perception that the decision was made autocratically and arbitrarily.

DISADVANTAGES OF GROUPS Of course, group decisions are not without drawbacks. Their major disadvantages include the following:

1. *Time consuming*. It takes time to assemble a group. The interaction that takes place once the group is in place is frequently inefficient. The result is that groups take more time to reach a solution than would be the case if an individual was making the decision. This can limit management's ability to act quickly and decisively when necessary.
2. *Pressures to conform*. As noted previously, there are social pressures in groups. The desire by group members to be accepted and considered an asset to the group can result in squashing any overt disagreement, thus encouraging conformity among viewpoints.
3. *Domination by the few*. Group discussion can be dominated by one or a few members. If this dominant coalition is composed of low- and medium-ability members, the group's overall effectiveness will suffer.
4. *Ambiguous responsibility*. Group members share responsibility, but who is actually accountable for the final outcome? In an individual decision, it is clear who is responsible. In a group decision, the responsibility of any single member is watered down.

EFFECTIVENESS AND EFFICIENCY Whether groups are more effective than individuals depends on the criteria you use for defining effectiveness. In terms of *accuracy*, group decisions tend to be more accurate. The evidence indicates that, on the average, groups make better quality decisions than individuals.[53] However, if decision effectiveness is defined in terms of *speed*, individuals are superior. If *creativity* is important, groups tend to be more effective than individuals. And if effectiveness means the degree of *acceptance* the final solution achieves, the nod again goes to the group.[54]

But effectiveness cannot be considered without also assessing efficiency. In terms of efficiency, groups almost always stack up as a poor second to the individual decision maker. With few exceptions, group decision making consumes more work hours than if an individual was to tackle the same problem alone. The exceptions tend to be those instances where, to achieve comparable quantities of diverse input, the single decision maker must spend a great deal of time reviewing files and talking to people. Because groups can include members from diverse areas, the time spent searching for information can be reduced. However, as we noted, these advantages in efficiency tend to be the exception. Groups are generally less efficient than individuals. In deciding whether to use groups, then, consideration should be given to assessing whether increases in effectiveness are more than enough to offset the losses in efficiency.

SUMMARY Groups offer an excellent vehicle for performing many of the steps in the decision-making process. They are a source of both breadth and depth of input for information gathering. If the group is composed of individuals with diverse backgrounds, the alternatives generated should be more extensive and the analysis more critical. When the final solution is agreed on, there are more people in a group decision to support and implement it. These pluses, however, can be more than offset by the time consumed by group decisions, the internal conflicts they create, and the pressures they generate toward conformity. Table 8-3 briefly outlines the group's assets and liabilities. It allows you to evaluate the net advantage or disadvantage that would accrue in a given situation when you have to choose between an individual and a group decision.

Groupthink and Groupshift

Two by-products of group decision making have received a considerable amount of attention by researchers in OB. As we'll show, these two phenomena have the potential to affect the group's ability to appraise alternatives objectively and arrive at quality decision solutions.

The first phenomenon, called **groupthink**, is related to norms. It describes situations in which group pressures for conformity deter the group from critically appraising unusual, minority, or unpopular views. Groupthink is a disease that attacks many groups and can dramatically hinder their performance. The second phenomenon we review is called **groupshift**. It indicates that in discussing a given set of alternatives and arriving at a solution, group members tend to exaggerate the initial positions they hold. In some situations, caution dominates, and there is a conservative shift. More often, however, the evidence indicates that groups tend toward a risky shift. Let's look at each of these phenomena in more detail.

groupthink
Phenomenon in which the norm for consensus overrides the realistic appraisal of alternative courses of action.

groupshift
A change in decision risk between the group's decision and the individual decision that members within the group would make; can be either toward conservatism or greater risk.

GROUPTHINK A number of years ago I had a peculiar experience. During a faculty meeting, a motion was placed on the floor stipulating each faculty member's responsibilities in regard to counseling students. The motion received a second, and the floor was opened for questions. There were none. After about 15 seconds of silence, the chairperson asked if he could "call for the question" (fancy terminology for permission to take the vote). No objections were voiced. When the chair asked for those in favor, a vast majority of the 32

Table 8-3 The Group Decision: Its Assets and Liabilities

Assets	Liabilities
Breadth of information	Time consuming
Diversity of information	Conformity
Acceptance of solution	Domination of discussion
Legitimacy of process	Ambiguous responsibility

faculty members in attendance raised their hands. The motion was passed, and the chair proceeded to the next item on the agenda.

Nothing in the process seemed unusual, but the story is not over. About 20 minutes following the end of the meeting, a professor came roaring into my office with a petition. The petition said that the motion on counseling students had been rammed through and requested the chairperson to replace the motion on the next month's agenda for discussion and a vote. When I asked this professor why he had not spoken up less than an hour earlier, he gave me a frustrated look. He then proceeded to tell me that in talking with people after the meeting, he realized there actually had been considerable opposition to the motion. He didn't speak up, he said, because he thought he was the only one opposed. Conclusion: The faculty meeting we had attended had been attacked by the deadly groupthink "disease."

Have you ever felt like speaking up in a meeting, classroom, or informal group, but decided against it? One reason may have been shyness. But you may have been a victim of groupthink, the phenomenon that occurs when group members become so enamored of seeking concurrence, the norm for consensus overrides the realistic appraisal of alternative courses of action and the full expression of deviant, minority, or unpopular views. It describes a deterioration in an individual's mental efficiency, reality testing, and moral judgment as a result of group pressures.[55]

We have all seen the symptoms of the groupthink phenomenon:

1. Group members rationalize any resistance to the assumptions they have made. No matter how strongly the evidence may contradict their basic assumptions, members behave so as to reinforce those assumptions continually.
2. Members apply direct pressures on those who momentarily express doubts about any of the group's shared views or who question the validity of arguments supporting the alternative favored by the majority.
3. Those members who have doubts or hold differing points of view seek to avoid deviating from what appears to be group consensus by keeping silent about misgivings and even minimizing to themselves the importance of their doubts.
4. There appears to be an illusion of unanimity. If someone doesn't speak, it's assumed he or she is in full accord. In other words, abstention becomes viewed as a "Yes" vote.[56]

In studies of historic American foreign policy decisions, these symptoms were found to prevail when government policymaking groups failed—unpreparedness at Pearl Harbor in 1941, the U.S. invasion of North Korea, the Bay of Pigs fiasco, and the escalation of the Vietnam War. Importantly, these four groupthink characteristics could not be found where group policy decisions were successful—the Cuban missile crisis and the formulation of the Marshall Plan.[57]

Groupthink appears to be closely aligned with the conclusions Asch drew in his experiments with a lone dissenter. Individuals who hold a position different from that of the dominant majority are under pressure to suppress, withhold, or modify their true feelings and beliefs. As members of a group, we find it more pleasant to be in agreement—to be a positive part of the group—than to be a disruptive force, even if disruption is necessary to improve the effectiveness of the group's decisions.

Are all groups equally vulnerable to groupthink? The evidence suggests not. Researchers have focused in on three moderating variables—the group's cohesiveness, its leader's behavior, and its insulation from outsiders—but the findings have not been consistent.[58] At this point, the most valid conclusions we can make are these: (1) highly cohesive groups have more discussion and bring out more information, but it's unclear whether such groups discourage dissent; (2) groups with impartial leaders who encourage member input generate and discuss more alternative solutions; (3) leaders should avoid expressing a preferred solution early in the group's discussion because this tends to limit critical analysis and significantly increase the likelihood the group will adopt this solution as the final choice; and (4) insulation of the group leads to fewer alternatives being generated and evaluated.

GROUPSHIFT In comparing group decisions with the individual decisions of members within the group, evidence suggests that there are differences.[59] In some cases, the group decisions are more conservative than the individual decisions. More often, the shift is toward greater risk.[60]

What appears to happen in groups is that the discussion leads to a significant shift in the positions of members toward a more extreme position in the direction toward which they were already leaning before the discussion. So conservative types become more cautious and the more aggressive types take on more risk. The group discussion tends to exaggerate the initial position of the group.

The groupshift can be viewed as actually a special case of groupthink. The decision of the group reflects the dominant decision-making norm that develops during the group's discussion. Whether the shift in the group's decision is toward greater caution or more risk depends on the dominant prediscussion norm.

The greater occurrence of the shift toward risk has generated several explanations for the phenomenon.[61] It's been argued, for instance, that the discussion creates familiarization among the members. As they become more comfortable with each other, they also become more bold and daring. Another argument is that our society values risk, we admire individuals who are willing to take risks, and group discussion motivates members to show they are at least as willing as their peers to take risks. The most plausible explanation of the shift toward risk, however, seems to be that the group diffuses responsibility. Group decisions free any single member from accountability for the group's final choice. Greater risk can be taken because even if the decision fails, no one member can be held wholly responsible.

So how should you use the findings on groupshift? Recognize that group decisions exaggerate the initial position of the individual members, the shift has been shown more often to be toward greater risk, and whether a group will shift toward greater risk or caution is a function of the members' prediscussion inclinations.

Group Decision-Making Techniques

The most common form of group decision making takes place in face-to-face **interacting groups**. But as our discussion of groupthink demonstrated, interacting groups often censor themselves and pressure individual members toward conformity of opinion. Brainstorming, nominal group and Delphi techniques, and electronic meetings have been proposed as ways to reduce many of the problems inherent in the traditional interacting group. We discuss each in this section.

interacting groups
Typical groups, where members interact with each other face-to-face.

brainstorming
An idea-generation process that specifically encourages any and all alternatives, while withholding any criticism of those alternatives.

BRAINSTORMING **Brainstorming** is meant to overcome pressures for conformity in the interacting group that retard the development of creative alternatives.[62] It does this by utilizing an idea generation process that specifically encourages any and all alternatives while withholding any criticism of those alternatives.

In a typical brainstorming session, a half dozen to a dozen people sit around a table. The group leader states the problem in a clear manner so it is understood by all participants. Members then free-wheel as many alternatives as they can in a given length of time. No criticism is allowed, and all the alternatives are recorded for later discussion and analysis. That one idea stimulates others and that judgments of even the most bizarre suggestions are withheld until later encourages group members to "think the unusual."

Brainstorming, however, is merely a process for generating ideas. The next three techniques go further by offering methods of actually arriving at a preferred solution.[63]

nominal group technique
A group decision-making method in which individual members meet face-to-face to pool their judgments in a systematic but independent fashion.

NOMINAL GROUP TECHNIQUE The **nominal group technique** restricts discussion or interpersonal communication during the decision-making process, hence the term *nominal*. Group members are all physically present, as in a traditional committee meeting, but members operate independently. Specifically, a problem is presented and then the following steps take place:

1. Members meet as a group but, before any discussion takes place, each member independently writes down his or her ideas on the problem.
2. This silent period is followed by each member presenting one idea to the group. Each member takes his or her turn, going around the table, presenting a single idea until all ideas have been presented and recorded (typically on a flip chart or chalkboard). No discussion takes place until all ideas have been recorded.
3. The group now discusses the ideas for clarity and evaluates them.
4. Each group member silently and independently rank-orders the ideas. The final decision is determined by the idea with the highest aggregate ranking.

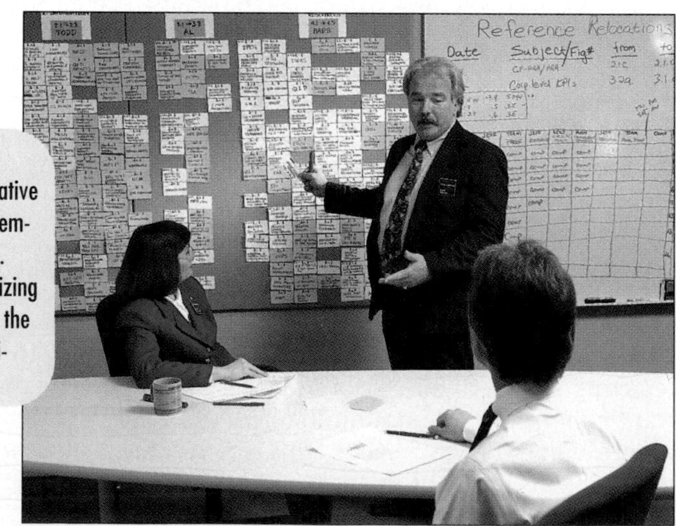

Office furniture maker Haworth Inc. is using brainstorming in applying for the Malcolm Baldrige National Quality Award. To ensure that the creative process flows uninterrupted and without criticism, Haworth has group members write their ideas on index cards that are tacked on a bulletin board. The group facilitator moves the cards around in organizing and reorganizing new and old ideas. Haworth finds that the use of mobile cards enhances the brainstorming process because it increases employee motivation to participate and continually stimulates other new ideas.

The chief advantage of the nominal group technique is that it permits the group to meet formally but does not restrict independent thinking, as does the interacting group.

DELPHI TECHNIQUE A more complex and time-consuming alternative is the **Delphi technique**. It is similar to the nominal group technique except it does not require the physical presence of the group's members. In fact, the Delphi technique never allows the group's members to meet face to face. The following steps characterize the Delphi technique.

Delphi technique
A group decision method in which individual members, acting separately, pool their judgments in a systematic and independent fashion.

1. The problem is identified and members are asked to provide potential solutions through a series of carefully designed questionnaires.
2. Each member anonymously and independently completes the first questionnaire.
3. Results of the first questionnaire are compiled at a central location, transcribed, and reproduced.
4. Each member receives a copy of the results.
5. After viewing the results, members are again asked for their solutions. The results typically trigger new solutions or cause changes in the original position.
6. Steps 4 and 5 are repeated as often as necessary until consensus is reached.

Like the nominal group technique, the Delphi technique insulates group members from the undue influence of others. Because it doesn't require the physical presence of the participants, the Delphi technique can be used for decision making among geographically scattered groups. For instance, Sony could use the technique to query its managers in Tokyo, Brussels, Paris, London, New York, Toronto, Rio de Janeiro, and Melbourne as to the best worldwide price for one of the company's products. The cost of bringing the executives together at a central location is avoided. Of course, the Delphi technique has its drawbacks. Because the method is extremely time consuming, it is frequently not applicable where a speedy decision is necessary. Additionally, the method may not develop the rich array of alternatives as the interacting or nominal group technique does. Ideas that might surface from the heat of face-to-face interaction may never arise.

ELECTRONIC MEETINGS The most recent approach to group decision making blends the nominal group technique with sophisticated computer technology.[64] It's called the *electronic meeting*.

IBM uses electronic meetings to bring people from diverse backgrounds in the company together. More than 7,000 IBMers have taken part in these meetings. Other organizations making wide use of the electronic meeting include public relations giant Hill & Knowlton, Marriott Corporation, and Westinghouse Electric.

Once the technology is in place, the concept is simple. Up to 50 people sit around a horseshoe-shaped table, empty except for a series of computer terminals. Issues are presented to participants and they type their responses onto their computer screen. Individual comments, as well as aggregate votes, are displayed on a projection screen in the room.

The major advantages of electronic meetings are anonymity, honesty, and speed. Participants can anonymously type any message they want and it flashes on the screen for all to see at the push of a participant's board key. It also allows people to be brutally honest without penalty. And it's fast because chitchat is eliminated, discussions don't digress, and many participants can "talk" at once without stepping on one another's toes.

Experts claim that electronic meetings are as much as 55 percent faster than traditional face-to-face meetings. Phelps Dodge Mining, for instance, used the approach to cut its annual planning meeting from several days down to 12 hours. Yet there are drawbacks to this technique. Those who can type fast can outshine those who are verbally eloquent but poor typists; those with the best ideas don't get credit for them; and the process lacks the information richness of face-to-face oral communication. But although this technology is currently in its infancy, the future of group decision making is very likely to include extensive use of electronic meetings.

SUMMARY: EVALUATING EFFECTIVENESS How do these various techniques stack up against the traditional interacting group? As we find so often, each technique has its own set of strengths and weaknesses. The choice of one technique over another will depend on what criteria you want to emphasize. For instance, as Table 8-4 indicates, the interacting group is good for building group cohesiveness, brainstorming keeps social pressures to a minimum, the Delphi technique minimizes interpersonal conflict, and electronic meetings process ideas fast. So the best technique is defined by the criteria you use to evaluate the group.

Table 8-4 Evaluating Group Effectiveness

Effectiveness Criteria	TYPE OF GROUP: Interacting	Brainstorming	Nominal	Delphi	Electronic
Number of ideas	Low	Moderate	High	High	High
Quality of ideas	Low	Moderate	High	High	High
Social pressure	High	Low	Moderate	Low	Low
Money costs	Low	Low	Low	Low	High
Speed	Moderate	Moderate	Moderate	Low	High
Task orientation	Low	High	High	High	High
Potential for interpersonal conflict	High	Low	Moderate	Low	Low
Feelings of accomplishment	High to low	High	High	Moderate	High
Commitment to solution	High	Not applicable	Moderate	Low	Moderate
Develops group cohesiveness	High	High	Moderate	Low	Low

Source: Based on J.K. Murnighan, "Group Decision Making: What Strategies Should You Use?", *Management Review* (February 1981), p. 61.

From Concepts to Skills

Conducting a Group Meeting

Group meetings have a reputation for inefficiency. For instance, noted economist John Kenneth Galbraith has said, "Meetings are indispensable when you don't want to do anything."

When you're responsible for conducting a meeting, what can you do to make it more efficient and effective? Follow these 12 steps:

1. *Prepare a meeting agenda.* An agenda defines what you hope to accomplish at the meeting. It should state the meeting's purpose; who will be in attendance; what, if any, preparation is required of each participant; a detailed list of items to be covered; the specific time and location of the meeting; and a specific ending time.
2. *Distribute the agenda in advance.* Participants should have the agenda enough ahead of time so they can adequately prepare for the meeting.
3. *Consult with participants before the meeting.* An unprepared participant can't contribute to his or her full potential. It is your responsibility to ensure that members are prepared, so check with them ahead of time.
4. *Get participants to go over the agenda.* The first thing to do at the meeting is to have participants review the agenda, make any changes, then approve the final agenda.
5. *Establish specific time parameters.* Meetings should begin on time and have a specific time for completion. It is your responsibility to specify these time parameters and to hold to them.
6. *Maintain focused discussion.* It is your responsibility to give direction to the discussion; to keep it focused on the issues; and to minimize interruptions, disruptions, and irrelevant comments.
7. *Encourage and support participation of all members.* To maximize the effectiveness of problem-oriented meetings, each participant must be encouraged to contribute. Quiet or reserved personalities need to be drawn out so their ideas can be heard.
8. *Maintain a balanced style.* The effective group leader pushes when necessary and is passive when need be.
9. *Encourage the clash of ideas.* You need to encourage different points of view, critical thinking, and constructive disagreement.
10. *Discourage the clash of personalities.* An effective meeting is characterized by the critical assessment of ideas, not attacks on people. When running a meeting, you must quickly intercede to stop personal attacks or other forms of verbal insult.
11. *Be an effective listener.* You need to listen with intensity, empathy, objectivity, and do whatever is necessary to get the full intended meaning from each participant's comments.
12. *Bring proper closure.* You should close a meeting by summarizing the group's accomplishments; clarifying what actions, if any, need to follow the meeting; and allocating follow-up assignments. If any decisions are made, you also need to determine who will be responsible for communicating and implementing them.

Should Management Seek Cohesive Work Groups?

It is often implied that effective work groups are cohesive. In this section, we want to determine whether cohesiveness, as a group characteristic, is desirable. More specifically, should management actively seek to create work groups that are highly cohesive?

cohesiveness
Degree to which group members are attracted to each other and are motivated to stay in the group.

Intuitively, it would appear that groups in which there is a lot of internal disagreement and a lack of cooperative spirit would be relatively less effective at completing their tasks than would groups in which individuals generally agree and cooperate and where members like each other. Research to test this intuition has focused on the concept of group **cohesiveness**, defined as the degree to which members are attracted to one another and are motivated to stay in the group.[65] In the following pages, we review the factors that have been found to influence group cohesiveness and then look at the effect of cohesiveness on group productivity.[66]

Determinants of Cohesiveness

What factors determine whether group members will be attracted to one another? Cohesiveness can be affected by such factors as time spent together, the severity of initiation, group size, the gender makeup of the group, external threats, and previous successes.

TIME SPENT TOGETHER If you rarely get an opportunity to see or interact with other people, you're unlikely to be attracted to them. The amount of time people spend together, therefore, influences cohesiveness. As people spend more time together, they become more friendly. They naturally begin to talk, respond, gesture, and engage in other interactions. These interactions typically lead to the discovery of common interests and increased attraction.[67]

The opportunity for group members to spend time together depends on their physical proximity. We would expect more close relationships among members who are located close to one another rather than far apart. People who live on the same block, ride in the same car pool, or share a common office are more likely to become a cohesive group because the physical distance between them is minimal. For instance, among clerical workers in one organization, it was found that the distance between their desks was the single most important determinant of the rate of interaction between any two of the clerks.[68]

SEVERITY OF INITIATION The more difficult it is to get into a group, the more cohesive that group becomes. The competition to be accepted into a good medical school results in first-year medical school classes that are highly cohesive. The common initiation rites—applications, test taking, interviews, and the long wait for a final decision—all contribute to creating this cohesiveness.

GROUP SIZE If group cohesiveness tends to increase with the time members are able to spend together, it seems logical that cohesiveness should decrease as group size increases, since it becomes more difficult for a member to interact with all the other members. This is generally what the research indicates.[69] As a group's size expands, interaction with all members becomes more difficult, as does the ability to maintain a common goal. Not surprisingly, too, as the group's size increases, the likelihood of cliques forming also increases. The creation of groups within groups tends to decrease overall cohesiveness.

GENDER OF MEMBERS A consistent finding in recent studies is that women report greater cohesion than men.[70] For example, in one study, all-female and mixed-sex six-person personal growth groups rated themselves higher on cohesion than did members of all-male groups.[71] In another study, female intercollegiate basketball players reported higher group cohesion than their male counterparts.[72] Just why this occurs is not evident. A reasonable hypothesis, however, is that women are less competitive and/or more cooperative with people they see as friends, colleagues, or teammates than men are, and this results in greater group bonding.

EXTERNAL THREATS Most of the research supports the proposition that a group's cohesiveness will increase if the group comes under attack from external sources.[73] Management threats frequently bring together an otherwise disarrayed union. Efforts by management to redesign unilaterally even one or two jobs or to discipline one or two employees occasionally grab local headlines because the entire work force walks out in support of the abused few. These examples illustrate the kind of cooperative phenomenon that can develop within a group when it is attacked from outside.

While a group generally moves toward greater cohesiveness when threatened by external agents, this does not occur under all conditions. If group members perceive that their group may not meet an attack well, then the group becomes less important as a source of security, and cohesiveness will not necessarily increase. Additionally, if members believe the attack is directed at the group merely because of its existence and that it will cease if the group is abandoned or broken up, there is likely to be a decrease in cohesiveness.[74]

PREVIOUS SUCCESSES If a group has a history of successes, it builds an esprit de corps that attracts and unites members. Successful firms find it easier to attract and hire new employees than unsuccessful ones. The same holds true for successful research teams, well-known and prestigious universities, and winning athletic teams. The recent successes of firms like Fidelity Investments and Microsoft make it easier for these companies to recruit "the best and the brightest." People who harbor ambitions of attending a top ten graduate school of business need to recognize that the success of these schools attracts large numbers of candidates—many have 20 or more applicants for every vacancy.

Effects of Cohesiveness on Group Productivity

The previous section indicates that, generally speaking, group cohesiveness is increased when members spend time together and undergo a severe initiation, when the group size is small and predominantly female, when external threats exist, and when the group has a history of previous successes. But is increased cohesiveness always desirable from the point of view of management? That is, is it related to increased productivity?

Research has generally shown that highly cohesive groups are more effective than those with less cohesiveness,[75] but the relationship is more complex than merely allowing us to say high cohesiveness is good. First, high cohesiveness is both a cause and an outcome of high productivity. Second, the relationship is moderated by performance-related norms.

Cohesiveness influences productivity and productivity influences cohesiveness. Camaraderie reduces tension and provides a supportive environment for the successful attainment of group goals. But as already noted, the successful attainment of group goals, and the members' feelings of having been a part of a successful unit, can serve to enhance the commitment of members. Basketball coaches, for example, are famous for their devotion to teamwork. They believe that if the team is going to win games, its members have to learn to

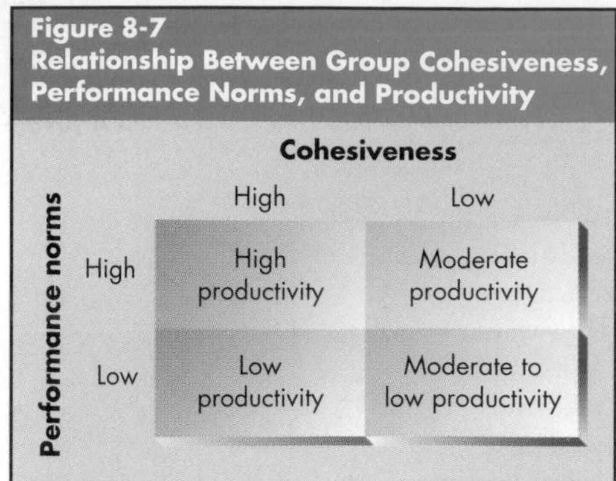

Figure 8-7
Relationship Between Group Cohesiveness, Performance Norms, and Productivity

play together. Popular coaching phrases include "There are no individuals on this team" and "We win together, or we lose together." The other side of this view is that winning reinforces camaraderie and leads to increased cohesiveness; that is, successful performance leads to increased intermember attractiveness and sharing.

More important has been the recognition that the relationship of cohesiveness and productivity depends on the performance-related norms established by the group.[76] The more cohesive the group, the more its members will follow its goals. If performance-related norms are high (for example, high output, quality work, cooperation with individuals outside the group), a cohesive group will be more productive than a less cohesive group. But if cohesiveness is high and performance norms are low, productivity will be low. If cohesiveness is low and performance norms are high, productivity increases, but less than in the high cohesiveness, high norms situation. Where cohesiveness and performance-related norms are both low, productivity will tend to fall into the low to moderate range. These conclusions are summarized in Figure 8-7.

Summary and Implications for Managers

We've covered a lot of territory in this chapter. Since we essentially organized our discussion around the group behavior model in Figure 8-4, let's use this model to summarize our findings regarding performance and satisfaction.

Performance

Any predictions about a group's performance must begin by recognizing that work groups are part of a larger organization and that factors such as the organization's strategy, authority structure, selection procedures, and reward system can provide a favorable or unfavorable climate for the group to operate within. For example, if an organization is characterized by distrust between management and workers, it is more likely work groups in that organization will develop norms to restrict effort and output than will work groups in an organization where trust is high. So managers shouldn't look at any group in isolation. Rather, they should begin by assessing the degree of support that external conditions provide the group. It is obviously a lot easier for any work group to be productive when the overall organization of which it is a part is growing and it has both top management's support and abundant resources. Similarly, a group is more likely to be productive when its members have the requisite skills to do the group's tasks and the personality characteristics that facilitate working well together.

A number of structural factors show a relationship to performance. Among the more prominent are role perception, norms, status inequities, the size of the group, its demographic makeup, the group's task, and cohesiveness.

There is a positive relationship between role perception and an employee's performance evaluation.[77] The degree of congruence that exists between an employee and his or her boss in the perception of the employee's job influences the degree to which that employee will be judged as an effective performer by the boss. To the extent the employee's role perception fulfills the boss's role expectations, the employee will receive a higher performance evaluation.

Norms control group member behavior by establishing standards of right and wrong. If managers know the norms of a given group, it can help explain the behaviors of its members. Where norms support high output, managers can expect individual performance to be markedly higher than where group norms aim to restrict output. Similarly, acceptable standards of absenteeism will be dictated by the group norms.

Status inequities create frustration and can adversely influence productivity and the willingness to remain with an organization. Among those individuals who are equity sensitive, incongruence is likely to lead to reduced motivation and an increased search for ways to bring about fairness (i.e., taking another job).

The impact of size on a group's performance depends on the type of task in which the group is engaged. Larger groups are more effective at fact-finding activities. Smaller groups are more effective at action-taking tasks. Our knowledge of social loafing suggests that if management uses larger groups, efforts should be made to provide measures of individual performance within the group.

We found the group's demographic composition to be a key determinant of individual turnover. Specifically, the evidence indicates that group members who share a common age or date of entry into the work group are less prone to resign.

The primary contingency variable moderating the relationship between group processes and performance is the group's task. The more complex and interdependent the tasks, the more inefficient processes will lead to reduced group performance.

Finally, we found that cohesiveness can play an important function in influencing a group's level of productivity. Whether or not it does depends on the group's performance-related norms.

Satisfaction

As with the role perception–performance relationship, high congruence between a boss and employee about the perception of the employee's job shows a significant association with high employee satisfaction.[78] Similarly, role conflict is associated with job-induced tension and job dissatisfaction.[79]

Most people prefer to communicate with others at their own status level or a higher one rather than with those below them.[80] As a result, we should expect satisfaction to be greater among employees whose job minimizes interaction with individuals who are lower in status than themselves.

The group size–satisfaction relationship is what one would intuitively expect: Larger groups are associated with lower satisfaction.[81] As size increases, opportunities for participation and social interaction decrease, as does the ability of members to identify with the group's accomplishments. At the same time, having more members also prompts dissension, conflict, and the formation of subgroups, which all act to make the group a less pleasant entity to be a part of.

For Review

1. Compare and contrast command, task, interest, and friendship groups.
2. What might motivate you to join a group?
3. Define *sociometry* and explain its value to managers.
4. What is the relationship between a work group and the organization of which it is a part?
5. What are the implications of Zimbardo's prison experiment for OB?
6. How do norms develop?
7. What are the implications of Whyte's restaurant study for OB?
8. How are status and norms related?
9. How can a group's demography help you predict turnover?
10. What is *groupthink*? What's its effect on decision-making quality?

For Discussion

1. How could you use the punctuated-equilibrium model to better understand group behavior?
2. Identify five roles you play. What behaviors do they require? Are any of these roles in conflict? If so, in what way? How do you resolve these conflicts?
3. "High cohesiveness in a group leads to higher group productivity." Do you agree or disagree? Explain.
4. What effect, if any, do you expect that work force diversity has on a group's performance and satisfaction?
5. If group decisions consistently achieve better quality outcomes than those achieved by individuals, how did the phrase "a camel is a horse designed by a committee" become so popular and ingrained in our culture?

Point

Designing Jobs Around Groups

It's time to take small groups seriously, that is, to use groups, rather than individuals, as the basic building blocks for an organization. I propose we should design organizations from scratch around small groups rather than the way we have traditionally done it—around individuals.

Why would management want to do such a thing? At least seven reasons can be identified. First, small groups seem to be good for people. They can satisfy important membership needs. They can provide a moderately wide range of activities for individual members. They can provide support in times of stress and crisis. They are settings in which people can learn not only cognitively but empirically to be reasonably trusting and helpful to one another. Second, groups seem to be good problem-finding tools. They seem to be useful in promoting innovation and creativity. Third, in a wide variety of decision situations, they make better decisions than individuals do. Fourth, they are great tools for implementation. They gain commitment from their members so group decisions are likely to be willingly carried out. Fifth, they can control and discipline individual members in ways that are often extremely difficult through impersonal quasi-legal disciplinary systems. Sixth, as organizations grow large, small groups appear to be useful mechanisms for fending off many of the negative effects of large size. They help prevent communication lines from growing too long, the hierarchy from growing too steep, and the individual from getting lost in the crowd. There is also a seventh, but altogether different, kind of argument for taking groups seriously. Groups are natural phenomena and facts of organizational life. They can be created, but their spontaneous development cannot be prevented.

Operationally, how would an organization that was truly designed around groups function? One answer to this question is merely to take the things that organizations do with individuals and apply them to groups. The idea would be to raise the level from the atom to the molecule and select groups rather than individuals, train groups rather than individuals, pay groups rather than individuals, promote groups rather than individuals, fire groups rather than individuals, and so on down the list of activities that organizations have traditionally carried on in order to use human beings in their organizations.

In the past, the human group has been primarily used for patching and mending organizations that were built around the individual. The time has come for management to discard the notion that individuals are the basic building blocks of organizations and to redesign organizations around groups. Importantly, a number of organizations seem to be moving in this direction. Peters and Waterman, for instance, in their search for high-performing organizations, found that "small groups are, quite simply, the basic organizational building blocks of excellent companies."* Similarly, hundreds of major companies, including Saturn Corp., Federal Express, and Microsoft, have essentially designed their current operations around small groups.

Based on H.J. Leavitt, "Suppose We Took Groups Seriously," in E.L. Cass and F.G. Zimmer (eds.), *Man and Work in Society* (New York: Van Nostrand Reinhold, 1975), pp. 67–77.

*T.J. Peters and R.H. Waterman, *In Search of Excellence* (New York: Harper & Row, 1982), p. 126.

counterPoint

Jobs Should Be Designed Around Individuals

The argument that organizations can and should be designed around groups might hold in a socialistic society, but not in capitalistic countries like the United States, Canada, Australia, Germany, and the United Kingdom. The following response directly relates to the United States and American workers, although it is probably generalizable to other economically advanced capitalistic countries. In fact, given the recent political changes in Eastern Europe and the increasing acceptance of profit-motivated businesses, the case for the individually oriented organization may be applicable throughout the world.

America was built on the ethic of the individual. This ethic has been pounded into Americans from birth. The result is that it is deeply embedded in the psyche of every American. They strongly value individual achievement. They praise competition. Even in team sports, they want to identify individuals for recognition. Sure, they enjoy group interaction. They like being part of a team, especially a winning team. But it is one thing to be a member of a work group while maintaining a strong individual identity and another to sublimate one's identity to that of the group. The latter is inconsistent with the values of American life.

The American worker likes a clear link between his or her individual effort and a visible outcome. It is not happenstance that the United States, as a nation, has a considerably larger proportion of high achievers than exists in socialistic countries. America breeds achievers, and achievers seek personal responsibility. They would be frustrated in job situations where their contribution is commingled and homogenized with the contributions of others.

Americans want to be hired based on their individual talents. They want to be evaluated on their individual efforts. They also want to be rewarded with pay raises and promotions based on their individual performances. Americans believe in an authority and status hierarchy. They accept a system where there are bosses and subordinates. They are not likely to accept a group's decision on such issues as their job assignments and wage increases. It's harder to imagine that they would be comfortable in a system where the sole basis for their promotion or termination would be the performance of their group.

One of the best examples of how fully the individual ethic has permeated the American psyche is the general lack of enthusiasm that college students display toward group term papers. For years I've offered students the option to write term papers individually or as members of a small group. I tell the class they can do the paper alone, in which case I would expect around 20 to 25 pages in length. Or they can do the paper in groups, but I'd expect the length to expand commensurately. The only qualifier I state is that we can't do both. The class has to decide whether they want to do individual or group papers, and everyone has to abide by that decision. I can tell you that I have never had a class where the majority voluntarily chose the group-paper option! But I'm not surprised. Isn't this consistent with the stereotype of the individualistic American, motivated by his or her self-interest? Of someone who wants to rise or fall based on his or her own work performance? Yes! Is this a future full-time employee who would be satisfied, and reach his or her full productive capacity, in a group-centered organization? I don't think so.

Learning About Yourself Exercise

Are You Attracted to the Group?

Most of us have had experience writing a term paper. Some of these have been individual assignments. That is, the instructor expected each student to hand in a separate paper and your grade was determined solely by your own effort and contribution. But sometimes instructors assign group term papers, where students must work together on the project and share in the grade.

Think back to your most recent experience in doing a group term paper. Now envision yourself at about the halfway point in the completion of that group assignment. Using your mind-set at this halfway point, answer the following 20 questions. This questionnaire measures your feelings about that work group.*

	Agree Disagree
1. I want to remain a member of this group.	1 2 3 4 5 6 7 8 9
2. I like my group.	1 2 3 4 5 6 7 8 9
3. I look forward to coming to the group.	1 2 3 4 5 6 7 8 9
4. I don't care what happens in this group.	1 2 3 4 5 6 7 8 9
5. I feel involved in what is happening in my group.	1 2 3 4 5 6 7 8 9
6. If I could drop out of the group now, I would.	1 2 3 4 5 6 7 8 9
7. I dread coming to this group.	1 2 3 4 5 6 7 8 9
8. I wish it were possible for the group to end now.	1 2 3 4 5 6 7 8 9
9. I am dissatisfied with the group.	1 2 3 4 5 6 7 8 9
10. If it were possible to move to another group at this time, I would.	1 2 3 4 5 6 7 8 9
11. I feel included in the group.	1 2 3 4 5 6 7 8 9
12. In spite of individual differences, a feeling of unity exists in my group.	1 2 3 4 5 6 7 8 9
13. Compared to other groups I know of, I feel my group is better than most.	1 2 3 4 5 6 7 8 9
14. I do not feel a part of the group's activities.	1 2 3 4 5 6 7 8 9
15. I feel it would make a difference to the group if I were not here.	1 2 3 4 5 6 7 8 9
16. If I were told my group would not meet today, I would feel bad.	1 2 3 4 5 6 7 8 9
17. I feel distant from the group.	1 2 3 4 5 6 7 8 9
18. It makes a difference to me how this group turns out.	1 2 3 4 5 6 7 8 9
19. I feel my absence would not matter to the group.	1 2 3 4 5 6 7 8 9
20. I would not feel bad if I had to miss a meeting of this group.	1 2 3 4 5 6 7 8 9

Turn to page A-28 for scoring directions and key.

*Reproduced from N.J. Evans and P.A. Jarvis, "The Group Attitude Scale: A Measure of Attraction to Group," *Small Group Behavior* (May 1986), pp. 203–16. With permission.

Working With Others Exercise

The Paper Tower Exercise

Step 1 Organize the class into groups of five to eight people.

Step 2 Each group will receive one 12-inch stack of newspapers and one roll of masking tape from your instructor. The groups have 20 minutes to plan a paper tower that will be judged on the basis of three criteria: height, stability, and beauty. No physical work is allowed during this planning period.

Step 3 Each group has thirty minutes for the actual construction of the paper tower.

Step 4 Each tower will be identified by a number assigned by your instructor. Each student is to individually examine all the paper towers. Your group is then to come to a consensus as to which tower is the winner. A spokesperson from your group should report its decision and the criteria the group used in reaching it.

Step 5 In your small groups, discuss the following questions:

a. What percentage of the plan did each member of your group contribute?

b. To what degree did your group follow the five-step group development model?

c. Did a single leader emerge from the group? If so, who? Why do you think this person became the leader?

d. In groups, someone typically assumes a task-oriented role, concerned with "getting the job done"; another takes a human relations role, making encouraging, friendly, and supportive comments. Did these roles emerge in your group? Did these roles aid or hinder the group's effectiveness?

e. How did the group generally respond to the ideas that were expressed?

f. List specific behaviors exhibited during the planning and building sessions that you felt were helpful to the group.

g. List specific behaviors exhibited during the planning and building sessions that you felt were dysfunctional to the group.

Step 6 Discuss the following questions with the entire class:

a. How did the groups' behavior differ?

b. What characterized the most effective groups?

c. How could the behavior of the less effective groups be improved?

Source: Adapted from P.L. Hunsaker and J.S. Hunsaker, "The Paper Tower Exercise: Experiencing Leadership and Group Dynamics," unpublished manuscript. With permission of the authors.

Ethical Dilemma Exercise

Should You Agree with Your Boss When You Don't?

The Asch conformity studies point up a related dilemma that many employees face: whether it is ethical to outwardly agree with your boss when, in actuality, you think he or she is wrong.

There is an old adage: The boss isn't always right, but (s)he's always the boss. The underlying message is you don't argue with your superior because that superior has authority over you. But what about when you know the boss is acting unethically? Would openly agreeing with the boss in those circumstances mean compromising your personal standards of integrity? What about merely suppressing your disagreement? That might be more politically astute, but would it mean you lack moral character?

The norms of conformity can be very strong in an organization. Individuals who openly challenge long-condoned but questionable practices may be labeled as disloyal or lacking in commitment to the organization. One perspective argues that conformance with group and organizational norms bonds people together. Such conformity facilitates cooperation and cohesiveness and contributes to standardizing behavior. These are qualities that can enhance organizational effectiveness. An opposite argument can be made that the suppression of dissent and the appearance of conformity don't improve organizational effectiveness, but rather plant the seeds for later hostilities and conflicts.

(1) What should you do when you disagree with your boss about an ethical issue? (2) If you were the boss, would you want your employees to openly disagree with you? If so, how would you want them to express their views? (3) What can organizations do to avoid encouraging individuals to unethically conform but, at the same time, encourage cohesiveness and commitment?

CASE INCIDENT

Games People Play in the Shipping Department

The Science Fiction Book Club (SFBC) sells a large list of science fiction books, at discount prices, entirely by mail order. In 1994 the club shipped over 370,000 books and generated revenues of $6.4 million. Anyone familiar with the mail-order business realizes it offers extremely high profit potential because under careful management, inventory costs and overhead can be kept quite low. The biggest problems in mail-order businesses are filling orders, shipping the merchandise, and billing the customers. At SFBC, the Packing and Shipping (P&S) Department employs eight full-time people:

- Ray, 44 years old, has worked in P&S for seven years.
- Al, 49, has worked in P&S for nine years.
- R.J., 53, has worked in P&S for 16 years. He was head of the department for two years back in the early 1980s, but stepped down voluntarily because of continuing stomach problems that doctors attributed to supervisory pressures.
- Pearl, 59, was the original employee hired by the founder. She has been at SFBC for 25 years and in P&S for 21 years.

- Margaret, 31, is the newest member of the department. She has been employed less than a year.
- Steve, 27, has worked in P&S for three years. He goes to college at nights and makes no effort to hide that he plans on leaving P&S and probably SFBC when he gets his degree next year.
- George, 46, is currently head of P&S. He has been with SFBC for ten years, and in P&S for six.
- Gary, 25, has worked in P&S for two years.

The jobs in a shipping department are uniformly dull and repetitive. Each person is responsible for wrapping, addressing, and making the bills out on anywhere from 100 to 200 books a day. Part of George's responsibilities are to make allocations to each worker and to ensure that no significant backlogs occur. However, George spends less than 10 percent of his time in supervisory activities. The rest of the time he wraps, addresses, and makes out bills just like everyone else.

Apparently to deal with the repetitiveness of their jobs, the department members have created a number of games they play among themselves. They seem almost childish, but it is obvious the games mean something to these people. Importantly, each is played regularly. Some of the ones we describe are played at least once a day. All are played a minimum of twice a week.

"The Stamp Machine Is Broken" is a game that belongs to Al. At least once a day, Al goes over to the postage meter in the office and unplugs it. He then proceeds loudly to attempt to make a stamp for a package. "The stamp machine is broken again," he yells. Either Ray or Gary, or both, will come over and spend 30 seconds or so trying to "fix" it, then "discover" that it's unplugged. The one who finds it unplugged then says, "Al, you're a mechanical spastic," and others in the office join in and laugh.

Gary is the initiator of the game "Steve, There's a Call for You." Usually played in the late afternoon, an hour or so before everyone goes home, Gary will pick up the phone and pretend there is someone on the line. "Hey, Steve, it's for you," he'll yell out. "It's Mr. Big [the president of SFBC]. Says he wants you to come over to his office right away. You're going to be the new vice president!" The game is an obvious sarcastic jab at Steve's going to college and his frequent comments about someday being a big executive.

R.J., although 53 years old, has never married and lives with his mother. The main interests in his life are telling stories, showing pictures of last year's vacation, and planning for this year's trip. Without exception, everyone finds R.J.'s vacation talk boring. But that doesn't stop Pearl or George from setting him up several times a week. "Hey R.J., can we see those pictures you took last year in Oregon again?" That question always gets R.J. to drop whatever he's doing and pull 75 to 100 pictures from his top drawer. "Hey, R. J., what are you planning to do on your vacation this year?" always gets R. J.'s eyes shining and invariably leads to the unfolding of maps he also keeps in his top drawer.

George's favorite game is "What's It Like to Be Rich?" which he plays with Pearl. Pearl's husband was a successful banker and died a half dozen years ago. He left her very well off financially. Pearl enjoys everyone knowing she doesn't have to work, has a large lovely home, buys a new car every two years, and includes some of the city's more prominent businesspeople and politicians among her friends. George will mention the name of some big shot in town, and Pearl never fails to take the bait. She proceeds to tell how he is a close friend of hers. George might also bring up money in some context in order to allow Pearl to complain about high taxes, the difficulty in finding good housekeepers, the high cost of traveling to Europe, or some other concern of the affluent.

Questions

1. Analyze the group's interactions using the group behavior model.
2. How do these games affect the department's performance?
3. Are these games functional? Dysfunctional? Explain.

The Prima Donna

They drive the people they have to work with nuts. They're pampered, they're spoiled, and they seem to always have to be the center of attention. Who are they? They're opera's main attraction—the prima donna.

The firing of prima donna Kathleen Battle by the Metropolitan Opera in New York City brought the public's attention to how difficult prima donnas can be to work with.

Battle was notorious for her arrogance and difficult behavior. According to the Met's general manager, Battle arrived late for rehearsals that had been rescheduled for her in the first place, she left early, and she demanded that other singers leave the stage when she was singing. *Newsweek*'s music critic Tim Page tells how Battle "insisted on being moved from hotel to hotel. At one of the hotels she moved because she thought somebody was looking at her funny. At another one they served her some spaghetti with some peas in it, and it turns out that she doesn't like peas. After she sang in San Francisco, members of the San Francisco chorus had T-shirts made up saying, 'I Survived the Battle.'"

While Battle has gotten a lot of attention for her behavior, she's not unique in her profession. Opera stars are notorious for being temperamental. For instance, Luciano Pavarotti was fired by the Lyric Opera of Chicago for missing 26 of 41 performances. In another instance, a Philadelphia opera director made the grave mistake of advertising one of his tenors as "the greatest tenor alive." All of his other tenors immediately canceled for that season. Even Beverly Sills, by all accounts one of the nicest people in the world of opera, had her difficult moments. "I was at La Scala," says Sills. "I kept asking to have my costume color changed, and the designer had agreed to it. And the woman who was head of the dressmaking department, who wears one of those great big scissors on a black ribbon, for some reason didn't want to go through the extra work of changing the costume. And I asked her and asked her, and she wouldn't pay attention. So, for the costume parade, they march it in front of the lights. It was still the same bad color. So I went over to her, I took the gown and folded it up in little pieces, took her great big scissors, and I cut it in four ways. And I said, 'Here. Now make me a new costume.'"

What makes these people behave this way? Singer Lisa Gasteen thinks it's the pressure of being out front. "The responsibility of singing front roles is really huge. It's important to be at your best when you're performing, and that is a huge pressure." Battle's former agent, Peter Gelb, thinks it relates to the quest for perfection. "I think Kathleen encountered some difficulties because she is incredibly difficult and demanding in search of perfection in her art, in the same way that Michael Jordan would have been in trying to hit 50 points in a basketball game." After all, opera is a business where even a small mistake can be perceived as failure, and success is defined as nothing less than perfection.

Questions

1. Does the job shape the personality or do certain personalities go into opera?
2. "Battle and other opera stars' behavior can be explained in terms of playing roles." Discuss.
3. CEOs are under pressure. Similarly, Garth Brooks and Whitney Houston sing in front of tens of thousands and are expected to perform without mistakes. What, if anything, differentiates these people from opera stars?

Source: "The Prima Donna—Temperamental Opera Stars," *Nightline* (February 11, 1994).

Suggestions for Further Reading

GEORGE, J.M., "Extrinsic and Intrinsic Origins of Perceived Social Loafing in Organizations," *Academy of Management Journal* (March 1992), pp. 191–202.

GUZZO, R.A., and G.P. SHEA, "Group Performance and Intergroup Relations in Organizations," in M.D. Dunnette and L.M. Hough, (eds.), *Handbook of Industrial & Organizational Pyschology*, Vol. 3 (Palo Alto, CA: Consulting Psychologists Press, 1992), pp. 269–313.

HACKMAN, J.R. (ed.), *Groups That Work (and Those That Don't)* (San Francisco: Jossey-Bass, 1990).

HACKMAN, J.R., "Group Influences on Individuals in Organizations," in M.D. Dunnette and L.M. Hough, (eds.), *Handbook of Industrial & Organizational Psychology*, Vol. 3 (Palo Alto, CA: Consulting Psychologists Press, 1992), pp. 199–267.

KIDWELL, R.E., JR. and N. BENNETT, "Employee Propensity to Withhold Effort: A Conceptual Model to Intersect Three Avenues of Research," *Academy of Management Review* (July 1993), pp. 429–56.

KRUGLANSKI, A.W., and O. MAYSELESS, "Classic and Current Social Comparison Research: Expanding the Perspective," *Psychological Bulletin* (July 1990), pp. 195–208.

LEVINE, J.M., and R.L. MORELAND, "Progress in Small Group Research," in M.F. Rosenzweig and L.W. Porter (eds.), *Annual Review of Psychology*, Vol. 41 (Palo Alto, CA: Annual Reviews, 1990), pp. 585–634.

PAULUS, P.B. (ed.), *Psychology of Group Influence*, 2nd ed. (Hillsdale, NJ: Erlbaum, 1989).

WIERSEMA, M.F., and A. BIRD, "Organizational Demography in Japanese Firms: Group Heterogeneity, Individual Dissimilarity, and Top Management Team Turnover," *Academy of Management Journal* (October 1993), pp. 996–1025.

WORCHEL, S., W. WOOD, and J.A. SIMPSON (eds.), *Group Process and Productivity* (Newbury Park, CA: Sage 1991).

Notes

[1] Based on M. Stevenson, "Be Nice for a Change," *Canadian Business* (November 1993), pp. 81–85.

[2] L.R. Sayles, "Work Group Behavior and the Larger Organization," in C. Arensburg et al. (eds.), *Research in Industrial Relations* (New York: Harper & Row, 1957), pp. 131–45.

[3] B.W. Tuckman, "Developmental Sequences in Small Groups," *Psychological Bulletin* (June 1965), pp. 384–99; B.W. Tuckman and M.C. Jensen, "Stages of Small-Group Development Revisited," *Group and Organizational Studies* (December 1977), pp. 419–27; and M.F. Maples, "Group Development: Extending Tuckman's Theory," *Journal for Specialists in Group Work* (Fall 1988), pp. 17–23.

[4] R.C. Ginnett, "The Airline Cockpit Crew," in J.R. Hackman (ed.), *Groups That Work (and Those That Don't)* (San Francisco: Jossey-Bass, 1990).

[5] C.J.G. Gersick, "Time and Transition in Work Teams: Toward a New Model of Group Development," *Academy of Management Journal* (March 1988), pp. 9–41; C.J.G. Gersick, "Marking Time: Predictable Transitions in Task Groups," *Academy of Management Journal* (June 1989), pp. 274–309; and E. Romanelli and M.L. Tushman, "Organizational Transformation as Punctuated Equilibrium: An Empirical Test," *Academy of Management* (October 1994), pp. 1141–66.

[6] See J.L. Moreno, "Contributions of Sociometry to Research

Methodology in Sociology," *American Sociological Review* (June 1947), pp. 287–92. Also J.W. Hart and R. Nath, "Sociometry in Business and Industry: New Developments in Historical Perspective," *Group Psychotherapy, Psychodrama and Sociometry*, Vol. 32 (1979), pp. 128–49.

[7] N.M. Tichy, M.L. Tushman, and C. Fombrun, "Social Network Analysis for Organizations," *Academy of Management Review* (October 1979), pp. 507–19; and N. Tichy and C. Fombrun, "Network Analysis in Organizational Settings," *Human Relations* (November 1979), pp. 923–65.

[8] D. Krackhardt and L.W. Porter, "The Snowball Effect: Turnover Embedded in Communication Networks," *Journal of Applied Psychology* (February 1986), pp. 50–55.

[9] R.E. Nelson, "The Strength of Strong Ties: Social Networks and Intergroup Conflict in Organizations," *Academy of Management Journal* (June 1989), pp. 377–401.

[10] H. Ibarra, "Personal Networks of Women and Minorities in Management: A Conceptual Framework," *Academy of Management Review* (January 1993), pp. 56–87.

[11] This model is substantially based on the work of P.S. Goodman, E. Ravlin, and M. Schminke, "Understanding Groups in Organizations," in L.L. Cummings and B. M. Staw (eds.), *Research in Organizational Behavior*, Vol. 9 (Greenwich, CT: JAI Press, 1987), pp. 124–28; J.R. Hackman, "The Design of Work Teams," in J.W. Lorsch (ed.), *Handbook of Organizational Behavior* (Englewood Cliffs, NJ: Prentice Hall, 1987), pp. 315–42; and G.R. Bushe and A.L. Johnson, "Contextual and Internal Variables Affecting Task Group Outcomes in Organizations," *Group and Organization Studies* (December 1989), pp. 462–82.

[12] F. Friedlander, "The Ecology of Work Groups," in J.W. Lorsch (ed.), *Handbook of Organizational Behavior*, pp. 301–14; P.B. Paulus and D. Nagar, "Environmental Influences on Groups," in P. Paulus (ed.), *Psychology of Group Influence*, 2nd ed. (Hillsdale, NJ: Erlbaum, 1989); and E. Sundstrom and I. Altman, "Physical Environments and Work-Group Effectiveness," in L.L. Cummings and B.M. Staw (eds.), *Research in Organizational Behavior*, Vol. 11 (Greenwich, CT: JAI Press, 1989), pp. 175–209.

[13] See, for example, J. Krantz, "Group Processes Under Conditions of Organizational Decline," *The Journal of Applied Behavioral Science*, Vol. 21, No. 1 (1985), pp. 1–17.

[14] Hackman, "The Design of Work Teams," pp. 325–26.

[15] See, for instance, G.R. Oldham and Y. Fried, "Employee Reactions to Workspace Characteristics," *Journal of Applied Psychology* (February 1987), pp. 75–80.

[16] A.D. Szilagyi, Jr., and M.J. Wallace, Jr., *Organizational Behavior and Performance*, 4th ed. (Glenview, IL: Scott, Foresman, 1987), p. 223.

[17] See M. Hill, "Group Versus Individual Performance. Are N + 1 Heads Better Than One?" *Psychological Reports* (April 1982), pp. 517–39; and A. Tziner and D. Eden, "Effects of Crew Composition on Crew Performance: Does the Whole Equal the Sum of Its Parts?" *Journal of Applied Psychology* (February 1985), pp. 85–93.

[18] M.E. Shaw, *Contemporary Topics in Social Psychology* (Morristown, NJ: General Learning Press, 1976), pp. 350–51.

[19] S. Lieberman, "The Effects of Changes in Roles on the Attitudes of Role Occupants," *Human Relations* (November 1956), pp. 385–402.

[20] See S.L. Robinson, M.S. Kraatz, and D.M. Rousseau, "Changing Obligations and the Psychological Contract: A Longitudinal Study," *Academy of Management Journal* (February 1994), pp. 137–52.

[21] E.H. Schein, *Organizational Psychology*, 3rd ed. (Englewood Cliffs, NJ: Prentice-Hall, 1980), p. 24.

[22] P.G. Zimbardo, C. Haney, W.C. Banks, and D. Jaffe, "The Mind Is a Formidable Jailer: A Pirandellian Prison," *New York Times* (April 8, 1973), pp. 38–60.

[23] For a recent review of the research on group norms, see J.R. Hackman, "Group Influences on Individuals in Organizations," in M.D. Dunnette and L.M. Hough (eds.), *Handbook of Industrial & Organizational Psychology*, 2nd ed., Vol. 3 (Palo Alto, CA: Consulting Psychologists Press, 1992), pp. 235–50.

[24] A. Harlan, J. Kerr, and S. Kerr, "Preference for Motivator and Hygiene Factors in a Hypothetical Interview Situation: Further Findings and Some Implications for the Employment Interview," *Personnel Psychology* (Winter 1977), pp. 557–66.

[25] Adapted from Goodman, Ravlin, and Schminke, "Understanding Groups in Organizations," p. 159.

[26] D.C. Feldman, "The Development and Enforcement of Group Norms," *Academy of Management Journal* (January 1984), pp. 47–53; and K.L. Bettenhausen and J.K. Murnighan, "The Development of an Intragroup Norm and the Effects of Interpersonal and Structural Challenges," *Administrative Science Quarterly* (March 1991), pp. 20–35.

[27] C.A. Kiesler and S.B. Kiesler, *Conformity* (Reading, MA: Addison-Wesley, 1969).

[28] Ibid., p. 27.

[29] S.E. Asch, "Effects of Group Pressure upon the Modification and Distortion of Judgments," in H. Guetzkow (ed.), *Groups, Leadership and Men* (Pittsburgh: Carnegie Press, 1951), pp. 177–90.

[30] R. Keyes, *Is There Life After High School?* (New York: Warner Books, 1976).

[31] W.F. Whyte, "The Social Structure of the Restaurant," *American Journal of Sociology* (January 1954), pp. 302–308.

[32] Cited in J.R. Hackman, "Group Influences on Individuals in Organizations," p. 236.

[33] O.J. Harvey and C. Consalvi, "Status and Conformity to Pressures in Informal Groups," *Journal of Abnormal and Social Psychology* (Spring 1960), pp. 182–87.

[34] J.A. Wiggins, F. Dill, and R.D. Schwartz, "On 'Status-Liability.'" *Sociometry* (April-May 1965), pp. 197–209.

[35] J. Greenberg, "Equity and Workplace Status: A Field Experiment," *Journal of Applied Psychology* (November 1988), pp. 606–13.

[36] E.J. Thomas and C.F. Fink, "Effects of Group Size," *Psychological Bulletin* (July 1963), pp. 371–84; A.P. Hare, *Handbook of Small Group Research* (New York: Free Press, 1976); and M.E. Shaw, *Group Dynamics: The Psychology of Small Group Behavior*, 3rd ed. (New York: McGraw-Hill, 1981).

[37] W. Moede, "Die Richtlinien der Leistungs-Psychologie," *Industrielle Psychotechnik*, Vol. 4 (1927), pp. 193–207. See also D.A. Kravitz and B. Martin, "Ringelmann Rediscovered: The

Original Article," *Journal of Personality and Social Psychology* (May 1986), pp. 936–41.

[38] See, for example, J.A. Shepperd, "Productivity Loss in Performance Groups: A Motivation Analysis," *Psychological Bulletin* (January 1993), pp. 67–81; and S.J. Karau and K.D. Williams, "Social Loafing: A Meta-Analytic Review and Theoretical Integration," *Journal of Personality and Social Psychology* (October 1993), pp. 681–706.

[39] S.G. Harkins and K. Szymanski, "Social Loafing and Group Evaluation," *Journal of Personality and Social Psychology* (December 1989), pp. 934–41.

[40] See P.C. Earley, "Social Loafing and Collectivism: A Comparison of the United States and the People's Republic of China," *Administrative Science Quarterly* (December 1989), pp. 565–81; and P.C. Earley, "East Meets West Meets Mideast: Further Explorations of Collectivistic and Individualistic Work Groups," *Academy of Management Journal* (April 1993), pp. 319–48.

[41] Thomas and Fink, "Effects of Group Size"; Hare, *Handbook; Shaw, Group Dynamics*; and P. Yetton and P. Bottger, "The Relationships Among Group Size, Member Ability, Social Decision Schemes, and Performance," *Organizational Behavior and Human Performance* (October 1983), pp. 145–59.

[42] See, for example, P.S. Goodman, E.C. Ravlin, and L. Argote, "Current Thinking About Groups: Setting the Stage for New Ideas," in P.S. Goodman and associates (eds.), *Designing Effective Work Groups* (San Francisco: Jossey-Bass, 1986), pp. 15–16; and R.A. Guzzo and G.P. Shea, "Group Performance and Intergroup Relations in Organizations," in M.D. Dunnette and L.M. Hough, (eds.), *Handbook of Industrial & Organizational Psychology*, 2nd ed., Vol. 3 (Palo Alto, CA: Consulting Psychologists Press, 1992), pp. 288–90.

[43] Shaw, *Contemporary Topics*, p. 356.

[44] W.E. Watson, K. Kumar, and L.K. Michaelsen, "Cultural Diversity's Impact on Interaction Process and Performance: Comparing Homogenous and Diverse Task Groups," *Academy of Management Journal* (June 1993), pp. 590–602.

[45] B.E. McCain, C.A. O'Reilly III, and J. Pfeffer, "The Effects of Departmental Demography on Turnover: The Case of a University," *Academy of Management Journal* (December 1983), pp. 626–41; W.G. Wagner, J. Pfeffer, and C.A. O'Reilly III, "Organizational Demography and Turnover in Top-Management Groups," *Administrative Science Quarterly* (March 1984), pp. 74–92; J. Pfeffer and C.A. O'Reilly III, "Hospital Demography and Turnover Among Nurses," *Industrial Relations* (Spring 1987), pp. 158–73; C.A. O'Reilly III, D.F. Caldwell, and W.P. Barnett, "Work Group Demography, Social Integration, and Turnover," *Administrative Science Quarterly* (March 1989), pp. 21–37; and S.E. Jackson, J.F. Brett, V.I. Sessa, D.M. Cooper, J.A. Julin, and K. Peyronnin, "Some Differences Make a Difference: Individual Dissimilarity and Group Heterogeneity as Correlates of Recruitment, Promotions, and Turnover," *Journal of Applied Psychology* (August 1991), pp. 675–89.

[46] I.D. Steiner, *Group Process and Productivity* (New York: Academic Press, 1972).

[47] R.B. Zajonc, "Social Facilitation," *Science* (March 1965), pp. 269–74.

[48] C.F. Bond, Jr. and L.J. Titus, "Social Facilitation: A Meta-Analysis of 241 Studies," *Psychological Bulletin* (September 1983), pp. 265–92.

[49] V.F. Nieva, E.A. Fleishman, and A. Rieck, "Team Dimensions: Their Identity, Their Measurement, and Their Relationships." Final Technical Report for Contract No. DAHC 19-C-0001 (Washington, DC: Advanced Research Resources Organizations, 1978).

[50] See, for example, J.R. Hackman and C.G. Morris, "Group Tasks, Group Interaction Process and Group Performance Effectiveness: A Review and Proposed Integration," in L. Berkowitz (ed.), *Advances in Experimental Social Psychology* (New York: Academic Press, 1975), pp. 45–99; and R. Saavedra, P.C. Earley, and L. Van Dyne, "Complex Interdependence in Task-Performing Groups," *Journal of Applied Psychology* (February 1993), pp. 61–72.

[51] J. Galbraith, *Organizational Design* (Reading, MA: Addison-Wesley, 1977).

[52] See N.R.F. Maier, "Assets and Liabilities in Group Problem Solving: The Need for an Integrative Function," *Psychological Review* (April 1967), pp. 239–49; G.W. Hill, "Group versus Individual Performance: Are N + 1 Heads Better Than One?" *Psychological Bulletin* (May 1982), pp. 517–39; and A.E. Schwartz and J. Levin, "Better Group Decision Making," *Supervisory Management* (June 1990), p. 4.

[53] See, for example, R.A. Cooke and J.A. Kernaghan, "Estimating the Difference Between Group versus Individual Performance on Problem-Solving Tasks," *Group & Organization Studies* (September 1987), pp. 319–42; and L.K. Michaelsen, W.E. Watson, and R.H. Black, "A Realistic Test of Individual versus Group Consensus Decision Making," *Journal of Applied Psychology* (October 1989), pp. 834–39.

[54] See, for example, W.C. Swap and associates, *Group Decision Making* (Newbury Park, CA: Sage, 1984).

[55] I.L. Janis, *Groupthink* (Boston: Houghton Mifflin, 1982).

[56] Ibid.

[57] Ibid.

[58] C. R. Leana, "A Partial Test of Janis' Groupthink Model: Effects of Group Cohesiveness and Leader Behavior on Defective Decision Making," *Journal of Management* (Spring 1985), pp. 5–17; and G. Moorhead and J.R. Montanari, "An Empirical Investigation of the Groupthink Phenomenon," *Human Relations* (May 1986), pp. 399–410.

[59] See D.J. Isenberg, "Group Polarization: A Critical Review and Meta-Analysis," *Journal of Personality and Social Psychology* (December 1986), pp. 1141–51; J.L. Hale and F.J. Boster, "Comparing Effect Coded Models of Choice Shifts," *Communication Research Reports* (April 1988), pp. 180–86; and P.W. Paese, M. Bieser, and M.E. Tubbs, "Framing Effects and Choice Shifts in Group Decision Making," *Organizational Behavior and Human Decision Processes* (October 1993), pp. 149–65.

[60] See, for example, N. Kogan and M. A. Wallach, "Risk Taking as a Function of the Situation, the Person, and the Group," in *New Directions in Psychology*, Vol. 3 (New York: Holt, Rinehart and Winston, 1967); and M.A. Wallach, N. Kogan, and D.J. Bem, "Group Influence on Individual Risk Taking," *Journal of Abnormal and Social Psychology*, Vol. 65 (1962), pp. 75–86.

[61] R.D. Clark III, "Group-Induced Shift Toward Risk: A Critical

Appraisal," *Psychological Bulletin* (October 1971), pp. 251–70.

[62] A.F. Osborn, *Applied Imagination: Principles and Procedures of Creative Thinking* (New York: Scribner's, 1941).

[63] See A.L. Delbecq, A.H. Van deVen, and D.H. Gustafson, *Group Techniques for Program Planning: A Guide to Nominal and Delphi Processes* (Glenview, IL: Scott, Foresman, 1975); and W.M. Fox, "Anonymity and Other Keys to Successful Problem-Solving Meetings," *National Productivity Review* (Spring 1989), pp. 145–56.

[64] See J. Bartimo, "At These Shouting Matches, No One Says a Word," *Business Week* (June 11, 1990), p. 78; M.S. Poole, M. Holmes, and G. DeSanctis, "Conflict Management in a Computer-Supported Meeting Environment," *Management Science* (August 1991), pp. 926–53; A.R. Dennis and J.S. Valacich, "Computer Brainstorms: More Heads Are Better Than One," *Journal of Applied Psychology* (August 1993), pp. 531–37; R.B. Gallupe and W.H. Cooper, "Brainstorming Electronically," *Sloan Management Review* (Fall 1993), pp. 27–36; and R.B. Gallupe, W.H. Cooper, M.L. Grise, and L.M. Bastianutti, "Blocking Electronic Brainstorms," *Journal of Applied Psychology* (February 1994), pp. 77–86.

[65] For some of the controversy surrounding the definition of cohesion, see J. Keyton and J. Springston, "Redefining Cohesiveness in Groups," *Small Group Research* (May 1990), pp. 234–54.

[66] See, for example, I. Summers, T. Coffelt, and R.E. Horton, "Work-Group Cohesion," *Psychological Reports* (October 1988), pp. 627–36.

[67] C. Insko and M. Wilson, "Interpersonal Attraction as a Function of Social Interaction," *Journal of Personality and Social Psychology* (December 1977), pp. 903–11.

[68] J.T. Gullahorn, "Distance and Friendship as Factors in the Gross Interaction Matrix," *Sociometry* (February-March 1952), pp. 123–34.

[69] E.J. Thomas and C.F. Fink, "Effects of Group Size," *Psychological Bulletin* (July 1963), pp. 371–84.

[70] K.L. Bettenhausen, "Five Years of Groups Research: What We Have Learned and What Needs to Be Addressed," *Journal of Management* (June 1991), p. 362.

[71] J.R. Taylor and D.S. Strassberg, "The Effects of Sex Composition on Cohesiveness and Interpersonal Learning in Short-Term Personal Growth Groups," *Psychotherapy* (Summer 1986), pp. 267–73.

[72] C.A. Wrisberg and M.V. Draper, "Sex, Sex Role Orientation, and the Cohesion of Intercollegiate Basketball Teams," *Journal of Sports Behavior* (March 1988), pp. 45–54.

[73] A. Stein, "Conflict and Cohesion: A Review of the Literature," *Journal of Conflict Resolution* (March 1976), pp. 143–72.

[74] A. Zander, "The Psychology of Group Processes," in M.R. Rosenzweig and L.W. Porter (eds.), *Annual Review of Psychology*, Vol. 30 (Palo Alto, CA: Annual Reviews, 1979), p. 436.

[75] See, for example, C.N. Greene, "Cohesion and Productivity in Work Groups," *Small Group Behavior* (February 1989), pp. 70–86; and B. Mullen and C. Copper, "The Relation Between Group Cohesiveness and Performance: An Integration," *Psychological Bulletin* (March 1994), pp. 210–27.

[76] See, for example, S. Schachter, N. Ellertson, D. McBride, and D. Gregory, "An Experimental Study of Cohesiveness and Productivity," *Human Relations* (March 1951), pp. 229–38; J. Darley, N. Gross, and W. Martin, "Studies of Group Behavior: Factors Associated with the Productivity of Groups," *Journal of Applied Psychology* (June 1952), pp. 396–403; and L. Berkowitz, "Group Standards, Cohesiveness, and Productivity," *Human Relations* (August 1954), pp. 509–19.

[77] T.P. Verney, "Role Perception Congruence, Performance, and Satisfaction," in D.J. Vredenburgh and R.S. Schuler (eds.), *Effective Management: Research and Application*, Proceedings of the 20th Annual Eastern Academy of Management (Pittsburgh, May 1983), pp. 24–27.

[78] Ibid.

[79] M. Van Sell, A.P. Brief, and R.S. Schuler, "Role Conflict and Role Ambiguity: Integration of the Literature and Directions for Future Research," *Human Relations* (January 1981), pp. 43–71; and A.G. Bedeian and A.A. Armenakis, "A Path-Analytic Study of the Consequences of Role Conflict and Ambiguity," *Academy of Management Journal* (June 1981), pp. 417–24.

[80] Shaw, *Group Dynamics*.

[81] B. Mullen, C. Symons, L. Hu, and E. Salas, "Group Size, Leadership Behavior, and Subordinate Satisfaction," *Journal of General Psychology* (April 1989), pp. 155–70.

CHAPTER

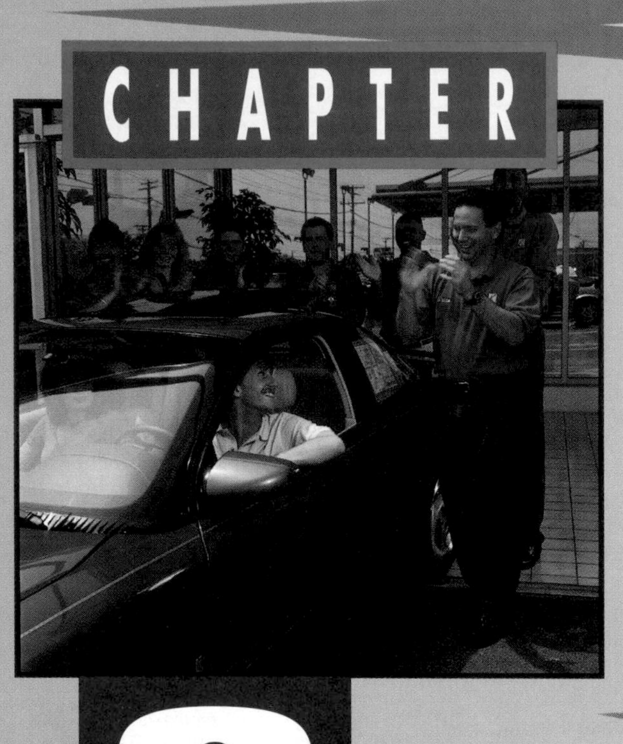

Teamwork at Saturn dealerships boosts employee morale and customer satisfaction. When buyers pick up their new Saturn, spirited team members from sales, service, parts, and reception give them a cheer, snap their picture, and hand them their keys. Working as a team, Saturn dealerships' employees are committed to achieving the company's goal of exceeding customer expectations.

9

UNDERSTANDING WORK TEAMS

CHAPTER OUTLINE

LEARNING OBJECTIVES

After studying this chapter, you should be able to:

1. Explain the growing popularity of teams in organizations
2. Contrast teams with groups
3. Identify three types of teams
4. Demonstrate the linkage between group concepts and high-performing teams
5. Identify ways managers can build trust among team members
6. Explain how organizations can create team players
7. Describe the current legal climate surrounding the use of teams in unionized settings
8. Explain how management can keep teams from becoming stagnant and rigid

Is it true that everyone's responsibility is, in reality, nobody's responsibility?
ANONYMOUS

The Boeing Co.'s senior management team (pictured above) has decided the future of aircraft design lies with replacing the firm's historical military-style hierarchy with self-regulating, cross-disciplinary work teams.[1]

As a case in point, the planning and development of Boeing's new 777-200 twin jet revolved around an internal collaboration of designers, production experts, maintenance people, customer service personnel, finance specialists, and even airline customers. Grouped into small teams of eight or ten, they were charged with the task of refining and meshing all aspects of the aircraft program right from the start. The intention was to have each team consider the aircraft as a whole and to act quickly on ideas, free from chain-of-command second guessing.

Boeing's past practice was to develop a plane sequentially, starting at the tail and working forward to the nose. First, suggestions would come from the designers, then the production people, then customer-support personnel, and so on. In the process, refinements snowballed. Worse, development costs soared just before the plane went into production as last-minute fixes were made. The inefficiencies of this system resulted in reduced productivity and increased costs.

By using teams on the 777 project, the company was able to "front-load" development costs. That is, it was able to get the bugs out of the aircraft before it ever got into production. For instance, the novel folding wingtips on the new 777 had one significant shortcoming: Airlines that wanted a traditional continuous wing couldn't get one. The company initially said that the best it could offer was a wing with foldable tips locked in place. Under the old Boeing way, the airlines would have had to accept the accompanying weight penalty. That's because a bureaucratic chasm separated workers who designed parts from those who made them. However, working closely with shop experts, 777 engineers devised a way to build the continuous wing on the same tool used to make the foldable wing—without disrupting the production work flow. Airline representatives ended up contributing more than 1,000 design changes. Similarly, Boeing's in-house maintenance experts offered hundreds of ideas that helped make the 777 cheaper to operate and faster to service.

Boeing's top management team believes the use of teams will allow the company to produce better products, faster, and at lower costs. They have decided to use the teamwork approach on the 737X, a passenger jet scheduled for delivery in 1997; and Boeing's defense group is using teams to design and build the F-22 fighter that is being planned for delivery to the U.S. Air Force in 2003.

Why Have Teams Become So Popular?

Twenty years ago, when companies like Volvo, Toyota, and General Foods introduced teams into their production processes, it made news because no one else was doing it. Today, it's just the opposite. It's the organization that *doesn't* use teams that has become newsworthy. Pick up almost any business periodical today and you'll read how teams have become an essential part of the way business is being done in companies like General Electric, AT&T, Hewlett-Packard, Motorola, Apple Computer, Shiseido, Federal Express, Chrysler, Saab, 3M Co., John Deere, Texas Instruments, Australian Airlines, Johnson & Johnson, Dayton Hudson, Shenandoah Life Insurance Co., Florida Power & Light, and Emerson Electric. Even the world-famous San Diego Zoo has restructured its native habitat zones around cross-departmental teams.

How do we explain the current popularity of teams? The evidence suggests that teams typically outperform individuals when the tasks being done require multiple skills, judgment, and experience.[2] As organizations have restructured themselves to compete more effectively and efficiently, they have turned

◆◆◆◆ OB in the News ◆◆◆◆

Building Teamwork in the Clinton Administration

One of the first things Bill Clinton did when he took over the U.S. presidency was to have his key administrative group go through some team-building exercises.

At Clinton's first cabinet meeting, which took place at a retreat in the woods at Camp David, two professional facilitators were brought in to help the new cabinet members learn to work more effectively with each other. Cabinet members were asked to bring their résumés and be prepared to talk about the passions in their lives. At the Saturday night session, they were also asked by the facilitators to talk about significant personal events they hadn't mentioned in their résumés. Clinton got the ball rolling by saying he had been fat as a boy, and the other kids had teased him.

The object of these team-building exercises is to get people to understand how they can use their own personal characteristics to contribute to the group. Since these cabinet members will be working closely together to solve numerous problems, Clinton and his staff decided they needed to learn more about each other and move from being just a group of people toward a coordinated team. This initial team-building experience was followed up by another four months later, then regular sessions every six months after that.

Using professional facilitators to make group meetings run smoother and to facilitate teamwork isn't new in the federal government. The Internal Revenue Service and the army have used them for years. But this is the first time this has been tried at the very top level of government.

Based on J.M. Perry, "Using 'Team Builders' May Become Common in Clinton Administration," *Wall Street Journal* (March 5, 1993), p. A7A.

to teams as a way to better utilize employee talents. Management has found that teams are more flexible and responsive to changing events than are traditional departments or other forms of permanent groupings. Teams have the capability to quickly assemble, deploy, refocus, and disband.

But don't overlook the motivational properties of teams. Consistent with our discussion in Chapter 7 of the role of employee involvement as a motivator, teams facilitate employee participation in operating decisions. For instance, some assembly-line workers at John Deere are part of sales teams that call on customers.[3] These workers know the products better than any traditional salesperson; and by traveling and speaking with farmers, these hourly workers develop new skills and become more involved in their jobs. So another explanation for the popularity of teams is that they are an effective means for management to democratize their organizations and increase employee motivation.

Teams vs. Groups: What's the Difference?

Groups and teams are not the same thing. In this section, we define and clarify the difference between a work group and a work team.[4]

In the last chapter, we defined a *group* as two or more individuals, interacting and interdependent, who have come together to achieve particular

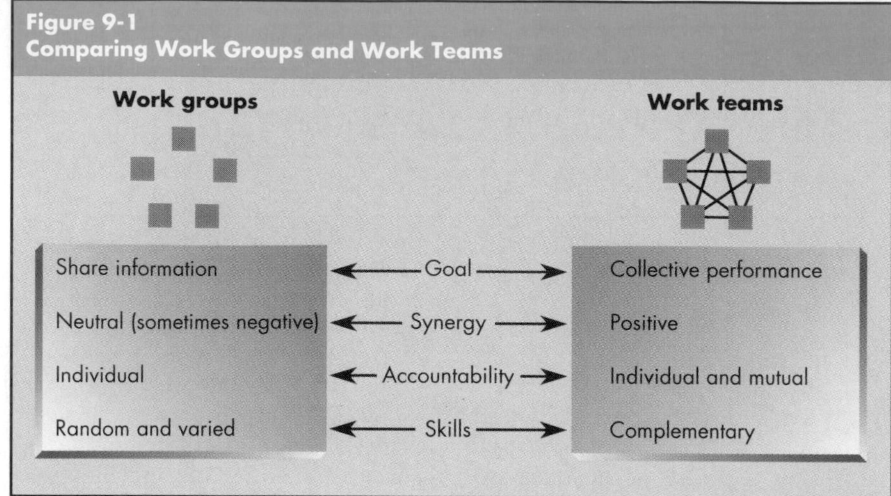

Figure 9-1
Comparing Work Groups and Work Teams

objectives. A **work group** is a group that interacts primarily to share information and to make decisions to help each member perform within his or her area of responsibility.

Work groups have no need or opportunity to engage in collective work that requires joint effort. So their performance is merely the summation of each group member's individual contribution. There is no positive synergy that would create an overall level of performance greater than the sum of the inputs.

work group
Group that interacts primarily to share information and to make decisions to help each member perform within his or her area of responsibility.

work team
Group whose individual efforts result in a performance that is greater than the sum of those individual inputs.

A **work team** generates positive synergy through coordinated effort. Their individual efforts result in a level of performance that is greater than the sum of those individual inputs. Figure 9-1 highlights the differences between work groups and work teams.

These definitions help clarify why so many organizations have recently restructured work processes around teams. Management is looking for that positive synergy that will allow their organizations to increase performance. The extensive use of teams creates the *potential* for an organization to generate greater outputs with no increase in inputs. Notice, however, we said "potential." Nothing inherently magical in the creation of teams assures the achievement of this positive synergy. Merely calling a *group* a *team* doesn't automatically increase its performance. As we show later in this chapter, successful or high-performing teams have certain common characteristics. If management hopes to gain increases in organizational performance through the use of teams, it will need to ensure that their teams possess these characteristics.

Types of Teams

Teams can be classified based on their objective. The three most common forms of teams you're likely to find in an organization are problem-solving teams, self-managed teams, and cross-functional teams (see Figure 9-2).

Problem-Solving Teams

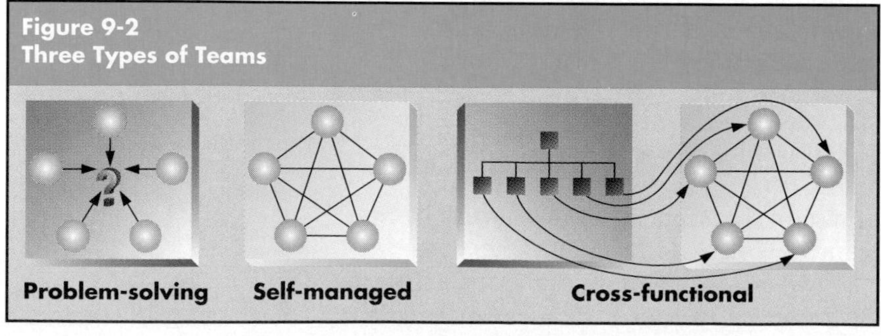

Figure 9-2
Three Types of Teams

If we look back 15 years or so, teams were just beginning to grow in popularity, and the form most of these teams took was similar. These were typically composed of 5 to 12 hourly employees from the same department who met for a few hours each week to discuss ways of improving quality, efficiency, and the work environment.[5] We call these **problem-solving teams**.

problem-solving teams
Groups of 5 to 12 employees from the same department who meet for a few hours each week to discuss ways of improving quality, efficiency, and the work environment.

In problem-solving teams, members share ideas or offer suggestions on how work processes and methods can be improved. Rarely, however, are these teams given the authority to unilaterally implement any of their suggested actions.

One of the most widely practiced application of problem-solving teams during the 1980s were quality circles.[6] As described in Chapter 7, these are work teams of eight to ten employees and supervisors who have a shared area of responsibility and meet regularly to discuss their quality problems, investigate causes of the problems, recommend solutions, and take corrective actions.

Self-Managed Work Teams

Problem-solving teams were on the right track, but they didn't go far enough in getting employees involved in work-related decisions and processes. This led to experimentations with truly autonomous teams that could not only solve problems but implement solutions and take full responsibility for outcomes.

Self-managed work teams are generally composed of 10 to 15 people who take on the responsibilities of their former supervisors.[7] Typically, this includes collective control over the pace of work, determination of work assignments, organization of breaks, and collective choice of inspection procedures. Fully self-managed work teams even select their own members and have the members evaluate each other's performance. As a result, supervisory positions take on decreased importance and may even be eliminated. At GE's locomotive-engine plant in Grove City, Pennsylvania, about 100 teams make most of the plant's decisions. They arrange the maintenance, schedule the work, and routinely authorize equipment purchases. One team spent $2 million and the plant manager never flinched. At the L-S Electrogalvanizing Co., in Cleveland, the entire plant is run by self-managed teams. They do their own scheduling, rotate jobs on their own, establish production targets, set pay scales that are linked to skills, fire coworkers, and do the hiring. "I never meet a new employee until his first day on the job," says the plant's general manager.[8]

self-managed work teams
Groups of 10 to 15 people who take on responsibilities of their former supervisors.

◆Teams have become an essential part of the way business is being done.

Xerox, General Motors, Coors Brewing, PepsiCo, Hewlett-Packard, Honeywell, M&M/Mars, and Aetna Life are just a few familiar names that have implemented self-managed work teams. Approximately one in five U.S. employers now use this form of teams, and experts predict that 40 to 50 percent of all U.S. workers could be managing themselves through such teams by the decade's end.[9]

Recent business periodicals have been chock full of articles describing successful applications of self-managed teams. Texas Instruments's defense group gives self-directed teams credit for helping it win the Malcolm Baldrige National Quality Award and for allowing it to achieve the same level of sales with 25 percent fewer employees.[10] Aid Association for Lutherans, one of the largest insurance and financial service companies in the United States, claims that self-managed teams were primarily responsible for helping increase employee satisfaction and allowing the company to increase business volume by 50 percent over a four-year period while cutting work force staff by 15 percent.[11] The Edy's Grand Ice Cream plant in Fort Wayne, Indiana, introduced self-managed teams in 1990, and attributes to them the plant's 39 percent reduction in costs and 57 percent increase in productivity.[12] Whole Foods Market, a health food

When the San Diego Zoo reorganized exhibits into bioclimatic zones that integrate animals and plants in cageless areas resembling their native habitat, it also changed the way employees work. Instead of operating the new exhibits the traditional way—where keepers tend the animals and gardeners tend the plants—the zoo formed self-managed teams and gave members joint responsibility for operating and maintaining their exhibit. The Tiger River exhibit shown here is self-managed by a team of mammal and bird specialists, horticulturalists, and maintenance and construction workers. Self-managed teams are helping the zoo achieve two of its key goals: enriching the visitor's experience and improving employees' quality of work life.

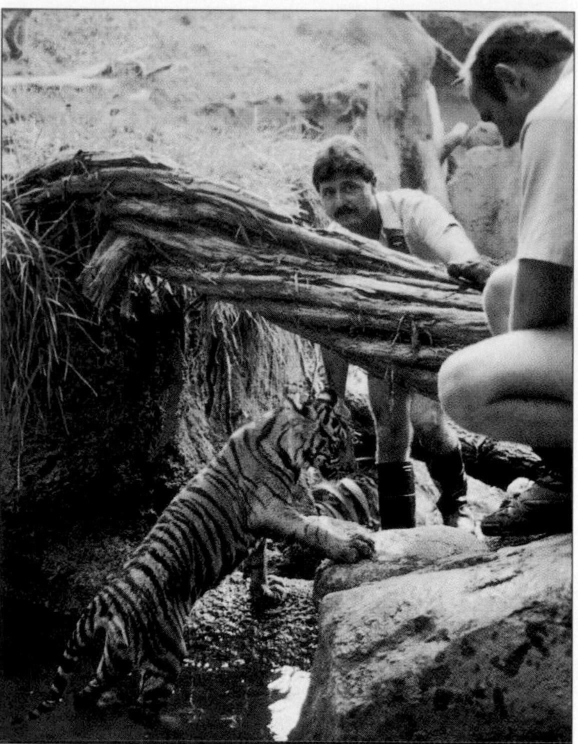

chain, claims self-managed teams are the main reason it doubled sales between 1989 and 1992, and is able to achieve a 3.7 percent operating margin compared to the average supermarket chain's 2.6.[13]

In spite of these impressive stories, a word of caution needs to be offered here. Some organizations have been disappointed with the results from self-managed teams. For instance, employees at Douglas Aircraft Co., which has been undergoing large layoffs, have revolted against self-managed teams. They've come to view cooperating with the team concept as an exercise in assisting one's own executioner.[14] The overall research on the effectiveness of self-managed work teams has not been uniformly positive.[15] For example, individuals on these teams do tend to report higher levels of job satisfaction. However, counter to conventional wisdom, employees on self-managed work teams seem to have higher absenteeism and turnover rates than do employees working in traditional work structures. The specific reasons for these findings are unclear, which implies a need for additional research.

Cross-Functional Teams

Our description of the Boeing Company's development efforts on the 777, at the opening of this chapter, illustrates the latest application of the team concept. This is the use of **cross-functional teams**. They are made up of employees from about the same hierarchical level, but from different work areas, who come together to accomplish a task.[16]

cross-functional teams
Employees from about the same hierarchical level, but from different work areas, who come together to accomplish a task.

Many organizations have used horizontal boundary-spanning groups for years. For example, IBM created a large task force in the 1960s—made up of employees from across departments in the company—to develop the highly successful System 360. And a **task force** is really nothing other than a temporary cross-functional team. Similarly, **committees** composed of members from across departmental lines are another example of cross-functional teams.

task force
Temporary cross-functional team.

committees
Groups made up of members from across departmental lines.

But the popularity of cross-discipline work teams exploded in the late 1980s. All the major automobile manufacturers—including Toyota, Honda, Nissan, BMW, GM, Ford, and Chrysler—have turned to these forms of teams in order to coordinate complex projects. For example, the Neon, Chrysler's ground-breaking subcompact, was developed completely by a cross-functional team. The new model was delivered in a speedy 42 months and for a fraction of what any other manufacturer's small car has cost.[17]

Motorola's Iridium Project illustrates why so many companies have turned to cross-functional teams.[18] This project is developing a huge network that will contain 66 satellites. "We realized at the beginning that there was no way we could manage a project of this size and complexity in the traditional way and still get it done on time," says the project's general manager. For the first year and a half of the project, a cross-functional team of 20 Motorola people met every morning. This has since been expanded to include diverse expertise from people in dozens of other companies as well, such as McDonnell Douglas, Raytheon, Russia's Khrunichev Enterprise, Martin Marietta, Scientific-Atlanta, and General Electric.

In summary, cross-functional teams are an effective way to allow people from diverse areas within an organization (or even between organizations) to exchange information, develop new ideas and solve problems, and coordinate complex projects. Of course, cross-functional teams are no picnic to manage.[19] Their early stages of development are often very time consuming as members learn to work with diversity and complexity. It takes time to build trust and teamwork, especially among people from different backgrounds, with different experiences and perspectives. Later in this chapter, we discuss ways managers can help facilitate and build trust among team members.

Tool giant Black & Decker spotted a big market opportunity in booming home improvement sales. So, in 1991, B&D formed a cross-functional team to develop Quantum, a new line of powerful mid-priced tools for the growing number of home repair enthusiasts. Charged with launching the new line in 1993, Team Quantum included 85 employees from design, engineering, marketing, finance, manufacturing, and other functions. In addition to crossing functions, the team spanned national boundaries, including employees from plants in the United States, Great Britain, Germany, Italy, and Switzerland. Here, Quantum team members display new products that they developed on schedule and that were racking up estimated sales of $30 to $40 million by the end of 1994.

◆◆◆◆ OB in the News ◆◆◆◆

Just Because You're Big, You Don't Have to Be Slow

The computer business lives and dies on new products produced in ever-shorter cycles. To survive in the industry, companies must continually develop innovative products and do so at lightning fast speed. One company that has learned how to do this successfully is Hewlett-Packard.

One of H-P's recent triumphs is something called the Kittyhawk Personal Storage Module. Weighing 1 ounce, and about the size of a matchbox, this tiny disk drive is powerful enough to store the equivalent of 20 long novels.

H-P brought the Kittyhawk to market in only 10 months, compared with the more traditional cycle time of about two years. And the secret to this speedy development process? Teams!

A tightly knit group of ten H-P engineers and marketers locked themselves up in a trailer separate from H-P's disk drive division in Boise, Idaho. Realizing they couldn't break the time barrier by doing everything alone, the team forged an unprecedented number of partnerships. AT&T's microelectronics group designed the Kittyhawk's circuitry. Read-Rite produced the head that reads and writes data. Citizen Watch of Japan helped design the manufacturing process—and today makes the Kittyhawk for H-P. Coordinating the entire project by using a team cut through the bureaucratic red tape that traditionally hinders large companies and allowed for diverse input and quick decision making.

Based on L. Grant, "Six Companies That Are Winning the Race," *Los Angeles Times* (January 17, 1993), p. D1.

Linking Teams and Group Concepts: Toward Creating High-Performance Teams

In the previous chapter, we introduced a number of basic group concepts. Let's now build on that introduction and look at how our knowledge of group processes can help us create more effective or high-performance teams.[20]

Size of Work Teams

The best work teams tend to be small. When they have more than about 10 to 12 members, it becomes difficult for them to get much done. They have trouble interacting constructively and agreeing on much. Large numbers of people usually can't develop the cohesiveness, commitment, and mutual accountability necessary to achieve high performance. So in designing effective teams, managers should keep them to under a dozen. If a natural working unit is larger and you want a team effort, consider breaking the group into subteams.

Abilities of Members

To perform effectively, a team requires three different types of skills. First, it needs people with *technical expertise*. Second, it needs people with the *problem-solving and decison-making skills* to be able to identify problems, generate alternatives, evaluate those alternatives, and make competent choices. Finally, teams need people with good listening, feedback, conflict resolution, and other *interpersonal skills.*

No team can achieve its performance potential without developing all three types of skills. The right mix is crucial. Too much of one at the expense of others will result in lower team performance. But teams don't need to have all the complementary skills in place at their beginning. It's not uncommon for one or more members to take responsibility to learn the skills in which the group is deficient, thereby allowing the team to reach its full potential.

Allocating Roles and Promoting Diversity

In Chapter 3, we demonstrated that people differ in terms of personality traits and that employee performance is enhanced when individuals are put into jobs that are compatible with their personalities. Well, the same thing is true with regard to filling positions on a work team. Teams have different needs and people should be selected for a team based on their personalities and preferences.

High-performing teams properly match people to various roles. For example, the basketball coaches that continually win over the long term have learned how to size up prospective players, identify their strengths and weaknesses, and then assign them to positions that best fit with their skills and allow them to contribute most to the overall team's performance. They recognize that winning teams need a variety of skills—for example, ball handlers, power scorers, three-point shooters, and shot blockers. Successful teams have people to fill all the key roles and have selected people to play in these roles based on their skills and preferences.

One stream of research has identified nine potential team roles that people prefer to play[21] (see Table 9-1). Let's briefly describe each and then consider their implications in creating high-performance teams.

CREATOR-INNOVATORS These are people who are usually imaginative and good at initiating ideas or concepts. They are typically very independent and prefer to work at their own pace in their own way and very often in their own time.

EXPLORER-PROMOTERS Explorer-Promoters like to take new ideas and champion their cause. They are good at picking up ideas from Creator-Innovators

Table 9-1 Nine Team Roles

Creator-Innovators: Initiate creative ideas.
Explorer-Promoters: Champion ideas after they're initiated.
Assessor-Developers: Analyze decision options.
Thruster-Organizers: Provide structure.
Concluder-Producers. Provide direction and follow through.
Controller-Inspectors: Check for details.
Upholder-Maintainers. Fight external battles.
Reporter-Advisers. Seek full information.
Linkers. Coordinate and integrate.

Source: C. Margerison and D. McCann, *Team Management: Practical New Approaches* (London: Mercury Books, 1990).

and finding the resources to promote these ideas. Their primary weakness is that they may not always have the patience and control skills to ensure the ideas are followed through in detail.

ASSESSOR-DEVELOPERS These individuals have strong analytical skills. They're at their best when given several different options to evaluate and analyze before a decision is made.

THRUSTER-ORGANIZERS Thruster-Organizers like to set up operating procedures to turn ideas into reality and get things done. They set goals, establish plans, organize people, and establish systems to ensure deadlines are met.

CONCLUDER-PRODUCERS Like Thruster-Organizers, Concluder-Producers are also concerned with results. Only their role focuses on insisting that deadlines are kept and ensuring that all commitments are followed through on. They take pride in producing a regular output to a standard.

CONTROLLER-INSPECTORS These are people with a high concern for establishing and enforcing rules and regulations. They are good at examining details and making sure that inaccuracies are avoided. They want to check all the facts and figures; they want to make sure the "i's are dotted" and the "t's are crossed."

UPHOLDERS-MAINTAINERS These people hold strong convictions about the way things should be done. They'll defend and fight the team's battles with outsiders while, at the same time, strongly supporting internal team members. Upholders-Maintainers are important because they provide team stability.

REPORTER-ADVISERS Reporter-Advisers are good listeners and don't tend to press their point of view on others. They tend to favor getting more information before making decisions. As such, they perform an important role in encouraging the team to seek additional information before making decisions and discouraging the team from making hasty decisions.

LINKERS The last role overlaps the others. It can be played by any of the previous eight. Linkers try to understand all views. They are coordinators and integrators. They dislike extremism and try to build cooperation among all team members. They recognize the various contributions that other team members can make and try to integrate people and activities despite the differences that may exist.

Although if forced to, most people can perform in any of these roles, most have two or three roles they strongly prefer. Managers need to understand the individual strengths that each person can bring to a team, select members with this in mind, and allocate work assignments that fit with members' preferred styles. By matching individual preferences with team role demands, managers increase the likelihood that the team members will work well together. The researchers who developed this framework argue that unsuccessful teams have an unbalanced portfolio of individual talents, with too much energy being expended in one area and not enough in other areas.

Having a Commitment to a Common Purpose

Does the team have a meaningful purpose that all members aspire to? This purpose is a vision. It's broader than specific goals. Effective teams have a common and meaningful purpose that provides direction, momentum, and commitment for members.

The development team at Apple Computer that designed the Macintosh, for example, were almost religiously committed to creating a user-friendly machine that would revolutionize the way people used computers. Production teams at Saturn Corp. are driven and united by the common purpose of building an American automobile that can successfully compete in terms of quality and price with the best of Japanese cars.

Members of successful teams put a tremendous amount of time and effort into discussing, shaping, and agreeing on a purpose that belongs to them both collectively and individually. This common purpose, when accepted by the team, becomes the equivalent of what celestial navigation is to a ship captain—it provides direction and guidance under any and all conditions.

Establishing Specific Goals

Successful teams translate their common purpose into specific, measurable, and realistic performance goals. Just as we demonstrated in Chapter 6 how goals lead individuals to higher performance, goals also energize teams. These specific goals facilitate clear communication. They also help teams maintain their focus on getting results. Thermos Corp., for example, created a cross-functional team in the fall of 1990 with the specific task of designing and building an innovative barbecue grill.[22] They agreed to create a new grill that looked like a handsome piece of furniture, didn't require pollutants like charcoal lighter, and cooked food that tasted good. The team also agreed on a rock solid deadline. They wanted to have their grill ready for the big National Hardware Show in August 1992. So they had a little less than two years to plan, design, and build their new product. And that's exactly what they did. They created the Thermos Thermal Electric Grill, which has since won four design awards and become one of the most successful new product launches in the company's history.

How did Thermos succeed in developing its new electric grill? Credit goes to Thermos CEO Monte Peterson, shown here (front) with the Lifestyle team that created the product. First, Peterson shared with employees his broad vision of product innovation, a vision that inspired employees to commit to developing a product completely different from competitors'. Then Peterson challenged employees by setting a specific goal: develop in two years a good-looking, easy-to-use, nonpolluting grill that gives food a barbequed flavor. Peterson provided the leadership and structure to achieve his vision by forming the flexible and cross-functional Lifestyle team from marketing, manufacturing, and engineering. The team replaced a bureaucratic structure organized by function.

Leadership and Structure

Goals define the team's end targets. But high-performance teams also need leadership and structure to provide focus and direction. Defining and agreeing on a common approach, for example, assures that the team is unified on the means for achieving its goals.

Team members must agree on who is to do what and ensure that all members contribute equally in sharing the workload. Additionally, the team needs to determine how schedules will be set, what skills need to be developed, how the group will resolve conflicts, and how the group will make and modify decisions. Agreeing on the specifics of work and how it fits together to integrate individual skills requires team leadership and structure. This, incidentally, can be provided directly by management or by the team members themselves as they fulfill Explorer-Promoter, Thruster-Organizer, Concluder-Producer, Upholder-Maintainer, and Linker roles.

Social Loafing and Accountability

We learned in the previous chapter that individuals can hide inside a group. They can engage in "social loafing" and coast on the group's effort because their individual contributions can't be identified. High-performing teams undermine this tendency by holding themselves accountable at both the individual and team level.

Successful teams make members individually and jointly accountable for the team's purpose, goals, and approach. They are clear on what they are individually responsible for and what they are jointly responsible for.

Appropriate Performance Evaluation and Reward Systems

How do you get team members to be both individually and jointly accountable? The traditional individually oriented evaluation and reward system must be modified to reflect team performance.[23]

Individual performance evaluations, fixed hourly wages, individual incentives, and the like, are not consistent with the development of high-performance teams. So in addition to evaluating and rewarding employees for their individual contribution, management should consider group-based appraisals, profit sharing, gain sharing, small-group incentives, and other system modifications that reinforce team effort and commitment.

Figure 9-3
Dimensions of Trust

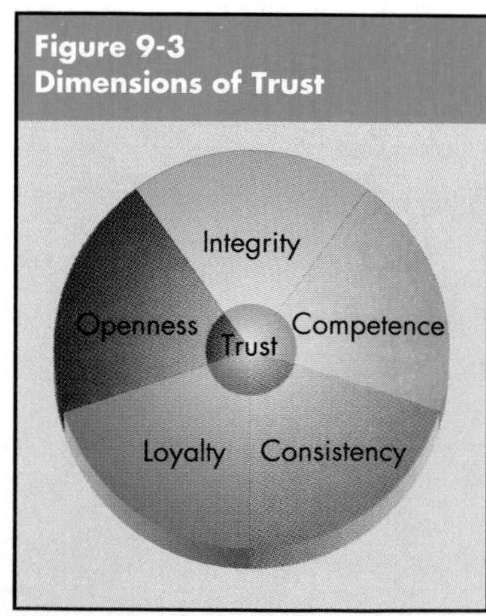

Developing High Mutual Trust

High-performance teams are characterized by high mutual **trust** among members. That is, members believe in the integrity, character, and ability of each other. But as you know from personal relationships, trust is fragile. It takes a long time to build, can be easily destroyed, and is hard to regain.[24] Also, since trust begets trust and distrust begets distrust, maintaining trust requires careful attention by management.

DIMENSIONS OF TRUST Recent research has identified five dimensions that underly the concept of trust (see Figure 9-3)[25]:

- **Integrity**: Honesty and truthfulness
- **Competence**: Technical and interpersonal knowledge and skills

- **Consistency**: Reliability, predictability, and good judgment in handling situations
- **Loyalty**: Willingness to protect and save face for a person
- **Openness**: Willingness to share ideas and information freely

In terms of trust among team members, it's been found that the importance of these five dimensions is relatively constant: integrity > competence > loyalty > consistency > openness.[26] Moreover, integrity and competence are the most critical characteristics that an individual looks for in determining another's trustworthiness. Integrity seems to be rated highest because "without a perception of the other's 'moral character' and 'basic honesty,' other dimensions of trust were meaningless."[27] The high ranking of competence is probably due to the need for peer interaction by team members in order to successfully complete their job responsibilities.

trust
Characteristic of high-performance teams where members believe in the integrity, character, and ability of each other.

integrity
Honesty and truthfulness.

competence
Technical and interpersonal knowledge and skills.

consistency
Reliability, predictability, and good judgment in handling situations.

loyalty
Willingness to protect and save face for a person.

openness
Willingness to share ideas and information freely.

HOW DO YOU BUILD TRUST? Managers and team leaders have a significant impact on a team's trust climate. As a result, managers and team leaders need to build trust between themselves and team members. The following summarizes ways you can build trust.[28]

Demonstrate you're working for others' interests as well as your own. All of us are concerned with our own self-interest. But if others see you using them, your job, or the organization for your personal goals to the exclusion of your team, department, and organization's interests, your credibility will be undermined.

Be a team player. Support your work team both through words and actions. Defend the team and team members when they're attacked by outsiders. This will demonstrate your loyalty to your work group.

Practice openness. Mistrust comes as much from what people don't know as from what they do know. Openness leads to confidence and trust. So keep people informed, explain your decisions, be candid about problems, and fully disclose relevant information.

Be fair. Before making decisions or taking actions, consider how others will perceive them in terms of objectivity and fairness. Give credit where it's due, be objective and impartial in performance evaluations, and pay attention to equity perceptions in reward distributions.

Speak your feelings. Managers and leaders who convey only hard facts come across as cold and distant. By sharing your feelings, others will see you as real and human. They will know who you are and will increase their respect for you.

Show consistency in the basic values that guide your decision making. Mistrust comes from not knowing what to expect. Take the time to think about your values and beliefs. Then let them consistently guide your decisions. When you know your central purpose, your actions will follow accordingly, and you'll project a consistency that earns trust.

Maintain confidences. You trust those you can confide in and rely on. So if people tell you something in confidence, they need to feel assured you won't discuss it with others or betray that confidence. If people perceive you as someone who leaks personal confidences or someone who can't be depended on, you won't be perceived as trustworthy.

Demonstrate competence. Develop the admiration and respect of others by demonstrating technical and professional ability and good business sense. Pay particular attention to developing and displaying your communication, team building, and other interpersonal skills.

Turning Individuals into Team Players

To this point, we've made a strong case for the value and growing popularity of teams. But many people are not inherently team players. They're loners or people who want to be recognized for their individual achievements. There are also a great many organizations that have historically nurtured individual accomplishments. They have created competitive work environments where only the strong survive. If these organizations adopt teams, what do they do about the selfish, "I-got-to-look-out-for-me" employees they've created? And finally, as we discussed in Chapter 2, countries differ in terms of how they rate on individualism and collectivism. Teams fit well with countries that score high on collectivism. But what if an organization wants to introduce teams into a work population that is made up largely of individuals born and raised in a highly individualistic society? As one writer so aptly put it in describing the role of teams in the United States, "Americans don't grow up learning how to function in teams. In school we never receive a team report card or learn the names of the team of sailors who traveled with Columbus to America."[29] This limitation would obviously be just as true of Canadians, British, Australians, and others from highly individualistic societies.

The Challenge

The previous points are meant to dramatize that one substantial barrier to using work teams is individual resistance. An employee's success is no longer defined in terms of individual performance. To perform well as team members, individuals must be able to communicate openly and honestly; to confront differences and resolve conflicts; and to sublimate personal goals for the good of the team. For many employees, this is a difficult—sometimes impossible—task.

The challenge of creating team players will be greatest where (1) the national culture is highly individualistic, and (2) the teams are being introduced

How can organizations turn individuals into team players? NASA knows how. Developing team players takes time and training. Astronauts are high-achieving individuals who undergo an extremely competitive selection process to become astronauts. But when they become part of a shuttle crew, astronauts must work harmoniously with other crew members to achieve their mission's goal. NASA shapes astronauts into team players by training them to work together—including brushing their teeth together—every day for a year or two before their shuttle mission. By stressing that the mission's success depends on effective teamwork, NASA teaches astronauts how to compromise and make decisions that benefit the entire team.

into an established organization that has historically valued individual achievement. This describes, for instance, what faced managers at AT&T, Ford, Motorola, and other large U.S.-based companies. These firms prospered by hiring and rewarding corporate stars; and they bred a competitive climate that encouraged individual achievement and recognition. Employees in these types of firms can be jolted by this sudden shift to the importance of team play.[30] One veteran employee of a large company, who had done very well by working alone, described the experience of joining a team: "I'm learning my lesson. I just had my first negative performance appraisal in 20 years."[31]

In contrast, the challenge for management is less demanding when teams are introduced where employees have strong collectivist values—such as in Japan or Mexico—or in new organizations that use teams as their initial form for structuring work. Saturn Corp., for instance, is an American organization and owned by General Motors. But the company was designed around teams from its inception. Everyone at Saturn was initially hired with the knowledge they would be working in teams. And the ability to be a good team player was a basic hiring qualification that all new employees had to meet.

Shaping Team Players

The following summarizes the primary options for managers who are trying to turn individuals into team players.

SELECTION Some people already possess the interpersonal skills to be effective team players. When hiring team members, in addition to the technical skills required to fill the job, care should be taken to ensure that candidates can fulfill their team roles as well as technical requirements.

But many job candidates don't have team skills. This is especially true for those socialized around individual contributions. When faced with such candidates, managers basically have three options. The candidates can undergo training to "make them into team players." If this isn't possible or doesn't work, the other two options are to transfer the individual to another unit within the organization without teams (if this possibility exists), or not to hire the candidate. In established organizations that decide to redesign jobs around teams, it should be expected that some employees will resist being team players and may be untrainable. Unfortunately, such people typically become casualties of the team approach.

TRAINING On a more optimistic note, a large proportion of people raised on the importance of individual accomplishment can be trained to become team players. Training specialists conduct exercises that allow employees to experience the satisfaction that teamwork can provide. They typically offer workshops to help employees improve their problem-solving, communication, negotiation, conflict management, and coaching skills. Employees also learn the five-stage group development model described in Chapter 8. At Bell Atlantic, for example, trainers focus on how a team goes through various stages before it finally gels. And employees are reminded of the importance of patience—because teams take longer to make decisions than if employees were acting alone.[32]

Emerson Electric's Speciality Motor Division in Missouri, for instance, has achieved remarkable success in getting its 650-member work force not only to accept, but to welcome, team training.[33] Outside consultants were brought in to give workers practical skills for working in teams. After less than a year, employees have enthusiastically accepted the value of teamwork.

REWARDS The reward system needs to be reworked to encourage cooperative efforts rather than competitive ones. For instance, Martin Marietta's Space Launch Systems Company has organized its 1,400 employees into teams. Rewards are structured to return a percentage increase in the bottom line to the team members based on the achievement of the team's performance goals.

Promotions, pay raises, and other forms of recognition should be given to individuals for how effective they are as a collaborative team member. This doesn't mean individual contribution is ignored, but rather that it is balanced with selfless contributions to the team. Examples of behaviors that should be rewarded include training new colleagues, sharing information with teammates, helping resolve team conflicts, and mastering new skills that your team needs but in which it's deficient.

Lastly, don't forget the intrinsic rewards that employees can receive from teamwork. Teams provide camaraderie. It's exciting and satisfying to be an integral part of a successful team. The opportunity to engage in personal development and to help teammates grow can be a very satisfying and rewarding experience for employees.

Contemporary Issues in Managing Teams

In this section, we address four issues related to managing teams: (1) How are federal laws undermining efforts to implement teams in unionized organizations? (2) How do teams facilitate the adoption of total quality management? (3) What are the implications of work force diversity on team performance? and (4) How does management reenergize stagnant teams?

Teams and Labor Law

Historically, the relationship between labor and management was built on conflict. The interests of management and labor were seen as basically at odds, each treating the other as the enemy.

But times have changed. Management has become increasingly aware that successful efforts to increase productivity, improve quality, and lower costs require employee involvement and commitment. Similarly, labor unions have come to recognize that they can help their members more by cooperating with management than by fighting them.

Ironically, current U.S. labor laws, passed in an era of mistrust and antagonism between management and labor, have become barriers to these parties putting their differences aside and becoming cooperative partners. As a case in point, the National Labor Relations Act was passed in 1935 to encourage collective bargaining and to balance workers' power against that of management. That legislation also sought to eliminate the then widespread practice of firms setting up company unions for the sole purpose of undermining efforts of outside unions to organize their employees. So the law prohibits employers from creating or supporting a "labor organization." Ironically, these outmoded labor laws are now working against management–labor cooperation. Specifically, they are making it difficult for companies to establish employee work teams.[34]

Recently, the National Labor Relations Board (NLRB), the federal agency that rules on labor disputes, decided against two firms—Electromation, Inc., a small Indiana electrical components manufacturer, and a Du Pont chemical plant in New Jersey—that had set up worker committees and empowered them to handle issues like pay and plant safety. The NLRB ruled that in both instances management dominated the formation and operation of the teams, which met the broad definition of labor organizations and thus behaved as company-run unions. For instance, in the Electromation case, the NLRB found that management clearly dominated the teams: Management had proposed them, defined their purpose, limited their authority, and helped determine their makeup.

The current legal environment doesn't outlaw work teams in the U.S. per se. What it does is require management to give its work teams independence. When work teams become dominated by management, they are likely to be interpreted as "sham unions"—groups that perform some functions of labor unions but are controlled by management.

What team behaviors would indicate that the team is *not* dominated by management? Some examples might include choosing team members through secret ballot elections, giving teams wide latitude in deciding what issues to deal with, permitting teams to meet apart from management, and specifying that employee teams are not susceptible to dissolution by management whim. The key theme the NLRB seems to be conveying is that where work teams are introduced, they must truly have the power to make decisions and act independent of management.

Table 9-2 suggests some key questions that might indicate a team violates national labor law.

Teams and Total Quality Management

One of the central characteristics of total quality management (TQM) is the use of teams. But why are teams an essential part of TQM?

The essence of TQM is process improvement, and employee involvement is the linchpin of process improvement. In other words, TQM requires management to give employees the encouragement to share ideas and act on what they suggest. As one author put it, "None of the various TQM processes and techniques will catch on and be applied except in work teams. All such techniques and processes require high levels of communication and contact, response and adaptation, and coordination and sequencing. They require, in short, the environment that can be supplied only by superior work teams."[35]

Teams provide the natural vehicle for employees to share ideas and to implement improvements. As stated by Gil Mosard, a TQM specialist at McDonnell

Table 9-2 When Teams Are Illegal in the United States

An affirmative answer to any one of the following questions could mean a team violates national labor law:

- Does management dominate the teams by controlling their formation, setting their goals, or deciding how they operate?
- Does the team address issues affecting other, nonteam, employees?
- Does the team deal with traditional bargaining issues such as wages and working conditions?
- Does the team deal with any supervisors, managers, or executives on any issue?

Source: Based on A. Bernstein, "Making Teamwork Work—and Appeasing Uncle Sam," *Business Week* (January 25, 1993), p. 101.

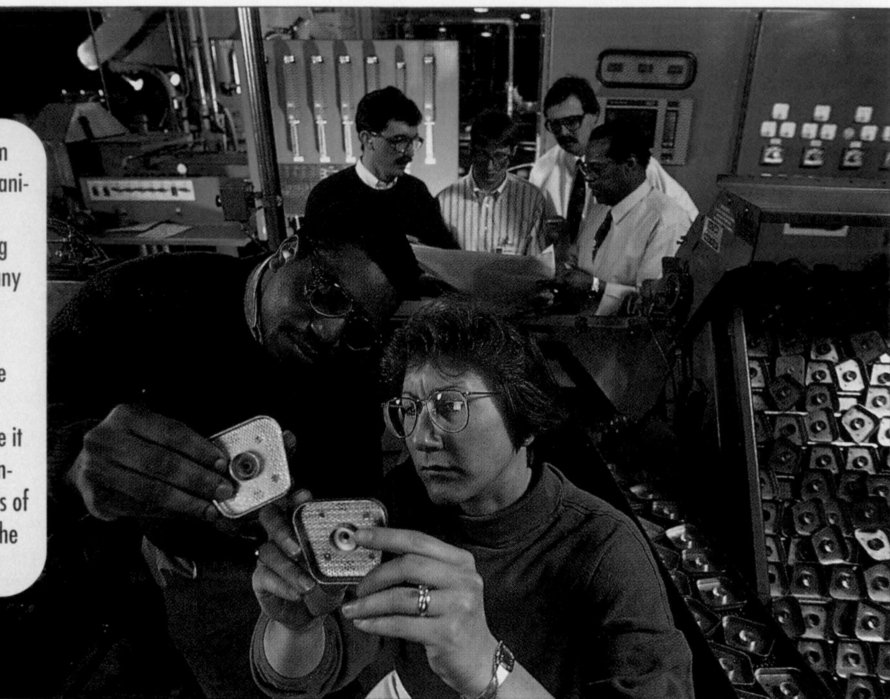

AlliedSignal initiated its total quality program by changing from a department-oriented organization to one governed by cross-functional teams focused on satisfying customers. During the first phase of its quality effort, the company trained teams to identify, design, implement, and measure process improvements. It then asked teams to find ways to drastically reduce the cycle times of their work processes. One Aerospace/Automotive team reduced the time it takes to produce and deliver aircraft brake linings from 90 days to 30 days. Here, members of the team inspect an assembly used to make the brake linings.

Douglas, "When your measurement system tells you your process is out of control, you need teamwork for structured problem-solving. Not everyone needs to know how to do all kinds of fancy control charts for performance tracking, but everybody does need to know where their process stands so they can judge if it is improving."[36] Examples from Ford Motor Co. and Amana Refrigeration, Inc. illustrate how teams are being used in TQM programs.[37]

Ford began its TQM efforts in the early 1980s with teams as the primary organizing mechanism. "Because this business is so complex, you can't make an impact on it without a team approach," noted one Ford manager. In designing their quality problem-solving teams, Ford's management identified five goals. The teams should (1) be small enough to be efficient and effective; (2) be properly trained in the skills their members will need; (3) be allocated enough time to work on the problems they plan to address; (4) be given the authority to resolve the problems and implement corrective action; and (5) each have a designated "champion" whose job it is to help the team get around roadblocks that arise.

At Amana, cross-functional task forces made up of people from different levels within the company are used to deal with quality problems that cut across departmental lines. The various task forces each have a unique area of problem-solving responsibility. For instance, one handles in-plant products, another deals with items that arise outside the production facility, and still another focuses its attention specifically on supplier problems. Amana claims the use of these teams has improved vertical and horizontal communication within the company and substantially reduced both the number of units that don't meet company specifications and the number of service problems in the field.

◆◆◆◆ OB in the News ◆◆◆◆

A Look at One of America's Best Performing Manufacturing Plants

The Pueblo, Colorado, plant of Unisys Corp.'s Government Systems Group makes printed circuit card assemblies, computers, and information processing systems for the Department of Defense and other government agencies. Opened in 1986, and now employing 550 people, the plant was recently recognized for being one of the highest performing manufacturing facilities in the United States.

The plant won accolades for the speed with which it was able to build the Weasel Attack Signal Processor, the computer aboard the F-4 Wild Weasel aircraft that knocks out surface-to-air missile launchers. The original contract called for the plant to deliver these computers to the Air Force in 18 months. But with the Persian Gulf War imminent, the Air Force wanted that shaved to 12 months.

Employee work teams at the Pueblo plant immediately began looking for ways to cut time. Teams were sent to vendors' facilities to help them shorten their lead times. Special teams were formed to cut assembly time in half. Still other teams were set up to trim test time. The plant ended up beating the Air Force deadline. They delivered the computers in a remarkable nine months!

Since the Gulf War, the plant has continued to demonstrate ongoing improvements in productivity. It has cut the cycle time for its printed circuit card assemblies from four weeks to only six or seven days. Over the last three years it has trimmed its work-in-process inventory by 71 percent, total inventory by 60 percent, and total costs by 50 percent. And productivity has soared 55 percent.

Management attributes a large part of the plant's success to strong communications among employees, the use of teams, and employee involvement.

Open communication contributes to the feeling of "family" that visitors to the plant quickly sense—a feeling that helps explain the plant's low turnover rate of 10.8 percent (8 percent below the industry average) and why only six employees chose to take advantage of the company's lucrative early retirement plan. "People like to work here," sums up Pamela White, a senior subcontract administrator. "They like the empowerment and ownership we have."

Today the Pueblo plant has 93 teams, which employees are allowed to form without management approval. The goal of Melvin Murray, the plant's manager, is to have the plant completely run by self-managing teams by 1998.

Based on W.H. Miller, "Unisys Corp.," *Industry Week* (October 18, 1993), pp. 33–34.

Teams and Work Force Diversity

Managing diversity on teams is a balancing act (see Table 9-3). Diversity typically provides fresh perspectives on issues but it makes it more difficult to unify the team and reach agreements.

Table 9-3 Advantages and Disadvantages of Diversity

Advantages	Disadvantages
Multiple perspectives	Ambiguity
Greater openness to new ideas	Complexity
Multiple interpretations	Confusion
Increased creativity	Miscommunication
Increased flexibility	Difficulty in reaching a single agreement
Increased problem-solving skills	Difficulty in agreeing on specific actions

Source: Adapted from N.J. Adler, *International Dimensions of Organizational Behavior*, 2nd ed. (Boston: PWS-Kent, 1991), p. 99.

The strongest case for diversity on work teams is when these teams are engaged in problem-solving and decision-making tasks.[38] Heterogeneous teams bring multiple perspectives to the discussion, thus increasing the likelihood that the team will identify creative or unique solutions. Additionally, the lack of a common perspective usually means diverse teams spend more time discussing issues, which decreases the chances that a weak alternative will be chosen. However, keep in mind that the positive contribution that diversity makes to decision-making teams undoubtedly declines over time. As we pointed out in the previous chapter, diverse groups have more difficulty working together and solving problems, *but this dissipates with time*. Expect the value-added component of diverse teams to increase as members become more familiar with each other and the team becomes more cohesive.

Studies tell us that members of cohesive teams have greater satisfaction, lower absenteeism, and lower attrition from the group.[39] Yet cohesiveness is likely to be lower on diverse teams.[40] So here is a potential negative of diversity: It is detrimental to group cohesiveness. But again referring back to the last chapter, we found that the relationship between cohesiveness and group productivity was moderated by performance-related norms. We suggest that if the norms of the team are supportive of diversity, then a team can maximize the value of heterogeneity while, at the same time, achieving the benefits of high cohesiveness.[41] This makes a strong case for team members to participate in diversity training.

Reinvigorating Mature Teams

Just because a team is performing well at a given point in time is no assurance that it will continue to do so.[42] Effective teams can become stagnant. Initial enthusiasm can give way to apathy. Time can diminish the positive value from diverse perspectives as cohesiveness increases.

In terms of the five-stage development model introduced in the previous chapter, teams don't automatically stay at the "performing stage." Familiarity breeds apathy. Success can lead to complacency. And maturity brings less openness to novel ideas and innovation.

Mature teams are particularly prone to suffer from groupthink. Members begin to believe they can read everyone's mind so they assume they know what everyone is thinking. As a result, team members become reluctant to express their thoughts and less likely to challenge each other.

Another source of problems for mature teams is that their early successes are often due to having taken on easy tasks. It's normal for new teams to begin by taking on those issues and problems they can handle most easily. But as time passes, the easy problems become solved and the team has to begin to confront more difficult issues. At this point, the team has typically developed entrenched processes and routines, and members are reluctant to change the "perfect" system they've already worked out. The results can often be disastrous. Internal team processes no longer work smoothly. Communication bogs down. Conflicts increase because problems are less likely to have obvious solutions. And team performance can drop dramatically.

What can be done to reinvigorate mature teams? We offer four suggestions: (1) *Prepare members to deal with the problems of maturity*. Remind team members that they're not unique—all successful teams have to confront maturity issues. They shouldn't feel let down or lose their confidence in the team concept when the initial euphoria subsides and conflicts surface. (2) *Offer refresher training*. When teams get into ruts, it may help to provide them with refresher training in communication, conflict resolution, team processes, and similar skills. This can help members regain confidence and trust in one another. (3) *Offer advanced training*. The skills that worked with easy problems may be insufficient for more difficult ones. So mature teams can often benefit from advanced training to help members develop stronger problem-solving, interpersonal, and technical skills. (4) *Encourage teams to treat their development as a constant learning experience*. Like TQM, teams should approach their own development as part of a search for continuous improvement. Teams should look for ways to improve, to confront member fears and frustrations, and to use conflict as a learning opportunity.

Summary and Implications for Managers

Few trends have influenced employee jobs as much as the massive movement to introduce teams into the workplace. The shift from working alone to working on teams requires employees to cooperate with others, share information, confront differences, and sublimate personal interests for the greater good of the team.

High-performing teams have been found to have common characteristics. They tend to be small. They contain people with three different types of skills: technical, problem-solving and decision-making, and interpersonal. They properly match people to various roles. These teams have a commitment to a common purpose, establish specific goals, and have the leadership and structure to provide focus and direction. They also hold themselves accountable at both the individual and team level by having well-designed evaluation and reward systems. Finally, high-performing teams are characterized by high mutual trust among members.

Because individualistic organizations and societies attract and reward individual accomplishment, it is more difficult to create team players in these environments. To make the conversion, management should try to select individuals with the interpersonal skills to be effective team players, provide training to develop teamwork skills, and reward individuals for cooperative efforts.

Once teams are mature and performing effectively, management's job isn't over. This is because mature teams can become stagnant and complacent. Managers need to support mature teams with advice, guidance, and training if these teams are to continue to improve.

For Review

1. Why did Boeing adopt teams to design the 777-200 twin jet?
2. How can teams increase employee motivation?
3. Contrast *self-managed* and *cross-functional* teams.
4. What are *problem-solving teams*?
5. List and describe the nine potential team roles.
6. How do high-performing teams minimize social loafing?
7. How do high-performing teams minimize groupthink?
8. What are the five dimensions that underlie the concept of trust?
9. How are federal laws undermining efforts to implement teams in the United States?
10. Contrast the pros and cons of having diverse teams.

For Discussion

1. Don't teams create conflict? Isn't conflict bad? Why, then, would management support the concept of teams?
2. Are there factors in the Japanese society that make teams more acceptable in the workplace than in the United States or Canada? Explain.
3. What problems might surface on teams at each stage in the five-stage group development model?
4. How do you think member expectation might affect team performance?
5. Would you prefer to work alone or as part of a team? Why? How do you think your answer compares with others in your class?

Point

The Value of Teams

The value of teams is now well known. Let's summarize the primary benefits that experts agree can result from the introduction of work teams.

Increased employee motivation. Work teams enhance employee involvement. They typically make jobs more interesting. They help employees meet their social needs. They also create social pressures on slackers to exert higher levels of effort in order to remain in the team's good graces. Consistent with the research on social facilitation, individuals are likely to perform better when they're in the presence of other people.

Higher levels of productivity. Teams have the potential to create positive synergy. In recent years, the introduction of teams in most organizations has been associated with cuts in staff. What management has done is to use the positive synergy to get the same or greater output from fewer people. This translates into higher levels of productivity.

Increased employee satisfaction. Employees have a need for affiliation. Working in teams can help meet this need by increasing worker interactions and creating camaraderie among team members. Moreover, people who are part of a satisfying team climate cope better with stress and enjoy their jobs more.

Common commitment to goals. Teams encourage individuals to sublimate their individual goals for those of the group. The process of developing a common purpose, committing to that purpose, and agreeing on specific goals—combined with the social pressures exerted by the team—result in a high unity of commitment to team goals.

Improved communication. Self-managed teams create interpersonal dependencies that require members to interact considerably more than when they work on jobs alone. Similarly, cross-functional teams create interfunctional dependencies and increase organizational-wide communication.

Expanded job skills. The implementation of teams almost always comes with expanded job training. Through this training, employees build their technical, decision-making, and interpersonal skills.

Organizational flexibility. Teams focus on processes rather than functions. They encourage cross training, so members can do each other's jobs, and expansion of skills. It's not unusual for compensation on teams to be based on the number of skills a member has acquired. This expansion of skills increases organizational flexibility. Work can be reorganized and workers allocated, as needed, to meet changing conditions.

Does the introduction of teams *always* achieve these benefits? No! For instance, a study by Ernst & Young found that forming teams to investigate and improve products and processes led to measurable improvement only in organizations that were performing poorly in their markets in terms of profit, productivity, and quality.* In medium-performing companies, the study found, bottom-line results were unaffected by team activities. In high-performing companies, the introduction of new team-based work systems actually lowered performance.

There are obviously contingency factors that influence the acceptance and success of teams. Some examples might be tasks that benefit from combining multiple skills; when the market will pay a premium for improved quality or innovation; with employees who value continual learning and enjoy complex tasks; and where management–employee relations already have a strong basis of mutual trust. Nevertheless, we can't ignore the reality that the team movement currently has tremendous momentum and reflects management's belief that teams can be successful in a wide range of settings.

*Cited in R. Zemke, "Rethinking the Rush to Team Up," *Training* (November 1993), p. 56.

counterPoint

The Tyranny of a Team Ideology

Beliefs about the benefits of teams have achieved an unquestioned place in the study of organizations. Teams, it's argued, are able to satisfy everything at once: individual needs (for sociability, self-actualization, job participation); organizational needs (for productivity, flexibility, effectiveness); and even society's needs for alleviating the malaise of alienation and other by-products of modern industrial society. We need to step back and take a harder look at teams and the assumptions that underlie the team ideology. The following assesses four of those assumptions.

Mature teams are task-oriented and have successfully minimized the negative influences of other group forces. Task-oriented teams still experience antitask behavior, and indeed have much in common with other types of groups. For instance, they often suffer from infighting over assignments and decision outcomes, low participation rates, and member apathy.

Individual, group, and organizational goals can all be integrated into common team goals. Contrary to what team advocates assume, people are not so simply motivated by the sociability and self-actualization supposedly offered by work teams. These teams suffer from competitiveness, conflict, and hostility. And rarely do team members support and help one another as difficult ideas and issues are worked through. Additionally, contrary to the notion that teams increase job satisfaction, the evidence suggests that individuals experience substantial and continuing stress as team members. Rarely is the team experience satisfying. Moreover, certain types of workers and certain types of work are better suited to solitary work situations, and individuals with particular work styles will never perform well on a team. For the hard-driving, competitive person who thrives on individual achievement, the cult of the team player is likely to produce only frustration and stress.

Participative or shared leadership is always effective. The team ideology oversimplifies the requirement for leadership. It downplays the importance of leadership by suggesting that high-performing teams can dispense with, or ignore, leadership concerns. It assumes that the team's commitment to a common goal unites all team action and thus reduces the need for leadership. Group process theorists are unanimous that all groups will experience phases of identifying with, rejecting, and working through relations with authority. This process cannot be eliminated simply by eliminating leaders from groups. The abdication of leadership can, in effect, paralyze teams.

The team environment drives out the subversive forces of politics, power, and conflict that divert groups from efficiently doing their work. Recipes for effective teams rate them on the quality of decision making, communication, cohesion, clarity and acceptance of goals, acceptance of minority views, and other criteria. Such recipes betray the fact that teams are made up of people with self-interests who are prepared to make deals, reward favorites, punish enemies, and engage in similar behaviors to further those self-interests. The result is that teams are political entities, where members play power games and engage in conflicts. Neither training nor organizational actions will alter the intrinsically political nature of teams.

The argument here has been that the team ideology, under the banner of benefits for all, ignores that teams are frequently used to camouflage coercion under the pretense of maintaining cohesion; conceal conflict under the guise of consensus; convert conformity into a semblance of creativity; delay action in the supposed interests of consultation; legitimize lack of leadership; and disguise expedient arguments and personal agendas. Teams do not necessarily provide fulfillment of individual needs, nor do they necessarily contribute to individual satisfaction and performance or organizational effectiveness. On the contrary, it is likely that the infatuation with teams and making every employee part of a team results in organizations not getting the best performance from many of their members.

Based on A. Sinclair, "The Tyranny of a Team Ideology," *Organization Studies*, Vol. 13, No. 4 (1992), pp. 611–26.

Learning About Yourself Exercise

Do Others See Me as Trustworthy?

To get some insight into how others may view your trustworthiness, complete this questionnaire. First, however, identify the person who will be evaluating you (e.g., a work colleague, friend, supervisor, team leader).

Use the following scale to score each question:

Strongly Disagree 1 2 3 4 5 6 7 8 9 10 Strongly Agree

	Score
1. I can be expected to play fair.	_____
2. You can confide in me and know I will keep what's told to me in confidence.	_____
3. I can be counted on to tell the truth.	_____
4. I would never intentionally misrepresent my point of view to others.	_____
5. If I promise to do a favor, I can be counted on to carry out that promise.	_____
6. If I have an appointment with someone, I can be counted on to show up promptly.	_____
7. If I'm lent money, I can be counted on to pay it back as soon as possible.	_____

Turn to page A-28 for scoring directions and key.

Source: Based on C. Johnson-George and W.C. Swap, "Measurement of Specific Interpersonal Trust: Construction and Validation of a Scale to Assess Trust in a Specific Other," *Journal of Personality and Social Psychology* (December 1982), pp. 1306–17.

Working with Others Exercise

Team Experience Exercise

1. Form into groups of four or five.
2. Each person in the group will share a *positive* experience he or she has had while participating on a team.
3. After step 2 is complete, each person in the group will share a *negative* experience he or she has had while participating on a team.
4. Group members will now analyze the shared responses:
   a. What common characteristics, if any, do you see when members described positive experiences? Negative experiences?
   b. What implications can the group draw from these shared experiences for the design of teams? For making teams more effective?

Ethical Dilemma Exercise

Do I Have to Be a Team Player?

After earning his bachelor's degree in economics from Princeton, Todd Donnelly took a job with the British Broadcasting Company (BBC) in London. He was assigned to the business group in the news division. His job was to provide producers and newspeople with research material for their on-air stories. Todd took the job knowing it wasn't how he wanted to spend his whole professional career. But he thought the job would be interesting, he'd gain some valuable business experience, and he'd get the opportunity to spend a few years in Europe.

During his third year at the BBC, Todd decided it was time to go back to school, get his MBA, and move into the fast track. He applied and was accepted at the Harvard Business School.

The two years Todd spent at Harvard were demanding but exciting. He flourished in Harvard's competitive environment. Todd relished the opportunity to analyze complex cases and argue the merits of his conclusions with his classmates. When graduation day came, Todd ranked in the top 10 percent of his class.

During his last semester at Harvard, Todd interviewed with a number of companies. In spite of several highly attractive offers from management consulting firms, Todd decided he wanted to get into the production side of a business. When Ford Motor Co. offered him a job in inventory management, Todd accepted.

"I'd been with Ford about four months when my boss told me that I was being assigned to a cross-functional team that would look at ways we could reduce inventory costs," Todd began. "This team would essentially be a permanent body. The other team members came from supplier relations, cost accounting, transportation, and production systems. Let me be honest with you. I was definitely upset with this decision.

"I'm not a team kind of guy. I didn't join clubs in high school. I was on the track team and I did well, but track is an individual sport. We were a team only in the sense that we rode together in the same bus to away meets. In college, I avoided the whole fraternity thing. Some people call me a loner. I don't think that's true. I can work well with others, but I hate meetings and committees. They waste so much time. And anytime you're working with a group, you've got all these different personalities that you have to adjust for. I'm an independent operator. Give me a job and I'll do it. I work harder than anyone I know. But I don't want my performance to be dependent on the other people in my group. They won't work as hard as I will. Someone is sure to try to shirk some of their responsibilities. I just don't want to be a team player."

Does Todd have a choice? Should his boss give him the option of joining the inventory cost reduction team? Or in the 1990s, should everyone be expected to be a team player? Is it unethical for a manager to *require* an employee to do his or her job as part of a team? What do *you* think?

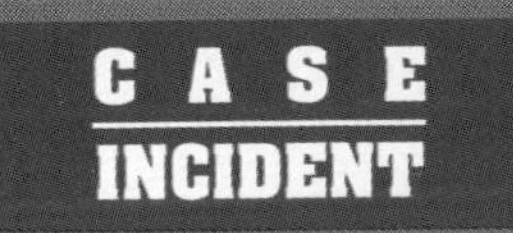

XEL Communications

XEL Communications is a small fish in a big pond. The company employs 180 people and manufactures custom circuit boards. It competes against the likes of Northern Telecom and AT&T.

Bill Sanko and his partners bought the company from GTE Corp. And GTE is its major customer. But Bill wants to cut down his dependence on GTE.

He needs to sell more to the Baby Bells and to big industrial customers that operate their own phone systems.

Bill's problem is that to compete successfully for new business he has to dramatically improve XEL's agility. He wants lightning turnaround of orders, quicker than any big company could manage. He wants speedy response to customer needs. All done with close attention to cost. Unfortunately, XEL is not designed for speed or flexibility. Its costs are also too high to give the firm a competitive advantage.

For example, on the shop floor, it takes XEL eight weeks to get a product through the production cycle—from start-up to finished product. This process ties up a lot of money in inventory and frustrates customers who want quick delivery. Sanko believes high-performing teams could cut production time down to four days or less. The company's structure is also burdensome. Line workers report to supervisors, who report to unit or departmental managers, who report on up the ladder to Sanko and a crew of top executives. This high vertical structure delays decision making and increases expenses. "If a hardware engineer needs some software help, he goes to his manager," Sanko says. "The manager says, 'Go write it up.' Then the hardware manager takes the software manager to lunch and they talk about it."

Sanko has decided to reorganize his company around self-managed teams. He thinks a well-designed team structure can help him better satisfy his customers by cutting cycle time from eight weeks down to four days, significantly improve quality, cut assembly costs by 25 percent, and reduce inventory costs by 50 percent. Ambitious goals? You bet! But Bill Sanko thinks it's possible. Moreover, achieving these goals might be necessary if his company is to survive.

Questions

1. Describe in detail the steps you think Sanko should take in planning and implementing self-managed teams.
2. What problems should Sanko be on the lookout for?

Source: Based on J. Case, "What the Experts Forgot to Mention," INC. (September 1993), pp. 66–78.

Assembly Line Teams at Square D

Square D is a manufacturer of electrical equipment. Their Lexington, Kentucky, plant introduced teams in 1988 in order to improve quality, speed orders, and increase productivity.

Every day begins with a team meeting at the Lexington plant. The 800 employees are divided into 20- to 30-person self-managed teams. Each team is like its own little factory within the factory. Team members control their own work and make decisions without checking with management. The teams are fully responsible for their products, from start to finish.

The decision by management to introduce teams in 1988 wasn't made in a vacuum. Management recognized that employees would need training in order to effectively convert from a system where people did narrow, specialized tasks on an assembly line and never saw the finished product they were working on. That training has included exercises to help employees learn how to work as part of a team, solve problems, handle new technology, and service customers better. The plant continues to spend 4 percent of its payroll on training.

The results at Lexington are impressive. Employees no longer have to wait for maintenance personnel when equipment breaks down. They've been trained in maintenance and can fix their own machines. Employees exhibit newfound pride in their work and greater commitment to doing a good job. And management is pleased with the 75 percent reduction in the rejection rate and the ability to process orders in an average of 3 days versus 6 weeks under the old system.

Questions

1. Not all efforts to introduce teams are successful. Is there anything in the case of Square D that suggests why this program is doing so well?
2. What is there about team processes that can explain how self-managed teams could dramatically cut rejection rates and processing time from what had existed previously with high specialization?

Source: "Assembly Line Teams Are Better Trained and More Efficient," *World News Tonight* (February 24, 1993).

Suggestions for Further Reading

ANCONA, D.G., and D.F. CALDWELL, "Bridging the Boundary: External Activity and Performance in Organizational Teams," *Administrative Science Quarterly* (December 1992), pp. 634–65.

BANTZ, C.R., "Cultural Diversity and Group Cross-Cultural Team Research," *Journal of Applied Communication Research* (February 1993), pp. 1–20.

DUMAINE, B., "The Trouble with Teams," *Fortune* (September 5, 1994), pp. 86–92.

GERSICK, C.J.G. (ed.), *Group Management: Current Issues in Practice and Research* (Brookfield, VT: Dartmouth, 1995).

GOODMAN, P.S., R. DEVADAS, and T.L. GRIFFITH-HUGHSON, "Groups and Productivity: Analyzing the Effectiveness of Self-Managing Teams," in J.P. Cambell, R.J. Campell, and associates (eds.), *Productivity in Organizations* (San Francisco: Jossey-Bass, 1988).

KATZENBACH, J.R., and D.K. SMITH, "The Discipline of Teams," *Harvard Business Review* (March-April 1993), pp. 111–20.

ORSBURN, J.D., L. MORAN, E. MUSSELWHITE, and J.H. ZENGER, *Self-Directed Work Teams: The New American Challenge* (Homewood, IL: Business One Irwin, 1990).

SHONK, J.H., *Team-Based Organizations* (Homewood, IL: Business One Irwin, 1992).

SUNDSTROM, E., K.P. DE MEUSE, and D. FUTRELL, "Work Teams: Applications and Effectiveness," *American Psychologist* (February 1990), pp. 120–33.

ZENGER, J.H., E. MUSSELWHITE, K. HURSON, and C. PERRIN, *Leading Teams: Mastering the New Role* (Homewood, IL: Business One Irwin, 1994).

Notes

[1] Based on B. Acohido, "Boeing Workforce Tries New Direction," *Dallas Morning News* (May 5, 1991), p. H8; D. Jones Yang, "When the Going Gets Tough, Boeing Gets Touchy-Feely," *Business Week* (January 17, 1994), pp. 65–66; and W.J. Cook, "The End of the Plain Plane," *U.S. News & World Report* (April 11, 1994), pp. 43–46.

[2] See, for example, D. Tjosvold, *Working Together to Get Things Done: Managing for Organizational Productivity* (Lexington, MA: Lexington Books, 1986); D. Tjosvold, *Team Organization: An Enduring Competitive Advantage* (Chichester, England: Wiley, 1991); J. Lipnack and J. Stamps, *The TeamNet Factor* (Essex Junction, VT: Oliver Wight, 1993); and J.R. Katzenbach and D.K. Smith, *The Wisdom of Teams* (Boston: Harvard Business School Press, 1993).

[3] K. Kelly, "The New Soul of John Deere," *Business Week* (January 31, 1994), pp. 64–66.

[4] This section is based on J.R. Katzenbach and D.K. Smith, *The Wisdom of Teams*, pp. 21, 45, 85; and D.C. Kinlaw, *Developing Superior Work Teams* (Lexington, MA: Lexington Books, 1991), pp. 3–21.

[5] J.H. Shonk, *Team-Based Organizations* (Homewood, IL: Business One Irwin, 1992); and M.A. Verespej, "When Workers Get New Roles," *Industry Week* (February 3, 1992), p. 11.

[6] M.L. Marks, P.H. Mirvis, E.J. Hackett, and J.F. Grady, Jr., "Employee Participation in a Quality Circle Program: Impact on Quality of Work Life, Productivity, and Absenteeism," *Journal of Applied Psychology* (February 1986), pp. 61–69; T.R. Miller, "The Quality Circle Phenomenon: A Review and Appraisal," *SAM Advanced Management Journal* (Winter 1989), pp. 4–7; and E.E. Adams, Jr., "Quality Circle Performance," *Journal of Management* (March 1991), pp. 25–39.

[7] See, for example, D. Barry, "Managing the Bossless Team," *Organizational Dynamics* (Summer 1991), pp. 31–47; and J.R. Barker, "Tightening the Iron Cage: Concertive Control in Self-Managing Teams," *Administrative Science Quarterly* (September 1993), pp. 408–37.

[8] J. Hillkirk, "Self-Directed Work Teams Give TI Lift," *USA Today* (December 20, 1993), p. 8B; and M.A. Verespej, "Worker-Managers," *Industry Week* (May 16, 1994), p. 30.

[9] J.S. Lublin, "Trying to Increase Worker Productivity, More Employers Alter Management Style," *Wall Street Journal* (February 13, 1992), p. B1.

[10] J. Hillkirk, "Self-Directed Work Teams."

[11] "A Conversation with Charles Dull," *Organizational Dynamics* (Summer 1993), pp. 57–70.

[12] T.B. Kirker, "Edy's Grand Ice Cream," *Industry Week* (October 18, 1993), pp. 29–32.

[13] W. Zellner, "Moving Tofu into the Mainstream," *Business Week* (May 25, 1992), p. 94.

[14] R. Zemke, "Rethinking the Rush to Team Up," *Training* (November 1993), pp. 55–61.

[15] See, for instance, T.D. Wall, N.J. Kemp, P.R. Jackson, and C.W. Clegg, "Outcomes of Autonomous Workgroups: A Long-Term Field Experiment," *Academy of Management Journal* (June 1986), pp. 280–304; and J.L. Cordery, W.S. Mueller, and L.M. Smith, "Attitudinal and Behavioral Effects of Autonomous Group Working: A Longitudinal Field Study," *Academy of Management Journal* (June 1991), pp. 464–76.

[16] J. Lipnack and J. Stamps, *The TeamNet Factor*, pp. 14–17.

[17] D. Woodruff, "Chrysler's Neon: Is This the Small Car Detroit Couldn't Build?" *Business Week* (May 3, 1993), pp. 116–26.

[18] T.B. Kinni, "Boundary-Busting Teamwork," *Industry Week* (March 21, 1994), pp. 72–78.

[19] "Cross-Functional Obstacles," *Training* (May 1994), pp. 125–26.

[20] This section is largely based on K. Hess, *Creating the High-Performance Team* (New York: Wiley, 1987); and J.R. Katzenbach and D.K. Smith, *The Wisdom of Teams*, pp. 43–64.

[21] Based on C. Margerison and D. McCann, *Team Management: Practical New Approaches* (London: Mercury Books, 1990).

[22] B. Dumaine, "Payoff from the New Management," *Fortune* (December 13, 1993), pp. 103–10.

[23] See S.T. Johnson, "Work Teams: What's Ahead in Work Design and Rewards Management," *Compensation & Benefits Review* (March-April 1993), pp. 35–41.

[24] F.K. Sonnenberg, "Trust Me . . . Trust Me Not," *Industry Week* (August 16, 1993), pp. 22–28.

[25] P.L. Schindler and C.C. Thomas, "The Structure of Interpersonal Trust in the Workplace," *Psychological Reports* (October 1993), pp. 563–73.

[26] Ibid.

[27] J.K. Butler Jr. and R.S. Cantrell, "A Behavioral Decision Theory Approach to Modeling Dyadic Trust in Superiors and Subordinates," *Psychological Reports* (August 1984), pp. 19–28.

[28] Based on F. Bartolome, "Nobody Trusts the Boss Completely—Now What?" *Harvard Business Review* (March-April 1989), pp. 135–42; and P. Pascarella, "15 Ways to Win People's Trust," *Industry Week* (February 1, 1993), pp. 47–51.

[29] D. Harrington-Mackin, *The Team Building Tool Kit* (New York: AMACOM, 1994), p. 53.

[30] T.D. Schellhardt, "To Be a Star Among Equals, Be a Team Player," *Wall Street Journal* (April 20, 1994), p. B1.

[31] Ibid.

[32] Ibid.

[33] "Teaming Up for Success," *Training* (January 1994), p. S41.

[34] See A. Bernstein, "Making Teamwork Work—And Appeasing Uncle Sam," *Business Week* (January 25, 1993), p. 101; K.G. Salwen, "DuPont Is Told It Must Disband Nonunion Panels," *Wall Street Journal* (June 7, 1993), p. A2; and "Study Commends Worker Participation, But Says Labor Laws May Be Limiting," *Wall Street Journal* (June 3, 1994), p. A2.

[35] D.C. Kinlaw, *Developing Superior Work Teams*, p. 43.

[36] B. Krone, "Total Quality Management: An American Odyssey," *The Bureaucrat* (Fall 1990), p. 37.

[37] *Profiles in Quality: Blueprints for Action from 50 Leading Companies* (Boston: Allyn & Bacon, 1991), pp. 71–72, 76–77.

[38] See the review of the literature in S.E. Jackson, V.K. Stone, and E.B. Alvarez, "Socialization Amidst Diversity: The Impact of Demographics on Work Team Oldtimers and Newcomers," in L.L. Cummings and B.M. Staw (eds.), *Research in Organizational Behavior*, Vol. 15 (Greenwich, CT: JAI Press, 1993), pp. 64.

[39] R.M. Stogdill, "Group Productivity, Drive, and Cohesiveness," *Organizational Behavior and Human Performance* (February 1972), pp. 36–43.

[40] J.E. McGrath, *Groups: Interaction and Performance* (Englewood Cliffs, NJ: Prentice-Hall, 1984).

[41] This idea is proposed in S.E. Jackson, V.K. Stone, and E.B. Alvarez, "Socialization Amidst Diversity," p. 68.

[42] This section is based on M. Kaeter, "Repotting Mature Work Teams," *Training* (April 1994) (Supplement), pp. 4–6.

CHAPTER

Rapid communication is key to customer excellence throughout Arco Chemical Company's European operations. Teams from multiple departments use feedback from customer surveys and visits to improve responsiveness to customer needs.

10

COMMUNICATION

CHAPTER OUTLINE

LEARNING OBJECTIVES

After studying this chapter, you should be able to:

1. Define *communication* and list its four functions.
2. Identify factors affecting the use of the grapevine.
3. List common barriers to effective communication.
4. Describe an effective communication program in an organization undergoing dramatic change.
5. Outline the behaviors related to effective active listening.
6. Contrast the meaning of talk for men versus women.
7. Describe potential problems in cross-cultural communication.
8. Discuss how technology is changing organizational communication.

I didn't say that I didn't say it. I said that I didn't say that I said it.
I want to make that very clear.
G. Romney

Can a few words literally mean the difference between life and death? They did on January 25, 1990. On that date, a communication breakdown between the pilots on Avianca Flight 52 and the air traffic controllers at New York's Kennedy airport resulted in a crash that killed 73 people.[1]

At 7:40 P.M. on January 25, Flight 52 was cruising at 37,000 feet above the southern New Jersey coast. The aircraft had enough fuel to last nearly two hours—a healthy cushion, since the plane was less than half an hour from touchdown. Then a series of delays began. First, at 8 P.M., the controllers at Kennedy told Flight 52 it would have to circle in a holding pattern because of heavy traffic. At 8:45, the Avianca copilot advised Kennedy they were "running low on fuel." The controller at Kennedy acknowledged the message, but the plane was not cleared to land until 9:24. In the interim, the Avianca crew relayed no information to Kennedy that an emergency was imminent, yet the cockpit crew spoke worriedly among themselves about their dwindling fuel supplies.

Flight 52's first attempt to land at 9:24 was aborted. The plane had come in too low and poor visibility made a safe landing uncertain. When the Kennedy controllers gave Flight 52's pilot new instructions for a second attempt, the crew again told them they were running low on fuel. But the pilot told the controllers that the newly assigned flight path was "OK." At 9:32, two of Flight 52's engines lost power. A minute later, the other two cut off. The plane, out of fuel, crashed on Long Island at 9:34 P.M.

When investigators reviewed cockpit tapes and talked with the controllers involved, they learned a communication breakdown caused this tragedy. A closer look at the events of that evening help to explain why a simple message was neither clearly transmitted nor adequately received.

First, the pilots kept saying they were "running low on fuel." Traffic controllers told investigators it is fairly common for pilots to use this phrase. In times of delay, controllers assume everyone has a fuel problem. However, had the pilots uttered the words "fuel emergency," the controllers would have been obligated to direct the jet ahead of all others and clear it to land as soon as possible. As one controller put it, if a pilot "declares an emergency, all rules go out the window and we get the guy to the airport as quickly as possible." Unfortunately, the pilots of Flight 52 never used the word *emergency*, so the people at Kennedy never understood the true nature of the pilots' problem.

Second, the vocal tone of the pilots on Flight 52 didn't convey the severity or urgency of the fuel problem to the air traffic controllers. Many of these controllers are trained to pick up subtle tones in a pilot's voice in such situations. While the crew of Flight 52 expressed considerable concern among themselves about the fuel problem, their voice tones in communicating to Kennedy were cool and professional.

Finally, the culture and traditions of pilots and airport authorities may have made the pilot of Flight 52 reluctant to declare an emergency. A pilot's expertise and pride can be at stake in such a situation. Declaration of a formal emergency requires the pilot to complete a wealth of paperwork. Moreover, if a pilot is found negligent in calculating how much fuel was needed for a flight, the Federal Aviation Administration can suspend his license. These negative reinforcers strongly discourage pilots from calling an emergency.

The Avianca Flight 52 tragedy demonstrates the importance of good communication to any group's or organization's effectiveness. In fact, research indicates that poor communication is probably the most frequently cited source of interpersonal conflict.[2] Because individuals spend nearly 70 percent of their waking hours communicating—writing, reading, speaking, listening—it seems reasonable to conclude that one of the most inhibiting forces to successful group performance is a lack of effective communication.

No group can exist without communication: the transference of meaning among its members. It is only through transmitting meaning from one person to another that information and ideas can be conveyed. Communication, however, is more than merely imparting meaning. It must also be understood. In a group where one member speaks only German and the others do not know German, the individual speaking German will not be fully understood. Therefore, **communication** must include both the *transference* and the *understanding of meaning*.

communication
The transference and understanding of meaning.

Figure 10-1
Source: *Business Week*, May 16, 1994, p. 8. Reprinted by special permission. Copyright © 1994 by McGraw-Hill, Inc.

An idea, no matter how great, is useless until it is transmitted and understood by others. Perfect communication, if there were such a thing, would exist when a thought or an idea was transmitted so the mental picture perceived by the receiver was exactly the same as that envisioned by the sender. Although elementary in theory, perfect communication is never achieved in practice, for reasons we expand on later.

> ◆An idea, no matter how great, is useless until it is transmitted and understood by others.

Before making too many generalizations concerning communication and problems in communicating effectively, we need to review briefly the functions that communication performs and describe the communication process.

Functions of Communication

Communication serves four major functions within a group or organization: control, motivation, emotional expression, and information.[3]

Communication acts to *control* member behavior in several ways. Organizations have authority hierarchies and formal guidelines that employees are required to follow. When employees, for instance, are required to first communi-

Founders of Home Depot keep employees informed and inspired during live "Breakfast with Bernie & Arthur" broadcasts. During the shows, Chief Executive Bernard Marcus (shown here) and President Arthur Blank speak directly to all employees, briefing them on new developments, sharing sales and profit results, and taking call-in questions. Home Depot's culture is based on candid, face-to-face communication. Marcus and Blank spend up to 40 percent of their time in stores talking with employees, who are encouraged to express differences of opinion without fear of being fired or demoted.

cate any job-related grievance to their immediate boss, to follow their job description, or to comply with company policies, communication is performing a control function. But informal communication also controls behavior. When work groups tease or harass a member who produces too much (and makes the rest of the group look bad), they are informally communicating with, and controlling, the member's behavior.

Communication fosters *motivation* by clarifying to employees what is to be done, how well they are doing, and what can be done to improve performance if it's subpar. We saw this operating in our review of goal-setting and reinforcement theories in Chapter 6. The formation of specific goals, feedback on progress toward the goals, and reinforcement of desired behavior all stimulate motivation and require communication.

For many employees, their work group is a primary source for social interaction. The communication that takes place within the group is a fundamental mechanism by which members show their frustrations and feelings of satisfaction. Communication, therefore, provides a release for the *emotional expression* of feelings and for fulfillment of social needs.

The final function that communication performs relates to its role in facilitating decision making. It provides the *information* that individuals and groups need to make decisions by transmitting the data to identify and evaluate alternative choices.

No one of these four functions should be seen as being more important than the others. For groups to perform effectively, they need to maintain some form of control over members, stimulate members to perform, provide a means for emotional expression, and make decision choices. You can assume almost every communication interaction that takes place in a group or organization performs one or more of these four functions.

The Communication Process

Communication can be thought of as a process or flow. Communication problems occur when there are deviations or blockages in that flow. In this section, we describe the process in terms of a communication model, consider how distortions can disrupt the process, and introduce the concept of communication apprehension as another potential disruption.

A Communication Model

Before communication can take place, a purpose, expressed as a message to be conveyed, is needed. It passes between a source (the sender) and a receiver. The message is encoded (converted to symbolic form) and is passed by way of some medium (channel) to the receiver, who retranslates (decodes) the message initiated by the sender. The result is a transference of meaning from one person to another.[4]

communication process
The steps between a source and a receiver that result in the transference and understanding of meaning.

encoding
Converting a communication message to symbolic form.

Figure 10-2 depicts the **communication process**. This model is made up of seven parts: (1) the communication source, (2) encoding, (3) the message, (4) the channel, (5) decoding, (6) the receiver, and (7) feedback.

The source initiates a message by **encoding** a thought. Four conditions have been described that affect the encoded message: skill, attitudes, knowledge, and the social-cultural system.

My success in communicating to you depends on my writing skills; if the authors of textbooks are without the requisite writing skills, their messages will

Figure 10-2
The Communication Process Model

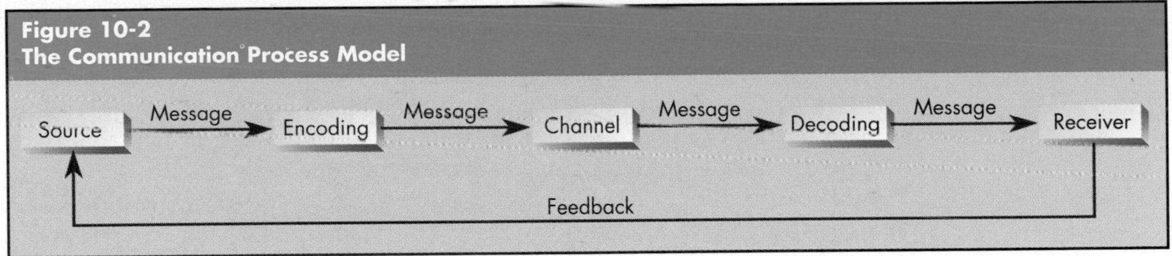

not reach students in the form desired. One's total communicative success includes speaking, reading, listening, and reasoning skills as well. As we discussed in Chapter 5, our attitudes influence our behavior. We hold predisposed ideas on numerous topics, and our communications are affected by these attitudes. Further, we are restricted in our communicative activity by the extent of our knowledge of the particular topic. We cannot communicate what we don't know, and should our knowledge be too extensive, it's possible our receiver will not understand our message. Clearly, the amount of knowledge the source holds about his or her subject will affect the message he or she seeks to transfer. And, finally, just as attitudes influence our behavior, so does our position in the social-cultural system in which we exist. Your beliefs and values, all part of your culture, act to influence you as a communicative source.

The **message** is the actual physical product from the source encoding. "When we speak, the speech is the message. When we write, the writing is the message. When we paint, the picture is the message. When we gesture, the movements of our arms, the expressions on our faces are the message."[5] Our message is affected by the code or group of symbols we use to transfer meaning, the content of the message itself, and the decisions we make in selecting and arranging both codes and content.

message
What is communicated.

The **channel** is the medium through which the message travels. It is selected by the source, who must determine which channel is formal and which one is informal. Formal channels are established by the organization and transmit messages that pertain to the job-related activities of members. They traditionally follow the authority network within the organization. Other forms of messages, such as personal or social, follow the informal channels in the organization.

channel
The medium through which a communication message travels.

The receiver is the object to whom the message is directed. But before the message can be received, the symbols in it must be translated into a form that can be understood by the receiver. This is the **decoding** of the message. Just as the encoder was limited by his or her skills, attitudes, knowledge, and social-cultural system, the receiver is equally restricted. Just as the source must be skillful in writing or speaking, the receiver must be skillful in reading or listening, and both must be able to reason. One's knowledge, attitudes, and cultural background influence one's ability to receive, just as they do the ability to send.

decoding
Retranslating a sender's communication message.

The final link in the communication process is a **feedback loop**. "If a communication source decodes the message that he encodes, if the message is put back into his system, we have feedback."[6] Feedback is the check on how successful we have been in transferring our messages as originally intended. It determines whether understanding has been achieved.

feedback loop
The final link in the communication process; puts the message back into the system as a check against misunderstandings.

Sources of Distortion

Unfortunately, most of the seven components in the process model have the potential to create distortion and, therefore, impinge on the goal of communicating perfectly. These sources of distortion explain why the message that is decoded by the receiver is rarely the exact message the sender intended.

If the encoding is done carelessly, the message decoded by the sender will have been distorted. The message itself can also cause distortion. The poor choice of symbols and confusion in the content of the message are frequent problem areas. Of course, the channel can distort a communication if a poor one is selected or if the noise level is high. The receiver represents the final potential source for distortion. His or her prejudices, knowledge, perceptual skills, attention span, and care in decoding are all factors that can result in interpreting the message somewhat differently than envisioned by the sender.

Communication Apprehension

communication apprehension Undue tension and anxiety about oral communication, written communication, or both.

Another major roadblock to effective communication is that some people—an estimated 5 to 20 percent of the population[7]—suffer from debilitating **communication apprehension** or anxiety. Although lots of people dread speaking in front of a group, communication apprehension is a more serious problem because it affects a whole category of communication techniques. People who suffer from it experience undue tension and anxiety in oral communication, written communication, or both.[8] For example, oral apprehensives may find it extremely difficult to talk with others face to face or become extremely anxious when they have to use the telephone. As a result, they may rely on memos or letters to convey messages when a phone call would not only be faster but more appropriate.

Studies demonstrate that oral-communication apprehensives avoid situations requiring them to engage in oral communication.[9] We should expect to find some self-selection in jobs so such individuals don't take positions, such as teacher, where oral communication is a dominant requirement.[10] But almost all jobs require some oral communication. And of greater concern is the evidence that high-oral-communication apprehensives distort the communication demands of their jobs in order to minimize the need for communication.[11] So we need to be aware of a set of people in organizations who severely limit their oral communication and rationalize this practice by telling themselves that more communication isn't necessary for them to do their job effectively.

Communication Fundamentals

A working knowledge of communication requires a basic understanding of some fundamental concepts. In this section, we review those concepts. Specifically, we look at the flow patterns of communication, compare formal and informal communication networks, describe the importance of nonverbal communication, consider how individuals select communication channels, and summarize the major barriers to effective communication.

Direction of Communication

Communication can flow vertically or laterally. The vertical dimension can be further divided into downward and upward directions.[12]

DOWNWARD Communication that flows from one level of a group or organization to a lower level is a downward communication.

When we think of managers communicating with subordinates, the downward pattern is the one we usually think of. It is used by group leaders and managers to assign goals, provide job instructions, inform underlings of policies and procedures, point out problems that need attention, and offer feedback about performance. But downward communication doesn't have to be oral or face-to-face contact. When management sends letters to employees' homes to advise them of the organization's new sick leave policy, it is using downward communication.

UPWARD Upward communication flows to a higher level in the group or organization. It is used to provide feedback to higher-ups, inform them of progress toward goals, and relay current problems. Upward communication keeps managers aware of how employees feel about their jobs, coworkers, and the organization in general. Managers also rely on upward communication for ideas on how things can be improved.

Some organizational examples of upward communication are performance reports prepared by lower management for review by middle and top management, suggestion boxes, employee attitude surveys, grievance procedures, superior–subordinate discussions, and informal gripe sessions where employees have the opportunity to identify and discuss problems with their boss or representatives of higher management.

For example, Federal Express prides itself on its computerized upward communication program.[13] All 68,000 employees annually complete climate surveys and reviews of management. This program was cited as a key human resources strength by the Malcom Baldrige National Quality Award examiners when Federal Express won the honor.

LATERAL When communication takes place among members of the same work group, among members of work groups at the same level, among managers at the same level, or among any horizontally equivalent personnel, we describe it as lateral communications.

Why would there be a need for horizontal communications if a group or organization's vertical communications are effective? The answer is that horizontal communications are often necessary to save time and facilitate

Top managers of Reliable Cartage Company aggressively seek employee feedback. They distribute a questionnaire to their 117 employees, asking them for their views of company wages, benefits, work policies, and working environment. Each month, Executive Vice President John Mooney (right) puts on a uniform and spends the day with a driver, listening to problems, complaints, and ideas for improvement. Reliable pays attention to the smallest details on employees' minds. President George Enguita (center) says, "Those little things have to be heard."

coordination. In some cases, these lateral relationships are formally sanctioned. Often, they are informally created to short-circuit the vertical hierarchy and expedite action. So lateral communications can, from management's viewpoint, be good or bad. Since strict adherence to the formal vertical structure for all communications can impede the efficient and accurate transfer of information, lateral communications can be beneficial. In such cases, they occur with the knowledge and support of superiors. But they can create dysfunctional conflicts when the formal vertical channels are breached, when members go above or around their superiors to get things done, or when bosses find out that actions have been taken or decisions made without their knowledge.

Formal vs. Informal Networks

communication networks
Channels by which information flows.

formal networks
Task-related communications that follow the authority chain.

informal network
The communication grapevine.

Communication networks define the channels by which information flows. These channels are one of two varieties—either formal or informal. **Formal networks** are typically vertical, follow the authority chain, and are limited to task-related communications. In contrast, the **informal network**—usually better known as the grapevine—is free to move in any direction, skip authority levels, and is as likely to satisfy group members' social needs as it is to facilitate task accomplishments.

FORMAL SMALL-GROUP NETWORKS Figure 10-3 illustrates three common small-group networks: the chain, wheel, and all channel. The chain rigidly follows the formal chain of command. The wheel relies on the leader to act as the central conduit for all the group's communication. The all-channel network permits all group members to actively communicate with each other.

As Table 10-1 demonstrates, the effectiveness of each network depends on the dependent variable you are concerned about. For instance, the structure of the wheel facilitates the emergence of a leader, the all-channel network is best if you are concerned with having high member satisfaction, and the chain is best if accuracy is most important. So Table 10-1 leads us to the conclusion that no single network is best for all occasions.

Figure 10-3
Three Common Small-Group Networks

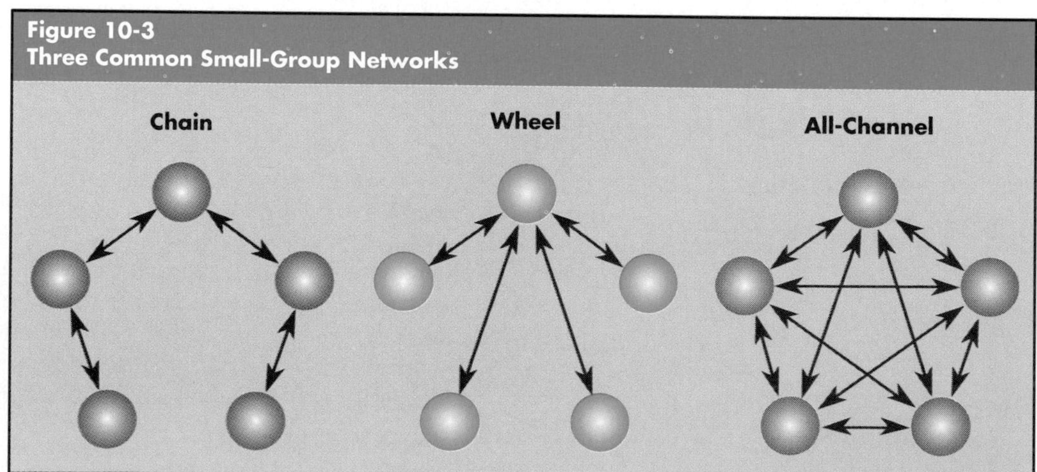

Table 10-1 Small-Group Networks and Effectiveness Criteria

	Networks		
Criteria	**Chain**	**Wheel**	**All-Channel**
Speed	Moderate	Fast	Fast
Accuracy	High	High	Moderate
Emergence of a leader	Moderate	High	None
Member satisfaction	Moderate	Low	High

THE INFORMAL NETWORK The previous discussion of networks emphasized formal communication patterns, but the formal system is not the only communication system in a group or between groups. Now let's turn our attention to the informal system, where information flows along the well-known grapevine and rumors can flourish.

The grapevine has three main characteristics.[14] First, it is not controlled by management. Second, it is perceived by most employees as being more believable and reliable than formal communiqués issued by top management. Third, it is largely used to serve the self-interests of those people within it.

One of the most famous studies of the grapevine investigated the communication pattern among 67 managerial personnel in a small manufacturing firm.[15] The basic approach used was to learn from each communication recipient how he first received a given piece of information and then trace it back to its source. It was found that, while the grapevine was an important source of information, only 10 percent of the executives acted as liaison individuals, that is, passed the information on to more than one other person. For example, when one executive decided to resign to enter the insurance business, 81 percent of the executives knew about it, but only 11 percent transmitted this information on to others.

Two other conclusions from this study are also worth noting. Information on events of general interest tended to flow between the major functional groups (that is, production, sales) rather than within them. Also, no evidence surfaced to suggest that members of any one group consistently acted as liaisons; rather, different types of information passed through different liaison persons.

An attempt to replicate this study among employees in a small state government office also found that only a small percentage (10 percent) acted as liaison individuals.[16] This is interesting, since the replication contained a wider spectrum of employees—including rank and file as well as managerial personnel. However, the flow of information in the government office took place within, rather than between, functional groups. It was proposed that this discrepancy might be due to comparing an executive-only sample against one that also included rank-and-file workers. Managers, for example, might feel greater pressure to stay informed and thus cultivate others outside their immediate functional group. Also, in contrast to the findings of the original study, the replication found that a consistent group of individuals acted as liaisons by transmitting information in the government office.

Is the information that flows along the grapevine accurate? The evidence indicates that about 75 percent of what is carried is accurate.[17] But what conditions foster an active grapevine? What gets the rumor mill rolling?

It is frequently assumed that rumors start because they make titillating gossip. Such is rarely the case. Rumors have at least four purposes: to structure and reduce anxiety; to make sense of limited or fragmented information; to serve as a vehicle to organize group members, and possibly outsiders, into coalitions; and to signal a sender's status ("I'm an insider and, with respect to this rumor, you're an outsider") or power ("I have the power to make you into an insider").[18] Research indicates that rumors emerge as a response to situations which are important to us, where there is ambiguity, and under conditions that arouse anxiety.[19] Work situations frequently contain these three elements, which explains why rumors flourish in organizations. The secrecy and competition that typically prevail in large organizations—around such issues as the appointment of new bosses, the relocation of offices, and the realignment of work assignments—create conditions that encourage and sustain rumors on the grapevine. A rumor will persist either until the wants and expectations creating the uncertainty underlying the rumor are fulfilled or until the anxiety is reduced.

What can we conclude from this discussion? Certainly the grapevine is an important part of any group or organization's communication network and well worth understanding.[20] It identifies for managers those confusing issues that employees consider important and anxiety provoking. It acts, therefore, as both a filter and a feedback mechanism, picking up the issues that employees consider relevant. Maybe more important, again from a managerial perspective, it seems possible to analyze grapevine information and to predict its flow, given that only a small set of individuals (around 10 percent) actively passes on information to more than one other person. By assessing which liaison individuals will consider a given piece of information to be relevant, we can improve our ability to explain and predict the pattern of the grapevine.

Can management entirely eliminate rumors? No! What management should do, however, is minimize the negative consequences of rumors by limiting their range and impact. Table 10-2 offers a few suggestions for minimizing those negative consequences.

Nonverbal Communications

Anyone who has ever paid a visit to a singles bar or a nightclub is aware that communication need not be verbal in order to convey a message. A glance, a stare, a smile, a frown, a provocative body movement—they all convey meaning. This example illustrates that no discussion of communication would be

Table 10-2 Suggestions for Reducing the Negative Consequences of Rumors

1. Announce timetables for making important decisions.
2. Explain decisions and behaviors that may appear inconsistent or secretive.
3. Emphasize the downside, as well as the upside, of current decisions and future plans.
4. Openly discuss worst case possibilities—it is almost never as anxiety provoking as the unspoken fantasy.

Source: Adapted from L. Hirschhorn, "Managing Rumors," in L. Hirschhorn (ed.), *Cutting Back* (San Francisco: Jossey-Bass, 1983), pp. 54–56. With permission.

complete without a discussion of **nonverbal communications**. This includes body movements, the intonations or emphasis we give to words, facial expressions, and the physical distance between the sender and receiver.

nonverbal communications Messages conveyed through body movements, the intonations or emphasis we give to words, facial expressions, and the physical distance between the sender and receiver.

The academic study of body motions has been labeled **kinesics**. It refers to gestures, facial configurations, and other movements of the body. But it is a relatively new field, and it has been subject to far more conjecture and popularizing than the research findings support. Hence, while we acknowledge that body movement is an important segment of the study of communication and behavior, conclusions must be necessarily guarded. Recognizing this qualification, let us briefly consider the ways in which body motions convey meaning.

kinesics The study of body motions.

It has been argued that every body movement has a meaning and no movement is accidental.[21] For example, through body language,

> [W]e say, "Help me, I'm lonely. Take me, I'm available. Leave me alone, I'm depressed." And rarely do we send our messages consciously. We act out our state of being with nonverbal body language. We lift one eyebrow for disbelief. We rub our noses for puzzlement. We clasp our arms to isolate ourselves or to protect ourselves. We shrug our shoulders for indifference, wink one eye for intimacy, tap our fingers for impatience, slap our forehead for forgetfulness.[22]

While we may disagree with the specific meaning of these movements, body language adds to and often complicates verbal communication. A body position or movement does not by itself have a precise or universal meaning, but when it is linked with spoken language, it gives fuller meaning to a sender's message.

If you read the verbatim minutes of a meeting, you could not grasp the impact of what was said in the same way you could if you had been there or saw the meeting on video. Why? There is no record of nonverbal communication. The emphasis given to words or phrases is missing. To illustrate how *intonations* can change the meaning of a message, consider the student in class who asks the instructor a question. The instructor replies, "What do you mean by that?" The student's reaction will be different depending on the tone of the instructor's response. A soft, smooth tone creates a different meaning from an intonation that is abrasive with strong emphasis placed on the last word.

The *facial expression* of the instructor will also convey meaning. A snarled face says something different from a smile. Facial expressions, along with intonations, can show arrogance, aggressiveness, fear, shyness, and other characteristics that would never be communicated if you read a transcript of what had been said.

The way individuals space themselves in terms of *physical distance* also has meaning. What is considered proper spacing largely depends on cultural norms. For example, what is "businesslike" distance in some European countries would be viewed as "intimate" in many parts of North America. If someone stands closer to you than is considered appropriate, it may indicate aggressiveness or sexual interest. If farther away than usual, it may mean disinterest or displeasure with what is being said.

It is important for the receiver to be alert to these nonverbal aspects of communication. You should look for nonverbal cues as well as listen to the literal meaning of a sender's words. You should particularly be aware of contradictions between the messages. The boss may say she is free to talk to you about that raise you have been seeking, but you may see nonverbal signals that suggest this is not the time to discuss the subject. Regardless of what is being said,

◆Actions speak louder (and more accurately) than words.

an individual who frequently glances at her wristwatch is giving the message she would prefer to terminate the conversation. We misinform others when we express one emotion verbally, such as trust, but nonverbally communicate a contradictory message that reads, "I don't have confidence in you." These contradictions often suggest that "actions speak louder (and more accurately) than words."

Choice of Communication Channel

Why do individuals choose one channel of communication over another—for instance, a phone call instead of a face-to-face talk? One answer might be anxiety! As you will remember, some people are apprehensive about certain kinds of communication. What about the 80 to 95 percent of the population who don't suffer from this problem? Is there any general insight we might be able to provide regarding choice of communication channel? The answer is a qualified "Yes." A model of media richness has been developed to explain channel selection among managers.[23]

channel richness
The amount of information that can be transmitted during a communication episode.

Recent research has found that channels differ in their capacity to convey information. Some are rich in that they have the ability to (1) handle multiple cues simultaneously, (2) facilitate rapid feedback, and (3) be very personal. Others are lean in that they score low on these three factors. As Figure 10–4 illustrates, face-to-face talk scores highest in terms of **channel richness** because it provides for the maximum amount of information to be transmitted during a communication episode. That is, it offers multiple information cues (words, posture, facial expressions, gestures, intonations), immediate feedback (both verbal and nonverbal), and the personal touch of being there. Impersonal written media such as bulletins and general reports rate lowest in richness.

Figure 10-4
Hierarchy of Channel Richness

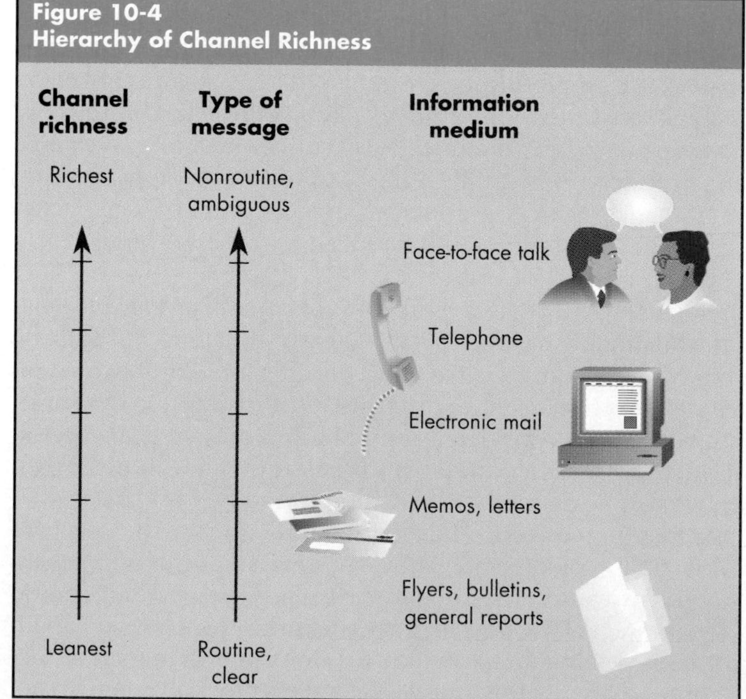

The choice of one channel over another depends on whether the message is routine or nonroutine. The former types of messages tend to be straightforward and have a minimum of ambiguity. The latter are likely to be complicated and have the potential for misunderstanding. Managers can communicate routine messages efficiently through channels that are lower in richness. However, they can communicate nonroutine messages effectively only by selecting rich channels.

The media richness model is consistent with organizational trends and practices during the past decade. It is not just coincidence that more and more senior managers have been using meetings to facilitate communication and regularly leaving the isolated sanctuary of their executive offices to manage by walking around. These executives are relying on richer channels of communication to transmit the more ambiguous messages they need to convey. The past decade has been characterized by organizations closing facilities, imposing large layoffs, restructuring, merging, consolidating, and introducing new products and services at an accelerated pace—all nonroutine messages high in ambiguity and requiring the use of channels that can convey a large amount of information. It is not surprising, therefore, to see the most effective managers expanding their use of rich channels.

Barriers to Effective Communication

We conclude our discussion of communication fundamentals by reviewing several of the more prominent barriers to effective communication of which you should be aware.

FILTERING **Filtering** refers to a sender manipulating information so it will be seen more favorably by the receiver. For example, when a manager tells her boss what she feels her boss wants to hear, she is filtering information. Does this happen much in organizations? Sure! As information is passed up to senior executives, it has to be condensed and synthesized by underlings so those on top don't become overloaded with information. The personal interests and perceptions of what is important by those doing the synthesizing are going to result in filtering. As a former group vice president of General Motors described it, the filtering of communications through levels at GM made it impossible for senior managers to get objective information because "lower-level specialists . . . provided information in such a way that they would get the answer they wanted. I know. I used to be down below and do it."[24]

filtering
A sender's manipulation of information so that it will be seen more favorably by the receiver.

The major determinant of filtering is the number of levels in an organization's structure. The more vertical levels in the organization's hierarchy, the more opportunities for filtering.

SELECTIVE PERCEPTION We have mentioned selective perception before in this book. It appears again because the receivers in the communication process selectively see and hear based on their needs, motivations, experience, background, and other personal characteristics. Receivers also project their interests and expectations into communications as they decode them. The employment interviewer who expects a female job applicant to put her family ahead of her career is likely to see that in female applicants, regardless of whether the applicants feel that way or not. As we said in Chapter 4, we don't see reality; rather, we interpret what we see and call it reality.

From Concepts to Skills

Effective Listening

Too many people take listening skills for granted.[25] They confuse hearing with listening. What's the difference? Hearing is merely picking up sound vibrations. Listening is making sense out of what we hear. That is, listening requires paying attention, interpreting, and remembering sound stimuli.

The average person normally speaks at the rate of 125 to 200 words per minute. However, the average listener can comprehend up to 400 words per minute. This leaves a lot of time for idle mind wandering while listening. For most people, it also means they've acquired a number of bad listening habits to fill in the "idle time."

The following eight behaviors are associated with effective listening skills. If you want to improve your listening skills, look to these behaviors as guides:

1. *Make eye contact.* How do you feel when somebody doesn't look at you when you're speaking? If you're like most people, you're likely to interpret this as aloofness or disinterest. We may listen with our ears, but others tend to judge whether we're really listening by looking at our eyes.
2. *Exhibit affirmative head nods and appropriate facial expressions.* The effective listener shows interest in what is being said. How? Through nonverbal signals. Affirmative head nods and appropriate facial expressions, when added to good eye contact, convey to the speaker you're listening.
3. *Avoid distracting actions or gestures.* The other side of showing interest is avoiding actions that suggest your mind is somewhere else. When listening, don't look at your watch, shuffle papers, play with your pencil, or engage in similar distractions. They make the speaker feel you're bored or uninterested. Maybe more importantly, they indicate you aren't fully attentive and may be missing

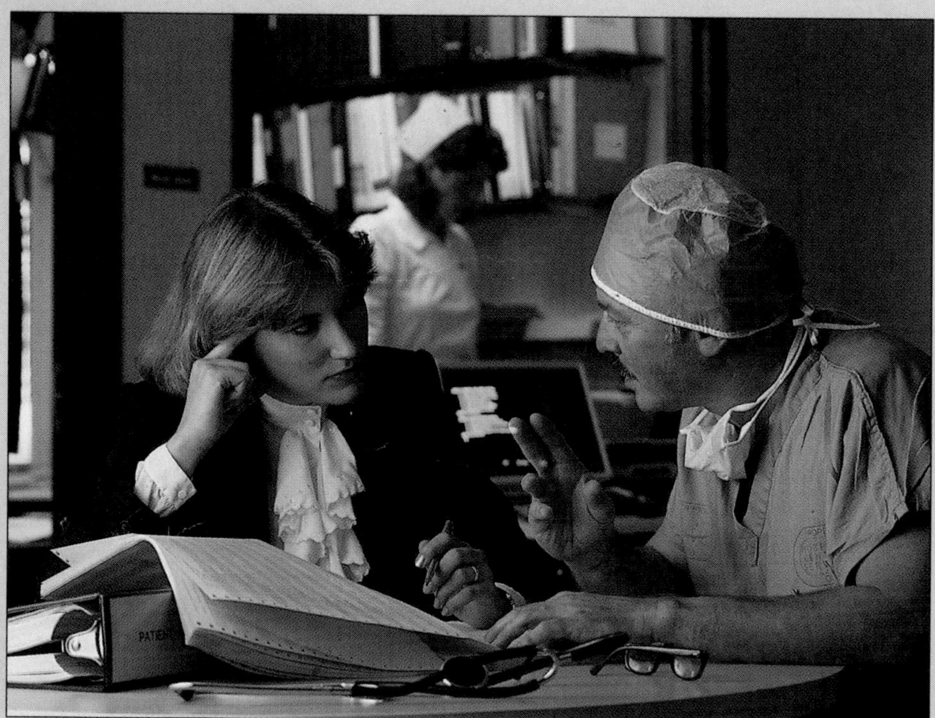

Listening skills are critical to the success of salespeople. Their job is listening to the "voice of the customer" to determine what the customer needs and wants.

part of the message the speaker wants to convey.

4. *Ask questions*. The critical listener analyzes what he or she hears and asks questions. This behavior provides clarification, ensures understanding, and assures the speaker you're listening.
5. *Paraphrase*. Paraphrasing means restating what the speaker has said in your own words. The effective listener uses phrases like "What I hear you saying is . . ." or "Do you mean . . .?" Why rephrase what's already been said? Two reasons! First, it's an excellent control device to check on whether you're listening carefully. You can't paraphrase accurately if your mind is wandering or if you're thinking about what you're going to say next. Second, it's a control for accuracy. By rephrasing what the speaker has said in your own words and feeding it back to the speaker, you verify the accuracy of your understanding.
6. *Avoid interrupting the speaker*. Let the speaker complete his or her thought before you try to respond. Don't try to second-guess where the speaker's thoughts are going. When the speaker is finished, you'll know it!
7. *Don't overtalk*. Most of us would rather speak our own ideas than listen to what someone else says. Too many of us listen only because it's the price we have to pay to get people to let us talk. While talking may be more fun and silence may be uncomfortable, you can't talk and listen at the same time. The good listener recognizes this fact and doesn't overtalk.
8. *Make smooth transitions between the roles of speaker and listener*. When you're a student sitting in a lecture hall, you find it relatively easy to get into an effective listening frame of mind. Why? Because communication is essentially one way: The teacher talks and you listen. But the teacher–student dyad is atypical. In most work situations, you're continually shifting back and forth between the roles of speaker and listener. The effective listener, therefore, makes transitions smoothly from speaker to listener and back to speaker. From a listening perspective, this means concentrating on what a speaker has to say and practicing not thinking about what you're going to say as soon as you get your chance.

EMOTIONS How the receiver feels at the time of receipt of a communication message will influence how he or she interprets it. The same message received when you're angry or distraught is likely to be interpreted differently when you're in a neutral disposition. Extreme emotions—such as jubilation or depression—are most likely to hinder effective communication. In such instances, we are most prone to disregard our rational and objective thinking processes and substitute emotional judgments.

LANGUAGE Words mean different things to different people. "The meanings of words are not in the words; they are in us."[26] Age, education, and cultural background are three of the more obvious variables that influence the language a person uses and the definitions he or she gives to words. Rap artist Snoop Doggy Dogg and political analyst/author William F. Buckley, Jr., both speak English. But the language each uses is vastly different from the other. In fact, the typical person on the street might have difficulty understanding either of these individuals' vocabulary.

In an organization, employees usually come from diverse backgrounds and, therefore, have different patterns of speech. Additionally, the grouping of employees into departments creates specialists who develop their own jargon or technical language. In large organizations, members are also frequently widely dispersed geographically—even operating in different countries—and individuals in each locale will use terms and phrases that are unique to their area.

The existence of vertical levels can also cause language problems. For instance, differences in meaning with regard to words such as *incentives* and *quotas* have been found at different levels in management. Top managers often speak about the need for incentives and quotas, yet these terms imply manipulation and create resentment among many lower managers.

The point is that while you and I speak a common language—English—our usage of that language is far from uniform. If we knew how each of us modified the language, communication difficulties would be minimized. The problem is that members in an organization usually don't know how others with whom they interact have modified the language. Senders tend to assume the words and terms they use mean the same to the receiver as they do to them. This, of course, is often incorrect, thus creating communication difficulties.

In Practice: Effective Employee Communication in Leading Companies Undergoing Dramatic Changes

As we've noted throughout this book, organizations around the world are restructuring in order to reduce costs and improve competitiveness. Almost all Fortune 100 companies, for instance, have scaled back the size of their labor force in the last five years through attrition and layoffs.

A recent study looked at employee communications programs in ten leading companies that had successfully undertaken major restructuring programs.[27] The companies were chosen because they had developed reputations for having excellent internal communication programs. The authors were interested in seeing if there were some common factors that determined the effectiveness of these firms' employee communications. The authors specifically chose companies that had undergone restructuring and reorganization because they believed the true test of a firm's communication effectiveness was how well it worked in times of major organizational change.

The authors found eight factors related to the effectiveness of employee communications in these ten firms. Since the companies studied came from a variety of industries and organizational settings, the authors propose that these eight characteristics should apply to many types of organizations.

Let's take a look at these eight factors because they provide some research-based guidance to managers in helping decide how best to communicate with employees.

The CEO Must Be Committed to the Importance of Communication

The most significant factor in a successful employee-communications program is the chief executive's leadership. He or she must be philosophically and behaviorally committed to the notion that communicating with employees is essential to the achievement of the organization's goals. If the organization's senior executive is committed to communication through his or her words and actions, it trickles down to the rest of the organization.

In addition to espousing a philosophical commitment to employee communications, the CEO must be a skilled and visible communications role model and be willing to personally deliver key messages. The CEOs in this study spent a significant amount of their time talking with employees, responding to questions, listening to their concerns, and conveying their vision of the company. Importantly, they tended to do this in person. They didn't delegate this task to other managers. By personally championing the cause of good communication, they lessen employee fears about changes that are being implemented and set the precedent for other managers to follow.

Managers Match Actions and Words

Closely related to CEO support and involvement is managerial action. As we've noted previously, actions speak louder than words. When the implicit messages that managers send contradict the official messages as conveyed in formal communications, the managers lose credibility with employees. Employees will listen to what management has to say regarding changes being made and where the company is going. But these words must be backed up by matching actions.

Commitment to Two-Way Communication

Ineffective programs are dominated by downward communication. Successful programs balance downward and upward communication.

How does a firm promote upward communication and stimulate employee dialogue? The company that displayed the highest commitment to two-way communication used interactive television broadcasts that allowed employees to call in questions and get responses from top management. Company publications had question-and-answer columns and employees were encouraged to submit questions. The company developed a grievance procedure that processed complaints quickly. Additionally managers were trained in feedback techniques and then were rewarded for using them.

Emphasis on Face-to-Face Communication

In times of uncertainty and change—which characterize major restructuring efforts—employees have lots of fears and concerns. Is their job in jeopardy? Will they have to learn new skills? Is their work group going to be disbanded? Consistent with our previous discussion of channel richness, these messages are nonroutine and ambiguous. The maximum amount of information can be transmitted through face-to-face conversation. Because the firms in this study were all undergoing significant changes, their senior executives got out and personally carried their messages to operating employees. Candid, open, face-

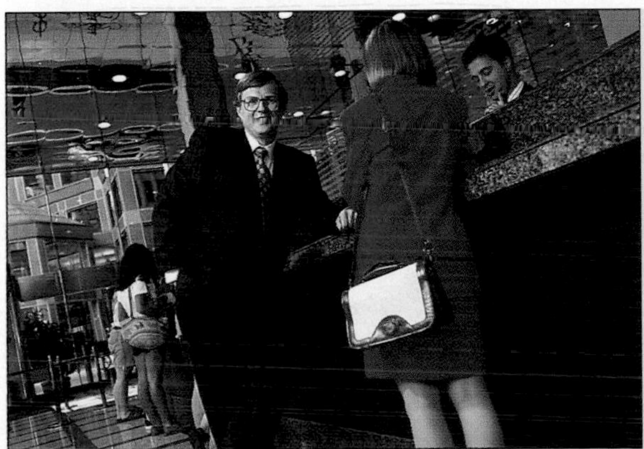

Ed Clark, president and CEO of Canada Trust, shows his commitment to communication by personally visiting CT's 400 branch locations. His philosophy is that you can't sit in an office and tell people what to do. He frequently holds pizza and ginger ale sessions with employees. Clark's approachable style and ability to explain complex issues without talking down to listeners has earned him the loyalty of employees.

to-face communication with employees presents executives as living, breathing people who understand the needs and concerns of the workers.

Shared Responsibility for Employee Communications

Top management provides the big picture—where the company is going. Supervisors link the big picture to their work group and to individual employees. Every manager has some responsibility in ensuring that employees are well informed, with the implications for changes becoming more specific as they flow down the organization hierarchy.

People prefer to hear about the changes that might affect them from their boss, not from their peers or from the grapevine. This requires top management to keep middle and lower managers fully apprised of planned changes. And it means middle and lower level managers must quickly share information with their work group in order to minimize ambiguity.

Dealing with Bad News

Organizations with effective employee communications aren't afraid to confront bad news. In fact, they typically have a high bad news to good news ratio. This doesn't mean these firms have more problems; rather, they don't penalize the bearer of bad news.

All organizations will, at times, have product failures, delivery delays, customer complaints, or similar problems. The issue is how comfortable people feel in communicating those problems. When bad news is candidly reported, a climate is created in which people aren't afraid to be truthful and good news gains increased credibility.

The Message Is Shaped for Its Intended Audience

Different people in the organization have different information needs. What is important to supervisors may not be so to middle managers. Similarly, what is interesting information to someone in product planning may be irrelevant to someone in accounting.

What information do individuals and groups want to know? When do they need to know it? In what form (at home, newsletter, E-mail, team meeting) is the best way for them to receive it? Employees vary in the type of information they need and the most effective way for them to receive it. Managers need to recognize this and design their communication program accordingly.

Treat Communication as an Ongoing Process

These leading companies viewed employee communications as a critical management process. This is illustrated by five common activities that these firms engaged in.

MANAGERS CONVEY THE RATIONALE UNDERLYING DECISIONS As change occurs more frequently, and their future becomes less certain, employees increasingly want to know the rationale underlying the decisions and changes that are being made. *Why* is this occurring? *How* will this affect me?

As the historical social contract that traded employee loyalty for job security has eroded, employees have new expectations from management.[28] In times of permanent employment, comprehensive explanations of management decisions weren't as critical for employees because no matter what the changes, their jobs were relatively secure. But under the new covenant, with workers assuming a much greater responsibility for their own careers, employees feel a need for more information so they can make intelligent career decisions. Employees are looking for something from management to make up the difference between what they used to have guaranteed and what they have now. One of those things is information.

TIMELINESS IS VITAL It's important for managers to communicate what they know, when they know it. Employees don't want to be treated as children,

◆◆◆◆ OB in the News ◆◆◆◆

Open-Book Management

John Davis is a vice president at Re:Member Data Services. His company sells data processing systems to credit unions, and Davis runs the department known as Conversions and Training in Re:Member's Memphis office. Once a sale is made, Davis's group converts the customer's database to the new system and then trains the customer's employees.

Until 1989, when Re:Member bought it, Davis's office was owned by a large Minneapolis firm that prided itself on keeping its employees in the dark. Davis would learn about a new job when it landed on his desk, deadline attached. He never knew which prospects were being courted or what the salesperson was promising them or how many jobs he and his colleagues would be faced with in the next month or three. Nor did Davis know how much money his department made or lost or, indeed, how the office itself was doing.

When Re:Member came in, Davis was made a vice president and thereby gained access to all the information he needed. But the frustrating experience of working in the dark stuck with him. What would happen, he wondered, if every employee knew as much as he knew now—about upcoming jobs, about how the department was doing, even about how much they themselves contributed to the business? Davis decided to let this kind of information permeate his office: He introduced open-book management.

Davis developed a detailed cost accounting system. It required each employee to keep a record of time spent on each job, materials costs, travel and entertainment, and so on. He had the computer track each employee's time, daily billing, salary costs, and expenses. Then he explained to his employees that each of them would now be responsible for his or her own profitability. Every month, Davis would provide his 12-person staff with printouts showing how much the company made or lost on each job. Every person would also get a printout showing how much money he or she had made or lost for the company that month.

The new system made some people nervous at first because they feared it would be found out they weren't making any money for the firm. But gradually those fears subsided. And with their newfound information, employees began coming up with ways their group could generate revenues, cut costs, and expand their skills to improve their individual accounts. In the first year of the program, Davis found that employee-initiated ideas saved the company $37,000. In addition, he believes he has made his office a more exciting and challenging place to work.

Based on J. Case, "The Open-Book Managers," *INC.* (September 1990), pp. 104–13.

parceled out bits of information piece by piece or kept from information for fear it might be misconstrued. Give people the facts as soon as they become available. This lessens the power of the grapevine and increases management's credibility. The cost of not communicating in a timely manner is disaffection, anger, and loss of trust.

COMMUNICATE CONTINUALLY Communication should be continual, particularly during periods of change or crisis. When employees need information and it's not forthcoming, they'll fall back on informal channels to fill the void, even if those channels provide only unsubstantiated rumors. In those organizations where management strives to keep the information continually flowing, employees are also more forgiving of the occasional error or omission.

LINK THE BIG PICTURE WITH THE LITTLE PICTURE Truly effective communication does not occur until employees understand how the big picture affects them and their jobs. Changes in the economy, among competitors in the industry, or in the organization as a whole must be translated into implications for each location, department, and employee. This responsibility falls most directly on employees' direct supervisor.

DON'T DICTATE THE WAY PEOPLE SHOULD FEEL ABOUT THE NEWS Employees don't want to be told how they should interpret and feel about change. Trust and openness is not enhanced by claims like "These new changes are really exciting!" or "You're going to like the way the department is being restructured!" More often than not, these attempts to sway opinion only provoke antagonistic responses.

It's more effective to communicate, "who, what, when, where, why, and how" and then let employees draw their own conclusions.

Current Issues in Communication

We close this chapter by addressing four current issues: Why do men and women often have difficulty communicating with each other? What are the implications of the politically correct movement on communications in organizations? How can individuals improve their cross-cultural communications? And how is electronics changing the way people communicate with each other in organizations?

Communication Barriers Between Women and Men

Research by Deborah Tannen provides us with some important insights into the differences between men and women in terms of their conversational styles.[29] In particular, she has been able to explain why gender often creates oral communication barriers.

> ◆Men use talk to emphasize status whereas women use it to create connection.

The essence of Tannen's research is that men use talk to emphasize status whereas women use it to create connection. Tannen states that communication is a continual balancing act, juggling the conflicting needs for intimacy and independence. Intimacy emphasizes closeness and commonalities. Independence emphasizes separateness and differences. But here's the kick: Women speak and hear a language of connection and intimacy; men speak and hear a language of status and independence. So, for many men, conversations

Kathy Knight (left), president of market research firm BAI, deals with power struggles and communication differences between men and women by instilling in her employees the value of direct, honest communication. Knight encourages honesty by assuring employees they are not at risk in losing face or their job by admitting mistakes. She focuses on mutual understanding rather than assigning blame or giving apologies. When a conflict arises, Knight tells the employees involved to confront each other directly instead of discussing it with twelve other workers at lunch.

are primarily a means to preserve independence and maintain status in a hierarchical social order. For many women, conversations are negotiations for closeness in which people try to seek and give confirmation and support. A few examples will illustrate Tannen's thesis.

Men frequently complain that women talk on and on about their problems. Women criticize men for not listening. What's happening is that when men hear a problem, they frequently assert their desire for independence and control by offering solutions. Many women, however, view telling a problem as a means to promote closeness. The women present the problem to gain support and connection, not to get the male's advice. Mutual understanding is symmetrical. But giving advice is asymmetrical—it sets the advice giver up as more knowledgeable, more reasonable, and more in control. This contributes to distancing men and women in their efforts to communicate.

Men are often more direct than women in conversation. A man might say, "I think you're wrong on that point." A woman might say, "Have you looked at the marketing department's research report on that point?" (the implication being that the report will show the error). Men frequently see female indirectness as "covert" or "sneaky," but women are not as concerned as men with the status and oneupmanship that directness often creates.

Finally, men often criticize women for seeming to apologize all the time. Men tend to see the phrase "I'm sorry" as a weakness because they interpret the phrase to mean the woman is accepting blame, when he knows she's not to blame. The woman also knows she is not to blame. The problem is that women typically use "I'm sorry" to express regret: "I know you must feel bad about this; I do, too."

"Politically Correct" Communication

What words do you use to describe a colleague who is wheelchair bound? What terms do you use in addressing a female customer? How do you communicate with a brand-new client who is not like you? The right answers can mean the difference between losing a client, an employee, a lawsuit, a harassment claim, or a job.[30]

Most of us are acutely aware of how our vocabulary has been modified to reflect political correctness. For instance, most of us have cleansed the words *handicapped*, *blind*, and *elderly* from our vocabulary, and replaced them with terms like *physically challenged*, *visually impaired*, and *senior*. The *Los Angeles*

Times, for instance, allows its journalists to use the term *old age* but cautions that the onset of old age varies from person to person, so not all 75-year-olds are necessarily old.[31]

We must be sensitive to others' feelings. Certain words can and do stereotype, intimidate, and insult individuals. In an increasingly diverse work force, we must be aware of how words might offend others. But there's a downside to political correctness. It's shrinking our vocabulary and making it more difficult for people to communicate. To illustrate, you probably know what these two terms mean: *death* and *women*. But both of these words have been found to offend one or more groups. They've been replaced with terms like *negative-patient-care outcome* and *people of gender*. The problem is that these terms are much less likely to convey a uniform message than the words they replaced. You know what death means; I know what death means; but can you be sure that "negative-patient-care outcome" will be consistently defined as synonymous with death? No! The phrase could also mean a longer stay than expected in the hospital or notification that your insurance company won't pay your hospital bill.

Some critics, for humor's sake, enjoy carrying political correctness to the extreme. Even those of us with thinning scalps, who aren't too thrilled at being labeled bald, have to smirk when we're referred to as "follically challenged." But our concern here is with how politically correct language is contributing a new barrier to effective communication.

Words are the primary means by which people communicate. When we eliminate words from usage because they're politically incorrect, we reduce our options for conveying messages in the clearest and most accurate form. For the most part, the larger the vocabulary used by a sender and a receiver, the greater the opportunity to transmit messages accurately. By removing certain words from our vocabulary, we make it harder to communicate accurately. When we further replace these words with new terms whose meanings are less well understood, we have reduced the likelihood that our messages will be received as we had intended them.

We must be sensitive to how our choice of words might offend others. But we also have to be careful not to sanitize our language to the point where it clearly restricts clarity of communication. There is no simple solution to this dilemma. However, you should be aware of the trade-offs and the need to find a proper balance.

Cross-Cultural Communication

Effective communication is difficult under the best of conditions. Cross-cultural factors clearly create the potential for increased communication problems.

One author has identified four specific problems related to language difficulties in cross-cultural communications.[32]

First, there are *barriers caused by semantics*. As we've noted previously, words mean different things to different people. This is particularly true for people from different national cultures. Some words, for instance, don't translate between cultures. Understanding the word *sisu* will help you in communicating with people from Finland, but this word is untranslatable into English. It means something akin to "guts" or "dogged persistence." Similarly, the new capitalists in Russia may have difficulty communicating with their British or Canadian counterparts because English terms such as *efficiency*, *free market*, and *regulation* are not directly translatable into Russian.

Second, there are *barriers caused by word connotations*. Words imply different things in different languages. Negotiations between Americans and Japanese executives, for instance, is made more difficult because the Japanese word *hai* translates as "yes," but its connotation may be "yes, I'm listening," rather than "yes, I agree."

Third are *barriers caused by tone differences*. In some cultures, language is formal, in others it's informal. In some cultures, the tone changes depending on the context: people speaking differently at home, in social situations, and at work. Using a personal, informal style in a situation where a more formal style is expected can be embarrassing and off-putting.

Fourth, there are *barriers caused by differences among perceptions*. People who speak different languages actually view the world in different ways. Eskimos perceive snow differently because they have many words for it. Thais perceive "no" differently than Americans because the former have no such word in their vocabulary.

When communicating with people from a different culture, what can you do to reduce misperceptions, misinterpretations, and misevaluations? Following these four rules can be helpful:[33]

1. *Assume differences until similarity is proven*. Most of us assume that others are more similar to us than they actually are. But people from different countries often are very different from us. So you are far less likely to make an error if you assume others are different from you rather than assuming similarity until difference is proven.
2. *Emphasize description rather than interpretation or evaluation*. Interpreting or evaluating what someone has said or done, in contrast to description, is based more on the observer's culture and background than on the observed situation. As a result, delay judgment until you've had sufficient time to observe and interpret the situation from the differing perspectives of all the cultures involved.
3. *Practice empathy*. Before sending a message, put yourself in the recipient's shoes. What are his or her values, experiences, and frames of reference? What do you know about his or her education, upbringing, and background that can give you added insight? Try to see the other person as he or she really is.
4. *Treat your interpretations as a working hypothesis*. Once you've developed an explanation for a new situation or think you empathize with someone from a foreign culture, treat your interpretation as a hypothesis that needs further testing rather than as a certainty. Carefully assess the feedback provided by recipients to see if it confirms your hypothesis. For important decisions or communiqués, you can also check with other foreign and home country colleagues to make sure your interpretations are on target.

Electronic Communications

Until the last 10 or 15 years, there were very few technological "breakthroughs" that significantly affected organizational communications. Early in this century, the telephone dramatically reduced personal face-to-face communication. The popularization of the photocopy machine in the late 1960s sounded the death knell for carbon paper and made the copying of documents faster and easier. But since the early 1980s, we've been subjected to an onslaught of new electronic technologies that are largely reshaping the way we communicate in organizations.[34] These include pagers, facsimile machines, video conferencing, electronic meetings, E-mail, cellular phones, voice messaging, and palm-sized personal communicators.

Electronic communications no longer make it necessary for you to be at your work station or desk to be available. Pagers, cellular phones, and personal communicators allow you to be reached when you're in a meeting, during your lunch break, while visiting in a customer's office across town, or during a golf game on Saturday morning. The line between an employee's work and nonwork life is no longer distinct. In the electronic age, all employees can theoretically be on call 24 hours a day.

Organizational boundaries become less relevant as a result of electronic communications. Why? Because networked computers—that is, computers interlinked to communicate with each other—allow employees to jump vertical levels within the organization, work full time at home or someplace other than an organizationally operated facility, and carry on communications with people in other organizations. The market researcher who wants to discuss an issue with the vice president of marketing (who is three levels up in the hierarchy), can bypass the people in between and send an E-mail message directly. And in so doing, the traditional status hierarchy, largely determined by level and access, becomes essentially negated. Or that same market researcher may choose to live in the Cayman Islands and work at home via telecommuting rather than do his or her job in the company's Chicago office. And when an employee's computer is linked to suppliers' and customers' computers, the boundaries separating organizations becomes further blurred. Hundreds of suppliers, for instance, are linked into Wal-Mart's computers. This allows people at companies like Levi Strauss to be able to monitor Wal-Mart's inventory of Levi jeans and to replace merchandise as needed, and clouds the distinction between Levi and Wal-Mart employees.

While the telephone allowed people to transmit verbal messages instantly, it's only been very recently that this same speed became available for the written word. In the mid-1960s, organizations depended almost completely on interoffice memos for internal on-site messages, and wire services and the post office for external messages. Then came overnight express delivery and fax machines. Today, with almost all organizations having introduced E-mail and an increasing number providing their employees with access to the

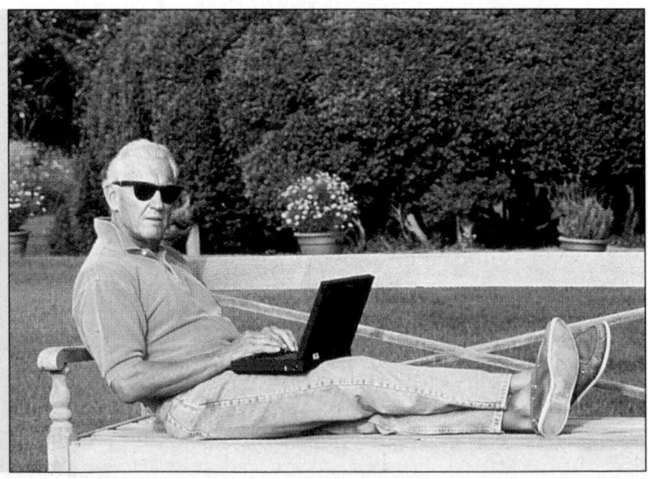

Sitting in an office moving papers around and stuffing information in drawers is not Jay Chiat's idea of creative work. So the chairman of Chiat/Day advertising agency is using electronic communications to change the way employees work. He gave employees cellular phones and E-mail-equipped notebook computers, freed them from a nine-to-five work schedule, and replaced individual work areas with open, common areas and meeting rooms. He installed fax machines, a central file server that manages the agency's shared information resources, and computerized editing rooms with communication software that instantly transfers words, pictures, sound, and video to any Chiat-Day office in the world. Chiat's vision is to create an agency without boundaries so employees can spend more time in clients' offices preparing ads for accounts that quickly change their products and images. Chiat is shown here using his laptop at home to answer his E-mail messages.

Internet, written communications can be transmitted with all the speed of the telephone.

Electronic communications have revolutionized both the ability to access other people and to reach them almost instantaneously. Unfortunately this access and speed has come with some costs. Electronic mail, for instance, doesn't provide the nonverbal communication component that the face-to-face meeting does. Nor does E-mail convey the emotions and nuances that come through from verbal intonations in telephone conversations. Similarly, it's been noted that meetings have historically served two distinct purposes: fulfilling a need for group affiliation and serving as a forum for completing task work.[35] Video conferences and electronic meetings do a good job at supporting tasks but don't address affiliation needs. For people with a high need for social contact, a heavy reliance on electronic communications is likely to lead to lower job satisfaction.

Summary and Implications for Managers

A careful review of this chapter finds a common theme regarding the relationship between communication and employee satisfaction: the less the uncertainty, the greater the satisfaction. Distortions, ambiguities, and incongruities all increase uncertainty and, hence, have a negative impact on satisfaction.[36]

The less distortion that occurs in communication, the more that goals, feedback, and other management messages to employees will be received as they were intended.[37] This, in turn, should reduce ambiguities and clarify the group's task. Extensive use of vertical, lateral, and informal channels will increase communication flow, reduce uncertainty, and improve group performance and satisfaction. We should also expect incongruities between verbal and nonverbal communiqués to increase uncertainty and reduce satisfaction.

Findings in the chapter further suggest that the goal of perfect communication is unattainable. Yet evidence demonstrates a positive relationship between effective communication (which includes factors such as perceived trust, perceived accuracy, desire for interaction, top management receptiveness, and upward information requirements) and worker productivity.[38] Choosing the correct channel, being an effective listener, and utilizing feedback may, therefore, make for more effective communication. But the human factor generates distortions that can never be fully eliminated. The communication process represents an exchange of messages, but the outcome is meanings that may or may not approximate those the sender intended. Whatever the sender's expectations, the decoded message in the mind of the receiver represents his or her reality. And it is this reality that will determine performance, along with the individual's level of motivation and his or her degree of satisfaction. The issue of motivation is critical, so we should briefly review how communication is central in determining an individual's degree of motivation.

You will remember from expectancy theory that the degree of effort an individual exerts depends on his or her perception of the effort–performance, performance–reward, and reward–goal satisfaction linkages. If individuals are not given the data necessary to make the perceived probability of these linkages high, motivation will suffer. If rewards are not made clear, if the criteria for determining and measuring performance are ambiguous, or if individuals are not relatively certain their effort will lead to satisfactory performance, then effort will be reduced. So communication plays a significant role in determining the level of employee motivation.

A final implication from the communication literature relates to predicting turnover. The use of realistic job previews acts as a communication device for clarifying role expectations (see the "Counterpoint" in Chapter 4). Employees who have been exposed to a realistic job preview have more accurate information about that job. Comparisons of turnover rates between organizations that use the realistic job preview versus either no preview or only presentation of positive job information show that those not using the realistic preview have, on average, almost 29 percent higher turnover.[39] This makes a strong case for managers to convey honest and accurate information about a job to applicants during the recruiting and selection process.

For Review

1. Describe the functions that communication provides within a group or organization. Give an example of each.
2. Contrast encoding and decoding.
3. Describe the communication process and identify its key components. Give an example of how this process operates with both oral and written messages.
4. Identify three common small-group networks and give the advantages of each.
5. What is *kinesics*? Why is it important?
6. What characterizes a communication that is rich in its capacity to convey information?
7. What conditions stimulate the emergence of rumors?
8. Describe how political correctness can hinder effective communication.
9. List four specific problems related to language difficulties in cross-cultural communication.
10. What are the managerial implications from the research contrasting male and female communication styles?

For Discussion

1. "Ineffective communication is the fault of the sender." Do you agree or disagree? Discuss.
2. What can you do to improve the likelihood your communiqués will be received and understood as you intend?
3. How might managers use the grapevine for their benefit?
4. Using the concept of channel richness, give examples of messages best conveyed by E-mail, by face-to-face communication, and on the company bulletin board.
5. Why do you think so many people are poor listeners?

Point

The Case for Mutual Understanding: The Johari Window

The Johari Window (named after its creators, Joseph Luft and Harry Ingram) is a popular model used by training specialists for assessing and categorizing communication styles. The essence of the model is the belief that mutual understanding improves perceptual accuracy and communication.

The model classifies an individual's tendencies to facilitate or hinder interpersonal communication along two dimensions: exposure and feedback. Exposure is defined as the extent to which an individual openly and candidly divulges feelings, experiences, and information when trying to communicate. Feedback is the extent to which an individual successfully elicits exposure from others. As shown in Figure 10-A, these dimensions translate into four "windows"—open, blind, hidden, and unknown. The *open* window is information known to you as well as others. The *blind* window encompasses certain things about you that are apparent to others but not to yourself. This is the result of no one ever telling you or because you're defensively blocking them out. The *hidden* window is information known by you and unknown by others. It encompasses those things or feelings that we're aware of but don't share with others for fear they'll think less of us or possibly use the information against us. And the *unknown* window includes feelings, experience, and information that neither you nor others are aware of.

While there is no substantive body of research to support the following conclusion, the Johari Window model argues for more open communication on the assumption that people understand each other better when the amount of information in the open area increases. If you accept this conclusion, how would you increase the open area? According to Luft and Ingram, through disclosure and feedback. By increasing self-disclosure, you reveal your inner feelings and experiences. In addition, the evidence suggests that self-disclosure encourages others to be similarly forthcoming and open. So disclosure breeds more disclosure. When others provide feedback on their insights into your behavior, you reduce your blind window.

While advocates of the Johari Window encourage a climate of openness, where individuals self-disclose freely with each other, they recognize conditions where guarded communication may be appropriate. These include transitory relationships, where one party has violated trust in the past, in competitive situations, or where the culture of the organization doesn't support openness. Although critics might argue that one or more of those conditions just about covers almost all communication situations in organizations, proponents of the Johari Window are more optimistic. They see openness, authenticity, and honesty to be valued qualities in interpersonal relationships. And while they don't say so directly, they imply it's in the self-interest of individuals to try to expand the size of the open window by increasing self-disclosure and by being willing to listen to feedback from others even if it's unflattering.

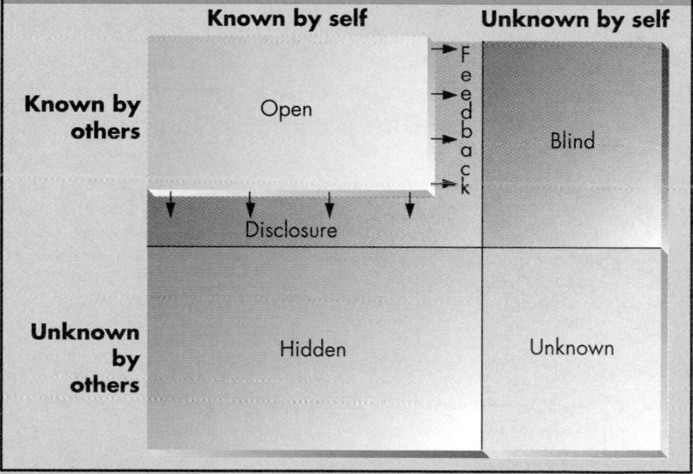

Based on J. Luft, *Group Processes*, 3rd ed. (Palo Alto, CA: Mayfield, 1984), pp. 11–20; and J. Hall, "Communication Revisited," *California Management Review* (Fall 1973), pp. 56–67.

Figure 10-A
The Johari Window

	Known by self	Unknown by self
Known by others	Open	Blind
Unknown by others	Hidden	Unknown

Feedback

Disclosure

counterPoint

The Case for Ambiguous Communication

The argument for mutual understanding and openness, while honorable, is incredibly naive. It assumes communicators actually want to achieve mutual understanding and that openness is the preferred means toward that end. Unfortunately, that argument overlooks a very basic fact: It's often in the sender's and/or receiver's best interest to keep communication ambiguous.

Lack of communication seems to have replaced original sin as the explanation for the ills of the world. We're continually hearing that problems would go away if we could "just communicate better." Some of the basic assumptions underlying this view need to be looked at carefully.

One assumption is the way in which poor communication resembles original sin: Both tend to get tangled up with control of the situation. If one defines communication as mutual understanding, this does not imply control for either party, and certainly not for both. However, equating good communication with control appears in the assumption that better communication will necessarily reduce strife and conflict. Each individual's definition of better communication, like his or her definition of virtuous conduct, becomes that of having the other party accept his or her views, which would reduce conflict at that party's expense. A better understanding of the situation might serve only to underline the differences rather than to resolve them. Indeed, many of the techniques thought of as poor communication were apparently developed with the aim of bypassing or avoiding confrontation.

Another assumption associated with this view is that when a conflict has existed for a long time and shows every sign of continuing, lack of communication must be one of the basic problems. Usually, if the situation is examined more carefully, plenty of communication will be found; the problem is, again, one of equating communication with agreement.

Still a third assumption, somewhat related but less squarely based on the equation of communication with control, is that it is always in the interest of at least one of the parties to an interaction, and often of both, to attain maximum clarity as measured by some more or less objective standard. Aside from the difficulty of setting up this standard—whose standard? and doesn't this give him or her control of the situation?—there are some sequences, and perhaps many of them, in which it is in the interests of both parties to leave the situation as fuzzy and undefined as possible. This is notably true in culturally or personally sensitive and taboo areas involving prejudices, preconceptions, and so on, but it can also be true when the area is merely a new one that could be seriously distorted by using old definitions and old solutions.

Too often we forget that keeping communications fuzzy cuts down on questions, permits faster decision making, minimizes objections, reduces opposition, makes it easier to deny one's earlier statements, preserves freedom to change one's mind, helps to preserve mystique and hide insecurities, allows one to say several things at the same time, permits one to say "No" diplomatically, and helps to avoid confrontation and anxiety.

If you want to see the fine art of ambiguous communication up close, all you have to do is watch a television interview with a politician who is running for office. The interviewer attempts to get specific information; the politician tries to retain multiple possible interpretations. Such ambiguous communications allow the politician to approach his or her ideal image of being "all things to all people."

Based on C.O. Kursh, "The Benefits of Poor Communication," *The Psychoanalytic Review* (Summer-Fall 1971), pp. 189–208; and E.M. Eisenberg and M.G. Witten, "Reconsidering Openness in Organizational Communication," *Academy of Management Review* (July 1987), pp. 418–26.

Learning About Yourself Exercise

Listening Self-Inventory

Go through this 15-item questionnaire twice. The first time, mark the yes or no box next to each question. Mark as truthfully as you can in light of your behavior in recent meetings or gatherings you have attended. The second time, mark a plus (+) next to your answer if you are satisfied with that answer, or a minus (−) next to the answer if you wish you could have answered that question differently.

	Yes	No	+ or −
1. I frequently attempt to listen to several conversations at the same time.		X	
2. I like people to give me only the facts and then let me make my own interpretations.		X	
3. I sometimes pretend to pay attention to people.		X	
4. I consider myself a good judge of nonverbal communications.	X		
5. I usually know what another person is going to say before he or she says it.		X	
6. I usually end conversations that don't interest me by diverting my attention from the speaker.		X	
7. I frequently nod, frown, or whatever to let the speaker know how I feel about what he or she is saying.	X		
8. I usually respond immediately when someone has finished talking.		X	
9. I evaluate what is being said while it is being said.		X	
10. I usually formulate a response while the other person is still talking.		X	
11. The speaker's delivery style frequently keeps me from listening to content.	X		
12. I usually ask people to clarify what they have said rather than guess at the meaning.	X		
13. I make a concerted effort to understand other people's point of view.	X		
14. I frequently hear what I expect to hear rather than what is said.		X	
15. Most people feel that I have understood their point of view when we disagree.		X	

Turn to page A-28 for scoring directions and key.

Source: E.C. Glenn and E.A. Pood, "Listening Self-Inventory," *Supervisory Management* (January 1989), pp. 12–15. With permission.

Working With Others Exercise

An Absence of Nonverbal Communication

This exercise will help you see the value of nonverbal communication to interpersonal relations.

1. The class is to split up into pairs (Party A and Party B).
2. Party A is to select a topic from the following list:
   a. Managing in the Middle East is significantly different from managing in North America.
   b. Employee turnover in an organization can be functional.
   c. Some conflict in an organization is good.
   d. Whistle-blowers do more harm than good for an organization.
   e. Bureaucracies are frustrating to work in.
   f. An employer has a responsibility to provide every employee with an interesting and challenging job.
   g. Everyone should register to vote.
   h. Organizations should require all employees to undergo regular tests for AIDS.
   i. Organizations should require all employees to undergo regular drug tests.
   j. Individuals who have majored in business or economics make better employees than those who have majored in history or English.
3. Party B is to choose his or her position on this topic (for example, arguing *against* the view that "some conflict in an organization is good"). Party A now must automatically take the opposite position.
4. The two parties have ten minutes in which to debate their topic.
   The catch is that individuals can only communicate verbally. They may *not* use gestures, facial movements, body movements, or any other nonverbal communication. It may help for each party to sit on his or her hands to remind them of their restrictions.
5. After the debate is over, the class should discuss the following:
   a. How effective was communication during these debates?
   b. What barriers to communication existed?
   c. What purposes does nonverbal communication serve?
   d. Relate the lessons learned in this exercise to problems that might occur when communicating on the telephone or through E-mail.

Ethical Dilemma Exercise

Is It Wrong to Tell a Lie?

When we were children, our parents told us, "It's wrong to tell a lie." Yet we all have told lies at one time or another. If most of us agree that telling lies is wrong, how do we justify continuing to do it? We often differentiate between "real lies" and "little white lies"—the latter being an acceptable, even necessary, part of social interaction. Since lying is so closely intertwined with interpersonal communication, let's look at a specific dilemma that managers regularly confront: Does a sound purpose justify intentionally distorting information?

You have just seen your division's sales report for last month. Sales are down considerably. Your boss, who works 2,000 miles away in another city, is unlikely to see last month's sales figures. You're optimistic that sales will pick up this month and next, so your quarterly number will be acceptable. You also know your boss is the type of person who hates to hear bad news. You're having a phone conversation today with your boss. He happens to ask, in passing, how last month's sales went. Do you tell him the truth?

A subordinate asks you about a rumor she's heard that your department and all its employees will be transferred from New York to Dallas. You know the rumor is true, but you would rather not let the information out just yet. You're fearful it could hurt departmental morale and lead to premature resignations. What do you say to your employee?

These two incidents illustrate dilemmas that managers face regarding evasion, distortion, and outright lying to others. Is it unethical to purposely distort communications to get a favorable outcome? Is distortion acceptable, but lying not? What about so-called little white lies that really don't hurt anybody? What do *you* think?

Affinity Groups on Apple's Electronic Message System

Electronic mail is a way of life at Apple Computer Inc. Not only do managers use it for sharing information and marketing directors use it to facilitate product introductions, but E-mail also provides a lifeline for seven groups of Apple employees.

These are the so-called affinity groups—gays and lesbians, Latinos, Asians, African-Americans, women, Vietnamese, and devotees of Jewish culture—that use Apple's AppleLink electronic message system to spread the word about meetings, seminars, and community events. This is all done with complete approval and support of Apple's top management.

Apple Computer isn't the only company to utilize its E-mail system to strengthen ties among affinity groups. Pacific Gas & Electric, Lotus Development, Levi Strauss, and Pacific Bell also encourage employees who are members of affinity groups to use E-mail as a communication tool.

There are no objective statistics on how widespread the use of E-mail by affinity groups is. However, worldwide, E-mail practitioners number at least 45 million. Approximately two-thirds of these practitioners have access to networks that reach beyond their immediate circle of colleagues, thus making E-mail an effective way for people with similar interests to maintain links across companies and national borders.

On the plus side, the use of E-mail by affinity groups facilitates communication, strengthens social contacts, and promotes workplace diversity. However, it can also build animosity among out-group members. Antigay employees at Pacific Gas & Electric, for instance, have used their system to communicate offensive messages toward gay and lesbian colleagues.

Questions

1. Is the use of E-mail by affinity groups an example of formal or informal communication? Explain.

2. "Apple's program to encourage affinity groups linked by E-mail doesn't improve organizational communication. It merely builds communication barriers between groups." Do you agree or disagree? Defend your position.
3. If you were a senior manager at Apple with the authority to approve an affinity group's access to the company's E-mail system, how would you respond to requests for E-mail access by employee groups promoting (a) animal rights; (b) the Republican party; (c) prolife issues; or (d) the rights of white males?

Based on M. Groves, "An Affinity for E-Mail," *Los Angeles Times* (May 16, 1994), pp. 9, 30.

Politically Correct Speech

Dr. Leonard Jeffries was chair of the black studies department at the City University of New York (CUNY) for 20 years. Then, in 1991, he gave a speech in Albany, New York. In that speech, he claimed, among other things, that Jews had helped finance the slave trade and that there is a conspiracy among Jews in Hollywood to systematically destroy black people. These remarks caused an uproar, and Jeffries was removed from his chair position by administrators at CUNY.

Jeffries sued. He asserted his removal was a blatant attack on his right to free speech. The university's position claimed he was incompetent in his administrative position and that was the reason for their action.

Many objective evaluators of Jeffries's speech concluded it was racist. However, not all felt this justified CUNY's action. Isn't an individual allowed, they asked, to say things others may not agree with or that others may find offensive?

Free speech is of absolutely no value if it applies only to concepts or points of view that are popular to begin with. The inherent value of free speech is that it affords those who hold unpopular opinions an equal right to be heard.

Frederick Starr, president of Oberlin College, says, "The issue is the protection of the university. Frankly, we have to be willing to tolerate some pretty outrageous things and really offensive things from time to time, in order to protect the freedom that has to go on to protect the genuinely unpopular but maybe insightful view."

Thomas Jefferson once argued we have nothing to fear from irresponsible speech if others are free to point out its errors. The question is: Should academic freedom give shoddy scholars or racists a place to hide?

Leon Botstein, president of Bard College, believes even racist views have a place on college campuses. He believes Jeffries's speech was racist, but that Jeffries should be put under serious scrutiny for the arguments behind his remarks rather than for the remarks themselves. "The university is precisely the place for people to express their prejudices and have the opportunity to have those prejudices heard, discerned, and defeated and taken apart."

Supporters of Jeffries believe he is being unfairly treated. He should be allowed to say what he wants and not be penalized for the content of his speech. Critics wonder if he isn't arguing for a double standard, where blacks can make racist comments with no penalty while racist comments by whites should not be allowed.

Questions

1. Do you think "free speech" extends to expressing racist remarks?
2. How does "political correctness" cloud critical discussion in this case?
3. "Professors should feel free to express controversial ideas without fear of retaliation. That's the essence of what a university is about." If this is true, does it extend to a professor's roles outside that of the university?

Source: "Offensive Speech: Is There a Double Standard?" *Nightline* (May 12, 1993).

Suggestions for Further Reading

CLAMPITT, P.G., *Communicating for Managerial Effectiveness* (Newbury Park, CA: Sage, 1991).

CUPACH, W.R., and B.H. SPITZBERG (eds.), *The Dark Side of Interpersonal Communication* (Hillsdale, NJ: Erlbaum, 1994).

DIFONZO, N., P. BORDIA, and R.L. ROSNOW, "Reining in Rumors," *Organizational Dynamics* (Summer 1994), pp. 47–62.

GARSIDE, S.G., and B.H. KLEINER, "Effective One-to-One Communication Skills," *Industrial and Commercial Training*, Vol. 23, No. 7, (1991), pp. 24–28.

GOLEN, S., "A Factors Analysis of Barriers to Effective Listening," *The Journal of Business Communication* (Winter 1990), pp. 25–36.

HEWES, D.E. (ed.), *The Cognitive Bases of Interpersonal Communication* (Hillsdale, NJ: Erlbaum, 1994).

KALBFLEISCH, P.J. (ed.), *Interpersonal Communication* (Hillsdale, NJ: Erlbaum, 1993).

KHARBANDA, O.P., and E.A. STALLWORTHY, "Verbal and Non-Verbal Communication," *Journal of Managerial Psychology*, Vol. 6, No. 4, (1991), pp. 10–13+.

TANNEN, D., *Talking from 9 to 5* (New York: William Morrow, 1994).

VICTOR, D.A., *International Business Communication* (New York: HarperCollins, 1992).

Notes

[1] Based on J. Cushman, "Avianca Flight 52: The Delays That Ended in Disaster," *New York Times* (February 5, 1990), p. B-1; and E. Weiner, "Right Word Is Crucial in Air Control," *New York Times* (January 29, 1990), p. B-5.

[2] See, for example, K.W. Thomas and W.H. Schmidt, "A Survey of Managerial Interests with Respect to Conflict," *Academy of Management Journal* (June 1976), p. 317.

[3] W.G. Scott and T.R. Mitchell, *Organization Theory: A Structural and Behavioral Analysis* (Homewood, IL: Richard D. Irwin, 1976).

[4] D. K. Berlo, *The Process of Communication* (New York: Holt, Rinehart and Winston, 1960), pp. 30–32.

[5] Ibid., p. 54.

[6] Ibid., p. 103.

[7] J.C. McCroskey, J.A. Daly, and G. Sorenson, "Personality Correlates of Communication Apprehension," *Human Communication Research* (Spring 1976), pp. 376–80.

[8] B.H. Spitzberg and M.L. Hecht, "A Competent Model of Relational Competence," *Human Communication Research* (Summer 1984), pp. 575–99.

[9] See, for example, L. Stafford and J.A. Daly, "Conversational Memory: The Effects of Instructional Set and Recall Mode on Memory for Natural Conversations," *Human Communication Research* (Spring 1984), pp. 379–402.

[10] J.A. Daly and J.C. McCrosky, "Occupational Choice and Desirability as a Function of Communication Apprehension," paper presented at the annual meeting of the International Communication Association, Chicago, 1975.

[11] J.A. Daly and M.D. Miller, "The Empirical Development of an Instrument of Writing Apprehension," *Research in the Teaching of English* (Winter 1975), pp. 242–49.

[12] R.L. Simpson, "Vertical and Horizontal Communication in Formal Organizations," *Administrative Science Quarterly* (September 1959), pp. 188–96; and B. Harriman, "Up and Down the Communications Ladder," *Harvard Business Review* (September-October 1974), pp. 143–51.

[13] B. Smith, "FedEx's Key to Success," *Management Review* (July 1993), pp. 23–24.

[14] See, for instance, J.W. Newstrom, R.E. Monczka, and W.E. Reif, "Perceptions of the Grapevine: Its Value and Influence," *Journal of Business Communication* (Spring 1974), pp. 12–20; and S.J. Modic, "Grapevine Rated Most Believable," *Industry Week* (May 15, 1989), p. 14.

[15] K. Davis, "Management Communication and the Grapevine," *Harvard Business Review* (September-October 1953), pp. 43–49.

[16] H. Sutton and L.W. Porter, "A Study of the Grapevine in a Governmental Organization," *Personnel Psychology* (Summer 1968), pp. 223–30.

[17] K. Davis, cited in R. Rowan, "Where Did That Rumor Come From?" *Fortune* (August 13, 1979), p. 134.

[18] L. Hirschhorn, "Managing Rumors," in L. Hirschhorn (ed.), *Cutting Back* (San Francisco: Jossey-Bass, 1983), pp. 49–52.

[19] R.L. Rosnow and G.A. Fine, *Rumor and Gossip: The Social Psychology of Hearsay* (New York: Elsevier, 1976).

[20] See, for instance, A. Zaremba, "Working with the Organizational Grapevine," *Personnel Journal* (July 1988), pp. 31–35; J.G. March and G. Sevon, "Gossip, Information and Decision Making," in J.G. March (ed.), *Decisions and Organizations* (Oxford: Blackwell, 1988), pp. 429–42; and M. Noon and R. Delbridge, "News from Behind My Hand: Gossip in Organizations," *Organization Studies*, Vol. 14, No. 1, (1993), pp. 23–36.

[21] R. L. Birdwhistell, *Introduction to Kinesics* (Louisville, KY: University of Louisville Press, 1952).

[22] J. Fast, *Body Language* (Philadelphia: M. Evan, 1970), p. 7.

[23] R.L. Daft and R.H. Lengel, "Information Richness: A New Approach to Managerial Behavior and Organization Design," in B.M. Staw and L.L. Cummings (eds.), *Research in Organizational Behavior*, Vol. 6 (Greenwich, CT: JAI Press, 1984), pp. 191–233; R.E. Rice and D.E. Shook, "Relationships of Job Categories and Organizational Levels to Use of Communication Channels, Including Electronic Mail: A Meta-Analysis and Extension," *Journal of Management Studies* (March 1990), pp. 195–229; G.S. Russ, R.L. Daft, and R.H. Lengel, "Media Selection and Managerial Characteristics in Organizational Communications," *Management Communication Quarterly* (November 1990), pp. 151–75; L.K. Trevino, R.H. Lengel, W. Bodensteiner, E. Gerloff, and N.K. Muir, "The Richness Imperative and Cognitive Style: The Role of Individual Differences in Media Choice Behavior," *Management Communication Quarterly* (November 1990), pp. 176–97; R.E. Rice, "Task Analyzability, Use of New Media, and Effectiveness," *Organization Science* (November 1992), pp. 475–500; and S.G. Straus and J.E. McGrath, "Does the Medium Matter? The Interaction of Task Type and Technology on Group Performance and Member Reaction," *Journal of Applied Psychology* (February 1994), pp. 87–97.

[24] J. DeLorean, quoted in S.P. Robbins, *The Administrative Process* (Englewood Cliffs, NJ: Prentice-Hall, 1976), p. 404.

[25] This box is based on S.P. Robbins, *Training in InterPersonal Skills: TIPS for Managing People at Work* (Englewood Cliffs, NJ: Prentice Hall, 1989), Chapter 3; and data in R.C. Huseman, J.M. Lahiff, and J.M. Penrose, *Business Communication: Strategies and Skills* (Chicago: Dryden Press, 1988), pp. 380, 425.

[26] S.I. Hayakawa, *Language in Thought and Action* (New York: Harcourt Brace Jovanovich, 1949), p. 292.

[27] M. Young and J.E. Post, "Managing to Communicate, Communicating to Manage: How Leading Companies Communicate with Employees," *Organizational Dynamics* (Summer 1993), pp. 31–43.

[28] B. O'Reilly, "The New Deal: What Companies and Employees Owe One Another," *Fortune* (June 13, 1994), pp. 44–52.

[29] D. Tannen, *You Just Don't Understand: Women and Men in Conversation* (New York: Ballantine Books, 1991).

[30] M.L. LaGanga, "Are There Words That Neither Offend Nor Bore?" *Los Angeles Times* (May 18, 1994), p. II-27.

[31] Cited in J. Leo, "Falling for Sensitivity," *U.S. News & World Report* (December 13, 1993), p. 27.

[32] See M. Munter, "Cross-Cultural Communication for Managers," *Business Horizons* (May-June 1993), pp. 75–76.

[33] N. Adler, *International Dimensions of Organizational Behavior*, 2nd ed. (Boston: PWS-Kent, 1991), pp. 83–84.

[34] See, for instance, R. Hotch, "Communication Revolution," *Nation's Business* (May 1993), pp. 20–28; G. Brockhouse, "I Have Seen the Future . . . ," *Canadian Business* (August 1993), pp. 43–45; R. Hotch, "In Touch Through Technology," *Nation's Business* (January 1994), pp. 33–35; and B. Filipczak, "The Ripple Effect of Computer Networking," *Training* (March 1994), pp. 40–47.

[35] A. LaPlante, "TeleConfrontationing," *Forbes ASAP* (September 13, 1993), p. 117.

[36] See, for example, R.S. Schuler, "A Role Perception Transactional Process Model for Organizational Communication-Outcome Relationships," *Organizational Behavior and Human Performance* (April 1979), pp. 268–91.

[37] J.P. Walsh, S.J. Ashford, and T.E. Hill, "Feedback Obstruc-

tion: The Influence of the Information Environment on Employee Turnover Intentions," *Human Relations* (January 1985), pp. 23–46.

[38] S.A. Hellweg and S.L. Phillips, "Communication and Productivity in Organizations: A State-of-the-Art Review," in *Proceedings of the 40th Annual Academy of Management Conference* (Detroit, 1980), pp. 188–92.

[39] R.R. Reilly, B. Brown, M.R. Blood, and C.Z. Malatesta, "The Effects of Realistic Previews: A Study and Discussion of the Literature," *Personnel Psychology* (Winter 1981), pp. 823–34.

CHAPTER

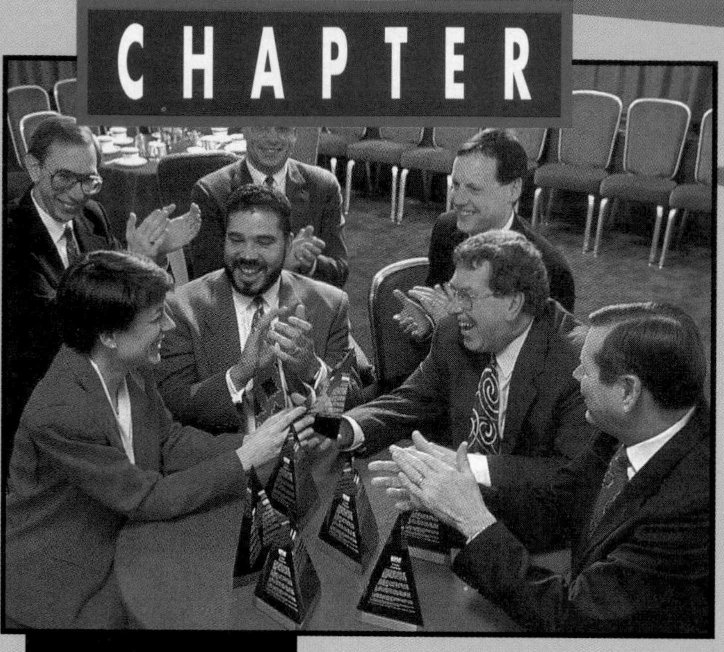

These managers at insurance company USF&G were rewarded for exhibiting what the company calls its "Seven C's of Leadership"—communication, confidence, character, comprehension, conviction, courage, and competency.

11

LEADERSHIP

CHAPTER OUTLINE

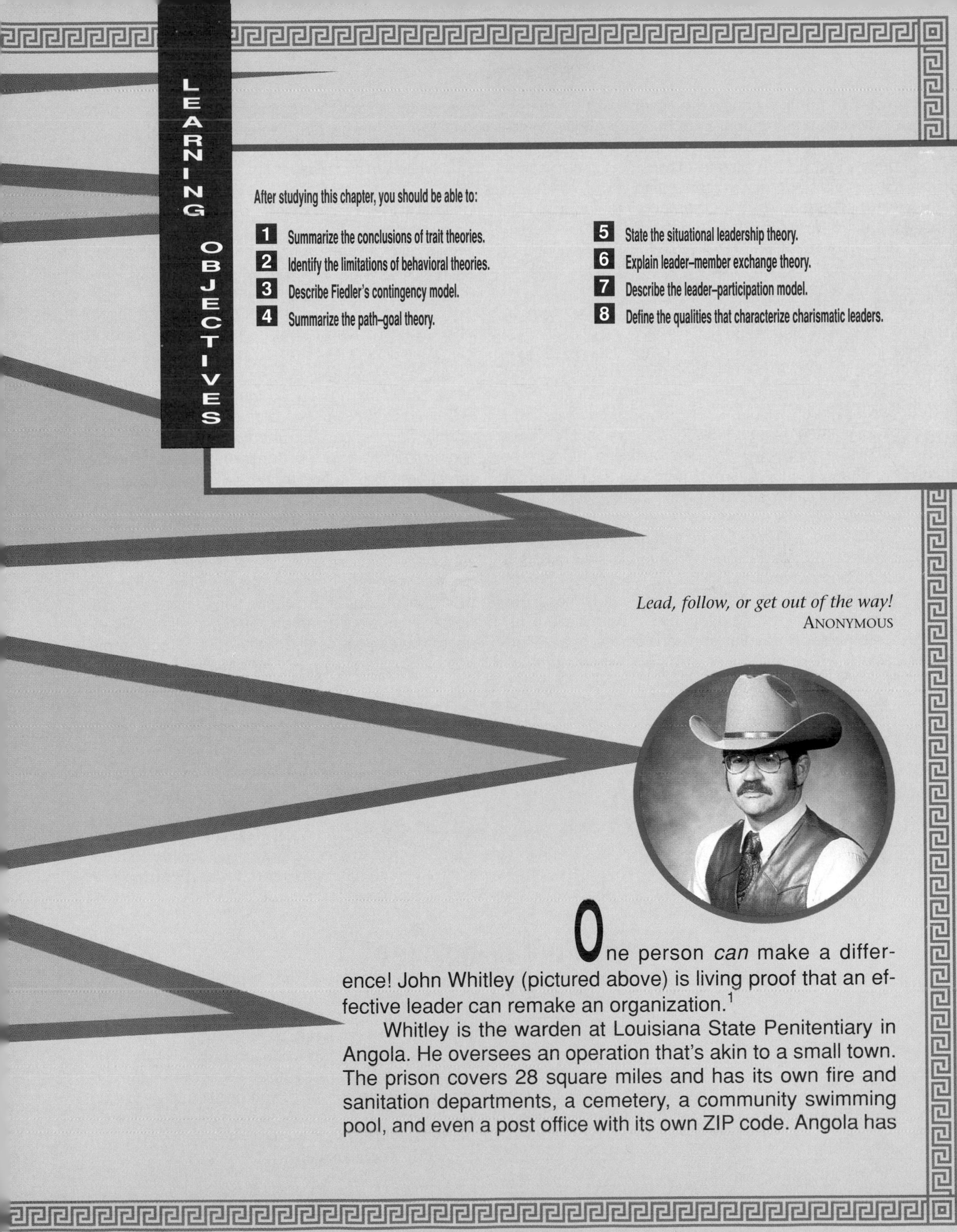

LEARNING OBJECTIVES

After studying this chapter, you should be able to:

1. Summarize the conclusions of trait theories.
2. Identify the limitations of behavioral theories.
3. Describe Fiedler's contingency model.
4. Summarize the path–goal theory.
5. State the situational leadership theory.
6. Explain leader–member exchange theory.
7. Describe the leader–participation model.
8. Define the qualities that characterize charismatic leaders.

Lead, follow, or get out of the way!
ANONYMOUS

One person *can* make a difference! John Whitley (pictured above) is living proof that an effective leader can remake an organization.[1]

Whitley is the warden at Louisiana State Penitentiary in Angola. He oversees an operation that's akin to a small town. The prison covers 28 square miles and has its own fire and sanitation departments, a cemetery, a community swimming pool, and even a post office with its own ZIP code. Angola has a staff of 1,545 to handle the prison's 5,200 inmates.

Whitley was brought in to head up Angola in the spring of 1990. He faced an awesome task. The prison had a long history of violence and prisoner discontent. Murders, suicides, and escape attempts were common. The mood among inmates could be summed up in a word: hopelessness. And morale among the staff was low. Trying to control an inmate population composed of mostly lifers made working at Angola tough.

In less than three years, Whitley turned Angola around. The number of stabbings, hangings, and escape attempts have dropped dramatically. The tension and uneasiness has lifted. In fact it's hard to find a Whitley detractor, even among the prisoners. "The warden's pretty cool people," says Curtis Kyles, one of 35 inmates on death row. "He sees people as individuals, not throwaways." One objective measure of the effect Whitley has had is the number of formal complaints filed with state prison authorities. They've dropped from 50 a month to fewer than 10.

What did John Whitley do that had such a positive influence on this prison? What leadership qualities did he bring to Angola that previous wardens hadn't? The answer seems to be decency and fairness. He is almost universally described in terms such as open-minded, impartial, and considerate. In a closed society, where authorities are the keepers and prisoners are the kept, Whitley has changed the rules. He essentially considers himself the prisoners' advocate within the system. He demands that his staff treat inmates as people, with feelings and needs. And when Whitley makes a mistake, he admits it. As one lifer noted, "Wardens just don't do that." To help prisoners make better use of their free time, Whitley has added basic reading and college-level computer and paralegal courses. To encourage good conduct, he has offered concrete rewards: increased visitation, telephone, and TV privileges.

One of the best illustrations of Whitley's leadership style was his reaction to the state legislature's strict deadline of October 1991 for inmates to challenge their convictions. Whitley, alone of Louisiana's 12 prison wardens, helped inmates beat the cutoff. He authorized the prison print shop to run off 5,000 appeal applications. He then instructed the prison radio station to hold a question-and-answer program, brought in a lawyer to field questions, and ordered all inmates to listen.

Don't conclude that because Whitley is humanistic he's soft on crime or wants to coddle prisoners. He favors the death penalty and believes executions would serve as a deterrent if they were carried out more swiftly. And if prisoners don't act responsibly, he has no qualms about enacting penalities. Curse a guard, forfeit your canteen privileges. Throw a meal tray in the cafeteria, lose your radio.

As John Whitley has demonstrated at Angola, leaders can make a difference. In this chapter, we look at the various studies on leadership to determine what makes an effective leader and what differentiates leaders from nonleaders. But first let's clarify what we mean by the term *leadership*.

What Is Leadership?

Few terms in OB inspire less agreement on definition than *leadership*. As one expert put it, "There are almost as many definitions of leadership as there are persons who have attempted to define the concept."[2]

While almost everyone seems to agree that leadership involves an influence process, differences tend to center around whether leadership must be noncoercive (as opposed to using authority, rewards, and punishments to exert influence over followers) and whether it is distinct from management.[3] The latter issue has been a particularly heated topic of debate in recent years, with most experts arguing that leadership and management are different.

For instance, Abraham Zaleznik of the Harvard Business School argues that leaders and managers are very different kinds of people.[4] They differ in motivation, personal history, and how they think and act. Zaleznik says that managers tend to adopt impersonal, if not passive, attitudes toward goals, whereas leaders take a personal and active attitude toward goals. Managers tend to view work as an enabling process involving some combination of people and ideas interacting to establish strategies and make decisions. Leaders work from high-risk positions—indeed, they are often temperamentally disposed to seek out risk and danger, especially when opportunity and reward appear high. Managers prefer to work with people; they avoid solitary activity because it makes them anxious. They relate to people according to the role they play in a sequence of events or in a decision-making process. Leaders, who are concerned with ideas, relate to people in more intuitive and empathic ways.

John Kotter, a colleague of Zaleznik at Harvard, also argues that leadership is different from management, but for different reasons.[5] Management, he proposes, is about coping with complexity. Good management brings about order and consistency by drawing up formal plans, designing rigid organization structures, and monitoring results against the plans. Leadership, in contrast, is about coping with change. Leaders establish direction by developing a vision of the future; then they align people by communicating this vision and inspiring them to overcome hurdles. Kotter sees both strong leadership and strong management as necessary for optimum organizational effectiveness. But he believes that most organizations are underled and overmanaged. He claims we need to focus more on developing leadership in organizations because the people in charge today are too concerned with keeping things on time and on budget and with doing what was done yesterday, only doing it 5 percent better.

So where do we stand? We use a broad definition of leadership, one that can encompass all the current approaches to the subject. Thus we define **leadership** as the ability to influence a group toward the achievement of goals. The source of this influence may be formal, such as that provided by the possession of managerial rank in an organization. Since management positions come with some degree of formally designated authority, a person may assume a leadership role simply because of the position he or she holds in the organization. But not all leaders are managers; nor, for that matter, are all managers leaders. Just because an organization provides its managers with certain formal rights is no assurance they will be able to lead effectively. We find that nonsanctioned leadership—that is, the ability to influence that arises outside the formal structure of the organization—is as important or more important than formal influence. In other words, leaders can emerge from within a group as well as by formal appointment to lead a group.

leadership
The ability to influence a group toward the achievement of goals.

◆Not all leaders are managers nor are all managers leaders.

Transition in Leadership Theories

The leadership literature is voluminous, and much of it is confusing and contradictory. In order to make our way through this forest, we consider four approaches to explaining what makes an effective leader. The first sought to find universal personality traits that leaders had to some greater degree than nonleaders. The second tried to explain leadership in terms of the behavior a person engaged in. Both approaches have been described as "false starts," based on their erroneous and oversimplified conception of leadership.[6] The third used contingency models to explain the inadequacies of previous leadership theories in reconciling and bringing together the diversity of research findings. Most recently, attention has returned to traits, but from a different perspective. Researchers are now attempting to identify the set of traits that people implicitly refer to when they characterize someone as a leader. This line of thinking proposes that leadership is as much style—projecting the appearance of being a leader—as it is substance. In this chapter, we present the contributions and limitations of each of these four approaches, introduce and review a number of contemporary issues related to applying leadership concepts, and conclude by considering the value of the leadership literature for practicing managers.

Trait Theories

When Margaret Thatcher was prime minister of Great Britain, she was regularly singled out for her leadership. She was described in terms such as confident, iron-willed, determined, and decisive. These terms are traits and, whether Thatcher's advocates and critics recognized it at the time, when they described her in such terms they became trait theorist supporters.

trait theories of leadership
Theories that sought personality, social, physical, or intellectual traits that differentiated leaders from nonleaders.

The media has long been a believer in **trait theories**. They identify people like Thatcher, Ronald Reagan, Nelson Mandela, Ted Turner, Barbara Jordan, and Jesse Jackson as leaders, and then describe them in terms such as *charismatic, enthusiastic*, and *courageous*. Well, the media isn't alone. The search for personality, social, physical, or intellectual attributes that would describe leaders and differentiate them from nonleaders goes back to the 1930s and research done by psychologists.

Research efforts at isolating leadership traits resulted in a number of dead ends. For instance, a review of 20 different studies identified nearly 80 leadership traits, but only 5 of these traits were common to 4 or more of the investigations.[7] If the search was intended to identify a set of traits that would always differentiate leaders from followers and effective from ineffective leaders, the search failed. Perhaps it was a bit optimistic to believe there could be consistent and unique traits that would apply universally to all effective leaders, no matter whether they were in charge of the Louisiana State Penitentiary in Angola, the Mormon Tabernacle Choir, General Electric, Ted's Malibu Surf Shop, the Brazilian National soccer team, or Oxford University.

If, however, the search was intended to identify traits that were consistently associated with leadership, the results can be interpreted in a more im-

What traits characterize leaders like Nelson Mandela? Research studies indicate six traits are consistently associated with leadership: ambition and energy, the desire to lead, honesty and integrity, self-confidence, intelligence, and job-relevant knowledge. Possessing these traits helped Mandela succeed in achieving his vision of ending apartheid in South Africa. Recognized worldwide as a courageous and enthusiastic leader, Mandela won the Nobel Peace Prize for his efforts in creating national unity.

pressive light. For example, six traits on which leaders tend to differ from nonleaders are ambition and energy, the desire to lead, honesty and integrity, self-confidence, intelligence, and job-relevant knowledge.[8] Additionally, recent research provides strong evidence that people who are high self-monitors—that is, are highly flexible in adjusting their behavior in different situations—are much more likely to emerge as leaders in groups than low self-monitors.[9] Overall, the cumulative findings from more than half a century of research lead us to conclude that some traits increase the likelihood of success as a leader, but none of the traits *guarantee* success.[10]

Why hasn't the trait approach proven more successful in explaining leadership? We can suggest at least four reasons. It overlooks the needs of followers, it generally fails to clarify the relative importance of various traits, it doesn't separate cause from effect (for example, are leaders self-confident or does success as a leader build self-confidence?), and it ignores situational factors. These limitations have led researchers to look in other directions. Although there has been some resurgent interest in traits during the past decade,[11] a major movement away from traits began as early as the 1940s. Leadership research from the late 1940s through the mid-1960s emphasized the preferred behavioral styles that leaders demonstrated.

Behavioral Theories

The inability to strike "gold" in the trait "mines" led researchers to look at the **behaviors** that specific leaders exhibited. They wondered if there was something unique in the way effective leaders behave. For example, Robert Crandall, chairman of American Airlines, and Paul B. Kazarian, the former chairman of Sunbeam-Oster, both have been very successful in leading their companies through difficult times.[12] And they both rely on a common leadership style—tough talking, intense, autocratic. Does this suggest autocratic behavior is a preferred style for *all* leaders? In this section, we look at four different behavioral theories in order to answer that question. First, however, let's consider the practical implications of the behavioral approach.

behavioral theories of leadership
Theories proposing that specific behaviors differentiate leaders from nonleaders.

If the behavioral approach to leadership were successful, it would have implications quite different from those of the trait approach. If trait research had been successful, it would have provided a basis for *selecting* the "right" person to assume formal positions in groups and organizations requiring leadership. In contrast, if behavioral studies were to turn up critical behavioral determinants of leadership, we could *train* people to be leaders. The difference between trait and behavioral theories, in terms of application, lies in their underlying assumptions. If trait theories were valid, then leadership is basically inborn: You either have it or you don't. On the other hand, if there were specific behaviors that identified leaders, then we could teach leadership—we could design programs that implanted these behavioral patterns in individuals who desired to be effective leaders. This was surely a more exciting avenue, for it meant the supply of leaders could be expanded. If training worked, we could have an infinite supply of effective leaders.

Ohio State Studies

The most comprehensive and replicated of the behavioral theories resulted from research that began at Ohio State University in the late 1940s.[13] These researchers sought to identify independent dimensions of leader behavior. Beginning with over 1,000 dimensions, they eventually narrowed the list into two categories that substantially accounted for most of the leadership behavior described by subordinates. They called these two dimensions *initiating structure* and *consideration*.

initiating structure
The extent to which a leader is likely to define and structure his or her role and those of subordinates in the search for goal attainment.

Initiating structure refers to the extent to which a leader is likely to define and structure his or her role and those of subordinates in the search for goal attainment. It includes behavior that attempts to organize work, work relationships, and goals. The leader characterized as high in initiating structure could be described in terms such as "assigns group members to particular tasks," "expects workers to maintain definite standards of performance," and "emphasizes the meeting of deadlines." Robert Crandall and Paul Kazarian exhibit high initiating structure behavior.

consideration
The extent to which a leader is likely to have job relationships characterized by mutual trust, respect for subordinates' ideas, and regard for their feelings.

Consideration is described as the extent to which a person is likely to have job relationships that are characterized by mutual trust, respect for subordinates' ideas, and regard for their feelings. He or she shows concern for followers' comfort, well-being, status, and satisfaction. A leader high in consideration could be described as one who helps subordinates with personal problems, is friendly and approachable, and treats all subordinates as equals. The current chairman of Southwest Airlines, Herb Kelleher, rates high on consideration behavior. His leadership style is very people oriented, emphasizing friendliness and empowerment.

Extensive research, based on these definitions, found that leaders high in initiating structure and consideration (a "high-high" leader) tended to achieve high subordinate performance and satisfaction more frequently than those who rated low on either consideration, initiating structure, or both. However, the "high-high" style did not always result in positive consequences. For example, leader behavior characterized as high on initiating structure led to greater rates of grievances, absenteeism, and turnover and lower levels of job satisfaction for workers performing routine tasks. Other studies found that high consideration was negatively related to performance ratings of the leader by his or her superior. In conclusion, the Ohio State studies suggested that the "high-high" style

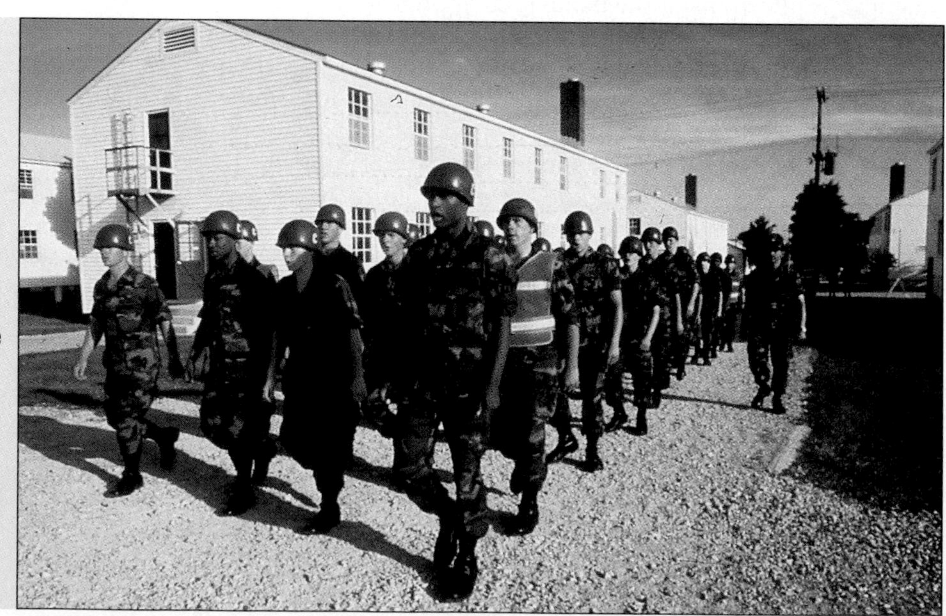

Army drill instructors exemplify individuals who are high in initiating structure. In boot camp, they give orders continuously and structure recruits' activities from sunrise to bedtime. Emphasis on task accomplishment takes precedence over the recruits' personal needs because much learning must be condensed into a short period and accepting authority and obeying orders is critical to the Army's operating efficiency.

generally resulted in positive outcomes, but enough exceptions were found to indicate that situational factors needed to be integrated into the theory.

University of Michigan Studies

Leadership studies undertaken at the University of Michigan's Survey Research Center, at about the same time as those being done at Ohio State, had similar research objectives: to locate behavioral characteristics of leaders that appeared to be related to measures of performance effectiveness.

The Michigan group also came up with two dimensions of leadership behavior that they labeled **employee oriented** and **production oriented**.[14] Employed-oriented leaders were described as emphasizing interpersonal relations; they took a personal interest in the needs of their subordinates and accepted individual differences among members. The production-oriented leaders, in contrast, tended to emphasize the technical or task aspects of the job: Their main concern was in accomplishing their group's tasks, and the group members were a means to that end.

employee-oriented leader One who emphasizes interpersonal relations.

production-oriented leader One who emphasizes technical or task aspects of the job.

The conclusions arrived at by the Michigan researchers strongly favored the leaders who were employee-oriented in their behavior. Employee-oriented leaders were associated with higher group productivity and higher job satisfaction. Production-oriented leaders tended to be associated with low group productivity and lower job satisfaction.

The Managerial Grid

A graphic portrayal of a two-dimensional view of leadership style was developed by Blake and Mouton.[15] They proposed a **Managerial Grid** based on the styles of "concern for people" and "concern for production," which essentially represent the Ohio State dimensions of consideration and initiating structure or the Michigan dimensions of employee oriented and production oriented.

Managerial Grid A nine-by-nine matrix outlining eighty-one different leadership styles.

The grid, depicted in Figure 11-1 on page 418, has 9 possible positions along each axis, creating 81 different positions in which the leader's style may fall. The grid does not show results produced but, rather, the dominating factors in a leader's thinking in regard to getting results.

Based on the findings of Blake and Mouton, managers were found to perform best under a 9,9 style, as contrasted, for example, with a 9,1 (authority type) or 1,9 (country club type) style.[16] Unfortunately, the grid offers a better framework for conceptualizing leadership style than for presenting any tangible new information in clarifying the leadership quandary, since there is little substantive evidence to support the conclusion that a 9,9 style is most effective in all situations.[17]

Scandinavian Studies

The three behavioral approaches we've just reviewed were essentially developed between the late 1940s and early 1960s. These approaches evolved during a time when the world was a far more stable and predictable place. In the belief that these studies fail to capture the more dynamic realities of today, researchers in Finland and Sweden have been reassessing whether there are only two dimensions that capture the essence of leadership behavior.[18] Their basic premise is that in a changing world, effective leaders would exhibit **development-oriented** behavior. These are leaders who value experimentation, seek new ideas, and generate and implement change.

development-oriented leader One who values experimentation, seeking new ideas, and generating and implementing change.

Figure 11-1
The Managerial Grid

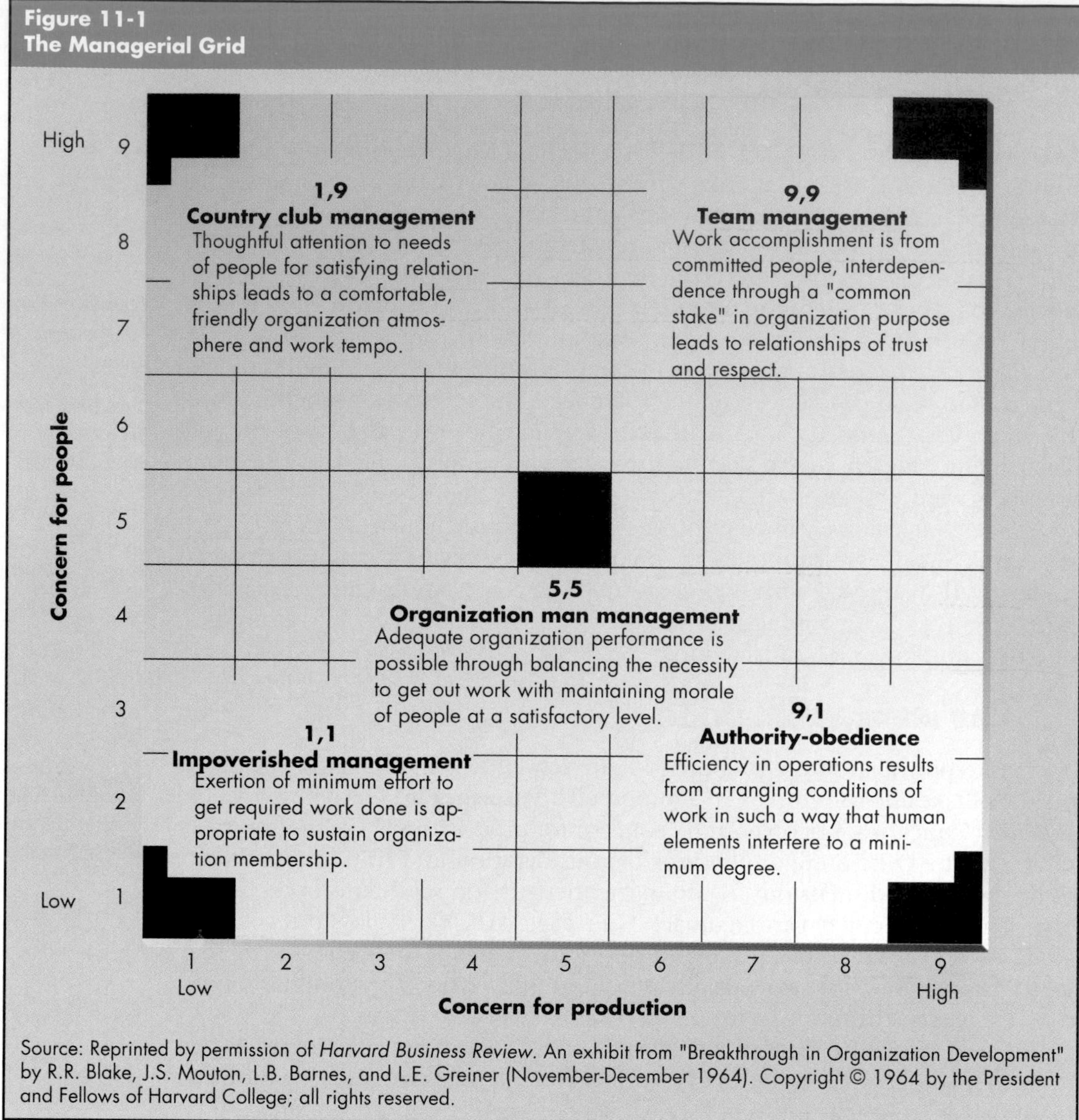

Source: Reprinted by permission of *Harvard Business Review.* An exhibit from "Breakthrough in Organization Development" by R.R. Blake, J.S. Mouton, L.B. Barnes, and L.E. Greiner (November-December 1964). Copyright © 1964 by the President and Fellows of Harvard College; all rights reserved.

For instance, these Scandinavian researchers went back and looked at the original Ohio State data. They found that the Ohio State people included development items such as "pushes new ways of doing things," "originates new approaches to problems," and "encourages members to start new activities." But these items, at the time, didn't explain much toward effective leadership. It could be, the Scandinavian researchers proposed, that this was because developing new ideas and implementing change wasn't critical *in those days*. In today's dynamic environment, this may no longer be true. So the Scandinavian researchers have been conducting new studies looking to see if there is a third dimension—development orientation—that is related to leader effectiveness.

The early evidence is positive. Using samples of leaders in Finland and Sweden, the researchers have found strong support for development-oriented leader behavior as a separate and independent dimension. That is, the previous behavioral approaches that focused in on only two behaviors may not appropriately capture leadership in the 1990s. Moreover, while initial conclusions need to be guarded without more confirming evidence, it also appears that leaders who demonstrate development-oriented behavior have more satisfied subordinates and are seen as more competent by those subordinates.

Summary of Behavioral Theories

We've described the most important of the attempts to explain leadership in terms of the behavior exhibited by the leader. In general, researchers have had modest success in identifying consistent relationships between patterns of leadership behavior and group performance. What seems to be missing is consideration of the *situational* factors that influence success or failure. For example, Robert Crandall and Herb Kelleher have both been effective leaders of airlines, yet their styles are almost diametrically opposed. How can that be? The answer is that American and Southwest are very different companies, operating in different markets with very different labor forces. The behavioral theories fail to take this into account. Jesse Jackson is certainly an effective leader of black causes in the *1990s*, but would his style have been equally effective in the *1890s*? Probably not! Situations change and leadership styles need to change with them. Unfortunately, the behavioral approaches don't recognize changes in situations.

Contingency Theories

Bob Knight, the men's head basketball coach at Indiana University, consistently uses an intense, task-oriented leadership style that intimidates players, officials, the media, and university administrators. But his style works with the Indiana teams he recruits. Knight has one of the most impressive win-loss records of any active major college basketball coach. But would this same style work if Bob Knight was counsel-general of the United Nations or project manager for a group of Ph.D. software designers at Microsoft? Probably not! Observations such as this have directed researchers to look at more adaptive approaches to leadership.

It became increasingly clear to those who were studying the leadership phenomenon that the predicting of leadership success was more complex than isolating a few traits or preferable behaviors. The failure to obtain consistent results led to a focus on situational influences. The relationship between leadership style and effectiveness suggested that under condition *a*, style *x* would be appropriate whereas style *y* would be more suitable for condition *b*, and style *z* for condition *c*. But what were the conditions *a*, *b*, *c*, and so forth? It was one thing to say that leadership effectiveness was dependent on the situation and another to be able to isolate those situational conditions.

No shortage of studies has attempted to isolate critical situational factors that affect leadership effectiveness. For instance, popular moderating variables used in the development of contingency theories include the degree of structure in the task being performed, the quality of leader-member relations, the leader's position power, subordinates' role clarity, group norms, information availability, subordinate acceptance of leader's decisions, and subordinate maturity.[19]

Several approaches to isolating key situational variables have proven more successful than others and, as a result, have gained wider recognition. We consider five of these: the Fiedler model, Hersey and Blanchard's situational theory, leader-member exchange theory, and the path-goal and leader-participation models.

◆◆◆◆ OB in the News ◆◆◆◆

Jack Croushore: From Tough Guy to Cream Puff

Jack Croushore used to be a "tough guy." During a 26-year career in the steel industry, he built a reputation as a hard-nosed boss. He took no guff. When workers got out of line, he didn't hesitate to hand out disciplinary slips and suspensions without pay.

"I was a very strict disciplinarian for 18 years," recalls Croushore, now president and CEO of CP Industries Inc., in McKeesport, Pennsylvania, a manufacturer of seamless pressure vessels for storing and transporting gasses. "I probably gave out more slips than anybody. I was very critical of the work force—even the foremen and general foremen who worked for me."

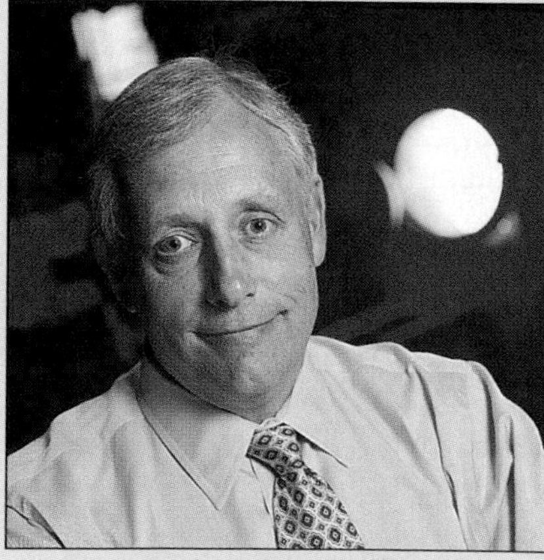

Jack Croushore learned that situational factors influence leadership effectiveness. He improved his relationship with employees by replacing his autocratic leadership style with a participative approach.

All that changed in 1984. He was working for U.S. Steel, and he had just participated in the closing of the company's National Works plant, where he had spent 18 years. According to Croushore, he had done "everything I was asked to do at National Works [as plant manager], and, in the end, I couldn't keep the plant open. I followed all the rules. I did what they said would work. And, in the end, they said, "We're going to shut it down." Six hundred workers lost their jobs.

In 1984 Croushore was reassigned to the company's smaller Christy Park Works, which later became CP Industries. When he arrived, "I told the fellow who'd hired me, 'Look, I'm not going to do things the way I did them down there—because they *don't work*. I'm going to try new things.'"

Those new things included a very different leadership style. Croushore traded in his autocratic approach for a trusting, participative style. His new guiding principle became the Golden Rule. "Usually, when I get into a situation, I think about how I would feel and how I would want to be treated if I were in that person's place." He avoids disciplinary actions, trusting that most workers will do the right thing. He encourages his employees to take responsibility and make decisions on their own. He has even empowered teams of hourly workers to oversee the hiring and development of new employees.

The "new" Jack Croushore doesn't penalize employees for absenteeism or insubordination. "We don't require anybody to do anything," he asserts. "You can't *make* people do things they don't want to do. There aren't enough supervisors, and there isn't enough time in the day." What's more, Croushore contends, disciplinary actions tend to be counterproductive, especially in a union atmosphere. The grievance process takes up valuable time of workers, foremen, and plant management. Productivity suffers and morale goes down the tubes.

Jack Croushore's revised leadership style has worked. The labor force at Christy (which is now CP Industries) has shrunk through attrition, and productivity has soared. In 1992 an hourly work force of just 89 people generated 20 percent more revenues than a 159-person work force had in 1984.

Based on J.H. Sheridan, "Jack Croushore: From Tough Guy to 'Cream Puff,'" *Industry Week* (December 6, 1993), pp. 11–16.

Fiedler Model

The first comprehensive contingency model for leadership was developed by Fred Fiedler.[20] The **Fiedler contingency model** proposes that effective group performance depends on the proper match between the leader's style of interacting with his or her subordinates and the degree to which the situation gives control and influence to the leader. Fiedler developed an instrument, which he called the **least preferred coworker (LPC) questionnaire**, that purports to measure whether a person is task or relationship oriented. Further, he isolated three situational criteria—leader-member relations, task structure, and position power—that he believes can be manipulated so as to create the proper match with the behavioral orientation of the leader. In a sense, the Fiedler model is an outgrowth of trait theory, since the LPC questionnaire is a simple psychological test. However, Fiedler goes significantly beyond trait and behavioral approaches by attempting to isolate situations, relating his personality measure to his situational classification, and then predicting leadership effectiveness as a function of the two.

Fiedler contingency model
The theory that effective groups depend upon a proper match between a leader's style of interacting with subordinates and the degree to which the situation gives control and influence to the leader.

least preferred co-worker (LPC) questionnaire
An instrument that purports to measure whether a person is task- or relationship-oriented.

This description of the Fiedler model is somewhat abstract. Let's now look at the model more closely.

IDENTIFYING LEADERSHIP STYLE Fiedler believes a key factor in leadership success is the individual's basic leadership style. So he begins by trying to find out what that basic style is. Fiedler created the LPC questionnaire for this purpose. It contains 16 contrasting adjectives (such as pleasant–unpleasant, efficient–inefficient, open–guarded, supportive–hostile). The questionnaire then asks the respondent to think of all the coworkers they have ever had and to describe the one person they *least enjoyed* working with by rating him or her on a scale of 1 to 8 for each of the 16 sets of contrasting adjectives. Fiedler believes that based on the respondents' answers to this LPC questionnaire, he can determine their basic leadership style. If the least preferred coworker is described in relatively positive terms (a high LPC score), then the respondent is primarily interested in good personal relations with this coworker. That is, if you essentially describe the person you are least able to work with in favorable terms, Fiedler would label you *relationship oriented.* In contrast, if the least preferred coworker is seen in relatively unfavorable terms (a low LPC score), the respondent is primarily interested in productivity and thus would be labeled *task oriented.* About 16 percent of respondents score in the middle range.[21] Such individuals cannot be classified as either relationship or task oriented and thus fall outside the theory's predictions. The rest of our discussion, therefore, relates to the 84 percent who score in either the high or low range of the LPC.

Fiedler assumes that an individual's leadership style is fixed. As we show in a moment, this is important because it means that if a situation requires a task-oriented leader and the person in that leadership position is relationship oriented, either the situation has to be modified or the leader removed and replaced if optimum effectiveness is to be achieved. Fiedler argues that leadership style is innate to a person—you *can't* change your style to fit changing situations!

DEFINING THE SITUATION After an individual's basic leadership style has been assessed through the LPC, it is necessary to match the leader with the situation. Fiedler has identified three contingency dimensions that, he argues, define the key situational factors that determine leadership effectiveness. These

Bob Knight, the highly successful basketball coach at Indiana University, generally confirms Fiedler's belief that a person's leadership style is fixed. Knight's intense, task-oriented style seems unvarying. He regularly argues with referees and once threw a chair across the floor to protest a call. In one season he benched all his starters in a key conference game because they weren't practicing intensely enough. He even kicked his own son off the team for a rules infraction.

leader–member relations
The degree of confidence, trust, and respect subordinates have in their leader.

task structure
The degree to which job assignments are procedurized.

position power
Influence derived from one's formal structural position in the organization; includes power to hire, fire, discipline, promote, and give salary increases.

are **leader–member relations**, **task structure**, and **position power**. They are defined as follows:

1. *Leader–member relations:* The degree of confidence, trust, and respect subordinates have in their leader
2. *Task structure:* The degree to which the job assignments are procedurized (that is, structured or unstructured)
3. *Position power:* The degree of influence a leader has over power variables such as hiring, firing, discipline, promotions, and salary increases

So the next step in the Fiedler model is to evaluate the situation in terms of these three contingency variables. Leader–member relations are either good or poor, task structure is either high or low, and position power is either strong or weak.

Fiedler states the better the leader–member relations, the more highly structured the job, and the stronger the position power, the more control or influence the leader has. For example, a very favorable situation (where the leader would have a great deal of control) might involve a payroll manager who is well respected and whose subordinates have confidence in her (good leader–member relations), where the activities to be done—such as wage computation, check writing, report filing—are specific and clear (high task structure), and the job provides considerable freedom for her to reward and punish her subordinates (strong position power). On the other hand, an unfavorable situation might be the disliked chairman of a voluntary United Way fundraising team. In this job, the leader has very little control. Altogether, by mixing the three contingency variables, there are potentially eight different situations or categories in which a leader could find him or herself.

MATCHING LEADERS AND SITUATIONS With knowledge of an individual's LPC and an assessment of the three contingency variables, the Fiedler model proposes matching them up to achieve maximum leadership effectiveness.[22]

Based on Fiedler's study of over 1,200 groups, in which he compared relationship- versus task-oriented leadership styles in each of the eight situational categories, he concluded that task-oriented leaders tend to perform better in situations that were *very favorable* to them and in situations that were *very unfavorable* (see Figure 11-2). So Fiedler would predict that when faced with a category I, II, III, VII, or VIII situation, task-oriented leaders perform better. Relationship-oriented leaders, however, perform better in moderately favorable situations: categories IV through VI.

Figure 11-2
Findings from Fiedler Model

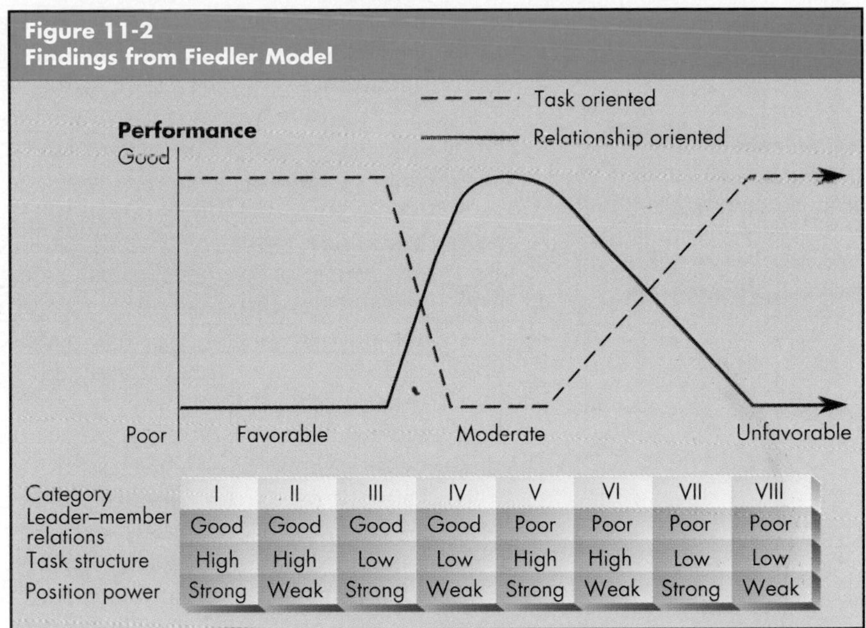

Category	I	II	III	IV	V	VI	VII	VIII
Leader–member relations	Good	Good	Good	Good	Poor	Poor	Poor	Poor
Task structure	High	High	Low	Low	High	High	Low	Low
Position power	Strong	Weak	Strong	Weak	Strong	Weak	Strong	Weak

Given Fiedler's findings, how would you apply them? You would seek to match leaders and situations. Individuals' LPC scores would determine the type of situation for which they were best suited. That "situation" would be defined by evaluating the three contingency factors of leader–member relations, task structure, and position power. But remember that Fiedler views an individual's leadership style as being fixed. Therefore, there are really only two ways in which to improve leader effectiveness.

First, you can change the leader to fit the situation—as in a baseball game, a manager can reach into his bullpen and put in a right-handed pitcher or a left-handed pitcher, depending on the situational characteristics of the hitter. So, for example, if a group situation rates as highly unfavorable but is currently led by a relationship-oriented manager, the group's performance could be improved by replacing that manager with one who is task oriented. The second alternative would be to change the situation to fit the leader. That could be done by restructuring tasks or increasing or decreasing the power of the leader to control factors such as salary increases, promotions, and disciplinary actions. To illustrate, assume a task-oriented leader is in a category IV situation. If this leader could increase his or her position power, then the leader would be operating in category III and the leader–situation match would be compatible for high group performance.

EVALUATION As a whole, reviews of the major studies undertaken to test the overall validity of the Fiedler model lead to a generally positive conclusion. That is, considerable evidence supports at least substantial parts of the model.[23] But additional variables are probably needed if an improved model is to fill in some of the remaining gaps. Moreover, problems with the LPC and the practical use of the model need to be addressed. For instance, the logic underlying the LPC is not well understood and studies have shown that respondents' LPC scores are not stable.[24] Also, the contingency variables are complex and difficult for practitioners to assess. It's often difficult in practice to determine how good the leader–member relations are, how structured the task is, and how much position power the leader has.[25]

cognitive resource theory
A theory of leadership that states that a leader obtains effective group performance by, first, making effective plans, decisions, and strategies, and then communicating them through directive behavior.

COGNITIVE RESOURCE THEORY: AN UPDATE ON FIEDLER'S CONTINGENCY MODEL In 1987, Fiedler and an associate, Joe Garcia, reconceptualized the former's original theory[26] to deal with "some serious oversights that need to be addressed."[27] Specifically, they are trying to explain the process by which a leader obtains effective group performance. They call this reconceptualization **cognitive resource theory**.

They begin by making two assumptions. First, intelligent and competent leaders formulate more effective plans, decisions, and action strategies than less intelligent and competent leaders. Second, leaders communicate their plans, decisions, and strategies through directive behavior. Fiedler and Garcia then show how stress and cognitive resources such as experience, tenure, and intelligence act as important influences on leadership effectiveness.

The essence of the new theory can be boiled down to three predictions: (1) directive behavior results in good performance only if linked with high intelligence in a supportive, nonstressful leadership environment; (2) in highly stressful situations, there is a positive relationship between job experience and performance; and (3) the intellectual abilities of leaders correlate with group performance in situations the leader perceives as nonstressful.

Fiedler and Garcia admit that their data supporting cognitive resource theory are far from overwhelming. And the limited number of studies to test the theory have, to date, generated mixed results.[28] Clearly, more research is needed. Yet, given the impact of Fiedler's original contingency model of leadership on organizational behavior, the new theory's link to this earlier model, and the new theory's introduction of the leader's cognitive abilities as an important influence on leadership effectiveness, cognitive resource theory should not be dismissed out of hand.

Hersey and Blanchard's Situational Theory

situational leadership theory
A contingency theory that focuses on followers' readiness.

Paul Hersey and Ken Blanchard have developed a leadership model that has gained a strong following among management development specialists.[29] This model—called **situational leadership theory**—has been used as a major training device at such Fortune 500 companies as BankAmerica, Caterpillar, IBM, Mobil Oil, and Xerox; it has also been widely accepted in all the military services.[30] Although the theory has undergone limited evaluation to test its validity, we include it here because of its wide acceptance and its strong intuitive appeal.

Situational leadership is a contingency theory that focuses on the followers. Successful leadership is achieved by selecting the right leadership style, which Hersey and Blanchard argue is contingent on the level of the followers' readiness or maturity. Before we proceed, we should clarify two points: Why focus on the followers? What is meant by the term *readiness*?

The emphasis on the followers in leadership effectiveness reflects the reality that it is they who accept or reject the leader. Regardless of what the leader does, effectiveness depends on the actions of his or her followers. This is an important dimension that has been overlooked or underemphasized in most leadership theories. The term *readiness*, as defined by Hersey and Blanchard, refers to the extent to which people have the ability and willingness to accomplish a specific task.

Situational leadership uses the same two leadership dimensions that Fiedler identified: task and relationship behaviors. However, Hersey and Blanchard go a step farther by considering each as either high or low and then combining them into four specific leader behaviors: telling, selling, participating, and delegating. They are described as follows:

◆ *Telling* (high task–low relationship). The leader defines roles and tells people what, how, when, and where to do various tasks. It emphasizes directive behavior.

◆ *Selling* (high task–high relationship). The leader provides both directive behavior and supportive behavior.

◆ *Participating* (low task–high relationship). The leader and follower share in decision making, with the main role of the leader being facilitating and communicating.

◆ *Delegating* (low task–low relationship). The leader provides little direction or support.

The final component in Hersey and Blanchard's theory is defining four stages of follower readiness:

R1. People are both unable and unwilling to take responsibility to do something. They are neither competent nor confident.

R2. People are unable but willing to do the necessary job tasks. They are motivated but currently lack the appropriate skills.

R3. People are able but unwilling to do what the leader wants.

R4. People are both able and willing to do what is asked of them.

Figure 11-3 integrates the various components into the situational leadership model. As followers reach high levels of readiness, the leader responds by not only continuing to decrease control over activities, but also by continuing to decrease relationship behavior as well. At stage R1, followers need clear and specific directions. At stage R2, both high-task and high-relationship behavior is needed. The high-task behavior compensates for the followers' lack of ability, and the high-relationship behavior tries to get the followers psychologically to buy into the leader's desires. R3 creates motivational problems that are best solved by a supportive, nondirective, participative style. Finally, at stage R4, the leader doesn't have to do much because followers are both willing and able to take responsibility.

The astute reader might have noticed the high similarity between Hersey and Blanchard's four leadership styles and the four extreme "corners" in the Managerial Grid. The telling style equates to the 9,1 leader; selling equals 9,9; participating is equivalent to 1,9; and delegating is the same as the 1,1 leader. Is situational leadership, then, merely the Managerial Grid with one major difference—the replacement of the 9,9

Figure 11-3
Hersey and Blanchard's Situational Leadership Model

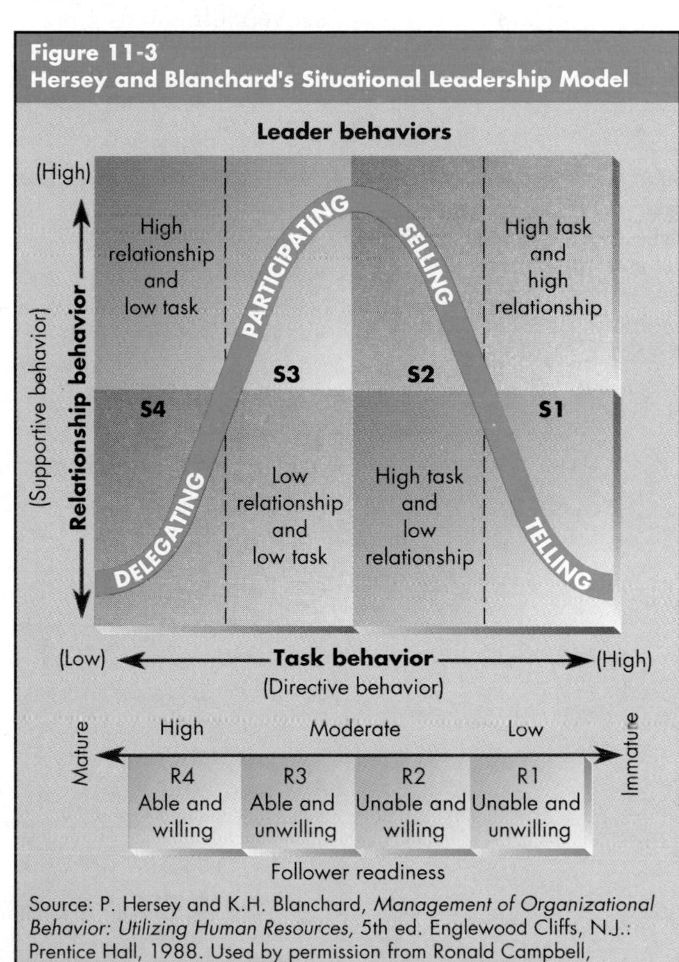

Source: P. Hersey and K.H. Blanchard, *Management of Organizational Behavior: Utilizing Human Resources,* 5th ed. Englewood Cliffs, N.J.: Prentice Hall, 1988. Used by permission from Ronald Campbell, President, Leadership Studies. Escondido, CA. September, 1991.

("one style for all occasions") contention with the recommendation that the "right" style should align with the readiness of the followers? Hersey and Blanchard say "No."[31] They argue that the grid emphasizes *concern* for production and people, which are attitudinal dimensions. Situational leadership, in contrast, emphasizes task and relationship *behavior*. In spite of Hersey and Blanchard's claim, this is a pretty minute differentiation. Understanding of the situational leadership theory is probably enhanced by considering it as a fairly direct adaptation of the grid framework to reflect four stages of follower readiness.

Finally, we come to the critical question: Is there evidence to support situational leadership theory? As noted earlier, the theory has received little attention from researchers,[32] but on the basis of the research to date, conclusions must be guarded. Some researchers provide partial support for the theory;[33] others find no support for its assumptions.[34] As a result, any enthusiastic endorsement should be cautioned against.

Leader–Member Exchange Theory

For the most part, the leadership theories we've covered to this point have largely assumed that leaders treat all their subordinates in the same manner. But think about your experiences in groups. Did you notice that leaders often act very differently toward different subordinates? Did the leader tend to have favorites who made up his or her "in" group? If you answered "Yes" to both these questions, you're acknowledging what George Graen and his associates have observed, which creates the foundation for their leader–member exchange theory.[35]

leader–member exchange (LMX) theory
Leaders create in-groups and out-groups, and subordinates with in-group status will have higher performance ratings, less turnover, and greater satisfaction with their superior.

The **leader–member exchange (LMX) theory** argues that because of time pressures, leaders establish a special relationship with a small group of their subordinates. These individuals make up the in-group—they are trusted, get a disproportionate amount of the leader's attention, and are more likely to receive special privileges. Other subordinates fall into the out-group. They get less of the leader's time, fewer of the preferred rewards that the leader controls, and have superior–subordinate relations based on formal authority interactions.

The theory proposes that early in the history of the interaction between a leader and a given subordinate, the leader implicitly categorizes the subordinate as an "in" or an "out" and that relationship is relatively stable over time.[36] Just precisely how the leader chooses who falls into each category is unclear, but there is evidence that leaders tend to choose in-group members because they have personal characteristics (for example, age, gender, attitudes) that are similar to the leader, a higher level of competence than out-group members, and/or an extroverted personality[37] (see Figure 11-4). LMX theory predicts that subordinates with in-group status will have higher performance ratings, less turnover, and greater satisfaction with their superior.

Research to test LMX theory has been generally supportive.[38] More specifically, the theory and research surrounding it provide substantive evidence that leaders do differentiate among subordinates, that these disparities are far from random, and that in-group and out-group status are related to employee performance and satisfaction.[39]

Path-Goal Theory

Currently, one of the most respected approaches to leadership is the path-goal theory. Developed by Robert House, path-goal theory is a contingency model

Figure 11-4
Leader-Member Exchange Theory

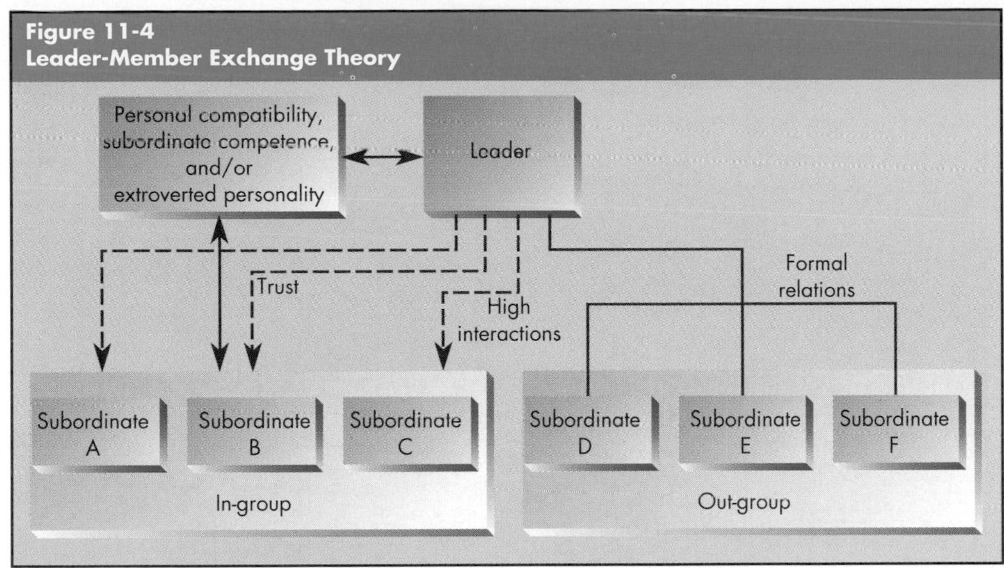

of leadership that extracts key elements from the Ohio State leadership research on initiating structure and consideration and the expectancy theory of motivation.[40]

The essence of the theory is that it's the leader's job to assist his or her followers in attaining their goals and to provide the necessary direction and/or support to ensure their goals are compatible with the overall objectives of the group or organization. The term *path-goal* is derived from the belief that effective leaders clarify the path to help their followers get from where they are to the achievement of their work goals and make the journey along the path easier by reducing roadblocks and pitfalls.

path-goal theory
The theory that a leader's behavior is acceptable to subordinates insofar as they view it as a source of either immediate or future satisfaction.

According to **path-goal theory**, a leader's behavior is *acceptable* to subordinates to the degree that it is viewed by them as an immediate source of satisfaction or as a means of future satisfaction. A leader's behavior is *motivational* to the degree it (1) makes subordinate need satisfaction contingent on effective performance, and (2) provides the coaching, guidance, support, and rewards that are necessary for effective performance. To test these statements, House identified four leadership behaviors. The *directive leader* lets subordinates know what is expected of them, schedules work to be done, and gives specific guidance as to how to accomplish tasks. This closely parallels the Ohio State dimension of initiating structure. The *supportive leader* is friendly and shows concern for the needs of subordinates. This is essentially synonymous with the Ohio State dimension of consideration. The *participative leader* consults with subordinates and uses their suggestions before making a decision. The *achievement-oriented leader* sets challenging goals and expects subordinates to perform at their highest level. In contrast to Fiedler's view of a leader's behavior, House assumes that leaders are flexible. Path-goal theory implies that the same leader can display any or all of these behaviors depending on the situation.

As Figure 11-5 illustrates, path-goal theory proposes two classes of situational or contingency variables that moderate the leadership behavior–outcome relationship: those in the environment that are outside the control of the subordinate (task structure, the formal authority system, and the work group) and those that are part of the personal characteristics of the subordinate (locus of control, experience, and perceived ability). Environmental factors determine

Figure 11-5
The Path-Goal Theory

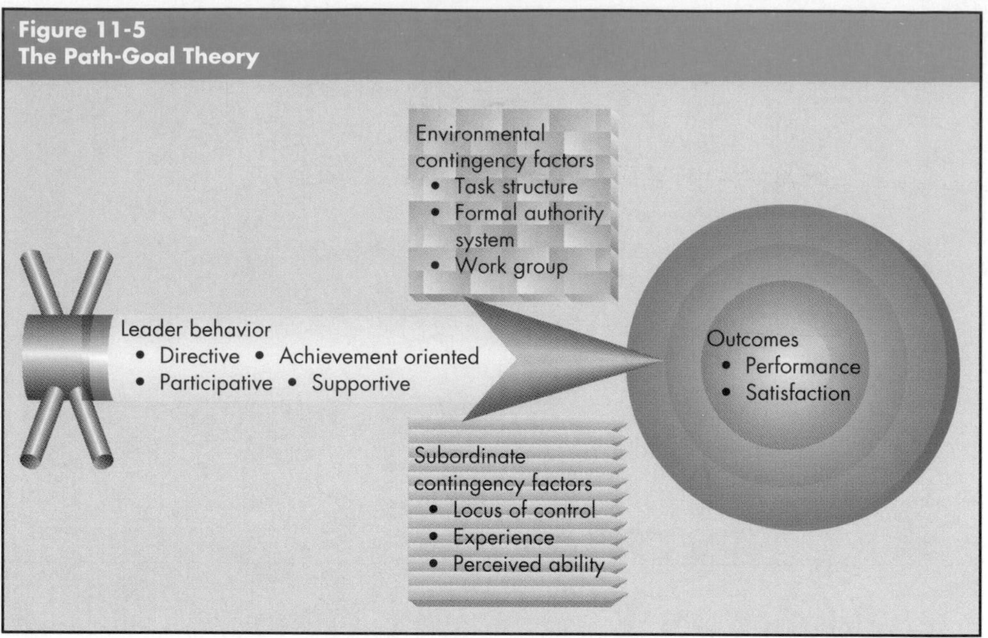

the type of leader behavior required as a complement if subordinate outcomes are to be maximized; personal characteristics of the subordinate determine how the environment and leader behavior are interpreted. So the theory proposes that leader behavior will be ineffective when it is redundant with sources of environmental structure or incongruent with subordinate characteristics.

The following are some examples of hypotheses that have evolved out of path-goal theory:

- Directive leadership leads to greater satisfaction when tasks are ambiguous or stressful than when they are highly structured and well laid out.
- Supportive leadership results in high employee performance and satisfaction when subordinates are performing structured tasks.
- Directive leadership is likely to be perceived as redundant among subordinates with high perceived ability or with considerable experience.
- The more clear and bureaucratic the formal authority relationships, the more leaders should exhibit supportive behavior and deemphasize directive behavior.
- Directive leadership will lead to higher employee satisfaction when there is substantive conflict within a work group.
- Subordinates with an internal locus of control (those who believe they control their own destiny) will be more satisfied with a participative style.
- Subordinates with an external locus of control will be more satisfied with a directive style.
- Achievement-oriented leadership will increase subordinates' expectancies that effort will lead to high performance when tasks are ambiguously structured.

Research to validate hypotheses such as these is generally encouraging.[41] The evidence supports the logic underlying the theory. That is, employee performance and satisfaction are likely to be positively influenced when the leader compensates for things lacking in either the employee or the work setting. However, the leader who spends time explaining tasks when those tasks are already clear or when the employee has the ability and experience to handle them without interference is likely to be ineffective because the employee will see such directive behavior as redundant or even insulting.

What does the future hold for path-goal theory? Its framework has been tested and appears to have moderate to high empirical support. We can, however, expect to see more research focused on refining and extending the theory by incorporating additional moderating variables.

Leader-Participation Model

leader-participation model
A leadership theory that provides a set of rules to determine the form and amount of participative decision making in different situations.

Back in 1973, Victor Vroom and Phillip Yetton developed a **leader-participation model** that related leadership behavior and participation to decision making.[42] Recognizing that task structures have varying demands for routine and nonroutine activities, these researchers argued that leader behavior must adjust to reflect the task structure. Vroom and Yetton's model was normative—it provided a sequential set of rules that should be followed for determining the form and amount of participation desirable in decision making, as dictated by different types of situations. The model was a complex decision tree incorporating seven contingencies (whose relevance could be identified by making "Yes" or "No" choices) and five alternative leadership styles.

More recent work by Vroom and Arthur Jago has resulted in a revision of this model.[43] The new model retains the same 5 alternative leadership styles but expands the contingency variables to 12, 10 of which are answered along a 5-point scale. Table 11-1 on page 430 lists the 12 variables.

The model assumes that any of five behaviors may be feasible in a given situation: Autocratic I (AI), Autocratic II (AII), Consultative I (CI), Consultative II (CII), and Group II (GII):

- AI. You solve the problem or make a decision yourself using information available to you at that time.
- AII. You obtain the necessary information from subordinates and then decide on the solution to the problem yourself. You may or may not tell subordinates what the problem is when getting the information from them. The role played by your subordinates in making the decision is clearly one of providing the necessary information to you rather than generating or evaluating alternative solutions.
- CI. You share the problem with relevant subordinates individually, getting their ideas and suggestions without bringing them together as a group. Then you make the decision, which may or may not reflect your subordinates' influence.
- CII. You share the problem with your subordinates as a group, collectively obtaining their ideas and suggestions. Then you make the decision that may or may not reflect your subordinates' influence.
- GII. You share the problem with your subordinates as a group. Together you generate and evaluate alternatives and attempt to reach an agreement (consensus) on a solution.

Vroom and Jago have developed a computer program that cuts through the complexity of the new model. But managers can still use decision trees to select their leader style if there are no shades of gray (that is, when the status of a variable is clear cut so a "Yes" or "No" response will be accurate), there are no

Table 11-1 Contingency Variables in the Revised Leader-Participation Model

QR: Quality Requirement

How important is the technical quality of this decision?

1	2	3	4	5
No Importance	Low Importance	Average Importance	High Importance	Critical Importance

CR: Commitment Requirement

How important is subordinate commitment to the decision?

1	2	3	4	5
No Importance	Low Importance	Average Importance	High Importance	Critical Importance

LI: Leader Information

Do you have sufficient information to make a high-quality decision?

1	2	3	4	5
No	Probably No	Maybe	Probably Yes	Yes

ST: Problem Structure

Is the problem well structured?

1	2	3	4	5
No	Probably No	Maybe	Probably Yes	Yes

CP: Commitment Probability

If you were to make the decision by yourself, is it reasonably certain your subordinates would be committed to the decision?

1	2	3	4	5
No	Probably No	Maybe	Probably Yes	Yes

GC: Goal Congruence

Do subordinates share the organizational goals to be attained in solving this problem?

1	2	3	4	5
No	Probably No	Maybe	Probably Yes	Yes

CO: Subordinate Conflict

Is conflict among subordinates over preferred solutions likely?

1	2	3	4	5
No	Probably No	Maybe	Probably Yes	Yes

SI: Subordinate Information

Do subordinates have sufficient information to make a high-quality decision?

1	2	3	4	5
No	Probably No	Maybe	Probably Yes	Yes

TC: Time Constraint

Does a critically severe time constraint limit your ability to involve subordinates?

1	5
No	Yes

GD: Geographical Dispersion

Are the costs involved in bringing together geographically dispersed subordinates prohibitive?

1	5
No	Yes

MT: Motivation–Time

How important is it to you to minimize the time it takes to make the decision?

1	2	3	4	5
No Importance	Low Importance	Average Importance	High Importance	Critical Importance

MD: Motivation–Development

How important is it to you to maximize the opportunities for subordinate development?

1	2	3	4	5
No Importance	Low Importance	Average Importance	High Importance	Critical Importance

Source: V.H. Vroom and A.G. Jago, *The New Leadership: Managing Participation in Organizations* (Englewood Cliffs, NJ: Prentice Hall, 1988), pp. 111–12. With permission.

critically severe time constraints, and subordinates are not geographically dispersed. Figure 11-6 illustrates one of these decision trees.

Research testing of the original leader–participation model was very encouraging.[44] Because the revised model is new, its validity still needs to be assessed. But the new model is a direct extension of the 1973 version and it's also consistent with our current knowledge of the benefits and costs of participation. So, at this time, we have every reason to believe that the revised model provides an excellent guide to help managers choose the most appropriate leadership style in different situations.

Two last points before we move on. First, the revised leader–participation model is very sophisticated and complex, which makes it impossible to describe in detail in a basic OB textbook. But the variables identified in Table 11-1 provide you with some solid insights about which contingency variables you need to consider when choosing your leadership style.

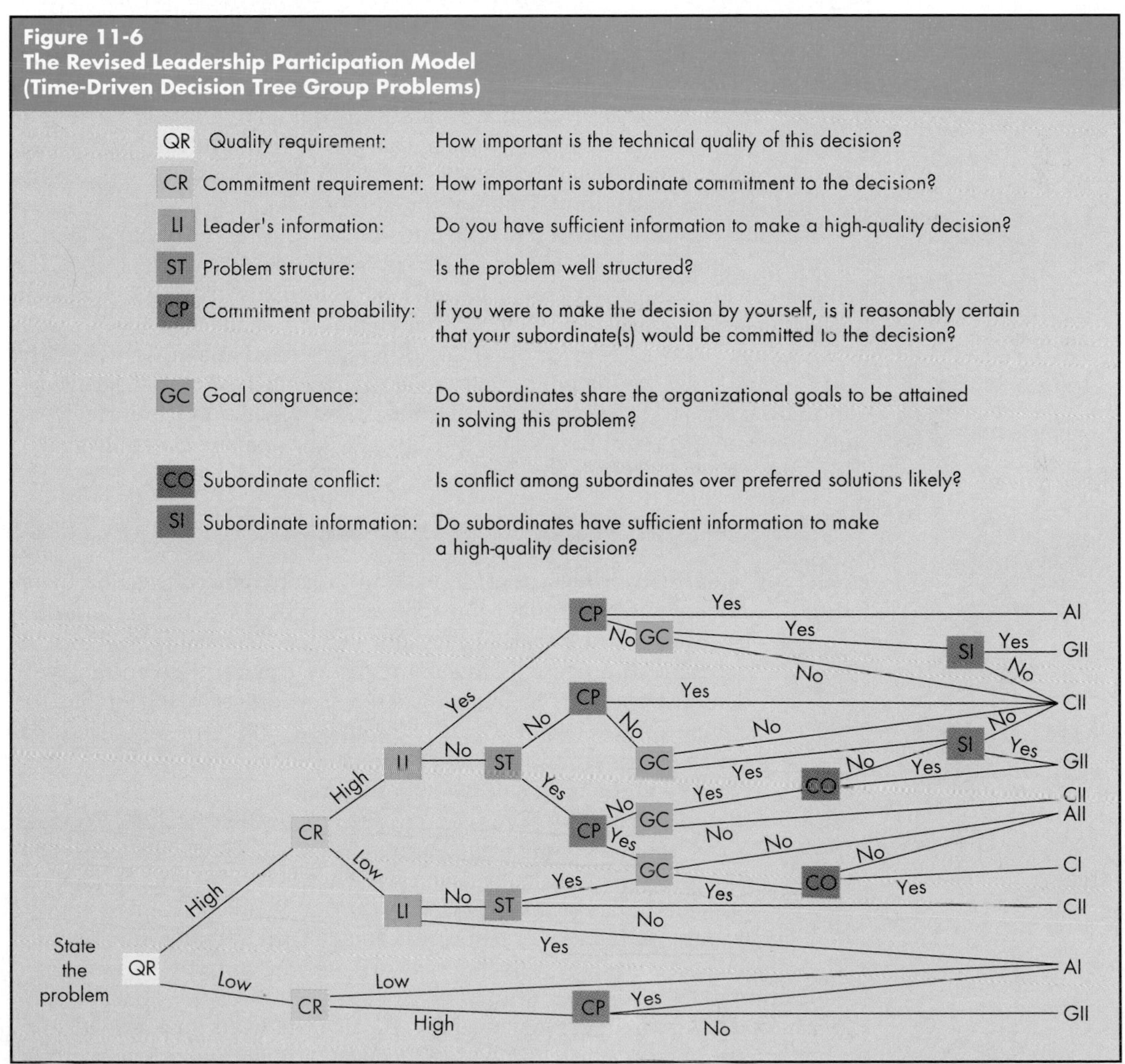
QR Quality requirement: How important is the technical quality of this decision?
CR Commitment requirement: How important is subordinate commitment to the decision?
LI Leader's information: Do you have sufficient information to make a high-quality decision?
ST Problem structure: Is the problem well structured?
CP Commitment probability: If you were to make the decision by yourself, is it reasonably certain that your subordinate(s) would be committed to the decision?
GC Goal congruence: Do subordinates share the organizational goals to be attained in solving this problem?
CO Subordinate conflict: Is conflict among subordinates over preferred solutions likely?
SI Subordinate information: Do subordinates have sufficient information to make a high-quality decision?
State the problem
QR
High
Low
CR
High
Low
LI
ST
CP
GC
CO
SI
Yes
No
AI
GII
CII
CI
AII

Figure 11-6
The Revised Leadership Participation Model (Time-Driven Decision Tree Group Problems)

Figure 11-7
Source: B. Parker and J. Hart, *Let There Be Reign* (Greenwich, CT: Fawcett Books, 1972).

Second, the leader–participation model confirms that leadership research should be directed at the situation rather than the person. It probably makes more sense to talk about autocratic and participative *situations* than about autocratic and participative *leaders*. As did House in his path-goal theory, Vroom, Yetton, and Jago argue against the notion that leader behavior is inflexible. The leader-participation model assumes the leader can adjust his or her style to different situations.

The cartoon in Figure 11-7 proposes adjusting the individual to the coat, rather than vice versa. In terms of leadership, we can think of "coat" as analogous to "situation." If an individual's leadership style range is very narrow, as Fiedler proposes, we are required to place that individual into the appropriate-size situation if he or she is to lead successfully. But there is another possibility: If House and Vroom-Yetton-Jago are right, the individual leader has to assess the situation that is available and adjust his or her style accordingly. Whether we should adjust the situation to fit the person or fix the person to fit the situation is an important issue. The answer is probably that it depends on the leader—specifically, on whether that person rates high or low on self-monitoring.[45] As we know, individuals differ in their behavioral flexibility. Some people show considerable ability to adjust their behavior to external, situational factors; they are adaptable. Others, however, exhibit high levels of consistency regardless of the situation. High self-monitors are generally able to adjust their leadership style to suit changing situations.

Sometimes Leadership Is Irrelevant!

In keeping with the contingency spirit, we want to conclude this section by offering this notion: the belief that some leadership style *will always* be effective *regardless* of the situation may not be true. Leadership may not always be important. Data from numerous studies collectively demonstrate that, in many situations, whatever behaviors leaders exhibit are irrelevant. Certain individual, job, and organizational variables can act as *substitutes* for leadership or *neutralize* the leader's effect to influence his or her subordinates.[46]

> ◆The belief that some leadership style *will always* be effective *regardless* of the situation may not be true.

Neutralizers make it impossible for leader behavior to make any difference to subordinate outcomes. They negate the leader's influence. Substitutes, however, make a leader's influence not only impossible but also unnecessary. They act as a replacement for the leader's influence. For instance, characteristics of subordinates such as their experience, training, "professional" orientation, or indifference toward organizational rewards can substitute for, or neutralize the effect of, leadership. Experience and training, for instance, can replace the need for a leader's support or ability to create structure and reduce task ambiguity. Jobs that are in-

Table 11-2 Substitutes and Neutralizers for Leadership

Defining Characteristics	Relationship-Oriented Leadership	Task-Oriented Leadership
Individual		
Experience/training	No effect on	Substitutes for
Professionalism	Substitutes for	Substitutes for
Indifference to rewards	Neutralizes	Neutralizes
Job		
Highly structured task	No effect on	Substitutes for
Provides its own feedback	No effect on	Substitutes for
Intrinsically satisfying	Substitutes for	No effect on
Organization		
Explicit formalized goals	No effect on	Substitutes for
Rigid rules and procedures	No effect on	Substitutes for
Cohesive work groups	Substitutes for	Substitutes for

Source: Based on S. Kerr and J.M. Jermier, "Substitutes for Leadership: Their Meaning and Measurement," *Organizational Behavior and Human Performance* (December 1978), p. 378.

herently unambiguous and routine or are intrinsically satisfying may place fewer demands on the leadership variable. Organizational characteristics like explicit formalized goals, rigid rules and procedures, and cohesive work groups can replace formal leadership (see Table 11-2).

This recent recognition that leaders don't always have an impact on subordinate outcomes should not be that surprising. After all, we have introduced a number of variables—attitudes, personality, ability, and group norms, to name but a few—that have been documented as having an effect on employee performance and satisfaction. Yet supporters of the leadership concept have tended to place an undue burden on this variable for explaining and predicting behavior. It is too simplistic to consider subordinates as guided to goal accomplishments solely by the behavior of their leader. It is important, therefore, to recognize explicitly that leadership is merely another independent variable in our overall OB model. In some situations, it may contribute a lot to explaining employee productivity, absence, turnover, and satisfaction, but in other situations, it may contribute little toward that end.

Looking for Common Ground: What Does It All Mean?

The topic of leadership certainly doesn't lack for theories. But from an overview perspective, what does it all mean? Let's identify commonalities among the leadership theories and determine what, if any, practical value the theories hold for application to organizations.

Careful examination discloses that the concepts of "task" and "people"—often expressed in more elaborate terms that hold substantially the same meaning—permeate most of the theories.[47] The task dimension is called just that by Fiedler, but it goes by the name of "initiating structure" for the Ohio State group, "directive leadership" by path-goal supporters, "production orientation" by the Michigan researchers, and "concern for production" by Blake and Mouton. The people dimension gets similar treatment, going under such aliases as "consideration," "employee-oriented," "supportive," or "relationship-oriented" leadership. With the obvious exception posed by the Scandinavian studies, leadership behavior tends to be reduced to two dimensions—task and people—but researchers continue to differ as to whether the orientations are two ends of a single continuum (you could be high on one or the other but not both) or two independent dimensions (you could be high or low on both).

Although one well-known scholar argues that virtually every theory has also "wrestled with the question of how much a leader should share power with subordinates in decision making,"[48] there is far less support for this contention. The situational leadership theory and the leader-participation model address this issue, but the task–people dichotomy appears to be far more encompassing.

Leadership theorists don't agree on the issue of whether a leader's style is fixed or flexible. For example, Fiedler takes the former position; Vroom, Yetton, and Jago argue for the latter. As previously noted, our position is that both are probably right—it depends on the leader's personality. High self-monitors are more likely to adjust their leadership style to changing situations than are low self-monitors.[49] So the need to adjust the situation to the leader in order to improve the leader–situation match seems to be necessary only with low self-monitoring individuals.

How should we interpret the findings presented so far in this chapter? Some traits have proved, over time, to be modest predictors of leadership effectiveness. But knowing a manager possesses intelligence, ambition, self-confidence, or the like would by no means assure us his or her subordinates would be productive and satisfied employees. The ability of these traits to predict leadership success is just not that strong.

The early task–people approaches (such as the Ohio State, Michigan, and Managerial Grid theories) also offer us little substance. The strongest statement one can make based on these theories is that leaders who rate high in people orientation should end up with satisfied employees. The research is too mixed to make predictions regarding employee productivity or the effect of a task orientation on productivity and satisfaction.

The most important contribution of the Fiedler model may well be that it initiated a more rigorous search to identify contingency variables in leadership. While this model is no longer at the cutting edge of leadership theories, several of the situational variables that Fiedler originally identified continue to surface in more recent contingency theories.

Hersey and Blanchard's situational leadership theory is straightforward, intuitively appealing, and important for its explicit recognition that the subordinate's ability and motivation are critical to the leader's success. Yet, in spite of its wide acceptance by practitioners, the mixed empirical support renders the theory, at least at this time, more speculative than substantive.

Leader–member exchange theory looks at leadership from a different angle. It focuses on in-groups and out-groups. Given the impressive evidence that in-group employees have higher performance and satisfaction than out-group members, the theory provides valuable insight for predicting leader effect as long as we know whether an employee is an "in" or an "out."

Studies testing the original Vroom-Yetton version of the leader-participation model were supportive. Given that the revised Vroom-Jago version is a sophisticated extension of the original model, we should expect it to be even

Tommye Jo Daves (right) manages the Levi Strauss sewing plant in Murphy, North Carolina, where 385 employees produce some 3 million pairs of jeans each year. Under Levi's traditional management structure, Daves was a directive leader, giving orders to employees who performed one or two tasks and scheduling their work. To make significant improvements in quality, manufacturing costs, and quick response to customer orders, Levi changed to a team management structure. Employee teams are now cross-trained for 36 tasks and are involved in running the plant and setting production goals and personnel policy. Consistent with the path-goal model, Daves changed from a directive to a participative leader as the skills and responsibilities of her employees expanded. "You can't lead a team by just barking orders," Daves says.

better. But the complexity of the model is a major limitation to its usage. With 5 styles and 12 contingency variables, it is difficult to use as a day-to-day guide for practicing managers. Still, leadership and decision making are complex issues requiring a complex process. To hope for some easy but valid model may be wishful thinking. The important conclusion here seems to be that where we find leaders who follow the model, we should expect also to find productive and satisfied employees.[50]

Finally, the path-goal model provides a framework for explaining and predicting leadership effectiveness that has developed a solid, empirical foundation. It recognizes that a leader's success depends on adjusting his or her style to the environment the leader is placed in, as well as to the individual characteristics of followers. In a limited way, path-goal theory validates contingency variables in other leadership theories. For example, its emphasis on task structure is consistent with the Fiedler contingency model and Vroom and Jago's leader-participation model (remember their question: Is the problem well structured?). Path-goal theory's recognition of individual characteristics is also consistent with Hersey and Blanchard's focus on the experience and ability of followers.

The Most Recent Approaches to Leadership

We conclude our review of leadership theories by presenting three more recent approaches to the subject: an attribution theory of leadership, charismatic leadership, and transactional versus transformational leadership. If there is one theme to the approaches in this section, it is that they all deemphasize theoretical complexity and look at leadership more the way the average layperson views the subject.

Attribution Theory of Leadership

In Chapter 4 we discussed attribution theory in relation to perception. Attribution theory has also been used to help explain the perception of leadership.

Attribution theory, as you remember, deals with people trying to make sense out of cause-effect relationships. When something happens, they want to attribute it to something. In the context of leadership, attribution theory says that leadership is merely an attribution that people make about other individuals.[51] Using the attribution framework, researchers have found that people characterize leaders as having such traits as intelligence, outgoing personality, strong verbal skills, aggressiveness, understanding, and industriousness.[52] Similarly, the high-high leader (high on both initiating structure and consideration) has been found to be consistent with attributions of what makes a good leader.[53] That is, regardless of the situation, a high-high leadership style tends to be perceived as best. At the organizational level, the attribution framework accounts for the conditions under which people use leadership to explain organizational outcomes. Those conditions are extremes in organizational performance. When an organization has either extremely negative or extremely positive performance, people are prone to make leadership attributions to explain the performance.[54] This helps account for the vulnerability of CEOs when their organizations suffer a major financial setback, regardless of whether they had much to do with it. It also accounts for why these CEOs tend to be given credit for extremely positive financial results—again, regardless of how much or how little they contributed.

attribution theory of leadership
Proposes that leadership is merely an attribution that people make about other individuals.

One of the more interesting themes in the **attribution theory of leadership** literature is the perception that effective leaders are generally considered consistent or unwavering in their decisions.[55] That is, one of the explanations for why Ronald Reagan (during his first term as president) was perceived as a leader was that he was fully committed, steadfast, and consistent in the decisions he made and the goals he set. Evidence indicates that a heroic leader is perceived as being someone who takes up a difficult or unpopular cause and, through determination and persistence, ultimately succeeds.[56]

Charismatic Leadership Theory

charismatic leadership
Followers make attributions of heroic or extraordinary leadership abilities when they observe certain behaviors.

Charismatic leadership theory is an extension of attribution theory. It says that followers make attributions of heroic or extraordinary leadership abilities when they observe certain behaviors.[57] Studies on charismatic leadership have, for the most part, been directed at identifying those behaviors that differentiate charismatic leaders from their noncharismatic counterparts. Some examples of individuals frequently cited as being charismatic leaders include Franklin D. Roosevelt, John F. Kennedy, Martin Luther King, Jr., Walt Disney, Mary Kay Ash (founder of Mary Kay Cosmetics), Ross Perot, Steve Jobs (cofounder of Apple Computer), Ted Turner, Lee Iacocca (former chairman of Chrysler), Jan Carlzon (chairman of SAS Airlines), and Gen. Norman Schwarzkopf.

Several authors have attempted to identify personal characteristics of the charismatic leader. Robert House (of path-goal fame) identified three: extremely high confidence, dominance, and strong convictions in his or her beliefs.[58] Warren Bennis, after studying 90 of the most effective and successful leaders in the United States, found they had four common competencies: They had a compelling vision or sense of purpose; they could communicate that vision in clear terms their followers could readily identify with; they demonstrated consistency and focus in the pursuit of their vision; and they knew their own strengths and capitalized on them.[59] The most comprehensive analysis, however, has been completed by Conger and Kanungo at McGill University.[60] Among their conclusions, they propose that charismatic leaders have an idealized goal they want to achieve, a strong personal commitment to their goal, are perceived as unconventional, are assertive and self-confident, and are perceived as agents of radical change rather than managers of the status quo. Table 11-3 summarizes the key characteristics that appear to differentiate charismatic leaders from noncharismatic ones.

Table 11-3 Key Characteristics of Charismatic Leaders

1. *Self-confidence.* They have complete confidence in their judgment and ability.
2. *A vision.* This is an idealized goal that proposes a future better than the status quo. The greater the disparity between this idealized goal and the status quo, the more likely that followers will attribute extraordinary vision to the leader.
3. *Ability to articulate the vision.* They are able to clarify and state the vision in terms that are understandable to others. This articulation demonstrates an understanding of the followers' needs and, hence, acts as a motivating force.
4. *Strong convictions about the vision.* Charismatic leaders are perceived as being strongly committed, and willing to take on high personal risk, incur high costs, and engage in self-sacrifice to achieve their vision.
5. *Behavior that is out of the ordinary.* Those with charisma engage in behavior that is perceived as being novel, unconventional, and counter to norms. When successful, these behaviors evoke surprise and admiration in followers.
6. *Perceived as being a change agent.* Charismatic leaders are perceived as agents of radical change rather than as caretakers of the status quo.
7. *Environment sensitivity.* These leaders are able to make realistic assessments of the environmental constraints and resources needed to bring about change.

Source: Based on J.A. Conger and R.N.Kanungo, "Behavioral Dimensions of Charismatic Leadership," in J.A. Conger and R.N. Kanungo, *Charismatic Leadership* (San Francisco: Jossey-Bass, 1988), p. 91.

Attention has recently focused on trying to determine how charismatic leaders actually influence followers. The process begins by the leader articulating an appealing vision. This vision provides a sense of continuity for followers by linking the present with a better future for the organization. The leader then communicates high performance expectations and expresses confidence that followers can attain them. This enhances follower self-esteem and self-confidence. Next, the leader conveys, through words and actions, a new set of values and, by his or her behavior, sets an example for followers to imitate. Finally, the charismatic leader makes self-sacrifices and engages in unconventional behavior to demonstrate courage and convictions about the vision.[61]

What can we say about the charismatic leader's effect on his or her followers? An increasing body of research shows impressive correlations between charismatic leadership and high performance and satisfaction among followers.[62] People working for charismatic leaders are motivated to exert extra work effort and, because they like their leader, express greater satisfaction.

If charisma is desirable, can people learn to be charismatic leaders? Or are charismatic leaders born with their qualities? While a small minority still think charisma cannot be learned, most experts believe individuals can be trained to exhibit charismatic behaviors and can thus enjoy the benefits that accrue to being labeled "a charismatic leader."[63] For instance, one set of authors proposes that a person can learn to become charismatic by following a three-step process.[64] First, an individual needs to develop the aura of charisma by maintaining an optimistic view, using passion as a catalyst for generating enthusiasm, and communicating with the whole body, not just with words. Second, an individual draws others in by creating a bond that inspires others to follow. And third, the individual brings out the potential in followers by tapping into their emotions. This approach seems to work as evidenced by researchers who've succeeded in actually scripting undergraduate business students to "play" charismatic.[65] The students were taught to articulate an overarching goal, communicate high performance expectations, exhibit confidence in the ability of subordinates to meet these expectations, and empathize with the needs of their subordinates; they learned to project a powerful, confident, and dynamic presence; and they practiced using a captivating and engaging voice tone. To further capture the dynamics and energy of charisma, the leaders were trained to evoke charismatic nonverbal characteristics: They alternated between pacing and sitting on the edges of their desks, leaned toward the subordinate, maintained direct eye contact, and had a relaxed posture and animated facial expressions. These researchers found that these students could learn how to project charisma. Moreover, subordinates of these leaders had higher task performance, task adjustment, and adjustment to the leader and to the group than did subordinates who worked under groups led by noncharismatic leaders.

One last word on this topic: Charismatic leadership may not always be needed to achieve high levels of employee performance. It may be most appropriate when the follower's task has an ideological component.[66] This may explain why, when charismatic leaders surface, it is more likely to be in politics, religion, wartime, or when a business firm is introducing a radically new product or facing a life threatening crisis. Such conditions tend to involve ideological concerns. Franklin D. Roosevelt offered a vision to get Americans out of the Great Depression. Steve Jobs achieved unwavering loyalty and commitment from the technical staff he oversaw at Apple Computer during the late 1970s and early 1980s by articulating a vision of personal computers that would dramatically change the way people lived. Gen. "Stormin Norman" Schwarzkopf's blunt, passionate style, absolute confidence in his troops, and a vision of total victory over Iraq made him a hero in the free world following Operation Desert Storm in 1991. Charismatic leaders, in fact, may become a liability to an organization once the crisis and need for dramatic change subside.[67] Why? Because then the charismatic leader's overwhelming self-confidence often becomes a liability. He or she is unable to listen to others, becomes uncomfortable when challenged by aggressive subordinates, and begins to hold an unjustifiable belief in his or her "rightness" on issues. Philippe Kahn's charismatic style, for instance, was an asset during the rapid growth years of software database company Borland International. But Borland's CEO became a liability as the company matured. His dictatorial style, arrogance, and reckless decision making have put the company's future in jeopardy.[68]

Transactional vs. Transformational Leadership

The final stream of research we touch on is the recent interest in differentiating transformational leaders from transactional leaders.[69] As you'll see, because transformational leaders are also charismatic, there is some overlap between this topic and our previous discussion of charismatic leadership.

transactional leaders
Leaders who guide or motivate their followers in the direction of established goals by clarifying role and task requirements.

transformational leaders
Leaders who provide individualized consideration and intellectual stimulation, and who possess charisma.

Most of the leadership theories presented in this chapter—for instance, the Ohio State studies, Fiedler's model, path-goal theory, and the leader–participation model—have concerned **transactional leaders**. These kinds of leaders guide or motivate their followers in the direction of established goals by clarifying role and task requirements. But there is another type of leader who inspires followers to transcend their own self-interests for the good of the organization, and who is capable of having a profound and extraordinary effect on his or her followers. These are **transformational leaders** like Leslie

Table 11-4 Characteristics of Transactional and Transformational Leaders

Transactional Leader

Contingent Reward: Contracts exchange of rewards for effort, promises rewards for good performance, recognizes accomplishments.

Management by Exception (active): Watches and searches for deviations from rules and standards, takes corrective action.

Management by Exception (passive): Intervenes only if standards are not met.

Laissez-Faire: Abdicates responsibilities, avoids making decisions.

Transformational Leader

Charisma: Provides vision and sense of mission, instills pride, gains respect and trust.

Inspiration: Communicates high expectations, uses symbols to focus efforts, expresses important purposes in simple ways.

Intellectual Stimulation: Promotes intelligence, rationality, and careful problem solving.

Individualized Consideration: Gives personal attention, treats each employee individually, coaches, advises.

Source: B.M. Bass, "From Transactional to Transformational Leadership: Learning to Share the Vision" by Professor Bernard Bass et al. in *Organizational Dynamics* (Winter 1990), p. 22. Copyright © 1989 by the American Management Association, New York. All rights reserved.

Wexner of The Limited retail chain and Jack Welch at General Electric. They pay attention to the concerns and developmental needs of individual followers; they change followers' awareness of issues by helping them look at old problems in new ways; and they are able to excite, arouse, and inspire followers to put out extra effort to achieve group goals. Table 11-4 briefly identifies and defines the four characteristics that differentiate these two types of leaders.

Transactional and transformational leadership should not, however, be viewed as opposing approaches to getting things done.[70] Transformational leadership is built *on top of* transactional leadership—it produces levels of subordinate effort and performance that go beyond what would occur with a transactional approach alone. Moreover, transformational leadership is more than charisma. "The purely charismatic [leader] may want followers to adopt the charismatic's world view and go no further; the transformational leader will attempt to instill in followers the ability to question not only established views but eventually those established by the leader."[71]

The evidence supporting the superiority of transformational leadership over the transactional variety is overwhelmingly impressive. For instance, a number of studies with U.S., Canadian, and German military officers found, at every level, that transformational leaders were evaluated as more effective than their transactional counterparts.[72] And managers at Federal Express who were rated by their followers as exhibiting more transformational leadership were evaluated by their immediate supervisors as higher performers and more promotable.[73] In summary, the overall evidence indicates that transformational leadership is more strongly correlated than transactional leadership with lower turnover rates, higher productivity, and higher employee satisfaction.[74]

◆◆◆◆ OB in the News ◆◆◆◆

Southwest Airlines's Charismatic Leader

Herb Kelleher, CEO at Southwest Airlines, began his airline in 1971 with a clear vision: Southwest would be a short-haul, high-frequency, low-fare, point-to-point carrier. The company made money in its second year and has remained profitable every year since—a record unmatched in the U.S. airline industry.

But don't confuse Herb Kelleher with any of those serious executives running American, Delta, and other major airlines. No, Herb Kelleher is one of a kind! He's the company hell-raiser, jokester, and cheerleader—all rolled into one. Give him the opportunity and he'll party with employees into the wee hours of the morning; dress up as Elvis or the Easter Bunny; or lead employees in company cheers. His unorthodox style, plus his unconditional commitment to his employees, has created a "family feeling" among Southwest's work force that translates into employees who are willing to pitch in wherever needed, to walk—or fly—the extra mile. Pilots sometimes work the boarding gate if things are running slow; ticket agents voluntarily haul luggage if it will help get planes into the air faster.

Kelleher has created a band of 12,000 loyalists. Says David Ridley, who arrived in 1988 at Southwest to direct marketing and sales after working at two more traditional companies, "I was pretty dubious at first, having been at places where everyone but two or three top people were considered commodities. But I have come to appreciate a place where kindness and the human spirit are nurtured."

Kelleher's "I care" style consistently wins points with employees. According to an executive at Northwest Airlines, "Herb has somehow managed to get union people to identify personally with his company." The following incident captures Kelleher's unique style of labor relations. A Wall Street analyst tells of the time he was having lunch in the company cafeteria. Kelleher, seated at a table across the room with several female employees, suddenly leapt to his feet, kissed one of the women with gusto, and began leading the entire crowd in a series of cheers. When the analyst asked what was going on, one of the executives at his table explained that Kelleher had at that moment negotiated a new contract with Southwest's flight attendants.

Based on K. Labich, "Is Herb Kelleher America's Best CEO?" *Fortune* (May 2, 1994), pp. 44–52.

Contemporary Issues in Leadership

Do men and women rely on different leadership styles? If so, is one style inherently superior to the other? How is the current popularity of *empowerment* affecting the way managers lead? Since leaders aren't leaders unless they have followers, what can managers do to make employees more effective followers? How does national culture affect the choice of leadership style? Is there a biological basis for leadership?

In this section, we briefly address these five contemporary issues in leadership.

Gender: Do Males and Females Lead Differently?

An extensive review of the literature suggests two conclusions regarding gender and leadership.[75] First, the similarities between men and women tend to out-

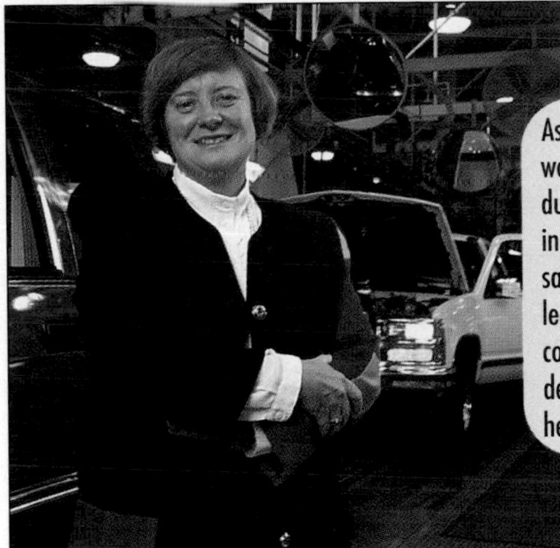

As the new president of General Motors of Canada Ltd., Maureen Kempston Darkes is the first woman to hold the company's top leadership position. Darkes downplays her gender, saying that during her 20 years with GM Canada she has never focused on the fact that she is a woman working in a male-dominated industry. Unlike most top auto executives who have backgrounds in sales, finance, or engineering, Darkes moved up the ranks of GM Canada through the company's legal and public policy departments. And, unlike many of her male contemporaries who feel most comfortable with an authoritarian style of leadership, Darkes uses a democratic style. Colleagues describe Darkes as the quintessential corporate leader—intelligent, ambitious, single-minded in her determination to succeed, a quick learner, and a tough negotiator.

weigh the differences. Second, what differences there are seem to be that women fall back on a more democratic leadership style whereas men feel more comfortable with a directive style.

The similarities among men and women leaders shouldn't be completely surprising. Almost all the studies looking at this issue have used managerial positions as being synonymous with leadership. As such, gender differences apparent in the general population don't tend to be as evident. Why? Because of career self-selection and organization selection. Just as people who choose careers in law enforcement or civil engineering have a lot in common, individuals who choose managerial careers also tend to have commonalities. People with traits associated with leadership—such as intelligence, confidence, and sociability—are more likely to be perceived as leaders and encouraged to pursue careers where they can exert leadership. This is true nowadays regardless of gender. Similarly, organizations tend to recruit and promote people into leadership positions who project leadership attributes. The result is that, regardless of gender, those who achieve formal leadership positions in organizations tend to be more alike than different.

In spite of the previous conclusion, studies indicate some differences in the inherent leadership styles between women and men. Women tend to adopt a more democratic leadership style. They encourage participation, share power and information, and attempt to enhance followers' self-worth. They prefer to lead through inclusion and rely on their charisma, expertise, contacts, and interpersonal skills to influence others. Men, however, are more likely to use a directive command and control style. They rely on the formal authority of their position for their influence base. However, consistent with our first conclusion, these findings need to be qualified. The tendency for female leaders to be more democratic than males declines when women are in male-dominated jobs. Apparently group norms and masculine stereotypes of leaders override personal preferences so women abandon their feminine styles in such jobs and act more autocratically.

Given that men have historically held the great majority of leadership positions in organizations, it's tempting to assume the existence of the noted differences between men and women would automatically work to favor men. It doesn't. In today's organizations, flexibility, teamwork, trust, and information sharing are replacing rigid structures, competitive individualism, control, and

From Concepts to Skills

Coaching

Effective managers are increasingly being described as *coaches* rather than *bosses*. They are expected to provide instruction, guidance, advice, and encouragement to help employees improve their job performance. If a manager wants to transform himself or herself into a coach, what needs to be done? More specifically, what actions characterize effective coaching?

Managers should exhibit three general skills if they are to help their employees generate breakthroughs in performance.[76] The following reviews these general skills and the specific behaviors associated with each.

1. *Ability to analyze ways to improve an employee's performance and capabilities.* A coach looks for opportunities for an employee to expand his or her capabilities and improve performance.
   - **a.** Observe your employee's behavior on a day-to-day basis.
   - **b.** Ask questions of the employee: Why do you do a task this way? Can it be improved? What other approaches might be used?
   - **c.** Show genuine interest in the person as an individual, not merely as an employee. Respect his or her individuality. More important than any technical expertise you can provide about improving job performance is the insight you have into the employee's uniqueness.
   - **d.** Listen to the employee. You can't understand the world from an employee's perspective unless you listen.
2. *Ability to create a supportive climate.* It's the coach's responsibility to reduce barriers to development and facilitate a climate that encourages performance improvement.
   - **a.** Create a climate that contributes to a free and open exchange of ideas.
   - **b.** Offer help and assistance. Give guidance and advice when asked.
   - **c.** Encourage your employees. Be positive and upbeat. Don't use threats.
   - **d.** Focus on mistakes as learning opportunities. Change implies risk and employees must not feel mistakes will be punished. When failure occurs, ask: "What did we learn that can help us in the future?"
   - **e.** Reduce obstacles. What factors do you control that, if eliminated, would help the employee improve his or her job performance?
   - **f.** Express to the employee the value of his or her contribution to the unit's goals.
   - **g.** Take personal responsibility for the outcome, but don't rob employees of their full responsibility. Validate the employees' efforts when they succeed, and point to what was missing when they fail. Never blame the employees for poor results.
3. *Ability to influence employees to change their behavior.* The ultimate test of coaching effectiveness is whether an employee's performance improves. But this is not a static concept. We are concerned with ongoing growth and development.
   - **a.** Encourage continual improvement. Recognize and reward small improvements and, consistent with TQM, treat coaching as helping employees to continually work toward improvement. There are no absolute upper limits to an employee's job performance.
   - **b.** Use a collaborative style. Employees will be more responsive to accepting change if they participate in identifying and choosing among improvement ideas.
   - **c.** Break difficult tasks down into simpler ones. By breaking down more complex jobs into a series of tasks of increasing difficulty, discouraged employees are more likely to experience success. Achieving success on simpler tasks encourages them to take on more difficult ones.
   - **d.** Model the qualities you expect from your employees. If you want openness, dedication, commitment, and responsibility from your employees, you must demonstrate these qualities yourself. Your employees will look to you as a role model so make sure your deeds match your words.

secrecy. The best managers listen, motivate, and provide support to their people. And many women seem to do those things better than men. As a specific example, the expanded use of cross-functional teams in organizations means that effective managers must become skillful negotiators. The leadership styles women typically use can make them better at negotiating, as they are less likely to focus on wins, losses, and competition, as do men. They tend to treat negotiations in the context of a continuing relationship—trying hard to make the other party a winner in its own and others' eyes.

Leading Through Empowerment

An important trend has developed over the past decade that has immense implications for leadership. That trend is for managers to embrace **empowerment**. More specifically, managers are being advised that effective leaders share power and responsibility with their employees.[77] The empowering leader's role is to show trust, provide vision, remove performance-blocking barriers, offer encouragement, motivate, and coach employees. The list of companies that have jumped on the "empowerment bandwagon" includes such world-famous corporations as General Electric, Intel, Ford, Saturn, Scandinavian Airline Systems, Harley-Davidson, NCR, Goodyear, and Conrail. Many have introduced empowerment as part of their corporatewide efforts in implementing total quality managment.[78]

Does this wholesale embracement of shared leadership strike you as a bit strange, given the attention that has been focused on contingency approaches to leadership? If it doesn't, it should. Why? Because empowerment proponents are essentially advocating a noncontingent approach to leadership. Directive, task-oriented, autocratic leadership is out, and empowerment is in.

The problem with the current empowerment movement is that it ignores the extent to which leadership can be shared and the conditions facilitating success of shared leadership. Because of factors such as downsizing, higher employee skills, commitment of organizations to continuous training, implementation of total quality management programs, and introduction of self-managed teams, no doubt an increasing number of situations call for a more empowering approach to leadership. But not *all* situations! Blanket acceptance of empowerment, or *any* universal approach to leadership, is inconsistent with the best and most current evidence we have on the subject.

What About Followership?

When someone was once asked what it took to be a great leader, he responded, "Great followers!" While the response may have seemed sarcastic, it has some truth. We have long known that many managers can't lead a horse to water. But, then again, many subordinates can't follow a parade.

Only recently have we begun to recognize that in addition to having leaders who can lead, successful organizations need followers who can follow.[79] In fact, it's probably fair to say that all organizations have far more followers than leaders, so ineffective followers may be more of a handicap to an organization than ineffective leaders.

What qualities do effective followers have? One writer focuses on four.[80]

1. *They manage themselves well.* They are able to think for themselves. They can work independently and without close supervision.
2. *They are committed to a purpose outside themselves.* Effective followers are committed to something—a cause, a product, a work team, an

THE FAR SIDE By GARY LARSON

"Well, what d'ya know! . . . *I'm* a follower, too!"

Figure 11-8

organization, an idea—in addition to the care of their own lives. Most people like working with colleagues who are emotionally, as well as physically, committed to their work.

3. *They build their competence and focus their efforts for maximum impact.* Effective followers master skills that will be useful to their organizations, and they hold higher performance standards than their job or work group requires.
4. *They are courageous, honest, and credible.* Effective followers establish themselves as independent, critical thinkers whose knowledge and judgment can be trusted. They hold high ethical standards, give credit where credit is due, and aren't afraid to own up to their mistakes.

National Culture as an Added Contingency Variable

One general conclusion that surfaced from our discussion of leadership is that effective leaders don't use any single style. They adjust their style to the situation. While not mentioned explicitly in any of the theories we presented, certainly national culture is an important situational factor determining which leadership style will be most effective.[81] We propose you consider it as another contingency variable.

National culture affects leadership style by way of the subordinate. Leaders cannot choose their styles at will. They are constrained by the cultural conditions their subordinates have come to expect. For example, a manipulative or autocratic style is compatible with high power distance, and we find high-power-distance scores in Arab, Far Eastern, and Latin countries. Power-distance rankings should also be good indicators of employee willingness to accept participative leadership. Participation is likely to be most effective in such low-power-distance cultures as exist in Norway, Finland, Denmark, and Sweden. Not incidentally, this may explain (1) why a number of leadership theories (the more obvious being ones like the University of Michigan behavioral studies and the leader–participation model) implicitly favor the use of a participative or people-oriented style; (2) the emergence of development-oriented leader behavior found by Scandinavian researchers; and (3) the recent enthusiasm in North America with empowerment. Remember that most leadership theories were developed by North Americans, using North American subjects; and the United States, Canada, and Scandinavian countries all rate below average on power distance.

Is There a Biological Basis for Leadership?

Is it possible that leader behavior lies in the body's hormones and in the brain's neurotransmitters? While this may take the study of leadership out of the behavioral laboratory and into the chemistry lab, increasing evidence indicates that leadership has biological roots.[82]

◆Increasing evidence indicates that leadership has biological roots.

A growing body of research suggests the best leaders are not necessarily the smartest, strongest, or most aggressive of a group but rather those who are most proficient at handling social interactions. That finding isn't particularly surprising. However, the researchers have found that effective leaders possess a unique biochemical mixture of hormones and brain chemistry that helps them build social alliances and cope with stress.

Two chemicals—serotonin and testosterone—have received most of the attention. Increased levels of the former appear to improve sociability and control aggression. Higher levels of the latter increase competitive drive.

Studies with monkeys find that (1) dominant monkeys—the leaders (whether male or female)—have a higher level of serotonin than do their subordinates; and (2) when that leader is removed from the group, the new leader that takes charge shows a marked increase in levels of serotonin. Researchers believe high levels of serotonin promote leadership by controlling aggressive and antisocial impulses, as well as reducing overreaction to petty or irrelevant stresses. The direction of causation, however, isn't clear: High levels of serotonin may stimulate leadership and/or leadership may result in a rise in serotonin.

Testosterone also seems to play a role in leadership. Studies with baboons finds that leaders experience a sudden rise in testosterone levels when legitimate threats appear. In subordinates, the level of testosterone goes down during a crisis.

But enough about monkeys. How about humans? A study in a college fraternity found males in the highest leadership positions had the highest level of serotonin. Researchers have also found that testosterone levels rise in top tennis players before competitive matches. The high levels seem to make the tennis players more assertive and motivated to win. It's been found that testosterone also rises *after* status-enhancing achievements such as winning a promotion or earning a degree, and women in professional jobs have higher levels of the hormone.

The step from laboratory to workplace isn't as far as you might think. The highly popular antidepressant Prozac, for instance, is one of a new class of drugs called serotonin reuptake inhibitors. It zeros in on one neurotransmitter, serotonin, lifting mood and lessening anxiety by keeping pools of the chemical available in the brain for nerve cells to use and reuse. Prozac raises serotonin and improves the sociability of its users. Similarly, patches—similar to those worn by people trying to quit smoking—are now available to help individuals increase testosterone levels. While we certainly aren't suggesting that individuals turn to pills or patches as a means to increase their leadership opportunities, the possibilities are nevertheless thought provoking.

Summary and Implications for Managers

Leadership plays a central part in understanding group behavior, for it's the leader who usually provides the direction toward goal attainment. Therefore, a more accurate predictive capability should be valuable in improving group performance.

In this chapter, we described a transition in approaches to the study of leadership—from the simple trait orientation to increasingly complex and sophisticated transactional models, such as path-goal and leader-participation models. With the increase in complexity has also come an increase in our ability to explain and predict behavior.

A major breakthrough in our understanding of leadership came when we recognized the need to include situational factors. Recent efforts have moved beyond mere recognition toward specific attempts to isolate these situational variables. We can expect further progress to be made with leadership models, but in the last decade, we have taken several large steps—large enough that we now can make moderately effective predictions as to who can best lead a group and explain under what conditions a given approach (such as task oriented or people oriented) is likely to lead to high employee performance and satisfaction.

In addition, the study of leadership has expanded to include more heroic and visionary approaches to leadership. As we learn more about the personal characteristics that followers attribute to charismatic and transformational leaders, and about the conditions that facilitate their emergence, we should be better able to predict when followers will exhibit extraordinary commitment and loyalty to their leaders and to those leaders' goals.

Finally, we addressed a number of contemporary issues in leadership. We learned, for instance, that male and female leadership styles tend to be more alike than different; but that women's propensity to rely on shared leadership is more in line with organizational needs in the 1990s than the directive style often preferred by men. Empowered leadership was shown to be increasingly popular, but managers should not assume that empowering employees is the ideal leadership style for all occasions. Also, consistent with the contingency approach, managers should be sure to consider national culture as an important variable in choosing a leadership style. Finally, recent evidence on the link between biology and leadership suggests the subject of leadership is not the sole province of psychologists and sociologists. In the future, improved understanding of the leadership phenomena may increasingly come from chemists or pharmacologists.

For Review

1. Trace the development of leadership research.
2. Describe the strengths and weaknesses in the trait approach to leadership.
3. What is the *Managerial Grid*? Contrast its approach to leadership with the approaches of the Ohio State and Michigan groups.
4. What was the contribution of the Scandinavian studies to the behavioral theories?
5. How do Hersey and Blanchard define *readiness*? Is this contingency variable included in any other contingency theory of leadership?
6. Describe the leader-participation model. What are its contingency variables?
7. When might leaders be irrelevant?

8. Contrast transactional and tranformational leaders.
9. Explain why empowerment has become so popular in North America.
10. What characteristics define an effective follower?
11. Explain the biological basis for leadership effectiveness.

For Discussion

1. Develop an example where you operationalize the Fiedler model.
2. Contrast the situational leadership theory with the Managerial Grid.
3. Develop an example where you operationalize path-goal theory.
4. Reconcile Hersey and Blanchard's situational leadership theory, path–goal theory, and substitutes for leadership.
5. What kind of activities could a full-time college student pursue that might lead to the perception that he or she is a charismatic leader? In pursuing those activities, what might the student do to enhance this perception of being charismatic?

Point

Leaders Make a Real Difference!

There can be little question that the success of an organization, or any group within an organization, depends largely on the quality of its leadership. Whether in business, government, education, medicine, or religion, the quality of an organization's leadership determines the quality of the organization itself. Successful leaders anticipate change, vigorously exploit opportunities, motivate their followers to higher levels of productivity, correct poor performance, and lead the organization toward its objectives.

The importance relegated to the leadership function is well known. Rarely does a week go by that we don't hear or read about some leadership concern: "President Fails to Provide the Leadership America Needs!" "The Republican Party Searches for New Leadership!" "Eisner Leads Disney Turnaround!" A review of the leadership literature led two academics to conclude that the research shows "a consistent effect for leadership explaining 20 to 45 percent of the variance on relevant organizational outcomes."*

Why is leadership so important to an organization's success? The answer lies in the need for coordination and control. Organizations exist to achieve objectives that are either impossible or extremely inefficient to achieve if done by individuals acting alone. The organization itself is a coordination and control mechanism. Rules, policies, job descriptions, and authority hierarchies are illustrations of devices created to facilitate coordination and control. But leadership, too, contributes toward integrating various job activities, coordinating communication between organizational subunits, monitoring activities, and controlling deviations from standard. No number of rules and regulations can replace the experienced leader who can make rapid and decisive decisions.

The importance of leadership is not lost on those who staff organizations. Corporations, government agencies, school systems, and institutions of all shapes and sizes cumulatively spend billions of dollars every year to recruit, select, evaluate, and train individuals for leadership positions. The best evidence, however, of the importance organizations place on leadership roles is exhibited in salary schedules. Leaders are routinely paid 10, 20, or more times the salary of those in nonleadership positions. The head of General Motors earns more than $1.5 million annually. The highest skilled autoworker, in contrast, earns under $50,000 a year. The president of this autoworker's union makes better than $100,000 a year. Police officers typically make around $30,000 to $45,000 a year. Their boss probably earns 25 percent more, and his or her boss another 25 percent. The pattern is well established. The more responsibility a leader has, as evidenced by his or her level in the organization, the more he or she earns. Would organizations voluntarily pay their leaders so much more than their nonleaders if they didn't strongly believe that leaders make a real difference?

*D.V. Day and R.G. Lord, "Executive Leadership and Organizational Performance: Suggestions for a New Theory and Methodology," *Journal of Management* (Fall 1988), pp. 453–64.

counterPoint

Leaders Don't Make a Difference

Given the resources that have been spent on studying, selecting, and training leaders, you'd expect there would be overwhelming evidence supporting the positive effect of leadership on organizational performance. But that's not the case!

Currently, the two most popular approaches to leadership are contingency models and the study of charisma. For the most part, both operate under the naive assumption that through selection and/or training, leaders can learn to exhibit certain behaviors that, when properly matched to the situation, will result in improved employee and organizational performance. There are a number of flaws in this assumption.

First, leaders exist in a social system that constrains their behavior. They have to live with role expectations which define behaviors that are acceptable and unacceptable. Pressures to conform to the expectations of peers, subordinates, and superiors all limit the range of behaviors a leader can exhibit.

Second, organizational rules, procedures, policies, and historical precedents all act to limit a leader's unilateral control over decisions and resources. Hiring decisions, for instance, must be made according to procedures. And budget allocations are typically heavily influenced by previous budget precedents.

Third, there are factors outside the organization that leaders can't control but have a large bearing on organizational performance. For example, consider the executive in a home construction firm. Costs are largely determined by the operations of the commodities and labor markets, and demand largely depends on interest rates, availability of mortgage money, and economic conditions that are affected by governmental policies over which the executive has little control. Or consider the case of school superintendents. They have little control over birthrates and community economic development, both of which profoundly affect school system budgets. While a leader may react to problems as they arise or attempt to forecast and anticipate external changes, he or she has little influence over the environment. On the contrary, the environment typically puts significant limits and constraints on the leader.

Finally, the trend in recent years is toward leaders playing a smaller and smaller role in organizational activities. Important decisions are increasingly made by committees, not individuals. Additionally, the widespread popularity of employee involvement programs, the empowerment movement, and self-managed work teams have all contributed to reducing any specific leader's influence.

There is a basic myth associated with leadership. We believe in attribution—when something happens, we believe something has *caused* it. Leaders play that role in organizations. And the fact that leaders earn higher pay than nonleaders is a symbolic gesture which organizations have created to further add to the impression that leaders make a difference. So while leaders may not really matter, the *belief* in leadership does. Although leaders take the credit for successes and the blame for failures, a more realistic conclusion would probably be that, except in times of rapid growth, change, or crisis, leaders don't make much of a difference in an organization's actual performance. But people want to believe that leadership is the cause of performance changes, particularly at the extremes.

Ideas in this argument came from J. Pfeffer, "The Ambiguity of Leadership," *Academy of Management Review* (January 1977), pp. 104–11; A.B. Thomas, "Does Leadership Make a Difference to Organizational Performance?" *Administrative Science Quarterly* (September 1988), pp. 388–400; C.C. Manz and H.P. Sims, Jr., "SuperLeadership: Beyond the Myth of Heroic Leadership," *Organizational Dynamics* (Spring 1991), pp. 18–35; and G. Gemmill and J. Oakley, "Leadership: An Alienating Social Myth?" *Human Relations* (February 1992), pp. 113–29.

Learning About Yourself Exercise

What's Your LPC Score?

Think of the person with whom you work least well. He or she may be someone you work with now, or may be someone you knew in the past. He or she does not have to be the person you like least well, but should be the person with whom you now have or have had the most difficulty in getting a job done. Describe this person as he or she appears to you by placing an "x" at that point you believe best describes that person. Do this for each pair of adjectives.

Pleasant	8	7	6	5	4	3	2	1	Unpleasant
Friendly	8	7	6	5	4	3	2	1	Unfriendly
Rejecting	8	7	6	5	4	3	2	1	Accepting
Helpful	8	7	6	5	4	3	2	1	Frustrating
Unenthusiastic	8	7	6	5	4	3	2	1	Enthusiastic
Tense	8	7	6	5	4	3	2	1	Relaxed
Distant	8	7	6	5	4	3	2	1	Close
Cold	8	7	6	5	4	3	2	1	Warm
Cooperative	8	7	6	5	4	3	2	1	Uncooperative
Supportive	8	7	6	5	4	3	2	1	Hostile
Boring	8	7	6	5	4	3	2	1	Interesting
Quarrelsome	8	7	6	5	4	3	2	1	Harmonious
Self-assured	8	7	6	5	4	3	2	1	Hesitant
Efficient	8	7	6	5	4	3	2	1	Inefficient
Gloomy	8	7	6	5	4	3	2	1	Cheerful
Open	8	7	6	5	4	3	2	1	Guarded

Turn to page A-29 for scoring directions and key.

Working With Others Exercise

Practicing To Be Charismatic

People who are charismatic engage in the following behaviors:

1. *Project a powerful, confident, and dynamic presence.* This has both verbal and nonverbal components. They use a captivating and engaging voice tone. They convey confidence. They also talk directly to people, maintaining direct eye contact, and holding their body posture in a way that says they are sure of themselves. They speak clearly, avoid stammering, and avoid sprinkling their sentences with noncontent phrases such as "ahhh" and "you know."
2. *Articulate an overarching goal.* They have a vision for the future, unconventional ways of achieving the vision, and the ability to communicate the vision to others.

   The vision is a clear statement of where they want to go and how they're going to get there. They are able to persuade others how the achievement of this vision is in the others' self-interest.

   They look for fresh and radically different approaches to problems. The road to achieving their vision is novel but also appropriate to the context.

   They not only have a vision but they're able to get others to buy into it. The real power of Martin Luther King, Jr. was not that he had a dream, but that he could articulate it in terms that made it accessible to millions.
3. *Communicate high performance expectations and confidence in others' ability to meet these expectations.* They demonstrate their confidence in people by stating ambitious goals for them individually and as a group. They convey absolute belief they will achieve their expectations.
4. *Are sensitive to the needs of followers.* Charismatic leaders get to know their followers individually. They understand their individual needs and are able to develop intensely personal relationships with each. They do this through encouraging followers to express their points of view, being approachable, genuinely listening to and caring about their followers' concerns, and by asking questions so they can learn what is really important to them.

Now that you know what charismatic leaders do, you get the opportunity to practice projecting charisma.

a. The class should break into pairs.
b. Student A's task is to "lead" Student B through a new-student orientation to your college. The orientation should last about 10 to 15 minutes. Assume Student B is new to your college and is unfamiliar with the campus. Remember, Student A should attempt to project himself or herself as charismatic.
c. Roles now reverse, and Student B's task is to "lead" Student A in a 10- to 15-minute program on how to study more effectively for college exams. Take a few minutes to think about what has worked well for

you and assume Student B is a new student interested in improving his or her study habits. Again, remember that Student B should attempt to project himself or herself as charismatic.

d. When both role plays are complete, each pair should assess how well they did in projecting charisma and how they might improve.

Source: This exercise is based on J.M. Howell and P.J. Frost, "A Laboratory Study of Charismatic Leadership," *Organizational Behavior and Human Decision Processes* (April 1989), pp. 243–69.

Ethical Dilemma Exercise

Using Drugs To Improve Sociability and Leadership Performance

Tim Lightner and a group of friends were sitting around consuming a couple of pizzas one afternoon. Tim was comfortable with the group. He felt he had their trust. So when the topic of moodiness and depression came up, Tim confided he had been taking the antidepressant drug Prozac for nearly three years.

Tim's friends were surprised. They'd only known him for a little more than a year—ever since he had moved to Atlanta from New Jersey. The Tim they knew was always friendly and outgoing. But Tim told them it hadn't always been this way. Since early childhood, he'd been quiet and shy. Then, three years ago, he read about Prozac. He learned that not only did the drug attack depression, it also made its users more outgoing and friendly. The side effects from the drug were minimal. So Tim decided Prozac might be able to help him become the personable and dynamic individual he always wanted to be. He made an appointment with a doctor, told that doctor he had long suffered from depression (which wasn't true), and asked to be given Prozac. The doctor agreed, and Tim joined the more than 10 million people worldwide who use the drug.

Tim confessed to his friends that the drug changed his personality. He was more outgoing, more self-confident, more sociable, and more popular. While five years ago he had almost no friends, he now has dozens. Before taking Prozac, his career was going nowhere. Now, three years later, he's had two promotions, including last year's move to Atlanta to become his company's southern regional district manager. Three years ago he was a salesman making $38,000 a year. Today Tim oversees a staff of 140 and earns $125,000 a year. He attributes all his recent successes—from new friends to new job responsibilities—to Prozac.

Has Tim done anything unethical? What do *you* think?

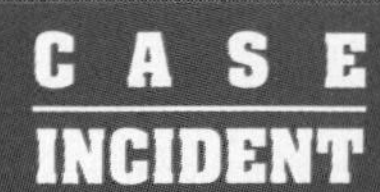

The Case Against "Vision"

Robert J. Eaton had big shoes to fill. In July 1993 he took the post of chairman at Chrysler Corp. that had previously been held by "Mr. Charisma," Lee Iacocca. Iacocca had taken over the top spot at Chrysler in 1980, when the company was on the verge of bankruptcy. In only a few short years, Iacocca had turned Chrysler into a money-making machine.

Iacocca's style was bold and visionary. He developed several grand strategies for Chrysler. To get the company immediately profitable, he created a basic compact model—the K car—and used its platform to create a host of new cars including the incredibly successful minivan. To fill the need for subcompacts, he began importing cars from Japan and putting Chrysler Corp. nameplates on them.

But that was then and this is now. Robert Eaton has joined an impressive group of chief executives who no longer buy the notion that leaders need to provide grand visions or long-term strategies for their companies. In its place, they are emphasizing the short-term bottom line.

"Internally, we don't use the word *vision*," says Eaton. "I believe in quantifiable short-term results—things we can all relate to—as opposed to some esoteric thing no one can quantify."

That view is also being articulated by CEOs at Apple Computer, IBM, Aetna Life & Casualty, and General Motors. When asked for his recipe for an IBM comeback, the recently appointed chairman, Louis V. Gerstner, said, "The last thing IBM needs right now is a vision."

It appears that, at least among some leaders, grand visions are out of fashion. They're concentrating on the nuts and bolts of running their businesses.

Questions

1. Isn't this short-term focus likely to hurt their companies in the longer term?
2. What's the purpose of a grand vision? What takes its place if a company's leader doesn't provide it?
3. Don't organizations need radical new ideas to win in the marketplace?
4. Eaton says his goal for Chrysler is "getting a little bit better every single day." Is that a viable goal for a real "leader"?

Source: Based on D. Lavin, "Robert Eaton Thinks 'Vision' Is Overrated and He's Not Alone," *Wall Street Journal* (October 4, 1993), p. A1.

Richard Branson of the Virgin Group

Richard Branson is Great Britain's answer to Ted Turner: brash, confident, unconventional, a self-promoter, a bold risk taker, a man with big ideas. Each is a billionaire who made his fortune through entrepreneurial activities. Both are also sportsmen. Turner made a reputation for himself in sailing. Branson made his in trans-Pacific ballooning.

Branson never graduated from high school. But he understood the taste of music consumers. He created Virgin Records and built it into a megacorporation. From there he ventured into producing music videos, running an island hotel, and creating an airline. His sale of Virgin Records for nearly a billion dollars gave him the deep pockets to pursue his current interest—Virgin Atlantic Airlines.

Virgin Atlantic has only eight 747s, but it has redefined transatlantic service. First class is out, replaced by upper class, which includes free limo service. Branson's airline has aggressively sought and captured a large share of the transatlantic business-traveler market. He's gotten it by merging technology and service. He was the first, for instance, to install a six-channel video monitor for every seat on his planes.

Branson is a fighter. He won't be intimidated by bigger foes. As a case in point, he went to court and charged British Airways (BA) with dirty tricks like dumping tickets on the market and calling Virgin customers at home. In February 1993 he won his case—receiving a multimillion dollar settlement and a public apology from BA.

Branson has a unique philosophy about business. Counter to current norms, he *doesn't* put the customer first. "Almost 100 percent of running a business is motivating your staff and the people around you. And if you can motivate them, then you can achieve anything. And too many companies have put shareholders first, customers second, staff way last. If you reverse that and you put your staff first, very quickly you find that the customers come first as well, and the shareholders come first as well."

Questions

1. Branson's leadership style is unusual. Describe the aspects of his style that you think make his management philosophy work.
2. Would you call Branson a charismatic leader? Why or why not?
3. Would you want to work for Richard Branson? Explain.
4. What effect do you think a Branson would have as CEO of Korean Airlines, Air Canada, or Delta Airlines?

Source: "Richard Branson," *Business World* (November 22, 1992).

Suggestions for Further Reading

BASS, B.M., *Bass and Stogdill's Handbook of Leadership: Theory, Research, and Managerial Applications*, 3rd ed. (New York: Free Press, 1990).

EDEN, D., "Leadership and Expectations: Pygmalion Effects and Other Self-Fulfilling Prophecies in Organizations," *Leadership Quarterly* (Winter 1992), pp. 271–305.

GASTIL, J., "A Meta-Analytic Review of the Productivity and Satisfaction of Democratic and Autocratic Leadership," *Small Group Research* (August 1994), pp. 384–410.

HOUSE, R.J., and J.M. HOWELL, "Personality and Charismatic Leadership," *Leadership Quarterly* (Summer 1992), pp. 81–108.

HUNT, J.G., *Leadership: A New Synthesis* (Newbury Park, CA: Sage, 1991).

KETS DE VRIES, M.F.R., "The Leadership Mystique," *Academy of Management Executive* (August 1994), pp. 73–89.

KOUZES, J.M., and B.Z. POSNER, *Credibility: How Leaders Gain and Lose It, Why People Demand It* (San Francisco: Jossey-Bass, 1993).

MALLOY, T.E., and C.L. JANOWSKI, "Perceptions and Metaperceptions of Leadership: Components, Accuracy, and Dispositional Correlates," *Personality and Social Psychology Bulletin* (December 1992), pp. 700–708.

WHEATLEY, M.J., *Leadership and the New Science* (San Francisco: Berrett-Koehler, 1992).

YUKL, G., *Leadership in Organizations*, 3rd ed. (Englewood Cliffs, NJ: Prentice Hall, 1994).

Notes

[1] J. Smolowe, "Bringing Decency into Hell," *Time* (December 14, 1992), pp. 60–62.

[2] R.M. Stogdill, *Handbook of Leadership: A Survey of the Literature* (New York: Free Press, 1974), p. 259.

[3] For a review of the controversies, see G. Yukl, "Managerial Leadership: A Review of Theory and Research," *Journal of Management* (June 1989), pp. 252–53.

[4] A. Zaleznik, "Excerpts from 'Managers and Leaders: Are They Different?'" *Harvard Business Review* (May-June 1986), p. 54.

[5] J.P. Kotter, "What Leaders Really Do," *Harvard Business Review* (May-June 1990), pp. 103–11; and J.P. Kotter, *A Force for Change: How Leadership Differs from Management* (New York: Free Press, 1990).

[6] V.H. Vroom, "The Search for a Theory of Leadership," in J.W. McGuire (ed.), *Contemporary Management: Issues and Viewpoints* (Englewood Cliffs, NJ: Prentice-Hall, 1974), p. 396.

[7] J. G. Geier, "A Trait Approach to the Study of Leadership in Small Groups," *Journal of Communication* (December 1967), pp. 316–23.

[8] S.A. Kirkpatrick and E.A. Locke, "Leadership: Do Traits Matter?" *Academy of Management Executive* (May 1991), pp. 48–60.

[9] G.H. Dobbins, W.S. Long, E.J. Dedrick, and T.C. Clemons, "The Role of Self-Monitoring and Gender on Leader Emergence: A Laboratory and Field Study," *Journal of Management* (September 1990), pp. 609–18.

[10] G. Yukl and D.D. Van Fleet, "Theory and Research on Leadership in Organizations," in M.D. Dunnette and L.M. Hough (eds.), *Handbook of Industrial & Organizational Psychology*, 2nd ed., Vol. 3 (Palo Alto, CA: Consulting Psychologists Press, 1992), p. 150.

[11] R.G. Lord, C.L. DeVader, and G.M. Alliger, "A Meta-Analysis of the Relation Between Personality Traits and Leadership Perceptions: An Application of Validity Generalization Procedures," *Journal of Applied Psychology* (August 1986), pp. 402–10; Dobbins, Long, Dedrick, and Clemons, "The Role of Self-Monitoring and Gender on Leader Emergence"; and Kirkpatrick and Locke, "Leadership."

[12] See T. Mulligan, "It's All a Matter of How to Crack the Whip," *Los Angeles Times* (April 3, 1993), p. D1.

[13] R.M. Stogdill and A.E. Coons (eds.), *Leader Behavior: Its Description and Measurement*, Research Monograph No. 88 (Columbus: Ohio State University, Bureau of Business Research, 1951). This research is updated in S. Kerr, C.A. Schriesheim, C.J. Murphy, and R.M. Stogdill, "Toward a Contingency Theory of Leadership Based upon the Consideration and Initiating Structure Literature," *Organizational Behavior and Human Performance* (August 1974), pp. 62–82; and B. M. Fisher, "Consideration and Initiating Structure and Their Relationships with Leader Effectiveness: A Meta-Analysis," F. Hoy (ed.), *Proceedings of the 48th Academy of Management Conference* (Anaheim, CA, 1988), pp. 201–205.

[14] R. Kahn and D. Katz, "Leadership Practices in Relation to Productivity and Morale," D. Cartwright and A. Zander (eds.), *Group Dynamics: Research and Theory*, 2nd ed. (Elmsford, NY: Row, Peterson, 1960).

[15] R.R. Blake and J.S. Mouton, *The Managerial Grid* (Houston: Gulf, 1964).

[16] See, for example, R.R. Blake and J.S. Mouton, "A Comparative Analysis of Situationalism and 9,9 Management by Principle," *Organizational Dynamics* (Spring 1982), pp. 20–43.

[17] See, for example, L.L. Larson, J.G. Hunt, and R.N. Osborn, "The Great Hi-Hi Leader Behavior Myth: A Lesson from Occam's Razor," *Academy of Management Journal* (December 1976), pp. 628–41; and P.C. Nystrom, "Managers and the Hi-Hi Leader Myth," *Academy of Management Journal* (June 1978), pp. 325–31.

[18] See G. Ekvall and J. Arvonen, "Change-Centered Leadership: An Extension of the Two-Dimensional Model," *Scandinavian Journal of Management*, Vol. 7, No. 1 (1991), pp. 17–26; M. Lindell and G. Rosenqvist, "Is There a Third Management Style?" *The Finnish Journal of Business Economics*, Vol. 3 (1992), pp. 171–98; and M. Lindell and G. Rosenqvist, "Management Behavior Dimensions and Development Orientation," *Leadership Quarterly* (Winter 1992), pp. 355–77.

[19] J.P. Howell, P.W. Dorfman, and S. Kerr, "Moderating Variables in Leadership Research," *Academy of Management Review* (January 1986), pp. 88–102.

[20] F.E. Fiedler, *A Theory of Leadership Effectiveness* (New York: McGraw-Hill, 1967).

[21] S. Shiflett, "Is There a Problem with the LPC Score in LEADER MATCH?" *Personnel Psychology* (Winter 1981), pp. 765–69.

[22] F.E. Fiedler, M.M. Chemers, and L. Mahar, *Improving Leadership Effectiveness: The Leader Match Concept* (New York: Wiley, 1977).

[23] L.H. Peters, D.D. Hartke, and J.T. Pohlmann, "Fiedler's Contingency Theory of Leadership: An Application of the Meta-Analysis Procedures of Schmidt and Hunter," *Psychological Bulletin* (March 1985), pp. 274–85; and C.A. Schriesheim, B.J. Tepper, and L.A. Tetrault, "Least Preferred Co-Worker Score, Situational Control, and Leadership Effectiveness: A Meta-Analysis of Contingency Model Performance Predictions," *Journal of Applied Psychology* (August 1994), pp. 561–73.

[24] See, for instance, R.W. Rice, "Psychometric Properties of the Esteem for the Least Preferred Coworker (LPC) Scale," *Academy of Management Review* (January 1978), pp. 106–18; C.A. Schriesheim, B.D. Bannister, and W.H. Money, "Psychometric Properties of the LPC Scale: An Extension of Rice's Review," *Academy of Management Review* (April 1979), pp. 287–90; and J.K. Kennedy, J.M. Houston, M.A. Korgaard, and D.D. Gallo, "Construct Space of the Least Preferred Co-Worker (LPC) Scale," *Educational & Psychological Measurement* (Fall 1987), pp. 807–14.

[25] See E.H. Schein, *Organizational Psychology*, 3rd ed. (Englewood Cliffs, NJ: Prentice-Hall, 1980), pp. 116–17; and B. Kabanoff, "A Critique of Leader Match and Its Implications for Leadership Research," *Personnel Psychology* (Winter 1981), pp. 749–64.

[26] F.E. Fiedler and J.E. Garcia, *New Approaches to Effective Leadership: Cognitive Resources and Organizational Performance* (New York: Wiley, 1987).

[27] Ibid., p. 6.

[28] See R.P. Vecchio, "Theoretical and Empirical Examination of Cognitive Resource Theory," *Journal of Applied Psychology* (April 1990), pp. 141–47; and F.W. Gibson, F.E. Fiedler, and K.M. Barrett, "Stress, Babble, and the Utilization of the Leader's Intellectual Abilities," *Leadership Quarterly* (Summer 1993), pp. 189–208.

[29] P. Hersey and K.H. Blanchard, "So You Want to Know Your Leadership Style?" *Training and Development Journal* (February 1974), pp. 1–15; and P. Hersey and K.H. Blanchard, *Management of Organizational Behavior: Utilizing Human Resources*, 5th ed. (Englewood Cliffs, NJ: Prentice Hall, 1988).

[30] Hersey and Blanchard, *Management of Organizational Behavior*, p. 171.

[31] P. Hersey and K.H. Blanchard, "Grid Principles and Situationalism: Both! A Response to Blake and Mouton," *Group & Organization Studies* (June 1982), pp. 207–10.

[32] R.K. Hambleton and R. Gumpert, "The Validity of Hersey and Blanchard's Theory of Leader Effectiveness," *Group & Organization Studies* (June 1982), pp. 225–42; C.L. Graeff, "The Situational Leadership Theory: A Critical View," *Academy of Management Review* (April 1983), pp. 285–91; R.P. Vecchio, "Situational Leadership Theory: An Examination of a Prescriptive Theory," *Journal of Applied Psychology* (August 1987), pp. 444–51; J.R. Goodson, G.W. McGee, and J.F. Cashman, "Situational Leadership Theory: A Test of Leadership Prescriptions," *Group & Organization Studies* (December 1989), pp. 446–61; W. Blank, J.R. Weitzel, and S.G. Green, "A Test of the Situational Leadership Theory," *Personnel Psychology* (Autumn 1990), pp. 579–97; and W.R. Norris and R.P. Vecchio, "Situational Leadership Theory: A Replication," *Group & Organization Management* (September 1992), pp. 331–42.

[33] Vecchio, "Situational Leadership Theory"; and Norris and Vecchio, "Situational Leadership Theory."

[34] W. Blank, J.R. Weitzel, and S.G. Green, "A Test of the Situational Leadership Theory."

[35] F. Dansereau, J. Cashman, and G. Graen, "Instrumentality Theory and Equity Theory as Complementary Approaches in Predicting the Relationship of Leadership and Turnover Among Managers," *Organizational Behavior and Human Performance* (October 1973), pp. 184–200; and G. Graen, M. Novak, and P. Sommerkamp, "The Effects of Leader-Member Exchange and Job Design on Productivity and Satisfaction: Testing a Dual Attachment Model," *Organizational Behavior and Human Performance* (August 1982), pp. 109–31.

[36] G. Graen and J. Cashman, "A Role-Making Model of Leadership in Formal Organizations: A Development Approach," in J.G. Hunt and L.L. Larson (eds.), *Leadership Frontiers* (Kent, OH: Kent State University Press, 1975), pp. 143–65; R. Liden and G. Graen, "Generalizability of the Vertical Dyad Linkage Model of Leadership," *Academy of Management Journal* (September 1980), pp. 451–65; and R.C. Liden, S.J. Wayne, and D. Stilwell, "A Longitudinal Study of the Early Development of Leader-Member Exchanges," *Journal of Applied Psychology* (August 1993), pp. 662–74.

[37] D.Duchon, S.G. Green, and T.D. Taber, "Vertical Dyad Linkage: A Longitudinal Assessment of Antecedents, Measures, and Consequences," *Journal of Applied Psychology* (February 1986), pp. 56–60; and R.C. Liden, S.J. Wayne, and D. Stilwell, "A Longitudinal Study on the Early Development of Leader–Member Exchanges;" R.J. Deluga and J.T. Perry, "The Role of Subordinate Performance and Ingratiation in

Leader–Member Exchanges," *Group & Organization Management* (March 1994), pp. 67–86; and A.S. Phillips and A.G. Bedeian, "Leader–Follower Exchange Quality: The Role of Personal and Interpersonal Attributes," *Academy of Management Journal* (August 1994), pp. 990–1001.

[38] See, for example, G. Graen, M. Novak, and P. Sommerkamp, "The Effects of Leader–Member Exchange"; T. Scandura and G. Graen, "Moderating Effects of Initial Leader–Member Exchange Status on the Effects of a Leadership Intervention," *Journal of Applied Psychology* (August 1984), pp. 428–36; R.P. Vecchio and B.C. Gobdel, "The Vertical Dyad Linkage Model of Leadership: Problems and Prospects," *Organizational Behavior and Human Performance* (August 1984), pp. 5–20; and T.M. Dockery and D.D. Steiner, "The Role of the Initial Interaction in Leader–Member Exchange," *Group & Organization Studies* (December 1990), pp. 395–413.

[39] A. Jago, "Leadership: Perspectives in Theory and Research," *Management Science* (March 1982), p. 331.

[40] R.J. House, "A Path-Goal Theory of Leader Effectiveness," *Administrative Science Quarterly* (September 1971), pp. 321–38; R.J. House and T.R. Mitchell, "Path-Goal Theory of Leadership," *Journal of Contemporary Business* (Autumn 1974), p. 86; and R.J. House, "Retrospective Comment," in L.E. Boone and D.D. Bowen (eds.), *The Great Writings in Management and Organizational Behavior*, 2nd ed. (New York: Random House, 1987), pp. 354–64.

[41] See J. Indik, "Path-Goal Theory of Leadership: A Meta-Analysis," paper presented at the National Academy of Management Conference, Chicago, August 1986; R.T. Keller, "A Test of the Path-Goal Theory of Leadership with Need for Clarity as a Moderator in Research and Development Organizations," *Journal of Applied Psychology* (April 1989), pp. 208–12; and J.C. Wofford and L.Z. Liska, "Path-Goal Theories of Leadership: A Meta-Analysis," *Journal of Management* (Winter 1993), pp. 857–76.

[42] V.H. Vroom and P.W. Yetton, *Leadership and Decision-Making* (Pittsburgh: University of Pittsburgh Press, 1973).

[43] V.H. Vroom and A.G. Jago, *The New Leadership: Managing Participation in Organizations* (Englewood Cliffs, NJ: Prentice Hall, 1988). See especially Chapter 8.

[44] See, for example, R.H.G. Field, "A Test of the Vroom-Yetton Normative Model of Leadership," *Journal of Applied Psychology* (October 1982), pp. 523–32; C.R. Leana, "Power Relinquishment versus Power Sharing: Theoretical Clarification and Empirical Comparison of Delegation and Participation," *Journal of Applied Psychology* (May 1987), pp. 228–33; J.T. Ettling and A.G. Jago, "Participation Under Conditions of Conflict: More on the Validity of the Vroom-Yetton Model," *Journal of Management Studies* (January 1988), pp. 73–83; and R.H.G. Field and R.J. House, "A Test of the Vroom-Yetton Model Using Manager and Subordinate Reports," *Journal of Applied Psychology* (June 1990), pp. 362–66.

[45] Dobbins, Long, Dedrick, and Clemons, "The Role of Self-Monitoring and Gender on Leader Emergence"; and S.J. Zaccaro, R.J. Foti, and D.A. Kenny, "Self-Monitoring and Trait-Based Variance in Leadership: An Investigation of Leader Flexibility Across Multiple Group Situations," *Journal of Applied Psychology* (April 1991), pp. 308–15.

[46] S. Kerr and J.M. Jermier, "Substitutes for Leadership: Their Meaning and Measurement," *Organizational Behavior and Human Performance* (December 1978), pp. 375–403; J.P. Howell and P.W. Dorfman, "Substitutes for Leadership: Test of a Construct," *Academy of Management Journal* (December 1981), pp. 714–28; J.P. Howell, P.W. Dorfman, and S. Kerr, "Leadership and Substitutes for Leadership," *Journal of Applied Behavioral Science*, Vol. 22, No. 1 (1986), pp. 29–46; J.P. Dorfman, P.W. Dorfman, and S. Kerr, "Moderator Variables in Leadership Research," *Academy of Management Review* (January 1986), pp. 88–102; N.J. Pitner, "Leadership Substitutes: Their Factorial Validity in Educational Organizations," *Educational & Psychological Measurement* (Summer 1988), pp. 307–15; J.P. Howell, D.E. Bowen, P.W. Dorfman, S. Kerr, and P.M. Podsakoff, "Substitutes for Leadership: Effective Alternatives to Ineffective Leadership," *Organizational Dynamics* (Summer 1990), pp. 21–38; P.M. Podsakoff, B.P. Niehoff, S.B. MacKenzie, and M.L. Williams, "Do Substitutes for Leadership Really Substitute for Leadership? An Empirical Examination of Kerr and Jermier's Situational Leadership Model," *Organizational Behavior and Human Decision Processes* (February 1993), pp. 1–44; and P.M. Podsakoff, S.B. MacKenzie, and R. Fetter, "Substitutes for Leadership and the Management of Professionals," *Leadership Quarterly* (Spring 1993), pp. 1–44.

[47] B. Karmel, "Leadership: A Challenge to Traditional Research Methods and Assumptions," *Academy of Management Review* (July 1978), pp. 477–79.

[48] Schein, *Organizational Psychology*, p. 132.

[49] See L.R. Anderson, "Toward a Two-Track Model of Leadership Training: Suggestions from Self-Monitoring Theory," *Small Group Research* (May 1990), pp. 147–67.

[50] C. Margerison and R. Glube, "Leadership Decision-Making: An Empirical Test of the Vroom and Yetton Model," *Journal of Management Studies* (February 1979), pp. 45–55.

[51] See, for instance, J.C. McElroy, "A Typology of Attribution Leadership Research," *Academy of Management Review* (July 1982), pp. 413–17; J.R. Meindl and S.B. Ehrlich, "The Romance of Leadership and the Evaluation of Organizational Performance," *Academy of Management Journal* (March 1987), pp. 91–109; J.C. McElroy and J.D. Hunger, "Leadership Theory as Causal Attribution of Performance," in J.G. Hunt, B.R. Baliga, H.P. Dachler, and C.A. Schriesheim (eds.), *Emerging Leadership Vistas* (Lexington, MA: Lexington Books, 1988); and B. Shamir, "Attribution of Influence and Charisma to the Leader: The Romance of Leadership Revisited," *Journal of Applied Social Psychology* (March 1992), pp. 386–407.

[52] R.G. Lord, C.L. DeVader, and G.M. Alliger, "A Meta-Analysis of the Relation Between Personality Traits and Leadership Perceptions."

[53] G.N. Powell and D.A. Butterfield, "The "High-High" Leader Rides Again!" *Group & Organization Studies* (December 1984), pp. 437–50.

[54] J.R. Meindl, S.B. Ehrlich, and J.M. Dukerich, "The Romance of Leadership," *Administrative Science Quarterly* (March 1985), pp. 78–102.

[55] J. Pfeffer, *Managing with Power* (Boston: Harvard Business School Press, 1992), p. 194; and M. Loeb, "An Interview with Warren Bennis: Where Leaders Come From," *Fortune* (September 19, 1994), p. 241.

[56] B.M. Staw and J. Ross, "Commitment in an Experimenting Society: A Study of the Attribution of Leadership from Administrative Scenarios," *Journal of Applied Psychology* (June 1980), pp. 249–60.

[57] J.A. Conger and R.N. Kanungo, "Behavioral Dimensions of Charismatic Leadership," in J.A. Conger, R.N. Kanungo and associates, *Charismatic Leadership* (San Francisco: Jossey-Bass, 1988), p. 79.

[58] R.J. House, "A 1976 Theory of Charismatic Leadership," in J.G. Hunt and L.L. Larson (eds.), *Leadership: The Cutting Edge* (Carbondale: Southern Illinois University Press, 1977), pp. 189–207.

[59] W. Bennis, "The 4 Competencies of Leadership," *Training and Development Journal* (August 1984), pp. 15–19.

[60] Conger and Kanungo, "Behavioral Dimensions of Charismatic Leadership," pp. 78–97.

[61] B. Shamir, R.J. House, and M.B. Arthur, "The Motivational Effects of Charismatic Leadership: A Self-Concept Theory," *Organization Science* (November 1993), pp. 577–94.

[62] R.J. House, J. Woycke, and E.M. Fodor, "Charismatic and Noncharismatic Leaders: Differences in Behavior and Effectiveness," in Conger and Kanungo, *Charismatic Leadership*, pp. 103–104; and D.A. Waldman, B.M. Bass, and F.J. Yammarino, "Adding to Contingent-Reward Behavior: The Augmenting Effect of Charismatic Leadership," *Group & Organization Studies* (December 1990), pp. 381–94.

[63] J.A. Conger and R.N. Kanungo, "Training Charismatic Leadership: A Risky and Critical Task," in Conger and Kanungo, *Charismatic Leadership*, pp. 309–23.

[64] R.J. Richardson and S.K. Thayer, *The Charisma Factor: How to Develop Your Natural Leadership Ability* (Englewood Cliffs, NJ: Prentice Hall, 1993).

[65] J.M. Howell and P.J. Frost, "A Laboratory Study of Charismatic Leadership," *Organizational Behavior and Human Decision Processes* (April 1989), pp. 243–69.

[66] House, "A 1976 Theory of Charismatic Leadership."

[67] J.A. Conger, *The Charismatic Leader: Behind the Mystique of Exceptional Leadership* (San Francisco: Jossey-Bass, 1989); and R. Hogan, R. Raskin, and D. Fazzini, "The Dark Side of Charisma," in K.E. Clark and M.B. Clark (eds.), *Measures of Leadership* (West Orange, NJ: Leadership Library of America, 1990).

[68] G.P. Zachary, "How 'Barbarian' Style of Philippe Kahn Led Borland into Jeopardy," *Wall Street Journal* (June 2, 1994), p. A1.

[69] See, for instance, J.M. Burns, *Leadership* (New York: Harper & Row, 1978); B.M. Bass, *Leadership and Performance Beyond Expectations* (New York: Free Press, 1985); B.M. Bass, "From Transactional to Transformational Leadership: Learning to Share the Vision," *Organizational Dynamics* (Winter 1990), pp. 19–31; F.J. Yammarino, W.D. Spangler, and B.M. Bass, "Transformational Leadership and Performance: A Longitudinal Investigation," *Leadership Quarterly* (Spring 1993), pp. 81–102; and J.M. Howell and B.J. Avolio, "Transformational Leadership, Transactional Leadership, Locus of Control, and Support for Innovation: Key Predictors of Consolidated-Business-Unit Performance," *Journal of Applied Psychology* (December 1993), pp. 891–902.

[70] B.M. Bass, "Leadership: Good, Better, Best," *Organizational Dynamics* (Winter 1985), pp. 26–40; and J. Seltzer and B.M. Bass, "Transformational Leadership: Beyond Initiation and Consideration," *Journal of Management* (December 1990), pp. 693–703.

[71] B.J. Avolio and B.M. Bass, "Transformational Leadership, Charisma and Beyond," working paper, School of Management, State University of New York, Binghamton, 1985, p. 14.

[72] Cited in B.M. Bass and B.J. Avolio, "Developing Transformational Leadership: 1992 and Beyond," *Journal of European Industrial Training* (January 1990), p. 23.

[73] J.J. Hater and B.M. Bass, "Supervisors' Evaluation and Subordinates' Perceptions of Transformational and Transactional Leadership," *Journal of Applied Psychology* (November 1988), pp. 695–702.

[74] Bass and Avolio, "Developing Transformational Leadership."

[75] The material in this section is based on J. Grant, "Women as Managers: What They Can Offer to Organizations," *Organizational Dynamics* (Winter 1988), pp. 56–63; S. Helgesen, *The Female Advantage: Women's Ways of Leadership* (New York: Doubleday, 1990); A.H. Eagly and B.T. Johnson, "Gender and Leadership Style: A Meta-Analysis," *Psychological Bulletin* (September 1990), pp. 233–56; A.H. Eagly and S.J. Karau, "Gender and the Emergence of Leaders: A Meta-Analysis," *Journal of Personality and Social Psychology* (May 1991), pp. 685–710. J.B. Rosener, "Ways Women Lead," *Harvard Business Review* (November-December 1990), pp. 119–25; "Debate: Ways Men and Women Lead," *Harvard Business Review* (January-February 1991), pp. 150–60; A.H. Eagly, M.G. Makhijani, and B.G. Klonsky, "Gender and the Evaluation of Leaders: A Meta-Analysis," *Psychological Bulletin* (January 1992), pp. 3–22; A.H. Eagly, S.J. Karau, and B.T. Johnson, "Gender and Leadership Style Among School Principals: A Meta-Analysis," *Educational Administration Quarterly* (February 1992), pp. 76–102; L.R. Offermann and C. Beil, "Achievement Styles of Women Leaders and Their Peers," *Psychology of Women Quarterly* (March 1992), pp. 37–56; T. Melamed and N. Bozionelos, "Gender Differences in the Personality Features of British Managers," *Psychological Reports* (December 1992), pp. 979–986; and G.N. Powell, *Women & Men in Management*, 2nd ed. (Thousand Oaks, CA: Sage, 1993).

[76] C.D. Orth, H.E. Wilkinson, and R.C. Benfari, "The Manager's Role as Coach and Mentor," *Organizational Dynamics* (Spring 1987), p. 67.

[77] See W.W. Burke, "Leadership as Empowering Others," in S. Srivastva and associates, *Executive Power* (San Francisco: Jossey-Bass, 1986); J.A. Conger and R.N. Kanungo, "The Empowerment Process: Integrating Theory and Practice," *Academy of Management Review* (July, 1988), pp. 471–82; J. Greenwald, "Is Mr. Nice Guy Back?" *Time* (January 27, 1992), pp. 42–44; J. Weber, "Letting Go Is Hard to Do," *Business Week* (November 1, 1993), pp. 218–19; and L. Holpp, "Applied Empowerment," *Training* (February 1994), pp. 39–44.

[78] See, for instance, D.A. Waldman, "A Theoretical Consideration of Leadership and Total Quality Management," *Leadership Quarterly* (Spring 1993), pp. 65–79.

[79] R.E. Kelley, "In Praise of Followers," *Harvard Business Review* (November-December 1988), pp. 142–48; and E.P. Hollander, "Leadership, Followership, Self, and Others," *Leadership Quarterly* (Spring 1992), pp. 43–54.

[80] Kelley, "In Praise of Followers."

[81] For a review of the cross-cultural applicability of the leadership literature, see R.S. Bhagat, B.L. Kedia, S.E. Crawford, and M.R. Kaplan, "Cross-Cultural Issues in Organizational Psychology: Emergent Trends and Directions for Research in the 1990s," in C.L. Cooper and I.T. Robertson (eds.), *International Review of Industrial and Organizational Psychology*, Vol. 5 (Chichester, England: Wiley, 1990), pp. 79–89.

[82] This section is based on R.M. Sapolsky and J.C. Ray, "Styles of Dominance and Their Endocrine Correlates Among Wild Olive Baboons," *American Journal of Primatology*, Vol. 18, No. 1 (1989), pp. 1–13; A. Booth, G. Shelley, A. Mazur, G. Tharp, and R. Kittok, "Testosterone, and Winning and Losing in Human Competition," *Hormones and Behavior* (December 1989), pp. 556–71; W.F. Allman, "Political Chemistry," *U.S. News & World Report* (November 2, 1992), pp. 62–65; E.L. Andrews, "A Skin Patch to Increase Testosterone," *New York Times* (November 2, 1992), p. C2; P.D. Kramer, *Listening to Prozac* (New York: Penguin, 1993); and M. Konner, "Out of the Darkness," *New York Times Magazine* (October 2, 1994), pp. 70–73.

CHAPTER 12

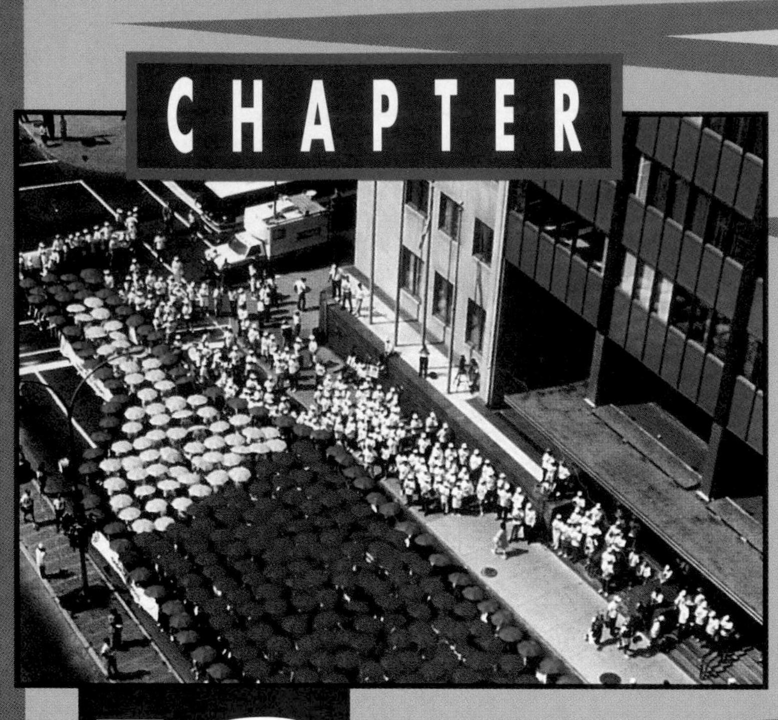

In an effort to influence federal and provincial governments, some 1,200 distillery employees joined forces to protest the high level of alcohol taxes in Canada. They claim the high tax encourages smuggling and is jeopardizing their jobs.

POWER AND POLITICS

CHAPTER OUTLINE

LEARNING OBJECTIVES

After studying this chapter, you should be able to:

1. Contrast *leadership* and *power*.
2. Define the four bases of power.
3. List seven power tactics and their contingencies.
4. Explain how sexual harassment is about the abuse of power.
5. List those individual and organizational factors that stimulate political behavior.
6. Identify seven techniques for managing the impression one makes on others.
7. Explain how defensive behaviors can protect an individual's self- interest.
8. List the three questions that can help determine if a political action is ethical.

You can get much farther with a kind word and a gun than you can with a kind word alone.
A. CAPONE

Michael Ovitz is widely acknowledged as the most powerful man in show business.[1] How powerful? *Time* magazine was doing a recent article on him. When the heads of two film studios and one of Ovitz's own employees were asked by a *Time* reporter what they thought of him, all three sang his praises. But they insisted on anonymity, for fear Ovitz might become upset that they said anything at all. Almost immediately after the interviews, further rethinking the wisdom of their actions, each of the three called Ovitz to confess preemptively that he had talked to a reporter.

Who is this guy Ovitz? And why is everyone in show business scared to death of him?

Michael Ovitz is cofounder and chairman of the Creative Artists Agency (CAA). The power he wields becomes self-evident if you consider two facts. First, the key people in the entertainment industry—producers, studio executives, heads of music companies, and the like—depend on talent to make their films, videos, and compact discs. Second, Ovitz and CAA control most of that talent. He represents almost every major movie star, musical artist, and film director in America. That client list includes Dustin Hoffman, Meryl Streep, Robert De Niro, Al Pacino, Eddie Murphy, Robert Redford, Robin Williams, Kevin Costner, Whoopi Goldberg, Tom Cruise, Warren Beatty, Barbra Streisand, Madonna, Michael Jackson, Eric Clapton, Steven Spielberg, Rob Reiner, Oliver Stone, Martin Scorsese, John Hughes, and Francis Ford Coppola. So you want to make a film? You want to sign a major recording artist to your label? You've got to come to Ovitz and his agency. When Ovitz talks, the people at companies like Columbia Pictures, Disney, and MCA/Universal have no choice but to listen!

Power has been described as the last dirty word. It is easier for most of us to talk about money or even sex than it is to talk about power. People who have it deny it, people who want it try not to appear to be seeking it, and those who are good at getting it are secretive about how they got it.[2] But OB researchers have learned a lot in the past decade or two about how people gain and use power in organizations. In this chapter, we present you with their findings.

◆Power has been described as the last dirty word.

A major theme throughout this chapter is that power is a natural process in any group or organization. As such, you need to know how it's acquired and exercised if you're going to fully understand organizational behavior. While you may have heard the phrase "power corrupts, and absolute power corrupts absolutely," power is not necessarily bad. As one author has noted, most medicines can kill if taken in the wrong amount and thousands die each year in automobile accidents, but we don't abandon chemicals or cars because of the dangers associated with them. Rather, we consider danger an incentive to get training and information that'll help us use these forces productively.[3] The same applies to *power*. It's a reality of organizational life and it's not going to go away. Moreover, by learning how power works in organizations, you'll be better able to use your knowledge to help you be a more effective manager.

A Definition of Power

power
A capacity that A has to influence the behavior of B so that B does things he or she would not otherwise do.

dependency
B's relationship to A when A possesses something that B requires.

Power refers to a capacity that A has to influence the behavior of B, so B does something he or she would not otherwise do. This definition implies (1) a *potential* that need not be actualized to be effective, (2) a *dependency* relationship, and (3) the assumption that B has some *discretion* over his or her own behavior. Let's look at each of these points more closely.

Power may exist but not be used. It is, therefore, a capacity or potential. One can have power but not impose it.

Probably the most important aspect of power is that it is a function of **dependency**. The greater B's dependence on A, the greater is A's power in the relationship. Dependence, in turn, is based on alternatives that B perceives and the importance that B places on the alternative(s) that A controls. A person can have power over you only if he or she controls something you desire. If you want a college degree and have to pass a certain course to get it, and your current instructor is the only faculty member in the college who teaches that course, he or she has power over you. Your alternatives are highly limited and you place a high degree of importance on obtaining a passing grade. Similarly, if you're attending college on funds totally provided by your parents, you probably recognize the power they hold over you. You're dependent on them for financial support. But once you're out of school, have a job, and are making a solid income, your parents' power is reduced significantly. Who among us, though, has not known or heard of the rich relative who is able to control a large number of family members merely through the implicit or explicit threat of "writing them out of the will"?

For A to get B to do something he or she otherwise would not do means B must have the discretion to make choices. At the extreme, if B's job behavior is so programmed he is allowed no room to make choices, he obviously is constrained in his ability to do something other than what he is doing. For instance, job descriptions, group norms, and organizational rules and regulations, as well as community laws and standards, constrain people's choices. As a nurse, you may be dependent on your supervisor for continued employment. But, in spite of this dependence, you're unlikely to comply with her request to perform heart surgery on a patient or steal several thousand dollars from petty cash. Your job description and laws against stealing constrain your ability to make these choices.

Contrasting Leadership and Power

A careful comparison of our description of power with our description of leadership in the previous chapter reveals that the two concepts are closely intertwined. Leaders use power as a means of attaining group goals. Leaders achieve goals, and power is a means of facilitating their achievement.

What differences are there between the two terms? One difference relates to goal compatibility. Power does not require goal compatibility, merely dependence. Leadership, on the other hand, requires some congruence between the goals of the leader and the led. A second difference relates to the direction of influence. Leadership focuses on the downward influence on one's subordinates. It minimizes the importance of lateral and upward influence patterns. Power does not. Still another difference deals with research emphasis. Leadership research, for the most part, emphasizes style. It seeks answers to such questions as: How supportive should a leader be? How much decision making should be shared with subordinates? In contrast, the research on power has tended to encompass a broader area and focus on tactics for gaining compliance. It has gone beyond the individual as exerciser because power can be used by groups as well as by individuals to control other individuals or groups.

Bases of Power

Where does power come from? What is it that gives an individual or a group influence over others? The answer to these questions is a five-category classifi-

Table 12-1 Measuring Bases of Power

Does a person have one or more of the five bases of power? Affirmative responses to the following statements can answer this question:

- The person can make things difficult for people, and you want to avoid getting him or her angry. [coercive power]
- The person is able to give special benefits or rewards to people, and you find it advantageous to trade favors with him or her. [reward power]
- The person has the right, considering his or her position and your job responsibilities, to expect you to comply with legitimate requests. [legitimate power]
- The person has the experience and knowledge to earn your respect, and you defer to his or her judgment in some matters. [expert power]
- You like the person and enjoy doing things for him or her. [referent power]

Source: G. Yukl and C.M. Falbe, "Importance of Different Power Sources in Downward and Lateral Relations," *Journal of Applied Psychology* (June 1991), p. 417. With permission.

cation scheme identified by French and Raven.[4] They proposed five bases or sources of power: coercive, reward, legitimate, expert, and referent (see Table 12-1).

Coercive Power

coercive power
Power that is based on fear.

The **coercive power** base is defined by French and Raven as being dependent on fear. One reacts to this power out of fear of the negative results that might occur if one failed to comply. It rests on the application, or the threat of application, of physical sanctions such as the infliction of pain, the generation of frustration through restriction of movement, or the controlling by force of basic physiological or safety needs.

In the 1930s, when John Dillinger went into a bank, held a gun to a teller's head, and asked for money, he was incredibly successful at getting compliance with his request. His power base was coercive. A loaded gun gives its holder power because others are fearful they will lose something they hold dear—their lives.

> Of all the bases of power available to man, the power to hurt others is possibly most often used, most often condemned, and most difficult to control . . . the state relies on its military and legal resources to intimidate nations, or even its own citizens. Businesses rely upon the control of economic resources. Schools and universities rely upon their rights to deny students formal education, while the church threatens individuals with loss of grace. At the personal level, individuals exercise coercive power through a reliance upon physical strength, verbal facility, or the ability to grant or withhold emotional support from others. These bases provide the individual with the means to physically harm, bully, humiliate, or deny love to others.[5]

At the organizational level, A has coercive power over B if A can dismiss, suspend, or demote B, assuming B values his or her job. Similarly, if A can assign B work activities that B finds unpleasant or treat B in a manner B finds embarrassing, A possesses coercive power over B.

Reward Power

The opposite of coercive power is **reward power**. People comply with the wishes or directives of another because it produces positive benefits; therefore, one who can distribute rewards that others view as valuable will have power over them. These rewards can be anything another person values. In an organizational context, we think of money, favorable performance appraisals, promotions, interesting work assignments, friendly colleagues, important information, and preferred work shifts or sales territories.

reward power Compliance achieved based on the ability to distribute rewards that others view as valuable.

Coercive and reward power are actually counterparts of each other. If you can remove something of positive value from another or inflict something of negative value upon him or her, you have coercive power over that person. If you can give someone something of positive value or remove something of negative value, you have reward power over that person. Again, as with coercive power, you don't need to be a manager to be able to exert influence through rewards. Rewards such as friendliness, acceptance, and praise are available to everyone in an organization. To the degree an individual seeks such rewards, your ability to give or withhold them gives you power over that individual.

Legitimate Power

In formal groups and organizations, probably the most frequent access to one or more of the power bases is one's structural position. This is called **legitimate power**. It represents the power a person receives as a result of his or her position in the formal hierarchy of an organization.

legitimate power The power a person receives as a result of his or her position in the formal hierarchy of an organization.

Positions of authority include coercive and reward powers. Legitimate power, however, is broader than the power to coerce and reward. Specifically, it includes acceptance by members of an organization of the authority of a position. When school principals, bank presidents, or army captains speak (assum-

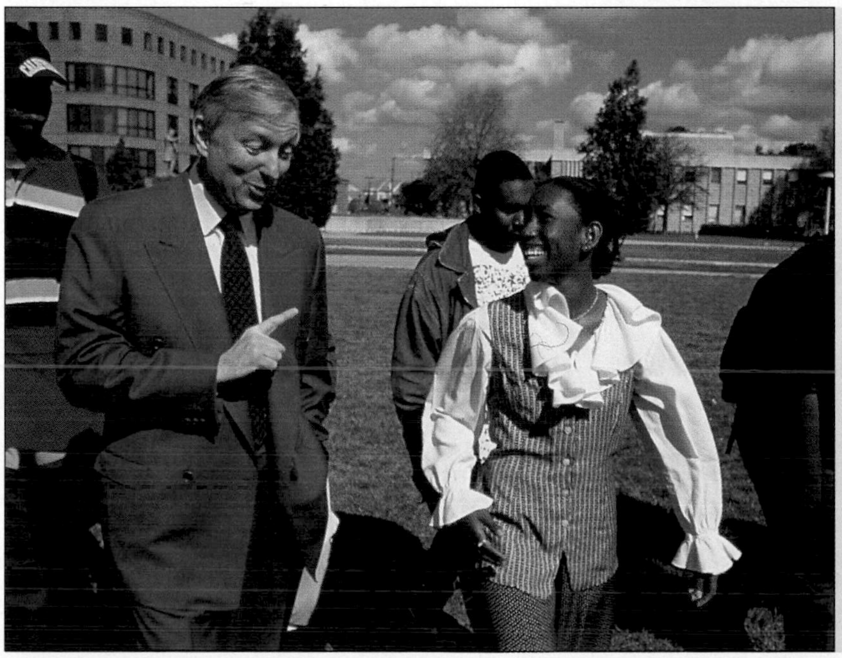

Diversity advocate Ernest Drew, CEO of Hoechst Celanese, is using legitimate and reward power to reach his goal of at least 34 percent representation of women and minorities at all levels of his company by 2001. Drew travels from plant to plant to discuss the value of a diverse work force with employees. He says, "When the CEO meets with employees, it signals diversity is important." Under Drew's direction, diversity is one of four performance criteria used in determining managers' salaries and bonuses. He requires his top 26 officers to join two organizations in which they are a minority. Drew put the policy in place to help managers break out of their comfort zones and give them experience of what it's like to be a minority so they learn "that all people are similar." Drew is a board member of black Hampton University and of SER-Jobs for Progress, a Hispanic association. He is shown here with students from Hampton.

"I was just going to say 'Well, I don't make the rules.' But, of course, I do make the rules."

Figure 12-1
Source: Drawing by Leo Cullum in *The New Yorker*. Copyright © 1986 The New Yorker Magazine. Reprinted by permission.

ing their directives are viewed to be within the authority of their positions), teachers, tellers, and first lieutenants listen and usually comply.

Expert Power

expert power
Influence based on special skills or knowledge.

Expert power is influence wielded as a result of expertise, special skill, or knowledge. Expertise has become one of the most powerful sources of influence as the world has become more technologically oriented. As jobs become more specialized, we become increasingly dependent on "experts" to achieve goals. So, while it is generally acknowledged that physicians have expertise and hence expert power—most of us follow the advice our doctor gives us—you should also recognize that computer specialists, tax accountants, solar engineers, industrial psychologists, and other specialists are able to wield power as a result of their expertise.

Referent Power

referent power
Influence based on possession by an individual of desirable resources or personal traits.

The last category of influence that French and Raven identified was **referent power**. Its base is identification with a person who has desirable resources or personal traits. If I admire and identify with you, you can exercise power over me because I want to please you.

Referent power develops out of admiration of another and a desire to be like that person. In a sense, then, it is a lot like charisma. If you admire someone to the point of modeling your behavior and attitudes after him or her, this person possesses referent power over you. Referent power explains why celebrities are paid millions of dollars to endorse products in commercials. Marketing research shows that people like Bill Cosby, Elizabeth Taylor, and Michael Jordan have the power to influence your choice of photo processors, perfume, and athletic shoes. With a little practice, you or I could probably deliver as smooth a sales pitch as these celebrities, but the buying public doesn't identify with you and me. In organizations, if you are articulate, domineering, physically imposing, or charismatic, you hold personal characteristics that may be used to get others to do what you want.

Dependency: The Key to Power

Earlier in this chapter we said that probably the most important aspect of power is that it is a function of dependence. In this section, we show how an understanding of dependency is central to furthering your understanding of power itself.

The General Dependency Postulate

Let's begin with a general postulate: *The greater B's dependency on A, the greater the power A has over B.* When you possess anything that others require but you alone control, you make them dependent on you and, therefore, you gain power over them.[6] Dependency, then, is inversely proportional to the alternative sources of supply. If something is plentiful, possession of it will not increase your power. If everyone is intelligent, intelligence gives no special advantage. Similarly, among the super rich, money is no longer power. But, as the old saying goes, "In the land of the blind, the one-eyed man is king!" If you can create a monopoly by controlling information, prestige, or anything others crave, they become dependent on you. Conversely, the more you can expand your options, the less power you place in the hands of others. This explains, for example, why most organizations develop multiple suppliers rather than give their business to only one. It also explains why so many of us aspire to financial independence. Financial independence reduces the power that others can have over us.

Joyce Fields provides an example of the role that dependency plays in a work group or organization.[7] In 1975 she took a job with the Times Mirror Company in its Los Angeles headquarters. Fields moved quickly up the organization ladder, eventually becoming treasurer of the company. Among her many accomplishments at Times Mirror has been setting up a full-scale commercial paper borrowing program from scratch and negotiating $1 billion of new debt to finance the company's media purchases. In 1988 Fields's husband was offered a promotion to chief financial officer at Paramount Communications in New York City. The job was too good to pass up, so the couple decided to pack up and move to Manhattan. However, Times Mirror didn't want to lose Fields to a New York company. So, in a tribute to her importance, top management at Times Mirror moved the company's entire treasury operations across the country to New York.

What Creates Dependency?

Dependency is increased when the resource you control is important, scarce, and nonsubstitutable.[8]

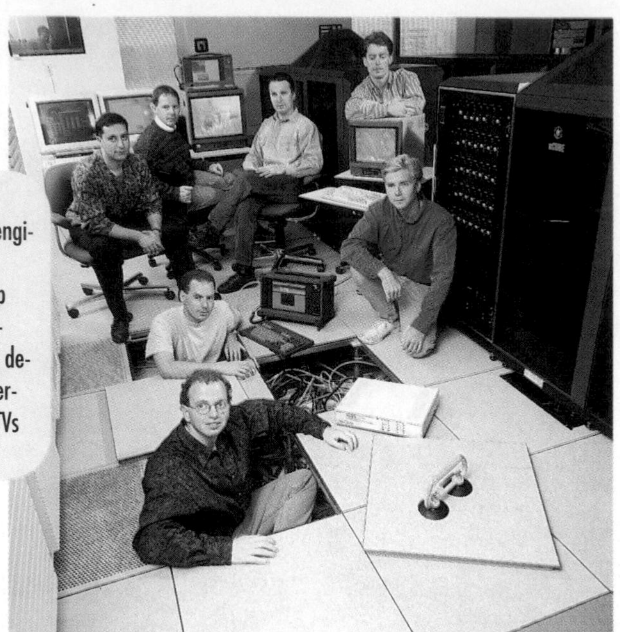

At Oracle Systems Corporation, engineers are important and powerful. The future of Oracle, a producer of software for corporate databases, depends on its engineers' technical expertise and inventiveness. Oracle plans to become a major player on the information highway and is depending on its engineers to develop the software that will make the communications and computer systems work together. Oracle's engineers have already designed software that makes video on demand a reality, enabling people to see movies at home at any time on their interactive TVs. Shown here is Oracle's video team testing hookups of computers to TVs in a company laboratory.

IMPORTANCE If nobody wants what you've got, it's not going to create dependency. To create dependency, therefore, the thing(s) you control must be perceived as being important. It's been found, for instance, that organizations actively seek to avoid uncertainty.[9] We should, therefore, expect that those individuals or groups who can absorb an organization's uncertainty will be perceived as controlling an important resource. For instance, a study of industrial organizations found that the marketing departments in these firms were consistently rated as the most powerful.[10] It was concluded by the researcher that the most critical uncertainty facing these firms was selling their products. This might suggest that during a labor strike, the organization's negotiating representatives have increased power, or that engineers, as a group, would be more powerful at Intel than at Procter & Gamble. These inferences appear to be generally valid. Labor negotiators do become more powerful within the personnel area and the organization as a whole during periods of labor strife. An organization such as Intel, which is heavily technologically oriented, is highly dependent on its engineers to maintain its products' technical advantages and quality. And, at Intel, engineers are clearly a powerful group. At Procter & Gamble, marketing is the name of the game, and marketers are the most powerful occupational group. These examples support not only the view that the ability to reduce uncertainty increases a group's importance and, hence, its power but also that what's important is situational. It varies between organizations and undoubtedly also varies over time within any given organization.

SCARCITY As noted previously, if something is plentiful, possession of it will not increase your power. A resource needs to be perceived as scarce to create dependency.

This can help to explain how low-ranking members in an organization who have important knowledge not available to high-ranking members gain power over the high-ranking members. Possession of a scarce resource—in this case, important knowledge—makes the high-ranking member dependent on the low-ranking member. This also helps make sense out of behaviors of low-ranking members that otherwise might seem illogical, such as destroying the procedure manuals that describe how a job is done, refusing to train people in their jobs or even to show others exactly what they do, creating specialized language and terminology that inhibits others from understanding their jobs, or operating in secrecy so an activity will appear more complex and difficult than it really is.

The scarcity–dependency relationship can further be seen in the power of occupational categories. Individuals in occupations in which the supply of personnel is low relative to demand can negotiate compensation and benefit packages far more attractive than can those in occupations where there is an abundance of candidates. College administrators have no problem today finding English instructors. The market for engineering teachers, in contrast, is extremely tight, with the demand high and the supply limited. The result is that the bargaining power of engineering faculty allows them to negotiate higher salaries, lower teaching loads, and other benefits.

NONSUBSTITUTABILITY The more a resource has no viable substitutes, the more power control over that resource provides. This is illustrated in a concept we call the **elasticity of power**.

elasticity of power
The relative responsiveness of power to changes in available alternatives.

In economics, considerable attention is focused on the elasticity of demand, which is defined as the relative responsiveness of quantity demanded to change in price. This concept can be modified to explain the strength of power.

Elasticity of power is defined as the relative responsiveness of power to change in available alternatives. One's ability to influence others is viewed as being dependent on how these others perceive their alternatives.

As shown in Figure 12-2, assume there are two individuals. Mr. A's power elasticity curve is relatively inelastic. This would describe, for example, an employee who believed he had a large number of employment opportunities outside his current organization. Fear of being fired would have only a moderate impact on Mr. A, for he perceives he has a number of other alternatives. Mr. A's boss finds that threatening A with termination has only a minimal impact on influencing his behavior. A reduction in alternatives (from X to X − 1) only increases the power of A's boss slightly (A′ to A″). However, Mr. B's curve is relatively elastic. He sees few other job opportunities. His age, education, present salary, or lack of contacts may severely limit his ability to find a job somewhere else. As a result, Mr. B is dependent on his present organization and boss. If B loses his job (Y to Y − 1), he may face prolonged unemployment, and it shows itself in the increased power of B's boss. As long as B perceives his options as limited and B's boss holds the power to terminate his employment, B's boss will hold considerable power over him. In such a situation, it is obviously important for B to get his boss to believe his options are considerably greater than they really are. If this is not achieved,

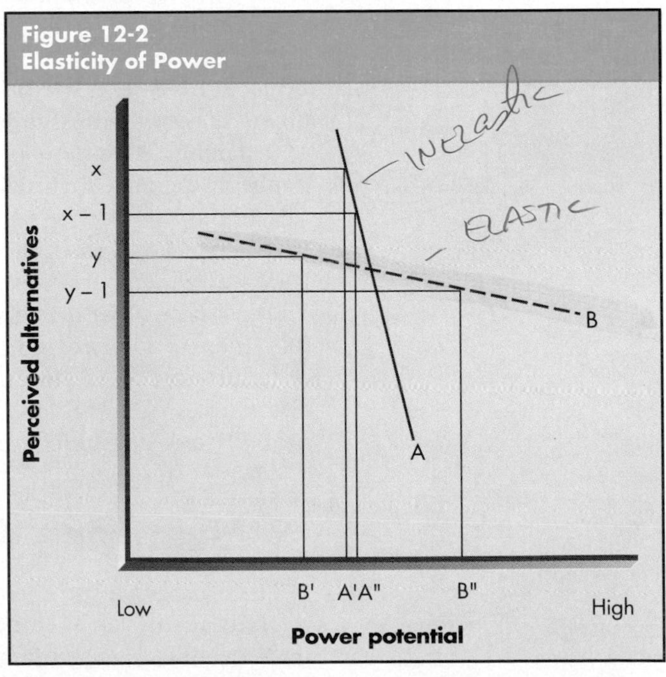

◆◆◆◆ OB in the News ◆◆◆◆

The Power of Subordinates

Watch out from below! Bosses aren't the only people in organizations with power. Subordinates have power too. They can effectively undermine your effectiveness and credibility with subtle actions like criticizing you to customers, peers, or bosses, or by excluding you from important decisions.

A New York advertising executive was hired to manage a major consumer-products account. He was chosen over Ms. Drew, an internal candidate, who had developed the account's brand strategy. Naively, the new executive assumed Drew, who was now one of his employees, would support him during his first big meeting with the client. He assumed wrong. At the meeting, he recommended against creating an extension of the brand. To his shock, Drew literally slumped in her chair, undermining him openly. Her efforts to undermine him didn't end there. She continued to defy the executive and hurt his ability to perform by using her strong ties to the other agency people he needed. One creative director, for instance, failed to attend a critical meeting with one of the executive's big customers—and the agency lost the account. Unable to gain credibility with his colleagues or clients, the executive was soon shuttled to another assignment. He quit a year later. And Drew? She got a promotion!

This incident illustrates that when a manager takes a new job or assignment, he or she needs to identify subversive subordinates early and take steps to win them over. Individuals who are particularly likely to become subversives include subordinates who had unsuccessfully sought the manager's job and close allies to the person the new manager is replacing. Also keep in mind that it may be easier for managers to win over subversives than fire them. These Benedict Arnolds often have formed powerful friendships with senior executives who will protect them in a "shoot-out." Moreover, these ties with senior executives can be used to convey negative information about the way their manager is performing his or her job.

Based on J.E. Rigdon, "Look Out Below for Deadly Hits on Your Career," *Wall Street Journal* (May 25, 1994), p. B1.

B places his fate in the hands of his boss and makes himself captive to almost any demands the boss devises.

Higher education provides an excellent example of how this elasticity concept operates. In universities where there are strong pressures for the faculty to publish, we can say a department head's power over a faculty member is inversely related to that member's publication record. The more recognition the faculty member receives through publication, the more mobile he or she is. That is, since other universities want faculty who are highly published and visible, there is an increased demand for his or her services. Although the concept of tenure can act to alter this relationship by restricting the department head's alternatives, those faculty members with little or no publications have the least mobility and are subject to the greatest influence from their superiors.

Identifying Where the Power Is

Mike Cisco got a summer job between his junior and senior years in college working in the lab at Phoenix Lutheran Hospital. As a chemistry major, Mike had never taken any courses in management or organizational behavior. But he had seen pictures of organization charts before. So on that first day at work, when the assistant in the human resources department gave Mike his orientation and showed him where the lab fit on the hospital's organization chart, he felt good. The lab ranked fairly high up on the chart.

After about a week or so at the hospital, Mike noticed the lab's manager didn't seem to have near the clout that the managers of marketing and finance had. And what puzzled Mike was that all three managers ranked at the same level on the hospital's organization chart.

Mike's first theory was that the marketing and finance managers were more aggressive individuals. But that clearly wasn't the case. It was obvious to almost everyone at the hospital that Mike's manager was smarter, more articulate, and more forceful than the other two managers. So Mike was at a loss to figure out why the marketing and finance managers seemed to be considered more important than his manager.

Mike got his answer over lunch during that second week. Traci Chou, a summer intern in the admissions office who was also working on her master's in business administration, clarified it for him. "The organization chart is deceptive. It doesn't tell you where the power is around here," Traci stated. "Ten years ago, the lab was equal to or maybe more important than finance or marketing. But not anymore. As competition has set in in the health-care industry, hospitals have had to learn how to cut costs, do more with less, and develop new sources of revenue. This has resulted in expanding the power of departments like finance and marketing around here."

How do you determine where the power is in an organization at any given point? We can answer this question from both the departmental and individual manager level.

At the departmental level, answers to the following questions will give you a good idea of how powerful that department is: What proportion of the organization's top-level managers came up through the department? Is the department represented on important interdepartmental teams and committees? How does the salary of the senior manager in the department compare with others at his or her level? Is the department located in the headquarters building? What's the average size of offices for people working in the department compared to offices in other departments? Has the department grown in number of employees relative to other departments? How does the promotion rate for people in the department compare to other units? Has the department's budget allocation been increasing relative to other departments?[11]

At the level of the individual manager, be on the lookout for certain symbols that suggest a manager has power.[12] These include the ability to intercede favorably on behalf of someone in trouble in the organization, to get approval for expenditures beyond the budget, to get items on the agenda at major meetings, and to get fast access to top decision makers in the organization.

Power Tactics

This section is a logical extension of our previous discussions. We've reviewed where power comes from. Now we move to the topic of **power tactics** to learn how employees translate their power bases into specific actions. Recent research indicates there are standardized ways by which powerholders attempt to get what they want.[13]

power tactics
Ways in which individuals translate power bases into specific actions.

When 165 managers were asked to write essays describing an incident in which they influenced their bosses, coworkers, or subordinates, a total of 370 power tactics grouped into 14 categories were identified. These answers were condensed, rewritten into a 58-item questionnaire, and given to over 750 employees. These respondents were not only asked how they went about influencing others at work but also the possible reasons for influencing the target person. The results, which are summarized here, give us considerable insight into power tactics—how managerial employees influence others and the conditions under which one tactic is chosen over another.[14]

The findings identified seven tactical dimensions or strategies:

- *Reason:* Use of facts and data to make a logical or rational presentation of ideas
- *Friendliness:* Use of flattery, creation of goodwill, acting humble, and being friendly prior to making a request
- *Coalition:* Getting the support of other people in the organization to back up the request
- *Bargaining:* Use of negotiation through the exchange of benefits or favors
- *Assertiveness:* Use of a direct and forceful approach such as demanding compliance with requests, repeating reminders, ordering individuals to do what is asked, and pointing out that rules require compliance
- *Higher authority:* Gaining the support of higher levels in the organization to back up requests
- *Sanctions:* Use of organizationally derived rewards and punishments such as preventing or promising a salary increase, threatening to give an unsatisfactory performance evaluation, or withholding a promotion

The researchers found that employees do not rely on the seven tactics equally. However, as shown in Table 12-2, the most popular strategy was the use of reason, regardless of whether the influence was directed upward or

Table 12-2 Usage of Power Tactics: From Most to Least Popular

	When Managers Influenced Superiors*	When Managers Influenced Subordinates
Most Popular ↑	Reason	Reason
	Coalition	Assertiveness
	Friendliness	Friendliness
	Bargaining	Coalition
	Assertiveness	Bargaining
	Higher authority	Higher authority
↓ Least Popular		Sanctions

*Sanctions is omitted in the scale that measures upward influence.

Source: Reprinted, by permission of the publisher, from "Patterns of Managerial Influence: Shotgun Managers, Tacticians, and Bystanders," by D. Kipnis et al., *Organizational Dynamics* (Winter 1984), p. 62.

downward. Additionally, the researchers uncovered four contingency variables that affect the selection of a power tactic: the manager's relative power, the manager's objectives for wanting to influence, the manager's expectation of the target person's willingness to comply, and the organization's culture.

A manager's relative power impacts the selection of tactics in two ways. First, managers who control resources that are valued by others, or who are perceived to be in positions of dominance, use a greater variety of tactics than do those with less power. Second, managers with power use assertiveness with greater frequency than do those with less power. Initially, we can expect that most managers will attempt to use simple requests and reason. Assertiveness is a backup strategy, used when the target of influence refuses or appears reluctant to comply with the request. Resistance leads to managers using more directive strategies. Typically, they shift from using simple requests to insisting their demands be met. But the manager with relatively little power is more likely to stop trying to influence others when he or she encounters resistance, because he or she perceives the costs associated with assertiveness as unacceptable.

Managers vary their power tactics in relation to their objectives. When managers seek benefits from a superior, they tend to rely on kind words and the promotion of pleasant relationships; that is, they use friendliness. In comparison, managers attempting to persuade their superiors to accept new ideas usually rely on reason. This matching of tactics to objectives also holds true for downward influence. For example, managers use reason to sell ideas to subordinates and friendliness to obtain favors.

The manager's expectations of success guide his or her choice of tactics. When past experience indicates a high probability of success, managers use simple requests to gain compliance. Where success is less predictable, managers are more tempted to use assertiveness and sanctions to achieve their objectives.

Finally, we know that cultures within organizations differ markedly—for example, some are warm, relaxed, and supportive; others are formal and conservative. The organizational culture in which a manager works, therefore, will have a significant bearing on defining which tactics are considered appropriate. Some cultures encourage the use of friendliness, some encourage reason, and still others rely on sanctions and assertiveness. So the organization itself will influence which subset of power tactics is viewed as acceptable for use by managers.

Power in Groups: Coalitions

Those "out of power" and seeking to be "in" will first try to increase their power individually. Why spread the spoils if one doesn't have to? But if this proves ineffective, the alternative is to form a coalition. There is strength in numbers.

The natural way to gain influence is to become a powerholder. Therefore, those who want power will attempt to build a personal power base. But, in many instances, this may be difficult, risky, costly, or impossible. In such cases, efforts will be made to form a coalition of two or more "outs" who, by joining together, can combine their resources to increase rewards for themselves.[15]

Historically, blue-collar workers in organizations who were unsuccessful in bargaining on their own behalf with management resorted to labor unions to bargain for them. In recent years, white-collar employees and professionals have increasingly turned to unions after finding it difficult to exert power individually to attain higher wages and greater job security.

Individuals had little success in attempting to influence local, state, and federal legislation to protect the rights of those suffering from AIDS. However, coalitions like ACTUP have successfully increased public awareness and lobbied for greater rights protection.

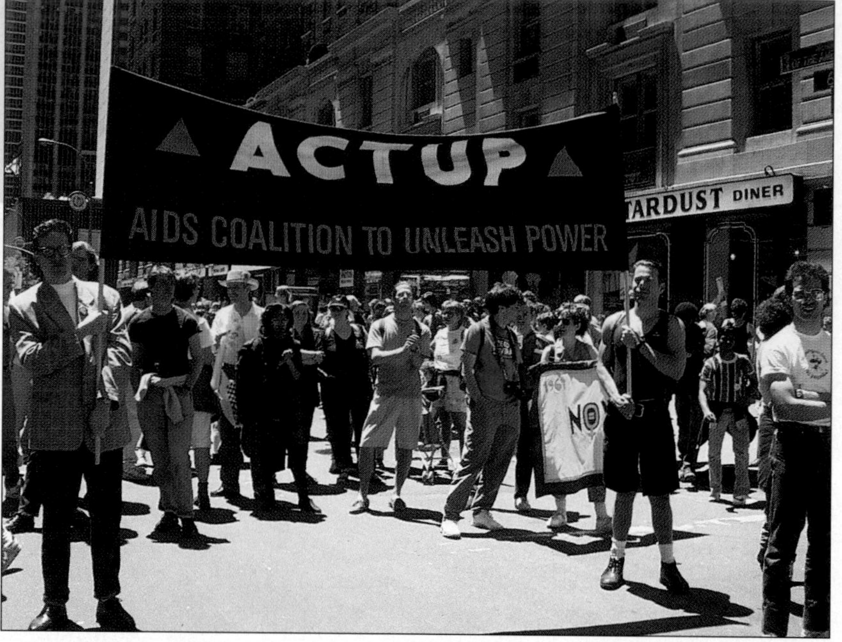

What predictions can we make about coalition formation?[16] First, coalitions in organizations often seek to maximize their size. In political science theory, coalitions move the other way—they try to minimize their size. They tend to be just large enough to exert the power necessary to achieve their objectives. But legislatures are different from organizations. Specifically, decision making in organizations does not end just with selection from among a set of alternatives. The decision must also be implemented. In organizations, the implementation of and commitment to the decision is at least as important as the decision itself. It's necessary, therefore, for coalitions in organizations to seek a broad constituency to support the coalition's objectives. This means expanding the coalition to encompass as many interests as possible. This coalition expansion to facilitate consensus building, of course, is more likely to occur in organizational cultures where cooperation, commitment, and shared decision making are highly valued. In autocratic and hierarchically controlled organizations, this search for maximizing the coalition's size is less likely to be sought.

Another prediction about coalitions relates to the degree of interdependence within the organization. More coalitions will likely be created where there is a great deal of task and resource interdependence. In contrast, there will be less interdependence among subunits and less coalition formation activity where subunits are largely self-contained or resources are abundant.

Finally, coalition formation will be influenced by the actual tasks that workers do. The more routine the task of a group, the greater the likelihood that coalitions will form. The more that the work people do is routine, the greater their substitutability for each other and, thus, the greater their dependence. To offset this dependence, they can be expected to resort to a coalition. We see, therefore, that unions appeal more to low-skill and nonprofessional workers than to skilled and professional types. Of course, where the supply of skilled and professional employees is high relative to their demand or where organizations have standardized traditionally nonroutine jobs, we would expect these incumbents to find unionization attractive.

Sexual Harassment: Unequal Power in the Workplace

The issue of sexual harassment got increasing attention by corporations and the media in the 1980s because of the growing ranks of female employees, especially in nontraditional work environments. But it was the congressional hearings in the fall of 1991 in which law professor Anita Hill graphically accused Supreme Court nominee Clarence Thomas of sexual harassment that challenged organizations to reassess their harassment policies and practices.[17]

Legally, **sexual harassment** is defined as unwelcome advances, requests for sexual favors, and other verbal or physical conduct of a sexual nature. A 1993 Supreme Court decision helped clarify this definition by adding that the key test for determining if sexual harassment has occurred is whether comments or behavior in a work environment "would reasonably be perceived, and

sexual harassment
Unwelcome advances, requests for sexual favors, and other verbal or physical conduct of a sexual nature.

A San Francisco jury awarded Rena Weeks $7.1 million in punitive damages for sexual harassment in a suit against Baker & McKenzie, the world's largest law firm. Weeks, a secretary in the law firm, testified that her boss, a partner in the firm, harassed her with physical touching and lewd comments. After she complained to her superiors, Weeks was transferred to another department and her boss was sent to counseling. During the trial, other former employees related similar harassment accounts that they reported to their superiors. Although Weeks' boss testified that his behavior wasn't done with malice or an intent to harm, the jury found him guilty and held the law firm responsible for not taking the complaints seriously and taking appropriate action. One juror said of the defense's testimony, "I got the feeling of power, arrogance, and outright lies." Shown here is Weeks with her lawyers after the trial.

is perceived, as hostile or abusive."[18] But there continues to be disagreement as to what *specifically* constitutes sexual harassment. Organizations have made considerable progress in the last few years toward limiting overt forms of sexual harassment of female employees. This includes unwanted physical touching, recurring requests for dates when it is made clear the woman isn't interested, and coercive threats that a woman will lose her job if she refuses a sexual proposition. The problems today are likely to surface around more subtle forms of sexual harassment: unwanted looks or comments; off-color jokes; sexual artifacts, like nude calendars, in the workplace; or misinterpretations of where the line between "being friendly" ends and "harassment" begins.

Most studies confirm that the concept of power is central to understanding sexual harassment.[19] This seems to be true whether the harassment comes from a supervisor, a coworker, or even a subordinate.

The supervisor–employee dyad best characterizes an unequal power relationship, where position power gives the supervisor the capacity to reward and coerce. Supervisors give subordinates their assignments, evaluate their performance, make recommendations for salary adjustments and promotions, and even decide whether an employee retains his or her job. These decisions give a supervisor power. Since subordinates want favorable performance reviews, salary increases, and the like, it's clear supervisors control resources that most subordinates consider important and scarce. It's also worth noting that individuals who occupy high-status roles (like management positions) sometimes believe that sexually harassing female subordinates is merely an extension of their right to make demands on lower status individuals. Because of power inequities, sexual harassment by one's boss typically creates the greatest difficulty for those who are being harassed. If there are no witnesses, it is her word against his. Are there others this boss has harassed and, if so, will they come forward? Because of the supervisor's control over resources, many of those who are harassed are afraid of speaking out for fear of retaliation by the supervisor.

While coworkers don't have position power, they can have influence and use it to sexually harass peers. In fact, although coworkers appear to engage in somewhat less severe forms of harassment than do supervisors, coworkers are the most frequent perpetrators of sexual harassment in organizations. How do coworkers exercise power? Most often it's by providing or withholding information, cooperation, and support. For example, the effective performance of most jobs requires interaction and support from coworkers. This is especially true nowadays as work is assigned to teams. By threatening to withhold or delay providing information that's necessary for the successful achievement of your work goals, coworkers can exert power over you.

Although it doesn't get nearly the attention that harassment by a supervisor does, women in positions of power can be subjected to sexual harassment from males who occupy less powerful positions within the organization. This is usually achieved by the subordinate devaluing the woman through highlighting traditional gender stereotypes (such as helplessness, passivity, lack of career commitment) that reflect negatively on the woman in power. Why would a subordinate engage in such practices? To attempt to gain some power over the higher ranking female or to minimize power differentials.

The topic of sexual harassment is about power. It's about an individual controlling or threatening another individual. It's wrong. Moreover, it's illegal. But you can understand how sexual harassment surfaces in organizations if you analyze it in power terms.

◆◆◆◆ OB in the News ◆◆◆◆

Many Companies Are Trying Hard to Stamp Out Sexual Harassment

Sexual harassment! No subject in recent memory has stirred so much confusion. Managers and employees are asking basic questions such as: Was it all right to say I liked her dress? Is it okay to ask him out to lunch to talk about that project? Should I just stop touching anybody, even if it's only a congratulatory pat on the back?

One point that all the experts seem to agree on is that sexual harassment is not really about sex. It's about power—more specifically, the abuse of power.

Ninety percent of Fortune 500 companies have dealt with sexual harassment complaints. More than a third have been sued at least once, and about a quarter have been sued over and over again.

What are organizations doing to eliminate sexual harassment? Most are taking a three-prong approach. First, they're establishing formal policies that show the company is serious about the problem. Honeywell, for instance, publicizes its policy against sexual harassment in a handbook given to every employee and on posters placed in conspicuous places. AT&T warns its employees that they can be fired for repeatedly making unwelcome sexual advances, using sexually degrading words to describe someone, or displaying sexually offensive pictures or objects at work. Second, organizations are investing in training. The most effective training appears to be workshops where participants get a chance to talk to each other, instead of just listening to a lecture or watching a video. In classes where men and women are asked to compare their impressions of the same hypothetical situation, real revelations can occur. Finally, organizations are establishing clear procedures for handling complaints when they arise. Typically, employers choose an impartial ombudsperson, usually in the human resources department, to hear and investigate charges before lawyers get involved. When complaints are found to be legitimate, organizations then are taking "immediate and appropriate action." Depending on the circumstances, this can range from transferring the harassed or the harasser to a different department, to docking the harasser a couple of weeks' pay, to firing the guilty party outright.

Based on A.B. Fisher, "Sexual Harassment: What to Do," *Fortune* (August 23, 1993), pp. 84–88.

Politics: Power in Action

When people get together in groups, power will be exerted. People want to carve out a niche from which to exert influence, to earn awards, and to advance their careers.[20] When employees in organizations convert their power into action, we describe them as being engaged in politics. Those with good political skills have the ability to use their bases of power effectively.[21]

Definition

There has been no shortage of definitions for organizational politics. Essentially, however, they have focused on the use of power to affect decision making in the organization or on behaviors by members that are self-serving and organizationally nonsanctioned.[22] For our purposes, we define **political behavior** in organizations as *those activities that are not required as part of one's formal role in the organization, but that influence, or attempt to influence, the distribution of advantages and disadvantages within the organization.*[23]

political behavior
Those activities that are not required as part of one's formal role in the organization, but that influence, or attempt to influence, the distribution of advantages and disadvantages within the organization.

This definition encompasses key elements from what most people mean when they talk about organizational politics. Political behavior is *outside* one's specified job requirements. The behavior requires some attempt to use one's *power* bases. Additionally, our definition encompasses efforts to influence the goals, criteria, or processes used for *decision making* when we state that politics is concerned with "the distribution of advantages and disadvantages within the organization." Our definition is broad enough to include such varied political behaviors as withholding key information from decision makers, whistleblowing, spreading rumors, leaking confidential information about organizational activities to the media, exchanging favors with others in the organization for mutual benefit, and lobbying on behalf of or against a particular individual or decision alternative. Table 12-3 provides a quick measure to help you assess how political your organization is.

legitimate political behavior
Normal everyday politics.

illegitimate political behavior
Extreme political behavior that violates the implied rules of the game.

A final comment relates to what has been referred to as the "legitimate–illegitimate" dimension in political behavior.[24] **Legitimate political behavior** refers to normal everyday politics—complaining to your supervisor, bypassing the chain of command, forming coalitions, obstructing organizational policies or decisions through inaction or excessive adherence to rules, and developing contacts outside the organization through one's professional activities. However, there are also **illegitimate political behaviors** that violate the implied rules of the game. Those who pursue such extreme activities are often described as individuals who play hardball. Illegitimate activities include sabotage, whistle-blowing, and symbolic protests such as wearing unorthodox dress or protest buttons and groups of employees simultaneously calling in sick.

Table 12-3 A Quick Measure of How Political Your Organization Is

How political is your organization? Answer the following five questions using the following scale:

SD = Strongly disagree
D = Disagree
U = Uncertain
A = Agree
SA = Strongly agree

1. Favoritism rather than merit determines who gets ahead. ____
2. There is no place for "yes people" around here; good ideas are desired even when it means disagreeing with supervisors. ____
3. You can get along around here by being a good guy, regardless of the quality of your work. ____
4. Employees are encouraged to speak out frankly even when they are critical of well established ideas. ____
5. There are "cliques" or "in-groups" that hinder the effectiveness around here. ____

Scoring: For items 1,3, and 5, give yourself 1 point for Strongly disagree; 2 points for Disagree; and so forth (through 5 points for Strongly agree). For items 2 and 4, reverse the score (i.e., 1 point for Strongly agree, etc.). Add up the total. The higher the total score, the greater degree of perceived organizational politics.

Source: G.R. Ferris and K.M. Kacmar, "Perceptions of Organizational Politics," *Journal of Management* (March 1992), p. 99. Copyright © 1992 by Southern Management Association. Reprinted by permission.

The vast majority of all organizational political actions are of the legitimate variety. The reasons are pragmatic: The extreme illegitimate forms of political behavior pose a very real risk of loss of organizational membership or extreme sanctions against those who use them and then fall short in having enough power to ensure they work.

The Reality of Politics

Politics is a fact of life in organizations. People who ignore this fact of life do so at their own peril. But why, you may wonder, must politics exist? Isn't it possible for an organization to be politics free? It's *possible*, but most unlikely.

◆Politics is a fact of life in organizations.

Organizations are made up of individuals and groups with different values, goals, and interests.[25] This sets up the potential for conflict over resources. Departmental budgets, space allocations, project responsibilities, and salary adjustments are just a few examples of the resources about whose allocation organizational members will disagree.

Resources in organizations are also limited, which often turns potential conflict into real conflict. If resources were abundant, then all the various constituencies within the organization could satisfy their goals. But because they are limited, not everyone's interests can be provided for. Further, whether true or not, gains by one individual or group are often *perceived* as being at the expense of others within the organization. These forces create a competition among members for the organization's limited resources.

Maybe the most important factor leading to politics within organizations is the realization that most of the "facts" used to allocate the limited resources are open to interpretation. What, for instance, is *good* performance? What's an *adequate* improvement? What constitutes an *unsatisfactory* job? The manager of any major league baseball team knows a .400 hitter is a high performer and a .125 hitter a poor performer. You don't need to be a baseball genius to know you should play your .400 hitter and send the .125 hitter back to the minors. But what if you have to choose between players who hit .280 and .290? Then other factors—less objective ones—come into play: fielding expertise, attitude, potential, ability to perform under pressure, loyalty to the team, and so on. More managerial decisions resemble choosing between a .280 and a .290 hitter than deciding between a .125 hitter and a .400 hitter. It is in this large and ambiguous middle ground of organizational life—where the facts *don't* speak for themselves—that politics flourish (see Table 12-4 on page 480).

Finally, because most decisions have to be made in a climate of ambiguity—where facts are rarely fully objective and thus are open to interpretation—people within organizations will use whatever influence they can to taint the facts to support their goals and interests. That, of course, creates the activities we call *politicking*.

So, to answer the earlier question—Isn't it possible for an organization to be politics free?—we can say, Yes, if all members of that organization hold the same goals and interests; if organizational resources are not scarce; and if performance outcomes are completely clear and objective. But that doesn't describe the organizational world most of us live in!

Factors Contributing to Political Behavior

Not all groups or organizations are equally political. In some organizations, for instance, politicking is overt and rampant; in others, politics plays a small role

Table 12-4 Politics Is in the Eye of the Beholder

A behavior that one person labels as "organizational politics" is very likely to be characterized as an instance of "effective management" by another. The fact is not that effective management is necessarily political, although in some cases it might be. Rather, a person's reference point determines what he or she classifies as organizational politics. Take a look at the following labels used to describe the same phenomenon. These suggest that politics, like beauty, is in the eye of the beholder.

"Political" label	"Effective management" label
1. Blaming others	1. Fixing responsibility
2. "Kissing up"	2. Developing working relationships
3. Apple polishing	3. Demonstrating loyalty
4. Passing the buck	4. Delegating authority
5. Covering your rear	5. Documenting decisions
6. Creating conflict	6. Encouraging change and innovation
7. Forming coalitions	7. Facilitating teamwork
8. Whistle-blowing	8. Improving efficiency
9. Scheming	9. Planning ahead
10. Overachieving	10. Competent and capable
11. Ambitious	11. Career minded
12. Opportunistic	12. Astute
13. Cunning	13. Practical minded
14. Arrogant	14. Confident
15. Perfectionist	15. Attentive to detail

This table is based on T.C. Krell, M.E. Mendenhall, and J. Sendry, "Doing Research in the Conceptual Morass of Organizational Politics," paper presented at the Western Academy of Management Conference, Hollywood, CA, April 1987.

in influencing outcomes. Why is there this variation? Recent research and observation have identified a number of factors that appear to encourage political behavior. Some are individual characteristics, derived from the unique qualities of the people the organization employs; others are a result of the organization's culture or internal environment. Figure 12-3 illustrates how both individual and organizational factors can increase political behavior and provide favorable outcomes (increased rewards and averted punishments) for both individuals and groups in the organization.

INDIVIDUAL FACTORS At the individual level, researchers have identified certain personality traits, needs, and other factors that are likely to be related to political behavior. In terms of traits, we find that employees who are high self-monitors, possess an internal locus of control, and have a high need for power are more likely to engage in political behavior.[26]

The high self-monitor is more sensitive to social cues, exhibits higher levels of social conformity, and is more likely to be highly skilled in political behavior than the low self-monitor. Individuals with an internal locus of control, because they believe they can control their environment, are more prone to take a proactive stance and attempt to manipulate situations in their favor. And, not surprisingly, the Machiavellian personality—which is characterized by the will to manipulate and the desire for power—is comfortable using politics as a means to further his or her self-interest.

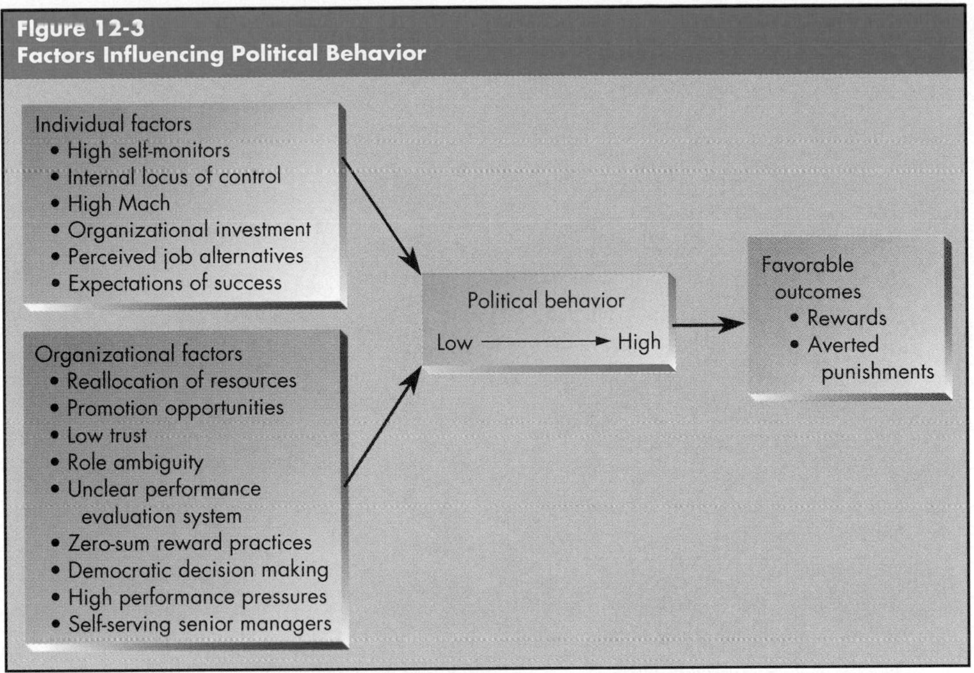

Figure 12-3
Factors Influencing Political Behavior

Additionally, an individual's investment in the organization, perceived alternatives, and expectations of success will influence the degree to which he or she will pursue illegitimate means of political action.[27] The more a person has invested in the organization in terms of expectations of increased future benefits, the more a person has to lose if forced out and the less likely he or she is to use illegitimate means. The more alternative job opportunities an individual has—due to a favorable job market or the possession of scarce skills or knowledge, a prominent reputation, or influential contacts outside the organization—the more likely he or she is to risk illegitimate political actions. Last, if an individual has a low expectation of success in using illegitimate means, it is unlikely he or she will attempt them. High expectations of success in the use of illegitimate means are most likely to be the province of both experienced and powerful individuals with polished political skills and inexperienced and naive employees who misjudge their chances.

ORGANIZATIONAL FACTORS Political activity is probably more a function of the organization's characteristics than of individual difference variables. Why? Because many organizations have a large number of employees with the individual characteristics we listed, yet the extent of political behavior varies widely.

While we acknowledge the role that individual differences can play in fostering politicking, the evidence more strongly supports that certain situations and cultures promote politics. More specifically, when an organization's resources are declining, when the existing pattern of resources is changing, and when there is opportunity for promotions, politics is more likely to surface.[28] In addition, cultures characterized by low trust, role ambiguity, unclear performance evaluation systems, zero-sum reward allocation practices, democratic decision making, high pressures for performance, and self-serving senior managers will create breeding grounds for politicking.[29]

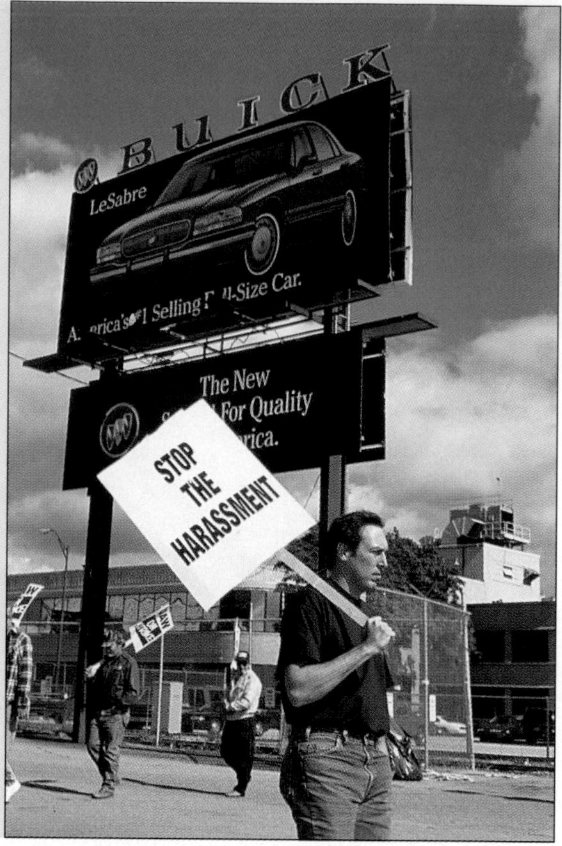

Exhausted by long hours of daily overtime and weekend work, employees at General Motors' Buick City plant in Flint, Michigan, took to politicking to rebel against the company's decision not to hire more permanent employees. Following downsizing layoffs that helped reduce costs and improve competitiveness, GM decided that paying existing employees for overtime was less expensive than the combined wage, fringe benefit, and training costs of hiring new workers. But employees said excessive overtime hours left them no time to spend with their families and that they were literally working themselves sick. At one point, more than 1,000 of the 11,500 plant employees were out on sick leave. Employees decided to strike in an attempt to force GM to hire more permanent workers to relieve the overtime crush. GM settled after a three-day walkout, promising to hire 779 more full-time workers.

When organizations cut back to improve efficiency, reductions in resources have to be made. Threatened with the loss of resources, people may engage in political actions to safeguard what they have. But any changes, especially those that imply significant reallocation of resources within the organization, are likely to stimulate conflict and increase politicking.

Promotion decisions have consistently been found to be one of the most political in organizations. The opportunity for promotions or advancement encourages people to compete for a limited resource and to try to positively influence the decision outcome.

The less trust there is within the organization, the higher the level of political behavior and the more likely the political behavior will be of the illegitimate kind. So high trust should suppress the level of political behavior in general and inhibit illegitimate actions in particular.

Role ambiguity means the prescribed behaviors of the employee are not clear. There are fewer limits, therefore, to the scope and functions of the employee's political actions. Since political activities are defined as those not required as part of one's formal role, the greater the role ambiguity, the more one can engage in political activity with little chance of it being visible.

The practice of performance evaluation is far from a perfected science. The more organizations use subjective criteria in the appraisal, emphasize a single outcome measure, or allow significant time to pass between the time of an action and its appraisal, the greater the likelihood an employee can get away with politicking. Subjective performance criteria create ambiguity. The use of a single outcome measure encourages individuals to do whatever is necessary to look good on that measure, but often at the expense of performing well on other important parts of the job that are being appraised. The amount of time that elapses between an action and its appraisal is also a relevant factor. The longer the time period, the more unlikely the employee will be held accountable for his or her political behaviors.

The more an organization's culture emphasizes the zero-sum or win-lose approach to reward allocations, the more employees will be motivated to engage in politicking. The zero-sum approach treats the reward pie as fixed so any gain one person or group achieves has to come at the expense of another person or group. If I win, you must lose! If $10,000 in annual raises is to be distributed among five employees, then any employee who gets more than $2,000 takes money away from one or more of the others. Such a practice encourages making others look bad and increasing the visibility of what you do.

In the last 25 years, there has been a general move in North America and among most developed nations toward making organizations less autocratic. Managers in these organizations are being asked to behave more democratically. They're told they should allow subordinates to advise them on decisions and should rely to a greater extent on group input into the decision process. Such moves toward democracy, however, are not necessarily embraced by all individual managers. Many managers sought their positions in order to have legitimate power so as to be able to make unilateral decisions. They fought hard and often paid high personal costs to achieve their influential positions. Sharing their power with others runs directly against their desires. The result is that managers—especially those who began their careers in the 1950s and 1960s—may use the required committees, conferences, and group meetings in a superficial way, as arenas for maneuvering and manipulating.

The more pressure that employees feel to perform well, the more likely they are to engage in politicking. When people are held strictly accountable for outcomes, this puts great pressure on them to look good. If a person perceives his or her entire career is riding on next quarter's sales figures or next month's plant productivity report, there is motivation to do whatever is necessary to make sure the numbers come out favorably.

Finally, when employees see the people on top engaging in political behavior, especially when they do so successfully and are rewarded for it, a climate is created that supports politicking. Politicking by top management, in a sense, gives permission to those lower in the organization to play politics by implying that such behavior is acceptable.

Impression Management

We know that people have an ongoing interest in how others perceive and evaluate them. For example, North Americans spend billions of dollars on diets, health club memberships, cosmetics, and plastic surgery—all intended to make them more attractive to others.[30] Being perceived positively by others should have benefits for people in organizations. It might, for instance, help them initially to get the jobs they want in an organization and, once hired, to get favorable evaluations, superior salary increases, and more rapid promotions. In a political context, it might help sway the distribution of advantages in their favor.

The process by which individuals attempt to control the impression others form of them is called **impression management**.[31] It's a subject that only quite recently has gained the attention of OB researchers.[32]

impression management The process by which individuals attempt to control the impression others form of them.

From Concepts to Skills

Politicking

Forget, for a moment, the ethics of politicking and any negative impressions you may have of people who engage in organizational politics. If you wanted to be more politically adept in your organization, what could you do? The following eight suggestions are likely to improve your political effectiveness.[33]

1. *Frame arguments in terms of organizational goals.* Effective politicking requires camouflaging your self-interest. No matter that your objective is self-serving; all the arguments you marshal in support of it must be framed in terms of the benefits that will accrue to the organization. People whose actions appear to blatantly further their own interests at the expense of the organization's are almost universally denounced, are likely to lose influence, and often suffer the ultimate penalty of being expelled from the organization.
2. *Develop the right image.* If you know your organization's culture, you understand what the organization wants and values from its employees—in terms of dress, associates to cultivate and those to avoid, whether to appear risk taking or risk aversive, the preferred leadership style, the importance placed on getting along well with others, and so forth. Then you are equipped to project the appropriate image. Because the assessment of your performance is not a fully objective process, style as well as substance must be attended to.
3. *Gain control of organizational resources.* The control of organizational resources that are scarce and important is a source of power. Knowledge and expertise are particularly effective resources to control. They make you more valuable to the organization, and therefore more likely to gain security, advancement, and a receptive audience for your ideas.
4. *Make yourself appear indispensable.* Since we're dealing with appearances rather than objective facts, you can enhance your power by appearing to be indispensable. That is, you don't have to really be indispensable as long as key people in the organization believe you are. If the organization's prime decision makers believe there is no ready substitute for what you are giving the organization, they are likely to go to great lengths to ensure your desires are satisfied.
5. *Be visible.* Since performance evaluation has a substantial subjective component, it's important your boss and those in power in the organization be made aware of your contribution. If you are fortunate enough to have a job that brings your accomplishments to the attention of others, it may not be necessary to take direct measures to increase your visibility. But your job may require you to handle activities that are low in visibility, or your specific contribution may be indistinguishable because you're part of a team endeavor. In such cases—*without appearing to be tooting your own horn or creating the image of a braggart*—you'll want to call attention to yourself by highlighting your successes in routine reports, having satisfied customers relay their appreciation to senior executives in your organization, being seen at social functions, being active in your professional associations, developing powerful allies who speak positively about your accomplishments, and similar tactics. Of course, the skilled politician actively and successfully lobbies to get those projects that will increase his or her visibility.
6. *Develop powerful allies.* It helps to have powerful people in your camp. Cultivate contacts with potentially influential people above you, at your own level, and in the lower ranks. They can provide you with important information that may not be available through normal channels. Additionally, there will be times when decisions will be made in favor of those with the greatest support. Having powerful allies can provide you with a coalition of support if and when you need it.
7. *Avoid "tainted" members.* Almost every organization has fringe members whose status is questionable. Their performance and/or loyalty is suspect. Keep your distance from such individuals. Given the reality that effectiveness has a large subjective component, your own effectiveness might be called into question if you're perceived as being too closely associated with tainted members.
8. *Support your boss.* Your immediate future is in the hands of your current boss. Since he or she evaluates your performance, you will typically want to do whatever is necessary to have your boss on your side. You should make every effort to help your boss succeed, make her look good, support her if she is under siege, and spend the time to find out what criteria she will be using to assess your effectiveness. Don't undermine your boss. And don't speak negatively of her to others.

Is everyone concerned with impression management (IM)? No! Who, then, might we predict to engage in IM? No surprise here! It's our old friend, the high self-monitor.[34] Low self-monitors tend to present images of themselves that are consistent with their personalities, regardless of the beneficial or detrimental effects for them. In contrast, high self-monitors are good at reading situations and molding their appearances and behavior to fit each situation.

Given that you want to control the impression others form of you, what techniques could you use? Table 12-5 summarizes some of the more popular IM techniques and provides an example of each.

Table 12-5 Impression Management (IM) Techniques

Conformity
Agreeing with someone else's opinion in order to gain his or her approval.
Example: A manager tells his boss, "You're absolutely right on your reorganization plan for the western regional office. I couldn't agree with you more."

Excuses
Explanations of a predicament-creating event aimed at minimizing the apparent severity of the predicament.
Example: Sales manager to boss, "We failed to get the ad in the paper on time, but no one responds to those ads anyway."

Apologies
Admitting responsibility for an undesirable event and simultaneously seeking to get a pardon for the action.
Example: Employee to boss, "I'm sorry I made a mistake on the report. Please forgive me."

Acclaiming
Explanation of favorable events to maximize the desirable implications for oneself.
Example: A salesperson informs a peer, "The sales in our division have nearly tripled since I was hired."

Flattery
Complimenting others about their virtues in an effort to make oneself appear perceptive and likable.
Example: New sales trainee to peer, "You handled that client's complaint so tactfully! I could never have handled that as well as you did."

Favors
Doing something nice for someone to gain that person's approval.
Example: Salesperson to prospective client, "I've got two tickets to the theater tonight that I can't use. Take them. Consider it a thank you for taking the time to talk with me."

Association
Enhancing or protecting one's image by managing information about people and things with which one is associated.
Example: A job applicant says to an interviewer, "What a coincidence. Your boss and I were roommates in college."

Source: Based on B.R. Schlenker, *Impression Management* (Monterey, CA: Brooks/Cole, 1980); W.L. Gardner and M.J. Martinko, "Impression Management in Organizations," *Journal of Management* (June 1988), p. 332; and R.B. Cialdini, "Indirect Tactics of Image Management: Beyond Basking," in R.A. Giacalone and P. Rosenfeld (eds.), *Impression Management in the Organization* (Hillsdale, NJ: Erlbaum, 1989), pp. 45–71.

Keep in mind that IM does not imply the impressions people convey are necessarily false (although, of course, they sometimes are).[35] Excuses and acclaiming, for instance, may be offered with sincerity. Referring to the examples used in Table 12-5, you can *actually* believe ads contribute little to sales in your region or that you are the key to the tripling of your division's sales. But misrepresentation can have a high cost. If the image claimed is false, you may be discredited.[36] If you cry wolf once too often, no one is likely to believe you when the wolf really comes. So the impression manager must be cautious not to be perceived as insincere or manipulative.[37]

Are there *situations* where individuals are more likely to misrepresent themselves or more likely to get away with it? Yes—situations that are characterized by high uncertainty or ambiguity.[38] These situations provide relatively little information for challenging a fraudulent claim and reduce the risks associated with misrepresentation.

Only a limited number of studies have been undertaken to test the effectiveness of IM techniques, and these have been essentially limited to determining whether IM behavior is related to job interview success. This makes a particularly relevant area of study because applicants are clearly attempting to present positive images of themselves and there are relatively objective outcome measures (written assessments and typically a hire–don't hire recommendation).

The evidence is that IM behavior works.[39] In one study, for instance, interviewers felt that those applicants for a position as a customer service representative who used IM techniques performed better in the interview, and they seemed somewhat more inclined to hire these people.[40] Moreover, when the researchers considered applicants' credentials, they concluded it was the IM techniques alone that influenced the interviewers. That is, it didn't seem to matter if applicants were well or poorly qualified. If they used IM techniques, they did better in the interview.

Another employment interview study looked at whether certain IM techniques work better than others.[41] The researchers compared applicants who

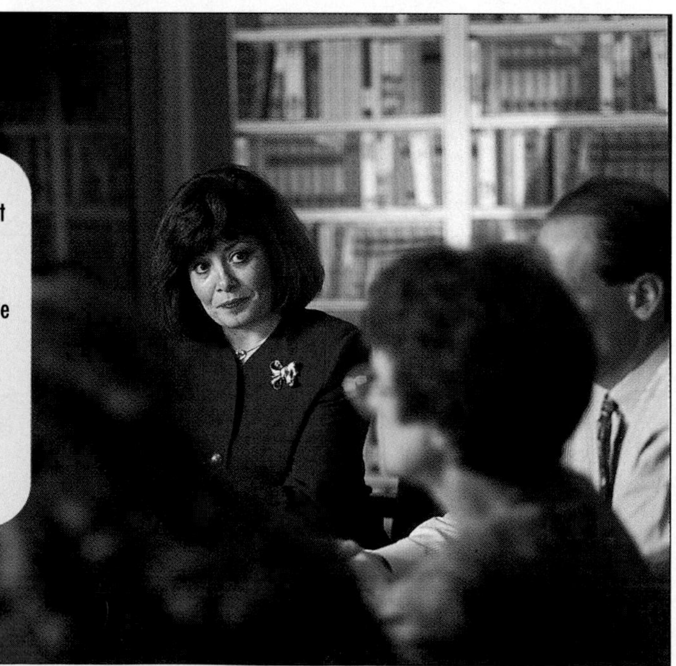

V. Cheryl Womack owns VCW, a company that sells insurance to 8,600 independent truckers. She expects her 70 employees to give 110 percent to their jobs. They must be willing to come in early frequently and work late during a crunch. Womack asks employees to write personal mission statements detailing their goals and to assess their progress annually. She depends on employee suggestions that help customers to fuel her company's growth. When Womack interviews job candidates, she is more interested in attitudes that reflect passion, flexibility, and excitement than in job credentials. Suppose you want to work for VCW. Which techniques of impression management would you use to influence Womack to hire you?

used IM techniques that focused the conversation on themselves (called a *controlling style*) to applicants who used techniques that focused on the interviewer (referred to as a *submissive style*). The researchers hypothesized that applicants who used the controlling style would be more effective because of the implicit expectations inherent in employment interviews. We tend to expect job applicants to use self-enhancement, self-promotion, and other active controlling techniques in an interview because they reflect self-confidence and initiative. The researchers predicted these active controlling techniques would work better for applicants than submissive tactics like conforming their opinions to those of the interviewer and offering favors to the interviewer. The results confirmed the researchers' predictions. Those applicants who used the controlling style were rated higher by interviewers on factors such as motivation, enthusiasm, and even technical skills—and they received more job offers.

Defensive Behaviors

Organizational politics includes protection of self-interest as well as promotion. Individuals often engage in reactive and protective "defensive" behaviors to avoid action, blame, or change.[42] This section discusses common varieties of **defensive behaviors**, classified by their objective.

defensive behaviors
Reactive and protective behaviors to avoid action, blame, or change.

AVOIDING ACTION Sometimes the best political strategy is to avoid action. That is, the best action is no action! However, role expectations typically dictate that one at least give the impression of doing something. Here are six popular ways to avoid action:

1. *Overconforming*. You strictly interpret your responsibility by saying things like, "The rules clearly state . . ." or "This is the way we've always done it." Rigid adherence to rules, policies, and precedents avoids the need to consider the nuances of a particular case.
2. *Passing the buck*. You transfer responsibility for the execution of a task or decision to someone else.
3. *Playing dumb*. This is a form of strategic helplessness. You avoid an unwanted task by falsely pleading ignorance or inability.
4. *Depersonalization*. You treat other people as objects or numbers, distancing yourself from problems and avoiding having to consider the idiosyncrasies of particular people or the impact of events on them. Hospital physicians often refer to patients by their room number or disease in order to avoid becoming too personally involved with them.
5. *Stretching and smoothing*. Stretching refers to prolonging a task so you appear to be occupied—for example, you turn a two-week task into a four-month job. Smoothing refers to covering up fluctuations in effort or output. Both these practices are designed to make you appear continually busy and productive.
6. *Stalling*. This foot-dragging tactic requires you to appear more or less supportive publicly while doing little or nothing privately.

AVOIDING BLAME What can you do to avoid blame for actual or anticipated negative outcomes? You can try one of the following six tactics:

1. *Buffing*. This is a nice way to refer to covering your rear. It describes the practice of rigorously documenting activity to project an image of competence and thoroughness. "I can't provide that information unless I get a formal written requisition from you" is an example.

2. *Playing safe.* This encompasses tactics designed to evade situations that may reflect unfavorably on you. It includes taking on only projects with a high probability of success, having risky decisions approved by superiors, qualifying expressions of judgment, and taking neutral positions in conflicts.
3. *Justifying.* This tactic includes developing explanations that lessen your responsibility for a negative outcome and/or apologizing to demonstrate remorse.
4. *Scapegoating.* This is the classic effort to place the blame for a negative outcome on external factors that are not entirely blameworthy. "I would have had the paper in on time but my computer went down—and I lost everything—the day before the deadline."
5. *Misrepresenting.* This tactic involves the manipulation of information by distortion, embellishment, deception, selective presentation, or obfuscation.
6. *Escalation of commitment.* One way to vindicate an initially poor decision and a failing course of action is to escalate support for the decision. By further increasing the commitment of resources to a previous course of action, you indicate that the previous decision was not wrong. When you "throw good money after bad," you demonstrate confidence in past actions and consistency over time.

AVOIDING CHANGE Finally, there are two forms of defensiveness frequently used by people who feel personally threatened by change:

1. *Resisting change.* This is a catch-all name for a variety of behaviors, including some forms of overconforming, stalling, playing safe, and misrepresenting.
2. *Protecting turf.* This is defending your territory from encroachment by others. As one purchasing executive commented, "Tell the people in production that it's our job to talk with vendors, not theirs."

EFFECTS OF DEFENSIVE BEHAVIOR In the short run, extensive use of defensiveness may well promote an individual's self-interest. But in the long run, it more often than not becomes a liability. This is because defensive behavior frequently becomes chronic or even pathological over time. People who constantly rely on defensiveness find that, eventually, it is the only way they know how to behave. At that point, they lose the trust and support of their peers, bosses, subordinates, and clients. In moderation, however, defensive behavior can be an effective device for surviving and flourishing in an organization because it is often deliberately or unwittingly encouraged by management.

In terms of the organization, defensive behavior tends to reduce effectiveness. In the short run, defensiveness delays decisions, increases interpersonal and intergroup tensions, reduces risk taking, makes attributions and evaluations unreliable, and restricts change efforts. In the long term, defensiveness leads to organizational rigidity and stagnation, detachment from the organization's environment, an organizational culture that is highly politicized, and low employee morale.

The Ethics of Behaving Politically

We conclude our discussion of politics by providing some ethical guidelines for political behavior. While there are no clear-cut ways to differentiate ethical from unethical politicking, there are some questions you should consider.

Figure 12-4
Is a Political Action Ethical?

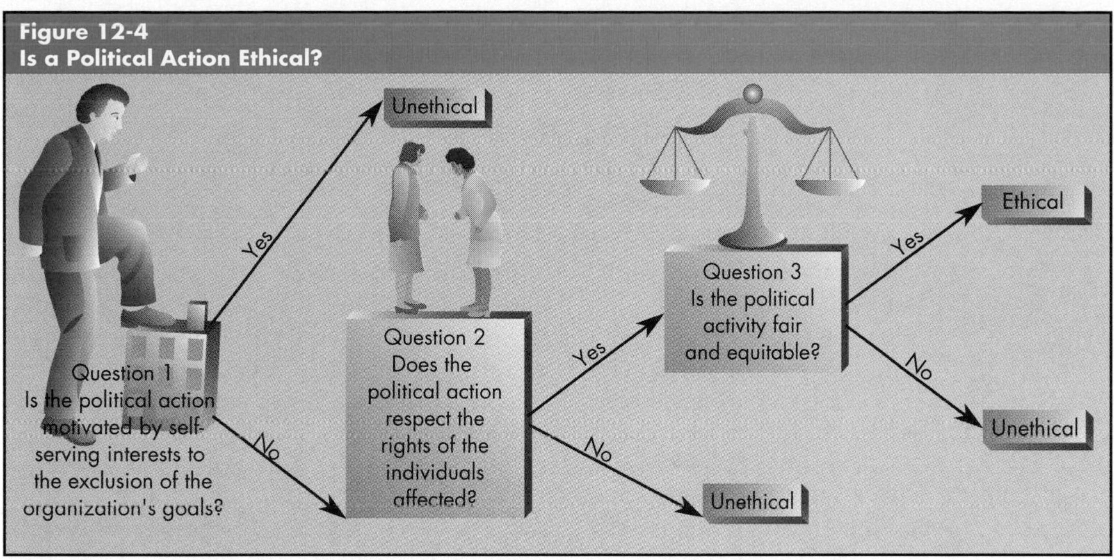
Question 1
Is the political action motivated by self-serving interests to the exclusion of the organization's goals?
Yes
No
Unethical
Question 2
Does the political action respect the rights of the individuals affected?
Yes
No
Unethical
Question 3
Is the political activity fair and equitable?
Yes
No
Ethical
Unethical

Figure 12-4 illustrates a decision tree to guide ethical actions.[43] The first question you need to answer addresses self-interest versus organizational goals. Ethical actions are consistent with the organization's goals. Spreading untrue rumors about the safety of a new product introduced by your company, in order to make that product's design team look bad, is unethical. However, there may be nothing unethical if a department head exchanges favors with her division's purchasing manager in order to get a critical contract processed quickly.

The second question concerns the rights of other parties. If the department head described in the previous paragraph went down to the mail room during her lunch hour and read through the mail directed to the purchasing manager—with the intent of "getting something on him" so he'll expedite your contract—she would be acting unethically. She would have violated the purchasing manager's right to privacy.

The final question that needs to be addressed relates to whether the political activity conforms to standards of equity and justice. The department head who inflates the performance evaluation of a favored employee and deflates the evaluation of a disfavored employee—then uses these evaluations to justify giving the former a big raise and nothing to the latter—has treated the disfavored employee unfairly.

Unfortunately, the answers to the questions in Figure 12-4 are often argued in ways to make unethical practices seem ethical. Powerful people, for example, can become very good at explaining self-serving behaviors in terms of the organization's best interests. Similarly, they can persuasively argue that unfair actions are really fair and just. Our point is that immoral people can justify almost any behavior. Those who are powerful, articulate, and persuasive are most vulnerable because they are likely to be able to get away with unethical practices successfully. When faced with an ethical dilemma regarding organizational politics, try to answer the questions in Figure 12-4 truthfully. And if you have a strong power base, recognize the ability of power to corrupt. Remember, it's a lot easier for the powerless to act ethically, for no other reason than they typically have very little political discretion to exploit.

Summary and Implications for Managers

If you want to get things done in a group or organization, it helps to have power. As a manager who wants to maximize your power, you will want to increase others' dependence on you. You can, for instance, increase your power in relation to your boss by developing knowledge or a skill he needs and for which he perceives no ready substitute. But power is a two-way street. You will not be alone in attempting to build your power bases. Others, particularly subordinates, will be seeking to make you dependent on them. The result is a continual battle. While you seek to maximize others' dependence on you, you will be seeking to minimize your dependence on others. And, of course, others you work with will be trying to do the same.

Few employees relish being powerless in their job and organization. It's been argued, for instance, that when people in organizations are difficult, argumentative, and temperamental it may be because they are in positions of powerlessness, where the performance expectations placed on them exceed their resources and capabilities.[44]

There is evidence that people respond differently to the various power bases.[45] Expert and referent power are derived from an individual's personal qualities. In contrast, coercion, reward, and legitimate power are essentially organizationally derived. Since people are more likely to enthusiastically accept and commit to an individual who they admire or whose knowledge they respect (rather than someone who relies on his or her position to reward or coerce them), the effective use of expert and referent power should lead to higher employee performance, commitment, and satisfaction. In fact, expert power has been found to be the most strongly and consistently related to effective employee performance.[46] For example, in a study of five organizations, knowledge was the most effective base for getting others to perform as desired.[47] Competence appears to offer wide appeal, and its use as a power base results in high performance by group members. The message here for managers seems to be: Develop and use your expert power base!

The power of your boss may also play a role in determining your job satisfaction. "One of the reasons many of us like to work for and with people who are powerful is that they are generally more pleasant—not because it is their native disposition, but because the reputation and reality of being powerful permits them more discretion and more ability to delegate to others."[48]

The effective manager accepts the political nature of organizations. By assessing behavior in a political framework, you can better predict the actions of others and use this information to formulate political strategies that will gain advantages for you and your work unit.

We can only speculate at this time on whether organizational politics is positively related to *actual* performance. However, there seems to be ample evidence that good political skills are positively related to high performance evaluations and, hence, to salary increases and promotions. We can comment more confidently on the relationship between politics and employee satisfaction. The more political that employees perceive an organization to be, the lower their satisfaction.[49] However, this conclusion needs to be moderated to reflect the employees' level in the organization.[50] Lower ranking employees, who lack the power base and the means of influence needed to benefit from the political game, perceive organizational politics as a source of frustration and indicate lower satisfaction. But higher ranking employees, who are in a better position to handle political behavior and benefit from it, don't tend to exhibit this negative attitude.

A final thought on organizational politics: Regardless of level in the organization, some people are just significantly more politically astute than are others. While there is little evidence to support or negate the following conclusion, it seems reasonable that the politically naive or inept are likely to exhibit lower job satisfaction than their politically astute counterparts. The politically naive and inept tend to feel continually powerless to influence those decisions that most affect them. They look at actions around them and are perplexed at why they are regularly shafted by colleagues, bosses, and the so-called system.

For Review

1. What is power? How is it different from leadership?
2. Contrast power tactics with power bases. What are some of the key contingency variables that determine which tactic a powerholder is likely to use?
3. Which of the five power bases lie with the individual? Which are derived from the organization?
4. State the general dependency postulate. What does it mean?
5. What's the "elasticity of power" concept?
6. What is a coalition? When is it likely to develop?
7. How are power and politics related?
8. Define political behavior. Why is politics a fact of life in organizations?
9. What factors contribute to political activity?
10. Define *sexual harassment*. Who is most likely to harass a female employee: her boss, coworker, or subordinate?

For Discussion

1. Based on the information presented in this chapter, what would you do as a recent college graduate entering a new job to maximize your power and accelerate your career progress?
2. "More powerful managers are good for an organization. It is the powerless, not the powerful, who are the ineffective managers." Do you agree or disagree with this statement? Discuss.
3. You're a sales representative for an international software company. After four excellent years, sales in your territory are off 30 percent this year. Describe three defensive responses you might use to reduce the potential negative consequences of this decline in sales.
4. "Sexual harassment should not be tolerated at the workplace." "Workplace romances are a natural occurrence in organizations." Are both of these statements true? Can they be reconciled?
5. Which impression management techniques have you used? What ethical implications are there, if any, in using impression management?

Point

It's a Political Jungle Out There!

Nick is a talented television camera operator. He has worked on a number of popular television shows—including *Designing Women*, *L.A. Law*, and *Northern Exposure*—over a ten-year period. But he's had trouble keeping those jobs. While most other camera operators and production employees are rehired from one season to the next, Nick seems to never get called back for a second year. It isn't that Nick isn't competent. Quite the contrary. His technical knowledge and formal education are typically more impressive than the directors he works for. Nick's problem is that he frequently disagrees with the camera angles that directors want him to set up, and he has no qualms about expressing his displeasure to those directors. He also feels some need to offer unsolicited suggestions to directors and producers on how camera placements and shots can be improved.

Roy is also a camera operator. Like Nick, Roy sees directors and producers regularly making decisions he doesn't agree with. But Roy holds his tongue and does what he's told. He recently finished his sixth straight year as the lead camera operator on one of television's most successful situation comedies.

Roy gets it. Nick doesn't. Nick has failed to recognize the reality that organizations are political systems. And while Roy is secure in his job, Nick's career continues to suffer because of his political naiveté.

It would be nice if all organizations or formal groups within organizations could be described in such terms as supportive, harmonious, objective, trusting, collaborative, or cooperative. A nonpolitical perspective can lead one to believe that employees will always behave in ways consistent with the interests of the organization, and that competence and high performance will always be rewarded. In contrast, a political view can explain much of what may seem to be irrational behavior in organizations. It can help to explain, for instance, why employees withhold information, restrict output, attempt to build empires, publicize their successes, hide their failures, distort performance figures to make themselves look better, and engage in similar activities that appear to be at odds with the organization's desire for effectiveness and efficiency.

For those who want tangible evidence that it's a political jungle out there in the real world, let's look at two studies. The first analyzed what it takes to get promoted fast in organizations. The second addressed the performance appraisal process.

As previously described in Chapter 1, Luthans and his associates* studied more than 450 managers. They found that these managers engaged in four managerial activities: traditional management (decision making, planning, and controlling); communication (exchanging routine information and processing paperwork); human resource management (motivating, disciplining, managing conflict, staffing, and training); and networking (socializing, politicking, and interacting with outsiders). Those managers who got promoted fastest spent 48 percent of their time networking. The average managers spent most of their efforts on traditional management and communication activities and only 19 percent of their time networking. We suggest that this provides strong evidence of the importance that social and political skills play in getting ahead in organizations.

Longenecker and his associates** held in-depth interviews with 60 upper-level executives to find out what went into performance ratings. What they found was that executives frankly admitted to deliberately manipulating formal appraisals for political purposes. Accuracy was not a primary concern of these executives. Rather, they manipulated the appraisal results in an intentional and systematic manner to get the outcomes they wanted.

*F. Luthans, R.M. Hodgetts, and S.A. Rosenkrantz, *Real Managers* (Cambridge, MA: Ballinger, 1988).

**C.O. Longenecker, D.A. Gioia, and H.P. Sims, Jr., "Behind the Mask: The Politics of Employee Appraisal," *Academy of Management Executive* (August 1987), pp. 183–94.

counterPoint

Corporate Politics: What You See Is What You Get!

Organizational behavior currently appears to be undergoing a period of fascination with workplace politics. Proponents argue that politics is inevitable in organizations, that power struggles, alliance formations, strategic maneuverings, and cutthroat actions are as endemic to organizational life as are planning, organizing, leading, and controlling.

But is organizational politics inevitable? A recent study suggests that it's more myth and interpretation than reality. One hundred and eighty experienced managers (92 men and 88 women) completed questionnaires for the study. They analyzed a series of decisions and indicated the degree to which they thought the decisions were influenced by politics. They also completed a measure that assessed political inevitability. This included items such as "Politics is a normal part of any decision-making process" and "Politics can have as many helpful outcomes for the organizations as harmful ones." Additionally, the questionnaire asked respondents their beliefs about power and control in the world at large. Finally, respondents provided data on their income, job responsibilities, and years of managerial experience.

The study found that beliefs about politics affected how respondents perceived organizational events. Those managers who held strong beliefs in politics' inevitability tended to see their own organization and the decision situations in the questionnaire in highly political terms. Moreover, there was evidence suggesting that these beliefs encompass not only beliefs about politics, but also about power and control in the world at large. Managers who viewed the world as posing difficult and complex problems and ruled by luck also tended to perceive events as highly politicized. That is, they perceived organizations as part of a disorderly and unpredictable world where politics is inevitable.

Interestingly, not *all* managers saw organizations as political jungles. It was typically the inexperienced managers, with lower incomes and more limited responsibilities, who held this view. The researchers concluded that because junior managers often lack clear understandings of how organizations really work, they tend to interpret events as irrational. It's through their attempts to make sense of their situations that these junior managers may come to make political attributions.

This study attempted to determine whether the corporate political jungle is myth, reality, or a matter of interpretation. The popular press often presents the political jungle as the dominant corporate reality where gamesmanship and manipulation are key to survival. However, the findings of this study suggest that a manager's political reality is somewhat mythical in nature, partially constructed through his or her beliefs about politics' inevitability and about power and control in the world. More specifically, it's the inexperienced managers—those who likely hold the fewest and least accurate interpretation of organizational events—who perceive the extent of organizational politics to be greatest.

So if there is a corporate political jungle, it appears to be mostly in the eyes of the young and inexperienced. Because they tend to have less understanding of organizational processes and less power to influence outcomes, they are more likely to see organizations through a political lens. More experienced and higher ranking managers, on the contrary, are more likely to see the corporate political jungle as a myth.

This argument is based on C. Kirchmeyer, "The Corporate Political Jungle: Myth, Reality, or a Matter of Interpretation," in C. Harris and C.C. Lundberg (eds.), *Proceedings of the 29th Annual Eastern Academy of Management* (Baltimore, 1992), pp. 161–64.

Learning About Yourself Exercise

How Political Are You?

To determine your political tendencies, answer the following questions. Check the answer that best represents your behavior or belief, even if that particular behavior or belief is not present all the time.

	True	False
1. You should make others feel important through an open appreciation of their ideas and work.	___	___
2. Because people tend to judge you when they first meet you, always try to make a good first impression.	___	___
3. Try to let others do most of the talking, be sympathetic to their problems, and resist telling people they are totally wrong.	___	___
4. Praise the good traits of the people you meet and always give people an opportunity to save face if they are wrong or make a mistake.	___	___
5. Spreading false rumors, planting misleading information, and backstabbing are necessary, if somewhat unpleasant, methods to deal with your enemies.	___	___
6. Sometimes it is necessary to make promises you know you will not or cannot keep.	___	___
7. It is important to get along with everybody, even with those who are generally recognized as windbags, abrasive, or constant complainers.	___	___
8. It is vital to do favors for others so you can call in these IOUs at times when they will do you the most good.	___	___
9. Be willing to compromise, particularly on issues that are minor to you, but major to others.	___	___
10. On controversial issues, it is important to delay or avoid your involvement if possible.	___	___

Turn to page A-29 for scoring directions and key.

Source: J.F. Byrnes, "The Political Behavior Inventory." With permission.

Working With Others Exercise

Understanding Power Dynamics

1. Creation of groups

Students turn in a dollar bill to the instructor and are divided into three groups based on criteria given by the instructor, assigned to their workplaces, and instructed to read the rules and task below. The money is divided into thirds, giving two-thirds of it to the top group, one-third to the middle group, and none to the bottom group.

2. Conduct exercise

Groups go to their assigned workplaces and have 30 minutes to complete their tasks.

Rules

a. Members of the top group are free to enter the space of either of the other groups and to communicate whatever they wish, whenever they wish. Members of the middle group may enter the space of the lower group when they wish but must request permission to enter the top group's space (which the top group can refuse). Members of the lower group may not disturb the top group in any way unless specifically invited by the top. The lower group does have the right to knock on the door of the middle group and request permission to communicate with them (which can also be refused).

b. The members of the top group have the authority to make any change in the rules they wish, at any time, with or without notice.

Tasks

a. Top Group: To be responsible for the overall effectiveness and learning from the exercise, and to decide how to use its money.

b. Middle Group: To assist the Top Group in providing for the overall welfare of the organization, and to decide how to use its money.

c. Bottom Group: To identify its resources and to decide how best to provide for learning and the overall effectiveness of the organization.

3. Debriefing

Each of the three groups chooses two representatives to go to the front of the class and discuss the following questions:

a. Summarize what occurred within and between the three groups.

b. What are some of the differences between being in the Top Group versus being in the Bottom Group?

c. What can we learn about power from this experience?

d. How accurate do you think this exercise is to the reality of resource allocation decisions in large organizations?

Source: This exercise is adapted from L. Bolman and T.E. Deal, *Exchange*, Vol. 3, No. 4 (1979), pp. 38–42. With permission.

Ethical Dilemma Exercise

Ethics in the Use of Power

Is it true that power corrupts and absolute power corrupts absolutely? Or is it that power corrupts, but *lack* of power corrupts absolutely? These concerns beg this question: Is it unethical for organizational members to use power? Many contemporary behavioral scientists would argue it isn't. They note that power is a natural part of human interactions—"we influence, or try to influence, other people every day under all sorts of conditions"—that carries into organizational life.*

Power really has two faces: one negative and the other positive.** The negative side is associated with abuse—when, for example, powerholders exploit others or use their power to merely accumulate status symbols. The positive side is characterized by a concern for group goals, helping the group to formulate its goals, and providing group members with the support they need to achieve those goals.

If you accept that using power is not unethical per se, then we should further inquire: Are certain *bases* of power more ethical than others? For instance, is reward power always more ethically preferable to coercive power? Is expertise preferable to legitimate power? What do *you* think?

*D.C. McClelland and D.H. Burnham, "Power Is the Great Motivator," *Harvard Business Review* (March-April 1976), pp. 100–10.
**Ibid.

CASE INCIDENT

Damned If You Do; Damned If You Don't

Fran Gilson has spent 15 years with the Thompson Grocery Company.* Starting out as a part-time cashier while attending college, Fran has risen up through the ranks of this 50-store grocery store chain. Today, at the age of 34, she is a regional manager, overseeing seven stores and earning nearly $80,000 a year. Fran also thinks she's ready to take on more responsibility. About five weeks ago, she was contacted by an executive-search recruiter inquiring about her interest in the position of vice president and regional manager for a national drugstore chain. She would be responsible for more than 100 stores in five states. She agreed to meet with the recruiter. This led to two meetings with top executives at the drugstore chain. The recruiter called Fran two days ago to tell her she was one of the two finalists for the job.

The only person at Thompson who knows Fran is looking at this other job is her good friend and colleague, Ken Hamilton. Ken is director of finance for the grocery chain. "It's a dream job," Fran told Ken. "It's a lot more responsibility and it's a good company to work for. The regional office is just 20 miles from here so I wouldn't have to move. And the pay is first rate. With the performance bonus, I could make nearly $200,000 a year. But best of all, the job provides terrific visibility. I'd be their only female vice president. The job would allow me to be a more visible role model for young women and give me a bigger voice in opening up doors for women and ethnic minorities in retailing management."

Since Fran considered Ken a close friend and wanted to keep the fact that she was looking at another job secret, she asked Ken last week if she could use his name as a reference. Said Ken, "Of course. I'll give you a great recommendation. We'd hate to lose you here, but you've got a lot of talent. They'd be lucky to get someone with your experience and energy." Fran passed Ken's name on to the executive recruiter as her only reference at Thompson. She made it very clear to the recruiter that Ken was the only person at Thompson who knew she was considering another job. Thompson's top management is old fashioned and places a high value on loyalty. If they heard she was talking to another company, it might seriously jeopardize her chances for promotion. But she trusted Ken completely. It's against this backdrop that this morning's incident became more than just a question of sexual harassment. It became a full-blown ethical and political dilemma for Fran.

Jennifer Chung has been a financial analyst in Ken's department for five months. Fran met Jennifer through Ken. The three have chatted together on a number of occasions down in the coffee room. Fran's impression of Jennifer is quite positive. In many ways, Jennifer strikes Fran as a lot like she was ten or so years ago. This morning, Fran came to work around 6:30 A.M. as she usually does. It allows her to get a lot accomplished before the troops roll in at 8 A.M. At about 6:45, Jennifer came into Fran's office. It was immediately evident that something was wrong. Jennifer was very nervous and uncomfortable, which was most unlike her. She asked Fran if they could talk. Fran sat her down and listened to her story.

What Fran heard was hard to believe, but she had no reason to think Jennifer was lying. Jennifer said that Ken began making off-color comments to her when they were alone within a month after Jennifer joined Thompson. From there it got progressively worse. Ken would leer at her. He put his arm over her shoulder when they were reviewing reports. He patted her rear. Every time one of these occurrences happened, Jennifer would ask him to stop and not do it again. But it fell on deaf ears. Yesterday, Ken reminded Jennifer that her six-month probationary review was coming up. "He told me that if I didn't sleep with him that I couldn't expect a very favorable evaluation." She told Fran that all she could do was go to the ladies' room and cry.

Jennifer said that she had come to Fran because she didn't know what to do or whom to turn to. "I came to you, Fran, because you're a friend of Ken's and the highest ranking woman here. Will you help me?" Fran had never heard anything like this about Ken before. About all she knew regarding his personal life was that he was in his late 30s, single, and involved in a long-term relationship.

Questions

1. Analyze Fran's situation in a purely legalistic sense. You might want to talk to friends or relatives who are in management or the legal profession for advice in this analysis.
2. Analyze Fran's dilemma in political terms.
3. Analyze Fran's situation in an ethical sense. What is the *ethically* right thing for her to do? Is that also the *politically* right thing to do?
4. If you were Fran, what would *you* do?

*The identity of this organization and the people described are disguised for obvious reasons.

Sexual Harassment in the FBI

After nine years with the Federal Bureau of Investigation, Suzanne Doucette decided to call it quits. It wasn't that she wanted to leave, but she says she finally got tired of the sexual harassment she suffered at the bureau. By quitting, she hoped to make her protest visible.

In the early years, all FBI agents were men. Only in the 1970s did the bureau begin hiring female agents. But today, even though 1,188 of its 10,443 agents are women, the FBI still has a macho culture where men question whether women agents can do their job.

Is Doucette's claim valid? There certainly is ample evidence that the FBI has historically discriminated against women and minorities. Internal studies find that 13 percent of female agents say they've been sexually harassed. In 1991 eight employees were disciplined for harassing a black agent. In 1992 the agency admitted it needed to increase agent diversity and that it planned to aggressively recruit black agents. And women appear to have been selectively kept out of senior administrative positions. The highest ranking woman at the FBI, for instance, runs a small office in Anchorage, Alaska.

Doucette claims that the agency intensified its harassment of her when she went public with her complaints that the agency tolerated sexual harassment. For instance, she says she was put on administrative leave, without pay, and denied promotions because she testified in front of Congress. Doucette claims the FBI is overly concerned with its image. When an agent tarnishes that image (for example, by claiming sexual harassment), the bureau considers it evidence of disloyalty. She says there are two informal norms at the FBI. First, don't embarrass the bureau. Second, admit nothing, deny everything, and make counterallegations.*

Questions

1. How is Doucette exercising power by going public with her resignation?
2. Are the politics in the FBI any different than one would find in any large corporation?
3. What can senior officials in the FBI do to make the agency less threatening to women and minorities?

Source: "Sexual Harassment in the FBI," *Nightline* (October 11, 1993).

* Epilogue: On January 31, 1995 the FBI agreed to pay Ms. Doucette $297,500 to settle the suit she filed against the bureau.

Suggestions for Further Reading

BRASS, D.J., and M.E. BURKHARDT, "Potential Power and Power Use: An Investigation of Structure and Behavior," *Academy of Management Journal* (June 1993), pp. 441–70.

DAVENPORT, T.H., R.G. ECCLES, and L. PRUSAK, "Information Politics," *Sloan Management Review* (Fall 1992), pp. 53–65.

DILENSCHNEIDER, R.L., *On Power* (New York: HarperBusiness, 1994).

FERRIS, G.R., and T.R. KING, "The Politics of Age Discrimination in Organizations," *Journal of Business Ethics* (May 1992), pp. 341–50.

GIOIA, D.A., and C.O. LONGENECKER, "Delving into the Dark Side: The Politics of Executive Appraisal," *Organizational Dynamics* (Winter 1994), pp. 47–58.

KACMAR, K.M., and G.R. FERRIS, "Politics at Work: Sharpening the Focus of Political Behavior in Organizations," *Business Horizons* (July-August 1993), pp. 70–74.

KEYS, B., and T. CASE, "How to Become an Influential Manager," *Academy of Management Executive* (November 1990), pp. 38–51.

MAINIERO, L.A., "On Breaking the Glass Ceiling: The Political Seasoning of Powerful Women Executives," *Organizational Dynamics* (Spring 1994), pp. 5–21.

OCASIO, W., "Political Dynamics and the Circulation of Power: CEO Succession in U.S. Industrial Corporations, 1960–1990," *Administrative Science Quarterly* (June 1994), pp. 285–312.

PFEFFER, J., "Understanding Power in Organizations," *California Management Review* (Winter 1992), pp. 29–50.

Notes

[1] Based on R. Grover, "Fear Not, Hollywood: Golden Boy Is Still Golden," *Business Week* (May 29, 1989), pp. 64–65; S. Andrews, "The Man Who Would Be Walt," *New York Times* (January 26, 1992), p. H1; and B. Weinraub, "Michael Ovitz + 3 Baby Bells = Entertainment," *New York Times* (October 26, 1994), p. C1.

[2] R.M. Kanter, "Power Failure in Management Circuits," *Harvard Business Review* (July-August 1979), p. 65.

[3] J. Pfeffer, "Understanding Power in Organizations," *California Management Review* (Winter 1992), p. 35.

[4] J.R.P. French, Jr., and B. Raven, "The Bases of Social Power," in D. Cartwright (ed.), *Studies in Social Power* (Ann Arbor: University of Michigan, Institute for Social Research, 1959), pp. 150–67. For an update on French and Raven's work, see D.E. Frost and A.J. Stahelski, "The Systematic Measurement of French and Raven's Bases of Social Power in Workgroups," *Journal of Applied Social Psychology* (April 1988), pp. 375–89; T.R. Hinkin and C.A. Schriesheim, "Development and Application of New Scales to Measure the French and Raven (1959) Bases of Social Power," *Journal of Applied Psychology* (August 1989), pp. 561–67; and G.E. Littlepage, J.L. Van Hein, K.M. Cohen, and L.L. Janiec, "Evaluation and Comparison of Three Instruments Designed to Measure Organizational Power and Influence Tactics," *Journal of Applied Social Psychology* (January 16–31, 1993), pp. 107–25.

[5] D. Kipnis, *The Powerholders* (Chicago: University of Chicago Press, 1976), pp. 77–78.

[6] R.E. Emerson, "Power-Dependence Relations," *American Sociological Review*, Vol. 27 (1962), pp. 31–41.

[7] Cited in *Business Month* (April 1989), p. 41.

[8] H. Mintzberg, *Power in and Around Organizations* (Englewood Cliffs, NJ: Prentice-Hall, 1983), p. 24.

[9] R.M. Cyert and J.G. March, *A Behavioral Theory of the Firm* (Englewood Cliffs, NJ: Prentice-Hall, 1963).

[10] C. Perrow, "Departmental Power and Perspective in Industrial Firms," in M.N. Zald (ed.), *Power in Organizations* (Nashville, TN: Vanderbilt University Press, 1970).

[11] Adapted from J. Pfeffer, *Managing with Power* (Boston: Harvard Business School Press, 1992), pp. 63–64.

[12] Adapted from R.M. Kanter, "Power Failure in Management Circuits," p. 67.

[13] See, for example, D. Kipnis, S.M. Schmidt, C. Swaffin-Smith, and I. Wilkinson, "Patterns of Managerial Influence: Shotgun Managers, Tacticians, and Bystanders," *Organizational Dynamics* (Winter 1984), pp. 58–67; T. Case, L. Dosier, G. Murkison, and B. Keys, "How Managers Influence Superiors: A Study of Upward Influence Tactics," *Leadership and Organization Development Journal*, Vol. 9, No. 4 (1988), pp. 25–31; D. Kipnis and S.M. Schmidt, "Upward-Influence Styles: Relationship with Performance Evaluations, Salary, and Stress," *Administrative Science Quarterly* (December 1988), pp. 528–42; T.R. Hinkin and C.A. Schriesheim, "Relationships Between Subordinate Perceptions of Supervisor Influence Tactics and Attributed Bases of Supervisory Power," *Human Relations* (March 1990), pp. 221–37; G. Yukl and C.M. Falbe, "Influence Tactics and Objectives in Upward, Downward, and Lateral Influence Attempts," *Journal of Applied Psychology* (April 1990), pp. 132–40; H.E. Chacko, "Methods of Upward Influence, Motivational Needs, and Administrators' Perceptions of Their Supervisors' Leadership Styles," *Group & Organization Studies* (September 1990), pp. 253–65; and B. Keys and T. Case, "How to Become an Influential Manager," *Academy of Management Executive* (November 1990), pp. 38–51.

[14] This section is adapted from Kipnis, Schmidt, Swaffin-Smith, and Wilkinson, "Patterns of Managerial Influence."

[15] P.P. Poole, "Coalitions: The Web of Power," in *Research and Application, Proceedings of the 20th Annual Eastern Academy of Management*, D.J. Vredenburgh and R.S. Schuler (eds.), *Effective Management:* (Pittsburgh, May 1983), pp. 79–82.

[16] See Pfeffer, *Power in Organizations*, pp. 155–57.

[17] For a recent review of the literature, see L.F. Fitzgerald and S.L. Shullman, "Sexual Harassment: A Research Analysis and Agenda for the 1990s," *Journal of Vocational Behavior* (February 1993), pp. 5–27.

[18] S. Silverstein and S. Christian, "Harassment Ruling Raises Free-Speech Issues," *Los Angeles Times* (November 11, 1993), p. D2.

[19] The following section is based on J.N. Cleveland and M.E. Kerst, "Sexual Harassment and Perceptions of Power: An Under-Articulated Relationship," *Journal of Vocational Behavior* (February 1993), pp. 49–67.

[20] S.A. Culbert and J.J. McDonough, *The Invisible War: Pursuing Self-Interest at Work* (New York: Wiley, 1980), p. 6.

[21] Mintzberg, *Power in and Around Organizations*, p. 26.

[22] D.J. Vredenburgh and J.G. Maurer, "A Process Framework of Organizational Politics," *Human Relations* (January 1984), pp. 47–66.

[23] D. Farrell and J.C. Petersen, "Patterns of Political Behavior in Organizations," *Academy of Management Review* (July 1982), p. 405. For a thoughtful analysis of the academic controversies underlying any definition of organizational politics, see A. Drory and T. Romm, "The Definition of Organizational Politics: A Review," *Human Relations* (November 1990), pp. 1133–54.

[24] Farrell and Petersen,"Patterns of Political Behavior," pp. 406–407; and A. Drory, "Politics in Organization and Its Perception Within the Organization," *Organization Studies*, Vol. 9, No. 2 (1988), pp. 165–79.

[25] Pfeffer, *Power in Organizations*.

[26] See, for example, G. Biberman, "Personality and Characteristic Work Attitudes of Persons with High, Moderate, and Low Political Tendencies," *Psychological Reports* (October 1985), pp. 1303–10; and G.R. Ferris, G.S. Russ, and P.M. Fandt, "Politics in Organizations," in R.A. Giacalone and P. Rosenfeld (eds.), *Impression Management in the Organization* (Hillsdale, NJ: Erlbaum, 1989), pp. 155–56.

[27] Farrell and Petersen, "Patterns of Political Behavior," p. 408.

[28] S.C. Goh and A.R. Doucet, "Antecedent Situational Conditions of Organizational Politics: An Empirical Investigation," paper presented at the Annual Administrative Sciences Association of Canada Conference, Whistler, B.C., May 1986; C. Hardy, "The Contribution of Political Science to Organizational Behavior," in J.W. Lorsch (ed.), *Handbook of Organizational Behavior* (Englewood Cliffs, NJ: Prentice Hall, 1987), p. 103; and G.R. Ferris and K.M. Kacmar, "Perceptions of Organizational Politics," *Journal of Management* (March 1992), pp. 93–116.

[29] See, for example, Farrell and Petersen, "Patterns of Political Behavior," p. 409; P.M. Fandt and G.R. Ferris, "The Management of Information and Impressions: When Employees Behave Opportunistically," *Organizational Behavior and Human Decision Processes* (February 1990), pp. 140–58; and Ferris, Russ, and Fandt, "Politics in Organizations," p. 147.

[30] M.R. Leary and R.M. Kowalski, "Impression Management: A Literature Review and Two-Component Model," *Psychological Bulletin* (January 1990), pp. 34–47.

[31] Ibid., p. 34.

[32] See, for instance, B.R. Schlenker, *Impression Management: The Self-Concept, Social Identity, and Interpersonal Relations* (Monterey, CA: Brooks/Cole, 1980); W.L. Gardner and M.J. Martinko, "Impression Management in Organizations," *Journal of Management* (June 1988), pp. 321–38; D.C. Gilmore and G.R. Ferris, "The Effects of Applicant Impression Management Tactics on Interviewer Judgments," *Journal of Management* (December 1989), pp. 557–64; Leary and Kowalski, "Impression Management: A Literature Review and Two-Component Model," pp. 34–47; S.J. Wayne and K.M. Kacmar, "The Effects of Impression Management on the Performance Appraisal Process," *Organizational Behavior and Human Decision Processes* (February 1991), pp. 70–88; and E.W. Morrison and R.J. Bies, "Impression Management in the Feedback-Seeking Process: A Literature Review and Research Agenda," *Academy of Management Review* (July 1991), pp. 522–41.

[33] S.P. Robbins, *Training in InterPersonal Skills: TIPS for Managing People at Work* (Englewood Cliffs, NJ: Prentice Hall, 1989), pp. 172–74.

[34] M. Snyder and J. Copeland, "Self-Monitoring Processes in Organizational Settings," in Giacalone and Rosenfeld, *Impression Management in the Organization*, p. 11; and E.D. Long and G.H. Dobbins, "Self-Monitoring, Impression Management, and Interview Ratings: A Field and Laboratory Study," in J.L. Wall and L.R. Jauch (eds.), *Proceedings of the 52nd Annual Academy of Management Conference* (Las Vegas, August 1992), pp. 274–78.

[35] Leary and Kowalski, "Impression Management," p. 40.

[36] Gardner and Martinko, "Impression Management in Organizations," p. 333.

[37] R.A. Baron, "Impression Management by Applicants During Employment Interviews: The 'Too Much of a Good Thing' Effect," in R.W. Eder and G.R. Ferris (eds.), *The Employment Interview: Theory, Research, and Practice* (Newbury Park, CA: Sage, 1989), pp. 204–15.

[38] Ferris, Russ, and Fandt, "Politics in Organizations."

[39] Baron, "Impression Management by Applicants During Employment Interviews"; Gilmore and Ferris, "The Effects of Applicant Impression Management Tactics on Interviewer Judgments"; and A.L. Kristof and C.K. Stevens, "Applicant Impression Management Tactics: Effects on Interviewer Evaluations and Interview Outcomes," in D.P. Moore (ed.), *Proceedings of the National Academy of Management Conference* (Dallas, TX, August 1994), pp. 127–31.

[40] Gilmore and Ferris, "The Effects of Applicant Impression Management Tactics on Interviewer Judgments."

[41] K.M. Kacmar, J.E. Kelery, and G.R. Ferris, "Effectiveness of the Use of Impression Management Tactics by Applicants on Employment Interview Outcomes," in D.F. Ray (ed.), *Proceedings of the Southern Management Association* (Orlando, FL, 1990), pp. 351–53.

[42] This section is based on B.E. Ashforth and R.T. Lee, "Defen-

sive Behavior in Organizations: A Preliminary Model," *Human Relations* (July 1990), pp. 621–48.

[43] This figure is based on G.F. Cavanagh, D.J. Moberg, and M. Valasquez, "The Ethics of Organizational Politics," *Academy of Management Journal* (June 1981), pp. 363–74.

[44] R.M. Kanter, *Men and Women of the Corporation* (New York: Basic Books, 1977).

[45] See, for instance, C.M. Falbe and G. Yukl, "Consequences for Managers of Using Single Influence Tactics and Combinations of Tactics," *Academy of Management Journal* (August 1992), pp. 638–52.

[46] See, for example, M.A. Rahim, "Relationships of Leader Power to Compliance and Satisfaction with Supervision: Evidence from a National Sample of Managers," *Journal of Management* (December 1989), pp. 545–56.

[47] J.G. Bachman, D.G. Bowers, and P.M. Marcus, "Bases of Supervisory Power: A Comparative Study in Five Organizational Settings," in A. S. Tannenbaum (ed.), *Control in Organizations* (New York: McGraw-Hill, 1968), p. 236.

[48] J. Pfeffer, *Managing with Power*, p. 137.

[49] G.R. Ferris and K.M. Kacmar, "Perceptions of Organizational Politics."

[50] A. Drory, "Perceived Political Climate and Job Attitudes," *Organization Studies*, Vol. 14, No. 1 (1993), pp. 59–71.

CHAPTER

When a conflict over management's firing of union members erupted in a strike against construction-equipment giant Caterpillar, Inc., 11,500 employees picketed and heckled the 4,000 employees who returned to work.

13

CONFLICT, NEGOTIATION, AND INTERGROUP BEHAVIOR

CHAPTER OUTLINE

LEARNING OBJECTIVES

After studying this chapter, you should be able to:

1. Define *conflict.*
2. Differentiate between the traditional, human relations, and interactionist views of conflict.
3. Outline the conflict process.
4. Describe the five conflict-handling intentions.
5. Contrast distributive and integrative bargaining.
6. Describe the five steps in the negotiation process.
7. Explain the factors that affect intergroup relations.
8. Identify methods for managing intergroup relations.

When two people in business always agree,
one of them is unnecessary.
W. WRIGLEY, JR.

Shea & Gould was one of New York's best known law firms.[1] It was founded in the mid-1960s by the man for whom Shea Stadium (home of the New York Mets) was named—William A. Shea, a confidant of governors, mayors, and corporate chieftains until his death in 1991—and Milton H. Gould. Among the firm's prestigious clients were the Mets, the New York Yankees, Apple Computer, Marine Midland Bank, and Toys "R" Us. In early 1994

Shea & Gould had 80 partners, 200 lawyers, and offices in New York, Los Angeles, Washington, and Miami.

Shea and Gould had complementary talents. Shea was known more for his leadership skills than legal prowess; Gould was a remarkably talented lawyer. Together they made a formidable team. Their firm grew and prospered in the 1970s and 1980s. At its peak, Shea & Gould had 350 lawyers and played a leading role in New York politics, banking, real estate, and sports.

A number of large- and medium-sized law firms have closed their doors in recent years as competition has increased and major clients have been lost. It isn't totally surprising, then, to learn that Shea & Gould's partners voted to dissolve their firm in January 1994. What is striking about this dissolution is that it had nothing to do with the firm's finances. Revenue in 1993 was $85 million, up from $83 million the year before. The firm, in fact, was still highly profitable for its partners. What brought the demise of Shea & Gould was that these partners couldn't get along with each other.

The problems at Shea & Gould began in the mid-1980s, when the founding partners began to cede control to younger lawyers. Some partners, accustomed to years of strong leadership by Shea and Gould, challenged the new power structure. Cliques and factions formed around legal disciplines, as well as age groups and clients. Lawyers specializing in securities litigation lobbied for their interests; lawyers who worked on legal matters for Big Six accounting firms fought for theirs. Younger partners clustered together against older partners. And no one group or alliance was strong enough to gain control over the whole firm. As the conflict escalated in December 1993, five partners resigned. A number of others were rumored to be actively looking at opportunities at other firms.

In January 1994 the partners gave up the fight and voted to dissolve the firm. A well-known consultant to the legal profession concluded that "this was a firm that had basic and principled differences among the partners that were basically irreconcilable." That same consultant also addressed the partners at their last meeting: "You don't have an economic problem," he said. "You have a personality problem. You hate each other!"

Conflict can be a serious problem in *any* organization. It might not bring about the demise of a firm—as happened at Shea & Gould—but it certainly can hurt an organization's performance as well as lead to the loss of many good employees. However, as we show in this chapter, all conflicts aren't bad. Conflict has a positive side as well as a negative. We explain the differences in this chapter and provide a guide to help you understand how conflicts develop. We also present two other topics in this chapter, both closely related to conflict: negotiation and intergroup relations. But let's begin by clarifying what we mean by conflict.

A Definition of Conflict

There has been no shortage of definitions of conflict.[2] But despite the divergent meanings the term has acquired, several common themes underlie most definitions. Conflict must be *perceived* by the parties to it; whether or not conflict exists is a perception issue. If no one is aware of a conflict, then it is generally agreed no conflict exists. Additional commonalities in the definitions are opposition or incompatibility and some form of interaction.[3] These factors set the conditions that determine the beginning point of the conflict process.

We can define **conflict**, then, as a process that begins when one party perceives that another party has negatively affected, or is about to negatively affect, something the first party cares about.[4]

conflict
A process that begins when one party perceives that another party has negatively affected, or is about to negatively affect, something that the first party cares about.

This definition is purposely broad. It describes that point in any ongoing activity when an interaction crosses over to become an interparty conflict. It encompasses the wide range of conflicts that people experience in organizations—incompatibility of goals, differences over interpretations of facts, disagreements based on behavioral expectations, and the like. Finally, our definition is flexible enough to cover the full range of conflict levels, from overt and violent acts to subtle forms of disagreement.

Transitions in Conflict Thought

It is entirely appropriate to say there has been "conflict" over the role of conflict in groups and organizations. One school of thought has argued that conflict must be avoided, that it indicates a malfunctioning within the group. We call this the *traditional* view. Another school of thought, the *human relations* view, argues that conflict is a natural and inevitable outcome in any group and that it need not be evil, but rather has the potential to be a positive force in determining group performance. The third, and most recent, perspective proposes not only that conflict *can* be a positive force in a group but explicitly argues that some conflict is *absolutely necessary* for a group to perform effectively. We label this third school the *interactionist* approach. Let's take a closer look at each of these views.

The Traditional View

The early approach to conflict assumed all conflict was bad. Conflict was viewed negatively, and it was used synonymously with such terms as *violence*, *destruction*, and *irrationality* to reinforce its negative connotation. Conflict, by definition, was harmful and was to be avoided.

The **traditional** view was consistent with the attitudes that prevailed about group behavior in the 1930s and 1940s. Conflict was seen as a dysfunctional outcome resulting from poor communication, a lack of openness and trust between people, and the failure of managers to be responsive to the needs and aspirations of their employees.

traditional view of conflict
The belief that all conflict is harmful and must be avoided.

The view that all conflict is bad certainly offers a simple approach to looking at the behavior of people who create conflict. Since all conflict is to be avoided, we need merely direct our attention to the causes of conflict and correct these malfunctionings in order to improve group and organizational performance. Although research studies now provide strong evidence to dispute that this approach to conflict reduction results in high group performance, many of us still evaluate conflict situations utilizing this outmoded standard. So, too, do many boards of directors.

The board of Sunbeam-Oster followed the traditional approach when they fired the company's chairman, Paul Kazarian, in 1993.[5] Three years earlier, Kazarian took over the company when it was in bankruptcy. He sold off losing businesses, restructured the remaining appliance operation, and turned a $40 million loss in 1990 into a $47 million profit in 1991. A few days before he was fired, the company reported a 40 percent jump in quarterly profits. But Kazarian's so-called crime was that he rubbed a lot of people in the company the wrong way. He aggressively confronted managers, employees, and suppliers. People complained that his style was abrasive. Kazarian, however, defended his actions as necessary: "You don't change a company in bankruptcy without making a few waves. I wasn't there to be a polite manager. I was there to create value for stockholders."

The Human Relations View

human relations view of conflict The belief that conflict is a natural and inevitable outcome in any group.

The **human relations** position argued that conflict was a natural occurrence in all groups and organizations. Since conflict was inevitable, the human relations school advocated acceptance of conflict. They rationalized its existence: It cannot be eliminated, and there are even times when conflict may benefit a group's performance. The human relations view dominated conflict theory from the late 1940s through the mid-1970s.

The Interactionist View

interactionist view of conflict The belief that conflict is not only a positive force in a group but that it is absolutely necessary for a group to perform effectively.

While the human relations approach accepted conflict, the **interactionist** approach encourages conflict on the grounds that a harmonious, peaceful, tranquil, and cooperative group is prone to becoming static, apathetic, and nonresponsive to needs for change and innovation. The major contribution of the interactionist approach, therefore, is encouraging group leaders to maintain an ongoing minimum level of conflict—enough to keep the group viable, self-critical, and creative.

Given the interactionist view—and it is the one we take in this chapter—it becomes evident that to say conflict is all good or bad is inappropriate and naive. Whether a conflict is good or bad depends on the type of conflict. Specifically, it's necessary to differentiate between functional and dysfunctional conflict.

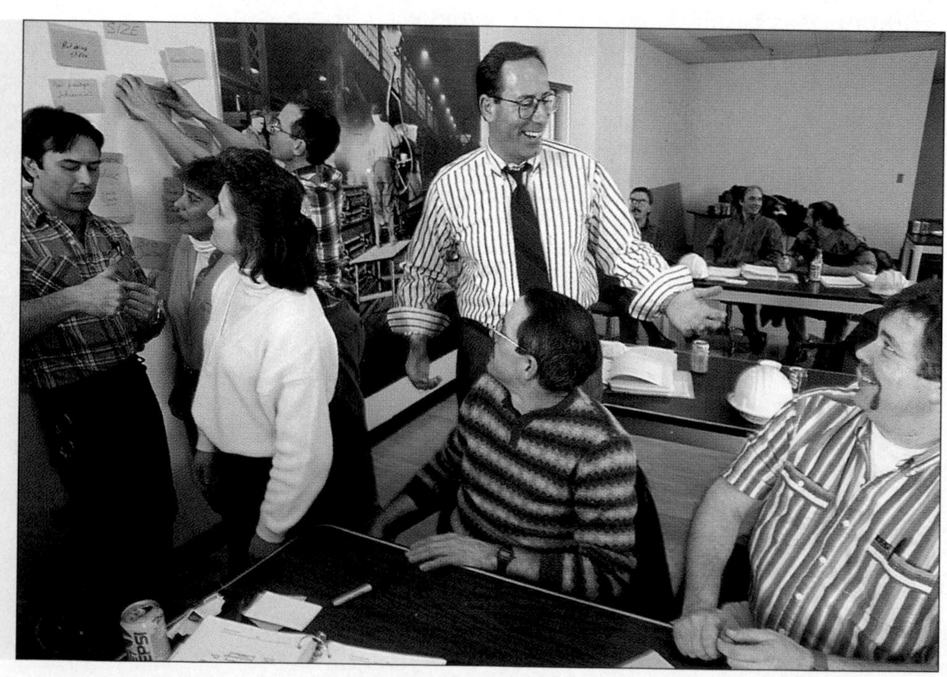

These employees of ME International, a manufacturer of metal grinding balls, illustrate the interactionist view of conflict. The president of ME challenged his workers to develop a statement of corporate values. He hired consultant Rob Lebow (standing, center) to maintain an ongoing minimum level of conflict during the process by encouraging employees to express personal beliefs and opinions and openly question and disagree with others' ideas. Such conflict kept employees self-critical and creative, improving their performance in determining a set of shared values and in choosing the words that best reflect those values.

Functional vs. Dysfunctional Conflict

The interactionist view does not propose *all* conflicts are good. Rather, some conflicts support the goals of the group and improve its performance; these are **functional**, constructive forms of conflict. Additionally, there are conflicts that hinder group performance; these are **dysfunctional**, or destructive forms of conflict. The conflict among partners at the law firm of Shea & Gould was clearly in the dysfunctional category.

functional conflict
Conflict that supports the goals of the group and improves its performance.

dysfunctional conflict
Conflict that hinders group performance.

Of course, it is one thing to argue that conflict can be valuable for the group, and another to be able to tell if a conflict is functional or dysfunctional. The demarcation between functional and dysfunctional is neither clear nor precise. No one level of conflict can be adopted as acceptable or unacceptable under all conditions. The type and level of conflict that creates healthy and positive involvement toward one group's goals today may, in another group or in the same group at another time, be highly dysfunctional.

The criterion that differentiates functional from dysfunctional conflict is group performance. Since groups exist to attain a goal or goals, it is the impact the conflict has on the group, rather than on any individual member, that determines functionality. Of course, the impact of conflict on the individual and its impact on the group are rarely mutually exclusive, so the ways that individuals perceive a conflict may have an important influence on its effect on the group. However, this need not be the case, and when it is not, our focus will be on the group. So whether an individual group member perceives a given conflict as being personally disturbing or positive is irrelevant. For example, a group member may perceive an action as dysfunctional, in that the outcome is personally dissatisfying to him or her. However, for our analysis, that action would be functional if it furthers the objectives of the group. So while many people at Sunbeam-Oster thought the conflicts created by Paul Kazarian were dysfunctional, Kazarian was convinced they were functional because they improved Sunbeam's performance.

The Conflict Process

The **conflict process** can be seen as comprising five stages: potential opposition or incompatibility, cognition and personalization, intentions, behavior, and outcomes. The process is diagrammed in Figure 13-1 on page 508.

conflict process
Five stages: potential opposition or incompatibility; cognition and personalization; intentions; behavior; and outcomes.

Stage I: Potential Opposition or Incompatibility

The first step in the conflict process is the presence of conditions that create opportunities for conflict to arise. They *need not* lead directly to conflict, but one of these conditions is necessary if conflict is to arise. For simplicity's sake, these conditions (which also may be looked at as causes or sources of conflict) have been condensed into three general categories: communication, structure, and personal variables.[6]

COMMUNICATION Susan had worked in purchasing at Bristol-Myers Squibb for three years. She enjoyed her work in large part because her boss, Tim McGuire, was a great guy to work for. Then Tim got promoted six months ago and Chuck Benson took his place. Susan says her job is a lot more frustrating now. "Tim and I were on the same wave length. It's not that way with Chuck.

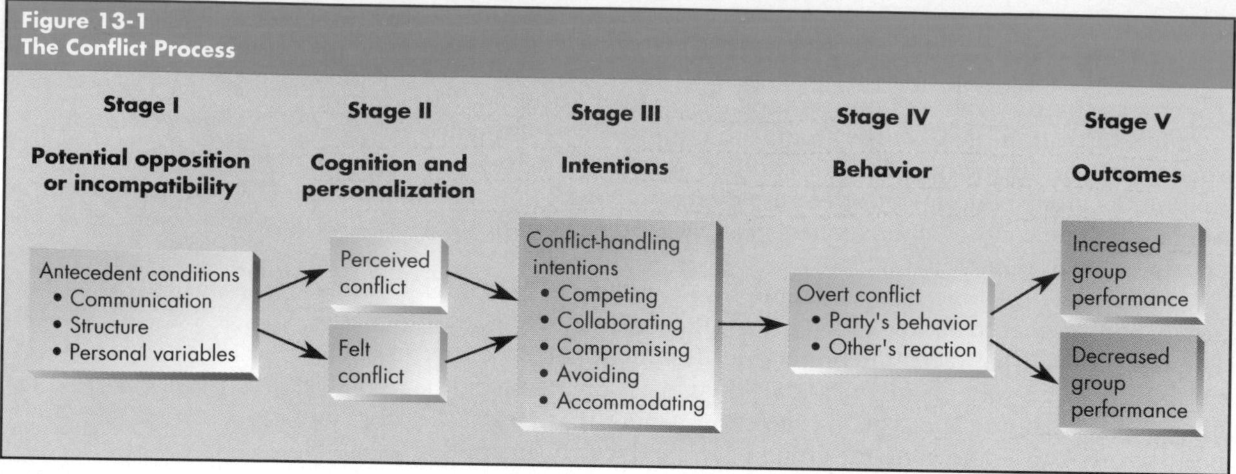

He tells me something and I do it. Then he tells me I did it wrong. I think he means one thing but says something else. It's been like this since the day he arrived. I don't think a day goes by when he isn't yelling at me for something. You know, there are some people you just find it easy to communicate with. Well, Chuck isn't one of those!"

Susan's comments illustrate that communication can be a source of conflict. It represents those opposing forces that arise from semantic difficulties, misunderstandings, and "noise" in the communication channels. You can relate much of this discussion back to our comments on communication in Chapter 10.

One of the major myths most of us carry around with us is that poor communication is the reason for conflicts: "If we could just communicate with each other, we could eliminate our differences." Such a conclusion is not unreasonable, given the amount of time each of us spends communicating. But, of course, poor communication is certainly not the source of all conflicts, although there is considerable evidence to suggest that problems in the communication process act to retard collaboration and stimulate misunderstanding.

> ◆One of the major myths that most of us carry around with us is that poor communication is the major reason for conflicts.

A review of the research suggests that semantic difficulties, insufficient exchange of information, and noise in the communication channel are all barriers to communication and potential antecedent conditions to conflict. Specifically, evidence demonstrates that semantic difficulties arise as a result of differences in training, selective perception, and inadequate information about others. Research has further demonstrated a surprising finding: The potential for conflict increases when either too little or too much communication takes place. Apparently, an increase in communication is functional up to a point, whereupon it is possible to overcommunicate, with a resultant increase in the potential for conflict. So, too much information as well as too little can lay the foundation for conflict. Further, the channel chosen for communicating can have an influence on stimulating opposition. The filtering process that occurs as information is passed between members and the divergence of communications from formal or previously established channels offer potential opportunities for conflict to arise.

STRUCTURE Charlotte and Teri both work at the Portland Furniture Mart, a large discount furniture retailer. Charlotte is a salesperson on the floor; Teri is the company credit manager. The two women have known each other for years and have much in common: They live within two blocks of each other, and their oldest daughters attend the same middle school and are best friends. In reality, if Charlotte and Teri had different jobs they might be best friends themselves. But these two women are consistently fighting battles with each other. Charlotte's job is to sell furniture and she does a great job. But most of her sales are made on credit. And Teri's job is to make sure the company minimizes credit losses. So she regularly has to turn down the credit application of a customer with whom Charlotte has just closed a sale. It's nothing personal between Charlotte and Teri—the requirements of their jobs just bring them into conflict.

The conflicts between Charlotte and Teri are structural in nature. The term *structure* is used, in this context, to include variables such as size, degree of specialization in the tasks assigned to group members, jurisdictional clarity, member–goal compatibility, leadership styles, reward systems, and the degree of dependence between groups.

Research indicates that size and specialization act as forces to stimulate conflict. The larger the group and the more specialized its activities, the greater the likelihood of conflict. Tenure and conflict have been found to be inversely related. The potential for conflict tends to be greatest where group members are younger and where turnover is high.

The greater the ambiguity in precisely defining where responsibility for actions lies, the greater the potential for conflict to emerge. Such jurisdictional ambiguities increase intergroup fighting for control of resources and territory.

Groups within organizations have diverse goals. For instance, purchasing is concerned with the timely acquisition of inputs at low prices, marketing's goals concentrate on disposing of outputs and increasing revenues, quality control's attention is focused on improving quality and ensuring that the organization's products meet standards, and production units seek efficiency of operations by maintaining a steady production flow. This diversity of goals among groups is a major source of conflict. Where groups within an organization seek diverse ends, some of which—like sales and credit at Portland Furniture Mart—are inherently at odds, there are increased opportunities for conflict.

There is some indication that a close style of leadership—tight and continuous observation with general control of others' behaviors—increases conflict potential, but the evidence is not particularly strong. Too much reliance on participation may also stimulate conflict. Research tends to confirm that participation and conflict are highly correlated, apparently because participation encourages the promotion of differences. Reward systems, too, are found to create conflict when one member's gain is at another's expense. Finally, if a group is dependent on another group (in contrast to the two being mutually independent) or if interdependence allows one group to gain at another's expense, opposing forces are stimulated.

PERSONAL VARIABLES Did you ever meet someone who you took an immediate disliking to? Most of the opinions they expressed, you disagreed with. Even insignificant characteristics—the sound of their voice, the smirk when they smiled, their personality—annoyed you. We've all met people like that. When you have to work with such individuals, there is often the potential for conflict.

So our last category of potential sources of conflict is personal factors. As indicated, they include each person's individual value systems and the personality characteristics that account for individual idiosyncrasies and differences.

The evidence indicates that certain personality types—for example, individuals who are highly authoritarian and dogmatic, and who demonstrate low esteem—lead to potential conflict. Most important, and probably the most overlooked variable in the study of social conflict, is differing value systems. Value differences, for example, are the best explanation of such diverse issues as prejudice, disagreements over one's contribution to the group and the rewards one deserves, and assessments of whether this particular book is any good. That John dislikes African-Americans and Dana believes John's position indicates his ignorance, that an employee thinks he is worth $35,000 a year but his boss believes him to be worth $30,000, and that Ann thinks this book is interesting to read while Jennifer views it as trash are all value judgments. And differences in value systems are important sources for creating the potential for conflict.

Stage II: Cognition and Personalization

If the conditions cited in Stage I negatively affect something that one party cares about, then the potential for opposition or incompatibility becomes actualized in the second stage. The antecedent conditions can only lead to conflict when one or more of the parties are affected by, and aware of, the conflict.

perceived conflict
Awareness by one or more parties of the existence of conditions that create opportunities for conflict to arise.

felt conflict
Emotional involvement in a conflict creating anxiety, tenseness, frustration, or hostility.

As we noted in our definition of conflict, perception is required. Therefore, one or more of the parties must be aware of the existence of the antecedent conditions. However, because a conflict is **perceived** does not mean it is personalized. In other words, "A may be aware that B and A are in serious disagreement . . . but it may not make A tense or anxious, and it may have no effect whatsoever on A's affection toward B."[7] It is at the **felt** level, when individuals become emotionally involved, that parties experience anxiety, tenseness, frustration, or hostility.

Keep in mind two points. First, Stage II is important because it's where conflict issues tend to be defined. This is the place in the process where the parties decide what the conflict is about.[8] And, in turn, this "sense making" is critical because the way a conflict is defined goes a long way toward establishing the sort of outcomes that might settle it. For instance, if I define our salary disagreement as a zero-sum situation—that is, if you get the increase in pay you want, there will be just that amount less for me—I am going to be far less willing to compromise than if I frame the conflict as a potential win-win situation (i.e., the dollars in the salary pool might be increased so both of us could get the added pay we want). So the definition of a conflict is important, for it typically delineates the set of possible settlements. Our second point is that emotions play a major role in shaping perceptions.[9] For example, negative emotions have been found to produce oversimplification of issues, reductions in trust, and negative interpretations of the other party's behavior.[10] In contrast, positive feelings have been found to increase the tendency to see potential relationships among the elements of a problem, to take a broader view of the situation, and to develop more innovative solutions.[11]

Stage III: Intentions

intentions
Decisions to act in a given way in a conflict episode.

Intentions intervene between people's perceptions and emotions and their overt behavior. These intentions are decisions to act in a given way.[12]

Why are intentions separated out as a distinct stage? You have to infer the other's intent in order to know how to respond to that other's behavior. A lot of conflicts are escalated merely by one party attributing the wrong intentions to the other party. Additionally, there is typically a great deal of slippage between intentions and behavior, so that behavior does not always accurately reflect a person's intentions.

Figure 13-2 represents one author's effort to identify the primary conflict-handling intentions. Using two dimensions—*cooperativeness* (the degree to which one party attempts to satisfy the other party's concerns) and *assertiveness* (the degree to which one party attempts to satisfy his or her own concerns)—five conflict-handling intentions can be identified: *competing* (assertive and uncooperative); *collaborating* (assertive and cooperative); *avoiding* (unassertive and uncooperative); *accommodating* (unassertive and cooperative); and *compromising* (midrange on both assertiveness and cooperativeness).[13]

Figure 13-2
Dimensions of Conflict—Handling Intentions

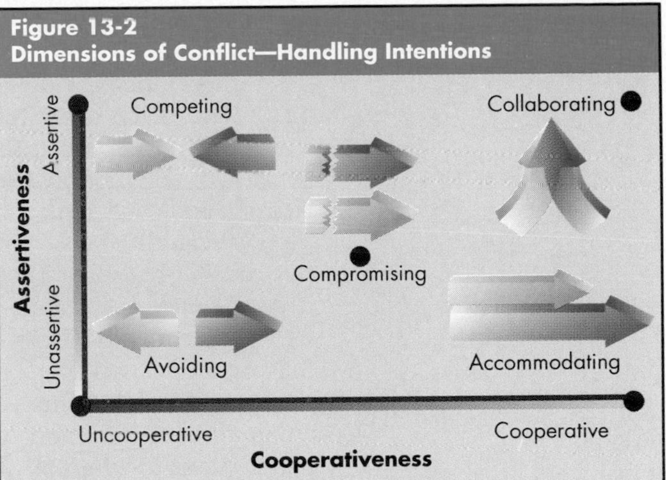

Source: K. Thomas, "Conflict and Negotiation Processes in Organizations," in M.D. Dunnette and L.M. Hough (eds.), *Handbook of Industrial and Organizational Psychology*, 2nd ed., Vol. 3 (Palo Alto, CA: Consulting Psychologists Press, 1992), p. 668. With permission.

COMPETING When one person seeks to satisfy his or her own interests, regardless of the impact on the other parties to the conflict, he or she is **competing**. Examples are intending to achieve your goal at the sacrifice of the other's goal, attempting to convince another your conclusion is correct and theirs is mistaken, and trying to make someone else accept blame for a problem.

competing
A desire to satisfy one's interests, regardless of the impact on the other party to the conflict.

COLLABORATING When the parties in conflict each desire to fully satisfy the concern of all parties, we have cooperation and the search for a mutually beneficial outcome. In **collaborating**, the intention of the parties is to solve the problem by clarifying differences rather than by accommodating various points of view. Examples are attempting to find a win-win solution that allows both parties' goals to be completely achieved and seeking a conclusion that incorporates the valid insights of both parties.

collaborating
A situation where the parties to a conflict each desire to satisfy fully the concerns of all parties.

AVOIDING A person may recognize that a conflict exists and want to withdraw from it or suppress it. Examples of **avoiding** are trying to just ignore a conflict and avoiding others with whom you disagree.

avoiding
The desire to withdraw from or suppress a conflict.

ACCOMMODATING When one party seeks to appease an opponent, that party may be willing to place the opponent's interests above his or her own. In other words, in order for the relationship to be maintained, one party is willing to be self-sacrificing. We refer to this intention as **accommodating**. Examples are a willingness to sacrifice your goal so the other party's goal can be attained, supporting someone else's opinion despite your reservations about it, and forgiving someone for an infraction and allowing subsequent ones.

accommodating
The willingness of one party in a conflict to place the opponent's interests above his or her own.

COMPROMISING When each party to the conflict seeks to give up something, sharing occurs, resulting in a compromised outcome. In **compromising**, there is no clear winner or loser. Rather, there is a willingness to ration the object of the conflict and accept a solution that provides incomplete satisfaction of both parties' concerns. The distinguishing characteristic of compromising, therefore, is that each party intends to give up something. Examples might be willingness to accept a raise of $1 an hour rather than $2, to acknowledge

compromising
A situation in which each party to a conflict is willing to give up something.

partial agreement with a specific viewpoint, and to take partial blame for an infraction.

Intentions provide general guidelines for parties in a conflict situation. They define each party's purpose. Yet people's intentions are not fixed. During the course of a conflict, they might change because of reconceptualization or because of an emotional reaction to the behavior of the other party. However, research indicates that people have an underlying disposition to handle conflicts in certain ways.[14] Specifically, individuals have preferences among the five conflict-handling intentions just described; these preferences tend to be relied on quite consistently; and a person's intentions can be predicted rather well from a combination of intellectual and personality characteristics. So it may be more appropriate to view the five conflict-handling intentions as relatively fixed rather than as a set of options from which individuals choose to fit an appropriate situation. That is, when confronting a conflict situation, some people want to win it all at any cost, some want to find an optimum solution, some want to run away, others want to be obliging, and still others want to split the difference.

Stage IV: Behavior

When most people think of conflict situations, they tend to focus on Stage IV. Why? Because this is where conflicts become visible. The behavior stage includes the statements, actions, and reactions made by the conflicting parties.

These conflict behaviors are usually overt attempts to implement each party's intentions. But these behaviors have a stimulus quality that is separate from intentions. As a result of miscalculations or unskilled enactments, overt behaviors sometimes deviate from original intentions.[15]

It helps to think of Stage IV as a dynamic process of interaction. For example, you make a demand on me; I respond by arguing; you threaten me; I threaten you back; and so on. Figure 13-3 provides a way of visualizing conflict behavior. All conflicts exist somewhere along this continuum. At the lower part of the continuum, we have conflicts characterized by subtle, indirect, and highly controlled forms of tension. An illustration might be a student questioning in class a point the instructor has just made. Conflict intensities escalate as they move upward along the continuum until they become highly destructive. Strikes, riots, and wars clearly fall in this upper range. For the most part, you should assume conflicts that reach the upper ranges of the continuum are almost always dysfunctional. Functional conflicts are typically confined to the lower range of the continuum.

Figure 13-3
Conflict Intensity Continuum

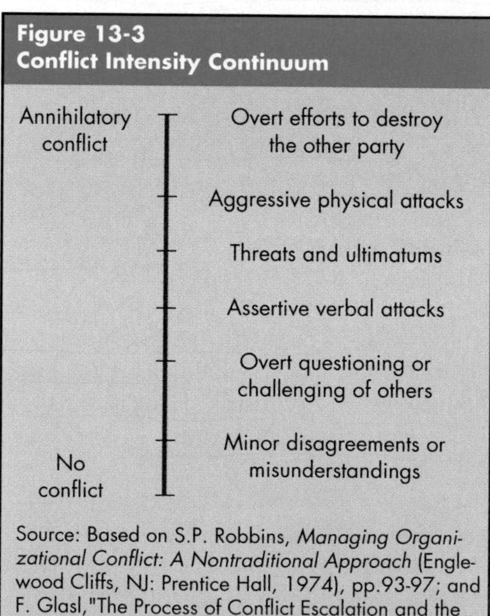

Source: Based on S.P. Robbins, *Managing Organizational Conflict: A Nontraditional Approach* (Englewood Cliffs, NJ: Prentice Hall, 1974), pp.93-97; and F. Glasl,"The Process of Conflict Escalation and the Roles of Third Parties," in G.B.J. Bomers and R. Peterson (eds.), *Conflict Management and Industrial Relations* (Boston: Kluwer-Nijhoff, 1982), pp.119-40.

If a conflict is dysfunctional, what can the parties do to deescalate it? Or, conversely, what options exist if conflict is too low and needs to be increased? This brings us to **conflict management** techniques. Table 13-1 lists the major resolution and stimulation techniques that allow managers to control

conflict management
The use of resolution and stimulation techniques to achieve the desired level of conflict.

Table 13-1 Conflict Management Techniques

Conflict Resolution Techniques	
Problem solving	Face-to-face meeting of the conflicting parties for the purpose of identifying the problem and resolving it through open discussion.
Superordinate goals	Creating a shared goal that cannot be attained without the cooperation of each of the conflicting parties.
Expansion of resources	When a conflict is caused by the scarcity of a resource—say, money, promotion opportunities, office space—expansion of the resource can create a win-win solution.
Avoidance	Withdrawal from, or suppression of, the conflict.
Smoothing	Playing down of differences while emphasizing common interests between the conflicting parties.
Compromise	Each party to the conflict gives up something of value.
Authoritative command	Management uses its formal authority to resolve the conflict and then communicates its desires to the parties involved.
Altering the human variable	Using behavioral change techniques such as human relations training to alter attitudes and behaviors that cause conflict.
Altering the structural variables	Changing the formal organization structure and the interaction patterns of conflicting parties through job redesign, transfers, creation of coordinating positions, and the like.
Conflict Stimulation Techniques	
Communication	Using ambiguous or threatening messages to increase conflict levels.
Bringing in outsiders	Adding employees to a group whose backgrounds, values, attitudes, or managerial styles differ from those of present members.
Restructuring the organization	Realigning work groups, altering rules and regulations, increasing interdependence, and making similar structural changes to disrupt the status quo.
Appointing a devil's advocate	Designating a critic to purposely argue against the majority positions held by the group.

Source: Based on S.P. Robbins, *Managing Organizational Conflict: A Nontraditional Approach* (Englewood Cliffs, NJ: Prentice-Hall, 1974), pp. 59–89.

conflict levels. Notice that several of the resolution techniques were earlier described as conflict-handling intentions. This, of course, shouldn't be surprising. Under ideal conditions, a person's intentions should translate into comparable behaviors.

Stage V: Outcomes

The action-reaction interplay between the conflicting parties results in consequences. As our model (see Figure 13-1) demonstrates, these outcomes may be functional, in that the conflict results in an improvement in the group's performance, or dysfunctional, in that it hinders group performance.

FUNCTIONAL OUTCOMES How might conflict act as a force to increase group performance? It is hard to visualize a situation where open or violent aggression could be functional. But there are a number of instances where it is possible to envision how low or moderate levels of conflict could improve the effectiveness of a group. Because people often find it difficult to think of instances where conflict can be constructive, let's consider some examples and then review the research evidence.

Conflict is constructive when it improves the quality of decisions, stimulates creativity and innovation, encourages interest and curiosity among group members, provides the medium through which problems can be aired and tensions released, and fosters an environment of self-evaluation and change. The evidence suggests that conflict can improve the quality of decision making by allowing all points, particularly the ones that are unusual or held by a minority, to be weighed in important decisions.[16] Conflict is an antidote for groupthink. It doesn't allow the group passively to rubber-stamp decisions that may be based on weak assumptions, inadequate consideration of relevant alternatives, or other debilities. Conflict challenges the status quo and therefore furthers the creation of new ideas, promotes reassessment of group goals and activities, and increases the probability that the group will respond to change.

For examples of companies that have suffered because they had too little functional conflict, you don't have to look further than Sears, Roebuck and General Motors.[17] Many of the problems that beset both of these companies throughout the 1970s and 1980s can be traced to a lack of functional conflict. They hired and promoted individuals who were "yes men," loyal to the organization to the point of never questioning company actions. Managers were, for the most part, conservative white Anglo-Saxon males raised in the midwestern United States who resisted change. They preferred looking back to past successes rather than forward to new challenges. Moreover, both firms kept their senior executives sheltered in their respective Chicago and Detroit headquarters' offices, protected from hearing anything they didn't want to hear, and a world away from the changes that were dramatically altering the retailing and automobile industries.

Research studies in diverse settings confirm the functionality of conflict. Consider the following findings.

The comparison of six major decisions made during the administration of four different U.S. presidents found that conflict reduced the chance that groupthink would overpower policy decisions. The comparisons demonstrated that conformity among presidential advisers was related to poor decisions, whereas an atmosphere of constructive conflict and critical thinking surrounded the well-developed decisions.[18]

The bankruptcy of the Penn Central Railroad has been generally attributed to mismanagement and the failure of the company's board of directors to question actions taken by management. The board was composed of outside directors who met monthly to oversee the railroad's operations. Few questioned decisions made by the operating management, although there was evidence that several board members were uncomfortable with many decisions made by them. Apathy and a desire to avoid conflict allowed poor decisions to stand unquestioned.[19] This, however, should not be surprising, since a review of the relationship between bureaucracy and innovation has found that conflict encourages innovative solutions.[20] The corollary of this finding also appears true: Lack of conflict results in a passive environment with reinforcement of the status quo.

Not only do better and more innovative decisions result from situations where there is some conflict, but evidence indicates that conflict can be positively related to productivity. It was demonstrated that, among established groups, performance tended to improve more when there was conflict among members than when there was fairly close agreement. The investigators observed that when groups analyzed decisions that had been made by the individual members of that group, the average improvement among the high-conflict groups was 73 percent greater than was that of those groups characterized by low-conflict conditions.[21] Others have found similar results: Groups composed of members with different interests tend to produce higher quality solutions to a variety of problems than do homogeneous groups.[22]

The preceding also leads us to predict that the increasing cultural diversity of the work force should provide benefits to organizations. And that's what the evidence indicates. Research demonstrates that heterogeneity among group and organization members can increase creativity, improve the quality of decisions, and facilitate change by enhancing member flexibility.[23] For example, researchers compared decision-making groups composed of all-Anglo individuals with groups that also contained members from Asian, Hispanic, and black ethnic groups. The ethnically diverse groups produced more effective and more feasible ideas and the unique ideas they generated tended to be of higher quality than the unique ideas produced by the all-Anglo group.

Similarly, studies of professionals—systems analysts and research and development scientists—support the constructive value of conflict. An investigation of 22 teams of systems analysts found that the more incompatible groups

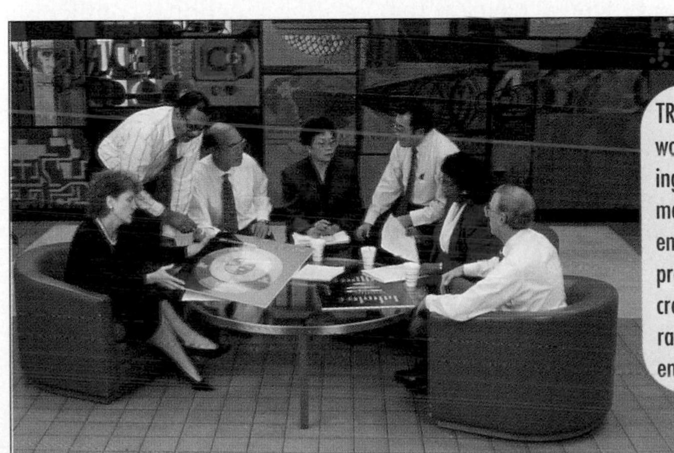

TRW is committed to the belief that an ethnically and culturally diverse work force will benefit the company's long-term competitiveness. Recognizing that diversity is a strength as it relates to problem solving and decision making, TRW is creating a work culture that makes the best use of each employee's uniqueness. It launched diversity training and communication programs in its automotive equipment, space/defense, and consumer credit businesses to help employees become aware of and learn to value racial, sexual, age, and cultural differences. Shown here is a group of employees discussing a diversity program.

were likely to be more productive.[24] Research and development scientists have been found to be most productive where there is a certain amount of intellectual conflict.[25]

Conflict can even be constructive on sports teams and in unions. Studies of sports teams indicate that moderate levels of group conflict contribute to team effectiveness and provide an additional stimulus for high achievement.[26] An examination of local unions found that conflict between members of the local was positively related to the union's power and to member loyalty and participation in union affairs.[27] These findings might suggest that conflict within a group indicates strength rather than, as in the traditional view, weakness.

DYSFUNCTIONAL OUTCOMES The destructive consequences of conflict on a group or organization's performance are generally well known. A reasonable summary might state the following: Uncontrolled opposition breeds discontent, which acts to dissolve common ties, and eventually leads to the destruction of the group. And, of course, a substantial body of literature documents how conflict—the dysfunctional varieties—can reduce group effectiveness.[28] Among the more undesirable consequences are a retarding of communication, reductions in group cohesiveness, and subordination of group goals to the primacy of infighting between members. At the extreme, conflict can bring group functioning to a halt and potentially threaten the group's survival.

This discussion has again returned us to the issue of what is functional and what is dysfunctional. Research on conflict has yet to clearly identify those situations where conflict is more likely to be constructive than destructive. However, growing evidence indicates that the type of group activity is a significant factor determining functionality.[29] The more nonroutine the tasks of the group, the greater the probability that internal conflict will be constructive. Groups that are required to tackle problems demanding new and novel approaches—as in research, advertising, and other professional activities—will benefit more from conflict than will groups performing highly routine activities—for instance, those of work teams on an automobile assembly line.

CREATING FUNCTIONAL CONFLICT We briefly mentioned conflict stimulation as part of Stage IV of the conflict process. Since the topic of conflict stimulation is relatively new and somewhat controversial, you might be wondering, If managers accept the interactionist view toward conflict, what can they do to encourage functional conflict in their organizations?[30]

There seems to be general agreement that creating functional conflict is a tough job, particularly in large American corporations. As one consultant put it, "A high proportion of people who get to the top are conflict avoiders. They don't like hearing negatives, they don't like saying or thinking negative things. They frequently make it up the ladder in part because they don't irritate people on the way up." Another suggests that at least 7 out of 10 people in American business keep quiet when their opinions are at odds with those of their superiors, allowing bosses to make mistakes even when they themselves know better.

Such anticonflict cultures may have been tolerable in the past, but not in today's fiercely competitive global economy. Those organizations that don't encourage and support dissent may not survive the 1990s. Let's look at some of the approaches organizations are taking to encourage their people to challenge the system and develop fresh ideas.

Hewlett-Packard rewards dissenters by recognizing go-against-the-grain types, or people who stay with the ideas they believe in even when those ideas are rejected by management. Herman Miller Inc., an office furniture manufacturer, has a formal system in which employees evaluate and criticize their bosses. IBM also has a formal system that encourages dissension. Employees can question their boss with impunity. If the disagreement can't be resolved, the system provides a third party for counsel.

Royal Dutch Shell Group, General Electric, and Anheuser-Busch build devil's advocates into the decision process. For instance, when the policy com-

◆◆◆◆ OB in the News ◆◆◆◆

Spectrum Associates Purposely Builds Conflict into Its Structure

Spectrum Associates is a small, but rapidly growing software company. In 1988, the company's first year of operations, revenues were only $404,000. In just five years, Spectrum's revenues have grown more than 6,000 percent to $25 million.

Spectrum's founders attribute a large part of the company success to the way it's structured. The firm is designed to create conflict. All product teams and support groups at Spectrum compete against each other for internal resources and outside markets. The founders sincerely believe in the free enterprise system and they have tried to create an organization that allows the fittest teams to grow and prosper while weaker ones fall by the wayside.

"We've kept the company growing by making sure nobody gets comfortable," says one of the founders. The company simulates internally what all companies face externally. By setting internal groups against each other, the company simulates "the pricing pressure, the delivery pressure, and the growth pressure that we encounter in the marketplace." The result is a work force in a perpetual state of readiness. "It keeps us healthy. A little insecurity can be very healthy."

The company only hires self-starters. New employees are told that "the company is not your parent. It's just a facility where you can come and lower your risks significantly because you have benefits, you have a base salary. But you're on your own." Recruits are encouraged to "grow your own business" within Spectrum. If it succeeds, you share in the wealth. If it fails, try again.

Spectrum's competitive culture is a shock for some. One employee, for example, said she wasn't prepared to have her own colleagues blocking her shots. "It took me a while to realize that meant convincing the salespeople to flip work to me instead of to someone else in the organization—that it meant bidding more aggressively to get a job. I had to get in the game."

But "it's not a free-for-all" says one cofounder. "Yeah, people compete, but they do it in groups. One individual is not out there trying to do in another person. It's groups vying to be the best." Reluctant to regulate, the two owners referee squabbles—such as a bidding war over a prospective employee—as they arise, but they refuse to formalize boundaries or set rules. "Behind it all there's a very healthy thing going on, which is a struggle to do what's right for the customer," argues one of the founders. "When I talk to customers, I can say, 'Look, what do you want? The best quality, the best price, and the best delivery. It so happens that we're organized in such a way that we can guarantee all that."

In essence what Spectrum has done is create a bunch of different businesses inside their company. And all are competing for the organization's limited financial and human resources. So, in contrast to the typical firm whose competition is with outside companies, Spectrum's people have to compete against products created by its own internal groups.

Based on A. Murphy, "The Enemy Within," *INC.* (March 1994), pp. 58–69.

mittee at Anheuser-Busch considers a major move, such as getting into or out of a business or making a major capital expenditure, it often assigns teams to make the case for each side of the question. This process frequently results in decisions and alternatives that previously hadn't been considered.

The governor of Maryland stimulates conflict and invigorates his organization by requiring state cabinet officials to swap jobs for one month every year, then write reports and suggestions based on their experiences.

One common ingredient in organizations that successfully create functional conflict is that they reward dissent and punish conflict avoiders. The president of Innovis Interactive Technologies, for instance, fired a top executive who refused to dissent. His explanation: "He was the ultimate yes-man. In this organization, I can't afford to pay someone to hear my own opinion." But the real challenge for managers is when they hear news they don't want to hear. The news may make their blood boil or their hopes collapse, but they can't show it. They have to learn to take the bad news without flinching. No tirades, no tight-lipped sarcasm, no eyes rolling upward, no gritting of teeth. Rather, managers should ask calm, even-tempered questions: "Can you tell me more about what happened?" "What do you think we ought to do?" A sincere "Thank you for bringing this to my attention" is likely to reduce the likelihood that managers will be cut off from similar communications in the future.

Negotiation

Negotiation permeates the interactions of almost everyone in groups and organizations. There's the obvious: Labor bargains with management. There's the not so obvious: Managers negotiate with subordinates, peers, and bosses; salespeople negotiate with customers; purchasing agents negotiate with suppliers. And there's the subtle: A worker agrees to answer a colleague's phone for a few minutes in exchange for some past or future benefit. In today's team-based organizations, where members are increasingly finding themselves having to work with colleagues over whom they have no direct authority and with whom they may not even share a common boss, negotiation skills become critical.

negotiation
A process in which two or more parties exchange goods or services and attempt to agree upon the exchange rate for them.

We define **negotiation** as a process in which two or more parties exchange goods or services and attempt to agree on the exchange rate for them.[31] Note that we use the terms *negotiation* and *bargaining* interchangeably.

In this section, we contrast two bargaining strategies, provide a model of the negotiation process, consider biases that hinder effective negotiation, ascertain the role of personality traits on bargaining, review cultural differences in negotiation, and take a brief look at third-party negotiations.

Bargaining Strategies

There are two general approaches to negotiation: *distributive bargaining* and *integrative bargaining*.[32] These are compared in Table 13-2.

distributive bargaining
Negotiation that seeks to divide up a fixed amount of resources; a win-lose situation.

DISTRIBUTIVE BARGAINING You see a used car advertised for sale in the newspaper. It appears to be just what you've been looking for. You go out to see the car. It's great and you want it. The owner tells you the asking price. You don't want to pay that much. The two of you then negotiate over the price. The negotiating strategy you're engaging in is called **distributive bargaining**. Its most identifying feature is that it operates under zero-sum conditions. That

Table 13-2 Distributive vs. Integrative Bargaining

Bargaining Characteristic	Distributive Bargaining	Integrative Bargaining
Available resources	Fixed amount of resources to be divided	Variable amount of resources to be divided
Primary motivations	I win, you lose	I win, you win
Primary interests	Opposed to each other	Convergent or congruent with each other
Focus of relationships	Short term	Long term

Source: Based on R.J. Lewicki and J.A. Litterer, *Negotiation* (Homewood, IL: Irwin, 1985), p. 280.

is, any gain I make is at your expense, and vice versa. Referring back to the used car example, every dollar you can get the seller to cut from the car's price is a dollar you save. Conversely, every dollar more he can get from you comes at your expense. So the essence of distributive bargaining is negotiating over who gets what share of a fixed pie.

Probably the most widely cited example of distributive bargaining is in labor–management negotiations over wages. Typically, labor's representatives come to the bargaining table determined to get as much money as possible out of management. Since every cent more that labor negotiates increases management's costs, each party bargains aggressively and treats the other as an opponent who must be defeated.

The essence of distributive bargaining is depicted in Figure 13-4. Parties A and B represent two negotiators. Each has a *target point* that defines what he or she would like to achieve. Each also has a *resistance point*, which marks the lowest outcome that is acceptable—the point below which they would break off negotiations rather than accept a less favorable settlement. The area between between these two points makes up each one's aspiration range. As long as there is some overlap between A and B's aspiration ranges, there exists a settlement range where each one's aspirations can be met.

Figure 13-4
Staking Out the Bargaining Zone

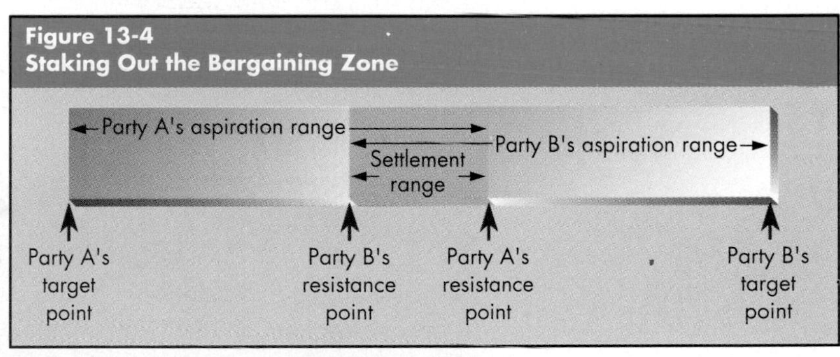

When engaged in distributive bargaining, one's tactics focus on trying to get one's opponent to agree to one's specific target point or to get as close to it as possible. Examples of such tactics are persuading your opponent of the impossibility of getting to his or her target point and the advisability of accepting a settlement near yours; arguing that your target is fair, but your opponent's isn't; and attempting to get your opponent to feel emotionally generous toward you and thus accept an outcome close to your target point.

INTEGRATIVE BARGAINING A sales representative for a women's sportswear manufacturer has just closed a $15,000 order from a small clothing retailer. The sales rep calls in the order to her firm's credit department. She is told the firm can't approve credit to this customer because of a past slow-pay record. The next day, the sales rep and the firm's credit manager meet to discuss the problem. The sales rep doesn't want to lose the business. Neither does the credit manager, but he also doesn't want to get stuck with an uncollectable debt. The two openly review their options. After considerable discussion, they agree on a solution that meets both their needs: The credit manager will approve the sale, but the clothing store's owner will provide a bank guarantee that will assure payment if the bill isn't paid within 60 days.

integrative bargaining Negotiation that seeks one or more settlements that can create a win-win solution.

This sales–credit negotiation is an example of **integrative bargaining**. In contrast to distributive bargaining, integrative problem solving operates under the assumption that there exists one or more settlements that can create a win-win solution.

In terms of intraorganizational behavior, all things being equal, integrative bargaining is preferable to distributive bargaining. Why? Because the former builds long-term relationships and facilitates working together in the future. It bonds negotiators and allows each to leave the bargaining table feeling he or she has achieved a victory. Distributive bargaining, on the other hand, leaves one party a loser. It tends to build animosities and deepen divisions when people have to work together on an ongoing basis.

Why, then, don't we see more integrative bargaining in organizations? The answer lies in the conditions necessary for this type of negotiation to succeed. These include parties who are open with information and candid about their concerns; a sensitivity by both parties to the other's needs; the ability to trust one another; and a willingness by both parties to maintain flexibility.[33] Since these conditions often don't exist in organizations, it isn't surprising that negotiations often take on a win-at-any-cost dynamic.

The Negotiation Process

Figure 13-5 provides a simplified model of the negotiation process. It views negotiation as made up of five steps: (1) preparation and planning; (2) definition of ground rules; (3) clarification and justification; (4) bargaining and problem solving; and (5) closure and implementation.[34]

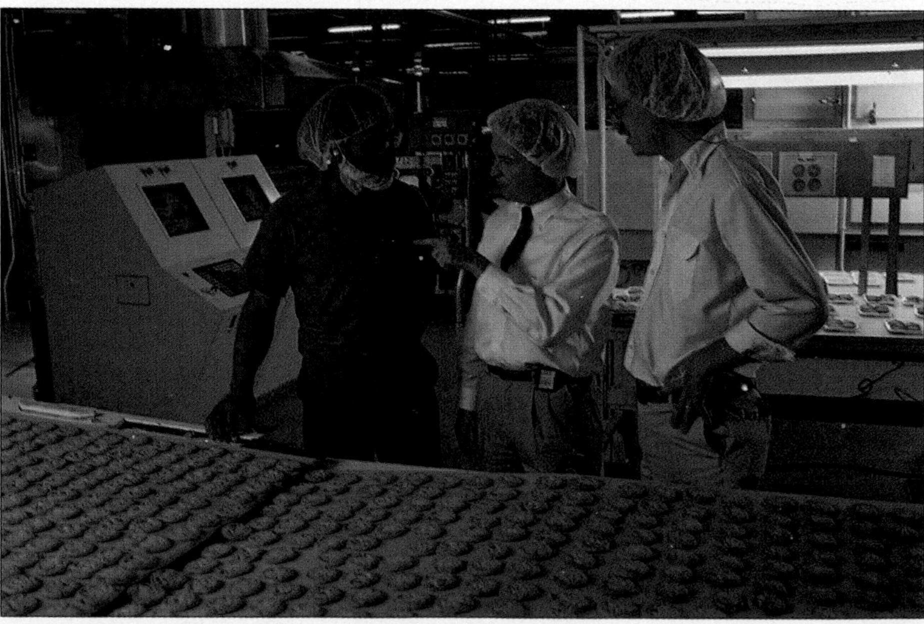

Nabisco Brands' management and the Bakery, Confectionary and Tobacco Workers International Union have been using integrative bargaining teams to settle work force disputes for several years. It has worked so well that Nabisco and the BCT recently won the U.S. government's first annual award for Excellence in Industrial Relations.

PREPARATION AND PLANNING Before you start negotiating, you need to do your homework. What's the nature of the conflict? What's the history leading up to this negotiation? Who's involved and what are their perceptions of the conflict?

What do you want from the negotiation? What are *your* goals? If you're a purchasing manager at Dell Computer, for instance, and your goal is to get a significant cost reduction from your supplier of keyboards, make sure this goal stays paramount in your discussions and doesn't get overshadowed by other issues. It often helps to put your goals in writing and develop a range of outcomes—from "most hopeful" to "minimally acceptable"—to keep your attention focused.

You also want to prepare an assessment of what you think the other party to your negotiation's goals are. What are they likely to ask for? How entrenched are they likely to be in their position? What intangible or hidden interests may be important to them? What might they be willing to settle on? When you can anticipate your opponent's position, you are better equipped to counter his or her arguments with the facts and figures that support your position.

Use the information you've gathered to develop a strategy. Like a chess match, expert chess players have a strategy. They know ahead of time how they will respond to any given situation. As part of your strategy, you should determine yours and the other side's *B*est *A*lternative *T*o a *N*egotiated *A*greement (**BATNA**).[35] Your BATNA determines the lowest value acceptable to you for a negotiated agreement. Any offer you receive that is higher than your BATNA is better than an impasse. Conversely, you shouldn't expect success in your negotiation effort unless you're able to make the other side an offer they find more attractive than their BATNA. If you go into your negotiation having a good idea of what the other party's BATNA is, even if you're not able to meet theirs, you might be able to get them to change it.

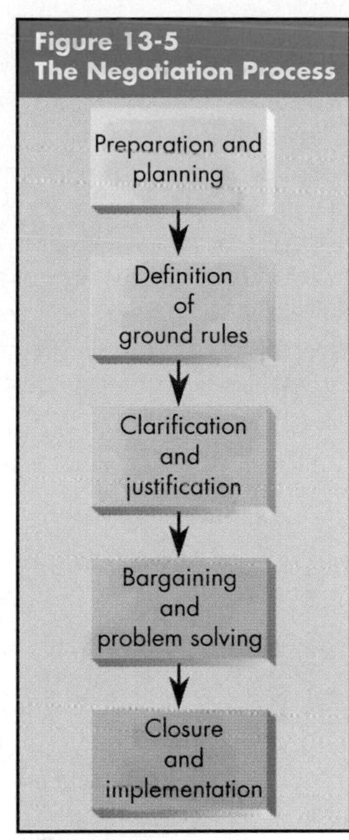

BATNA
The best alternative to a negotiated agreement; the lowest acceptable value to an individual for a negotiated agreement.

DEFINITION OF GROUND RULES Once you've done your planning and developed a strategy, you're ready to begin defining the ground rules and procedures with the other party over the negotiation itself. Who will do the negotiating? Where will it take place? What time constraints, if any, will apply? What issues will negotiation be limited to? Will there be a specific procedure to follow if an impasse is reached? During this phase, the parties will also exchange their initial proposals or demands.

CLARIFICATION AND JUSTIFICATION When initial positions have been exchanged, both you and the other party will explain, amplify, clarify, bolster, and justify your original demands. This needn't be confrontational. Rather, it is an opportunity for educating and informing each other on the issues, why they're important, and how each arrived at their initial demands. This is the point where you might want to provide the other party with any documentation that helps support your position.

BARGAINING AND PROBLEM SOLVING The essence of the negotiation process is the actual give-and-take in trying to hash out an agreement. Concessions will undoubtedly need to be made by both parties. The "From Concepts to Skills" box (see page 524) on negotiating directly addresses some of the actions you should take to improve the likelihood you can achieve a good agreement.

CLOSURE AND IMPLEMENTATION The final step in the negotiation process is formalizing the agreement that has been worked out and developing any

Negotiations over a shortened work week ended when Chrysler Canada Ltd.'s minivan plant in Windsor, Ontario, and the Canadian Auto Workers union signed a new labor-management contract. The union agreed to Chrysler's goal of adding a third daily shift of more than 800 new assembly-line workers. The additional shift moves the plant into 7-day, 24-hour production, enabling Chrysler to meet the booming consumer demand for its minivans. In return, Chrysler agreed to the union's proposal of reduced hours without a wage reduction. To accommodate the third shift, Chrysler reduced assemblers' work day from 8 to 7½ hours and agreed to continue to pay them for an 8-hour day and to increase their $20.48-an-hour wage by one percent.

procedures necessary for implemention and monitoring. For major negotiations—which would include everything from labor–management negotiations, to bargaining over lease terms, to buying a piece of real estate, to negotiating a job offer for a senior management position—this will require hammering out the specifics in a formal contract. For most cases, however, closure of the negotiation process is nothing more formal than a handshake.

Issues in Negotiation

We conclude our discussion of negotiation by reviewing four contemporary issues in negotiation: decision-making biases; the role of personality traits; the effect of cultural differences on negotiating styles; and the use of third parties to help resolve differences.

DECISION-MAKING BIASES THAT HINDER EFFECTIVE NEGOTIATION All of us have had negotiating experiences where the results have been less than we had hoped for. Why? We tend to be blind to opportunities that prevent us from getting as much as possible out of a negotiation. The following identifies seven decision-making biases that can blind us.[36]

1. *Irrational escalation of commitment.* People tend to continue a previously selected course of action beyond what rational analysis would recommend. Such misdirected persistence can lead to wasting a great deal of time, energy, and money. Time and money already invested are sunk costs. They *cannot* be recovered and should *not* be considered when selecting future courses of action.
2. *The mythical fixed pie.* Bargainers assume their gain must come at the expense of the other party. As noted with integrative bargaining, that needn't be the case. There are often win-win solutions. By assuming a zero-sum game, you preclude opportunities to find options that can allow multiple victories.
3. *Anchoring and adjustments.* People often have a tendency to anchor their judgments on irrelevant information, such as an initial offer. Many factors influence the initial positions people take when entering a negotiation. They are often meaningless. Effective negotiators don't let an initial anchor minimize the amount of information and the depth of thinking they use to evaluate a situation, and don't give too much weight to their opponent's initial offer too early in the negotiation.

4. *Framing negotiations.* People tend to be overly affected by the way information is presented to them. For instance, in a labor–management contract negotiation, assume your employees are currently making $15 an hour but the union is seeking a $4 raise. You are prepared to go to $17. The union's response is likely to be different if you can successfuly frame this as a $2 an hour gain (in comparison to the current wage) rather than a $2 an hour loss (when compared against the union's demand).

5. *Availability of information.* Negotiators often rely too much on readily available information while ignoring more relevant data. Things or events that people have encountered more often are usually easy to remember—they're more "available" in their memory. It's also easier to remember or imagine more vivid events. Information that is easily recalled because it's familiar or vivid may be interpreted as being reliable when it's not. So effective negotiators learn to distinguish what's emotionally familiar to them from what's reliable and relevant.

6. *The winner's curse.* A friend went in to a local dealership to buy a new luxury sports car. The list price was $42,300. My friend estimated that the dealer probably paid around $35,000 for the car. My friend was prepared to go as high as $41,000, but he made an initial offer of $38,000. To his surprise, the dealer accepted his offer. Two hours later he was driving home in his new car. That night he couldn't sleep. Even though he had paid $3,000 less than he expected, he felt he still may have paid too much.

   My friend experienced "winner's curse," or the regret one feels after closing a negotiation. Because your opponent accepted your offer, you become concerned that you offered too much. This postnegotiation reaction is not unusual. In most negotiations, one side (usually the seller) has much better information than the other. Yet people often tend to act in a negotiation as if their opponent is inactive and ignore the valuable information that can be learned by thinking about the other side's decisions. You can reduce the curse by gaining as much information as possible and putting yourself in your opponent's shoes.

7. *Overconfidence.* Many of the previous biases can combine to inflate a person's confidence in his or her judgment and choices. When people hold certain beliefs and expectations, they tend to ignore information that contradicts them. The result is that negotiators tend to be overconfident. This, in turn, lessens the incentive to compromise. Considering the suggestions of qualified advisers or seeking objective assessment about your position from a neutral party are two ways to temper this tendency.

THE ROLE OF PERSONALITY TRAITS IN NEGOTIATION Can you predict an opponent's negotiating tactics if you know something about his or her personality? It's tempting to answer "Yes" to this question. For instance, you might assume that high risk takers would be more aggressive bargainers who make fewer concessions. Surprisingly, the evidence doesn't support this intuition.[37]

Overall assessments of the personality–negotiation relationship finds that personality traits have no significant direct effect on either the bargaining process or negotiation outcomes. This conclusion is important. It suggests that you should concentrate on the issues and the situational factors in each bargaining episode and not on your opponent and his or her characteristics.

From Concepts to Skills

Negotiating

Once you've taken the time to assess your own goals, consider the other party's goals and interests, and develop a strategy, you're ready to begin actual negotiations. The following suggestions should improve your negotiating skills.[38]

- *Begin with a positive overture*. Studies on negotiation show that concessions tend to be reciprocated and lead to agreements. As a result, begin bargaining with a positive overture—perhaps a small concession—and then reciprocate your opponent's concessions.
- *Address problems, not personalities*. Concentrate on the negotiation issues, not on the personal characteristics of your opponent. When negotiations get tough, avoid the tendency to attack your opponent. It's your opponent's ideas or position that you disagree with, not him or her personally. Separate the people from the problem, and don't personalize differences.
- *Pay little attention to initial offers*. Treat an initial offer as merely a point of departure. Everyone has to have an initial position. These initial offers tend to be extreme and idealistic. Treat them as such.
- *Emphasize win-win solutions*. Inexperienced negotiators often assume their gain must come at the expense of the other party. As noted with integrative bargaining, that needn't be the case. There are often win-win solutions. But assuming a zero-sum game means missed opportunities for trade-offs that could benefit both sides. So if conditions are supportive, look for an integrative solution. Frame options in terms of your opponent's interests and look for solutions that can allow your opponent, as well as yourself, to declare a victory.
- *Create an open and trusting climate*. Skilled negotiators are better listeners, ask more questions, focus their arguments more directly, are less defensive, and have learned to avoid words and phrases that can irritate an opponent (i.e., "generous offer," "fair price," "reasonable arrangement"). In other words, they are better at creating the open and trusting climate necessary for reaching an integrative settlement.

CULTURAL DIFFERENCES IN NEGOTIATIONS While there appears to be no significant direct relationship between an individual's personality and negotiation style, cultural background does seem to be relevant. Negotiating styles clearly vary between national cultures.[39]

The French like conflict. They frequently gain recognition and develop their reputations by thinking and acting against others. As a result, the French tend to take a long time in negotiating agreements and they aren't overly concerned about whether their opponents like or dislike them.[40] The Chinese also draw out negotiations but that's because they believe negotiations never end. Just when you think you've pinned down every detail and reached a final solution with a Chinese executive, that executive might smile and start the process all over again. Like the Japanese, the Chinese negotiate to develop a relationship and a commitment to work together rather than to tie up every loose end.[41] Americans are known around the world for their impatience and their desire to be liked. Astute negotiators from other countries often turn these characteristics to their advantage by dragging out negotiations and making friendship conditional on the final settlement.

The cultural context of the negotiation significantly influences the amount and type of preparation for bargaining, the relative emphasis on task versus interpersonal relationships, the tactics used, and even where the negotiation should be conducted. To further illustrate some of these differences, let's look at two studies comparing the influence of culture on business negotiations.

The first study compared North Americans, Arabs, and Russians.[42] Among the factors that were looked at were their negotiating style, how they responded to an opponent's arguments, their approach to making concessions, and how they handled negotiating deadlines. North Americans tried to persuade by relying on facts and appealing to logic. They countered opponents' arguments with objective facts. They made small concessions early in the negotiation to establish a relationship, and usually reciprocated opponents' concessions. North Americans treated deadlines as very important. The Arabs tried to persuade by appealing to emotion. They countered opponents' arguments with subjective feelings. They made concessions throughout the bargaining process and almost always reciprocated opponents' concessions. Arabs approached deadlines very casually. The Russians based their arguments on asserted ideals. They made few, if any, concessions. Any concession offered by an opponent was viewed as a weakness and almost never reciprocated. Finally, the Russians tended to ignore deadlines.

The second study looked at verbal and nonverbal negotiation tactics exhibited by North Americans, Japanese, and Brazilians during half-hour bargaining sessions.[43] Some of the differences were particularly interesting. For instance, the Brazilians on average said "No" 83 times, compared to 5 times for the Japanese and 9 times for the North Americans. The Japanese displayed more than five periods of silence lasting longer than 10 seconds during the 30-minute sessions. North Americans averaged 3.5 such periods; the Brazilians had none. The Japanese and North Americans interrupted their opponent about the same number of times, but the Brazilians interrupted 2½ to 3 times more often than the North Americans and the Japanese. Finally, while the Japanese and the North Americans had no physical contact with their opponents during negotiations except for handshaking, the Brazilians touched each other almost five times every half hour.

THIRD-PARTY NEGOTIATIONS To this point, we've discussed bargaining in terms of direct negotiations. Occasionally, however, individuals or group representatives reach a stalemate and are unable to resolve their differences through direct negotiations. In such cases, they may turn to a third party to help them find a solution. There are four basic third-party roles: mediator, arbitrator, conciliator, and consultant.[44]

A **mediator** is a neutral third party who facilitates a negotiated solution by using reasoning and persuasion, suggesting alternatives, and the like. Mediators are widely used in labor–management negotiations and in civil court disputes.

mediator
A neutral third party who facilitates a negotiated solution by using reasoning, persuasion, and suggestions for alternatives.

The overall effectiveness of mediated negotiations is fairly impressive. The settlement rate is approximately 60 percent, with negotiator satisfaction at about 75 percent. But the situation is the key to whether mediation will succeed; the conflicting parties must be motivated to bargain and resolve their conflict. Additionally, conflict intensity can't be too high; mediation is most effective under moderate levels of conflict. Finally, perceptions of the mediator are important; to be effective, the mediator must be perceived as neutral and noncoercive.

An **arbitrator** is a third party with the authority to dictate an agreement. Arbitration can be voluntary (requested) or compulsory (forced on the parties by law or contract).

arbitrator
A third party to a negotiation who has the authority to dictate an agreement.

The authority of the arbitrator varies according to the rules set by the negotiators. For instance, the arbitrator might be limited to choosing one of the negotiator's last offers or to suggesting an agreement point that is nonbinding, or free to choose and make any judgment he or she wishes.

The big plus of arbitration over mediation is that it always results in a settlement. Whether there is a negative side depends on how heavy-handed the arbitrator appears. If one party is left feeling overwhelmingly defeated, that party is certain to be dissatisfied and unlikely to graciously accept the arbitrator's decision. Hence the conflict may resurface at a later time.

conciliator
A trusted third party who provides an informal communication link between the negotiator and the opponent.

A **conciliator** is a trusted third party who provides an informal communication link between the negotiator and the opponent. This role was made famous by Robert Duval in the first *Godfather* film. As Don Corleone's adopted son and a lawyer by training, Duval acted as an intermediary between the Corleone family and the other mafioso families.

Conciliation is used extensively in international, labor, family, and community disputes. Comparing its effectiveness to mediation has proven difficult because the two overlap a great deal. In practice, conciliators typically act as more than mere communication conduits. They also engage in fact-finding, interpreting messages, and persuading disputants to develop agreements.

consultant as negotiator
An impartial third party, skilled in conflict management, who attempts to facilitate creative problem solving through communication and analysis.

A **consultant** is a skilled and impartial third party who attempts to facilitate problem solving through communication and analysis, aided by his or her knowledge of conflict management. In contrast to the previous roles, the consultant's role is not to settle the issues but, rather, to improve relations between the conflicting parties so they can reach a settlement themselves. Instead of putting forward specific solutions, the consultant tries to help the parties learn to understand and work with each other. Therefore, this approach has a longer term focus: to build new and positive perceptions and attitudes between the conflicting parties.

◆◆◆◆ OB in the News ◆◆◆◆

Ombudsmen Proliferate in the Workplace

Many companies are increasingly turning to informal problem solvers, known as ombudsmen, to reduce tensions and deter litigation in the work force.

Use of ombudsmen at medium-sized and large companies more than doubled between 1988 and 1993. About 500 companies, most with 500 or more workers, now employ ombudsmen.

The ombudsmen—most of whom aren't lawyers—listen to work complaints ranging from benefits mixups, to conflicts between workers and supervisors, to workplace violence, and then try to help solve the problems before they get out of hand. They're different from other staff relations and grievance officials because they're neutral, rather than representatives of management. Also, their conversations with employees, and any mediation sessions, are confidential unless the employees involved say otherwise.

Where do these companies find their ombudsmen? Typically right inside their firms. "Just look for the person that everybody already goes to for advice," says Eugene T. Herbert, a consulting ombudsman to the International Monetary Fund.

Based on J. Woo, "Ombudsmen Proliferate in the Workplace," *Wall Street Journal* (February 19, 1993), p. B12.

Intergroup Relations

For the most part, the concepts we've discussed from Chapter 8 on have dealt with intragroup activities. For instance, the previous material in this chapter emphasized interpersonal and intragroup conflict as well as interpersonal negotiations. But we need to understand relationships between groups as well as within groups. In this section, we focus on intergroup relationships. These are the coordinated bridges that link two distinct organizational groups.[45] As we show, the efficiency and quality of these relationships can have a significant bearing on one or both of the groups' performances and their members' satisfaction.

Factors Affecting Intergroup Relations

Successful intergroup performance is a function of a number of factors. The umbrella concept that overrides these factors is *coordination*. Each of the following can affect efforts at coordination.

INTERDEPENDENCE The first overriding question we need to ask is: Do the groups really need coordination? The answer to this question lies in determining the degree of interdependence that exists between the groups. That is, do the groups depend on each other and, if so, how much? The three most frequently identified types of interdependence are pooled, sequential, and reciprocal.[46] Each requires an increasing degree of group interaction (see Figure 13-6 on page 528).

When two groups function with relative independence but their combined output contributes to the organization's overall goals, **pooled interdependence** exists. At a firm such as Apple Computer, for instance, this would describe the relationship between the product development department and the shipping department. Both are necessary if Apple is to develop new prod-

pooled interdependence
Where two groups function with relative independence but their combined output contributes to the organization's overall goals.

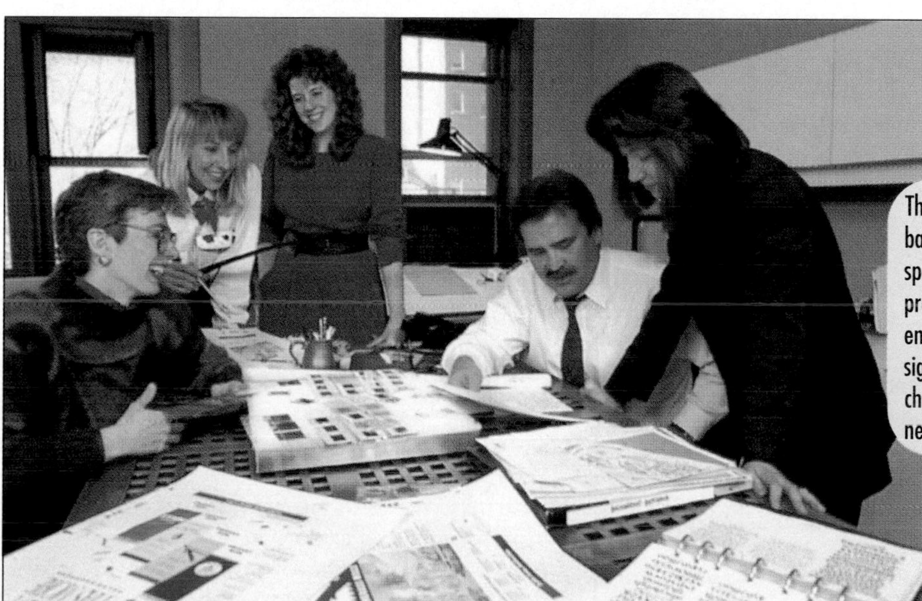

The work of designers at Chadick & Kimball, a Washington, D.C. design firm that specializes in developing corporate identity programs, requires reciprocal interdependence with the firm's marketing staff. Design and marketing people need to exchange information in order to meet client needs.

ucts and get those products into consumers' hands, but each is essentially separate and distinct from the other. All else being equal, coordination requirements between groups linked by pooled interdependence are less than with sequential or reciprocal interdependence.

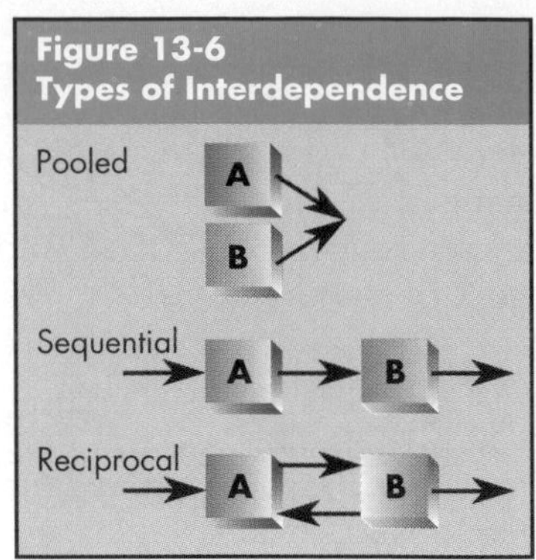

Figure 13-6
Types of Interdependence

sequential interdependence
One group depends on another for its input but the dependency is only one way.

The purchasing and parts assembly departments at Apple are **sequentially interdependent**. One group—parts assembly—depends on another—purchasing—for its inputs, but the dependency is only one way. Purchasing is not directly dependent on parts assembly for its inputs. In sequential interdependence, if the group that provides the input doesn't perform its job properly, the group that is dependent on the first will be significantly affected. In our Apple example, if purchasing fails to order an important component that goes into the assembly process, then the parts assembly department may have to slow down or temporarily close its assembly operations.

reciprocal interdependence
Where groups exchange inputs and outputs.

The most complex form of interdependence is **reciprocal**. In these instances, groups exchange inputs and outputs. For example, sales and product development groups at Apple are reciprocally interdependent. Salespeople, in contact with customers, acquire information about their future needs. Sales then relays this back to product development so they can create new computer products. The long-term implications are that if product development doesn't come up with new products that potential customers find desirable, sales personnel are not going to get orders. So there is high interdependence—product development needs sales for information on customer needs so it can create successful new products, and sales depends on the product development group to create products it can successfully sell. This high degree of dependency translates into greater interaction and increased coordination demands.

TASK UNCERTAINTY The next coordination question is: What type of tasks are the groups involved in? For simplicity's sake, we can think of a group's tasks as ranging from highly routine to highly nonroutine[47] (see Figure 13-7).

Highly routine tasks have little variation. Problems that group members face tend to contain few exceptions and are easy to analyze. Such group activities lend themselves to standardized operating procedures. For example, manufacturing tasks in a tire factory are made up of highly routine tasks. At the other extreme are nonroutine tasks. These are unstructured activities, with many exceptions and problems that are hard to analyze. Many of the tasks undertaken by marketing research and product development groups are of this variety. Of course, a lot of group tasks fall somewhere in the middle or combine both routine and nonroutine tasks.

task uncertainty
The greater the uncertainty in a task, the more custom the response. Conversely, low uncertainty encompasses routine tasks with standardized activities.

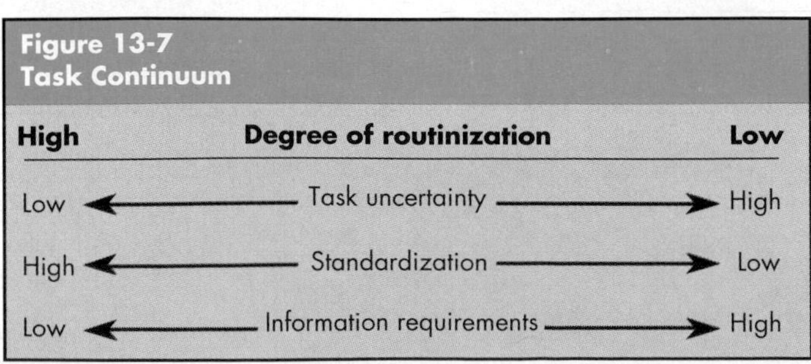

Figure 13-7
Task Continuum

The key to **task uncertainty** is that nonroutine tasks require considerably more processing of information. Tasks with low uncertainty tend to be standardized. Further, groups that do standardized tasks do not have to interact much with other groups. In contrast, groups that undertake tasks high in uncertainty face problems that require custom responses. This, in turn, leads to a need for more and better information. We would expect the people in the marketing research department at Goodyear Tire & Rubber to interact much more with other departments and constituencies—marketing, sales, product design, tire dealers, advertising agencies, and the like—than would people in Goodyear's manufacturing group.

TIME AND GOAL ORIENTATION How different are the groups in terms of their members' background and thinking? This is the third question relevant to the degree of coordination necessary between groups. Research demonstrates that a work group's perceptions of what is important may differ on the basis of the time frame that governs their work and their goal orientation.[48] This can make it difficult for groups with different perceptions to work together.

Why might work groups have different time and goal orientations? Top management historically divided work up by putting common tasks into common functional groups and assigning these groups specific goals. Then people were hired with the appropriate background and skills to complete the tasks and help the group achieve its goals. This differentiation of tasks and hiring of specialists made it easier to coordinate intragroup activities. But it made it increasingly difficult to coordinate interaction between groups.

To illustrate how orientations differ between work groups, manufacturing personnel have a short-term time focus. They worry about today's production

Figure 13-8

Source: CATHY copyright Cathy Guisewite. Reprinted with permission of Universal Press Syndicate.

schedule and this week's productivity. In contrast, people in research and development focus on the long run. They're concerned about developing new products that may not be produced for several years. Similarly, work groups often have different goal orientations. As we noted earlier in the chapter, sales typically wants to sell anything and everything. Their goals center on sales volume and increasing revenue and market share. Their customers' ability to pay for the sales they make are not their concern. But people in the credit department want to ensure that sales are made only to creditworthy customers. These differences in goals often make it difficult for sales and credit to communicate. It also makes it harder to coordinate their interactions.

Methods for Managing Intergroup Relations

What coordination methods are available for managing intergroup relations? There are a number of options; we identify the seven most frequently used in Figure 13-9. These seven are listed on a continuum, in order of increasing cost.[49] They also are cumulative in the sense that succeeding methods higher on the continuum add to, rather than are substituted for, lower methods. In most organizations, the simpler methods listed at the lower end of the continuum are used in conjunction with the more complex methods listed at the upper end. For instance, if a manager is using teams to coordinate intergroup relations, that manager is also likely to be using rules and procedures.

◆ The most simple and least costly method for managing intergroup relations is to establish rules and procedures.

RULES AND PROCEDURES The most simple and least costly method for managing intergroup relations is to establish, in advance, a set of formalized rules and procedures that will specify how group members are to interact with each other. In large organizations, for example, standard operating procedures are likely to specify that when additional permanent staff are needed in any department, a "request for new staff" form is to be filed with the human resources department. Upon receipt of this form, human resources begins a standardized process to fill the request. Notice that such rules and procedures minimize the need for interaction and information flow between the departments or work groups. The major drawback to this method is that it works well only when intergroup activities can be anticipated ahead of time and when they recur often enough to justify establishing rules and procedures for handling them. Under conditions of high uncertainty and change, rules and procedures alone may not be adequate to guarantee effective coordination of intergroup relations.

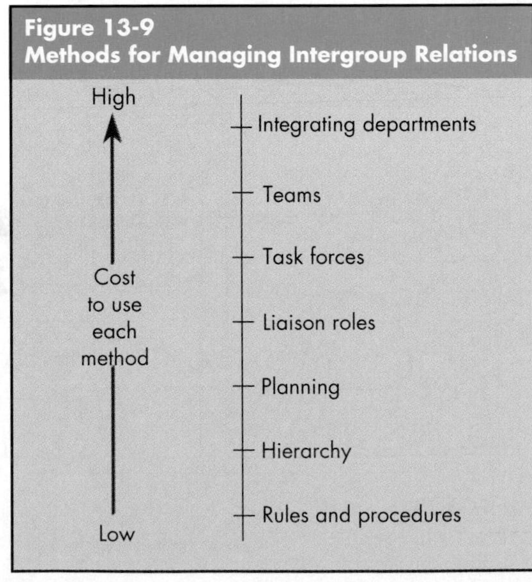

Figure 13-9
Methods for Managing Intergroup Relations

HIERARCHY If rules and procedures are inadequate, the use of the organization's hierarchy becomes the primary method for managing intergroup relations. What this means is that coordination is achieved by referring problems to a common superior higher in the organization. In a college, if the chairpersons for the English and speech communication departments can't agree on where the new courses in debate will be taught, they can take the issue to the college dean for a resolution. The major limitation to this method is that it increases demands on the common superior's time. If all differences were resolved by this means, the organization's chief executive would be overwhelmed with resolving intergroup problems, leaving little time for other matters.

PLANNING The next step up the continuum is the use of planning to facilitate coordination. If each work group has specific goals for which it is responsible, then each knows what it is supposed to do. Intergroup tasks that create problems are resolved in terms of the goals and contributions of each group. In a state motor vehicle office, each of the various work groups—testing and examinations, driving permits, vehicle registration, cashiering, and the like—has a set of goals that defines its area of responsibility and acts to reduce intergroup conflicts. Planning tends to break down as a coordination device where work groups don't have clearly defined goals or where the volume of contacts between groups is high.

LIAISON ROLES Liaison roles are specialized roles designed to facilitate communication between two interdependent work units. In one organization, where accountants and engineers had a long history of conflict, management hired an engineer with an MBA degree and several years of experience in public accounting. This person could speak the language of both groups and understood their problems. After this new liaison role was established, conflicts that had previously made it difficult for the accounting and engineering departments to coordinate their activities were significantly reduced. The major drawback to this coordination device is that there are limits to any liaison person's ability to handle information flow between interacting groups, especially where the groups are large and interactions are frequent.

TASK FORCES A task force is a temporary group made up of representatives from a number of departments. It exists only long enough to solve the problem it was created to handle. After a solution is reached, task force participants return to their normal duties.

Task forces are an excellent device for coordinating activities when the number of interacting groups is more than two or three. For example, when Audi began receiving numerous complaints about its cars accelerating when the transmission was put in reverse, even though drivers swore their feet were firmly on the brakes, the company created a task force to assess the problem and develop a solution. Representatives from design, production, legal, and engineering departments were brought together. After a solution was determined, the task force was disbanded.

TEAMS As tasks become more complex, additional problems arise during the act of execution. Previous coordination devices are no longer adequate. If the delays in decisions become long, lines of communication become ex-

Merck & Co., the world's largest pharmaceutical company, created a human resources task force after it acquired Medco Containment Services Inc., a pharmacy benefits management firm. The temporary team worked on a wide range of issues related to the firms' cultural, managerial, and business integration. For example, task force members shared information about compensation and benefits, employee relations, employee development, management approaches, and work environments. Shown here are task force members Katherine Harrison of Merck (left) and Cynthia Gilhooly of Medco.

tended, and top managers are forced to spend more time on day-to-day operations, the next response is to use permanent teams. They are typically formed around frequently occurring problems—with team members maintaining a responsibility to both their primary functional department and to the team. When the team has accomplished its task, each member returns full time to his or her functional assignment.

Boeing uses a cross-functional team to coordinate investigations of air crashes. When a Boeing aircraft is involved in an accident, the company immediately dispatches a team made up of members from various departments—including design, production, legal, and public relations. Whenever an accident occurs, designated members of the team immediately drop their current departmental tasks, go directly to the accident site, and join the other team members to begin their investigation.

INTEGRATING DEPARTMENTS When intergroup relations become too complex to be coordinated through plans, task forces, teams, and the like, organizations may create integrating departments. These are permanent departments with members formally assigned to the task of integration between two or more groups. Although they're permanent and expensive to maintain, they tend to be used when an organization has a number of groups with conflicting goals, nonroutine problems, and intergroup decisions that have a significant impact on the organization's total operations. They are also excellent devices to manage intergroup conflicts for organizations facing long-term retrenchments. When organizations are forced to shrink in size—as has recently occurred in a wide range of industries—conflicts over how cuts are to be distributed and how the smaller resource pie is to be allocated become major and ongoing dilemmas. The use of integrating departments in such cases can be an effective means for managing these intergroup relations.

Summary

It may help to put this discussion in perspective by considering methods for managing intergroup relations in terms of effectiveness.

Researchers state that the effectiveness of intergroup relations can be evaluated in terms of efficiency and quality.[50] Efficiency considers the costs to the organization of transforming an intergroup conflict into actions agreed to by the groups. Quality refers to the degree to which the outcome results in a well-defined and enduring exchange agreement. Using these definitions, the seven methods introduced in this section were presented, in order, from most efficient to least efficient. That is, ignoring outcomes for a moment, rules and procedures are less costly to implement than hierarchy, hierarchy is less costly than planning, and so forth. But, of course, keeping costs down is only one consideration. The other element of effectiveness is quality, or how well the coordination device works in facilitating interaction and reducing dysfunctional conflicts. As we've shown, the least costly alternative may not be adequate. So managers have a number of options at their disposal for managing intergroup relations. But since they tend to be cumulative, with costs rising as you move up the continuum in Figure 13-9, the most effective coordination device will be the one lowest on the continuum that facilitates an enduring integrative exchange.

Summary and Implications for Managers

Many people automatically assume that conflict is related to lower group and organizational performance. This chapter has demonstrated that this assumption is frequently incorrect. Conflict can be either constructive or destructive to the functioning of a group or unit. As shown in Figure 13-10 on page 534, levels of conflict can be either too high or too low. Either extreme hinders peformance. An optimal level is where there is enough conflict to prevent stagnation, stimulate creativity, allow tensions to be released, and initiate the seeds for change, yet not so much as to be disruptive or deter coordination of activities.

Inadequate or excessive levels of conflict can hinder the effectiveness of a group or an organization, resulting in reduced satisfaction of group members, increased absence and turnover rates, and, eventually, lower productivity. However, when conflict is at an optimal level, complacency and apathy should be minimized, motivation should be enhanced through the creation of a challenging and questioning environment with a vitality that makes work interesting, and there should be the amount of turnover needed to rid the organization of misfits and poor performers.

What advice can we give managers faced with excessive conflict and need to reduce it? Don't assume one conflict-handling intention will always be best!

Figure 13-10
Conflict and Unit Performance

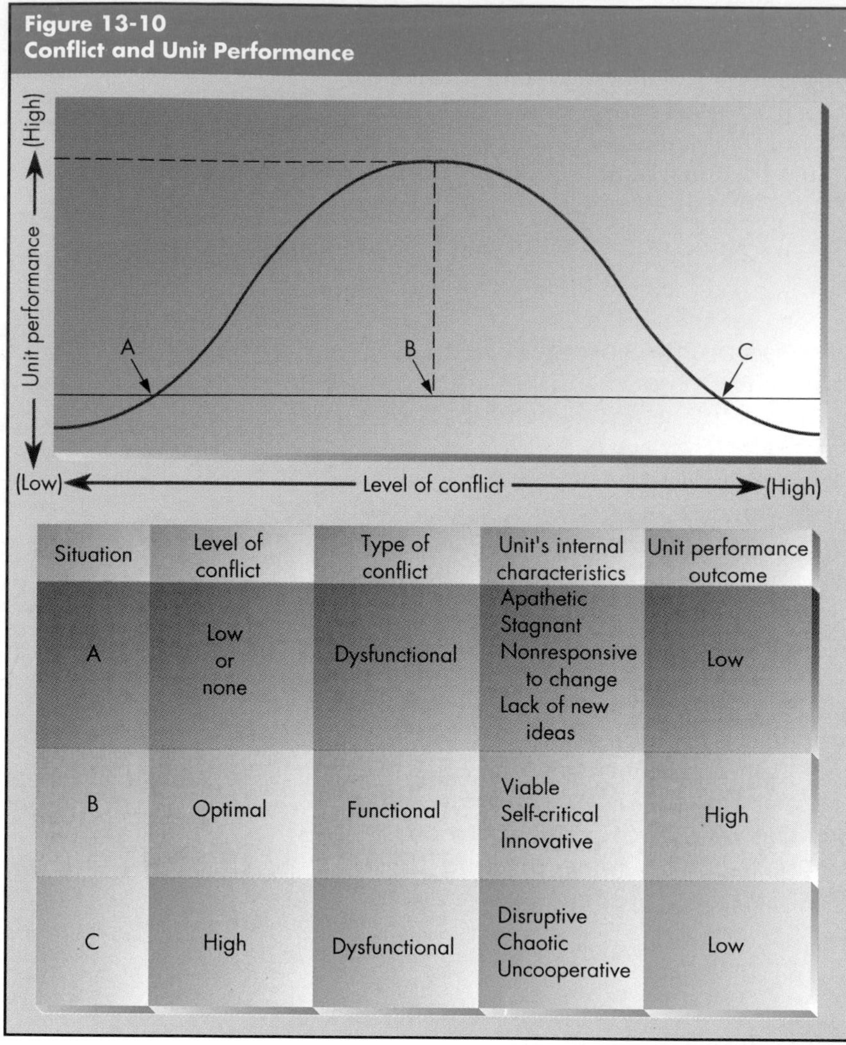

Situation	Level of conflict	Type of conflict	Unit's internal characteristics	Unit performance outcome
A	Low or none	Dysfunctional	Apathetic Stagnant Nonresponsive to change Lack of new ideas	Low
B	Optimal	Functional	Viable Self-critical Innovative	High
C	High	Dysfunctional	Disruptive Chaotic Uncooperative	Low

You should select an intention appropriate for the situation. The following provides some guidelines:[51]

- Use *competition* when quick, decisive action is vital (in emergencies); on important issues, where unpopular actions need implementing (in cost cutting, enforcing unpopular rules, discipline); on issues vital to the organization's welfare when you know you're right; and against people who take advantage of noncompetitive behavior.
- Use *collaboration* to find an integrative solution when both sets of concerns are too important to be compromised; when your objective is to learn; to merge insights from people with different perspectives; to gain commitment by incorporating concerns into a consensus; and to work through feelings that have interfered with a relationship.
- Use *avoidance* when an issue is trivial, or more important issues are pressing; when you perceive no chance of satisfying your concerns; when potential disruption outweighs the benefits of resolution; to let people cool down and regain perspective; when gathering information supersedes immediate decisions; when others can resolve the conflict more effectively; and when issues seem tangential or symptomatic of other issues.
- Use *accommodation* when you find you're wrong and to allow a better position to be heard, to learn, and to show your reasonableness; when issues are more important to others than yourself and to satisfy others and maintain cooperation; to build social credits for later issues; to minimize loss when you are outmatched and losing; when harmony and stability are especially important; and to allow subordinates to develop by learning from mistakes.
- Use *compromise* when goals are important, but not worth the effort of potential disruption of more assertive approaches; when opponents with equal power are committed to mutually exclusive goals; to achieve temporary settlements to complex issues; to arrive at expedient solutions under time pressure; and as a backup when collaboration or competition is unsuccessful.

Negotiation was shown to be an ongoing activity in groups and organizations. Distributive bargaining can resolve disputes but it often negatively affects one or more negotiators' satisfaction because it is focused on the short term and is confrontational. Integrative bargaining, in contrast, tends to provide outcomes that satisfy all parties and to build lasting relationships.

Intergroup conflicts can also affect an organization's performance. Emphasis at this level, however, has tended to focus on dysfunctional conflicts and methods for managing them. Where organizational performance depends on effective group relations and where there is high interdependence between groups, management needs to ensure that the proper integrative device is put in place. However, consistent with the interactionist perspective on conflict, there is no reason to believe all intergroup conflicts are dysfunctional. Some minimal levels of conflict can facilitate critical thinking between group members, make a group more responsive to the need for change, and provide similar benefits that can enhance group and organizational performance.

For Review

1. What are the disadvantages to conflict? What are its advantages?
2. What is the difference between functional and dysfunctional conflict? What determines functionality?
3. Under what conditions might conflict be beneficial to a group?
4. Identify various types of conflict.
5. What are the components in the conflict process model? From your own experiences, give an example of how a conflict proceeded through the five stages.
6. How could a manager stimulate conflict in his or her department?
7. What defines the settlement range in distributive bargaining?
8. Why isn't integrative bargaining more widely practiced in organizations?
9. What can you do to improve your negotiating effectiveness?
10. How do you assess the effectiveness of intergroup relations?

For Discussion

1. Do you think competition and conflict are different? Explain.
2. "Participation is an excellent method for identifying differences and resolving conflicts." Do you agree or disagree? Discuss.
3. Assume a Canadian had to negotiate a contract with someone from Spain. What problems might he or she face? What suggestions would you make to help facilitate a settlement?
4. From your own experience, describe a situation you were involved in where the conflict was dysfunctional. Describe another example from your experience where the conflict was functional. Now analyze how other parties in both conflicts might have interpreted the situation in terms of whether the conflicts were functional or dysfunctional.
5. Discuss the mechanisms for resolving intergroup conflicts between students and faculty on your campus. Are they effective? How could they be improved?

Point

Conflict Is Good for an Organization

We've made considerable progress in the last 25 years toward overcoming the negative stereotype given to conflict. Most behavioral scientists and an increasing number of practitioners now accept that the goal of effective management is not to eliminate conflict. Rather, it's to create the right intensity of conflict so as to reap its functional benefits.

Since conflict can be good for an organization, it is only logical to acknowledge that there may be times when managers will purposely want to increase its intensity. Let's briefly review how stimulating conflict can provide benefits to the organization.

- *Conflict is a means by which to bring about radical change.* It's an effective device by which management can drastically change the existing power structure, current interaction patterns, and entrenched attitudes.
- *Conflict facilitates group cohesiveness.* Whereas conflict increases hostility between groups, external threats tend to cause a group to pull together as a unit. Intergroup conflicts raise the extent to which members identify with their own group and increase feelings of solidarity, while, at the same time, internal differences and irritations dissolve.
- *Conflict improves group and organizational effectiveness.* The stimulation of conflict initiates the search for new means and goals and clears the way for innovation. The successful solution of a conflict leads to greater effectiveness, to more trust and openness, to greater attraction of members for each other, and to depersonalization of future conflicts. In fact, it has been found that as the number of minor disagreements increases, the number of major clashes decreases.
- *Conflict brings about a slightly higher, more constructive level of tension.* This enhances the chances of solving the conflicts in a way satisfactory to all parties concerned. When the level of tension is very low, the parties are not sufficiently motivated to do something about a conflict.

These points are clearly not comprehensive. As noted in the chapter, conflict provides a number of benefits to an organization. However, groups or organizations devoid of conflict are likely to suffer from apathy, stagnation, groupthink, and other debilitating diseases. In fact, more organizations probably fail because they have *too little* conflict, not because they have too much. Take a look at a list of large organizations that have failed or suffered serious financial setbacks over the past decade or two. You see names like E.F. Hutton, Sears, General Motors, Western Union, Gimbel's, Eastern Airlines, IBM, Greyhound, and Digital Computer. The common thread through these companies is that they stagnated. Their managements became complacent and unable or unwilling to facilitate change. These organizations could have benefited by having had more conflict—the functional kind.

The points presented here were influenced by E. Van de Vliert, "Escalative Intervention in Small-Group Conflicts," *Journal of Applied Behavioral Science* (Winter 1985), pp. 19–36.

counterPoint

All Conflicts Are Dysfunctional!

It may be true that conflict is an inherent part of any group or organization. It may not be possible to eliminate it completely. However, just because conflicts exist is no reason to deify them. All conflicts are dysfunctional, and it is one of management's major responsibilities to keep conflict intensity as low as humanly possible. The following points support this case.

- *The negative consequences from conflict can be devastating*. The list of negatives associated with conflict are awesome. The most obvious are increased turnover, decreased employee satisfaction, inefficiencies between work units, sabotage, labor grievances and strikes, and physical aggression.
- *Effective managers build teamwork*. A good manager builds a coordinated team. Conflict works against such an objective. A successful work group is like a successful sports team; each member knows his or her role and supports his or her teammates. When a team works well, the whole becomes greater than the sum of the parts. Management creates teamwork by minimizing internal conflicts and facilitating internal coordination.
- *Competition is good for an organization, but not conflict*. Competition and conflict should not be confused with each other. Conflict is behavior directed against another party, whereas competition is behavior aimed at obtaining a goal without interference from another party. Competition is healthy; it's the source of organizational vitality. Conflict, on the other hand, is destructive.
- *Managers who accept and stimulate conflict don't survive in organizations*. The whole argument on the value of conflict may be moot as long as the majority of senior executives in organizations view conflict from the traditional view. In the traditional view, any conflict will be seen as bad. Since the evaluation of a manager's performance is made by higher level executives, those managers who do not succeed in eliminating conflicts are likely to be appraised negatively. This, in turn, will reduce opportunities for advancement. Any manager who aspires to move up in such an environment will be wise to follow the traditional view and eliminate any outward signs of conflict. Failure to follow this advice might result in the premature departure of the manager.

Learning About Yourself Exercise

What Is Your Primary Conflict-Handling Intention?

Indicate how often you rely on each of the following tactics by circling the number you feel is most appropriate.

	Rarely				Always
1. I argue my case with my coworkers to show the merits of my position.	1	2	3	4	5
2. I negotiate with my coworkers so that a compromise can be reached.	1	2	3	4	5
3. I try to satisfy the expectations of my coworkers.	1	2	3	4	5
4. I try to investigate an issue with my coworkers to find a solution acceptable to us.	1	2	3	4	5
5. I am firm in pursuing my side of the issue.	1	2	3	4	5
6. I attempt to avoid being put on the spot and try to keep my conflict with my coworkers to myself.	1	2	3	4	5
7. I hold on to my solution to a problem.	1	2	3	4	5
8. I use give-and-take so a compromise can be made.	1	2	3	4	5
9. I exchange accurate information with my coworkers to solve a problem together.	1	2	3	4	5
10. I avoid open discussion of my differences with my coworkers.	1	2	3	4	5
11. I accommodate the wishes of my coworkers.	1	2	3	4	5
12. I try to bring all our concerns out in the open so the issues can be resolved in the best possible way.	1	2	3	4	5
13. I propose a middle ground for breaking deadlocks.	1	2	3	4	5
14. I go along with the suggestions of my coworkers.	1	2	3	4	5
15. I try to keep my disagreements with my coworkers to myself in order to avoid hard feelings.	1	2	3	4	5

Turn to page A-29 for scoring directions and key.

Source: This is an abbreviated version of a 35-item instrument described in M. A. Rahim, "A Measure of Styles of Handling Interpersonal Conflict," *Academy of Management Journal* (June 1983), pp. 368–76.

Working With Others Exercise

A Negotiation Role Play

This role play is designed to help you develop your negotiating skills. The class is to break into pairs. One person will play the role of Terry, the department supervisor. The other person will play Dale, Terry's boss.

The Situation: Terry and Dale work for Nike in Portland, Oregon. Terry supervises a research laboratory. Dale is the manager of research and development (R&D). Terry and Dale are former college runners who have worked for Nike for more than six years. Dale has been Terry's boss for two years.

One of Terry's employees, Lisa Roland, has greatly impressed Terry. Lisa was hired 11 months ago. She is 24 years old and holds a master's degree in mechanical engineering. Her entry-level salary was $32,500 a year. She was told by Terry that, in accordance with corporation policy, she would receive an initial performance evaluation at six months and a comprehensive review after one year. Based on her performance record, Lisa was told she could expect a salary adjustment at the time of the one-year evaluation.

Terry's evaluation of Lisa after six months was very positive. Terry commented on the long hours Lisa was putting in, her cooperative spirit, the fact that others in the lab enjoyed working with her, and that she was making an immediate positive contribution to the project she had been assigned. Now that Lisa's first anniversary is coming up, Terry has again reviewed Lisa's performance. Terry thinks Lisa may be the best new person the R&D group has ever hired. After only a year, Terry has rated Lisa as the number 3 ranked performer in a department of 11.

Salaries in the department vary greatly. Terry, for instance, has a basic salary of $57,000, plus eligibility for a bonus that might add another $5,000 to $8,000 a year. The salary range of the 11 department members is $26,400 to $51,350. The lowest salary is a recent hire with a bachelor's degree in physics. The two people that Terry has rated above Lisa earn base salaries of $47,700 and $51,350. They're both 27 years old and have been at Nike for three and four years, respectively. The median salary in Terry's department is $42,660.

Terry's Role: You want to give Lisa a big raise. Although she's young, she has proven to be an excellent addition to the department. You don't want to lose her. More importantly, she knows in general what other people in the department are earning and she thinks she's underpaid. The company typically gives one-year raises of 5 percent, although 10 percent is not unusual and 20 to 30 percent increases have been approved on occasion. You'd like to get Terry as large an increase as Dale will approve.

Dale's Role: All your supervisors typically try to squeeze you for as much money as they can for their people. You understand this because you did the same thing when you were a supervisor. But your boss wants to keep a lid on costs. He wants you to keep raises for recent hires generally in the 5 to 8 percent range. In fact, he's sent a memo to all managers and supervisors saying this. However, your boss is also very concerned with equity and paying people what they're worth. You feel assured he will support any salary recommendation you make, as long as it can be justified. Your goal, consistent with cost reduction, is to keep salary increases as low as possible.

The Negotiation: Terry has a meeting scheduled with Dale to discuss Lisa's performance review and salary adjustment. Take a couple of minutes to think through the facts in this exercise and to prepare a strategy. Then you have up to 15 minutes to conduct your negotiation. When your negotiation is complete, the class will compare the various strategies used and pair outcomes.

Ethical Dilemma Exercise

Is Stimulating Conflict Unethical?

The research demonstrates that conflict can, at times, actually improve a group or an organization's performance. So managers may find themselves in situations where the conflict level in their unit is too low and in need of stimulation. In spite of this conclusion, North Americans tend to view conflict negatively. They prefer cooperation to conflict. As a result, they are likely to take a dim view of someone who purposely seeks to increase conflict levels, regardless of how good that person's intentions may be.

These opposing facts—the positive potential of conflict for organizational performance and the negative view of it held by most North Americans—place U.S. and Canadian managers in a difficult position. Do they try to stifle all conflicts in order to stay in step with society's preferences? Or do they ignore societal norms and do what is best for their organizations? Managers who decide in favor of the organization then face another ethical issue: Is it wrong to deceive others?

Since employees are likely to negatively interpret any efforts to overtly stimulate conflict, managers may be tempted to mask their intentions. Why? Because managers aren't likely to endear themselves to their staffs by admitting they are "purposely trying to increase conflict levels."

Is it unethical to try to increase conflict for organizational ends? Is it wrong to do so by masking one's true intentions? What do *you* think?

Tip Says "No Way"

CASE INCIDENT

Marc Lattoni is supervisor of an eight-member cost accounting department in a large metals fabricating plant in Albuquerque, New Mexico. He was promoted about six months ago to his supervisory position after only a year as an accountant, largely because of his education: He has an MBA, whereas no one else in the department has a college degree. The transition to supervisor went smoothly, and there were hardly any problems until this morning.

The need for another cost accountant in the office had been obvious to Marc for over a month. Overtime had become commonplace and was putting a strain on department members as well as the department's budget (overtime was computed at time and a half). Marc had his eye on one particular individual in production control who he thought would fit his needs quite well. He had talked with the production control supervisor and the personnel manager, and the three had agreed a young African-American clerk in production named Ralph might be a good candidate to move into cost accounting and help with the increased departmental workload. Ralph had been with the company for eight months, shown above average potential, and was only six units shy of a bachelor's degree (with a major in accounting) that he was earning at night at the University of New Mexico.

Marc had discussed the cost accounting position with Ralph earlier in the week, and Ralph had been enthusiastic. Marc had said that, while he could make no promises, he thought he would recommend Ralph for the job. However, Marc emphasized it would be a week or so before a final decision was made and the announcement made official.

When Marc came into his office this morning, he was confronted by Tip O'Malley, a 58-year-old cost accountant who has been at the plant since its opening over 24 years ago. Tip, born and raised in a small town in the Deep South, had heard a rumor that Ralph would be coming up and working in the cost department. Tip minced no words: "I've never worked with a black and I never will." Tip's face was red, and it was obvious this was an emotionally charged issue for him. His short one-way confrontation closed with the statement: "I have no intention of working in the same department as that fellow."

Questions

1. What is the source of this conflict?
2. Assume you're Marc. Which conflict-handling intention is most appropriate for this situation? Why?
3. Describe, in detail, what you would say to Tip.
4. Do you think your approach has permanently resolved this conflict? Explain.

Conflict in the New York City Schools

Joseph Fernandez, chancellor of the New York City school system, was fired in 1993, in spite of his record for cutting costs and improving student performance.

Fernandez was born in New York City. His family was poor. He dropped out of high school and joined the Air Force. At some point, he managed to turn his life around. He got his high school diploma and eventually his doctorate in education. Fernandez rose to prominence as head of the Miami school system. Based on his success in Miami, New York City lured him away to head its school system in 1990.

By most objective standards, Fernandez made improvements in the New York system. He cut bureaucracy by 30 percent, math and science test scores of students rose, and dropout rates leveled off. But his successes couldn't offset the controversial stands he took. Some battles you confront, and some you walk away from. Fernandez apparently chose to take on the wrong battles.

Fernandez argues that problems in schools today are different than they were 20 or 25 years ago. "We have to deal with bias and intolerance, AIDS. We have to deal with children that don't come from the traditional family of two parents . . . plus violence. It's different from the '50s and the '40s, where chewing gum or talking out of turn was the big problem. We're dealing with some real serious issues now."

Fernandez's solution was to confront some of these social issues. For instance, he promoted AIDS education, availability of condoms in the schools, and programs that taught first and second grade children tolerance for gays and lesbians.

School board members did not look favorably on a lot of what Fernandez was trying to do. The ousted chancellor sees the decision in political terms. He thinks the board doesn't want schools to deal with social issues. His critics agree, but add that Fernandez's arrogance was also a major factor in their decision. Fernandez's response: "Look, I am what I am. I think that most people that have worked with me will tell you that I'm impatient and I think that's a good characteristic. I don't think it's a bad one. I don't think we can afford to lose another generation of kids."

Questions

1. What's the source of this conflict?
2. If you had been a concerned member of the school board and wanted to resolve this conflict prior to Fernandez's firing, what actions might you have taken?

Source: "Joseph Fernandez, Fired NY School Chancellor," *World News Tonight* (February 12, 1993).

Suggestions for Further Reading

HALL L.(ed.), *Negotiation: Strategies for Mutual Gain* (Newbury Park, CA: Sage, 1993).

JACKSON, J.W., "Realistic Group Conflict Theory: A Review and Evaluation of the Theoretical and Empirical Literature," *The Psychological Record* (Summer 1993), pp. 395–414.

KRAMER, R.M., "Intergroup Relations and Organizational Dilemmas," in L.L. Cummings and B.M. Staw (eds.), *Research in Organizational Behavior*, Vol. 13 (Greenwich, CT: JAI Press, 1991), pp. 191–228.

NEALE, M.A., and M.H. BAZERMAN, "Negotiating Rationally: The Power and Impact of the Negotiator's Frame," *Academy of Management Executive* (August 1992), pp. 42–51.

PUTNAM, L.L., and M.E. ROLOFF (eds.), *Communication and Negotiation* (Newbury Park, CA: Sage, 1992).

RAHIM, M.A., *Theory and Research in Conflict Management* (New York: Praeger, 1990).

SITKIN, S.B., and R.J. BIES, "Social Accounts in Conflict Situations: Using Explanations to Manage Conflict," *Human Relations* (March 1993), pp. 349–70.

STEVENS, C.K., A.G. BAVETTA, and M.E. GIST, "Gender Differences in the Acquisition of Salary Negotiation Skills: The Role of Goals, Efficacy, and Perceived Control," *Journal of Applied Psychology* (October 1993), pp. 723–35.

TJOSVOLD, D., *The Conflict Positive Organization* (Reading, MA: Addison-Wesley, 1991).

TUNG, R., "Handshakes Across the Sea: Cross-Cultural Negotiating for Business Success," *Organizational Dynamics* (Winter 1991), pp. 30–40.

Notes

[1] J. Barron, "Shea & Gould Partners Vote to Break Up the Law Firm," *New York Times* (January 29, 1994), p. 17; and M. Geyelin and E. Felsenthal, "Irreconcilable Differences Force Shea & Gould Closure," *Wall Street Journal* (January 31, 1994), p. B1.

[2] See, for instance, C.F. Fink, "Some Conceptual Difficulties in the Theory of Social Conflict," *Journal of Conflict Resolution* (December 1968), pp. 412–60.

[3] L.L. Putnam and M.S. Poole, "Conflict and Negotiation," in F.M. Jablin, L.L. Putnam, K.H. Roberts, and L.W. Porter (eds.), *Handbook of Organizational Communication: An Interdisciplinary Perspective* (Newbury Park, CA: Sage, 1987), pp. 549–99.

[4] K.W. Thomas, "Conflict and Negotiation Processes in Organizations," in M.D. Dunnette and L.M. Hough (eds.), *Handbook of Industrial and Organizational Psychology*, 2nd ed., Vol. 3 (Palo Alto, CA: Consulting Psychologists Press, 1992), pp. 651–717.

[5] G. Smith, "How to Lose Friends and Influence No One," *Business Week* (January 25, 1993), pp. 42–43.

[6] This section is based on S.P. Robbins, *Managing Organizational Conflict: A Nontraditional Approach* (Englewood Cliffs, NJ: Prentice Hall, 1974), pp. 31–55.

[7] L.R. Pondy, "Organizational Conflict: Concepts and Models," *Administrative Science Quarterly* (September 1967), p. 302.

[8] See, for instance, R.L. Pinkley, "Dimensions of Conflict Frame: Disputant Interpretations of Conflict," *Journal of Applied Psychology* (April 1990), pp. 117–26; and R.L. Pinkley and G.B. Northcraft, "Conflict Frames of Reference: Implications for Dispute Processes and Outcomes," *Academy of Management Journal* (February 1994), pp. 193–205.

[9] R. Kumar, "Affect, Cognition and Decision Making in Negotiations: A Conceptual Integration," in M.A. Rahim (ed.), *Managing Conflict: An Integrative Approach* (New York: Praeger, 1989), pp. 185–94.

[10] Ibid.

[11] P.J.D. Carnevale and A.M. Isen, "The Influence of Positive Affect and Visual Access on the Discovery of Integrative Solutions in Bilateral Negotiations," *Organizational Behavior and Human Decision Processes* (February 1986), pp. 1–13.

[12] Thomas, "Conflict and Negotiation Processes in Organizations."

[13] Ibid.

[14] See R.J. Sternberg and L.J. Soriano, "Styles of Conflict Resolution," *Journal of Personality and Social Psychology* (July 1984), pp. 115–26; and R.A. Baron, "Personality and Organizational Conflict: Effects of the Type A Behavior Pattern and Self-Monitoring," *Organizational Behavior and Human Decision Processes* (October 1989), pp. 281–96.

[15] Thomas, "Conflict and Negotiation Processes in Organizations."

[16] See, for instance, R.A. Cosier and C.R. Schwenk, "Agreement and Thinking Alike: Ingredients for Poor Decisions," *Academy of Management Executive* (February 1990), pp. 69–74.

[17] See, for instance, C.J. Loomis, "Dinosaurs?," *Fortune* (May 3, 1993), pp. 36–42.

[18] I. L. Janis, *Victims of Groupthink* (Boston: Houghton Mifflin, 1972).

[19] P. Binzen and J.R. Daughen, *Wreck of the Penn Central* (Boston: Little, Brown, 1971).

[20] V.A. Thompson, "Bureaucracy and Innovation," *Administrative Science Quarterly* (March 1965), pp. 1–20.

[21] J. Hall and M.S. Williams, "A Comparison of Decision-Making Performances in Established and Ad-Hoc Groups," *Journal of Personality and Social Psychology* (February 1966), p. 217.

[22] R.L. Hoffman, "Homogeneity of Member Personality and Its Effect on Group Problem-Solving," *Journal of Abnormal and Social Psychology* (January 1959), pp. 27–32; and R.L. Hoffman and N.R. F. Maier, "Quality and Acceptance of Problem Solutions by Members of Homogeneous and Heterogeneous Groups," *Journal of Abnormal and Social Psychology* (March 1961), pp. 401–407.

[23] See T.H. Cox and S. Blake, "Managing Cultural Diversity: Implications for Organizational Competitiveness," *Academy of Management Executive* (August 1991), pp. 45–56; T.H. Cox, S.A. Lobel, and P.L. McLeod, "Effects of Ethnic Group Cultural Differences on Cooperative Behavior on a Group Task," *Academy of Management Journal* (December 1991), pp. 827–47; P.L. McLeod and S.A. Lobel, "The Effects of Ethnic Diversity on Idea Generation in Small Groups," paper presented at the Annual Academy of Management Conference, Las Vegas, August 1992; and C. Kirchmeyer and A. Cohen, "Multicultural Groups: Their Performance and Reactions with Constructive Conflict," *Group & Organization Management* (June 1992), pp. 153–70.

[24] R.E. Hill, "Interpersonal Compatibility and Work Group Performance Among Systems Analysts: An Empirical Study," *Proceedings of the Seventeenth Annual Midwest Academy of Management Conference* (Kent, OH, April 1974), pp. 97–110.

[25] D.C. Pelz and F. Andrews, *Scientists in Organizations* (New York: John Wiley, 1966).

[26] H. Lenk, "Konflikt und Leistung in Spitzensportmannschafter: Isozometrische Strukturen von WettKampfachtern in Ruden," *Soziale Welt*, Vol. 15 (1964), pp. 307–43.

[27] A. Tannenbaum, "Control Structure and Union Functions," *American Journal of Sociology* (May 1956), pp. 127–40.

[28] For an excellent source of studies that focus on the dysfunctional consequences of conflict, see the *Journal of Conflict Resolution*.

[29] K. Jehn, "Enhancing Effectiveness: An Investigation of Advantages and Disadvantages of Value Based Intragroup Conflict," *International Journal of Conflict Management* (July 1994), pp. 223–38.

[30] This section is based on F. Sommerfield, "Paying the Troops to Buck the System," *Business Month* (May 1990), pp. 77–79; W. Kiechel III, "How to Escape the Echo Chamber," *Fortune* (June 18, 1990), pp. 129–30; and B. Angelo, "Musical Chairs in Maryland," *Time* (August 26, 1991), p. 21. See also E. van de Vliert and C.K.W. de Dreu, "Optimizing Performance by Conflict Stimulation," *International Journal of Conflict Management*, forthcoming.

[31] J.A. Wall, Jr., *Negotiation: Theory and Practice* (Glenview, IL: Scott, Foresman, 1985).

[32] R.E. Walton and R.B. McKersie, *A Behavioral Theory of Labor Negotiations: An Analysis of a Social Interaction System* (New York: McGraw-Hill, 1965).

[33] Thomas, "Conflict and Negotiation Processes in Organizations."

[34] This model is based on R.J. Lewicki, "Bargaining and Negotiation," *Exchange: The Organizational Behavior Teaching Journal*, Vol. 6, No. 2 (1981), pp. 39–40; and B.S. Moskal, "The Art of the Deal," *Industry Week* (January 18, 1993), p. 23.

[35] M.H. Bazerman and M.A. Neale, *Negotiating Rationally* (New York: Free Press, 1992), pp. 67–68.

[36] Ibid.

[37] J.A. Wall, Jr. and M.W. Blum, "Negotiations," *Journal of Management* (June 1991), pp. 276–78.

[38] These suggestions are based on J.A. Wall, Jr. and M.W. Blum, "Negotiations," pp. 278–82.

[39] See N.J. Adler, *International Dimensions of Organizational Behavior*, 2nd ed. (Boston: PWS-Kent, 1991), pp. 179–217.

[40] K.D. Schmidt, *Doing Business in France* (Menlo Park, CA: SRI International, 1987).

[41] S. Lubman, "Round and Round," *Wall Street Journal* (December 10, 1993), p. R3.

[42] E.S. Glenn, D. Witmeyer, and K.A. Stevenson, "Cultural Styles of Persuasion," *Journal of Intercultural Relations* (Fall 1977), pp. 52–66.

[43] J. Graham, "The Influence of Culture on Business Negotiations," *Journal of International Business Studies* (Spring 1985), pp. 81–96.

[44] J.A. Wall, Jr. and M.W. Blum, "Negotiations," pp. 283–87.

[45] J.M. Brett and J.K. Rognes, "Intergroup Relations in Organizations," in P.S. Goodman and associates (eds.), *Designing Effective Work Groups* (San Francisco: Jossey-Bass, 1986), p. 205.

[46] J. D. Thompson, *Organizations in Action* (New York: McGraw-Hill, 1967), pp. 54–55.

[47] C. Perrow, "A Framework for the Comparative Analysis of Organizations," *American Sociological Review* (April 1967), pp. 194–208.

[48] P.R. Lawrence and J.W. Lorsch, *Organization and Environment* (Homewood, IL: R.D. Irwin, 1969), pp. 34–39.

[49] J. Galbraith, *Designing Complex Organizations* (Reading, MA: Addison-Wesley, 1973).

[50] Brett and Rognes, "Intergroup Relations in Organizations," p. 212.

[51] K.W. Thomas, "Toward Multidimensional Values in Teaching: The Example of Conflict Behaviors," *Academy of Management Review* (July 1977), p. 487.

PROGRESSIVE CASE
◆ PART THREE ◆
THE GROUP

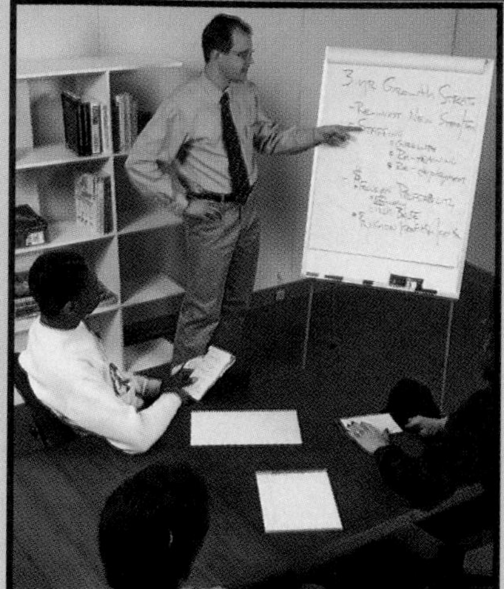

ROB PANCO: MANAGING GROUPS AND TEAMS

"I'm a big fan of teams," says Rob Panco. "When I came to Aslett, things were not organized as well as they could have been. Of course, we were quite a bit smaller then. I decided to use teams as an organizing device for three reasons. First, functional specialization made teaming easy. I could take the separators or desk-top-publishing people and group them into common teams very easily. Second, teams allowed me greater control. And third, teams are good for the kind of work we do. We work around projects. I thought cross-functional teams would be an effective way for us to meet our project goals." When asked if he had any people who weren't team players and, if so, how he handled it, Rob said, "I inherited one guy, Nick, who couldn't work well with others. No one wanted to work with him. I told him he didn't have to be a team member but he had a responsibility to respect other projects. I isolated him as a team of one! Nick's a high maintenance person for me. He has a talent I can't duplicate. He hurts morale when he cops his attitude. But I need him and he's respected around here for his job competence."

On the subject of communication, Rob noted that he and his people are making increased use of electronics. Employees use an internal network to E-mail messages between each other. Rob works with a consultant in the United Kingdom and communicates regularly with him via fax and E-mail as well as the telephone. But Rob is not an uncritical supporter of E-mail. "At AT&T I got so much E-mail, I couldn't read it all. It can become a party line with a lot of noise. From my standpoint, I think E-mail works well as a motivation tool. I can use it on Monday, for instance, to summarize the previous week's performance and to set this week's goals." The UK example also reminded Rob of internal communication problems created by employees who come from different cultures. One of his British employees, for example, has difficulty with the looseness and informality of his American peers. He views them as behaving "less than proper."

On leadership, Rob had some insightful comparisons between his managerial roles at AT&T versus Aslett. "At AT&T, I had responsibility but no authority because I managed peers. To be effective, I had to rely a lot on horse trading. Now I have real authority." But he's had some problems adjusting to this authority. "I'm friendly by nature. I have trouble creating distance between myself and my staff. This apparently confuses people. They'll say, 'One minute Rob is my pal and then the next minute he's asking me where the pages are or why I missed a deadline.' I haven't figured out how to walk this tightrope very well." Rob also used the topic of leadership to explain his philosophy on empowering employees. "Realistically, there are some people I just can't delegate to. So I practice *selective* empowerment. But I think it's critical for our people to take the ball and run with it. This is because empowerment is necessary if we're to continue growing. I look at empowerment as an alternative to adding another level of management."

While Rob doesn't consider himself a political animal, he clearly understands the importance of building a power base. For example, he noted that selection to the Leadership Continuity Program at AT&T gave him the clout to get the transfers he wanted when he wanted them. It also gave him influence with managers above him. But at a cost: Peers were jealous and it created conflicts with them. When asked if he did anything to increase his power at AT&T, he quickly admitted to volunteering for committees and visible assignments. "Early in my career at AT&T, a boss told me to volunteer to work with upper managers. I asked 'why?' He said, 'It'll help at performance appraisal time. The people who will be evaluating you and ranking you against others will know who you are.'"

Rob made a point to contrast politicking at Aslett and AT&T. "Look, politics occur everywhere. A certain amount is appropriate. At AT&T, however, it was individually oriented. People kissed up to their boss to improve their personal status—to get a promotion or a salary increase. At Aslett, politics is more team directed. It's used to get attention for a team or to protect the team's self-interest."

Rob is currently in the process of developing a company policy on sexual harassment. "I think this is a really important issue. I took a course on the subject, then I held a couple of meetings to talk about what I learned." Rob's plan is to first set the policy; then conduct employee training sessions on the subject; and finally have everyone sign a copy of the sexual harassment policy, indicating they understand and accept it.

On the topic of how Rob handles conflict in his organization, there was an obvious linkage back to his decision-making style. "When I see conflicts bubbling up, I sit back and analyze them. I don't do anything hastily. I want to think before I act. You can be too confrontational and make a situation worse. I want to get all the facts. So I'll talk privately with each individual involved in the conflict and ask him or her, 'What's going on?' Then I validate the information. Only then will I bring the parties together and try to find a resolution."

Questions

1. Evaluate Rob's solution to the problem of an employee who doesn't work well on teams.
2. Is there a conflict between being "boss" and being friendly with your staff? Discuss.
3. What do you think Rob means when he says empowerment can be an alternative to adding another level of management?
4. Is team-based politicking more functional to an organization than individually based politicking? What do you think?
5. What do you think of Rob's conflict-handling orientation?

Boston Chicken's owners created a flat, decentralized structure based on the power of information. Regional managers use networking software to collaborate on team projects like changing menus, planning restaurant expansion, and handling customer complaints.

14

FOUNDATIONS OF ORGANIZATION STRUCTURE

CHAPTER OUTLINE

LEARNING OBJECTIVES

After studying this chapter, you should be able to:

1. Identify the six key elements that define an organization's structure.
2. Describe a simple structure.
3. Explain the characteristics of a bureaucracy.
4. Describe a matrix organization.
5. Explain the characteristics of a "virtual" organization.
6. Summarize why managers want to create boundaryless organizations.
7. List the factors that favor different organization structures.
8. Explain the behavioral implications of different organizational designs.

The dinosaur's eloquent lesson is that if some bigness is good, an overabundance of bigness is not necessarily better.
E.A. JOHNSTON

Oticon A/S is the third largest hearing aid manufacturer in the world.[1] In 1987, according to the Danish firm's managing director, Lars Kolind, Oticon was also one of the world's most conservative and aristocratic companies. "We had hardwood paneling on the walls, Jaguars in the garage, and the steepest of hierarchies," says Kolind. But this conservatism and rigid structure was contributing to the company's demise. In 1987 alone, Oticon lost 40 million DKK.

Oticon's competitors were large and aggressive. As noted by one executive, "It would be difficult for us to develop chips for digital sound processing better than Sony, but we had to try to do something better." Management decided "something better" would be to develop a unique organizational structure that would give Oticon a flexibility its competitors didn't have. Among the changes that were implemented were a redesign of jobs, the elimination of departments, and the creation of flexible work spaces.

Today, people at Oticon no longer have single jobs. They have a constantly changing set of jobs they choose for themselves. For example, an engineer might have a primary job designing new integrated circuits, but also might sign up to do a market study or prepare the company newsletter. The company now benefits from the part-time use of many skills that were unavailable with the old structure.

Oticon's management eliminated all the functional departments at the company's head office. They did away with all titles and created a structure with no bosses and no managers. In the place of departments and formal bosses are teams that work for a common cause. To keep the chaos under control, management makes sure everyone knows the company's plans and strategies. With everyone united behind a single vision, management claims the chances are significantly increased that actions taken independently will align with and support each other.

Oticon's physical office layout has almost been completely revamped. Everyone now has exactly the same amount of space, and no one has a fixed desk. Everyone has a portable work station—a low file cabinet with a desk drawer on wheels. To work together, a project team chooses a number of adjacent tables, and each member wheels his or her work station up to one of the tables, which then becomes that person's "desk." On each table there is already a computer that gives whoever signs on access to personal files, E-mail, and company databases. And since everyone carries mobile phones, people can be reached regardless of where they are.

Coffee bars are sprinkled throughout Oticon's headquarters with counters for "stand-up meetings" (see photo on page 549), because according to a senior executive, "people think and work better, faster, and more flexibly while they're standing up."

The new structure gives Oticon tremendous flexibility. For instance, it has resulted in cutting the time-to-market on new products in half. Sales grew 13 percent in 1992 and another 23 percent in 1993; meanwhile, profits climbed to industry records in 1993 and 1994. And employees seem to like the new structure. Despite a reduction in staff of 15 percent, attitude surveys indicate that employee satisfaction is at record highs.

The theme of this chapter is that organizations have different structures and that these structures have a bearing on employee attitudes and behavior. More specifically, in the following pages, we define the key components that make up an organization's structure, present half a dozen or so structural design options which managers can choose from, identify the contingency factors that make certain structural designs preferable in varying situations, and conclude by considering the different effects of various organizational designs on employee behavior.

What Is Organizational Structure

organizational structure How job tasks are formally divided, grouped, and coordinated.

An **organizational structure** defines how job tasks are formally divided, grouped, and coordinated. Oticon, for instance, changed its structure from one where employees performed narrow specialized tasks in separate departments, under the direct guidance of a department manager, to a team-based structure that did away with functional departments and managers.

Managers need to address six key elements when they design their organization's structure: work specialization, departmentalization, chain of command, span of control, centralization and decentralization, and formalization.[2]

Table 14-1 Six Key Questions That Managers Need to Answer in Designing the Proper Organization Structure

The Key Question	The Answer Is Provided by
1. To what degree are tasks subdivided into separate jobs?	*Work specialization*
2. On what basis will jobs be grouped together?	*Departmentalization*
3. To whom do individuals and groups report?	*Chain of command*
4. How many individuals can a manager efficiently and effectively direct?	*Span of control*
5. Where does decision-making authority lie?	*Centralization and decentralization*
6. To what degree will there be rules and regulations to direct employees and managers?	*Formalization*

Table 14-1 presents each of these elements as answers to an important structural question. The following sections describe these six elements of structure.

Work Specialization

Early in this century, Henry Ford became rich and famous by building automobiles on an assembly line. Every Ford worker was assigned a specific, repetitive task. For instance, one person would just put on the right-front wheel and someone else would install the right-front door. By breaking jobs up into small standardized tasks, which could be performed over and over again, Ford was able to produce cars at the rate of one every ten seconds while using employees who had relatively limited skills.

Ford demonstrated that work can be performed more efficiently if employees are allowed to specialize. Today we use the term **work specialization**, or *division of labor* to describe the degree to which tasks in the organization are subdivided into separate jobs.

work specialization
The degree to which tasks in the organization are subdivided into separate jobs.

The essence of work specialization is that, rather than an entire job being done by one individual, it is broken down into a number of steps, each step being completed by a separate individual. In essence, individuals specialize in doing part of an activity rather than the entire activity.

By the late 1940s, most manufacturing jobs in industrialized countries were being done with high work specialization. Management saw this as a way to make the most efficient use of its employees' skills. In most organizations, some tasks require highly developed skills; others can be performed by the untrained. If all workers were engaged in each step of, say, an organization's manufacturing process, all would have to have the skills necessary to perform both the most demanding and the least demanding jobs. As a result, except when performing the most skilled or highly sophisticated tasks, employees would be working below their skill levels. And since skilled workers are paid more than unskilled workers and their wages tend to reflect their highest level of skill, paying highly skilled workers to do easy tasks represents an inefficient usage of organizational resources.

Managers also looked for other efficiencies that could be achieved through work specialization. Employee skills at performing a task successfully increase through repetition. Less time is spent in changing tasks, in putting away one's tools and equipment from a prior step in the work process, and in getting ready for another. Equally important, training for specialization is more

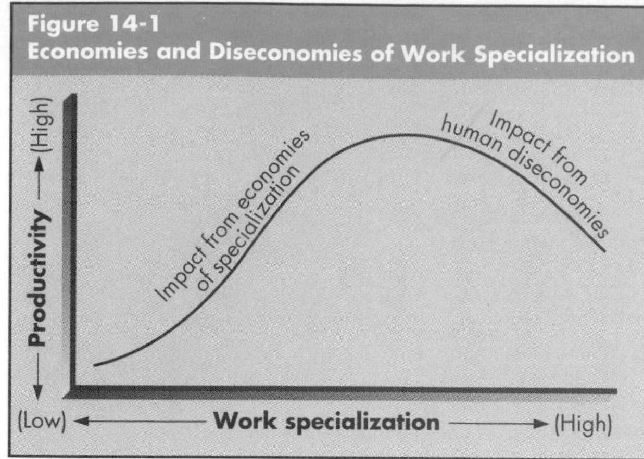

efficient from the organization's perspective. It is easier and less costly to find and train workers to do specific and repetitive tasks. This is especially true of highly sophisticated and complex operations. For example, could Cessna produce one Citation jet a year if one person had to build the entire plane alone? Finally, work specialization increases efficiency and productivity by encouraging the creation of special inventions and machinery.

For much of the first half of this century, managers viewed work specialization as an unending source of increased productivity. And they were probably right. Because specialization was not widely practiced, its introduction almost always generated higher productivity. But by the 1960s, increasing evidence showed a good thing can be carried too far. The point had been reached in some jobs where the human diseconomies from specialization—which surface as boredom, fatigue, stress, low productivity, poor quality, increased absenteeism, and high turnover—more than offset the economic advantages (see Figure 14-1). In such cases, productivity could be increased by enlarging, rather than narrowing, the scope of job activities. Additionally, a number of companies found that by giving employees a variety of activities to do, allowing them to do a whole and complete job, and by putting them into teams with interchangeable skills, they often achieved significantly higher output with increased employee satisfaction.

EDS Corp., a wholly-owned subsidiary of General Motors, coordinates and directs the voice, video, and data communications for more than 7,000 customers around the world. The information technology services provided by management information specialists at the company's Information Management Center (shown here) increase the efficiency and productivity of EDS and its customers. Specialization has helped EDS evolve from a local Dallas company to a global corporation.

Most managers today neither see work specialization as obsolete nor an unending source of increased productivity. Rather, managers recognize the economies it provides in certain types of jobs and the problems it creates when it's carried too far. You'll find, for example, high work specialization being used by McDonald's to efficiently make and sell hamburgers and fries, and by medical specialists in most health maintenance organizations. However, companies like Oticon A/S and the Saturn Corporation have had success by broadening the scope of jobs and reducing specialization.

Departmentalization

Once you've divided jobs up through work specialization, you need to group these jobs together so common tasks can be coordinated. The basis by which jobs are grouped together is called **departmentalization**.

departmentalization
The basis by which jobs are grouped together.

One of the most popular ways to group activities is by *functions* performed. A manufacturing manager might organize his or her plant by separating engineering, accounting, manufacturing, personnel, and purchasing specialists into common departments. Of course, departmentalization by function can be used in all types of organizations. Only the functions change to reflect the organization's objectives and activities. A hospital might have departments devoted to research, patient care, accounting, and so forth. A professional football franchise might have departments for player personnel, ticket sales, and travel and accommodations. The major advantage to this type of grouping is obtaining efficiencies from putting like specialists together. Functional departmentalization seeks to achieve economies of scale by placing people with common skills and orientations into common units.

Tasks can also be departmentalized by the type of *product* the organization produces. At Sun Petroleum Products, for instance, each of the three major product areas in the corporation (fuels, lubricants and waxes, and chemicals) is placed under the authority of a vice president who is a specialist in, and responsible for, everything having to do with his or her product line. Each, for example, would have his or her own manufacturing and marketing group. The major advantage to this type of grouping is increased accountability for product performance, since all activities related to a specific product are under the direction of a single manager. If an organization's activities are service rather than product related, each service would be autonomously grouped. For instance, an accounting firm could have departments for tax, management consulting, auditing, and the like. Each would offer a common array of services under the direction of a product or service manager.

Another way to departmentalize is on the basis of *geography* or territory. The sales function, for instance, may have western, southern, midwestern, and eastern regions. Each of these regions is, in effect, a department organized around geography. If an organization's customers are scattered over a large geographic area, then this form of departmentalization can be valuable.

At a Reynolds Metals aluminum tubing plant in upstate New York, production is organized into five departments: casting; press; tubing; finishing; and inspect, pack, and ship. This is an example of *process* departmentalization because each department specializes in one specific phase in the production of aluminum tubing. The metal is cast in huge furnaces; sent to the press department, where it is extruded into aluminum pipe; transferred to the tube mill, where it is stretched into various sizes and shapes of tubing; moved to finishing, where it is cut and cleaned; and finally arrives in the inspect, pack, and ship department. Since each process requires different skills, this method offers a basis for the homogeneous categorizing of activities.

Process departmentalization can be used for processing customers as well as products. If you've ever been to a state motor vehicle office to get a driver's license, you probably went through several departments before receiving your license. In one state, applicants must go through three steps, each handled by a separate department: (1) validation, by the motor vehicles division; (2) processing, by the licensing department; and (3) payment collection, by the treasury department.

A final category of departmentalization is to use the particular type of *customer* the organization seeks to reach. The sales activities in an office supply firm, for instance, can be broken down into three departments to service retail, wholesale, and government customers. A large law office can segment its staff on the basis of whether they service corporate or individual clients. The assumption underlying customer departmentalization is that customers in each department have a common set of problems and needs that can best be met by having specialists for each.

Large organizations may use all of the forms of departmentalization we've described. A major Japanese electronics firm, for instance, organizes each of its divisions along functional lines and its manufacturing units around processes; it departmentalizes sales around seven geographic regions; and divides each sales region into four customer groupings. Two general trends, however, seem to be gaining momentum in the 1990s. First, customer departmentalization is growing in popularity. In order to better monitor the needs of customers and to be better able to respond to changes in those needs, many organizations have given greater emphasis to customer departmentalization. Xerox, for example,

◆◆◆◆ OB in the News ◆◆◆◆

Organizing Around Work Processes

Companies such as AT&T, Boeing, British Telecommunications, Ericsson, Canadian Imperial Bank of Commerce, Hallmark Cards, Sun Life Assurance of Canada, Xerox, and Volvo are completely overhauling the way they do business in order to achieve the productivity, speed, and customer satisfaction they need to thrive. They've carefully examined how their work is carried out, then reorganized their corporations around work processes.

At Sun Life Assurance's U.S. office in Wellesley, Massachusetts, only one business process was identified: serving customers. Upscale buyers of the company's life insurance policies wanted to deal with Sun Life quickly and effectively. In response, Sun Life representatives have been reorganized into eight-person teams trained to expedite all requests. With this new approach, Sun Life no longer irritates customers by switching their calls from one specialist to another.

At Hallmark Cards, editors, writers, artists, and production specialists join with representatives from manufacturing, graphic arts, sales, and distribution to oversee everything from new ideas to customer deliveries. This teamwork has cut production time for new versions of Hallmark's Shoebox Greeting cards from nine to three months.

Based on L. Grant, "New Jewel in the Crown," *U.S. News & World Report* (February 28, 1994), pp. 55–57.

has eliminated its corporate marketing staff and placed marketing specialists out in the field.[3] This allows the company to better understand who their customers are and to respond faster to their requirements. The second trend is that rigid functional departmentalization is being complemented by teams that cross over traditional departmental lines. As we described in Chapter 9, as tasks have become more complex and more diverse skills are needed to accomplish those tasks, management has turned to cross-functional teams.

Chain of Command

Twenty years ago, the chain-of-command concept was a basic cornerstone in the design of organizations. As you'll see, it has far less importance today. But contemporary managers should still consider its implications when they decide how best to structure their organizations.

chain of command
The unbroken line of authority that extends from the top of the organization to the lowest eschelon and clarifies who reports to whom.

The **chain of command** is an unbroken line of authority that extends from the top of the organization to the lowest echelon and clarifies who reports to whom. It answers questions for employees such as "Who do I go to if I have a problem?" and "Whom am I responsible to?"

authority
The rights inherent in a managerial position to give orders and expect the orders to be obeyed.

You can't discuss the chain of command without discussing two complementary concepts: authority and unity of command. **Authority** refers to the rights inherent in a managerial position to give orders and expect the orders to be obeyed. To facilitate coordination, each managerial position is given a place in the chain of command; and each manager is given a degree of authority in order to meet his or her responsibilities. The **unity of command** principle helps preserve the concept of an unbroken line of authority. It states that a person should have one and only one superior to whom he or she is directly responsible. If the unity of command is broken, a subordinate might have to cope with conflicting demands or priorities from several superiors.

> ◆The concepts of chain of command, authority, and unity of command have substantially less relevance today because of advancements in computer technology and the trend toward empowering employees.

Times change and so do the basic tenets of organization design. The concepts of chain of command, authority, and unity of command have substantially less relevance today because of advancements in computer technology and the trend toward empowering employees. Just how different things are today is illustrated in the following excerpt from a recent article in *Business Week*:

unity of command
A subordinate should have only one superior to whom he or she is directly responsible.

> Puzzled, Charles Chaser scanned the inventory reports from his company's distribution centers one Wednesday morning in mid-March. According to the computer printouts, stocks of Rose Awakening Cutex nail polish were down to three days' supply, well below the three-and-a-half week stock Chesebrough-Pond's Inc. tries to keep on hand. But Chaser knew his Jefferson City (Missouri) plant had shipped 346 dozen bottles of the polish just two days before. Rose Awakening must be flying off store shelves, he thought. So Chaser turned to his terminal next to the production line and typed in instructions to produce 400 dozen more bottles on Thursday morning.
>
> All in a day's work for a scheduling manager, right? Except for one detail: Chaser isn't management. He's a line worker—officially a "line coordinator"—one of hundreds who routinely tap the plant's computer network to track shipments, schedule their own workloads, and generally perform functions that used to be the province of management.[4]

A low-level employee today can access information in seconds that, 20 years ago, was available only to top managers. Similarly, computer technology increasingly allows employees anywhere in an organization to communicate with anyone else without going through formal channels. Moreover, the concepts of authority and maintaining the chain of command are increasingly less relevant as operating employees are being empowered to make decisions that previously were reserved for management. Add to this the popularity of self-managed and cross-functional teams and the creation of new structural designs that include multiple bosses, and the unity-of-command concept takes on less relevance. Many organizations, of course, still find they can be most productive by enforcing the chain of command. There just seem to be fewer of them nowadays.

Span of Control

span of control
The number of subordinates a manager can efficiently and effectively direct.

How many subordinates can a manager efficiently and effectively direct? This question of **span of control** is important because, to a large degree, it determines the number of levels and managers an organization has. All things being equal, the wider or larger the span, the more efficient the organization. An example can illustrate the validity of this statement.

Assume we have two organizations, both of which have approximately 4,100 operative-level employees. As Figure 14-2 illustrates, if one has a uniform span of four and the other a span of eight, the wider span would have two fewer levels and approximately 800 fewer managers. If the average manager made $40,000 a year, the wider span would save $32 million a year in management salaries! Obviously, wider spans are more efficient in terms of cost. However, at some point wider spans reduce effectiveness. That is, when the span becomes too large, employee performance suffers because supervisors no longer have the time to provide the necessary leadership and support.

Small spans have their advocates. By keeping the span of control to five or six employees, a manager can maintain close control.[5] But small spans have three major drawbacks. First, as already described, they're expensive because they add levels of management. Second, they make vertical communication in the organization more complex. The added levels of hierarchy slow down decision making and tend to isolate upper management. Third, small spans of control encourage overly tight supervision and discourage employee autonomy.

The trend in recent years has been toward larger spans of control. For example, the span for managers at companies such as General Electric and Reynolds Metals has expanded to 10 or 12 subordinates—twice the number of 15 years ago.[6] Tom Smith, a regional manager with Carboline Co., oversees 27 people. His counterpart of 20 years ago would have typically managed 12 employees.[7]

Wide spans of control are consistent with recent efforts by companies to reduce costs, cut overhead, speed up decision making, increase flexibility, get closer to customers, and empower employees. However, to ensure that performance doesn't suffer because of these wider spans, organizations have been investing heavily in employee training. Managers recognize they can handle a wider span when employees know their jobs inside and out or can turn to their coworkers when they have questions.

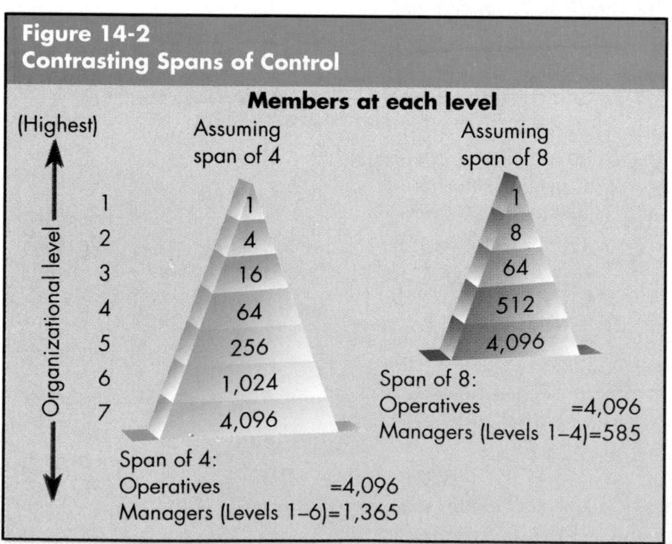

Figure 14-2 Contrasting Spans of Control

Owens-Corning, a building supply manufacturer and retailer, is increasing its sales managers' span of control by equipping its sales force with computers loaded with software providing up-to-date information about their company, customers, and marketplace trends. The information empowers salespeople to manage their own territories by making on-the-spot decisions on their own. Charles Causey (left), a regional sales manager for Owens-Corning's insulation products, expects the sales automation system to increase his span of control from nine salespeople to fifteen. Wider span of control is helping Owens-Corning achieve its goal of increasing sales reps' attention to customers.

Centralization and Decentralization

In some organizations, top managers make all the decisions. Lower level managers merely carry out top management's directives. At the other extreme are organizations where decision making is pushed down to those managers who are closest to the action. The former organizations are highly centralized; the latter are decentralized.

The term **centralization** refers to the degree to which decision making is concentrated at a single point in the organization. The concept includes only formal authority, that is, the rights inherent in one's position. Typically, it's said that if top management makes the organization's key decisions with little or no input from lower level personnel, then the organization is centralized. In contrast, the more that lower-level personnel provide input or are actually given the discretion to make decisions, the more **decentralization** there is.

centralization
The degree to which decision making is concentrated at a single point in the organization.

decentralization
Decision discretion is pushed down to lower-level employees.

An organization characterized by centralization is an inherently different structural animal from one that is decentralized. In a decentralized organization, action can be taken more quickly to solve problems, more people provide input into decisions, and employees are less likely to feel alienated from those who make the decisions that affect their work lives.

Consistent with recent management efforts to make organizations more flexible and responsive, there has been a marked trend toward decentralizing decision making. In large companies, lower level managers are closer to the action and typically have more detailed knowledge about problems than do top managers. Big retailers like Sears and J.C. Penney have given their store managers considerably more discretion in choosing what merchandise to stock. This allows those stores to compete more effectively against local merchants. Similarly, the Bank of Montreal has grouped its 1,164 Canadian branches into 236 "communities"—that is, a group of branches within a limited geographical area.[8] Each community is led by a community area manager, who typically works within a 20-minute drive of the other branches. This area manager can respond faster and more intelligently to problems in his or her community than could some senior executive in Montreal. IBM Europe's chairman Renato Riverso has similarly sliced the Continent into some 200 autonomous business units, each with its own profit plan, employee incentives, and customer focus. "We used to manage from the top, like an army," says Riverso. "Now, we're trying to create entities that drive themselves."[9]

From Concepts to Skills

Delegating Authority

If you're a manager and want to delegate some of your authority to someone else, how do you go about it? The following summarizes the primary steps you need to take.

1. *Clarify the assignment.* The place to begin is to determine what is to be delegated and to whom. You need to identify the person best capable of doing the task, then determine if he or she has the time and motivation to do the job.

Assuming you have a willing and able subordinate, it is your responsibility to provide clear information on what is being delegated, the results you expect, and any time or performance expectations you hold.

Unless there is an overriding need to adhere to specific methods, you should delegate only the end results. That is, get agreement on what is to be done and the end results expected, but let the subordinate decide on the means.

2. *Specify the subordinate's range of discretion.* Every act of delegation comes with constraints. You're delegating authority to act, but not *unlimited* authority. What you're delegating is authority to act on certain issues and, on those issues, within certain parameters. You need to specify what those parameters are so subordinates know, in no uncertain terms, the range of their discretion.

3. *Allow the subordinate to participate.* One of the best sources for determining how much authority will be necessary to accomplish a task is the subordinate who will be held accountable for that task. If you allow employees to participate in determining what is delegated, how much authority is needed to get the job done, and the standards by which they'll be judged, you increase employee motivation, satisfaction, and accountability for performance.

4. *Inform others that delegation has occurred.* Delegation should not take place in a vacuum. Not only do you and the subordinate need to know specifically what has been delegated and how much authority has been granted, but anyone else who may be affected by the delegation act also needs to be informed.

5. *Establish feedback controls.* The establishment of controls to monitor the subordinate's progress increases the likelihood that important problems will be identified early and that the task will be completed on time and to the desired specifications. For instance, agree on a specific time for completion of the task, and then set progress dates when the subordinate will report back on how well he or she is doing and any major problems that have surfaced. This can be supplemented with periodic spot checks to ensure that authority guidelines are not being abused, organization policies are being followed, and proper procedures are being met.

Formalization

formalization
The degree to which jobs within the organization are standardized.

Formalization refers to the degree to which jobs within the organization are standardized. If a job is highly formalized, then the job incumbent has a minimum amount of discretion over what is to be done, when it is to be done, and how he or she should do it. Employees can be expected always to handle the same input in exactly the same way, resulting in a consistent and uniform output. There are explicit job descriptions, lots of organizational rules, and clearly defined procedures covering work processes in organizations where there is high formalization. Where formalization is low, job behaviors are relatively nonprogrammed and employees have a great deal of freedom to exercise discretion in their work. Since an individual's discretion on the job is inversely related to the amount of behavior in that job that is preprogrammed by the organization, the greater the standardization, the less input the employee has into how his or her work is to be done. Standardization not only eliminates the possibility of employees engaging in alternative behaviors, but it even removes the need for employees to consider alternatives.

The degree of formalization can vary widely between organizations and within organizations. Certain jobs, for instance, are well known to have little formalization. College book travelers—the representatives of publishers who call on professors to inform them of their company's new publications—have a great deal of freedom in their jobs. They have no standard sales spiel, and the extent of rules and procedures governing their behavior may be little more than the requirement that they submit a weekly sales report and some suggestions on what to emphasize for the various new titles. At the other extreme are clerical and editorial positions in the same publishing houses where employees are required to clock in at their work stations by 8 A.M.. or be docked a half hour of pay and, once at that work station, to follow a set of precise procedures dictated by management.

Common Organizational Designs

We now turn to describing three of the more common organizational designs found in use: the simple structure, the bureaucracy, and the matrix structure.

The Simple Structure

What do a small retail store, an electronics firm run by a hard-driving entrepreneur, a new Planned Parenthood office, and an airline in the midst of a companywide pilot's strike have in common? They probably all utilize the **simple structure**.

simple structure
A structure characterized by a low degree of departmentalization, wide spans of control, authority centralized in a single person, and little formalization.

The simple structure is said to be characterized most by what it is not rather than what it is. The simple structure is not elaborated.[10] It has a low degree of departmentalization, wide spans of control, authority centralized in a single person, and little formalization. The simple structure is a "flat" organization; it usually has only two or three vertical levels, a loose body of employees, and one individual in whom the decision-making authority is centralized.

The simple structure is most widely practiced in small businesses in which the manager and the owner are one and the same. This organizational design is illustrated in Figure 14-3 on page 560, an organization chart for a retail men's store. Jack Gold owns and manages this store. Although Jack Gold employs five full-time salespeople, a cashier, and extra personnel for weekends and holidays, he runs the show.

The strength of the simple structure lies in its simplicity. It's fast, flexible, inexpensive to maintain, and accountability is clear. One major weakness is that it's difficult to maintain in anything other than small organizations. It becomes increasingly inadequate as an organization grows because its low formalization and high centralization tend to create information overload at the top. As size increases, decision making typically becomes slower and can eventually come to a standstill as the single executive tries to continue making all the decisions. This often proves to be the undoing of many small businesses. When an organization begins to employ 50 or 100 people, it's very difficult for the owner-manager to make all the choices. If the structure isn't changed and

Figure 14-3
A Simple Structure (Jack Gold's Men's Store)

made more elaborate, the firm often loses momentum and can eventually fail. The simple structure's other weakness is that it's risky: Everything depends on one person. One heart attack can literally destroy the organization's information and decision-making center.

The simple structure isn't strictly limited to small organizations, it's just harder to make it work effectively in larger firms. One large company that seems to have succeeded with the simple structure is Nucor Corp., a $2.3 billion steel company that operates minimills in Indiana and Arkansas.[11] Its headquarters in Charlotte, North Carolina, employs just 24 people. And there are only three levels between the company's president and mill workers. This lean structure has helped Nucor to become the most profitable steelmaker in the United States.

The Bureaucracy

Standardization! That's the key concept underlying all bureaucracies. Take a look at the bank where you keep your checking account; the department store where you buy your clothes; or the government offices that collect your taxes, enforce health regulations, or provide local fire protection. They all rely on standardized work processes for coordination and control.

bureaucracy
A structure with highly routine operating tasks achieved through specialization, very formalized rules and regulations, tasks that are grouped into functional departments, centralized authority, narrow spans of control, and decision making that follows the chain of command.

The **bureaucracy** is characterized by highly routine operating tasks achieved through specialization, very formalized rules and regulations, tasks that are grouped into functional departments, centralized authority, narrow spans of control, and decision making that follows the chain of command.

The primary strength of the bureaucracy lies in its ability to perform standardized activities in a highly efficient manner. Putting like specialities together in functional departments results in economies of scale, minimum duplication of personnel and equipment, and employees who have the opportunity to talk the same language among their peers. Further, bureaucracies can get by nicely with less talented—and, hence, less costly—middle- and lower-level managers. The pervasiveness of rules and regulations substitute for managerial discretion. Standardized operations, coupled with high formalization,

"I'm sorry, dear, but you knew I was a bureaucrat when you married me."

Figure 14-4
Drawing by Weber in *The New Yorker.* Copyright © 1980 by The New Yorker Magazine. Reprinted by permission.

allow decision making to be centralized. There is little need, therefore, for innovative and experienced decision makers below the level of senior executives.

One of the major weaknesses of bureaucracy is illustrated in the following dialogue between four executives in one company: "Ya know, nothing happens in this place until we *produce* something," said the production executive. "Wrong," commented the research and development manager, "nothing happens until we *design* something!" "What are you talking about?" asked the marketing executive. "Nothing happens here until we *sell* something!" Finally, the exasperated accounting manager responded, "It doesn't matter what you produce, design, or sell. No one knows what happens until we *tally up the results*!" This conversation points up the fact that specialization creates subunit conflicts. Functional unit goals can override the overall goals of the organization.

The other major weakness of bureaucracy is something we've all experienced at one time or another when having to deal with people who work in these organizations: obsessive concern with following the rules. When cases arise that don't precisely fit the rules, there is no room for modification. The bureaucracy is efficient only as long as employees confront problems they have previously encountered and for which programmed decision rules have already been established.

The peak of bureaucracy's popularity was probably in the 1950s and 1960s. At that time, for instance, just about every major corporation in the world—firms such as IBM, General Electric, Volkswagen, Matsushita, and Royal Dutch Shell—was organized as a bureaucracy. Although the bureaucracy is out of fashion in the 1990s—critics argue it can't respond rapidly to change and hinders employee initiative[12]—the majority of large organizations still take on basic bureaucratic characteristics, particularly specialization and high formalization. However, spans of control have generally been widened, authority has become more decentralized, and functional departments have been supplemented with an increased use of teams. Another trend is toward breaking bureaucracies up into smaller, although fully functioning, mini-bureaucracies. These smaller versions, with 150 to 250 people, each have their own mission and profit goals. It's been estimated that about 15 percent of large corporations have taken this direction.[13] For instance, Eastman Kodak has transformed over 100 production units into separate businesses.

The Matrix Structure

matrix structure
A structure that creates dual lines of authority; combines functional and product departmentalization.

Another popular organizational design option is the **matrix structure**. You'll find it being used in advertising agencies, aerospace firms, research and development laboratories, construction companies, hospitals, government agencies, universities, management consulting firms, and entertainment companies.[14] Essentially, the matrix combines two forms of departmentalization: functional and product.

The strength of functional departmentalization lies in putting like specialists together, which minimizes the number necessary, while it allows the pooling and sharing of specialized resources across products. Its major disadvantage is the difficulty of coordinating the tasks of diverse functional specialists so their activities are completed on time and within budget. Product departmentalization, on the contrary, has exactly the opposite benefits and disadvantages. It facilitates coordination among specialties to achieve on-time completion and meet budget targets. Further, it provides clear responsibility for all activities related to a product, but with duplication of activities and costs. The matrix attempts to gain the strengths of each while avoiding their weaknesses.

The most obvious structural characteristic of the matrix is that it breaks the unity-of-command concept. Employees in the matrix have two bosses—their functional department managers and their product managers. Therefore, the matrix has a dual chain of command.

Figure 14-5 shows the matrix form as used in a college of business administration. The academic departments of accounting, marketing, and so forth,

Zurich, Switzerland-based Asea Brown Boveri Ltd. uses a global matrix structure in managing its 1,300 separate companies in Asia, Europe, and the Americas. ABB primarily produces large, power engineering components such as the generator shown here, which ABB makes in Poland for power plant equipment it assembles at plants in Germany and Switzerland. ABB's matrix of 25,000 managers includes global managers who focus on developing a global competitive strategy; business-area managers who coordinate the design, manufacture, and distribution of product lines worldwide; and country managers who develop a nation's specialized talents and resources. A matrix structure gives ABB enormous global market clout. It eliminates costly duplication of business operations, allows managers to tap quickly into the best technology and expertise of specialists, and increases flexibility and responsiveness to serve customers better.

Figure 14-5
Matrix Structure for a College of Business Administration

Academic departments \ Programs	Undergraduate	Master's	Ph. D.	Research	Executive development	Community service
Accounting						
Administrative studies						
Finance						
Information and decision sciences						
Marketing						
Organizational behavior						
Quantitative methods						

are functional units. Additionally, specific programs (that is, products) are overlaid on the functions. In this way, members in a matrix structure have a dual assignment—to their functional department and to their product groups. For instance, a professor of accounting teaching an undergraduate course reports to the director of undergraduate programs as well as to the chairperson of the accounting department.

The strength of the matrix lies in its ability to facilitate coordination when the organization has a multiplicity of complex and interdependent activities. As an organization gets larger, its information processing capacity can become overloaded. In a bureaucracy, complexity results in increased formalization. The direct and frequent contact between different specialties in the matrix can make for better communication and more flexibility. Information permeates the organization and more quickly reaches those people who need to take account of it. Further, the matrix reduces bureaupathologies. The dual lines of authority reduce tendencies of departmental members to become so busy protecting their little worlds that the organization's overall goals become secondary.

There is also another advantage to the matrix. It facilitates the efficient allocation of specialists. When individuals with highly specialized skills are lodged in one functional department or product group, their talents are monopolized and underutilized. The matrix achieves the advantages of economies of scale by providing the organization with both the best resources and an effective way of ensuring their efficient deployment.

The major disadvantages of the matrix lie in the confusion it creates, its propensity to foster power struggles, and the stress it places on individuals.[15] When you dispense with the unity-of-command concept, ambiguity is significantly increased and ambiguity often leads to conflict. For example, it's frequently unclear who reports to whom, and it is not unusual for product managers to fight over getting the best specialists assigned to their products. Confusion and ambiguity also create the seeds of power struggles. Bureaucracy reduces the potential for power grabs by defining the rules of the game. When those rules are up for grabs, power struggles between functional and product managers result. For individuals who desire security and absence from ambiguity, this work climate can produce stress. Reporting to more than one boss introduces role conflict, and unclear expectations introduce role ambiguity. The comfort of bureaucracy's predictability is absent, replaced by insecurity and stress.

New Design Options

Since the early 1980s, senior managers in a number of organizations have been working to develop new structural options that can better help their firms compete effectively. In this section, we describe four such structural designs: the team structure, the virtual organization, the boundaryless organization, and the feminine organization.

The Team Structure

team structure
The use of teams as the central device to coordinate work activities.

As described in Chapter 9, teams have become an extremely popular means around which to organize work activities. When management uses teams as its central coordination device, you have a **team structure**. The primary characteristics of the team structure are that it breaks down departmental barriers and decentralizes decision making to the level of the work team. Team structures also require employees to be generalists as well as specialists.[16]

In smaller companies, the team structure can define the entire organization. For instance, Imedia, a 30-person marketing firm in New Jersey, is organized completely around teams that have full responsibility for most operational issues and client services.[17]

More often, particularly among larger organizations, the team structure complements what is typically a bureaucracy. This allows the organization to achieve the efficiency of bureaucracy's standardization while gaining the flexibility that teams provide. To improve productivity at the operating level, for instance, companies like Chrysler, Saturn, Motorola, and Xerox have made extensive use of self-managed teams. When companies like Boeing or Hewlett-Packard need to design new products or coordinate major projects, however, they'll structure activities around cross-functional teams.

The Virtual Organization

virtual organization
A small, core organization that outsources major business functions.

Why own when you can rent? That's the essence of the **virtual organization**, a small, core organization that outsources major business functions.[18] In structural terms, the virtual organization is highly centralized, with little or no departmentalization.

Magicorp runs a small shop that makes graphics transparencies. It relies on other companies for the rest of its operations. People who use graphics software on their personal computers send data by phone lines to Magicorp's office in Wilmington, Ohio. Why is Magicorp in Wilmington? Because the Airborne Express hub is there, making fast turnarounds possible. Rather than do its own marketing, Magicorp relies on graphics software vendors to promote its services, paying these vendors on a royalty basis.

Companies like Nike, Reebok, Liz Claiborne, Emerson Radio, and Dell Computer are just a few of the thousands of companies that have found they can do hundreds of millions of dollars in business without owning manufacturing facilities. Dell Computer, for instance, owns no plants and merely assembles computers from outsourced parts. National Steel Corp. contracts out its mail room operations. AT&T farms out its credit card processing. Mobil Corp. has turned over maintenance of its refineries to another firm.

What's going on here? A quest for maximum flexibility. These "virtual" organizations have created networks of relationships that allow them to contract out manufacturing, distribution, marketing, or any other business function where management feels others can do it better or cheaper.

Figure 14-6
A Virtual Organization

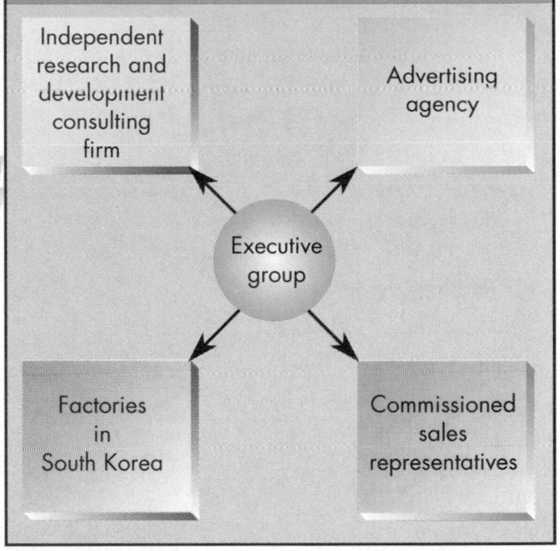

The virtual organization stands in sharp contrast to the typical bureaucracy that has many vertical levels of management and where control is sought through ownership. In such organizations, research and development are done in house, production occurs in company-owned plants, and sales and marketing are performed by the company's own employees. To support all this, management has to employ extra personnel including accountants, human resource specialists, and lawyers. The virtual organization, however, outsources many of these functions and concentrates on what it does best. For most U.S. firms, that means focusing on design or marketing. Emerson Radio Corporation, for example, designs and engineers its TVs, stereos, and other consumer electronic products, but it contracts out their manufacture to Asian suppliers.

Figure 14-6 shows a virtual organization in which management outsources all of the primary functions of the business. The core of the organization is a small group of executives. Their job is to oversee directly any activities that are done in house and to coordinate relationships with the organizations that manufacture, distribute, and perform other crucial functions for the virtual organization. The arrowed lines in Figure 14-6 represent those relationships, typically maintained under contracts. In essence, managers in virtual structures spend most of their time coordinating and controlling external relations, typically by way of computer network links.

The major advantage to the virtual organization is its flexibility. For instance, it allows someone with an innovative idea and little money—such as Michael Dell and his Dell Computer firm—to successfully compete against large companies like IBM. The primary drawback to this structure is that it reduces management's control over key parts of its business.

The Boundaryless Organization

boundaryless organization
An organization that seeks to eliminate the chain of command, have limitless spans of control, and replace departments with empowered teams.

General Electric chairman Jack Welch coined the term **boundaryless organization** to describe his idea of what he wanted GE to become. Welch wanted to turn his company into a "$60 billion family grocery store."[19] That is, in spite of its monstrous size, he wanted to eliminate *vertical* and *horizontal* boundaries within GE and breakdown *external* barriers between the company and its customers and suppliers. The boundaryless organization seeks to eliminate the chain of command, have limitless spans of control, and replace departments with empowered teams.

◆GE wants to become the $60 billion family grocery store.

While GE hasn't yet achieved this boundaryless state—and probably never will—it has made significant progress toward this end. So have other companies like Hewlett-Packard, AT&T, and Mo-

General Electric describes boundaryless behavior as breaking down walls and layers that "cramp people, inhibit creativity, waste time, restrict visions, smother dreams, and, above all, slow things down." GE is breaking down barriers by fostering teamwork and rewarding employees who share ideas to improve every aspect of company operations. This photo illustrates boundaryless behavior in action. Labor and management at GE's Appliance Park complex in Louisville, Kentucky, are joining together to improve the plant's profitability. With a combination of labor practice changes and GE investment, thousands of highly involved employees are coming up with ideas and putting them into action to "Save the Park."

torola. Let's take a look at what a boundaryless organization would look like and what some firms are doing to make it a reality.[20]

By removing *vertical* boundaries, management flattens the hierarchy. Status and rank are minimized. And the organization looks more like a silo than a pyramid, where the grain at the top is no different than the grain at the bottom. Cross-hierarchical teams (which include top executives, middle managers, supervisors, and operative employees), participative decision-making practices, and the use of 360-degree performance appraisals (where peers and others above and below the employee evaluate his or her performance) are examples of what GE is doing to break down vertical boundaries.

Functional departments create *horizontal* boundaries. The way to reduce these barriers is to replace functional departments with cross-functional teams and to organize activities around processes. For instance, Xerox now develops new products through multidisciplinary teams that work in a single process instead of around narrow functional tasks. Similarly, some AT&T units are now doing annual budgets based not on functions or departments but on processes such as the maintenance of a worldwide telecommunications network. Another way management can cut through horizontal barriers is to use lateral transfers and rotate people into and out of different functional areas. This turns specialists into generalists.

When fully operational, the boundaryless organization also breaks down barriers to *external* constituencies and barriers created by geography. Globalization, strategic alliances, customer–organization linkages, and telecommuting are all examples of practices that reduce external boundaries. Coca-Cola, for instance, sees itself as a global corporation, not a U.S. or Atlanta company. Firms like NEC Corp., Boeing, and Apple Computer each have strategic alliances or joint partnerships with dozens of companies. These alliances blur the distinction between one organization and another as employees work on joint projects. Companies like AT&T and Northwest Airlines are allowing customers to perform functions that previously were done by management. For instance, some AT&T units are receiving bonuses based on customer evaluations of the teams that serve them. Northwest gives its frequent fliers ten $50 award certificates each year and tells these customers to distribute these awards to Northwest employees when they see them do something good. This practice, in essence, allows Northwest's customers to participate in employee appraisals. Finally, we suggest that telecommuting is blurring organizational boundaries. The security analyst with Merrill Lynch who does his job from his ranch in Montana or the software designer who works for a San Francisco company but does her job in Boulder, Colorado, are just two examples of the millions of workers who are now doing their jobs outside the physical boundaries of their employers' premises.

The one common technological thread that makes the boundaryless organization possible is networked computers. They allow people to communicate across intraorganizational and interorganizational boundaries.[21] Electronic mail, for instance, enables hundreds of employees to share information simultaneously and allows rank-and-file workers to communicate directly with senior executives. And interorganizational networks now make it possible for Wal-Mart suppliers like Procter & Gamble and Levi Strauss to monitor inventory levels of laundry soap and jeans, respectively, because P&G and Levi's computer systems are networked to Wal-Mart's system.

The Feminine Organization

One of the more controversial issues currently related to organization design is whether gender differences have created a preference among women for a feminine or feminist organization.

Beginning in the 1980s, some organization theorists began to look for links between female values and structural preferences. The primary finding was that women preferred organizations that emphasized relatedness and connecting with others.[22] This finding, according to theorists, was essentially a re-

Husband and wife team Joyce Roberts and Vic Williams (center) operate their company as a feminine organization. They own Architectural Support Services Inc., an Atlanta firm that provides computer-aided design services for architects, designers, and engineers. Roberts and Williams nurture the personal growth of their young work force by involving them in every aspect of the business. They allow employees to train each other, form their own project teams, deal directly with all of ASSI's clients, and choose their own job titles. Given these opportunities, employees not only expand their technical skills quickly but also acquire breadth of experience well beyond their young age.

sult of the way women have been socialized. "Few could argue with the conclusion that for the most part, females have been socialized for their role in the family, a role that teaches the value of supporting and nurturing others, of protecting long-term (familial) relationships, of seeking solutions where everyone wins and, wherever possible, of forging a mutuality of interests."[23]

feminine organization
An organization characterized by humanistic treatment of individuals, nonopportunism, careers defined through service to others, commitment to employee growth, creation of a caring community, and power sharing.

Organizational sociologist Joyce Rothschild has summarized the research and developed a model of the **feminine organization** that has six characteristics:[24]

1. *Members are valued as individual human beings*. People are treated as individuals, with individual values and needs, rather than as occupants of roles or offices.
2. *Nonopportunistic.* Relationships are seen as possessing value in themselves, not just as formal means to the achievement of organizational goals.
3. *Careers are defined in terms of service to others*. Whereas organization members in a bureaucracy define career success in terms of promotions, acquisition of power, and pay increases, organization members in the feminine model measure success in terms of service to others.
4. *Commitment to employee growth*. Feminine organizations create extensive personal growth opportunities for their members. Rather than emphasizing specialization and the development of narrow expertise, these organizations expand member skills and broaden employee competencies by offering new learning experiences.
5. *Creation of a caring community*. Members become closely bound in a community sense, much as in small towns where people have learned to trust and care for their neighbors.
6. *Power sharing*. In the traditional bureaucracy, information and decision-making authority are coveted and hierarchically allocated. In the feminine organization, information is generously shared. All members who will be affected by a decision are given the opportunity to participate in that decision.

According to Rothschild, the feminine model may be more effective and the model of choice in organizations that are essentially managed by and for women. This would include, but certainly not be limited to, rape crisis centers, battered women's shelters, and entrepreneurial firms that sell products directed to the female market such as Mary Kay Cosmetics. For instance, Rothschild studied several "new wave" clerical trade unions that were led by women and had mostly female members.[25] She found that (1) their organizational structure more closely resembled the feminine model than a bureaucracy, and (2) they succeeded in organizing female clerical and service sector employees where the bureaucratically designed AFL-CIO unions had failed.

Why Do Structures Differ?

mechanistic model
A structure characterized by extensive departmentalization, high formalization, a limited information network, and centralization.

In the previous sections, we described a variety of organizational designs. They ranged from the highly structured and standardized bureaucracy to the loose and amorphous boundaryless organization. The other designs we discussed tend to exist somewhere between these two extremes.

Figure 14-7 reconceptualizes our previous discussions by presenting two extreme models of organization design. One extreme we call the **mechanistic**

Figure 14-7
Mechanistic vs. Organic Models

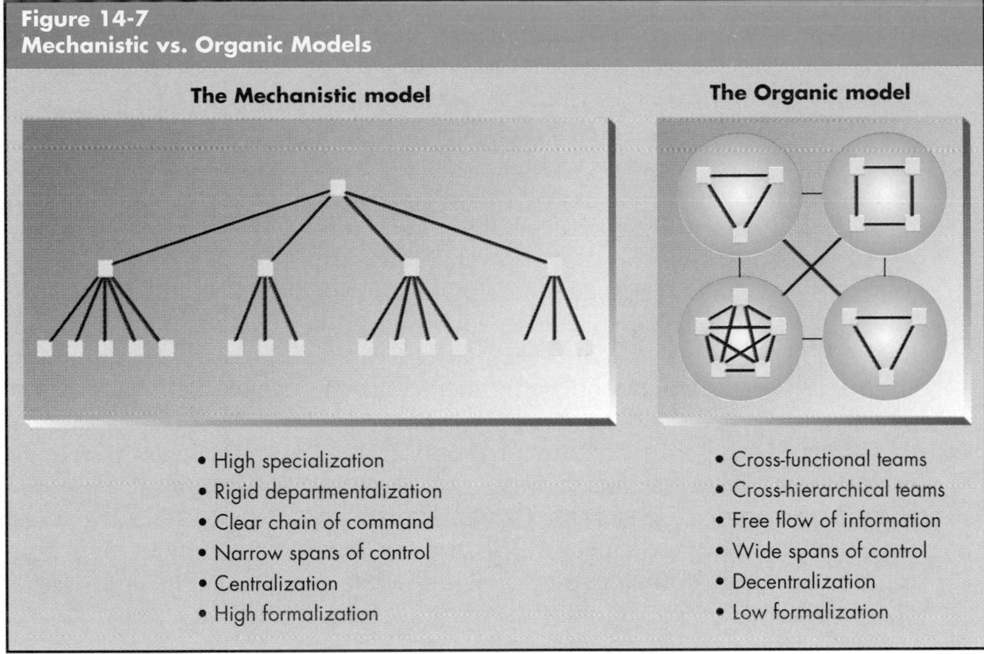

The Mechanistic model	The Organic model
• High specialization	• Cross-functional teams
• Rigid departmentalization	• Cross-hierarchical teams
• Clear chain of command	• Free flow of information
• Narrow spans of control	• Wide spans of control
• Centralization	• Decentralization
• High formalization	• Low formalization

model. It is generally synonymous with the bureaucracy in that it has extensive departmentalization, high formalization, a limited information network (mostly downward communication), and little participation by low-level members in decision making. At the other extreme is the **organic model**. This model looks a lot like the boundaryless organization. It's flat, uses cross-hierarchical and cross-functional teams, has low formalization, possesses a comprehensive information network (utilizing lateral and upward communication as well as downward), and it involves high participation in decision making.[26]

organic model A structure that is flat, uses cross-hierarchical and cross-functional teams, has low formalization, possesses a comprehensive information network, and relies on participative decision making.

With these two models in mind, we're now prepared to address this question: Why are some organizations structured along more mechanistic lines while others follow organic characteristics? What are the forces influencing the design that is chosen? In the following pages, we present the major forces that have been identified as causes or determinants of an organization's structure.[27]

Strategy

An organization's structure is a means to help management achieve its objectives. Since objectives are derived from the organization's overall strategy, it is only logical that strategy and structure should be closely linked. More specifically, structure should follow strategy. If management makes a significant change in its organization's strategy, the structure will need to be modified to accommodate and support this change.[28] Most current strategy frameworks focus on three strategic options—innovation, cost minimization, and imitation—and the structural design that works best with each.[29]

To what degree does an organization introduce major new products or services? An **innovation strategy** does not mean a strategy merely for simple or cosmetic changes from previous offerings but rather one for meaningful and unique innovations. Obviously, not all firms pursue innovation. This strategy may appropriately characterize 3M Co., but it certainly is not a strategy pursued by Reader's Digest.

innovation strategy A strategy that emphasizes the introduction of major new products and services.

cost-minimization strategy
A strategy that emphasizes tight cost controls, avoidance of unnecessary innovation or marketing expenses, and price-cutting.

imitation strategy
A strategy that seeks to move into new products or new markets only after their viability has already been proven.

An organization pursuing a **cost-minimization strategy** tightly controls costs, refrains from incurring unnecessary innovation or marketing expenses, and cuts prices in selling a basic product. This would describe the strategy pursued by Office Depot or the sellers of generic grocery products.

Organizations following an **imitation strategy** try to capitalize on the best of both of the previous strategies. They seek to minimize risk and maximize opportunity for profit. Their strategy is to move into new products or new markets only after viability has been proven by innovators. They take the successful ideas of innovators and copy them. Manufacturers of mass-marketed fashion goods that are rip-offs of designer styles follow the imitation strategy. This label also probably characterizes such well-known firms as IBM and Caterpillar. They essentially follow their smaller and more innovative competitors with superior products, but only after their competitors have demonstrated the market is there.

Table 14-2 describes the structural option that best matches each strategy. Innovators need the flexibility of the organic structure; cost minimizers seek the efficiency and stability of the mechanistic structure. Imitators combine the two structures. They use a mechanistic structure in order to maintain tight controls and low costs in their current activities while at the same time they create organic subunits in which to pursue new undertakings.

Organization Size

A quick glance at the organizations we deal with regularly in our lives would lead most of us to conclude that size would have some bearing on an organization's structure. The more than 800,000 employees of the U.S. Postal Service, for example, do not neatly fit into one building, or into several departments supervised by a couple of managers. It's hard to envision 800,000 people being organized in any manner other than one that contains a great deal of specialization, departmentalization, uses a large number of procedures and regulations to ensure uniform practices, and follows a high degree of decentralized decision making. But a local messenger service that employs ten people and generates less than $300,000 a year in service fees is not likely to need decentralized decision making or formalized procedures and regulations.

Considerable evidence supports the idea that an organization's size significantly affects its structure.[30] For instance, large organizations—those typically employing 2,000 or more people—tend to have more specialization, more departmentalization, more vertical levels, and more rules and regulations than do small organizations. However, the relationship isn't linear. Rather, size affects

Table 14-2 The Strategy-Structure Thesis

Strategy	Structural Option
Innovation	**Organic**: A loose structure; low specialization, low formalization, decentralized
Cost minimization	**Mechanistic**: Tight control; extensive work specialization, high formalization, high centralization
Imitation	**Mechanistic and organic**: Mix of loose with tight properties; tight controls over current activities and looser controls for new undertakings

structure at a decreasing rate. The impact of size becomes less important as an organization expands. Why is this? Essentially, once an organization has around 2,000 employees, it's already fairly mechanistic. An additional 500 employees will not have much impact. However, adding 500 employees to an organization that has only 300 members is likely to result in a shift toward a more mechanistic structure.

Technology

The term **technology** refers to how an organization transfers its inputs into outputs. Every organization has at least one technology for converting financial, human, and physical resources into products or services. The Ford Motor Co., for instance, predominantly uses an assembly-line process to make its products. Colleges, in contrast, may use a number of instruction technologies—the ever-popular formal lecture method, the case analysis method, the experiential exercise method, the programmed learning method, and so forth. In this section we show how organization structures adapt to their technology.

technology How an organization transfers its inputs into outputs.

Numerous studies have been carried out on the technology–structure relationship.[31] The details of those studies are quite complex, so let's go straight to the bottom line and attempt to summarize what we know.

The common theme differentiating technologies is their *degree of routineness*. By this we mean that technologies tend toward either routine or nonroutine activities. The former are characterized by automated and standardized operations. Nonroutine activities are customized. They include such varied operations as furniture restoring, custom shoemaking, and genetic research.

What relationships have been found between technology and structure? Although the relationship is not overwhelmingly strong, we find that routine tasks are associated with taller and more departmentalized structures. The relationship between technology and formalization, however, is stronger. Studies consistently show routineness to be associated with the presence of rule manuals, job descriptions, and other formalized documentation. Finally, there has been found to be an interesting relationship between technology and centralization. It seems logical that routine technologies would be associated with a centralized structure, whereas nonroutine technologies, which rely more heavily on the knowledge of specialists, would be characterized by delegated decision authority. This position has met with some support. However, a more generalizable conclusion is that the technology–centralization relationship is moderated by the degree of formalization. Formal regulations and centralized decision making are both control mechanisms, and management can substitute one for the other. Routine technologies should be associated with centralized control if there is a minimum of rules and regulations. However, if formalization is high, routine technology can be accompanied by decentralization. So, we would predict that routine technology would lead to centralization, but only if formalization is low.

Environment

An organization's **environment** is composed of those institutions or forces that are outside the organization and potentially affect the organization's performance. These typically include suppliers, customers, competitors, government regulatory agencies, public pressure groups, and the like.

environment Those institutions or forces outside the organization that potentially affect the organization's performance.

Why should an organization's structure be affected by its environment? Because of environmental uncertainty. Some organizations face relatively static environments—few forces in their environment are changing. There are, for example, no new competitors, no new technological breakthroughs by current competitors, or little activity by public pressure groups to influence the organization. Other organizations face very dynamic environments—rapidly changing government regulations affecting their business, new competitors, difficulties in acquiring raw materials, continually changing product preferences by customers, and so on. Static environments create significantly less uncertainty for managers than do dynamic ones. And since uncertainty is a threat to an organization's effectiveness, management will try to minimize it. One way to reduce environmental uncertainty is through adjustments in the organization's structure.[32]

Recent research has helped clarify what is meant by environmental uncertainty. Three key dimensions to any organization's environment have been found: capacity, volatility, and complexity.[33]

The *capacity* of an environment refers to the degree to which it can support growth. Rich and growing environments generate excess resources, which can buffer the organization in times of relative scarcity. Abundant capacity, for example, leaves room for an organization to make mistakes; scarce capacity does not. In 1995 firms operating in the multimedia software business had relatively abundant environments, whereas those in the full-service brokerage business faced relative scarcity.

The degree of instability in an environment is captured in the *volatility* dimension. Where there is a high degree of unpredictable change, the environment is dynamic. This makes it difficult for management to predict accurately the probabilities associated with various decision alternatives. At the other extreme is a stable environment. The accelerated changes in Eastern Europe and the demise of the Cold War had dramatic effects on the defense industry in the early 1990s. This moved the environment of major defense contractors like McDonnell-Douglas, General Dynamics, and Northrop from relatively stable to dynamic.

Finally, the environment needs to be assessed in terms of *complexity*, that is, the degree of heterogeneity and concentration among environmental elements. Simple environments are homogeneous and concentrated. This might describe the tobacco industry, since there are relatively few players. It's easy for firms in this industry to keep a close eye on the competition. In contrast, environments characterized by heterogeneity and dispersion are called complex. This is essentially the current environment in the on-line computer data services business. Every day there seems to be another "new kid on the block" with whom established data services firms have to deal.

Figure 14-8
Three-Dimensional Model of the Environment

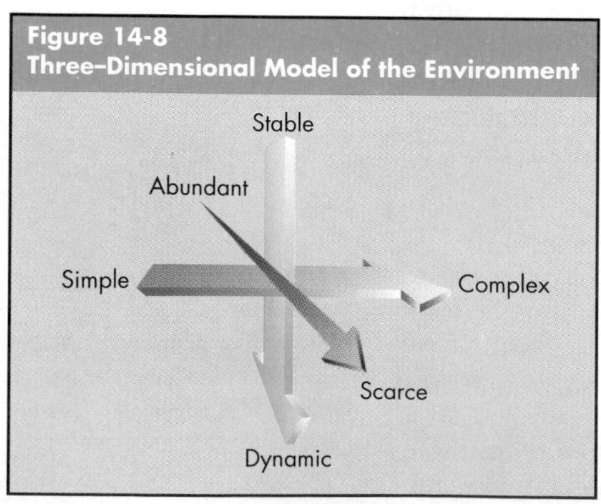

Figure 14-8 summarizes our definition of the environment along its three dimensions. The arrows in this figure indicate movement toward higher uncertainty. So organizations that operate in environments characterized as scarce, dynamic, and complex face the greatest degree of uncertainty. Why? Because they have little room for error, high unpredictability, and a diverse set of elements in the environment to constantly monitor.

Given this three-dimensional definition of environment, we can offer some general conclusions. There is evidence that relates the degrees of environmental uncertainty to different structural arrangements. Specifically, the more scarce, dynamic, and complex the environment, the more organic a structure should be. The more abundant, stable, and simple the environment, the more the mechanistic structure will be preferred.

Summary

We've shown that four variables—strategy, size, technology, and environment—are the primary forces determining whether an organization is mechanistic or organic. Now let's use our previous analysis to explain the evolution of structural designs throughout this century.

The industrial revolution encouraged economies of scale and the rise of the modern large corporation. As companies grew from their original simple structures, they took on mechanistic characteristics and became bureaucracies. The rise of bureaucracy, to become the dominant structure in industrialized nations from the 1920s through the 1970s, can be largely explained by three facts. First, the environment was relatively stable and certain over this period. The monopoly power of the large corporations, coupled with little international competition, kept environmental uncertainty to a minimum. Second, economies of scale and minimal competition allowed these corporations to introduce highly routine technologies. And third, most of these large corporations chose to pursue cost minimization or imitation strategies, leaving innovation to the little guys. Combine these strategies with large size, routine technologies, and relatively abundant, stable, and simple environments, and you have a reasonably clear explanation for the rise and domination of the bureaucracy.

Things began to change in the 1970s, when the environment became significantly more uncertain. Oil prices quadrupled literally overnight in 1973. Inflation exploded into double digits in 1978 and 1979. Advances in computer technology—especially the availability of increasingly powerful systems at dramatically falling prices—began to lessen the advantage that accrued to large size. And, of course, competition moved to the global arena. To compete effectively, top management responded by restructuring their organizations. Some went to the matrix to give their companies increased flexibility. Some added team structures so they could respond more rapidly to change. Today, senior managers in most large corporations are debureaucratizing their organizations—making them more organic by reducing staff, cutting vertical levels, decentralizing authority, and the like—primarily because the environment continues to be uncertain. Managers realize that in a dynamic and changing environment, inflexible organizations end up as bankruptcy statistics.

Organizational Designs and Employee Behavior

We opened this chapter by implying that an organization's structure can have profound effects on its members. In this section, we directly assess just what those effects might be.

A review of the evidence linking organizational structures to employee performance and satisfaction leads to a clear conclusion: You can't generalize! Not everyone prefers the freedom and flexibility of organic structures. Some people are most productive and satisfied when work tasks are standardized and ambiguity is minimized—that is, in mechanistic structures. So any discussion of the effect of organization design on employee behavior has to address individual differences. To illustrate this point, let's consider employee preferences for work specialization, span of control, and centralization.[34]

The evidence generally indicates that *work specialization* contributes to higher employee productivity but at the price of reduced job satisfaction. However, this statement ignores individual differences and the type of job tasks people do.

As we noted previously, work specialization is not an unending source of higher productivity. Problems start to surface, and productivity begins to suffer, when the human diseconomies of doing repetitive and narrow tasks overtake the economies of specialization. As the work force has become more highly educated and desirous of jobs that are intrinsically rewarding, the point where productivity begins to decline seems to be reached more quickly than in decades past.

While more people today are undoubtedly turned off by overly specialized jobs than were their parents or grandparents, it would be naive to ignore the reality that there is still a segment of the work force that prefers the routine and repetitiveness of highly specialized jobs. Some individuals want work that makes minimal intellectual demands and provides the security of routine. For these people, high work specialization is a source of job satisfaction. The empirical question, of course, is whether this represents 2 percent of the work force or 52 percent. Given that there is some self-selection operating in the choice of careers, we might conclude that negative behavioral outcomes from high specialization are most likely to surface in professional jobs occupied by individuals with high needs for personal growth and diversity.

A review of the research indicates that it is probably safe to say no evidence supports a relationship between *span of control* and employee performance. While it is intuitively attractive to argue that large spans might lead to higher employee performance because they provide more distant supervision and more opportunity for personal initiative, the research fails to support this notion. At this point it is impossible to state that any particular span of control is best for producing high performance or high satisfaction among subordinates. The reason is, again, probably individual differences. That is, some people like to be left alone, whereas others prefer the security of a boss who is quickly available at all times. Consistent with several of the contingency theories of leadership discussed in Chapter 11, we would expect factors such as employees' experiences and abilities and the degree of structure in their tasks to explain when wide or narrow spans of control are likely to contribute to their performance and job satisfaction. However, some evidence indicates that a *manager's* job satisfaction increases as the number of subordinates he or she supervises increases.

We find fairly strong evidence linking *centralization* and job satisfaction. In general, organizations that are less centralized have a greater amount of participative decision making. And the evidence suggests that participative decision making is positively related to job satisfaction. But, again, individual differences surface. The decentralization–satisfaction relationship is strongest with employees who have low self-esteem. Because low self-esteem individuals have less confidence in their abilities, they place a higher value on shared decision making, which means they're not held solely responsible for decision outcomes.

Our conclusion: To maximize employee performance and satisfaction, individual differences—such as experience, personality, and the work task—

should be taken into account. For simplicity's sake, it might help to keep in mind that individuals with a high degree of bureaucratic orientation (see "Learning About Yourself Exercise" at the end of this chapter) tend to place a heavy reliance on higher authority, prefer formalized and specific rules, and prefer formal relationships with others on the job. These people seem better suited to mechanistic structures. Those individuals with a low degree of bureaucratic orientation would probably fit better in organic structures.

Summary and Implications for Managers

The theme of this chapter has been that an organization's internal structure contributes to explaining and predicting behavior. That is, in addition to individual and group factors, the structural relationships in which people work have an important bearing on employee attitudes and behavior.

What's the basis for the argument that structure has an impact on both attitudes and behavior? To the degree an organization's structure reduces ambiguity for employees and clarifies such concerns as "What am I supposed to do?" "How am I supposed to do it?" "Whom do I report to?" and "Whom do I go to if I have a problem?", it shapes their attitudes and facilitates and motivates them to higher levels of performance.

Of course, structure also constrains employees to the extent it limits and controls what they do. For example, organizations structured around high levels of formalization and specialization, strict adherence to the chain of command, limited delegation of authority, and narrow spans of control give employees little autonomy. Controls in such organizations are tight and behavior will tend to vary within a narrow range. In contrast, organizations that are structured around limited specialization, low formalization, wide spans of control, and the like, provide employees greater freedom and, thus, will be characterized by greater behavioral diversity.

Figure 14-9 visually summarizes what we've discussed in this chapter. Strategy, size, technology, and environment determine the type of structure an organization will have. For simplicity's sake, we can classify structural designs around one of two models: mechanistic or organic. The specific effect of structural designs on performance and satisfaction is moderated by employees' individual preferences.

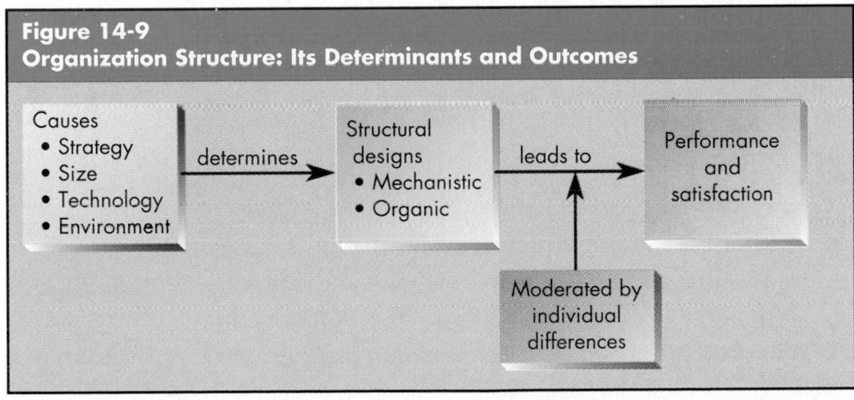

Figure 14-9
Organization Structure: Its Determinants and Outcomes

One last point: Managers need to be reminded that structural variables like work specialization, span of control, formalization, and centralization are objective characteristics that can be measured by organizational researchers. The findings and conclusions we've offered in this chapter, in fact, are directly a result of the work of these researchers. But employees don't objectively measure these structural characteristics! They observe things around them in an unscientific fashion and then form their own implicit models of what the organization's structure is like. How many people did they have to interview with before they were offered their jobs? How many people work in their departments and buildings? Is there an organization policy manual? If so, is it readily available and do people follow it closely? How is the organization and its top management described in newspapers and periodicals? Answers to questions such as these, when combined with an employee's past experiences and comments made by peers, leads members to form an overall subjective image of what their organization's structure is like. This image, though, may in no way resemble the organization's actual objective structural characteristics.

The importance of these *implicit models of organization structure* should not be overlooked. As we noted in Chapter 4, people respond to their perceptions rather than objective reality. The research, for instance, on the relationship between many structural variables and subsequent levels of performance or job satisfaction is far from consistent. We explained some of this as being attributable to individual differences. However, an additional contributing cause to these inconsistent findings might be diverse perceptions of the objective characteristics. Researchers typically focus on actual levels of the various structural components, but these may be irrelevant if people interpret similar components differently. The bottom line, therefore, is to understand how employees interpret their organization's structure. That should prove a more meaningful predictor of their behavior than the objective characteristics themselves.

For Review

1. Why isn't work specialization an unending source of increased productivity?
2. All things being equal, which is more efficient, a wide or narrow span of control? Why?
3. In what ways can management departmentalize?
4. What is a *matrix structure*? When would management use it?
5. Contrast the network organization with the boundaryless organization.
6. What type of structure works best with an innovation strategy? A cost-minimization strategy? An imitation strategy?
7. Summarize the size–structure relationship.
8. Define and give an example of what is meant by the term *technology*.
9. Summarize the environment–structure relationship.
10. What is the importance of this statement? "Employees form implicit models of organization structure."

For Discussion

1. "Employees prefer to work in flat, decentralized organizations." Do you agree or disagree? Discuss.
2. Do you think most employees prefer high formalization? Support your position.
3. If you were an employee in a matrix structure, what pluses do you think the structure would provide? What about minuses?
4. Do *you* think there is such a thing as a "feminine organization"? Explain.
5. What behavioral predictions would you make about people who worked in a "pure" boundaryless organization (if such a structure were ever to exist)?

Point

Small Is Beautiful

The Davids are beating up on the Goliaths. Big corporations are going the way of the dinosaurs because they're overly rigid, technologically obsolete, and too bureaucratic. They're being replaced by small agile companies. These small organizations are the technology innovators, able to respond quickly to changing market opportunities, and have become the primary job generators in almost all developed countries.

In almost every major industry, the smaller and more agile firms are outperforming their larger competitors. In the airlines, little Southwest Air continually outperforms the likes of American and United. CNN has taken on ABC, CBS, and NBC with impressive results. In steel, small minimill operators like Nucor have proven to be far more efficient and responsive to change than big producers like U.S. Steel. And in the computer industry, giants like IBM and Digital are fighting for their lives against hundreds of small entrepreneurial firms.

What's going on? The law of economies of scale is being repealed! The law of economies of scale argued that larger operations drove out smaller ones because, with large size, came greater efficiency. Fixed costs, for instance, could be spread over more units. Large companies could use standardization and mass production to produce the lowest cost products. But that no longer applies because of market fragmentation, strategic alliances, and technology.

Customers of Intellection would agree that small is beautiful. The 30-employee firm specializes in a niche market, making software for manufacturers that models an entire production line, from raw materials to finished goods. When a customer puts in an order, Intellection delivers with speed and agility. Intellection president Sanjiv Sidhu (right) keeps the entrepreneurial spirit alive by bouncing around new ideas with his development team.

Niche markets have taken away the advantages of large size. Southwest can compete successfully against American and United because it doesn't try to match the big guys' full-service strategy. It doesn't use hubs, it doesn't transfer baggage, it doesn't compete in every market, it doesn't offer meals, and it provides no reserved seats.

Strategic alliances offer small firms the opportunity to share others' expertise and development costs, allowing little companies to compete with big ones. For example, many small book publishers don't have the money to develop marketing operations and sales staffs in Australia or Asia. By joining forces with publishers in those countries to market their books, they can behave like the big guys.

Technology is also taking away a lot of the advantage that used to go to size. Computer and satellite linkage and flexible manufacturing systems are examples of such technology. Quick & Reilly or Charles Schwab can execute orders as efficiently as Dean Witter or Merrill Lynch through computer links to exchanges, even though they are a fraction of the size.

In today's increasingly dynamic environment, large size has become a serious handicap. It restricts the creativity to develop new products and services. It also limits job growth. More specifically, it's the small organizations that innovate and create jobs. For instance, consultant David Birch estimates that very small firms—those with fewer than 20 employees—created 88 percent of all net jobs in the United States between 1981 and 1985. Additionally, Birch claims that between 1988 and 1991, small firms created virtually all new jobs in the United States.

Big companies are getting the message. They're laying off tens of thousands of employees. They're selling businesses that don't fit with their core competencies. And they're restructuring themselves to be more agile and responsive.

This argument is based on J. Case, "The Disciples of David Birch," *INC.* (January 1989), pp. 39–45; T. Peters, "Rethinking Scale," *California Management Review* (Fall 1992), pp. 7–28; I. Sager, "The Great Equalizer," *BusinessWeek/The Information Revolution* (1994), pp. 100–10; and J. Naisbitt, *Global Paradox* (New York: William Morrow, 1994).

counterPoint

"Small Is Beautiful" Is a Myth!

It's now become the conventional wisdom to acknowledge that large organizations are at a disadvantage in today's dynamic environment. Their large size limits their agility. Additionally, competitive and technological forces have ganged up to take away the economies that derived from scale. Well, the conventional wisdom is wrong! The hard evidence shows that the importance of small businesses as job generators and as engines of technological dynamism has been greatly exaggerated. Moreover, large organizations have discovered how to become less rigid, more entrepreneurial, and less hierarchical—while still maintaining the advantages that accrue to large size.

First, the research showing that small companies have been the prime job generator in recent years is flawed. The early data that was used exaggerated the incidence of start-ups and covered too short a period. It also failed to recategorize companies once they grew or shrunk, which systematically inflated the relative importance of small firms. Using the more common definition of small companies as those with fewer than 100 employees, the evidence indicates that the share of jobs held by small companies has remained virtually unchanged since the 1960s. The vast majority of job creation over time is contributed by a tiny fraction of new firms. Among the 245,000 U.S. businesses begun in 1985, 75 percent of the employment gains three years later were made by 735 companies (or .003 percent) of the group. And all of those 735 companies had more than 100 employees to begin with. This same pattern—new firms that are successful start out big—also holds in the United Kingdom.

People like to cite computers as a high-tech industry dominated by innovative small firms. It isn't true. Only 5 percent of U.S. computer companies employ 500 workers or more (which includes companies like Intel and Microsoft), yet this 5 percent accounts for more than 90 percent of both jobs and sales in the industry. Incidentally, in Japan, computers have always been dominated by giants such as NEC, Toshiba, and Fujitsu.

It's true the typical organization is getting smaller. The average American business establishment has shrunk dramatically during the last quarter century—from 1,100 employees in 1967 to 665 in 1985. But what these numbers don't reveal is that these smaller establishments are increasingly part of a large multilocation firm with the financial and technological resources to compete in a global marketplace. In other words, these smaller organizations are a de facto part of the large enterprise. And this practice is going on throughout the world. For example, a study found that the 32 largest German manufacturing companies had in excess of a thousand legally independent subsidiaries, and the number grew by almost 50 percent between 1971 and 1983.

Second, technology favors the big guys. Studies demonstrate that small firms turn out to be systematically backward when it comes to technology. For example, on every continent, the big companies are far more likely than the small ones to invest in computer-controlled factory automation.

Third, everyone agrees that large organizations are improving their flexibility by increasing their use of strategic alliances, interorganizational networks, and similar devices. For instance, Siemens, the huge German multinational, has strategic alliances with Fujitsu to make robotics, GTE in telecommunications, Philips to produce semiconductors, and with Microsoft to develop software. This worldwide trend, coupled with efforts to widen spans of control, decentralize decision making, cut vertical levels, and sell off or close operations that don't fit with the organization's primary purpose, have made large firms increasingly agile and responsive.

This argument is based on B. Harrison, *Lean and Mean: The Changing Landscape of Corporate Power in the Age of Flexibility* (New York: Basic Books, 1994).

Learning About Yourself Exercise

Bureaucratic Orientation Test

Instructions: For each statement, check the response (either Mostly agree or Mostly disagree) that best represents your feelings.

	Mostly agree	Mostly disagree
1. I value stability in my job.	✓	
2. I like a predictable organization.	✓	
3. The best job for me would be one in which the future is uncertain.		✓
4. The federal government would be a nice place to work.	✓	
5. Rules, policies, and procedures tend to frustrate me.		✓
6. I would enjoy working for a company that employed 85,000 people worldwide.	✓	
7. Being self-employed would involve more risk than I'm willing to take.	✓	✓
8. Before accepting a job, I would like to see an exact job description.	✓	
9. I would prefer a job as a free-lance house painter to one as a clerk for the Department of Motor Vehicles.		✓
10. Seniority should be as important as performance in determining pay increases and promotion.		✓
11. It would give me a feeling of pride to work for the largest and most successful company in its field.		✓
12. Given a choice, I would prefer to make $40,000 per year as a vice president in a small company to $45,000 as a staff specialist in a large company.		✓
13. I would regard wearing an employee badge with a number on it as a degrading experience.		✓
14. Parking spaces in a company lot should be assigned on the basis of job level.	✓	
15. If an accountant works for a large organization, he or she cannot be a true professional.		✓
16. Before accepting a job (given a choice), I would want to make sure the company had a very fine program of employee benefits.	✓	
17. A company will probably not be successful unless it establishes a clear set of rules and procedures.		✓

18. Regular working hours and vacations are more important to me than finding thrills on the job. ___ ✓
19. You should respect people according to their rank. ___ ✓
20. Rules are meant to be broken. ___ ✓

Turn to page A-29 for scoring directions and key.

Source: A.J. DuBrin, *Human Relations: A Job Oriented Approach* © 1978, pp. 687–88. Reprinted with permission of Reston Publishing Co., a Prentice Hall Co., 11480 Sunset Hills Road, Reston, VA 22090.

Working With Others Exercise

Authority Figures

Purpose: To learn about one's experiences with, and feelings about, authority.

Time: Approximately seventy-five minutes.

Procedure:

1. Your instructor will separate class members into groups based on their birth order. Groups are formed consisting of "Only children," "Eldest," "Middle," and "Youngest," according to placement in families. Larger groups will be broken into smaller ones, with four or five members, to allow for freer conversation.
2. Each group member should talk about how he or she "typically reacts to the authority of others." Focus should be on specific situations that offer general information about how individuals deal with authority figures (for example, bosses, teachers, parents, or coaches). The group has 25 minutes to develop a written list of how the group generally deals with others' authority. Be sure to separate tendencies that group members share and those they do not.
3. Repeat step 2, except this time discuss how group members "typically are as authority figures." Again make a list of shared characteristics.
4. Each group will share its general conclusions with the entire class.
5. Class discussion will focus on questions such as these:
   a. What patterned differences have surfaced between the groups?
   b. What may account for these differences?
   c. What hypotheses might explain the connection between how individuals react to the authority of others and how they are as authority figures?

Source: This exercise is adapted from W.A. Kahn, "An Exercise of Authority," *Organizational Behavior Teaching Review*, Vol. XIV, Issue 2 (1989–90), pp. 28–42.

Ethical Dilemma Exercise

Employee Monitoring: How Far Is Too Far?

When does management's effort to control the actions of its employees become an invasion of privacy? Consider two cases.[35]

Employees at General Electric's Answering Center handle telephone inquiries from customers all day long. Those conversations are taped by GE and occasionally reviewed by its management.

The Internal Revenue Service's internal audit group monitors a computer log that shows employee access to taxpayer's accounts. This monitoring activity allows management to check and see what employees are doing on their computers.

Are either of these cases—monitoring telephone calls or computer activities—an invasion of employee privacy? When does management overstep the bounds of decency and privacy by silently (even covertly) scrutinizing the behavior of its employees?

Managers at GE and the IRS defend their practice in terms of ensuring quality, productivity, and proper employee behavior. GE can point to U.S. government statistics estimating that 6 million workers are being electronically monitored on their jobs. And silent surveillance of telephone calls can be used to help employees do their jobs better. One IRS audit of its southeastern regional offices found that 166 employees took unauthorized looks at the tax returns of friends, neighbors, or celebrities.

When does management's need for information about employee performance cross over the line and interfere with a worker's right to privacy? For example, must employees be notified ahead of time they will be monitored? Does management's right to protect its interests extend to electronic monitoring of every place a worker might be—bathrooms, locker rooms, and dressing rooms?

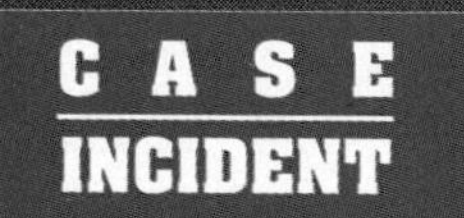

Organizing the Clinton Administration

Richard Haass, a former Bush aide, thinks the Clinton administration is organized wrong. According to Haass, the structure Bill Clinton and his people have chosen promotes new ideas, but it also wastes time, saps morale, and invites disaster.

The Clinton administration has organized itself as an adhocracy—an organic structure that minimizes reliance on regularized and systematic patterns of providing advice and instead relies heavily on the president to distribute assignments and select whom he listens to and when. Haass claims that an adhocracy has six drawbacks: (1) It tends to discourage debate and dissent. Important meetings—where sensitive information is discussed and decisions made—may include only those the powers-to-be want there. Adhocracy thus discourages truthfulness, for people fear being left out. (2) It leads to inconsistency because no one is given full responsibility for a policy. (3) Adhocracy undermines morale. Those with titles but no power feel slighted. (4) This structural form is error prone. The lack of standardized procedures increases the likelihood of mistakes. (5) The lack of standardization also increases the probability of scandals. The emphasis on personal relationships leads individuals to think too much about protecting the boss; the absence of formal procedures lets them get away with it. (6) Finally, adhocracy ends up misallocating the president's time. The president becomes his own chief of staff, taking time away from his primary task of providing leadership for the country.

Haass notes that the president's kitchen cabinet of old friends, consultants, and favored appointees have created "government by inner circle," which favors people over positions. Clinton listens to this favored group more than those in formal positions. And because Clinton and his senior advisers neither trust nor respect standing bureaucracies, they rely heavily on task forces (run by presidential intimates) to handle issues like health care or welfare reform.

Haass argues that many of President Clinton's problems can be attributed to this adhocratic structure. Foreign policy, according to Haass, suffers from a lack of direction. Relations with Congress falter due to inconsistent directives from the administration.

Questions

1. Haass dwells on the drawbacks of adhocracy. What do you think its strengths are?
2. A dynamic environment demands flexibility and adhocracy is flexible. Why, then, isn't this structure an ideal mechanism for managing government?
3. "The structure of an administration should compensate for weaknesses in the president." Do you agree or disagree with this statement? What would the implications of this statement be for the Clinton administration?
4. Contrast Clinton's role in leading a country with the CEO's job at a multibillion-dollar corporation. Is Clinton merely implementing a "boundaryless organization" in government the way, say, Jack Welch is at General Electric?

This case is based on R.N. Haass, "Bill Clinton's Adhocracy," *New York Times Magazine* (May 29, 1994), pp. 40–41.

Big Brother IS Watching You!

Some corporations have been spying on employees. Sheraton Hotel has been doing it. So has Kmart. This spying brings into question just how far a company's authority goes and the line between corporate control and personal freedom.

Francklin Etienne and Brad Fair were among dozens of employees secretly videotaped at Sheraton. And not just while they were doing their job. Brad, for instance, was taped undressing in the employees' locker room! Francklin was *caught* reading a book on his break. Sheraton officials defend their actions by saying secret videotaping did result in catching one drug-dealing employee. An immigrant from Haiti, Etienne couldn't reconcile this action by his employer and America's preoccupation with freedom. "When I found out that I was on the tape, I said to myself, 'Where is the privacy that they're always talking about? Where is the freedom they're always talking about?'"

Lewis Hubble's experience at Kmart was more personal. He learned that two coworkers he had befriended were actually private investigators hired by

Kmart to compile reports on its employees by going to local taverns with them, visiting them at their homes, and the like. These reports contained information that had little or nothing to do with the employees' jobs. For instance, one said an employee had fathered another employee's child—and it named names. Kmart management would not speak on the record, but they say they used the investigators to break up an inside theft ring. Said Marva Plumley, a Kmart warehouse employee: "What takes place in that warehouse, they have a right to know. They do not have a right to know what goes on in my bedroom, in my living room."

These are not isolated examples. One government estimate indicates that at least 6 million American workers are spied on at work each year. It takes various forms—listening in on phone calls, videotaping work areas, reviewing computer entries, monitoring E-mail. And there is little employees can do to stop management from spying on company property or off. Historically, the courts have ruled in favor of a company's right to collect information on workers without their knowledge. There is a federal law to keep employers from listening to workers' personal phone calls, but aside from that almost no laws guarantee employees protection from prying eyes on the job.

Management has an obligation to protect its assets and to monitor its premises for illegal activities. On-the-job drug abuse and employee stealing, for example, cost American businesses billions of dollars each year. It is for these reasons that management justifies spying on employees.

Questions

1. Is spying a substitute for direct managerial leadership or formal regulations? Discuss.
2. When does spying cross the line from effective management controls to invasion of employee privacy?

3. Would you think any better of Sheraton or Kmart's management if they had told employees ahead of time their companies might videotape employees anywhere or hired undercover private investigators to monitor illegal activities by employees? Discuss.
4. Do you think the loss in employee morale and organizational commitment as a result of these spying practices are offset by reductions in property loss and gains in productivity (for example, by identifying and removing employees who abuse drugs)?

Source: "Employers Spying on Employees," *World News Tonight* (March 28, 1994).

Suggestions for Further Reading

CAPPELLI, P., and P.D. SHERER, "The Missing Role of Context in OB: The Need for a Meso-Level Analysis," in L.L. Cummings and B.M. Staw (eds.), *Research in Organizational Behavior,* Vol. 13 (Greenwich, CT: JAI Press, 1991), pp. 55–110.

GALBRAITH, J.R., and E.E. LAWLER, III, *Organizing for the Future: The New Logic for Managing Complex Organizations* (San Francisco: Jossey-Bass, 1993).

HIRSCHHORN, L., and T. GILMORE, "The New Boundaries of the 'Boundaryless' Company," *Harvard Business Review* (May-June 1992), pp. 104–15.

JACQUES, E., "In Praise of Hierarchy," *Harvard Business Review* (January-February 1990), pp. 127–33.

LAWLER, E.E., III, *The Ultimate Advantage: Creating the High-Involvement Organization* (San Francisco: Jossey-Bass, 1992).

MILLER, D., "Organizational Configurations: Cohesion, Change, and Prediction," *Human Relations* (August 1990), pp. 771–89.

MITROFF, I.I., R.O. MASON, and C.M. PEARSON, "Radical Surgery: What Will Tomorrow's Organizations Look Like?" *Academy of Management Executive* (May 1994), pp. 11–21.

PARTHASARTHY, R., and S.B. SETHI, "The Impact of Flexible Automation on Business Strategy and Organizational Structure," *Academy of Management Review* (January 1992), pp. 86–111.

PINCHOT, G., and E. PINCHOT, *The End of Bureaucracy and the Rise of the Intelligent Organization* (San Francisco: Berrett-Koehler, 1994).

ROBBINS, S.P., *Organization Theory: Structure, Design, and Applications,* 3rd ed. (Englewood Cliffs, NJ: Prentice Hall, 1990).

Notes

[1] G. Pinchot and E. Pinchot, "Oticon A/S: A De-Stalinized Company," *At Work* (January-February 1994), p. 1; and P. LaBarre, "The Dis-Organization of Oticon," *Industry Week* (July 18, 1994), pp. 23–28.

[2] See, for instance, R.L. Daft, *Organization Theory and Design*, 5th ed. (St. Paul, MN: West, 1995).

[3] J.H. Sheridan, "Sizing Up Corporate Staffs," *Industry Week* (November 21, 1988), p. 47.

[4] J.B. Treece, "Breaking the Chains of Command," *Business Week/The Information Revolution 1994*, p. 112.

[5] See, for instance, L. Urwick, *The Elements of Administration* (New York: Harper & Row, 1944), pp. 52–53.

[6] J.S. McClenahen, "Managing More People in the '90s," *Industry Week* (March 20, 1989), p. 30.

[7] J.R. Brandt, "Middle Management: Where the Action Will Be," *Industry Week* (May 2, 1994), p. 31.

[8] A. Ross, "BMO's Big Bang," *Canadian Business* (January 1994), pp. 58–63.

[9] J.B. Levine, "For IBM Europe, 'This Is the Year of Truth,'" *Business Week* (April 19, 1993), p. 45.

[10] H. Mintzberg, *Structure in Fives: Designing Effective Organizations* (Englewood Cliffs, NJ: Prentice-Hall, 1983), p. 157.

[11] S. Baker, "Can Nucor Forge Ahead—and Keep Its Edge?" *Business Week* (April 4, 1994), p. 108.

[12] See, for instance, the interview with Edward Lawler in "Bureaucracy Busting," *Across the Board* (March 1993), pp. 23–27.

[13] Cited in *At Work* (May-June 1993), p. 3.

[14] K. Knight, "Matrix Organization: A Review," *Journal of Management Studies* (May 1976), pp. 111–30; and L.R. Burns and D.R. Wholey, "Adoption and Abandonment of Matrix Management Programs: Effects of Organizational Characteristics and Interorganizational Networks," *Academy of Management Journal* (February 1993), pp. 106–38.

[15] See, for instance, S.M. Davis and P.R. Lawrence, "Problems of Matrix Organization," *Harvard Business Review* (May-June 1978), pp. 131–42.

[16] M. Kaeter, "The Age of the Specialized Generalist," *Training* (December 1993), pp. 48–53.

[17] L. Brokaw, "Thinking Flat," *INC.* (October 1993), p. 88.

[18] See, for instance, C.C. Snow, R.E. Miles, and H.J. Coleman, Jr., "Managing 21st Century Network Organizations," *Organizational Dynamics* (Winter 1992), pp. 5–20; S. Tully, "The Modular Corporation," *Fortune* (February 8, 1993), pp. 106–16; E.O. Welles, "Virtual Realities," *INC.* (August 1993), pp. 50–58; and E.A. Gargan, "'Virtual' Companies Leave the Manufacturing to Others," *New York Times* (July 17, 1994), p. F5.

[19] "GE: Just Your Average Everyday $60 Billion Family Grocery Store," *Industry Week* (May 2, 1994), pp. 13–18.

[20] This section is based on L. Grant, "The Management Model That Jack Built," *Los Angeles Times Magazine* (May 9, 1993), pp. 20–22, 34–36; and J.A. Byrne, "The Horizontal Corporation," *Business Week* (December 20, 1993), pp. 76–81.

[21] See J. Lipnack and J. Stamps, *The TeamNet Factor* (Essex Junction, VT: Oliver Wight, 1993); J.R. Wilke, "Computer Links Erode Hierarchical Nature of Workplace Culture," *Wall Street Journal* (December 9, 1993), p. A1; and T.A. Stewart, "Managing in a Wired Company," *Fortune* (July 11, 1994), pp. 44–56.

[22] See, for instance, C. Hyde, "A Feminist Model for Macro-Practice: Promises and Problems," *Administration in Social Work*, Vol. 13, No. 3/4 (1989), pp. 145–81; and J.K. Fletcher, "Castrating the Female Advantage," *Journal of Management Inquiry* (March 1994), pp. 74–82.

[23] J. Rothschild and C. Davies, "Organizations Through the Lens of Gender: Introduction to the Special Issue," *Human Relations* (Summer 1994), p. 588.

[24] J. Rothschild, "Towards a Feminine Model of Organization," working paper, Department of Sociology, Virginia Polytechnic Institute and State University, 1991.

[25] Ibid.

[26] T. Burns and G.M. Stalker, *The Management of Innovation* (London: Tavistock, 1961); and J.A. Courtright, G.T. Fairhurst, and L.E. Rogers, "Interaction Patterns in Organic and Mechanistic Systems," *Academy of Management Journal* (December 1989), pp. 773–802.

[27] This analysis is referred to as a contingency approach to organization design. See, for instance, J.M. Pennings, "Structural Contingency Theory: A Reappraisal," in B.M. Staw and L.L. Cummings (eds.), *Research in Organizational Behavior*, Vol. 14 (Greenwich, CT: JAI Press, 1992), pp. 267–309.

[28] The strategy-structure thesis was originally proposed in A.D. Chandler, Jr., *Strategy and Structure: Chapters in the History of the Industrial Enterprise* (Cambridge, MA: MIT Press, 1962).

[29] See R.E. Miles and C.C. Snow, *Organizational Strategy, Structure, and Process* (New York: McGraw-Hill, 1978); D. Miller, "The Structural and Environmental Correlates of Business Strategy," *Strategic Management Journal* (January-February 1987), pp. 55–76; and D.C. Galunic and K.M. Eisenhardt, "Renewing the Strategy-Structure-Performance Paradigm," in B.M. Staw and L.L. Cummings (eds.), *Research in Organizational Behavior*, Vol. 16 (Greenwich, CT: JAI Press, 1994), pp. 215–55.

[30] See, for instance, P.M. Blau and R.A. Schoenherr, *The Structure of Organizations* (New York: Basic Books, 1971); D.S. Pugh, "The Aston Program of Research: Retrospect and Prospect," in A.H. Van de Ven and W.F. Joyce (eds.), *Perspectives on Organization Design and Behavior* (New York: Wiley, 1981), pp. 135–66; R.Z. Gooding and J.A. Wagner III, "A Meta-Analytic Review of the Relationship Between Size and Performance: The Productivity and Efficiency of Organizations and Their Subunits," *Administrative Science Quarterly* (December 1985), pp. 462–81; and A.C. Bluedorn, "Pilgrim's Progress: Trends and Convergence in Research on Organizational Size and Environments," *Journal of Management* (Summer 1993), pp. 163–92.

[31] See J. Woodward, *Industrial Organization: Theory and Practice* (London: Oxford University Press, 1965); C. Perrow, "A Framework for the Comparative Analysis of Organizations," *American Sociological Review* (April 1967), pp. 194–208; J.D. Thompson, *Organizations in Action* (New York: McGraw-Hill, 1967); J. Hage and M. Aiken, "Routine Technology, Social Structure, and Organizational Goals," *Administrative Science Quarterly* (September 1969), pp. 366–77; and C.C. Miller, W.H. Glick, Y. Wang, and G.P. Huber, "Understanding Technology–Structure Relationships: Theory Development and Meta-Analytic Theory Testing," *Academy of Management Journal* (June 1991), pp. 370–99.

[32] See F.E. Emery and E. Trist, "The Causal Texture of Organizational Environments," *Human Relations* (February 1965), pp. 21–32; P. Lawrence and J.W. Lorsch, *Organization and Environment: Managing Differentiation and Integration* (Boston: Harvard Business School, Division of Research, 1967); and A.C. Bluedorn, "Pilgrim's Progress."

[33] G.G. Dess and D.W. Beard, "Dimensions of Organizational Task Environments," *Administrative Science Quarterly* (March 1984), pp. 52–73; and E.A. Gerloff, N.K. Muir, and W.D. Bodensteiner, "Three Components of Perceived Environment Uncertainty: An Exploratory Analysis of the Effects of Aggregation," *Journal of Management* (December 1991), pp. 749–68.

[34] See, for instance, L.W. Porter and E.E. Lawler, III, "Properties of Organization Structure in Relation to Job Attitudes and Job Behavior," *Psychological Bulletin* (July 1965), pp. 23–51; L.R. James and A.P. Jones, "Organization Structure: A Review of Structural Dimensions and Their Conceptual Relationships with Individual Attitudes and Behavior," *Organizational Behavior and Human Performance* (June 1976), pp. 74–113; D.R. Dalton, W.D. Todor, M.J. Spendolini, G.J. Fielding, and L.W. Porter, "Organization Structure and Performance: A Critical Review," *Academy of Management Review* (January 1980), pp. 49–64; W. Snizek and J.H. Bullard, "Perception of Bureaucracy and Changing Job Satisfaction: A Longitudinal Analysis," *Organizational Behavior and Human Performance* (October 1983), pp. 275–87; and D.B. Turban and T.L. Keon, "Organizational Attractiveness: An Interactionist Perspective," *Journal of Applied Psychology* (April 1994), pp. 184–93.

[35] G. Bylinsky, "How Companies Spy on Employees," *Fortune* (November 4, 1991), pp. 131–40; D. Warner, "The Move to Curb Worker Monitoring," *Nation's Business* (December 1993), pp. 37–38; and M. Picard, "Working Under an Electronic Thumb," *Training* (February 1994), pp. 47–51.

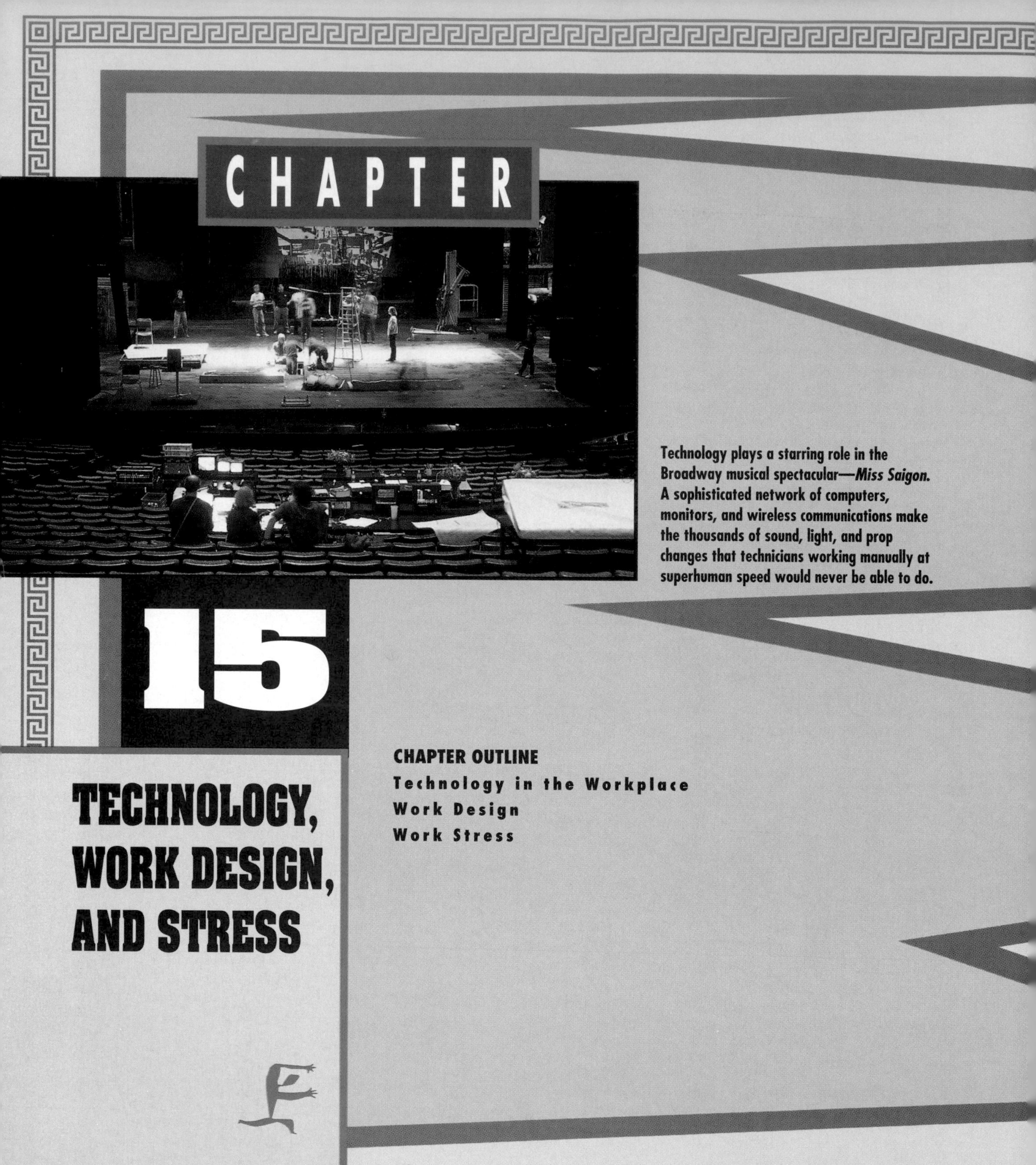

CHAPTER 15

TECHNOLOGY, WORK DESIGN, AND STRESS

Technology plays a starring role in the Broadway musical spectacular—*Miss Saigon.* A sophisticated network of computers, monitors, and wireless communications make the thousands of sound, light, and prop changes that technicians working manually at superhuman speed would never be able to do.

CHAPTER OUTLINE

LEARNING OBJECTIVES

After studying this chapter, you should be able to:

1. Describe the role of the PDCA Cycle in continuous improvement
2. Explain the current popularity of reengineering and contrast it with TQM
3. Describe the implications of flexible manufacturing systems for people who work within them
4. Identify who is affected by worker obsolescence
5. Contrast the job characteristics model with the social information processing model
6. Identify the characteristics of a family-friendly organization
7. Describe potential sources of stress
8. Explain individual difference variables that moderate the stress–outcome relationship

Robinson Crusoe started the 40-hour week. He had all the work done by Friday.

— L. Fechtner

The Federal National Mortgage Association (better known as Fannie Mae) is the largest U.S. buyer of home mortgages. As you might expect, Fannie Mae relies heavily on computers to process huge amounts of loan information and to help the firm package its loans into easily marketable securities.

Until the early 1990s, Fannie Mae relied on dozens of mainframe computers and a highly centralized management system to get its work done. But this system couldn't keep up with the company's growing volume of business. So management remade work processes in the organization, breaking down old centralized departments and replacing them with work teams that linked financial, marketing, and computer experts. To tie everything together, management replaced its centralized computer system with a network of more than 2,000 personal computers and new software that made the machines accessible to workers with a minimum of training.

The $10 million that Fannie Mae spent on new computers and revising work processes proved to be money well spent. When interest rates dropped in 1992, refinancings surged and Fannie Mae's volume soared. Not only could the new system handle the large increase in volume, it generated a significant improvement in average employee productivity. That is, Fannie Mae was able to do lots more work with just a few more people. Between 1991 and 1992, volume nearly doubled to $257 billion. This was achieved, however, by adding only 100 new employees to its work force of nearly 3,000. "If we had not used this technology," says Vice Chairman Franklin D. Raines, shown in the photo on page 71, "our business would have collapsed." Instead, Fannie Mae profits jumped 13 percent, to $1.6 billion.[1]

This chapter looks at three interrelated topics: technology, the design of work, and work stress. We show how technology is changing organizations and the jobs that people do. We also show how management is redesigning jobs and work schedules in the belief that such actions can increase employee productivity and satisfaction. Finally, we demonstrate that technology and work design are two factors contributing to increased stress levels among some employees.

Technology in the Workplace

We introduced the term *technology* in the previous chapter's discussion of why structures differ. We said it was how an organization transfers its inputs into outputs. In recent years, the term has become widely used by economists, managers, consultants, and business analysts to describe machinery and equipment that utilizes sophisticated electronics and computers to produce those outputs.

The common theme among new technologies in the workplace is that they substitute machinery for human labor in transforming inputs into outputs. This substitution of capital for labor has been going on essentially nonstop since the Industrial Revolution in the mid-1800s. For instance, the introduction of electricity allowed textile factories to introduce mechanical looms that could produce cloth far faster and cheaper than was previously possible when the looms were powered by individuals. But it's been the computerization of equipment and machinery in the last quarter century that has been the prime mover in reshaping the twentieth-century workplace. Automated teller machines (ATMs), for example, have replaced thousands of human tellers in banks. Ninety-eight percent of the spot welds on new Ford Tauruses are performed by robots, not people. Many cars now come equipped with on-board computers that diagnose problems in seconds that used to take hours for mechanics. IBM has built a plant in Austin, Texas, that can produce laptop computers without the help of a single worker. Everything from the time parts

Drug distributor McKesson literally arms its order fillers with technology. Warehouse staff wear a 12 ounce device consisting of a computer, laser scanner, and two-way radio. The device receives customers' order from a central computer and displays it on a tiny computer screen, which tells the order fillers where the products are and plans the most efficient product-retrieval route through the 22,000-item warehouse. When an order is complete, the mini-computer radios the warehouse's central computer, updating inventory numbers and the customer's invoice.

arrive at the IBM plant to the final packing of finished products is completely automated. And our opening Fannie Mae example illustrates how companies have utilized personal computers to decentralize decison making and generate enormous increases in productivity.

This book is concerned with the behavior of people at work. No coverage of this topic today would be complete without discussing how recent advances in technology are changing the workplace and affecting the work lives of employees. In this section, we look at four specific issues related to technology and work: total quality management (TQM) and continuous improvement processes, reengineering, flexible manufacturing systems, and worker obsolescence.

Quality and Continuous Improvement Processes

In Chapter 1, we described TQM as a philosophy of management that's driven by the constant attainment of customer satisfaction through the continuous improvement of all organizational processes. Managers in many organizations, especially in North America, have been criticized for accepting a level of performance below perfection. TQM, however, argues that *good* isn't *good enough*! To dramatize this point, it's easy to assume that 99.9 percent error-free performance represents the highest standards of excellence. Yet it doesn't look so impressive when you recognize this standard would result in the U.S. Post Office losing 2,000 pieces of mail per hour, or U.S. doctors performing 500 incorrect surgical operations per week, or two plane crashes per day at O'Hare Airport in Chicago![2]

TQM programs seek to achieve continuous process improvements so variability is constantly reduced. When you eliminate variations, you increase the uniformity of the product or service. This, in turn, results in lower costs and higher quality. For instance, Advanced Filtration Systems Inc., of Champaign, Illinois, recently cut the number of product defects—as determined by a customer quality audit—from 26.5 per 1,000 units to zero over four years. And that occurred during a period when monthly unit production tripled and the number of workers declined by 20 percent.

Continuous improvement runs counter to the more typical American management approach of seeing work projects as being linear—with a beginning and

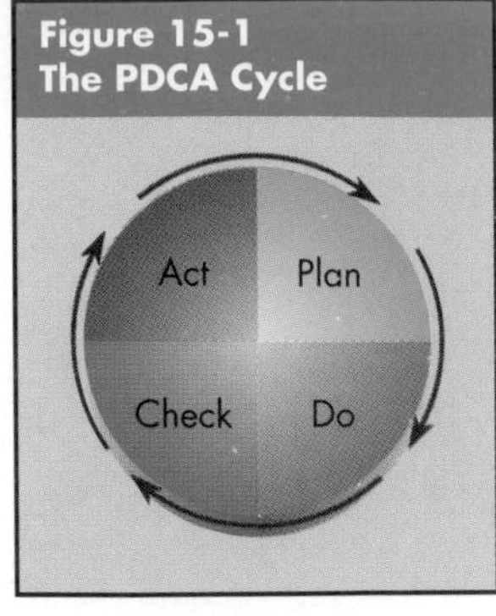

Figure 15-1
The PDCA Cycle

an end. For example, American managers have traditionally looked at cost cutting as a short-term project. They set a goal of cutting costs by 20 percent, achieve it, and then say, "Whew! Our cost cutting is over." The Japanese, on the other hand, have regarded cost control as something that never ends. The search for continual improvement creates a race without a finish line.

The search for never-ending improvement requires a circular approach rather than a linear one. This is illustrated in the Plan-Do-Check-Act (PDCA) Cycle shown in Figure 15-1.[3] Management plans a change, does it, checks the results, and, depending on the outcome, acts to standardize the change or begin the cycle of improvement again with new information. This cycle treats all organizational processes as being in a constant state of improvement.

Eaton Corporation, a major manufacturer of automobile components, has adopted the PDCA Cycle throughout the company.[4] Management encourages its workers to take thousands of small steps to incrementally improve the products they make and the processes used to make them. This extends to office workers who haggle over utility rates, challenge local tax assessments, scrutinize inventories, and eliminate paperwork. Continuous improvement has helped Eaton increase its annual productivity between 1983 and 1992 by 3 percent a year compared to the U.S. average of 1.9 percent.

As literally tens of thousands of organizations introduce TQM and continuous process improvement, what does it mean for employees and their jobs? It means they're no longer able to rest on their previous accomplishments and successes. So, for some people, they may experience increased stress from a work climate that no longer accepts complacency with the status quo. A race with no finish line means a race that's never over—which creates constant tension. While this tension may be positive for the organization (remember *functional conflict* from Chapter 13?), the pressures from an unrelenting search for process improvements can create anxiety and stress in some employees. But probably the most significant implication for employees is that management will look to them as the prime source of improvement ideas. Employee involvement programs, therefore, are part and parcel of TQM. Empowered work teams who have hands-on involvement in process improvement, for instance, are widely used in those organizations that have introduced TQM.

◆The search for continual improvement creates a race without a finish line.

Reengineering Work Processes

We also introduced reengineering in Chapter 1. We described it as considering how things would be done if you could start all over from scratch.

The term *reengineering* comes from the historical process of taking apart an electronics product and designing a better version. Michael Hammer coined the term for organizations. When he found companies using computers simply to automate outdated processes, rather than finding fundamentally better ways of doing things, he realized the same principles could be applied to business. So, as applied to organizations, reengineering means management should start with a clean sheet of paper—rethinking and redesigning those processes by which the organization creates value and does work, ridding itself of operations that have become antiquated in the computer age.[5]

KEY ELEMENTS Three key elements of reengineering are identifying an organization's distinctive competencies, assessing core processes, and reorganizing horizontally by process.

An organization's **distinctive competencies** define what it is that the organization is more superior at delivering than its competition. Examples might include superior store locations, a more efficient distribution system, higher quality products, more knowledgeable sales personnel, or superior technical support. Dell Computer, for instance, differentiates itself from its competitors by emphasizing high-quality hardware, comprehensive service and technical support, and low prices. Why is identifying distinctive competencies so important? Because it guides decisions regarding what activities are crucial to the organization's success.

distinctive competencies
Define what it is that the organization is more superior at delivering than its competition.

Management also needs to assess the core processes that clearly add value to the organization's distinctive competencies. These are the processes that transform materials, capital, information, and labor into products and services the customer values. When the organization is viewed as a series of processes, ranging from strategic planning to after-sales customer support, management can determine to what degree each adds value. Not surprisingly, this **process value analysis** typically uncovers a whole lot of activities that add little or nothing of value and whose only justification is "we've always done it this way."

process value analysis
Determination to what degree each organizational process adds value to the organization's distinctive competencies.

Reengineering requires management to reorganize around horizontal processes. This means cross-functional and self-managed teams. It means focusing on processes rather than functions. So, for instance, the vice president of marketing might become the "process owner of finding and keeping customers."[6] And it also means cutting out levels of middle management. As Hammer points out, "Managers are not value-added. A customer never buys a product because of the caliber of management. Management is, by definition, indirect. So if possible, less is better. One of the goals of reengineering is to minimize the necessary amount of management."[7]

WHY REENGINEERING NOW? Isn't reengineering something management should have been doing all along? Why has it become such a hot topic in the 1990s? The answers, according to Michael Hammer, are a changing global environment and organizational structures that had gotten top heavy.[8]

Traditional mechanistic organizations worked fine in times of stable growth. Activities could be fragmented and specialized to gain economic efficiencies. This described the environment faced by most North American organizations in the 1950s, 1960s, and much of the 1970s. But most organizations today operate in global conditions of overcapacity. Customers are much more informed and sophisticated than they were 30 years ago. Moreover, markets, production, and capital are all globally mobile. Investors in Australia, for example, can put their money into opportunities in Japan, Canada, or anywhere else in the world if they see better returns than they can get at home. Global customers now demand quality, service, and low cost. If *you* can't provide it, they'll get it from someone else.

Work specialization, functional departments, narrow spans of control, and the like, drove down direct labor costs, but the bureaucracies they created had massive overhead costs. That is, to coordinate all the fragmentation and specialization, the organization had to create numerous levels of middle managment to glue together the fragmented pieces. So while bureaucracies drove down costs at the operating level, they required increasingly expensive coordinating systems. Those organizations that introduced teams, decentralized decisions, widened spans of control, and flattened structures became more efficient and challenged the traditional ways of doing things.

REENGINEERING VS. TQM Is reengineering just another term for TQM? No! They do have some common characteristics.[9] They both, for instance, emphasize processes and satisfying the customer. After that, they diverge radically. This is evident in their goals and the means they use for achieving their goals.

TQM seeks incremental improvements; reengineering looks for quantum leaps in performance. That is, the former is essentially about improving something that is basically OK; the latter is about taking something that is irrelevant, throwing it out, and starting over. And the means the two approaches use are totally different. TQM relies on bottom-up, participative decision making in both the planning of a TQM program and its execution. Reengineering, on the other hand, is initially driven by top management. When reengineering is complete, the workplace is largely self-managed. But getting there is a very autocratic, nondemocratic process. Reengineering's supporters argue it has to be this way because the level of change the process demands is highly threatening to people and they aren't likely to accept it voluntarily. When top management commits to reengineering, employees have no choice. As Hammer is fond of saying, "You either get on the train, or we'll run over you with the train."[10]

IMPLICATIONS FOR EMPLOYEES Reengineering is rapidly gaining momentum in business and industry.[11] A recent survey found that, among manufacturing firms, 44 percent of respondents indicated they are now reengineering or considering doing so. Among utilities and insurance companies, the responses were 48 and 52 percent, respectively.

Some of the companies that have implemented reengineering in at least some of their divisions include Motorola, Xerox, Ford, Banc One, Banca di America e di Italia, AT&T, Siemens, KPMG Peat Marwick, Hallmark, and the Commonwealth life insurance group. Hallmark, for instance, cut the time it

Top management at Union Carbide's industrial chemicals division led the drive to reengineer work processes in plant and equipment maintenance, which accounted for 30 percent of costs. Directed to work in teams and to set ambitious cost-cutting goals, employees (shown here) worked out the details of their new work process by developing new repair and maintenance procedures. The reengineering effort saved Union Carbide $20 million, 50 percent more than management's target. Companywide, Union Carbide has used reengineering to cut $400 million out of fixed costs over a recent three-year period.

takes to get a new product to market down from two years to a few months.[12] And Commonwealth now has 1,100 people doing the work 1,900 used to do, even though its business has risen 25 percent.[13]

Reengineering's popularity isn't surprising. In today's highly competitive global marketplace, companies are finding they're forced to reengineer their work processes if they're going to survive. And employees will have to "get on the train."

Lots of people are going to lose their jobs as a direct result of reengineering efforts. Just how many depends on the pace at which organizations adopt the new techniques. Some experts say that reengineering will eliminate between a million and 2.5 million jobs each year for the foreseeable future.[14] Regardless of the number, the impact won't be uniform across the organization. Staff support jobs, especially middle managers, will be most vulnerable. So, too, will clerical jobs in service industries. For instance, one knowledgeable observer predicts that reengineering will reduce employment in commerical banks and thrift institutions by 30 to 40 percent by the year 2000.[15]

Those employees that keep their jobs after reengineering will find they aren't the same jobs any longer. These new jobs will typically require a wider range of skills, include more interaction with customers and suppliers, offer greater challenge, contain increased responsibilities, and provide higher pay. However, the three- to five-year period it takes to implement reengineering is usually tough on employees. They suffer from uncertainty and anxiety associated with taking on new tasks and having to discard long-established work practices and formal social networks.

Flexible Manufacturing Systems

They look like something out of a science fiction movie in which remote-controlled carts deliver a basic casting to a computerized machining center. With robots positioning and repositioning the casting, the machining center calls on its hundreds of tools to perform varying operations that turn the casting into a finished part. Completed parts, each a bit different from the others, are finished at a rate of one every 90 seconds. Neither skilled machinists nor conventional machine tools are used. Nor are there any costly delays for changing dies or tools in this factory. A single machine can make dozens or even hundreds of different parts in any order management wants. Welcome to the world of **flexible manufacturing systems**.[16]

flexible manufacturing system
Integration of computer-aided design, engineering, and manufacturing to produce low-volume products at mass production costs.

In a global economy, those manufacturing organizations that can respond rapidly to change have a competitive advantage. They can, for instance, better meet the diverse needs of customers and deliver products faster than their competitors. When customers were willing to accept standardized products, fixed assembly lines made sense. But nowadays, flexible technologies are increasingly necessary to compete effectively.

The unique characteristic of flexible manufacturing systems is that by integrating computer-aided design, engineering, and manufacturing, they can produce low-volume products for customers at a cost comparable to what had been previously possible only through mass production. Flexible manufacturing systems are, in effect, repealing the laws of economies of scale. Management no longer has to mass produce thousands of identical products to achieve low per-unit production costs. With flexible manufacturing, when management wants to produce a new part, it doesn't change machines—it just changes the computer program.

Some automated plants can build a wide variety of flawless products and switch from one product to another on cue from a central computer. John Deere, for instance, has a $1.5 billion automated factory that can turn out ten basic tractor models with as many as 3,000 options without plant shutdowns for retooling. National Bicycle Industrial Co., which sells its bikes under the Panasonic brand, uses flexible manufacturing to produce any of 11,231,862 variations on 18 models of racing, road, and mountain bikes in 199 color patterns and an almost unlimited number of sizes. This allows Panasonic to provide almost customized bikes at mass-produced prices.[17]

What do flexible manufacturing systems mean for people who have to work within them? They require a different breed of industrial employee.[18] Workers in flexible manufacturing plants need more training and higher skills. This is because there are fewer employees, so each has to be able to do a greater variety of tasks. For instance, at a flexible Carrier plant in Arkansas, which makes compressors for air conditioners, all employees undergo six weeks of training before they start their jobs. This training includes learning to read blueprints, math such as fractions and metric calculations, statistical process-control methods, some computer skills, and solving the problems involved in dealing with fellow workers. In addition to higher skills, employees in flexible plants are typically organized into teams and given considerable decision-making discretion. Consistent with the objective of high flexibility, these plants tend to have organic structures. They decentralize authority into the hands of the operating teams.

Worker Obsolescence

Changes in technology have cut the shelf life of most employees' skills. A factory worker or clerical employee in the 1950s could learn one job and be reasonably sure his or her skills would be adequate to do that job for most of his or her work life. That certainly is no longer true. New technologies driven by computers, reengineering, TQM, and flexible manufacturing systems are changing the demands of jobs and the skills employees need to do them.

Repetitive tasks—like those traditionally performed on assembly lines and by low-skilled office clerks—will continue to be automated. And a good number of jobs will be upgraded. For instance, as most managers and professionals take on the task of writing their own memos and reports using word processing software, the traditional secretary's job will be upgraded to become more of an administrative assistant. Those secretaries unequipped to take on these expanded roles will be displaced.

Reengineering, as we previously noted, is producing significant increases in employee productivity. The redesign of work processes is achieving higher output with fewer workers. And these reengineered jobs require different skills. Employees who are computer illiterate, have poor interpersonal skills, or can't work autonomously will increasingly find themselves ill prepared for the demands of new technologies.

Finally, keep in mind that the obsolescence phenomenon doesn't exclude the managerial ranks. Those middle managers who merely acted as conduits in the chain of command between top management and the operating floor are being eliminated. And those managers who believe that employees only respond to directive leadership, tight controls, and intimidation will either change or find themselves on the street. The new model for effective managers will be one that emphasizes good listening, coaching, motivation, and team-support skills.

Work Design

The way tasks are combined to create individual jobs, the degree of flexibility employees have on their jobs, and the presence or absence of organizational support systems (like on-site day care and family leave) all have a direct influence on employee performance and satisfaction. In this section, we look at task characteristics theories, job redesign, work schedule options, and family-friendly work environments. Then we conclude by suggesting that, as we approach the twenty-first century, we need to begin completely rethinking what a job is. In 20 or 25 years, it's very possible that few of us will be doing anything that looks like what we have traditionally called *a job*.

Task Characteristics Theories

"Every day was the same thing," Frank Greer began. "Put the right passenger seat into Jeeps as they came down the assembly line, pop in four bolts locking the seat frame to the car body, then tighten the bolts with my electric wrench. Thirty cars and 120 bolts an hour, eight hours a day. I didn't care that they were paying me $18 an hour, I was going crazy. I did it for almost a year and a half. Finally, I just said to my wife that this isn't going to be the way I'm going to spend the rest of my life. My brain was turning to Jello on that job. So I quit. Now I work in a print shop and I make less than $12 an hour. But let me tell you, the work I do is really interesting. It challenges me! I look forward every morning to going to work again."

Frank Greer is acknowledging two facts we all know: (1) jobs are different, and (2) some are more interesting and challenging than others. These facts have not gone unnoticed by OB researchers. They have responded by developing a number of **task characteristics theories** that seek to identify task characteristics of jobs, how these characteristics are combined to form different jobs, and the relationship of these task characteristics to employee motivation, satisfaction, and performance.

task characteristics theories Seek to identify task characteristics of jobs, how these characteristics are combined to form different jobs, and their relationship to employee motivation, satisfaction, and performance.

There are at least seven different task characteristics theories.[19] Fortunately, there is a significant amount of overlap between them.[20] For instance, Herzberg's motivation-hygiene theory and the research on the achievement need (both discussed in Chapter 6) are essentially task characteristics theories. You'll remember that Herzberg argued that jobs which provided opportunities for achievement, recognition, responsibility, and the like, would increase employee satisfaction. Similarly, McClelland demonstrated that high achievers performed best in jobs that offered personal responsibility, feedback, and moderate risks.

In this section, we review the three most important task characteristics theories: requisite task attributes theory, the job characteristics model, and the social information processing model.

REQUISITE TASK ATTRIBUTES THEORY The task characteristics approach began with the pioneering work of Turner and Lawrence in the mid-1960s.[21] They developed a research study to assess the effect of different kinds of jobs on employee satisfaction and absenteeism. They predicted employees would prefer jobs that were complex and challenging; that is, such jobs would increase satisfaction and result in lower absence rates. They defined job complexity in terms of six task characteristics: (1) variety, (2) autonomy, (3) responsibility, (4) knowledge and skill, (5) required social interaction, and (6) optional social interaction. The higher a job scored on these characteristics, according to Turner and Lawrence, the more complex it was.

Their findings confirmed their absenteeism prediction. Employees in high-complexity tasks had better attendance records. But they found no general correlation between task complexity and satisfaction—until they broke their data down by the background of employees. When individual differences in the form of urban-versus-rural background were taken into account, employees from urban settings were shown to be more satisfied with low-complexity jobs. Employees with rural backgrounds reported higher satisfaction in high-complexity jobs. Turner and Lawrence concluded that workers in larger communities had a variety of nonwork interests and thus were less involved and motivated by their work. In contrast, workers from smaller towns had fewer nonwork interests and were more receptive to the complex tasks of their jobs.

Turner and Lawrence's requisite task attributes theory was important for at least three reasons. First, they demonstrated that employees did respond differently to different types of jobs. Second, they provided a preliminary set of task attributes by which jobs could be assessed. And third, they focused attention on the need to consider the influence of individual differences on employees' reaction to jobs.

THE JOB CHARACTERISTICS MODEL Turner and Lawrence's requisite task attributes theory laid the foundation for what is today the dominant framework for defining task characteristics and understanding their relationship to employee motivation, performance, and satisfaction: Hackman and Oldham's **job characteristics model** (JCM).[22]

According to the JCM, any job can be described in terms of five core job dimensions, defined as follows:

1. **Skill variety**: The degree to which the job requires a variety of different activities so the worker can use a number of different skills and talents
2. **Task identity**: The degree to which the job requires completion of a whole and identifiable piece of work
3. **Task significance**: The degree to which the job has a substantial impact on the lives or work of other people
4. **Autonomy**: The degree to which the job provides substantial freedom, independence, and discretion to the individual in scheduling the work and in determining the procedures to be used in carrying it out
5. **Feedback**: The degree to which carrying out the work activities required by the job results in the individual obtaining direct and clear information about the effectiveness of his or her performance

job characteristics model (JCM)
Identifies five job characteristics and their relationship to personal and work outcomes.

skill variety
Degree to which a job requires a variety of different activities so the worker can use a number of different skills and talents.

task identity
Degree to which a job requires completion of a whole and identifiable piece of work.

task significance
Degree to which a job has a substantial impact on the lives or work of other people.

task autonomy
Degree to which a job provides substantial freedom, independence, and discretion to the individual in scheduling the work and in determining the procedures to be used in carrying it out.

feedback
Degree to which carrying out the work activities required by a job results in the individual obtaining direct and clear information about the effectiveness of his or her performance.

Table 15–1 offers examples of job activities that rate high and low for each characteristic.

Figure 15-2 presents the model. Notice how the first three dimensions—skill variety, task identity, and task significance—combine to create meaningful work. That is, if these three characteristics exist in a job, we can predict the incumbent will view the job as being important, valuable, and worthwhile. Notice, too, that jobs possessing autonomy give the job incumbent a feeling of personal responsibility for the results and that, if a job provides feedback, the employee will know how effectively he or she is performing. From a motivational standpoint, the model says that internal rewards are obtained by an in-

Table 15-1 Examples of High and Low Job Characteristics

Skill Variety	
High variety	The owner-operator of a garage who does electrical repair, rebuilds engines, does body work, and interacts with customers
Low variety	A body shop worker who sprays paint eight hours a day
Task Identity	
High identity	A cabinetmaker who designs a piece of furniture, selects the wood, builds the object, and finishes it to perfection
Low identity	A worker in a furniture factory who operates a lathe solely to make table legs
Task Significance	
High significance	Nursing the sick in a hospital intensive care unit
Low significance	Sweeping hospital floors
Autonomy	
High autonomy	A telephone installer who schedules his or her own work for the day, makes visits without supervision, and decides on the most effective techniques for a particular installation
Low autonomy	A telephone operator who must handle calls as they come according to a routine, highly specified procedure
Feedback	
High feedback	An electronics factory worker who assembles a radio and then tests it to determine if it operates properly
Low feedback	An electronics factory worker who assembles a radio and then routes it to a quality control inspector who tests it for proper operation and makes needed adjustments

Source: G. Johns, *Organizational Behavior: Understanding Life at Work*, 3rd ed. (New York: HarperCollins, 1992), p. 216. With permission.

dividual when she *learns* (knowledge of results) that she *personally* (experienced responsibility) has performed well on a task she *cares* about (experienced meaningfulness).[23] The more these three psychological states are present, the greater will be the employee's motivation, performance, and satisfaction, and the lower his or her absenteeism and likelihood of leaving the organization. As Figure 15-2 shows, the links between the job dimensions and the outcomes are moderated or adjusted by the strength of the individual's growth need, that is, by the employee's desire for self-esteem and self-actualization. This means that individuals with a high growth need are more likely to experience the psychological states when their jobs are enriched than are their counterparts with a low growth need. Moreover, they will respond more positively to the psychological states when they are present than will low-growth-need individuals.

The core dimensions can be combined into a single predictive index, called the **motivating potential score** (MPS). Its computation is shown in Figure 15-3 on page 82.

motivating potential score (MPS) Predictive index suggesting the motivation potential in a job.

Jobs high on motivating potential must be high on at least one of the three factors that lead to experienced meaningfulness, and they must be high on both autonomy and feedback. If jobs score high on motivating potential, the model predicts that motivation, performance, and satisfaction will be positively affected, and the likelihood of absence and turnover will be lessened.

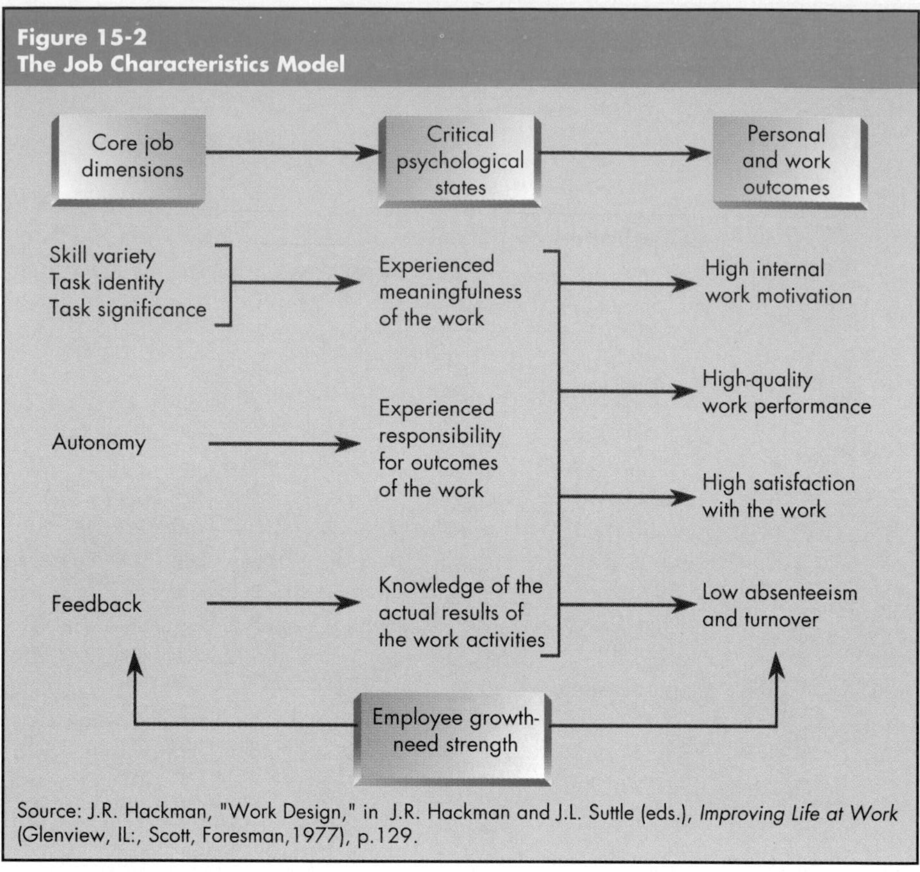

Figure 15-2
The Job Characteristics Model

Source: J.R. Hackman, "Work Design," in J.R. Hackman and J.L. Suttle (eds.), *Improving Life at Work* (Glenview, IL:, Scott, Foresman, 1977), p.129.

The job characteristics model has been well researched. Most of the evidence supports the general framework of the theory—that is, there is a multiple set of job characteristics and these characteristics impact behavioral outcomes.[24] But there is still considerable debate around the five specific core dimensions in the JCM, the multiplicative properties of the MPS, and the validity of growth-need strength as a moderating variable.

There is some question whether task identity adds to the model's predictive ability,[25] and evidence suggests that skill variety may be redundant with autonomy.[26] Further, a number of studies have found that by adding all the variables in the MPS, rather than adding some and multiplying by others, the MPS

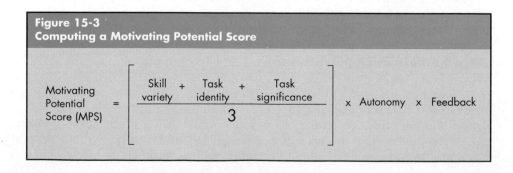

Figure 15-3
Computing a Motivating Potential Score

$$\text{Motivating Potential Score (MPS)} = \left[\frac{\text{Skill variety} + \text{Task identity} + \text{Task significance}}{3}\right] \times \text{Autonomy} \times \text{Feedback}$$

◆◆◆◆ OB in the News ◆◆◆◆

Increasing Job Autonomy

In 1988 Dave Wiegand was about 90 days away from closing up his telecommunications company—Advanced Network Design Inc., of La Mirada, California. An admitted control freak, Wiegand's autocratic style was single-handedly killing his company. The more he pushed, the less productive his 35 employees became.

In a last-ditch effort, Wiegand hired a consultant. The consultant's advice? Make sure people are properly trained to do their jobs, then give them authority and responsibility. The consultant said the likely results would be stronger employee motivation, better work quality, higher job satisfaction, and lower turnover.

Reluctantly, Wiegand remade the jobs in his company to increase employee autonomy. For each job, managers and employees identify the four or five tasks generating the majority of that job's results. If the employee isn't already proficient in those tasks, the employee undergoes training. Then, once employees have shown they can master a task, it's turned over to them. After that, they just report to management on a weekly or monthly basis.

Employees like the new system. "It's much more productive," says Carmen Pugliese, a client services representative. "My supervisor used to dictate all my weekly and monthly goals. Now I set my own goals, and I can prioritize them better, so the flow is smoother. And if you see something that needs to be done, you do it. Job satisfaction is much stronger now."

It took Wiegand two years to feel comfortable giving employees so much freedom. But he has to like the results. Business is better than ever. And he now has 20 employees handling more work than the 35 had done previously.

Interestingly, the results at Advanced Network Design are consistent with data from national surveys. In a recent poll, when workers were asked what they valued most in a job, 64 percent gave the highest rating to "ability to work independently." That even beat out "high income" and "chances for promotion."

Based on J. Finegan, "People Power," *INC.* (July 1993), pp. 62–63.

becomes a better predictor of work outcomes.[27] Finally, the strength of an individual's growth needs as a meaningful moderating variable has recently been called into question.[28] Other variables—such as the presence or absence of social cues, perceived equity with comparison groups, and propensity to assimilate work experience[29]—may be more valid in moderating the job characteristics–outcome relationship. Given the current state of research on moderating variables, one should be cautious in unequivocally accepting growth-need strength as originally included in the JCM.

Where does this leave us? Given the current state of evidence, we can make the following statements with relative confidence: (1) People who work on jobs with high-core job dimensions are generally more motivated, satisfied, and productive than are those who do not; and (2) Job dimensions operate through the psychological states in influencing personal and work outcome variables rather than influencing them directly.[30]

SOCIAL INFORMATION PROCESSING MODEL At the beginning of this section on task characteristics theories, do you remember Frank Greer complaining about his former job on the Jeep assembly line? Would it surprise you to know that one of Frank's best friends, Russ Wright, is still working at Jeep, doing the same job Frank did, and Russ thinks his job is perfectly fine? Probably not! Why? Because, consistent with our discussion of perception in Chapter 4, we recognize that people can look at the same job and evaluate it differently. The fact that people respond to their jobs as *they perceive them* rather than to the *objective* jobs themselves is the central thesis in our third task characteristics theory. It's called the **social information processing (SIP) model**.[31]

social information processing model
Employees adopt attitudes and behaviors in response to the social cues provided by others with whom they have contact.

The SIP model argues that employees adopt attitudes and behaviors in response to the social cues provided by others with whom they have contact. These others can be coworkers, supervisors, friends, family members, or customers. For instance, Gary Ling got a summer job working in a British Columbia sawmill. Since jobs were scarce and this one paid particularly well, Gary arrived on his first day of work highly motivated. Two weeks later, however, his motivation was quite low. What happened was that his coworkers consistently bad-mouthed their jobs. They said the work was boring, having to clock in and out proved management didn't trust them, and supervisors never listened to their opinions. The objective characteristics of Gary's job had not changed in the two-week period; rather, Gary had reconstructed reality based on messages he had received from others.

A number of studies generally confirm the validity of the SIP model.[32] For instance, it has been shown that employee motivation and satisfaction can be manipulated by such subtle actions as a coworker or boss commenting on the existence or absence of job features like difficulty, challenge, and autonomy. So managers should give as much (or more) attention to employees' perceptions of their jobs as to the actual characteristics of those jobs. They might spend more time telling employees how interesting and important their jobs are. And managers should also not be surprised that newly hired employees and people transferred or promoted to a new position are more likely to be receptive to social information than are those with greater seniority.

Work Redesign

What are some of the options managers have at their disposal if they want to redesign or change the makeup of employee jobs? The following discusses three of those options: job rotation, job enlargement, and job enrichment.

job rotation
Periodic shifting of a worker from one task to another.

JOB ROTATION If employees suffer from overroutinization of their work, one alternative is to use **job rotation** (or what many now call *cross-training*). When an activity is no longer challenging, the employee is rotated to another job, at the same level, that has similar skill requirements.[33]

G.S.I. Transcomm Data Systems Inc. in Pittsburgh uses job rotation to keep its staff of 110 people from getting bored.[34] Over a recent two-year period, nearly 20 percent of Transcomm's employees made lateral job switches. Management believes the job rotation program has been a major contributor to cutting employee turnover from 25 percent to less than 7 percent a year. Brazil's Semco SA makes extensive use of job rotation. "Practically no one," says Semco's president, "stays in the same position for more than two or three years. We try to motivate people to move their areas completely from time to time so they don't get stuck to the technical solutions, to ways of doing things in which they have become entrenched."[35] Mike Conway, CEO of America West Airlines, describes how his company fully cross-trains their customer service representatives. He says America West does it "to give the employees a better job, to give them more job variety. It's more challenging, and for those who are interested in upward mobility, it exposes them to about 16 different areas of the company versus the one they would be exposed to if we specialized."[36]

The strengths of job rotation are that it reduces boredom and increases motivation through diversifying the employee's activities. Of course, it can also have indirect benefits for the organization, since employees with a wider range of skills give management more flexibility in scheduling work, adapting to changes, and filling vacancies. On the other hand, job rotation is not without its drawbacks. Training costs are increased, and productivity is reduced by moving a worker into a new position just when his or her efficiency at the prior job was creating organizational economies. Job rotation also creates disruptions. Members of the work group have to adjust to the new employee. The supervisor may also have to spend more time answering questions and monitoring the work of the recently rotated employee. Finally, job rotation can demotivate ambitious trainees who seek specific responsibilities in their chosen specialty.

JOB ENLARGEMENT More than 30 years ago, the idea of expanding jobs horizontally, or what we call **job enlargement**, grew in popularity. Increasing the number and variety of tasks that an individual performed resulted in jobs with more diversity. Instead of only sorting the incoming mail by department, for instance, a mail sorter's job could be enlarged to include physically delivering the mail to the various departments or running outgoing letters through the postage meter.

job enlargement
Horizontal expansion of jobs.

Efforts at job enlargement met with less than enthusiastic results.[37] As one employee who experienced such a redesign on his job remarked, "Before I had one lousy job. Now, through enlargement, I have three!" However, there have been some successful applications of job enlargement. For example, U.S. Shoe Co. created modular work areas to replace production lines in over half of their factories. In these work areas, workers perform two or three shoe-making steps instead of only one, as in traditional production lines. The result has been footwear produced more efficiently and with greater attention to quality.[38]

So, while job enlargement attacked the lack of diversity in overspecialized jobs, it did little to instill challenge or meaningfulness to a worker's activities. Job enrichment was introduced to deal with the shortcomings of enlargement.

JOB ENRICHMENT **Job enrichment** refers to the vertical expansion of jobs. It increases the degree to which the worker controls the planning, execution, and evaluation of his or her work. An enriched job organizes tasks so as to allow the worker to do a complete activity, increases the employee's freedom and independence, increases responsibility, and provides feedback, so an individual will be able to assess and correct his or her own performance.

job enrichment
Vertical expansion of jobs.

How does management enrich an employee's job? The following suggestions, based on the job characteristics model, specify the types of changes in jobs that are most likely to lead to improving their motivating potential (see Figure 15-4 on the next page).

1. *Combine tasks.* Managers should seek to take existing and fractionalized tasks and put them back together to form a new and larger module of work. This increases skill variety and task identity.
2. *Create natural work units.* The creation of natural work units means the tasks an employee does form an identifiable and meaningful whole.

To motivate employees to provide excellent customer service, Marriott Corporation is enriching jobs. Once only a doorman at the Marriott Hotel in Schaumburg, Illinois, Tony Prsyszlak (in red blazer) is now a guest service associate, or GSA, who performs the entire task of getting guests to their room. He greets them at the door, carries their bags, checks them into the hotel, and escorts them to their room. He is also responsible for handling guest requests and problems that he previously referred to his supervisor or another department. Prsyszlak says of his enriched job: "I'm a bellman, a doorman, a front-desk clerk, and a concierge all rolled into one. I have more responsibilities. I feel better about my job, and the guest gets better service."

This increases employee "ownership" of the work and improves the likelihood that employees will view their work as meaningful and important rather than as irrelevant and boring.

3. *Establish client relationships*. The client is the user of the product or service that the employee works on (and may be an "internal customer" as well as someone outside the organization). Wherever possible, managers should try to establish direct relationships between workers and their clients. This increases skill variety, autonomy, and feedback for the employee.
4. *Expand jobs vertically*. Vertical expansion gives employees responsibilities and control that were formerly allocated to management. It seeks to partially close the gap between the "doing" and the "controlling" aspects of the job, and it increases employee autonomy.
5. *Open feedback channels*. By increasing feedback, employees not only learn how well they are performing their jobs, but also whether their performance is improving, deteriorating, or remaining at a constant level. Ideally, this feedback about performance should be received directly as the employee does the job, rather than from management on an occasional basis.[39]

Figure 15-4
Guidelines for Enriching a Job

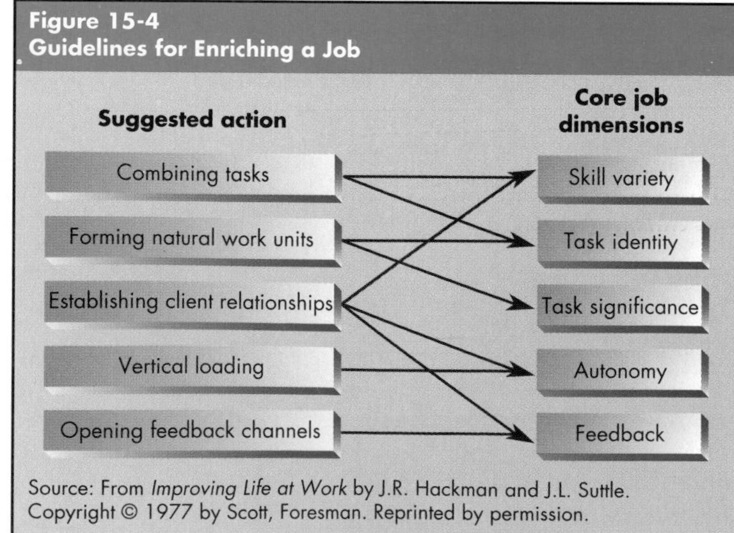

Source: From *Improving Life at Work* by J.R. Hackman and J.L. Suttle. Copyright © 1977 by Scott, Foresman. Reprinted by permission.

Lawrence Buettner used the suggestions just listed to design a job enrichment program for his international-trade banking department at First Chicago Corporation.[40] His department's chief product is commercial letters of credit—essentially a bank guarantee to stand behind huge import and export transactions. When he took over the department of 300 employees, he found paperwork crawling along a document "assembly line," with errors creeping in at each handoff. And employees did little to hide the boredom they were experiencing in their jobs. Buettner replaced the narrow specialized tasks that employees were doing with enriched jobs. Each clerk is now a trade expert who can handle a customer from start to finish. After 200 hours of training in finance and law, the clerks became full-service advisers who could turn around documents in a day while advising clients on such arcane matters as bank procedures in Turkey and U.S. munitions' export controls. And the results? Productivity has more than tripled, employee satisfaction has soared, and transaction volume has risen more than 10 percent a year. Additionally, increased skills have translated into higher pay for the employees who are performing the enriched jobs. These trade-service representatives, some of whom had come to the bank directly out of high school, now earn from $25,000 to $50,000 a year.

The First Chicago example shouldn't be taken as a blanket endorsement of job enrichment. The overall evidence generally shows that job enrichment reduces absenteeism and turnover costs and increases satisfaction; but on the critical issue of productivity, the evidence is inconclusive.[41] In some situations, such as at First Chicago, job enrichment increases productivity; in others, it decreases it. However, even when productivity goes down, there does seem to be consistently more conscientious use of resources and a higher quality of product or service.

Alternative Work Schedule Options

Susan Ross is your classic morning person. She rises each day at 5 A.M. sharp, full of energy. But, as she puts it, "I'm usually ready for bed right after the 7 P.M. news."

Susan's work schedule as a claims processor at Hartford Insurance is flexible. It allows her some degree of freedom as to when she comes to work and when she leaves. Her office opens at 6 A.M. and closes at 7 P.M. It's up to her how she schedules her 8-hour day within this 13-hour period. Because Susan is a morning person and also has a 7-year-old son who gets out of school at 3 P.M. every day, she opts to work from 6 A.M. to 3 P.M. "My work hours are perfect. I'm at the job when I'm mentally most alert, and I can be home to take care of Sean after he gets out of school."

Most people work an eight-hour day, five days a week. They start at a fixed time and leave at a fixed time. But a number of organizations have introduced alternative work schedule options as a way to improve employee motivation, productivity, and satisfaction.

COMPRESSED WORKWEEK The most popular form of the **compressed workweek** is four 10-hour days. The 4–40 program was conceived to allow workers more leisure time and shopping time, and to permit them to travel to and from work at non-rush-hour times. Supporters suggest that such a program can increase employee enthusiasm, morale, and commitment to the organization; increase productivity and reduce costs; reduce machine downtime in manufacturing; reduce overtime, turnover, and absenteeism; and make it easier for the organization to recruit employees. Currently about 25 percent of major U.S. companies offer this scheduling option.[42]

compressed workweek
Four-day week, with employees working 10 hours a day.

Proponents argue that the compressed workweek may positively affect productivity in situations in which the work process requires significant start-up and shutdown periods.[43] When start-up and shutdown times are a major factor, productivity standards take these periods into consideration in determining the time required to generate a given output. Consequently, in such cases, the compressed workweek will increase productivity even though worker performance is not affected, simply because the improved work scheduling reduces nonproductive time.

The evidence on 4–40 program performance is generally positive.[44] While some employees complain of fatigue near the end of the day, and about the difficulty of coordinating their jobs with their personal lives—the latter a problem especially for working mothers—most like the 4–40 program. In one study, for instance, when employees were asked whether they wanted to continue their 4–40 program, which had been in place for six months, or go back to a traditional five-day week, 78 percent wanted to keep the shorter workweek.[45]

SHORTER WORKWEEK How does a reduced four-day, 32-hour workweek sound? What if it included a 20 percent cut in pay? A number of Western European countries are considering the former. But if unions have their way, it won't be with any pay cut.[46]

Western Europe has 20 million unemployed workers. In an effort to deal with this problem, countries such as Germany, France, Spain, and Belgium are seriously considering spreading the available work among more people by cutting the workweek 20 percent.

With the jobless rate nearly 12 percent and rising in France and Germany, political pressures are building for this proposal. Volkswagen, for instance, has given an ultimatum to the union that represents its 103,000 workers: Accept a four-day workweek with a 20 percent drop in pay, or nearly every third job will be cut.

It's not clear at this point whether the 32-hour workweek will become the new standard in Western Europe. Moreover, even if it does, it isn't certain that employees will have to take a commensurate cut in pay. Proposals currently being considered at the federal level include having employers absorb the full cost—paying workers for 40 hours, even if they work only 32; having the government pick up the tab; or some combination of cost sharing among workers, employers, and government.

The impact on employees of a shorter workweek can only be speculative at this time. While the program would create more jobs, employees are likely to focus on how it affects them individually rather than the positive effect on their country's employment. A 20 percent cut in hours, with no cut in pay, should have generally positive effects on employee satisfaction and negative effects on productivity. If the cut in hours are matched with a 20 percent reduction in pay, satisfaction is likely to drop.

FLEXTIME Flextime is a scheduling option that allows employees, within specific parameters, to decide when to go to work. Susan Ross's work schedule at Hartford Insurance is an example of flextime. But what specifically is flextime?

flextime
Employees work during a common core time period each day but have discretion in forming their total workday from a flexible set of hours outside the core.

Flextime is short for flexible work hours. It allows employees some discretion over when they arrive and leave work. Employees have to work a specific number of hours a week, but they are free to vary the hours of work within certain limits. As shown in Figure 15-5, each day consists of a common core, usually six hours, with a flexibility band surrounding the core. For example, exclusive of a one-hour lunch break, the core may be 9 A.M. to 3 P.M., with the office actually opening at 6 A.M. and closing at 6 P.M. All employees are required to be at their jobs during the common core period, but they are allowed to accumulate their other two hours before and/or after the core time. Some flextime programs allow extra hours to be accumulated and turned into a free day off each month.

Are employees more happy, loyal, productive, and satisfied with their jobs when allowed flexibility in scheduling their work hours? Laura Henderson believes so. When she founded Prospect Associates, a health research and communications firm, Henderson (left) created an environment to support her belief that employees are a company's most valuable asset. In addition to offering her employees flextime, telecommuting, and part-time options, Henderson allows them to bring children to work when necessary and will realign employees' jobs to help them cope with difficult times in their lives. Henderson believes flexible scheduling helps her attract and keep the best employees, giving her small business a competitive advantage.

Of all work schedule options, flextime seems to currently be the most widely accepted. A survey of 1,000 major companies found flextime was offered by 73 percent.[47] At Metropolitan Life, for instance, 90 percent of the company's 28,000 administrative employees use the flextime program, starting between 7:30 A.M. and 10 A.M.[48]

The benefits claimed for flextime are numerous. They include reduced absenteeism, increased productivity, reduced overtime expenses, a lessening in hostility toward management, reduced traffic congestion around work sites, elimination of tardiness, and increased autonomy and responsibility for employees that may increase employee job satisfaction.[49] But beyond the claims, what's flextime's record?

Most of the performance evidence stacks up favorably. Flextime tends to reduce absenteeism and frequently improves worker productivity,[50] probably for several reasons. Employees can schedule their work hours to align with personal demands, thus reducing tardiness and absences, and employees can adjust their work activities to those hours in which they are individually more productive.

Flextime's major drawback is that it's not applicable to every job. It works well with clerical tasks where an employee's interaction with people outside his or her department is limited. It is not a viable option for receptionists, sales

Figure 15-5
Example of a Flextime Schedule

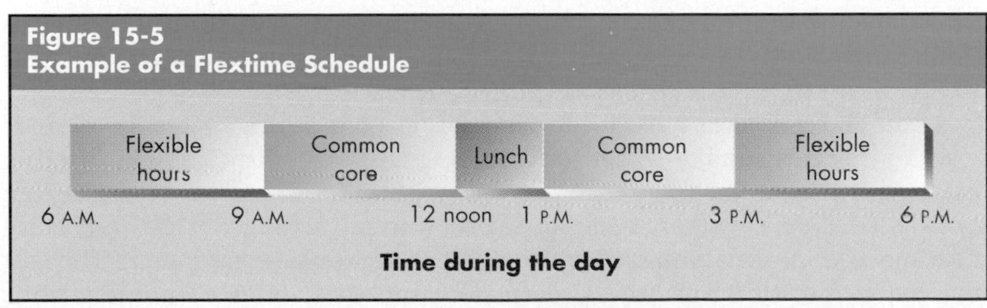

personnel in retail stores, or similar jobs where comprehensive service demands that people be at their work stations at predetermined times.

job sharing
Practice of having two or more people split a 40-hour-a-week job.

JOB SHARING A recent work-scheduling innovation is **job sharing**. It allows two or more individuals to split a traditional 40-hour-a-week job. So, for example, one person might perform the job from 8 A.M. to noon, and another performs the same job from 1 P.M. to 5 P.M.; or the two could work full, but alternate, days.

Xerox is one of the thousands of large companies that permit job sharing. Laura Meier and Lori Meagher, for instance, share a sales management position at Xerox.[51] Both are mothers of preschoolers and wanted greater flexibility. But they didn't want to give up their managerial careers at Xerox. So now Laura oversees their eight sales reps on Thursdays and Fridays, Lori has the job on Mondays and Tuesdays, and the two women work alternate Wednesdays.

From management's standpoint, job sharing allows the organization to draw on the talents of more than one individual in a given job. It also opens up the opportunity to acquire skilled workers—for instance, women with young children and retirees—who might not be available on a full-time basis. From the employee's viewpoint, job sharing increases flexibility. As such, it can increase motivation and satisfaction for those for whom a 40-hour-a-week job is just not practical.

telecommuting
Employees do their work at home on a computer that is linked to their office.

TELECOMMUTING It might be close to the ideal job for many people. No commuting, flexible hours, freedom to dress as you please, and little or no interruptions from colleagues. It's called **telecommuting**, and refers to employees who do their work at home on a computer linked to their office.[52] Currently, over 6.6 million people work at home in the United States (about 5.3 percent of the work force) doing tasks like taking orders over the phone, filling out reports and other forms, and processing or analyzing information. It's presently one of the fastest growing trends in work scheduling.[53]

American Express Travel Services is one organization whose experience with telecommuting has been very positive.[54] In 1993, 100 AmEx travel agents in 15 locations were telecommuters. The company can connect these people's homes to American Express's phone and data lines for a modest onetime expense of $1,300 each, including hardware. Once in place, calls to AmEx's reservation service are seamlessly routed to workers at home, where they can look up fares and book reservations on PCs. The typical telecommuting agent at AmEx handles 26 percent more calls at home than at the office. Why? One agent thinks it's an absence of distractions: "I don't feel like I'm working any harder. It's just that I don't have Suzy next to me telling me her husband is a jerk. I'm not worried about who's going into the boss's office, or noticing who's heading to the bathroom for the tenth time today." Additionally, as more agents become telecommuters and free up office space, the company will generate substantial savings in rent. For instance, in New York City, it costs AmEx nearly $4,400 a year to rent the 125 square feet of space each travel agent occupies.

Not all employees embrace the idea of telecommuting. After the massive Los Angeles earthquake in January 1994, many L.A. firms began offering telecommuting for their workers.[55] It was popular for a week or two, but that soon faded. Many workers complained they were missing out on important meetings and informal interactions that led to new policies and ideas. The vast majority were willing to put up with two- and three-hour commutes while bridges and freeways were being rebuilt in order to maintain their social contacts at work.

The long-term future of telecommuting depends on some questions for which we don't yet have definitive answers. For instance, will employees who do their work at home be at a disadvantage in office politics? Might they be less likely to be considered for salary increases and promotions? Is being out of sight equivalent to being out of mind? Will non-work-related distractions like children, neighbors, and the close proximity of the refrigerator significantly reduce productivity for those without superior willpower and discipline?

Family-Friendly Organizations

Forty-six percent of the U.S. work force is now female. More and more fathers want to actively participate in the care and raising of their children. As the baby-boom generation ages, many are finding themselves having to care for elderly parents. These three facts translate into an increasing number of employees who are attempting to juggle family obligations along with their job responsibilities. In the United States, the federal government acknowledged this fact when, in 1993, Congress passed the Family and Medical Leave Act. Its key provision is up to 12 weeks of unpaid leave for employees following childbirth or adoption, or to care for a seriously ill child, spouse, or parent. The act also requires employers to continue health benefits during this leave and guarantees employees the same or a comparable job upon return. In much of Western Europe, such family-leave laws have been in place for decades.

Companies like Aetna, Corning, IBM, Johnson & Johnson, and Quaker Oats are leading the way in establishing themselves as **family-friendly organizations**. They offer an umbrella of work/family programs such as on-site day care, child-care and elder-care referrals, flexible hours, compressed workweeks, job sharing, telecommuting, temporary part-time employment, and relocation assistance for employees' family members.[56]

family-friendly organizations Companies that offer an umbrella of work/family programs such as on-site day care, child-care and elder-care referrals, flexible hours, compressed workweeks, job sharing, telecommuting, temporary part-time employment, and relocation assistance for employees' family members.

Creating a family-friendly work climate was initially motivated by management's concern to improve employee morale and productivity and to reduce absenteeism. At Quaker Oats, for instance, 60 percent of employees admitted being absent at least three days a year because of children's illnesses, and 56 percent said they were unable to attend company-related functions or work overtime because of child-care problems.[57] However, the overall evidence indicates the major benefit to creating a family-friendly organization is that it makes it easier for employers to recruit and retain first-class workers.[58]

But increasing evidence shows there is a lot more talk about family friendliness than action.[59] For instance, a survey of employees at 80 major companies revealed that fewer than 2 percent of eligible employees actually took advantage of job sharing, telecommuting, and part-time work options.[60] Why the low usage? There seem to be three reasons. First, many managers find that giving employees increased flexibility to handle family obligations makes it harder to assign and schedule departmental work assignments. In spite of corporate policies that allow employees increased flexibility, supervisors frequently discourage their use and even punish those who insist on taking leaves or going on flextime. Second, coworkers often resent peers who aren't around. In some cases, family-friendly programs merely mean that other workers have to put in longer hours to make up the difference. So peer pressure discourages some employees from making use of family-friendly programs. Third, employees are frequently reluctant to take advantage of some of these programs—especially ones like

NEGATIVE ASPECTS

leaves of absence, telecommuting, and part-time employment—for fear they will be perceived as dispensable by upper management. At a time when so many organizations are laying off workers, employees don't want to give the impression they're not committed or suggest their job might be a good one for elimination.

Changing the Way We Look at Jobs: A Provocative Perspective

The changes we've described throughout this book have led one observer to predict that the whole notion of *jobs* may be becoming obsolete.[61]

Prior to 1800, very few people had a job. People worked hard raising food or making things at home. They had no regular hours, no job descriptions, no bosses, and no employee benefits. Instead, they put in long hours on shifting clusters of tasks, in a variety of locations, on a schedule set by the sun and the weather and the needs of the day. It was the Industrial Revolution and the creation of large manufacturing companies that brought about the concept of what we have come to think of as *jobs*. But the conditions that created "the job" are disappearing. Customized production is pushing out mass production; most workers now handle information, not physical products; and competitive conditions are demanding rapid response to changing markets. While economists and social analysts continue to talk about the disappearance of jobs in certain countries or industries, they're missing a more relevant point: What's actually disappearing is *the job itself.*

In a fast-moving economy, jobs are rigid solutions to an elastic problem. We can rewrite a person's job description occasionally, but not every week. When the work that needs doing changes constantly—which increasingly describes today's world—organizations can't afford the inflexibility that traditional jobs bring with it.

In 25 years or so it's possible that very few people will have jobs as we have come to know them. In place of jobs, there will be part-time and temporary work situations. Organizations will be transformed from a structure built out of jobs into a field of work needing to be done. And these organizations will be essentially made up of hired guns—contingent employees (temporaries, part-timers, consultants, and contract workers) who join project teams created to complete a specific task. When that task is finished, the team disbands. People will work on more than one team at a time, keeping irregular hours, and may be never meeting their coworkers face to face. Computers, pagers, cellular phones, modems, and the like, will allow people to work for multiple employers, at the same time, in locations throughout the world.[62] Few of these employees will be working nine to five at specific work spots. And they'll have little of the security their grandparents—who worked for U.S. Steel, General Motors, Sears, Bank of America, or similar large bureaucracies—had. In place of security and predictability, they'll have flexibility and autonomy. They'll be able to put together their own place-time combinations to support their diverse work, family, lifestyle, and financial needs.

◆In 25 years or so it's possible that very few people will have jobs as we have come to know them.

Is this jobless scenario realistic? Certainly pressures in the environment encourage employers to move in this direction. However, we should expect labor unions and others with a vested interest in the status quo to fight hard to protect the security and predictability that traditional jobs provide. Yet there are already companies—for instance, Intel and Microsoft—that are moving toward creating these jobless work environments. Employees in these firms are typically assigned to a project when they're hired. As the project changes over time, employee responsibilities and tasks change with it. As projects evolve and new projects are developed, employees are added to and dropped from various projects. At any given time, most employees are working on multiple projects, under several team leaders, keeping different schedules, being in various places, and performing a number of different tasks. These employees don't look to job descriptions or a supervisor for direction. Instead, they take their cues for what they should do from the changing demands of the specific project they're working on.

Work Stress

Between 1983 and 1993, 34 people were killed and 20 wounded in 12 post office-related shootings in the United States. Job-related tensions were said to be a factor in all the incidents.[63] Union leaders in the Postal Service cite the pressures on postal employees—such as sorting letters on machines at a rate of one per second, making deliveries at a pace management sets, and coping with authoritarian supervisors.

Across North America, the majority of large companies are reducing staff. Those employees who survive these layoffs are being expected to absorb the increased workload. The result is increased stress levels.

A recent sample of 600 U.S. workers found that 46 percent said their jobs were highly stressful and 34 percent reported the stress was so bad they were thinking of quitting.[64]

The Japanese call it *karoshi.* It means sudden death by a heart attack or stroke triggered by overwork.[65] In a land where 16-hour workdays are not uncommon, experts estimate that 10,000 Japanese die each year from *karoshi.*

The facts just cited demonstrate that work stress is a serious problem in organizations. In this section we look at the causes and consequences of stress, and then consider what individuals and organizations can do to reduce it.

One point of clarification is necessary before we proceed. The topic of stress has individual and group-level relevance as well as organization system implications. As we'll show, an individual's stress level can be increased by such varied factors as his or her personality, role conflicts, and the job's design. So work stress, even though presented in Part IV of this book, The Organization System, is a multilevel concept.

What Is Stress?

Stress is a dynamic condition in which an individual is confronted with an opportunity, constraint, or demand related to what he or she desires and for which the outcome is perceived to be both uncertain and important.[66] This is a complicated definition. Let's look at its components more closely.

stress
A dynamic condition in which an individual is confronted with an opportunity, constraint, or demand related to what he or she desires and for which the outcome is perceived to be both uncertain and important.

Stress is not necessarily bad in and of itself. While stress is typically discussed in a negative context, it also has positive value. It is an opportunity when it offers potential gain. Consider, for example, the superior performance that an athlete or stage performer gives in "clutch" situations. Such individuals often use stress positively to rise to the occasion and perform at or near their maximum.

◆◆◆◆ OB in the News ◆◆◆◆

The Stress of Being a Manager in the 1990s

As corporations cut staff and restructure, they are forcing managers through one of the most harrowing stress tests in business history. It's more than just the rapid pace of change that makes bosses feel pressured—it's what's happening where their business touches their lives every day. The sales and production quotas they have to meet go up relentlessly, but everything else about their careers seems headed down: operating budgets, travel allowances, expense accounts, salary increases, and opportunities for promotion. Most painful of all, managers who were trained to build are now being paid to tear down. Instead of adding staff, they're having to fire people.

For most managers, firing employees as a result of downsizing or reengineering is so traumatic that it leads to burnout. Donald Rosen (seated left), senior associate at the Menninger Clinic, helps managers deal with the trauma of firing subordinates. He conducts week-long seminars during which managers break from their routine, reflect on their work, and learn how to cope with the challenges of terminating workers.

A growing number of line managers, senior staff, and other executives suffer some stage of burnout. Although not a precisely defined medical condition, burnout has recognizable symptoms and is a result of prolonged stress, says Donald E. Rosen, a psychiatrist at the famed Menninger Clinic. "Victims are lethargic, feel empty, no longer able to take satisfaction in what they once enjoyed," says Rosen. "They have a deep questioning of the value of the tasks they perform." In everyday parlance, they hate to go to work, not just on an occasional morning but on most mornings.

L. Smith, "Burned-Out Bosses," *Fortune* (July 25, 1994), p. 44

constraints
Forces that prevent individuals from doing what they desire.

demands
Loss of something desired.

More typically, stress is associated with **constraints** and **demands**. The former prevent you from doing what you desire. The latter refers to the loss of something desired. So when you take a test at school or you undergo your annual performance review at work, you feel stress because you confront opportunities, constraints, and demands. A good performance review may lead to a promotion, greater responsibilities, and a higher salary. But a poor review may prevent you from getting the promotion. An extremely poor review might even result in your being fired.

Two conditions are necessary for potential stress to become actual stress.[67] There must be uncertainty over the outcome and the outcome must be important. Regardless of the conditions, it is only when there is doubt or uncertainty regarding whether the opportunity will be seized, the constraint removed, or the loss avoided that there is stress. That is, stress is highest for those individuals who perceive they are uncertain as to whether they will win or lose and lowest for those individuals who think that winning or losing is a certainty. But importance is also critical. If winning or losing is an unimportant outcome, there is no stress. If keeping your job or earning a promotion doesn't hold any importance for you, you have no reason to feel stress over having to undergo a performance review.

Understanding Stress and Its Consequences

What causes stress? What are its consequences for individual employees? Why is it that the same set of conditions which creates stress for one person seems to have little or no effect on another person? Figure 15-7 provides a model that can help to answer questions such as these.[68]

The model identifies three sets of factors—environmental, organizational, and individual—that act as *potential* sources of stress. Whether they lead to *actual* stress depends on individual differences such as job experience and personality. When stress is experienced by an individual, its symptoms can surface as physiological, psychological, and behavioral outcomes.

Potential Sources of Stress

The model in Figure 15-7 shows three categories of potential stressors: environmental, organizational, and individual. Let's take a look at each.[69]

ENVIRONMENTAL FACTORS Just as environmental uncertainty influences the design of an organization's structure, it also influences stress levels among employees in that organization.

Changes in the business cycle create *economic uncertainties*. When the economy is contracting, people become increasingly anxious about their security. It was not a chance occurrence that suicide rates skyrocketed during the Great Depression of the 1930s. Minor recessions, too, increase stress levels. Downward swings in the economy are often accompanied by permanent reductions in the work force, temporary layoffs, reduced pay, shorter workweeks, and the like.

Political uncertainties don't tend to create stress among North Americans as they do for employees in countries like Haiti or Iraq. The obvious reason is that the United States and Canada have stable political systems where change is typically implemented in an orderly manner. Yet political threats and changes, even in countries like the United States and Canada, can be stress inducing. Efforts by Quebec officials to negotiate an agreement with the rest of Canada that would recognize and preserve Quebec's unique French culture have increased political uncertainty in Canada. Failure to arrive at a mutually acceptable arrangement might precipitate Quebec's separation from the rest of Canada. Until fully resolved, this difficult problem increases stress among many Canadians, especially among those living in Quebec with little or no skills in the French language.

New innovations can make an employee's skills and experience obsolete in a very short period of time. *Technological uncertainty*, therefore, is a third type of environmental factor that can cause stress. Computers, robotics, automation, and other forms of technological innovation are a threat to many people and cause them stress.

ORGANIZATIONAL FACTORS Numerous factors within the organization can cause stress. Pressures to

Figure 15-6
THE FAR SIDE copyright 1990 & 1991 FARWORKS, INC./Dist. by UNIVERSAL PRESS SYNDICATE. Reprinted with permission. All rights reserved.

Figure 15-7
A Model of Stress

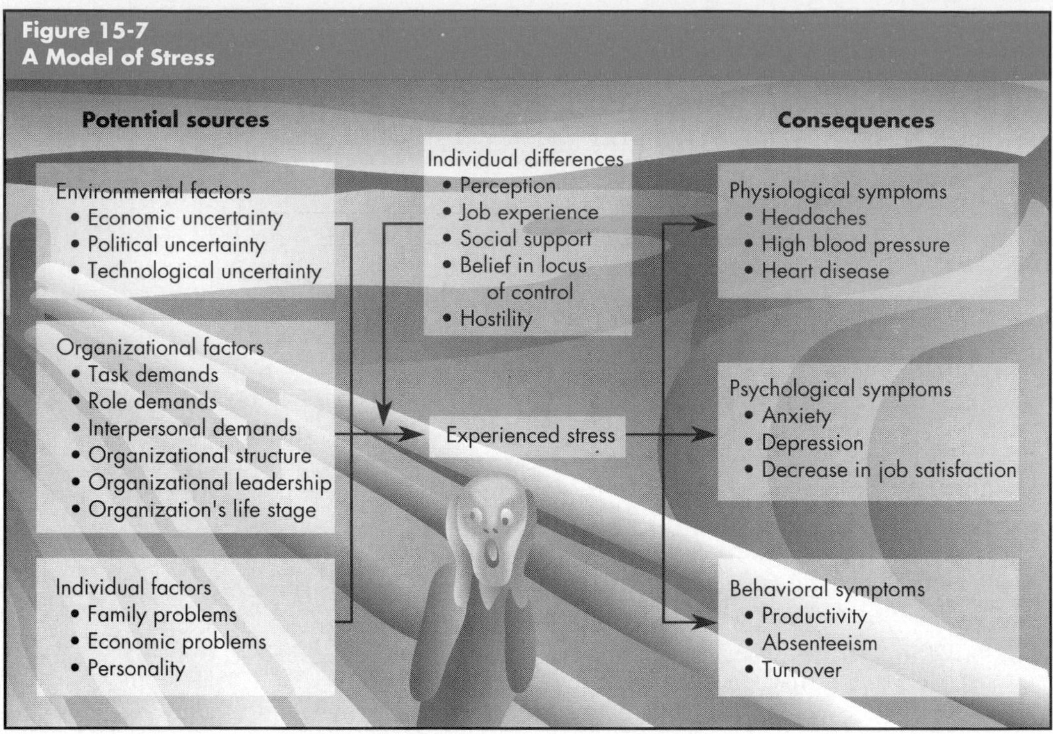

avoid errors or complete tasks in a limited time period, work overload, a demanding and insensitive boss, and unpleasant coworkers are a few examples (see Table 15–2). We've categorized these factors around task, role, and interpersonal demands, organization structure, organizational leadership, and the organization's life stage.[70]

Task demands are factors related to a person's job. They include the design of the individual's job (autonomy, task variety, degree of automation), working conditions, and the physical work layout. Assembly lines can put pressure on people when their speed is perceived as excessive. The more interdependence between a person's tasks and the tasks of others, the more potential stress there

Table 15-2 Primary Causes of Stress at Work

What factors cause the most stress on the job? A *Wall Street Journal* survey reported the following:

Factor	Percentage Response*
Not doing the kind of work I want to	34
Coping with current job	30
Working too hard	28
Colleagues at work	21
A difficult boss	18

*Percentages exceed 100 as a result of some multiple responses.

Source: "Worries at Work," *Wall Street Journal* (April 7, 1988), p. 27. Reprinted by permission of *Wall Street Journal*, is. Autonomy, however, tends to lessen stress. Jobs where temperatures, noise, or other working conditions are dangerous or undesirable can increase anxiety. So, too, can working in an overcrowded room or in a visible location where interruptions are constant.

Role demands relate to pressures placed on a person as a function of the particular role he or she plays in the organization. Role conflicts create expectations that may be hard to reconcile or satisfy. Role overload is experienced when the employee is expected to do more than time permits. Role ambiguity is created when role expectations are not clearly understood and the employee is not sure what he or she is to do.

Interpersonal demands are pressures created by other employees. Lack of social support from colleagues and poor interpersonal relationships can cause considerable stress, especially among employees with a high social need.

Organization structure defines the level of differentiation in the organization, the degree of rules and regulations, and where decisions are made. Excessive rules and lack of participation in decisions that affect an employee are examples of structural variables that might be potential sources of stress.

Organizational leadership represents the managerial style of the organization's senior executives. Some chief executive officers create a culture characterized by tension, fear, and anxiety. They establish unrealistic pressures to perform in the short run, impose excessively tight controls, and routinely fire employees who don't measure up. For instance, Procter & Gamble chairman Edwin Artzt has built a reputation for browbeating his managers.[71] Insiders say meetings with Artzt often turn into humiliating public hazings.

Organizations go through a cycle. They're established, they grow, become mature, and eventually decline. An *organization's life stage*—that is, where it is in this four-stage cycle—creates different problems and pressures for employees. The establishment and decline stages are particularly stressful. The former is characterized by a great deal of excitement and uncertainty, whereas the latter typically requires cutbacks, layoffs, and a different set of uncertainties. Stress tends to be least in maturity where uncertainties are at their lowest point.

INDIVIDUAL FACTORS The typical individual only works about 40 to 50 hours a week. The experiences and problems that people encounter in those other 120-plus nonwork hours each week can spill over to the job. Our final category, then, encompasses factors in the employee's personal life. Primarily, these factors are family issues, personal economic problems, and inherent personality characteristics.

National surveys consistently show that people hold *family* and personal relationships dear. Marital difficulties, the breaking off of a relationship, and discipline troubles with children are examples of relationship problems that create stress for employees and aren't left at the front door when they arrive at work.

Economic problems created by individuals overextending their financial resources is another set of personal troubles that can create stress for employees and distract their attention from their work. Regardless of income level—people who make $80,000 a year seem to have as much trouble handling their finances as those who earn $18,000—some people are poor money managers or have wants that always seem to exceed their earning capacity.

Recent research in three diverse organizations found that stress symptoms reported prior to beginning a job accounted for most of the variance in stress symptoms reported nine months later.[72] This led the researchers to conclude that some people may have an inherent tendency to accentuate negative aspects of the world in general. If true, then a significant individual factor influencing stress is a person's basic dispositional nature. That is, stress symptoms expressed on the job may actually originate in the person's *personality*.

STRESSORS ARE ADDITIVE A fact that tends to be overlooked when stressors are reviewed individually is that stress is an additive phenomenon.[73] Stress builds up. Each new and persistent stressor adds to an individual's stress level. A single stressor may seem relatively unimportant in and of itself, but if it is added to an already high level of stress, it can be the straw that breaks the camel's back. If we want to appraise the total amount of stress an individual is under, we have to sum up his or her opportunity stresses, constraint stresses, and demand stresses.

Individual Differences

Some people thrive on stressful situations; others are overwhelmed by them. What is it that differentiates people in terms of their ability to handle stress? What individual difference variables moderate the relationship between *potential* stressors and *experienced* stress? At least five variables—perception, job experience, social support, belief in locus of control, and hostility—have been found to be relevant moderators.

PERCEPTION In Chapter 4 we demonstrated that employees react in response to their perception of reality rather than to reality itself. Perception, therefore, will moderate the relationship between a potential stress condition and an employee's reaction to it. One person's fear that he'll lose his job because his company is laying off personnel may be perceived by another as an opportunity to get a large severance allowance and start his own business. Similarly, what one employee perceives as an efficient and challenging work environment may be viewed as threatening and demanding by others. So the stress potential in environmental, organizational, and individual factors doesn't lie in their objective condition. Rather, it lies in an employee's interpretation of those factors.

JOB EXPERIENCE Experience is said to be a great teacher. It can also be a great stress reducer. Think back to your first date or your first few days in college. For most of us, the uncertainty and newness of these situations created stress. But as we gained experience, that stress disappeared or at least significantly decreased. The same phenomenon seems to apply to work situations. That is, experience on the job tends to be negatively related to work stress. Two explanations have been offered.[74] First is the idea of selective withdrawal. Voluntary turnover is more probable among people who experience more stress. Therefore, people who remain with the organization longer are those with more stress-resistant traits or those who are more resistant to the stress characteristics of their organization. Second, people eventually develop coping mechanisms to deal with stress. Because this takes time, senior members of the organization are more likely to be fully adapted and should experience less stress.

SOCIAL SUPPORT Increasing evidence shows that social support—that is, collegial relationships with co-workers or supervisors—can buffer the impact of stress.[75] The logic underlying this moderating variable is that social support acts as a palliative, mitigating the negative effects of even high-strain jobs.

For individuals whose work associates are unhelpful or even actively hostile, social support may be found outside the job. Involvement with family, friends, and community can provide the support—especially for those with a high social need—that is missing at work and this can make job stressors more tolerable.

BELIEF IN LOCUS OF CONTROL Locus of control was introduced in Chapter 3 as a personality attribute. Those with an internal locus of control believe they control their own destiny. Those with an external locus believe their lives are controlled by outside forces. Evidence indicates that internals perceive their jobs to be less stressful than do externals.[76]

When internals and externals confront a similar stressful situation, the internals are likely to believe they can have a significant effect on the results. They, therefore, act to take control of events. Externals are more likely to be passive and defensive. Rather than do something to reduce the stress, they acquiesce. So externals, who are more likely to feel helpless in stressful situations, are also more likely to experience stress.

HOSTILITY For much of the 1970s and 1980s, a great deal of attention was directed at the Type A personality.[77] In fact, throughout the 1980s, it was undoubtedly the most frequently used moderating variable related to stress.

As noted in Chapter 3, the Type A personality is characterized by feeling a chronic sense of time urgency and by an *excessive* competitive drive. A Type A individual is "*aggressively* involved in a *chronic, incessant* struggle to achieve more and more in less and less time, and if required to do so, against the opposing efforts of other things or other persons."[78]

Until quite recently, researchers believed Type A's were more likely to experience stress on and off the job. More specifically, Type A's were widely believed to be at higher risk for heart disease. A closer analysis of the evidence, however, has produced new conclusions.[79] By looking at various components of Type A behavior, it's been found that only the hostility and anger associated with Type A behavior is actually related to heart disease. The chronically angry, suspicious, and mistrustful person is the one at risk.

So just because a person is a workaholic, rushes around a lot, and is impatient or competitive does not mean he or she is unduly susceptible to heart disease or the other negative effects of stress. Rather, it's the quickness to anger, the persistently hostile outlook, and the cynical mistrust of others that are harmful.

Consequences of Stress

Stress shows itself in a number of ways. For instance, an individual who is experiencing a high level of stress may develop high blood pressure, ulcers, irritability, difficulty in making routine decisions, loss of appetite, accident proneness, and the like. These can be subsumed under three general categories: physiological, psychological, and behavioral symptoms.[80]

PHYSIOLOGICAL SYMPTOMS Most of the early concern with stress was directed at physiological symptoms. This was primarily because the topic was researched by specialists in the health and medical sciences. This research led to the conclusion that stress could create changes in metabolism, increase heart and breathing rates, increase blood pressure, bring on headaches, and induce heart attacks.

The link between stress and particular physiological symptoms is not clear. There are few, if any, consistent relationships.[81] This is attributed to the complexity of the symptoms and the difficulty of objectively measuring them. But of greater relevance is the fact that physiological symptoms have the least direct relevance to students of OB. Our concern is with behaviors and attitudes. Therefore, the two other categories of symptoms are more important to us.

PSYCHOLOGICAL SYMPTOMS Stress can cause dissatisfaction. Job-related stress can cause job-related dissatisfaction. Job dissatisfaction, in fact, is "the simplest and most obvious psychological effect" of stress.[82] But stress shows itself in other psychological states—for instance, tension, anxiety, irritability, boredom, and procrastination.

The evidence indicates that when people are placed in jobs that make multiple and conflicting demands or in which there is a lack of clarity as to the incumbent's duties, authority, and responsibilities, both stress and dissatisfaction are increased.[83] Similarly, the less control people have over the pace of their work, the greater the stress and dissatisfaction. While more research is needed to clarify the relationship, the evidence suggests that jobs providing a low level of variety, significance, autonomy, feedback, and identity to incumbents create stress and reduce satisfaction and involvement in the job.[84]

BEHAVIORAL SYMPTOMS Behaviorally related stress symptoms include changes in productivity, absence, and turnover, as well as changes in eating habits, increased smoking or consumption of alcohol, rapid speech, fidgeting, and sleep disorders.

A significant amount of research has investigated the stress–performance relationship. The most widely studied pattern in the stress–performance literature is the inverted-U relationship.[85] This is shown in Figure 15-8.

The logic underlying the inverted U is that low to moderate levels of stress stimulate the body and increase its ability to react. Individuals then often perform their tasks better, more intensely, or more rapidly. But too much stress places unattainable demands or constraints on a person, which results in lower performance. This inverted-U pattern may also describe the reaction to stress over time, as well as to changes in stress intensity. That is, even moderate levels of stress can have a negative influence on performance over the long term as the continued intensity of the stress wears down the individual and saps his or her energy resources. An athlete may be able to use the positive effects of stress to obtain a higher performance during every Saturday's game in the fall season, or a sales executive may be able to psych herself up for her presentation at the annual national meeting. But moderate levels of stress experienced continually over long periods of time—as typified by the emergency room staff in a large urban hospital—can result in lower performance. This may explain why emergency room staffs at such hospitals are frequently rotated and why it is unusual to

Figure 15-8
Inverted-U Relationship Between Stress and Job Performance

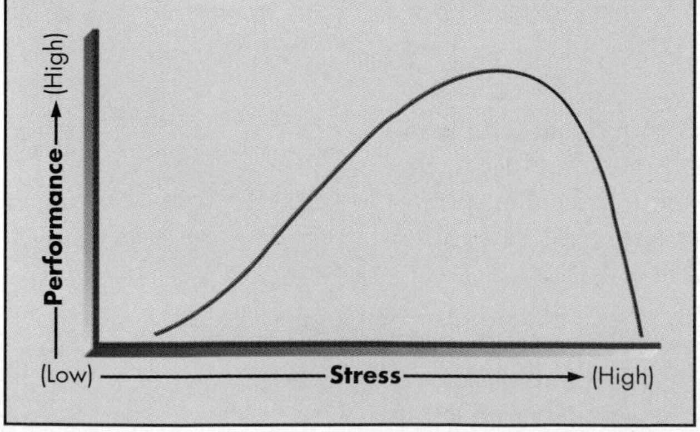

find individuals who have spent the bulk of their career in such an environment. In effect, to do so would expose the individual to the risk of career burnout.

In spite of the popularity and intuitive appeal of the inverted-U model, it doesn't get a lot of empirical support.[86] At this point, managers should be careful in assuming this model accurately depicts the stress–performance relationship.

Managing Stress

From the organization's standpoint, management may not be concerned when employees experience low to moderate levels of stress. The reason, as we showed earlier, is that such levels of stress may be functional and lead to higher employee performance. But high levels of stress, or even low levels sustained over long periods of time, can lead to reduced employee performance and, thus, require action by management.

While a limited amount of stress may benefit an employee's performance, don't expect employees to see it that way. From the individual's standpoint, even low levels of stress are likely to be perceived as undesirable. It's not unlikely, therefore, for employees and management to have different notions of what constitutes an acceptable level of stress on the job. What management may consider as "a positive stimulus that keeps the adrenaline running" is very likely to be seen as "excessive pressure" by the employee. Keep this in mind as we discuss individual and organizational approaches toward managing stress.[87]

INDIVIDUAL APPROACHES An employee can take personal responsibility for reducing his or her stress level. Individual strategies that have proven effective include implementing time-management techniques, increasing physical exercise, relaxation training, and expanding the social support network.

Many people manage their time poorly. The things they have to accomplish in any given day or week are not necessarily beyond completion if they manage their time properly. The well-organized employee, like the well-organized student, can often accomplish twice as much as the person who is poorly organized. So an understanding and utilization of basic *time-management* principles can help individuals better cope with tensions created by job demands.[88] A few of the more well-known time-management principles are (1) making daily lists of activities to be accomplished; (2) prioritizing activities by importance and urgency; (3) scheduling activities according to the priorities set; and (4) knowing your daily cycle and handling the most demanding parts of your job during the high part of your cycle when you are most alert and productive.[89]

Noncompetitive physical exercise such as aerobics, walking, jogging, swimming, and riding a bicycle have long been recommended by physicians as a way to deal with excessive stress levels. These forms of *physical exercise* increase heart capacity, lower at-rest heart rate, provide a mental diversion from work pressures, and offer a means to let off steam.[90]

Individuals can teach themselves to reduce tension through *relaxation techniques* such as meditation, hypnosis, and biofeedback. The objective is to reach a state of deep relaxation, where one feels physically relaxed, somewhat detached from the immediate environment, and detached from body sensations.[91] Fifteen or 20 minutes a day of deep relaxation releases tension and provides a person with a pronounced sense of peacefulness. Importantly, significant changes in heart rate, blood pressure, and other physiological factors result from achieving the deep relaxation condition.

As we noted earlier in this chapter, having friends, family, or work colleagues to talk to provides an outlet when stress levels become excessive. Expanding your social support network, therefore, can be a means for tension reduction. It provides you with someone to hear your problems and a more objective perspective on the situation. Research also demonstrates that social support moderates the stress–burnout relationship.[92] That is, high support reduces the likelihood that heavy work stress will result in job burnout.

ORGANIZATIONAL APPROACHES Several of the factors that cause stress—particularly task and role demands, and organization structure—are controlled by management. As such, they can be modified or changed. Strategies that management might want to consider include improved personnel selection and job placement, use of realistic goal setting, redesigning of jobs, increased employee involvement, improved organizational communication, and establishment of corporate wellness programs.

While certain jobs are more stressful than others, we learned earlier in this chapter that individuals differ in their response to stress situations. We know, for example, that individuals with little experience or an external locus of control tend to be more stress prone. *Selection and placement* decisions should take these facts into consideration. Obviously, although management shouldn't restrict hiring to only experienced individuals with an internal locus, such individuals may adapt better to high-stress jobs and perform those jobs more effectively.

We discussed *goal setting* in Chapter 6. Based on an extensive amount of research, we concluded that individuals perform better when they have specific and challenging goals and receive feedback on how well they are progressing toward these goals. The use of goals can reduce stress as well as provide motivation. Specific goals that are perceived as attainable clarify performance expectations. Additionally, goal feedback reduces uncertainties as to actual job performance. The result is less employee frustration, role ambiguity, and stress.

Redesigning jobs to give employees more responsibility, more meaningful work, more autonomy, and increased feedback can reduce stress because these factors give the employee greater control over work activities and lessen dependence on others. But as we noted in our discussion of work design, not all employees want enriched jobs. The right job redesign, then, for employees with a low need for growth might be less responsibility and increased specialization. If individuals prefer structure and routine, reducing skill variety should also reduce uncertainties and stress levels.

Role stress is detrimental to a large extent because employees feel uncertain about goals, expectations, how they'll be evaluated, and the like. By giving these employees a voice in those decisions that directly affect their job performances, management can increase employee control and reduce this role stress. So managers should consider increasing *employee involvement* in decision making.[93]

Increasing formal *organizational communication* with employees reduces uncertainty by lessening role ambiguity and role conflict. Given the importance that perceptions play in moderating the stress–response relationship, management can also use effective communications as a means to shape employee perceptions. Remember that what employees categorize as demands, threats, or opportunities are merely an interpretation, and that interpretation can be affected by the symbols and actions communicated by management.

wellness programs
Organizationally supported programs that focus on the employee's total physical and mental condition.

Our final suggestion is to offer organizationally supported **wellness programs**. These programs focus on the employee's total physical and mental con-

Adolph Coors Company is a corporate leader in wellness programs, thanks to the vision of chairman and CEO Bill Coors. The company established its wellness center in 1981 because of Bill Coors' desire to have the healthiest employees in the Rocky Mountain area. The 23,000-square-foot center includes exercise equipment (shown here) and is open 97 hours a week to employees and their family members. Coors' wellness program also includes mental-health services, an on-site medical center that gives flu shots and mammograms, an on-site dental center that provides routine checkups and cleanings at no cost, on-site cardiac- and back-rehabilitation programs, and smoking-cessation and weight-loss classes.

dition.[94] For example, they typically provide workshops to help people quit smoking, control alcohol use, lose weight, eat better, and develop a regular exercise program. The assumption underlying most wellness programs is that employees need to take personal responsibility for their physical and mental health. The organization is merely a vehicle to facilitate this end.

Organizations, of course, aren't altruistic. They expect a payoff from their investment in wellness programs. And most of those firms that have introduced wellness programs have found the benefits to exceed the costs. For instance, Du Pont saw a 14 percent decline in sick days among employees at 41 plants; nonhospital health-care costs shrank 43 percent at Tenneco Inc.; and the average annual employee health claim at Steelcase Inc. fell from $1,155 to $537.[95] Adolph Coors, the beer company, estimates it saves $6.15 for each dollar spent on wellness.[96]

Summary and Implications for Managers

Technology is changing people's jobs and their work behavior. TQM and its emphasis on continuous process improvement can increase employee stress as individuals find that performance expectations are constantly being increased. Reengineering is eliminating millions of jobs and completely reshaping the jobs of those who remain. Flexible manufacturing systems require employees to learn new skills and accept increased responsibilities. And technology is making many job skills obsolete and shortening the life span of almost all skills—technical, administrative, and managerial.

An understanding of work design can help managers design jobs that positively affect employee motivation. For instance, jobs that score high in motivating potential increase an employee's control over key elements in his or her work. Therefore, jobs that offer autonomy, feedback, and similar complex task characteristics help satisfy the individual goals of those employees who desire greater control over their work. Of course, consistent with the social information processing model, the perception that task characteristics are complex is probably more important in influencing an employee's motivation than the objective task characteristics themselves. The key, then, is to provide employees with cues suggesting their jobs score high on factors such as skill variety, task identity, autonomy, and feedback.

We found that the existence of work stress, in and of itself, need not imply lower performance. The evidence indicates that stress can be either a positive or negative influence on employee performance. For many people, low to moderate amounts of stress enable them to perform their jobs better, by increasing their work intensity, alertness, and ability to react. However, a high level of stress, or even a moderate level sustained over a long period of time, eventually takes its toll and performance declines. The impact of stress on satisfaction is far more straightforward. Job-related tension tends to decrease general job satisfaction.[97] Even though low to moderate levels of stress may improve job performance, employees find stress dissatisfying.

For Review

1. What are the implications for employees of a continuous improvement program?
2. What are the implications for employees of a reengineering program?
3. What are flexible manufacturing systems?
4. What are the implications of the social information processing model for predicting employee behavior?
5. What are the advantages of flextime from an employee's perspective? From management's perspective?
6. From an employee's perspective, what are the pros and cons of telecommuting?
7. How is the concept of a *job* changing?
8. How are opportunities, constraints, and demands related to stress? Give an example of each.
9. Describe the three sources of potential stress. Which of these are controllable by management?
10. What can organizations do to reduce employee stress?

For Discussion

1. Reengineering needs to be autocratically imposed in order to overcome employee resistance. This runs directly counter to the model of a contemporary manager who is a good listener, a coach, motivates through employee involvement, and who possesses strong team-support skills. Can these two positions be reconciled?
2. How has technology changed the manager's job over the past 20 years?
3. Would you want a full-time job telecommuting? How do you think most of your friends would feel about such a job? Do you think telecommuting has a future?
4. "If it were to look like the jobless society was to become a widespread reality, politicians would be under strong pressure to create legislation to outlaw it." Do you agree or disagree with this statement? Explain your position.
5. With very few exceptions, labor unions have not been receptive to stress management programs. Why do you suppose this is true? What can management do that might gain a union's support for an organizationally sponsored stress management program?

Point

Employee Stress Isn't a Management Problem!

The recent attention given employee stress by behavioral scientists has been blown totally out of proportion. Undoubtedly a small proportion of the working population suffers from stress. These people have ongoing headaches, ulcers, high blood pressure, and the like. They may even turn to alcohol and drugs as an outlet to deal with their stress. But if there is a problem, it's a medical one. It's not a management problem. In support of this position, I argue that (1) stress is not that important because human beings are highly adaptive; (2) most stress that employees experience is of the positive type; and (3) even if the first two points weren't relevant, a good portion of what causes excessive work stress tends to be uncontrollable by management anyway.

Those who seem to be so concerned about employee stress forget that people are more adaptable than we traditionally give them credit for. Individuals are amazingly resilient. Most successfully adjust to illnesses, misfortune, and other changes in their lives. All through their school years, they adapted to the demands that dozens of teachers put on them. They survived the trials of puberty, dating, beginning and ending relationships, and leaving home—to name a few of the more potentially stressful times we have all gone through. By the time individuals enter the work force, they have experienced many difficult situations and, for the most part, they have adjusted to each. There is no reason to believe this ability to adapt to changing or uncomfortable conditions breaks down once people begin their working careers.

Stress, like conflict, has a positive as well as a negative side. But that positive side tends to be overshadowed by concern with the negative. A life without stress is a life without challenge, stimulation, or change. Many positive and exciting life events—marriage, the birth of a child, inheriting a large sum of money, buying a new home, a job promotion, vacations—have been found to create stress. Does that mean these positive events should be avoided? The answer is obviously "No." Unfortunately, when most people talk about stress and the need to reduce it, they tend to overlook its positive side.

Finally, there is the reality that many sources of employee stress are outside the control of management. Management can't control environmental factors. If stress is due to an inherent personality characteristic, here again, the source lies outside management's control. Most other individual factors, too, are outside management's influence. Even if stresses created by such individual factors as family and economic problems can be influenced by managerial actions, there remains the ethical question: Does management have the right to interfere in an employee's personal life? Undoubtedly, a good portion of any employee's total stress level is created by factors that are uncontrollable by management—marital problems, divorce, children who get into trouble, poor personal financial management, uncertainty over the economy, societal norms to achieve and acquire material symbols of success, pressures of living in a fast-paced, urban world, and the like. The actions of management didn't create these stressors. Most are just part of modern living. More importantly, employers can do little to lessen these stressors without extending their influence beyond the organization and into the employee's personal life. That's something most of us would agree is outside the province of the employer-employee relationship.

counterPoint

Stress Creates Real Costs to Organizations

Those who think management should ignore the problem of employee stress need to take a look at what stress is costing organizations.*

The total cost of work-related accidents in the United States is approximately $32 billion per year. It is estimated that at least three-quarters of all industrial accidents are caused by the inability of employees to cope with emotional distress.

Stress-related absenteeism, organizational medical expenses, and lost productivity are estimated to cost business more than $150 billion a year or nearly $1,500 per worker. In California, mental stress claims are the most rapidly increasing type of workers' compensation cases, having risen 700 percent in a decade. Stress-related headaches are the leading cause of lost work time in U.S. industry.

Coronary heart disease is a leading killer of Americans. Over 1 million Americans suffer heart attacks each year, and half of them are fatal. One out of every five average healthy male Americans will suffer a heart attack before he reaches the age of 65. Heart disease causes an annual loss of more than 135 million workdays. The premature loss of valued employees means the loss of experienced personnel and the additional cost of replacing these people. These facts are important because there now exists a wealth of research that links stress to heart disease.

More than 60 percent of long-term disability is related to psychological or psychosomatic problems often brought on or made worse by stress. State workers' compensation boards are increasingly awarding compensation for physical- and mental-stress claims. A single claim for permanent total disability can cost in excess of $250,000. Since each employer's workers' compensation costs are based on claims against that employer, any increase in awards is an added cost of doing business.

Two facts about stress cannot be ignored. First, people get sick from stress at work. Second, the costs associated with stress are significant to every employer. They include lost time, increased accidents, higher insurance premiums and health-care costs, and lower productivity. The only natural conclusion one can draw is that managers cannot ignore the stress issue and must actively seek to do something about it. It is in management's self-interest to take an active stance because, if for no other reason, it provides a basis for defending the organization against claims that its jobs and working conditions are stress creating and the primary cause for compensable emotional problems.

*These figures come from "Stress: Can We Cope?" *Time* (June 6, 1983), pp. 48–54; J. W. Jones, "A Cost Evaluation for Stress Management," *EAP Digest* (November-December 1984), p. 34; "Stress Claims Are Making Business Jumpy," *Business Week* (October 14, 1985), pp. 152–54; M. J. McCarthy, "Stressed Employees Look for Relief in Workers' Compensation Claims," *Wall Street Journal* (April 7, 1988), p. 27; "Stress: The Test Americans Are Failing," *Business Week* (April 18, 1988), p. 74; and T.F. O'Boyle, "Fear and Stress in the Office Take Toll," *Wall Street Journal* (November 6, 1990), p. B1.

Learning About Yourself Exercise

What's Your Stress Personality?

Using the numerical scale here, indicate how strongly you agree with each of the following statements; then tally your score.

4 = All the time
3 = Often
2 = Sometimes
1 = Never

1. I'm exhausted by daily demands at work, college, and home. ___

2. My stress is caused by outside forces beyond my control. ___

3. I'm trapped by circumstances that I just have to live with. ___

4. No matter how hard I work to stay on top of my schedule, I can't get caught up. ___

5. I have financial obligations I can't seem to meet. ___

6. I dislike my work, but I can't take the risk of making a career change (or, if not working: I dislike college, but I can't take the risk of dropping out). ___

7. I'm dissatisfied with my personal relationships. ___

8. I feel responsible for the happiness of people around me. ___

9. I'm embarrassed to ask for help. ___

10. I do not know what I want out of life. ___

11. I'm disappointed that I have not achieved what I had hoped for. ___

12. No matter how much success I have, I feel empty. ___

13. If the people around me were more competent, I would feel happier. ___

14. People let me down. ___

15. I stew in my anger rather than express it. ___

16. I become enraged and resentful when I am hurt. ___

17. I can't take criticism. ___

18. I'm afraid I'll lose my job (or fail out of school). ___

19. I don't see the value of expressing sadness or grief. ___

20. I don't trust that things will work out. ___

Turn to page A-30 for scoring directions and key.

Source: Adapted from R.S. Eliot, *From Stress to Strength: How to Lighten Your Load and Save Your Life* (New York: Bantam, 1994).

Working with Others Exercise

Analyzing and Redesigning Jobs

Break into groups of five to seven members each. Each student should describe the worst job he or she has ever had. Use any criteria you want to select one of these jobs for analysis by the group.

Members of the group will analyze the job selected by determining how well it scores on the job characteristics model. Use the following scale for your analysis of each job dimension:

7 = Very high
6 = High
5 = Somewhat high
4 = Moderate
3 = Somewhat low
2 = Low
1 = Very low

Here are some sample questions that can guide the group in its analysis of the job in question:

- *Skill variety*: Describe the different identifiable skills required to do this job. What is the nature of the oral, written, and/or quantitative skills needed? Physical skills? Does the jobholder get the opportunity to use all of his or her skills?
- *Task identity*: What is the product the jobholder creates? Is he or she involved in its production from beginning to end? If not, is he or she involved in a particular phase of its production from beginning to end?
- *Task significance*: How important is the product? How important is the jobholder's role in producing it? How important is the jobholder's contribution to the people he or she works with? If the jobholder's job was eliminated, how inferior would the product be?
- *Autonomy*: How much independence does the jobholder have? Does he or she have to follow a strict schedule? How closely is he or she supervised?
- *Feedback*: Does the jobholder get regular feedback from his or her supervisor? From peers? From subordinates? From customers? How about intrinsic performance feedback when doing the job?

Using the formula in Figure 15-3, calculate the job's motivating potential. Then using the suggestions offered in the chapter for redesigning jobs, describe specific actions management could take to increase this job's motivating potential.

Calculate the costs to management of redesigning the job in question. Do the benefits exceed the costs?

Conclude the exercise by having a representative of each group share his or her group's analysis and redesign suggestions with the entire class. Possible topics for class discussion might include similarities in the jobs chosen; problems in rating job dimensions; and the cost-benefit assessment of design changes.

Source: This exercise is based on W.P. Ferris, "Enlivening the Job Characteristics Model," in C. Harris and C.C. Lundberg (eds.), *Proceedings of the 29th Annual Eastern Academy of Management Meeting* (Baltimore, MD: May 1992), pp. 125–28.

Ethical Dilemma Exercise

What's the Right Balance Between Work and Family?

More employees are bringing family matters into their working lives, and more managers are trying to accommodate them. As the line between work and family blurs, managers must address many questions. What's your position on each of the following questions? Compare your answers with others in your class.

1. Is it OK for someone to bring his or her baby to work on an emergency basis?
2. An employee works from home part of the time, putting in the same hours as colleagues at the office. But whenever the boss calls, the boss can hear the sound of children in the background. The boss knows that any business callers will hear the same noises. Is that a problem?
3. A divorced father, who doesn't get to see his 8-year-old daughter often, wants to bring her into the office after her early school dismissal every Wednesday at 2 P.M., as well as on her vacations. She is perfectly well behaved, reading quietly by his desk. Should she be allowed to come to the office?
4. Should a boss ask subordinates if they want to buy her daughter's Girl Scout cookies?
5. Should a woman promise to return from maternity leave, even though she isn't sure she will?
6. Is it OK for a worker to interrupt a conversation with a subordinate or peer to take a call from her spouse? How about from her children? How about from her best friend?
7. Is it OK for a boss to schedule regular Friday staff meetings at 7:30 A.M.?
8. Is it OK for an employee to cover his work area with pictures of his newborn or drawings scrawled by his young children? Assume clients occasionally meet with the employee in his work area.
9. A worker is asked to spend several months away from home, solving a problem at a factory. He can fly home on the weekends at the company's expense. Should the company pay for accommodations big enough for his wife and two children to accompany him?
10. If clients complain about a job-sharing arrangement because they want full-time service by one representative, should the company eliminate the job sharing? Assume the company believes there is no reduction in service as a result of the job sharing.

Based on "No Easy Answers," *Wall Street Journal* (June 21, 1993), p. R3.

Reengineering the College Experience

At the turn of the century, less than 2 percent of high school graduates went on to college. For the most part, college in those days was an elitist experience reserved for children of the upper class. Today, in places like the United States, approximately 60 percent of high school graduates continue on to college. In the 1990s, in much of the world, higher education has become a product for the masses.

While higher educational institutions now serve a much broader and diverse audience, the structure of colleges and their basic curricula have not changed much since the turn of the century. Critics claim that the typical undergraduate experience—four years of course work, broken down into 8 or 12 terms, with students taking three to six courses per term, taught mostly by full-time instructors who lecture to their classes—makes little sense today. For example, we realize knowledge isn't compartmentalized by narrow departmental specialties or into three-unit segments, but that's how it tends to be taught. Additionally, while lecturing made sense a century ago, it is a rather outdated means for transferring information when students have ready access to libraries and on-line databases. Critics also challenge a number of other well-established practices of colleges and universities: expansive campuses with dormitories and other facilities for resident students when, in fact, most students commute; accreditation processes that legitimize the faculty's academic credentials, the importance of research, the use of full-time over part-time faculty, and the granting of tenure; the heavy subsidizing of public education by taxpayers; and the unresponsiveness of faculty and administrators to the need for change.

What would a college look like if it were reengineered? Vermont's Bennington College, for instance, recently announced it was eliminating tenure for new faculty. National University in San Diego breaks its curriculum into monthly courses that are offered all-year round and taught almost entirely by working practitioners rather than full-time faculty. And some colleges are experimenting with team-teaching classes with faculty from diverse disciplines. But these represent only incremental changes. True reengineering would require creating an entire new structure and curriculum from scratch.

Questions

1. List as many characteristics of your college as you can that you think hinder its effectiveness in the 1990s.
2. What do you think a reengineered college structure and curriculum would look like?
3. In times of dramatic societal change, colleges and universities remain relatively stable. College campuses haven't changed much from those your parents or grandparents might have experienced. What changes have occurred have either been incremental or introduced by newly developed colleges. Why, in times when almost every business firm is having to completely overhaul its traditional practices, do most established colleges and universities continue to operate as they always have?

GM Workers Go on Strike Demanding *Less Money!*

You pick up the morning newspaper and all you read about are companies laying off employees, replacing full-time workers with part-timers, and qualified job applicants who are frustrated because they can't find permanent work. It might seem strange, then, to see workers at GM's Flint, Michigan plant going on strike to protest having to work *too much*. These workers say they want less money, not more, and less work, too.

A few years ago, when GM car sales were stagnating and the company was drastically cutting its workforce, most GM hourly employees would have jumped at the chance to work 60-plus-hour weeks and earn thousands of dollars in overtime pay. But now that business is strong, GM has decided to make overtime mandatory in order to meet increased customer demand for its cars. Sixty-six hour workweeks are not unusual. What's motivating GM to require hourly workers to put in such extensive overtime? The high cost of employee benefits such as health care and pensions. An average GM hourly employee earns about $53,000 a year in wages and gets another $35,000 in benefits. GM can save a lot of money by paying overtime rather than hiring additional permanent workers.

But these long hours are taking a heavy toll on workers. Employees complain of being tired all the time. Their stress levels are up as they try to balance their off-work responsibilities with long hours on the job. As one worker put it, "About the only thing you do is work, sleep, eat, and go back to work."

Questions

1. Do you think GM's strategy is good for the long-term interest of the company? Explain your answer.
2. Can you think of alternative solutions that would be acceptable to employees and GM's management?
3. Analyze this case in terms of the stress model in this chapter.

Source: "Overworked GM Employees Strike at Flint Plant," *ABC World News Tonight* (September 29, 1994).

Suggestions for Further Reading

BARLEY, S.R. and D.B. KNIGHT, "Toward a Cultural Theory of Stress Complaints," in B.M. Staw and L.L. Cummings (eds.), *Research in Organizational Behavior*, Vol. 14 (Greenwich, CT: JAI Press, 1992), pp. 1–48.

CAMPION, M.A. and C.L. MCCLELLAND, "Interdisciplinary Examination of the Costs and Benefits of Enlarged Jobs: A Job Design Quasi-Experiment," *Journal of Applied Psychology* (April 1991), pp. 186–98.

FISHER, A.B., "Welcome to the Age of Overwork," *Fortune* (November 30, 1992), pp. 64–71.

HALL, G., J. ROSENTHAL, and J. WADE, "How to Make Reengineering Really Work," *Harvard Business Review* (November-December 1993), pp. 119–31.

HOTCH, R., "Managing from a Distance," *Nation's Business* (February 1993), pp. 24–26.

IRONSON, G.H., "Job Stress and Health," in C.J. CRANNY, P.C. SMITH, and E.F. STONE, (eds.) *Job Satisfaction* (New York: Lexington Books, 1992), pp. 219–39.

JOHNS, G., J.L. XIE, and Y FANG, "Mediating and Moderating Effects in Job Design," *Journal of Management* (December 1992), pp. 657–76.

SCHAUBROECK, J., D.C. GANSTER, and M.L. FOX, "Dispositional Affect and Work-Related Stress," *Journal of Applied Psychology* (June 1992), pp. 322–35.

SPECTOR, P.E. and S.M. JEX, "Relations of Job Characteristics from Multiple Data Sources with Employee Affect, Absence, Turnover Intentions, and Health," *Journal of Applied Psychology* (February 1991), pp. 46–53.

TRENT, J.T., A.L. SMITH, and D.L. WOOD, "Telecommuting: Stress and Social Support," *Psychological Reports* (June 1994), pp. 1312–14.

Notes

[1] Based on H. Gleckman, "The Technology Payoff," *Business Week* (June 14, 1993), p. 57.

[2] See, for example, T.H. Berry, *Managing the Total Quality Transition* (New York: McGraw-Hill, 1991); D. Ciampa, *Total Quality* (Reading, MA: Addison-Wesley, 1992); and W.H. Schmidt and J.P. Finnegan, *The Race Without a Finish Line* (San Francisco: Jossey-Bass, 1992).

[3] M. Sashkin and K.J. Kiser, *Putting Total Quality Management to Work* (San Francisco: Berrett-Koehler, 1993), p. 44.

[4] T.F. O'Boyle, "A Manufacturer Grows Efficient by Soliciting Ideas from Employees," *Wall Street Journal* (June 5, 1992), p. A1.

[5] M. Hammer and J. Champy, *Re-Engineering the Corporation: A Manifesto for Business Revolution* (New York: HarperBusiness, 1993).

[6] R. Karlgaard, "ASAP Interview: Mike Hammer," *Forbes ASAP* (September 13, 1993), p. 70.

[7] Ibid.

[8] "The Age of Reengineering," *Across the Board* (June 1993), pp. 26–33.

[9] Ibid., p. 29.

[10] Ibid., p. 33.

[11] Cited in "The Bigger Picture: Reorganizing Work," *Industry Week* (August 2, 1993), p. 24.

[12] "The Age of Reengineering," p. 31.

[13] A. Ehrbar, "'Re-Engineering' Gives Firms New Efficiency, Workers the Pink Slip," *Wall Street Journal* (March 16, 1993), p. A1.

[14] Ibid.

[15] Ibid.

[16] See, for instance, P.L. Nemetz and L.W. Fry, "Flexible Manufacturing Organizations: Implications for Strategy Formulation and Organization Design," *Academy of Management Review* (October 1988), pp. 627–38; A. De Meyer et al., "Flexibility: The Next Competitive Battle the Manufacturing Futures Survey," *Strategic Management Journal* (March-April 1989), pp. 135–44; O. Port, "Moving Past the Assembly Line," *Business Week/Reinventing America Special Issue* (November 1992), pp. 177–80; and D.M. Upton, "The Management of Manufacturing Flexibility," *California Management Review* (Winter 1994), pp. 72–89.

[17] S. Moffat, "Japan's New Personalized Production," *Fortune* (October 22, 1990), p. 44.

[18] See E. Norton, "Small, Flexible Plants May Play Crucial Role in U.S. Manufacturing," *Wall Street Journal* (January 13, 1993), p. A1.

[19] R.M. Steers and R.T. Mowday, "The Motivational Properties of Tasks," *Academy of Management Review* (October 1977), pp. 645–58.

[20] D.G. Gardner and L.L. Cummings, "Activation Theory and Job Design: Review and Reconceptualization," in B.M. Staw and L.L. Cummings (eds.), *Research in Organizational Behavior*, Vol. 10 (Greenwich, CT: JAI Press, 1988), p. 100.

[21] A.N. Turner and P.R. Lawrence, *Industrial Jobs and the Worker* (Boston: Harvard University Press, 1965).

[22] J.R. Hackman and G.R. Oldham, "Motivation Through the Design of Work: Test of a Theory," *Organizational Behavior and Human Performance* (August 1976), pp. 250–79.

[23] J.R. Hackman, "Work Design," in J.R. Hackman and J.L. Suttle (eds.), *Improving Life at Work* (Santa Monica, CA: Goodyear, 1977), p. 129.

[24] See "Job Characteristics Theory of Work Redesign," in J.B. Miner, *Theories of Organizational Behavior* (Hinsdale, IL: Dryden Press, 1980), pp. 231–66; B.T. Loher, R.A. Noe, N.L. Moeller, and M.P. Fitzgerald, "A Meta-Analysis of the Relation of Job Characteristics to Job Satisfaction," *Journal of Applied Psychology* (May 1985), pp. 280–89; W.H. Glick, G.D. Jenkins, Jr., and N. Gupta, "Method versus Substance: How Strong Are Underlying Relationships Between Job Characteristics and Attitudinal Outcomes?" *Academy of Management Journal* (September 1986), pp. 441–64; Y. Fried and G.R. Ferris, "The Validity of the Job Characteristics Model: A Review and Meta-Analysis," *Personnel Psychology* (Summer 1987), pp. 287–322; and S.J. Zaccaro and E.F. Stone, "Incremental Validity of an Empirically Based Measure of Job Characteristics," *Journal of Applied Psychology* (May 1988), pp. 245–52.

[25] See R.B. Dunham, "Measurement and Dimensionality of Job Characteristics," *Journal of Applied Psychology* (August 1976), pp. 404–409; J. L. Pierce and R. B. Dunham, "Task Design: A Literature Review," *Academy of Management Review* (January 1976), pp. 83–97; and D. M. Rousseau, "Technological Differences in Job Characteristics, Employee Satisfaction, and Motivation: A Synthesis of Job Design Research and Sociotechnical Systems Theory," *Organizational Behavior and Human Performance* (October 1977), pp. 18–42.

[26] Ibid.; and Y. Fried and G. R. Ferris, "The Dimensionality of Job Characteristics: Some Neglected Issues," *Journal of Applied Psychology* (August 1986), pp. 419–26.

[27] See, for instance, Fried and Ferris, "The Dimensionality of Job Characteristics"; and M.G. Evans and D.A. Ondrack, "The Motivational Potential of Jobs: Is a Multiplicative Model Really Necessary?" in S.L. McShane (ed.), *Organizational Behavior*, ASAC Conference Proceedings, Vol. 9, Part 5 (Halifax, Nova Scotia: 1988), pp. 31–39.

[28] R.B. Tiegs, L.E. Tetrick, and Y. Fried, "Growth Need Strength and Context Satisfactions as Moderators of the Relations of the Job Characteristics Model," *Journal of Management* (September 1992), pp. 575–93.

[29] C. A. O'Reilly and D. F. Caldwell, "Informational Influence as a Determinant of Perceived Task Characteristics and Job Satisfaction," *Journal of Applied Psychology* (April 1979), pp. 157–65; R. V. Montagno, "The Effects of Comparison Others and Prior Experience on Responses to Task Design," *Academy of Management Journal* (June 1985), pp. 491–98; and P. C. Bottger and I. K-H. Chew, "The Job Characteristics Model and Growth Satisfaction: Main Effects of Assimilation of Work Experience and Context Satisfaction," *Human Relations* (June 1986), pp. 575–94.

[30] Hackman, "Work Design," pp. 132–33.

[31] G.R. Salancik and J. Pfeffer, "A Social Information Processing Approach to Job Attitudes and Task Design," *Administrative Science Quarterly* (June 1978), pp. 224–53; J. G. Thomas and R. W. Griffin, "The Power of Social Information in the Workplace," *Organizational Dynamics* (Autumn 1989), pp. 63–75; and M. D. Zalesny and J. K. Ford, "Extending the Social Information Processing Perspective: New Links to Attitudes, Behaviors, and Perceptions," *Organizational Behavior and Human Decision Processes* (December 1990), pp. 205–46.

[32] See, for instance, J. Thomas and R.W. Griffin, "The Social Information Processing Model of Task Design: A Review of the Literature," *Academy of Management Journal* (October 1983), pp. 672–82; and M.D. Zalesny and J.K. Ford, "Extending the Social Information Processing Perspective: New Links to Attitudes, Behaviors, and Perceptions," *Organizational Behavior and Human Decision Processes* (December 1990), pp. 205–46. For a discussion of the reciprocal nature of the perception-satisfaction relationship, see J.E. Mathieu, D.A. Hofmann, and J.L. Farr, "Job Perception-Job Satisfaction Relations: An Empirical Comparison of Three Competing Theories," *Organizational Behavior and Human Decision Processes* (December 1993), pp. 370–87.

[33] J.E. Rigdon, "Using Lateral Moves to Spur Employees," *Wall Street Journal* (May 26, 1992), p. B1.

[34] B. G. Posner, "Role Changes," *INC.* (February 1990), pp. 95–98.

[35] C. Garfield, "Creating Successful Partnerships with Employees," *At Work* (May/June 1992), p. 8.

[36] Ibid.

[37] See, for instance, data on task enlargement described in M.A. Campion and C.L. McClelland, "Follow-Up and Extension of the Interdisciplinary Costs and Benefits of Enlarged Jobs," *Journal of Applied Psychology* (June 1993), pp. 339–51.

[38] Related in personal communication with the author.

[39] J.R. Hackman, "Work Design," in J.R. Hackman and J.L. Suttle (eds.), *Improving Life at Work* (Santa Monica, CA: Goodyear, 1977), pp. 132–33.

[40] Cited in *U.S. News & World Report* (May 31, 1993), p. 63.

[41] See, for example, J.R. Hackman and G.R. Oldham, *Work Redesign* (Reading, MA: Addison-Wesley, 1980); J. B. Miner, *Theories of Organizational Behavior* (Hinsdale, IL: Dryden Press, 1980), pp. 231–66; R.W. Griffin, "Effects of Work Redesign on Employee Perceptions, Attitudes, and Behaviors: A Long-Term Investigation," *Academy of Management Journal* (June 1991), pp. 425–35; and J.L. Cotton, *Employee Involvement* (Newbury Park, CA: Sage, 1993), pp. 141–72.

[42] Cited in G. Fuchsberg, "Four-Day Workweek Has Become a Stretch for Some Employees," *Wall Street Journal* (August 3, 1994), p. A1.

[43] E. J. Calvasina and W. R. Boxx, "Efficiency of Workers on the Four-Day Workweek," *Academy of Management Journal* (September 1975), pp. 604–10.

[44] See, for example, J.C. Latack and L.W. Foster, "Implementation of Compressed Work Schedules: Participation and Job Redesign as Critical Factors for Employee Acceptance," *Personnel Psychology* (Spring 1985), pp. 75–92; and J.W. Seybolt and J.W. Waddoups, "The Impact of Alternative Work Schedules on Employee Attitudes: A Field Experiment," paper presented at the Western Academy of Management meeting, Hollywood, CA, April 1987.

[45] J.C. Goodale and A.K. Aagaard, "Factors Relating to Varying Reactions to the 4-Day Work Week," *Journal of Applied Psychology* (February 1975), pp. 33–38.

[46] This section is based on T. Roth, "Europe Ponders the Shorter Workweek," *Wall Street Journal* (November 12, 1993), p. A11.

[47] Cited in "Flextime Favored."

[48] Cited in "Flexible Work Arrangements Continue to Find a Home at Companies," *Wall Street Journal* (January 19, 1993), p. A1.

[49] W.F. Glueck, "Changing Hours of Work: A Review and Analysis of the Research," *The Personnel Administrator* (March 1979), pp. 44–47.

[50] See, for example, D.A. Ralston and M.F. Flanagan, "The Effect of Flextime on Absenteeism and Turnover for Male and Female Employees," *Journal of Vocational Behavior* (April 1985), pp. 206–17; D.A. Ralston, W.P. Anthony, and D.J. Gustafson, "Employees May Love Flextime, but What Does It Do to the Organization's Productivity?" *Journal of Applied Psychology* (May 1985), pp. 272–79; J.B. McGuire and J.R. Liro, "Flexible Work Schedules, Work Attitudes, and Perceptions of Productivity," *Public Personnel Management* (Spring 1986), pp. 65–73; P. Bernstein, "The Ultimate in Flextime: From Sweden, by Way of Volvo," *Personnel* (June 1988), pp. 70–74; and D.R. Dalton and D.J. Mesch, "The Impact of Flexible Scheduling on Employee Attendance and Turnover," *Administrative Science Quarterly* (June 1990), pp. 370–87.

[51] "Teaming Up to Manage," *Working Woman* (September 1993), pp. 31–32.

[52] See, for example, T. H. Willard, "Telecommuting: Some Myths and Hits," *Los Angeles Times* (April 17, 1991), p. D3; R. Hotch, "Managing from a Distance," *Nation's Business* (February 1993), pp. 24-26; and R. Maynard, "The Growing Appeal of Telecommuting," *Nation's Business* (August 1994), pp. 61–62.

[53] A. Bianchi, "New Businesses," *INC.* (December 1992), p. 57; and "Telecommuting on the Increase," *INC.* (November 1993), p. 142.

[54] "American Express: Telecommuting," *Fortune* (Autumn 1993), pp. 24–28.

[55] S. Silverstein, "Telecommuting Boomlet Has Few Follow-Up Calls," *Los Angeles Times* (May 16, 1994), p. A1.

[56] See A. Saltzman, "Family Friendliness," *U.S. News & World Report* (February 22, 1993), pp. 59–66; S. Shellenbarger, "So Much Talk, So Little Action," *Wall Street Journal* (June 21, 1993), p. R1; J. Fierman, "Are Companies Less Family-Friendly?" *Fortune* (March 21, 1994), pp. 64–67; R. Sharpe, "Family Friendly Firms Don't Always Promote Females," *Wall Street Journal* (March 29, 1994), p. B1; and C.M. Solomon, "Work/Family's Failing Grade: Why Today's Initiatives Aren't Enough," *Personnel Journal* (May 1994), pp. 72–82.

[57] Cited in M.A. Verespej, "People-First Policies," *Industry Week* (June 21, 1993), p. 20.

[58] S. Shellenbarger, "Data Gap," *Wall Street Journal* (June 21, 1993), p. R6.

[59] A. Saltzman, "Family Friendliness."

[60] Cited in J. Fierman, "Are Companies Less Family-Friendly?"

[61] W. Bridges, "Why Jobs as We Know Them Are Vanishing," *USA Today* (December 21, 1993), p. 11A; and W. Bridges, *Job-Shift* (Reading, MA: Addison-Wesley, 1994).

[62] M.A. Verespej, "Anytime, Anyplace Workplace," *Industry Week* (July 4, 1994), pp. 37–40.

[63] B. Billiter, "Stress, Bad Management Cited in Violence," *Los Angeles Times* (May 7, 1993), p. A36; and P.T. Kilborn, "Inside Post Offices, the Mail Is Only Part of the Pressure," *New York Times* (May 17, 1993), p. A1.

[64] Cited in A. Farnham, "Who Beats Stress Best—and How," *Fortune* (October 7, 1991), p. 71.

[65] K.L. Miller, "Now, Japan Is Admitting It: Work Kills Executives," *Business Week* (August 3, 1992), p. 17.

[66] Adapted from R. S. Schuler, "Definition and Conceptualization of Stress in Organizations," *Organizational Behavior and Human Performance* (April 1980), p. 189. For an updated review of definitions, see R.L. Kahn and P. Byosiere, "Stress in Organizations," in M.D. Dunnette and L.M. Hough (eds.), *Handbook of Industrial and Organizational Psychology*, 2nd ed., Vol. 3 (Palo Alto, CA: Consulting Psychologists Press, 1992), pp. 573–80.

[67] R.S. Schuler, "Definition and Conceptualization of Stress in Organizations" p. 191.

[68] This model is based on D.F. Parker and T.A. DeCotiis, "Organizational Determinants of Job Stress," *Organizational Behavior and Human Performance* (October 1983), p. 166; S. Parasuraman and J.A. Alutto, "Sources and Outcomes of Stress in Organizational Settings: Toward the Development of a Structural Model," *Academy of Management Journal* (June 1984), p. 333; and R.L. Kahn and P. Byosiere, "Stress in Organizations," p. 592.

[69] This section is adapted from C.L. Cooper and R. Payne, *Stress at Work* (London: Wiley, 1978); and Parasuraman and Alutto, "Sources and Outcomes of Stress in Organizational Settings," pp. 330–50.

[70] See, for example, D.R. Frew and N.S. Bruning, "Perceived Organizational Characteristics and Personality Measures as Predictors of Stress/Strain in the Work Place," *Journal of Management* (Winter 1987), pp. 633–46; and M.L. Fox, D.J. Dwyer, and D.C. Ganster, "Effects of Stressful Job Demands and Control of Physiological and Attitudinal Outcomes in a Hospital Setting," *Academy of Management Journal* (April 1993), pp. 289–318.

[71] C. Hymowitz and G. Stern, "At Procter & Gamble, Brands Face Pressure and So Do Executives," *Wall Street Journal* (May 10, 1993), p. A1.

[72] D. L. Nelson and C. Sutton, "Chronic Work Stress and Coping: A Longitudinal Study and Suggested New Directions," *Academy of Management Journal* (December 1990), pp. 859–69.

[73] H. Selye, *The Stress of Life*, rev. ed. (New York: McGraw-Hill, 1956).

[74] S.J. Motowidlo, J.S. Packard, and M.R. Manning, "Occupational Stress: Its Causes and Consequences for Job Performance," *Journal of Applied Psychology* (November 1987), pp. 619–20.

[75] See, for instance, J.J. House, *Work Stress and Social Support* (Reading, MA: Addison-Wesley, 1981); S. Jayaratne, D. Himle, and W.A. Chess, "Dealing with Work Stress and Strain: Is the Perception of Support More Important Than Its Use?" *The Journal of Applied Behavioral Science*, Vol. 24, No. 2, (1988), pp. 191–202; and R. C. Cummings, "Job Stress and the Buffering Effect of Supervisory Support," *Group & Organization Studies* (March 1990), pp. 92–104.

[76] See L.R. Murphy, "A Review of Organizational Stress Management Research," *Journal of Organizational Behavior Management* (Fall-Winter 1986), pp. 215–27.

[77] M. Friedman and R.H. Rosenman, *Type A Behavior and Your Heart* (New York: Knopf, 1974).

[78] Ibid., p. 84.

[79] R. Williams, *The Trusting Heart: Great News About Type A Behavior* (New York: Times Books, 1989).

[80] Schuler, "Definition and Conceptualization of Stress," pp. 200–205; and R.L. Kahn and P. Byosiere, "Stress in Organizations," pp. 604–10.

[81] See T.A. Beehr and J.E. Newman, "Job Stress, Employee Health, and Organizational Effectiveness: A Facet Analysis, Model, and Literature Review," *Personnel Psychology* (Winter 1978), pp. 665–99; and B.D. Steffy and J.W. Jones, "Workplace Stress and Indicators of Coronary-Disease Risk," *Academy of Management Journal* (September 1988), pp. 686–98.

[82] B.D. Steffy and J.W. Jones, "Workplace Stress and Indicators of Coronary-Disease Risk," p. 687.

[83] C.L. Cooper and J. Marshall, "Occupational Sources of Stress: A Review of the Literature Relating to Coronary Heart Disease and Mental Ill Health," *Journal of Occupational Psychology*, Vol. 49, No. 1 (1976), pp. 11–28.

[84] J.R. Hackman and G.R. Oldham, "Development of the Job Diagnostic Survey," *Journal of Applied Psychology* (April 1975), pp. 159–70.

[85] See, for instance, J.M. Ivancevich and M.T. Matteson, *Stress and Work* (Glenview, IL: Scott, Foresman, 1981); and R.D. Allen, M.A. Hitt, and C.R. Greer, "Occupational Stress and Perceived Organizational Effectiveness in Formal Groups: An Examination of Stress Level and Stress Type," *Personnel Psychology* (Summer 1982), pp. 359–70.

[86] S.E. Sullivan and R.S. Bhagat, "Organizational Stress, Job Satisfaction and Job Performance: Where Do We Go from Here?" *Journal of Management* (June 1992), pp. 361–64.

[87] The following discussion has been influenced by J.E. Newman and T.A. Beehr, "Personal and Organizational Strategies for Handling Job Stress," *Personnel Psychology* (Spring 1979), pp. 1–38; A.P. Brief, R.S. Schuler, and M. Van Sell, *Managing Job Stress*; R.L. Rose and J.F. Veiga, "Assessing the Sustained Effects of a Stress Management Intervention on Anxiety and Locus of Control," *Academy of Management Journal* (March 1984), pp. 190–98; J.M. Ivancevich and M.T. Matteson, "Organizational Level Stress Management Interventions: A Review and Recommendations," *Journal of Organ-*

izational Behavior Management (Fall-Winter 1986), pp. 229–48; M.T. Matteson and J.M. Ivancevich, "Individual Stress Management Interventions: Evaluation of Techniques," *Journal of Management Psychology* (January 1987), pp. 24–30; J.M. Ivancevich, M.T. Matteson, S.M. Freedman, and J.S. Phillips, "Worksite Stress Management Interventions," *American Psychologist* (February 1990), pp. 252–61; R. Maturi, "Stress *Can* Be Beaten," *Industry Week* (July 20, 1992), pp. 23–26; and P. Froiland, "What Cures Job Stress?" *Training* (December 1993), pp. 32–36.

[88] T.H. Macan, "Time Management: Test of a Process Model," *Journal of Applied Psychology* (June 1994), pp. 381–91.

[89] See, for example, M.E. Haynes, *Practical Time Management: How to Make the Most of Your Most Perishable Resource* (Tulsa, OK: PennWell Books, 1985).

[90] J. Kiely and G. Hodgson, "Stress in the Prison Service: The Benefits of Exercise Programs," *Human Relations* (June 1990), pp. 551–72.

[91] E.J. Forbes and R.J. Pekala, "Psychophysiological Effects of Several Stress Management Techniques," *Psychological Reports* (February 1993), pp. 19–27; and G. Smith, "Meditation, the New Balm for Corporate Stress," *Business Week* (May 10, 1993), pp. 86–87.

[92] D. Etzion, "Moderating Effects of Social Support on the Stress-Burnout Relationship," *Journal of Applied Psychology* (November 1984), pp. 615–22; and Jackson, Schwab, and Schuler, "Toward an Understanding of the Burnout Phenomenon."

[93] S.E. Jackson, "Participation in Decision Making as a Strategy for Reducing Job-Related Strain," *Journal of Applied Psychology* (February 1983), pp. 3–19; and P. Froiland, "What Cures Job Stress?"

[94] See, for instance, R. A. Wolfe, D. O. Ulrich, and D. F. Parker, "Employee Health Management Programs: Review, Critique, and Research Agenda," *Journal of Management* (Winter 1987), pp. 603–15; D.L. Gebhardt and C.E. Crump, "Employee Fitness and Wellness Programs in the Workplace," *American Psychologist* (February 1990), pp. 262–72; and C.E. Beadle, "And Let's Save 'Wellness.' It Works," *New York Times* (July 24, 1994), p. F9.

[95] C.E. Beadle, "And Let's Save 'Wellness.'"

[96] "Don't Forget Wellness," *Industry Week* (May 2, 1994), p. 61.

[97] R.L. Kahn and P. Byosiere, "Stress in Organizations," pp. 605–608.

CHAPTER 16

Hilton Hotels' investment in employee training pays big dividends. Its work force is the benchmark for service excellence in the hospitality industry. Employee feedback helped Hilton develop its video-based training series (shown here).

HUMAN RESOURCE POLICIES AND PRACTICES

CHAPTER OUTLINE

Selection Practices
Training and Development Programs
Performance Evaluation
Reward Systems
The Union–Management Interface
International Human Resource Practices: Selected Issues

LEARNING OBJECTIVES

After studying this chapter, you should be able to:

1. Identify the key skills for effective interviewing.
2. List the advantages of performance simulation tests over written tests.
3. Define three skill categories.
4. Summarize the four stages in a career.
5. Identify the advantages of using behaviors rather than traits in evaluating performance.
6. Describe the potential problems in performance evaluation and actions that can correct these problems.
7. Outline the various types of rewards.
8. Clarify how the existence of a union affects employee behavior.

After listening to my employees, I have to conclude that I have only three types of people working for me: stars, all-stars, and superstars! How is it possible for all my people to be above average?

AN ANONYMOUS BOSS

John Merriman, manager of the Gates Rubber plant in Siloam Springs, Arkansas, has developed a multistage screening-and-interviewing process as a means to improve the quality of new hires and to reduce turnover in his 650-employee plant.[1]

Every successful job applicant has to go through four steps. The first is a general interview with the human resources department. That's followed up three days later with a second interview by someone else from human resources to verify information and impressions from the first meeting. The third stage consists of a panel interview with three people (including Merriman) from different parts of the plant. "We're evaluating communications skills, work attitudes, and general confidence levels," says Merriman. "Since all the work of the plant is done in teams, we're also focusing on an applicant's ability to respond well in a group setting." If the panel approves the candidate, the human resources department checks references. If these prove satisfactory, the candidate is invited back for a fourth, and final, meeting.

This final meeting typically takes place on a Friday evening, lasts two hours, and includes spouses or significant others—of the candidate as well as those of the three plant people. From 7 to 9 P.M. the candidate and his or her spouse watch a 20-minute video on the history of Gates Rubber, are briefed on the company's benefits program, and discuss what it means to be part of a self-managed work team. "This is the most revealing part of the process," states Merriman. "We're looking at the interaction between the candidate and his spouse. Did he tell her about working on the night shift? Did he explain the level of commitment we require? How did they react when we explain how we don't think unions are needed here? Any sign of trouble and we pass on the candidate."

Merriman attributes this elaborate selection process to screening out misfits and significantly cutting employee turnover. Annual turnover at the Arkansas plant is now only 8 percent, compared to 100 percent at a comparable plant owned by another company in town.

The lower turnover at Gates's Siloam Springs's plant illustrates how human resource policies and practices—in this case, the plant's use of a four-stage screening-and-interview process for employee selection—can affect important organizational behavior outcomes. In this chapter, we discuss a number of human resource concerns that add important pieces to our puzzle as we attempt to explain and predict employee behavior. Specifically, we look at selection practices, training and career development programs, performance evaluation, reward systems, and union–management relations.

Selection Practices

The objective of effective selection is to match individual characteristics (ability, experience, and so on) with the requirements of the job.[2] When management fails to get a proper match, both employee performance and satisfaction suffer. In this search to achieve the right individual–job fit, where does management begin? The answer is to assess the demands and requirements of the job. The process of assessing the activities within a job is called job analysis.

Job Analysis

job analysis
Developing a detailed description of the tasks involved in a job, determining the relationship of a given job to other jobs, and ascertaining the knowledge, skills, and abilities necessary for an employee to perform the job successfully.

Job analysis involves developing a detailed description of the tasks involved in a job, determining the relationship of a given job to other jobs, and ascertaining the knowledge, skills, and abilities necessary for an employee to successfully perform the job.[3]

How is this information attained? Table 16-1 describes the more popular job analysis methods.

Information gathered by using one or more of the job analysis methods results in the organization being able to create a **job description** and

Table 16-1 Popular Job Analysis Methods

1. **Observation Method.** An analyst watches employees directly or reviews films of workers on the job.
2. **Individual Interview Method.** Selected job incumbents are extensively interviewed, and the results of a number of these interviews are combined into a single job analysis.
3. **Group Interview Method.** Same as individual except that a number of job incumbents are interviewed simultaneously.
4. **Structured Questionnaire Method.** Workers check or rate the items they perform in their jobs from a long list of possible task items.
5. **Technical Conference Method.** Specific characteristics of a job are obtained from "experts," who typically are supervisors with extensive knowledge of the job.
6. **Diary Method.** Job incumbents record their daily activities in a diary.

job specification. The former is a written statement of what a jobholder does, how it is done, and why it is done. It should accurately portray job content, environment, and conditions of employment. The job specification states the minimum acceptable qualifications that an employee must possess to perform a given job successfully. It identifies the knowledge, skills, and abilities needed to do the job effectively. So job descriptions identify characteristics of the job; job specifications identify characteristics of the successful job incumbent.

job description
A written statement of what a jobholder does, how it is done, and why it is done.

job specification
States the minimum acceptable qualifications that an employee must possess to perform a given job successfully.

The job description and specification are important documents for guiding the selection process. The job description can be used to describe the job to potential candidates. The job specification keeps the attention of those doing the selection on the list of qualifications necessary for an incumbent to perform a job and assists in determining whether or not candidates are qualified.

Selection Devices

What do application forms, interviews, employment tests, background checks, and personal letters of recommendation have in common? Each is a device for obtaining information about a job applicant that can help the organization determine whether the applicant's skills, knowledge, and abilities are appropriate for the job in question. In this section, we review the more important of these selection devices: interviews, written tests, and performance simulation tests.

INTERVIEWS Do you know anyone who has gotten a job without at least one interview? You may have an acquaintance who got a part-time or summer job through a close friend or relative without having to go through an interview, but such instances are rare. Of all the selection devices that organizations use to differentiate candidates, the interview continues to be the one most frequently used.[4]

The interview also seems to carry a great deal of weight. That is, not only is it widely used, but its results tend to have a disproportionate amount of influence on the selection decision. The candidate who performs poorly in the employment interview is likely to be cut from the applicant pool, regardless of his or her experience, test scores, or letters of recommendation. Conversely, "all too often, the person most polished in job-seeking techniques, particularly

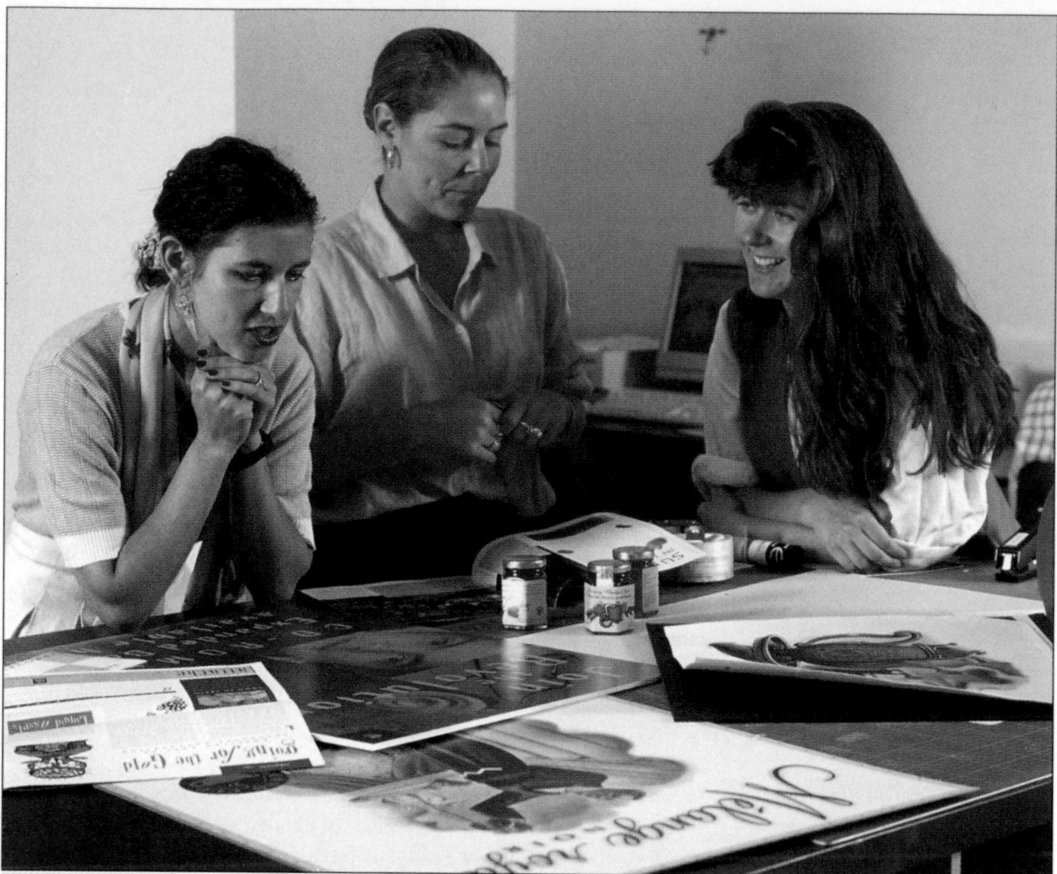

Ellie Rubin (left) uses job interviews to select candidates who are what she calls "professional eclectics." Rubin is a founding partner of Canada's The Bulldog Group, a Toronto marketing firm that specializes in new communications vehicles such as interactive kiosks and CD-ROM publishing. Rubin interviews qualified applicants who have backgrounds in graphic design or video production. They must demonstrate technical proficiency in at least four, but preferably nine, specialized software programs. In addition to specialized technical skills, applicants must also convince Rubin they possess a host of generalist skills. Rubin's ideal employee is creative, flexible, analytical, communicative, thinks independently but interrelates with team members, and is willing to learn.

those used in the interview process, is the one hired, even though he or she may not be the best candidate for the position."[5]

These findings are important because of the unstructured manner in which the selection interview is frequently conducted. The unstructured interview—short in duration, casual, and made up of random questions—has been proven to be an ineffective selection device.[6] The data gathered from such interviews are typically biased and often unrelated to future job performance. Without structure, a number of biases can distort results. These biases include interviewers tending to favor applicants who share their attitudes, giving unduly high weight to negative information, and allowing the order in which applicants are interviewed to influence evaluations.[7] By having interviewers use a standardized set of questions, providing interviewers with a uniform method of recording information, and standardizing the rating of the applicant's qualifications, the variability in results across applicants is reduced and the validity of the interview as a selection device is greatly enhanced.

From Concepts to Skills

Selection Interviewing

The interview is made up of four stages. It begins with preparation, followed by the opening, a period of questioning and discussion, and a conclusion.[8]

1. *Preparation.* Prior to meeting the applicant, you should review his or her application form and résumé. You also should review the job description and job specification for the position the applicant is interviewing for.

Next, structure the agenda for the interview. Specifically, use the standardized questions provided to you or prepare a set of questions you want to ask the applicant. Choose questions that can't be merely answered with only a yes or no. Inquiries that begin with *how* or *why* tend to stimulate extended answers. Avoid leading questions that telegraph the desired response (such as "Would you say you have good interpersonal skills?") and bipolar questions that require the applicant to select an answer from only two choices (such as "Do you prefer working with people or working alone?"). In most cases, questions relating to marital and family status, age, race, religion, gender, ethnic background, credit rating, and arrest record are prohibited by law unless you can demonstrate they are in some way related to job performance. So avoid them. In place of asking "Are you married?" or "Do you have children?" you might ask, "Are there any reasons why you might not be able to work overtime several times a month?" Of course, to avoid discrimination, you have to ask this question of both male and female candidates.

2. *Opening.* Assume the applicant is tense and nervous. If you're going to get valid insights into what the applicant is really like, you'll need to put him or her at ease. Introduce yourself. Be friendly. Begin with a few simple questions or statements that can break the ice; for example, "Did you run into much traffic coming over?"

Once the applicant is fairly relaxed, you should provide a brief orientation. Preview what topics will be discussed, how long the interview will take, and explain if you'll be taking notes. Encourage the applicant to ask questions.

3. *Questioning and discussion.* The questions you developed during the preparation stage will provide a general road map to guide you. Make sure you cover them all. Additional questions should arise from the answers to the standardized questions. Select follow-up questions that naturally flow from the answers given.

Follow-up questions should seek to probe deeper into what the applicant says. If you feel the applicant's response is superficial or inadequate, seek elaboration. Ask a question like, "Tell me more about that issue." If you need to clarify information, say something like, "You said working overtime was okay *sometimes*. Can you tell me specifically when you'd be willing to work overtime?" If the applicant doesn't directly answer your question, follow up by repeating the question or paraphrasing it. Finally, never underestimate the power of silence in an interview. One of the biggest errors that inexperienced interviewers make is to talk too much. You're not learning anything about the candidate when you're doing the talking. Pause for at least a few seconds after the applicant appears to have finished an answer. Your silence encourages the applicant to continue talking.

4. *Concluding.* Once you're through with the questions and discussions, you're ready to wrap up the interview. Let the applicant know this fact with a statement like, "Well, that covers all the questions I have. Is there anything about the job or our organization that I haven't answered for you?" Then, let the applicant know what's going to happen next. When can he or she expect to hear from you? Will you write or phone? Are there likely to be more follow-up interviews?

Before you consider the interview complete, write your evaluation while it is fresh in your mind. Ideally, you kept notes or recorded the applicant's answers to your questions and made comments of your impressions. Now that the applicant is gone, take the time to assess the applicant's responses.

The evidence indicates that interviews are most valuable for assessing an applicant's intelligence, level of motivation, and interpersonal skills.[9] Where these qualities are related to job performance, the validity of the interview as a selection device is increased. For example, these qualities have demonstrated relevance for performance in upper managerial positions. This may explain why applicants for senior management positions typically undergo dozens of interviews with executive recruiters, board members, and other company executives before a final decision is made. It can also explain why organizations that design work around teams, like the Gates Rubber plant described at the beginning of this chapter, may similarly put applicants through an unusually large number of interviews.

WRITTEN TESTS Typical written tests are tests of intelligence, aptitude, ability, interest, and integrity. Long popular as selection devices, they have generally declined in use since the late 1960s. The reason is that such tests have frequently been characterized as discriminating, and many organizations have not validated, or cannot validate, such tests as being job related.

Tests of intellectual ability, spatial and mechanical ability, perceptual accuracy, and motor ability have shown to be moderately valid predictors for many semiskilled and unskilled operative jobs in industrial organizations.[10] Intelligence tests are reasonably good predictors for supervisory positions.[11] But the burden is on management to demonstrate that any test used is job related. Since the characteristics that many of these tests tap are considerably removed from the actual performance of the job itself, getting high validity coefficients has often been difficult. The result has been a decreased use of traditional written tests.

One exception has been the recent interest in integrity tests. These are paper-and-pencil tests that measure factors such as dependability, carefulness, responsibility, and honesty. The evidence is impressive that these tests are powerful in predicting supervisory ratings of job performance and counterproductive employee behavior on the job such as theft, discipline problems, and excessive absenteeism.[12]

PERFORMANCE SIMULATION TESTS What better way is there to find out if an applicant can do a job successfully than by having him or her do it? That is precisely the logic of performance simulation tests.

> ◆What better way is there to find out if an applicant can do a job successfully than by having him or her do it?

Performance simulation tests have increased significantly in popularity during the past two decades. Undoubtedly, the enthusiasm for these tests comes from the fact that they are based on job analysis data and, therefore, should more easily meet the requirement of job relatedness than do written tests. Performance simulation tests are made up of actual job behaviors rather than surrogates, as are written tests.

The two best known performance simulation tests are work sampling and assessment centers. The former is suited to routine jobs, whereas the latter is relevant for the selection of managerial personnel.

work sampling
Creating a miniature replica of a job to evaluate the performance abilities of job candidates.

Work sampling is an effort to create a miniature replica of a job. Applicants demonstrate they possess the necessary talents by actually doing the tasks. By carefully devising work samples based on job analysis data, the knowledge, skills, and abilities needed for each job are determined. Then each work sample element is matched with a corresponding job performance element. For instance, a work sample for a job where the employee has to use computer spreadsheet software would require the applicant to actually solve a problem using a spreadsheet.

The results from work sample experiments are impressive. Studies almost consistently demonstrate that work samples yield validities superior to written aptitude and personality tests.[13]

A more elaborate set of performance simulation tests, specifically designed to evaluate a candidate's managerial potential, is administered in **assessment centers**. In assessment centers, line executives, supervisors, and/or trained psychologists evaluate candidates as they go through two to four days of exercises that simulate real problems they would confront on the job. Based on a list of descriptive dimensions the actual job incumbent has to meet, activities might include interviews, in-basket problem-solving exercises, group discussions, and business decision games.

assessment centers
A set of performance simulation tests designed to evaluate a candidate's managerial potential.

The evidence on the effectiveness of assessment centers is extremely impressive. They have consistently demonstrated results that predict later job performance in managerial positions.[14] Although they are not cheap—AT&T, which has assessed more than 200,000 employees, computes its assessment costs at $800 to $1,500 per employee—the selection of an ineffective manager is unquestionably far more costly.

Training and Development Programs

Competent employees don't remain competent forever. Skills deteriorate and can become obsolete. That's why organizations spend billions of dollars each year on formal training. One recent study, for instance, found that U.S. organizations with 100 or more employees spent $48 billion in a single year on formal training for 47.2 million workers.[15] Xerox alone spends over $300 million a year on training and retraining its employees.[16] Motorola, Federal Express, Andersen Consulting, Corning, and Singapore Airlines all spend a minimum of 3 percent of their payroll costs on training.[17] And thousands of small companies are investing heavily in employee training.[18]

Intensified competition, technological changes, and the search for improved productivity is motivating management to increase expenditures for training. Engineers need to update their knowledge of mechanical and electri-

Singapore Airlines maintains its reputation as one of the best airlines in the world with the highest levels of service by investing heavily in employee training. In a recent year, Singapore Airlines invested almost $53 million on employee training, or $2,225 for each of its 23,787 employees. Cabin crew members go through a rigorous four-month initial training program, including learning emergency safety procedures (as shown here) and are retrained every two years. Training encompasses beauty tips, discussions of fine wine and gourmet food, the art of conversation, reading body language, and appreciating cultural differences among passengers. Crew members also learn ways to memorize passengers' names easily, to discern which passengers want to be talked to and which want to be left alone, and to anticipate what passengers want before they ask for it.

cal systems. Hourly workers attend seminars on problem solving, quality improvement, and team-building skills. Clerical personnel take courses to learn how to fully utilize the latest software programs on their computers. And executives themselves participate in workshops to learn how to become more effective leaders or develop strategic plans for their divisions. In the 1990s, people at all levels in organizations are involved in formal training.

In this section, we look at the type of skills that training can improve; then we review various skill training methods, as well as the career development programs that can prepare employees for a future that's different from today.

Skill Categories

We can dissect skills into three categories: technical, interpersonal, and problem solving. Most training activities seek to modify one or more of these skills.

TECHNICAL Most training is directed at upgrading and improving an employee's technical skills. This applies as much to white-collar as to blue-collar jobs. Jobs change as a result of new technologies and improved methods. Postal sorters have had to undergo technical training in order to learn to operate automatic sorting machines. Many auto repair personnel have had to undergo extensive training to fix and maintain recent models with front-wheel-drive trains, electronic ignitions, fuel injection, and other innovations. Not many clerical personnel during the past decade have been unaffected by the computer. Literally millions of such employees have had to be trained to operate and interface with a computer terminal.

INTERPERSONAL Almost all employees belong to a work unit. To some degree, their work performance depends on their ability to effectively interact with their coworkers and their boss. Some employees have excellent interpersonal skills, but others require training to improve theirs. This includes learning how to be a better listener, how to communicate ideas more clearly, and how to be a more effective team player.

One of the fastest growing areas of interpersonal skill development is diversity training.[19] The two most popular types of this training focus on increasing awareness and building skills. *Awareness training* tries to create an understanding of the need for, and meaning of, managing and valuing diversity. *Skill-building training* educates employees about specific cultural differences in the workplace. Companies leading the way in diversity training include American Express, Avon, Corning, Hewlett-Packard, Monsanto, Motorola, Pacific Gas & Electric, U.S. West, and Xerox.

PROBLEM SOLVING Managers, as well as many employees who perform nonroutine tasks, have to solve problems on their job. When people require these skills, but are deficient, they can participate in problem-solving training. This would include activities to sharpen their logic, reasoning, and problem-defining skills, as well as their abilities to assess causation, develop alternatives, analyze alternatives, and select solutions. Problem-solving training has become a basic part of almost every organizational effort to introduce self-managed teams or implement TQM.

◆◆◆◆ OB in the News ◆◆◆◆

Diversity Training Grows at Small Firms

For more than a year, two of Emma Colquitt's employees had argued about religion. Then one of them, a Hispanic Roman Catholic woman, approached her office manager with a complaint: The other worker, a black follower of Jehovah's Witnesses, had listened sympathetically as a customer "bashed" Catholicism.

While Colquitt's firm, Cardiac Concepts, Inc., a Texas outpatient laboratory that specializes in cardiovascular tests, employs only 11 people, she can't afford these kinds of conflicts. Moreover, most of her 11 employees are women and minority members, representing half a dozen faiths. "I have three employees in that office, and when two-thirds are arguing with each other, that is not cost effective," says Colquitt.

Emma Colquitt decided to do what many small-business owners now are doing to ease internal tensions created by diversity. She hired a consultant to give her staff a workshop on appreciating differences and learning how to get along.

For Cardiac Concepts, that training lasted only four hours and emphasized role-playing activities and exercises focusing on individual employee's backgrounds and beliefs. For instance, one exercise required employees to pair off and make lists of stereotypes of other ethnic groups present. It helped make employees aware of the values and lifestyles of their colleagues from other cultures—and to acknowledge their own prejudices.

The cost for this workshop—$3,000—was high for a small firm like Cardiac Concepts, whose annual sales are only $1 million. But Colquitt considers the money well spent. She says there have been no diversity-related squabbles since the workshop took place. And working relationships between the Hispanic Catholic and the black follower of Jehovah's Witnesses have become "less strained," she says.

Based on M. Lee, "Diversity Training Grows at Small Firms," *Wall Street Journal* (September 2, 1993), p. B2.

Training Methods

Most training takes place on the job. This preference can be attributed to the simplicity and, usually, lower cost of on-the-job training methods. However, on-the-job training can disrupt the workplace and result in an increase in errors as learning proceeds. Also, some skill training is too complex to learn on the job. In such cases, it should take place outside the work setting.[20]

ON-THE-JOB TRAINING Popular on-the-job training methods include job rotation and understudy assignments. *Job rotation* involves lateral transfers that enable employees to work at different jobs. Employees get to learn a wide variety of jobs and gain increased insight into the interdependency between jobs and a wider perspective on organizational activities. New employees frequently learn their jobs by understudying a seasoned veteran. In the trades, this is usually called an *apprenticeship*. In white-collar jobs, it is called a *coaching*, or *mentor*, relationship. In each, the understudy works under the observation of an experienced worker, who acts as a model the understudy attempts to emulate.

Both job rotation and understudy assignments apply to the learning of technical skills. Interpersonal and problem-solving skills are acquired more effectively by training that takes place off the job.

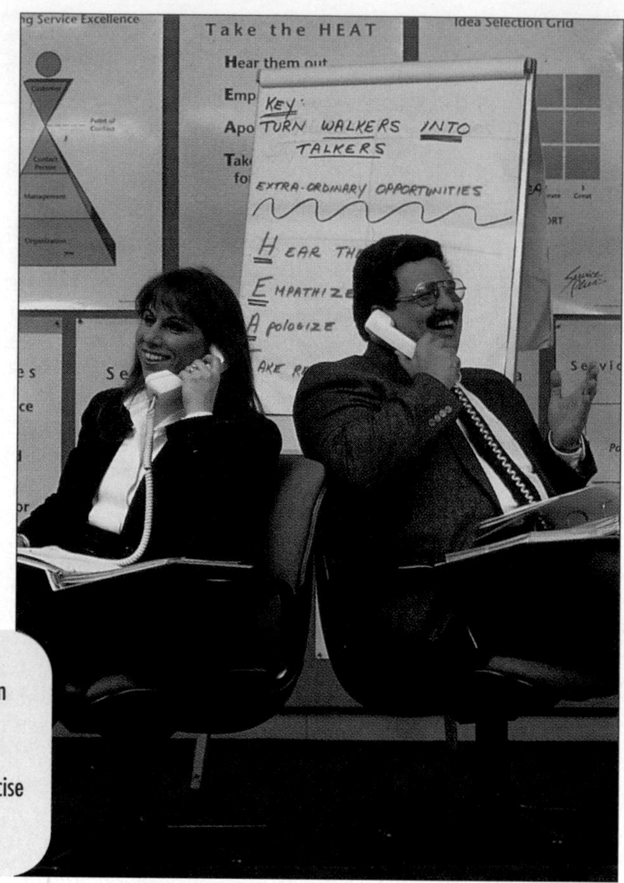

Off-the-job training at Philadelphia Newspapers, Inc. includes simulation exercises. Here, Chris Bonanducci (left), employee relations manager, participates in a role-playing exercise with Ed Delfin, circulation training manager.

OFF-THE-JOB TRAINING There are a number of off-the-job training methods that managers may want to make available to employees. The more popular are classroom lectures, videos, and simulation exercises. *Classroom lectures* are well suited for conveying specific information. They can be used effectively for developing technical and problem-solving skills. *Videos* can also be used to explicitly demonstrate technical skills that are not easily presented by other methods. Interpersonal and problem-solving skills may be best learned through *simulation exercises* such as case analyses, experiential exercises, role playing, and group interaction sessions. Complex computer models, such as those used by airlines in the training of pilots, are another kind of simulation exercise, which in this case is used to teach technical skills. So, too, is *vestibule training*, in which employees learn their jobs on the same equipment they will be using, only the training is conducted away from the actual work floor. Table 16-2 describes the results from a survey of off-the-job instructional methods used for employee training.

Off-the-job training can rely on outside consultants, local college faculty, or in-house personnel. Granite Rock, Inc., a producer of construction and paving materials that spends nearly 1 percent of gross sales and a whopping 4.2 percent of payroll on training, has even created its own internal university.[21] Granite Rock University offers more than 50 courses and seminars for company employees on everything from enhancing self-esteem to the mechanics of mobile hydraulic equipment.

Table 16-2 Popularity Among Instructional Methods

Method	Percentage
Percentage of organizations using these methods for employee training	
Videotapes	95
Lectures	93
One-on-one instruction	76
Role plays	63
Games	58
Computer-based training	58
Audiotapes	54
Self-assessment/self-testing instruments	53
Case studies	52

Based on a national survey of U.S. companies with at least 100 employees.

Source: P. Froiland, "Who's Getting Trained?" *Training* (October 1993), p. 53.

Career Development

Career development is a way for an organization to sustain or increase its employees' current productivity, while at the same time preparing them for a changing world.

Twenty years ago, when a person was more likely to spend his or her entire work years with the same employer, most medium-sized and large organizations engaged in extensive employee career planning. It focused exclusively on developing employees for opportunities within the specific organization. For instance, management would develop sophisticated replacement charts that would identify potential promotion candidates for key internal positions. They'd also offer a wide range of in-house career development programs to prepare employees for promotions. Companies like Aetna Life, General Electric, Merrill Lynch, and Toshiba still invest heavily in this form of career planning. But as more and more organizations downsize their operations, reengineer processes, and restructure themselves to increase flexibility, they're shifting career development responsibility to their employees.[22] Consistent with the employee empowerment movement, an increasing number of organizations are empowering employees to manage their own careers. Apple Computer, for instance, supports employees with workshops, career counseling, and tuition reimbursement programs. But employees are told they have to take responsibility for planning their personal career track. It's not their manager's or the company's job to define their future. In those cases where it becomes evident an employee's personal goals can't be fulfilled at Apple, company counselors even help the individual prepare for a future outside Apple.

In spite of this shifting of responsibility trend, definite benefits accrue to organizations that offer career development programs.[23] These include ensuring the right people will be available for meeting changing staffing requirements, increasing work force diversity, and providing employees with more realistic job expectations. In this section, we briefly review some basic career concepts and offer suggestions for creating an effective career development program.

career
A sequence of positions occupied by a person during the course of a lifetime.

CAREER STAGES A **career** is a "sequence of positions occupied by a person during the course of a lifetime."[24] This definition does not imply advancement or success or failure. Any work, paid or unpaid, pursued over an extended period of time, can constitute a career. In addition to formal job work, it may include schoolwork, homemaking, or volunteer work.[25]

career stages
The four steps most people go through in their careers: exploration, establishment, midcareer, and late career.

Careers can be more easily understood if we think of them as proceeding through **career stages**.[26] Most of us have gone or will go through four stages: exploration, establishment, midcareer, and late career.

Exploration begins prior to even entering the work force on a paid basis and ends for most of us in our mid-twenties as we make the transition from school to our primary work interest. It's a time of self-exploration and an assessment of alternatives. The *establishment* stage includes being accepted by our peers, learning the job, and gaining tangible evidence of successes or failures in the "real world." Most people don't face their first severe career dilemmas until they reach the *midcareer* stage, a stage that is typically reached between the ages of 35 and 50. This is a time where one may continue to improve one's performance, level off, or begin to deteriorate. At this stage, the first dilemma is accepting the fact that you're no longer seen as a "learner." Mistakes carry greater penalties. At this point in a career, you are expected to have moved beyond apprenticeship to journeyman status. For those who continue to grow through the midcareer stage, the *late career* usually is a pleasant time when you are allowed the luxury to relax a bit and enjoy playing the part of the elder statesperson. For those who have stagnated or deteriorated during the previous stage, the late career brings the reality they will not have a lasting impact or change the world as they once thought. It is a time when individuals recognize they have decreased work mobility and may be locked into their current jobs. They begin to look forward to retirement and the opportunities to do something different.

If employees are to remain productive, career development and training programs need to be available that can support an employee's task and emotional needs at each stage. Table 16-3 identifies the more important of these needs.

CAREER ANCHORS In addition to stages, another concept that can help to understand people in their jobs is that of career anchors.[27]

Just as boats put down anchors to keep them from drifting too far, people put down anchors to stabilize their career decisions and keep them within constraints. **Career anchors**, then, are distinct patterns of self-perceived talents and abilities, motives and needs, and attitudes and values that guide and stabilize a person's career after several years of real-world experience and feedback.

career anchors
Distinct patterns of self-perceived talents and abilities, motives and needs, and attitudes and values that guide and stabilize a person's career after several years of real-world experience and feedback.

As people reach their late twenties and early thirties, they have to begin making decisions about which jobs to pursue and how to balance personal and work life. To avoid erratic or random decisions, they develop career anchors. If they sense a job or job situation will not be consistent with their talents, needs, and values, their anchor pulls them back into situations that are more congruent with their self-image.

Research has identified five specific patterns:

TECHNICAL/FUNCTIONAL COMPETENCE This anchor focuses on the actual content of a person's work. Someone with an accounting degree and a CPA certificate might find jobs outside of accounting a challenge to her feelings of competence yet inconsistent with her basic occupational self-concept.

Table 16-3 Training Needs Within Career Stages

Stage	Task Needs	Emotional Needs
Exploration	1. Varied job activities	1. Make preliminary job choices
	2. Self-exploration	2. Settling down
Establishment	1. Job challenge	1. Deal with rivalry and competition; face failures
	2. Develop competence in a specialty area	2. Deal with work/ family conflicts
	3. Develop creativity and innovation	3. Support
	4. Rotate into new area after three to five years	4. Autonomy
Midcareer	1. Technical updating	1. Express feelings about midlife
	2. Develop skills in training and coaching others (younger employees)	2. Reorganize thinking about self in relation to work, family, community
	3. Rotation into new job requiring new skill	3. Reduce self-indulgence and competitiveness
	4. Develop broader view of work and own role in organization	
Late career	1. Plan for retirement	1. Support and counseling to see one's work as a platform for others
	2. Shift from power role to one of consultation and guidance	2. Develop sense of identity in extra-organizational activities
	3. Identify and develop successors	
	4. Begin activities outside the organization	

Source: Adapted from D.T. Hall and M. Morgan, "Career Development and Planning," in K. Perlman, F.L. Schmidt, and W.C. Hamner (eds.), *Contemporary Problems in Personnel* (3rd ed.). Copyright © 1983 by John Wiley & Sons. Reprinted by permission of John Wiley & Sons.

MANAGERIAL COMPETENCE This anchor emphasizes holding and exercising managerial responsibility. These people seek situations where they can be analytical, utilize their interpersonal skills, and exercise power.

SECURITY For some people, a key factor in career decision making is work stability. A new position with great opportunities and challenges, but little job security, would be incongruent with these people's needs. They prefer job and organizational stability, employment contracts, good employment benefits, attractive pension plans, and the like.

AUTONOMY The overriding factor for some people in career decisions is to maintain their independence and freedom. They seek to minimize organizational constraints. These people, not surprisingly, prefer small organic types of organizations in which to work.

CREATIVITY These people are driven by an overarching desire to create something that is entirely of their own making. For creativity-anchored people, starting a new business, working in a research laboratory, being a major player on a new project's team, and similar activities are important to their self-worth.

The career anchor perspective has both selection and motivational implications. For example, it can help to explain why dramatic changes in career focus are so difficult for people to make. They require great effort and are not likely to occur very frequently. The perspective also helps to explain why individuals may have very different reactions to similar jobs. Any understanding of how job characteristics will affect an individual has to take into consideration the dynamics between the job's task attributes and the career anchors of the person in that job.

EFFECTIVE CAREER DEVELOPMENT PRACTICES What kind of practices would characterize an organization that understood the value of career development? The following summarizes a few of the more effective practices.

An increasing body of evidence indicates that employees who receive especially *challenging job assignments* early in their careers do better on later jobs.[28] More specifically, the degree of stimulation and challenge in a person's initial job assignment tends to be significantly related to later career success and retention in the organization.[29] Apparently, initial challenges, particularly if they are successfully met, stimulate a person to perform well in subsequent years.

To provide information to all employees about job openings, job opportunities should be posted. *Job postings* list key job specification data—abilities, experience, and seniority requirements to qualify for vacancies—and are typically communicated through bulletin board displays or organizational publications.

One of the most logical parts of career development is *career counseling*. An effective program helps employees identify career goals and expectations, and determines specific self-development activities that will lead to goal achievement. Consistent with the new workplace environment, counseling should also emphasize helping employees cope with ambiguity and constant change.[30]

Organizations can offer group *workshops* to facilitate career development. By bringing together groups of employees with their supervisors and managers, problems and misperceptions can be identified and, it is hoped, resolved. These workshops can be general, or they can be designed to deal with problems common to certain groups of employees—new members, minorities, older workers, and so forth.

Periodic job changes can prevent obsolescence and stimulate career growth. The changes can be lateral transfers, vertical promotions, or temporary assignments. The important element in periodic job changes is that they give the employee a variety of experiences that offer diversity and new challenges. For individuals seeking upper-level management positions, foreign experience is rapidly becoming essential. Larry Holleran, human resources vice president at FMC Corp., believes "no one will be in a general management job by the end of the decade who didn't have international exposure and experience."[31]

Performance Evaluation

Would you study differently or exert a different level of effort for a college course graded on a pass–fail basis than for one where letter grades from A to F are used? When I ask that question of students, I usually get an affirmative answer. Students typically tell me they study harder when letter grades are at stake. Additionally, they tell me that when they take a course on a pass–fail basis, they tend to do just enough to ensure a passing grade.

This finding illustrates how performance evaluation systems influence behavior. Major determinants of your in-class behavior and out-of-class studying effort in college are the criteria and techniques your instructor uses to evaluate your performance. Of course, what applies in the college context also applies to employees at work. In this section, we show how the choice of a performance evaluation system and the way it's administered can be an important force influencing employee behavior.

Purposes of Performance Evaluation

Performance evaluation serves a number of purposes in organizations (see Table 16-4 for survey results on primary uses of evaluations).[32] Management uses evaluations for general *human resource decisions*. Evaluations provide input into such important decisions as promotions, transfers, and terminations. Evaluations *identify training and development needs*. They pinpoint employee skills and competencies that are currently inadequate but for which programs can be developed to remedy. Performance evaluations can be used as a *criterion against which selection and development programs are validated*. Newly hired employees who perform poorly can be identified through performance evaluation. Similarly, the effectiveness of training and development programs can be determined by assessing how well those employees who have participated do on their performance evaluation. Evaluations also fulfill the purpose of *providing feedback to employees* on how the organization views their performance. Further, performance evaluations are used as the *basis for reward allocations*. Decisions as to who gets merit pay increases and other rewards are frequently determined by performance evaluations.

Each of these functions of performance evaluation is important. Yet their importance to us depends on the perspective we're taking. Several are clearly

Table 16-4 Primary Uses of Performance Evaluations

Use	Percentage*
Compensation	85.6
Performance feedback	65.1
Training	64.3
Promotion	45.3
Human resource planning	43.1
Retention/discharge	30.3
Research	17.2

*Based on responses from 600 organizations.

Source: Based on "Performance Appraisal: Current Practices and Techniques," *Personnel* (May-June 1984), p. 57.

relevant to human resource management decisions. But our interest is in organizational behavior. As a result, we emphasize performance evaluation in its role as a mechanism for providing feedback and as a determinant of reward allocations.

Performance Evaluation and Motivation

In Chapter 6, considerable attention was given to the expectancy model of motivation. We argued that this model currently offers one of the best explanations of what conditions the amount of effort an individual will exert on his or her job. A vital component of this model is performance, specifically the effort–performance and performance–reward linkages.

But what defines *performance*? In the expectancy model, it's the individual's performance evaluation. To maximize motivation, people need to perceive that the effort they exert leads to a favorable performance evaluation and that the favorable evaluation will lead to the rewards they value.

Following the expectancy model of motivation, if the objectives that employees are expected to achieve are unclear, if the criteria for measuring those objectives are vague, and if the employees lack confidence their efforts will lead to a satisfactory appraisal of their performance or believe there will be an unsatisfactory payoff by the organization when their performance objectives are achieved, we can expect individuals to work considerably below their potential.

What Do We Evaluate?

The criteria or criterion that management chooses to evaluate, when appraising employee performance, will have a major influence on what employees do. The two examples that follow illustrate this.

In a public employment agency, which served workers seeking employment and employers seeking workers, employment interviewers were appraised by the number of interviews they conducted. Consistent with the thesis that the evaluating criteria influence behavior, interviewers emphasized the *number* of interviews conducted rather than the *placements* of clients in jobs.[33]

A management consultant specializing in police research noticed that, in one community, officers would come on duty for their shift, proceed to get into their police cars, drive to the highway that cut through the town, and speed back and forth along this highway for their entire shift. Clearly this fast cruising had little to do with good police work, but this behavior made considerably more sense once the consultant learned the community's City Council used mileage on police vehicles as an evaluative measure of police effectiveness.[34]

These examples demonstrate the importance of criteria in performance evaluation. This, of course, begs the question: What should management evaluate? The three most popular sets of criteria are individual task outcomes, behaviors, and traits.

INDIVIDUAL TASK OUTCOMES If ends count, rather than means, then management should evaluate an employee's task outcomes. Using task outcomes, a plant manager could be judged on criteria such as quantity produced, scrap generated, and cost per unit of production. Similarly, a salesperson could be assessed on overall sales volume in his or her territory, dollar increase in sales, and number of new accounts established.

BEHAVIORS In many cases, it's difficult to identify specific outcomes that can be directly attributable to an employee's actions. This is particularly true of personnel in staff positions and individuals whose work assignments are intrinsically part of a group effort. In the latter case, the group's performance may be readily evaluated, but the contribution of each group member may be difficult or impossible to identify clearly. In such instances, it is not unusual for management to evaluate the employee's *behavior*. Using the previous examples, behaviors of a plant manager that could be used for performance evaluation purposes might include promptness in submitting his or her monthly reports or the leadership style that the manager exhibits. Pertinent salesperson behaviors could be average number of contact calls made per day or sick days used per year.

TRAITS The weakest set of criteria, yet one still widely used by organizations, is individual traits.[35] We say they are weaker than either task outcomes or behaviors because they are farthest removed from the actual performance of the job itself. Traits such as having "a good attitude," showing "confidence," being "dependable" or "cooperative," "looking busy," or possessing "a wealth of experience" may or may not be highly correlated with positive task outcomes, but only the naive would ignore the reality that such traits are frequently used in organizations as criteria for assessing an employee's level of performance.

Who Should Do the Evaluating?

Who should evaluate an employee's performance? The obvious answer would seem to be his or her immediate boss! By tradition, a manager's authority typically has included appraising subordinates' performance. The logic behind this tradition seems to be that since managers are held responsible for their subordinates' performance, it only makes sense that these managers do the evaluating of that performance. But that logic may be flawed. Others may actually be able to do the job better.

IMMEDIATE SUPERIOR As we implied, about 95 percent of all performance evaluations at the lower and middle levels of the organization are conducted by the employee's immediate boss.[36] Yet a number of organizations are recognizing the drawbacks to using this source of evaluation. For instance, many bosses feel unqualified to evaluate the unique contributions of each of their subordinates. Others resent being asked to "play God" with their employees' careers. Additionally, in the 1990s, when many organizations are using self-managed teams, telecommuting, and other organizing devices that distance bosses from their employees, an employee's immediate superior may not be a reliable judge of that employee's performance.

PEERS Peer evaluations are one of the most reliable sources of appraisal data. Why? First, peers are close to the action. Daily interactions provide them with a comprehensive view of an employee's job performance. Second, using peers as raters results in a number of independent judgments. A boss can offer only a single evaluation, but peers can provide multiple appraisals. And the average of several ratings is often more reliable than a single evaluation. On the downside, peer evaluations can suffer from coworkers' unwillingness to evaluate one another and from friendship-based biases.

SELF-EVALUATION Having employees evaluate their own performance is consistent with values such as self-management and empowerment. Self-evaluations get high marks from employees themselves; they tend to lessen employees' defensiveness about the appraisal process; and they make excellent vehicles for stimulating job performance discussions between employees and their superiors. However, as you might guess, they suffer from overinflated assessment and self-serving bias. Moreover, self-evaluations are often low in agreement with superiors' ratings.[37] Because of these serious drawbacks, self-evaluations are probably better suited to developmental uses than evaluative purposes.

IMMEDIATE SUBORDINATES A fourth judgment source is an employee's immediate subordinates. For instance, Datatec Industries, a maker of in-store computer systems, uses this form of appraisal.[38] The company's president says it's consistent with the firm's core values of honesty, openness, and employee empowerment.

Immediate subordinates' evaluations can provide accurate and detailed information about a manager's behavior because the evaluators typically have frequent contact with the evaluatee. The obvious problem with this form of rating is fear of reprisal from bosses given unfavorable evaluations. Therefore, respondent anonymity is crucial if these evaluations are to be accurate.

THE COMPREHENSIVE APPROACH: 360-DEGREE EVALUATIONS The latest approach to performance evaluation is the use of 360-degree evaluations.[39] It provides for performance feedback from the full circle of daily contacts that an employee might have, ranging from mail room personnel to customers to bosses to peers. The number of appraisals can be as few as 3 or 4 evaluations or as many as 25; with most organizations collecting 5 to 10 per employee.

A recent survey found 26 percent of U.S. companies using some form of 360-degree feedback as part of the review process.[40] This includes companies like Alcoa, Du Pont, Levi Strauss, Honeywell, UPS, Sprint, Amoco, AT&T, and W.L. Gore & Associates.

What's the appeal of 360-degree evaluations? They fit well into organizations that have introduced teams, employee involvement, and TQM programs. By relying on feedback from coworkers, customers, and subordinates, these organizations are hoping to give everyone more of a sense of participation in the review process and gain more accurate readings on employee performance.

Raychem, an electronics and electrical equipment company, is one of the growing number of firms using the 360-degree evaluation to improve its managers' performance. Raychem CEO Robert Saldich (standing) was told by his team of top executives that he fell short in the area of contingency planning. Saldich was aware of the shortcoming but believed he had kept it well hidden.

OB in the News

At Hampton Pension Services, Everybody Evaluates Everybody!

Hampton Pension Services, a pension administration and consulting company located in Ohio, has taken 360-degree evaluations to their extreme. The company's 40-odd employees rate every employee in the firm, including themselves, on how well each satisfies 10 performance statements.

In 1989 a team of employees from all levels developed the 10 performance statements. They consider factors such as placing organization above self, treating others with respect and consideration, accepting responsibility for errors, and whether "if I was starting a business, I would want this person to work for my company." These questions "reflect what the firm as a whole wants the company culture to be," says founder and president Walter Bettinger II.

To maintain confidentiality, all evaluations are prepared on computers using a standard format. Employees copy their evaluations to disks, which are then anonymously returned for compilation by a small team of employees. An evaluation report is prepared for each employee and every manager, including the company's president. This report includes the numerical rankings for every individual as judged by the company as a whole. It also includes breakdowns of the evaluations based on the rater's job level. So an employee can see how he or she is viewed by management separately from how he or she is seen by peers. The numerical totals from these evaluations are used to determine the percentage of the annual raise and bonus pool received by each employee and manager.

To date, this comprehensive evaluation system seems to be working well. Employees speak positively about the specific performance feedback they get. As the senior vice president noted, "When 40 people are telling you something, it has real impact." The program also has been given primary credit for keeping the company's employee turnover rate significantly below industry norms.

Based on T.B. Kinni, "Judge and Be Judged," *Industry Week* (August 2, 1993), pp. 45–48.

Methods of Performance Evaluation

The previous sections explained *what* we evaluate and *who* should do the evaluating. Now we ask, *How* do we evaluate an employee's performance? That is, what are the specific techniques for evaluation? This section reviews the major performance evaluation methods.

WRITTEN ESSAYS Probably the simplest method of evaluation is to write a narrative describing an employee's strengths, weaknesses, past performance, potential, and suggestions for improvement. The written essay requires no complex forms or extensive training to complete. But the results often reflect the ability of the writer. A good or bad appraisal may be determined as much by the evaluator's writing skill as by the employee's actual level of performance.

critical incidents Evaluating those behaviors that are key in making the difference between executing a job effectively and executing it ineffectively.

CRITICAL INCIDENTS **Critical incidents** focus the evaluator's attention on those behaviors that are key in making the difference between executing a job effectively and executing it ineffectively. That is, the appraiser writes down anecdotes describing what the employee did that was especially effective or ineffective. The key here is that only specific behaviors, not vaguely defined personality traits, are cited. A list of critical incidents provides a rich set of examples from which the employee can be shown those behaviors that are desirable and those that call for improvement.

graphic rating scales
An evaluation method where the evaluator rates performance factors on an incremental scale.

GRAPHIC RATING SCALES One of the oldest and most popular methods of evaluation is the use of **graphic rating scales**. In this method, a set of performance factors, such as quantity and quality of work, depth of knowledge, cooperation, loyalty, attendance, honesty, and initiative, are listed. The evaluator then goes down the list and rates each on incremental scales. The scales typically specify five points, so a factor like *job knowledge* might be rated 1 ("poorly informed about work duties") to 5 ("has complete mastery of all phases of the job").

Why are graphic ratings scales so popular? Although they don't provide the depth of information that essays or critical incidents do, they are less time consuming to develop and administer. They also allow for quantitative analysis and comparison.

behaviorally anchored rating scales
An evaluation method where actual job-related behaviors are rated along a continuum.

BEHAVIORALLY ANCHORED RATING SCALES **Behaviorally anchored rating scales** (BARS) combine major elements from the critical incident and graphic rating scale approaches: The appraiser rates the employees based on items along a continuum, but the points are examples of actual behavior on the given job rather than general descriptions or traits.

BARS specify definite, observable, and measurable job behavior. Examples of job-related behavior and performance dimensions are found by asking participants to give specific illustrations of effective and ineffective behavior regarding each performance dimension. These behavioral examples are then translated into a set of performance dimensions, each dimension having varying levels of performance. The results of this process are behavioral descriptions, such as *anticipates, plans, executes, solves immediate problems, carries out orders*, and *handles emergency situations*.

MULTIPERSON COMPARISONS Multiperson comparisons evaluate one individual's performance against the performance of one or more others. It is a relative rather than an absolute measuring device. The three most popular comparisons are group order ranking, individual ranking, and paired comparisons.

group order ranking
An evaluation method that places employees into a particular classification such as quartiles.

The **group order ranking** requires the evaluator to place employees into a particular classification, such as top one-fifth or second one-fifth. This method is often used in recommending students to graduate schools. Evaluators are asked whether the student ranks in the top 5 percent of the class, the next 5 percent, the next 15 percent, and so forth. But when used by managers to appraise employees, managers deal with all their subordinates. Therefore, if a rater has 20 subordinates, only 4 can be in the top fifth and, of course, 4 must also be relegated to the bottom fifth.

individual ranking
An evaluation method that rank-orders employees from best to worst.

paired comparison
An evaluation method that compares each employee with every other employee and assigns a summary ranking based on the number of superior scores that the employee achieves.

The **individual ranking** approach rank-orders employees from best to worst. If the manager is required to appraise 30 subordinates, this approach assumes the difference between the first and second employee is the same as that between the 21st and 22nd. Even though some of the employees may be closely grouped, this approach allows for no ties. The result is a clear ordering of employees, from the highest performer down to the lowest.

The **paired comparison** approach compares each employee with every other employee and rates each as either the superior or the weaker member of the pair. After all paired comparisons are made, each employee is assigned a summary ranking based on the number of superior scores he or she achieved. This approach ensures that each employee is compared against every other, but it can obviously become unwieldy when many employees are being compared.

Multiperson comparisons can be combined with one of the other methods to blend the best from both absolute and relative standards. For example, a college might use the graphic rating scale and the individual ranking method to provide more accurate information about its students' performance. The student's relative rank in the class could be noted next to an absolute grade of A, B, C, D, or F. A prospective employer or graduate school could then look at two students who each got a B in their different financial accounting courses and draw considerably different conclusions about each because next to one grade it says "ranked 4th out of 26," while next to the other it says "ranked 17th out of 30." Obviously, the latter instructor gives out a lot more high grades!

Potential Problems

While organizations may seek to make the performance evaluation process free from personal biases, prejudices, and idiosyncrasies, a number of potential problems can creep into the process. To the degree that the following factors are prevalent, an employee's evaluation is likely to be distorted.

SINGLE CRITERION The typical employee's job is made up of a number of tasks. An airline flight attendant's job, for example, includes welcoming passengers, seeing to their comfort, serving meals, and offering safety advice. If performance on this job was assessed by a single criterion measure—say, the time it took to provide food and beverages to 100 passengers—the result would be a limited evaluation of that job. More important, flight attendants whose performance evaluation included assessment on only this single criterion would be motivated to ignore those other tasks in their job. Similarly, if a football quarterback was appraised only on his percentage of completed passes, he would be likely to throw short passes and only in situations where he felt assured they would be caught. Our point is that where employees are evaluated on a single job criterion, and where successful performance on that job requires good performance on a number of criteria, employees will emphasize the single criterion to the exclusion of other job-relevant factors.

LENIENCY ERROR Every evaluator has his or her own value system that acts as a standard against which appraisals are made. Relative to the true or actual performance an individual exhibits, some evaluators mark high and others low. The former is referred to as positive **leniency error**, and the latter as negative leniency error. When evaluators are positively lenient in their appraisal, an individual's performance becomes overstated, that is, rated higher than it actually should be. This results in inflated evaluations—a problem widely acknowledged to exist in U.S. organizations.[41] A negative leniency error understates performance, giving the individual a lower appraisal than deserved.

leniency error
The tendency to evaluate a set of employees too high (positive) or too low (negative).

If all individuals in an organization were appraised by the same person, there would be no problem. Although there would be an error factor, it would be applied equally to everyone. The difficulty arises when we have different raters with different leniency errors making judgments. For example, assume Jones and Smith are performing the same job for different supervisors, but they have absolutely identical job performance. If Jones's supervisor tends to err toward positive leniency, while Smith's supervisor errs toward negative leniency, we might be confronted with two dramatically different evaluations.

HALO ERROR The halo effect or error, as we noted in Chapter 4, is the tendency for an evaluator to let the assessment of an individual on one trait influence his or her evaluation of that person on other traits. For example, if an employee tends to be dependable, we might become biased toward that individual to the extent we rate him or her high on many desirable attributes.[42]

People who design teaching appraisal forms for college students to fill out to evaluate the effectiveness of their instructors each semester must confront the halo error. Students tend to rate a faculty member as outstanding on all criteria when they are particularly appreciative of a few things he or she does in the classroom. Similarly, a few bad habits—like showing up late for lectures, for example, or being slow in returning papers, or assigning an extremely demanding reading requirement—might result in students' evaluating the instructor as poor across the board.

similarity error
Giving special consideration when rating others to those qualities that the evaluator perceives in himself or herself.

SIMILARITY ERROR When evaluators rate other people giving special consideration to those qualities they perceive in themselves, they are making a **similarity error**. For example, the evaluator who perceives himself as aggressive may evaluate others by looking for aggressiveness. Those who demonstrate this characteristic tend to benefit, while others are penalized.[43]

Again, this error would tend to wash out if the same evaluator appraised all the people in the organization. However, interrater reliability obviously suffers when various evaluators are utilizing their own similarity criteria.

LOW DIFFERENTIATION It's possible that, regardless of whom the appraiser evaluates and what traits are used, the pattern of evaluation remains the same. It's possible that the evaluator's ability to appraise objectively and accurately has been impeded by social differentiation—that is, the evaluator's style of rating behavior.

It has been suggested that evaluators may be classified as (1) high differentiators, who use all or most of the scale; or (2) low differentiators, who use a limited range of the scale.[44]

Low differentiators tend to ignore or suppress differences, perceiving the universe as being more uniform than it really is. High differentiators, in contrast, tend to utilize all available information to the utmost extent and thus are better able to perceptually define anomalies and contradictions than are low differentiators.[45]

This finding tells us that evaluations made by low differentiators need to be carefully inspected and that the people working for a low differentiator have a high probability of being appraised as being significantly more homogeneous than they really are.

FORCING INFORMATION TO MATCH NONPERFORMANCE CRITERIA While rarely advocated, it is not an infrequent practice to find the formal evaluation taking place *following* the decision as to how the individual has been performing. This may sound illogical, but it merely recognizes that subjective, yet formal, decisions are often arrived at prior to the gathering of objective information to support those decisions.[46] For example, if the evaluator believes the evaluation should not be based on performance, but rather on seniority, he or she may be unknowingly adjusting each "performance" evaluation so as to bring it into line with the employee's seniority rank. In this and other similar cases, the evaluator is increasing or decreasing performance appraisals to align with the nonperformance criteria actually being utilized.

Overcoming the Problems

Just because organizations can encounter problems with performance evaluations should not lead managers to give up on the process. Some things can be done to overcome most of the problems we have identified.[47]

USE MULTIPLE CRITERIA Since successful performance on most jobs requires doing a number of things well, all those "things" should be identified and evaluated. The more complex the job, the more criteria that will need to be identified and evaluated. But everything need not be assessed. The critical activities that lead to high or low performance are the ones that need to be evaluated.

EMPHASIZE BEHAVIORS RATHER THAN TRAITS Many traits often considered to be related to good performance may, in fact, have little or no performance relationship. For example, traits like loyalty, initiative, courage, reliability, and self-expression are intuitively appealing as desirable characteristics in employees. But the relevant question is, Are individuals who are evaluated as high on those traits higher performers than those who rate low? We can't answer this question easily. We know there are employees who rate high on these characteristics and are poor performers. We can find others who are excellent performers but do not score well on traits such as these. Our conclusion is that traits like loyalty and initiative may be prized by managers, but there is no evidence to support that certain traits will be adequate synonyms for performance in a large cross section of jobs.

Another weakness of trait evaluation is the judgment itself. What is "loyalty"? When is an employee "reliable"? What you consider "loyalty," I may not. So traits suffer from weak interrater agreement.

DOCUMENT PERFORMANCE BEHAVIORS IN A DIARY By keeping a diary of specific critical incidents for each employee, evaluations tend to be more accurate.[48] Diaries, for instance, tend to reduce leniency and halo errors because they encourage the evaluator to focus on performance-related behaviors rather than traits.

USE MULTIPLE EVALUATORS As the number of evaluators increases, the probability of attaining more accurate information increases. If rater error tends to follow a normal curve, an increase in the number of appraisers will tend to find the majority congregating about the middle. You see this approach being used in athletic competitions in such sports as diving and gymnastics. A set of evaluators judges a performance, the highest and lowest scores are dropped, and the final performance evaluation is made up from the cumulative scores of those remaining. The logic of multiple evaluators applies to organizations as well.

If an employee has had ten supervisors, nine having rated her excellent and one poor, we can discount the value of the one poor evaluation. Therefore, by moving employees about within the organization so as to gain a number of evaluations or by using multiple assessors (as provided in 360-degree appraisals), we increase the probability of achieving more valid and reliable evaluations.

EVALUATE SELECTIVELY It has been suggested that appraisers should evaluate only those areas in which they have some expertise.[49] If raters make evaluations on only those dimensions on which they are in a good position to rate, we increase the interrater agreement and make the evaluation a more valid process. This approach also recognizes that different organizational levels often have different orientations toward ratees and observe them in different settings. In general, therefore, we would recommend that appraisers should be as close as possible, in terms of organizational level, to the individual being evaluated. Conversely, the more levels that separate the evaluator and evaluatee, the less opportunity the evaluator has to observe the individual's behavior and, not surprisingly, the greater the possibility for inaccuracies.

The specific application of these concepts would result in having immediate supervisors, coworkers, subordinates, or some combination of these people provide the major input into the appraisal and having them evaluate those factors they are best qualified to judge. For example, it has been suggested that when professors are evaluating secretaries within a university, they use such criteria as judgment, technical competence, and conscientiousness, whereas peers (other secretaries) use such criteria as job knowledge, organization, cooperation with coworkers, and responsibility.[50] Using both professors and peers as appraisers is a logical and reliable approach, since it results in having people appraise only those dimensions on which they are in a good position to make judgments.

TRAIN EVALUATORS If you can't *find* good evaluators, the alternative is to *make* good evaluators. There is substantial evidence that training evaluators can make them more accurate raters.[51]

Common errors such as halo and leniency have been minimized or eliminated in workshops where managers practice observing and rating behaviors. These workshops typically run from one to three days, but allocating many hours to training may not always be necessary. One case has been cited where both halo and leniency errors were decreased immediately after exposing evaluators to explanatory training sessions lasting only five minutes.[52] But the effects of training do appear to diminish over time.[53] This suggests the need for regular refresher sessions.

Providing Performance Feedback

For many managers, few activities are more unpleasant than providing performance feedback to employees. In fact, unless pressured by organizational policies and controls, managers are likely to ignore this responsibility.[54]

Why the reluctance to give performance feedback? There seem to be at least three reasons. First, managers are often uncomfortable discussing performance weaknesses with employees. Given that almost every employee could stand to improve in some areas, managers fear a confrontation when presenting negative feedback. Second, many employees tend to become defensive when their weaknesses are pointed out. Instead of accepting the feedback as constructive and a basis for improving performance, some employees challenge the evaluation by criticizing the manager or redirecting blame to someone else.

Finally, employees tend to have an inflated assessment of their own performance. Statistically speaking, half of all employees must be below-average performers. But the evidence indicates that the average employee's estimate of his or her own performance level generally falls around the 75th percentile.[55] So even when managers are providing good news, employees are likely to perceive it as not good enough!

◆The average employee's estimate of his or her own performance level generally falls around the 75th percentile.

The solution to the performance feedback problem is not to ignore it, but to train managers how to conduct constructive feedback sessions. An effective review—one in which the employee perceives the appraisal as fair, the manager as sincere, and the climate as constructive—can result in the employee leaving the interview in an upbeat mood, informed about the performance areas in which he or she needs to improve and determined to correct the deficiencies.[56] Additionally, the performance review should be designed more as a counseling activity than a judgment process. This can best be accomplished by allowing the review to evolve out of the employee's own self-evaluation.

What About Team Performance Evaluations?

Performance evaluation concepts have been almost exclusively developed with only individual employees in mind. This reflects the historic belief that individuals are the core building block around which organizations are built. But as we've described throughout this book, more and more organizations are restructuring themselves around teams. In those organizations using teams, how should they evaluate performance? Four suggestions have been offered for designing a system that supports and improves the performance of teams.[57]

1. *Tie the team's results to the organization's goals.* It's important to find measurements that apply to important goals the team is supposed to accomplish.
2. *Begin with the team's customers and the work process the team follows to satisfy their needs.* The final product the customer receives can be evaluated in terms of the customer's requirements. The transactions between teams can be evaluated based on delivery and quality. And the process steps can be evaluated based on waste and cycle time.
3. *Measure both team and individual performance.* Define the roles of each team member in terms of accomplishments that support the team's work process. Then assess each member's contribution and the team's overall performance.
4. *Train the team to create its own measures.* Having the team define its objectives and those of each member ensures everyone understands their role on the team and helps the team develop into a more cohesive unit.

Reward Systems

Our knowledge of motivation tells us that people do what they do to satisfy needs. Before they do anything, they look for the payoff or reward. Many of these rewards—salary increases, employee benefits, preferred job assignments—are organizationally controlled. While we previously discussed some organizational reward programs in Chapter 7, we should spend a moment to describe rewards that are under managerial discretion and the important role they can play in influencing employee behavior.[58]

The types of rewards an organization can allocate are more complex than is generally thought. Obviously, there is direct compensation. But there are also indirect compensation and nonfinancial rewards. Each of these types of rewards can be distributed on an individual, group, or organizationwide basis. Figure 16-1 presents a structure for looking at rewards.

intrinsic rewards
The pleasure or value one receives from the content of a work task.

Intrinsic rewards are those that individuals receive for themselves. They are largely a result of the worker's satisfaction with his or her job. As we noted in the previous chapter, techniques like job enrichment and efforts to redesign or restructure work to increase its personal worth to the employee may make the work more intrinsically rewarding.

extrinsic rewards
Rewards received from the environment surrounding the context of the work.

Extrinsic rewards include direct compensation, indirect compensation, and nonfinancial rewards. Of course, an employee expects some form of direct compensation: a basic wage or salary, overtime and holiday premium pay, bonuses based on performance, profit sharing, and/or opportunities to purchase stock options. Employees will expect their direct compensation generally to align with their assessment of their contribution to their work group and the organization and, additionally, will expect it to be comparable to the direct compensation given to other employees with similar abilities and performance.

The organization will provide employees with indirect compensation: insurance, pay for holidays and vacations, services, and perquisites. Inasmuch as these are generally made uniformly available to all employees at a given job level, regardless of performance, they are really not motivating rewards. However, where indirect compensation is controllable by management and is used to reward performance, then it clearly needs to be considered as a motivating reward. To illustrate, if a company-paid membership in a country club is not available to all middle- and upper-level executives, but only to those who have shown particular performance ratings, then it is a motivating reward. Similarly, if company-owned automobiles and aircraft are made available to certain employees based on their performance rather than their "entitlement," we should view these indirect compensations as motivating rewards for those who might deem these forms of compensation attractive.

The classification of nonfinancial rewards tends to be a smorgasbord of desirable "things" that are potentially at the disposal of the organization. The creation of nonfinancial rewards is limited only by managers' ingenuity and ability to assess "payoffs" that individuals in the organization find desirable and are within the managers' discretion.

The old saying "One man's food is another man's poison" certainly applies to rewards. What one employee views as highly desirable, another finds superfluous. Therefore *any* reward may not get the desired result; however, where selection has been done assiduously, the benefits to the organization by way of higher worker performance should be impressive.

Some workers are very status conscious. A paneled office, a carpeted floor, a large walnut desk, or a private bathroom may be just the office furnishing that stimulates them toward top performance. Status-oriented employees may also value an impressive job title, their own secretary, or a well-located parking space with their name clearly painted underneath the "Reserved" sign.

Some employees value having their lunch at, say 1 to 2 P.M. If lunch is normally from 11 A.M. to 12 noon, the benefit of being able to take their lunch at another, more desirable time can be viewed as a reward. Having a chance to

Figure 16-1
Types of Rewards

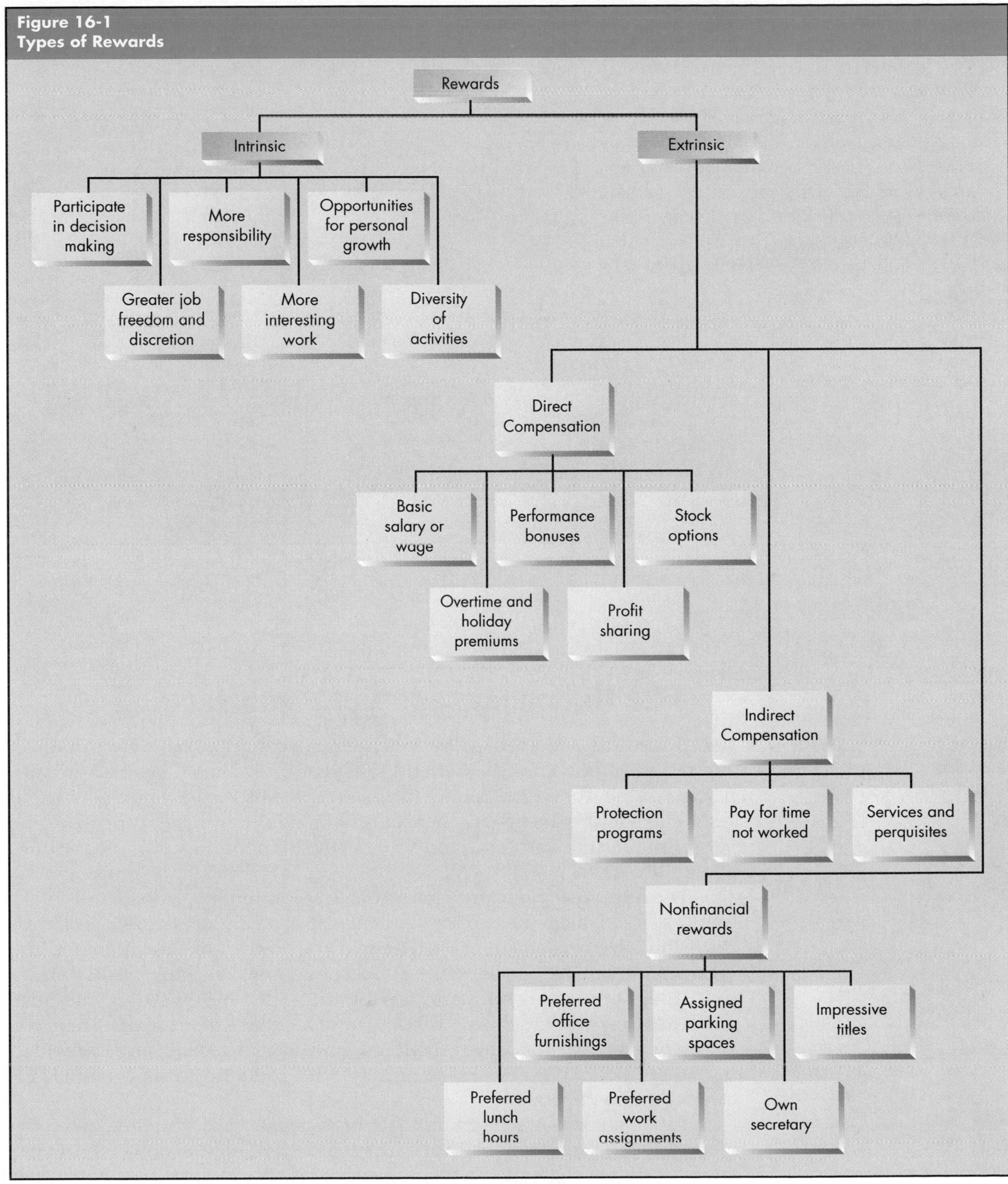

work with congenial colleagues, achieving a desired work assignment, and getting an assignment where the worker can operate without close supervision are all rewards that are within the discretion of management and, when carefully aligned to individual needs, can provide stimulus for improved performance.

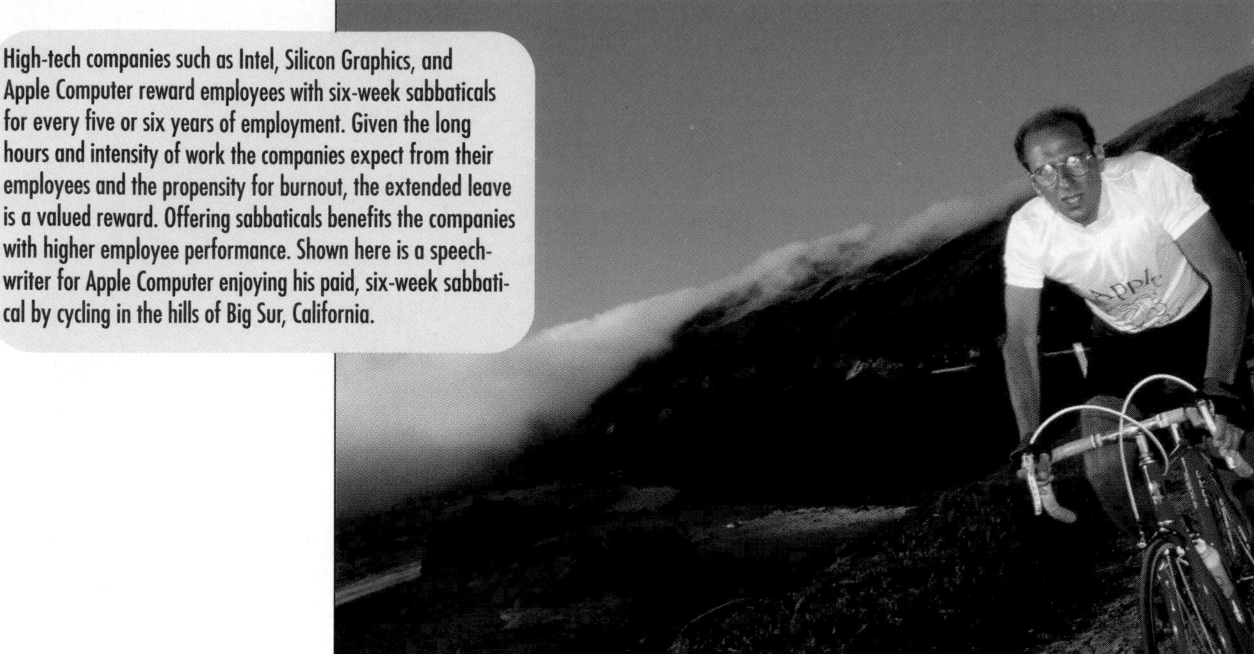

High-tech companies such as Intel, Silicon Graphics, and Apple Computer reward employees with six-week sabbaticals for every five or six years of employment. Given the long hours and intensity of work the companies expect from their employees and the propensity for burnout, the extended leave is a valued reward. Offering sabbaticals benefits the companies with higher employee performance. Shown here is a speechwriter for Apple Computer enjoying his paid, six-week sabbatical by cycling in the hills of Big Sur, California.

The Union-Management Interface

labor union
An organization, made up of employees, that acts collectively to protect and promote employee interests.

Labor unions are a vehicle by which employees act collectively to protect and promote their interests. Currently, in the United States, approximately 15 percent of the work force belongs to and is represented by a union. This number is considerably higher in other countries. For instance, in Japan, Germany, Great Britain, and Canada, typically 30 to 40 percent of the labor force belongs to a union.

For employees who are members of a labor union, wage levels and conditions of employment are expiicitly articulated in a contract that is negotiated, through collective bargaining, between representatives of the union and the organization's management. But the impact of unions on employees is broader than their minority representation figure might imply. This is because nonunionized employees benefit from the gains that unions make. There is a spillover effect so the wages, benefits, and working conditions provided nonunionized employees tend to mirror—with some time lag—those negotiated for union members.

Labor unions influence a number of organizational activities.[59] Recruitment sources, hiring criteria, work schedules, job design, redress procedures, safety rules, and eligibility for training programs are examples of activities that are influenced by unions. The most obvious and pervasive area of influence, of course, is wage rates and working conditions. Where unions exist, performance evaluation systems tend to be less complex because they play a relatively small part in reward decisions. Wage rates, when determined through collective bargaining, emphasize seniority and downplay performance differences.

Figure 16-2 shows what impact a union has on an employee's performance and job satisfaction. The union contract affects motivation through determination of wage rates, seniority rules, layoff procedures, promotion criteria, and security provisions. Unions can influence the competence with which employees perform their jobs by offering special training programs to their members, by requiring apprenticeships, and by allowing members to gain leadership experience through union organizational activities. The actual level of employee performance will be further influenced by collective bargaining restrictions placed on the amount of work produced, the speed with which work can be done, overtime allowances per worker, and the kind of tasks a given employee is allowed to perform.

The research evaluating the specific effect of unions on productivity is mixed.[60] Some studies found that unions had a positive effect on productivity as a result of improvements in labor–management relations as well as improvements in the quality of the labor force. In contrast, other studies have shown that unions negatively impact on productivity by reducing the effectiveness of some productivity-enhancing managerial practices and by contributing to a poorer labor–management climate. The evidence, then, is too inconsistent to draw any meaningful conclusions.

Are union members more satisfied with their jobs than their nonunion counterparts? The answer to this question is more complicated than a simple "Yes" or "No." The evidence consistently demonstrates that unions have only indirect effects on job satisfaction.[61] They increase pay satisfaction, but negatively affect satisfaction with the work itself (by decreasing job scope perceptions), satisfaction with coworkers and supervision (through less favorable perceptions of supervisory behavior), and satisfaction with promotions (through the lower importance placed on promotions).

Figure 16-2
The Union's Impact on Employee Performance and Job Satisfaction

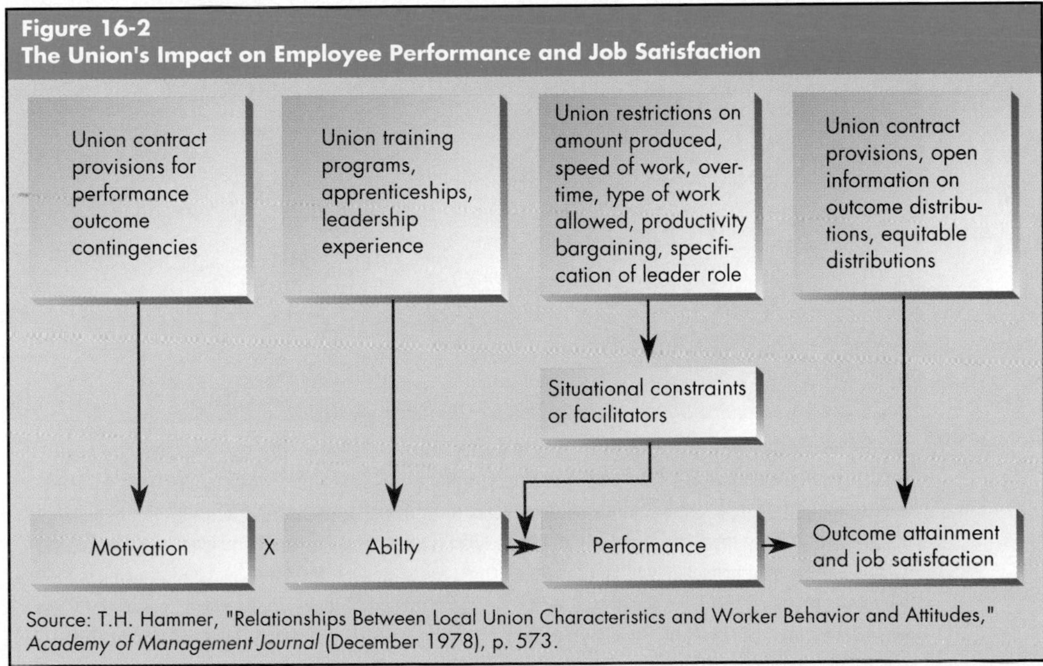

Source: T.H. Hammer, "Relationships Between Local Union Characteristics and Worker Behavior and Attitudes," *Academy of Management Journal* (December 1978), p. 573.

International Human Resource Practices: Selected Issues

Many of the human resource policies and practices discussed in this chapter have to be modified to reflect societal differences.[62] To illustrate this point, let's briefly look at the problem of selecting managers for foreign assignments and the importance of performance evaluation in different cultures.

Selection

The global corporation increasingly needs managers who have experience in diverse cultures and who are sensitive to the challenges of international operations. At Ford Motor Co., for instance, an international assignment is a requirement for a rising executive's career. But many domestic managers don't have the attitudes or characteristics associated with successful international executives. One selection technique that an increasing number of companies are using is the Overseas Assignment Inventory (OAI). This 85-item questionnaire assesses 15 predictors: motivations, expectations, open-mindedness, respect for others' beliefs, trust in people, flexibility, tolerance, personal control, patience, adaptability, self-confidence/initiative, sense of humor, interpersonal interest, interpersonal harmony, and spouse/family communication. Results are compared against a database of more than 10,000 previous test takers. Research indicates that using the OAI as a prescreening device eliminates about 40 percent of traditional overseas assignment problems.[63]

International experience is a requirement for top management positions at The Coca-Cola Company. Coke grooms international talent by challenging managers with difficult assignments in different countries. John Hunter, an Australian, became Coke's top international executive after successfully building strong relationships with bottlers in many countries. For example, when Hunter served as Coke's regional manager for the Philippines, he spearheaded a plan that reversed Pepsi's two-to-one market share lead by forming a joint-venture partnership with Coke's bottler. As executive vice president for Coke's international business, Hunter travels the world to achieve his company's goal of increasing international volume by 8 to 10 percent. In this photo, Hunter mingles with customers in Mexico, a market that offers Coke significant growth potential.

Performance Evaluation

Earlier in the chapter, we examined the role that performance evaluation plays in motivation and in affecting behavior. Caution must be used, however, in generalizing across cultures. Why? Because many cultures are not particularly concerned with performance appraisal or, if they are, they don't look at it the same way as do managers in the United States or Canada.

Let's look at three cultural dimensions discussed in Chapter 2: a person's relationship to the environment, time orientation, and focus of responsibility.

U.S. and Canadian organizations hold people responsible for their actions because people in these countries believe they can dominate their environment. In Middle Eastern countries, however, performance evaluations aren't likely to be widely used, since managers in these countries tend to see people as subjugated to their environment.

Some countries, such as the United States, have a short-term time orientation. Performance evaluations are likely to be frequent in such a culture—at least once a year. In Japan, however, where people hold a long-term time frame, performance appraisals may occur only every five or ten years.

Israel's culture values group activities much more than does the United States or Canada. So, while North American managers emphasize the individual in performance evaluations, their counterparts in Israel are much more likely to emphasize group contributions and performance.

Summary and Implications for Managers

An organization's human resource policies and practices represent important forces for shaping employee behavior and attitudes. In this chapter, we specifically discussed the influence of selection practices, training and development programs, performance evaluation systems, reward systems, and the existence of a union.

Selection Practices

An organization's selection practices determine who gets hired. If properly designed, they identify competent candidates and accurately match them to the job. The use of the proper selection devices increases the probability the right person will be chosen to fill a slot.

While employee selection is far from a science, some organizations fail to design their selection systems so as to maximize the likelihood that the right person–job fit will be achieved. When errors are made, the chosen candidate's performance may be less than satisfactory. Training may be necessary to improve the candidate's skills. At the worst, the candidate will prove unacceptable and a replacement will need to be found. Similarly, where the selection process results in the hiring of less qualified candidates or individuals who don't fit into the organization, those chosen are likely to feel anxious, tense, and uncomfortable. This, in turn, is likely to increase dissatisfaction with the job.

Training and Development Programs

Training programs can affect work behavior in two ways. The most obvious is by directly improving the skills necessary for the employee to successfully complete his or her job. An increase in ability improves the employee's potential to perform at a higher level. Of course, whether that potential becomes realized is largely an issue of motivation.

A second benefit from training is that it increases an employee's self-efficacy. As you'll remember from Chapter 6, self-efficacy is a person's expectation that he or she can successfully execute the behaviors required to produce an outcome.[64] For employees, those behaviors are work tasks and the outcome is effective job performance. Employees with high self-efficacy have strong expectations about their abilities to perform successfully in new situations. They're confident and expect to be successful. Training, then, is a means to positively affect self-efficacy because employees may be more willing to undertake job tasks and exert a high level of effort. Or in expectancy terms (see Chapter 6), individuals are more likely to perceive their effort as leading to performance.

We also discussed career development programs in this chapter. Organizations that provide formal career development activities and match them to needs that employees experience at various stages in their careers reduce the likelihood that productivity will decrease as a result of obsolescence or that job frustrations will create reduced satisfaction.[65]

In today's work environment—with cutbacks, increasingly wider spans of control, and reduced promotion opportunities—employees will increasingly confront the reality of career plateaus. Out of frustration, employees may look for other jobs. Organizations with well-designed career programs will have employees with more realistic expectations and career tracking systems that will lessen the chance good employees will leave because of inadequate opportunities.

Performance Evaluation

A major goal of performance evaluation is to assess accurately an individual's performance contribution as a basis for making reward allocation decisions. If the performance evaluation process emphasizes the wrong criteria or inaccurately appraises actual job performance, employees will be over- or underrewarded. As demonstrated in Chapter 6 in our discussion of equity theory, this can lead to negative consequences such as reduced effort, increases in absenteeism, or search for alternative job opportunities. In addition, the content of the performance evaluation has been found to influence employee performance and satisfaction.[66] Specifically, performance and satisfaction are increased when the evaluation is based on behavioral, results-oriented criteria; when career issues as well as performance issues are discussed; and when the subordinate has an opportunity to participate in the evaluation.

Reward Systems

If employees perceive that their efforts will be accurately appraised, and if they further perceive the rewards they value are closely linked to their evaluations, management will have optimized the motivational properties from the organization's evaluation and reward procedures and policies. More specifically, based on the contents of this chapter and our discussion of motivation in Chapters 6 and 7, we can conclude that rewards are likely to lead to high employee performance and satisfaction when they are (1) perceived as being equitable by the employee, (2) tied to performance, and (3) tailored to the needs of the individual. These conditions should foster a minimum of dissatisfaction among employees, reduce withdrawal patterns, and increase organizational commitment. Employee benefits like flexible work hours, paternity leaves, and daycare centers may be most relevant for the impact they have on reducing absenteeism and improving job satisfaction. These rewards reduce barriers that many employees—particularly those with significant responsibilities outside the job—find get in the way of being at work on time or even making it to work at all. To the degree these benefits lessen an employee's worries over outside responsibilities, they may increase satisfaction with the job and the organization.

Union-Management Interface

The existence of a union in an organization adds another variable in our search to explain and predict employee behavior. The union has been found to be an important contributor to employees' perceptions, attitudes, and behavior.

The power of the union surfaces in the collective bargaining agreement it negotiates with management. Much of what an employee can and cannot do on the job is formally stipulated in this agreement. In addition, the informal norms that union cohesiveness fosters can encourage or discourage high productivity, organizational commitment, and morale.

For Review

1. What is job analysis? How is it related to those the organization hires?
2. What are assessment centers? Why are they more effective for selecting managers than traditional written tests?
3. Describe several on-the-job training methods and several off-the-job methods.
4. What would an effective career development program look like?
5. What effect do career anchors have on employee behavior?
6. Why do organizations evaluate employees?
7. What are the advantages and disadvantages of the following performance evaluation methods: (a) written essays, (b) graphic rating scales, and (c) behaviorally anchored rating scales?
8. How can management effectively evaluate individuals when they work as part of a team?
9. How can an organization's performance evaluation system affect employee behavior?
10. What impact do unions have on an organization's reward system?

For Discussion

1. If you were the dean of a college of business, how would you determine which job candidates would be effective teachers?
2. If you were the dean of a college of business, how would you evaluate the performance of your faculty members?
3. What relationship, if any, is there between job analysis and performance evaluation?
4. What problems, if any, can you see developing as a result of using 360-degree evaluations?
5. Some organizations have a personnel policy that pay information be kept secret. Not only is pay information not given out by management, but employees are also discouraged from talking about their pay with coworkers. How do you think this practice affects employee behavior?

Point

Capitalism, Control, and the Deskilling of Labor

A pervasive tendency in contemporary capitalistic countries is to reorganize jobs at increasingly lower skill levels. Managers systematically destroy all-around skills where they exist and replace them with skills and occupations that fit management's needs. This deskilling of work allows management to cut costs, increase profits, and impose control over labor.

These statements constitute the central thesis proposed in the mid-1970s by Harry Braverman.* His controversial views, clearly Marxist in origin, have gained little attention from OB scholars in business schools. But they have been enthusiastically adopted by many organizational sociologists.** The basic elements of Braverman's thesis can be briefly summarized as follows.

Control is the central concept of all management systems. Therefore, it is not surprising that management seeks to control labor. It does this by deskilling jobs. And managers in twentieth-century capitalistic countries have been able to impose deskilling on the labor force without significant resistance.

Deskilling reduces management's dependence on its workers. Work specialization, for instance, leads to the eradication of craft or skilled work. So, too, does mechanization. Additionally, deskilling creates a two-class system—an informed management cadre and an uninformed labor force. By hoarding knowledge (through centralized decision making) and imposing secrecy requirements, management ensures that labor will be powerless. By deskilling jobs, management has "appropriated" the intellectual skills once held by craft labor.

Interestingly, Braverman understands that work specialization is prevalent in all social groups. Citing Karl Marx, he notes that the social division of labor allows species to capitalize on their inherent strengths—"the spider weaves, the bear fishes, the beaver builds dams and houses" (p. 72). But while the social division of labor merely subdivides *society*, Braverman believes that the extreme division of labor enforced in modern organizations subdivides *human beings*. Although "the subdivision of society may enhance the individual and the species, the subdivision of the individual, when carried on without regard to human capabilities and needs, is a crime against the person and against humanity" (p. 73).

Braverman doesn't ignore contemporary trends toward employee involvement and the humanization of work, but he dismisses them as superficial—"allowing the worker to adjust a machine, replace a light bulb, move from one fractional job to another, and to have the illusion of making decisions by choosing among fixed and limited alternatives designed by a management which deliberately leaves insignificant matters open to choice" (p. 39).

Proponents of Braverman's thesis might add another dimension to his argument that he, understandably, overlooked at the time he was writing. That's the widespread introduction by management of computerized information processing controls. Management is increasingly monitoring the work of employees who use computers through the use of sophisticated software that, for instance, can calculate the average number of keystrokes made per minute, the average number of forms processed per hour, the number of "nonprocessing" minutes per day, and the like, for each worker.

*H. Braverman, *Labor and Monopoly Capital: The Degradation of Work in the Twentieth Century* (New York: Monthly Review Press, 1974).

**See, for instance, S. Wood (ed.), *The Transformation of Work?* (London: Unwin Hyman, 1989).

counterPoint

The Myth of Deskilling in Capitalistic Societies

Braverman's analysis has a number of flaws. The following paragraphs highlight some of them.

The assumption that deskilling is pervasive in capitalistic societies is false. Ample evidence indicates that the profit motive sometimes dictates a higher skilled (and higher paid) work force. High-skilled employees are, in some jobs, more productive and cost effective than those with lower skills. A good example of this is the rapid growth of high-skilled professional jobs in the areas of health, education, high-technology industries, and government. Braverman has minimized the importance of the new high-skilled intellectual jobs.

He has also overlooked the fact that specialization through division of labor does not necessarily imply a lessening of skill. Dermatologists, neurosurgeons, endocrinologists, and other medical specialists are clearly not less skilled than general practitioners.

Braverman underrates the knowledge needed by "unskilled" workers. Even routinized machine-paced work demands a considerable amount of conceptual and practical knowledge. He understates the extent of mental work in modern jobs. Moreover, he ignores the common practice in organizations of transferring the simplest tasks of highly paid craft workers to lower paid noncraft workers. What this practice does is to moderately upgrade the work of the noncraft worker and reserve the more complex tasks for the craft worker. So rather than deskilling jobs, this practice actually upgrades the jobs of both the high skilled and the low skilled.

Braverman further errs in ignoring the evidence that some people prefer routine, deskilled jobs. He assumes all individuals want jobs composed of complex and sophisticated tasks, and this is clearly untrue. Some portion of the labor force prefers and seeks work that makes minimal demands on their intellectual capabilities.

Braverman argues that managers impose their will on the work force without significant resistance. This claim ignores the role and influence of labor unions. Unions have actively fought management's efforts to dominate the labor force.

While automation and mechanization have certainly replaced a significant number of workers during this century, this does not necessarily result in deskilling, for automation typically only replaces already deskilled, repetitious labor. So, in fact, automation has decreased the number of deskilled jobs and improved the overall quality of the remaining jobs.

Finally, Braverman's thesis runs counter to recent trends by management to enrich jobs, create self-managed work teams, decentralize work units, and implement other improvements that empower employees and give control of jobs back to the workers.

This argument is substantially based on P. Attewell, "The Deskilling Controversy," *Work and Occupations* (August 1987), pp. 323–46.

Learning About Yourself Exercise

Career Assessment Test

Complete the following questionnaire by circling the answer that best describes your feelings about each statement. For each item, circle your response according to the following:

SA = Strongly Agree, A = Agree, D = Disagree, SD = Strongly Disagree.

1. I would leave my company rather than be promoted out of my area of expertise. SA A D SD
2. Becoming highly specialized and highly competent in some specific functional or technical area is important to me. SA A D SD
3. A career that is free from organization restriction is important to me. SA A D SD
4. I have always sought a career in which I could be of service to others. SA A D SD
5. A career that provides a maximum variety of types of assignments and work projects is important to me. SA A D SD
6. To rise to a position in general management is important to me. SA A D SD
7. I like to be identified with a particular organization and the prestige that accompanies that organization. SA A D SD
8. Remaining in my present geographical location rather than moving because of a promotion is important to me. SA A D SD
9. The use of my skills in building a new business enterprise is important to me. SA A D SD
10. I would like to reach a level of responsibility in an organization where my decisions really make a difference. SA A D SD
11. I see myself more as a generalist as opposed to being committed to one specific area of expertise. SA A D SD
12. An endless variety of challenges in my career is important to me. SA A D SD
13. Being identified with a powerful or prestigious employer is important to me. SA A D SD
14. The excitement of participating in many areas of work has been the underlying motivation behind my career. SA A D SD
15. The process of supervising, influencing, leading, and controlling people at all levels is important to me. SA A D SD
16. I am willing to sacrifice some of my autonomy to stabilize my total life situation. SA A D SD
17. An organization that will provide security through guaranteed work, benefits, a good retirement, and so forth, is important to me. SA A D SD

18. During my career I will be mainly concerned with my own sense of freedom and autonomy. SA A D SD
19. I will be motivated throughout my career by the number of products that I have been directly involved in creating. SA A D SD
20. I want others to identify me by my organization and job. SA A D SD
21. Being able to use my skills and talents in the service of an important cause is important to me. SA A D SD
22. To be recognized by my title and status is important to me. SA A D SD
23. A career that permits a maximum of freedom and autonomy to choose my own work, hours, and so forth, is important to me. SA A D SD
24. A career that gives me a great deal of flexibility is important to me. SA A D SD
25. To be in a position in general management is important to me. SA A D SD
26. It is important for me to be identified by my occupation. SA A D SD
27. I will accept a management position only if it is in my area of expertise. SA A D SD
28. It is important for me to remain in my present geographical location rather than move because of a promotion or new job assignment. SA A D SD
29. I would like to accumulate a personal fortune to prove to myself and others that I am competent. SA A D SD
30. I want to achieve a position that gives me the opportunity to combine analytical competence with supervision of people. SA A D SD
31. I have been motivated throughout my career by using my talents in a variety of different areas of work. SA A D SD
32. An endless variety of challenges is what I really want from my career. SA A D SD
33. An organization that will give me long-run stability is important to me. SA A D SD
34. To be able to create or build something that is entirely my own product or idea is important to me. SA A D SD
35. Remaining in my specialized area, as opposed to being promoted out of my area of expertise, is important to me. SA A D SD
36. I do not want to be constrained by either an organization or the business world. SA A D SD
37. Seeing others change because of my efforts is important to me. SA A D SD
38. My main concern in life is to be competent in my area of expertise. SA A D SD
39. The chance to pursue my own lifestyle and not be constrained by the rules of an organization is important to me. SA A D SD
40. I find most organizations to be restrictive and intrusive. SA A D SD

41. Remaining in my area of expertise, rather than being promoted into general management, is important to me. SA A D SD
42. I want a career that allows me to meet my basic needs through helping others. SA A D SD
43. The use of my interpersonal and helping skills in the service of others is important to me. SA A D SD
44. I like to see others change because of my efforts. SA A D SD

Turn to page A-30 for scoring directions and key.

Source: Adapted, by permission of the publisher, from "Reexamining the Career Anchor Model," by T.J. Delong, PERSONNEL (May-June 1982), pp. 56–57.

Working With Others Exercise

Evaluating Performance and Providing Feedback

Objective To experience the assessment of performance and observe the providing of performance feedback.

Time Approximately 30 minutes.

Procedure A class leader is to be selected. He or she may be either a volunteer or someone chosen by your instructor. The class leader will preside over class discussion and perform the role of manager in the evaluation review.

Your instructor will leave the room. The leader is then to spend up to 15 minutes helping the class evaluate your instructor. Your instructor understands this is only a class exercise and is prepared to accept criticism (and, of course, any praise you may want to convey). Your instructor also recognizes the leader's evaluation is actually a composite of many students' input. So be open and honest in your evaluation and have confidence your instructor will not be vindictive.

Research has identified seven performance dimensions to the college instructor's job: (1) instructor knowledge, (2) testing procedures, (3) student–teacher relations, (4) organizational skills, (5) communication skills, (6) subject relevance, and (7) utility of assignments. The discussion of your instructor's performance should focus on these seven dimensions. The leader may want to take notes for personal use, but will not be required to give your instructor any written documentation.

When the 15-minute class discussion is complete, the leader will invite the instructor back into the room. The performance review will begin as soon as the instructor walks through the door, with the class leader becoming the manager and the instructor playing him or herself.

When completed, class discussion will focus on performance evaluation criteria and how well your class leader did in providing performance feedback.

Ethical Dilemma Exercise

Ethics Training: Smoke or Substance?

Approximately 80 percent of the largest U.S. corporations have formal ethics programs, and 44 percent of these firms provide ethics training.* Most college and university programs in business now require courses in ethics or have added an ethics component to their courses in marketing, finance, and management.

What do proponents of ethics training expect to achieve with these programs? Ethics educators include among their goals: stimulating moral thought, recognizing ethical dilemmas, creating a sense of moral obligation, developing problem-solving skills, and tolerating or reducing ambiguity. But can you teach ethics in college? The evidence is mixed. Let's briefly review the evidence presented by both sides.

Critics argue that ethics are based on values, and value systems are fixed at an early age. By the time people reach college, their ethical values are already established. The critics also claim that ethics cannot be formally "taught," but must be learned by example. Leaders set ethical examples by what they say and do. If this is true, then ethics training is relevant only as part of leadership training.

Supporters of ethics training argue that values can be learned and changed after early childhood. And even if they couldn't, ethics training would be effective because it gets employees to think about ethical dilemmas and become more aware of the ethical issues underlying their actions. Supporters of ethics training point to the research evidence on the last point: A comprehensive analysis of the effectiveness of ethics training programs found that they improved students' ethical awareness and reasoning skills.

Can colleges and universities teach ethics? Should business firms be spending money on ethics training programs? What do *you* think?

*The information in this exercise is from G. L. Pamental, "The Course in Business Ethics: Can It Work?" *Journal of Business Ethics* (July 1989), pp. 547–51; P.F. Miller and W.T. Coady, "Teaching Work Ethics," *Education Digest* (February 1990), pp. 54–55; D. Rice and C. Dreilinger, "Rights and Wrongs of Ethics Training," *Training and Development Journal* (May 1990), pp. 103–108; and J. Weber, "Measuring the Impact of Teaching Ethics to Future Managers: A Review, Assessment, and Recommendations," *Journal of Business Ethics* (March 1990), pp. 183–90.

CRST's Struggle to Hire and Retain Truck Drivers

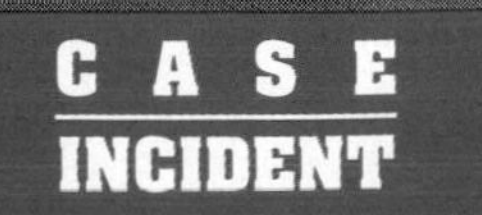

For the past half-dozen years, all we seem to read about in business periodicals is downsizing and layoffs. But not *all* companies are cutting staff. The management at CRST International, a Cedar Rapids, Iowa, long-haul trucking company, is pulling out its hair trying to find and keep good truck drivers.

The problems started for the U.S. trucking industry when it was deregulated in 1980. Carriers turned to cheaper, nonunion truck drivers and no-frills trucks. Excess capacity and constant pressure on rates also spurred trucking firms to squeeze more out of their equipment and employees by keeping them on the road longer. While companies succeeded in achieving better utilization of their trucks, drivers found themselves going anywhere and on any day of the week.

The current work environment at CRST and other trucking firms has led to a wave of defections and resignations. Drivers complain about being overworked, underpaid, and required to load and unload tremendous amounts of freight. One driver, for instance, quit the long-haul business to drive a dump truck for a local quarry. Although he made $32,000 a year doing long hauls, he calculates that if he added up all the hours he spent in the truck, either driving, sleeping or waiting at docks, "I was making less than minimum wage. It just wasn't worth the stress and abuse."

Fewer people seem to be willing to spend weeks in a truck. Ward Wright quit driving for CRST after six weeks on the road. "My wife was shedding tears on the phone, and my daughters said, 'Come home, Dad.' It weighs on you," says Mr. Wright, who is looking for a local job. The erratic lifestyle also frustrates drivers. "I had no control over anything," said one. Dispatchers also don't seem to help much. They focus on efficient use of the trucks rather than personal concerns of drivers.

With the demand for drivers exceeding the supply, truckers like CRST are losing revenues to railroads, facing service disruptions and unhappy customers, and having to deal with annual driver turnover rates of nearly 100 percent.

So many trucking recruiters attended a recent job fair in Oklahoma that Mark Deere, CRST's director of driver development, says, "We spent all our time talking to each other." Companies can't hire anyone under 21. Salaries are attractive: Inexperienced drivers who go to work for CRST can earn $20,000 to $25,000 in their first year; rising to $32,000 to $39,000 in their second. But laid off workers from other industries don't make first-rate candidates. "The guy in his mid- to late-40s who spent 20 years in an auto plant, went to work every day at the same time and bowled every Tuesday night doesn't necessarily adapt well to this industry," said a CRST vice president.

"Over the next 10 years, my biggest concern isn't the marketplace, but how are we going to recruit, train, and retain drivers," says CRST's chief executive. He calls the supply of drivers the "Achilles" heel of the trucking industry. CRST has had to idle 30 rigs and cancel an order for 100 new trucks because it couldn't find drivers.

Questions

1. What would an effective selection process look like for filling truck driving positions?
2. If you were CRST's chief executive, what would you do to deal with the problem you face?

This case is based on D. Machalaba, "Trucking Firms Find It Is a Struggle to Hire and Retain Drivers," *Wall Street Journal* (December 28, 1993), p. A1.

Will-Burt Is Educating Its Workers

VIDEO CASE

Will-Burt Manufacturing Corp., a machine parts company in Orville, Ohio, is blending business and education. Management at Will-Burt has come to recognize that spending money educating its workers can pay hefty dividends.

The company supports and encourages its employees to take courses in subjects such as algebra, trigonometry, calculus, and business management. Originally, the management's motivation was to improve product quality. What has transpired, however, is the creation of a whole new organizational culture. Will-Burt's new culture treats employees like intelligent individuals. They're assumed to have ideas and to be able to make knowledgeable decisions. In order to compete in the global marketplace, Will-Burt needs employees who are self-disciplined and who are able to do their jobs at a highly efficient level. Education is the key. The educated worker can solve his or her own problems, and doesn't require managers to give them directives.

Will-Burt's commitment to education has allowed the company to thrive in a highly competitive environment. The new culture has resulted in a significant reduction in mistakes and defective parts. Communication among workers has improved greatly. And absenteeism is down from 9 percent to 2 percent.

Questions

1. How could courses in algebra or business management contribute to higher productivity among factory workers?
2. Is there a difference between training and education? The management at Will-Burt think so, and they're investing in the latter. Why?
3. Is the Will-Burt experience generalizable to other manufacturing firms? Why or why not?

Source: "Look at Company Making Profits After Schooling Workers," *World News Tonight* (May 12, 1993).

Suggestions for Further Reading

BAKER, H.G., and M.S. SPIER, "The Employment Interview: Guaranteed Improvement in Reliability," *Public Personnel Management* (Spring 1990), pp. 85–87.

CASCIO, W.F., *Applied Psychology in Personnel Management* (Englewood Cliffs, NJ: Prentice Hall, 1991).

DECENZO, D.A., and S.P. ROBBINS, *Human Resource Management*, 5th ed. (New York: Wiley, 1996).

DULEWICZ, V., "Improving Assessment Centers," *Personnel Management* (June 1991), pp. 50–55.

FERRIS, G.R., and K.M. ROWLAND (eds.), *Performance Evaluation, Goal Setting, and Feedback* (Greenwich, CT: JAI Press, 1990).

MAINIERO, L.A., "Getting Anointed for Advancement: The Case of Executive Women," *Academy of Management Executive* (May 1994), pp. 53–67.

NEWTON, L.A., and L.M. SHORE, "A Model of Union Membership: Instrumentality, Commitment, and Opposition," *Academy of Management Review* (April 1992), pp. 275–98.

ORNSTEIN, S., and L.A. ISABELLA, "Making Sense of Careers: A Review 1989–1992," *Journal of Management* (Summer 1993), pp. 243–67.

SCOTT, W.R., and J.W. MEYER, "The Rise of Training Programs in Firms and Agencies: An Institutional Perspective," in L.L. Cummings and B.M. Staw (eds.), *Research in Organizational Behavior*, Vol. 13 (Greenwich, CT: JAI Press, 1991).

ZALESNY, M.D., and S. HIGHHOUSE, "Accuracy in Performance Evaluation," *Organizational Behavior and Human Decision Processes* (February 1992), pp. 22–50.

Notes

[1] "Best Practices: Hiring," *INC.* (March 1994), p. 10.

[2] See, for instance, C.T. Dortch, "Job-Person Match," *Personnel Journal* (June 1989), pp. 49–57; and S. Rynes and B. Gerhart, "Interviewer Assessments of Applicant 'Fit': An Exploratory Investigation," *Personnel Psychology* (Spring 1990), pp. 13–34.

[3] See, for example, J.V. Ghorpade, *Job Analysis: A Handbook for the Human Resource Director* (Englewood Cliffs, NJ: Prentice Hall, 1988).

[4] R.L. Dipboye, *Selection Interviews: Process Perspectives* (Cincinnati: South-Western, 1992), p. 6.

[5] T.J. Hanson and J.C. Balestreri-Spero, "An Alternative to Interviews," *Personnel Journal* (June 1985), p. 114.

[6] See A.I. Huffcutt and W. Arthur, Jr., "Hunter and Hunter (1984) Revisited: Interview Validity for Entry-Level Jobs," *Journal of Applied Psychology* (April 1994), pp. 184–90; and M.A. McDaniel, D.L. Whetzel, F.L. Schmidt, and S.D. Maurer, "The Validity of Employment Interviews: A Comprehensive Review and Meta-Analysis," *Journal of Applied Psychology* (August 1994), pp. 599–616.

[7] R.L. Dipboye, Selection Interviews, pp. 42–44.

[8] This box is based on W.C. Donaghy, *The Interview: Skills and Applications* (Glenview, IL: Scott, Foresman, 1984), pp. 245–80.

[9] W.F. Cascio, *Applied Psychology in Personnel Management*, 4th ed. (Englewood Cliffs, NJ: Prentice Hall, 1991), p. 271.

[10] E.E. Ghiselli, "The Validity of Aptitude Tests in Personnel Selection," *Personnel Psychology* (Winter 1973), p. 475.

[11] G. Grimsley and H.F. Jarrett, "The Relation of Managerial Achievement to Test Measures Obtained in the Employment Situation: Methodology and Results," *Personnel Psychology* (Spring 1973), pp. 31–48; and A.K. Korman, "The Prediction of Managerial Performance: A Review," *Personnel Psychology* (Summer 1968), pp. 295–322.

[12] D.S. Ones, C. Viswesvaran, and F.L. Schmidt, "Comprehensive Meta-Analysis of Integrity Test Validities: Findings and Implications for Personnel Selection and Theories of Job Performance," *Journal of Applied Psychology* (August 1993), pp. 679–703.

[13] J.J. Asher and J.A. Sciarrino, "Realistic Work Sample Tests: A Review," *Personnel Psychology* (Winter 1974), pp. 519–33; and I.T. Robertson and R.S. Kandola, "Work Sample Tests: Validity, Adverse Impact and Applicant Reaction," *Journal of Occupational Psychology* (Spring 1982), pp. 171–82.

[14] G.C. Thornton, *Assessment Centers in Human Resource Management* (Reading, MA: Addison-Wesley, 1992).

[15] "Industry Report," *Training* (October 1993), p. 30.

[16] Cited in J.C. Szabo, "Training Workers for Tomorrow," *Nation's Business* (March 1993), pp. 22–32.

[17] R. Henkoff, "Companies That Train Best," *Fortune* (March 22, 1993), p. 64; and "How SIA Nurtures High Fliers," *Asian Business* (December 1993), p. 44.

[18] M.E. Mangelsdorf, "Ground-Zero Training," *INC.* (February 1993), pp. 82–93.

[19] See, for instance, S.E. Jackson (ed.), *Diversity in the Workplace* (New York: Guilford Press, 1992); R.B. Johnson and J. O'-Mara, "Shedding New Light on Diversity Training," *Training & Development Journal* (May 1992), pp. 45–52; and B. Hagerty, "Trainers Help Expatriate Employees Build Bridges to Different Cultures," *Wall Street Journal* (June 14, 1993), p. B1.

[20] For an extended discussion of on-the-job and off-the-job training methods, see D. DeCenzo and S.P. Robbins, *Human Resource Management*, 4th ed. (New York: Wiley, 1994), pp. 260–65.

[21] Cited in N.K. Austin, "Where Employee Training Works," *Working Woman* (May 1993), p. 23.

[22] S. Sherman, "A Brave New Darwinian Workplace," *Fortune* (January 25, 1993), pp. 50–56.

[23] See, for example, P.O. Benham, Jr., "Developing Organizational Talent: The Key to Performance and Productivity," *SAM Advanced Management Journal*, January 1993, pp. 34–39.

[24] D.E. Super and D.T. Hall, "Career Development: Exploration and Planning," in M.R. Rosenzweig and L.W. Porter (eds.), *Annual Review of Psychology*, Vol. 29 (Palo Alto, CA: Annual Reviews, 1978), p. 334.

[25] D.T. Hall, *Careers in Organizations* (Santa Monica, CA: Goodyear, 1976), pp. 3–4.

[26] See, for example, D.E. Super, *The Psychology of Careers* (New York: Harper & Row, 1957); and E.H. Schein, "The Individual, the Organization, and the Career: A Conceptual Scheme," *Journal of Applied Behavioral Science* (August 1971), pp. 401–26.

[27] E.H. Schein, "How Career Anchors Hold Executives to Their Career Paths," *Personnel* (May 1975), pp. 11–24; and E.H. Schein, *Career Dynamics: Matching Individual and Organizational Needs* (Reading, MA: Addison-Wesley, 1978).

[28] D.E. Berlew and D.T. Hall, "The Socialization of Managers: Effects of Expectations on Performance," *Administrative Science Quarterly* (September 1966), pp. 207–23; and D.W. Bray, R.J. Campbell, and D.L. Grant, *Formulative Years in Business: A Long-Term AT&T Study of Managerial Lives* (New York: Wiley, 1974).

[29] See Super and Hall, "Career Development: Exploration and Planning," p. 362.

[30] See A. Bennett, "Path to Top Job Now Twists and Turns," *Wall Street Journal* (March 15, 1993), p. B1.

[31] Ibid., p. B3.

[32] See J.N. Cleveland, K.R. Murphy, and R.E. Williams, "Multiple Uses of Performance Appraisal: Prevalence and Correlates," *Journal of Applied Psychology* (February 1989), pp. 130–35.

[33] P.M. Blau, *The Dynamics of Bureaucracy*, rev. ed. (Chicago: University of Chicago Press, 1963).

[34] "The Cop-Out Cops," *National Observer* (August 3, 1974).

[35] A.H. Locher and K.S. Teel, "Appraisal Trends," *Personnel Journal* (September 1988), pp. 139–45.

[36] G.P. Latham and K.N. Wexley, *Increasing Productivity*

Through Performance Appraisal (Reading, MA: Addison-Wesley, 1981), p. 80.

[37] See review in R.D. Bretz, Jr., G.T. Milkovich, and W. Read, "The Current State of Performance Appraisal Research and Practice: Concerns, Directions, and Implications," *Journal of Management* (June 1992), p. 326.

[38] "Appraisals: Reverse Reviews," *INC.* (October 1992), p. 33.

[39] See, for instance, R.J. Newman, "Job Reviews Go Full Circle," *U.S. News & World Report* (November 1, 1993), pp. 42–43; J.A. Lopez, "A Better Way?" *Wall Street Journal* (April 13, 1994), p. R6; M.S. Hirsch, "360 Degrees of Evaluation," *Working Woman* (August 1994), pp. 20–21; and B. O'Reilly, "360 Feedback Can Change Your Life," *Fortune* (October 17, 1994), pp. 93–100.

[40] Cited in R.J. Newman, "Job Reviews Go Circle."

[41] R.D. Bretz, Jr., G.T. Milkovich, and W. Read, "The Current State of Performance Appraisal Research and Practice," p. 333.

[42] For a recent review of the role of halo error in performance evaluations, see W.K. Balzer and L.M. Sulsky, "Halo and Performance Appraisal Research: A Critical Evaluation," *Journal of Applied Psychology* (December 1992), pp. 975–85.

[43] See T.A. Judge and G.R. Ferris, "Social Context of Performance Evaluation Decisions," *Academy of Management Journal* (February 1993), pp. 80–105.

[44] A. Pizam, "Social Differentiation—A New Psychological Barrier to Performance Appraisal," *Public Personnel Management* (July-August 1975), pp. 244–47.

[45] Ibid., pp. 245–46.

[46] See D.J. Woehr and J. Feldman, "Processing Objective and Question Order Effects on the Causal Relation Between Memory and Judgment in Performance Appraisal: The Tip of the Iceberg," *Journal of Applied Psychology* (April 1993), pp. 232–41.

[47] See, for example, W.M. Fox, "Improving Performance Appraisal Systems," *National Productivity Review* (Winter 1987–88), pp. 20–27.

[48] See J. Greenberg, "Determinants of Perceived Fairness of Performance Evaluations," *Journal of Applied Psychology* (May 1986), pp. 340–42; and B.P. Maroney and M.R. Buckely, "Does Research in Performance Appraisal Influence the Practice of Performance Appraisal? Regretfully Not!" *Public Personnel Management* (Summer 1992), pp. 185–96.

[49] W.C. Borman, "The Rating of Individuals in Organizations: An Alternate Approach," *Organizational Behavior and Human Performance* (August 1974), pp. 105–24.

[50] Ibid.

[51] See, for instance, D.E. Smith, "Training Programs for Performance Appraisal: A Review," *Academy of Management Review* (January 1986), pp. 22–40; D.C. Martin and K. Bartol, "Training the Raters: A Key to Effective Performance Appraisal," *Public Personnel Management* (Summer 1986), pp. 101–109; and T.R. Athey and R.M. McIntyre, "Effect of Rater Training on Rater Accuracy: Levels-of-Processing Theory and Social Facilitation Theory Perspectives," *Journal of Applied Psychology* (November 1987), pp. 567–72.

[52] H.J. Bernardin, "The Effects of Rater Training on Leniency and Halo Errors in Student Rating of Instructors," *Journal of Applied Psychology* (June 1978), pp. 301–08.

[53] Ibid.; and J.M. Ivancevich, "Longitudinal Study of the Effects of Rater Training on Psychometric Error in Ratings, *Journal of Applied Psychology* (October 1979), pp. 502–508.

[54] Much of this section is based on H.H. Meyer, "A Solution to the Performance Appraisal Feedback Enigma," *Academy of Management Executive* (February 1991), pp. 68–76.

[55] R.J. Burke, "Why Performance Appraisal Systems Fail," *Personnel Administration* (June 1972), pp. 32–40.

[56] B.R. Nathan, A.M. Mohrman, Jr., and J. Milliman, "Interpersonal Relations as a Context for the Effects of Appraisal Interviews on Performance and Satisfaction: A Longitudinal Study," *Academy of Management Journal* (June 1991), pp. 352–69.

[57] J. Zigon, "Making Performance Appraisal Work for Teams," *Training* (June 1994), pp. 58–63.

[58] See E.E. Lawler, III and G.D. Jenkins, Jr., "Strategic Reward Systems," in M.D. Dunnette and L.M. Hough (eds.), *Handbook of Industrial and Organizational Psychology*, Vol. 3 (Palo Alto, CA: Consulting Psychologists Press, 1992), pp. 1009–49.

[59] This material was adapted from T.H. Hammer, "Relationship Between Local Union Characteristics and Worker Behavior and Attitudes," *Academy of Management Journal* (December 1978), pp. 560–77.

[60] See J.B. Arthur and J.B. Dworkin, "Current Topics in Industrial and Labor Relations Research and Practice," *Journal of Management* (September 1991), pp. 530–32.

[61] See, for example, C.J. Berger, C.A. Olson, and J.W. Boudreau, "Effects of Unions on Job Satisfaction: The Role of Work-Related Values and Perceived Rewards," *Organizational Behavior and Human Performance* (December 1983), pp. 289–324; and M.G. Evans and D.A. Ondrack, "The Role of Job Outcomes and Values in Understanding the Union's Impact on Job Satisfaction: A Replication," *Human Relations* (May 1990), pp. 401–18.

[62] See, for instance, M. Mendonca and R.N. Kanungo, "Managing Human Resources: The Issue of Cultural Fit," *Journal of Management Inquiry* (June 1994), pp. 189–205.

[63] W. Lobdell, "Who's Right for an Overseas Position?" *World Trade* (April-May 1990), pp. 20–26.

[64] A. Bandura, "Self-Efficacy: Towards a Unifying Theory of Behavioral Change," *Psychological Review* (March 1977), pp. 191–215; and P.C. Earley, "Self or Group? Cultural Effects of Training on Self-Efficacy and Performance," *Administrative Science Quarterly* (March 1994), pp. 89–117.

[65] M.K. Mount, "Managerial Career Stage and Facets of Job Satisfaction," *Journal of Vocational Behavior* (June 1984), pp. 340–54; and C.S. Granrose and J.D. Portwood, "Matching Individual Career Plans and Organizational Career Management," *Academy of Management Journal* (December 1987), pp. 699–720.

[66] B.R. Nathan, A.M. Mohrman, Jr., and J. Milliman, "Interpersonal Relations as a Context for the Effects of Appraisal Interviews on Performance and Satisfaction: A Longitudinal Study."

CHAPTER 17

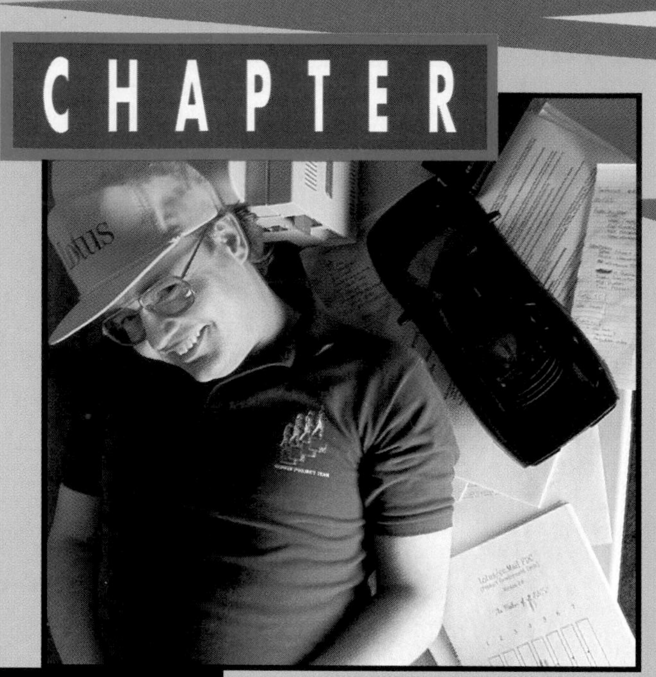

Steve Turner, a vice president at software producer Lotus Development Corporation, symbolizes the company's culture of creativity, innovation, and risk taking. All Lotus employees are given freedom of expression in the way they dress, decorate their offices, and structure their work.

ORGANIZATIONAL CULTURE

CHAPTER OUTLINE

LEARNING OBJECTIVES

After studying this chapter, you should be able to:

1. Describe institutionalization and its relationship to organizational culture.
2. Define the common characteristics making up organizational culture.
3. Contrast strong and weak cultures.
4. Identify the functional and dysfunctional effects of organizational culture on people and the organization.
5. Explain the factors determining an organization's culture.
6. List the factors that maintain an organization's culture.
7. Clarify how culture is transmitted to employees.
8. Outline the various socialization alternatives available to management.

In any organization, there are the ropes to skip and the ropes to know.
R. RITTI AND G. FUNKHOUSER

Automatic Data Processing (ADP), a computer services company that processes payroll checks, tax statements, and other forms for 300,000 companies, has a profit record any management team would envy. The company has increased earnings per share by 10 percent or more every quarter for the past 132 quarters—or for 33 years! When ADP's chairman and chief executive, Josh Weston, was asked how his company does it, he summed it up in one word: "Culture."[1]

Weston attributes much of ADP's success to creating a strong organizational culture that fosters decentralized decision making, a motivated work force, accessible senior managers, and what he calls "strong central awareness."

Even though ADP employs 22,000 people, its corporate staff numbers only 250. This small staff can handle only a small portion of decisions that need to be made. The result: Employees lower in the organization become empowered to make important decisions, and enjoy the satisfaction and motivation that comes from being able to actively control work-related decisions that affect them.

Weston makes himself easy to find. All 300,000 clients have his direct-line phone number, and his secretary answers only if he doesn't pick it up in the first three rings. "The humorous thing about it," he says, "is that if angry clients call and I answer the phone, it usually takes the steam right out of them. They say, 'Gee, I'm sorry to bother you, but . . .'"

Weston is also accessible to employees. As shown in the photo on the previous page, he meets regularly with employees to share and assess new ideas.

Finally, people at ADP know that little things matter. Weston calls this emphasis on the details "strong central awareness." For instance, about one-fifth of the 250-member corporate staff are financial professionals, who carefully monitor performance in the company's many processing data-processing locations around the United States and in Europe. To reinforce the importance of looking for little ways to make ADP more effective, once a month Weston asks the finance organization to hand him a stack of 40 to 50 randomly selected ADP accounts payable receipts, which he studies for ways to cut costs.

A strong organizational culture like that found at ADP provides employees with a clear understanding of "the way things are done around here." In this chapter, we show that every organization has a culture and, depending on its strength, culture can have a significant influence on the attitudes and behaviors of organization members.

Institutionalization: A Forerunner of Culture

The idea of viewing organizations as cultures—where there is a system of shared meaning among members—is a relatively recent phenomenon. Twenty years ago, organizations, for the most part, were simply thought of as rational means by which to coordinate and control a group of people. They had vertical levels, departments, authority relationships, and so forth. But organizations are more. They have personalities too, just like individuals. They can be rigid or flexible, unfriendly or supportive, innovative or conservative. General Electric offices and people *are* different from the offices and people at General Mills. Harvard and MIT are in the same business—education—and separated only by the width of the Charles River, but each has a unique feeling and character beyond its structural characteristics. Organizational theorists, in recent years, have begun to acknowledge this by recognizing the important role that culture plays in the lives of organization members. Interestingly, though, the origin of culture as an independent variable affecting an employee's attitudes and behavior can be traced back nearly 50 years ago to the notion of **institutionalization**.[2]

institutionalization
When an organization takes on a life of its own, apart from any of its members, and acquires immortality.

When an organization becomes institutionalized, it takes on a life of its own, apart from its founders or any of its members. Ross Perot created Electronic Data Systems (EDS) in the early 1960s; but he left in 1987 to found a new company, Perot Systems. EDS, now part of General Motors, has continued to thrive in spite of the departure of its founder. Sony, Eastman Kodak, and Timex Corporation are examples of organizations that have existed beyond the life of any one member.

Additionally, when an organization becomes institutionalized, it becomes valued for itself, not merely for the goods or services it produces. It acquires immortality. If its original goals are no longer relevant, it doesn't go out of business. Rather, it redefines itself. When the demand for Timex's watches declined, the company merely redirected itself into the consumer electronics business—making, in addition to watches, clocks, computers, and health-care products such as digital thermometers and blood pressure testing devices. Timex took on an existence that went beyond its original mission to manufacture low-cost mechanical watches.

Institutionalization operates to produce common understandings among members about what is appropriate and, fundamentally, meaningful behavior.[3] So when an organization takes on institutional permanence, acceptable modes of behavior become largely self-evident to its members. As we'll see, this is essentially the same thing that organizational culture does. So an understanding of what makes up an organization's culture, and how it is created, sustained, and learned, will enhance our ability to explain and predict the behavior of people at work.

What Is Organizational Culture?

A few years back, I asked an executive to tell me what he thought *organizational culture* meant and he gave me essentially the same answer a Supreme Court Justice once gave in attempting to define pornography: "I can't define it, but I know it when I see it." This executive's approach to defining organizational culture isn't acceptable for our purposes. We need a basic definition to provide a point of departure for our quest to better understand the phenomenon. In this section, we propose a specific definition and review several peripheral issues that revolve around this definition.

A Definition

There seems to be wide agreement that **organizational culture** refers to a system of shared meaning held by members that distinguishes the organization from other organizations.[4] This system of shared meaning is, on closer examination, a set of key characteristics that the organization values. The most recent research suggests the following seven primary characteristics that, in aggregate, capture the essence of an organization's culture:[5]

organizational culture A common perception held by the organization's members; a system of shared meaning.

1. *Innovation and risk taking.* The degree to which employees are encouraged to be innovative and take risks.

2. *Attention to detail.* The degree to which employees are expected to exhibit precision, analysis, and attention to detail.

3. *Outcome orientation.* The degree to which management focuses on results or outcomes rather than on the techniques and processes used to achieve these outcomes.

4. *People orientation.* The degree to which management decisions take into consideration the effect of outcomes on people within the organization.

5. *Team orientation.* The degree to which work activities are organized around teams rather than individuals.
6. *Aggressiveness.* The degree to which people are aggressive and competitive rather than easygoing.
7. *Stability.* The degree to which organizational activities emphasize maintaining the status quo in contrast to growth.

Each of these characteristics exists on a continuum from low to high. Appraising the organization on these seven characteristics, then, gives a compos-

Table 17-1 Contrasting Organizational Cultures

Organization A

This organization is a manufacturing firm. Managers are expected to fully document all decisions; and "good managers" are those who can provide detailed data to support their recommendations. Creative decisions that incur significant change or risk are not encouraged. Because managers of failed projects are openly criticized and penalized, they try not to implement ideas that deviate much from the status quo. One lower level manager quoted an often used phrase in the company: "If it ain't broke, don't fix it."

There are extensive rules and regulations in this firm that employees are required to follow. Managers supervise employees closely to ensure there are no deviations. Management is concerned with high productivity, regardless of the impact on employee morale or turnover.

Work activities are designed around individuals. There are distinct departments and lines of authority, and employees are expected to minimize formal contact with other employees outside their functional area or line of command. Performance evaluations and rewards emphasize individual effort, although seniority tends to be the primary factor in the determination of pay raises and promotions.

Organization B

This organization is also a manufacturing firm. Here, however, management encourages and rewards risk taking and change. Decisions based on intuition are valued as much as those that are well rationalized. Management prides itself on its history of experimenting with new technologies and its success in regularly introducing innovative products. Managers or employees who have a good idea are encouraged to "run with it." And failures are treated as "learning experiences." The company prides itself on being market driven and rapidly responsive to the changing needs of its customers.

There are few rules and regulations for employees to follow, and supervision is loose because management believes its employees are hardworking and trustworthy. Management is concerned with high productivity, but believes this comes through treating its people right. The company is proud of its reputation as being a good place to work.

Job activities are designed around work teams, and team members are encouraged to interact with people across functions and authority levels. Employees talk positively about the competition between teams. Individuals and teams have goals, and bonuses are based on achievement of these outcomes. Employees are given considerable autonomy in choosing the means by which the goals are attained.

ite picture of the organization's culture. This picture becomes the basis for feelings of shared understanding that members have about the organization, how things are done in it, and the way members are supposed to behave. Table 17-1 demonstrates how these characteristics can be mixed to create highly diverse organizations.

Cultural Typologies

Jeffrey Sonnenfeld of Emory University has developed a labeling schema that can help us see differences between organizational cultures and the importance of properly matching people to cultures. From his study of organizations, he has identified four cultural "types": *academy, club, baseball team,* and *fortress*.[6]

ACADEMY An academy is the place for steady climbers who want to thoroughly master each new job they hold. These companies like to recruit young college graduates, provide them with much special training, and then carefully steer them through a myriad of specialized jobs within a particular function. According to Sonnenfeld, IBM is a classic academy. So, too, are Coca-Cola, Procter & Gamble, and General Motors.

CLUB According to Sonnenfeld, clubs place a high value on fitting in, on loyalty, and on commitment. Seniority is the key at clubs. Age and experience count. In contrast to an academy, the club grooms managers as generalists. Examples of clubs are United Parcel Service, Delta Airlines, the Bell operating companies, government agencies, and the military.

- AAI somewhat

◆◆◆◆ OB in the News ◆◆◆◆

Creating a Risk-Taking Culture

Microsoft seeks to hire people who have made mistakes and learned from them. "We look for somebody who learns, adapts, and is active in the process of learning from mistakes," says Michael Mapes, Microsoft's executive vice president. In the hiring process, "We always ask, what was a major failure you had? What did you learn from it?"

Take Craig Mundie, for example. He cofounded Alliant Computer Systems in 1982. Ten years later, unable to meet his payroll, his company went bankrupt. Yet Microsoft hired Mundie in December 1992 to head a division charged with figuring out how to put new technology to work in consumer products. What Microsoft saw in Mundie was someone who not only had technical and managerial experience, but someone with the guts to bet on a vision—even though it turned out to be flawed. People at Microsoft will tell you: Betting on visions is what the company is all about. That many of these visions will ultimately fail is less important than that they be tried.

In its search for visionary risk takers, Microsoft likes to take chances on people who have dealt successfully with failure and setbacks. "There's a lot of internal failure that's accepted here," says one executive. "You can't let [employees] think that if it doesn't work out they're going to get fired. Otherwise nobody would take those jobs."

At Microsoft, it's better to take chances and fail than never to take chances at all.

Based on B. McMenamin, "The Virtue of Making Mistakes," *Forbes* (May 9, 1994), pp. 192–94.

BASEBALL TEAM These organizations are entrepreneurially oriented havens for risk takers and innovators. Baseball teams seek out talented people of all ages and experiences, then reward them for what they produce. Because they offer huge financial incentives and great freedom to their star performers, job hopping among these organizations is commonplace. Organizations that fit the baseball team description are common in accounting, law, investment banking, and consulting firms; advertising agencies; software developers; and bioresearch concerns.

FORTRESS While baseball teams prize inventiveness, fortresses are preoccupied with survival. Many were once academies, clubs, or baseball teams, but fell on hard times and are now seeking to reverse their sagging fortunes. Fortresses offer little job security, yet they can be exciting places to work for those who like the challenge of a turnaround. Fortress organizations include large retailers, forest products companies, and natural gas exploration firms.

Sonnenfeld found that many organizations can't be neatly categorized into one of the four categories either because they have a blend of cultures or because they are in transition. General Electric, for instance, was found to have distinctly different cultures within its different units, and Apple Computer started out as a baseball team but is maturing into an academy.

Sonnenfeld found that each of the four cultural types tends to attract certain personalities, and the personality–organizational culture match affects how far and how easily a person will move up the management ranks. For instance, a risk taker will thrive at a baseball team, but fall flat at an academy.

Culture Is a Descriptive Term

Organizational culture is concerned with how employees perceive the characteristics of an organization's culture, not with whether or not they like them. That is, it is a descriptive term. This is important because it differentiates this concept from that of job satisfaction.

Research on organizational culture has sought to measure how employees see their organization: Does it encourage teamwork? Does it reward innovation? Does it stifle initiative?

In contrast, job satisfaction seeks to measure affective responses to the work environment. It is concerned with how employees feel about the organization's expectations, reward practices, and the like. Although the two terms undoubtedly have overlapping characteristics, keep in mind that the term *organizational culture* is descriptive; *job satisfaction* is evaluative.

Do Organizations Have Uniform Cultures?

Organizational culture represents a common perception held by the organization's members. This was made explicit when we defined culture as a system of *shared* meaning. We should expect, therefore, that individuals with different backgrounds or at different levels in the organization will tend to describe the organization's culture in similar terms.[7]

Acknowledgment that organizational culture has common properties does not mean, however, that there cannot be subcultures within any given culture. Most large organizations have a dominant culture and numerous sets of subcultures.[8]

A **dominant culture** expresses the core values that are shared by a majority of the organization's members. When we talk about an *organization's* culture, we are referring to its dominant culture. It is this macro view of culture that gives an organization its distinct personality. **Subcultures** tend to develop in large organizations to reflect common problems, situations, or experiences that members face. These subcultures are likely to be defined by department designations and geographical separation. The purchasing department, for example, can have a subculture that is uniquely shared by members of that department. It will include the **core values** of the dominant culture plus additional values unique to members of the purchasing department. Similarly, an office or unit of the organization that is physically separated from the organization's main operations may take on a different personality. Again, the core values are essentially retained but modified to reflect the separated unit's distinct situation.

dominant culture
Expresses the core values that are shared by a majority of the organization's members.

subcultures
Minicultures within an organization, typically defined by department designations and geographical separation.

core values
The primary or dominant values that are accepted throughout the organization.

If organizations had no dominant culture and were composed only of numerous subcultures, the value of organizational culture as an independent variable would be significantly lessened because there would be no uniform interpretation of what represented appropriate and inappropriate behavior. It is the "shared meaning" aspect of culture that makes it such a potent device for guiding and shaping behavior. But we cannot ignore the reality that many organizations also have subcultures that can influence the behavior of members.

Strong vs. Weak Cultures

It has become increasingly popular to differentiate between strong and weak cultures.[9] The argument here is that strong cultures have a greater impact on employee behavior and are more directly related to reduced turnover.

In a **strong culture**, the organization's core values are both intensely held and widely shared.[10] The more members who accept the core values and the greater their commitment to those values, the stronger the culture is. Consistent with this definition, a strong culture will have a great influence on the behavior of its members because the high degree of sharedness and intensity creates an internal climate of high behavioral control. For example, Seattle-based

strong cultures
Cultures where the core values are intensely held and widely shared.

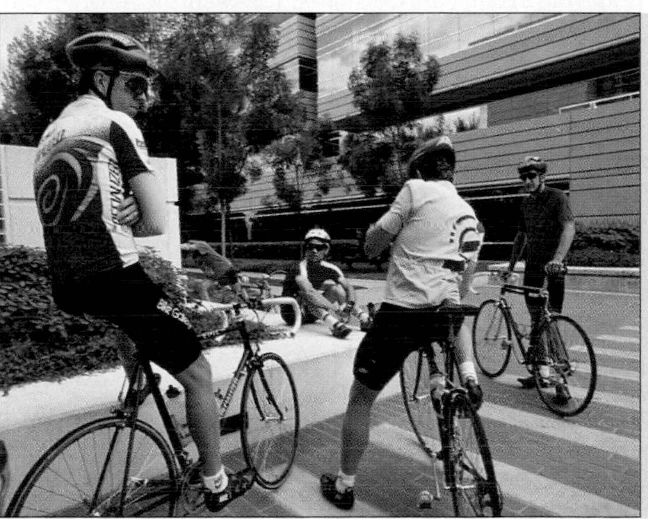

Nike, Inc. has a strong sports-oriented culture instilled by its founder Philip Knight. Nike's corporate goal is "to enhance people's lives through sports and fitness." Recognized worldwide as "an athlete's company," Nike is run by former pro, college, and Olympic athletes who design and market shoes and clothing for sports enthusiasts. Nike headquarters in Beaverton, Oregon, is a 74-acre World Campus with walking and jogging trails and buildings named after Nike heroes such as the Joan Benoit Samuelson Center, the Bo Jackson Fitness Center, and the Joe Paterno Day Care Center. The company practices that promote health and fitness include paying employees extra for biking to work instead of driving.

Nordstrom has developed one of the strongest service cultures in the retailing industry. Nordstrom employees know in no uncertain terms what is expected of them and these expectations go a long way in shaping their behavior.

One specific result of a strong culture should be lower employee turnover. A strong culture demonstrates high agreement among members about what the organization stands for. Such unanimity of purpose builds cohesiveness, loyalty, and organizational commitment. These qualities, in turn, lessen employees' propensity to leave the organization.[11]

Culture vs. Formalization

◆A strong organizational culture increases behavioral consistency.

A strong organizational culture increases behavioral consistency. In this sense, we should recognize that a strong culture can act as a substitute for formalization.

In Chapter 14, we discussed how formalization's rules and regulations act to regulate employee behavior. High formalization in an organization creates predictability, orderliness, and consistency. Our point is that a strong culture achieves the same end without the need for written documentation. Therefore, we should view formalization and culture as two different roads to a common destination. The stronger an organization's culture, the less management need be concerned with developing formal rules and regulations to guide employee behavior. Those guides will be internalized in employees when they accept the organization's culture.

Organizational Culture vs. National Culture

This chapter takes the anthropologist's concept of societal cultures and applies it at the organizational level. Our main thesis is that members of an organization develop common perceptions that, in turn, affect their attitudes and behavior. The strength of that effect, however, depends on the strength of the organization's culture.

Throughout this book we've argued that national differences—that is, national cultures—must be taken into account if accurate predictions are to be made about organizational behavior in different countries. It seems appropriate at this point, then, to ask this question: Does national culture override an organization's culture? Is an IBM facility in Germany, for example, more likely to reflect German ethnic culture or IBM's corporate culture?

The research indicates that national culture has a greater impact on employees than does their organization's culture.[12] German employees at an IBM facility in Munich, therefore, will be influenced more by German culture than by IBM's culture. This means that as influential as organizational culture is to understanding the behavior of people at work, national culture is even more so.

Our conclusion has to be qualified to reflect the self-selection that goes on at the hiring stage. IBM, for example, may be less concerned with hiring the "typical Italian" for its Italian operations than in hiring an Italian who fits within the IBM way of doing things.[13] Italians who have a high need for autonomy are more likely to go to Olivetti than IBM. Why? Because Olivetti's organizational culture is informal and nonstructured. It allows employees considerably more freedom than IBM does.[14] In fact, Olivetti seeks to hire individuals who are impatient, risk taking, and innovative—qualities in job candidates that IBM's Italian operations would purposely seek to exclude in new hires.

What Does Culture Do?

We've alluded to organizational culture's impact on behavior. We've also explicitly argued that a strong culture should be associated with reduced turnover. In this section, we more carefully review the functions that culture performs and assess whether culture can be a liability for an organization.

Culture's Functions

Culture performs a number of functions within an organization. First, it has a boundary-defining role; that is, it creates distinctions between one organization and others. Second, it conveys a sense of identity for organization members. Third, culture facilitates the generation of commitment to something larger than one's individual self-interest. Fourth, it enhances social system stability. Culture is the social glue that helps hold the organization together by providing appropriate standards for what employees should say and do. Finally, culture serves as a sense-making and control mechanism that guides and shapes the attitudes and behavior of employees. It is this last function that is of particular interest to us. As the following quote makes clear, culture defines the rules of the game:

> Culture by definition is elusive, intangible, implicit, and taken for granted. But every organization develops a core set of assumptions, understandings, and implicit rules that govern day-to-day behavior in the workplace. . . . Until newcomers learn the rules, they are not accepted as full-fledged members of the organization. Transgressions of the rules on the part of high-level executives or front-line employees result in universal disapproval and powerful penalties. Conformity to the rules becomes the primary basis for reward and upward mobility.[15]

The role of culture in influencing employee behavior appears to be increasingly important in the 1990s. As organizations have widened spans of control, flattened structures, introduced teams, reduced formalization, and empowered employees, the *shared meaning* provided by a strong culture ensures that everyone is pointed in the same direction.

As we show later in this chapter, who receives a job offer to join the organization, who is appraised as a high performer, and who gets the promotion are strongly influenced by the individual–organization "fit"—that is, whether the applicant or employee's attitudes and behavior are compatible with the culture. It's not a coincidence that employees at Disneyland and Disney World appear to be almost universally attractive, clean, and wholesome looking, with bright smiles. That's the image Disney seeks. The company selects employees who will maintain that image. And once on the job, a strong culture, supported by formal rules and regulations, ensure that Disney employees will act in a relatively uniform and predictable way.

Culture as a Liability

We are treating culture in a nonjudgmental manner. We haven't said it's good or bad, only that it exists. Many of its functions, as outlined, are valuable for both the organization and the employee. Culture enhances organizational commitment and increases the consistency of employee behavior. These are clearly benefits to an organization. From an employee's standpoint, culture is valuable because it reduces ambiguity. It tells employees how things are done and what's important. But we shouldn't ignore the potentially dysfunctional aspects of culture, especially a strong one, on an organization's effectiveness.

BARRIER TO CHANGE Culture is a liability where the shared values are not in agreement with those that will further the organization's effectiveness. This is most likely to occur when the organization's environment is dynamic. When the environment is undergoing rapid change, the organization's entrenched culture may no longer be appropriate. So consistency of behavior is an asset to an organization when it faces a stable environment. It may, however, burden the organization and make it difficult to respond to changes in the environment. This helps to explain the challenges that executives at companies like IBM, Eastman Kodak, and General Dynamics have had in recent years in adapting to upheavals in their environment. These companies have strong cultures that worked well for them in the past. But these strong cultures become barriers to change when "business as usual" is no longer effective. For many organizations with strong cultures, practices that led to previous successes can lead to failure when those practices no longer match up well with environmental needs.[16]

BARRIER TO DIVERSITY Hiring new employees who, because of race, gender, ethnic, or other differences, are not like the majority of the organization's members creates a paradox.[17] Management wants new employees to accept the organization's core cultural values. Otherwise, these employees are unlikely to fit in or be accepted. But at the same time, management wants to openly acknowledge and demonstrate support for the differences these employees bring to the workplace.

Strong cultures put considerable pressure on employees to conform. They limit the range of values and styles that are acceptable. Obviously, this creates a dilemma. Organizations hire diverse individuals because of the alternative strengths these people bring to the workplace. Yet these diverse behaviors and strengths are likely to diminish in strong cultures as people attempt to fit in. Strong cultures, therefore, can be liabilities when they effectively eliminate those unique strengths that people of different backgrounds bring to the organization.

BARRIER TO MERGERS AND ACQUISITIONS Historically, the key factors that management looked at in making merger or acquisition decisions were related to financial advantages or product synergy. In recent years, cultural compatibility has become the primary concern.[18] While a favorable financial statement or product line may be the initial attraction of an acquisition candidate, whether the acquisition actually works seems to have more to do with how well the two organizations' cultures match up.

BankAmerica's acquisition of discount broker Charles Schwab & Co. provides a vivid illustration. BankAmerica bought Schwab in 1983 as part of its strategy of diversifying into a broader range of financial products. But the companies were a terrible match. BA was conservative; Schwab was aggressive and risk taking. One of the most obvious symbols of the differences between these two firms was in the cars their executives drove. BA executives were provided with four-door Fords and Buicks. Top executives at Schwab also drove company cars but theirs were Ferraris, Porsches, and BMWs. In spite of Schwab being a profitable enterprise and expanding BA's product line, the Schwab people couldn't fit into the BA way of doing things. The marriage was dissolved in 1987, when Charles Schwab bought his company back from BankAmerica.

Creating and Sustaining Culture

An organization's culture doesn't pop out of thin air. Once established, it rarely fades away. What forces influence the creation of a culture? What reinforces and sustains these forces once they are in place? We answer both of these questions in this section.

How a Culture Begins

An organization's current customs, traditions, and general way of doing things are largely due to what it has done before and the degree of success it has had with those endeavors. This leads us to the ultimate source of an organization's culture: its founders.[19]

The founders of an organization traditionally have a major impact on that organization's early culture. They have a vision of what the organization should be. They are unconstrained by previous customs or ideologies. The small size that typically characterizes new organizations further facilitates the founders' imposition of their vision on all organizational members.

Microsoft's culture is largely a reflection of cofounder and current CEO, Bill Gates. Gates is personally aggressive, competitive, and highly disciplined. Those are the same characteristics often used to describe the software giant he heads. Other contemporary examples of founders who have had an immeasurable impact on their organization's culture are Akio Morita at Sony, Ted Turner at Turner Broadcasting Systems, Fred Smith at Federal Express, Mary Kay at Mary Kay Cosmetics, Steve Jobs at Apple Computer, and Richard Branson at the Virgin Group.

McDonald's founder Ray Kroc died in 1984. But his philosophy of providing customers with quality, service, cleanliness, and value is preserved on tape. McDonald's managers throughout the world learn about Kroc's vision and guiding principles at one of five Hamburger University training centers in the United States, Germany, England, Japan, and Australia.

◆◆◆◆ OB in the News ◆◆◆◆

Chung Ju Yung and the Company He Created: Hyundai

Hyundai is a $45 billion-a-year business empire made up of more than 40 companies in fields ranging from ships to semiconductors, motor vehicles to computers, engineering to robots, petrochemicals to department stores. The Hyundai group is a disciplined militaristic organization. The man who made it this way is Chung Ju Yung.

Chung was born in 1915, one of seven children from an impoverished peasant farm family. Following World War II, Chung set up an auto repair business. He called it "Hyundai," which means *modern* in Korean. From this small beginning, the giant empire began. Throughout the company's growth, Chung's style shaped its culture. Family loyalty and authoritarianism reign. "The boss is still the boss," says Kim Yung Duc, president of Hyundai Corp. U.S.A.

At the height of his powers, Chung was a fearsome figure. There are rumors that a stretcher used to be a fixture in Hyundai's executive board room because Chung would sometimes punch out underlings who wouldn't listen to him or do what he wanted.

Hyundai may represent an extreme in feudal obedience, but it evolved into what Chung's executives call the "Hyundai Spirit." A manual given to new recruits states, "The hard work of the creator [Chung] and the courage of the pioneer have helped us open the way for the expansion, sophistication and internationalization of the industrial society of our country." In Hyundai lore and literature, Chung is quoted nearly as much as the Chinese, two decades ago, invoked Mao Zedong.

"Everything at Hyundai is run on a fairly military basis," says a U.S. consultant. "They have an armory in the yard. The guys who are educated all know what they have to do if war breaks out."

If you want to understand Hyundai's fierce, competitive style, its feudal obedience, or its disciplined, militaristic nature, you don't need to go any further than looking at its founder, Chung Ju Yung.

Based on D. Kirk, "The Humbling of Chairman Chung," *Asia, Inc.* (April 1994), pp. 24–29.

Keeping a Culture Alive

Once a culture is in place, practices within the organization act to maintain it by giving employees a set of similar experiences.[20] For example, many of the human resource practices we discussed in Chapter 16 reinforce the organization's culture. The selection process, performance evaluation criteria, reward practices, training and career development activities, and promotion procedures ensure that those hired fit in with the culture, reward those who support it, and penalize (and even expel) those who challenge it. Three forces play a particularly important part in sustaining a culture: selection practices, the actions of top management, and socialization methods. Let's take a closer look at each.

SELECTION The explicit goal of the selection process is to identify and hire individuals who have the knowledge, skills, and abilities to perform the jobs within the organization successfully. But, typically, more than one candidate will be identified who meets any given job's requirements. When that point is reached, it would be naive to ignore that the final decision as to who is hired will be significantly influenced by the decision maker's judgment of how well the candidates will fit into the organization. This attempt to ensure a proper match, whether purposely or inadvertently, results in the hiring of people who have values essentially consistent with those of the organization, or at least a good portion of those values.[21] Additionally, the selection process provides information to applicants about the organization. Candidates learn about the organization, and, if they perceive a conflict between their values and those of the organization, they can self-select themselves out of the applicant pool. Selection, therefore, becomes a two-way street, allowing either employer or applicant to abrogate a marriage if there appears to be a mismatch. In this way, the selection process sustains an organization's culture by selecting out those individuals who might attack or undermine its core values.

Applicants for entry-level positions in brand management at Procter & Gamble experience an exhaustive application and screening process. Their interviewers are part of an elite cadre who have been selected and trained extensively via lectures, videotapes, films, practice interviews, and role plays to identify applicants who will successfully fit in at P&G. Applicants are interviewed in depth for such qualities as their ability to "turn out high volumes of excellent work," "identify and understand problems," and "reach thoroughly substantiated and well-reasoned conclusions that lead to action." P&G values rationality and seeks applicants who think that way. College applicants receive two interviews and a general knowledge test on campus, before being flown to Cincinnati for three more one-on-one interviews and a group interview at lunch. Each encounter seeks corroborating evidence of the traits the firm believes correlate highly with "what counts" for success at P&G.[22]

Applicants for positions at Compaq Computer are carefully chosen for their ability to fit into the company's teamwork-oriented culture. As one executive put it, "We can find lots of people who are competent. . . . The No. 1 issue is whether they fit into the way we do business."[23] At Compaq, that means job candidates who are easy to get along with and who feel comfortable with the company's consensus management style. To increase the likelihood that loners and those with big egos get screened out, it's not unusual for an applicant to be interviewed by 15 people, who represent all departments of the company and a variety of seniority levels.[24]

TOP MANAGEMENT The actions of top management also have a major impact on the organization's culture.[25] Through what they say and how they behave, senior executives establish norms that filter down through the organization, for example, whether risk taking is desirable; how much freedom managers should give their subordinates; what is appropriate dress; and what actions will pay off in terms of pay raises, promotions, and other rewards.

For example, look at Xerox Corp.[26] Its chief executive from 1961 to 1968 was Joseph C. Wilson. An aggressive entrepreneurial type, he oversaw Xerox's staggering growth on the basis of its 914 copier, one of the most successful products in American history. Under Wilson, Xerox had an entrepreneurial environment, with an informal, high-camaraderie, innovative, bold, risk-taking culture. Wilson's replacement as CEO was C. Peter McColough, a Harvard MBA with a formal management style. He instituted bureaucratic controls and a major change in Xerox's culture. When McColough stepped down in 1982, Xerox had become stodgy and formal, with lots of politics and turf battles and layers of watchdog managers. His replacement was David T. Kearns. He believed the culture he inherited hindered Xerox's ability to compete. To increase the company's competitiveness, Kearns trimmed Xerox down by cutting

The success of computer chip maker Intel Corporation hinges on its ability to be the first to market innovative products. To achieve speed and innovation, Intel's CEO Andy Grove fosters an egalitarian culture in which all employees feel their ideas are respected and valued. Through his actions and policies, Grove breaks down communication barriers that cause discomfort and inhibit the free-flowing exchange of ideas and information. At Intel, all employees, including Grove (shown here), work in small, open cubicles. Grove reduces power struggles by eliminating status symbols such as private dining rooms for executives and reserved spaces in company parking lots.

15,000 jobs, delegated decision making downward, and refocused the organization's culture around a simple theme: boosting the quality of Xerox products and services. By his actions and those of his senior managerial cadre, Kearns conveyed to everyone at Xerox that the company valued and rewarded quality and efficiency. When Kearns retired in 1990, Xerox still had its problems. The copier business was mature and Xerox had fared badly in developing computerized office systems. The current CEO, Paul Allaire, has again sought to reshape Xerox's culture. Specifically, he has reorganized the corporation around a worldwide marketing department, has unified product development and manufacturing divisions, and has replaced half of the company's top management team with outsiders. Allaire seeks to reshape Xerox's culture to focus on innovative thinking and outhustling the competition.

SOCIALIZATION No matter how good a job the organization does in recruiting and selection, new employees are not fully indoctrinated in the organization's culture. Maybe most important, because they are unfamiliar with the organization's culture, new employees are potentially likely to disturb the beliefs and customs that are in place. The organization will, therefore, want to help new employees adapt to its culture. This adaptation process is called **socialization**.[27]

socialization
The process that adapts employees to the organization's culture.

All Marines must go through boot camp, where they "prove" their commitment. Of course, at the same time, the Marine trainers are indoctrinating new recruits in the "Marine way." New Sanyo employees go through an intensive five-month training program (trainees eat and sleep together in company-subsidized dorms and are required to vacation together at company-owned resorts) where they learn the Sanyo way of doing everything—from how to speak to superiors to proper grooming and dress.[28] The company considers this program essential for transforming young employees, fresh out of school, into dedicated *kaisha senshi*, or corporate warriors.

As we discuss socialization, keep in mind that the most critical socialization stage is at the time of entry into the organization. This is when the organization seeks to mold the outsider into an employee "in good standing." Those employees who fail to learn the essential or pivotal role behaviors risk being labeled "nonconformists" or "rebels," which often leads to expulsion. But the organization will be socializing every employee, although maybe not as explicitly, throughout his or her entire career in the organization. This further contributes to sustaining the culture.

Socialization can be conceptualized as a process made up of three stages: prearrival, encounter, and metamorphosis.[29] The first stage encompasses all the learning that occurs before a new member joins the organization. In the second stage, the new employee sees what the organization is really like and confronts the possibility that expectations and reality may diverge. In the third stage, the relatively long-lasting changes take place. The new employee masters the skills required for his or her job, successfully performs his or her new roles, and makes the adjustments to his or her work group's values and norms.[30] This three-stage process impacts on the new employee's work productivity, commitment to the organization's objectives, and eventual decision to stay with the organization. Figure 17–1 depicts this process.

The **prearrival stage** explicitly recognizes that each individual arrives with a set of values, attitudes, and expectations. These cover both the work to be done and the organization. For instance, in many jobs, particularly professional work, new members will have undergone a considerable degree of prior socialization in training and in school. One major purpose of a business school, for example, is to socialize business students to the attitudes and behaviors that business firms want. If business executives believe successful employees value the profit ethic, are loyal, will work hard, desire to achieve, and willingly accept directions from their superiors, they can hire individuals out of business schools who have been premolded in this pattern. But prearrival socialization goes beyond the specific job. The selection process is used in most organizations to inform prospective employees about the organization as a whole. In addition, as noted previously, the selection process also acts to ensure the inclusion of the "right type"—those who will fit in. "Indeed, the ability of the individual to present the appropriate face during the selection process determines his ability to move into the organization in the first place. Thus, success depends on the degree to which the aspiring member has correctly anticipated the expectations and desires of those in the organization in charge of selection."[31]

prearrival stage
The period of learning in the socialization process that occurs before a new employee joins the organization.

Upon entry into the organization, the new member enters the **encounter stage**. Here the individual confronts the possible dichotomy between her expectations—about her job, her coworkers, her boss, and the organization in general—and reality. If expectations prove to have been more or less accurate, the encounter stage merely provides for a reaffirmation of the perceptions gained earlier. However, this is often not the case. Where expectations and reality differ, the new employee must undergo socialization that will detach her from her previous assumptions and replace them with another set that the organization deems desirable. At the extreme, a new member may be-

encounter stage
The stage in the socialization process in which a new employee sees what the organization is really like and confronts the possibility that expectations and reality may diverge.

Figure 17-1
A Socialization Model

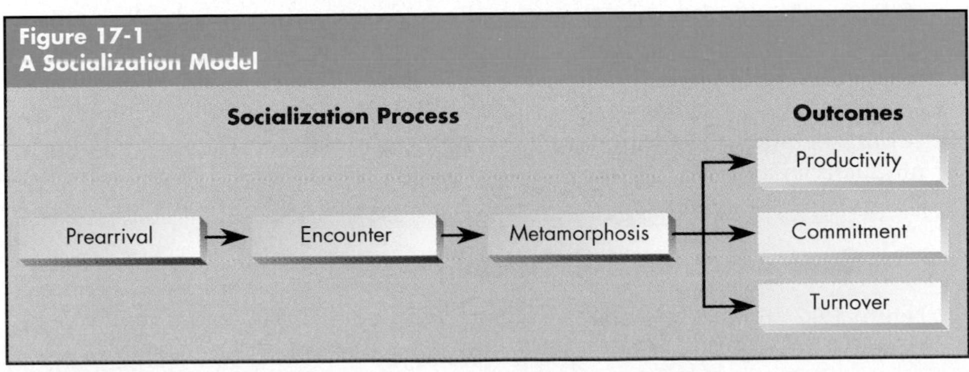

During the encounter stage of socialization, Toshiba indoctrinates new employees in its organization's culture. Recruits not only learn about the company's history and core values, they are also required to learn the company song.

come totally disillusioned with the actualities of her job and resign. Proper selection should significantly reduce the probability of the latter occurrence.

metamorphosis stage
The stage in the socialization process in which a new employee adjusts to his or her work group's values and norms.

Finally, the new member must work out any problems discovered during the encounter stage. This may mean going through changes—hence, we call this the **metamorphosis stage**. The options presented in Table 17-2 are alternatives designed to bring about the desired metamorphosis. Note, for example, that the more management relies on socialization programs that are formal, collective, fixed, serial, and emphasize divestiture, the greater the likelihood that newcomers' differences and perspectives will be stripped away and replaced by standardized and predictable behaviors. Careful selection by management of newcomers' socialization experiences can—at the extreme—create conformists who maintain traditions and customs, or inventive and creative individualists who consider no organizational practice sacred.

We can say that metamorphosis and the entry socialization process is complete when the new member has become comfortable with the organization and his or her job. She has internalized the norms of the organization and her work group, and understands and accepts these norms. The new member feels accepted by her peers as a trusted and valued individual, is self-confident she has the competence to complete the job successfully, and understands the system—not only her own tasks, but the rules, procedures, and informally accepted practices as well. Finally, she knows how she will be evaluated, that is, what criteria will be used to measure and appraise her work. She knows what is expected, and what constitutes a job "well done." As Figure 17-1 shows, successful metamorphosis should have a positive impact on the new employee's productivity and her commitment to the organization, and reduce her propensity to leave the organization.

Summary: How Cultures Form

Figure 17-2 summarizes how an organization's culture is established and sustained. The original culture is derived from the founder's philosophy. This, in

Table 17-2 Entry Socialization Options

Formal vs. Informal The more a new employee is segregated from the ongoing work setting and differentiated in some way to make explicit his or her newcomer's role, the more formal socialization is. Specific orientation and training programs are examples. Informal socialization puts the new employee directly into his or her job, with little or no special attention.

Individual vs. Collective New members can be socialized individually. This describes how it's done in many professional offices. They can also be grouped together and processed through an identical set of experiences, as in military boot camp.

Fixed vs. Variable This refers to the time schedule in which newcomers make the transition from outsider to insider. A fixed schedule establishes standardized stages of transition. This characterizes rotational training programs. It also includes probationary periods, such as the 8- to 10-year "associate" status used by accounting and law firms before deciding on whether a candidate is made a partner. Variable schedules give no advanced notice of their transition timetable. Variable schedules describe the typical promotion system, where one is not advanced to the next stage until he or she is "ready."

Serial vs. Random Serial socialization is characterized by the use of role models who train and encourage the newcomer. Apprenticeship and mentoring programs are examples. In random socialization, role models are deliberately withheld. The new employee is left on his or her own to figure things out.

Investiture vs. Divestiture Investiture socialization assumes the newcomer's qualities and qualifications are the necessary ingredients for job success, so these qualities and qualifications are confirmed and supported. Divestiture socialization tries to strip away certain characteristics of the recruit. Fraternity and sorority pledges go through divestiture socialization to shape them into the proper role.

Source: Based on J. Van Maanen, "People Processing: Strategies of Organizational Socialization," *Organizational Dynamics* (Summer 1978), pp. 19–36; and E.H. Schein, "Organizational Culture," *American Psychologist* (February 1990), p. 116.

turn, strongly influences the criteria used in hiring. The actions of the current top management set the general climate of what is acceptable behavior and what is not. How employees are to be socialized will depend both on the degree of success achieved in matching new employees' values to those of the organization's in the selection process and on top management's preference for socialization methods.

Figure 17-2
How Organization Cultures Form

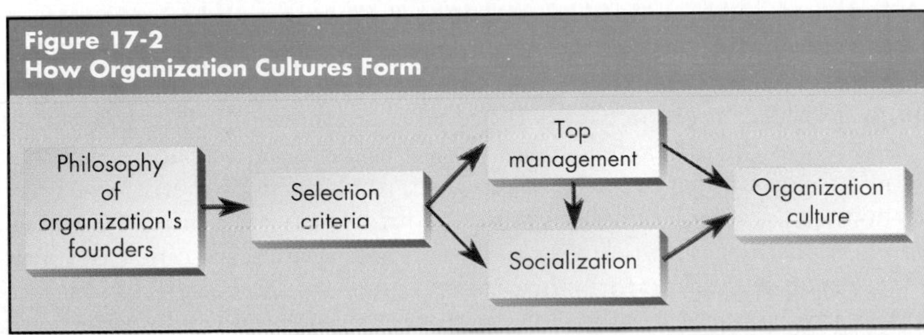

How Employees Learn Culture

Culture is transmitted to employees in a number of forms, the most potent being stories, rituals, material symbols, and language.

Stories

During the days when Henry Ford II was chairman of the Ford Motor Co., one would have been hard pressed to find a manager who hadn't heard the story about Mr. Ford reminding his executives, when they got too arrogant, that "it's my name that's on the building." The message was clear: Henry Ford II ran the company!

Nordstrom employees are fond of the following story. It strongly conveys the company's policy toward customer returns: When this specialty retail chain was in its infancy, a customer came in and wanted to return a set of automobile tires. The sales clerk was a bit uncertain how to handle the problem. As the customer and sales clerk spoke, Mr. Nordstrom walked by and overheard the conversation. He immediately interceded, asking the customer how much he had paid for the tires. Mr. Nordstrom then instructed the clerk to take the tires back and provide a full cash refund. After the customer had received his refund and left, the perplexed clerk looked at the boss. "But Mr. Nordstrom, we don't sell tires!" "I know," replied the boss, "but we do whatever we need to do to make the customer happy. I mean it when I say we have a no-questions-asked return policy." Nordstrom then picked up the telephone and called a friend in the auto parts business to see how much he could get for the tires.

Stories such as these circulate through many organizations. They typically contain a narrative of events about the organization's founders, rule breaking, rags-to-riches successes, reductions in the work force, relocation of employees, reactions to past mistakes, and organizational coping.[32] These stories anchor the present in the past and provide explanations and legitimacy for current practices.[33]

Rituals

rituals
Repetitive sequences of activities that express and reinforce the key values of the organization, what goals are most important, which people are important and which are expendable.

Rituals are repetitive sequences of activities that express and reinforce the key values of the organization, what goals are most important, which people are important and which are expendable.[34]

College faculty members undergo a lengthy ritual in their quest for permanent employment—tenure. Typically, the faculty member is on probation for six years. At the end of that period, the member's colleagues must make one of two choices: extend a tenured appointment or issue a one-year terminal contract. What does it take to obtain tenure? It usually requires satisfactory teaching performance, service to the department and university, and scholarly activity. But, of course, what satisfies the requirements for tenure in one department at one university may be appraised as inadequate in another. The key is that the tenure decision, in essence, asks those who are tenured to assess whether the candidate has demonstrated, based on six years of performance, whether he or she fits in. Colleagues who have been socialized properly will have proved themselves worthy of being granted tenure. Every year, hundreds of faculty members at colleges and universities are denied tenure. In some cases, this action is a result of poor performance across the board. More often, however, the decision can be traced to the faculty member's not doing well in those areas the tenured faculty believe are important. The instructor who spends dozens of

An annual ritual at Sun Microsystems in Mountain View, California, is an elaborate April Fool's Day hoax. Each year a team of engineers mastermind a prank that targets a member of the company's top management. One year the target was Wayne "Scuba" Rosing, vice-president of Sun Microsystems Laboratories, Inc. Shown here is a life-size replica of Rosing's office that company engineers built at the bottom of a shark tank in a San Francisco aquarium. Top managers view the ritual as a tribute to the company's engineering prowess and willingness to have fun. They believe the humorous events encourage teamwork and camaraderie and boost morale. The rituals are videotaped so employees at other company locations in the United States and 18 countries can share in the fun.

hours each week preparing for class and achieves outstanding evaluations by students, but neglects his or her research and publication activities, may be passed over for tenure. What has happened, simply, is that the instructor has failed to adapt to the norms set by the department. The astute faculty member will assess early on in the probationary period what attitudes and behaviors his or her colleagues want and will then proceed to give them what they want. And, of course, by demanding certain attitudes and behaviors, the tenured faculty have made significant strides toward standardizing tenure candidates.

One of the best known corporate rituals is Mary Kay Cosmetics's annual award meeting.[35] Looking like a cross between a circus and a Miss America pageant, the meeting takes place over a couple of days in a large auditorium, on a stage in front of a large cheering audience, with all the participants dressed in glamorous evening clothes. Saleswomen are rewarded with an array of flashy gifts—gold and diamond pins, fur stoles, pink Cadillacs—based on success in achieving sales quota. This "show" acts as a motivator by publicly recognizing outstanding sales performance. In addition, the ritual aspect reinforces Mary Kay's personal determination and optimism, which enabled her to overcome personal hardships, found her own company, and achieve material success. It conveys to her salespeople that reaching their sales quota is important and that through hard work and encouragement they too can achieve success.

Material Symbols

Tandem Computers's headquarters in Cupertino, California, doesn't look like your typical head office operation. It has jogging trails, a basketball court, space for dance and yoga classes, and a large swimming pool—all for its employees' enjoyment. Every Friday afternoon at 4:30, employees partake in the weekly beer bust, courtesy of the company. This informal corporate headquarters conveys to employees that Tandem values openness and equality.

Figure 17-3
Drawing by Mick Stevens in *The New Yorker*, October 3, 1994. Copyright © 1994 by The New Yorker Magazine, Inc. Reprinted by permission.

"I don't know how it started, either. All I know is that it's part of our corporate culture."

Some corporations provide their top executives with chauffeur-driven limousines and, when they travel by air, unlimited use of the corporate jet. Others may not get to ride in limousines or private jets but they might still get a car and air transportation paid for by the company. Only the car is a Chevrolet (with no driver) and the jet seat is in the economy section of a commercial airliner.

The layout of corporate headquarters, the types of automobiles top executives are given, and the presence or absence of corporate aircraft are a few examples of material symbols. Others include the size and layout of offices, the elegance of furnishings, executive perks, and dress attire.[36] These material symbols convey to employees who is important, the degree of egalitarianism desired by top management, and the kinds of behavior (for example, risk taking, conservative, authoritarian, participative, individualistic, social) that are appropriate.

Language

Many organizations and units within organizations use language as a way to identify members of a culture or subculture. By learning this language, members attest to their acceptance of the culture and, in so doing, help to preserve it.

> ◆By learning an organization's language, members attest to their acceptance of the culture and, in so doing, help to preserve it.

The following are examples of terminology used by employees at Dialog, a California-based data redistributor: *accession number* (a number assigned each individual record in a database); *KWIC* (a set of key-words-in-context); and *relational operator* (searching a database for names or key terms in some order). Librarians are a rich source of terminology foreign to people outside their profession. They sprinkle their conversations liberally with acronyms like ARL (Association for Research Libraries), OCLC (a center in Ohio that does cooperative cataloging), and OPAC (for on-line patron accessing catalog). When Louis Gerstner left RJR Nabisco to head up IBM, he had to learn a whole new vocabulary that included *the Orchard* (IBM's Armonk, New York corporate headquarters, which was once an apple orchard); *big iron* (mainframe computers); *hypo* (a high-potential employee); *a one performer* (an employee with IBM's top performance rating); and *PROFS* (Professional Office Systems, IBM's internal electronic mail system).[37]

Organizations, over time, often develop unique terms to describe equipment, offices, key personnel, suppliers, customers, or products that relate to its business. New employees are frequently overwhelmed with acronyms and jargon that, after six months on the job, have become fully part of their language. Once assimilated, this terminology acts as a common denominator that unites members of a given culture or subculture.

Organizational Culture in Action

We now turn our attention to three specific organizations and their cultures: the Walt Disney Co., MCI Communications, and Time Warner. They are of interest for different reasons. Disney is fascinating because of its culture's strength; MCI because it is so untraditional; and Time Warner as an illustration of what happens when diverse cultures merge.

The Walt Disney Co.

The Walt Disney Co. is made up of three main divisions: filmed entertainment, consumer products, and theme parks and resorts. Currently, the company's theme parks in California, Florida, Tokyo, and Paris account for 56 percent of Disney's revenues and 64 percent of its operating profits. Since these theme parks are the part of the Disney operation most of us know best—and where the Disney culture is strongest—let's take a look at how management creates and sustains that "Disney look."[38]

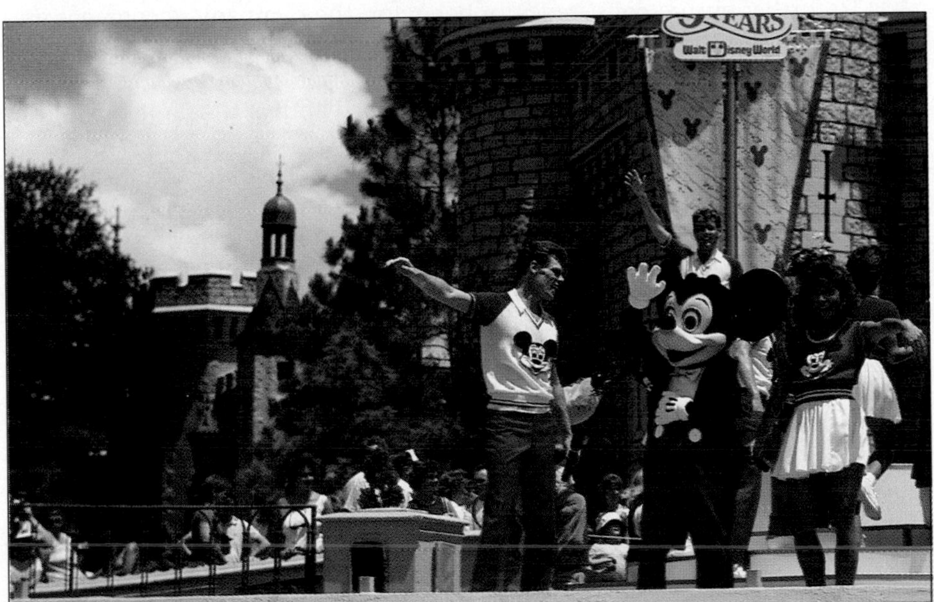

This photo of Disney World employees depicts the Disney "look." Both the young man and woman are clean cut, slim, and healthy-looking. Cast members—whether they are food servers, parade marchers, souvenir sellers, bus drivers, or room cleaners—are selected to reinforce the wholesome Disney image. During Traditions, Disney's initial training session, new hires receive a 36-page appearance guide detailing everything from length and style of hair to proper quantities of cosmetics. Equally important as appearance is the Disney "personality." Interviewers choose candidates who are enthusiastic, have pride in their work, are able to take charge of a situation, and are team players.

Suppose you wanted a summer job at Disneyland. You'd increase your chance of getting that job if you knew someone already working in the organization. Disney has found that personal links reduce social variability in the hiring pool. All final hirees get at least two personal interviews with park representatives. Emphasis is placed on identifying people who conform to Disney's highly specific standards of appearance—complexion, height and weight, straightness and color of teeth, and the like. It's not by chance that most Disneyland employees are single, in their early twenties, of healthy appearance, without facial blemishes, of above-average height and below-average weight, with conservative grooming standards. The lengthy hiring process reduces the likelihood that "misfits" will be selected.

Once hired, new employees undergo entry socialization that is formal, collective, and serial. Incoming identities are not so much dismantled as they are set aside as employees are schooled in their new identities. They receive 8 hours of orientation, followed by 40 hours or so of apprenticeship training on park grounds.

One of the essential parts of the Disney orientation is learning the language. There are no employees, only "cast members." People don't have jobs, they're cast in roles. In fact, the company has a whole language of its own. Customers are "guests," rides are called "attractions," law enforcement personnel are "security hosts," uniforms are "costumes," accidents are "incidents," people aren't working but are "onstage"—the list goes on and on.

Of course, new hires also learn the company's history, Walt Disney's philosophy, and the standards of guest service. Values such as "everyone is a child at heart when at Disneyland" are emphasized.

To further ensure consistency of behavior, the company encourages employees to spend their off-work hours together. Disneyland's softball and volleyball leagues, its official picnics, employee nights at the park, and beach parties provide a busy social scene for those interested and, at the same time, limit exposure to non-Disney values.

Once trained, Disneyland employees come to believe they are really "onstage" while working. The ease with which they glide into their user-friendly roles and the everyday acting skill they display in bringing off these roles—whether as a ride operator at Space Mountain, a candy merchant on "Main Street," or Donald Duck himself—are, in large measure, feats of social engineering.

MCI Communications

The late Bill McGowan founded MCI Communications in 1968. From its inception, MCI was a renegade operation. This was the company that, with annual sales of only a few million dollars in the early 1970s, had the audacity to attempt to break up the world's largest corporation by going to court and attacking AT&T's phone monopoly. And, in one of the great "David slays Goliath" stories in business history, it succeeded. In 1993 MCI had revenues of $11.9 billion and earned $627 million in profits.

In contrast to most successful executives, who create organization out of chaos, McGowan shaped MCI's culture to create chaos out of organization.[39] The company reflects McGowan's belief that both seniority and corporate loyalty are unimportant. Five-year pins and ten-year pins are nonexistent. Why? They imply that people who have been with the company longer are somehow better. McGowan said, "The opposite is almost always the truth. It's the newcomers, the young people, who bring the fresh ideas and the energy." Consistent with these values, the company has an official goal of filling at least half of all job openings from outside. Moreover, people who quit MCI aren't treated as traitors, as they are at most large companies. Instead, they're given parties and reminded that MCI will hire them back.

The same amount of effort that Disney exerts to standardize the behavior of its theme park employees is exerted at MCI to encourage individuals to be unique. MCI wants its employees to be free and flexible. McGowan cringed at the thought of rewarding employees for adhering to standardized rules and procedures. At annual companywide meetings, he was fond of saying, "I know that somewhere, someone out there is trying to write up a manual on procedures. Well, one of these days I'm going to find out who you are, and when I do, I'm going to fire you."

Time Warner

As we noted earlier in this chapter, when an acquisition succeeds or fails, cultural compatibility has increasingly been looked to for an explanation. While a favorable financial statement or product synergy may be the initial attraction of an acquisition candidate, whether the acquisition actually works may have more to do with how well the two organizations' cultures match up. The case of Time Warner illustrates this point.[40]

Time Warner is one of the world's largest media companies, with annual revenues of $14.5 billion. It was created by Time Inc.'s acquisition of Warner Communications in 1989. Time brought an impressive list of publication properties—such as *Sports Illustrated*, *People*, *Time*, and *Fortune* magazines—to the marriage. Warner contributed movie, cable television, and music businesses. The underlying logic behind the merger of these two giants was the creation of an integrated media conglomerate.

In its first five years, Time's acquisition of Warner has not proved to be the success that management and stockholders had hoped for. In 1990 Time Warner lost $227 million. In 1993 it was still losing $164 million. Certainly a number of factors have contributed to these losses—particularly heavy interest expenses from debt incurred in the buyout—but the merger of two very different organizational cultures has clearly been a major problem.

From its founding by Henry Luce, Time prospered by isolating editorial concerns from those of business. Time's culture was conservative and paternalistic. Consistent with journalistic values, the company fostered a strong belief in integrity. Time provided its employees with a stable work environment, a feeling of family, and as close to lifetime employment as one could find in an American corporation.

Warner, however, was a firm that lived in a world of deal making. Its products—music, TV series, recordings—recreate themselves constantly as a new deal to be made. Hollywood and entertainment industry values blurred Warner's corporate morality. Warner experienced considerable turnover, as one might expect in a "high-risk, high-reward" climate. Time veterans regularly use the word *sleazy* when speaking of Warner's Hollywood deal makers. While Time's people grew up in a company that encouraged and rewarded caution, Warner's people survived by moving fast and taking risks.

Can two such diverse cultures live happily ever after? Excuse the pun, but Time will tell!

Summary and Implications for Managers

Figure 17-4 depicts organizational culture as an intervening variable. Employees form an overall subjective perception of the organization based on such factors as degree of risk tolerance, team emphasis, and support of people. This overall perception becomes, in effect, the organization's culture or personality. These favorable or unfavorable perceptions then affect employee performance and satisfaction, with the impact being greater for stronger cultures.

Just as people's personalities tend to be stable over time, so too do strong cultures. This makes strong cultures difficult for managers to change. When a culture becomes mismatched to its environment, management will want to change it. But as the Point-Counterpoint debate for this chapter demonstrates, changing an organization's culture is a long and difficult process. The result, at least in the short term, is that managers should treat their organization's culture as relatively fixed.

One of the more important managerial implications of organizational culture relates to selection decisions. Hiring individuals whose values don't align with those of the organization are likely to lead to employees who lack motivation and commitment and who are dissatisfied with their jobs and the organization.[41] Not surprisingly, employee "misfits" have considerably higher turnover rates than individuals who perceive a good fit.[42]

We should also not overlook the influence of socialization on employee performance. An employee's performance depends to a considerable degree on knowing what he or she should or should not do. Understanding the right way to do a job indicates proper socialization. Further, the appraisal of an individual's performance includes how well the person fits into the organization. Can he or she get along with coworkers? Does he or she have acceptable work habits, and demonstrate the right attitude? These qualities differ between jobs and organizations. For instance, on some jobs, employees will be evaluated more favorably if they are aggressive and outwardly indicate they are ambitious. On another job, or on the same job in another organization, such an approach may be evaluated negatively. As a result, proper socialization becomes a significant factor in influencing both actual job performance and how it's perceived by others.

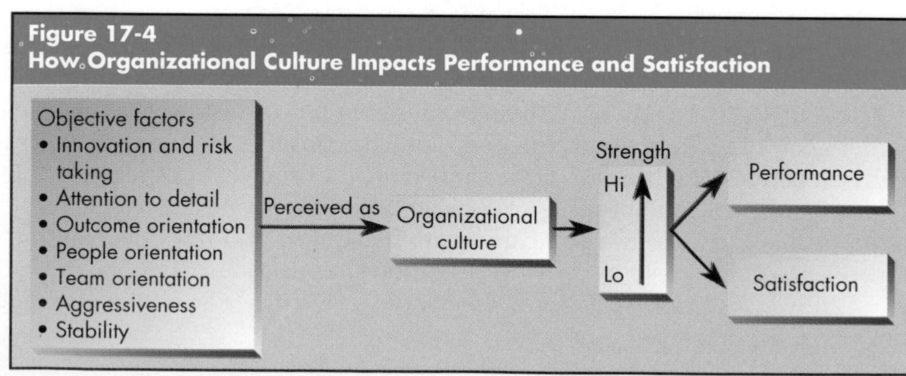

Figure 17-4
How Organizational Culture Impacts Performance and Satisfaction

For Review

1. What is the relationship between institutionalization, formalization, and organizational culture?
2. What's the difference between job satisfaction and organizational culture?
3. Can an employee survive in an organization if he or she rejects its core values? Explain.
4. List and compare four cultural typologies.
5. What defines an organization's subcultures?
6. Contrast organizational culture with national culture.
7. How can culture be a liability to an organization?
8. How is an organization's culture maintained?
9. What benefits can socialization provide for the organization? For the new employee?
10. Contrast the organizational cultures of Disney and MCI.

For Discussion

1. Contrast individual personality and organizational culture. How are they similar? How are they different?
2. Is socialization brainwashing? Explain.
3. If management sought a culture characterized as innovative and autonomous, what might its socialization program look like?
4. Can you identify a set of characteristics that describes your college's culture? Compare your list with several of your peers. How closely do they agree?
5. "We should be opposed to the manipulation of individuals for organizational purposes, but a degree of social uniformity enables organizations to work better." Do you agree or disagree with this statement? Discuss.

Point

The Case Against Cultural Change

That an organization's culture is made up of relatively stable characteristics would imply culture is very difficult for management to change. Such a conclusion would be correct.

An organization's culture develops over many years and is rooted in deeply held values to which employees are strongly committed. In addition, there are several forces continually operating to maintain a given culture. These would include written statements about the organization's mission and philosophy, the design of physical spaces and buildings, the dominant leadership style, hiring criteria, past promotion practices, entrenched rituals, popular stories about key people and events, the organization's historic performance evaluation criteria, and the organization's formal structure.

Selection and promotion policies are particularly important devices that work against cultural change. Employees chose the organization because they perceived their values to be a "good fit" with the organization. They become comfortable with that fit and will strongly resist efforts to disturb the equilibrium. The serious difficulties that organizations like IBM, Sears, General Motors, AT&T, and the U.S. Postal Service have had in trying to reshape their cultures attests to this dilemma.* These organizations historically tended to attract individuals who desired and flourished in situations that were stable and highly structured. Those in control in organizations will also select senior managers who will continue the current culture. Even attempts to change a culture by going outside the organization to hire a new chief executive are unlikely to be effective. The evidence indicates that the culture is more likely to change the executive than the other way around. Why? It's too entrenched, and change becomes a potential threat to member self-interest. In fact, a more pragmatic view of the relationship between an organization's culture and its chief executive would be to note that the practice of filling senior-level management positions from current managerial employees ensures that those who run the organization have been fully indoctrinated in the organization's culture. Promoting from within provides stability and lessens uncertainty. When Exxon's board of directors selects as a new chief executive officer an individual who has spent 30 years in the company, it virtually guarantees the culture will continue unchanged.

Our argument, however, should not be viewed as saying culture can never be changed. In the unusual case when an organization confronts a survival-threatening crisis—a crisis universally acknowledged as a true life-or-death situation—members of the organization will be responsive to efforts at cultural change. For instance, it was only when executives from General Motors'and AT&T were able to successfully convey to employees the crises faced from competitors that these organizations' cultures began to show signs of adaptation. However, anything less than a crisis is unlikely to be effective in bringing about cultural change.

*See, for instance, K. Kerwin, "Can Jack Smith Fix GM?" *Business Week* (November 1, 1993), pp. 126–31; and L. Hays, "Gerstner Is Struggling as He Tries to Change Ingrained IBM Culture," *Wall Street Journal* (May 13, 1994), p. A1.

counterPoint

How to Change an Organization's Culture

Changing an organization's culture is extremely difficult, but cultures *can* be changed. For example, Lee Iacocca came to Chrysler Corp. in 1978, when the company appeared to be only weeks away from bankruptcy. It took him about five years but, in what is now a well-worn story, he took Chrysler's conservative, inward-looking, and engineering-oriented culture and changed it into an action-oriented, market-responsive culture.

The evidence suggests that cultural change is most likely to take place when most or all of the following conditions exist:

A dramatic crisis. This is the shock that undermines the status quo and calls into question the relevance of the current culture. Examples of these crises might be a surprising financial setback, the loss of a major customer, or a dramatic technological breakthrough by a competitor. Executives at Pepsi-Cola and Ameritech even admit to creating crises in order to stimulate cultural change in their organizations.*

Turnover in leadership. New top leadership, which can provide an alternative set of key values, may be perceived as more capable of responding to the crisis. This would definitely be the organization's chief executive but also might need to include all senior management positions. The hiring of outside CEOs at IBM (Louis Gerstner) and General Motors (Jack Smith) illustrate attempts to introduce new leadership.

Young and small organization. The younger the organization, the less entrenched its culture will be. Similarly, it's easier for management to communicate its new values when the organization is small. This again helps explain the difficulty that multibillion-dollar corporations have in changing their cultures.

Weak culture. The more widely held a culture is and the higher the agreement among members on its values, the more difficult it will be to change. Conversely, weak cultures are more amenable to change than strong ones.

If conditions support cultural change, you should consider the following suggestions:

1. Have top management people become positive role models, setting the tone through their behavior.
2. Create new stories, symbols, and rituals to replace those currently in vogue.
3. Select, promote, and support employees who espouse the new values that are sought.
4. Redesign socialization processes to align with the new values.
5. Change the reward system to encourage acceptance of a new set of values.
6. Replace unwritten norms with formal rules and regulations that are tightly enforced.
7. Shake up current subcultures through transfers, job rotation, and/or terminations.
8. Work to get peer group consensus through utilization of employee participation and creation of a climate with a high level of trust.

Implementing most or all of these suggestions will not result in an immediate or dramatic shift in the organization's culture. In the final analysis, cultural change is a lengthy process—measured in years rather than months. But if the question is, "Can culture be changed?" the answer is "Yes!"

*B. Dumaine, "Times Are Good? Create a Crisis," *Fortune* (June 28, 1993), pp. 123–30.

Learning About Yourself Exercise

What Kind of Organizational Culture Fits You Best?

For each of the following statements, circle the level of agreement or disagreement that you personally feel:

SA = Strongly Agree
A = Agree
U = Uncertain
D = Disagree
SD = Strongly disagree

1. I like being part of a team and having my performance assessed in terms of my contribution to the team. SA A U D SD
2. No person's needs should be compromised in order for a department to achieve its goals. SA A U D SD
3. I like the thrill and excitement from taking risks. SA A U D SD
4. If a person's job performance is inadequate, it's irrelevant how much effort he or she made. SA A U D SD
5. I like things to be stable and predictable. SA A U D SD
6. I prefer managers who provide detailed and rational explanations for their decisions. SA A U D SD
7. I like to work where there isn't a great deal of pressure and where people are essentially easygoing. SA A U D SD

Turn to page A-31 for scoring directions and key.

Working With Others Exercise

Rate Your Classroom Culture

Listed here are ten statements. Score each statement by indicating the degree to which you agree with it. If you strongly agree, give it a 5. If you strongly disagree, give it a 1.

1. My classmates are friendly and supportive. _____
2. My instructor is friendly and supportive. _____
3. My instructor encourages me to question and challenge him or her as well as other students. _____
4. My instructor clearly expresses his or her expectations to the class. _____
5. I think the grading system used by my instructor is based on clear standards of performance. _____

6. My instructor's behavior during examinations demonstrates his or her belief that students are honest and trustworthy. _____
7. My instructor provides regular and rapid feedback on my performance. _____
8. My instructor uses a strict bell curve to allocate grades. _____
9. My instructor is open to suggestions on how the course might be improved. _____
10. My instructor makes me want to learn. _____

Add up your score for all the statements except number eight. For number eight, reverse the score (strongly agree = 1; strongly disagree = 5) and add it to your total. Your score will fall between ten and fifty.

A high score (thirty-seven or above) describes an open, warm, human, trusting, and supportive culture. A low score (twenty-five or below) describes a closed, cold, task-oriented, autocratic, and tense culture.

Form groups of 5 to 7 members each. Compare your scores. How close do they align? Discuss and resolve discrepancies.

Ethical Dilemma Exercise

Cultural Factors and Unethical Behavior

An organization's culture socializes people. It subtly conveys to members that certain actions are acceptable, even though they are illegal. For instance, when executives at General Electric, Westinghouse, and other manufacturers of heavy electrical equipment illegally conspired to set prices in the early 1960s, the defendants invariably testified that they came new to their jobs, found price fixing to be an established way of life, and simply entered into it as they did into other aspects of their job. One GE manager noted that every one of his bosses had directed him to meet with the competition: "It had become so common and gone on for so many years that I think we lost sight of the fact that it was illegal."*

The strength of an organization's culture has an influence on the ethical behavior of its managers. A strong culture will exert more influence on managers than a weak one. If the culture is strong and supports high ethical standards, it should have a very powerful positive influence on a manager's ethical behavior. However, in a weak culture, managers are more likely to rely on subculture norms to guide their behavior. So work groups and departmental standards will more strongly influence ethical behavior in organizations that have weak overall cultures.

It is also generally acknowledged that the content of a culture effects ethical behavior. Assuming this is true, what would a culture look like that would shape high ethical standards? What could top management do to strengthen that culture? Do you think it's possible for a manager with high ethical standards to uphold those standards in an organizational culture that tolerates, or even encourages, unethical practices?

*As described in P.C. Yeager, "Analyzing Corporate Offenses: Progress and Prospects," in W.C. Frederick and L.E. Preston (eds.), *Business Ethics: Research Issues and Empirical Studies* (Greenwich, CT: JAI Press, 1990), p. 174.

The Levi Strauss Culture

Levi Strauss is the world's largest apparel maker. In 1993 it earned $492 million on sales of $5.9 billion. But after record sales and earnings for five of the six years between 1988 and 1993, the company is having troubles. Its primary problem is that it has been too slow developing new products and getting them into retail outlets. Haggar Apparel and Farah Manufacturing, for instance, beat Levi to market with wrinkle-free slacks by more than a year. Some critics put part of the blame on Levi's unique culture.

Levi Strauss is embarked on a grand social experiment. It is trying to fulfill a vision created by its CEO, Robert D. Haas, the great-great-grandnephew of the company's founder. Haas believes Levi should be an ethical creature—able to make substantial profits and, at the same time, make the world a better place to live. This vision is conveyed in a set of corporate "aspirations" that have been written by top management. They include the following:

Openness. Management must demonstrate directness, openness, commitment to the success of others, and willingness to acknowledge its own contributions to problems.

Diversity. The company values work force diversity at all levels of the organization. Differing points of view will be sought; diversity will be valued and honestly rewarded, not surppressed.

Ethics. Management will provide clear expectations, practice the stated standards of ethical behavior, and enforce these standards throughout the company.

Empowerment. Management must push authority down in the organization to those closest to the products and customers.

Levi will not do business with suppliers who violate Levi's strict standards regarding work environment and ethics. One-third of an employee's evaluation is based on how well he or she achieves "aspirational" behavior. If high-performing employees ignore issues such as diversity and empowerment, they might not get a raise.

Some critics raise the question of whether Levi's emphasis on values is distracting. Haas, not surprisingly, thinks things would be worse if it weren't for the company's free exchange of ideas and commitment to diversity and empowerment.

Questions

1. Describe Levi's culture using the seven characteristics described in this chapter.
2. Levi's management believes their culture gives them a competitive advantage in the marketplace. Do you think this might be true?
3. Would you want to work for Levi Strauss? Would you want to own stock in the company? Explain your answers.

Source: Based on R. Mitchell, "Managing by Values," *Business Week* (August 1, 1994), pp. 46–52.

Microsoft's Workaholic Culture

In the old days it was so simple. Dad went to work and Mom stayed home and cared for the kids. As we know, those traditional roles are now the exception. Today Mom is likely to hold a full-time job outside the home and Dad is likely to play a major role in doing household chores and raising the children. But have organizational policies changed to reflect these new roles? In a number of companies, the answer seems to be "no." Ironically, today's organizational policies may better reflect the needs of working mothers than the needs of fathers who want to balance family and work responsibilities. There are risks for fathers who choose "the daddy track."

Take the case of Jeff Coulter. Jeff had a sales job with Microsoft, a company known for expecting long hours from its employees. This is illustrated by the story of a Microsoft programmer who ran into the company's CEO, Bill Gates, one evening when the former was leaving for home. It was 8 P.M. Gates asked the employee where he was going. "Home," he replied. "I've been here for twelve hours." "Oh," responded Gates, "only working half day?" Microsoft's culture embraces a relentless work ethic. "Complaining about how hard you work at Microsoft," says one manager, "is like complaining about the weather in Seattle."

Coulter put in 50-hour workweeks at Microsoft. But, in order to get his work completed and get home in time for dinner, he would come in early. His coworkers and boss, who came in after he did in the mornings, only noticed that Coulter was leaving at 5 or 5:30 each evening. Coulter was eventually fired. The company said it was for inadequate performance. Coulter thinks otherwise. He says Microsoft discriminated against him because of his family status.

The following excerpts from Coulter's boss were secretly recorded by him during conversations with her: "Microsoft hires everybody who's killing themselves, so everyone who's killing themselves is competing against other people who are killing themselves and it's like survival of the fittest. . . . You picked a company where it's a disadvantage to be married. It's a disadvantage to have any other priority other than work." Microsoft's position is that these comments were taken out of context. Coulter, meanwhile, continues to believe his family cost him his job.

Questions

1. Is it unrealistic for a company like Microsoft to expect employees to put their careers ahead of their families? Do you think organizations need to change in response to changing family roles and values?
2. Working long hours is a widely recognized part of Microsoft's culture. Do you think Microsoft needs to change its culture to meet the needs of family-oriented employees like Jeff Coulter, or do you think workers like Jeff need to change to fit into Microsoft's culture?
3. Is there a double standard where organizations provide flextime, child care, and other family-friendly options to reduce career–family conflict for women while men put their careers at risk if they want to spend time with their family?

Source: "Joys and Risks of the Daddy Track," *Nightline* (August 14, 1991).

Suggestions for Further Reading

DENISON, D.R., *Corporate Culture and Organizational Effectiveness* (New York: Wiley, 1990).

GORDON, G.G., "Industry Determinants of Organizational Culture," *Academy of Management Review* (April 1991), pp. 396–415.

GREY, R.J., and T.J.F. THONE, "Differences Between North American and European Corporate Cultures," *Canadian Business Review* (Autumn 1990), pp. 26–30.

HATCH, M.J., "The Dynamics of Organizational Culture," *Academy of Management Review* (October 1993), pp. 657–93.

HOFSTEDE, G., M.H. BOND, and C-L. LUK, "Individual Perceptions of Organizational Cultures: A Methodological Treatise on Levels of Analysis," *Organization Studies*, Vol. 14, No. 4 (1993), pp. 483–502.

KENNEDY, C., "Changing the Company Culture at Ciba-Geigy," *Long Range Planning* (February 1993), pp. 18–27.

MARCOULIDES, G.A., and R.H. HECK, "Organizational Culture and Performance: Proposing and Testing a Model," *Organization Science* (May 1993), pp. 209–25.

QUICK, J., "Crafting an Organizational Culture: Herb's Hand at Southwest Airlines," *Organizational Dynamics* (Winter 1993), pp. 45–56.

SCHNEIDER, B., S.K. GUNNARSON, and K. NILES-JOLLY, "Creating the Climate and Culture of Success," *Organizational Dynamics* (Summer 1994), pp. 17–29.

TRICE, H.M., and J.M. BEYER, *The Cultures of Work Organizations* (Englewood Cliffs, NJ: Prentice Hall, 1993).

Notes

[1] P. Nulty, "Making Money Like Clockwork," *Fortune* (September 20, 1993), pp. 80–82.

[2] P. Selznick, "Foundations of the Theory of Organizations," *American Sociological Review* (February 1948), pp. 25–35.

[3] L.G. Zucker, "Organizations as Institutions," in S.B. Bacharach (ed.), *Research in the Sociology of Organizations* (Greenwich, CT: JAI Press, 1983), pp. 1–47; and A.J. Richardson, "The Production of Institutional Behaviour: A Constructive Comment on the Use of Institutionalization Theory in Organizational Analysis," *Canadian Journal of Administrative Sciences* (December 1986), pp. 304–16.

[4] See, for example, H.S. Becker, "Culture: A Sociological View," *Yale Review* (Summer 1982), pp. 513–27; and E.H. Schein, *Organizational Culture and Leadership* (San Francisco: Jossey-Bass, 1985), p. 168.

[5] C.A. O'Reilly III, J. Chatman, and D.F. Caldwell, "People and Organizational Culture: A Profile Comparison Approach to Assessing Person-Organization Fit," *Academy of Management Journal* (September 1991), pp. 487–516; and J.A. Chatman and K.A. Jehn, "Assessing the Relationship Between Industry Characteristics and Organizational Culture: How Different Can You Be," *Academy of Management Journal* (June 1994), pp. 522–53.

[6] C. Hymowitz, "Which Culture Fits You?" *Wall Street Journal* (July 17, 1989), p. B1.

[7] The view that there will be consistency among perceptions of organizational culture has been called the "integration" perspective. For a review of this perspective and conflicting approaches, see D. Meyerson and J. Martin, "Cultural Change: An Integration of Three Different Views," *Journal of Management Studies* (November 1987), pp. 623–47; and P.J. Frost, L.F. Moore, M.R. Louis, C.C. Lundberg, and J. Martin (eds.), *Reframing Organizational Culture* (Newbury Park, CA: Sage, 1991).

[8] See J.M. Jermier, J.W. Slocum, Jr., L.W. Fry, and J. Gaines, "Organizational Subcultures in a Soft Bureaucracy: Resistance Behind the Myth and Facade of an Official Culture," *Organization Science* (May 1991), pp. 170–94; and S.A. Sackmann, "Culture and Subcultures: An Analysis of Organizational Knowledge," *Administrative Science Quarterly* (March 1992), pp. 140–61.

[9] See, for example, G.G. Gordon and N. DiTomaso, "Predicting Corporate Performance from Organizational Culture," *Journal of Managment Studies* (November 1992), pp. 793–98.

[10] Y. Wiener, "Forms of Value Systems: A Focus on Organizational Effectiveness and Cultural Change and Maintenance," *Academy of Management Review* (October 1988), p. 536.

[11] R.T. Mowday, L.W. Porter, and R.M. Steers, *Employee-Organization Linkages: The Psychology of Commitment, Absenteeism, and Turnover* (New York: Academic Press, 1982).

[12] See N.J. Adler, *International Dimensions of Organizational Behavior*, 2nd ed. (Boston: PWS-Kent, 1991), pp. 58–60.

[13] S.C. Schneider, "National vs. Corporate Culture: Implications for Human Resource Management," *Human Resource Management* (Summer 1988), p. 239.

[14] Ibid.

[15] T.E. Deal and A.A. Kennedy, "Culture: A New Look Through Old Lenses," *Journal of Applied Behavioral Science* (November 1983), p. 501.

[16] See, for instance, D. Miller, "What Happens After Success: The Perils of Excellence," *Journal of Management Studies* (May 1994), pp. 11–38.

[17] See C. Lindsay, "Paradoxes of Organizational Diversity: Living Within the Paradoxes," in L.R. Jauch and J.L. Wall (eds.), *Proceedings of the 50th Academy of Management Conference* (San Francisco, 1990), pp. 374–78; and T. Cox, Jr., *Cultural Diversity in Organizations: Theory, Research & Practice* (San Francisco: Berrett-Koehler, 1993), pp. 162–70.

[18] A.F. Buono and J.L. Bowditch, *The Human Side of Mergers and Acquisitions: Managing Collisions Between People, Cultures, and Organizations* (San Francisco: Jossey-Bass, 1989); and S. Cartwright and C.L. Cooper, "The Role of Culture Compatibility in Successful Organizational Marriages," *Academy of Management Executive* (May 1993), pp. 57–70.

[19] E.H. Schein, "The Role of the Founder in Creating Organizational Culture," *Organizational Dynamics* (Summer 1983), pp. 13–28.

[20] See, for example, J.R. Harrison and G.R. Carroll, "Keeping the Faith: A Model of Cultural Transmission in Formal Organizations," *Administrative Science Quarterly* (December 1991), pp. 552–82.

[21] See B. Schneider, "The People Make the Place," *Personnel Psychology* (Autumn 1987), pp. 437–53; J.A. Chatman, "Matching People and Organizations: Selection and Socialization in Public Accounting Firms," *Administrative Science Quarterly* (September 1991), pp. 459–84; and D.E. Bowen, G.E. Ledford, Jr., and B.R. Nathan, "Hiring for the Organization, Not the Job," *Academy of Management Executive* (November 1991), pp. 35–51.

[22] R. Pascale, "The Paradox of 'Corporate Culture': Reconciling Ourselves to Socialization," *California Management Review* (Winter 1985), pp. 26–27.

[23] "Who's Afraid of IBM?" *Business Week* (June 29, 1987), p. 72.

[24] Ibid.

[25] D.C. Hambrick and P.A. Mason, "Upper Echelons: The Organization as a Reflection of Its Top Managers," *Academy of Management Review* (April 1984), pp. 193–206; B.P. Niehoff, C.A. Enz, and R.A. Grover, "The Impact of Top-Management Actions on Employee Attitudes and Perceptions," *Group and Organization Studies* (September 1990), pp. 337–52; and H.M. Trice and J.M. Beyer, "Cultural Leadership in Organizations," *Organization Science* (May 1991), pp. 149–69.

[26] "Culture Shock at Xerox," *Business Week* (June 22, 1987), pp. 1, 6–10; and T. Vogel, "At Xerox, They're Shouting 'Once More into the Breach,'" *Business Week* (July 23, 1990), pp. 62–63.

[27] See, for instance, R.L. Falcione and C.E. Wilson, "Socialization Processes in Organizations," in G.M. Goldhar and G.A. Barnett (eds.), *Handbook of Organizational Communication* (Norwood, NJ: Ablex, 1988), pp. 151–70; N.J. Allen and J.P. Meyer, "Organizational Socialization Tactics: A Longitudinal Analysis of Links to Newcomers' Commitment and Role Orientation," *Academy of Management Journal* (December 1990), pp. 847–58; V.D. Miller and F.M. Jablin, "Information Seeking During Organizational Entry: Influences, Tactics, and a Model of the Process," *Academy of Management Review* (January 1991), pp. 92–120; and Chatman, "Matching People and Organizations: Selection and Socialization in Public Accounting Firms."

[28] J. Impoco, "Basic Training, Sanyo Style," *U.S. News & World Report* (July 13, 1992), pp. 46–48.

[29] J. Van Maanen and E.H. Schein, "Career Development," in J.R. Hackman and J.L. Suttle (eds.), *Improving Life at Work* (Santa Monica, CA: Goodyear, 1977), pp. 58–62.

[30] D.C. Feldman, "The Multiple Socialization of Organization Members," *Academy of Management Review* (April 1981), p. 310.

[31] Van Maanen and Schein, "Career Development," p. 59.

[32] D.M. Boje, "The Storytelling Organization: A Study of Story Performance in an Office-Supply Firm," *Administrative Science Quarterly* (March 1991), pp. 106–26; and C.H. Deutsch, "The Parables of Corporate Culture," *New York Times* (October 13, 1991), p. F25.

[33] A.M. Pettigrew, "On Studying Organizational Cultures," *Administrative Science Quarterly* (December 1979), p. 576.

[34] Ibid.

[35] Cited in J.M. Beyer and H.M. Trice, "How an Organization's Rites Reveal Its Culture," *Organizational Dynamics* (Spring 1987), p. 15.

[36] A. Rafaeli and M.G. Pratt, "Tailored Meanings: On the Meaning and Impact of Organizational Dress," *Academy of Management Review* (January 1993), pp. 32–55.

[37] "LOB, Anyone?" *Business Week* (October 4, 1993), p. 94.

[38] This section is based on C. Knowlton, "How Disney Keeps the Magic Going," *Fortune* (December 4, 1989), pp. 111–32; C.M. Solomon, "How Does Disney Do It?" *Personnel Journal* (December 1989), pp. 50–57; J. Van Maanen and G. Kunda, "'Real Feelings': Emotional Expression and Organizational Culture," in L.L. Cummings and B.M. Staw (eds.), *Research in Organizational Behavior*, Vol. 11 (Greenwich, CT: JAI Press, 1989), pp. 58–70; and J. Van Maanen, "The Smile Factory: Work at Disneyland," in P.J. Frost, L.F. Moore, M.R. Louis, C.C. Lundberg, and J. Martin (eds.), *Reframing Organizational Culture* (Newbury Park, CA: Sage, 1991), pp. 58–75.

[39] E.L. Andrews, "Out of Chaos," *Business Month* (December 1989), p. 33; and "The Forbes 500 Annual Directory," *Forbes* (April 25, 1994), p. 282.

[40] J. Marchese, "Time Warp," *Business Month* (September 1990), pp. 32–40; P.M. Reilly, "Time Warner Posts a Narrowed Loss of $62 Million for the Third Quarter," *Wall Street Journal* (October 22, 1991), p. A8; M. Lander, "Time and Warner May Now Become Time Warner," *Business Week* (March 9, 1992), pp. 31–32; and J.L. Roberts, "Time Warner Loss Shrank in Period; Cable Hurt Results," *Wall Street Journal* (October 18, 1994), p. B9.

[41] J.A. Chatman, "Matching People and Organizations: Selection and Socialization in Public Accounting Firms," pp. 459–84; and B.Z. Posner, "Person-Organization Values Congruence: No Support for Individual Differences as a Moderating Influence," *Human Relations* (April 1992), pp. 351–61.

[42] J.E. Sheridan, "Organizational Culture and Employee Retention," *Academy of Management Journal* (December 1992), pp. 1036–56.

PROGRESSIVE CASE
PART FOUR
THE ORGANIZATION SYSTEM

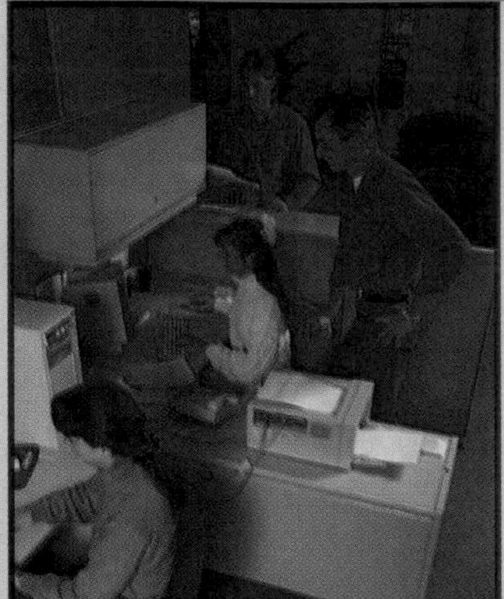

ROB PANCO: WORKING WITHIN THE ORGANIZATION SYSTEM

"The structure of AT&T and Aslett are as different as night and day," Rob Panco said. "AT&T was pure hierarchy. Everyone was very cognizant of your rank in the organization. It wasn't unusual for someone to say to me, for instance, 'You're only second level. Be careful about challenging fourth levels in a meeting.' Rank was everything. In fact, I remember traveling with a higher-level manager one time. When we picked up our rent-a-car at the airport, he said, 'You're the grunt. You drive.' At AT&T, they never let you forget where you are in the pecking order. In contrast, Aslett is very informal. We're a flat organization. People can come to me and not get their heads cut off. I don't pay much attention to rank. Then again, I'm in charge here. If I had been Bob Allen [CEO of AT&T], I might have thought AT&T was a lot less hierarchical. My perspective was from down below."

Most people are familiar with how large companies like AT&T go about the selection process. These companies historically hired young people for entry-level positions and let them grow up through the ranks. College grades and aptitude test scores were given a great deal of weight in the selection decision. During the past decade, AT&T has undergone major changes as a result of deregulation. Tens of thousands of people have been laid off. And, in contrast to past practices, new hires have often come from the outside to fill middle- and upper-level managerial slots because the necessary skills and perspectives weren't available inside AT&T. For instance, in 1990, the company hired Richard Bodman, president of Washington National Insurance, to become AT&T's senior vice president in charge of corporate strategy and development. In 1991, Alex Mandl, former chairman of Sea-Land Service, joined AT&T as its chief financial officer; and Jerre Stead, chairman of Square D Co., was brought in as president of AT&T's Business Communications Systems unit.

Aslett's small size and project form of structure allows Rob Panco to hire in a much more informal and direct way. About half of Aslett's new hires come from current employee referrals. Once hired, the referral typically becomes the new employee's sponsor. That is, the sponsor helps the new employee adjust to his or her job. Most other new hires come from the pool of freelancers the company uses. When an opening comes up, the best freelancers are usually looked at first as possible full-time employees. By hiring from this pool, Rob says he already has firsthand evidence of their performance capability so he doesn't have to do much screening. Their prior work becomes the test. But among referrals, Rob relies on work samples. For instance, candidates for jobs as designers and electronic page makers have to take a half-hour test where they can demonstrate their skills. Rob noted that all new hires from the freelancer pool also will have sponsors. They're usually the team leader from the freelancer's previous project. All new employees are told explicitly what is expected of them. They are then on probation for six months. At the end of six months, they are reviewed. Performance reviews after that are on their service anniversary.

The way AT&T and Aslett conduct performance evaluations also provides a good illustration of the differences between the two organizations. According to Rob, "Evaluations are a game at AT&T. They have great tools but they don't teach managers how to use them." The evaluation procedure is fairly standardized: Individuals are rated by their boss and ranked from 1 to n in their group. A modified bell curve is used. Ten percent are allocated to the highest category (outstanding performers), with 5 percent having to be labeled as low performers and placed on probation. Of course, there is considerable politicking and negotiating over rankings. Time in rank, for instance, carries a lot of weight."

"I'm a wimp. I don't like rating people," confides Rob. "I use a metric system of ratings because it's better than subjective appraisals, but I don't like ranking people." Rob then described the standardized form he uses, which breaks employee performance down into four categories: personal (individual) performance; teammanship; contribution to quality; and personal development. "The first three are about equal—they're worth about 30 percent each. Personal development is a tiebreaker." Within each category, Rob makes a list and rates people on (1) accomplishments made during the period and (2) areas for improvement. "I'll admit that I might be handling the process wrong. I don't ask employees for their input until the end of the review session. I should begin by asking people for a self-appraisal."

Aslett's small size creates very different problems for Rob than for managers at AT&T. "At a company the size of AT&T, no one person makes that much of a difference," Rob stated. "But in a small company like ours, each person is critical. If someone doesn't come to work, it can really affect the whole organization. This makes each person at Aslett close to the heart. My people here need to buy into the organization more than is necessary at an AT&T. That's why, for instance, I'm spending a lot of time working on a profit-based reward plan. Our people have to feel like partners. I'd like them to behave as if they were owners. That's the only way we're going to be able to grow at the rate we're striving for."

According to Rob, Aslett's rapid growth has created a great deal of stress among employees, especially at those critical times when projects are coming to completion. "People have to put in a lot of overtime. The hours are long. At the end of a project, it can get pretty crazy for members of a team. I don't assume stress is normal. I want to help my people relieve it. As it gets close to crunch time, I'll bring the team together and ask them to open up and tell me of any potential personal problems—like a child's christening they have to attend or a parent who has an upcoming operation. I want to know all the problems ahead of time so we can focus full attention on the project deadline. And when the deadline nears, I often bring in snacks, lunch, and similar things to break the tension and show I'm concerned. If someone becomes too stressed out, I'll send them home early with pay. Once a major project is over, I frequently tell people to take a couple of days off, again with pay. I want them to spend the time necessary to get their personal lives back in order."

Questions

1. Is it a law of structural design that large size (like AT&T) must result in a hierarchical-driven organization? Discuss.
2. Assess the pros and cons of filling job vacancies with referrals made by current employees.
3. Contrast the ways that structure constrains low-level employees at AT&T with operating personnel at Aslett.
4. Evaluate the effectiveness of the performance appraisal system Rob has put in place at Aslett. Does it help or hinder employee motivation? Discuss.
5. How can "sponsors" influence the attitudes and behavior of new hires?
6. What can Rob do to manage Aslett's culture?

PART FIVE
ORGANIZATIONAL DYNAMICS

CHAPTER

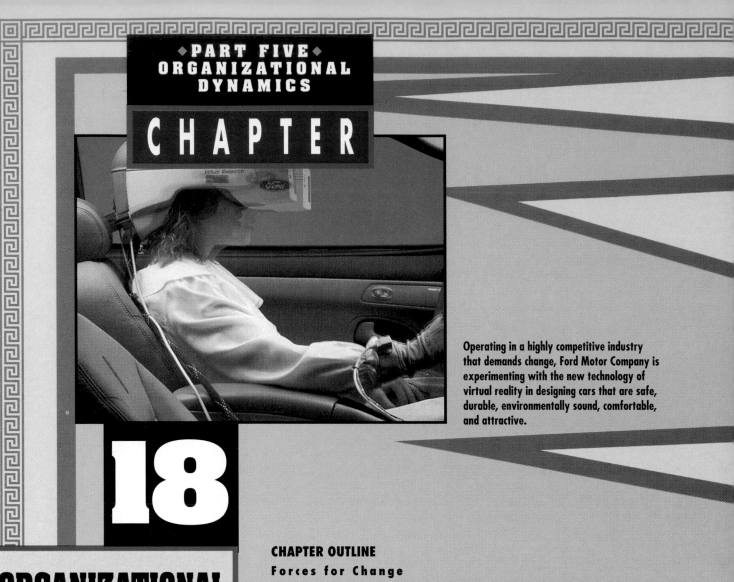

Operating in a highly competitive industry that demands change, Ford Motor Company is experimenting with the new technology of virtual reality in designing cars that are safe, durable, environmentally sound, comfortable, and attractive.

18

ORGANIZATIONAL CHANGE AND DEVELOPMENT

CHAPTER OUTLINE

- Forces for Change
- Managing Planned Change
- What Can Change Agents Change?
- Resistance to Change
- Approaches to Managing Organizational Change
- Key Change Issues for Management in the 1990s
- Organizational Development
- A Final Thought on Managing Change: It's Culture Bound!

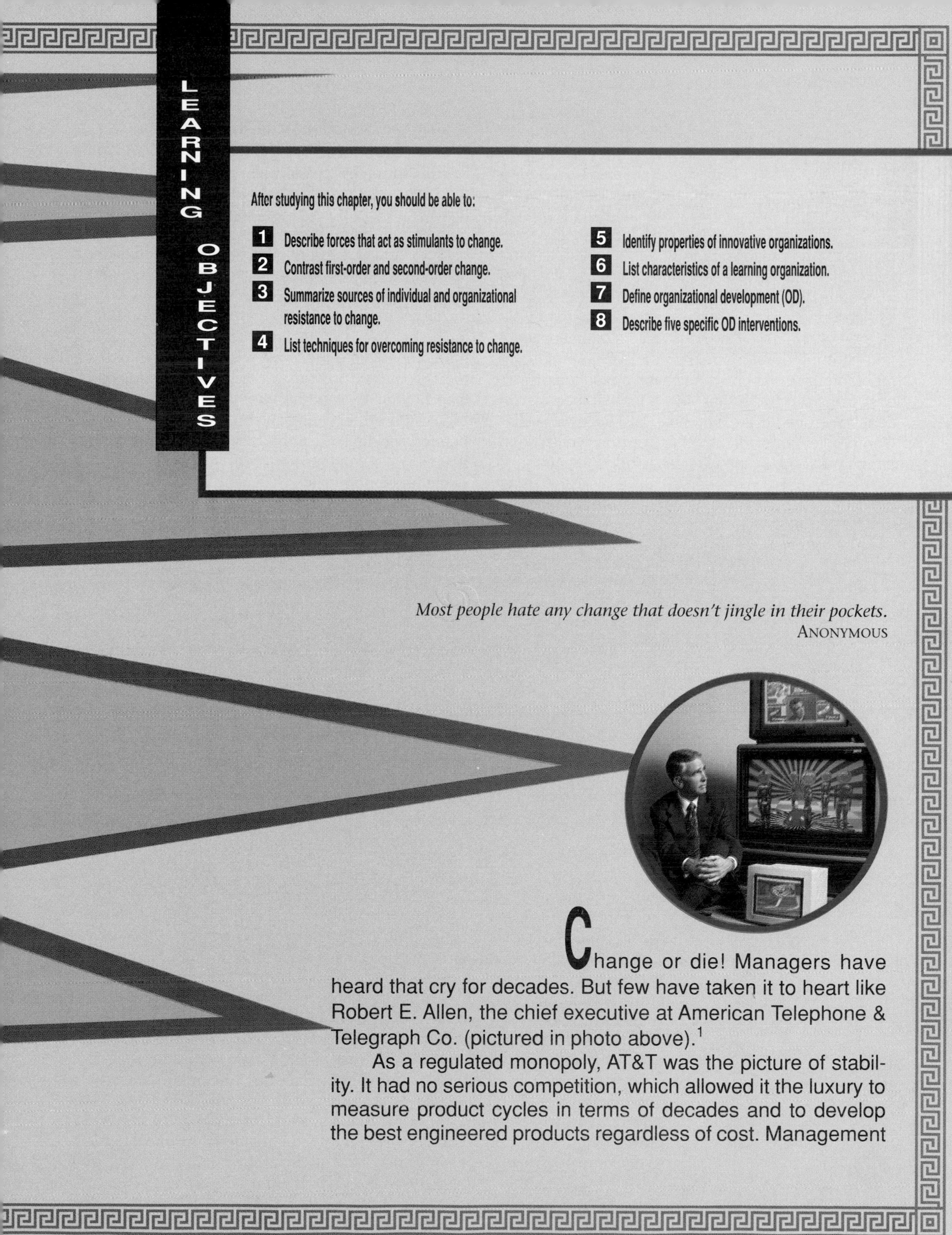

LEARNING OBJECTIVES

After studying this chapter, you should be able to:

1. Describe forces that act as stimulants to change.
2. Contrast first-order and second-order change.
3. Summarize sources of individual and organizational resistance to change.
4. List techniques for overcoming resistance to change.
5. Identify properties of innovative organizations.
6. List characteristics of a learning organization.
7. Define organizational development (OD).
8. Describe five specific OD interventions.

Most people hate any change that doesn't jingle in their pockets.
ANONYMOUS

Change or die! Managers have heard that cry for decades. But few have taken it to heart like Robert E. Allen, the chief executive at American Telephone & Telegraph Co. (pictured in photo above).[1]

As a regulated monopoly, AT&T was the picture of stability. It had no serious competition, which allowed it the luxury to measure product cycles in terms of decades and to develop the best engineered products regardless of cost. Management jobs were also relatively easy because thick manuals spelled out precise procedures for every eventuality. But in 1984 that all came to an end when the U.S. government broke up the company. No longer a monopoly, AT&T had to undergo massive changes if it was going to survive in a competitive marketplace. Allen has moved decisively to reinvent the old phone company and prepare it for the fast-moving, all-digital multimedia, anytime-anywhere communications market he wants to conquer.

Allen has created a strong vision to guide his change efforts. AT&T plans to build a global network and fill it full of every voice, data, video, entertainment, or any other communication option that develops. Consistent with that vision, for instance, he recently negotiated the purchase of McCaw Cellular Communications for $11.5 billion to give AT&T a strong presence in the wireless telephone market.

Allen has also overseen a massive restructuring of AT&T. The company has cut tens of thousands of jobs, and he's reorganized the company into approximately 20 independent business units. Allen has also set up and oversees a half-dozen cross-unit teams that meet regularly to address technical and marketing issues in emerging fields. Additionally, in contrast to the old AT&T, which filled almost all key management slots from inside the company, Allen has gone outside to bring in executives who held no loyalties to old practices and who were more marketing and entrepreneurially oriented.

Allen's remaking of AT&T is far from over. But so far he seems to be well on his way toward turning the company into the world's most successful high-technology corporation. For instance, those decade-long product cycles have been cut to only months, profits are up, and employees are increasingly understanding that AT&T's survival depends on product innovation and moving quickly to take advantage of market opportunities.

This chapter is about organizational change. We describe environmental forces that are requiring managers like Robert Allen to implement comprehensive change programs. We also consider why people and organizations often resist change and how this resistance can be overcome. We review various processes for managing organizational change. We discuss two major change themes for the 1990s: stimulating innovation and creating a learning organization. Finally, we present the concept of organizational development as a systemwide approach to change.

Forces for Change

More and more organizations today face a dynamic and changing environment that, in turn, requires these organizations to adapt. Table 18-1 summarizes six specific forces that are acting as stimulants for change.

In a number of places in this book, we've discussed the changing *nature of the work force.* For instance, almost every organization is having to adjust to a multicultural environment. Human resource policies and practices have to change in order to attract and keep this more diverse work force. And many companies are having to spend large amounts of money on training to upgrade reading, math, computer, and other skills of employees.

As we noted in Chapter 15, *technology* is changing jobs and organizations. The substitution of computer control for direct supervision, for instance, is resulting in wider spans of control for managers and flatter organizations. Sophisticated information technology is also making organizations more responsive. Companies like AT&T, Motorola, General Electric, and Chrysler can now

Table 18-1 Forces for Change

Force	Examples
Nature of the work force	• More cultural diversity • Increase in professionals • Many new entrants with inadequate skills
Technology	• More computers and automation • TQM programs • Reengineering programs
Economic shocks	• Security market crashes • Interest rate fluctuations • Foreign currency fluctuations
Competition	• Global competitors • Mergers and consolidations • Growth of specialty retailers
Social trends	• Increase in college attendance • Delayed marriages by young people • Increase in divorce rate
World politics	• Collapse of Soviet Union • Iraq's invasion of Kuwait • Overthrow of Haitian dictator

develop, make, and distribute their products in a fraction of the time it took them a decade ago. And, as organizations have had to become more adaptable, so too have their employees. As we observed in our discussion of groups and organization design, many jobs are being reshaped. Individuals doing narrow, specialized, and routine jobs are being replaced by work teams whose members can perform multiple tasks and actively participate in team decisions.

We live in an "age of discontinuity." In the 1950s and 1960s, the past was a fairly good prologue to the future. Tomorrow was essentially an extended trend line from yesterday. That's no longer true. Beginning in the early 1970s, with the overnight quadrupling of world oil prices, *economic shocks* have continued to impose changes on organizations. In recent years, for instance, the U.S. dollar has declined sharply against Japanese and German currencies. And as U.S. interest rates rose rapidly in 1994, the price of bonds collapsed. While these economic shocks affect some industries and firms harder than others, they can be critical when they hit. As a case in point, many mortgage brokerage firms had to lay off large numbers of employees in 1994 because as interest rates rose the market for new home loans and refinancings dried up.

Competition is changing. The global economy means competitors are as likely to come from across the ocean as from across town. Heightened competition also means established organizations need to defend themselves against both traditional competitors who develop new products and services and small entrepreneurial firms with innovative offerings. Successful organizations will be the ones that can change in response to the competition. They'll be fast on their feet, capable of developing new products rapidly and getting them to market quickly. They'll rely on short production runs, short product cycles, and an ongoing stream of new products. In other words, they'll be flexible. They will require an equally flexible and responsive work force that can adapt to rapidly and even radically changing conditions.

Take a look at *social trends* during the 1970s and 1980s. They suggest changes for the 1990s that organizations have to adjust for. For instance, there has been a clear trend in marriage and divorce during the past two decades. Young people are delaying marriage, and half of all marriages are ending in divorce. One obvious result of this social trend is an increasing number of single households and demand for housing by singles. If you're in the house building business, this is an important factor in determining the size and design of homes. Similarly, the expansion of single households has increased demand for single-portion quantities of frozen meals, which is highly relevant to organizations like ConAgra's Healthy Choice division or Pillsbury's Green Giant.

In Chapter 2, we argued strongly for the importance of seeing OB in a global context. We then reinforced the argument in following chapters. While business schools have been preaching a global perspective since the early 1980s, no one—not even the strongest proponents of globalization—could have imagined how world *politics* would change in recent years. A few examples make the point: the fall of the Berlin Wall; the reunification of Germany; Iraq's invasion of Kuwait; and the breakup of the Soviet Union. Almost every major U.S. defense contractor, for instance, has had to rethink its business and make serious changes in response to the demise of the Soviet Union and a shrinking Pentagon budget. Since 1991, Hughes Aircraft has laid off more than 21,000 employees; Martin Lockheed has cut 15,000 workers; and McDonnell Douglas has eliminated more than 10,000 jobs.

Managing Planned Change

A group of employees who work in a small retail women's clothing store confronted the owner: "The air pollution in this store from cigarette smoking has gotten awful," said their spokeswoman. "We won't continue to work here if you allow smoking in the store. We want you to post no smoking signs on the entrance doors and not allow any employee to smoke on the floor. If people have to smoke, they can go into the mall." The owner listened thoughtfully to the group's ultimatum and agreed to their request. The next day the owner posted the no smoking signs and advised all of her employees of the new rule.

A major automobile manufacturer spent several billion dollars to install state-of-the-art robotics. One area that would receive the new equipment was quality control. Sophisticated computer-controlled equipment would be put in place to significantly improve the company's ability to find and correct defects. Because the new equipment would dramatically change the jobs of the people working in the quality control area, and since management anticipated considerable employee resistance to the new equipment, executives were developing a program to help people become familiar with the equipment and to deal with any anxieties they might be feeling.

change
Making things different.

planned change
Change activities that are intentional and goal-oriented.

Both of the previous scenarios are examples of **change**. That is, both were concerned with making things different. However, only the second scenario described a planned change. In this section, we want to clarify what we mean by planned change, describe its goals, contrast first-order and second-order change, and consider who is responsible for bringing about **planned change** in an organization.

Many changes in organizations are like the one that occurred in the retail clothing store—they just happen. Some organizations treat all change as an accidental occurrence. However, we're concerned with change activities that are proactive and purposeful. In this chapter, we address change as an intentional, goal-oriented activity.

What are the goals of planned change? Essentially there are two. First, it seeks to improve the ability of the organization to adapt to changes in its environment. Second, it seeks to change employee behavior.

If an organization is to survive, it must respond to changes in its environment. When competitors introduce new products or services, government agencies enact new laws, important sources of supply go out of business, or similar environmental changes take place, the organization needs to adapt. As you'll see in the rest of this chapter, efforts to stimulate innovation, empower employees, and introduce work teams are examples of planned-change activities directed at responding to changes in the environment.

Since an organization's success or failure is essentially due to the things its employees do or fail to do, planned change also is concerned with changing the behavior of individuals and groups within the organization. In this chapter, we review a number of techniques that organizations can use to get people to behave differently in the tasks they perform and in their interactions with others.

It also helps to think of planned change in terms of order of magnitude.[2] **First-order change** is linear and continuous. It implies no fundamental shifts in the assumptions that organizational members hold about the world or how the organization can improve its functioning. In contrast, **second-order change** is a multidimensional, multilevel, discontinuous, radical change involving reframing of assumptions about the organization and the world in which it operates. Mikio Kitano, director of all production engineering at Toyota, is introducing first-order change in his company.[3] He's pursuing slow, subtle, incremental changes in production processes to improve the efficiency of

first-order change
Linear and continuous.

second-order change
Change that is multidimensional, multilevel, discontinuous, and radical.

In 1993, Anheuser-Busch established a joint venture with Japan's Kirin Brewery to form Budweiser Japan Company, Ltd., which controls the marketing, sales, and distribution of Budweiser in Japan. The agreement didn't just happen. It was the result of a long-term planned change effort. Anheuser-Busch spent 12 years slowly laying the groundwork for expansion in Japan and other international beer markets. A-B's planned change efforts included developing a core of international executives and building relationships with management of leading brewers around the world. Shown here is a Japanese ceremony that was part of launching the joint venture, which A-B hopes will help it achieve its goal of making Budweiser a mainstream brand in Japan within 10 years.

Toyota's plants. In contrast, Boeing's top executives have recently committed themselves to radically reinventing their company.[4] Responding to a massive airline slump, aggressive competition from Airbus, and the threat of Japanese competitors, this second-order change process at Boeing includes slashing costs by up to 30 percent, reducing the time it takes to make a 737 from 13 months to 6 months, dramatically cutting inventories, putting the company's entire work force through a 4-day course in "competitiveness," and bringing customers and suppliers into the once secret process of designing new planes.

change agents
Persons who act as catalysts and assume the responsibility for managing change activities.

Who in organizations is responsible for managing change activities? The answer is **change agents**. Change agents can be managers or nonmanagers, employees of the organization or outside consultants.

Typically we look to senior executives as agents of change. Bob Allen has been a primary change agent at AT&T. Mikio Kitano is one at Toyota. The primary change agents at Boeing are Frank Shrontz and Philip Condit, the company's chairman and president, respectively.

For major change efforts, top managers are increasingly turning to temporary outside consultants with specialized knowledge in the theory and methods of change. Consultant change agents can offer a more objective perspective than insiders can. However, they are disadvantaged in that they often have an inadequate understanding of the organization's history, culture, operating procedures, and personnel. Outside consultants are also more willing to initiate second-order changes—which can be a benefit or a disadvantage—because they don't have to live with the repercussions. In contrast, internal staff specialists or managers, especially those who've spent many years with the organization, are often more cautious because they fear offending long-term friends and associates.

What Can Change Agents Change?

What can a change agent change? The options essentially fall into four categories: structure, technology, physical setting, and people[5] (see Figure 18–1). Changing *structure* involves making an alteration in authority relations, coordination mechanisms, job redesign, or similar structural variables. Changing *technology* encompasses modifications in the way work is processed and in the methods and equipment used. Changing the *physical setting* covers altering the space and layout arrangements in the workplace. Changing *people* refers to changes in employee attitudes, skills, expectations, perceptions, and/or behavior.

Changing Structure

In Chapter 14 we discussed structural issues such as work specialization, span of control, and various organizational designs. But organizational structures are not set in concrete. Changing conditions demand structural changes. As a result, the change agent might need to modify the organization's structure.

An organization's structure is defined as how tasks are formally divided, grouped, and coordinated. Change agents can alter one or more of the key elements in an organization's design. For instance, departmental responsibilities can be combined, vertical layers removed, and spans of control widened to make the organization flatter and less bureaucratic. More rules and procedures can be implemented to increase standardization. An increase in decentralization can be made to speed up the decision-making process.

Figure 18-1
Change Options

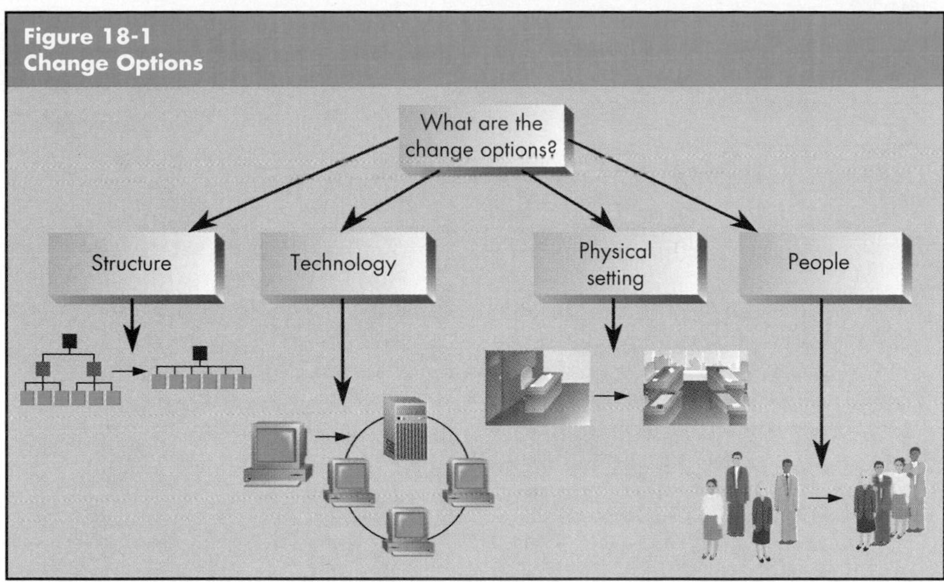

Change agents can also introduce major modifications in the actual structural design. This might include a shift from a simple structure to a team-based structure or the creation of a matrix design. Change agents might consider redesigning jobs or work schedules. Job descriptions can be redefined, jobs enriched, or flexible work hours introduced. Still another option is to modify the organization's compensation system. Motivation could be increased by, for example, introducing performance bonuses or profit sharing.

Changing Technology

Most of the early studies in management and organizational behavior dealt with efforts aimed at technological change. At the turn of the century, for example, scientific management sought to implement changes based on time-and-motion studies that would increase production efficiency. Today, major technological changes usually involve the introduction of new equipment, tools, or methods; automation; or computerization.

Competitive factors or innovations within an industry often require change agents to introduce new equipment, tools, or operating methods. For example, many aluminum companies have significantly modernized their plants in recent years to compete more effectively. More efficient handling equipment, furnaces, and presses have been installed to reduce the cost of manufacturing a ton of aluminum.

Automation is a technological change that replaces people with machines. It began in the Industrial Revolution and continues as a change option today. Examples of automation are the introduction of automatic mail sorters by the U.S. Postal Service and robots on automobile assembly lines.

As we noted in previous chapters, the most visible technological change in recent years has been expanding computerization. Many organizations now have sophisticated management information systems. Large supermarkets have converted their cash registers into input terminals and linked them to computers to provide instant inventory data. The office of 1995 is dramatically different from its counterpart of 1975, predominantly because of computerization. This is typified by desktop microcomputers that can run hundreds of business

◆◆◆◆ OB in the News ◆◆◆◆

Implementing Major Changes at Geon, Inc.

Until April 1993 Geon, a division of B.F. Goodrich Co., manufactured polyvinyl chloride (PVC). It was a money-losing operation—the division lost $135 million on sales of $1.2 billion in 1991—so Goodrich sold off Geon to the public.

William Patient was appointed to the top job at the new independent Geon. His task: Turn the company around. In his first 12 months as head of Geon, Patient implemented a radical change program. The results he's achieved have been nothing less than sensational.

Patient concluded that Goodrich had made a strategic mistake in trying to make Geon a specialty chemical maker. He saw Geon as the high-cost producer of a commodity product. It was spending a lot of money on research and development when it should have been concentrating on being a commodity producer and paring costs to the bone.

The change program that Patient introduced at Geon was comprehensive. He cut the work force by more than a third and instituted incentive profit sharing and stock award plans for those who survived. He carved $27 million out of staff functions such as human resources and purchasing and began using outside suppliers for many functions Geon had previously done internally. Patient eliminated private offices for most of Geon's plant managers in order to get managers closer to the workers. He closed 3 of the company's 8 plants, reducing PVC production capacity by 25 percent. And he reorganized the remaining plants, giving employees greater autonomy. The result: His 5 plants are now producing more than the original 8. Patient additionally reworked his product line, eliminating slow-selling products and significantly reducing the number of raw materials used in production.

In its first 12 months as an independent company, ending in April 1994, Geon posted profits of $31.8 million on sales of $1 billion. This compared to the previous year's loss of $27 million on sales of $906 million. Thus, on a sales gain of less than $100 million, Patient's change program produced a $58 million swing in profit.

Based on D. Machan, "Starting Over," *Forbes* (July 4, 1994), pp. 53–56.

Geon's inaugural annual report featured employees who contributed to the company's successful first year. The caption read "Here are some of the people of Geon, who through their teamwork, dedication, leadership, and hard work, are bringing this company to new levels of accomplishment."

software packages and network systems that allow these computers to communicate with one another.

Changing the Physical Setting

The layout of work space should not be a random activity. Typically, management thoughtfully considers work demands, formal interaction requirements, and social needs when making decisions about space configurations, interior design, equipment placement, and the like.

For example, by eliminating walls and partitions and opening up an office design, it becomes easier for employees to communicate with each other. Similarly, management can change the quantity and types of lights, the level of heat or cold, the levels and types of noise, and the cleanliness of the work area, as well as interior design dimensions like furniture, decorations, and color schemes.

The evidence indicates that change in the physical setting, in and of itself, doesn't have a substantial impact on organizational or individual performance.[6] But it can make certain employee behaviors easier or harder to perform. In this way, employee and organizational performance may be enhanced or reduced.[7]

Changing People

The final area in which change agents operate is in helping individuals and groups within the organization to work more effectively together. This category typically involves changing the attitudes and behaviors of organizational members through processes of communication, decision making, and problem solving. As you'll see near the end of this chapter, the concept of *organizational development* has come to encompass an array of interventions that are designed to change people and the nature and quality of their work relationships. We review these people-changing interventions in our discussion of organizational development.

Resistance to Change

One of the most well-documented findings from studies of individual and organizational behavior is that organizations and their members resist change. In a sense, this is positive. It provides a degree of stability and predictability to behavior. If there weren't some resistance, organizational behavior would take on characteristics of chaotic randomness. Resistance to change can also be a source of functional conflict. For example, resistance to a reorganization plan or a change in a product line can stimulate a healthy debate over the merits of the idea and result in a better decision. But there is a definite downside to resistance to change. It hinders adaptation and progress.

> ◆One of the most well-documented findings from studies of individual and organizational behavior is that organizations and their members resist change.

Resistance to change doesn't necessarily surface in standardized ways. Resistance can be overt, implicit, immediate, or deferred. It is easiest for management to deal with resistance when it is overt and immediate. For instance, a change is proposed and employees quickly respond by voicing complaints, engaging in a work slowdown, threatening to go on strike, or the like. The greater challenge is managing resistance that is implicit or deferred. Implicit resistance efforts are more subtle—loss of loyalty to the organization, loss of motivation to work, increased errors or mistakes, increased absenteeism due to "sickness"—and hence more difficult to recognize. Similarly, deferred actions cloud the link between the source of the resistance and the reaction to it. A change may produce what appears to be only a minimal reaction at the time it is initiated, but then resistance surfaces weeks, months, or even years later. Or a single change that in and of itself might have little impact becomes the straw that breaks the camel's back. Reactions to change can build up and then explode in some response that seems totally out of proportion to the change action it follows. The resistance, of course, has merely been deferred and stockpiled. What surfaces is a response to an accumulation of previous changes.

Let's look at the sources of resistance. For analytical purposes, we've categorized them by individual and organizational sources. In the real world, the sources often overlap.

Individual Resistance

Individual sources of resistance to change reside in basic human characteristics such as perceptions, personalities, and needs. The following summarizes five reasons why individuals may resist change (see Figure 18-2).

Figure 18-2
Sources of Individual Resistance to Change

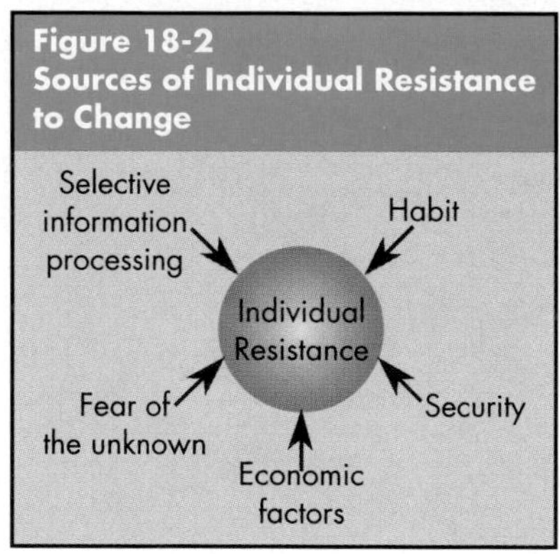

HABIT Every time you go out to eat, do you try a different restaurant? Probably not. If you're like most people, you find a couple of places you like and return to them on a somewhat regular basis.

As human beings, we're creatures of habit. Life is complex enough; we don't need to consider the full range of options for the hundreds of decisions we have to make every day. To cope with this complexity, we all rely on habits or programmed responses. But when confronted with change, this tendency to respond in our accustomed ways becomes a source of resistance. So when your department is moved to a new office building across town, it means you're likely to have to change many habits: waking up ten minutes earlier, taking a new set of streets to work, finding a new parking place, adjusting to the new office layout, developing a new lunchtime routine, and so on.

SECURITY People with a high need for security are likely to resist change because it threatens their feeling of safety. When Sears announces it's laying off 50,000 people or Ford introduces new robotic equipment, many employees at these firms may fear their jobs are in jeopardy.

ECONOMIC FACTORS Another source of individual resistance is concern that changes will lower one's income. Changes in job tasks or established work routines also can arouse economic fears if people are concerned they won't be able to perform the new tasks or routines to their previous standards, especially when pay is closely tied to productivity.

FEAR OF THE UNKNOWN Changes substitute ambiguity and uncertainty for the known. Regardless of how much you may dislike attending college, at least you know what is expected of you. But when you leave college and venture out into the world of full-time employment, regardless of how much you want to get out of college, you have to trade the known for the unknown.

Employees in organizations hold the same dislike for uncertainty. If, for example, the introduction of TQM means production workers will have to learn statistical process control techniques, some may fear they'll be unable to do so. They may, therefore, develop a negative attitude toward TQM or behave dysfunctionally if required to use statistical techniques.

SELECTIVE INFORMATION PROCESSING As we learned in Chapter 4, individuals shape their world through their perceptions. Once they have created this world, it resists change. So individuals are guilty of selectively processing information in order to keep their perceptions intact. They hear what they want to hear. They ignore information that challenges the world they've created. To return to the production workers who are faced with the introduction of TQM, they may ignore the arguments their bosses make in explaining why a knowledge of statistics is necessary or the potential benefits the change will provide them.

Organizational Resistance

Organizations, by their very nature, are conservative.[8] They actively resist change. You don't have to look far to see evidence of this phenomenon. Government agencies want to continue doing what they have been doing for years, whether the need for their service changes or remains the same. Organized religions are deeply entrenched in their history. Attempts to change church doctrine require great persistence and patience. Educational institutions, which exist to open minds and challenge established doctrine, are themselves extremely resistant to change. Most school systems are using essentially the same teaching technologies today as they were 50 years ago. The majority of business firms, too, appear highly resistant to change.

Six major sources of organizational resistance have been identified.[9] They are shown in Figure 18-3.

Figure 18-3
Sources of Organizational Resistance to Change

STRUCTURAL INERTIA Organizations have built-in mechanisms to produce stability. For example, the selection process systematically selects certain people in and certain people out. Training and other socialization techniques reinforce specific role requirements and skills. Formalization provides job descriptions, rules, and procedures for employees to follow.

The people who are hired into an organization are chosen for fit; they are then shaped and directed to behave in certain ways. When an organization is confronted with change, this structural inertia acts as a counterbalance to sustain stability.

LIMITED FOCUS OF CHANGE Organizations are made up of a number of interdependent subsystems. You can't change one without affecting the others. For example, if management changes the technological processes without simultaneously modifying the organization's structure to match, the change in technology is not likely to be accepted. So limited changes in subsystems tend to get nullified by the larger system.

GROUP INERTIA Even if individuals want to change their behavior, group norms may act as a constraint. An individual union member, for instance, may be willing to accept changes in his job suggested by management. But if union norms dictate resisting any unilateral change made by management, he's likely to resist.

THREAT TO EXPERTISE Changes in organizational patterns may threaten the expertise of specialized groups. The introduction of decentralized personal computers, which allow managers to gain access to information directly from a company's mainframe, is an example of a change that was strongly resisted by many information systems departments in the early 1980s. Why? Because decentralized end-user computing was a threat to the specialized skills held by those in the centralized information systems departments.

THREAT TO ESTABLISHED POWER RELATIONSHIPS Any redistribution of decision-making authority can threaten long established power relationships within the organization. The introduction of participative decision making or self-managed work teams is the kind of change that is often seen as threatening by supervisors and middle managers.

THREAT TO ESTABLISHED RESOURCE ALLOCATIONS Those groups in the organization that control sizable resources often see change as a threat. They tend to be content with the way things are. Will the change, for instance, mean a reduction in their budgets or a cut in their staff size? Those that most benefit from the current allocation of resources often feel threatened by changes that may affect future allocations.

Overcoming Resistance to Change

Six tactics have been suggested for use by change agents in dealing with resistance to change.[10] Let's review them briefly.

EDUCATION AND COMMUNICATION Resistance can be reduced through communicating with employees to help them see the logic of a change. This tactic basically assumes the source of resistance lies in misinformation or poor communication: If employees receive the full facts and get any misunderstandings cleared up, resistance will subside. Communication can be achieved through one-on-one discussions, memos, group presentations, or reports. Does it work? It does, provided the source of resistance is inadequate communication and that management–employee relations are characterized by mutual trust and credibility. If these conditions don't exist, the change is unlikely to succeed.

> ◆It's difficult for individuals to resist a change decision in which they participated.

PARTICIPATION It's difficult for individuals to resist a change decision in which they participated. Prior to making a change, those opposed can be brought into the decision process. Assuming the participants have the expertise to make a meaningful contribution, their involvement can reduce resistance, obtain commitment, and increase the quality of the change decision. However, against these advantages are the negatives: potential for a poor solution and great time consumption.

FACILITATION AND SUPPORT Change agents can offer a range of supportive efforts to reduce resistance. When employees' fear and anxiety are high, employee counseling and therapy, new-skills training, or a short paid leave of absence may facilitate adjustment. The drawback of this tactic is that, as with the others, it is time consuming. Additionally, it's expensive, and its implementation offers no assurance of success.

NEGOTIATION Another way for the change agent to deal with potential resistance to change is to exchange something of value for a lessening of the resistance. For instance, if the resistance is centered in a few powerful individuals, a specific reward package can be negotiated that will meet their individual needs. Negotiation as a tactic may be necessary when resistance comes from a powerful source. Yet one cannot ignore its potentially high costs. Additionally, there is the risk that, once a change agent negotiates with one party to avoid resistance, he or she is open to the possibility of being blackmailed by other individuals in positions of power.

MANIPULATION AND COOPTATION Manipulation refers to covert influence attempts. Twisting and distorting facts to make them appear more attractive, withholding undesirable information, and creating false rumors to get employees to accept a change are all examples of manipulation. If corporate management threatens to close down a particular manufacturing plant if that plant's employees fail to accept an across-the-board pay cut, and if the threat is actually untrue, management is using manipulation. Cooptation, however, is a form of both manipulation and participation. It seeks to buy off the leaders of a resistance group by giving them a key role in the change decision. The leaders' advice is sought, not to seek a better decision, but to get their endorsement. Both manipulation and cooptation are relatively inexpensive and easy ways to gain the support of adversaries, but the tactics can backfire if the targets become aware they are being tricked or used. Once discovered, the change agent's credibility may drop to zero.

COERCION Last on the list of tactics is coercion, that is, the application of direct threats or force on the resisters. If the corporate management mentioned in the previous discussion really is determined to close a manufacturing plant if employees don't acquiesce to a pay cut, then coercion would be the label attached to its change tactic. Other examples of coercion are threats of transfer, loss of promotions, negative performance evaluations, and a poor letter of recommendation. The advantages and drawbacks of coercion are approximately the same as those mentioned for manipulation and cooptation.

The Politics of Change

No discussion of resistance to change would be complete without a brief mention of the politics of change. Because change invariably threatens the status quo, it inherently implies political activity.[11]

Internal change agents typically are individuals high in the organization who have a lot to lose from change. They have, in fact, risen to their positions of authority by developing skills and behavioral patterns that are favored by the organization. Change is a threat to those skills and patterns. What if they are no longer the ones the organization values? This creates the potential for others in the organization to gain power at their expense.

Politics suggests that the impetus for change is more likely to come from individuals who are new to the organization (and have less invested in the status quo) or from executives slightly removed from the main power structure. Those managers who have spent their entire careers with a single organization and eventually achieve a senior position in the hierarchy are often major impediments to change. Change, itself, is a very real threat to their status and position. Yet they may be expected to implement changes to demonstrate they're

From Concepts to Skills

Assessing the Climate for Change

Why do some change programs succeed and others fail? One major factor is change readiness.[12] Research by Symmetrix, a Massachusetts consulting firm, identified 17 key elements to successful change. The more affirmative answers you get to the following questions, the greater the likelihood that change efforts will succeed.

1. Is the sponsor of change high up enough to have power to effectively deal with resistance?
2. Is day-to-day leadership supportive of the change and committed to it?
3. Is there a strong sense of urgency from senior management about the need for change and is it shared by the rest of the organization?
4. Does management have a clear vision of how the future will look different from the present?
5. Are there objective measures in place to evaluate the change effort, and are reward systems explicitly designed to reinforce them?
6. Is the specific change effort consistent with other changes going on within the organization?
7. Are functional managers willing to sacrifice their personal self-interest for the good of the organization as a whole?
8. Does management pride itself on closely monitoring changes and actions taken by competitors?
9. Is the importance of the customer and a knowledge of customer needs well accepted by everyone in the work force?
10. Are managers and employees rewarded for taking risks, being innovative, and looking for new solutions?
11. Is the organization structure flexible?
12. Are communication channels open both downward and upward?
13. Is the organization's hierarchy relatively flat?
14. Has the organization successfully implemented major changes in the recent past?
15. Is employee satisfaction and trust in management high?
16. Is there a high degree of cross-boundary interactions and cooperation between units in the organization?
17. Are decisions made quickly, taking into account a wide variety of suggestions?

not merely caretakers. By acting as change agents, they can symbolically convey to various constituencies—stockholders, suppliers, employees, customers—that they are on top of problems and adapting to a dynamic environment. Of course, as you might guess, when forced to introduce change, these long-time power holders tend to implement first-order changes. Radical change is too threatening.

Power struggles within the organization will determine, to a large degree, the speed and quantity of change. You should expect that long-time career executives will be sources of resistance. This, incidentally, explains why boards of directors who recognize the imperative for the rapid introduction of second-order change in their organizations frequently turn to outside candidates for new leadership.[13]

Approaches to Managing Organizational Change

Now we turn to several popular approaches to managing change. Specifically, we discuss Lewin's classic three-step model of the change process and present the action research model.

Lewin's Three-Step Model

Kurt Lewin argued that successful change in organizations should follow three steps: **unfreezing** the status quo, *movement* to a new state, and **refreezing** the new change to make it permanent[14] (see Figure 18-4). You can see the value of this model in the following example when the management of a large oil company decided to reorganize its marketing function in the western United States.

unfreezing
Change efforts to overcome the pressures of both individual resistance and group conformity.

refreezing
Stabilizing a change intervention by balancing driving and restraining forces.

The oil company had three divisional offices in the West, located in Seattle, San Francisco, and Los Angeles. The decision was made to consolidate the divisions into a single regional office to be located in San Francisco. The reorganization meant transferring over 150 employees, eliminating some duplicate managerial positions, and instituting a new hierarchy of command. As you might guess, a move of this magnitude was difficult to keep secret. The rumor of its occurrence preceded the announcement by several months. The decision itself was made unilaterally. It came from the executive offices in New York. Those people affected had no say whatsoever in the choice. For those in Seattle or Los Angeles, who may have disliked the decision and its consequences—the problems inherent in transferring to another city, pulling youngsters out of school, making new friends, having new coworkers, undergoing the reassignment of responsibilities—their only recourse was to quit. In actuality, less than 10 percent did.

Figure 18-4
Lewin's Three-Step Change Model

The status quo can be considered to be an equilibrium state. To move from this equilibrium—to overcome the pressures of both individual resistance and group conformity—unfreezing is necessary. It can be achieved in one of three ways (see Figure 18-5). The **driving forces**, which direct behavior away from the status quo, can be increased. The **restraining forces**, which hinder movement from the existing equilibrium, can be decreased. A third alternative is to *combine the first two approaches*.

driving forces
Forces that direct behavior away from the status quo.

restraining forces
Forces that hinder movement away from the status quo.

The oil company's management could expect employee resistance to the consolidation. To deal with that resistance, management could use positive incentives to encourage employees to accept the change. For instance, increases in pay can be offered to those who accept the transfer. Very liberal moving expenses can be paid by the company. Management might offer low-cost mortgage funds to allow employees to buy new homes in San Francisco. Of course, management might also consider unfreezing acceptance of the status quo by removing restraining forces. Employees could be counseled individually. Each employee's concerns and apprehensions could be heard and specifically clarified. Assuming most of the fears are unjustified, the counselor could assure the employees there was nothing to fear and then demonstrate,

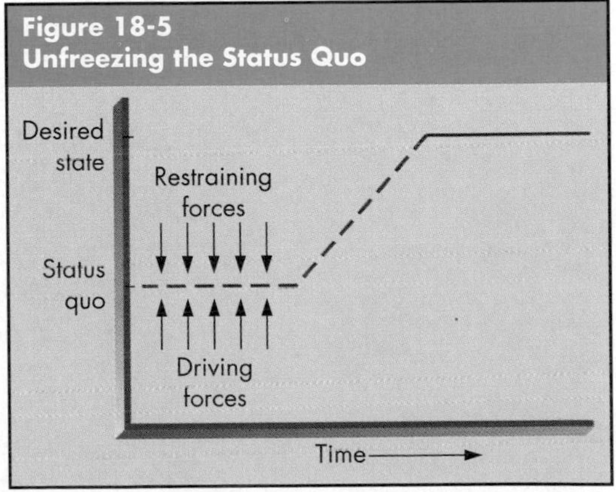

Figure 18-5
Unfreezing the Status Quo

through tangible evidence, that restraining forces are unwarranted. If resistance is extremely high, management may have to resort to both reducing resistance and increasing the attractiveness of the alternative if the unfreezing is to be successful.

Once the consolidation change has been implemented, if it is to be successful, the new situation needs to be refrozen so it can be sustained over time. Unless this last step is taken, there is a very high chance the change will be short lived and that employees will attempt to revert to the previous equilibrium state. The objective of refreezing, then, is to stabilize the new situation by balancing the driving and restraining forces.

How could the oil company's management refreeze their consolidation change? By systematically replacing temporary forces with permanent ones. For instance, they might impose a permanent upward adjustment of salaries or permanently remove time clocks to reinforce a climate of trust and confidence in employees. The formal rules and regulations governing behavior of those affected by the change should also be revised to reinforce the new situation. Over time, of course, the work group's own norms will evolve to sustain the new equilibrium. But until that point is reached, management will have to rely on more formal mechanisms.

Action Research

action research
A change process based on systematic collection of data and then selection of a change action based on what the analyzed data indicate.

Action research refers to a change process based on systematic collection of data and then selection of a change action based on what the analyzed data indicates.[15] Its importance lies in providing a scientific methodology for managing planned change.

The process of action research consists of five steps: diagnosis, analysis, feedback, action, and evaluation. You'll note that these steps closely parallel the scientific method.

DIAGNOSIS The change agent, often an outside consultant in action research, begins by gathering information about problems, concerns, and needed changes from members of the organization. This diagnosis is analogous to the physician's search to find what specifically ails a patient. In action research, the change agent asks questions, interviews employees, reviews records, and listens to the concerns of employees.

ANALYSIS The information gathered during the diagnostic stage is then analyzed. What problems do people key in on? What patterns do these problems seem to take? The change agent synthesizes this information into primary concerns, problem areas, and possible actions.

FEEDBACK Action research includes extensive involvement of the change targets. That is, the people who will be involved in any change program must be actively involved in determining what the problem is and participating in creating the solution. So the third step is sharing with employees what has been found from steps 1 and 2. The employees, with the help of the change agent, develop action plans for bringing about any needed change.

ACTION Now the "action" part of action research is set in motion. The employees and the change agent carry out the specific actions to correct the problems that have been identified.

EVALUATION Finally, consistent with the scientific underpinnings of action research, the change agent evaluates the effectiveness of the action plans. Using the initial data gathered as points of reference, any subsequent changes can be compared and evaluated.

Action research provides at least two specific benefits for an organization. First, it's problem focused. The change agent objectively looks for problems, and the type of problem determines the type of change action. While this may seem intuitively obvious, a lot of change activities aren't done this way. Rather, they're solution centered. The change agent has a favorite solution—for example, implementing flextime, teams, or a management by objectives program—and then seeks out problems his or her solution fits. Second, because action research so heavily involves employees in the process, resistance to change is reduced. In fact, once employees have actively participated in the feedback stage, the change process typically takes on a momentum of its own. The employees and groups that have been involved become an internal source of sustained pressure to bring about the change.

Key Change Issues for Management in the 1990s

Talk to managers. Read the popular business periodicals. You'll find that two issues have risen above the rest as current change topics: stimulating organizational *innovation* and creating a *learning organization.* In the following pages, we take a look at these topics.

Innovation

The relevant question is, How can an organization become more innovative? The standard toward which many organizations strive is that achieved by the 3M Co.[16] It has developed a reputation for being able to stimulate innovation

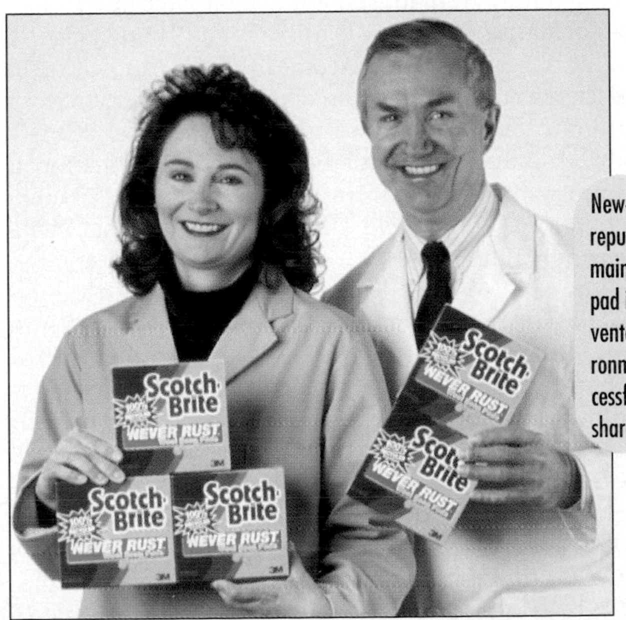

New-product successes like the Scotch-Brite Never Rust Wool Soap Pad fuel 3M's reputation as a paragon of innovation. Soap-filled steel wool scouring pads had remained virtually unchanged for 75 years until 3M introduced the new nonrusting pad in 1993. 3M scientists Connie Hubbard and Raymond Heyer (shown here) invented the pad, which is made from 100 percent recycled materials and uses environmentally safe phosphorous-free and biodegradable soap. One of the most successful product launches in 3M history, the pad achieved a 20 percent market share in its first year on the market.

over a long period of time. 3M has a stated objective that 25 percent of each division's profits are to come from products developed in the prior five years. In one recent year alone, 3M launched more than 200 new products.

What's the secret of 3M's success? What can other organizations do to clone 3M's track record for innovation? While there is no guaranteed formula, certain characteristics surface again and again when researchers study innovative organizations. We've grouped them into structural, cultural, and human resource categories. Our message to change agents is that they should consider introducing these characteristics into their organization if they want to create an innovative climate. Before we look at these characteristics, however, let's clarify what we mean by innovation.

innovation
A new idea applied to initiating or improving a product, process, or service.

DEFINITION We said change refers to making things different. Innovation is a more specialized kind of change. **Innovation** is a new idea applied to initiating or improving a product, process, or service.[17] So all innovations involve change, but not all changes necessarily involve new ideas or lead to significant improvements. Innovations in organizations can range from small incremental improvements, such as RJR Nabisco's extension of the Oreo product line to include double stuffs and chocolate-covered Oreos, up to radical breakthroughs, such as McGraw-Hill's recent creation of customized textbooks that utilize computer networks to link bookstore laser printers to McGraw's central database of text material. Keep in mind that while our examples are mostly of product innovations, the concept of innovation also encompasses new production process technologies, new structures or administrative systems, and new plans or programs pertaining to organizational members.

SOURCES OF INNOVATION *Structural variables* have been the most studied potential source of innovation.[18] A comprehensive review of the structure–innovation relationship leads to the following conclusions.[19] First, organic structures positively influence innovation. Because they're lower in vertical differentiation, formalization, and centralization, organic organizations facilitate the flexibility, adaptation, and cross-fertilization that make the adoption of innovations easier. Second, long tenure in management is associated with innovation. Managerial tenure apparently provides legitimacy and knowledge of how to accomplish tasks and obtain desired outcomes. Third, innovation is nurtured where there are slack resources. Having an abundance of resources allows an organization to afford to purchase innovations, bear the cost of instituting innovations, and absorb failures. Finally, interunit communication is high in innovative organizations.[20] These organizations are high users of committees, task forces, cross-functional teams, and other mechanisms that facilitate interaction across departmental lines.

Innovative organizations tend to have similar *cultures*. They encourage experimentation. They reward both successes and failures. They celebrate mistakes. Unfortunately, in too many organizations, people are rewarded for the absence of failures rather than for the presence of successes. Such cultures extinguish risk taking and innovation. People will suggest and try new ideas only where they feel such behaviors exact no penalties.

Within the *human resources* category, we find that innovative organizations actively promote the training and development of their members so they keep current, offer high job security so employees don't fear getting fired for making mistakes, and encourage individuals to become champions of change. Once a new idea is developed, champions of change actively and enthusiasti-

◆◆◆◆ OB in the News ◆◆◆◆

Rubbermaid Knows How to Innovate

For a company that makes some of the most mundane products you can imagine—things like dustpans, mops, spatulas, ice cube trays, dish strainers, and mailboxes—Rubbermaid is not likely to be a name that would come to your mind when you think of "America's most admired company." But in 1993, that was the case. A survey by *Fortune* magazine had Rubbermaid beating out far more well-known firms such as Coca-Cola and drug giant Merck.

The primary characteristic that has pushed Rubbermaid to the top of *Fortune*'s most admired list is the company's ability to innovate. Year in and year out, Rubbermaid has continued to develop new products and make small improvements to its lineup of more than 5,000 current products. In 1993, as an example, the company turned out new (not just improved) products at the unbelievable rate of one a day (yes, that's 365 a year)! Just as importantly, few of these failed in the marketplace. Nine out of 10 hit their commercial targets. Top management has recently set goals of entering a new product category every 12 to 18 months (most recently this includes hardware cabinets and garden sheds), achieving one-third of its sales from products introduced in the previous five years, and increasing non-U.S. sales from 18 percent to 25 percent of total revenues.

Gardening is the favorite hobby of Rubbermaid's CEO Wolfgang Schmitt. From his study of the structure of plants, Schmitt came up with the idea of organizing cross-functional teams to develop new products. Schmitt observed that each part of a plant replicates the structure of the entire plant. At Rubbermaid, he constructed a series of teams that replicate the management structure of the parent, like leaves on a plant.

How does Rubbermaid consistently chalk up its impressive innovation successes? It has created a culture that values and rewards risk taking and the constant search for ways to improve products. But management attributes most of its new product ideas to a structural device: cross-functional teams. Twenty of these teams, each made up of 5 to 7 members from marketing, manufacturing, R&D, finance, and other departments, focus on specific product lines such as bathroom accessories. Dick Gates, head of Rubbermaid business development, says, "If we weren't organized that way [around teams], who would be thinking about ice cube trays? Who would be thinking about johnny mops?"

Based on A. Farnham, "America's Most Admired Company," *Fortune* (February 7, 1994), pp. 50–54.

cally promote the idea, build support, overcome resistance, and ensure the innovation is implemented.[21] Recent research finds that champions have common personality characteristics: extremely high self-confidence, persistence, energy, and a tendency to risk taking. Champions also display characteristics associated with transformational leadership. They inspire and energize others with their vision of the potential of an innovation and through their strong personal conviction in their mission. They are also good at gaining the commitment of others to support their mission. Additionally, champions have jobs that provide considerable decision-making discretion. This autonomy helps them introduce and implement innovations in organizations.[22]

Given the status of 3M as a premier product innovator, we would expect it to have most or all of the properties we've identified. And it does. The company is so highly decentralized that it has many of the characteristics of small organic organizations. All of 3M's scientists and managers are challenged to "keep current." Idea champions are created and encouraged by allowing scientists and engineers to spend up to 15 percent of their time on projects of their own choosing. The company encourages its employees to take risks—and rewards the failures as well as the successes. And very importantly, 3M doesn't hire and fire with the business cycle. For instance, during the 1991–92 recession, while almost all major companies cut costs by firing employees, 3M initiated no layoffs.

Creating a Learning Organization

What TQM was to the 1980s and reengineering was to the early 1990s, the learning organization has become to the mid-1990s. It has developed a groundswell of interest from managers and organization theorists looking for new ways to successfully respond to a world of interdependence and change.[23] In this section, we describe what a learning organization looks like and methods for managing learning.

learning organization
An organization that has developed the continuous capacity to adapt and change.

single-loop learning
Errors are corrected using past routines and present policies.

double-loop learning
Errors are corrected by modifying the organization's objectives, policies, and standard routines.

WHAT'S A LEARNING ORGANIZATION? A **learning organization** is an organization that has developed the continuous capacity to adapt and change. Just as individuals learn, so too do organizations. "All organizations learn, whether they consciously choose to or not—it is a fundamental requirement for their sustained existence."[24] However, some organizations—such as Xerox, Corning, Federal Express, Ford, Clorox, General Electric, Motorola, Wal-Mart—just do it better than others.

Most organizations engage in what has been called **single-loop learning**.[25] When errors are detected, the correction process relies on past routines and present policies. In contrast, learning organizations use **double-loop learning**. When an error is detected, it's corrected in ways that involve the modification of the organization's objectives, policies, and standard routines. Like second-order change described at the beginning of this chapter, double-loop learning challenges deep-rooted assumptions and norms within an organization. In this way, it provides opportunities for radically different solutions to problems and dramatic jumps in improvement.

Table 18-2 summarizes the five basic characteristics of a learning organization. It's an organization where people put aside their old ways of thinking, learn to be open with each other, understand how their organization really works, form a plan or vision that everyone can agree on, and then work together to achieve that vision.[26]

Proponents of the learning organization envision it as a remedy for the three fundamental problems inherent in traditional organizations: fragmentation, competition, and reactiveness.[27] First, *fragmentation* based on specialization creates "walls" and "chimneys" that separate different functions into independent and often warring fiefdoms. Second, an overemphasis on *competition* often undermines collaboration. Members of the management

Table 18-2 Characteristics of a Learning Organization

1. There exists a shared vision that everyone agrees on.
2. People discard their old ways of thinking and the standard routines they use for solving problems or doing their jobs.
3. Members think of all organizational processes, activities, functions, and interactions with the environment as part of a system of interrelationships.
4. People openly communicate with each other (across vertical and horizontal boundaries) without fear of criticism or punishment.
5. People sublimate their personal self-interest and fragmented departmental interests to work together to achieve the organization's shared vision.

Source: Based on P.M. Senge, *The Fifth Discipline* (New York: Doubleday, 1990).

team compete with one another to show who is right, who knows more, or who is more persuasive. Divisions compete with one another when they ought to cooperate to share knowledge. Team project leaders compete to show who is the best manager. And third, *reactiveness* misdirects management's attention to problem solving rather than creation. The problem solver tries to make something go away; a creator tries to bring something new into being. An emphasis on reactiveness pushes out innovation and continuous improvement and, in its place, encourages people to run around "putting out fires."

It may help to better understand what a learning organization is if you think of it as an *ideal* model that builds on a number of *previous OB concepts*. No company has, or probably ever will, successfully achieved all the characteristics described in Table 18-2. As such, you should think of a learning organization as an ideal to strive toward rather than a realistic description of structured activity. Notice, too, how learning organizations draw on previous OB concepts such as TQM, organizational culture, the boundaryless organization, functional conflict, and transformational leadership. For instance, the learning organization adopts TQM's commitment to continuous improvement. Learning organizations are also characterized by a specific culture that values risk taking, openness, and growth. It seeks "boundarylessness" through breaking down barriers created by hierarchical levels and fragmented departmentation. A learning organization supports the importance of disagreements, constructive criticism, and other forms of functional conflict. And transformational leadership is needed in a learning organization to implement the shared vision.

MANAGING LEARNING How do you change an organization to make it into a continual learner? What can managers do to make their firms learning organizations?

- *Establish a strategy*. Management needs to make explicit its commitment to change, innovation, and continuous improvement.
- *Redesign the organization's structure*. The formal structure can be a serious impediment to learning. By flattening the structure, eliminating or combining departments, and increasing the use of cross-functional teams, interdependence is reinforced and boundaries between people are reduced.

The Clorox Company is an example of a learning organization. It has set a long-term average growth goal of 12 percent per year, a target designated as the Clorox Value Measure, and is asking all employees to work together to achieve the goal. Clorox is committed to the growth and development of all employees, from the office to the factory floor, so they can learn new behaviors that add value to their work. Part of the company's integrated program of people development and training is a game employees play that helps them learn how their decisions about the use of capital for plant, equipment, and inventories can help the company reach its growth target.

- *Reshape the organization's culture.* As we noted earlier, learning organizations are characterized by risk taking, openness, and growth. Management sets the tone for the organization's culture by both what it says (strategy) and what it does (behavior). Managers need to demonstrate by their actions that taking risks and admitting failures are desirable traits. That means rewarding people who take chances and make mistakes. And management needs to encourage functional conflict. "The key to unlocking real openness at work," says one expert on learning organizations, "is to teach people to give up having to be in agreement. We think agreement is so important. Who cares? You have to bring paradoxes, conflicts, and dilemmas out in the open, so collectively we can be more intelligent than we can be individually."[28]

Organizational Development

organizational development
A collection of planned-change interventions, built on humanistic-democratic values, that seek to improve organizational effectiveness and employee well-being.

No discussion of managing change would be complete without inclusion of organizational development. **Organizational development (OD)** is not an easily definable single concept. Rather, it's a term used to encompass a collection of planned-change interventions, built on humanistic democratic values, that seek to improve organizational effectiveness and employee well-being.[29]

OD Values

The OD paradigm values human and organizational growth, collaborative and participative processes, and a spirit of inquiry.[30] The change agent may be directive in OD; however, there is a strong emphasis on collaboration. Concepts such as power, authority, control, conflict, and coercion are held in relatively low esteem among OD change agents. The following briefly identifies the underlying values in most OD efforts:

1. *Respect for people.* Individuals are perceived as being responsible, conscientious, and caring. They should be treated with dignity and respect.
2. *Trust and support.* The effective and healthy organization is characterized by trust, authenticity, openness, and a supportive climate.
3. *Power equalization.* Effective organizations deemphasize hierarchical authority and control.

4. *Confrontation.* Problems shouldn't be swept under the rug. They should be openly confronted.
5. *Participation.* The more that people who will be affected by a change are involved in the decisions surrounding that change, the more they will be committed to implementing those decisions.

OD Interventions

What are some of the OD techniques or interventions for bringing about change? In the following pages, we present five interventions that change agents might consider using.

SENSITIVITY TRAINING It can go by a variety of names—laboratory training, **sensitivity training**, encounter groups, or T-groups (training groups)—but all refer to a method of changing behavior through unstructured group interaction. Members are brought together in a free and open environment in which participants discuss themselves and their interactive processes, loosely directed by a professional behavioral scientist. The group is process oriented, which means individuals learn through observing and participating rather than being told. The professional creates the opportunity for participants to express their ideas, beliefs, and attitudes. He or she does not accept—in fact, overtly rejects—any leadership role.

sensitivity training
Training groups that seek to change behavior through unstructured group interaction.

The objectives of the T-groups are to provide the subjects with increased awareness of their own behavior and how others perceive them, greater sensitivity to the behavior of others, and increased understanding of group processes. Specific results sought include increased ability to empathize with others, improved listening skills, greater openness, increased tolerance of individual differences, and improved conflict resolution skills.

If individuals lack awareness of how others perceive them, then the successful T-group can effect more realistic self-perceptions, greater group cohesiveness, and a reduction in dysfunctional interpersonal conflicts. Further, it will ideally result in a better integration between the individual and the organization.

SURVEY FEEDBACK One tool for assessing attitudes held by organizational members, identifying discrepancies among member perceptions, and solving these differences is the **survey feedback** approach.

survey feedback
The use of questionnaires to identify discrepancies among member perceptions; discussion follows and remedies are suggested.

Everyone in an organization can participate in survey feedback, but of key importance is the organizational family—the manager of any given unit and those employees who report directly to him or her. A questionnaire is usually completed by all members in the organization or unit. Organization members may be asked to suggest questions or may be interviewed to determine what issues are relevant. The questionnaire typically asks members for their perceptions and attitudes on a broad range of topics, including decision-making practices; communication effectiveness; coordination between units; and satisfaction with the organization, job, peers, and their immediate supervisor.

The data from this questionnaire are tabulated with data pertaining to an individual's specific "family" and to the entire organization and distributed to employees. These data then become the springboard for identifying problems and clarifying issues that may be creating difficulties for people. In some cases, the manager may be counseled by an external change agent about the meaning of the responses to the questionnaire and may even be given suggested guidelines for leading the organizational family in group discussion of the results. Particular attention is given to the importance of encouraging discussion and ensuring that discussions focus on issues and ideas and not on attacking individuals.

Finally, group discussion in the survey feedback approach should result in members identifying possible implications of the questionnaire's findings. Are people listening? Are new ideas being generated? Can decision making, interpersonal relations, or job assignments be improved? Answers to questions like these, it is hoped, will result in the group agreeing on commitments to various actions that will remedy the problems that are identified.

process consultation
Consultant gives a client insights into what is going on around the client, within the client, and between the client and other people; identifies processes that need improvement.

PROCESS CONSULTATION No organization operates perfectly. Managers often sense their unit's performance can be improved, but they are unable to identify what can be improved and how it can be improved. The purpose of **process consultation** is for an outside consultant to assist a client, usually a manager, "to perceive, understand, and act upon process events" with which he or she must deal.[31] These might include work flow, informal relationships among unit members, and formal communication channels.

Process consultation (PC) is similar to sensitivity training in its assumption that organizational effectiveness can be improved by dealing with interpersonal problems and in its emphasis on involvement. But PC is more task directed than sensitivity training.

Consultants in PC are there to "give the client 'insight' into what is going on around him, within him, and between him and other people."[32] They do not solve the organization's problems. Rather, the consultant is a guide or coach who advises on the process to help the client solve his or her own problems.

The consultant works with the client in *jointly* diagnosing what processes need improvement. The emphasis is on "jointly" because the client develops a skill at analyzing processes within his or her unit that can be continually called on long after the consultant is gone. Additionally, by having the client actively participate in both the diagnosis and the development of alternatives, there will be greater understanding of the process and the remedy and less resistance to the action plan chosen.

Importantly, the process consultant need not be an expert in solving the particular problem that is identified. The consultant's expertise lies in diagnosis and developing a helping relationship. If the specific problem uncovered requires technical knowledge outside the client and consultant's expertise, the consultant helps the client to locate such an expert and then instructs the client in how to get the most out of this expert resource.

team building
High interaction among team members to increase trust and openness.

TEAM BUILDING As we've noted in numerous places throughout this book, organizations are increasingly relying on teams to accomplish work tasks. **Team building** utilizes high interaction group activities to increase trust and openness among team members.[33]

Team building can be applied within groups or at the intergroup level where activities are interdependent. For our discussion, we emphasize the intragroup level and leave intergroup development to the next section. As a result, our interest concerns applications to organizational families (command groups), as well as to committees, project teams, self-managed teams, and task groups.

Not all group activity has interdependence of functions. To illustrate, consider a football team and a track team:

> Although members on both teams are concerned with the team's total output, they function differently. The football team's output depends synergistically on how well each player does his particular job in concert with his teammates. The quarterback's performance depends on the performance of his linemen and receivers, and ends on how well the quarterback throws the ball, and so on. On the other hand, a track team's performance is determined largely by the mere addition of the performances of the individual members.[34]

Team building is applicable to the case of interdependence, such as in football. The objective is to improve coordinative efforts of members that will result in increasing the team's performance.

The activities considered in team building typically include goal setting, development of interpersonal relations among team members, role analysis to clarify each member's role and responsibilities, and team process analysis. Of course, team building may emphasize or exclude certain activities depending on the purpose of the development effort and the specific problems with which the team is confronted. Basically, however, team building attempts to use high interaction among members to increase trust and openness.

It may be beneficial to begin by having members attempt to define the goals and priorities of the team. This will bring to the surface different perceptions of what the team's purpose may be. Following this, members can evaluate the team's performance—how effective are they in structuring priorities and achieving their goals? This should identify potential problem areas. This self-

Chrysler Corporation has used team building to reduce historical conflicts with unionized employees. This group of employees from Chrysler's Newark assembly plant in Delaware implemented the first modern operating agreement negotiated between Chrysler and the United Auto Workers. It allows more flexibility and communication in the workplace and helps labor and management function as a team.

critique discussion of means and ends can be done with members of the total team present or, where large size impinges on a free interchange of views, may initially take place in smaller groups followed up by the sharing of their findings with the total team.

Team building can also address itself to clarifying each member's role on the team. Each role can be identified and clarified. Previous ambiguities can be brought to the surface. For some individuals, it may offer one of the few opportunities they have had to think through thoroughly what their job is all about and what specific tasks they are expected to carry out if the team is to optimize its effectiveness.

Still another team-building activity can be similar to that performed by the process consultant; that is, to analyze key processes that go on within the team to identify the way work is performed and how these processes might be improved to make the team more effective.

INTERGROUP DEVELOPMENT A major area of concern in OD is the dysfunctional conflict that exists between groups. As a result, this has been a subject to which change efforts have been directed.

intergroup development
OD efforts to change the attitudes, stereotypes, and perceptions that groups have of each other.

Intergroup development seeks to change the attitudes, stereotypes, and perceptions that groups have of each other. For example, in one company, the engineers saw the accounting department as composed of shy and conservative types, and the human resources department as having a bunch of "ultra-liberals who are more concerned that some protected group of employees might get their feelings hurt than with the company making a profit." Such stereotypes can have an obvious negative impact on the coordinative efforts between the departments.

Although there are several approaches for improving intergroup relations,[35] a popular method emphasizes problem solving.[36] In this method, each group meets independently to develop lists of its perception of itself, the other group, and how it believes the other group perceives it. The groups then share their lists, after which similarities and differences are discussed. Differences are clearly articulated, and the groups look for the causes of the disparities.

Are the groups' goals at odds? Were perceptions distorted? On what basis were stereotypes formulated? Have some differences been caused by misunderstandings of intentions? Have words and concepts been defined differently by each group? Answers to questions like these clarify the exact nature of the conflict. Once the causes of the difficulty have been identified, the groups can move to the integration phase—working to develop solutions that will improve relations between the groups.

Subgroups, with members from each of the conflicting groups, can now be created for further diagnosis and to begin to formulate possible alternative actions that will improve relations.

A Final Thought on Managing Change: It's Culture Bound!

A number of the issues addressed in this chapter are culture bound. To illustrate, let's briefly look at four questions: (1) Do people believe change is possible? (2) If it is possible, how long will it take to bring it about? (3) Is resistance to change greater in some cultures than in others? (4) Does culture influence how change efforts will be implemented?

Do people believe change is possible? Remember that cultures vary in terms of beliefs about their ability to control their environment. In cultures where people believe they can dominate their environment, individuals will take a proactive view of change. This would describe the United States and Canada. In other countries, such as Iran and Saudi Arabia, people see themselves as subjugated to their environment and thus will tend to take a passive approach toward change.

If change is possible, how long will it take to bring it about? A culture's time orientation can help us answer this question. Societies that focus on the long term, such as Japan, will demonstrate considerable patience while waiting for positive outcomes from change efforts. In societies with a short-term focus, such as the United States and Canada, people expect quick improvements and will seek change programs that promise fast results.

Is resistance to change greater in some cultures than in others? Resistance to change will be influenced by a society's reliance on tradition. Italians, as an example, focus on the past; Americans emphasize the present. Italians, therefore, should generally be more resistant to change efforts than their American counterparts.

Does culture influence how change efforts will be implemented? Power distance can help with this issue. In high-power-distance cultures, such as the Philippines or Venezuela, change efforts will tend to be autocratically implemented by top management. In contrast, low-power-distance cultures value democratic methods. We'd predict, therefore, a greater use of participation in countries such as Denmark and Israel.

Summary and Implications for Managers

The need for change has been implied throughout this text. "A casual reflection on change should indicate that it encompasses almost all our concepts in the organizational behavior literature. Think about leadership, motivation, organizational environment, and roles. It is impossible to think about these and other concepts without inquiring about change."[37]

If environments were perfectly static, if employees' skills and abilities were always up to date and incapable of deteriorating, and if tomorrow was always exactly the same as today, organizational change would have little or no relevance to managers. But the real world is turbulent, requiring organizations and their members to undergo dynamic change if they are to perform at competitive levels.

Managers are the primary change agent players in most organizations. By the decisions they make and their role-modeling behaviors, they shape the organization's change culture. For instance, management decisions related to structural design, cultural factors, and human resource policies largely determine the level of innovation within the organization. Similarly, management decisions, policies, and practices determine the degree to which the organization learns and adapts to changing environmental factors.

For Review

1. What is meant by the phrase "we live in an age of discontinuity"?
2. What can change agents affect?
3. "Resistance to change is an irrational response." Do you agree or disagree? Explain.
4. Why is participation considered such an effective technique for lessening resistance to change?
5. Why does change so frequently become a political issue in organizations?
6. How does Lewin's three-step model of change deal with resistance to change?
7. Describe the action research process.
8. What changes can an organization that has a history of "following the leader" make to foster innovation?
9. "Learning organizations attack fragmentation, competitiveness, and reactiveness." Explain this statement.
10. What characteristics distinguish organizational development?

For Discussion

1. How have changes in the work force during the past 20 years affected organizational policies?
2. "Managing today is easier than at the turn of the century because the years of real change took place between the Civil War and World War I." Do you agree or disagree? Discuss.
3. Are all managers change agents? Discuss.
4. Discuss the link between learning theories discussed in Chapter 3 and the issue of organizational change.
5. Discuss the link between second-order change and double-loop learning.

Point

Change Is an Episodic Activity

The study of planned organizational change has, with very few exceptions, viewed it as an episodic activity. That is, it starts at some point, proceeds through a series of steps, and culminates in some outcome that those involved hope is an improvement over the starting point. When change is seen as an episodic activity, it has a beginning, a middle, and an end.

Both Lewin's three-step model and action research follow this perspective. In the former, change is seen as a break in the organization's equilibrium. The status quo has been disturbed, and change is necessary to establish a new equilibrium state. The objective of refreezing is to stabilize the new situation by balancing the driving and restraining forces. Action research begins with a diagnostic assessment in which problems are identified. These problems are then analyzed and shared with those who are affected, solutions are developed, and action plans are initiated. The process is brought to closure by an evaluation of the action plan's effectiveness. Even though supporters of action research recognize the cycle may need to go through numerous iterations, the process is still seen as a cycle with a beginning and an end.

Some experts have argued that organizational change should be thought of as balancing a system made up of five interacting variables within the organization: people, tasks, technology, structure, and strategy. A change in any one variable has repercussions on one or more of the others. Again, this perspective is episodic in that it treats organizational change as essentially an effort to sustain an equilibrium. A change in one variable begins a chain of events that, if properly managed, requires adjustments in the other variables to achieve a new state of equilibrium.

Another way to conceptualize the episodic way of looking at change is to think of managing change as analogous to captaining a ship. The organization is like a large ship traveling across the calm Mediterranean Sea to a specific port. The ship's captain has made this exact trip hundreds of times before with the same crew. Every once in a while, however, a storm will appear, and the crew has to respond. The captain will make the appropriate adjustments—that is, implement changes—and, having maneuvered through the storm, will return to calm waters. Managing an organization should therefore be seen as a journey with a beginning and an end, and implementing change as a response to a break in the status quo and needed only in occasional situations.

counterPoint

Change Is an Ongoing Activity

The episodic approach may be the dominant paradigm for handling planned organizational change, but it has become obsolete. It applies to a world of certainty and predictability. The episodic approach was developed in the 1950s and 1960s, and it reflects the environment of those times. It treats change as the occasional disturbance in an otherwise peaceful world. However, this paradigm has little resemblance to the 1990s' environment of constant and chaotic change.

If you want to understand what it's like to manage change in today's organizations, think of it as equivalent to permanent white-water rafting.* The organization is not a large ship, but more akin to a 40-foot raft. Rather than sailing a calm sea, this raft must traverse a raging river made up of an uninterrupted flow of permanent white-water rapids. To make things worse, the raft is manned by ten people who have never worked together or traveled the river before, much of the trip is in the dark, the river is dotted by unexpected turns and obstacles, the exact destination of the raft is not clear, and at irregular intervals the raft needs to pull to shore, where some new crew members are added and others leave. Change is a natural state and managing change is a continual process. That is, managers never get the luxury of escaping the white-water rapids.

To get a feeling for what managers are facing, think of what it would be like to attend a college that had the following structure: Courses vary in length. When you sign up for a course, however, you don't know how long it will last. It might go for 2 weeks or 30 weeks. Furthermore, the instructor can end a course any time he or she wants, with no prior warning. If that isn't frustrating enough, the length of the class changes each time it meets—sometimes it lasts 20 minutes, while other times it runs for 3 hours—and determination of when the next class meeting will take place is set by the instructor during the previous class. And one more thing: The exams are all unannounced, so you have to be ready for a test at any time.

A growing number of managers are coming to accept that their jobs are much like what a student would face in such a college. The stability and predictability of the episodic perspective don't exist. Nor are disruptions in the status quo only occasional, temporary, and followed by a return to an equilibrium state. Managers today face constant change, bordering on chaos. They are being forced to play a game they've never played before, governed by rules that are created as the game progresses. To manage in this dynamic arena, they are moving toward creating learning organizations.

*This perspective is based on P.B. Vaill, *Managing as a Performing Art: New Ideas for a World of Chaotic Change*. Copyright © 1989 by Jossey-Bass Publishers. Reprinted by permission.

Learning About Yourself Exercise

Managing-in-a-Turbulent-World Tolerance Test

Instructions

Listed here are some statements a 37-year-old manager made about his job at a large successful corporation. If your job had these characteristics, how would you react to them? After each statement are five letters, A to E. Circle the letter that best describes how you think you would react according to the following scale:

A *I would enjoy this very much: it's completely acceptable.*
B *This would be enjoyable and acceptable most of the time.*
C *I'd have no reaction to this feature one way or another, or it would be about equally enjoyable and unpleasant.*
D *This feature would be somewhat unpleasant for me.*
E *This feature would be very unpleasant for me.*

1. I regularly spend 30 to 40 percent of my time in meetings. A B C D E

2. A year and a half ago, my job did not exist, and I have been essentially inventing it as I go along. A B C D E

3. The responsibilities I either assume or am assigned consistently exceed the authority I have for discharging them. A B C D E
4. At any given moment in my job, I have on the average about a dozen phone calls to be returned. A B C D E
5. There seems to be very little relation in my job between the quality of my performance and my actual pay and fringe benefits. A B C D E
6. About two weeks a year of formal management training is needed in my job just to stay current. A B C D E
7. Because we have very effective equal employment opportunity in my company and because it is thoroughly multinational, my job consistently brings me into close working contact at a professional level with people of many races, ethnic groups, nationalities, and of both sexes. A B C D E

8. There is no objective way to measure my effectiveness. A B C D E
9. I report to three different bosses for different aspects of my job, and each has an equal say in my performance appraisal. A B C D E

10. On average, about a third of my time is spent dealing with unexpected emergencies that force all scheduled work to be postponed. A B C D E
11. When I have to have a meeting of the people who report to me, it takes my secretary most of a day to find a time when we are all available, and even then, I have yet to have a meeting where everyone is present for the entire meeting. A B C D E

12. The college degree I earned in preparation for this type of work is now obsolete, and I probably should go back for another degree. A B C D E

13. My job requires that I absorb 100 to 200 pages per week of technical materials. A B C D E

14. I am out of town overnight at least one night per week. A B C D E
15. My department is so interdependent with several other departments in the company that all distinctions about which departments are responsible for which tasks are quite arbitrary. A B C D E
16. I will probably get a promotion in about a year to a job in another division that has most of these same characteristics. A B C D E
17. During the period of my employment here, either the entire company or the division I worked in has been reorganized every year or so. A B C D E
18. While there are several possible promotions I can see ahead of me, I have no real career path in an objective sense. A B C D E
19. While there are several possible promotions I can see ahead of me, I think I have no realistic chance of getting to the top levels of the company. A B C D E
20. While I have many ideas about how to make things work better, I have no direct influence on either the business policies or the personnel policies that govern my division. A B C D E
21. My company has recently put in an "assessment center" where I and all other managers will be required to go through an extensive battery of psychological tests to assess our potential. A B C D E
22. My company is a defendant in an antitrust suit, and if the case comes to trial, I will probably have to testify about some decisions that were made a few years ago. A B C D E
23. Advanced computer and other electronic office technology is continually being introduced into my division, necessitating constant learning on my part. A B C D E
24. The computer terminal and screen I have in my office can be monitored in my bosses' offices without my knowledge. A B C D E

Turn to page A-31 for scoring directions and key.

Source: From P.B. Vaill, *Managing as a Performing Art: New Ideas for a World of Chaotic Change* (San Francisco: Jossey-Bass, 1989), pp. 8–9.

Working With Others Exercise

The Beacon Aircraft Co.

Objectives

1. To illustrate how forces for change and stability must be managed in organizational development programs.
2. To illustrate the effects of alternative change techniques on the relative strength of forces for change and forces for stability.

The Situation

The marketing division of the Beacon Aircraft Co. has gone through two reorganizations in the past two years. Initially, its structure changed from a functional to a matrix form. But the matrix structure did not satisfy some functional managers. They complained the structure confused the authority and responsibility relationships.

In reaction to these complaints, the marketing manager revised the structure back to the functional form. This new structure maintained market and project groups, which were managed by project managers with a few general staff personnel. But no functional specialists were assigned to these groups.

After the change, some problems began to surface. Project managers complained they could not obtain adequate assistance from functional staffs. It not only took more time to obtain necessary assistance, but it also created problems in establishing stable relationships with functional staff members. Since these problems affected their services to customers, project managers demanded a change in the organizational structure—probably again toward a matrix structure. Faced with these complaints and demands from project managers, the vice president is pondering another reorganization. He has requested an outside consultant to help him in the reorganization plan.

The Procedure

1. Divide yourselves into groups of five to seven and take the role of consultants.
2. Each group identifies the driving and resisting forces found in the firm. List these forces here.

The Driving Forces	The Resisting Forces
____________________	____________________
____________________	____________________
____________________	____________________
____________________	____________________
____________________	____________________
____________________	____________________

3. Each group develops a set of strategies for increasing the driving forces and another set for reducing the resisting forces.
4. Each group prepares a list of changes it wants to introduce.
5. The class reassembles and hears each group's recommendations.

Source: Adapted from K.H. Chung and L.C. Megginson, *Organizational Behavior* (New York: Harper & Row, 1981), pp. 498–99.

Ethical Dilemma Exercise

Ethical Issues in OD Interventions

OD interventions typically are based on humanistic democratic values. They rely heavily on processes such as participation, collaboration, and confrontation. OD interventions are viewed as effective to the degree to which they increase openness, trust, risk taking, autonomy, and respect for people, and how far they go to equalize power within the organization. The assumption by OD proponents is that these outcomes are desirable and lead to more effective organizational performance.

Some writers have noted, however, that when OD change agents use humanistic processes to achieve democratic outcomes, they are imposing their values on organizational participants.* For example, if employees in a given department have had trouble working with one another over a fairly long period of time, an OD change agent might recommend the department members get together in an informal session and openly discuss their perceptions of one another, the sources of their disagreements, and similar issues. But some people don't feel comfortable participating in a process that requires them to be open about their feelings and attitudes. OD interventions that demand openness reduce the privacy and freedom of such individuals. Even if participation is voluntary, the decision not to participate might carry negative connotations, result in lower performance appraisals, and have adverse career effects. Moreover, what if an employee does participate, is authentically open, reveals to the group some very personal fears and concerns, and then someone in the group uses this information vindictively against that employee at some later date? And doesn't even voluntary participation in an OD intervention imply control by the change agent over participants? What do *you* think?

*See, for example, G.A. Walter, "Organizational Development and Individual Rights," *Journal of Applied Behavioral Science* (November 1984), pp. 423–39.

Quantum Change at Alcoa

On a recent summer day in downtown Pittsburgh, CEO Paul O'Neill unveiled his plans for Aluminum Co. of America (Alcoa), the basic materials giant. What he presented was nothing short of a complete overhaul of a corporation that employs more than 63,000 people across 22 countries. He proposed a new structure that would focus on Alcoa customers and business units—"not Pittsburgh, not the vice presidents who service them, not the chairman—but business units." Pooled corporate resources would exist for the sole purpose of linking and supporting the company's 22 business units.

Corporate structure wasn't the only thing about to change. By way of introducing the company's new strategy, O'Neill challenged the popular notion of continuous improvement. That approach may work for companies that are market leaders, he asserted, but "it's a terrible idea if you are lagging the world-leadership benchmark. It is probably a disastrous idea if you are far behind the world standard."

In Alcoa's case, they seemed to be laggards. O'Neill argued that the company needed rapid quantum leaps in improvement, rather than slow and incremental changes. O'Neill's challenge to his people was this: Close the gap between current practices and world benchmarks by a minimum of 80 percent in two years.

"Waiting until outside events force change is at best reactive administration and, at worst, management cowardice," he told his team. Leadership has nothing to do with "change that is forced on an organization by performance that is so pitiful that shareholders have to clamor for change."

Questions

1. What do you think of O'Neill's approach to implementing change?
2. Is O'Neill suggesting that continuous improvement, a basic tenet of TQM, is mismatched for dynamic times?
3. Do you agree or disagree with O'Neill's perspective on leadership? Support your position.

Source: Based on T.E. Benson, "Paul O'Neill: True Innovation, True Values, True Leadership," *Industry Week* (April 19, 1993), pp. 25–28.

Defense Workers and Their Future

What happens to the millions of soldiers, scientists, and defense industry workers who have and will lose their jobs as the U.S. defense budget is slashed and the Cold War economy becomes history? Federal authorities suggest that these resources can be smoothly transferred to protecting the environment. This begs the question: Is it possible to develop a realistic conversion plan that reassigns many defense scientists to environment projects, encourages defense companies to build new products that don't pollute, and lets environmental researchers piggyback on work the military is already doing?

The federal government thinks it is possible. For instance, it suggests nuclear submarines can help global warming scientists measure ice thickness at the arctic ice cap; supercomputers previously used by the military could be redirected to help monitor weather and calculate if the earth's climate is changing; robots designed by defense scientists could be used to move toxic canisters; and workers who used to build fighter planes could build electric vehicles.

Questions

1. What problems would you expect managers at defense contractors like Martin Lockheed and McDonnell Douglas to have in converting to the environmental protection business?
2. How might a learning organization in the defense industry respond to a massive loss in its primary line of business?
3. "Employees of defense contractors are different from typical business employees because they've never had to operate in a true free-market climate. They never had to be efficient because, in the defense business, cost is no object." Do you agree or disagree with this statement? What, if any, implications does it have for managing human resources in defense firms?

Source: "New Career for Defense Workers: Protect the Environment," *World News Tonight* (March 3, 1993).

Suggestions for Further Reading

BENNETT, J.K., and M.J. O'BRIEN, "The Building Blocks of the Learning Organization," *Training* (June 1994), pp. 41–49.

BURKE, W.W., and G.H. LITWIN, "A Causal Model of Organizational Performance and Change," *Journal of Management* (September 1992), pp. 523–45.

FILIPCZAK, B., "Weathering Change: Enough Already!" *Training* (September 1994), pp. 23–29.

FORD, J.D., and L.W. FORD, "Logics of Identity, Contradiction, and Attraction in Change," *Academy of Management Review* (October 1994), pp. 756–85.

GOODSTEIN, L.D., and W.W. BURKE, "Creating Successful Organizational Change," *Organizational Dynamics* (Spring 1991), pp. 5–17.

KANTER, R.M., "Transcending Business Boundaries: 12,000 World Managers View Change," *Harvard Business Review* (May-June 1991), pp. 151–64.

MARSHAK, R.J., "Managing the Metaphors of Change," *Organizational Dynamics* (Summer 1993), pp. 44–56.

SCOTT, S.G., and R.A. BRUCE, "Determinants of Innovative Behavior: A Path Model of Individual Innovation in the Workplace," *Academy of Management Journal* (June 1994), pp. 580–607.

SLOCUM, J.W., JR., M. MCGILL, and D.T. LEI, "The New Learning Strategy: Anytime, Anything, Anywhere," *Organizational Dynamics* (Autumn 1994), pp. 33–47.

WOODMAN, R.W., and W.A. PASMORE (eds.), *Research in Organizational Change and Development*, Vol. 8 (Greenwich, CT: JAI Press, 1994).

Notes

1 G. Slutsker, "The Tortoise and the Hare," *Forbes* (February 1, 1993), pp. 66–69; and J.W. Verity, "How AT&T Thrives—as Other Giants Falter," *Business Week* (August 30, 1993), p. 32.

2 A. Levy, "Second-Order Planned Change: Definition and Conceptualization," *Organizational Dynamics* (Summer 1986), pp. 4–20.

3 K.L. Miller, "The Factory Guru Tinkering with Toyota," *Business Week* (May 17, 1993), pp. 95–97.

4 D.J. Yang and A. Rothman, "Reinventing Boeing: Radical Change and Crisis," *Business Week* (March 1, 1993), pp. 60–67.

5 Based on H.J. Leavitt, "Applied Organization Change in Industry," in W. Cooper, H. Leavitt, and M. Shelly (eds.), *New Perspectives on Organization Research* (New York: Wiley, 1964); and P.J. Robertson, D.R. Roberts, and J.I. Porras, "Dynamics of Planned Organizational Change: Assessing Empirical Support for a Theoretical Model," *Academy of Management Journal* (June 1993), pp. 619–34.

6 F. Steele, *Making and Managing High-Quality Workplaces: An Organizational Ecology* (New York: Teachers College Press, 1986).

7 J.I. Porras and P.J. Robertson, "Organizational Development: Theory, Practice, and Research," in M.D. Dunnette and L.M. Hough (eds.), *Handbook of Industrial & Organizational Psychology*, 2nd ed., Vol. 3 (Palo Alto: Consulting Psychologists Press, 1992), p. 734.

8 R.H. Hall, *Organizations: Structures, Processes, and Outcomes*, 4th ed. (Englewood Cliffs, NJ: Prentice Hall, 1987), p. 29.

9 D. Katz and R.L. Kahn, *The Social Psychology of Organizations*, 2nd ed. (New York: Wiley, 1978), pp. 714–15.

10 J.P. Kotter and L.A. Schlesinger, "Choosing Strategies for Change," *Harvard Business Review* (March-April 1979), pp. 106–14.

11 See J. Pfeffer, *Managing With Power: Politics and Influence in Organizations* (Boston: Harvard Business School Press, 1992), pp. 7, 318–20.

12 This box is based on T.A. Stewart, "Rate Your Readiness to Change," *Fortune* (February 7, 1994), pp. 106–10.

13 See, for instance, W. Ocasio, "Political Dynamics and the Circulation of Power: CEO Succession in U.S. Industrial Corporations, 1960–1990," *Administrative Science Quarterly* (June 1994), pp. 285–312.

14 K. Lewin, *Field Theory in Social Science* (New York: Harper & Row, 1951).

15 See, for example, A.B. Shani and W.A. Pasmore, "Organization Inquiry: Towards a New Model of the Action Research Process," in D.D. Warrick (ed.), *Contemporary Organization Development: Current Thinking and Applications* (Glenview, IL: Scott, Foresman, 1985), pp. 438–48.

16 Discussions of the 3M Co. in this chapter are based on K. Labich, "The Innovators," *Fortune* (June 6, 1988), p. 49; R. Mitchell, "Masters of Innovation," *Business Week* (April 10, 1989), p. 58; K. Kelly, "3M Run Scared? Forget About It," *Business Week* (September 16, 1991), pp. 59–62; and K. Kelly, "The Drought Is Over at 3M," *Business Week* (November 7, 1994), pp. 140–41.

[17] See, for instance, A. Van de Ven, "Central Problems in the Management of Innovation," *Management Science*, Vol. 32 (1986), pp. 590–607; and R.M. Kanter, "When a Thousand Flowers Bloom: Structural, Collective, and Social Conditions for Innovation in Organizations," in B.M. Staw and L.L. Cummings (eds.), *Research in Organizational Behavior*, Vol. 10 (Greenwich, CT: JAI Press, 1988), pp. 169–211.

[18] F. Damanpour, "Organizational Innovation: A Meta-Analysis of Effects of Determinants and Moderators," *Academy of Management Journal* (September 1991), p. 557.

[19] Ibid., pp. 555–90.

[20] See also P.R. Monge, M.D. Cozzens, and N.S. Contractor, "Communication and Motivational Predictors of the Dynamics of Organizational Innovation," *Organization Science* (May 1992), pp. 250–74.

[21] J.M. Howell and C.A. Higgins, "Champions of Change," *Business Quarterly* (Spring 1990), pp. 31–32; and D.L. Day, "Raising Radicals: Different Processes for Championing Innovative Corporate Ventures," *Organization Science* (May 1994), pp. 148–72.

[22] J.M. Howell and C.A. Higgins, "Champions of Change."

[23] See, for example, P.M. Senge, *The Fifth Discipline* (New York: Doubleday, 1990); G.P. Huber, "Organizational Learning: The Contributing Processes and the Literatures," *Organization Sciences* (February 1991), pp. 88–115; M. Dodgson, "Organizational Learning: A Review of Some Literatures," *Organization Studies*, Vol. 14, No. 3 (1993); and B. Dumaine, "Mr. Learning Organization," *Fortune* (October 17, 1994), pp. 147–57.

[24] D.H. Kim, "The Link Between Individual and Organizational Learning," *Sloan Management Review* (Fall 1993), p. 37.

[25] C. Argyris and D.A. Schon, *Organizational Learning* (Reading, MA: Addison-Wesley, 1978).

[26] B. Dumaine, "Mr. Learning Organization," p. 148.

[27] F. Kofman and P.M. Senge, "Communities of Commitment: The Heart of Learning Organizations," *Organizational Dynamics* (Autumn 1993), pp. 5–23.

[28] B. Dumaine, "Mr. Learning Organization," p. 154.

[29] For a sampling of various OD definitions, see J.I. Porras and P.J. Robertson, "Organizational Development: Theory, Practice, and Research," pp. 721–23.

[30] L.D. Brown and J.G. Covey, "Development Organizations and Organization Development: Toward an Expanded Paradigm for Organization Development," in R.W. Woodman and W.A. Pasmore (eds.), *Research in Organizational Change and Development*, Vol. 1 (Greenwich, CT: JAI Press, 1987), p. 63; and W.A. Pasmore and M.R. Fagans, "Participation, Individual Development, and Organizational Change: A Review and Synthesis," *Journal of Management* (June 1992), pp. 375–97.

[31] E.H. Schein, *Process Consultation: Its Role in Organizational Development* (Reading, MA: Addison-Wesley, 1969), p. 9.

[32] Ibid.

[33] See, for instance, P.F. Buller, "The Team Building–Task Performance Relation: Some Conceptual and Methodological Refinements," *Group and Organization Studies* (September 1986), pp. 147–68; and D. Eden, "Team Development: Quasi-Experimental Confirmation Among Combat Companies," *Group and Organization Studies* (September 1986), pp. 133–46.

[34] N. Margulies and J. Wallace, *Organizational Change: Techniques and Applications* (Glenview, IL: Scott, Foresman, 1973), pp. 99–100.

[35] See, for example, E.H. Neilsen, "Understanding and Managing Intergroup Conflict," in J.W. Lorsch and P.R. Lawrence (eds.), *Managing Group and Intergroup Relations* (Homewood, IL: Irwin-Dorsey, 1972), pp. 329–43.

[36] R.R. Blake, J.S. Mouton, and R.L. Sloma, "The Union–Management Intergroup Laboratory: Strategy for Resolving Intergroup Conflict," *Journal of Applied Behavioral Science*, No. 1 (1965), pp. 25–57.

[37] P.S. Goodman and L.B. Kurke, "Studies of Change in Organizations: A Status Report," in P.S. Goodman (ed.), *Change in Organizations* (San Francisco: Jossey-Bass, 1982), pp. 1–2.

PROGRESSIVE CASE ◆PART FIVE◆ ORGANIZATIONAL DYNAMICS

ROB PANCO: MANAGING CHANGE

"If it ain't broke and it ain't outdated, leave it alone. We change when we have to." That, according to Rob Panco, is his philosophy toward change. Yet in a growing company like M.E. Aslett, changes are going on all the time. As Rob put it, "We're a constantly evolving company. We never reach a point of equilibrium." He contrasted Aslett with AT&T.

"AT&T and Bell Labs have been going through a great deal of change since the federal government deregulated the phone monopoly. Since Bob Allen took over, he's done some terrific things. I have a lot of respect for him. The first thing he did was create autonomous divisions with their own presidents and decentralize decision-making authority. My impression, however, is that the commitment for change at AT&T was high at both the very top of the company and among lower-level managers. The problem was middle management. The typical 55-year-old middle manager, with 30 years in the company, was threatened by the changes Allen proposed. There was considerable factional resistance to change. For instance, product managers and sales teams were very resistant. It's not a coincidence that the company used downsizing in the early 1990s to retire a lot of those rigid middle managers."

At Aslett, Rob has tried to create a climate that supports the growth and changes that are going on. "In our firm, there are really two elements of change. First, we're introducing new technologies all the time. Our business, for instance, now relies heavily on desk-top publishing, digital technology, CD-ROM formats, and the like. So people have to adapt to these technological changes. Second, rapid growth itself creates change. We're hiring new people and taking on more projects. Much of our growth is coming from expanding the breadth of our product line. We're increasing vertical integration. Innovation through breadth of services means we're doing new things, not just more of what we were doing."

With all this growth, Rob says he tries to make people feel more secure. His job, he says, is made easier because so many of the present staff are relatively new to Aslett and aren't locked in to any old ways of doing things. The longest tenure at Aslett is a person with 17 years in the firm. Next is someone with 10 years. Four others have been there at least 5 years. Everybody else's tenure is 3 years or less. "When I interview job candidates now, I show them our growth chart," Rob confided. "I tell them where we've been and where we're going. And I stress that they have to live with growth and change here. I recently interviewed someone who told me she was looking for a place where she could bring her skills and routinely do her work. I knew she wasn't for us."

Questions

1. What do you think about Rob's philosophy toward change?
2. Contrast the challenges of implementing change at Aslett with implementing change at AT&T.
3. What would Rob need to do to make Aslett into a learning organization? Or is it already a learning organization?

APPENDIX A
THE HISTORICAL EVOLUTION OF ORGANIZATIONAL BEHAVIOR

Why study history? Oliver Wendell Holmes answered that question succinctly when he said, "When I want to understand what is happening today or try to decide what will happen tomorrow, I look back." By *looking back* at the history of organizational behavior, you gain a great deal of insight into how the field got to where it is today. It'll help you understand, for instance, how management came to impose rules and regulations on employees, why many workers in organizations do standardized and repetitive tasks on assembly lines, and why a number of organizations in recent years have replaced their assembly lines with team-based work units. In this appendix, you'll find a brief description of how the theory and practice of organizational behavior has evolved.

So where do we start? Human beings and organized activities have been around for thousands of years, but we needn't go back beyond the eighteenth or nineteenth century to find OB's roots.

Early Practices

There is no question that hundreds of people helped to plant the "seeds" from which the OB "garden" has grown.[1] Three individuals, however, were particularly important in promoting ideas that would eventually have a major influence in shaping the direction and boundaries of OB: Adam Smith, Charles Babbage, and Robert Owen.

Adam Smith

Adam Smith is more typically cited by economists for his contributions to classical economic doctrine, but his discussion in *The Wealth of Nations*,[2] published in 1776, included a brilliant argument on the economic advantages that organizations and society would reap from the division of labor (also called work specialization). Smith used the pin-manufacturing industry for his examples. He noted that ten individuals, each doing a specialized task, could produce about 48,000 pins a day among them. He proposed, however, that if each were working separately and independently, the ten workers together would be lucky to make ten pins in one day. If each had to draw the wire, straighten it, cut it, pound heads for each pin, sharpen the point, and solder the head and pin shaft, it would be quite a feat to produce ten pins a day!

Smith concluded that division of labor raises productivity by increasing each worker's skill and dexterity, by saving time that is commonly lost in changing tasks, and by encouraging the creation of labor-saving inventions and machinery. The extensive development of assembly-line production processes during this century has undoubtedly been stimulated by the economic advantages of work specialization cited over 200 years ago by Adam Smith.

Charles Babbage

Charles Babbage was a British mathematics professor who expanded on the virtues of division of labor first articulated by Adam Smith. In his book *On the Economy of Machinery and Manufactures*,[3] published in 1832, Babbage added the following to Smith's list of the advantages that accrue from division of labor:

1. It reduces the time needed for learning a job.
2. It reduces the waste of material during the learning stage.
3. It allows for the attainment of high skill levels.
4. It allows a more careful matching of people's skills and physical abilities with specific tasks.

Moreover, Babbage proposed that the economies from specialization should be as relevant to doing mental work as physical labor. Today, for example, we take specialization for granted among professionals. When we have a skin rash, we go to a dermatologist. When we buy a home, we consult a lawyer who specializes in real estate. The professors you encounter in your business school classes specialize in areas such as tax accounting, entrepreneurship, marketing research, and organizational behavior. These applications of division of labor were unheard of in eighteenth-century England. But contemporary organizations around the world—in both manufacturing and service industries—make wide use of division of labor.

Robert Owen

Robert Owen was a Welsh entrepreneur who bought his first factory in 1789, at the age of 18. He is important in the history of OB because he was one of the first industrialists to recognize how the growing factory system was demeaning to workers.

Repulsed by the harsh practices he saw in factories—such as the employment of young children (many under the age of 10), 13-hour workdays, and miserable working conditions—Owen became a reformer. He chided factory owners for treating their equipment better than their employees. He criticized them for buying the best machines, but then employing the cheapest labor to run them. Owen argued that money spent on improving labor was one of the best investments that business executives could make. He claimed that showing concern for employees both was profitable for management and would relieve human misery.

For his time, Owen was an idealist. What he proposed was a utopian workplace that would reduce the suffering of the working class. He was more than 100 years ahead of his time when he argued, in 1825, for regulated hours of work for all, child labor laws, public education, company-furnished meals at work, and business involvement in community projects.[4]

The Classical Era

The classical era covered the period from about 1900 to the mid-1930s. It was during this time that the first general theories of management began to evolve. The classical contributors—who include Frederick Taylor, Henri Fayol, Max Weber, Mary Parker Follett, and Chester Barnard—laid the foundation for contemporary management practices.

Scientific Management

The typical United Parcel Service driver today makes 120 stops during his or her work shift. Every step on that driver's daily route has been carefully studied by UPS industrial engineers to maximize efficiency. Every second taken up by stoplights, traffic, detours, doorbells, walkways, stairways, and coffee breaks has been documented by their engineers so as to cut wasted time. It's no accident, for instance, that all UPS drivers tap their horns when they approach a stop in hopes the customer will hurry to the door seconds sooner. It's also no accident that all UPS drivers walk to a customer's door at the brisk pace of 3 feet per second and knock first lest seconds be lost searching for the doorbell.

Today's UPS drivers are following principles that were laid down more than 85 years ago by Frederick W. Taylor in his *Principles of Scientific Management*.[5] In this book, Taylor described how the scientific method could be used to define the "one best way" for a job to be done. In this section, we review his work.

As a mechanical engineer at the Midvale and Bethlehem Steel companies in Pennsylvania, Taylor was consistently appalled at the inefficiency of workers. Employees used vastly different techniques to do the same job. They were prone to "taking it easy" on the job. Taylor believed worker output was only about one-third of what was possible. Therefore, he set out to correct the situation by applying the scientific method to jobs on the shop floor. He spent more than two decades pursuing with a passion the "one best way" for each job to be done.

It's important to understand what Taylor saw at Midvale Steel that aroused his determination to improve the way things were done in the plant. At the time, there were no clear concepts of worker and management responsibilities. Virtually no effective work standards existed. Employees purposely worked at a slow pace. Management decisions were based on hunch and intuition. Workers were placed on jobs with little or no concern for matching their abilities and aptitudes with the tasks they were required to do. Most important, management and workers considered themselves to be in continual conflict. Rather than cooperating to their mutual benefit, they perceived their relationship as a zero-sum game—any gain by one would be at the expense of the other.

Taylor sought to create a mental revolution among both the workers and management by defining clear guidelines for improving production efficiency. He defined four principles of management, listed in Table A-1; he argued that following these principles would result in the prosperity of both management and workers. Workers would earn more pay, and management more profits.

Probably the most widely cited example of scientific management has been Taylor's pig iron experiment. The average daily output of 92-pound pigs loaded onto rail cars was 12.5 tons per worker. Taylor was convinced that by

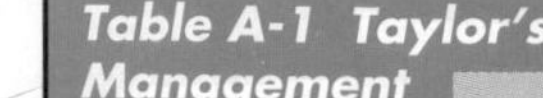

Table A-1 Taylor's Four Principles of Management

1. Develop a science for each element of an individual's work. (Previously, workers used the "rule-of-thumb" method.)
2. Scientifically select and then train, teach, and develop the worker. (Previously, workers chose their own work and trained themselves as best they could.)
3. Heartily cooperate with the workers so as to ensure all work is done in accordance with the principles of the science that has been developed. (Previously, management and workers were in continual conflict.)
4. Divide work and responsibility almost equally between management and workers. Management takes over all work for which it is better fitted than the workers. (Previously, almost all the work and the greater part of the responsibility were thrown on the workers.)

analyzing the job scientifically to determine the one best way to load pig iron, the output could be increased to between 47 and 48 tons per day.

Taylor began his experiment by looking for a physically strong subject who placed a high value on the dollar. The individual Taylor chose was a big, strong Dutch immigrant, whom he called Schmidt. Schmidt, like the other loaders, earned $1.15 a day, which even at the turn of the century was barely enough for a person to survive on. As the following quotation from Taylor's book demonstrates, Taylor used money—the opportunity to make $1.85 a day—as the primary means to get workers like Schmidt to do exactly as they were told:

> "Schmidt, are you a high-priced man?" "Vell, I don't know vat you mean." "Oh, yes you do. What I want to know is whether you are a high-priced man or not." "Vell, I don't know vat you mean." "Oh, come now, you answer my questions. What I want to find out is whether you are a high- priced man or one of these cheap fellows here. What I want to know is whether you want to earn $1.85 a day or whether you are satisfied with $1.15, just the same as all those cheap fellows are getting." "Did I vant $1.85 a day? Vas dot a high-priced man? Vell, yes. I vas a high-priced man."[6]

Using money to motivate Schmidt, Taylor went about having him load the pig irons, alternating various job factors to see what impact the changes had on Schmidt's daily output. For instance, on some days Schmidt would lift the pig irons by bending his knees, whereas on other days he would keep his legs straight and use his back. He experimented with rest periods, walking speed, carrying positions, and other variables. After a long period of trying various combinations of procedures, techniques, and tools scientifically, Taylor succeeded in obtaining the level of productivity he thought possible. By putting the right person on the job with the correct tools and equipment, by having the worker follow his instructions exactly, and by motivating the worker through the economic incentive of a significantly higher daily wage, Taylor was able to reach his 48-ton objective.

Another Taylor experiment dealt with shovel sizes. Taylor noticed that every worker in the plant used the same size shovel, regardless of the material he was moving. This made no sense to Taylor. If there was an optimum weight that would maximize a worker's shoveling output over an entire day, then Taylor thought the size of the shovel should vary depending on the weight of the material being moved. After extensive experimentation, Taylor found that 21 pounds was the optimum shovel capacity. To achieve this optimum weight, heavy material like iron ore would be moved with a small-faced shovel and light material like coke with a large-faced shovel. Based on Taylor's findings, supervisors would no longer merely tell a worker to "shovel that pile over there." Depending on the material to be moved, the supervisor would now have to determine the appropriate shovel size and assign that size to the worker. The result, of course, was again significant increases in worker output.

Using similar approaches in other jobs, Taylor was able to define the one best way for doing each job. He could then, after selecting the right people for the job, train them to do it precisely in this one best way. To motivate workers, he favored incentive wage plans. Overall, Taylor achieved consistent improvements in productivity in the range of 200 percent or more. He reaffirmed the role of managers to plan and control and that of workers to perform as they were instructed. *The Principles of Scientific Management*, as well as papers that Taylor wrote and presented, spread his ideas not only in the United States, but also in France, Germany, Russia, and Japan. One of the biggest boosts in interest in scientific management in the United States came during a 1910 hearing on railroad rates before the Interstate Commerce Commission. Appearing before the commission, an efficiency expert claimed that railroads could save a million dollars a day (equivalent to about $15 million a day in 1996 dollars) through the application of scientific management! The early acceptance of scientific management techniques by U.S. manufacturing companies, in fact, gave them a comparative advantage over foreign firms that made U.S. manufacturing efficiency the envy of the world—at least for 50 years or so!

Administrative Theory

Administrative theory describes efforts to define the universal functions that managers perform and principles that constitute good management practice. The major contributor to administrative theory was a French industrialist named Henri Fayol.

Writing at about the same time as Taylor, Fayol proposed that all managers perform five management functions: They plan, organize, command, coordinate, and control.[7] The importance of this simple insight is underlined when we acknowledge that almost every introductory management textbook today uses these same five functions, or a very close variant of them, as a basic framework for describing what managers do.

In addition, Fayol described the practice of management as something distinct from accounting, finance, production, distribution, and other typical business functions. He argued that management was an activity common to all human undertakings in business, in government, and even in the home. He then proceeded to state 14 principles of management that could be taught in schools and universities. These principles are shown in Table A-2.

Structural Theory

Whereas Taylor was concerned with management at the shop level (or what we today would describe as the job of a supervisor) and Fayol focused on general management functions, the German sociologist Max Weber (pronounced *Vayber*) was developing a theory of authority structures and describing organiza-

Table A-2 Fayol's 14 Principles of Management

1. *Division of Work.* This principle is the same as Adam Smith's "division of labor." Specialization increases output by making employees more efficient.
2. *Authority.* Managers must be able to give orders. Authority gives them this right. Along with authority, however, goes responsibility. Wherever authority is exercised, responsibility arises.
3. *Discipline.* Employees must obey and respect the rules that govern the organization. Good discipline is the result of effective leadership, a clear understanding between management and workers regarding the organization's rules, and the judicious use of penalties for infractions of the rules.
4. *Unity of Command.* Every employee should receive orders from only one superior.
5. *Unity of Direction.* Each group of organizational activities that have the same objective should be directed by one manager using one plan.
6. *Subordination of Individual Interests to the General Interests.* The interests of any one employee or group of employees should not take precedence over the interests of the organization as a whole.
7. *Remuneration.* Workers must be paid a fair wage for their services.
8. *Centralization.* Centralization refers to the degree to which subordinates are involved in decision making. Whether decision making is centralized (to management) or decentralized (to subordinates) is a question of proper proportion. The problem is to find the optimum degree of centralization for each situation.
9. *Scalar Chain.* The line of authority from top management to the lowest ranks represents the scalar chain. Communications should follow this chain. However, if following the chain creates delays, cross-communications can be allowed if agreed to by all parties and superiors are kept informed.
10. *Order.* People and materials should be in the right place at the right time.
11. *Equity.* Managers should be kind and fair to their subordinates.
12. *Stability of Tenure of Personnel.* High employee turnover is inefficient. Management should provide orderly personnel planning and ensure that replacements are available to fill vacancies.
13. *Initiative.* Employees who are allowed to originate and carry out plans will exert high levels of effort.
14. *Esprit de Corps.* Promoting team spirit will build harmony and unity within the organization.

tional activity as based on authority relations.[8] He was one of the first to look at management and organizational behavior from a structural perspective.

Weber described an ideal type of organization that he called a bureaucracy. Bureaucracy was a system characterized by division of labor, a clearly defined hierarchy, detailed rules and regulations, and impersonal relationships. Weber recognized this "ideal bureaucracy" didn't exist in reality but, rather, represented a selective reconstruction of the real world. He meant it to be taken as a basis for theorizing about work and how work could be done in large groups. His theory became the design prototype for large organizations. The detailed features of Weber's ideal bureaucratic structure are outlined in Table A-3.

Table A-3 Weber's Ideal Bureaucracy

1. *Job Specialization.* Jobs are broken down into simple, routine, and well-defined tasks.
2. *Authority Hierarchy.* Offices or positions are organized in a hierarchy, each lower one being controlled and supervised by a higher one.
3. *Formal Selection.* All organizational members are to be selected on the basis of technical qualifications demonstrated by training, education, or formal examination.
4. *Formal Rules and Regulations.* To ensure uniformity and to regulate the actions of employees, managers must depend heavily on formal organizational rules.
5. *Impersonality.* Rules and controls are applied uniformly, avoiding involvement with personalities and personal preferences of employees.
6. *Career Orientation.* Managers are professional officials rather than owners of the units they manage. They work for fixed salaries and pursue their careers within the organization.

"Social Man" Theory

People like Taylor, Fayol, and Weber could be faulted for forgetting that human beings are the central core of every organization and that human beings are social animals. Mary Parker Follett and Chester Barnard were two theorists who saw the importance of the social aspects of organizations. Their ideas were born late in the scientific management period but didn't achieve any large degree of recognition until the 1930s.[9]

MARY PARKER FOLLETT Mary Parker Follett was one of the earliest writers to recognize that organizations could be viewed from the perspective of individual and group behavior.[10] A transitionalist writing during the time when scientific management dominated, Follett was a social philosopher who proposed more people-oriented ideas. Her ideas had clear implications for organizational behavior. Follett thought that organizations should be based on a group ethic rather than individualism. Individual potential, she argued, remains only potential until released through group association. The manager's job is to harmonize and coordinate group efforts. Managers and workers should view themselves as partners—as part of a common group. Therefore, managers should rely more on their expertise and knowledge than on the formal authority of their position to lead subordinates.

Follett's humanistic ideas have influenced the way we look at motivation, leadership, power, and authority today. In fact, Japanese organization and management styles, which came into vogue in North America and Europe in the late 1970s, are indebted to Follett. They place a heavy emphasis on group togetherness and team effort.

CHESTER BARNARD Like Henri Fayol, Chester Barnard was a practitioner. He joined the American Telephone and Telegraph system in 1909 and became president of New Jersey Bell in 1927. Barnard had read Weber and was influenced by his writings. But unlike Weber, who had a mechanistic and impersonal view of organizations, Barnard saw organizations as social systems that require human cooperation. He expressed his views in *The Functions of the Executive,*[11] published in 1938.

Barnard viewed organizations as made up of people who have interacting social relationships. Managers' major roles were to communicate and to stimulate subordinates to high levels of effort. A major part of an organization's success, as Barnard saw it, depended on obtaining cooperation from its personnel. Barnard also argued that success depended on maintaining good relations with people and institutions outside the organization with whom the organization regularly interacted. By recognizing the organization's dependence on investors, suppliers, customers, and other external constituencies, Barnard introduced the idea that managers had to examine the environment and then adjust the organization to maintain a state of equilibrium. So, for instance, regardless of how efficient an organization's production might be, if management failed to ensure a continuous input of materials and supplies or to find markets for its outputs, then the organization's survival would be threatened. Much of the current interest in how the environment affects organizations and their employees can be traced to ideas initially suggested by Barnard.

The Behavioral Era

The "people side" of organizations came into its own during the period we call the behavioral era. As we show, this era was marked by the human relations movement and the widespread application in organizations of behavioral science research. While this behavioral era really didn't begin to roll until the 1930s, two earlier events deserve brief mention because they played an important part in the application and development of organizational behavior. These are the birth of the "personnel office" around the turn of the century and the creation of the field of industrial psychology with the publication of Hugo Münsterberg's textbook in 1913.

The Birth of the "Personnel Office"

In response to the growth of trade unionism at the turn of the century, a few firms—for example, H.J. Heinz, Colorado Fuel & Iron, and International Harvester—created the position of "welfare secretary." Welfare secretaries were supposed to assist workers by suggesting improvements in working conditions, housing, medical care, educational facilities, and recreation. These people, who were the forerunners of today's personnel or human resource management directors, acted as a buffer between the organization and its employees. The B. F. Goodrich Co. developed the first employment department in 1900, but its responsibilities consisted only of hiring. In 1902 the National Cash Register Company established the first comprehensive labor department responsible for wage administration, grievances, employment and working conditions, health conditions, recordkeeping, and worker improvement.

The Birth of Industrial Psychology

Hugo Münsterberg created the field of industrial psychology with the publication of his text *Psychology and Industrial Efficiency*[12] in 1913. In it, he argued for the scientific study of human behavior to identify general patterns and to explain individual differences. Interestingly, Münsterberg saw a link between scientific management and industrial psychology. Both sought increased efficiency through scientific work analyses and through better alignment of individual skills and abilities with the demands of various jobs.

Münsterberg suggested the use of psychological tests to improve employee selection, the value of learning theory in the development of training methods, and the study of human behavior in order to understand what techniques are most effective for motivating workers. Much of our current knowledge of selection techniques, employee training, work design, and motivation is built on Münsterberg's work.

The Magna Carta of Labor

Following the stock market crash of 1929, the United States and much of the world's economy entered the Great Depression. To help relieve the effects of the Depression on the U.S. labor force, President Franklin Roosevelt supported the Wagner Act, which was passed in 1935. This act recognized unions as the authorized representatives of workers, able to bargain collectively with employers in the interests of their members. The Wagner Act would prove to be the Magna Carta of labor. It legitimized the role of trade unions and encouraged rapid growth in union membership. In response to this legislation, managers in industry became much more open to finding new ways to handle their employees. Having lost the battle to keep unions out of their factories, management began to try to improve working conditions and seek better relations with their work force. A set of studies done at Western Electric's Hawthorne plant would be the prime stimulus for the human relations movement that swept American industry from the late 1930s through the 1950s.

Human Relations

The essence of the human relations movement was the belief that the key to higher productivity in organizations was increasing employee satisfaction. In addition to the Hawthorne studies, three people played important roles in conveying the message of human relations: Dale Carnegie, Abraham Maslow, and Douglas McGregor. In this section, we briefly review each man's contribution. But first, we briefly describe the very influential Hawthorne studies.

THE HAWTHORNE STUDIES Without question, the most important contribution to the human relations movement within organizational behavior came out of the Hawthorne studies undertaken at the Western Electric Company's Hawthorne Works in Cicero, Illinois. These studies, originally begun in 1924 but eventually expanded and carried on through the early 1930s, were initially devised by Western Electric industrial engineers to examine the effect of various illumination levels on worker productivity. Control and experimental groups were established. The experimental group was presented with varying illumination intensities; while the control group worked under a constant intensity. The engineers had expected individual output to be directly related to the intensity of light. However, they found that as the light level was increased in the experimental group, output for both groups rose. To the surprise of the engineers, as the light level was dropped in the experimental group, productivity continued to increase in both groups. In fact, a productivity decrease was observed in the experimental group only when the light intensity had been reduced to that of moonlight. The engineers concluded that illumination intensity was not directly related to group productivity, but they could not explain the behavior they had witnessed.

The Western Electric engineers asked Harvard professor Elton Mayo and his associates in 1927 to join the study as consultants. Thus began a relationship that would last through 1932 and encompass numerous experiments covering the redesign of jobs, changes in the length of the workday and workweek, introduction of rest periods, and individual versus group wage plans.[13] For example, one experiment was designed to evaluate the effect of a group piecework incentive pay system on group productivity. The results indicated that the incentive plan had less effect on a worker's output than did group pressure and acceptance and the concomitant security. Social norms or standards of the group, therefore, were concluded to be the key determinants of individual work behavior.

Scholars generally agree that the Hawthorne studies had a large and dramatic impact on the direction of organizational behavior and management practice. Mayo's conclusions were that behavior and sentiments are closely related, group influences significantly affect individual behavior, group standards establish individual worker output, and money is less a factor in determining output than group standards, group sentiments, and security. These conclusions led to a new emphasis on the human factor in the functioning of organizations and the attainment of their goals. They also led to increased paternalism by management.

The Hawthorne studies have not been without critics. Attacks have been made on their procedures, analyses of findings, and the conclusions they drew.[14] However, from a historical standpoint, it's of little importance whether the studies were academically sound or their conclusions justified. What is important is that they stimulated an interest in human factors.

DALE CARNEGIE Dale Carnegie's book *How to Win Friends and Influence People*[15] was read by millions during the 1930s, 1940s, and 1950s. During this same period, tens of thousands of managers and aspiring managers attended his management speeches and seminars. So Carnegie's ideas deserve attention because of the wide audience they commanded.

Carnegie's essential theme was that the way to success is through winning the cooperation of others. He advised his audience to (1) make others feel important through a sincere appreciation of their efforts; (2) strive to make a good first impression; (3) win people to your way of thinking by letting others do the talking, being sympathetic, and "never telling a man he is wrong"; and (4) change people by praising their good traits and giving the offender the opportunity to save face.[16]

ABRAHAM MASLOW Few college students have not been exposed to the ideas of Abraham Maslow. A humanistic psychologist, Maslow proposed a theoretical hierarchy of five needs: physiological, safety, social, esteem, and self-actualization.[17] From a motivation standpoint, Maslow argued that each step in the hierarchy must be satisfied before the next can be activated, and that once a need is substantially satisfied, it no longer motivates behavior. Moreover, he believed that self-actualization—that is, achieving one's full potential—is the summit of a human being's existence. Managers who accepted Maslow's hierarchy attempted to alter their organizations and management practices to reduce barriers to employees' self-actualization.

DOUGLAS MCGREGOR Douglas McGregor is best known for his formulation of two sets of assumptions—Theory X and Theory Y—about human nature.[18] Briefly, Theory X rests on an essentially negative view of people. It assumes they have little ambition, dislike work, want to avoid responsibility, and need to be closely directed to work effectively. Theory Y, on the contrary, rests on a positive view of people. It assumes they can exercise self-direction, accept responsibility, and consider work to be as natural as rest or play. McGregor personally believed Theory Y assumptions best capture the true nature of workers and should guide management practice. As a result, he argued that managers should free up their employees to unleash their full creative and productive potential.

Behavioral Science Theorists

The final category within the behavioral era encompasses a group of researchers who, as Taylor did in scientific management, relied on the scientific method for the study of organizational behavior. Unlike members of the human relations movement, the behavioral science theorists engaged in objective research of human behavior in organizations. They carefully attempted to keep their personal beliefs out of their work. They sought to develop rigorous research designs that could be replicated by other behavioral scientists in the hope a science of organizational behavior could be built.

A full review of the contributions made by behavioral science theorists would cover hundreds of pages, since their work makes up a large part of today's foundations of organizational behavior. But to give you the flavor of their work, we briefly summarize the contributions of a few of the major theorists.

JACOB MORENO Jacob Moreno created an analytical technique called *sociometry* for studying group interactions.[19] Members of a group were asked whom they liked or disliked, and whom they wished to work with or not work with. From these data, collected in interviews, Moreno was able to construct sociograms that identified attraction, repulsion, and indifference patterns among group members. Moreno's sociometric analysis has been used in organizations to create cohesive and high-performing work teams.

B.F. SKINNER Few behavioral scientists' names are more familiar to the general public than that of B. F. Skinner. His research on operant conditioning and behavior modification had a significant effect on the design of organizational training programs and reward systems.[20]

Essentially, Skinner demonstrated that behavior is a function of its consequences. He found that people will most likely engage in desired behavior if they are rewarded for doing so; these rewards are most effective if they immediately follow the desired response; and behavior that is not rewarded, or is punished, is less likely to be repeated.

DAVID MCCLELLAND Psychologist David McClelland tested the strength of individual achievement motivation by asking subjects to look at a set of somewhat ambiguous pictures and to write their own story about each picture. Based on these projective tests, McClelland found he was able to differentiate people with a high need to achieve—individuals who had a strong desire to succeed or achieve in relation to a set of standards—from people with a low need to achieve.[21] His research has been instrumental in helping organizations better match people with jobs and in redesigning jobs for high achievers so as to maximize their motivation potential. In addition, McClelland and his associates have successfully trained individuals to increase their achievement drive. For instance, in India, people who underwent achievement training worked longer hours, initiated more new business ventures, made greater investments in productive assets, employed a larger number of workers, and saw a greater increase in their gross incomes than did a similar group who did not undergo achievement training.

FRED FIEDLER Leadership is one of the most important and extensively researched topics in organizational behavior. The work of Fred Fiedler on the subject is significant for its emphasis on the situational aspects of leadership as well as for its attempt to develop a comprehensive theory of leadership behavior.[22]

From the mid-1960s through the late 1970s, Fiedler's contingency model dominated leadership research. He developed a questionnaire to measure an individual's inherent leadership orientation and identified three contingency variables that, he argued, determined what type of leader behavior is most effective. In testing his model, Fiedler and his associates studied hundreds of groups. Dozens of researchers have attempted to replicate his results. Although some of the predictions from the model have not stood up well under closer analysis, Fielder's model has been a major influence on current thinking and research about leadership.

FREDERICK HERZBERG With the possible exception of the Hawthorne studies, no single stream of research has had a greater impact on undermining the recommendations of scientific management than the work of Frederick Herzberg.[23]

Herzberg sought an answer to the question: What do individuals want from their jobs? He asked hundreds of people that question in the late 1950s, and then carefully analyzed their responses. He concluded that people prefer jobs that offer opportunities for recognition, achievement, responsibility, and growth. Managers who concern themselves with issues like company policies, employee pay, creating narrow and repetitive jobs, and developing favorable working conditions might placate their workers, but they wouldn't motivate them. According to Herzberg, if managers want to motivate their people, they should redesign jobs to allow workers to perform more and varied tasks. Much of the current interest in enriching jobs and improving the quality of work life can be traced to Herzberg's research.

J. RICHARD HACKMAN AND GREG OLDHAM While Herzberg's conclusions were greeted with enthusiasm, the methodology he used for arriving at those conclusions was far less enthusiastically embraced. It would be the work of J. Richard Hackman and Greg Oldham in the 1970s that would provide an explanation of how job factors influence employee motivation and satisfaction, and would offer a valid framework for analyzing jobs.[24] Hackman and Oldham's research also uncovered the core job dimensions—skill variety, task identity, task significance, autonomy, and feedback—that have stood up well as guides in the design of jobs. More specifically, Hackman and Oldham found that among individuals with strong growth needs, jobs that score high on these five core dimensions lead to high employee performance and satisfaction.

OB Today: A Contingency Perspective

We've demonstrated in this appendix that the present state of organizational behavior encompasses ideas introduced dozens, and sometimes hundreds, of years ago. So don't think of one era's concepts as *replacing* an earlier era's; rather, view them as *extensions* and *modifications* of earlier ideas. As United Parcel Service demonstrates, many of Taylor's scientific management principles can be applied today with impressive results. Of course, that doesn't mean those principles will work as well in other organizations. If there is anything we've learned over the last quarter of a century, it's that few ideas—no matter how attractive—are applicable to *all* organizations or to *all* jobs or to *all* types of employees. Today, organizational behavior must be studied and applied in a contingency framework.

Baseball fans know that a batter doesn't *always* try for a home run. It depends on the score, the inning, whether runners are on base, and similar contingency variables. Similarly, you can't say that students always learn more in small classes than in large ones. An extensive body of educational research tells us that *contingency* factors such as course content and teaching style of the instructor influence the relationship between class size and learning effectiveness. Applied to organizational behavior, contingency theory recognizes there is no "one best way" to manage people in organizations and no single set of simple principles that can be applied universally.[25]

A contingency approach to the study of OB is intuitively logical. Why? Because organizations obviously differ in size, objectives, and environmental uncertainty. Similarly, employees differ in values, attitudes, needs, and experiences. So it would be surprising to find that there are universally applicable principles that work in *all* situations. But, of course, it's one thing to say "it all depends" and another to say *what* it all depends on.

The most popular OB topics for research investigation in recent years have been theories of motivation, leadership, work design, and job satisfaction.[26] But while the 1960s and 1970s saw the development of new theories, the emphasis since has been on refining existing theories, clarifying previous assumptions, and identifying relevant contingency variables.[27] That is, researchers have been trying to identify the "what" variables and which ones are relevant for understanding various behavioral phenomena. This essentially reflects the maturing of OB as a scientific discipline. The near-term future of OB research is likely to continue to focus on fine-tuning current theories so as to better help us understand those situations where they're most likely to be useful.

Summary

While the seeds of organizational behavior were planted more than 200 years ago, current OB theory and practice are essentially products of the twentieth century.

Frederick Taylor's principles of scientific management were instrumental in engineering precision and standardization into people's jobs. Henri Fayol defined the universal functions that all managers perform and the principles that constitute good management practice. Max Weber developed a theory of authority structures and described organizational activity based on authority relations.

The "people side" of organizations came into its own in the 1930s, predominately as a result of the Hawthorne studies. These studies led to a new emphasis on the human factor in organizations and increased paternalism by management. In the late 1950s, managers' attention was caught by the ideas of people like Abraham Maslow and Douglas McGregor, who proposed that organization structures and management practices had to be altered so as to bring out the full productive potential of employees. Motivation and leadership theories offered by David McClelland, Fred Fiedler, Frederick Herzberg, and other behavioral scientists during the 1960s and 1970s provided managers with still greater insights into employee behavior.

Almost all contemporary management and organizational behavior concepts are contingency based. That is, they provide various recommendations dependent on situational factors. As a maturing discipline, current OB research is emphasizing the refinement of existing theories.

Notes

[1] See, for instance, D.A. Wren, *The Evolution of Management Thought*, 3rd ed. (New York: Wiley, 1987), especially Chapters 4, 9, 13–15, 17, and 20.

[2] A. Smith, *An Inquiry into the Nature and Causes of the Wealth of Nations* (New York: Modern Library, 1937; orig. pub. 1776).

[3] C. Babbage, *On the Economy of Machinery and Manufactures* (London: Charles Knight, 1832).

[4] R.A. Owen, *A New View of Society* (New York: E. Bliss & White, 1825).

[5] F.W. Taylor, *Principles of Scientific Management* (New York: Harper & Brothers, 1911).

[6] Ibid., p. 44.

[7] H. Fayol, *Industrial and General Administration* (Paris: Dunod, 1916).

[8] M. Weber, *The Theory of Social and Economic Organizations*, ed. T. Parsons, trans. A.M. Henderson and T. Parsons (New York: Free Press, 1947).

[9] Wren, *The Evolution of Management Thought*, p. 234.

[10] See, for example, M.P. Follett, *The New State: Group Organization the Solution of Popular Government* (London: Longmans, Green & Co., 1918).

[11] C.I. Barnard, *The Functions of the Executive* (Cambridge, MA: Harvard University Press, 1938).

[12] H. Münsterberg, *Psychology and Industrial Efficiency* (Boston: Houghton Mifflin, 1913).

[13] E. Mayo, *The Human Problems of an Industrial Civilization* (New York: Macmillan, 1933); and F.J. Roethlisberger and W.J. Dickson, *Management and the Worker* (Cambridge, MA: Harvard University Press, 1939).

[14] See, for example, A. Carey, "The Hawthorne Studies: A Radical Criticism," *American Sociological Review* (June 1967), pp. 403–16; R.H. Franke and J. Kaul, "The Hawthorne Experiments: First Statistical Interpretations," *American Sociological Review* (October 1978), pp. 623–43; B. Rice, "The Hawthorne Defect: Persistence of a Flawed Theory," *Psychology Today* (February 1982), pp. 70–74; J.A. Sonnenfeld, "Shedding Light on the Hawthorne Studies," *Journal of Occupational Behavior* (April 1985), pp. 111–30; and S.R.G. Jones, "Was There a Hawthorne Effect?" *American Journal of Sociology* (November 1992), pp. 451–68.

[15] D. Carnegie, *How to Win Friends and Influence People* (New York: Simon & Schuster, 1936).

[16] Wren, *The Evolution of Management Thought*, p. 422.

[17] A. Maslow, *Motivation and Personality* (New York: Harper & Row, 1954).

[18] D. McGregor, *The Human Side of Enterprise* (New York: McGraw-Hill, 1960).

[19] J.L. Moreno, "Contributions of Sociometry to Research Methodology in Sociology," *American Sociological Review* (June 1947), pp. 287–92.

[20] See, for instance, B.F. Skinner, *Science and Human Behavior* (New York: Free Press, 1953); and B.F. Skinner, *Beyond Freedom and Dignity* (New York: Knopf, 1972).

[21] D.C. McClelland, *The Achieving Society* (New York: Van Nostrand Reinhold, 1961); and D.C. McClelland and D.G. Winter, *Motivating Economic Achievement* (New York: Free Press, 1969).

[22] F.E. Fiedler, *A Theory of Leadership Effectiveness* (New York: McGraw-Hill, 1967).

[23] F. Herzberg, B. Mausner, and B. Snyderman, *The Motivation to Work* (New York, Wiley, 1959); and F. Herzberg, *The Managerial Choice: To Be Efficient or to Be Human*, rev. ed (Salt Lake City: Olympus, 1982).

[24] J.R. Hackman and G.R. Oldham, "Development of the Job Diagnostic Survey," *Journal of Applied Psychology* (April 1975), pp. 159–70.

[25] See, for instance, J.M. Shepard and J.G. Hougland, Jr., "Contingency Theory: 'Complex Man' or 'Complex Organization'?" *Academy of Management Review* (July 1978), pp. 413–27; and H.L. Tosi, Jr., and J.W. Slocum, Jr., "Contingency Theory: Some Suggested Directions," *Journal of Management* (Spring 1984), pp. 9–26.

[26] C.A. O'Reilly III, "Organizational Behavior: Where We've Been, Where We're Going," in M.R. Rosenzweig and L.W. Porter (eds.), *Annual Review of Psychology*, Vol. 42 (Palo Alto, CA: Annual Reviews, 1991), pp. 429–30.

[27] Ibid., pp. 427–58.

APPENDIX B
RESEARCH IN ORGANIZATIONAL BEHAVIOR

A few years back, a friend was all excited because he had read about the findings from a research study that finally, once and for all, resolved the question of what it takes to make it to the top in a large corporation. I doubted there was any simple answer to this question but, not wanting to dampen his enthusiasm, I asked him to tell me what he had read. The answer, according to my friend, was *participation in college athletics*. To say I was skeptical of his claim is a gross understatement, so I asked him to tell me more.

The study encompassed 1,700 successful senior executives at the 500 largest U.S. corporations. The researchers found that half of these executives had played varsity-level college sports.[1] My friend, who happens to be good with statistics, informed me that since fewer than 2 percent of all college students participate in intercollegiate athletics, the probability of this finding occurring by mere chance is less than 1 in 10 million! He concluded his analysis by telling me that, based on this research, I should encourage my management students to get into shape and to make one of the varsity teams.

My friend was somewhat perturbed when I suggested his conclusions were likely to be flawed. These executives were all males who attended college in the 1940s and 1950s. Would his advice be meaningful to females in the 1990s? These executives also weren't your typical college students. For the most part, they had attended elite private colleges like Princeton and Lehigh, where a large proportion of the student body participates in intercollegiate sports. And these "jocks" hadn't necessarily played football or basketball; many had participated in golf, tennis, baseball, cross-country running, crew, rugby, and similar minor sports. Moreover, maybe the researchers had confused the direction of causality. That is, maybe individuals with the motivation and ability to make it to the top of a large corporation are drawn to competitive activities like college athletics.

My friend was guilty of misusing research data. Of course, he is not alone. We are all continually bombarded with reports of experiments that link certain substances to cancer in mice and surveys that show changing attitudes toward sex among college students, for example. Many of these studies are carefully designed, with great caution taken to note the implications and limitations of the findings. But some studies are poorly designed, making their conclusions at best suspect, and at worst meaningless.

Rather than attempting to make you a researcher, the purpose of this appendix is to increase your awareness as a consumer of behavioral research. A

knowledge of research methods will allow you to appreciate more fully the care in data collection that underlies the information and conclusions presented in this text. Moreover, an understanding of research methods will make you a more skilled evaluator of those OB studies you will encounter in business and professional journals. So an appreciation of behavioral research is important because (1) it's the foundation on which the theories in this text are built, and (2) it will benefit you in future years when you read reports of research and attempt to assess their value.

Purpose of Research

Research is concerned with the systematic gathering of information. Its purpose is to help us in our search for the truth. While we will never find ultimate truth—in our case, that would be to know precisely how any person would behave in any organizational context—ongoing research adds to our body of OB knowledge by supporting some theories, contradicting others, and suggesting new theories to replace those that fail to gain support.

Research Terminology

Researchers have their own vocabulary for communicating among themselves and with outsiders. The following briefly defines some of the more popular terms you're likely to encounter in behavioral science studies.[2]

VARIABLE A *variable* is any general characteristic that can be measured and that changes in either amplitude, intensity, or both. Some examples of OB variables found in this text are job satisfaction, employee productivity, work stress, ability, personality, and group norms.

HYPOTHESIS A tentative explanation of the relationship between two or more variables is called a *hypothesis*. My friend's statement that participation in college athletics leads to a top executive position in a large corporation is an example of a hypothesis. Until confirmed by empirical research, a hypothesis remains only a *tentative* explanation.

DEPENDENT VARIABLE A *dependent variable* is a response affected by an independent variable. In terms of the hypothesis, it is the variable the researcher is interested in explaining. Referring back to our opening example, the dependent variable in my friend's hypothesis was executive succession. In organizational behavior research, the most popular dependent variables are productivity, absenteeism, turnover, job satisfaction, and organizational commitment.[3]

INDEPENDENT VARIABLE An *independent variable* is the presumed cause of some change in the dependent variable. Participating in varsity athletics was the independent variable in my friend's hypothesis. Popular independent variables studied by OB researchers include intelligence, personality, job satisfaction, experience, motivation, reinforcement patterns, leadership style, reward allocations, selection methods, and organization design.

You may have noticed we said that job satisfaction is frequently used by OB researchers as both a dependent and an independent variable. This is not an error. It merely reflects that the label given to a variable depends on its place in the hypothesis. In the statement "Increases in job satisfaction lead to reduced turnover," job satisfaction is an independent variable. However, in the statement "Increases in money lead to higher job satisfaction," job satisfaction becomes a dependent variable.

MODERATING VARIABLE A *moderating variable* abates the effect of the independent variable on the dependent variable. It might also be thought of as the contingency variable: If X (independent variable), then Y (dependent variable) will occur, but only under conditions Z (moderating variable). To translate this into a real-life example, we might say that if we increase the amount of direct supervision in the work area (X), then there will be an increase in worker productivity (Y), but this effect will be moderated by the complexity of the tasks being performed (Z).

CAUSALITY A hypothesis, by definition, implies a relationship. That is, it implies a presumed cause and effect. This direction of cause and effect is called *causality*. Changes in the independent variable are assumed to *cause* changes in the dependent variable. However, in behavioral research, it's possible to make an incorrect assumption of causality when relationships are found. For example, early behavioral scientists found a relationship between employee satisfaction and productivity. They concluded that a happy worker was a productive worker. Follow-up research has supported the relationship, but disconfirmed the direction of the arrow. The evidence more correctly suggests that high productivity leads to satisfaction rather than the other way around.

CORRELATION COEFFICIENT It's one thing to know there is a relationship between two or more variables. It's another to know the *strength* of that relationship. The term *correlation coefficient* is used to indicate that strength, and is expressed as a number between −1.00 (a perfect negative relationship) to +1.00 (a perfect positive correlation).

When two variables vary directly with one another, the correlation will be expressed as a positive number. When they vary inversely—that is, one increases as the other decreases—the correlation will be expressed as a negative number. If the two variables vary independently of each other, we say that the correlation between them is zero.

For example, a researcher might survey a group of employees to determine the satisfaction of each with his or her job. Then, using company absenteeism reports, the researcher could correlate the job satisfaction scores against individual attendance records to determine whether employees who are more satisfied with their jobs have better attendance records than their counterparts who indicated lower job satisfaction. Let's suppose the researcher found a correlation coefficient between satisfaction and attendance of +0.50. Would that be a strong association? There is, unfortunately, no precise numerical cutoff separating strong and weak relationships. A standard statistical test would need to be applied to determine whether or not the relationship was a significant one.

A final point needs to be made before we move on: A correlation coefficient measures only the strength of association between two variables. A high value does *not* imply causality. The length of women's skirts and stock market prices, for instance, have long been noted to be highly correlated, but one should be careful not to infer that a causal relationship between the two exists. In this instance, the high correlation is more happenstance than predictive.

THEORY The final term we introduce in this section is *theory*. Theory describes a set of systematically interrelated concepts or hypotheses that purport to explain and predict phenomena. In OB, theories are also frequently referred to as *models*. We use the two terms interchangeably.

There are no shortages of theories in OB. For instance, we have theories to describe what motivates people, the most effective leadership styles, the best way to resolve conflicts, and how people acquire power. In some cases, we have half a dozen or more separate theories that purport to explain and predict a given phenomenon. In such cases, is one right and the others wrong? No! They tend to reflect science at work—researchers testing previous theories, modifying them, and, when appropriate, proposing new models that may prove to have higher explanatory and predictive powers. Multiple theories attempting to explain common phenomena merely attest that OB is an active discipline, still growing and evolving.

Evaluating Research

As a potential consumer of behavioral research, you should follow the dictum of caveat emptor—let the buyer beware! In evaluating any research study, you need to ask three questions.[4]

Is it valid? Is the study actually measuring what it claims to be measuring? Many psychological tests have been discarded by employers in recent years because they have not been found to be valid measures of the applicants' ability to successfully do a given job. But the validity issue is relevant to all research studies. So, if you find a study that links cohesive work teams with higher productivity, you want to know how each of these variables were measured and whether they are actually measuring what they are supposed to be measuring.

Is it reliable? Reliability refers to consistency of measurement. If you were to have your height measured every day with a wooden yardstick, you'd get highly reliable results. If you were measured each day by an elastic tape measure, however, there would probably be considerable disparity between your height measurements from one day to the next. Your height, of course, doesn't change from day to day. The variability is due to the unreliability of the measuring device. So if a company asked a group of its employees to complete a reliable job satisfaction questionnaire, and then repeat the questionnaire six months later, we'd expect the results to be very similar—provided nothing changed in the interim that might significantly affect employee job satisfaction.

Is it generalizable? Are the results of the research study generalizable to groups of individuals other than those who participated in the original study? Be aware, for example, of the limitations that might exist in research that uses college students as subjects. Are the findings in such studies generalizable to full-time employees in real jobs? Similarly, how generalizable to the overall work population are the results from a study that assesses job stress among ten nuclear power plant engineers in the hamlet of Mahone Bay, Nova Scotia?

Research Design

Doing research is an exercise in trade-offs. Richness of information typically comes with reduced generalizability. The more a researcher seeks to control for confounding variables, the less realistic his or her results are likely to be. High precision, generalizability, and control almost always translate into higher costs. When researchers make choices about whom they'll study, where their research will be done, the methods they'll use to collect data, and so on, they must make some concessions. Good research designs are not perfect, but they do carefully reflect the questions being addressed. Keep these facts in mind as we review the strengths and weaknesses of five popular research designs: case studies, field surveys, laboratory experiments, field experiments, and aggregate quantitative reviews.

CASE STUDY You pick up a copy of Soichiro Honda's autobiography. In it he describes his impoverished childhood; his decisions to open a small garage, assemble motorcycles, and eventually build automobiles; and how this led to the creation of one of the largest and most successful corporations in the world. Or you're in a business class and the instructor distributes a 50-page handout covering two companies: Apple Computer and Digital Equipment Corporation (DEC). The handout details the two firms' histories, describes their product lines, production facilities, management philosophies, and marketing strategies, and includes copies of their recent balance sheets and income statements. The instructor asks the class members to read the handout, analyze the data, and determine why Apple has been more successful in recent years than DEC.

Soichiro Honda's autobiography and the Apple and DEC handouts are case studies. Drawn from real-life situations, case studies present an in-depth analysis of one setting. They are thorough descriptions, rich in details about an individual, a group, or an organization. The primary source of information in case studies is obtained through observation, occasionally backed up by interviews and a review of records and documents.

Case studies have their drawbacks. They're open to the perceptual bias and subjective interpretations of the observer. The reader of a case is captive to what the observer/case writer chooses to include and exclude. Cases also trade off generalizability for depth of information and richness of detail. Since it's always dangerous to generalize from a sample of one, case studies make it difficult to prove or reject a hypothesis. On the other hand, you can't ignore the in-depth analysis that cases often provide. They are an excellent device for initial exploratory research and for evaluating real-life problems in organizations.

FIELD SURVEY A questionnaire made up of approximately a dozen items sought to examine the content of supervisory training programs in billion dollar corporations. Copies of the questionnaire, with a cover letter explaining the nature of the study, were mailed to the corporate training officers at 250 corporations randomly selected from the Fortune 500 list; 155 officers responded to it. The results of this survey found, among other things, that the most common training topic was providing performance evaluation feedback to employees (92 percent of the surveyed companies selected this topic as the most common aspect of their program). This was closely followed by developing effective delegation skills (90 percent) and listening skills (83 percent).[5]

The preceding study illustrates a typical field survey. A sample of respondents (in this case, 250 corporate training officers) was selected to represent a larger group that was under examination (corporate training officers in Fortune 500 firms). The respondents were then surveyed using a questionnaire or interviewed to collect data on particular characteristics (the content of supervisory training programs) of interest to the researcher. The standardization of response items allows for data to be easily quantified, analyzed, and summarized, and for the researcher to make inferences from the representative sample about the larger population.

The field survey provides economies for doing research. It's less costly to sample a population than to obtain data from every member of that population. Moreover, as the supervisory training program example illustrates, field surveys provide an efficient way to find out how people feel about issues or how they say they behave. These data can then be easily quantified. But the field survey has a number of potential weaknesses. First, mailed questionnaires rarely obtain 100 percent returns. Low response rates call into question whether conclusions based on respondents' answers are generalizable to nonrespondents. Second, the format is better at tapping respondents' attitudes and perceptions than behaviors. Third, responses can suffer from social desirability, that is, people saying what they think the researcher wants to hear. Fourth, since field surveys are designed to focus on specific issues, they're a relatively poor means of acquiring depth of information. Finally, the quality of the generalizations is largely a factor of the population chosen. Responses from executives at Fortune 500 firms, for instance, tell us nothing about small- or medium-sized firms or not-for-profit organizations. In summary, even a well-designed field survey trades off depth of information for breadth, generalizability, and economic efficiencies.

LABORATORY EXPERIMENT The following study is a classic example of the laboratory experiment: A researcher, Stanley Milgram, wondered how far individuals would go in following commands. If subjects were placed in the role of a teacher in a learning experiment and told by an experimenter to administer a shock to a learner each time that learner made a mistake, would the subjects follow the commands of the experimenter? Would their willingness to comply decrease as the intensity of the shock was increased?

To test these hypotheses, Milgram hired a set of subjects. Each was led to believe the experiment was to investigate the effect of punishment on memory. Their job was to act as teachers and administer punishment whenever the learner made a mistake on the learning test.

Punishment was administered by an electric shock. The subject sat in front of a shock generator with 30 levels of shock—beginning at zero and progressing in 15-volt increments to a high of 450 volts. The demarcations of these positions ranged from "Slight Shock" at 15 volts to "Danger: Severe Shock" at 450 volts. To increase the realism of the experiment, the subjects received a sample shock of 45 volts and saw the learner—a pleasant, mild-mannered man about 50 years old—strapped into an "electric chair" in an adjacent room. Of course, the learner was an actor and the electric shocks were phony, but the subjects didn't know this.

Taking his seat in front of the shock generator, the subject was directed to begin at the lowest shock level and to increase the shock intensity to the next level each time the learner made a mistake or failed to respond.

When the test began, the shock intensity rose rapidly because the learner made many errors. The subject got verbal feedback from the learner: At 75 volts, the learner began to grunt and moan; at 150 volts, he demanded to be released from the experiment; at 180 volts, he cried out that he could no longer stand the pain; and at 300 volts, he insisted he be let out, yelled about his heart condition, screamed, and then failed to respond to further questions.

Most subjects protested and, fearful they might kill the learner if the increased shocks were to bring on a heart attack, insisted they could not go on with their job. Hesitations or protests by the subject were met by the experimenter's statement, "You have no choice, you must go on! Your job is to punish the learner's mistakes." Of course, the subjects did have a choice. All they had to do was stand up and walk out.

The majority of the subjects dissented. But dissension isn't synonymous with disobedience. Sixty-two percent of the subjects increased the shock level to the maximum of 450 volts. The average level of shock administered by the remaining 38 percent was nearly 370 volts.[6]

In a laboratory experiment such as that conducted by Milgram, an artificial environment is created by the researcher. Then the researcher manipulates an independent variable under controlled conditions. Finally, since all other things are held equal, the researcher is able to conclude that any change in the dependent variable is due to the manipulation or change imposed on the independent variable. Note that, because of the controlled conditions, the researcher is able to imply causation between the independent and dependent variables.

The laboratory experiment trades off realism and generalizability for precision and control. It provides a high degree of control over variables and precise measurement of those variables. But findings from laboratory studies are often difficult to generalize to the real world of work. This is because the artificial laboratory rarely duplicates the intricacies and nuances of real organizations. Additionally, many laboratory experiments deal with phenomena that cannot be reproduced or applied to real-life situations.

FIELD EXPERIMENT The following is an example of a field experiment: The management of a large company is interested in determining the impact that a four-day workweek would have on employee absenteeism. To be more specific, they want to know if employees working four 10-hour days have lower absence rates than similar employees working the traditional five-day week of 8 hours each day. Because the company is large, it has a number of manufacturing plants that employ essentially similar work forces. Two of these are chosen for the experiment, both located in the greater Cleveland area. Obviously, it would not be appropriate to compare two similar-sized plants if one is in rural Mississippi and the other is in urban Copenhagen, because factors such as national culture, transportation, and weather might be more likely to explain any differences found than changes in the number of days worked per week.

In one plant, the experiment was put into place—workers began the four-day week. At the other plant, which became the control group, no changes were made in the employees' five-day week. Absence data was gathered from the company's records at both locations for a period of 18 months. This extended time period lessened the possibility that any results would be distorted by the mere novelty of changes being implemented in the experimental plant. After 18 months, management found that absenteeism had dropped by 40 percent at the experimental plant, and by only 6 percent in the control plant. Because of the design of this study, management believed the larger drop in absences at the experimental plant was due to the introduction of the compressed workweek.

The field experiment is similar to the laboratory experiment, except it is conducted in a real organization. The natural setting is more realistic than the laboratory setting, and this enhances validity but hinders control. Additionally, unless control groups are maintained, there can be a loss of control if extraneous forces intervene—for example, an employee strike, a major layoff, or a corporate restructuring. Maybe the greatest concern with field studies has to do with organizational selection bias. Not all organizations are going to allow outside researchers to come in and study their employees and operations. This is especially true of organizations that have serious problems. Therefore, since most published studies in OB are done by outside researchers, the selection bias might work toward publication of studies conducted almost exclusively at successful and well-managed organizations.

Our general conclusion is that, of the four research designs we've discussed, the field experiment typically provides the most valid and generalizable findings and, except for its high cost, trades off the least to get the most.

AGGREGATE QUANTITATIVE REVIEWS What relationship, if any, is there between employee gender and occupational stress? There have been a number of individual field surveys and qualitative reviews of these surveys that have sought to throw light on this question. Unfortunately, these various studies produced conflicting results.

To try to reconcile these conflicts, researchers at Michigan State University identified all published correlations between gender and stress in work-related contexts.[7] After discarding reports that had inadequate information, nonquantitative data, and failed to include both men and women in their sample, the researchers narrowed their set to 15 studies that included data on 9,439 individuals. Using an aggregating technique called *meta-analysis*, the researchers were able to integrate the studies quantitatively and conclude there are no differences in experienced stress between men and women in a work setting.

The gender–stress review done by the Michigan State researchers illustrates the use of meta-analysis, a quantitative form of literature review that enables researchers to look at validity findings from a comprehensive set of individual studies, and then apply a formula to them to determine if they consistently produced similar results.[8] If results prove to be consistent, it allows researchers to conclude more confidently that validity is generalizable. Meta-analysis is a means for overcoming the potentially imprecise interpretations of qualitative reviews. Additionally, the technique enables researchers to identify potential moderating variables between an independent and a dependent variable.

In the past 10 to 15 years, there's been a surge in the popularity of this research method. Why? It appears to offer a more objective means for doing traditional literature reviews. While the use of meta-analysis requires researchers to make a number of judgment calls, which can introduce a considerable amount of subjectivity into the process, there is no arguing that meta-analysis reviews have now become widespread in the OB literature.

Ethics in Research

Researchers are not always tactful or candid with subjects when they do their studies. For instance, questions in field surveys may be perceived as embarrassing by respondents or as an invasion of privacy. Also, researchers in laboratory studies have been known to deceive participants as to the true purpose of their experiment "because they felt deception was necessary to get honest responses."[9]

The "learning experiments" conducted by Stanley Milgram were widely criticized by psychologists on ethical grounds. He lied to subjects, telling them his study was investigating learning, when, in fact, he was concerned with obedience. The shock machine he used was a fake. Even the "learner" was an accomplice of Milgram's who had been trained to act as if he were hurt and in pain.

Professional associations like the American Psychological Association, the American Sociological Association, and the Academy of Management have published formal guidelines for the conduct of research. Yet the ethical debate continues. On one side are those who argue that strict ethical controls can damage the scientific validity of an experiment and cripple future research. Deception, for example, is often necessary to avoid contaminating results. Moreover, proponents of minimizing ethical controls note that few subjects have been appreciably harmed by deceptive experiments. Even in Milgram's highly manipulative experiment, only 1.3 percent of the subjects reported negative feelings about their experience. The other side of this debate focuses on the rights of participants. Those favoring strict ethical controls argue that no procedure should ever be emotionally or physically distressing to subjects, and that, as professionals, researchers are obliged to be completely honest with their subjects and to protect the subjects' privacy at all costs.

Now, let's take a look at a sampling of ethical questions relating to research. Do you think Milgram's experiment was unethical? Would you judge it unethical for a company to anonymously survey its employees with mail questionnaires on their intentions to quit their present job? Would your answer be any different if the company coded the survey responses to identify those who didn't reply so they could send them follow-up questionnaires? Would it be unethical for management to hide a video camera on the production floor to study group interaction patterns (with the goal of using the data to design more effective work teams) without first telling employees that they were subjects of research?

Summary

The subject of organizational behavior is composed of a large number of theories that are research based. Research studies, when cumulatively integrated, become theories; and theories are proposed and followed by research studies designed to validate them. The concepts that make up OB, therefore, are only as valid as the research that supports them.

The topics and issues in this text are—for the most part—largely research derived. They represent the result of systematic information gathering rather than merely hunch, intuition, or opinion. This doesn't mean, of course, that we have all the answers to OB issues. Many require far more corroborating evidence. The generalizability of others is limited by the research methods used. But new information is being created and published at an accelerated rate. To keep up with the lastest findings, we strongly encourage you to review regularly the latest research in organizational behavior. The more academic work can be found in journals such as the *Academy of Management Journal*, *Academy of Management Review*, *Administrative Science Quarterly*, *Journal of Applied Psychology*, *Journal of Management*, and *Leadership Quarterly*. For more practical interpretations of OB research findings, you may want to read the *Academy of Management Executive*, *California Management Review*, *Harvard Business Review*, *Organizational Dynamics*, and the *Sloan Management Review*.

Notes

[1] J.A. Byrne, "Executive Sweat," *Forbes* (May 20, 1985), pp. 198–200.

[2] This discussion is based on material presented in E. Stone, *Research Methods in Organizational Behavior* (Santa Monica, CA: Goodyear, 1978).

[3] B.M. Staw and G.R. Oldham, "Reconsidering Our Dependent Variables: A Critique and Empirical Study," *Academy of Management Journal* (December 1978), pp. 539–59; and B.M. Staw, "Organizational Behavior: A Review and Reformulation of the Field's Outcome Variables," in M.R. Rosenzweig and L.W. Porter (eds.), *Annual Review of Psychology*, Vol. 35 (Palo Alto, CA: Annual Reviews, 1984), pp. 627–66.

[4] R.S. Blackburn, "Experimental Design in Organizational Settings," in J.W. Lorsch (ed.), *Handbook of Organizational Behavior* (Englewood Cliffs, NJ: Prentice Hall, 1987), pp. 127–28.

[5] G.G. Alpander, "Supervisory Training Programmes in Major U.S. Corporations," *Journal of Management Development*, Vol. 5, No. 5 (1986), pp. 3–22.

[6] S. Milgram, *Obedience to Authority* (New York: Harper & Row, 1974). For a critique of this research, see T. Blass, "Understanding Behavior in the Milgram Obedience Experiment: The Role of Personality, Situations, and Their Interactions," *Journal of Personality and Social Psychology* (March 1991), pp. 398–413.

[7] J.J. Martocchio and A.M. O'Leary, "Sex Differences in Occupational Stress: A Meta-Analytic Review," *Journal of Applied Psychology* (June 1989), pp. 495–501.

[8] See, for example, R.A. Guzzo, S.E. Jackson, and R.A. Katzell, "Meta-Analysis Analysis," in L.L. Cummings and B.M. Staw (eds.), *Research in Organizational Behavior*, Vol. 9 (Greenwich, CT: JAI Press, 1987), pp. 407–42; A.L. Beaman, "An Empirical Comparison of Meta-Analytic and Traditional Reviews," *Personality and Social Psychology Bulletin* (June 1991), pp. 252–57; and G.E. Ledford, Jr. and E.E. Lawler, III, "Research on Employee Participation: Beating a Dead Horse?" *Academy of Management Review* (October 1994), pp. 633–36.

[9] For more on ethical issues in research, see T.L. Beauchamp, R.R. Faden, R.J. Wallace, Jr., and L. Walters (eds.), *Ethical Issues in Social Science Research* (Baltimore, MD: Johns Hopkins University Press, 1982); and D. Baumrind, "Research Using Intentional Deception," *American Psychologist* (February 1985), pp. 165–74.

APPENDIX C

SCORING KEYS FOR "LEARNING ABOUT YOURSELF" EXERCISES

Chapter 1: How Does Your Ethical Behavior Rate?

Give yourself 1 point for each N answer, 2 points for each S answer, 3 points for each O answer, and 4 points for each R answer. Now total your score. It will fall somewhere between 15 and 60 points. Since all of items in this exercise are considered unethical, the lower your score the higher your ethical standards.

Chapter 2: What's Your International Culture I.Q.?

The correct answers are (1) a; (2) b; (3) e (Portuguese); (4) b; (5) d; (6) a; (7) d; (8) d; (9) b; (10) b. Scores of eight correct answers or more indicate you are relatively knowledgeable about customs, practices, and facts regarding different countries. Scores of 4 or less suggest considerable room for expanding your knowledge of other people and lands.

Chapter 3: How Important Is Success to You?

Add up your total points. The authors of this instrument suggest the following guidelines in interpreting your score:

Scores of 10 to 22. You have a fairly strong need for success. You like to win. Many people in this group demonstrate a strong fear of failure; they hate losing and have an internalized fear they may not succeed.

Scores of 23 to 35. You have a moderate need for success.

Scores of 36 to 50. You tend to suffer from "fear of success." You may be apprehensive about possible negative outcomes associated with success (as opposed to failure). You may feel unworthy about winning or uncomfortable with public recognition of your accomplishments.

Chapter 4: Decison-Making Style Questionnaire

Mark each of your responses on the following scales. Then use the point value column to arrive at your score. For example, if you answered *a* to the first question, you would check *1a* in the feeling column.

This response receives zero points when you add up the point value column. Instructions for classifying your scores are indicated below the scales.

Sensation	Point Value	Intuition	Point Value	Thinking	Point Value	Feeling	Point Value
2b ___	1	2a ___	2	1b ___	1	1a ___	0
4a ___	1	4b ___	1	3b ___	2	3a ___	1
5a ___	1	5b ___	1	7b ___	1	7a ___	1
6b ___	1	6a ___	0	8a ___	0	8b ___	1
9b ___	2	9a ___	2	10b ___	2	10a ___	1
12a ___	1	12b ___	0	11a ___	2	11b ___	1
15a ___	1	15b ___	1	13b ___	1	13a ___	1
16b ___	2	16a ___	0	14b ___	0	14a ___	1
Maximum Point Value	(10)		(7)		(9)		(7)

Write *intuition* if your intuition score is equal to or greater than your sensation score. Write *sensation* if your sensation score is greater than your intuition score. Write *feeling* if your feeling score is greater than your thinking score. Write *thinking* if your thinking score is greater than your feeling score.

A high score on *intuition* indicates you see the world in holistic terms. You tend to be creative. A high score on *sensation* indicates you are realistic and see the world in terms of facts. A high score on *feeling* means you make decisions based on gut feeling. A high score on *thinking* indicates a highly logical and analytical approach to decision making.

Chapter 5: What Do You Value?

Transfer the numbers for each of the 16 items to the appropriate column; then add up the two numbers in each column.

	Professional	Financial	Family	Social
	1. ___	2. ___	3. ___	4. ___
	9. ___	10. ___	11. ___	12. ___
Totals	___	___	___	___

	Community	Spiritual	Physical	Intellectual
	5. ___	6. ___	7. ___	8. ___
	13. ___	14. ___	15. ___	16. ___
Totals	___	___	___	___

The higher the total in any value dimension, the higher the importance you place on that value set. The closer the numbers are in all eight dimensions, the more well rounded you are.

Chapter 6: What Motivates You?

To determine your dominant needs—and what motivates you—place the number 1 through 5 that represents your score for each statement next to the number for that statement.

	Achievement	Power	Affiliation
	1. ___	2. ___	3. ___
	4. ___	5. ___	6. ___
	7. ___	8. ___	9. ___
	10. ___	11. ___	12. ___
	13. ___	14. ___	15. ___
Totals:	___	___	___

Add up the total of each column. The sum of the numbers in each column will be between 5 and 25 points. The column with the highest score tells you your dominant need.

Chapter 7: How Equity Sensitive Are You?

Sum up the points you allocated to the following items: 1B; 2A; 3B; 4A; and 5B. Your total will be between zero and 50.

Researchers have identified three equity sensitivity groups. They are labeled and defined as follows:

- Benevolents: Individuals who prefer their outcome/input ratios be less than the comparison others.
- Equity Sensitives: Individuals who prefer outcome/input ratios to be equal.
- Entitleds: Individuals who prefer their outcome/input ratios exceed those of the comparison others.

Based on data from more than 3,500 respondents, the researchers have found that scores less than 29 are classified as Entitleds; those between 29 and 32 are Equity Sensitives; and those with scores above 32 are Benevolents.

What does all this mean? First, not all individuals are equity sensitive. Second, equity theory predictions are most accurate with individuals in the Equity Sensitive group. And third, Benevolents actually prefer lower outcome/input ratios and tend to provide higher levels of inputs than either Equity Sensitives or Entitleds.

Chapter 8: Are You Attracted to the Group?

Add up your scores for items 4,6,7,8,9,10,14,17,19, and 20. Obtain a corrected score by subtracting the score for each of the remaining questions from 10. For example, if you marked 3 for item 1, you would obtain a corrected score of 7 (10 − 3). Add the corrected scores together with the total obtained on the ten items scored directly. The higher your score, the more positive are your feelings about the group.

Chapter 9: Do Others See Me as Trustworthy?

Add up your total score for the seven statements. The following provides general guidelines for interpreting your score.

57–70 points = You're seen as highly trustworthy.
21–56 points = You're seen as moderately trustworthy.
7–20 points = You're rated low on this characteristic.

Chapter 10: Listening Self-Inventory

The correct answers to the 15 questions, based on listening theory, are as follows: (1) No; (2) No; (3) No; (4) Yes; (5) No; (6) No; (7) No; (8) No; (9) No; (10) No; (11) No; (12) Yes; (13) Yes; (14) No; (15) Yes. To determine your score, add up the number of incorrect answers, multiply by 7, and subtract that total from 105. If you scored between 91 and 105, you have good listening habits. Scores of 77 to 90 suggest significant room for improvement. Scores below 76 indicate you're a poor listener and need to work hard on improving this skill.

Chapter 11: What's Your LPC Score?

Your score on the LPC scale is a measure of your leadership style. More specifically, it indicates your primary motivation or goal in a work setting.

To determine your LPC score, add up the points (1 through 8) for each of the 16 items. If your score is 64 or above, you're a *high* LPC person or *relationship* oriented. If your score is 57 or below, you're a *low* LPC person or *task* oriented. If your score falls between 58 and 63, you'll need to determine for yourself in which category you belong.

According to Fiedler, knowing your LPC score can allow you to find a situational match and, therefore, help you to be a more effective leader.

Chapter 12: How Political Are You?

According to the author of this instrument, a complete organizational politician will answer "true" to all 10 questions. Organizational politicians with fundamental ethical standards will answer "false" to questions 5 and 6, which deal with deliberate lies and uncharitable behavior. Individuals who regard manipulation, incomplete disclosure, and self-serving behavior as unacceptable will answer "false" to all or almost all of the questions.

Chapter 13: What Is Your Primary Conflict-Handling Intention?

To determine your primary conflict-handling intention, place the number 1 through 5 that represents your score for each statement next to the number for that statement. Then total up the columns.

	Competing	Collaborating	Avoiding	Accommodating	Compromising
	1. 3	4. 4	6. 4	3. 5	2. 4
	5. 2	9. 5	10. 4	11. 3	8. 4
	7. 3	12. 4	15. 4	14. 3	13. 4
Totals	8	13	12	11	12

Your primary conflict-handling intention is the category with the highest total. Your fall-back intention is the category with the second highest total.

Chapter 14: Bureaucratic Orientation Test

Give yourself one point for each statement for which you responded in the bureaucratic direction:

1. Mostly agree
2. Mostly agree
3. Mostly disagree
4. Mostly agree
5. Mostly disagree
6. Mostly disagree
7. Mostly agree
8. Mostly agree
9. Mostly disagree
10. Mostly agree
11. Mostly agree
12. Mostly disagree
13. Mostly disagree
14. Mostly agree
15. Mostly disagree
16. Mostly agree
17. Mostly disagree
18. Mostly agree
19. Mostly agree
20. Mostly disagree

A very high score (15 or over) suggests you would enjoy working in a bureaucracy. A very low score (5 or lower) suggests you would be frustrated by working in a bureaucracy, especially a large one.

Chapter 15: What's Your Stress Personality?

Total your score for the 20 items. The authors of this test provide the following analysis of your result:

20–29. You are your own best ally, with a high degree of control, self-esteem, and identity.

30–49. You have a healthy sense of control over your life, but occasionally negative self-talk causes you to feel anxious in stressful situations.

50–69. Your options are often clouded and you feel trapped because of frequent negative self-talk.

70–80. Life has become one crisis and struggle after another.

Chapter 16: Career Assessment Test

This instrument is an expanded version of Schein's five career anchors. It adds service, identity, and variety anchors. Score your responses by writing the number that corresponds to your response (SA = 4, A = 3, D = 2, SD = 1) to each question in the space next to the item number.

1 2	2 2	3 2	4 3	5 3	6 2
7 3	8 2	9 2	10 4	11 3	12 3
13 2	14 2	15 2	16 3	17 3	18 2
19 2	20 2	21 3	22 2	23 2	24 3
25 2	26 2	27 2	28 2	29 2	30 3
31 3	32 3	33 3	34 2	35 2	36 3
37 3	38 2	39 2	40 2	41 2	42 3
43 3	44 3				

Now obtain subscale scores by adding your scores on the items indicated and then divide by the number of items in the scale, as shown:

Technical Competence	numbers 1, 2, 27, 35, 38, 41	÷ 6 =	2
Autonomy	numbers 3, 18, 23, 36, 39, 40	÷ 6 =	2.17
Service	numbers 4, 21, 37, 42, 43, 44	÷ 6 =	3
Identity	numbers 7, 13, 20, 22, 26	÷ 5 =	2.2
Variety	numbers 5, 12, 14, 24, 31, 32	÷ 6 =	2.83
Managerial Competence	numbers 6, 10, 11, 15, 25, 30	÷ 6 =	2.67
Security	numbers 8, 16, 17, 28, 33	÷ 5 =	2.60
Creativity	numbers 9, 19, 29, 34	÷ 4 =	2.00

Briefly, the eight career anchors mean the following:

- *Technical competence*. You organize your career around the challenge of the actual work you're doing.
- *Autonomy*. You value freedom and independence.
- *Service*. You're concerned with helping others or working on an important cause.
- *Identity*. You're concerned with status, prestige, and titles in your work.
- *Variety*. You seek an endless variety of new and different challenges.
- *Managerial competence*. You like to solve problems and want to lead and control others.
- *Security*. You want stability and career security.
- *Creativity*. You have a strong need to create something of your own.

The higher your score on a given anchor, the stronger your emphasis. You'll function best when your job fits with your career anchor. Lack of fit between anchor and a job can cause you to leave the organization or suffer excessive stress.

Ask yourself now: On which anchor did I receive the highest score? What jobs fit best with this anchor? You can use your analysis to help you select the right job and career for you.

Chapter 17: What Kind of Organizational Culture Fits You Best?

For items 5 and 6, score as follows:

Strongly agree	=	+2
Agree	=	+1
Uncertain	=	0
Disagree	=	−1
Strongly disagree	=	−2

For items 1,2,3,4, and 7, reverse the score (Strongly agree = −2, and so on). Add up your total. Your score will fall somewhere between +14 and −14.

What does your score mean? The higher your score (positive), the more comfortable you'll be in a formal, mechanistic, rule-oriented, and structured culture. This is often associated with large corporations and government agencies. Negative scores indicate a preference for informal, humanistic, flexible, and innovative cultures, which are more likely to be found in research units, advertising firms, high-tech companies, and small businesses.

Chapter 18: Managing-in-a-Turbulent-World Tolerance Test

Score 4 points for each A, 3 for each B, 2 for each C, 1 for each D, and 0 for each E. Compute the total, divide by 24, and round to one decimal place.

While the results are not intended to be more than suggestive, the higher your score, the more comfortable you seem to be with change. The test's author suggests analyzing scores as if they were grade-point averages. In this way, a 4.0 average is an A, a 2.0 is a C, and scores below 1.0 flunk.

Using replies from nearly 500 MBA students and young managers, the range of scores was found to be narrow—between 1.0 and 2.2. The average score was between 1.5 and 1.6—equivalent to a D+/C− grade! If these scores are generalizable to the work population, clearly people are not very tolerant of the kind of changes that come with a turbulent environment. However, this sample is now nearly a decade old. We should expect average scores today to be higher as people have become more accustomed to living in a dynamic environment.

GLOSSARY

The number in parentheses following each term indicates the chapter in which the term was defined.

Ability (3) An individual's capacity to perform the various tasks in a job.
Absenteeism (1) Failure to report to work.
Accommodating (13) The willingness of one party in a conflict to place the opponent's interests above his or her own.
Achievement need (6) The drive to excel, to achieve in relation to a set of standards, to strive to succeed.
Action research (18) A change process based on systematic collection of data and then selection of a change action based on what the analyzed data indicate.
Adjourning (8) The final stage in group development for temporary groups, characterized by concern with wrapping up activities rather than task performance.
Affective component of an attitude (5) The emotional or feeling segment of an attitude.
Affiliation need (6) The desire for friendly and close interpersonal relationships.
Affirmative action programs (2) Programs that enhance the organizational status of members of protected groups.
Agreeableness (3) A personality dimension that describes someone who is good-natured, cooperative, and trusting.
Arbitrator (13) A third party to a negotiation who has the authority to dictate an agreement.
Assessment centers (16) A set of performance simulation tests designed to evaluate a candidate's managerial potential.
Attitudes (5) Evaluative statements or judgments concerning objects, people, or events.
Attitude surveys (5) Eliciting responses from employees through questionnaires about how they feel about their jobs, work groups, supervisors, and/or the organization.
Attribution theory (4) When individuals observe behavior, they attempt to determine whether it is internally or externally caused.
Attribution theory of leadership (11) Proposes that leadership is merely an attribution that people make about other individuals.
Authority (14) The rights inherent in a managerial position to give orders and expect the orders to be obeyed.
Autonomy (15) The degree to which the job provides substantial freedom and discretion to the individual in scheduling the work and in determining the procedures to be used in carrying it out.
Avoiding (13) The desire to withdraw from or suppress a conflict.

BATNA (13) The Best Alternative To a Negotiated Agreement; the lowest acceptable value to an individual for a negotiated agreement.
Behavioral component of an attitude (5) An intention to behave in a certain way toward someone or something.
Behavioral theories of leadership (11) Theories proposing that specific behaviors differentiate leaders from nonleaders.
Behaviorally anchored rating scales (16) An evaluation method where actual job-related behaviors are rated along a continuum.
Biographical characteristics (3) Personal characteristics—such as age, gender, and marital status—that are objective and easily obtained from personnel records.
Board representatives (7) A form of representative participation; employees sit on a company's board of directors and represent the interests of the firm's employees.
Boundaryless organization (14) An organization that seeks to eliminate the chain of command, have limitless spans of control, and replace departments with empowered teams.
Bounded rationality (4) Individuals make decisions by constructing simplified models that extract the essential features from problems without capturing all their complexity.
Brainstorming (8) An idea-generation process that specifically encourages any and all alternatives, while withholding any criticism of those alternatives.
Bridges (8) Individuals in a social network who serve as linking pins by belonging to two or more clusters.
Bureaucracy (14) A structure with highly routine operating tasks achieved through specialization, very formalized rules and regulations, tasks that are grouped into functional departments, centralized authority, narrow spans of control, and decision making that follows the chain of command.

Career (16) A sequence of positions occupied by a person during the course of a lifetime.
Career anchors (16) Distinct patterns of self-perceived talents and abilities, motives and needs, and attitudes and values that guide and stabilize a person's career after several years of real-world experience and feedback.
Career stages (16) The four steps most people go through in their careers: exploration, establishment, midcareer, and late career.
Centralization (14) The degree to which decision making is concentrated at a single point in the organization.
Chain of command (14) The unbroken line of authority that extends

from the top of the organization to the lowest eschelon and clarifies who reports to whom.

Change (18) Making things different.

Change agents (18) Persons who act as catalysts and assume the responsibility for managing change activities.

Channel (10) The medium through which a communication message travels.

Channel richness (10) The amount of information that can be transmitted during a communication episode.

Charismatic leadership (11) Followers make attributions of heroic or extraordinary leadership abilities when they observe certain behaviors.

Classical conditioning (3) A type of conditioning where an individual responds to some stimulus that would not invariably produce such a response.

Cliques (8) Relatively permanent informal groups that involve friendship.

Clusters (8) Groups that exist within social networks.

Coalitions (8) Clusters of individuals who temporarily come together to achieve a specific purpose.

Coercive power (12) Power that is based on fear.

Cognitive component of an attitude (5) The opinion or belief segment of an attitude.

Cognitive dissonance (5) Any incompatibility between two or more attitudes or between behavior and attitudes.

Cognitive evaluation theory (6) Allocating extrinsic rewards for behavior that had been previously intrinsically rewarded tends to decrease the overall level of motivation.

Cognitive resource theory (11) A theory of leadership that states that a leader obtains effective group performance by, first, making effective plans, decisions, and strategies, and then communicating them through directive behavior.

Cohesiveness (8) Degree to which group members are attracted to each other and are motivated to stay in the group.

Cohorts (8) Individuals who, as part of a group, hold a common attribute.

Collaborating (13) A situation where the parties to a conflict each desire to satisfy fully the concerns of all parties.

Collectivism (2) A national culture attribute that describes a tight social framework in which people expect others in groups of which they are a part to look after them and protect them.

Command group (8) A manager and his or her immediate subordinates.

Committees (9) A group made up of members from across departmental lines.

Communication (10) The transference and understanding of meaning.

Communication apprehension (10) Undue tension and anxiety about oral communication, written communication, or both.

Communication networks (10) Channels by which information flows.

Communication process (10) The steps between a source and a receiver that result in the transference and understanding of meaning.

Comparable worth (7) A doctrine that holds that jobs equal in value to an organization should be equally compensated, whether or not the work content of those jobs is similar.

Competence (9) Technical and interpersonal knowledge and skill.

Competing (13) A desire to satisfy one's interests, regardless of the impact on the other party to the conflict.

Compressed workweek (15) A four-day week, with employees working ten hours a day.

Compromising (13) A situation in which each party to a conflict is willing to give up something.

Conceptual skills (1) The mental ability to analyze and diagnose complex situations.

Conciliator (13) A trusted third party who provides an informal communication link between the negotiator and the opponent.

Conflict (13) A process that begins when one party perceives that another party has negatively affected, or is about to negatively affect, something that the first party cares about.

Conflict management (13) The use of resolution and stimulation techniques to achieve the desired level of conflict.

Conflict process (13) Five stages: potential opposition or incompatibility; cognition and personalization; intentions; behavior; and outcomes.

Conformity (8) Adjusting one's behavior to align with the norms of the group.

Conscientiousness (3) A personality dimension that describes someone who is responsible, dependable, persistent, and achievement oriented.

Consideration (11) The extent to which a leader is likely to have job relationships characterized by mutual trust, respect for subordinates' ideas, and regard for their feelings.

Consistency (9) Reliability, predictability, and good judgment in handling situations.

Constraints (15) Forces that prevent individuals from doing what they desire.

Consultant as negotiator (13) An impartial third party, skilled in conflict management, who attempts to facilitate creative problem solving through communication and analysis.

Contingency variables (1) Situational factors; variables that moderate the relationship between the independent and dependent variables and improve the correlation.

Continuous reinforcement (3) A desired behavior is reinforced each and every time it is demonstrated.

Contrast effects (4) Evaluations of a person's characteristics that are affected by comparisons with other people recently encountered who rank higher or lower on the same characteristics.

Controlling (1) Monitoring activities to ensure they are being accomplished as planned and correcting any significant deviations.

Core values (17) The primary or dominant values that are accepted throughout the organization.

Cost-minimization strategy (14) A strategy that emphasizes tight cost controls, avoidance of unnecessary innovation or marketing expenses, and price-cutting.

Critical incidents (16) Evaluating those behaviors that are key in making the difference between executing a job effectively and executing it ineffectively.

Cross-functional teams (9) Employees from about the same hierarchical level, but from different work areas, who come together to accomplish a task.

Culture shock (2) Confusion, disorientation, and emotional upheaval caused by being immersed in a new culture.

Decentralization (14) Decision discretion is pushed down to lower-level employees.

Decisions (4) The making of choices from among two or more alternatives.

Decoding (10) Retranslating a sender's communication message.

Defensive behaviors (12) Reactive and protective behaviors to avoid action, blame, or change.

Delphi technique (8) A group decision method in which individual members, acting separately, pool their judgments in a systematic and independent fashion.

Demands (15) The loss of something desired.

Departmentalization (14) The basis by which jobs are grouped together.

Dependency (12) B's relationship to A when A possesses something that B requires.

Dependent variable (1) A response that is affected by an independent variable.

Development-oriented leader (11) One who values experimentation, the seeking of new ideas, and the generating and implementing of change.

Distinctive competencies (15) Defines what it is that the organization is more superior at delivering than its competition.

Distributive bargaining (13) Negotiation that seeks to divide up a fixed amount of resources; a win-lose situation.

Distributive justice (6) Perceived fairness of the amount and allocation of rewards among individuals.

Dominant culture (17) Expresses the core values that are shared by a majority of the organization's members.

Double-loop learning (18) Errors are corrected by modifying the organization's objectives, policies, and standard routines.

Driving forces (18) Forces that direct behavior away from the status quo.

Dysfunctional conflict (13) Conflict that hinders group performance.

Effectiveness (1) Achievement of goals.

Efficiency (1) The ratio of effective output to the input required to achieve it.

Elasticity of power (12) The relative responsiveness of power to changes in available alternatives.

Emergent clusters (8) Informal, unofficial groups.

Emotional stability (3) A personality dimension that characterizes someone who is calm, enthusiastic, secure (positive) to tense, nervous, depressed, and insecure (negative).

Employee involvement (7) A participative process that uses the entire capacity of employees and is designed to encourage increased commitment to the organization's success.

Employee-oriented leader (11) One who emphasizes interpersonal relations.

Employee stock ownership plans (ESOPs) (7) Company-established benefit plans in which employees acquire stock as part of their benefits.

Empowerment (1) Putting employees in charge of what they do.

Encoding (10) Converting a communication message to symbolic form.

Encounter stage (17) The stage in the socialization process in which a new employee sees what the organization is really like and confronts the possibility that expectations and reality may diverge.

Environment (14) Those institutions or forces outside the organization that potentially affect the organization's performance.

Equity theory (6) Individuals compare their job inputs and outcomes with those of others and then respond so as to eliminate any inequities.

ERG theory (6) There are three groups of core needs: existence, relatedness, and growth.

Escalation of commitment (4) An increased commitment to a previous decision in spite of negative information.

Ethical dilemma (1) Situations where an individual is required to define right and wrong conduct.

Ethnocentric views (2) The belief that one's cultural values and customs are superior to all others.

European Union (2) A common market made up of 15 nations: France, Denmark, Belgium, Greece, Ireland, Italy, Luxembourg, the Netherlands, Portugal, Spain, the United Kingdom, Austria, Finland, Sweden, and Germany.

Extraversion (3) A personality dimension describing someone who is sociable, talkative, and assertive.

Exit (5) Dissatisfaction expressed through behavior directed toward leaving the organization.

Expectancy theory (6) The strength of a tendency to act in a certain way depends on the strength of an expectation that the act will be followed by a given outcome and on the attractiveness of that outcome to the individual.

Expert power (12) Influence based on special skills or knowledge.

Externals (3) Individuals who believe that what happens to them is controlled by outside forces such as luck or chance.

Extrinsic rewards (16) Rewards received from the environment surrounding the context of the work.

Family-friendly organizations (15) Companies that offer an umbrella of work/family programs such as on-site day-care, child-care and elder-care referrals, flexible hours, compressed workweeks, job sharing, telecommuting, temporary part-time employment, and relocation assistance for employees' family members.

Feedback (15) The degree to which carrying out the work activities required by a job results in the individual obtaining direct and clear information about the effectiveness of his or her performance.

Feedback loop (10) The final link in the communication process; puts the message back into the system as a check against misunderstandings.

Felt conflict (13) Emotional involvement in a conflict creating anxiety, tenseness, frustration, or hostility.

Feminine organization (14) An organization characterized by humanistic treatment of individuals, nonopportunism, careers defined through service to others, commitment to employee growth, creation of a caring community, and power sharing.

Fiedler contingency model (11) The theory that effective groups depend upon a proper match between a leader's style of interacting with subordinates and the degree to which the situation gives control and influence to the leader.

Filtering (10) A sender's manipulation of information so that it will be seen more favorably by the receiver.

First-order change (18) Linear and continuous.

Fixed-interval schedule (3) Rewards are spaced at uniform time intervals.

Fixed-ratio schedule (3) Rewards are initiated after a fixed or constant number of responses.

Flexible benefits (7) Employees tailor their benefit program to meet their personal needs by picking and choosing from a menu of benefit options.

Flexible manufacturing system (15) Integration of computer-aided design, engineering, and manufacturing to produce low-volume products at mass-production costs.

Flextime (15) Employees work during a common core time period each day but have discretion in forming their total workday from a flexible set of hours outside the core.

Formal group (8) A designated work group defined by the organization's structure.

Formal networks (10) Task-related communications that follow the authority chain.

Formalization (14) The degree to which jobs within the organization are standardized.

Forming (8) The first stage in group development, characterized by much uncertainty.

Friendship group (8) Those brought together because they share one or more common characteristics.

Functional conflict (13) Conflict that supports the goals of the group and improves its performance.

Fundamental attribution error (4) The tendency to underestimate the influence of external factors and overestimate the influence of internal factors when making judgments about the behavior of others.

Gainsharing (7) An incentive plan where improvements in group productivity determine the total amount of money that is allocated.

Goal-setting theory (6) The theory that specific and difficult goals lead to higher performance.

Graphic rating scales (16) An evaluation method where the evaluator rates performance factors on an incremental scale.

Group (8) Two or more individuals, interacting and interdependent, who have come together to achieve particular objectives.

Group demography (8) The degree to which members of a group share a common demographic attribute, such as age, gender, race, educational level, or length of service in the organization, and the impact of this attribute on turnover.

Group order ranking (16) An evaluation method that places employees into a particular classification such as quartiles.

Groupshift (8) A change in decision risk between the group's decision and the individual decision that members within the group would make; can be either toward conservatism or greater risk.

Groupthink (8) Phenomenon in which the norm for consensus overrides the realistic appraisal of alternative courses of action.

Halo effect (4) Drawing a general impression about an individual based on a single characteristic.

Hierarchy of needs theory (6) There is a hierarchy of five needs—physiological, safety, social, esteem, and self-actualization—and as each need is sequentially satisfied, the next need becomes dominant.

Higher-order needs (6) Needs that are satisfied internally; social, esteem, and self-actualization needs.

Human relations view of conflict (13) The belief that conflict is a natural and inevitable outcome in any group.

Human skills (1) The ability to work with, understand, and motivate other people, both individually and in groups.

Hygiene factors (6) Those factors—such as company policy and administration, supervision, and salary—that, when adequate in a job, placate workers. When these factors are adequate, people will not be dissatisfied.

Illegitimate political behavior (12) Extreme political behavior that violates the implied rules of the game.

Imitation strategy (14) A strategy that seeks to move into new products or new markets only after their viability has already been proven.

Implicit favorite model (4) A decision-making model where the decision maker implicitly selects a preferred alternative early in the decision process and biases the evaluation of all other choices.

Impression management (12) The process by which individuals attempt to control the impression others form of them.

Independent variable (1) The presumed cause of some change in the dependent variable.

Individual ranking (16) An evaluation method that rank-orders employees from best to worst.

Individualism (2) A national culture attribute describing a loosely knit social framework in which people emphasize only the care of themselves and their immediate family.

Informal group (8) A group that is neither formally structured nor organizationally determined; appears in response to the need for social contact.

Informal network (10) The communication grapevine.

Initiating structure (11) The extent to which a leader is likely to define and structure his or her role and those of subordinates in the search for goal attainment.

Innovation (18) A new idea applied to initiating or improving a product, process, or service.

Innovation strategy (14) A strategy that emphasizes the introduction of major new products and services.

Institutionalization (17) When an organization takes on a life of its own, apart from any of its members, and acquires immortality.

Instrumental values (5) Preferable modes of behavior or means of achieving one's terminal values.

Integrative bargaining (13) Negotiation that seeks one or more settlements that can create a win-win solution.

Integrity (9) Honesty and truthfulness.

Intellectual ability (3) That required to do mental activities.
Intentions (13) Decisions to act in a given way in a conflict episode.
Interacting groups (8) Typical groups, where members interact with each other face-to-face.
Interactionist view of conflict (13) The belief that conflict is not only a positive force in a group but that it is absolutely necessary for a group to perform effectively.
Interest group (8) Those working together to attain a specific objective with which each is concerned.
Intergroup development (18) OD efforts to change the attitudes, stereotypes, and perceptions that groups have of each other.
Intermittent reinforcement (3) A desired behavior is reinforced often enough to make the behavior worth repeating, but not every time it is demonstrated.
Internals (3) Individuals who believe that they control what happens to them.
Intrinsic rewards (16) The pleasure or value one receives from the content of a work task.
Intuition (1) A feeling not necessarily supported by research.
Intuitive decision making (4) An unconscious process created out of distilled experience.
Isolates (8) Individuals who are not connected to a social network.

Job analysis (16) Developing a detailed description of the tasks involved in a job, determining the relationship of a given job to other jobs, and ascertaining the knowledge, skills, and abilities necessary for an employee to perform the job successfully.
Job characteristics model (15) Identifies five job characteristics and their relationship to personal and work outcomes.
Job description (16) A written statement of what a jobholder does, how it is done, and why it is done.
Job enlargement (15) The horizontal expansion of jobs.
Job enrichment (15) The vertical expansion of jobs.
Job involvement (5) The degree to which a person identifies with his or her job, actively participates in it, and considers his or her performance important to self-worth.
Job rotation (15) The periodic shifting of a worker from one task to another.
Job satisfaction (1) A general attitude toward one's job; the difference between the amount of rewards workers receive and the amount they believe they should receive.
Job sharing (15) The practice of having two or more people split a forty-hour-a-week job.
Job specification (16) States the minimum acceptable qualifications that an employee must possess to perform a given job successfully.

Kinesics (10) The study of body motions.

Labor union (16) An organization, made up of employees, that acts collectively to protect and promote employee interests.
Leader–member exchange (LMX) theory (11) Leaders create in-groups and out-groups, and subordinates with in-group status will have higher performance ratings, less turnover, and greater satisfaction with their superior.
Leader–member relations (11) The degree of confidence, trust, and respect subordinates have in their leader.
Leader-participation model (11) A leadership theory that provides a set of rules to determine the form and amount of participative decision making in different situations.
Leadership (11) The ability to influence a group toward the achievement of goals.
Leading (1) Includes motivating subordinates, directing others, selecting the most effective communication channels, and resolving conflicts.
Learning (3) Any relatively permanent change in behavior that occurs as a result of experience.
Learning organization (18) An organization that has developed the continuous capacity to adapt and change.
Least preferred co-worker (LPC) questionnaire (11) An instrument that purports to measure whether a person is task- or relationship-oriented.
Legitimate political behavior (12) Normal everyday politics.
Legitimate power (12) The power a person receives as a result of his or her position in the formal hierarchy of an organization.
Leniency error (16) The tendency to evaluate a set of employees too high (positive) or too low (negative).
Liaisons (8) Individuals in a social network who connect two or more clusters but are not members of any cluster.
Locus of control (3) The degree to which people be-lieve they are masters of their own fate.
Lower-order needs (6) Needs that are satisfied externally; physiological and safety needs.
Loyalty (5) Dissatisfaction expressed by passively waiting for conditions to improve.

Machiavellianism (3) Degree to which an individual is pragmatic, maintains emotional distance, and believes that ends can justify means.
McClelland's theory of needs (6) Achievement, power, and affiliation are three important needs that help to understand motivation.
Management by objectives (MBO) (7) A program that encompasses specific goals, participatively set, for an explicit time period, with feedback on goal progress.
Managerial Grid (11) A nine-by-nine matrix outlining eighty-one different leadership styles.
Managers (1) Individuals who achieve goals through other people.
Matrix structure (14) A structure that creates dual lines of authority; combines functional and product departmentalization.
Mechanistic model (14) A structure characterized by extensive departmentalization, high formalization, a limited information network, and centralization.
Mediator (13) A neutral third party who facilitates a negotiated solution by using reasoning, persuasion, and suggestions for alternatives.
Message (10) What is communicated.
Metamorphosis stage (17) The stage in the socialization process in which a new employee adjusts to his or her work group's values and norms.
Model (1) Abstraction of reality; simplified representation of some real-world phenomenon.

Motivating potential score (15) A predictive index suggesting the motivation potential in a job.
Motivation (6) The willingness to exert high levels of effort toward organizational goals, conditioned by the effort's ability to satisfy some individual need.
Motivation-hygiene theory (6) Intrinsic factors are related to job satisfaction, while extrinsic factors are associated with dissatisfaction.
Multinational corporations (2) Companies that maintain significant operations in two or more countries simultaneously.
Myers-Briggs Type Indicator (MBTI) (3) A personality test that taps 4 characteristics and classifies people into one of 16 personality types.

National culture (2) The primary values and practices that characterize a particular country.
Need (6) Some internal state that makes certain outcomes appear attractive.
Neglect (5) Dissatisfaction expressed through allowing conditions to worsen.
Negotiation (13) A process in which two or more parties exchange goods or services and attempt to agree upon the exchange rate for them.
Nominal group technique (8) A group decision-making method in which individual members meet face-to-face to pool their judgments in a systematic but independent fashion.
Nonverbal communications (10) Messages conveyed through body movements, the intonations or emphasis we give to words, facial expressions, and the physical distance between the sender and receiver.
Norming (8) The third stage in group development, characterized by close relationships and cohesiveness.
Norms (8) Acceptable standards of behavior within a group that are shared by the group's members.
North American Free Trade Agreement (NAFTA) (2) An agreement that phases out tariffs on most goods traded among the U.S., Canada, and Mexico.

OB Mod (7) A program where managers identify performance-related employee behaviors and then implement an intervention strategy to strengthen desirable performance behaviors and weaken undesirable behaviors.
Openness (9) Willingness to share ideas and information freely.
Openness to experience (3) A personality dimension that characterizes someone who is imaginative, artistically sensitive, and intellectual.
Operant conditioning (3) A type of conditioning in which desired voluntary behavior leads to a reward or prevents a punishment.
Opportunity to perform (6) High levels of performance are partially a function of an absence of obstacles that constrain the employee.
Optimizing model (4) A decision-making model that describes how individuals should behave in order to maximize some outcome.
Organic model (14) A structure that is flat, uses cross-hierarchical and cross-functional teams, has low formalization, possesses a comprehensive information network, and relies on participative decision making.
Organization (1) A consciously coordinated social unit, composed of two or more people, that functions on a relatively continuous basis to achieve a common goal or set of goals.
Organizational structure (14) How job tasks are formally divided, grouped, and coordinated.
Organizational behavior (OB) (1) A field of study that investigates the impact that individuals, groups, and structure have on behavior within organizations, for the purpose of applying such knowledge toward improving an organization's effectiveness.
Organizational commitment (5) The degree to which an employee identifies with a particular organization and its goals, and wishes to maintain membership in the organization.
Organizational culture (17) A common perception held by the organization's members; a system of shared meaning.
Organizational development (18) A collection of planned-change interventions, built on humanistic-democratic values, that seek to improve organizational effectiveness and employee well-being.
Organizing (1) Determining what tasks are to be done, who is to do them, how the tasks are to be grouped, who reports to whom, and where decisions are to be made.

Paired comparison (16) An evaluation method that compares each employee with every other employee and assigns a summary ranking based on the number of superior scores that the employee achieves.
Parochialism (2) A narrow view of the world; an inability to recognize differences between people.
Participative management (7) A process where subordinates share a significant degree of decision-making power with their immediate superiors.
Path-goal theory (11) The theory that a leader's behavior is acceptable to subordinates insofar as they view it as a source of either immediate or future satisfaction.
Perceived conflict (13) Awareness by one or more parties of the existence of conditions that create opportunities for conflict to arise.
Perception (4) A process by which individuals organize and interpret their sensory impressions in order to give meaning to their environment.
Performing (8) The fourth stage in group development, when the group is fully functional.
Personality (3) The sum total of ways in which an individual reacts and interacts with others.
Personality-job fit theory (3) Identifies 6 personality types and proposes that the fit between personality type and occupational environment determines satisfaction and turnover.
Personality traits (3) Enduring characteristics that describe an individual's behavior.
Physical ability (3) That required to do tasks demanding stamina, dexterity, strength, and similar skills.
Piece-rate pay plans (7) Workers are paid a fixed sum for each unit of production completed.
Planned change (18) Change activities that are intentional and goal-oriented.
Planning (1) Includes defining goals, establishing strategy, and developing plans to coordinate activities.
Political behavior (12) Those activities that are not required as part of one's formal role in the organization, but that influence, or attempt to influence, the distribution of advan-

tages and disadvantages within the organization.

Pooled interdependence (13) Where two groups function with relative independence but their combined output contributes to the organization's overall goals.

Position power (11) Influence derived from one's formal structural position in the organization; includes power to hire, fire, discipline, promote, and give salary increases.

Power (12) A capacity that A has to influence the behavior of B so that B does things he or she would not otherwise do.

Power distance (2) A national culture attribute describing the extent to which a society accepts that power in institutions and organizations is distributed unequally.

Power need (6) The desire to make others behave in a way that they would not otherwise have behaved in.

Power tactics (12) Ways in which individuals translate power bases into specific actions.

Prearrival stage (17) The period of learning in the socialization process that occurs before a new employee joins the organization.

Prescribed clusters (8) Formal groups like departments, work teams, task forces, or committees.

Problem (4) A discrepancy between some current state of affairs and some desired state.

Problem-solving teams (9) Groups of 5 to 12 employees from the same department who meet for a few hours each week to discuss ways of improving quality, efficiency, and the work environment.

Procedural justice (6) The perceived fairness of the process used to determine the distribution of rewards.

Process consultation (18) Consultant gives a client insights into what is going on around the client, within the client, and between the client and other people; identifies processes that need improvement.

Process value analysis (15) Determination to what degree each organizational process adds value to the organization's distinctive competencies.

Production-oriented leader (11) One who emphasizes technical or task aspects of the job.

Productivity (1) A performance measure including effectiveness and efficiency.

Profit-sharing plans (7) Organization-wide programs that distribute compensation based on some established formula designed around a company's profitability.

Projection (4) Attributing one's own characteristics to other people.

Psychological contract (8) An unwritten agreement that sets out what management expects from the employee, and vice versa.

Quality circle (7) A work group of employees who meet regularly to discuss their quality problems, investigate causes, recommend solutions, and take corrective actions.

Quality of life (2) A national culture attribute that emphasizes relationships and concern for others.

Quantity of life (2) A national culture attribute describing the extent to which societal values are characterized by assertiveness and materialism.

Rationality (4) Choices that are consistent and value-maximizing.

Reciprocal interdependence (13) Where groups exchange inputs and outputs.

Reengineering (1) Reconsiders how work would be done and the organization structured if they were being created from scratch.

Referent power (12) Influence based on possession by an individual of desirable resources or personal traits.

Refreezing (18) Stabilizing a change intervention by balancing driving and restraining forces.

Reinforcement theory (6) Behavior is a function of its consequences.

Representative participation (7) Workers participate in organizational decision making through a small group of representative employees.

Restraining forces (18) Forces that hinder movement away from the status quo.

Reward power (12) Compliance achieved based on the ability to distribute rewards that others view as valuable.

Rituals (17) Repetitive sequences of activities that express and reinforce the key values of the organization, what goals are most important, which people are important and which are expendable.

Role (8) A set of expected behavior patterns attributed to someone occupying a given position in a social unit.

Role conflict (8) A situation in which an individual is confronted by divergent role expectations.

Role expectations (8) How others believe a person should act in a given situation.

Role identity (8) Certain attitudes and behaviors consistent with a role.

Role perception (8) An individual's view of how he or she is supposed to act in a given situation.

Satisficing model (4) A decision-making model where a decision maker chooses the first solution that is "good enough"; that is, satisfactory and sufficient.

Second-order change (18) Change that is multidimensional, multilevel, discontinuous, and radical.

Selective perception (4) People selectively interpret what they see based on their interests, background, experience, and attitudes.

Self-actualization (6) The drive to become what one is capable of becoming.

Self-efficacy (6) The individual's belief that he or she is capable of performing a task.

Self-esteem (3) Individuals' degree of liking or disliking for themselves.

Self-fulfilling prophecy (4) When one person inaccurately perceives a second person and the resulting expectations cause the second person to behave in ways consistent with the original perception.

Self-managed work teams (9) Groups of 10 to 15 people who take on responsibilities of their former supervisors.

Self-management (3) Learning techniques that allow individuals to manage their own behavior so that less external management control is necessary.

Self-monitoring (3) A personality trait that measures an individual's ability to adjust his or her behavior to external, situational factors.

Self-perception theory (5) Attitudes are used after the fact to make sense out of an action that has already occurred.

Self-serving bias (4) The tendency for individuals to attribute their own successes to internal factors while putting the blame for failures on external factors.

Sensitivity training (18) Training groups that seek to change behavior through unstructured group interaction.

Sequential interdependence (13) One group depends on another for its input but the dependency is only one way.

Sexual harassment (12) Unwelcome advances, requests for sexual favors, and other verbal or physical conduct of a sexual nature.

Shaping behavior (3) Systematically reinforcing each successive step that moves an individual closer to the desired response.

Similarity error (16) Giving special consideration when rating others to those qualities that the evaluator perceives in himself or herself.

Simple structure (14) A structure characterized by a low degree of departmentalization, wide spans of control, authority centralized in a single person, and little formalization.

Single-loop learning (18) Errors are corrected using past routines and present policies.

Situational leadership theory (11) A contingency theory that focuses on followers' readiness.

Skill-based pay (7) Pay levels are based on how many skills employees have or how many jobs they can do.

Skill variety (15) The degree to which the job requires a variety of different activities.

Socialization (17) The process that adapts employees to the organization's culture.

Social information-processing model (15) Employees adopt attitudes and behaviors in response to the social cues provided by others with whom they have contact.

Social-learning theory (3) People can learn through observation and direct experience.

Social loafing (8) The tendency for individuals to expend less effort when working collectively than when working individually.

Social networks (8) A specific set of linkages among a defined set of individuals.

Sociogram (8) A diagram that graphically maps the preferred social interactions obtained from interviews or questionnaires.

Sociometry (8) An analytical technique for studying group interactions.

Span of control (14) The number of subordinates a manager can efficiently and effectively direct.

Stages of moral development (4) An assessment of a person's capacity to judge what is morally right.

Stars (8) Individuals with the most linkages in a network.

Status (8) A socially defined position or rank given to groups or group members by others.

Stereotyping (4) Judging someone on the basis of one's perception of the group to which that person belongs.

Storming (8) The second stage in group development, characterized by intragroup conflict.

Stress (15) A dynamic condition in which an individual is confronted with an opportunity, constraint, or demand related to what he or she desires and for which the outcome is perceived to be both uncertain and important.

Strong cultures (17) Cultures where the core values are intensely held and widely shared.

Subcultures (17) Minicultures within an organization, typically defined by department designations and geographical separation.

Survey feedback (18) The use of questionnaires to identify discrepancies among member perceptions; discussion follows and remedies are suggested.

Synergy (8) An action of two or more substances that results in an effect that is different from the individual summation of the substances.

Systematic study (1) Looking at relationships, attempting to attribute causes and effects, and drawing conclusions based on scientific evidence.

Task characteristic theories (15) Seek to identify task characteristics of jobs, how these characteristics are combined to form different jobs, and their relationship to employee motivation, satisfaction, and performance.

Task force (9) A temporary cross-functional team

Task group (8) Those working together to complete a job task.

Task identity (15) The degree to which the job requires completion of a whole and identifiable piece of work.

Task significance (15) The degree to which the job has a substantial impact on the lives or work of other people.

Task structure (11) The degree to which job assignments are procedurized.

Task uncertainty (13) The greater the uncertainty in a task, the more custom the response. Conversely, low uncertainty encompasses routine tasks with standardized activities.

Team building (18) High interaction among team members to increase trust and openness.

Team structure (14) The use of teams as the central device to coordinate work activities.

Technical skills (1) The ability to apply specialized knowledge or expertise.

Technology (14) How an organization transfers its inputs into outputs.

Telecommuting (15) Employees do their work at home on a computer that is linked to their office.

Terminal values (5) Desirable end-states of existence; the goals that a person would like to achieve during his or her lifetime.

Theory X (6) The assumption that employees dislike work, are lazy, dislike responsibility, and must be coerced to perform.

Theory Y (6) The assumption that employees like work, are creative, seek responsibility, and can exercise self-direction.

Total quality management (TQM) (1) A philosophy of management that is driven by the constant attainment of customer satisfaction through the continuous improvement of all organizational processes.

Traditional view of conflict (13) The belief that all conflict is harmful and must be avoided.

Trait theories of leadership (11) Theories that sought personality, social, physical, or intellectual traits that differentiated leaders from nonleaders.

Transactional leaders (11) Leaders who guide or motivate their followers in the direction of established goals by clarifying role and task requirements.

Transformational leaders (11) Leaders who provide individualized consideration and intellectual stimulation, and who possess charisma.

Trust (9) A characteristic of high performance teams where members believe in the integrity, character, and ability of each other.

Turnover (1) Voluntary and involuntary permanent withdrawal from the organization.

Type A personality (3) Aggressive involvement in a chronic, incessant struggle to achieve more and more in less and less time and, if necessary, against the opposing efforts of other things or other people.

Uncertainty avoidance (2) A national culture attribute describing the extent to which a society feels threatened by uncertain and ambiguous situations and tries to avoid them.

Unfreezing (18) Change efforts to overcome the pressures of both individual resistance and group conformity.

Unity of command (14) A subordinate should have only one superior to whom he or she is directly responsible.

Utilitarianism (4) Decisions are made so as to provide the greatest good for the greatest number.

Value system (5) A hierarchy based on a ranking of an individual's values in terms of their intensity.

Values (5) Basic convictions that a specific mode of conduct or end-state of existence is personally or socially preferable to an opposite or converse mode of conduct or end-state of existence.

Variable-pay programs (7) A portion of an employee's pay is based on some individual and/or organizational measure of performance.

Variable-interval schedule (3) Rewards are distributed in time so that reinforcements are unpredictable.

Variable-ratio schedule (3) The reward varies relative to the behavior of the individual.

Virtual organization (14) A small, core organization that outsources major business functions.

Voice (5) Dissatisfaction expressed through active and constructive attempts to improve conditions.

Wellness programs (15) Organizationally supported programs that focus on the employee's total physical and mental condition.

Whistle-blowers (4) Individuals who report unethical practices by their employers to authorities inside and/or outside the organization.

Work force diversity (1) The increasing heterogeneity of organizations with the inclusion of different groups.

Work group (9) A group who interact primarily to share information and to make decisions to help each other perform within his or her area of responsibility.

Work sampling (16) Creating a miniature replica of a job to evaluate the performance abilities of job candidates.

Work team (9) A group whose individual efforts result in a performance that is greater than the sum of those individual inputs.

Work specialization (14) The degree to which tasks in the organization are subdivided into separate jobs.

Works councils (7) Groups of nominated or elected employees who must be consulted when management makes decisions involving personnel.

ILLUSTRATION CREDITS

Chapter 1

2 Louis Psihoyos/Matrix International; **3** Marilyn Adler; **5** William Taufic; **12** Jay Dickman; **15** Jim Sims; **17** Alan Levenson; **27** Linda Sue Scott; **37** Mark Jenkinson

Chapter 2

42 Arthur Meyerson. All rights reserved; **43** Peter Redman/Financial Post photo; **46** Munshi Ahmed; **48** Ann States/Saba Press Photos, Inc.; **51** E. Elder/Ponopress, Intl; **54** Courtesy United Airlines; **59** Alon Reininger/Contact Press; **65** Courtesy of John Hancock Financial Services; **77** Courtesy of Rob Panco

Chapter 3

80 Michael L. Abramson; **81** Eden Robbins; **83** Kevin Horan/Picture Group; **91** Mary Beth Camp/Matrix International; **107** Printed in Business Week-11/14/94 p.5+63/Rahn & Assoc.; **109** Courtesy of Siemans Corporation; **114** David Walberg; **117** Scott Goldsmith

Chapter 4

130 Andy Freeberg; **131** Superstock; **137** Maejima - Jan, 12, 1995/Pan-Asia Newspaper Alliance; **140** Bayne Stanley; **142** Courtesy of AMP Incorporated; **149** Doug Wilson/Black Star; **155** Terry Ashe/ Gamma-Liaison, Inc; 159 Munshi Ahmed

Chapter 5

172 Courtesy of Pep Boys; **173** David Schlabowske; **179** Ian Howart/Adventure Photo; **182** Andrew Vracin Photography; **184** Dave Buston; **189** Courtesy of Meridan Bancorp, Inc. Reading, PA; **193** Courtesy of Walgreen Co.; **195** Max Aguilera Hellweg

Chapter 6

210 Nina Berman/Sipa Press; **211** Courtesy Lincoln Electric Company; **215** Steve Woit; **220** Rhoda Baer; **224** Grant M. Jamieson; **228** Steve Dun/Allsport; **235** Charlesworth/Saba Press Photos, Inc.; **243** Rich Mays Photography

Chapter 7

250 James Schnepf/Gamma-Liaison, Inc.; **251** Courtesy of Donnelly Corporation; **258** Sandy May; **262** Courtesy of Brunswick Corporation; **265** Hestoft/Saba Press Photos, Inc.; **268** Courtesy of Mayflower Transit, Inc.; **271** Courtesy of McDonnell Douglas/Helicopter Systems; **273** National Institute of Health; **289** Frank Labua

Chapter 8

292 Courtesy of Magnetek, Inc.; **293** AP/Wide World Photos; **305** Courtesy of Pfizer Inc.; **307** Philip G. Zimbardo/Stanford University; **313** Fritz Hoffmann; **316** Paul Lowe/Magnum Photos, Inc.; **324** Courtesy of Haworth, Inc., Holland, MI; **325** Katherine Lambert

Chapter 9

344 David Graham; 345 Rex Rystedt; **350** Ron Garrison/ San Diego Zoological Society; **351** John Abbott Photography; **355** James Schnepf; **358** NASA; **362** Ted Horowitz

Chapter 10

374 Peter Vidor; **375** Ed Wheeler/Stock Market; **377** Anne States/Saba Press Photos, Inc.; **381** David B. Sutton; **388** Chuck Keeler/Tony Stone Worldwide; **391** Eden Robbins; **395** Arnold Adler Photography; **398** Donatella Brun

Chapter 11

410 Courtesy of USF&G Corpotation; **411** Courtesy of John P. Whitley; **414** Greg Mainovich/Matrix Inernational; **416** Courtesy of the U.S. Army; **420** Roger Mastroianni; **422** Jim Gund/Allsport; **435** Michael A. Schwarz; **441** Erin Elder

Chapter 12

460 Courtesy Edelman Houston Group/Montreal, Quebec; **461** David Strick/Onyx Enterprises, Inc.; **465** Vincent J. Musi; **468** Louis Psihoyos/ Matrix International; **474** Laima Druskis; **475** AP/Wide World Photos; **482** Duane Burleson/Sygma; **486** Eli Reichman

Chapter 13

502 Marc Pokempner/Impact Visuals Photo & Graphics, Inc.; **503** Richard Sandler; **506** Steve Woit; **515** TRW, Inc.; **520** Charlie Archambault; **522** Grant Black; **527** T. Michael Kesa/Nation's Business; **532** Courtesy of Merck & Co., Inc.; **546** Frank Labua

Chapter 14

548 Edward Gajdel Photography; **549** Courtesy of Oticon A/S; **552** Courtesy of EDS Corporation, Dallas, Texas; **557** Rob Nelson/Black Star; **562** Peter Korniss; **566** Ted Sanford/Courtesy of General Electric/Corporate Graphics Resource Inc.; **567** David Strick/Onyx Enterprises, Inc.; **578** Steven Pumphrey

Chapter 15

588 Ray Ng; **589** Manuello Paganelli Photography; **591** Ovak Arslanian; **594** J. Chiasson/Gamma-Liaison, Inc; **604** Kenneth Jarecke/Contact Press Images; **607** T. Michael Keza/Nation's Business; **612** Max Aquilera-Hellweg; **621** Courtesy of Coors Brewing Company

Chapter 16

634 Courtesy of Hilton Hotels Corporation; **635** Courtesy The Gates Rubber Company, Siloam Springs, Arkansas; **638** Peter Breggs/Maclean;s; **641** Munshi Ahmed Photography; **644** Courtesy Knight-Ridder; **652** Andy Freeberg; **662** Jeff Mermelstein; **664** Sergio Dorantes

Chapter 17

678 Rick Friedman/Black Star; **679** Vickers & Beechler/Time Life Books; **685** Burk Uzzle; **689** Kevin Horan; **691** Jeff Mermelstein; **694** R. Wallis/SIPA- PRESS; **697** Marc Costantini; **699** Stephen R. Swinburne/Stock, Boston **712**; Frank Labua

Chapter 18

714 Courtesy of Ford Motor Company; **715** Ted Hardin; **719** Courtesy Anheuser Busch Companies, Inc.; **722** Courtesy of Geon; **731** Steve Niedorf; **733** Michael L. Abramson; **736** Robert Day for the Clorox Company; **739** Courtesy Chrysler; **752** Frank Labua

INDEX

Name Index

Organization Index

Subject Index

STUDENT'S GUIDE TO USING

ORGANIZATIONAL BEHAVIOR

SEVENTH EDITION

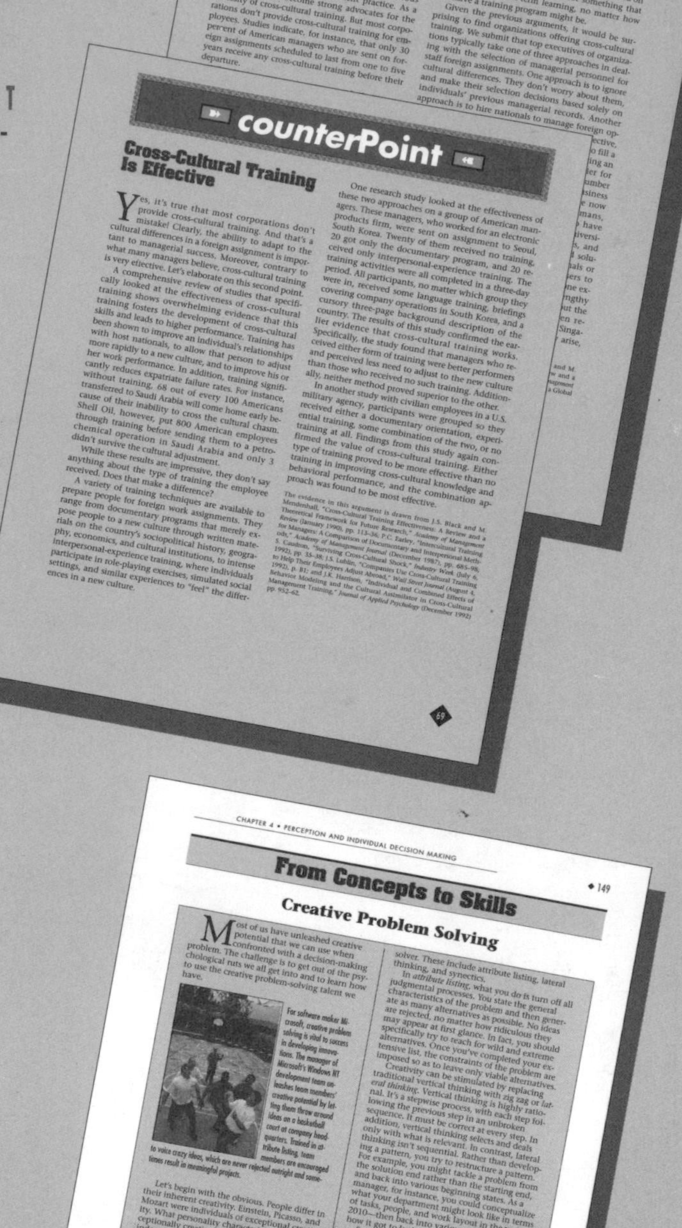

Point

Cross-Cultural Training Doesn't Work

counterPoint

Cross-Cultural Training Is Effective

POINT–COUNTERPOINT

Presents key OB issues in a debate-style format to help you develop your critical–thinking skills.

OB IN THE NEWS

Recreates articles from business periodicals to show the relevance of OB concepts to daily business activities.

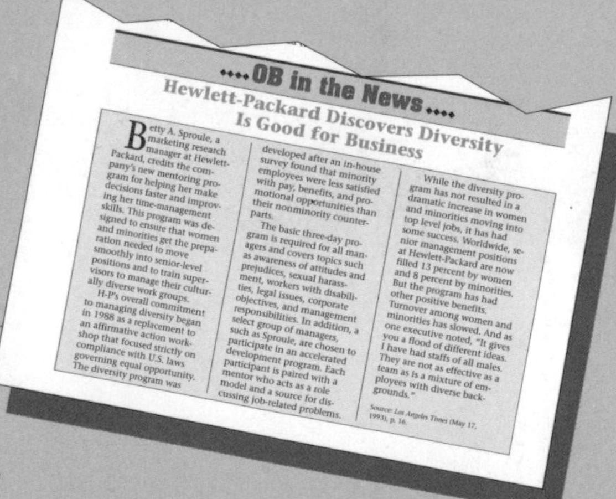

....OB in the News....

Hewlett-Packard Discovers Diversity Is Good for Business

CHAPTER 4 • PERCEPTION AND INDIVIDUAL DECISION MAKING

From Concepts to Skills

Creative Problem Solving

FROM CONCEPTS TO SKILLS

Illustrates how you can translate OB concepts into effective on–the–job skills.